Student Resources

Students! Your text is the first place for you to turn to begin your studies of Organizational Behavior. In addition, there is a wealth of other resources including study aids, practice tests, and downloads for your iPod® or MP3 player for studying on the go!

You don't have to wait for your instructor to assign practice tests or give you extra study aids. We've provided them on the Web site for your text at **www.mhhe.com/kreitner**

Throughout the text, you'll find boxes that suggest exercises for individuals and groups that will help you master the content of the text. You'll find these exercises and more at the Online Learning Center.

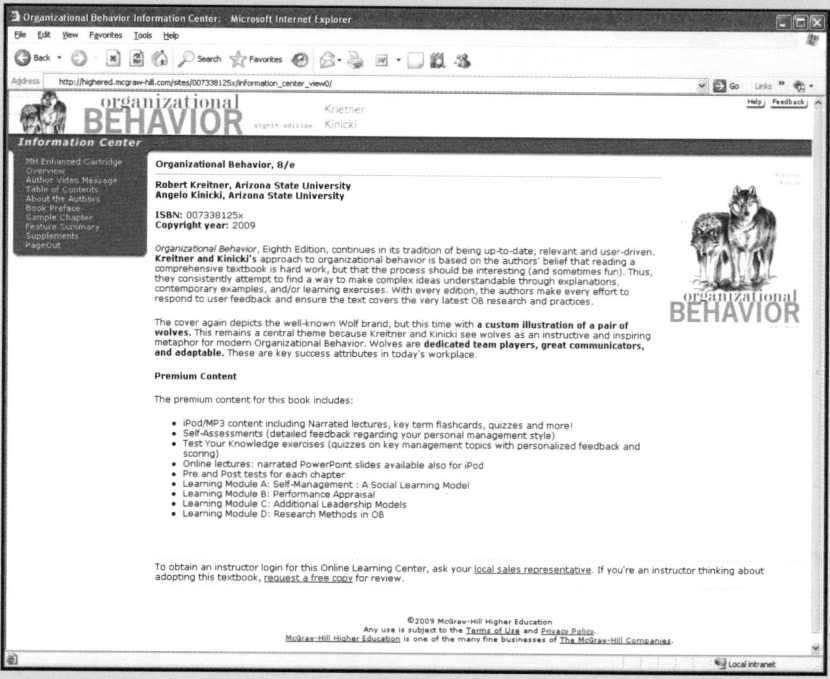

Study on the Go!

Our new iPod downloads are perfect for studying on the go! For just $10, you will have access to narrated chapter lectures, videos, and practice quizzes that can be downloaded to an iPod or MP3 player. These downloads can be purchased at the Online Learning Center.

Along with the downloads, your $10 will also get you additional practice testing, self-assessment exercises and more!

Courtesy of Apple

Organizational Behavior

Eighth Edition

Organizational Behavior
Eighth Edition

Robert Kreitner

Angelo Kinicki

Both of Arizona State University

McGraw-Hill Irwin

Boston   Burr Ridge, IL   Dubuque, IA   Madison, WI   New York   San Francisco   St. Louis
Bangkok   Bogotá   Caracas   Kuala Lumpur   Lisbon   London   Madrid   Mexico City
Milan   Montreal   New Delhi   Santiago   Seoul   Singapore   Sydney   Taipei   Toronto

The McGraw·Hill Companies

McGraw-Hill
Irwin

ORGANIZATIONAL BEHAVIOR

Published by McGraw-Hill/Irwin, a business unit of The McGraw-Hill Companies, Inc., 1221 Avenue of the Americas, New York, NY, 10020. Copyright © 2008 by The McGraw-Hill Companies, Inc. All rights reserved. No part of this publication may be reproduced or distributed in any form or by any means, or stored in a database or retrieval system, without the prior written consent of The McGraw-Hill Companies, Inc., including, but not limited to, in any network or other electronic storage or transmission, or broadcast for distance learning.

Some ancillaries, including electronic and print components, may not be available to customers outside the United States.

This book is printed on acid-free paper.

2 3 4 5 6 7 8 9 0 TWP/TWP 0 9 8
Printed in Singapore

ISBN: 978-0-07-338125-1
MHID: 0-07-338125-X

Publisher: *Paul Ducham*
Executive editor: *John Weimeister*
Developmental editor: *Donielle Xu*
Editorial assistant: *Heather Darr*
Marketing manager: *Margaret A. Beamer*
Media producer: *Greg Bates*
Project manager: *Dana M. Pauley*
Lead production supervisor: *Michael R. McCormick*
Senior designer: *Cara David*
Senior photo research coordinator: *Jeremy Cheshareck*
Photo researcher: *Jennifer Blankenship*
Senior media project manager: *Lynn M. Bluhm*
Cover illustration: *David J. Rogers*
Typeface: *10/12 Times Roman*
Compositor: *International Typesetting and Composition*
Printer: *Tien Wah Press*

Library of Congress Cataloging-in-Publication Data

Kreitner, Robert.
      Organizational behavior / Robert Kreitner, Angelo Kinicki. — 8th ed.
          p. cm.
      Includes index.
      ISBN-13: 978-0-07-338125-1 (alk. paper)
      ISBN-10: 0-07-338125-X (alk. paper)
      1. Organizational behavior. I. Kinicki, Angelo. II. Title.
   HD58.7.K766 2008
   658.3—dc22   2007026325

www.mhhe.com

About the Authors

Robert Kreitner, PhD (pictured left) is a professor emeritus of management at Arizona State University and a member of ASU's W P Carey School of Business Faculty Hall of Fame. Prior to joining ASU in 1975, Bob taught at Western Illinois University. He also taught organizational behavior at Thunderbird. Bob is a popular speaker who has addressed a diverse array of audiences worldwide on management topics. Bob has authored articles for journals such as *Organizational Dynamics, Business Horizons,* and *Journal of Business Ethics.* He also is the co-author (with Fred Luthans) of the award-winning book *Organizational Behavior Modification and Beyond: An Operant and Social Learning Approach,* and the author of *Management,* 10th edition, a best-selling introductory management text.

Among his consulting and executive development clients have been American Express, SABRE Computer Services, Honeywell, Motorola, Amdahl, the Hopi Indian Tribe, State Farm Insurance, Goodyear Aerospace, Doubletree Hotels, Bank One–Arizona, Nazarene School of Large Church Management, US Steel, and Allied-Signal. In 1981–82 he served as chairman of the Academy of Management's Management Education and Development Division. Bob grew up in western New York state. After a four-year enlistment in the US Coast Guard, including service on the icebreaker EASTWIND in Antarctica, Bob attended the University of Nebraska–Omaha on a football scholarship. Bob also holds an MBA from the University of Nebraska–Omaha and a PhD from the University of Nebraska–Lincoln. While working on his PhD in business at Nebraska, he spent six months teaching management courses for the University in Micronesia. In 1996, Bob taught two courses in Albania's first-ever MBA program (funded by the US Agency for International Development and administered by the University of Nebraska–Lincoln). He taught a summer leadership program in Switzerland from 1995 to 1998. Bob and his wife, Margaret, live in Phoenix with their two cats. They enjoy world travel, lots of hiking, and a little fishing.

Angelo Kinicki is a professor of management at the W P Carey School of Business at Arizona State University. He was awarded the Weatherup/Overby Chair in Leadership in 2005. He has held his current position since receiving his doctorate in organizational behavior from Kent State University in 1982.

Angelo is recognized for both his teaching and research. As a teacher, Angelo has been the recipient of several awards, including the John W Teets Outstanding Graduate Teacher Award (2004–05), Graduate Teaching Excellence Award (1998–99), Continuing Education Excellence Award (1991–92), and Undergraduate Teaching Excellence Award (1987–88). He also was selected into *Who's Who of American Colleges and Universities* and *Beta Gamma Sigma.* He has published more than 80 articles in a variety of leading academic and professional journals and has coauthored six college textbooks (19 including revisions). His textbooks have been used by hundreds of universities around the world and have been translated into multiple languages. Angelo's experience as a researcher resulted in his selection to serve on the editorial review boards for the *Academy of Management Journal*, the *Journal of Management*, and the *Journal of Vocational Behavior*. He also received the All-Time Best Reviewer Award from the *Academy of Management Journal* for the period of 1996 to 1999. Angelo's current research interests include the study of leadership, organizational culture, and coping with organizational change and involuntary job loss.

Angelo is an active international consultant who works with management groups to create organizational change aimed at increasing organizational effectiveness and profitability. He enjoys delivering a variety of executive development programs on many topics related to organizational behavior. He has worked with many *Fortune* 500 firms as well as numerous entrepreneurial organizations in diverse industries. His work on leadership development led to the creation of a 360-degree leadership feedback instrument called the Performance Management Leadership Survey (PMLS) that has been used by companies throughout the United States and Europe.

One of Angelo's strengths is his ability to teach students at all levels within a university. He uses an interactive environment to enhance undergraduates' understanding about management and organizational behavior. He focuses MBAs on applying management concepts to solve complex problems; PhD students learn the art and science of conducting scholarly research.

Angelo and his wife, Joyce, have enjoyed living in the beautiful Arizona desert for 25 years but are natives of Cleveland, Ohio. They enjoy traveling, golfing, and spoiling Nala, their golden retriever.

Preface

Things move very fast in today's Internet-linked global economy. Competition is intense. Speed, cost, and quality are no longer the trade-offs they once were (meaning improvement in one came at the expense of one or both of the others). Today's customers want immediate access to high-quality products and services at a reasonable price. Thus, managers are challenged to simultaneously speed up the product creation and delivery cycle, cut costs, and improve quality. (And to do so in an ethical manner.) Regardless of the size and purpose of the organization and the technology involved, *people* are the common denominator when facing this immense challenge. Success or failure hinges on the ability to attract, develop, retain, motivate, and lead a diverse array of appropriately skilled people. *The human factor drives everything*. To know more about workplace behavior is to gain a valuable competitive edge. The purpose of this textbook is to help present and future organizational participants better understand and manage people at work.

Although this eighth edition of *Organizational Behavior* is aimed at undergraduate business students in similarly named courses, previous editions have proven highly versatile. *Organizational Behavior* has been used effectively in MBA programs, executive education and management development programs, and industrial and organizational psychology programs around the world. (Note: special Canadian and European editions are available.)

This textbook is the culmination of our combined 60 years of teaching experience and research of organizational behavior and management in the United States, Pacific Rim, and Europe. Thanks to detailed feedback from students, professors, and practicing managers, this eighth edition is shorter, more refined, and better organized. Many new changes have been made in this edition, reflecting new research evidence, new management techniques, and the fruits of our own learning process.

Organizational Behavior, eighth edition, is *user driven* (as a result of carefully listening to our readers). It was developed through close *teamwork* between the authors and the publisher and is the product of *continuous improvement*. This approach has helped us achieve a difficult combination of balances. Among them are balances between theory and practice, solid content and interesting coverage, and instructive detail and readability. Students and instructors say they want an up-to-date, relevant, and interesting textbook that actively involves the reader in the learning process. Our efforts toward this end are evidenced by many new topics, 799 source material references dated 2006 and 552 dated 2007, many new real-life examples, a stimulating art program, timely new cases and boxed inserts, and end-of-chapter experiential exercises for both individuals and teams. We realize that reading a comprehensive textbook is hard work, but we also firmly believe the process should be interesting (and sometimes fun).

GUIDED TOUR

New and Expanded Coverage

Our readers and reviewers have kindly told us how much they appreciate our efforts to keep this textbook up-to-date and relevant. Toward that end, you will find the following important new and significantly improved coverage in the eighth edition:

Chapter 1
Major new section titled "The Ethics Challenge" includes coverage of Sarbanes-Oxley Act of 2002; a model of individual ethical behavior; Carroll's global model of corporate social responsibility and ethics; whistle-blowing; and a personal call to action. New key terms: *corporate social responsibility* and *whistle-blowing*.

Chapter 2
Updated data on demographic statistics and new examples of corporate diversity initiatives. New Ethical Dilemma feature.

Chapter 3
Discussion of sustainability as a corporate value, and new key term. Major new section on types of organizational culture revolves around the competing values framework (CVF). Key terms presented for the four types of organizational culture underlying the CVF: *clan culture, adhocracy culture, market culture,* and *hierarchy culture.* New discussion regarding the process of culture change, including key terms for vision and strategic plan. New examples for how organizations embed organizational culture.

Chapter 4
New discussion of Muslim-Americans and ethnocentrism.

Chapter 5
New coverage and key terms: *resiliency* and *impostor syndrome.* New section titled "Abilities and the Need for Sleep." New Ethical Dilemma feature.

Chapter 6
New examples and research pertaining to values, attitudes, and job satisfaction.

Chapter 7
New coverage of managerial implications of the perception process: workplace aggression and antisocial behavior, physical and psychological well-being; and designing Web pages. New recommendations for reducing commonly found perceptual errors. New key term for *implicit cognition* and a discussion of its role in stereotyping. New Ethical Dilemma feature.

Chapter 8
New examples and research pertaining to all models of motivation. New discussion of employee needs by different age groups. New coverage and key term for repetitive motion disorders.

Chapter 9
New coverage and key term: *line of sight* (to strategic goals). Coverage of goal orientation updated to reflect new research. New discussion of feedback versus performance appraisals. New Ethical Dilemma feature.

Chapter 10
New discussion of the challenge of being both a manager and a friend. More discussion of Sarbanes-Oxley Act of 2002. New Ethical Dilemma feature.

Chapter 11
Cooperation as a service quality strategy at Ritz-Carlton. New critique of team-building exercises. New Ethical Dilemma feature.

Chapter 12
New coverage and key terms for *nonrational model* of decision making and the *garbage can model* of decision making. Expanded discussion of decision-making biases now contains new material pertaining to the confirmation bias, the anchoring bias, the overconfidence bias, the hindsight bias, and the framing bias. New section devoted to ethical decision making, including the presentation of an ethical decision-making tree. New key term for *decision tree.* New Ethical Dilemma feature.

Chapter 13
New discussion and key term: *day of contemplation* (one-time-only day with pay to reflect on need for performance improvement). New Ethical Dilemma feature.

Chapter 14
Material on barriers to effective communication has been revised and restructured, including new coverage and key terms for *personal barriers, semantics,* and *jargon.* New coverage and key term for management by walking around, a form of informal communication. The section on communicating in the computerized information age is much more practical. There is new material about the costs of cybercrime and a table summarizing the benefits, drawbacks, and suggestions for managing e-mail. New Ethical Dilemma feature.

Chapter 15
Expanded coverage of charisma, relative to referent power. Advice for new college graduates who want to make a good impression on the job. New Ethical Dilemma feature.

Chapter 16
New examples and research for all leadership theories. New discussion of the takeaways from situational theories and transformational leadership.

Chapter 17
Organizational decline at Dell. Making a merger work with a people-centered approach. New Ethical Dilemma feature.

Chapter 18
New discussion of how an organizational crisis is an external force of change. New table presenting five types of organizational development interventions.

AACSB Coverage

In keeping with the curriculum recommendations for AACSB International (the Association to Advance Collegiate Schools of Business, www.aacsb.edu) for greater attention to managing in a global economy, managing cultural diversity, improving product/service quality, and making ethical decisions, we feature this coverage:

- A full chapter on international organizational behavior and cross-cultural management (Chapter 4). Comprehensive coverage from the landmark GLOBE project. To ensure integrated coverage of international topics, 12 of the Real World/Real People boxed inserts have a global theme.
- A full chapter on managing diversity (Chapter 2) offers comprehensive and up-to-date coverage of managing diversity. Fourteen of the Real World/Real People boxed inserts have a diversity theme.
- Principles of total quality management (TQM) and the legacy of W Edwards Deming are discussed in Chapter 1 to establish a quality-improvement context for the entire textbook. Also, many quality-related examples have been integrated into the textual presentation.
- As outlined next, the eighth edition includes comprehensive coverage of ethics-related concepts, cases, and issues. Seventeen of the Real World/Real People boxed inserts have an ethics theme, with specific attention called out by an ethics icon.
- *New!* The eighth edition test bank provided in the Instructor's Resource CD will have each question tagged to the AACSB knowledge category it covers.

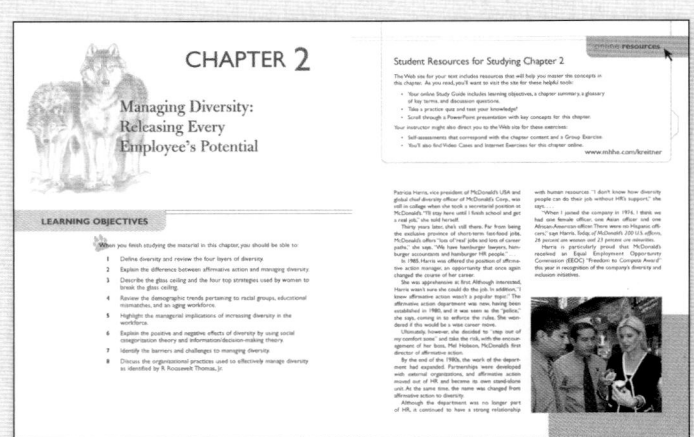

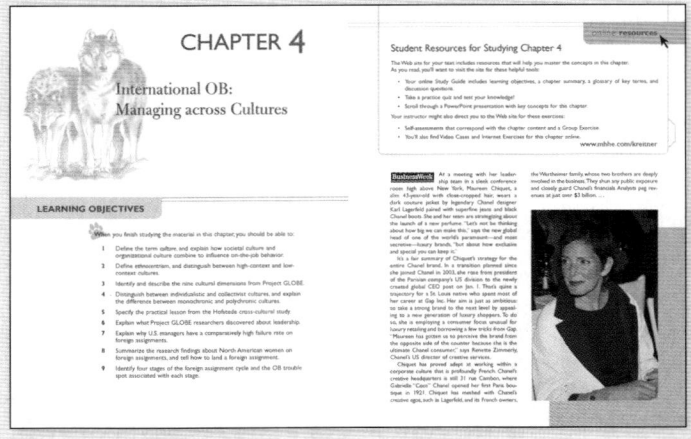

Comprehensive Ethics Coverage

Ethics is covered early and completely in Chapter 1 to set a proper moral tone for managing people at work. Ethical issues are raised throughout the text, with additional significant coverage of the Ethical Decision-Making Tree in Chapter 12. In nearly every chapter, one or two of the Real World/Real People boxed inserts are ethically based and are highlighted with the new ethics icon. Also in this eighth edition are 18 Ethical Dilemmas (one following each chapter). They raise hard-hitting ethical issues and ask tough questions, virtually guaranteeing a lively discussion/debate for cooperative learning. These Ethical Dilemmas (11 are new to this edition), along with the Real World/Real People boxes, are constant reminders of the importance of ethical management.

The contingency approach encourages managers to view organizational behavior within a situational context. According to this modern perspective, evolving situations, not hard-and-fast rules, determine when and where various management techniques are appropriate. Harvard's Clayton Christensen put it this way: "Many of the widely accepted principles of good management are only situationally appropriate."[67] For example, as discussed in Chapter 16, contingency researchers have determined that there is no single best style of leadership. Organizational behavior specialists embrace the contingency approach because it helps them realistically interrelate individuals, groups, and evolving circumstances inside and outside the organization.[68] Moreover, the contingency approach sends a clear message to managers in today's global economy: Carefully read the situation and then be flexible enough to adapt.

The Ethics Challenge

Here are six reasons to be concerned about business ethics:

- Bernard Ebbers, former CEO of WorldCom, serving a 25-year prison sentence for fraud and conspiracy.
- Jeffrey Skilling, former CEO of Enron, serving a 24-year prison sentence for securities fraud and insider trading.
- John Rigas, former CEO of Aldelphia Communications, serving a 15-year prison sentence for conspiracy and bank fraud.
- Sanjay Kumar, former CEO of Computer Associates, serving a 12-year prison sentence for securities fraud and obstruction of justice.
- Dennis Kozlowski, former CEO of Tyco, serving an 8-year prison sentence for grand larceny and falsifying business records.
- Andrew Fastow, former chief financial officer of Enron, serving a 6-year prison sentence for wire fraud.[69]

Thanks to the highly publicized criminal acts of these and other executives, corporate officers in the United States are now subject to high accountability standards and harsh penalties under the Sarbanes-Oxley Act of 2002.[70] The general public and elected officials (who have their own criminal hall of shame) have called for greater attention to ethical conduct. The challenge is immense because unethical behavior is pervasive.

A nationwide survey of 581 human resource professionals revealed that 62% of the respondents occasionally observed unethical behavior at their companies.[71] Unethical behavior occurs from the bottom to the top of organizations. For example, a survey of job applicants for executive positions indicated that 64% had been misinformed about the financial condition of potential employers, and 58% of these individuals were negatively affected by this misinformation.[72] It is very likely that some of these affected individuals moved their families and left their friends only to find out the promise of a great job in a financially stable organization was a lie. Job applicants, for their part, also have ethical lapses. An analysis of 2.6 million background checks by ADP Screening and Selection Services, revealed that "44% of applicants lied about their work histories, 41% lied about their education, and 23% falsified credentials or licenses."[73]

Experts estimated that US companies lose about $600 billion a year from unethical and criminal behavior.[74] Studies in the United States and the United Kingdom further demonstrated that corporate commitment to ethics can be profitable. Evidence

---

Road Map to Ethical Decision Making: A Decision Tree

In Chapter 1 we discussed the importance of ethics and the growing concern about the lack of ethical behavior among business leaders. For example, a US Roper poll revealed that 72% of respondents perceived that corporate wrongdoing was rampant, and only 2% believed that leaders of large organizations were trustworthy.[49] While this trend partially explains the passage of laws to regulate ethical behavior in corporate America, we believe that ethical acts ultimately involve individual or group decisions. It thus is important to consider the issue of ethical decision making. Harvard Business School professor Constance Bagley suggests that a decision tree can help managers to make more ethical decisions.[50] A **decision tree** is a graphical representation of the process underlying decisions and it shows the resulting consequences of making various choices. Decision trees are used as an aid in decision making.

Decision tree
Graphical representation of process underlying decision making.

Ethical decision making frequently involves trade-offs, and a decision tree helps managers to navigate through them. The decision tree shown in Figure 12–3 can be applied to any type of decision or action that an individual manager or corporation is contemplating. Looking at the tree, the first question to ask is whether or not the proposed action is legal. If the action is illegal, do not do it. If the action is legal, then consider the impact of the action on shareholder value. A decision maximizes shareholder value when it results in a more favorable financial position (e.g., increased profits) for an organization. Whether or not an action maximizes shareholder value, the decision tree shows that managers still need to consider the ethical implications of the decision or action. For example, if an action maximizes shareholder value, the next question to consider is whether or not the action is ethical. The answer to this question is based on considering the positive effect of the action on an organization's other key constituents (i.e., customers, employees, the community, the environment, and suppliers) against the benefit to the shareholders. According to the decision tree framework, managers should make the decision to engage in an action if the benefits to the shareholders exceed the benefits to the other key constituents. Managers should not engage in the action if the other key constituents would benefit more from the action than shareholders.

Figure 12–3 illustrates that managers use a slightly different perspective when their initial conclusion is that an action does not maximize shareholder value. In this case, the question becomes Would it be ethical not to take action? This question necessitates that a manager consider the *harm or cost* of an action to shareholders against the *costs or benefits* to other key constituents. If the costs to shareholders from a managerial decision exceed the costs or benefits to other constituents, the manager or company should not engage in the action. Conversely, the manager or company should take action when the perceived costs or benefits to the other constituents are greater than the costs to shareholders. Let us apply this decision tree to IBM's decision to raise the amount of money it required retirees to contribute to their health benefits.[51] The company made this decision in order to save money.

Is it legal for a company to decrease its contribution to retiree health care benefits while simultaneously raising retirees' contributions? The answer is yes. Does an organization maximize shareholder value by decreasing its retiree health care expenses? Again, the answer is yes. We now have to consider the overall benefits to shareholders against the overall benefits to other key constituents. The answer to this question is more complex than it appears and is contingent on an organization's corporate values.

Chris De Buyssher Uses Intuition to Detect the Shipping of Counterfeit Goods

His skills are a low-tech blend of old-fashioned gumshoe detective work and intuition. On a recent trip to Algeria, Mr De Buysscher singled out a shipping container from China for checking at the port of Oran. It was supposed to contain shoes—and it did—fake Nikes. . . .

Part of his expertise comes from knowing brand-name goods. He visits outlet malls to study the products of Nike and Oscar de la Renta. He knows how things are packed in certain countries. . . . He's also up on fashion and can recognize 10 perfumes by nose alone, he says. "Chanel, Dior and Yves Saint Laurent smells are trademarked, just like the bottles they're in. . . .

The growth of the $500 billion counterfeit goods industry is one of the biggest economic challenges facing European and American companies as they relocate production to Asia.

Are there better ways to catch crooks than by using intuition?

SOURCE: J W Miller, "Gumshoe's Intuition: Spotting Counterfeits at Port of Antwerp," *The Wall Street Journal,* December 14, 2006, p A1.

Ethical Dilemma

Should the Principal of Westwood High Allow an Exception to the Graduation Dress Code?[90]

This dilemma involves a situation faced by Helen Riddle, the principal of Mesa, Arizona's Westwood High. "Westwood High has 225 Native American students, including 112 from the Salt River Pima-Maricopa Indian Community, most of which lies within the boundaries of the Mesa United School District." Districtwide, there are 452 Native American high school students, 149 of whom are from the Salt River Reservation. Here is the situation.

Native American students asked the principal for permission to wear eagle feathers during their graduation ceremony. While this may seem like a reasonable request given these students' customs and traditions, Westwood High had a rule stating that "students were only allowed to wear a traditional cap and gown for graduation with no other adornments or clothing, including military uniforms. The rules were based on past practice and tradition at schools, not School Board policy."

Advocates for the Native American students argued that students should be allowed to wear the eagle feathers because they represent a significant achievement in the lives of those individuals. In contrast, one school board member opposed the exception to the rule because "it would open the door for other students wanting to display symbols of their own culture or background."

Pedagogical Features

The eighth edition of *Organizational Behavior* is designed to be a complete teaching/learning tool that captures the reader's interest and imparts useful knowledge. Some of the most significant pedagogical features of this text are the following:

- Classic and modern topics are given balanced treatment in terms of the latest and best available theoretical models, research evidence, and practical applications. Each chapter follows a Theory-Research-Practice approach. Students reading each chapter will be given an understanding of the basic theories about OB, whether or not the theories work by drawing on research to make summary conclusions, and will be able to apply the theories and research to real-world examples.

- Several concise learning objectives open each chapter to focus the reader's attention and serve as a comprehensive check. New to this edition is a design feature calling attention to each learning objective within the text. Look for numbered paw prints where the new learning objective begins. Additionally, the chapter summary is written to correlate with chapter learning objectives.

- A colorful and lively art program includes captioned photographs, figures, and cartoons.

- Hundreds of real-world examples involving large and small, public and private organizations have been incorporated into the textual material to make this edition up-to-date, interesting, and relevant.

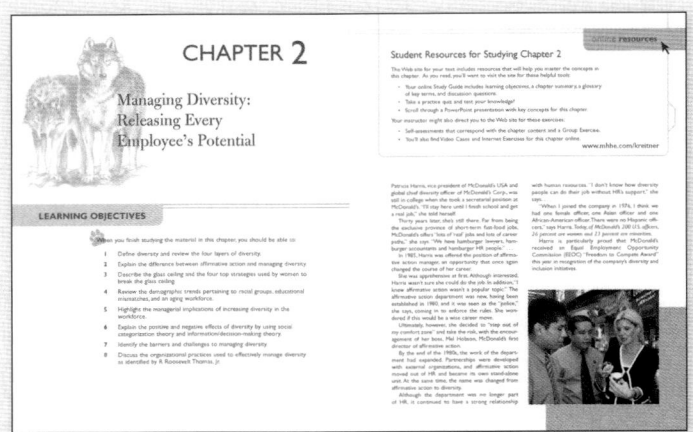

Streamlined End-of-Chapter Materials

The end-of-chapter materials for the eighth edition of *Organizational Behavior* were carefully selected for their use as a study guide for students. Each chapter contains

- A Summary of Key Concepts correlating with the Learning Objectives for that chapter
- A list of Key Terms (with text page notations)
- A new or updated OB in Action Case Study
- An Ethical Dilemma
- A reminder about the resources available on the Web

Note that the popular Personal Growth Exercises and Group Exercises, along with Group Discussion Questions, which were printed in the previous edition's end-of-chapter material, can now be found on the book's Web site. Instructors will be able to assign those exercises that specifically apply to your classroom needs, and are given more freedom to choose only those exercises that apply.

Summary of Key Concepts

1. *Explain how a work group becomes a team.* A team is a mature group where leadership is shared, accountability is both individual and collective, the members have developed their own purpose, problem solving is a way of life, and effectiveness is measured by collective outcomes.

2. *Identify and describe four types of work teams.* Advice teams provide information for managerial decisions. Production teams perform an organization's day-to-day operations. Project teams apply specialized knowledge to solve problems needed to complete a specific project. Action teams are highly skilled and highly coordinated to provide peak performance on demand.

3. *Explain the model of effective work teams, and specify the two criteria of team effectiveness.* Work teams need three things: (a) a team-friendly organization to provide a support system; (b) individuals with teamwork competencies; and (c) effective teamwork. The two team effectiveness criteria are performance (getting the job done) and team viability (satisfied members who are willing to continue contributing to the team).

4. *Identify five teamwork competences team members need to possess.* They are (a) orients team to problem-solving situation; (b) organizes and manages team performance; (c) promotes a positive team environment; (d) facilitates and manages task conflict; and (e) appropriately promotes perspective.

5. *Discuss why teams fail.* Teams fail because unrealistic expectations cause frustration and failure. Common management mistakes include weak strategies, creating a hostile environment for teams, faddish use of teams, not learning from team experience, vague team assignments, poor team staffing, inadequate training, and lack of trust.

Team members typically try too much too soon, experience conflict over differing work styles and personalities, ignore important group dynamics, resist change, exhibit poor interpersonal skills and chemistry, and display a lack of trust.

6. *List at least four things managers can do to build trust.* Six recommended ways to build trust are through communication, support, respect (especially delegation), fairness, predictability, and competence.

7. *Distinguish two types of group cohesiveness, and summarize cohesiveness research findings.* Cohesive groups have a shared sense of togetherness or a "we" feeling. Socio-emotional cohesiveness involves emotional satisfaction. Instrumental cohesiveness involves goal-directed togetherness. There is a small but significant relationship between cohesiveness and performance. The effect is stronger for smaller groups. Commitment to task among group members strengthens the cohesiveness-performance linkage. Success can build group cohesiveness. Cohesiveness is not a cure-all for group problems. Too much cohesiveness can lead to groupthink.

8. *Define virtual teams and self-managed teams.* Virtual teams are physically dispersed work groups that conduct their business via modern information technologies such as the Internet, e-mail, and videoconferences. Self-managed teams are work groups that perform their own administrative chores such as planning, scheduling, and staffing.

9. *Describe high-performance teams.* Eight attributes of high-performance teams are participative leadership, shared responsibility, aligned on purpose, high communication, future focused for growth, focused on task, creative talents applied, and rapid response.

Key Terms

Team 306
Team viability 309
Trust 317
Propensity to trust 318
Cohesiveness 319
Socio-emotional cohesiveness 319

Instrumental cohesiveness 319
Virtual team 322
Self-managed teams 324
Cross-functionalism 325
Team building 326
Self-management leadership 329

OB in Action Case Study

In the Trenches at VF Boot Camp[53]

BusinessWeek Nanette Byrnes, *BusinessWeek* reporter: There were six of us, squinting down the length of a conference table at a single laptop. It was past 9 p.m., and what we could make out on the screen wasn't encouraging. We'd all met just 13 hours earlier—when I was thrown together with five fast-climbing executives at apparel maker VF Corp. for an exercise in management boot camp. Over the four days of

Ethical Dilemma

Protects Like Armor, Fits Like Armani[54]

"Who here hasn't been shot?"

Miguel Caballero is walking around his company's showroom in Bogotá, Colombia, holding a .38-caliber revolver. "You!" he says, pointing to German Gonzalez, a 20-something salesman who's been on the job for just two weeks. "You're next."

Gonzalez wiggles nervously into an $850 brown suede winter jacket and zips it up to the collar. A foot or so away, the smiling Caballero lowers the weapon and takes aim.

"One!" Gonzalez takes a deep breath and stares up at the ceiling. "Two! . . ." A deafening blast sends Gonzalez lurching backward—and then screaming out in relief, clutching at the hole in the jacket where the bullet has come to a safe stop.

No, this isn't some cruel corporate hazing ritual. For Caballero, founder and CEO of the company that carries his name, this is just a showman's way of demonstrating his products. Caballero sells a line of armored clothing that fits like Armani but deflects point-blank gunfire like the Popemobile. Last year the 38-year-old entrepreneur sold an estimated $7 million worth of bulletproof trench coats, business suits, suede jackets, and denim casuals to executives, political leaders, undercover agents, and other VIPs—people who demand more than a bodyguard for protection and don't like the bulk or SWAT-team look of flak jackets and vests. "There are hundreds of companies that make bulletproof vests," Caballero says. "We make bulletproof fashion."

Situation: The president of your company witnessed this demonstration on a recent visit to Colombia and now wants you, the marketing director, to develop a similar marketing campaign as a North American distributor. **What is your response and its ethical implications?**

1. Talk about getting the customer's attention, this is great marketing! Let's go with live demonstrations. Who wants to take a bullet for the team?

2. A live demonstration is too dangerous and out of the question. Besides many cities have laws against firing guns within city limits. Let's go with a video demonstration. Who wants to take a bullet for the team?

3. What happens in Colombia should stay in Colombia. Have Miguel Caballero make a demonstration video, in Colombia, just like the one described above for use in foreign markets.

4. Live models in any sort of demonstration are out of the question. Too controversial. Let's create a promotional video in the safety of a shooting range with a mannequin wearing the bullet-proof jacket.

5. Invent other options. Discuss.

Web Resources

For study material and exercises that apply to this chapter, visit our Web site, www.mhhe.com/kreitner

Fresh Cases and Updated Research

Our continuing commitment to a timely and relevant textbook is evidenced by the number of new chapter-opening vignettes and chapter-closing cases. The vignettes and cases highlight male and female role models, public and private organizations, and US and foreign companies such as Patagonia, McDonald's, Safeway, Starbucks, Google, Chanel, PricewaterhouseCoopers, JP Morgan Chase, Nucor, Ford, Home Depot, Microsoft, Disney, Avon, Wal-Mart, ExxonMobil, and Best Buy.

Every chapter opens with a real-name, real-world vignette to provide a practical context for the material at hand. Seventeen of the chapter-opening vignettes are new.

This eighth edition is filled with current and relevant examples from both a research and a practice perspective. In fact, 799 source material references are dated 2006 and 552 are dated 2007.

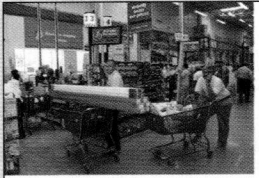

The only way over it, he decided, was through it. So Blake penned a heartfelt and repentant online letter to all Home Depot customers, essentially copping to the company's less-than-stellar service. He promised to increase staffing and begged for the chance to make good. He created a site to deal specifically with service. He thanked Scott Burns.

In crisis-management circles, the gamble was viewed as a win.¹

FOR DISCUSSION

Are bloggers creating more harm than good for organizations?

Home Depot's reported poor service caused an avalanche of Internet postings. CEO Francis Blake felt compelled to reply.

In his best-selling book *The World Is Flat*, Thomas L. Friedman concluded that information technology is transforming and connecting people's lives around the world. The chapter-opening vignette reinforces that claim. It shows how the Internet is being used to instantaneously communicate all types of information to anyone with access to a computer. Unfortunately, this information may be accurate or inaccurate. It thus is important for all of us to understand how information technology is affecting the way individuals communicate and how this technology influences organizational behavior as a whole. The final section of this chapter is devoted to examining these issues.

More broadly, the study of communication is important because every managerial function and activity involves some form of direct or indirect communication. Whether planning and organizing or directing and leading, managers find themselves communicating with and through others. This implies that everyone's communication skills affect both personal and organizational effectiveness.² For example, one study found that 70% of "preventable hospital mishaps" resulted from a lack of communication between employees, particularly during handoffs of patient care.³ Another polling of 336 organizations revealed that 66% of the respondents did not know or understand their organization's mission and business strategy, which subsequently led them to feel disengaged at work. This apparent lack of communication is a problem because employee disengagement is associated with lower productivity and product quality, and higher labor costs and turnover.⁴

This chapter will help you to better understand how managers can both improve their communication skills and design more effective communication programs. We discuss (1) basic dimensions of the communication process, focusing on a perceptual process model and barriers to effective communication; (2) interpersonal communication; (3) organizational communication; and (4) communicating in the computerized information age.

Basic Dimensions of the Communication Process

Communication
Interpersonal exchange of information and understanding.

Communication is defined as "the exchange of information between a sender and a receiver, and the inference (perception) of meaning between the individuals involved."⁵ Managers who understand this process can analyze their own communication patterns as well as design communication programs that fit organizational needs. This section

---

Real World/Real People

While theory and research are important to the study of OB, current examples of real people in real organizational situations are needed to bring OB to life for the reader. The eighth edition contains 64 Real World/Real People boxed inserts strategically located throughout the text. They are up-to-date (mostly drawn from 2006 or 2007 sources), often provocative, and definitely interesting. The Real World/Real People features tend to be short, for quick reading, and tightly linked to the accompanying textual discussion. They show real people at their best and sometimes at their worst.

New in this edition, the Real World/Real People boxes that address ethical issues are highlighted with a new ethics logo. Based on reviewer feedback, we've also included a discussion question with each box that ties it to the chapter content, to serve as a learning aid and class discussion starter.

Among the important and interesting topics and insights in the Real World/Real People features are building social capital, green corporations, worldwide employee shortages, corporate spying, Muslim-Americans and ethnocentrism, hiring military veterans, values, revenge in the workplace, CEO pay, coaching, blind conformity, project teams in MBA programs, co-worker support for cancer victims, pros and cons of team building, intuition, innovation, functional conflict, cubicle etiquette, semantic barriers, facial expressions, videoconferencing, employee wellness programs, empowerment, leadership development and effectiveness, shared leadership, open-system thinking, organizational decline, how to make a merger work, and resistance to change.

Organizations featured in the Real World/Real People boxes include Hackensack (NJ) University Medical Center, Microsoft, Unilever, Bank of America, Motorola, Hewlett-Packard, Home Depot, Xerox, Trane, NCR, PricewaterhouseCoopers, AMD, Raving Brands, Samsung, Grand Circle Corp., Toro, BET Networks, Wipro, Cisco Systems, IBM, Harrah's, Scotts, Goldman Sachs, eBay, Starbucks, and Dell.

REAL WORLD | real people ethics

Starbucks' Founder and Chairman, Howard Schultz, Brewed Up a Grand Vision

I wanted to build a different kind of company—a company that had a conscience. So it wasn't only that I needed people with skills and discipline and business acumen that complemented my own qualities, but most important, I needed to attract and retain people with like-minded values. What tied us together was not our respective disciplines, and it was not chasing an exit strategy driven by money. What tied us together was the dream of building a company that would achieve the fragile balance of profitability, shareholder value, a sense of benevolence, and a social conscience.

SOURCE: As quoted in "The Best Advice I Ever Got," *Fortune*, March 21, 2005, p 98.

Take It to the Web

Students are increasingly using the Internet for study resources and research. In this edition of *Organizational Behavior,* we have called more attention to the resources that are available for students at our Online Learning Center (the OLC). We heard from reviewers that the Web address wasn't highlighted enough, so we've added reminders in every chapter of the resources that are available online.

The set of tools that has been developed for both instructors and students on the OLC are an important supplement to the book. Based on reviewer feedback, instructors like to have the freedom to choose exercises that are applicable to them. In this edition, we've posted our hallmark exercise package online (including the in-text OB Exercises from the prior edition), thus providing freedom to choose only those exercises that make sense in your classroom.

Each of the exercises is advertised in the text with a unique design feature shown here. We've placed these advertisements in the text where we believe the exercise best matches the content.

---

online resources

Student Resources for Studying Chapter 10

The Web site for your text includes resources that will help you master the concepts in this chapter. As you read, you'll want to visit the site for these helpful tools:

- Your online Study Guide includes learning objectives, a chapter summary, a glossary of key terms, and discussion questions.
- Take a practice quiz and test your knowledge!
- Scroll through a PowerPoint presentation with key concepts for this chapter.

Your instructor might also direct you to the Web site for these exercises:

- Self-assessments that correspond with the chapter content and a Group Exercise.
- You'll also find Video Cases and Internet Exercises for this chapter online. **www.mhhe.com/kreitner**

Just when you think you've had a pretty good look at the office of Olson Sundberg Kundig Allen Architects, it shape-shifts. The pivoting walls in the conference room, you realize, are set at completely different angles than they were a few hours earlier. The huge white panel in the stairwell has suddenly been etched with a new abstraction of shadows. . . . And that skylight—that wasn't open before, was it? Even the staff itself scatters and shuffles. In fact, everything about this Seattle office is a work in progress, from the zealous use of raw materials to the firm's unique collaborative philosophy. It's never the same place twice. . . .

Like the cogs and wheels driving the skylight, the workings of the human machinery here are apparent as well. "This space shows our process of working rather than the finished product," [founder Jim] Olson says. "In our last space, we had all the interns in a back room, but now we've brought them out and put them right in the middle of everything. That's because this space itself is more like the back room."

The inside-out nature of the firm's culture is most evident during "the Crit," a Thursday afternoon tradition gathering the entire staff in one of the convertible cork-paneled conference rooms. The Crit allows staff members to explain their current projects, practice their presentation skills, or simply sort through a design problem using the studio's collective brain. The exploratory vibe helps the staff feel comfortable with their own less-than-perfect ideas. "There's nothing precious about this joint," says partner Rick Sundberg. "It's messy, it's dirty, it's funky. The process of creating is transparent, and it's right out there for everyone to see."[1]

FOR DISCUSSION

Why has it taken so long to fit workspaces to people, rather than vice versa?

The idea of marrying architecture and group dynamics, as illustrated in the opening vignette, promises to be fruitful in terms of more people-friendly workspaces and greater innovation. Organizations, by definition, are collections of people constantly interacting to achieve something greater than what can be achieved by individuals acting alone. Workspaces that encourage productive interaction leverage the social skills of organization members. Research consistently reveals the importance of social skills for both individual and organizational success.

For example, a recent study of 1,040 managers employed by 100 manufacturing and service organizations in the United States found 15 reasons why managers fail in the face of rapid change. The top two reasons were "ineffective communication skills/practices" and "poor work relationships/interpersonal skills."[2] Relationships *do* matter in the workplace, just as they do elsewhere.[3]

---

go to the Web for the Group Exercise: Stakeholder Audit Team

The Ever-Present Threat of Organizational Decline

Sadly, there are many examples of organizational decline and failure in the wake of the recent corporate scandals and the continuing pressure of globalization. (General Motors and Ford have been especially hard hit by the latter trend.)[45] Some failed because of illegal acts. Enron, for one, had the dubious honor of going from number seven on the 2001 *Fortune* 500 list to bankruptcy within a single year! During that time, Enron shareholders saw their shares plummet from $83 a share to 67 cents, when the stock was finally delisted. Thousands of Enron jobs evaporated and employee retirement plans and dreams were wiped out.[46] Other companies have tripped over strategic blunders and bad luck (see the Real World/Real People feature on page 513). Although the problems at these particular companies varied, both of them turned the corner from success to decline rather suddenly and dramatically.[47] Donald N Sull, a strategy professor at the London Business School, added this perspective:

> One of the most common business phenomena is also one of the most perplexing: when successful companies face big changes in their environment, they often fail to respond effectively. Unable to defend themselves against competitors armed with new products, technologies, or strategies, they watch their sales and profits erode, their best people leave, and their stock valuations tumble. Some ultimately manage to recover—usually after painful rounds of downsizing and restructuring—but many don't.[48]

Organizational decline
Decrease in organization's resource base (money, customers, talent, innovations).

Researchers call this downward spiral **organizational decline** and define it as "a decrease in an organization's resource base."[49] The term *resource* is used very broadly in this context, encompassing money, talent, customers, and innovative ideas and products. Managers seeking to maintain organizational effectiveness need to be alert to the problem because experts tell us "decline is almost unavoidable unless deliberate steps are taken to prevent it."[50] The first key step is to recognize the early warning signs of organizational decline.

Early Warning Signs of Decline Short of illegal conduct, there are 14 early warning signs of organizational decline:

1. Excess personnel.
2. Tolerance of incompetence.
3. Cumbersome administrative procedures.
4. Disproportionate staff power (e.g., technical staff specialists politically overpower line managers, whom they view as unsophisticated and too conventional).
5. Replacement of substance with form (e.g., the planning process becomes more important than the results achieved).
6. Scarcity of clear goals and decision benchmarks.
7. Fear of embarrassment and conflict (e.g., formerly successful executives may resist new ideas for fear of revealing past mistakes).
8. Loss of effective communication.
9. Outdated organizational structure.[51]
10. Increased scapegoating by leaders.

We hope you'll find the OLC easy to navigate and find exactly what you are looking for. A sampling of some of the features that you'll find at www.mhhe.com/kreitner is shown here. In our supplements section of this guide, we've outlined other features of the OLC as well.

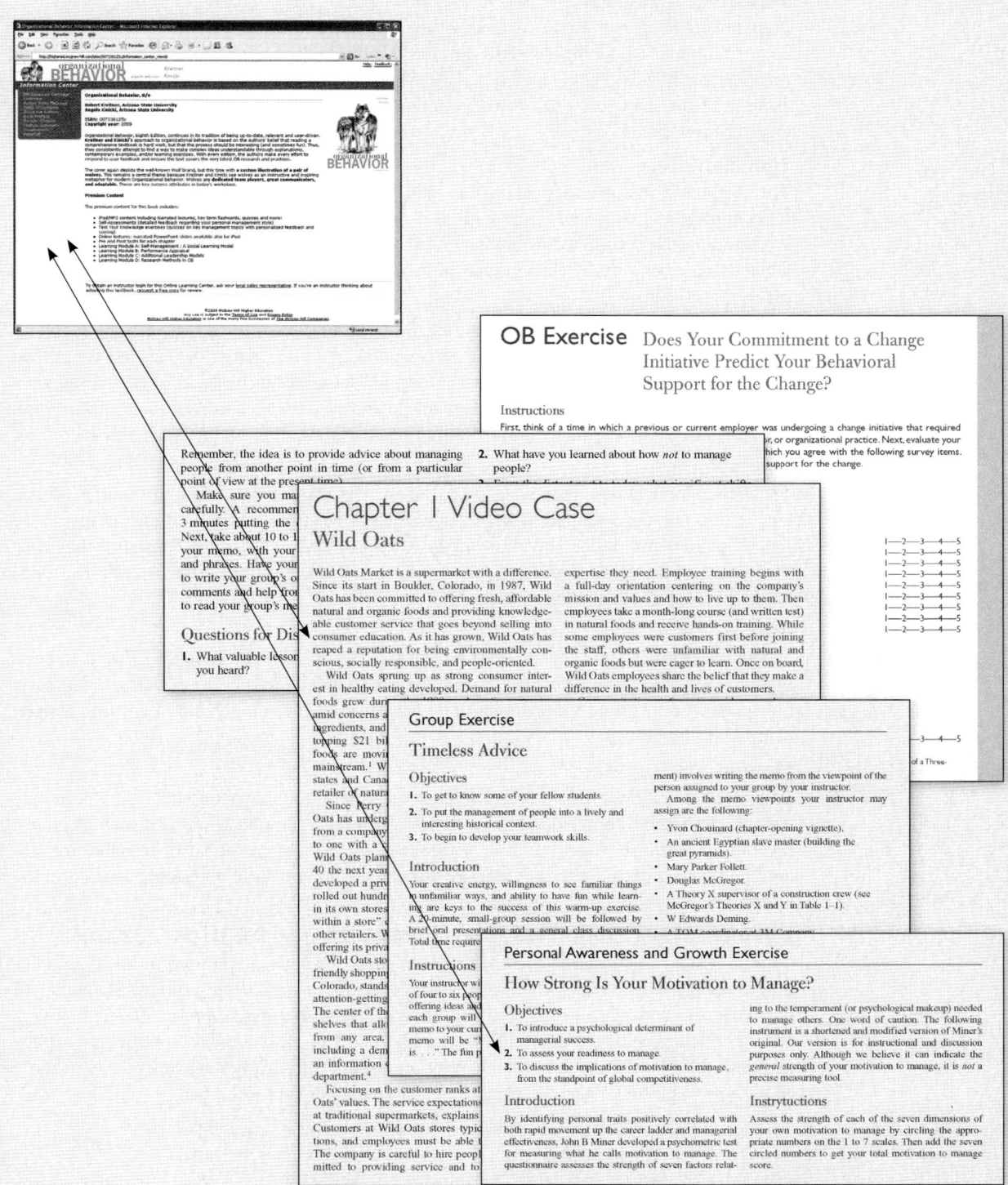

Comprehensive Supplements for Instructors and Students

Instructor's Resource CD
The all-in-one IRCD (13 ISBN: 9780073337272; 10 ISBN: 0073337277) includes the Instructor's Manual, Test Bank, EZ Test, and PowerPoint.

Instructor's Manual
Prepared by Professor Bryan Bonner of the University of Utah, each chapter includes a chapter summary, opening-vignette solution, lecture outline, discussion question solutions for Real World/Real People boxed inserts, OB in Action Case solution, notes on using the exercises from the OLC, one or two lecturettes, additional exercises, and integrative video case teaching notes.

Test Bank
The test bank includes approximately 100 test questions per chapter, including true-false, multiple choice, and essay with answers, page references, and Bloom's Taxonomy level coding. New to this edition, each test question will also be tagged to the Learning Objective it covers in the chapter and the AACSB Learning Standard it falls under.

EZ Test
McGraw-Hill's flexible and easy-to-use electronic testing program allows instructors to create tests from book-specific items. It accommodates a wide range of question types, and instructors may add their own questions. Multiple versions of the test can be created, and any test can be exported for use with course management systems such as WebCT or BlackBoard. EZ Test Online allows you to administer EZ Test-created exams and quizzes online.

PowerPoint
The PowerPoint slides have been prepared by Professor Paige Wolf of George Mason University and are designed to be meaningful lessons for students that encourage active thinking and participation and allow the instructor to have at his or her fingertips the information he or she wants to convey for each slide. eInstruction discussion questions (CPS) are included in the PowerPoint slides.

Videos
Videos are available on DVD (13 ISBN: 9780073337289; 10 ISBN: 0073337285), and one video is provided for each of the 18 chapters. Each video has a corresponding video case, now posted at the OLC. Video topics and companies feature timely and interesting people, companies, and issues.

Manager's Hot Seat
This interactive, video-based software puts students in the manager's hot seat where they have to apply their knowledge to make decisions on the spot on hot issues such as ethics, diversity, working in teams, and the virtual workplace. This resource is available for student purchase with the Kreitner text. Resources to support these videos are located in the Group and Video Resource Manual.

BusinessWeek Edition (13 ISBN: 9787229214; 10 ISBN: 0077229215)
Your students can subscribe to *BusinessWeek* for a specially priced rate of $8.25 in addition to the price of the text when instructors order the *BusinessWeek* edition. Students will receive a pass code shrink-wrapped with their new text. The card directs students to a Web site where they enter the code and then gain access to *BusinessWeek*'s registration page to enter address info and set up their print and online subscription as well. To learn more about how to get this package, please contact your sales representative.

Enhanced Cartridge with iPod Content

The Enhanced Cartridge is developed to help you get your course up and running in WebCT, BlackBoard, and other course management systems. The content, enhanced with more assignments and more study materials than a standard cartridge, is **prepopulated** into appropriate chapters and content categories. Now there's not a need to cut and paste our content into your course—it's already there! But, you can still choose to hide content we provide and add your own – just as you have before in WebCT and BlackBoard.

Every Enhanced Cartridge contains iPod/MP3 content, chapter pre-and post-tests, discussion boards, additional assignments, personalized graphics/banners/icons for your school, and grade book functionality.

The enhanced cartridge with iPod content will either be sold with a password card included in the book, or students can purchase the content via the book's Web site www.mhhe.com/kreitner for just $10.

Online Learning Center

The Online Learning Center (OLC), www.mhhe.com/kreitner, is a Web site that follows the text chapter-by-chapter. As noted earlier, students will be encouraged to visit the OLC at certain points in the chapter for Self and Group exercises. They will also be able to take self-grading quizzes, review chapter material, and work through interactive exercises. Also included are the popular Test Your Knowledge exercises and Self-Assessment Quizzes from the Group and Video Resource Manual and additional Learning Modules A–D. Professors and students can access all of this information in a variety of ways: directly through www.mhhe.com/kreitner, through PageOut, or within a course management system.

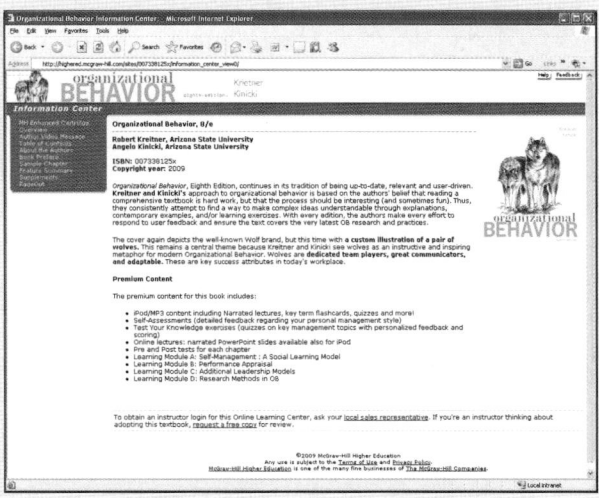

Group and Video Resource Manual: An Instructor's Guide to an Active Classroom (13 ISBN: 9780073044347; ISBN: 0073044342)

This manual for instructors created by co-author Angelo Kinicki contains everything needed to successfully integrate activities into your classroom. It is organized into 25 topics such as ethics, decision making, change, and leadership for easy inclusion in your lecture. Included are 20 Self-Assessment Exercises, 38 Test Your Knowledge quizzes, 23 Group Exercises, and 15 of the Manager's Hot Seat Video exercises all located in one manual along with teaching notes and PowerPoint slides.

Page Out

PageOut is McGraw-Hill's unique point-and-click course Web site tool, enabling you to create a full-featured, professional-quality course Web site without knowing HTML coding. With PageOut you can post your syllabus online, assign McGraw-Hill Online Learning Center or eBook content, add links to important off-site resources, and maintain student results in the online grade book. You can send class announcements, copy your course site to share with colleagues, and upload original files. PageOut is free for every McGraw-Hill/Irwin user.

McGraw-Hill Primis Online Digital Database

You can customize this text. McGraw-Hill Primis Online digital database offers you the flexibility to customize your course, including the material from the largest online collection of textbooks, readings, and cases. Primis leads the way in customized eBooks with hundreds of titles available at prices that save your students more than 20% off bookstore prices. Additional information is available at 800-228-0634.

Words of Appreciation

This textbook is the fruit of many people's labor. Our colleagues at Arizona State University have been supportive from the start. Through the years, our organizational behavior students at ASU, Thunderbird, and the University of Tirana (Albania) have been enthusiastic and candid academic "customers." We are grateful for their feedback and we hope we have done it justice in this new edition. Sincere appreciation goes to Bryan Bonner of the University of Utah, for his skillful and dedicated work on the *Instructor's Resource Manual* and *Test Bank.* Thank you to Paige Wolf of George Mason University for creating the unique and dynamic PowerPoint presentation. Thank you to Natalie Giboney of freelancepermissions.com for a very professional job of managing our permissions.

To the manuscript reviewers spanning the prior seven editions go our gratitude and thanks. Their feedback was thoughtful, rigorous, constructive, and above all, essential to our goal of *kaizen* (continuous improvement). Our reviewers and focus group participants for this edition were:

Berrin Erdogan
Portland State University

Bryan Bonner
University of Utah-Salt Lake City

Christy Weer
Radford University

Denise Potosky
Penn State University-Malvern

Ed Von Leffern
California State Poly University-Pomona

Floyd Ormsbee
Clarkson University

Holly Schroth
University of California-Berkeley

John Bingham
Brigham Young University-Provo

Leslie Shore
Metropolitan State University

Michael Scheuermann
Drexel University

Tom Keefe
Indiana University Southeast

Lynda Fuller
Wilmington College – New Castle

Janet Henquinet
Metropolitan State University

Howard Rudd
College of Charleston

Amelia Island Focus Group Participants:

Stella Anderson
Appalachian State University

Dick Blackburn
University of North Carolina

Deborah Butler
Georgia State University

Mark Cordano
Ithaca College

Dick DeFrank
University of Houston

Marty Fogelman
SUNY Albany

Nell Hartley
Robert Morris University

Mathew Hayward
University of Colorado at Boulder

John Keeling
Old Dominion University

Floyd Ormsbee
Clarkson University

Denise Potosky
Penn State University

Paul Timm
Brigham Young University

Special thanks go to our dedicated "pack" at McGraw-Hill/Irwin: Our editors, John Weimeister, Donielle Xu, and Heather Darr; our marketing manager, Margaret Beamer; and our design and production team, Cara David, Dana Pauley, Lynn Bluhm, Greg Bates, Michael McCormick, Jeremy Cheshareck, and Jen Blankenship.

Finally, we would like to thank our wives, Margaret and Joyce, for being tough and caring "first customers" of our work. This book has been greatly enhanced by their common sense, reality testing, and managerial experience. Thanks in large measure to their love and moral support, this project again was completed on time and it strengthened rather than strained a treasured possession–our friendship.

We hope you enjoy this textbook. Best wishes for success and happiness!

Bob Kreitner
Angelo Kinicki

Brief Contents

Contents

xxiii

Chapter Twelve
Individual and Group Decision Making   334

Chapter Thirteen
Managing Conflict and Negotiation   368

Part I

The World of Organizational Behavior

CHAPTER 1

Organizational Behavior: The Quest for People-Centered Organizations and Ethical Conduct

BusinessWeek Southern Californian Scott Robinson had quite a résumé when he returned from studying in France last Christmas. The 26-year-old had an undergraduate degree from Bucknell University, two MBAs, and internships at two of Europe's most respected corporations, Nestlé and Unilever Group. Yet, when it came time to take the next career step, he chose a job as a stock handler in a surf shop in Cardiff-by-the-Sea, California. Actually, he begged for the job. What gives? Simple, he says: "I wanted to work for a company that's driven by values."

The company is Patagonia Inc., a Ventura, California seller of outdoor clothing and equipment that has a reputation as an enlightened employer and champion of the environment. On his return from France, Robinson read *Let My People Go Surfing,* a memoir and manifesto of sustainable business practices by Patagonia founder and chairman Yvon Chouinard. The company's goal is as simple as it is challenging: to produce the highest-quality products while doing the least possible harm to the environment.

That mission is a daily inspiration for Patagonia's 1,275 employees, from Chouinard to the flip-flop-wearing guy who answers the phone in the headquarters lobby. Most corporate mission statements are empty platitudes. This one guides every decision. And it's the centerpiece of a set of management practices that have helped Patagonia grow at a healthy rate and retain what is arguably the best reputation in its industry even while it faces increasing competition from much larger companies.

Patagonia's philosophy is the handiwork of Chouinard, a gruff yet funny outdoorsman who,

despite his 67 years and arthritic hands, hasn't slowed down much. He helped pioneer modern rock-climbing techniques in his youth and now prowls the globe in search of outdoor adventures and product ideas. That is, when he's not shaking up his 33-year-old company, helping to preserve the environment, or advocating radical changes in the way Americans do business. "Most people want to do good things, but don't. At Patagonia, it's an essential part of your life," says Chouinard.

At a time when companies must adapt to an ever-quickening competitive pace, a highly motivated workforce can provide a crucial edge. Until now,

People line up to work at outdoor clothing and equipment maker Patagonia, founded by Yvon Chouinard (pictured here).

there have been two primary approaches to keeping employees at the top of their game. At the high-stress workplace, bosses rule by fear, kicking ass, and taking names. At feel-good places, managers try to motivate employees with kind words and generous benefits. Neither approach is optimal. In a recent Gallup poll, only one-third of Americans considered themselves passionate about their jobs.

A few companies have found a better way. "There are companies that stress continuous improvement and being way better than the competition but also make people feel comfortable," says Stanford University professor Jeffrey Pfeffer. These companies range from publicly traded giants such as FedEx and Southwest Airlines to a small fry like Patagonia. They are meritocracies with ambitious goals that trust their employees to do the right thing—and give them the tools and time they need to do it.

Patagonia, with 39 stores in seven countries, works hard at achieving that delicate balance. It offers an on-site day-care center at its headquarters and full medical benefits to all employees, including part-timers. When the surf's up, Chouinard himself urges people to hit the beach. At the same time, the company demands hard work, creativity, collaboration, and results. Management isn't shy about axing employees who aren't up to snuff. . . .

Patagonia enjoys an unrivaled reputation among outdoor aficionados, and its green philosophy is gaining broader appeal as more Americans embrace sustainable consumption. Chouinard's goal for Patagonia's own sustainability: "I look at this company as an experiment to see if we can run it so it's here 100 years from now and always makes the best-quality stuff," he says. That means keeping growth relatively slow but steady, at about 5% per year. Revenues were up a healthy 7% last year, to $260 million. Operating margins typically come in at the high end of the 12% to 15% industry average, according to people who have seen the numbers, and that's after it donates 1% of revenues to environmental groups. Patagonia, which declined to comment on its financials, is owned by a Chouinard family trust. . . .

Few Patagonians are in it just for the money. The company recently raised salaries to adjust for the cost of living, and everybody gets an annual bonus based on profits, but, overall, Patagonia pays at, or just slightly above, the market rate. However, the most significant rewards aren't monetary. One popular perk is a program that allows employees to take off up to two months at full pay and work for environmental groups. Lisa Myers, who works on the company's giving programs, tracked wolves in Yellowstone National Park during her sabbatical. The company also pays 50% of her college expenses as she pursues a wildlife biology degree. "It's easy to go to work when you get paid to do what you love to do," she says.

Patagonia's culture makes it a magnet for talented people. The company receives an average of 900 résumés for every job opening, so it can afford to be picky. . . .

Can others capture some of Patagonia's magic? Most companies—especially ones with demanding public shareholders—simply can't let employees take a surfing break. They can, however, foster creativity and provide a sense of purpose. Perhaps the most valuable and easily applied lesson from Patagonia's experience is this: To think outside the box, sometimes you need to get out of the cubicle.[1]

FOR DISCUSSION

Why aren't more companies managed like Patagonia?

Patagonia's leaders do more than talk about the importance of their people; they trust, empower, and listen to them. They have created what Stanford University's Jeffrey Pfeffer calls a "people-centered" organization. Research evidence from companies in both the United States and Germany shows the following seven *people-centered practices* to be strongly associated with much higher profits and significantly lower employee turnover:

1. Job security (to eliminate fear of layoffs).
2. Careful hiring (emphasizing a good fit with the company culture).
3. Power to the people (via decentralization and self-managed teams).
4. Generous pay for performance.
5. Lots of training.

6. Less emphasis on status (to build a "we" feeling).

7. Trust building (through the sharing of critical information).[2]

Importantly, these factors are a *package* deal, meaning they need to be installed in a coordinated and systematic manner—not in bits and pieces.

According to Pfeffer, only 12% of today's organizations have the systematic approaches and persistence to qualify as true people-centered organizations, thus giving them a competitive advantage.[3] James McNerney, CEO of aircraft maker Boeing, knows what it takes. He recently told *Fortune* magazine:

> I start with people's growth, my own growth included. I don't start with the company's strategy or products. I start with people's growth because I believe that if the people who are running and participating in a company grow, then the company's growth will in many respects take care of itself.[4]

To us, an 88% shortfall in the quest for people-centered organizations represents a tragic waste of human and economic potential. There are profound ethical implications as well. Each of us needs to accept the challenge to do better, whatever our role(s) in society—employer/entrepreneur, employee, manager, stockholder, student, teacher, voter, elected official, social/political activist. Toward that end, the mission of this book is to help increase the number of people-centered and ethically managed organizations around the world to improve the general quality of life.[5]

The purpose of this first chapter is to define organizational behavior (OB); examine its contemporary relevance; explore its historical, managerial, and ethical contexts; and introduce a topical roadmap for the balance of this book.

Welcome to the World of OB

Organizational behavior deals with how people act and react in organizations of all kinds. Think of the many organizations that touch your life on a regular basis; organizations that employ, educate, serve, inform, feed, heal, protect, and entertain you. Cradle to grave, we interface with organizations at every turn. According to Chester I Barnard's classic definition, an **organization** is "a system of consciously coordinated activities or forces of two or more persons."[6] Organizations are a social invention helping us to achieve things collectively that we could not achieve alone. For better or for worse, they extend our reach. Consider the inspiring example of the World Health Organization (WHO):

> In 1967, 10 to 15 million people around the globe were struck annually by smallpox. That year, the World Health Organization set up its smallpox-eradication unit. In 13 years it was able to declare the world free of the disease. In 1988, 350,000 people were afflicted by polio when the WHO set up a similar eradication unit. Since then it has spent $3 billion and received the help of 20 million volunteers from around the world. The result: in 2003 there were only 784 reported cases of polio.[7]

On the other hand, organizations such as *Al Qaeda* kill and terrorize, and others such as Enron squander our resources. Organizations are the chessboard upon which the game of life is played. To know more about *organizational* behavior—life within organizations—is to know more about the nature, possibilities, and rules of that game.

1 Organizational Behavior: An Interdisciplinary Field

Organizational behavior, commonly referred to as OB, is an interdisciplinary field dedicated to better understanding and managing people at work. By definition, organizational

Organization
System of consciously coordinated activities of two or more people.

Organizational behavior
Interdisciplinary field dedicated to better understanding and managing people at work.

behavior is both research and application oriented. Three basic levels of analysis in OB are individual, group, and organizational. OB draws upon a diverse array of disciplines, including psychology, management, sociology, organization theory, social psychology, statistics, anthropology, general systems theory, economics, information technology, political science, vocational counseling, human stress management, psychometrics, ergonomics, decision theory, and ethics. This rich heritage has spawned many competing perspectives and theories about human work behavior. By 2003, one researcher had identified 73 distinct theories about behavior within the field of OB.[8]

Some FAQs about Studying OB

Through the years we (and our colleagues) have fielded some frequently asked questions (FAQs) from our students about our field. Here are the most common ones, along with our answers.

Why Study OB?
If you thoughtfully study this book, you will learn more about yourself, how to interact effectively with others, and how to thrive (not just survive) in organizations. Lots of insights about your own personality, emotions, values, job satisfaction, perceptions, needs, and goals are available in Part Two. Relative to your interpersonal effectiveness, you will learn about being a team player, building trust, managing conflict, negotiating, communicating, and influencing and leading others. We conclude virtually every major topic with practical how-to-do-it instructions. The idea is to build your skills in areas such as self-management, making ethical decisions, avoiding groupthink, listening, coping with organizational politics, handling change, and managing stress. Respected OB scholar Edward E Lawler III created the "virtuous career spiral" in Figure 1–1 to illustrate how OB-related skills point you toward career success. "It shows that increased skills and performance can lead to better jobs and higher rewards."[9]

If I'm an Accounting (or Other Technical Major), Why Should I Study OB?
Many students in technical fields such as accounting, finance, computer science, and engineering consider OB to be a "soft" discipline with little or no relevance. You may indeed start out in a narrow specialty, but eventually your hard-won success will catch up with you and you will be tapped for some sort of supervisory or leadership position. Your so-called "soft" people skills will make or break your career at that point. Also, in today's team-oriented and globalized workplace, your teamwork, cross-cultural, communication, conflict handling, and negotiation skills and your powers of persuasion will be needed early and often. Jack Welch, the legendary CEO of General Electric, and Suzy Welch, the former editor of *Harvard Business Review,* recently offered this answer to a business school professor's question about how best to prepare students for today's global business environment:

> We'd make the case that the nitty-gritty of managing people should rank higher in the educational hierarchy. In the past two years we've visited 35 B-schools around the world and have been repeatedly surprised by how little classroom attention is paid to hiring, motivating, team-building, and firing. Instead, B-schools seem far more invested in teaching brainiac concepts—disruptive technologies, complexity modeling, and the like. Those may be useful, particularly if you join a consulting firm, but real managers need to know how to get the most out of people. . . .
>
> We hope you have the clout to make sure people management is front and center at your university. If you do, you'll launch your students' careers with a real head start.[10]

Figure 1–1   *OB-Related Skills Are the Ticket to Ride the Virtuous Career Spiral*

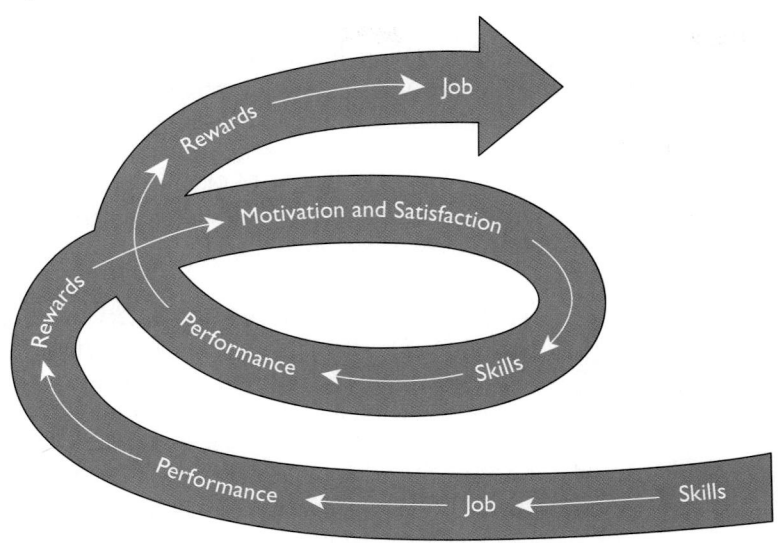

Can I Get a Job in OB? Organizational behavior is an academic designation. With the exception of teaching/research positions, OB is not an everyday job category such as accounting, marketing, or finance. Students of OB typically do not get jobs in organizational behavior, per se. This reality in no way demeans OB or lessens its importance in effective organizational management. OB is a *horizontal* discipline cutting across virtually every job category, business function, and professional specialty. Anyone who plans to make a living in a large or small, public or private, organization needs to study organizational behavior.

A Historical Perspective of OB

A historical perspective of the study of people at work helps in studying organizational behavior. According to a management history expert, this is important because

> Historical perspective is the study of a subject in light of its earliest phases and subsequent evolution. Historical perspective differs from history in that the object of historical perspective is to sharpen one's vision of the present, not the past.[11]

In other words, we can better understand where the field of OB is today and where it appears to be headed by appreciating where it has been and how it is being redirected.[12] Let us examine four significant landmarks in the understanding and management of people in the workplace.

1. The human relations movement.
2. The quality movement.
3. The e-business revolution.
4. The age of human and social capital.

The Human Relations Movement

A unique combination of factors during the 1930s fostered the human relations movement. First, following legalization of union–management collective bargaining in the United States in 1935, management began looking for new ways of handling employees. Second, behavioral scientists conducting on-the-job research started calling for more attention to the "human" factor. Managers who had lost the battle to keep unions out of their factories heeded the call for better human relations and improved working conditions. One such study, conducted at Western Electric's Chicago-area Hawthorne plant, was a prime stimulus for the human relations movement. Ironically, many of the Hawthorne findings have turned out to be more myth than fact.

These relay assembly test room employees in the classic Hawthorne Western Electric studies turned in record performance. Why? No one knows for certain, and debate continues to this day. Supportive supervision was long believed to be the key factor. Whatever the reason, Hawthorne gave the budding human relations movement needed research credibility.

The Hawthorne Legacy Interviews conducted decades later with three subjects of the Hawthorne studies and reanalysis of the original data with modern statistical techniques do not support initial conclusions about the positive effect of supportive supervision. Specifically, money, fear of unemployment during the Great Depression, managerial discipline, and high-quality raw materials—not supportive supervision—turned out to be responsible for high output in the relay assembly test room experiments.[13] Nonetheless, the human relations movement gathered momentum through the 1950s, as academics and managers alike made stirring claims about the powerful effect that individual needs, supportive supervision, and group dynamics apparently had on job performance.

The Writings of Mayo and Follett Essential to the human relations movement were the writings of Elton Mayo and Mary Parker Follett. Australian-born Mayo, who headed the Harvard researchers at Hawthorne, advised managers to attend to employees' emotional needs in his 1933 classic, *The Human Problems of an Industrial Civilization.* Follett was a true pioneer, not only as a woman management consultant in the male-dominated industrial world of the 1920s, but also as a writer who saw employees as complex combinations of attitudes, beliefs, and needs. Mary Parker Follett was way ahead of her time in telling managers to motivate job performance instead of merely demanding it, a "pull" rather than "push" strategy. She also built a logical bridge between political democracy and a cooperative spirit in the workplace.[14]

McGregor's Theory Y In 1960, Douglas McGregor wrote a book entitled *The Human Side of Enterprise,* which has become an important philosophical base for the modern view of people at work.[15] Drawing upon his experience as a management consultant, McGregor formulated two sharply contrasting sets of assumptions about human nature (see Table 1–1). His Theory X assumptions were pessimistic and negative and, according to McGregor's interpretation, typical of how managers traditionally perceived employees. To help managers break with this negative tradition, McGregor formulated his **Theory Y,** a modern and positive set of assumptions about people. McGregor believed managers could accomplish more through others by viewing them as self-energized, committed, responsible, and creative beings.[16]

Theory Y

McGregor's modern and positive assumptions about employees being responsible and creative.

Table 1-1   *McGregor's Theory X and Theory Y*

OUTDATED (THEORY X) ASSUMPTIONS ABOUT PEOPLE AT WORK	MODERN (THEORY Y) ASSUMPTIONS ABOUT PEOPLE AT WORK
1. Most people dislike work; they avoid it when they can.	1. Work is a natural activity, like play or rest.
2. Most people must be coerced and threatened with punishment before they will work. People require close direction when they are working.	2. People are capable of self-direction and self-control if they are committed to objectives.
3. Most people actually prefer to be directed. They tend to avoid responsibility and exhibit little ambition. They are interested only in security.	3. People generally become committed to organizational objectives if they are rewarded for doing so.
	4. The typical employee can learn to accept and seek responsibility.
	5. The typical member of the general population has imagination, ingenuity, and creativity.

SOURCE: Adapted from D McGregor, *The Human Side of Enterprise,* McGraw-Hill, © 1960, Ch 4. Reprinted by permission of The McGraw-Hill Companies, Inc.

According to this overview from *HR Magazine,* McGregor's Theory Y is still a distant vision in the American workplace:

> With strikingly similar statistics, several highly respected research and consulting organizations have found that there's a huge population of workers—roughly half of all Americans in the workforce—who show up, do what's expected of them, but don't go that extra mile, don't turn on the creative juices, don't get inspired to create great products or services.
>
> Perhaps the most significant finding: These are people, for the most part, who want to go above and beyond, to be an integral part of the company's success. Something— often a disconnect with an immediate supervisor or a feeling that the organization doesn't care about them—is getting in the way. There is a huge, untapped potential that many executives, managers and employees do not recognize and, therefore, have not addressed. And it's sapping organizations' potential.
>
> "We're running as an economy at 30% efficiency" because so many workers are not contributing as much as they could, says Curt Coffman [from the Gallup Organization].[17]

New Assumptions about Human Nature Unfortunately, unsophisticated behavioral research methods caused the human relationists to embrace some naive and misleading conclusions.[18] For example, human relationists believed in the axiom, "A satisfied employee is a hardworking employee." Subsequent research, as discussed later in this book, shows the satisfaction—performance linkage to be more complex than originally thought.

Despite its shortcomings, the human relations movement opened the door to more progressive thinking about human nature. Rather than continuing to view employees as passive economic beings, managers began to see them as active social beings and took steps to create more humane work environments.

The Quality Movement

In 1980, NBC aired a television documentary titled "If Japan Can . . . Why Can't We?" It was a wake-up call for North American companies to dramatically improve product quality or continue losing market share to Japanese electronics and automobile companies. A full-fledged movement ensued during the 1980s and 1990s. Much was written, said, and done about improving the quality of both goods and services.[19] Thanks to the concept of *total quality management* (TQM) and Six Sigma programs, the quality of the goods and services we purchase today is significantly better than in years past. Six Sigma was developed in 1986 at Motorola by engineer Bill Smith to achieve an astounding 99.9997% quality target by eliminating defects and cutting waste. It was licensed to companies such as General Electric that became avid users. An estimated 35% of U.S. companies have adopted Six Sigma.

> Six Sigma, broadly speaking, expresses a way of thinking about business problems that encourages precision and predictability. The mantra of Six Sigma "black belts" is DMAIC, for "define, measure, analyze, improve, control." The "sigma" refers to the Greek letter, which in statistics is used to measure how far something deviates from perfection. The "six" comes from the goal to be no more than six standard deviations away from that perfect measure.[20]

The underlying principles of TQM and Six Sigma are more important than ever given customers' steadily rising expectations:

> Establish a reputation for great value, top quality, or pulling late-night miracles in time for crucial client meetings, and soon enough, the goalposts move. "Greatness" lasts only as long as someone fails to imagine something better. Inevitably, the exceptional becomes the expected.
>
> Call it the performance paradox: If you deliver, you only qualify to deliver more. Great companies and their employees have always endured this treadmill of expectations. But these days, the brewing forces of technology, productivity, and transparency have accelerated the cycle to breakneck speed.[21]

The quality movement has profound practical implications for managing people today.[22]

Total quality management

An organizational culture dedicated to training, continuous improvement, and customer satisfaction.

What Is TQM? Experts on the subject offered this definition of **total quality management:**

> TQM means that the organization's culture is defined by and supports the constant attainment of customer satisfaction through an integrated system of tools, techniques, and training. This involves the continuous improvement of organizational processes, resulting in high-quality products and services.[23]

Quality consultant Richard J Schonberger sums up TQM as "continuous, customer-centered, employee-driven improvement."[24] TQM is necessarily employee driven because product/service quality cannot be continuously improved without the active learning and participation of *every* employee. Thus, in successful quality improvement programs, TQM principles are embedded in the organization's culture. In fact, according to the results of a field experiment, bank customers had higher satisfaction after interacting with bank employees who had been trained to provide excellent service.[25]

Quality Is the Rx at New Jersey's Hackensack University Medical Center

In the ER—and throughout the 781-bed hospital—staff have scrutinized every process, looking for ways to save time and avoid errors. . . . [For instance, they] consolidated all the medications needed to treat a heart attack into one tackle box. They have reserved a stretcher just for patients with chest pain, to avoid making them wait.

Hospital staff review their cases daily, looking for the causes of any mistakes and delays.

By the time [patient David] Ferrell had his heart attack, the ER team had perfected its routine. . . . [They] shocked Ferrell back to life and performed an EKG, a test of his heart rhythm, only seven minutes after his arrival—three minutes sooner than the hospital's goal. Within 70 minutes, a cardiologist had inflated a balloon within the arteries around Ferrell's heart, clearing three blockages that had deprived his heart of oxygen. That's 20 minutes sooner than a Medicare pilot program's rigorous new goal.

Have you ever thought about quality improvement in such stark life-and-death terms before?

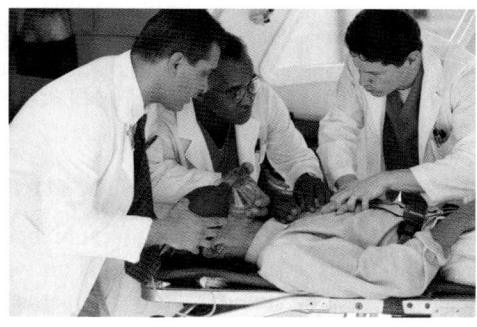

SOURCE: Excerpted from L Szabo, "Hallmark of Quality Care: Efficiency," *USA Today,* October 20, 2006, p 3B.

The Deming Legacy Quality is in the corporate DNA today thanks in large part to the pioneering work of W Edwards Deming.[26] Ironically, the mathematician credited with Japan's post–World War II quality revolution rarely talked in terms of quality. He instead preferred to discuss "good management" during the hard-hitting seminars he delivered right up until his death at age 93 in 1993.[27] Although Deming's passion was the statistical measurement and reduction of variations in industrial processes, he had much to say about how employees should be treated. Regarding the human side of quality improvement, Deming called for the following:

- Formal training in statistical process control techniques and teamwork.
- Helpful leadership, rather than order giving and punishment.
- Elimination of fear so employees will feel free to ask questions.
- Emphasis on continuous process improvements rather than on numerical quotas.
- Teamwork.
- Elimination of barriers to good workmanship.[28]

One of Deming's most enduring lessons for managers is his 85–15 rule.[29] Specifically, when things go wrong, there is roughly an 85% chance the *system* (including management, machinery, and rules) is at fault. Only about 15% of the time is the individual employee at fault. Unfortunately, as Deming observed, the typical manager spends most of his or her time wrongly blaming and punishing individuals for system failures. Statistical analysis is required to uncover system failures.

2 **Principles of TQM** Despite variations in the language and scope of TQM programs, it is possible to identify four common TQM principles:

1. Do it right the first time to eliminate costly rework and product recalls.

2. Listen to and learn from customers and employees.

3. Make continuous improvement an everyday matter (see Real World/Real People on page 11).

4. Build teamwork, trust, and mutual respect.[30]

Deming's influence is clearly evident in this list. Once again, as with the human relations movement, we see *people* as the key factor in organizational success.

In summary, TQM advocates have made a valuable contribution to the field of OB by providing a *practical* context for managing people. The case for TQM is strong because, as discovered in two comprehensive studies, *it works!*[31] When people are managed according to TQM principles, more of them are likely to get the employment opportunities and high-quality goods and services they demand.[32] As you will see many times in later chapters, this book is anchored to Deming's philosophy and TQM principles.

 # 3 The Internet and E-Business Revolution

E-business

Running the *entire* business via the Internet.

Experts on the subject draw an important distinction between *e-commerce* (buying and selling goods and services over the Internet) and **e-business,** using the Internet to facilitate *every* aspect of running a business.[33] Says one industry observer: "Strip away the highfalutin talk, and at bottom, the Internet is a tool that dramatically lowers the cost of communication. That means it can radically alter any industry or activity that depends heavily on the flow of information."[34] Relevant information includes everything from customer needs and product design specifications to prices, schedules, finances, employee performance data, and corporate strategy. Intel has taken this broad view of the Internet to heart. The computer-chip giant is striving to become what it calls an e-corporation, one that relies primarily on the Internet to not only buy and sell things, but to facilitate all business functions, exchange knowledge among its employees, and build partnerships with outsiders as well. Intel is on the right track according to this survey finding: "firms that embraced the Internet averaged a 13.4% jump in productivity . . . compared with 4.9% for those that did not."[35]

E-business has significant implications for OB because it eventually will seep into every corner of life both on and off the job. Thanks to Web 2.0, we are empowered to be in more than one place at once and collaborate at will. *BusinessWeek* recently offered this perspective:

> Web 2.0 portends a sea change on the Internet. Web 2.0 sites are not so much online places to visit as services to get something done, usually with other people. Call it the Live Web. From Yahoo! Inc.'s photo-sharing site Flickr to the group-edited online reference source Wikipedia to the teen hangout MySpace.com, they all demand active participation and social interaction. . . .
>
> As employees realize that Web 2.0-style networking and collaboration can help them in their jobs, they're slowly but surely starting to bring them inside the walls of their companies. . . .
>
> The young and the wired know the value of Web 2.0, but corporate executives will need to get a quick education. That's because the nature of these services will challenge the command-and-control mindset of the corporation, already in the throes of tech-driven transformations such as globalization and outsourcing. Web 2.0 could flatten a raft of organizational boundaries—between managers and employees and between the company and its partners and customers.[36]

In short, organizations and organizational life will never be the same because of e-mail, e-learning,[37] e-management, e-leadership (see Table 1–2), virtual teams, and virtual organizations.

Table 1–2   *The Brave New World of E-Leadership*

Because it involves electronically mediated interactions, in combination with the traditional face-to-face variety, experts say e-leadership raises these major issues for modern management:

1. Leaders and followers have more access to information and each other, and this is changing the nature and content of their interactions.

2. Leadership is migrating to lower and lower organizational levels and out through the boundaries of the organization to both customers and suppliers.

3. Leadership creates and exists in networks that go across traditional organizational and community boundaries.

4. Followers know more at earlier points in the decision-making process, and this is potentially affecting the credibility and influence of leaders.

5. Unethical leaders with limited resources can now impact negatively a much broader audience of potential followers.

6. The amount of time and contact that even the most senior leaders can have with their followers has increased, although the contact is not in the traditional face-to-face mode.

Making wise hiring and job assignment decisions, nurturing productive relationships, and building trust are more important than ever in the age of e-leadership.

SOURCE: Six implications excerpted from *Organizational Dynamics,* vol. 4, B J Avolio, and S S Kahai, "Adding the 'E' to E-Leadership: How It May Impact Your Leadership," p 333, © 2003, with permission from Elsevier.

 The Age of Human and Social Capital

Knowledge workers, those who add value by using their brains rather than the sweat off their backs, are more important than ever in today's global economy. What you know and whom you know increasingly are the keys to both personal and organizational success[38] (see Figure 1–2). In the United States, the following "perfect storm" of current and emerging trends heightens the importance and urgency of building human and social capital:

• Spread of advanced technology to developing countries with rapidly growing middle classes (e.g., China, India, Russia, and Brazil).

• Offshoring of increasingly sophisticated jobs (e.g., product design, architecture, medical diagnosis).

• Comparatively poor math and science skills among America's youth.

• Post-9/11 decline in highly skilled immigrants and graduate students.

• Massive brain drain caused by retiring post–World War II baby-boom generation.[39]

What Is Human Capital? (Hint: Think BIG) A team of human resource management authors recently offered this perspective:

We're living in a time when a new economic paradigm—characterized by speed, innovation, short cycle times, quality, and customer satisfaction—is highlighting the importance of intangible assets, such as brand recognition, knowledge, innovation, and particularly human capital.[40]

Figure 1–2   *The Strategic Importance and Dimensions of Human and Social Capital*

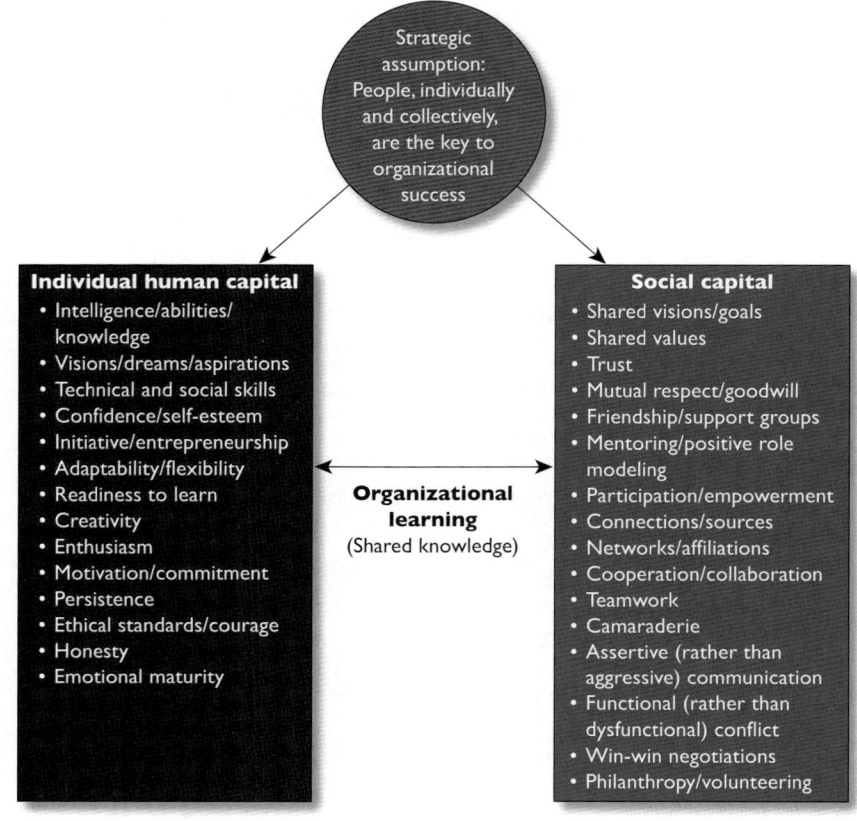

SOURCES: Based on discussions in P S Adler and S Kwon, "Social Capital: Prospects for a New Concept," *Academy of Management Review*, January 2002, pp 17–40; and C A Bartlett and S Ghoshal, "Building Competitive Advantage through People," *MIT Sloan Management Review*, Winter 2002, pp 34–41.

Human capital

The productive potential of one's knowledge and actions.

Human capital is the productive potential of an individual's knowledge and actions.[41] *Potential* is the operative word in this intentionally broad definition. When you are hungry, money in your pocket is good because it has the potential to buy a meal. Likewise, a present or future employee with the right combination of knowledge, skills, and motivation to excel represents human capital with the potential to give the organization a competitive advantage. Again Intel, a good example, is a high-tech company whose future depends on innovative engineering. It takes years of math and science studies to make world-class engineers. Not wanting to leave the future supply of engineers to chance, Intel annually spends millions of dollars funding education at all levels. The company encourages youngsters to study math and science and sponsors science competitions with generous scholarships for the winners.[42] Additionally, Intel encourages its employees to volunteer at local schools by giving the schools $200 for every 20 hours contributed.[43] Will all of the students end up working for Intel? No. That's not the point. The point is much bigger—namely, to build the *world's* human capital.

Social capital

The productive potential of strong, trusting, and cooperative relationships.

What Is Social Capital? Our focus now shifts from the individual to social units (e.g., friends, family, company, group or club, nation). Think *relationships*. **Social capital** is productive potential resulting from strong relationships, goodwill,

Bill Gates Tells How Microsoft Builds Social Capital Inside and Outside the Company

From the very earliest days at Microsoft, we used our United Way campaign to draw employees together and help them to see outside our world—to see the entire community and understand the needs of the most vulnerable people in it. We wanted to make this outward-looking worldview a part of our culture. In the last few years, we've developed a tool that helps our employees look for volunteer opportunities and instituted a program that matches their philanthropic giving. Last year, with these matching funds, the people at Microsoft donated more than $68 million and more than 100,000 hours of their own time. Many of the people who have volunteered and made donations have taken on major roles with charitable organizations. In the end, these experiences make them better employees.

Why is this outward-focused approach to building organizational social capital a good (or bad) idea?

SOURCE: Excerpted from Bill Gates, "The Way We Give," *Fortune*, January 22, 2007, pp 41–46.

Melinda and Bill Gates in Africa.

---

trust, and cooperative effort.[44] Again, the word *potential* is key. According to experts on the subject: "It's true: the social capital that used to be a given in organizations is now rare and endangered. But the social capital we can build will allow us to capitalize on the volatile, virtual possibilities of today's business environment."[45] Relationships do matter. In a general survey, 77% of the women and 63% of the men rated "Good relationship with boss" extremely important. Other factors—including good equipment, resources, easy commute, and flexible hours—received lower ratings.[46]

Building Human and Social Capital Various dimensions of human and social capital are listed in Figure 1–2. They are a preview of what lies ahead in this book, including our discussion of organizational learning in Chapter 17. Formal organizational learning and *knowledge management* programs, as discussed in Chapter 12, need social capital to leverage individual human capital for the greater good (see Real World/Real People). It is a straightforward formula for success. Growth depends on the timely sharing of valuable knowledge. After all, what good are bright employees who do not network, teach, and inspire? [47]

5 The Managerial Context: Getting Things Done with and through Others

Like the organizations they run, managers touch our lives in many ways. Schools, hospitals, government agencies, and large and small businesses all require systematic management. Formally defined, **management** is the process of working with and through others to achieve organizational objectives in an efficient and ethical manner. From the standpoint of organizational behavior, the central feature of this definition is "working with and through others." Managers play a constantly evolving role.[48] Today's successful managers are no longer the I've-got-everything-under-control

Management
Process of working with and through others to achieve organizational objectives efficiently and ethically.

order givers of yesteryear. Rather, they need to creatively envision and actively sell bold new directions in an ethical and people-friendly manner. Effective managers are team players empowered by the willing and active support of others who are driven by conflicting self-interests. Each of us has a huge stake in how well managers carry out their evolving role. Henry Mintzberg, a respected management scholar, observed: "No job is more vital to our society than that of the manager. It is the manager who determines whether our social institutions serve us well or whether they squander our talents and resources."[49]Consider the predicament of Europe's Airbus, as reported by *USA Today* in 2007:

> Missed deadlines can mean big losses and ruined careers. Airbus ... is running 22 months behind on production of its new A380 superjumbo jet, the company's flagship product. The delays have wrought senior management shake-ups at Airbus, canceled orders and untold millions of dollars in delay compensation [penalty payments] to customers.[50]

Airbus's main competitor Boeing, meanwhile, is thriving under the leadership of new CEO Jim McNerney. As always, quality of management makes a big difference.

Let us take a closer look at the skills managers need to perform and the future direction of management.

What Do Managers Do? A Skills Profile

Observational studies by Mintzberg and others have found the typical manager's day to be a fragmented collection of brief episodes.[51] Interruptions are commonplace, while large blocks of time for planning and reflective thinking are not. In one particular study, four top-level managers spent 63% of their time on activities lasting less than nine minutes each. Only 5% of the managers' time was devoted to activities lasting more than an hour.[52] But what specific skills do effective managers perform during their hectic and fragmented workdays?

Many attempts have been made over the years to paint a realistic picture of what managers do.[53] Diverse and confusing lists of managerial functions and roles have been suggested. Fortunately, a stream of research over the past 20 years by Clark Wilson and others has given us a practical and statistically validated profile of managerial *skills*[54] (see Table 1–3). Wilson's managerial skills profile focuses on 11 observable categories of managerial behavior. This is very much in tune with today's emphasis on managerial competency.[55] Wilson's unique skills-assessment technique goes beyond the usual self-report approach with its natural bias. In addition to surveying a given manager about his or her 11 skills, the Wilson approach also asks those who report directly to the manager to answer questions about their boss's skills. According to Wilson and his colleagues, the result is an assessment of skill *mastery,* not simply skill awareness.[56] The logic behind Wilson's approach is both simple and compelling. Who better to assess a manager's skills than the people who experience those behaviors on a day-to-day basis—those who report directly to the manager?

The Wilson managerial skills research yields four useful lessons:

1. Dealing effectively with *people* is what management is all about. The 11 skills in Table 1–3 constitute a goal creation/commitment/feedback/reward/accomplishment cycle with human interaction at every turn.

2. Managers with high skills mastery tend to have better subunit performance and employee morale than managers with low skills mastery.[57]

3. *Effective* female and male managers *do not* have significantly different skill profiles,[58] contrary to claims in the popular business press in recent years.[59]

Table 1–3   *Skills Exhibited by an Effective Manager*

1. **Clarifies goals and objectives** for everyone involved.
2. **Encourages participation,** upward communication, and suggestions.
3. **Plans and organizes** for an orderly work flow.
4. Has **technical and administrative expertise** to answer organization-related questions.
5. **Facilitates work** through team building, training, coaching, and support.
6. **Provides feedback** honestly and constructively.
7. **Keeps things moving** by relying on schedules, deadlines, and helpful reminders.
8. **Controls details** without being overbearing.
9. Applies reasonable **pressure for goal accomplishment.**
10. **Empowers and delegates** key duties to others while maintaining goal clarity and commitment.
11. **Recognizes good performance** with rewards and positive reinforcement.

SOURCES: Adapted from material in F Shipper, "A Study of the Psychometric Properties of the Managerial Skill Scales of the Survey of Management Practices," *Educational and Psychological Measurement,* June 1995, pp 468–79; and C L Wilson, *How and Why Effective Managers Balance Their Skills: Technical, Teambuilding, Drive* (Columbia, MD: Rockatech Multimedia Publishing, 2003).

4. At all career stages, *derailed* managers (those who failed to achieve their potential) tended to be the ones who *overestimated* their skill mastery (rated themselves higher than their employees did).[60] This prompted the following conclusion from the researcher: "when selecting individuals for promotion to managerial positions, those who are arrogant, aloof, insensitive, and defensive should be avoided."[61]

go to the Web for the Self-Exercise: How Strong Is Your Motivation to Manage?

6 21st-Century Managers

Today's workplace is indeed undergoing immense and permanent changes.[62] Organizations have been "reengineered" for greater speed, efficiency, and flexibility.[63] Teams are pushing aside the individual as the primary building block of organizations.[64] Command-and-control management is giving way to participative management and empowerment.[65] Ego-centered leaders are being replaced by customer-centered leaders. Employees increasingly are being viewed as internal customers. All this creates a mandate for a new kind of manager in the 21st century. After conducting a Gallup Organization survey of 80,000 managers and doing follow-up studies of the top performers, Marcus Buckingham came to this conclusion:

> I've found that while there are as many styles of management as there are managers, there is one quality that sets truly great

© 2002 Ted Goff

"So what's the problem with morale now?"

Copyright © 2002 Ted Goff. Reprinted with permission.

Table 1–4   *Evolution of the 21st-Century Manager*

	PAST MANAGERS	**FUTURE MANAGERS**
Primary role	Order giver, privileged elite, manipulator, controller	Facilitator, team member, teacher, advocate, sponsor, coach
Learning and knowledge	Periodic learning, narrow specialist	Continuous life-long learning, generalist with multiple specialties
Compensation criteria	Time, effort, rank	Skills, results
Cultural orientation	Monocultural, monolingual	Multicultural, multilingual
Primary source of influence	Formal authority	Knowledge (technical and interpersonal)
View of people	Potential problem	Primary resource; human capital
Primary communication pattern	Vertical	Multidirectional
Decision-making style	Limited input for individual decisions	Broad-based input for joint decisions
Ethical considerations	Afterthought	Forethought
Nature of interpersonal relationships	Competitive (win–lose)	Cooperative (win–win)
Handling of power and key information	Hoard and restrict access	Share and broaden access
Approach to change	Resist	Facilitate

managers apart from the rest: They discover what is unique about each person and then capitalize on it. Average managers play checkers, while great managers play chess. The difference? In checkers, all the pieces are uniform and move in the same way; they are interchangeable. You need to plan and coordinate their movements, certainly, but they all move at the same pace, on parallel paths. In chess, each type of piece moves in a different way, and you can't play if you don't know how each piece moves. More important, you won't win if you don't think carefully about how you move the pieces. Great managers know and value the unique abilities and even the eccentricities of their employees, and they learn how best to integrate them into a coordinated plan of attack.[66]

Table 1–4 contrasts the characteristics of past and future managers. As the balance of this book will demonstrate, the managerial shift in Table 1–4 is not just a good idea, it is an absolute necessity in the new workplace.

Contingency approach

Using management tools and techniques in a situationally appropriate manner; avoiding the one-best-way mentality.

The Contingency Approach to Management

Scholars have wrestled for many years with the problem of how best to apply the diverse and growing collection of management tools and techniques. Their answer is the contingency approach. The **contingency approach** calls for using management techniques in a situationally appropriate manner, instead of trying to rely on "one best way" or "one size fits all."

The contingency approach encourages managers to view organizational behavior within a situational context. According to this modern perspective, evolving situations, not hard-and-fast rules, determine when and where various management techniques are appropriate. Harvard's Clayton Christensen put it this way: "Many of the widely accepted principles of good management are only situationally appropriate."[67] For example, as discussed in Chapter 16, contingency researchers have determined that there is no single best style of leadership. Organizational behavior specialists embrace the contingency approach because it helps them realistically interrelate individuals, groups, and evolving circumstances inside and outside the organization.[68] Moreover, the contingency approach sends a clear message to managers in today's global economy: Carefully read the situation and then be flexible enough to adapt.

The Ethics Challenge

Here are six reasons to be concerned about business ethics:

- Bernard Ebbers, former CEO of WorldCom, serving a 25-year prison sentence for fraud and conspiracy.
- Jeffrey Skilling, former CEO of Enron, serving a 24-year prison sentence for securities fraud and insider trading.
- John Rigas, former CEO of Aldelphia Communications, serving a 15-year prison sentence for conspiracy and bank fraud.
- Sanjay Kumar, former CEO of Computer Associates, serving a 12-year prison sentence for securities fraud and obstruction of justice.
- Dennis Kozlowski, former CEO of Tyco, serving an 8-year prison sentence for grand larceny and falsifying business records.
- Andrew Fastow, former chief financial officer of Enron, serving a 6-year prison sentence for wire fraud.[69]

Thanks to the highly publicized criminal acts of these and other executives, corporate officers in the United States are now subject to high accountability standards and harsh penalties under the Sarbanes-Oxley Act of 2002.[70] The general public and elected officials (who have their own criminal hall of shame) have called for greater attention to ethical conduct. The challenge is immense because unethical behavior is pervasive.

A nationwide survey of 581 human resource professionals revealed that 62% of the respondents occasionally observed unethical behavior at their companies.[71] Unethical behavior occurs from the bottom to the top of organizations. For example, a survey of job applicants for executive positions indicated that 64% had been misinformed about the financial condition of potential employers, and 58% of these individuals were negatively affected by this misinformation.[72] It is very likely that some of these affected individuals moved their families and left their friends only to find out the promise of a great job in a financially stable organization was a lie. Job applicants, for their part, also have ethical lapses. An analysis of 2.6 million background checks by ADP Screening and Selection Services, revealed that "44% of applicants lied about their work histories, 41% lied about their education, and 23% falsified credentials or licenses."[73]

Experts estimated that US companies lose about $600 billion a year from unethical and criminal behavior.[74] Studies in the United States and the United Kingdom further demonstrated that corporate commitment to ethics can be profitable. Evidence

The Greening of Unilever

Under conventional notions of how to run a conglomerate like Unilever, CEO Patrick Cescau should wake up each morning with a laserlike focus: how to sell more soap and shampoo than Procter & Gamble Co. But ask Cescau about the $52 billion Dutch-British giant's biggest strategic challenges for the 21st century, and the conversation roams from water-deprived villages in Africa to the planet's warming climate.

The world is Unilever's laboratory. In Brazil, the company operates a free community laundry in a São Paulo slum, provides financing to help tomato growers convert to eco-friendly "drip" irrigation, and recycles 17 tons of waste annually at a toothpaste factory. Unilever funds a floating hospital that offers free medical care in Bangladesh, a nation with just 20 doctors for every 10,000 people. In Ghana, it teaches palm oil producers to reuse plant waste while providing potable water to deprived communities. In India, Unilever staff help thousands of women in remote villages start micro-enterprises. And responding to green activists, the company discloses how much carbon dioxide and hazardous waste its factories spew out around the world.

As Cescau sees it, helping such nations wrestle with poverty, water scarcity, and the effects of climate change is vital to staying competitive in coming decades. Some 40% of the company's sales and most of its growth now take place in developing nations. Unilever food products account for roughly 10% of the world's crops of tea and 30% of all spinach. It is also one of the world's biggest buyers of fish. As environmental regulations grow tighter around the world, Unilever must invest in green technologies or its leadership in packaged foods, soaps, and other goods could be imperiled. "You can't ignore the impact your company has on the community and environment," Cescau says. CEOs used to frame thoughts like these in the context of moral responsibility, he adds. But now, "it's also about growth and innovation. In the future, it will be the only way to do business."

Is all this an ethical high-water mark for corporations or just a slick public relations campaign?

SOURCE: Excerpted from P Engardio, "Beyond the Green Corporation," *BusinessWeek*, January 29, 2007, pp 50–64.

---

suggested that profitability is enhanced by a reputation for honesty and corporate citizenship.[75] Ethics can also impact the quality of people who apply to work in an organization. A recent online survey of 1,020 individuals indicated that 83% rated a company's record of business ethics as "very important" when deciding to accept a job offer. Only 2% rated it as "unimportant."[76]

Clearly, *everyone* needs to join in the effort to stem this tide of unethical conduct. There are a variety of individual and organizational factors that contribute to unethical behavior. OB is an excellent vantage point for better understanding and improving workplace ethics. If OB can provide insights about managing human work behavior, then it can teach us something about avoiding *misbehavior*.

Ethics

Study of moral issues and choices.

Ethics involves the study of moral issues and choices. It is concerned with right versus wrong, good versus bad, and the many shades of gray in supposedly black-and-white issues. Moral implications spring from virtually every decision, both on and off the job. Managers are challenged to have more imagination and the courage to do the right thing to make the world a better place (see Real World/Real People).

To enhance our understanding of ethics within an OB context, we will discuss (1) a global model of corporate social responsibility, (2) a model of individual ethical behavior, (3) general moral principles for managers, and (4) how to improve an organization's ethical climate.

Figure 1–3   *Carroll's Global Corporate Social Responsibility Pyramid*

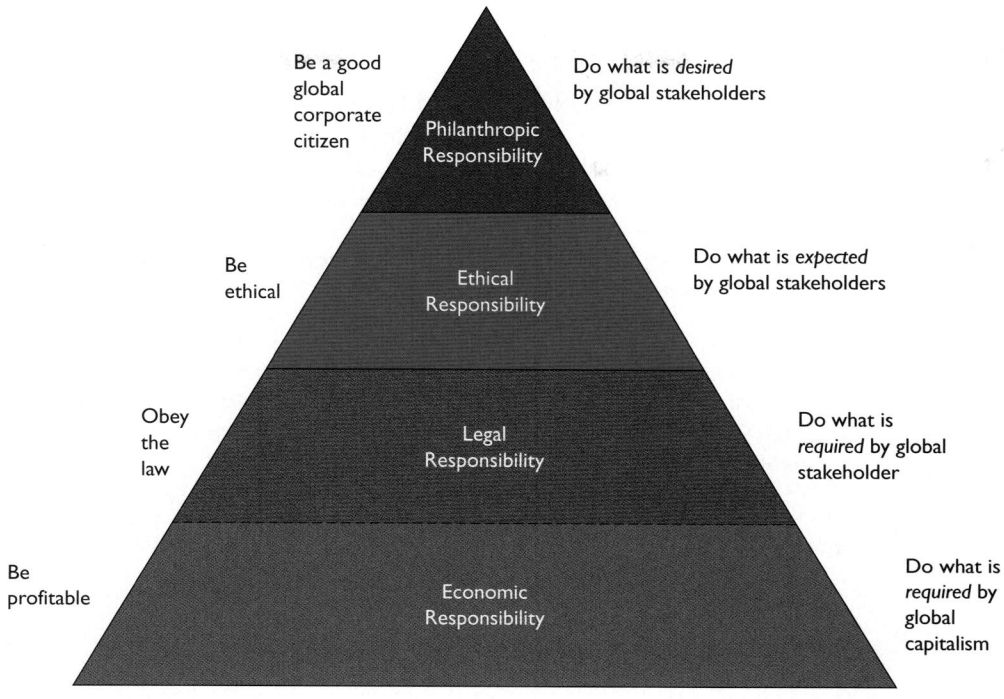

Be a good
global
corporate
citizen

Do what is *desired*
by global stakeholders

Philanthropic
Responsibility

Be
ethical

Do what is *expected*
by global stakeholders

Ethical
Responsibility

Obey
the
law

Do what is
required by global
stakeholder

Legal
Responsibility

Be
profitable

Do what is
required by
global
capitalism

Economic
Responsibility

7 A Global Model of Corporate Social Responsibility and Ethics

Corporate social responsibility (CSR) is defined as "the notion that corporations have an obligation to constituent groups in society other than stockholders and beyond that prescribed by law or union contract."[77] CSR challenges businesses to go above and beyond just making a profit to serve the interests and needs of "stakeholders," including past and present employees, customers, suppliers, and countries and communities where facilities are located. Accordingly, some use the term *corporate citizenship*.[78] A good deal of controversy surrounds the drive for greater CSR because classical economic theory says businesses are responsible for producing goods and services to make profits, not solving the world's social, political, and environmental ills.[79] What is your opinion?

University of Georgia business ethics scholar Archie B Carroll views CSR in broad terms. So broad, in fact, that he recently offered a model of CSR/business ethics with the global economy and multinational corporations in mind (see Figure 1–3). This model is very timely because it effectively triangulates three major trends: (1) economic globalization, (2) expanding CSR expectations, and (3) the call for improved business ethics. Carroll's global CSR pyramid, from the bottom up, advises organizations in the global economy to:

- *Make a profit* consistent with expectations for international businesses.
- *Obey the law* of host countries as well as international law.

Corporate social responsibility

Corporations are expected to go above and beyond following the law and making a profit.

- *Be ethical in its practices,* taking host-country and global standards into consideration.
- *Be a good corporate citizen,* especially as defined by the host country's expectations.[80]

In keeping with the pyramid idea, Carroll emphasizes that each level needs to be solid if the structure is to stand. A pick-and-choose approach to CSR is inappropriate. The top level of the pyramid, according to Carroll, reflects "global society's expectations that business will engage in social activities that are not mandated by law nor generally expected of business in an ethical sense."[81] The spirit of Carroll's global corporate social responsibility pyramid was recently voiced by Tachi Kiuchi, managing director of Japan's Mitsubishi Corp.:

> People talk about businesses needing to be responsible as if it's something new we need to do on top of everything else. But the whole essence of business should be responsibility. My philosophy is, we don't run companies to earn profits. We earn profits to run companies. Our companies need meaning and purpose if they're to fit into the world, or why should they live at all?[82]

Our chapter-opening case on Patagonia is another example. With this global CSR perspective in mind, we now turn to an individual and personal perspective of ethics.

A Model of Individual Ethical Behavior

Ethical and unethical conduct is the product of a complex combination of influences (see Figure 1–4). At the center of the model in Figure 1–4 is the individual decision maker. He or she has a unique combination of personality characteristics, values,

Figure 1–4   *A Model of Individual Ethical Behavior in the Workplace*

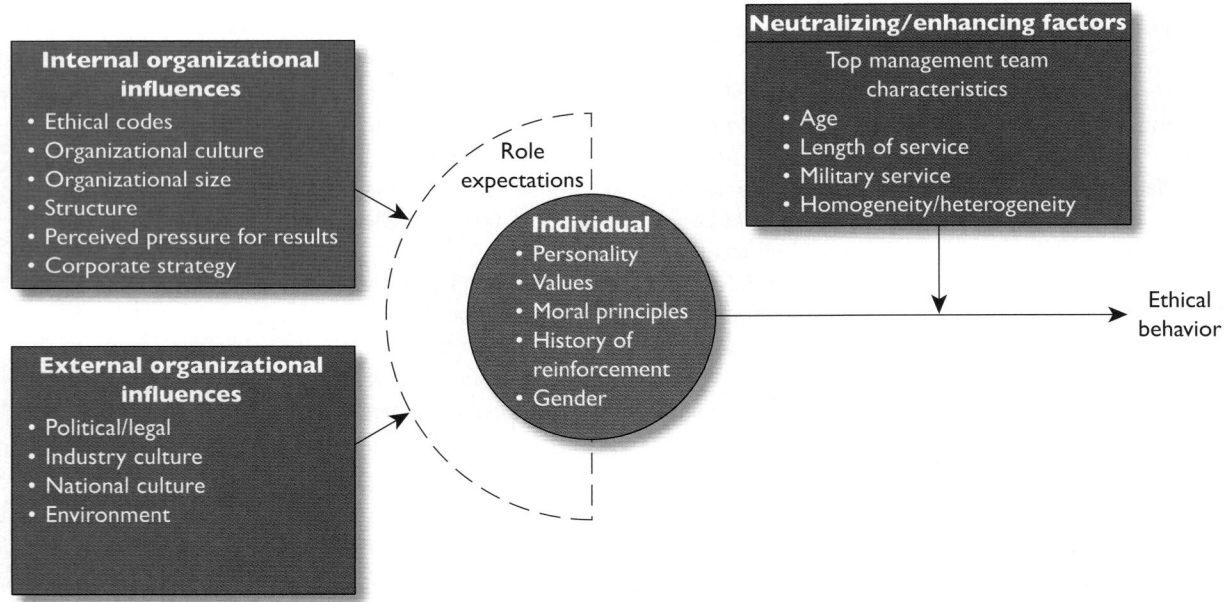

and moral principles, leaning toward or away from ethical behavior. Personal experience with being rewarded or reinforced for certain behaviors and punished for others also shapes the individual's tendency to act ethically or unethically. Finally, gender may play an important role in explaining ethical behavior. A traditional belief is that women and men have different moral orientations.[83] But a meta-analysis of 113 studies found that women were not more compassionate and caring (a *care* perspective) and less interested in rights and rules (a *justice* perspective) than men.[84] Importantly, this clarifies but does not rule out gender differences in moral reasoning.

Next, Figure 1–4 illustrates two major sources of influence on one's role expectations. People assume many roles in life, including those of employee or manager. One's expectations for how those roles should be played are shaped by a combination of internal and external organizational factors. Let us now examine how various internal and external organizational influences impact ethical behavior and how these effects are neutralized or enhanced by characteristics possessed by an organization's top management team.

Internal Organizational Influences
Figure 1–4 shows six key internal organizational influences on ethical behavior.[85] Corporate ethical codes of conduct and organizational culture, discussed in Chapter 2, clearly contribute to reducing the frequency of unethical behavior. Consider the example of Rudder Finn, the world's largest privately owned public relations agency.

> Rudder Finn established an ethics committee early on in its history because the founders maintain that public relations professionals have a special obligation to believe in what they are doing. David Finn, co-founder and CEO, chairs every ethics committee meeting to demonstrate how seriously he takes this issue. In part, these meetings perform the function of a training program in that all members of staff are invited to participate in an open forum, during which actual ethical problems are freely discussed and an outside adviser provides objectivity. "Employees have to trust that if they go to a line manager to discuss a delicate situation or seek advice, they can do so without fear of repercussions," says Finn.[86]

This example also illustrates the importance of top management support in creating an ethical work environment.

A number of studies have uncovered a positive relationship between organizational size and unethical behavior: Larger firms are more likely to behave illegally. Interestingly, research also reveals that managers are more likely to behave unethically in decentralized organizations. Unethical behavior is suspected to occur in this context because lower-level managers want to "look good" for the corporate office. In support of this conclusion, many studies have found a tendency among middle- and lower-level managers to act unethically in the face of perceived pressure for results. Further, this tendency is particularly pronounced when individuals are rewarded for accomplishing their goals.[87] By fostering a pressure-cooker atmosphere for results, managers can unwittingly set the stage for unethical shortcuts by employees who seek to please and be loyal to the company. Unfortunately, the seeds of this problem are planted early in life. A recent survey of 787 youngsters ages 13 to 18 found "that 44% of teens feel they're under strong pressure to succeed in school, no matter the cost. Of those, 81% believe the pressure will be the same or worse in the workplace."[88] Sixty-nine percent of the students admitted to lying in the past year (with 27% confessing they even lied on the survey!) and "22% said they cheated on a test."[89]

An annual right of passage for US highschoolers, sweating out the SAT exam.

External Organizational Influences Figure 1–4 identifies four key external influences on role expectations and ethical behavior. The political/legal system clearly impacts ethical behavior. As previously mentioned, the US political/legal system is demanding and monitoring corporate ethical behavior. The official tolerance of corruption varies from country to country. Also, the prevailing norms of conduct in some industries incubate unethical conduct. Globe-trotting businesspeople need to prepare accordingly.

Moreover, Figure 1–4 shows that national culture affects ethical behavior (national cultures are discussed in Chapter 4).[90] This conclusion was supported in a multination study (including the United States, Great Britain, France, Germany, Spain, Switzerland, India, China, and Australia) of management ethics. Managers from each country were asked to judge the ethicality of 12 questionable behaviors, including such things as giving and accepting gifts, passing blame, sharing confidential information, and concealing errors. Results revealed significant differences across the 10 nations in the study. That is, managers in some countries approved of practices that were frowned upon in other countries.[91] Finally, the external environment influences ethical behavior. For example, unethical behavior is more likely to occur in environments that are characterized by less generosity and when industry profitability is declining.

Neutralizing/Enhancing Factors

In their search for understanding the causes of ethical behavior, OB researchers uncovered several factors that may weaken or strengthen the relationship between the internal and external influences shown in Figure 1–4 and ethical behavior. These factors all revolve around characteristics possessed by an organization's top management team (TMT): A TMT consists of the CEO and his or her direct reports.[92] The relationship between ethical influences and ethical behavior is weaker with increasing average age and increasing tenure among the TMT. This result suggests that an older and more experienced group of leaders is less likely to allow unethical behavior to occur. Further, the ethical influences are less likely to lead to unethical behavior as the number of TMT members with military experience increases and when the TMT possesses heterogenous characteristics (e.g., diverse in terms of gender, age, race, religion, etc.). This conclusion has two important implications.

First, it appears that prior military experience favorably influences the ethical behavior of executives. While OB researchers are uncertain about the cause of this relationship, it may be due to the military's practice of indoctrinating recruits to endorse the values of duty, discipline, and honor. Regardless of the cause, military experience within a TMT is positively related to ethical behavior. Organizations thus should consider the merits of including military experience as one of its selection criteria when hiring or promoting managers. Second, organizations are encouraged to increase the diversity of its TMT if they want to reduce the chances of unethical decision making. Chapter 2 thoroughly discusses how employee diversity can increase creativity, innovation, group problem solving, and productivity.

8 General Moral Principles

Management consultant and writer Kent Hodgson has helpfully taken managers a step closer to ethical decisions by identifying seven general moral principles (see Table 1–5). Hodgson calls them "the magnificent seven" to emphasize their timeless

Table 1–5   *The Magnificent Seven: General Moral Principles for Managers*

1. *Dignity of human life:* The lives of people are to be respected. Human beings, by the fact of their existence, have value and dignity. We may not act in ways that directly intend to harm or kill an innocent person. Human beings have a right to live; we have an obligation to respect that right to life. Human life is to be preserved and treated as sacred.

2. *Autonomy:* All persons are intrinsically valuable and have the right to self-determination. We should act in ways that demonstrate each person's worth, dignity, and right to free choice. We have a right to act in ways that assert our own worth and legitimate needs. We should not use others as mere "things" or only as means to an end. Each person has an equal right to basic human liberty, compatible with a similar liberty for others.

3. *Honesty:* The truth should be told to those who have a right to know it. Honesty is also known as integrity, truth telling, and honor. One should speak and act so as to reflect the reality of the situation. Speaking and acting should mirror the way things really are. There are times when others have the right to hear the truth from us; there are times when they do not.

4. *Loyalty:* Promises, contracts, and commitments should be honored. Loyalty includes fidelity, promise keeping, keeping the public trust, good citizenship, excellence in quality of work, reliability, commitment, and honoring just laws, rules, and policies.

5. *Fairness:* People should be treated justly. One has the right to be treated fairly, impartially, and equitably. One has the obligation to treat others fairly and justly. All have the right to the necessities of life—especially those in deep need and the helpless. Justice includes equal, impartial, unbiased treatment. Fairness tolerates diversity and accepts differences in people and their ideas.

6. *Humaneness:* There are two parts: (1) Our actions ought to accomplish good, and (2) we should avoid doing evil. We should do good to others and to ourselves. We should have concern for the well-being of others; usually, we show this concern in the form of compassion, giving, kindness, serving, and caring.

7. *The common good:* Actions should accomplish the "greatest good for the greatest number" of people. One should act and speak in ways that benefit the welfare of the largest number of people, while trying to protect the rights of individuals.

SOURCE: From Kent Hodgson, *A Rock and a Hard Place: How to Make Ethical Business Decisions When the Choices Are Tough,* © 1992. Used by permission of the author.

and worldwide relevance. Both the justice and care perspectives are clearly evident in the magnificent seven, which are more detailed and, hence, more practical. Importantly, according to Hodgson, there are no absolute ethical answers for decision makers. The goal for managers should be to rely on moral principles so their decisions are *principled, appropriate,* and *defensible.*[93]

How to Improve the Organization's Ethical Climate

A team of management researchers recommended the following actions for improving on-the-job ethics.[94]

- *Behave ethically yourself.* Managers are potent role models whose habits and actual behavior send clear signals about the importance of ethical conduct. Ethical behavior is a top-to-bottom proposition.

- *Screen potential employees.* Surprisingly, employers are generally lax when it comes to checking references, credentials, transcripts, and other information on applicant résumés More diligent action in this area can screen out those given to fraud and misrepresentation. Integrity testing is fairly valid but is no panacea.[95]

- *Develop a meaningful code of ethics.* Codes of ethics can have a positive impact if they satisfy these four criteria:

  1. They are *distributed* to every employee.
  2. They are firmly *supported* by top management.
  3. They refer to *specific* practices and ethical dilemmas likely to be encountered by target employees (e.g., salespersons paying kickbacks, purchasing agents receiving payoffs, laboratory scientists doctoring data, or accountants "cooking the books").
  4. They are evenly *enforced* with rewards for compliance and strict penalties for noncompliance.

- *Provide ethics training.* Employees can be trained to identify and deal with ethical issues during orientation and through seminar, video, and Internet training sessions.[96]

- *Reinforce ethical behavior.* Behavior that is reinforced tends to be repeated, whereas behavior that is not reinforced tends to disappear. Ethical conduct too often is ignored or even punished while unethical behavior is rewarded.

- *Create positions, units, and other structural mechanisms to deal with ethics.* Ethics needs to be an everyday affair, not a one-time announcement of a new ethical code that gets filed away and forgotten. A growing number of large companies in the United States have chief ethics officers who report directly to the CEO, thus making ethical conduct and accountability priority issues.

Whistle-blowing

Reporting unethical/ illegal acts to outside third parties.

- *Create a climate in which whistle-blowing becomes unnecessary.* **Whistle-blowing** occurs when an employee reports a perceived unethical and/or illegal activity to a third party such as government agencies, news media, or public-interest groups. Enron's Sherron Watkins was a highly publicized whistle-blower.[97] Organizations can reduce the need for whistle-blowing by encouraging free and open expression of dissenting viewpoints and giving employees a voice through fair grievance procedures and/or anonymous ethics hot lines.

A Personal Call to Action

In the final analysis, ethics comes down to individual motivation. Organizational climate, role models, structure, and rewards all can point employees in the right direction. But individuals must *want* to do the right thing. Bill George, the respected former CEO of Medtronic, the maker of life-saving devices such as heart pacemakers, gave us this call to action: "Each of us needs to determine . . . where our ethical boundaries are and, if asked to violate (them), refuse. . . . If this means refusing a direct order, we must be prepared to resign."[98] Rising to this challenge requires strong personal *values* (more about values in Chapter 6) and the *courage* to adhere to them during adversity.[99]

Learning about OB: Research and a Road Map

OB is a broad and growing field. We have a lot of ground to cover. To make the trip as instructive and efficient as possible, we use a theory→research→practice strategy. For virtually all major topics in this book, we begin by presenting the underlying theoretical framework (often with graphical models showing how key variables are related) and defining key terms. Next, we tap the latest research findings for valuable insights. Finally, we round out the discussion with illustrative practical examples and, when applicable, how-to-do-it advice.

 ## 9 Five Sources of OB Research Insights

OB gains its credibility as an academic discipline by being research driven. Scientific rigor pushes aside speculation, prejudice, and untested assumptions about workplace behavior. We systematically cite "hard" evidence from five different categories. Worthwhile evidence was obtained by drawing upon the following *priority* of research methodologies:

- *Meta-analyses*. A **meta-analysis** is a statistical pooling technique that permits behavioral scientists to draw general conclusions about certain variables from many different studies.[100] It typically encompasses a vast number of subjects, often reaching the thousands. Meta-analyses are instructive because they focus on general patterns of research evidence, not fragmented bits and pieces or isolated studies.[101]

- *Field studies*. In OB, a **field study** probes individual or group processes in an organizational setting. Because field studies involve real-life situations, their results often have immediate and practical relevance for managers.

- *Laboratory studies*. In a **laboratory study,** variables are manipulated and measured in contrived situations. College students are commonly used as subjects. The highly controlled nature of laboratory studies enhances research precision. But generalizing the results to organizational management requires caution.

- *Sample surveys*. In a **sample survey,** samples of people from specified populations respond to questionnaires. The researchers then draw conclusions about the relevant population. Generalizability of the results depends on the quality of the sampling and questioning techniques.

- *Case studies,* A **case study** is an in-depth analysis of a single individual, group, or organization, Because of their limited scope, case studies yield realistic but not very generalizable results.

Meta-analysis
Pools the results of many studies through statistical procedure.

Field study
Examination of variables in real-life settings.

Laboratory study
Manipulation and measurement of variables in contrived situations.

Sample survey
Questionnaire responses from a sample of people.

Case study
In-depth study of a single person, group, or organization.

Figure 1–5   *A Topical Model for What Lies Ahead*

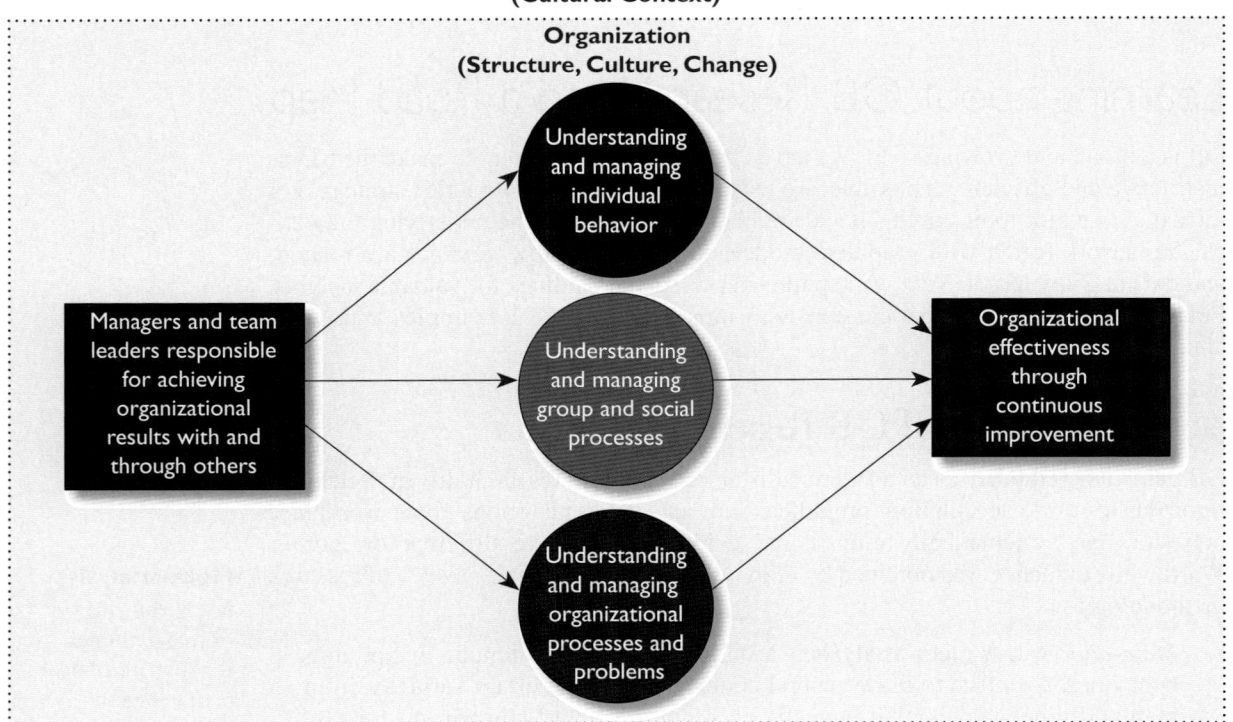

A Topical Model for Understanding and Managing OB

Figure 1–5 is a topical road map for our journey through this book. Our destination is organizational effectiveness through continuous improvement. Four different criteria for determining whether or not an organization is effective are discussed in Chapter 17. The study of OB can be a wandering and pointless trip if we overlook the need to translate OB lessons into effective and efficient organized endeavor.

At the far left side of our topical road map are managers and team leaders, those who are responsible for accomplishing organizational results with and through others. The three circles at the center of our road map correspond to Parts Two, Three, and Four of this text. Logically, the flow of topical coverage in this book (following introductory Part One) goes from individuals, to group processes, to organizational processes. Around the core of our topical road map in Figure 1–5 is the organization. Accordingly, we end our journey with organization-related material in Part Four. Organizational structure and design are covered there in Chapter 17 to establish and develop the *organizational* context of organizational behavior. Rounding out our organizational context is a discussion of organizational change in Chapter 18. Chapters 3 and 4 provide a *cultural* context for OB.

The dotted line represents a permeable boundary between the organization and its environment. Energy and influence flow both ways across this permeable boundary. Truly, no organization is an island in today's highly interactive and interdependent world.

Relative to the *external* environment, international cultures are explored in Chapter 4. Organization–environment contingencies are examined in Chapter 17.

Chapter 2 examines the OB implications of significant demographic and social trends. These discussions provide a realistic context for studying and managing people at work.

Bon voyage! Enjoy your trip through the challenging, interesting, and often surprising world of OB.

Summary of Key Concepts

1. *Define the term organizational behavior, and contrast McGregor's Theory X and Theory Y assumptions about employees.* Organizational behavior (OB) is an interdisciplinary field dedicated to better understanding and managing people at work. It is both research and application oriented. Theory X employees, according to traditional thinking, dislike work, require close supervision, and are primarily interested in security. According to the modern Theory Y view, employees are capable of self-direction, of seeking responsibility, and of being creative.

2. *Identify the four principles of total quality management (TQM).* (a) Do it right the first time to eliminate costly rework. (b) Listen to and learn from customers and employees. (c) Make continuous improvement an everyday matter. (d) Build teamwork, trust, and mutual respect.

3. *Define the term e-business, and specify at least three OB-related issues raised by e-leadership.* E-business involves using the Internet to more effectively and efficiently manage every aspect of a business. Six OB-related issues raised by the advent of e-leadership are (a) greater access to information for everyone, (b) leadership is migrating to lower levels and outside the organization, (c) development of nontraditional leadership networks, (d) followers have more information earlier in the decision-making process, (e) greater influence for unethical leaders with limited resources, and (f) more contact between senior leaders and their followers.

4. *Contrast human and social capital, and explain why we need to build both.* The first involves *individual* characteristics, the second involves *social* relationships. Human capital is the productive potential of an individual's knowledge and actions. Dimensions include such things as intelligence, visions, skills, self-esteem, creativity, motivation, ethics, and emotional maturity. Social capital is productive potential resulting from strong relationships, goodwill, trust, and cooperative effort. Dimensions include such things as shared visions and goals, trust, mutual respect, friendships, empowerment, teamwork, win-win negotiations, and volunteering. Social capital is necessary to tap

individual human capital for the good of the organization through knowledge sharing and networking.

5. *Define the term management, and identify at least five of the eleven managerial skills in Wilson's profile of effective managers.* Management is the process of working with and through others to achieve organizational objectives in an efficient and ethical manner. According to the Wilson skills profile, an effective manager (a) clarifies goals and objectives, (b) encourages participation, (c) plans and organizes, (d) has technical and administrative expertise, (e) facilitates work through team building and coaching, (f) provides feedback, (g) keeps things moving, (h) controls details, (i) applies reasonable pressure for goals accomplishment, (j) empowers and delegates, and (k) recognizes and rewards good performance.

6. *Characterize 21st-century managers.* They will be team players who will get things done cooperatively by relying on joint decision making, their knowledge instead of formal authority, and their multicultural skills. They will engage in life-long learning and be compensated on the basis of their skills and results. They will facilitate rather than resist change, share rather than hoard power and key information, and be multidirectional communicators. Ethics will be a forethought instead of an afterthought. They will be generalists with multiple specialties.

7. *Describe Carroll's global corporate social responsibility pyramid, and give an overview of the model of individual ethical behavior.* From bottom to top, the four levels of corporate responsibility in Carroll's pyramid are: *economic* (make a profit); *legal* (obey the law); *ethical* (be ethical in its practices); and *philanthropic* (be a good corporate citizen). Progress needs to be made on all levels. An individual's ethical behavior is the product of interaction among the *individual* (personality, values, moral principles, history of reinforcement, and possibly gender), his or her *role expectations* as shaped by internal influences (e.g., ethical codes and organizational culture and strategy) and external influences (e.g., laws and national culture), and *neutralizing/enhancing factors* (e.g., age, length

of service, military service, and diversity among the top management team).

8. *Identify four of the seven general ethical principles, and explain how to improve an organization's ethical climate.* The "magnificent seven" moral principles are (*a*) dignity of human life, (*b*) autonomy, (*c*) honesty, (*d*) loyalty, (*e*) fairness, (*f*) humaneness (by doing good and avoiding evil), and (*g*) the common good (accomplishing the greatest good for the greatest number of people). An organization's ethical climate can be improved by managers being good role models, carefully screening job applicants, creating and firmly enforcing a code of ethics mentioning specific practices, providing ethics training, rewarding ethical behavior, creating ethics-related positions and structures, and reducing the need for whistle-blowing (reporting unethical conduct to outside third parties) through open and honest debate.

9. *Describe the sources of organizational behavior research evidence.* Five sources of OB research evidence are meta-analyses (statistically pooled evidence from several studies), field studies (evidence from real-life situations), laboratory studies (evidence from contrived situations), sample surveys (questionnaire data), and case studies (observation of a single person, group, or organization).

Key Terms

Organization 5
Organizational behavior 5
Theory Y 8
Total quality management 10
E-business 12
Human capital 14
Social capital 14
Management 15
Contingency approach 18

Ethics 20
Corporate social responsibility 21
Whistle-blowing 26
Meta-analysis 27
Field study 27
Laboratory study 27
Sample survey 27
Case study 27

OB in Action Case Study

IBM's Donna Riley Strives for "Collaborative Influence"[102]

BusinessWeek It was at a client meeting in San Francisco in October 2002 that Sam Palmisano, IBM's new CEO, first unveiled the initiative he hoped would transform his company. His idea: The Internet really did change everything (the crash of the New Economy notwithstanding). In a hyperconnected world, IBM's clients needed to become "on-demand" companies, their every business process exquisitely calibrated to respond instantly to whatever got thrown at them. And to help them, IBM would have to do exactly the same thing.

When she heard about the new strategy, Donna Riley, IBM's vice president of global talent, remembers wondering whether the company had the right managers for its new direction. "If leadership is stuck in the past, and the business has changed, we have a problem," she says. By the spring of 2003, Palmisano and his leadership development team realized the strategy would indeed demand a new breed of boss—leaders who were as sensitive to changes in their environment as Indian scouts.

For help, Riley turned to the Hay Group, a consultancy that specializes in executive development. Hay had done work for IBM before, most notably in 1994 when, at former CEO Lou Gerstner's behest, the firm had interviewed a group of the company's top managers. As part of his turnaround strategy for the troubled company, Gerstner wanted to develop a new style of leader who could help transform its failed culture. Ultimately, Hay distilled 11 competencies from the interviews that would guide IBMers' performance as they pulled off one of the most remarkable corporate rebounds in history.

In the summer of 2003, Hay Group returned to conduct another set of interviews with 33 executives who had been identified as outstanding leaders in the new on-demand era—the folks who really got the new strategy and who were on the cutting edge in a high-performance culture. They were drawn from every division of the business, every part of the world, united by their extraordinary ability to get the job done. The plan was to put these top players under a microscope, to divine how they thought about their jobs and the company; how they interacted with clients, peers, and subordinates; how they set goals and went about meeting them—in short, to extract the best practices from the best leaders to see if they could be duplicated.

In a series of three-and-a-half-hour interviews, the managers discussed circumstances in which they had been successful—or not. The interviews were supplemented by surveys of the people they worked with. Researchers then combed through the stories and accompanying data, looking for characteristics and qualities that distinguished these high performers.

The results were stunning. "The experts predicted maybe a third of the competencies would be the same, a third would be slightly different, and a third would be brand new," says Riley. "Much to their surprise—and ours—we found it truly is a new book," requiring all new skills.

To begin with, the best executives no longer thought of the folks to whom they sold stuff as customers; they saw them as clients. The difference? "A customer is transactional," says Harris Ginsberg, IBM's director of global executive and organization capability. "A client is somebody with whom you have a longstanding relationship and a personal investment." It's no longer enough to sell a customer a server. An IBMer should be so focused on becoming a long-term trusted partner that she might even discourage a client from buying some new piece of hardware if it's in the client's best interest to hold off.

The 33 leaders were also adept at a skill IBM calls "collaborative influence." In a highly complex world, where multiple groups might need to unite to solve a client's problems, old-style siloed thinking just won't cut it, and command-and-control leadership doesn't work. "It's really about winning hearts and minds—and getting people whose pay you don't control to do stuff," says Mary Fontaine, vice president and general manager of Hay's McClelland Center for Research and Innovation.

For example, Frank Squillante, an IBM vice president, has only four direct reports. To do his job—devising the strategy for the company's intranet, and then developing and deploying applications for 325,000 people and 100,000 business partners—he must be a master at cajoling people over whom he has no real power. "I use 'collaborative influence' every minute of every day," he says. "If I tried to pull one of these, 'I'm in charge so you have to do this' maneuvers, the whole thing would break down."

Riley's team is now training IBM's executives in the new competencies. This year, only top management will be assessed against them. The next group—some 4,000 executives—will have a year to study the goals before being held accountable. But the new approach has already spurred some more flexible, collaborative efforts. Cross-functional teams from IBM's global services, software, and systems groups have helped Mobil Travel Guides transform itself from a travel content provider to a real-time, customized travel-planning service; a team of staffers from Big Blue's research, software, and consulting services helped Nextel dramatically improve its customer-care services.

In an interconnected world, such horizontal, collaborative networks of people clearly make more sense than rigid hierarchies. And leading in such a challenging environment is an acquired skill. "Leadership is a personal journey for each person," says Riley, "but I think having a culture that says this stuff matters—particularly when it's linked to your business strategy—is a very powerful combination."

Questions for Discussion

1. What role, if any, does McGregor's Theory Y play in IBM's drive to create a new breed of manager/leader?
2. What evidence of the e-leadership issues presented in Table 1–2 can you detect in this case? Explain.
3. How does the building of human and social capital (Figure 1–2) factor into this case?
4. Which three or four of Wilson's 11 managerial skills (Table 1–3) will be most important for IBM's managers in the years ahead? Explain your choices.
5. What is the linkage between the 21st-century manager, profiled in Table 1–4, and IBM's notion of collaborative influence?

Ethical Dilemma

You Mean Cheating Is Wrong?

College students are disturbed by recent corporate scandals: Some 84% believe the United States is having a business crisis, and 77% think CEOs should be held personally responsible for it.

But when the same students are asked about their own ethics, it's another story. Some 59% admit cheating on a test (66% of men, 54% of women). And only 19% say they would report a classmate who cheated (23% of men, but 15% of women—even though recent whistle-blowers have been women).

The survey of 1,100 students on 27 US campuses was conducted by Students in Free Enterprise (SIFE), a nonprofit that teams up with corporations to teach students ethical business practices. "There's a lack of understanding about ethics and how ethics are applied in real life," says Alvin Rohrs, SIFE'S CEO. "We have to get young people to stop and think about ethics and the decisions they're making." Otherwise, today's students may be tomorrow's criminals.[103]

How Should We Interpret This Hypocritical Double Standard?

1. Don't worry, most students know the difference between school and real life. They'll do the right thing when it really counts. Explain your rationale.

2. Whether in the classroom or on the job, pressure for results is the problem. People tend to take shortcuts and bend the rules when they're pressured. Explain.

3. A cheater today is a cheater tomorrow. Explain.

4. College professors need to do a better job with ethics education. How?

5. Both students and managers need to be held personally accountable for their unethical behavior. How?

6. Invent other interpretations or options. Discuss.

Web Resources

For study material and exercises that apply to this chapter, visit our Web site,

www.mhhe.com/kreitner

CHAPTER 2

Managing Diversity: Releasing Every Employee's Potential

LEARNING OBJECTIVES

When you finish studying the material in this chapter, you should be able to:

1. Define diversity and review the four layers of diversity.

2. Explain the difference between affirmative action and managing diversity.

3. Describe the glass ceiling and the four top strategies used by women to break the glass ceiling.

4. Review the demographic trends pertaining to racial groups, educational mismatches, and an aging workforce.

5. Highlight the managerial implications of increasing diversity in the workforce.

6. Explain the positive and negative effects of diversity by using social categorization theory and information/decision-making theory.

7. Identify the barriers and challenges to managing diversity.

8. Discuss the organizational practices used to effectively manage diversity as identified by R Roosevelt Thomas, Jr.

online **resources**

Student Resources for Studying Chapter 2

The Web site for your text includes resources that will help you master the concepts in this chapter. As you read, you'll want to visit the site for these helpful tools:

- Your online Study Guide includes learning objectives, a chapter summary, a glossary of key terms, and discussion questions.
- Take a practice quiz and test your knowledge!
- Scroll through a PowerPoint presentation with key concepts for this chapter.

Your instructor might also direct you to the Web site for these exercises:

- Self-assessments that correspond with the chapter content and a Group Exercise.
- You'll also find Video Cases and Internet Exercises for this chapter online.

www.mhhe.com/kreitner

Patricia Harris, vice president of McDonald's USA and global chief diversity officer of McDonald's Corp., was still in college when she took a secretarial position at McDonald's. "I'll stay here until I finish school and get a real job," she told herself.

Thirty years later, she's still there. Far from being the exclusive province of short-term fast-food jobs, McDonald's offers "lots of 'real' jobs and lots of career paths," she says. "We have hamburger lawyers, hamburger accountants and hamburger HR people." . . .

In 1985, Harris was offered the position of affirmative action manager, an opportunity that once again changed the course of her career.

She was apprehensive at first. Although interested, Harris wasn't sure she could do the job. In addition, "I knew affirmative action wasn't a popular topic." The affirmative action department was new, having been established in 1980, and it was seen as the "police," she says, coming in to enforce the rules. She wondered if this would be a wise career move.

Ultimately, however, she decided to "step out of my comfort zone" and take the risk, with the encouragement of her boss, Mel Hobson, McDonald's first director of affirmative action.

By the end of the 1980s, the work of the department had expanded. Partnerships were developed with external organizations, and affirmative action moved out of HR and became its own stand-alone unit. At the same time, the name was changed from affirmative action to diversity.

Although the department was no longer part of HR, it continued to have a strong relationship with human resources. "I don't know how diversity people can do their job without HR's support," she says. . . .

"When I joined the company in 1976, I think we had one female officer, one Asian officer and one African-American officer. There were no Hispanic officers," says Harris. *Today, of McDonald's 200 U.S. officers, 26 percent are women and 23 percent are minorities.*

Harris is particularly proud that McDonald's received an Equal Employment Opportunity Commission (EEOC) "Freedom to Compete Award" this year in recognition of the company's diversity and inclusion initiatives.

The EEOC specifically cited McDonald's employee networks, which include the African-American Council, the Hispanic Employee Network, the Asian Employee Network, the Women's Leadership Network (which is global now) and the Gays, Lesbians and Allies at McDonald's. Each group provides networking opportunities for its members and offers an avenue for sharing ideas with management.

Harris still remembers the first networking meetings she attended as a new employee. Those early sessions were somewhat ad hoc and casual, she says, but they started becoming more formal in the early 1980s.

"We're in a different place today," says Harris, and the networks are continuing to evolve. They offer seminars on career management and leadership skills development as well as provide opportunities to network and to share best practices.

While the early groups focused more on social aspects of networking, the primary focus today is on the business. Each network has a diversity goal and a plan that complements the organization's customer-centric approach to business. To prevent silos among the networks, cross-functional teams of network leaders share information and ideas. . . .

Earlier this year, Harris was promoted to global chief diversity officer, and she has already begun to meet with HR leaders from McDonald's country areas around the world to enlist their help in ensuring that diversity reaches all levels of the organization across the globe. "Diversity has so many dimensions," she says. "It means different things to different countries." As she takes on this exciting new role, she says happily, "I feel like I'm starting over again, and I love it."[1]

FOR DISCUSSION

What are the key components of McDonald's diversity programs?

The McDonald's example highlights two key reasons why it is important for managers to effectively manage diversity. Effectively managing diversity is not only a good thing to do in order to attract and retain the most talented employees, but it makes good business sense. Unfortunately, however, some organizations are missing the mark when it comes to managing diversity, and the result can be costly lawsuits. Consider the following examples:

- Seven Afghan Muslim employees at two car dealerships in Solano County, California, said they had been harassed and were called offensive names such as "the bin Laden gang," "sand niggers," "terrorists," and "camel jockeys." Their suit resulted in a $500,000 settlement with the dealerships.

- An 18-year-old male salesclerk for a baby products retailer in New Jersey alleged that he was subjected to a sexually hostile environment—he was called "fag," "faggot," and "happy pants," and he was forcefully stripped of his trousers by co-workers. The retailer settled for $205,000.[2]

- Janet Orlando, a former employee at Alarm One, a home security firm in Fresno, California, was awarded $1.7 million by a jury "after she was spanked in front of her colleagues in what her employer called a camaraderie-building exercise. Sales teams were encouraged to compete, and the losers were made fun of, forced to eat baby food, required to wear diapers and spanked with a rival company's yard signs, according to court documents."[3]

It is important to note that these things occurred in these companies despite the existence of laws that prohibit such behaviors. As you will learn in this chapter, managing diversity entails much more than following laws and creating policies and procedures proscribing equal treatment of employees.

Managing diversity is a sensitive, potentially volatile, and sometimes uncomfortable issue. Yet managers are required to deal with it in the name of organizational survival. Accordingly, the purpose of this chapter is to help you get a better understanding of this important context for organizational behavior. We begin by defining diversity. Next, we build the business case for diversity and then discuss the barriers and challenges associated with managing diversity. The chapter concludes by describing the organizational practices used to manage diversity effectively.

Defining Diversity

Diversity represents the multitude of individual differences and similarities that exist among people. Target Corporation offers a practical application of this definition.

> When we talk about diversity within Target, we define it inclusively as individuality. This individuality may include a wide spectrum of attributes such as personal style, age, race, gender, ethnicity, sexual orientation, language, physical ability, religion, family, citizenship status, socio-economic circumstances, education and life experiences. To us, diversity is any attribute that makes an individual unique that does not interfere with effective job performance.[4]

Target's application underscores a key issue about managing diversity. Diversity pertains to everybody. Diversity also does not pit white males against all other groups of people. Diversity pertains to the host of individual differences that make all of us unique and different from others.

This section begins our journey into managing diversity by first reviewing the key dimensions of diversity. Because many people associate diversity with affirmative action, this section compares affirmative action with managing diversity. They are not the same.

Layers of Diversity

Like seashells on a beach, people come in a variety of shapes, sizes, and colors. This variety represents the essence of diversity. Lee Gardenswartz and Anita Rowe, a team of diversity experts, identified four layers of diversity to help distinguish the important ways in which people differ (see Figure 2–1). Taken together, these layers define your personal identity and influence how each of us sees the world.

Figure 2–1 shows that personality is at the center of the diversity wheel. Personality is at the center because it represents a stable set of characteristics that is responsible for a person's identity. The dimensions of personality are discussed later in Chapter 5. The next layer of diversity consists of a set of internal dimensions that are referred to as surface-level dimensions of diversity. These dimensions, for the most part, are not within our control, but they strongly influence our attitudes and expectations and assumptions about others, which, in turn, influence our behavior. Take the encounter experienced by an African-American woman in middle management while vacationing at a resort:

> While I was sitting by the pool, "a large 50-ish white male approached me and demanded that I get him extra towels. I said, 'Excuse me?' He then said, 'Oh, you don't work here,' with no shred of embarrassment or apology in his voice."[5]

Stereotypes regarding one or more of the surface-level dimensions of diversity most likely influenced this man's behavior toward the woman.

Diversity

The host of individual differences that make people different from and similar to each other.

Figure 2–1   *The Four Layers of Diversity*

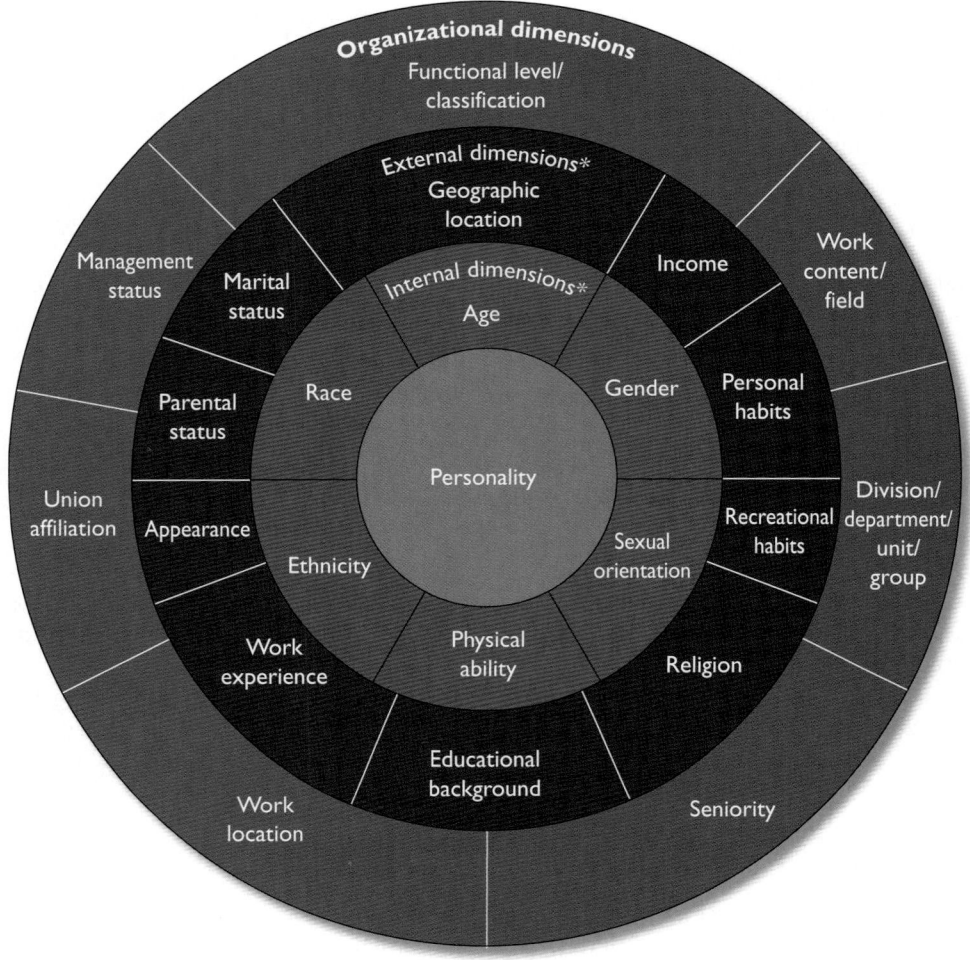

*Internal dimensions and external dimensions are adapted from Loden and Rosener, *Workforce America!* (Homewood, IL: Business One Irwin, 1991).

SOURCE: L Gardenswartz and A Rowe, *Diverse Teams at Work: Capitalizing on the Power of Diversity* (New York: McGraw-Hill, 1994), p. 33. © 1994.

Figure 2–1 reveals that the next layer of diversity is composed of external influences, which are referred to as secondary dimensions of diversity. They represent individual differences that we have a greater ability to influence or control. Examples include where you grew up and live today, your religious affiliation, whether you are married and have children, and your work experiences. These dimensions also exert a significant influence on our perceptions, behavior, and attitudes.

Consider religion as an illustration. Given that Islam is expected to surpass Judaism as the second-most commonly practiced religion in the United States (Christianity is first), organizations need to consider Muslim employees when implementing their policies, procedures, and programs. Ford Motor Company, for example, proactively conducted a series of Islam 101 training sessions in Dearborn, Michigan, after the September 11 terrorist attacks. It did this because the Dearborn area is home to one of the largest Arab-American and Middle Eastern communities in the United States and the company wanted to raise awareness about the Islamic faith.[6]

The Ford example illustrates that an organization's level of awareness about the external layer of diversity can foster positive feelings among employees. The final layer of diversity includes organizational dimensions such as seniority, job title and function, and work location.

go to the Web for the Self-Exercise: How Does Your Diversity Profile Affect Your Relationships with Other People?

2 Affirmative Action and Managing Diversity

Effectively managing diversity requires organizations to adopt a new way of thinking about differences among people. Rather than pitting one group against another, managing diversity entails recognition of the unique contribution every employee can make. As found at Designer Blinds, a 170-employee company located in Omaha, Nebraska, with a turnover rate of 167%, effectively managing diversity lowered turnover and increased productivity and quality.

> Top managers began by viewing recruiting and retention strategically and quantitatively. An entirely new approach to hiring was launched. One aspect was networking with representatives of various cultures, including the local Sudanese community, which had not been well represented in the workforce. Company supervisors and co-workers studied the culture and embraced it. The firm also identified Hispanics as the fastest-growing group in the area and made a sincere effort to welcome members of the community and to provide English-as-a-second-language classes.
>
> The diversification of the workplace has produced good results for several years, especially the last two. Employee efficiency and productivity is skyrocketing, quality is a benchmark for the industry, and turnover has plunged from stratospheric highs to 8% a year.[7]

The management philosophies used at Designer Blinds earned the company an Optimas Award for excellence in people management and are much different from the management philosophies associated with affirmative action. This section highlights the differences between affirmative action and managing diversity.

Affirmative Action Affirmative action is an outgrowth of equal employment opportunity (EEO) legislation. The goal of this legislation is to outlaw discrimination and to encourage organizations to proactively prevent discrimination. **Discrimination** occurs when employment decisions about an individual are due to reasons not associated with performance or are not related to the job. Table 2–1 provides a review of major federal laws pertaining to equal employment opportunity. As you can see from this table, many forms of discrimination are outlawed. For example, organizations cannot discriminate on the basis of race, color, religion, national origin, sex, age, physical and mental disabilities, and pregnancy. Many of these federal laws are enforced by the Equal Employment Opportunity Commission (EEOC), and individuals may sue for back pay and punitive damages when they feel that they have been discriminated against.[8]

In contrast to the proactive perspective of EEO legislation, **affirmative action** is an artificial intervention aimed at giving management a chance to correct an imbalance, an injustice, a mistake, or outright discrimination that occurred in the past.

Discrimination
Occurs when employment decisions are based on factors that are not job related.

Affirmative action
Focuses on achieving equality of opportunity in an organization.

Table 2–1   *Some Important US Federal Laws and Regulations Protecting Employees*

YEAR	LAW OR REGULATION	PROVISIONS
LABOR RELATIONS		
1974	Privacy Act	Gives employees legal right to examine letters of reference concerning them
1986	Immigration Reform & Control Act	Requires employers to verify the eligibility for employment of all their new hires (including U.S. citizens)
1988	Polygraph Protection Act	Limits employer's ability to use lie detectors
1988	Worker Adjustment & Retraining Notification Act	Requires organizations with 100 or more employees to give 60 days' notice for mass layoffs or plant closings
2003	Sarbanes-Oxley Act	Prohibits employers from demoting or firing employees who raise accusations of fraud to a federal agency
COMPENSATION AND BENEFITS		
1974	Employee Retirement Income Security Act (ERISA)	Sets rules for managing pension plans; provides federal insurance to cover bankrupt plans
1993	Family & Medical Leave Act	Requires employers to provide 12 weeks of unpaid leave for medical and family reasons, including for childbirth, adoption, or family emergency
1996	Health Insurance Portability & Accountability Act (HIPPA)	Allows employees to switch health insurance plans when changing jobs and receive new coverage regardless of preexisting health conditions; prohibits group plans from dropping ill employees
HEALTH AND SAFETY		
1970	Occupational Safety & Health Act (OSHA)	Establishes minimum health and safety standards in organizations
1985	Consolidated Omnibus Budget Reconciliation Act (COBRA)	Requires an extension of health insurance benefits after termination
EQUAL EMPLOYMENT OPPORTUNITY		
1963	Equal Pay Act	Requires men and women be paid equally for performing equal work
1964, amended 1972	Civil Rights Act, Title VII	Prohibits discrimination on basis of race, color, religion, national origin, or sex
1967, amended 1978 and 1986	Age Discrimination in Employment Act (ADEA)	Prohibits discrimination in employees over 40 years old; restricts mandatory retirement

1978	Pregnancy Discrimination Act	Broadens discrimination to cover pregnancy, childbirth, and related medical conditions; protects job security during maternity leave
1990	Americans with Disabilities Act (ADA)	Prohibits discrimination against essentially qualified employees with physical or mental disabilities or chronic illness; requires "reasonable accommodation" be provided so they can perform duties
1991	Civil Rights Act	Amends and clarifies Title VII, ADA, and other laws; permits suits against employers for punitive damages in cases of intentional discrimination

SOURCE: A Kinicki and B Williams, *Management: A Practical Introduction,* 3rd ed, McGraw-Hill, 2008, p 293. Reprinted by permission of McGraw-Hill Companies, Inc.

Affirmative action does not legitimize quotas. Quotas are illegal. They can only be imposed by judges who conclude that a company has engaged in discriminatory practices. It also is important to note that under no circumstances does affirmative action require companies to hire unqualified people.

Although affirmative action created tremendous opportunities for women and minorities, it does not foster the type of thinking that is needed to effectively manage diversity. For example, a recent meta-analysis summarizing 35 years of research involving 29,000 people uncovered the following results: (1) affirmative action plans are perceived more negatively by white males than women and minorities because it is perceived to work against their own self-interests; (2) affirmative action plans are viewed more positively by people who are liberals and Democrats than conservatives and Republicans; and (3) affirmative action plans are not supported by people who possess racist or sexist attitudes.[9]

Affirmative action programs also were found to negatively affect the women and minorities expected to benefit from them. Research demonstrated that women and minorities, supposedly hired on the basis of affirmative action, felt negatively stigmatized as unqualified or incompetent. They also experienced lower job satisfaction and more stress than employees supposedly selected on the basis of merit.[10] Another study, however, showed that these negative consequences were reduced for women when a merit criterion was included in hiring decisions. In other words, women hired under affirmative action programs felt better about themselves and exhibited higher performance when they believed they were hired because of their competence rather than their gender.[11]

Managing Diversity

Managing diversity entails enabling people to perform up to their maximum potential. It focuses on changing an organization's culture and infrastructure such that people provide the highest productivity possible. Wegmans, a grocery chain with 71 stores in five states that was ranked as the third best company to work for in America in 2007 by *Fortune,* is a good example of a company that effectively manages diversity (see the Real World/Real People feature on page 42).[12] Ann Morrison, a diversity expert, conducted a study of 16 organizations that successfully

Managing diversity

Creating organizational changes that enable all people to perform up to their maximum potential.

Wegmans Effectively Manages Diversity

Wegmans' hourly wages and annual salaries are at the high end of the market.... But salaries aren't the whole story. The company has shelled out $54 million for college scholarships to more than 17,500 full- and part-time employees over the past 20 years. It thinks nothing of sending, say, cheese manager Terri Zodarecky on a 10-day sojourn to cheesemakers in London, Paris, and Italy....

A common denominator of passionate customer service sets Wegmans workers apart from those at other retailers. Simply put, no customer is allowed to leave unhappy. To ensure that, employees are encouraged to do just about anything, on the spot, without consulting a higher-up.... Empowering employees goes beyond making house calls, though—it also means creating an environment where they can shine, unburdened by hierarchies.

What are the pros and cons of using college Scholarships to manage diversity?

SOURCE: Excerpted from M Boyle, "The Wegman's Way," *Fortune,* January 24, 2005, pp 66, 68.

Buying pastries can be a fun and tasty experience at Wegmans. Ranked as the third best American company to work for by *Fortune* in 2007, Wegmans fosters employee effort and commitment by effectively managing diversity.

---

managed diversity. Her results uncovered three key strategies for success: education, enforcement, and exposure. She describes them as follows:

> The education component of the strategy has two thrusts: one is to prepare nontraditional managers for increasingly responsible posts, and the other is to help traditional managers overcome their prejudice in thinking about and interacting with people who are of a different sex or ethnicity. The second component of the strategy, enforcement, puts teeth in diversity goals and encourages behavior change. The third component, exposure to people with different backgrounds and characteristics, adds a more personal approach to diversity by helping managers get to know and respect others who are different.[13]

In summary, both consultants and academics believe that organizations should strive to manage diversity rather than simply using affirmative action. This conclusion was supported by a study of 200 African-American and white males and females employed in retail stores. Results revealed that employees viewed leaders as more accepting of diversity and more desirable to work for when they demonstrated behaviors consistent with managing diversity as opposed to affirmative action.[14] More is said about managing diversity later in this chapter.

Bank of America Targets Illegal Immigrants as Source of Revenue Growth

In the latest sign of the U.S. banking industry's aggressive pursuit of the Hispanic market, Bank of America Corp. has quietly begun offering credit cards aimed at illegal immigrants. . . .

The new Bank of America program is open to people who lack both a Social Security number and a credit history, as long as they have held a checking account with the bank for three months without an overdraft. Most adults in the U.S. who don't have a Social Security number are undocumented immigrants.

The Charlotte, N.C. banking giant tested the program last year at five branches in Los Angeles, and last week expanded it to 51 branches in Los Angeles County, home to the largest concentration of illegal immigrants in the U.S. The bank hopes to roll out the program nationally later this year.

Do you think Bank of America is acting ethically? Why or why not?

SOURCE: Excerpted from M Jordan and B Bauerlein, "Bank of America Casts Wider Net for Hispanics," *The Wall Street Journal*, February 13, 2007, p A1.

Building the Business Case for Managing Diversity

The rationale for managing diversity goes well beyond legal, social, and moral reasons. Quite simply, the primary reason for managing diversity is the ability to grow and maintain a business in an increasingly competitive marketplace. Many companies understand and endorse this proposition. For example, IBM, PepsiCo, and Nordstrom's decided to focus on hiring and promoting diverse employees in order to help create and market products to a broader and more diverse customer base.[15] Research indirectly supports the logic of this strategy. For example, a study of 1,000 companies suggests that a diverse top management team can contribute to corporate profits. Results revealed that sales growth averaged 22.9%, 20.2%, and 13% for companies whose senior management team contained a majority of women, included people of color, and consisted of a majority of white men, respectively.[16] Goldman Sachs, on the other hand, is trying to increase its revenue stream by creating a new business unit that caters to the marketing and advertising of products to the growing Hispanic and Latino population. According to the Pew Hispanic Center in Washington, DC, the majority of all growth in the 18- to 34-year-old demographic between 2007 and 2010 will come from Hispanics.[17] It looks like Goldman will be well situated to penetrate this market. In contrast to the approach being used by Goldman, Bank of America is trying to target the Hispanic market by offering credit cards to illegal immigrants (see the Real World/Real People feature above).

Diverse team members like this work better together when an organization effectively manages diversity. Why is it that some organizations have trouble managing diversity?

Organizations cannot use diversity as a strategic advantage if employees fail to contribute their full talents, abilities, motivation, and commitment. It is thus essential for an organization to create an environment or culture that allows all employees to reach their full potential. Managing diversity is a critical component of creating such an organization.

This section explores the business need to manage diversity by first reviewing the demographic trends that are creating an increasingly diverse workforce. We then review evidence pertaining to the positive and negative effects associated with diverse work environments.

Increasing Diversity in the Workforce

Workforce demographics

Statistical profiles of adult workers.

Workforce demographics, which are statistical profiles of the characteristics and composition of the adult working population, are an invaluable human-resource planning aid. They enable managers to anticipate and adjust for surpluses or shortages of appropriately skilled individuals. Consider the implications associated with an aging population that will be retiring in record numbers over the next decade, a US birthrate that is too low to provide enough workers to meet future demand, a 57.4% increase in foreign-born immigrants from 1990 to 2000, over 7.5 million illegal immigrants working in the United States and another 700,000 to 850,000 predicted to arrive each coming year, a 33% drop out rate from high school, and a population under age 45 that will begin shrinking 6% annually in 2010.[18] Experts predict that these demographic trends will create a serious shortage of skilled workers in the future. In turn, these shortages will increase the amount of work that is outsourced to other countries around the world. Unfortunately, these predictions already are occurring. For example, a survey of 500 employers in Florida indicated that 52% were experiencing a lack of skilled workers and the Bureau of Labor Statistics estimated a shortfall of 10 million knowledge workers in the United States by 2010.[19]

Moreover, general population demographics give managers a preview of the values and motives of current and future employees. Demographic changes in the US workforce during the last two or three decades have immense implications for organizational behavior. This section explores four demographic-based characteristics of the workforce that have implications for organizational behavior: (1) women are encountering a glass ceiling, (2) racial groups are encountering a glass ceiling and perceived discrimination, (3) there is a mismatch between workers' educational attainment and occupational requirements, and (4) the workforce is aging.

3 Women Are Encountering a Glass Ceiling In spite of the fact that women constituted 46% of the labor force in 1996 and are expected to represent 48% by 2010, they continue to encounter the **glass ceiling.** The glass ceiling represents an invisible barrier that separates women and minorities from advancing into top management positions. Women, therefore, find themselves stuck in lower level jobs, ones that do not have profit-and-loss responsibility, and those with less visibility and influence. In general, these positions result in a lack of power because the job holder does not have control over others, resources, or technology. The end result is that women face legitimate power deficits while trying to climb the corporate ladder.

Glass ceiling

Invisible barrier blocking women and minorities from top management positions.

There are a variety of statistics that support the existence of a glass ceiling. As of March 2006, women were still underpaid relative to men: Women received 77% of men's earnings.[20] Even when women are paid the same as men, they may suffer in other areas of job opportunities. For example, a study of 69 male and female executives from a large multinational financial services corporation revealed no differences in base salary or bonus. However, the women in this sample received fewer stock options than the male executives, even after controlling for level of education, performance, and job function, and reported less satisfaction with future career opportunities.[21] A follow-up study of 13,503 female managers and 17,493 male managers from the same organization demonstrated that women at higher levels in the managerial hierarchy received fewer promotions than males at comparable positions.[22] Would you be motivated if you were a woman working in this organization?

Women still have not broken into the highest echelon of corporate America to a significant extent. For example, there were only 10 and 23 female CEOs in the *Fortune* 500 and *Fortune* 1000 as of February 2007, respectively. Women also accounted for only 15.6% of corporate-officer positions at *Fortune* 500 companies in 2006.[23] Further, the majority of women in top jobs are working in staff rather than line positions. In general, roles associated with line jobs contain more power and influence than staff positions.

Why does the glass ceiling exist for women? A team of researchers attempted to answer this question by surveying 461 executive women who held titles of vice president or higher in *Fortune* 1000 companies and all of the *Fortune* 1000 CEOs. Respondents were asked to evaluate the extent to which they used 13 different career strategies to break through the glass ceiling.

Findings indicated that the top nine strategies were central to the advancement of these female executives. Within this set, however, four strategies were identified as critical toward breaking the glass ceiling: consistently exceeding performance expectations, developing a style with which male managers are comfortable, seeking out difficult or challenging assignments, and having influential mentors.[24] These results are consistent with comments made by Sara Lee's CEO, Brenda Barnes, when asked by a reporter whether she saw any significance in being named CEO the same week Carly Fiorina was forced out at Hewlett-Packard. Barnes said, "The way I see it, CEOs are supposed to drive performance. That comes with the territory, male or female. The fact that we are both female is interesting, but the job is what it is. You have to do the job."[25]

Results from the survey further demonstrated that the CEOs and female executives differed in their assessment of the barriers preventing women from advancing to positions of corporate leadership. CEOs concluded that women do not get promoted because (1) they lack significant general management or line experience and (2) women have not been in the executive talent pool for a long enough period of time to get selected. In contrast, the female executives indicated that (1) male stereotyping and preconceptions and (2) exclusion from informal networks were the biggest inhibitors to their promotability. These findings suggest that it is important to sensitize CEOs to the corporate culture faced by female employees. Breaking the glass ceiling will only occur when senior management has a good understanding of the unique experiences associated with being in the minority.

4 Racial Groups Are Encountering a Glass Ceiling and Perceived Discrimination

Historically, the United States has been a black-and-white country. The percentage change in US population between 2000 and 2050 by race reveals that this pattern no longer exists (see Figure 2–2). Figure 2–2 shows that Asians and Hispanics are expected to have the largest growth in population between 2000 and 2050. The Asian population will triple

As was true for women, many people of color encounter the glass ceiling. Rudolpho Lorenzo, who was the recipient of a $5,000.00 micro loan to expand his grocery store, escaped the glass ceiling by starting his own business. The number of minority-owned businesses is on the rise, and the number of Hispanic-owned businesses partially fueled this growth. Can you recommend other strategies people of color can use to break the glass ceiling?

Figure 2–2   *Percentage Change in US Population by Race*

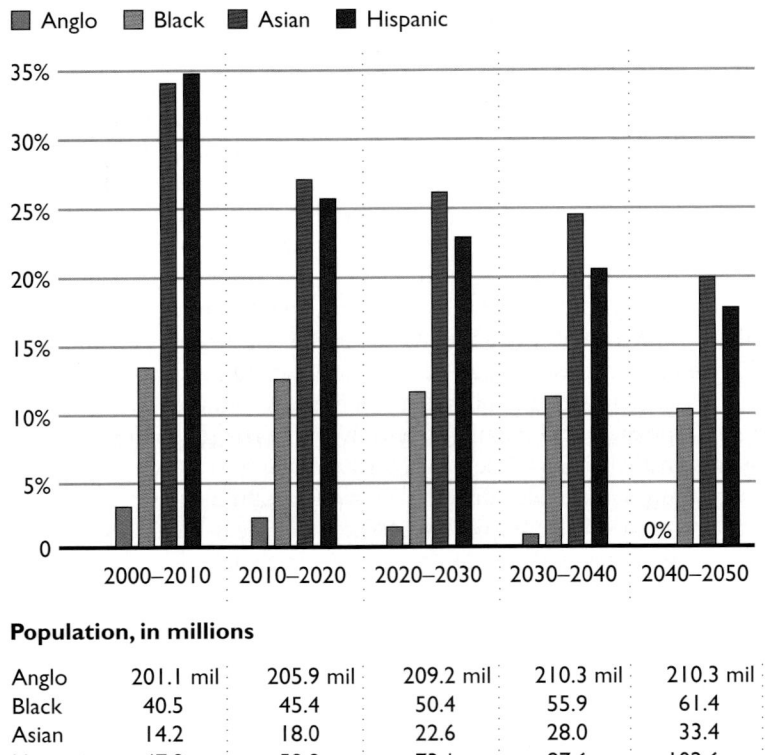

| Anglo ▣ | Black ▣ | Asian ▣ | Hispanic ■ |

Population, in millions

	2000–2010	2010–2020	2020–2030	2030–2040	2040–2050
Anglo	201.1 mil	205.9 mil	209.2 mil	210.3 mil	210.3 mil
Black	40.5	45.4	50.4	55.9	61.4
Asian	14.2	18.0	22.6	28.0	33.4
Hispanic	47.8	59.8	73.1	87.6	102.6

Source: US Census Bureau   Associated Press

SOURCE: G C Armas, "Almost Half of US Likely to Be Minorities by 2050," *Arizona Republic,* March 18, 2004, p A5. US Census Bureau, Tbl. 1a., "Projected Population of the US by Race and Hispanic Origin: 2000–2050 (www.census.gov/ipc/www/usinterimproj/), March 2004. Used by permission of the Associated Press.

to 33 million by 2050, and the Hispanics will increase their ranks by 118% to 102.6 million. Hispanics will account for 25% of the population in 2050. All told, the so-called minority groups will constitute 49.9% of the population in 2050 according to the Census Bureau.[26]

Unfortunately, three additional trends suggest that current-day minority groups are experiencing their own glass ceiling. First, minorities in general are advancing less in the managerial and professional ranks than whites. For example, whites, blacks, Asians, and Hispanics or Latinos held 35.6%, 26.5%, 45.2%, and 17.3% of all managerial and professional jobs in the United States in 2004.[27] Second, the number of race-based charges of discrimination that were deemed to show reasonable cause by the US Equal Employment Opportunity Commission increased from 294 in 1995 to 1,016 in 2006. Companies paid a total of $61.4 million to resolve these claims outside of litigation in 2006.[28] Third, minorities also tend to earn less personal income than whites. Median household income in 2005 was $48,977, $34,241, and $30,134 for whites, blacks, and Hispanics, respectively. Interestingly, Asians had the highest median income in the United States—$57,518.[29]

In addition to a racially based glass ceiling, a number of research studies showed that minorities experienced more perceived discrimination than whites. For example, telephone interviews with 635 blacks, 567 whites, and 314 Hispanics from around the United States demonstrated that blacks perceived that they experienced more discrimination and had a harder time getting ahead than did whites or Hispanics.[30] In support of these perceptual results, another study of 44 black managers and 80 white managers revealed that black managers experienced slower rates of promotion and less psychological support than white managers.[31] It thus is not surprising that the turnover rate for black executives is 40% higher than for their white counterparts. Finally, several studies have shown that blacks experience significant amounts of racism-related stress, which in turn affects their physical and psychological well-being.[32]

go to the Web for the Self-Exercise: What Are the Strategies for Breaking the Glass Ceiling?

Mismatch between Educational Attainment and Occupational Requirements

Approximately 27% of the labor force has a college degree, and it pays to graduate from college (see Figure 2–3). At the same time, however, three trends suggest a mismatch between educational attainment and the knowledge and skills needed by employers. First, recent studies show that college graduates, while technically and functionally competent, are lacking in terms of teamwork skills, critical thinking, and analytic reasoning. Second, there is a shortage of college graduates in technical fields related to science, math, and engineering. Third, organizations are finding that high school graduates working in entry-level positions do not possess the basic skills needed

Figure 2–3   *Education and Personal Income (2006)*

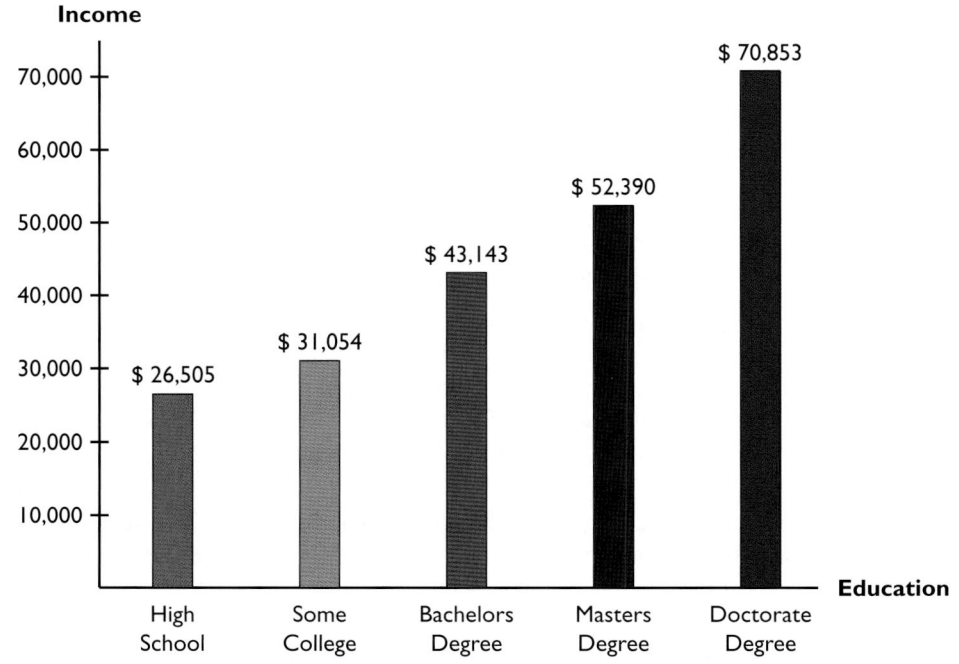

SOURCE: Data were obtained from "Personal Income in the United States," *Wikipedia*, http://en.wikipedia. org/wiki/Personal_income_in_the_United_States, last modified February 20, 2007.

to perform effectively.[33] This latter trend is partly due to a national high-school dropout rate estimated at 33% and the existence of about 90 million functionally illiterate adults in the United States. Literacy is defined as "an individual's ability to read, write, and speak English, compute and solve problems at levels of proficiency necessary to function on the job and in society, to achieve one's goals, and develop one's knowledge and potential."[34] Illiteracy costs corporate America around $60 billion a year in lost productivity.[35] These statistics are worrisome to both government officials and business leaders.

The key issue confronting organizations in the United States, and any country that wants to compete in a global economy, is whether or not the population has the skills and abilities needed to drive economic growth. Unfortunately, results from a study commissioned by the National Center on Education and the Economy suggests that the United States is losing ground on this issue. Findings were summarized in a book titled *Tough Choice or Tough Times: The Report of the New Commission on the Skills of the American Workforce*. The authors arrived at the following conclusions based on their analysis.

> Whereas for most of the 20th century the United States could take pride in having the best-educated workforce in the world, that is no longer true. Over the past 30 years, one country after another has surpassed us in the proportion of their entering workforce with the equivalent of a high school diploma, and many more are on the verge of doing so. Thirty years ago, the United States could lay claim to having 30 percent of the world's population of college students. Today that proportion has fallen to 14 percent and is continuing to fall.
>
> While our international counterparts are increasingly getting more education, their young people are getting a better education as well. American students and young adults place anywhere from the middle to the bottom of the back in all three continuing comparative studies of achievement in mathematics, science, and general literacy in the advanced industrial nations.
>
> While our relative position in the world's education league tables has continued its long slow decline, the structure of the global economy has continued to evolve. Every day, more and more of the work that people do ends up in a digitized form. From X-rays used for medical diagnostic purposes, to songs, movies, architectural drawings, technical papers, and novels, that work is saved on a hard disk and transmitted instantly over the Internet to someone near or far who makes use of it in an endless variety of ways. Because this is so, employers everywhere have access to a worldwide workforce composed of people who do not have to move to participate in work teams that are truly global. Because this is so, a swiftly rising number of American workers at every skill level are in direct competition with workers in every corner of the globe.[36]

These conclusions underscore the fact that the mismatch between educational attainment and occupational requirements have both short- and long-term implications for organizations and countries alike. American companies are more likely to outsource technical work to countries like India and China, to hire more immigrants to fill entry-level positions, and to spend more money on employee training.[37]

The Aging Workforce   America's population and workforce are getting older. Between 1995 and 2020, the number of individuals in the United States over age 65 will increase by 60%, the 45-to 64-year-old population by 34%, and those between ages 18 and 44 by 4%.[38] Life expectancy is increasing as well. The number of people living into their 80s is increasing rapidly, and this group disproportionately suffers from chronic illness. The United States is not the only country with an aging population. Germany, China, Japan, Russia, Brazil, Italy, and other countries in both eastern and western Europe, for

Figure 2–4   *Retirees per 100 Workers around the Globe**

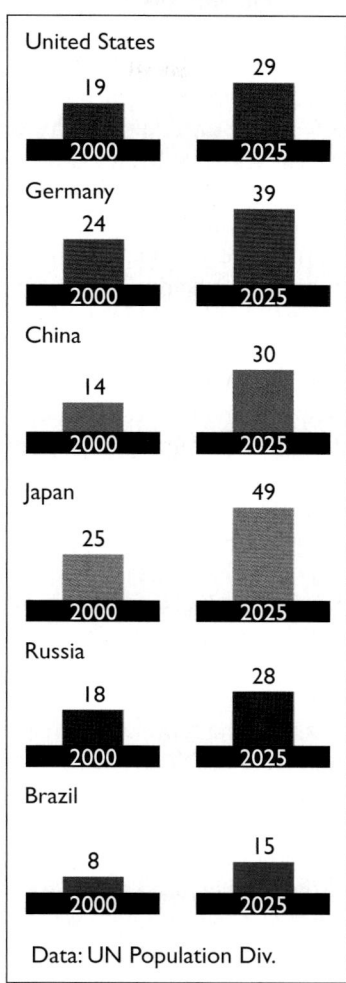

Data: UN Population Div.

*Retirees over age 65.

SOURCE: P Engardio, C Matlack, G Edmondson, I Rowley, C Barraclough, and G Smith, "Now the Geezer Glut," *BusinessWeek*, January 31, 2005, p 45.

example, are expected to encounter significant economic, social, and political problems due to an aging population.[39] Figure 2–4 provides a good illustration. It shows the number of retirees per 100 workers across various countries for the years of 2000 and 2025. The key conclusion derived from this data is that the greater the number of retirees that must be supported by a country's workforce, the greater the burden put on current workers to financially support the country's retirees. Relatively speaking, workers in Germany, China, and Japan are more likely to pay increased taxes in 2025 to support retirees than are workers in the United States, Russia, and Brazil based on data presented in Figure 2–4.

An aging population in the United States also underscores a potential skill gap in the future. As those employees in the baby-boom generation retire—the 76 million people born between 1946 and 1964—the US workforce will lose the skills, knowledge, experience, and relationships possessed by the more than a quarter of all Americans. This situation will likely create skill shortages in fast-growing technical fields.

5 Managerial Implications of Demographic Diversity

5 Managerial Implications of Demographic Diversity Regardless of gender, race, or age, all organizations need employees who possess the skills and abilities needed to successfully complete their jobs. To attract the best workers, companies need to adopt policies and procedures that meet the needs of all employees. Programs such as day care, elder care, flexible work schedules, and benefits such as paternal leaves, less rigid relocation policies, concierge services, and mentoring programs are likely to become more popular.[40] Pfizer, for example, offers on-site child care at four locations and elder care.[41] That said, however, special effort is needed to eliminate the glass ceiling that has impacted women and minorities. Ernst & Young, for instance, followed this recommendation after recognizing that the turnover rate among female employees was higher than male peers and that there were very few female partners: The cost of turnover averaged 150% of a departing employee's annual salary.

Organizations can also help women to break through the glass ceiling by making sure that they have the developmental assignments that prepare them for promotional opportunities.[42] Laura Desmond, CEO of Starcom Media Veset/the Americas, suggests that women need to help themselves advance to senior-level positions. She believes that "getting to the top requires setting goals and persevering—along with a willingness to seek stretch assignments that challenge and yield broader experiences." Andrea Jung, chairman and CEO of Avon Products, further recommends that women should find a company or industry that they love because "the hard work and sacrifices required are only possible if you are fully engaged in your company and enjoy what you do."[43]

Given the projected increase in the number of Hispanics entering the workforce over the next 25 years, managers should consider progressive methods to recruit, retain, and integrate this segment of the population into their organizations. For example, Diversified Investment Advisors, a retirement investment firm located in Purchase, New York, is providing financial education in Spanish to its employees. The organization found that this program increased employee participation in its retirement and health care programs while also increasing employee satisfaction and loyalty.[44] Research further reveals that the retention and career progression of minorities can be significantly enhanced through effective mentoring.

David Thomas, a researcher from Harvard University, conducted a three-year study of mentoring practices at three US corporations: a manufacturer, an electronics company, and a high-tech firm. His results revealed that successful people of color who advanced the furthest had a strong network of mentors and sponsors who nurtured their professional development. Findings also demonstrated that people of color should be mentored differently than their white counterparts. He recommended that organizations

> should provide a range of career paths, all uncorrelated with race, that lead to the executive suite.... Achieving this system, however, would require integrating the principles of opportunity, development, and diversity into the fabric of the organization's management practices and human resource systems. And an important element in the process would be to identify potential mentors, train them, and ensure that they are paired with promising professionals of color.[45]

Mismatches between the amount of education needed to perform current jobs and the amount of education possessed by members of the workforce are growing around the world (see the Real World/Real People feature on page 51). This trend creates three potential problems for organizations. First, there will be a shortage of qualified people in technical fields.[46] To combat this issue, both Lockheed Martin and

There Is a Shortage of Talent around the World

Employers in some unlikely places say they're having trouble filling jobs. Factory managers in Ho Chi Minh City report many of their $62-a-month workers went home for the Tet holiday in February and never came back. In Bulgaria, computer experts are in such demand they can't be bothered to answer the want ads of a Los Angeles movie studio. And in Peoria, Caterpillar Inc. is struggling to train enough service technicians. The problem in each case: not enough people who are both able and willing to do the work for the posted pay. "We've got a global problem . . . and it's only going to continue to get worse," says Stephen Hitch, a human resource manager at Caterpillar. . . .

"It's not just a U.S. phenomenon," says Jeffrey A. Joerres, CEO of Manpower Inc., the staffing agency. On Mar. 29, Manpower was to release the results of a survey of nearly 37,000 employers in 27 countries. The study found that 41% of them are having trouble hiring the people they need.

How might the shortage of talent in China affect the country's economic growth?

SOURCE: Excerpted from P Coy and J Ewing, "Where Are All the Workers?" *BusinessWeek*, April 9, 2007, p 28.

Agilent Technologies offer some type of paid apprenticeship or internship to attract high-school students interested in the sciences.[47] Second, on-the-job remedial skills and literacy training will be necessary to help the growing number of dropouts and illiterates cope with job demands. For example, US organizations spent $56 billion on training in 2006.[48] Finally, organizations will continue to be asked to help resolve the educational problems in the United States.[49]

Advanced Micro Devices in Sunnyvale, California, for example, devotes more than half its corporate contributions to education programs. Hewlett-Packard (HP) also makes significant contributions aimed at encouraging school reform and equipping school systems with the technology needed for technical education. HP also created the HP Scholar Program to support high-school minority students who are planning to major in computer science and electrical and computer engineering in college. The chosen students receive up to $40,000 in equipment to support their studies.[50] Supporting education is good for business and society at large. A better education system not only contributes to the United States' ability to compete internationally, but it facilitates a better quality of life for all its population.

As the baby-boom generation reaches retirement age after the turn of the century, the workforce will be top-heavy with older employees, creating the problem of career plateauing for younger workers. **Career plateauing** is defined "as that point in a career [at] which future hierarchical mobility seems unlikely."[51] Career plateauing is associated with stress and dissatisfaction.[52] Unfortunately, this problem is intensified by the fact that organizations are flattening—and reducing the number of managerial jobs—in order to save costs and increase efficiency. Managers will thus need to find alternatives other than promotions to help employees satisfy their needs and to feel successful, and employees will need to take a much more active role in managing their careers.

There are three additional recommendations for managing an aging workforce. The first involves the need to help employees deal with personal issues associated with elder care. Elder care is a critical issue for employees that have aging parents, and failing to deal with it can drive up an employer's costs. For example, MetLife estimates that a lack of elder care costs organizations at least $11 billion a year in lost productivity and increased absenteeism, workday interruptions, and turnover.[53] Second, employers need

Career plateauing
The end result when the probability of being promoted is very small.

to make a concerted effort to keep older workers engaged and committed and their skills current. The following seven initiatives can help accomplish this objective.[54]

1. Provide challenging work assignments that make a difference to the firm.
2. Give the employee considerable autonomy and latitude in completing a task.
3. Provide equal access to training and learning opportunities when it comes to new technology.
4. Provide frequent recognition for skills, experience, and wisdom gained over the years.
5. Provide mentoring opportunities whereby older workers can pass on accumulated knowledge to younger employees.
6. Ensure that older workers receive sensitive, high-quality supervision.
7. Design a work environment that is both stimulating and fun.

Employees from Chick Fil-A are working out at an organizationally sponsored health club at the headquarters in Hapeville, Georgia. Organizations fund such facilities because employee fitness helps to reduce the costs of healthcare. Would you like to work for an organization that has a fitness center?

The final recommendation involves the process of managing the cost of health care, which has risen at an average annual rate of 14% and is likely to increase as the population ages.[55] One option used by many companies is to drop different types of coverage or pass the expenses onto employees. Alternatively, other organizations have tried to lower health care costs by offering benefits that encourage employees to adopt a healthier life style. For example, SAS, the Cary, North Carolina, software company, encourages employees to use its 10-lane swimming pool, ping-pong tables, volleyball courts, soccer fields, tennis courts, and putting green. Adobe Systems in San Jose similarly offers its employees a fitness center with trainer and a combination of basketball and bocce courts.[56] Smoking cessation and weight loss programs are other popular benefits that have been found to lower the cost of health care. Experts estimate that smoking causes more than $157 billion in annual heath-related losses. Some organizations, such as Schweitzer Engineering Laboratories in Pullman, Washington, and Weyco Inc., in Okemos, Michigan, have gone so far as to implement a policy of not hiring smokers. This drastic step must be pursued with caution, however, as several states prohibit employers from making nonsmoking a condition of employment. Although the proactive approach of offering lifestyle-related benefits increases costs in the short-run, experience shows that the benefits can exceed the costs over time.[57]

6 The Positive and Negative Effects of Diverse Work Environments

Earlier in this chapter we stated that effectively managing diversity is not only a good thing to do in order to attract and retain the most talented employees, but it makes good business sense. Although one can easily find testimonials from managers and organizations supporting this conclusion, we need to examine the validity of this claim by considering the evidence provided by OB research. As you will learn shortly, this research reveals that there are both positive and negative effects of diversity on important work outcomes. Organizational behavior researchers have explained these conflicting results by integrating two competing explanations of how diversity impacts employee attitudes, behavior, and performance. These explanations are based on what is called *social categorization theory* and *information/decision-making* theory. This section focuses on helping you understand how to garner the positive benefits of diversity by presenting a process model of diversity that integrates these two explanations.

Social Categorization Theory

A team of OB researchers describe the **social categorization theory** of diversity as follows:

> The social categorization perspective holds that similarities and differences are used as a basis for categorizing self and others into groups, with ensuing categorizations distinguishing between one's own in-group and one or more out-groups. People tend to like and trust in-group members more than out-group members and thus generally tend to favor in-groups over out-groups.… [W]ork group members are more positively inclined toward their group and the people within it if fellow group members are similar rather than dissimilar to the self.[58]

This perspective further implies that similarity leads to liking and attraction, thereby fostering a host of positive outcomes. If this were the case, one would expect that the more homogeneous a work group, the higher the member commitment and group cohesion, and the lower the amount of interpersonal conflicts. There is a large body of research supporting propositions derived from the social categorization model.[59]

For example, past research revealed that people who were different from their work units in racial or ethnic background were less psychologically committed to their organizations, less satisfied with their careers.[60] Additional studies showed that demographic diversity was associated with less cooperation among team members and more negative impressions toward people who were demographically different.[61] Finally, recent studies demonstrated that demographic diversity was associated with higher employee turnover and employee deviance (i.e., exhibiting behavior that violates norms and threatens the well-being of the organization) and lower profits.[62] All told then, the social categorization model supports the idea that homogeneity is better than heterogeneity in terms of affecting work-related attitudes, behavior, and performance.

Information/Decision-Making Theory

The second theoretical point of view, referred to as **information/decision-making theory,** arrives at opposite predictions, proposing that diverse groups should outperform homogenous groups. The logic of this theory was described as follows:

> The idea is that diverse groups are more likely to possess a broader range of task-relevant knowledge, skills, and abilities that are distinct and nonredundant and to have different opinions and perspectives on the task at hand. This not only gives diverse groups a larger pool of resources, but may also have other beneficial effects.[63]

This perspective highlights three positive effects of diverse work groups.[64] First, diverse groups are expected to do a better job in earlier phases of problem solving because they are more likely to use their diverse backgrounds to generate a more comprehensive view of a problem. For example, gender and ethnic diversity can help work teams to better understand the needs and perspectives of a multicultural customer base. Second, the existence of diverse perspectives can help groups to brainstorm or uncover more novel alternatives during problem-solving activities. Finally, diversity can enhance the number of contacts a group or work unit has at its disposal. This broad network enables groups to gain access to new information

Social categorization theory
Similarity leads to linking and attraction.

Information/ decision-making theory
Diversity leads to better task-relevant processes and decision making.

and expertise, which results in more support for decisions than homogenous groups. Research supports this theory of diversity.

Team performance was positively related to a team's diversity in gender, ethnicity, age, and education.[65] Heterogeneous groups also were found to produce better-quality decisions and demonstrated higher productivity than homogenous groups.[66] Preliminary research also supports the idea that workforce diversity promotes creativity and innovation. This occurs through the sharing of diverse ideas and perspectives. Rosabeth Moss-Kanter, a management expert, was one of the first to investigate this relationship. Her results indicated that innovative companies deliberately used heterogeneous teams to solve problems, and they employed more women and minorities than less innovative companies. She also noted that innovative companies did a better job of eliminating racism, sexism, and classism.[67] A summary of 40 years of diversity research supported Moss-Kanter's conclusion that diversity can promote creativity and improve a team's decision making.[68]

Reconciling the Effects of Diverse Work Environments
Our previous discussion about social categorization theory and information/decision-making theory revealed that there are both positive and negative effects associated with diversity. The model in Figure 2–5 summarizes the process underlying these effects. Consistent with social categorization theory, there is a negative relationship between the amount of diversity in a work group and the quality of interpersonal processes and group dynamics within a work group (path A in Figure 2–5). This negative relationship ultimately results in negative outcomes because of the positive relationship between the quality of interpersonal processes and group dynamics and outcomes (path C). For example, gender and racial diversity in a work group foster more interpersonal conflict, which in turn results in lower job satisfaction, higher turnover, and lower productivity.

In contrast, research regarding the information/decision-making theory tells us that the amount of diversity in a work group is positively associated with task-relevant processes and decision making (path B), which in turn fosters positive outcomes

Figure 2–5   *A Process Model of Diversity*

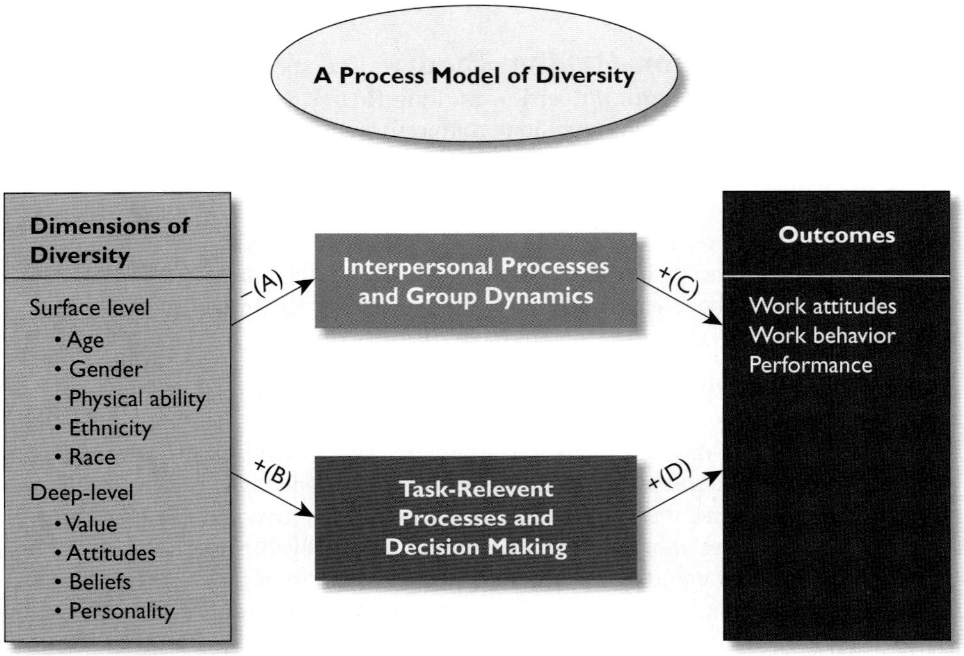

(path D). Gender and racial diversity in this case lead to positive outcomes because they lead to improved task-related processes and decision making.

Given that work-group diversity is associated with positive and negative outcomes, we need to consider what management can do to reduce the potential negative effects of diversity. First, organizations can target training to improve the inherent negative relationship between a work group's diversity and its interpersonal processes and group dynamics (path A in Figure 2–5). For example, training can be used to help employees develop interpersonal skills and a greater appreciation for diversity. This training might focus on conflict management, interpersonal influence, giving feedback, communication, and valuing differences. IBM, for instance, uses a program labeled "Shades of Blue" to help employees understand how differences in deep-level dimensions of diversity like values and beliefs influence social interactions at work.[69] Second, managers can seek ways to help employees ease the tensions of working in diverse groups. Such efforts might include the creation of support groups.[70] Finally, steps could be taken to reduce the negative effects of unconscious stereotyping and increase the use of group goals in heterogenous groups. Rewarding groups to accomplish group goals might encourage group members to focus on their common objectives rather than on demographic differences that are unrelated to performance.[71]

7 Barriers and Challenges to Managing Diversity

We introduced this chapter by noting that diversity is a sensitive, potentially volatile, and sometimes uncomfortable issue. It is therefore not surprising that organizations encounter significant barriers when trying to move forward with managing diversity. The following is a list of the most common barriers to implementing successful diversity programs;[72]

1. *Inaccurate stereotypes and prejudice.* This barrier manifests itself in the belief that differences are viewed as weaknesses. In turn, this promotes the view that diversity hiring will mean sacrificing competence and quality.

2. *Ethnocentrism.* The ethnocentrism barrier represents the feeling that one's cultural rules and norms are superior or more appropriate than the rules and norms of another culture. This barrier is thoroughly discussed in Chapter 4.

3. *Poor career planning.* This barrier is associated with the lack of opportunities for diverse employees to get the type of work assignments that qualify them for senior management positions.

4. *An unsupportive and hostile working environment for diverse employees.* Sexual, racial, and age harassment are common examples of hostile work environments. Whether perpetrated against women, men, or older individuals, hostile environments are demeaning, unethical, and appropriately called "work environment pollution." Moreover, the EEOC holds employers legally accountable for behavior that creates a hostile work environment. An expert on the subject explains:

   > An employer violates Title VII of the Civil Rights of 1964 (see Table 2–1) if it engages in unlawful discrimination by maintaining a hostile work environment. To prove a hostile work environment claim involving co-workers, an employee must show that she was subject to unwelcome harassment based on a protected characteristic [e.g., race, color, religion, national origin, sex, age] and that the harassment was severe or pervasive enough to create a hostile or abusive working environment. In addition, the employee must show that the employer knew or should have known about the environment and failed to act promptly to prevent or end the harassment.[73]

Sexual Harassment Is a Growing Problem in China

The phrase "sexual harassment" didn't exist in the Chinese language a decade ago. Now lawmakers are hoping to eliminate the action it describes. On March 4, [2005] female Communist Party leaders introduced legislation to make sexual harassment illegal.

The problem has become widespread in China as more women join the workforce. In a recent newspaper survey, 86% of women say they have been hassled by co-workers. In 2003, male officials in Sichuan Province were barred from having female assistants in order to curb incidents.

There is no specific law under which victims can get redress, so most sexual harassment suits in China are dismissed. The only two plaintiffs to win cases—one a man—did so by citing a law protecting their "human dignity." Each got $250 and an apology.

SOURCE: Excerpted from "Gender Watch: Now No Means No in China," *BusinessWeek*, March 28, 2005, p 12.

The increasing number of female employees in the workforce in China has led to an increase in sexual harassment throughout the country. To what extent will this problem influence China's expanding economic growth?

Sexual harassment, which we discuss in Chapter 11 under the context of men and women working together in groups, is the most frequent type of hostile environment charge filed with the EEOC. Sexual harassment also happens to be an international problem (see the Real World/Real People feature above).

5. *Lack of political savvy on the part of diverse employees.* Diverse employees may not get promoted because they do not know how to "play the game" of getting along and getting ahead in an organization. Research reveals that women and people of color are excluded from organizational networks.[74]

6. *Difficulty in balancing career and family issues.* Women still assume the majority of the responsibilities associated with raising children. This makes it harder for women to work evenings and weekends or to frequently travel once they have children. Even without children in the picture, household chores take more of a woman's time than a man's time.

7. *Fears of reverse discrimination.* Some employees believe that managing diversity is a smoke screen for reverse discrimination. This belief leads to very strong resistance because people feel that one person's gain is another's loss.

8. *Diversity is not seen as an organizational priority.* This leads to subtle resistance that shows up in the form of complaints and negative attitudes. Employees may complain about the time, energy, and resources devoted to diversity that could have been spent doing "real work."

9. *The need to revamp the organization's performance appraisal and reward system.* Performance appraisals and reward systems must reinforce the need to effectively manage diversity. This means that success will be based on a new set of criteria. For example, General Electric evaluates the extent to which its managers are inclusive of employees with different backgrounds. These evaluations are used in salary and promotion decisions.[75]

10. *Resistance to change.* Effectively managing diversity entails significant organizational and personal change. As discussed in Chapter 18, people resist change for many different reasons.

In summary, managing diversity is a critical component of organizational success.

go to the Web for the Group Exercise: Managing Diversity-Related Interactions

8 Organizational Practices Used to Effectively Manage Diversity

So what are organizations doing to effectively manage diversity? Answering this question requires that we provide a framework for categorizing organizational initiatives. Researchers and practitioners have developed relevant frameworks. One was developed by R Roosevelt Thomas, Jr, a diversity expert. He identified eight generic action options that can be used to address any type of diversity issue. This section reviews Thomas's framework in order to provide you with a broad understanding about how organizations are effectively managing diversity.

R Roosevelt Thomas, Jr's Generic Action Options

Thomas identified eight basic responses for handling any diversity issue. After describing each action option, we discuss relationships among them.[76]

Option 1: Include/Exclude This choice is an outgrowth of affirmative action programs. Its primary goal is to either increase or decrease the number of diverse people at all levels of the organizations. Shoney's restaurant represents a good example of a company that attempted to include diverse employees after settling a discrimination lawsuit. The company subsequently hired African-Americans into positions of dining-room supervisors and vice presidents, added more franchises owned by African-Americans, and purchased more goods and services from minority-owned companies.[77]

Option 2: Deny People using this option deny that differences exist. Denial may manifest itself in proclamations that all decisions are color, gender, and age blind and that success is solely determined by merit and performance. Consider State Farm Insurance, for example. "Although it was traditional for male agents and their regional managers to hire male relatives, State Farm Insurance avoided change and denied any alleged effects in a nine-year gender-bias suit that the company lost."[78]

Option 3: Assimilate The basic premise behind this alternative is that all diverse people will learn to fit in or become like the dominant group. It only takes time and reinforcement for people to see the light. Organizations initially assimilate employees through their recruitment practices and the use of company orientation programs. New hires generally are put through orientation programs that aim to provide employees with the organization's preferred values and a set of standard operating procedures. Employees then are encouraged to refer to the policies and procedures manual when they are confused about what to do in a specific situation. These practices create homogeneity among employees.

Option 4: Suppress

Differences are squelched or discouraged when using this approach. This can be done by telling or reinforcing others to quit whining and complaining about issues. The old "you've got to pay your dues" line is another frequently used way to promote the status quo.

Option 5: Isolate

This option maintains the current way of doing things by setting the diverse person off to the side. In this way the individual is unable to influence organizational change. Managers can isolate people by putting them on special projects. Entire work groups or departments are isolated by creating functionally independent entities, frequently referred to as "silos." Shoney Inc's employees commented to a *Wall Street Journal* reporter about isolation practices formerly used by the company:

> White managers told of how Mr Danner [previous chairman of the company] told them to fire blacks if they became too numerous in restaurants in white neighborhoods; if they refused, they would lose their jobs, too. Some also said that when Mr Danner was expected to visit their restaurant, they scheduled black employees off that day or, in one case, hid them in the bathroom. Others said blacks' applications were coded and discarded.[79]

Option 6: Tolerate

Toleration entails acknowledging differences but not valuing or accepting them. It represents a live-and-let-live approach that superficially allows organizations to give lip service to the issue of managing diversity. Toleration is different from isolation in that it allows for the inclusion of diverse people. However, differences are not really valued or accepted when an organization uses this option.

Option 7: Build Relationships

This approach is based on the premise that good relationships can overcome differences. It addresses diversity by fostering quality relationships—characterized by acceptance and understanding—among diverse groups. Rockwell Collins, Inc, a producer of aviation electronics in Cedar Rapids, Iowa, is a good example of a company attempting to use this diversity option. Rockwell is motivated to purse this option because it needs to hire around 7,000 employees between 2005 and 2010 in order to meet its revenue goals. The problem in recruiting is that the state is about 6% nonwhite. To attract minority candidates the company "is building closer relationships with schools that have strong engineering programs as well as sizable minority populations. It also is working more closely with minority-focused professional societies."[80] The city of Cedar Rapids is also getting involved in the effort by trying to offer more cultural activities and ethnic-food stores that cater to a more diverse population base.

Option 8: Foster Mutual Adaptation

In this option, people are willing to adapt or change their views for the sake of creating positive relationships with others. This implies that employees and management alike must be willing to accept differences, and most important, agree that everyone and everything is open for change. Companies can foster mutual adaptation through their recruitment and retention strategies as well their benefit packages. Consider the amount of mutual adaptation that has occurred with respect to the issue of sexual preferences. In 1990, for example, Cracker Barrel fired 11 gay employees because it did not want to employ people whose "sexual preferences fail to demonstrate normal heterosexual values."[81] As an aside, it is important to note that it is legal to fire employees simply for being gay in 34 states. In contrast, 263 firms in the *Fortune* 500 provided domestic partner benefits in 2006 whereas only 28 did in 1996. Hayward Bell, Chief Diversity Officer at Raytheon, offers keen insight about why organizations should consider fostering mutual adaptation. "Over the next ten years we're going to need anywhere from 30,000 to 40,000 new employees" and "we can't afford to turn our backs on anyone in the talent pool."[82]

Conclusions about Action Options Although the action options can be used alone or in combination, some are clearly better than others. Exclusion, denial, assimilation, suppression, isolation, and toleration are among the least preferred options. Inclusion, building relationships, and mutual adaptation are the preferred strategies.[83] That said, Thomas reminds us that mutual adaptation is the only approach that unquestionably endorses the philosophy behind managing diversity. In closing this discussion, it is important to note that choosing how to best manage diversity is a dynamic process that is determined by the context at hand. For instance, some organizations are not ready for mutual adaptation. The best one might hope for in this case is the inclusion of diverse people.

Raytheon is a good example of a company that is trying to eliminate the barriers to managing diversity. With a large number of employees needed in the near future, the Chief Diversity Officer has claimed that they won't be turning their backs on anyone.

Summary of Key Concepts

1. *Define diversity and review the four layers of diversity.* Diversity represents the individual differences that make people different from and similar to each other. Diversity pertains to everybody. It is not simply an issue of age, race, gender, or sexual orientation. The layers of diversity define an individual's personal identity and constitute a perceptual filter that influences how we interpret the world. Personality is at the center of the diversity wheel. The second layer of diversity consists of a set of internal dimensions that are referred to as surface-level dimensions of diversity. The third layer is composed of external influences and is called secondary dimensions of diversity. The final layer of diversity includes organizational dimensions.

2. *Explain the difference between affirmative action and managing diversity.* Affirmative action is an outgrowth of equal employment opportunity legislation and is an artificial intervention aimed at giving management a chance to correct past discrimination. Managing diversity entails creating a host of organizational changes that enable all people to perform up to their maximum potential.

3. *Explain the glass ceiling and the four top strategies used by women to break the glass ceiling.* The glass ceiling is an invisible barrier blocking women and minorities from top management positions. The top four strategies used by women included the following: consistently exceed performance expectations, develop a style with which male managers are comfortable, seek out difficult or challenging assignments, and find influential mentors.

4. *Review the demographic trends pertaining to racial groups, educational mismatches, and an aging workforce.* With respect to racial groups, Asians and Hispanics are expected to have the largest growth in the population between 2000 and 2050, and minority groups will constitute 49.9% of the population in 2050. Minority groups also are experiencing a glass ceiling. There is a mismatch between workers' educational attainment and occupational requirements. The workforce is aging.

5. *Highlight the managerial implications of increasing diversity in the workforce.* There are eight broad managerial implications: (a) To attract the best workers, companies need to adopt policies and programs that meet the needs of all employees; (b) managers should consider progressive methods to recruit, retain, and integrate Hispanic workers into their organizations; (c) mentoring programs are needed to help minorities advance within the organizational hierarchy; (d) there will be a shortage of qualified people in technical fields; (e) on-the-job remedial skills and literacy training will be needed to help the growing number of dropouts and illiterates cope with job demands; (f) organizations will need to provide tangible support education if the United States is to remain globally competitive; (g) the problem of career plateauing needs to be managed; and (h) there are three broad recommendations for managing an aging workforce.

6. *Explain the positive and negative effects of diversity by using social categorization theory and information/decision-making theory.* Social categorization theory implies that similarity leads to liking and attraction, thereby fostering a host of positive outcomes. This theory supports the idea that homogeneity is better than heterogeneity because diversity causes negative interpersonal processes and group dynamics. The information/ decision-making theory is based on

the notion that diverse groups should outperform homogenous groups because diversity is positively associated with task-relevant processes and decision making.

7. *Identify the barriers and challenges to managing diversity.* There are 10 barriers to successfully implementing diversity initiatives: (*a*) inaccurate stereotypes and prejudice, (*b*) ethnocentrism, (*c*) poor career planning, (*d*) an unsupportive and hostile working environment for diverse employees, (*e*) lack of political savvy on the part of diverse employees, (*f*) difficulty in balancing career and family issues, (*g*) fears of reverse discrimination, (*h*) diversity is not seen as an organizational priority, (*i*) the need to revamp the organization's

performance appraisal and reward system, and (*j*) resistance to change.

8. *Discuss the organizational practices used to effectively manage diversity as identified by R Roosevelt Thomas, Jr.* There are many different practices organizations can use to manage diversity. R. Roosevelt Thomas, Jr, identified eight basic responses for handling any diversity issue: include/exclude, deny, assimilate, suppress, isolate, tolerate, build relationships, and foster mutual adaptation. Exclusion, denial, assimilation, suppression, isolation, and toleration are among the least preferred options. Inclusion, building relationships, and mutual adaptation are the preferred strategies.

Key Terms

Diversity 37
Discrimination 39
Affirmative action 39
Managing diversity 41
Workforce demographics 44

Glass ceiling 44
Career plateauing 51
Social categorization theory 53
Information/decision-making theory 53

OB in Action Case Study

Safeway's Diversity Initiatives Break the Glass Ceiling and Improve Corporate Earnings[84]

BusinessWeek Ten years ago, Safeway began facing increasingly stiff competition from upmarket specialty grocers on one end and cut-rate pricing on the other from big box stores such as Wal-Mart and Target. To meet these market challenges, the company began exploring programs to attract, develop and retain its best talent, and to position Safeway as an employer of choice.

Since 70 percent of its customers are women, the retail grocery giant also wanted to broaden the diversity of its workforce to reflect the customer base. The company recognized that a diverse workforce would help it better understand and respond to the needs of its customers, and that would give Safeway a competitive advantage in the market place.

Male leadership has long been the norm in the retail grocery industry, so the new programs required a real culture shift. Kim Farnham, director of HR planning, says Safeway took a series of steps aimed at changing the corporate culture to "a culture of development," one that focused on helping women—including women of color—advance into management.

The foundation of today's diversity initiative was laid down in 1997, says Farnham. A diversity workshop to educate managers was designed, balanced workforce goals were created, and a system that holds managers accountable for meeting those goals was developed. Metrics to track their success were put in place.

The goal throughout the planning phase was "to do it right, not to be first on the block," says Farnham. The result-

ing women's initiative, "Championing Change for Women: An Integrated Strategy," was fully implemented in 2000 as the first piece of Safeway's overall diversity initiative.

The diversity strategy includes effective communication of the business case for diversity and programs that focus on leadership development, mentoring and work/life balance. A rigorous accountability system for measuring and tracking balanced workforce goals alerts the company to any potential problems.

Larree Renda, executive vice president, chief strategist and administrative officer, says communicating the business case effectively to the entire organization starts with "visible leadership at the top. You need executives who talk the talk and also walk the walk, and I think we've been very good at that." For example, CEO Steve Burd talks regularly with employees about diversity issues in live discussions and at town hall meetings and conferences.

He also makes a point of discussing diversity via taped satellite broadcasts, part of a program of weekly broadcasts that are sent to store managers and that frequently cover diversity. Managers are expected to make the broadcasts available to their employees. The programs, which can spark discussions at staff meetings in each store, are shown on monitors in the staff break room. In addition, employees can view the broadcasts on their computers, Renda says. . . .

Safeway likes to promote from within and has traditionally focused on the retail level as a source of potential managers. Many current executives came up from entry-level positions in Safeway stores through the Retail Leadership Development (RLD) program, a formal, full-time career development program.

When the women's initiative was implemented in 2000, the RLD program began to focus particularly on women and people of color, and targets were established to increase the number of women and minorities who go through the training. Employees who are interested in becoming store managers can apply for the program by taking an entrance exam that tests such basic retail knowledge as understanding gross margins. Applicants also write an essay explaining how they would solve a business problem.

Those who successfully complete the 26-week program are immediately assigned to a store as an assistant manager—a position that can lead to corporate-level jobs.

Safeway's efforts to encourage women to advance don't end there, however. Recognizing that women often need to coordinate work schedules with family responsibilities, the company ensures that all qualified employees—including part-timers and those who work flexible schedules—have the same opportunities for coaching, development and advancement as those who work more traditional hours. . . . Another resource for women interested in advancing into management is the women's leadership network, established 10 years ago as part of the women's initiative.

The group sponsors such events as the "Women's Road Show," a series of presentations at Safeway locations throughout the country that highlight the success of individual Safeway women and provide learning and networking opportunities.

Wherever the "Road Show" executives speak, they also meet with women in the area who've been identified as likely candidates for management positions and targeted for developmental opportunities in stores. In discussions with these high-potential women about their career interests, the executives suggest potential job opportunities and encourage them to apply for so-called "stretch positions" that can help them advance to the next level.

Today there are five network groups, including groups for blacks, Asians, Hispanics, and lesbian, gay, bisexual and transgendered employees. Each is open to all employees and regularly offers a variety of educational activities and events. . . . A strong mentoring program is critical to the success of the company's leadership development efforts. Every Safeway manager, from the CEO on down, is expected to mentor his or her own employees, plus several others.

Because there is a serious lack of female and minority mentors, says Renda, it is expected that a manager's first mentee should be a woman, the next a person of color of either sex, "and then you can have a [white] man, in that order." . . .

Managers are responsible for driving the company's diversity efforts throughout the organization, so education and training begins with them. All new managers, starting at the top, attend the Managing Diversity Workshop, an eight-hour session cofacilitated by a line manager and HR. Farnham says she intentionally involves line managers to avoid the perception that the workshop is "just an HR program. It's integrated into the business," she says.

While each manager attends the workshop only once, "we recognize that diversity education is not complete in one eight-hour session." Farnham says the education continues through events sponsored by the network groups and diversity advisory boards, through video productions such as a "Women in Management" DVD, and through regular diversity discussions in staff meetings. A toolkit designed to guide managers in incorporating diversity discussions into their staff meetings is available on the company intranet.

"Safeway is a data-driven company," says Farnham. "We track census data to identify the demographics of each geographic area," and this data is used to set each manager's specific targets for developing women.

Managers are evaluated on their success in meeting the diversity goals via balanced scorecard data and performance evaluations from their supervisors, employees and customers. And there are big incentives for managers to reach their diversity targets: High marks all around can increase a manager's bonus by up to 10 percent, and consistently high ratings are critical to advancement in the company.

Conversely, those who have trouble meeting their goals will be coached by senior leaders, and their bonuses can be reduced. . . . The following metrics offer mounting proof of the success of the women's initiative programs. Since 2000, says Farnham, the number of female store managers has increased by 42 percent. Within that group, the number of white females rose 31 percent and the number of women of color shot up a whopping 92 percent.

In addition, Safeway's diversity efforts have garnered praise from global investment bank Lehman Brothers. A research report prepared by the bank's independent analysts points out that Safeway's diversity programs have not only "led to substantial advancement for women and minorities both at the stores and at the corporate office," but also increased the company's sales and earnings. (In an industry with razor-thin margins, Safeway today is a highly profitable $40 billion company with 200,000 employees throughout the United States and Canada.) "Diversity is good for business," concludes the report.

Questions for Discussion

1. What is the business case that is driving Safeway's interest in managing diversity? Discuss.

2. Which layers of diversity is Safeway targeting in its overall diversity initiative?

3. Compare and contrast the extent to which Safeway is using principles from affirmative action and managing diversity. Explain your rationale.

4. Which of R Roosevelt Thomas Jr's eight generic diversity options is Safeway using to manage diversity? Explain.

5. While Safeway's diversity initiative is clearly working, what recommendations would you make for improving their program? Explain.

Ethical Dilemma

Should Wal-Mart Pull the Plug on Ningbo Beifa Group?[85]

TANG YINGHONG WAS CAUGHT IN AN IMPOSSIBLE squeeze. For years, his employer, Ningbo Beifa Group, had prospered as a top supplier of pens, mechanical pencils, and highlighters to Wal-Mart Stores and other major retailers. But late last year, Tang learned that auditors from Wal-Mart, Beifa's biggest customer, were about to inspect labor conditions at the factory in the Chinese coastal city of Ningbo where he worked as an administrator. Wal-Mart had already on three occasions caught Beifa paying its 3,000 workers less than China's minimum wage and violating overtime rules, Tang says. Under the U.S. chain's labor rules, a fourth offense would end the relationship.

Help arrived suddenly in the form of an unexpected phone call from a man calling himself Lai Mingwei. The caller said he was with Shanghai Corporate Responsibility Management & Consulting Co., and for a $5,000 fee, he'd take care of Tang's Wal-Mart problem. "He promised us he could definitely get us a pass for the audit," Tang says.

Lai provided advice on how to create fake but authentic-looking records and suggested that Beifa hustle any workers with grievances out of the factory on the day of the audit, Tang recounts. The consultant also coached Beifa managers on what questions they could expect from Wal-Mart's inspectors, says Tang. After following much of Lai's advice, the Beifa factory in Ningbo passed the audit earlier this year, Tang says, even though the company didn't change any of its practices.

For more than a decade, major American retailers and name brands have answered accusations that they exploit "sweatshop" labor with elaborate codes of conduct and on-site monitoring. But in China many factories have just gotten better at concealing abuses. Internal industry documents reviewed by *BusinessWeek* reveal that numerous Chinese factories keep double sets of books to fool auditors and distribute scripts for employees to recite if they are questioned. And a new breed of Chinese consultant has sprung up to assist companies like Beifa in evading audits. "Tutoring and helping factories deal with audits has become an industry in China," says Tang, 34, who recently left Beifa of his own volition to start a Web site for workers.

A lawyer for Beifa, Zhou Jie, confirms that the company employed the Shanghai consulting firm but denies any dishonesty related to wages, hours, or outside monitoring. Past audits had "disclosed some problems, and we took necessary measures correspondingly," he explains in a letter responding to questions. The lawyer adds that Beifa has "become the target of accusations" by former employees "whose unreasonable demands have not been satisfied." Reached by cell phone, a man identifying himself as Lai says that the Shanghai consulting firm helps suppliers pass audits, but he declines to comment on his work for Beifa.

BusinessWeek has informed executives at Wal-Mart about these allegations. What would you do if you were an executive at Wal-Mart?

1. Ningbo Beifa Group passed the most recent audit, so I would let these results stand for now.

2. What is done is done. However, I would investigate the allegations and then improve the future auditing procedures based on the results.

3. Investigate the allegations and discontinue working with Beifa if they are true.

4. Invent other options. Discuss.

Web Resources

For study material and exercises that apply to this chapter, visit our Web site,

www.mhhe.com/kreitner

CHAPTER 3

Organizational Culture, Socialization, and Mentoring

LEARNING OBJECTIVES

When you finish studying the material in this chapter, you should be able to:

1 Define organizational culture and discuss its three layers.

2 Discuss the difference between espoused and enacted values.

3 Describe the four functions of organizational culture.

4 Discuss the four types of organizational culture associated with the competing values framework.

5 Summarize the three key conclusions derived from research about the outcomes associated with organizational culture.

6 Review the three caveats about culture change.

7 Summarize the methods used by organizations to change organizational culture.

8 Describe the three phases in Feldman's model of organizational socialization.

9 Discuss the various socialization tactics used to socialize employees.

10 Explain the four developmental networks associated with mentoring.

online **resources**

Student Resources for Studying Chapter 3

The Web site for your text includes resources that will help you master the concepts in this chapter. As you read, you'll want to visit the site for these helpful tools:

- Your online Study Guide includes learning objectives, a chapter summary, a glossary of key terms, and discussion questions.
- Take a practice quiz and test your knowledge!
- Scroll through a PowerPoint presentation with key concepts for this chapter.

Your instructor might also direct you to the Web site for these exercises:

- Self-assessments that correspond with the chapter content and a Group Exercise.
- You'll also find Video Cases and Internet Exercises for this chapter online.

www.mhhe.com/kreitner

There's no doubt, developing *and* maintaining the right culture is a lot of work, but it can be done. Take Starbucks Coffee Canada. It does something 65% of the executives surveyed say their companies don't do: it regularly measures the status of its corporate culture. Every 18 months, the coffee chain asks its employees to spend 15 minutes filling out a Partner View Survey (every staff member is a "partner," in Starbucks lingo). Among other topics, participants answer questions about their overall job satisfaction and commitment to the company, using a five-point scale from "very dissatisfied" to "very satisfied." These questions are designed to gauge Starbucks progress toward one of its key values, providing a great work environment where people treat each other with respect and dignity.

The survey is voluntary, but the most recent Canadian one, in March, boasted a 90%-plus participation rate. The reason? The company makes it easy for staff members to fill out the questionnaire by allowing them to complete it online at the store, and Starbucks pays employees for their time. The senior management team also encourages employees to take part. But the biggest factor for the high participation rate is likely that the organization actually does something with the data. "People have seen tangible results from providing us feedback," says Colin Moore, president of Starbucks Coffee Canada, in Toronto. For example, the company recently learned its employees wanted to better understand career progression through the organization. Turns out, employees knew how a barista becomes a store manager but were less clear about how to land a job at the Toronto head office or one of the regional offices. "Our response was that we held career fairs in Vancouver, Calgary and Toronto," says Moore, "where we rented halls and staffed them with our department heads and other people across our company who spoke about their roles and job opportunities within the organization."

The Partner View Survey also serves as a two-way communications tool. Employees provide feedback; management reports the findings. During these discussions, the Canadian operation compares itself against operations in other countries and the entire Starbucks organization. Since the business tracks the results over time, it can see if it's making improvements every 18 months. Stores, district managers and functional departments of the company can also view the data and form workgroups to address specific issues and opportunities. "What the survey does," says Moore, "is give us another forum to talk to our people."

It seems to work. Even though one of Starbucks Coffee Canada's biggest challenges remains finding and keeping high-quality people, turnover is between 40% to 60% better than at many retail chains, says Moore. That's in spite of an aging population with fewer teenagers to take on junior positions. Make no mistake, part of what attracts people to the company are its well-known perks, such as extending benefits to part-time employees, giving employees the option to buy company stock at a discount and its commitment to social responsibility. But it's the company's culture that keeps them from leaving. "The Partner View Survey is a quantitative way for us to continue to ensure we're doing things that are consistent with our guiding principles and what we say we're going to do," says Moore.[1]

FOR DISCUSSION

How would you describe the organizational culture at Starbucks Coffee Canada?

The opening vignette highlights three key conclusions about organizational culture. First, an organization's culture can impact employee motivation, satisfaction, and turnover. Starbucks Canada was able to lower its employee turnover below industry average and increase employee satisfaction by creating a positive, employee-focused culture. The same can be said about the top five companies to work for in America in 2007 according to *Fortune*—Google, Genentech, Wegmans Food Markets, Container Store, and Whole Foods Market.[2] Second, organizational culture can be a source of competitive advantage. Southwest Airlines, for example, relies on its employees and customer-focused culture to produce sustained profits and high productivity.[3] Google and Genentech similarly use organizational culture to drive innovation and growth.[4] Finally, managers can influence organizational culture. Starbucks Canada, for instance, actively influenced or shaped its culture by using results from employee surveys.

This chapter will help you better understand how managers can use organizational culture as a competitive advantage. After defining and discussing the context of organizational culture, we examine (1) the dynamics of organizational culture, (2) the process of culture change, (3) the organization socialization process, and (4) the embedding of organizational culture through mentoring.

Organizational Culture: Definition and Context

Organizational culture

Shared values and beliefs that underlie a company's identity.

Organizational culture is "the set of shared, taken-for-granted implicit assumptions that a group holds and that determines how it perceives, thinks about, and reacts to its various environments."[5] This definition highlights three important characteristics of organizational culture. First, organizational culture is passed on to new employees through the process of socialization, a topic discussed later in this chapter. Second,

Figure 3–1   *A Conceptual Framework for Understanding Organizational Culture*

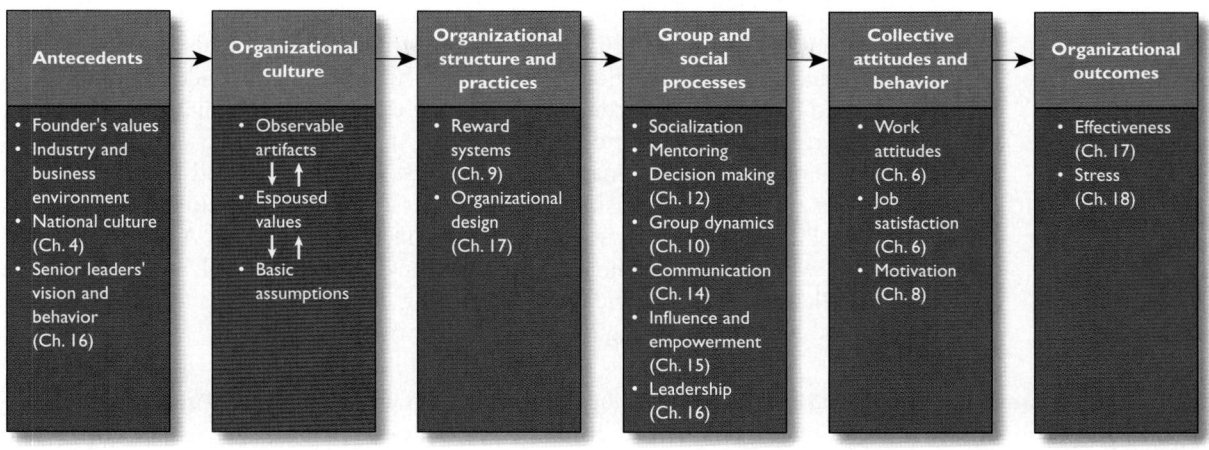

SOURCE: Adapted in part from C Ostroff, A Kinicki, and M Tamkins, "Organizational Culture and Climate," in *Handbook of Psychology*, vol. 12, ed Weiner, p 565–93, © 2003 John Wiley & Sons, Inc. Reprinted with permission of John Wiley & Sons, Inc.

organizational culture influences our behavior at work. Finally, organizational culture operates at different levels.

Figure 3–1 provides a conceptual framework for reviewing the widespread impact organizational culture has on organizational behavior. It also shows the linkage between this chapter—culture, socialization, and mentoring—and other key topics in this book. Figure 3–1 reveals organizational culture is shaped by four key components: the founder's values, the industry and business environment, the national culture, and the senior leaders' vision and behavior[6]: The impact of national culture on organizational behavior is discussed in detail in Chapter 4. In turn, organizational culture influences the type of organizational structure adopted by a company and a host of practices, policies, and procedures implemented in pursuit of organizational goals. These organizational characteristics then affect a variety of group and social processes. This sequence ultimately affects employees' attitudes and behavior and a variety of organizational outcomes. All told, Figure 3–1 reveals that organizational culture is a contextual variable influencing individual, group, and organizational behavior.

Dynamics of Organizational Culture

To gain a better understanding of how organizational culture is formed and used by employees, this section begins by discussing the layers of organizational culture. We then review the four functions of organizational culture, types of organizational culture, and outcomes associated with organizational culture.

Layers of Organizational Culture

Figure 3–1 shows the three fundamental layers of organizational culture: observable artifacts, espoused values, and basic assumptions. Each level varies in terms of outward visibility and resistance to change, and each level influences another level.

Observable Artifacts At the more visible level, culture represents observable artifacts. Artifacts consist of the physical manifestation of an organization's culture. Organizational examples include acronyms, manner of dress, awards, myths and stories told about the organization, published lists of values, observable rituals and ceremonies, special parking spaces, decorations, and so on. This level also includes visible behaviors exhibited by people and groups. Artifacts are easier to change than the less visible aspects of organizational culture. JCPenney Co., for example, is trying to revamp a culture based on tradition and hierarchy to one that is less formal and flexible by using the following artifacts: "Emphasizing the use of first names among colleagues and their superiors; selling the company's art collection—including work by AndyWahol—and replacing it with employee photos; reemphasizing business-casual attire during the week, and allowing jeans on Fridays; and allowing employees access to all parts of the headquarters' campus, including the executive suite and its elevator."[7]

Values
Enduring belief in a mode of conduct or end-state.

2 Espoused Values Values possess five key components. "**Values** (1) are concepts or beliefs, (2) pertain to desirable end-states or behaviors, (3) transcend situations, (4) guide selection or evaluation of behavior and events, and (5) are ordered by relative importance."[8]It is important to distinguish between values that are espoused versus those that are enacted.

Espoused values
The stated values and norms that are preferred by an organization.

Espoused values represent the explicitly stated values and norms that are preferred by an organization. They are generally established by the founder of a new or small company and by the top management team in a larger organization. Consider, for example, the espoused values of Williams-Sonoma, Inc. (see the Real World/Real People feature on page 69). This specialty retailer of home furnishings was founded in 1956 and has experienced substantial growth since its inception.

Sustainability
Meeting humanity's needs without harming future generations.

On a positive note, more and more companies are espousing the value of sustainability. **Sustainability** represents the belief that organizations should meet "humanity's needs without harming future generations." A recent article in *BusinessWeek* identified 24 companies committed to sustainability (e.g, Toyota, Nokia, Hewlett-Packard, ING, SONY, and Glaxo-SmithKline) and 7 that were seriously lagging behind (e.g., Allegheny Energy, General Motors, Petrochina, and Wal-Mart).[9] As mentioned in Chapter 1, Unilever is a great example of a company committed to this important value.

> The world is Unilever's laboratory. In Brazil, the company operates a free community laundry in a São Paulo slum, provides financing to help tomato growers convert to eco-friendly "drip" irrigation, and recycle 17 tons of waste annually at a toothpaste factory. Unilever funds a floating hospital that offers free medical care in Bangladesh, a nation with just 20 doctors for every 10,000 people. In Ghana, it teaches palm oil producers to reuse plant waste while providing potable water to deprived communities. In India, Unilever staff help thousands of women in remote villages start micro-enterprises. And responding to green activists, the company discloses how much carbon dioxide and hazardous waste its factories spew out around the world.[10]

Because espoused values represent aspirations that are explicitly communicated to employees, managers hope that those values will directly influence employee behavior. Unfortunately, aspirations do not automatically produce the desired behaviors because people do not always "walk the talk."

Enacted values
The values and norms that are exhibited by employees.

Enacted values, on the other hand, represent the values and norms that actually are exhibited or converted into employee behavior. They represent the values that employees ascribe to an organization based on their observations of what occurs on a daily basis. The following two examples are excellent representations of the difference between espoused and enacted values.

Williams-Sonoma's Espoused Values Focus on Employees, Customers, Shareholders, and Ethical Behavior

People First

We believe the potential of our company has no limit and is driven by our associates and their imagination. We are committed to an environment that attracts, motivates and recognizes high performance.

Customers

We are here to please our customers—without them nothing else matters.

Quality

We must take pride in everything we do. From our people, to our products and in our relationships with business partners and our community, quality is our signature.

Shareholders

We must provide a superior return to our shareholders. It's everyone's job.

Ethical Sourcing

Williams-Sonoma, Inc., and all of its brands are committed to maintaining the highest level of integrity and honesty throughout all aspects of our business, and strive to ensure that our business associates, including agents, vendors and suppliers, share our commitment to socially responsible employment conditions.

Environmental Paper Procurement Policy

Williams-Sonoma, Inc., is committed to environmental stewardship, and more specifically, to sound paper procurement practices that ensure the sustainability of forests and other natural resources.

To what extent are these values consistent with your own values? Would you like to work at Williams-Sonoma?

SOURCE: Excerpted from "Corporate Values," www. williams-sonomainc.com/car/car_val.cfm, accessed March 11, 2007.

A major international corporation hung signs in its hallways proclaiming that "trust" was one of its driving principles. Yet that same company searched employees' belongings each time they entered or exited the building. In another case, a multinational corporation that claimed to be committed to work/life values drew up an excellent plan to help managers incorporate work/life balance into the business. The company gathered its top 80 officers to review the plan—but scheduled the meetings on a weekend.[11]

The first company espoused that it valued trust and then behaved in an untrusting manner by checking employees' belongings. The second company similarly created a mismatch between espoused and enacted values by promoting work/life balance while simultaneously asking managers to attend weekend meetings.

It is important for managers to reduce gaps between espoused and enacted values because they can significantly influence employee attitudes and organizational performance. For example, a survey administered by the Ethics Resource Center showed that employees were more likely to behave ethically when management behaved in a way that set a good ethical example and kept its promises and commitments.[12] Another study of 312 British rail drivers revealed that employees were more cynical about safety when they believed that senior managers' behavior was inconsistent with the stated values regarding safety.[13] Managers can use a "cultural fit assessment" survey to determine the match between espoused and enacted values.

Basic Assumptions Basic underlying assumptions are unobservable and represent the core of organizational culture. They constitute organizational values that have become so taken for granted over time that they become assumptions that guide organizational behavior. They thus are highly resistant to change. When basic assumptions are widely held among employees, people will find behavior based on an inconsistent value inconceivable. Southwest Airlines, for example, is noted for operating according to basic assumptions that value employees' welfare and providing high-quality service. Employees at Southwest Airlines would be shocked to see management act in ways that did not value employees' and customers' needs.

Practical Application of Research on Values Organizations subscribe to a constellation of values rather than to only one and can be profiled according to their values. This enables managers to determine whether or not the organization's values are consistent and supportive of its corporate goals and initiatives. Organizations are less likely to accomplish their corporate goals when employees perceive an inconsistency between espoused values (e.g., honesty) and the behaviors needed to accomplish the goals (e.g., shredding financial documents). Similarly, organizational change is unlikely to succeed if it is based on a set of values highly inconsistent with employees' individual values.

Four Functions of Organizational Culture

As illustrated in Figure 3–2, an organization's culture fulfills four functions. To help bring these four functions to life, let us consider how each of them has taken shape at Southwest Airlines. Southwest is a particularly instructive example because it has grown to become the largest carrier in the United States based on scheduled departures since its inception in 1971 and has achieved 34 consecutive years of profitability. *Fortune* has ranked Southwest in the top five of the Best Companies to Work For in America from 1997 to 2000; Southwest has chosen not to participate in this ranking process since 2000. Southwest also was ranked as the third most admired company in the United States by *Fortune* in 2006, partly due to its strong and distinctive culture.[14]

1. *Give members an organizational identity.* Southwest Airlines is known as a fun place to work that values employee satisfaction and customer loyalty over corporate profits. Herb Kelleher, former CEO and current executive chairman, commented on this issue:

    > Who comes first? The employees, customers, or shareholders? That's never been an issue to me. The employees come first. If they're happy, satisfied, dedicated, and energetic, they'll take real good care of the customers. When the customers are happy, they come back. And that makes the shareholders happy.[15]

    The company also has a catastrophe fund based on voluntary contributions for distribution to employees who are experiencing serious personal difficulties. Southwest's people-focused identity is reinforced by the fact that it is an employer of choice. For example, Southwest received 284,827 résumés and hired 3,363 new employees in 2006. The company also was rated as providing outstanding opportunities for women and Hispanics by *Professional Women* magazine and *Hispanic* magazine, respectively, and *Business Ethics* ranked Southwest among the 100 Best Corporate Citizens seven years in a row.

2. *Facilitate collective commitment.* The mission of Southwest Airlines "is dedication to the highest quality of Customer Service delivered with a sense of warmth,

Figure 3–2   *Four Functions of Organizational Culture*

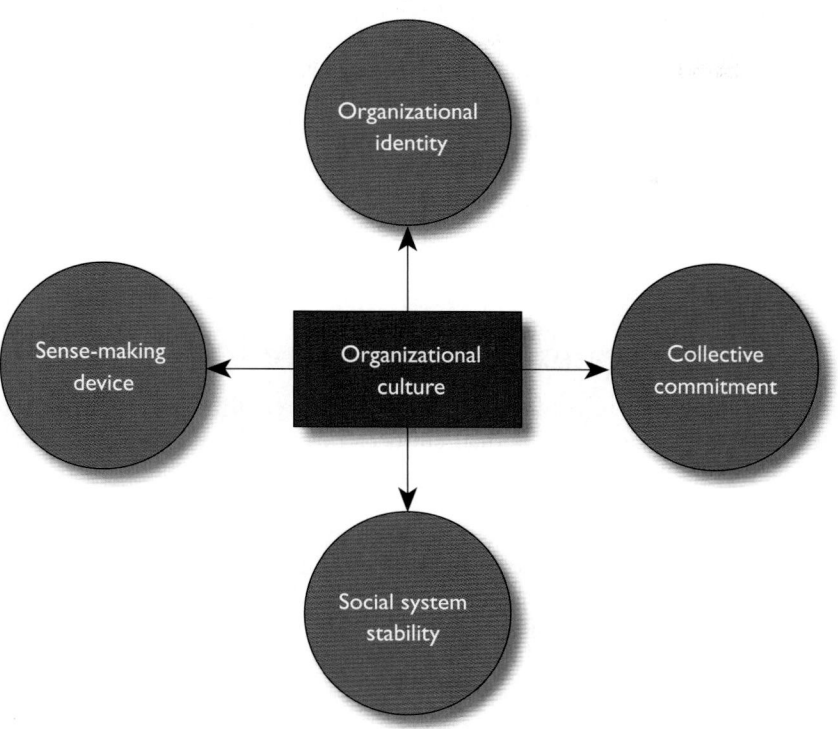

SOURCE: Adapted from discussion in L Smircich, "Concepts of Culture and Organizational Analysis," *Administrative Science Quarterly,* September 1983, pp 339–58. Reproduced by permission of John Wiley & Sons, Inc.

friendliness, individual pride, and Company Spirit."[16] Southwest's more than 32,000 employees are committed to this mission. The Department of Transportation's Air Travel Consumer Report reported Southwest was ranked number one in fewest customer complaints since 1987.

3. *Promote social system stability.* Social system stability reflects the extent to which the work environment is perceived as positive and reinforcing, and the extent to which conflict and change are effectively managed. Southwest is noted for its philosophy of having fun, having parties, and celebrating. For example, each city in which the firm operates is given a budget for parties. Southwest also uses a variety of performance based awards and service awards to reinforce employees. The company's positive and enriching environment is supported by the lowest turnover rates in the airline industry and the employment of 1,133 married couples.

4. *Shape behavior by helping members make sense of their surroundings.* This function of culture helps employees understand why the organization does what it does and how it intends to accomplish its long-term goals. Keeping in mind

This Southwest Airlines employee has a good reason to be smiling. The company boasts a low employee turnover rate attributed in part to its philosophy of having fun, having parties, and celebrating.

that Southwest's leadership originally viewed ground transportation as their main competitor in 1971, employees come to understand why the airline's primary vision is to be the best primarily short-haul, low-fare, high-frequency, point-to-point carrier in the United States. Employees understand they must achieve exceptional performance, such as turning a plane in 20 minutes, because they must keep costs down in order to compete against Greyhound and the use of automobiles. In turn, the company reinforces the importance of outstanding customer service and high performance expectations by using performance-based awards and profit sharing. Employees own about 8% of the company stock.

4 Types of Organizational Culture

Organizational behavior researchers have proposed three different frameworks to capture the various types of organizational culture: the Organizational Culture Inventory, the Competing Values Framework, and the Organizational Culture Profile.[17] This section discusses the Competing Values Framework because it is the most widely used approach for classifying organizational culture. It also was named as one of the 40 most important frameworks in the study of organizations and has been shown to be a valid approach for classifying organizational culture.[18]

Competing values framework

A framework for categorizing organizational culture.

The **competing values framework** (CVF) provides a practical way for managers to understand, measure, and change organizational culture. It was originally developed by a team of researchers who were trying to classify different ways to assess organizational effectiveness. This research showed that measures of organizational effectiveness vary along two fundamental dimensions or axes. One axis pertains to whether an organization focuses its attention and efforts on internal dynamics and employees or outward toward its external environment and its customers and shareholders. The second is concerned with an organization's preference for flexibility and discretion or control and stability. Combining these two axes creates four types of organizational culture that are based on different core values and different sets of criteria for accessing organizational effectiveness. The CVF is shown in Figure 3–3.[19]

Figure 3–3 shows the strategic thrust associated with each cultural type along with the means used to accomplish this thrust and the resulting ends or goals pursued by each cultural type. Before beginning our exploration of the CVF, it is important to note that organizations can possess characteristics associated with each culture type. That said, however, organizations tend to have one type of culture that is more dominant than the others. Let us begin our discussion of culture types by starting in the upper-left-hand quadrant of the CVF.

Clan culture

A culture that has an internal focus and values flexibility rather than stability and control.

Clan Culture A **clan culture** has an internal focus and values flexibility rather than stability and control. It resembles a family-type organization in which effectiveness is achieved by encouraging collaboration between employees. This type of culture is very "employee-focused" and strives to instill cohesion through consensus and job satisfaction and commitment through employee involvement. Clan organizations devote considerable resources to hiring and developing their employees, and they view customers as partners. Valero Energy Corp. is a good example of a company with a clan culture. Here is what Bill Greehey, Chairman of Valero Energy Corp., had to say about the company's culture after it was named the third best company to work for in America in 2006 by *Fortune* magazine.

Figure 3–3 *Competing Values Framework*

<table>
<tr><td colspan="2" align="center">**Flexibility and discretion**</td></tr>
<tr>
<td>

Clan

Thrust: Collaborate

Means: Cohesion, participation, communication, empowerment

Ends: Morale, people development, commitment

</td>
<td>

Adhocracy

Thrust: Create

Means: Adaptability, creativity, agility

Ends: Innovation, Growth, cutting-edge output

</td>
</tr>
<tr>
<td>

Hierarchy

Thrust: Control

Means: Capable processes, consistency, process control, measurement

Ends: Efficiency, timeliness, smooth functioning

</td>
<td>

Market

Thrust: Compete

Means: Customer focus, productivity, enhancing competitiveness

Ends: Market share, profitability, goal achievement

</td>
</tr>
<tr><td colspan="2" align="center">**Stability and control**</td></tr>
</table>

Internal focus and integration (left) **External focus and differentiation** (right)

SOURCE: Adapted from K S Cameron, R E Quinn, J Degraff, and A V Thakor, *Competing Values Leadership* (Northampton, MA: Edward Elgar, 2006), p 32.

> I think the reason that we are No. 3 on the list is that we truly do put our employees first. We've never had a layoff in our company's history. We offer the best salaries and the best benefits, and we give stock options down to the lowest level in the company. All nonexempt employees are eligible for stock options, and everyone has received at least one month's pay with our all-employee bonuses for the past several years....We're all part of the same team at Valero. Everyone is treated equally with equal respect, and no one is ever talked down to.... The caring attitude is truly a part of our corporate culture, and it is something that we not only preach but we live every day.[20]

Southwest Airlines and Nucor represent other good examples of successful companies with clan cultures.[21]

Adhocracy Culture An **adhocracy culture** has an external focus and values flexibility. This type of culture fosters the creation of innovative products and services by being adaptable, creative, and fast to respond to changes in the marketplace. Adhocracy cultures do not rely on the type of centralized power and authority relationships that are part of market and hierarchical cultures. They also encourage employees to take risks, think outside the box, and experiment with new ways of getting things done. This type of culture is well suited for start-up companies, those in industries undergoing constant change, and those in mature industries that are in need of innovation to enhance growth. Consider how Jeff Immelt, CEO of General Electric, is trying to instill characteristics of an adhocracy in order to fuel revenue growth.

Adhocracy culture

A culture that has an external focus and values flexibility.

> The company, which is well-known for sharing best practices across its many units, has recently begun formally discussing failures, too. Last September the company set up a two-hour conference call for managers of eight "imagination breakthroughs" that didn't

live up to expectations and were being shelved, or "retired," in GE's parlance. ("Imagination breakthrough"—Ibs—are new businesses or products that have potential sales of $100 million within three to five years.)

Such discussions can be nerve-racking, especially in companies where failure has traditionally been met with tough consequences. . . ."I had some offline conversations with some of the IB leaders reassuring them that this was not a call where they were going to get their pink slips," says Patia McGrath, a GE marketing director who helped put together the call. "The notion of taking big swings, and that it's O.K. to miss the swing, is something that's quite new with Jeff."[22]

W. L. Gore and Intel are two other companies that possess cultural characteristics consistent with an Adhocracy.

Home Depot is an example of a company focused on competition and results due to the actions of former CEO, Robert Nardelli. What other companies do you think fit into a Market Culture?

Market culture
A culture that has a strong external focus and values stability and control.

Market Culture
A **market culture** has a strong external focus and values stability and control. Organizations with this culture are driven by competition and a strong desire to deliver results and accomplish goals. Because this type of culture is focused on the external environment, customers and profits take precedence over employee development and satisfaction. The major goal of managers is to drive towards productivity, profits, and customer satisfaction. Employees are expected to react fast, work hard, and deliver quality work on time. Organizations with this culture tend to reward people who deliver results. Robert Nardelli, former CEO of Home Depot, decided that the company needed to eliminate some of its adhocracy characteristics and replace them with those associated with a market culture in order to grow its business.

He reduced store managers' autonomy and centralized the purchasing function. Nardelli also created common performance metrics that were used during Monday morning conference calls with his top 15 executives. These meetings were used to reinforce accountability for results and to increase information sharing about operations, markets, and competitive conditions. He further reinforced the thrust of competition by conducting an annual eight-day planning session that was followed up with quarterly business reviews. He ultimately rewarded high performers and fired those who did not meet their goals. Although Home Depot's revenue climbed during Nardelli's tenure from $46 billion in 2000 to $80 billion in 2005, he resigned in January 2007. He was under pressure from stockholders regarding his hefty pay package and the company's poor stock performance.[23]

Hierarchy culture
A culture that has an internal focus and values stability and control over flexibility.

Hierarchy Culture
Control is the driving force within a hierarchical culture. The **hierarchy culture** has an internal focus, which produces a more formalized and structured work environment, and values stability and control over flexibility. This orientation leads to the development of reliable internal processes, extensive measurement, and the implementation of a variety of control mechanisms. For example, companies with a hierachical culture are more likely to use the type of Total Quality Management (TQM) programs discussed in Chapter 1. Effectiveness in a company with this type of culture is likely to be assessed with measures of efficiency, timeliness, and reliability of producing and delivering products and services. Exelon, the No. 1 U.S. nuclear power generator, and Dell are good examples of companies with hierarchical cultures. Both companies focus on efficiency and cost-cutting in order to compete.[24]

Nortel Networks Attempts to Balance Innovation and Production Efficiency

Six Sigma, broadly speaking, expresses a way of thinking about business problems that encourages precision and predictability. . . . Innovation, by contrast, can be messy. It is hard to sum up in a simple statistic and requires a healthy tolerance of failure. . . . At Nortel Networks, CEO Mike S. Zafirovski, a veteran of both Motorola and Six Sigma stalwart General Electric Co., has installed his own version of the program, one that marries concepts from Toyota Motor's lean production system. The point says Joel Hackney, Nortel's Six Sigma guru, is to use Six Sigma

thinking to take superfluous steps out of operations. Running a more efficient shop, he argues, will free up workers to innovate. . . .

Six Sigma's success will only come in a culture that not only welcomes creative types and the metrics-obsessed, but one that makes them both better.

Why is it hard to have a culture that is high on adhocracy and hierarchy at the same time?

SOURCE: Excerpted From R O Crockett, "Six Sigma Still Pays Off at Motorola," *BusinessWeek*, December 4, 2006, p 50.

Cultural Types Represent Competing Values It is important to note that certain cultural types reflect opposing core values. These contradicting cultures are found along the two diagonals in Figure 3–2. For example, the Clan culture—upper-left quadrant—is represented by values that emphasize an internal focus and flexibility, whereas the market culture—bottom-right quadrant—has an external focus and concern for stability and control. You can see the same conflict between an adhocracy culture that values flexibility and an external focus and a hierarchical culture that endorses stability and control along with an internal focus. Why are these contradictions important?

They are important because an organization's success may depend on its ability to possess core values that are associated with competing cultural types. While this is difficult to pull off, it can be done. Consider Nortel Networks, for example. The company is trying to encourage innovation at the same time it is trying to implement Six Sigma—recall our discussion in Chapter 1 (see the Real World/Real People feature above). The Ritz-Carlton, a high-end luxury hotel, has similarly found a way to overcome competing values associated with clan and market cultures. The company spends 10% of its payroll on employee training and empowers its employees to determine the best way to provide customer service. At the same time, the company is fiercely focused on providing world-class customer service.[25]

go to the Web for the Group Exercise: Assessing the Organizational Culture at Your School

 5 Outcomes Associated with Organizational Culture

Both managers and academic researchers believe that organizational culture can be a driver of employee attitudes and organizational effectiveness and performance. To test this possibility, various measures of organizational culture have been correlated with a variety of individual and organizational outcomes. So what have we learned? First, several studies demonstrated that organizational culture was significantly correlated with employee behavior and attitudes. For example, a clan culture was positively associated with employees' job satisfaction, organizational commitment, intentions to stay at the company, and the quality of communication received from one's supervisor. Employees in clan cultures also reported having more positive relationships with their managers than employees working in organizations with an external focus, such as those with adhocracy or market cultures. Employees working in organizations with hierarchical or market-based cultures also reported lower job satisfaction and organizational commitment, and greater intentions to quit their jobs.[26] These results suggest that employees prefer to work in organizations that value flexibility over stability and control and those that are more concerned with satisfying employees' needs than customer or shareholder desires. Second, results from several studies revealed that the congruence between an individual's values and the organization's values was significantly associated with organizational commitment, job satisfaction, intention to quit, and turnover.[27]

Third, there is not a clear pattern of relationships between organizational culture and outcomes such as service quality, customer satisfaction, and an organization's financial performance. For example, organizations with a market culture have been shown to exhibit both higher and lower levels of financial performance.[28] While the aforementioned conclusion is supported by data obtained from employees' assessments of organizational culture, it must be tempered by results from two recent studies. A study of 200 companies in more than 40 industries showed that an organization's financial performance was significantly related to customer satisfaction.[29] These results imply that it is important for organizations to have an external focus on its customers if they want to make money. In contrast, a recent meta-analysis of 92 studies revealed that a firm's financial performance was positively associated with the extent to which it employed high performance work practices. High performance work practices reflect an internal cultural orientation and include such things as incentive compensation, employee involvement, employee training, and the use of flexible work schedules.[30] All told, these results suggest that it is important for managers to effectively accommodate the potential conflict between cultures that have both an internal and external focus.

This conclusion is consistent with findings from a study of 207 companies in 22 industries over an 11-year period. Results demonstrated that an organization's financial performance was higher among companies that had adaptive or flexible cultures.[31] Stated differently, successful companies modified their cultures over time so that they were appropriate or consistent with the market or business situation at hand. We encourage managers to evaluate the extent to which their organization's culture is aligned with its business or strategic context and to respond accordingly. As discussed previously in this chapter, companies such as Motorola and the Ritz Carlton are following this recommendation.

Finally, studies of mergers indicated that they frequently failed due to incompatible cultures. Due to the increasing number of corporate mergers around the world, and the conclusion that 7 out of 10 mergers and acquisitions failed to meet their financial promise, managers within merged companies would be well advised to consider the role of organizational culture in creating a new organization.[32]

In summary, research underscores the significance of organizational culture. It also reinforces the need to learn more about the process of cultivating and changing an organization's culture. An organization's culture is not determined by fate. It is formed and shaped by the combination and integration of everyone who works in the organization. A change-resistant culture, for instance, can undermine the effectiveness of any type of organizational change. Although it is not an easy task to change an organization's culture, the next section provides a preliminary overview of how this might be done.

6 The Process of Culture Change

Before describing the specific ways in which managers can change organizational culture, let us review three caveats about culture change. First, it is possible to change an organization's culture, and the process essentially begins with targeting one of the three layers of organizational culture previously discussed—observable artifacts, espoused values, and basic assumptions—for change. Ultimately, culture change involves changing people's minds and their behavior.[33] Second, it is important to consider the extent to which the current culture is aligned with the organization's vision and strategic plan before attempting to change any aspect of organizational culture. A **vision** represents a long-term goal that describes "what" an organization wants to become. For example, Walt Disney's original vision for Disneyland included the following components.

> Disneyland will be something of a fair, an exhibition, a playground, a community center, a museum of living facts, and a showplace of beauty and magic. It will be filled with the accomplishments, the joys and hopes of the world we live in. And it will remind and show us how to make those wonders part of our lives.[34]

A **strategic plan** outlines an organization's long-term goals and the actions necessary to achieve these goals. Mark Fields, executive vice president, Ford Motor Company, and president, The Americas, firmly believes that culture, vision, and strategic plans should be aligned. According to Fields, "Culture eats strategy for breakfast. You can have the best plan in the world, and if the culture isn't going to let it happen, it's going to die on the vine."[35]

Finally, it is important to use a structured approach when implementing culture change. Chapter 18 can help you in this regard as it presents several models that provide specific steps to follow when implementing any type of organizational change. Let us now consider the specific methods or techniques that managers can use to change an organization's culture.

Vision
Long-term goal describing "what" an organization wants to become.

Strategic plan
A long-term plan outlining actions needed to achieve desired results.

7

Edgar Schein, a well-known OB scholar, notes that changing organizational culture involves a teaching process. That is, organizational members teach each other about the organization's preferred values, beliefs, norms, expectations, and behaviors. This is accomplished by using one or more of the following mechanisms:[36]

1. *Formal statements of organizational philosophy, mission, vision, values, and materials used for recruiting, selection, and socialization.* Sam Walton, the founder of Wal-Mart, established three basic beliefs or values that represent the core of the organization's culture. They are (1) respect for the individual, (2) service to our customer, and (3) striving for excellence. Further, Nucor Corp. attempts to emphasize the value it places on its people by including every employee's name on the cover of the annual report. This practice also reinforces the clan type of culture the company wants to encourage.[37] Would you like to work at Nucor?

2. *The design of physical space, work environments, and buildings.* Consider how Acordia Inc. attempted to create a more entrepreneurial culture by building a new one-floor facility.

> The building facilitated interactive workflow procedures. Interactions among new-venture team members and among independent teams became grounded in forming and sharing tacit knowledge. Positive feelings surfacing from these interactions and the knowledge they fostered created positive morale in individuals and between employees and their vice president.[38]

3. *Slogans, language, acronyms, and sayings.* For example, Robert Mittelstaedt, Dean of the W.P. Carey School of Business at Arizona State University, promotes his vision of having one of the best business schools in the world through the slogan "Top-of-mind business school." Employees are encouraged to engage in activities that promote the quality and reputation of the school's academic programs.

4. *Deliberate role modeling, training programs, teaching, and coaching by managers and supervisors.* Boeing's CEO, Jim McNerney, leads by example. "He wins praise from co-workers for paying attention to the small things like remembering people's names, listening closely to their presentations, and not embarrassing underlings in public."[39]

5. *Explicit rewards, status symbols (e.g., titles), and promotion criteria.* Boeing is revising its reward system in order to reform its culture. "In the old days, no points were awarded for collaborating with other units or following ethics rules. Now pay and bonuses are directly linked to how well executives embrace a set of six leadership attributes such as 'Living Boeing Values.' That includes new criteria such as promoting integrity and avoiding abusive behavior."[40]

6. *Stories, legends, or myths about key people and events.* Goldman Sachs's culture is reinforced through a story that is passed on by business school students who applied to work at the organization.

   > One of the legends any MBA student is likely to hear is that of Goldman Sachs's signature recruitment experience. Successive cohorts of B-school students worldwide pass along the tale of the MBA student who went through 60 interviews before being hired. That story isn't an urban myth. The selection process is truly an endurance test, requiring enormous resources. In a given year, about 5,000 applicants speak to ten members of the firm, and the top 2,500 speak to more than 30. Each year, Goldman Sachs invests more than 100,000 man-hours in conversations with prospective employees.
   >
   > The seemingly endless interviews are not designed to ferret out candidates' intellectual prowess or previous work experiences—that's what GMAT scores and applications forms are for. The process is a reflection of the company's deep commitment to internal collaboration and networking and serves as a preview of life in the firm.[41]

7. *The organizational activities, processes, or outcomes that leaders pay attention to, measure, and control.* Consider the behavior of Jamie Dimon, CEO of J.P. Morgan Chase.

   > He has imposed rigorous pay-for-performance metrics and requires managers to present exhaustive monthly reviews, then grills them on the data for hours at a time. . . . To be sure he's getting the real story, Dimon button holes staffers in the elevators and calls suppliers out of the blue like a hyperactive gumshoe, collecting scraps of information he can throw back at executives. . . . He yanked Bank One's sponsorship of the Masters golf tournament because the country club hosting the event doesn't accept women members.[42]

8. *Leader reactions to critical incidents and organizational crises.* Consider the cultural messages sent by Mark Hurd, CEO of Hewlett-Packard Co., when he responded to the crisis involving an investigation of press leaks from board members by then chairman, Patricia Dunn (see Real World/Real People feature on page 79). His behavior shows that he was more concerned about performance than ethics prior to this crisis. The California charges against Ms. Dunn were dismissed in March 2007.[43]

Mark Hurd's Response to a Crisis Underscores Hewlett-Packard's Culture

To hear Hurd tell it, when HP's then board chairman, Patricia C Dunn, authorized an investigation into press leaks from the board, he also trusted that she and the company's legal and security personnel would handle it properly. Hurd figured he had enough work resurrecting the company. On September 25 [2006], red-eyed and clearly humbled, Hurd explained to *BusinessWeek:* "I'm a detail-oriented guy by trade. But when you have a place of this scale, you have to pick your spots where you're going to go dive. Compliance wasn't the first process I was going to go look at. I was going to go look at the performance of the company."

Even if Hurd is right about being mostly out of the loop, it's a decision he surely regrets. On September 22 he stood before a room of reporters and read a statement apologizing for the spying tactics that HP officials and security subcontractors used to track down the source of leaks. Hurd admitted that he was not paying close enough attention to spot some of the actions, which he called "very disturbing." . . .

Already, the scandal is filtering into Hurd's day-to-day management style in surprising ways. He says half-jokingly that he finds himself repeatedly telling employees in meetings that whatever they do has to be "legal and ethical." "We're going to have to regain the world's confidence one person at a time to prove that this is the company they thought it was."

What cultural messages did Hurd show through his comments and behavior?

SOURCE: Excerpted from P Burrows, "Controlling the Damage at HP," *Business Week,* October 9, 2006, pp 38–39.

---

9. *The workflow and organizational structure.* Hierarchical structures are more likely to embed an orientation toward control and authority than a flatter organization. Leaders from many organizations are increasingly reducing the number of organizational layers in an attempt to empower employees (see Chapter 17) and increase employee involvement.

10. *Organizational systems and procedures.* Baptist Health Care, for example, is using a creative procedure derived from the Ritz Carlton to reinforce a customer service orientation within the hospital. Every day 500 leaders conduct a lineup on the floor with their staffs.

"The eight- to 10-minute long briefings held around the clock to accommodate three shifts include a corporate message, updates and a discussion question that revolves around a weekly topic, which can range from communication to financial stewardship. The session ends with an inspirational quote. And so the things don't get stale, the lineups feature everything from skits to survey questions to the Hokey Pokey to Trivial Pursuit board game questions. Often, Bilbrey says [Pam Bilbrey is the president of Baptist Health Care's Leadership Institute], staff members share personal stories or stories about something standout that their co-workers have done, which fosters healthy competition. "It really sets the tone and in a lot of ways sets the bar because if you're telling stories about people who are doing extraordinary things, it sends the message, 'Well, I need to be doing extraordinary things, too.'"[44]

A daily floor line-up with staff at Baptist Health Care reinforces their commitment to a customer service orientation at the hospital.

11. *Organizational goals and the associated criteria used for recruitment, selection, development, promotion, layoffs, and retirement of people.* Aflac, for example, has spent considerable time establishing performance expectations for its employees in pursuit of a market-based culture that focuses on customer service.

> Aflac has embarked on a process to quantify service expectations for all positions, and Sharon Douglas, vice president and chief people officer, has been integrally involved in this process. . . . The process involved focus groups and quantitative studies involving customers, staff and managers. . . . Douglas stresses that expectations should be specific and explicitly stated, not assumed. For example, at Aflac there is an expectation that when employees field a phone call that is not directly related to their area of expertise, they will not transfer the call. "We expect them to take in all of the information and then go back to find the proper response," Douglas says.[45]

The Organizational Socialization Process

Organizational socialization

Process by which employees learn an organization's values, norms, and required behaviors.

Organizational socialization is defined as "the process by which a person learns the values, norms, and required behaviors which permit him to participate as a member of the organization."[46] As previously discussed, organization socialization is a key mechanism used by organizations to embed their organizational cultures. In short, organizational socialization turns outsiders into fully functioning insiders by promoting and reinforcing the organization's core values and beliefs. This section introduces a three-phase model of organizational socialization and examines the practical application of socialization research.

8 A Three-Phase Model of Organizational Socialization

One's first year in a complex organization can be confusing. There is a constant swirl of new faces, strange jargon, conflicting expectations, and apparently unrelated events. Some organizations treat new members in a rather haphazard, sink-or-swim manner. More typically, though, the socialization process is characterized by a sequence of identifiable steps.

"We're in awe of your ability to fit in here, Ms. Stoughton."

Ted Goff. Reprinted by permission.

Organizational behavior researcher Daniel Feldman has proposed a three-phase model of organizational socialization that promotes deeper understanding of this important process. As illustrated in Figure 3–4, the three phases are (1) anticipatory socialization, (2) encounter, and (3) change and acquisition. Each phase has its associated perceptual and social processes. Feldman's model also specifies behavioral and affective outcomes that can be used to judge how well an individual has been socialized. The entire three-phase sequence may take from a few weeks to a year to complete, depending on individual differences and the complexity of the situation.

Phase 1: Anticipatory Socialization The **anticipatory socialization phase** occurs before an individual actually joins an organization. It is represented by the information people have learned about different careers, occupations, professions, and organizations. For example, anticipatory socialization partially explains

Figure 3–4   *A Model of Organizational Socialization*

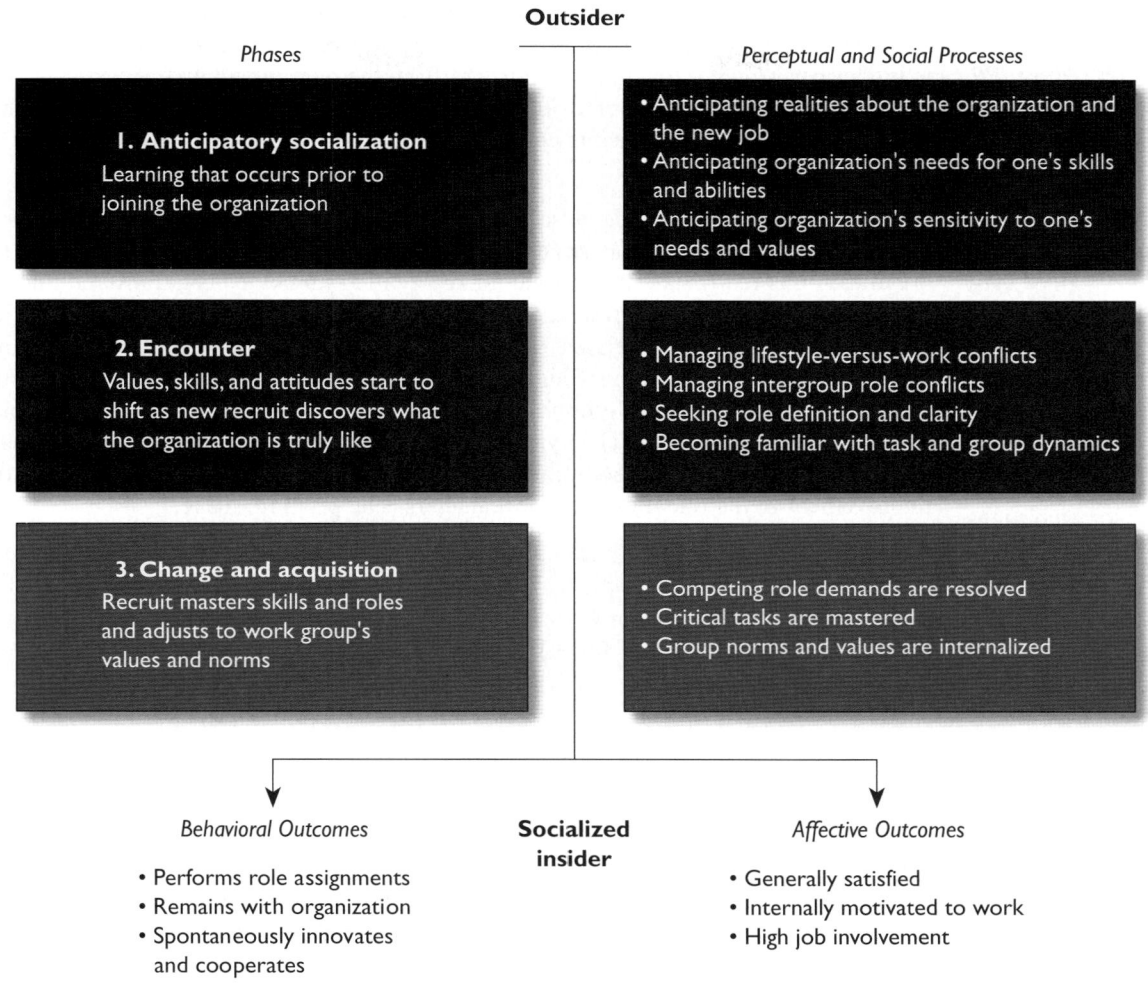

SOURCE: Adapted from material in D C Feldman, "The Multiple Socialization of Organization Members," *Academy of Management Review*, April 1981, pp 309–18. Reprinted by permission of The Academy of Management via The Copyright Clearance Center.

the different perceptions you might have about working for the US government versus a high-technology company like Intel or Microsoft. Anticipatory socialization information comes from many sources. An organization's current employees are a powerful source of anticipatory socialization. The recruiting or wooing of parents is another anticipatory socialization technique used by a variety of companies. "Merrill Lynch & Co. invited interns' parents to visit company offices. Ernst & Young LLP is packaging company information for parents. Vanguard Group Inc. sends letters to recruits' parents and has advertised on the parents sections of college Web sites. Deloitte & Touche and other big recruiters are weighing similar moves."[47] Anecdotal evidence shows that this technique is particularly helpful in recruiting highly valued prospects who have parents who take an active involvement in their child's postcollege plans.

Unrealistic expectations about the nature of the work, pay, and promotions are often formulated during phase 1. Because employees with unrealistic expectations are more likely to quit their jobs in the future, organizations may want to use realistic

Anticipatory socialization phase

Occurs before an individual joins an organization, and involves the information people learn about different careers, occupations, professions, and organizations.

Realistic job preview
Presents both positive and negative aspects of a job.

job previews.[48] A **realistic job preview** (RJP) involves giving recruits a realistic idea of what lies ahead by presenting both positive and negative aspects of the job. RJPs may be verbal, in booklet form, audiovisual, or hands-on. Research supports the practical benefits of using RJPs. A meta-analysis of 40 studies revealed that RJPs were related to higher performance and to lower attrition from the recruitment process. Results also demonstrated that RJPs lowered job applicants' initial expectations and led to lower turnover among those applicants who were hired.[49]

Encounter phase
Employees learn what the organization is really like and reconcile unmet expectations.

Onboarding
Programs aimed at helping employees integrate, assimilate, and transition to new jobs.

Phase 2: Encounter
This second phase begins when the employment contract has been signed. During the **encounter phase** employees come to learn what the organization is really like. It is a time for reconciling unmet expectations and making sense of a new work environment. Many companies use a combination of orientation and training programs to socialize employees during the encounter phase. Onboarding is one such technique. **Onboarding** programs help employees to integrate, assimilate, and transition to new jobs by making them familiar with corporate policies, procedures, and culture and by clarifying work role expectations and responsibilities.[50] Bristol-Myers Squibb's onboarding program, for example, resulted in substantial improvement in the retention rate for managers. The program makes

> new executives the object of a laserlike focus during the first 30 to 60 days of their employment, providing guidelines, clarifying roles, setting up meetings with influential colleagues and fostering each newcomer's understanding of the company's cultural norms. Follow-up meetings are held during the executive's first year to check progress and resolve problems.[51]

Change and acquisition phase
Requires employees to master tasks and roles and to adjust to work group values and norms.

Phase 3: Change and Acquisition
The **change and acquisition phase** requires employees to master important tasks and roles and to adjust to their work group's values and norms. Table 3–1 presents a list of socialization processes or tactics used by organizations to help employees through this adjustment process. Trilogy, for example, uses a variety of these tactics in its renowned socialization program. The three-month program takes place at the organization's corporate university, called Trilogy University.

> **Month one.** When you arrive at Trilogy University, you are assigned to a section and to an instruction track. Your section, a group of about 20, is your social group for the duration of TU.... Tracks are designed to be microcosms of future work life at Trilogy.... The technical challenges in such exercises closely mimic real customer engagements, but the time frames are dramatically compressed. The assignments pile up week after week for the first month, each one successively more challenging than the last. During that time, you're being constantly measured and evaluated, as assignment grades and comments are entered into a database monitoring your progress....
>
> **Month two.** Month two is TU project month.... In teams of three to five people, they have to come up with an idea, create a business model for it, build the product, and develop the marketing plan. In trying to launch bold new ideas in a hyperaccelerated time frame, they gain a deep appreciation of the need to set priorities, evaluate probabilities, and measure results. Mind you, these projects are not hypothetical—they're the real thing....
>
> **Month three.** Month three at Trilogy University is all about finding your place and having a broader impact in the larger organization. A few students continue with their TU projects, but most move on to "graduation projects," which generally are assignments within various Trilogy business units. People leave TU on a rolling basis as they find sponsors out in the company who are willing to take them on.[52]

Table 3–1   *Socialization Tactics*

TACTIC	DESCRIPTION
Collective vs. individual	Collective socialization consists of grouping newcomers and exposing them to a common set of experiences rather than treating each newcomer individually and exposing him or her to more or less unique experiences.
Formal vs. informal	Formal socialization is the practice of segregating a newcomer from regular organization members during a defined socialization period versus not clearly distinguishing a newcomer from more experienced members. Army recruits must attend boot camp before they are allowed to work alongside established soldiers.
Sequential vs. random	Sequential socialization refers to a fixed progression of steps that culminate in the new role, compared to an ambiguous or dynamic progression. The socialization of doctors involves a lock-step sequence from medical school, to internship, to residency before they are allowed to practice on their own.
Fixed vs. variable	Fixed socialization provides a timetable for the assumption of the role, whereas a variable process does not. American university students typically spend one year apiece as freshmen, sophomores, juniors, and seniors.
Serial vs. disjunctive	A serial process is one in which the newcomer is socialized by an experienced member, whereas a disjunctive process does not use a role model.
Investiture vs. divestiture	Investiture refers to the affirmation of a newcomer's incoming global and specific role identities and attributes. Divestiture is the denial and stripping away of the newcomer's existing sense of self and the reconstruction of self in the organization's image. During police training, cadets are required to wear uniforms and maintain an immaculate appearance, they are addressed as "officer," told they are no longer ordinary citizens but are representatives of the police force.

SOURCE: Descriptions were taken from B E Ashforth, *Role Transitions in Organizational Life: An Identity-Based Perspective* (Mahwah, NJ: Lawrence Erlbaum Associates, 2001), pp 149–83.

The change and acquisition phase at Trilogy is stressful, exhilarating, and critical for finding one's place within the organization. How would you like to work there? Returning to Table 3–1, can you identify the socialization tactics used by Trilogy?

Go to the Web for the Self-Exercise: Have You Been Adequately Socialized?

Practical Application of Socialization Research

Past research suggests six practical guidelines for managing organizational socialization.

1. A recent survey of executives from 100 companies revealed that 65% did an average or poor job of socializing new hires.[53] This reinforces the conclusion that managers should avoid a haphazard, sink-or-swim approach to organizational socialization because formalized socialization tactics positively affect new hires. Formalized or institutionalized socialization tactics were found to positively help employees in both domestic and international operations.[54]

2. Organizations like the United States Military Academy at West Point use socialization tactics to reinforce a culture that promotes ethical behavior. Managers are encouraged to consider how they might best set expectations regarding ethical behavior during all three phases of the socialization process.[55]

3. Managers play a key role during the encounter phase. Studies of newly hired accountants demonstrated that the frequency and type of information obtained during their first six months of employment significantly affected their job performance, their role clarity, and the extent to which they were socially integrated[56] Managers need to help new hires integrate within the organizational culture. Consider the approach used by John Chambers, CEO of Cisco Systems: "He meets with groups of new hires to welcome them soon after they start, and at monthly breakfast meetings workers are encouraged to ask him tough questions.[57]

4. Support for stage models is mixed. Although there are different stages of socialization, they are not identical in order, length, or content for all people or jobs.[58] Managers are advised to use a contingency approach toward organizational socialization. In other words, different techniques are appropriate for different people at different times.

5. The organization can benefit by training new employees to use proactive socialization behaviors. Socialization tactics should encourage new employees to seek information as they proceed through the encounter and change and acquisition phases of socialization. For example, a study of 140 co-op university students showed that the use of formalized socialization tactics was associated with newcomers feedback-seeking and information-seeking behaviors.[59]

6. Managers should pay attention to the socialization of diverse employees. Research demonstrated that diverse employees, particularly those with disabilities, experienced different socialization activities than other newcomers. In turn, these different experiences affected their long-term success and job satisfaction.[60]

Mentoring
Process of forming and maintaining developmental relationships between a mentor and a junior person.

Embedding Organizational Culture through Mentoring

The modern word *mentor* derives from Mentor, the name of a wise and trusted counselor in Greek mythology. Terms typically used in connection with mentoring are *teacher, coach, sponsor,* and *peer.* **Mentoring** is defined as the process of forming and maintaining intensive and lasting developmental relationships between a variety of developers (i.e., people

In today's high-technology work environments, helping or coaching others on the use of computer programs is a key function of mentoring. This type of mentoring is important in embedding an organization's culture because it contributes to a sense of oneness and it enhances employees' feelings of competence.

who provide career and psychosocial support) and a junior person (the protégé, if male; or protégée, if female).[61] Mentoring can serve to embed an organization's culture when developers and the protégé/protégée work in the same organization for two reasons. First, mentoring contributes to creating a sense of oneness by promoting the acceptance of the organization's core values throughout the organization. Second, the socialization aspect of mentoring also promotes a sense of membership.

Not only is mentoring important as a tactic for embedding organizational culture, but research suggests it can significantly influence the protégé/protégée's future career. For example, a meta-analysis revealed that mentored employees had higher compensation and more promotions than nonmentored employees. Mentored employees also reported higher job and career satisfaction and organizational commitment and lower turnover.[62] This section focuses on how people can use mentoring to their advantage. We discuss the functions of mentoring, the developmental networks underlying mentoring, and the personal and organizational implications of mentoring.

Functions of Mentoring

Kathy Kram, a Boston University researcher, conducted in-depth interviews with both members of 18 pairs of senior and junior managers. As a by-product of this study, Kram identified two general functions—career and psychosocial—of the mentoring process. Five *career functions* that enhanced career development were sponsorship, exposure-and-visibility, coaching, protection, and challenging assignments. Four *psychosocial functions* were role modeling, acceptance-and-confirmation, counseling, and friendship. The psychosocial functions clarified the participants' identities and enhanced their feelings of competence.[63]

10 Developmental Networks Underlying Mentoring

Historically, it was thought that mentoring was primarily provided by one person who was called a mentor. Today, however, the changing nature of technology, organizational structures, and marketplace dynamics requires that people seek career information and support from many sources. Mentoring is currently viewed as a process in which protégés and protégées seek developmental guidance from a network of people, who are referred to as developers. Lori McKee, a project manager with Chubb Group of Insurance Cos., is a good example of someone who used a network of people to advance her career. She started a book club at the company, and 19 Chubb Group women across the country meet via teleconference once a month to discuss career issues associated with books they have read. "As a result of her increased visibility at the company, the 31-year-old Ms McKee says she has been offered bigger assignments, including one to help upgrade the company's financial systems worldwide. 'The way I got it was through these discussions and getting mentoring from other women in the group,' she says."[64] This example implies that the diversity and strength of one's network of relationships is instrumental in obtaining the type of career assistance needed to manage one's career. Figure 3–5 presents a developmental network typology based on integrating the diversity and strength of developmental relationships.[65]

The **diversity of developmental relationships** reflects the variety of people within the network an individual uses for developmental assistance. There are two

Diversity of developmental relationships The variety of people in a network used for developmental assistance.

Figure 3–5   *Developmental Networks Associated with Mentoring*

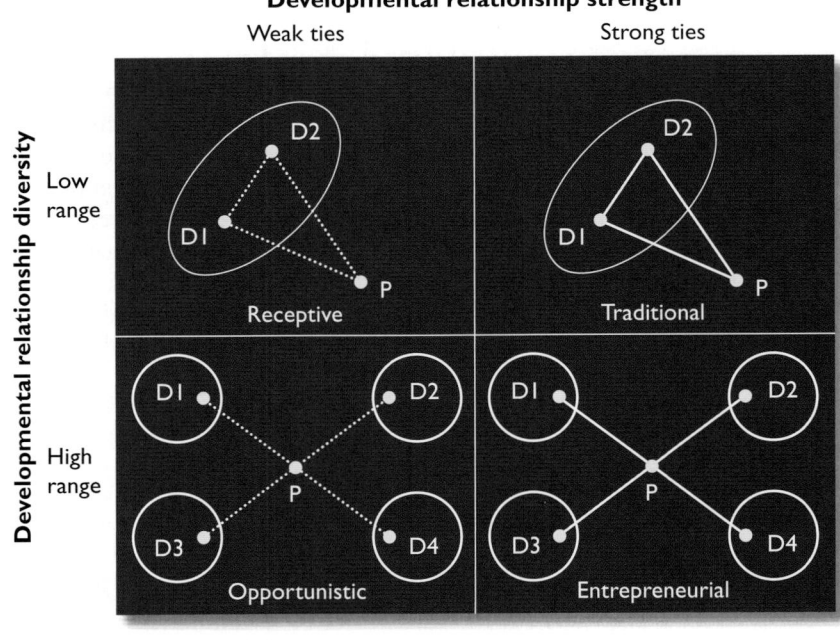

Key: D, developer; P, protégé

SOURCE: M Higgins and K Kram, "Reconceptualizing Mentoring at Work: A Developmental Network Perspective," *Academy of Management Review*, April 2001, p 270. Reprinted by permission of The Academy of Management via The Copyright Clearance Center.

subcomponents associated with network diversity: (1) the number of different people the person is networked with and (2) the various social systems from which the networked relationships stem (e.g., employer, school, family, community, professional associations, and religious affiliations). As shown in Figure 3–5, developmental relationship diversity ranges from low (few people or social systems) to high (multiple people or social systems).

Developmental relationship strength

The quality of relationships among people in a network.

Developmental relationship strength reflects the quality of relationships among the individual and those involved in his or her developmental network. For example, strong ties are reflective of relationships based on frequent interactions, reciprocity, and positive affect. Weak ties, in contrast, are based more on superficial relationships. Together, the diversity and strength of developmental relationships results in four types of developmental networks (see Figure 3–5): receptive, traditional, entrepreneurial, and opportunistic.

A *receptive* developmental network is composed of a few weak ties from one social system such as an employer or a professional association. The single oval around D1 and D2 in Figure 3–5 is indicative of two developers who come from one social system. In contrast, a *traditional* network contains a few strong ties between an employee and developers that all come from one social system. An entrepreneurial network, which is the strongest type of developmental network, is made up of strong ties among several developers (D1–D4) who come from four different social systems. Finally, an opportunistic network is associated with having weak ties with multiple developers from different social systems.

Personal and Organizational Implications

There are five key personal implications to consider. First, job and career satisfaction are likely to be influenced by the consistency between an individual's career goals and the type of developmental network at his or her disposal. For example, people with an entrepreneurial developmental network are more likely to experience change in their careers and to benefit from personal learning than people with receptive, traditional, and opportunistic networks. If this sounds attractive to you, you should try to increase the diversity and strength of your developmental relationships. In contrast, lower levels of job satisfaction are expected when employees have receptive developmental networks and they desire to experience career advancement in multiple organizations. Receptive developmental networks, however, can be satisfying to someone who does not desire to be promoted up the career ladder.[66] Second, a developer's willingness to provide career and psychosocial assistance is a function of the protégé/protégée's ability, potential, and the quality of the interpersonal relationship.[67] This implies that you must take ownership for enhancing your skills, abilities, and developmental networks if you desire to experience career advancement throughout your life.[68]

Third, put effort into finding a mentor. A study of 4,559 leaders and 944 human resource professionals from 42 countries showed that 91% of those who used a mentor found the experience moderately or greatly beneficial to their career success.[69] That said, another recent study showed that the success of a mentoring relationship from a protégé/protégée's perspective is partly determined by the skills and abilities of the mentor.[70] This leads to the fourth recommendation. If you believe that your mentor is ineffective, or worse yet, causing more harm than benefit, find a new mentor. Finally, although mentoring can help your career, and some mediocre people advance because of a strong mentor, don't be fooled into thinking that "who you know" is a replacement for talent, knowledge, and motivation.[71] We strongly encourage you to use your own passion, motivation, talents, and networking skills to accomplish your personal and professional goals.

Research also supports the organizational benefits of mentoring. For example, mentoring enhances the effectiveness of organizational communication. Specifically, mentoring increases the amount of vertical communication both up and down an organization, and it provides a mechanism for modifying or reinforcing organizational culture.

Summary of Key Concepts

1. *Define organizational culture and discuss its three layers.* Organizational culture represents the shared assumptions that a group holds. It influences employees' perceptions and behavior at work. The three layers of organizational culture include observable artifacts, espoused values, and basic assumptions. Artifacts are the physical manifestations of an organization's culture. Espoused values represent the explicitly stated values and norms that are preferred by an organization. Basic underlying assumptions are unobservable and represent the core of organizational culture.

2. *Discuss the difference between espoused and enacted values.* Espoused values represent the explicitly stated values and norms that are preferred by an organization. Enacted values, in contrast, reflect the values and norms that actually are exhibited or converted into employee behavior. Employees become cynical when management espouses one set of values and norms and then behaves in an inconsistent fashion.

3. *Describe the four functions of organizational culture.* Four functions of organizational culture are organizational identity, collective commitment, social system stability, and sense-making device.

4. *Discuss the four types of organizational culture associated with the competing values framework.* The competing values framework identifies four different types of organizational culture. A clan culture has an internal focus and values flexibility rather than stability and control. An adhocracy culture has an external focus and values flexibility. A market culture has a strong external focus and values stability and control. A hierarchy culture has an internal focus and values stability and control over flexibility.

5. *Summarize the three key conclusions derived from research about the outcomes associated with organizational culture.* Employees prefer to work in organizations that value flexibility and discretion over stability and control and those that are more concerned with satisfying employees' needs than customer or shareholder desires. Second, the congruence between an individual's values and the organization's values is significantly associated with organizational commitment, job satisfaction, intention to quit, and turnover. Third, there is not a clear pattern of relationships between organizational culture and outcomes such as service quality, customer satisfaction, and an organization's financial performance. These results in turn suggest that it is important for managers to effectively accommodate the potential conflict between cultures that have both an internal and external focus.

6. *Review the three caveats about culture change.* First, it is possible to change an organization's culture, and the process essentially begins with targeting one of the three layers of culture for change. Second, it is important to consider the extent to which the current culture is aligned with the organization's vision and strategic plans before attempting to change any aspect of organizational culture. Finally, it is important to use a structured approach when implementing culture change.

7. *Summarize the methods used by organizations to change organizational culture.* Changing culture amounts to teaching employees about the organization's preferred values, beliefs, expectations, and behaviors. This is accomplished by using one or more of the following 11 mechanisms: (*a*) formal statements of organizational philosophy, mission, vision, values, and materials used for recruiting, selection, and socialization; (*b*) the design of physical space, work environments, and buildings; (*c*) slogans, language, acronyms, and sayings; (*d*) deliberate role modeling, training programs, teaching, and coaching by managers and supervisors; (*e*) explicit rewards, status symbols, and promotion criteria; (*f*) stories, legends, and myths about key people and events; (*g*) the organizational activities, processes, or outcomes that leaders pay attention to, measure, and control; (*h*) leader reactions to critical incidents and organizational crises; (*i*) the workflow and organizational structure; (*j*) organizational systems and procedures; and (*k*) organizational goals and associated criteria used for recruitment, selection, development, promotion, layoffs, and retirement of people.

8. *Describe the three phases in Feldman's model of organizational socialization.* The three phases of Feldman's model are anticipatory socialization, encounter, and change and acquisition. Anticipatory socialization begins before an individual actually joins the organization. The encounter phase begins when the employment contract has been signed. Phase 3 involves the period in which employees master important tasks and resolve any role conflicts.

9. *Discuss the various socialization tactics used to socialize employees.* There are six key socialization tactics. They are collective versus individual, formal versus informal, sequential versus random, fixed versus variable, serial versus disjunctive, and investiture versus divestiture (see Table 3–1). Each tactic provides organizations with two opposing options for socializing employees.

10. *Explain the four developmental networks associated with mentoring.* The four developmental networks are based on integrating the diversity and strength of an individual's developmental relationships. The four resulting developmental networks are receptive, traditional, entrepreneurial, and opportunistic. A receptive network is composed of a few weak ties from one social system. Having a few strong ties with developers from one social system is referred to as a traditional network. An entrepreneurial network is made up of strong ties among several developers; and an opportunistic network is associated with having weak ties from different social systems.

Key Terms

Organizational culture 66
Values 68
Espoused values 68
Sustainability 68
Enacted values 68
Competing values framework (CVF) 72
Clan culture 72
Adhocracy culture 73
Market culture 74
Hierarchy culture 74
Vision 77

Strategic plan 77
Organizational socialization 80
Anticipatory socialization phase 81
Realistic job preview 82
Encounter phase 82
Onboarding 82
Change and acquisition phase 82
Mentoring 84
Diversity of developmental relationships 85
Developmental relationship
    strength 86

Google's Culture Is Truly Unique[72]

BusinessWeek **AT Google** it always comes back to the food. For human resources director Stacy Sullivan, it's the Irish oatmeal with fresh berries at the Plymouth Rock Café, located in building 1550 near the "people operations" group. "I sometimes dream about it," she says. "Seriously." As a seven-year veteran of the company, engineer Jen Fitzpatrick has developed a more sophisticated palate, preferring the raw bar at the Basque-themed Café Pintxo, a tapas joint in building 47. Her mother is thrilled she's eating well at work: "She came in for lunch once and thanked the chef," says Fitzpatrick. Joshua Bloch, an expert on the Java software language, swears by the roast quail at haute eatery Café Seven, professing *it* to be the best meal on campus. "It's uniformly excellent," he raves.

I found that to be a gross distortion of the facts. The roasted black bass with parsley pesto and bread crumbs had a delicate flavor, superior mouth feel, and a light yet satisfying finish that seemed to me unmatched among the 11 free gourmet cafeterias Google runs at its Mountain View, Calif., headquarters. . . .

Says co-founder Sergey Brin: "I mean, the cafés have always been pretty healthy, but the snacks are not, and the efforts to fix that have been remarkably challenging."

Though company lore has it that Brin and co-founder Larry Page believe no worker should be more than 150 feet from a food source, clearly not all food is equal. "A lot of people like their M&Ms. But the easy access is actually what's bad for them," he says.

Of course, when it comes to America's new Best Company to Work For, the food is, well, just the appetizer. At Google you can do your laundry; drop off your dry cleaning; get an oil change, then have your car washed; work out in the gym; attend subsidized exercise classes; get a massage; study Mandarin, Japanese, Spanish, and French; and ask a personal concierge to arrange dinner reservations. Naturally you can get haircuts onsite. Want to buy a hybrid car? The company will give you $5,000 toward that environmentally friendly end. Care to refer a friend to work at Google? Google would like that too, and it'll give you a $2,000 reward. Just have a new baby? Congratulations! Your employer will reimburse you for up to $500 in takeout food to ease your first four weeks at home. Looking to make new friends? Attend a weekly TGIF party, where there's usually a band playing. Five onsite doctors are available to give you a checkup, free of charge.

Many Silicon Valley companies provide shuttle-bus transportation from area train stations. Google operates free, Wi-Fi enabled coaches from five Bay Area locations. Lactation rooms are common in corporate America; Google provides breast pumps so that nursing moms don't have to haul the equipment to work. Work is such a cozy place that it's sometimes difficult for Google employees to leave the office, which is precisely how the company justifies the expenses, none of which it breaks out of its administrative costs.

The people at Google, it should be stated, almost universally see themselves as the most interesting people on the planet. Googlers tend to be happy-go-lucky on the outside, but Type A at their core. Ask one what he or she is doing, and it's never "selling ads" or "writing code." No, they're on a quest "to organize the world's information and make it universally accessible and useful." That's from the actual mission statement, by the way, which employees can and do cite with cloying frequency. . . .

I'm sitting on a heated toilet in my pajamas. I'm in engineering building 40 at Google on "pajama day," and directly in front of me, attached to the inside door of the toilet stall, is a one-page flier, printed on plain white paper, titled "Testing on the Toilet, Episode 21." The document, which is designed to prod the brains of engineers who test software code, explores such subjects as "lode coverage" and reminds engineers that even biobreaks need not interrupt their work. Presuming that one's stay here isn't sufficient to process that lesson, the sheet provides a link to two internal websites http://tott/ (for Testing on the Toilet) and http://botw/ (Bug of the Week). Not being a software engineer, I understand little of what I'm reading. Yet it reminds me of the first two sentences of the now famous founders' letter Page and Brin distributed to prospective Google shareholders before the company's 2004 IPO: "Google is not a conventional company. We do not intend to become one." Mission accomplished. . . .

Google's employment roster is now pushing 10,000, and the company has burgeoning offices in Bangalore, New York City, and Irvine, Calif., among many other cities, but the campus still feels like the brainiest university imaginable—one, however, in which every kid can afford a sports car (though geeky hybrids are cooler here than hot rods). . . .

Hours are long—typical for Silicon Valley— and it's not unusual for engineers to be seen in the hallways at 3 A.M. debating some esoteric algorithmic conundrum. "Hardcore geeks are here because there's no place they'd rather be," says Dennis Hwang, a Google webmaster who doubles as the artist who draws all the fancifully dressed-up versions of Google's home-page logo, called Doodles.

Teamwork is the norm, especially for big projects. . . . Google engineers are famously required to devote 20% of their time to pursuing projects they dream up that will help the company. The projects actually have a realistic chance of being adopted too. Google News,

Gmail, and the Google Finance site all sprouted from 20% time. Nontech ideas Googlers dream up have a shot at adoption as well.

The Google shuttle bus exists today because Carrie Spivak, who used to work on the company's book-search product, got sick of driving to work, scouted out a bus company, then plotted out the routes a shuttle might take. She brought the idea to senior management only after she'd done all the research. Any other company Google's size would form a cross-divisional transportation feasibility committee to study the issue. Google just did it.

That's not to say that anything goes at Google, where even the smallest issues are open to academic-style debate.

Questions for Discussion

1. What are the observable artifacts, espoused values, and basic assumptions associated with Google's culture? Explain.

2. Use the competing values framework to diagnose Google's culture. To what extent does it possess characteristics associated with a clan, adhocracy, market, and hierarchical cultures? Discuss.

3. What is Google's mission statement? Is the culture type you identified in question 2 consistent with the accomplishment of this mission? Explain.

4. What techniques for changing organizational culture has Google used to form its culture? Discuss.

5. Would you like to work at Google? Explain your rationale.

Ethical Dilemma

Would You Fire John Browne, CEO of BP?[73]

EXECUTIVES AT BP'S HEADquarters on London's leafy St. James's Square are marking their calendars with grim resignation. In mid-January, a panel led by former U.S. Secretary of State James A. Baker III is due to release a long-awaited report on a series of mishaps at the energy giant. The study could further bruise BP's already battered reputation and might hasten the departure of CEO John Browne, until recently one of Britain's most celebrated corporate chieftains.

If the findings are as harsh as some BP insiders fear, it will probably refocus attention on Browne. In 11 years as CEO, he has transformed BP from a middling player into an intensely competitive money machine. Browne consummated five big deals in five years, including the $62 billion takeover of Amoco in 1998 and a $32 billion buyout of Arco in 2000. But in his quest to boost financial returns, Browne may have overlooked problems for which he has paid dearly. In 2005, a refinery accident in Texas City, Tex., killed 15 people, sparking a firestorm of lawsuits. Last June, U.S. regulators alleged that BP manipulated the propane gas market. Then in August, BP was forced to cut production in Alaska's Prudhoe Bay field after inspectors discovered corroded and leaking pipelines.

The Baker report is likely to criticize top management for being lulled into complacency. While safety statistics showed improvement, the report is expected to say not enough was done to ensure correct procedures were followed. Browne might not disagree. "We learned a lot from what happened at Texas City," he says. "We are redoubling our efforts in safety processes." . . .

Executives privately say that problems were allowed to fester in a few of the less glamorous corners of the BP empire. Industry insiders say this may be partly due to Browne's view of the oil industry as a kind of three-dimensional chess game against rivals, particularly Shell and Exxon. "He has a restlessness; he is only interested in new ground," a close associate once said. Refining clearly didn't fall into the category of "new ground." It tends to be a low-margin business, and BP's focus has been keeping a lid on costs. BP executives say they recognized that the Texas refinery needed fixing, but the company did too little too late. . . .

Yet Browne's intense drive for results combined with BP's entrepreneurial culture may have also played a role in the company's woes. While Browne puts his managers through tough, detailed reviews each quarter, BP is less of a command-and-control company than rivals. It operates with a decentralized structure designed to reward individual initiative, and managers are expected to use their own judgment in running their operations. One source says Browne may have been guilty of "naivete" in trusting that managers in Texas and Alaska could achieve his demanding financial goals without compromising operations.

Some put it more bluntly. BP "is a financial culture gone wild," says Bernard Picchi, an analyst at Wall Street Access in New York, "The company has been doing deals for the sake of doing deals with an almost maniacal focus on the bottom line, to the [detriment] of normal operating standards."

Assume that you are member of BP's board. What would you do in light of the facts in this case?

1. Vigorously defend John Browne. He has transformed the company and it is making money. He also promises to look into the safety problems.

2. Given Browne one to two years to change the culture and clean up the problem. He will have to create more of a hierarchical culture while also reducing BP's orientation toward an adhocracy.

3. Fire him. He has exposed the company to tremendous liability under his leadership. His leadership is too strongly oriented toward results and not enough toward safety and concern for employees.
Invent other options.

Web Resources

Additional tools and resources are available to help you master the content of this chapter on the Web site at **www.mhhe.com/kreitner**

CHAPTER 4

International OB: Managing across Cultures

LEARNING OBJECTIVES

When you finish studying the material in this chapter, you should be able to:

1   Define the term *culture*, and explain how societal culture and organizational culture combine to influence on-the-job behavior.

2   Define *ethnocentrism*, and distinguish between high-context and low-context cultures.

3   Identify and describe the nine cultural dimensions from Project GLOBE.

4   Distinguish between individualistic and collectivist cultures, and explain the difference between monochronic and polychronic cultures.

5   Specify the practical lesson from the Hofstede cross-cultural study.

6   Explain what Project GLOBE researchers discovered about leadership.

7   Explain why U.S. managers have a comparatively high failure rate on foreign assignments.

8   Summarize the research findings about North American women on foreign assignments, and tell how to land a foreign assignment.

9   Identify four stages of the foreign assignment cycle and the OB trouble spot associated with each stage.

Student Resources for Studying Chapter 4

The Web site for your text includes resources that will help you master the concepts in this chapter. As you read, you'll want to visit the site for these helpful tools:

- Your online Study Guide includes learning objectives, a chapter summary, a glossary of key terms, and discussion questions.
- Take a practice quiz and test your knowledge!
- Scroll through a PowerPoint presentation with key concepts for this chapter.

Your instructor might also direct you to the Web site for these exercises:

- Self-assessments that correspond with the chapter content and a Group Exercise.
- You'll also find Video Cases and Internet Exercises for this chapter online.

www.mhhe.com/kreitner

BusinessWeek At a meeting with her leadership team in a sleek conference room high above New York, Maureen Chiquet, a slim 43-year-old with close-cropped hair, wears a dark couture jacket by legendary Chanel designer Karl Lagerfeld paired with superfine jeans and black Chanel boots. She and her team are strategizing about the launch of a new perfume. "Let's not be thinking about how big we can make this," says the new global head of one of the world's paramount—and most secretive—luxury brands, "but about how exclusive and special you can keep it."

It's a fair summary of Chiquet's strategy for the entire Chanel brand. In a transition planned since she joined Chanel in 2003, she rose from president of the Parisian company's US division to the newly created global CEO post on Jan. 1. That's quite a trajectory for a St. Louis native who spent most of her career at Gap Inc. Her aim is just as ambitious: to take a strong brand to the next level by appealing to a new generation of luxury shoppers. To do so, she is employing a consumer focus unusual for luxury retailing and borrowing a few tricks from Gap. "Maureen has gotten us to perceive the brand from the opposite side of the counter because she is the ultimate Chanel consumer," says Renette Zimmerly, Chanel's US director of creative services.

Chiquet has proved adept at working within a corporate culture that is profoundly French. Chanel's creative headquarters is still 31 rue Cambon, where Gabrielle "Coco" Chanel opened her first Paris boutique in 1921. Chiquet has meshed with Chanel's creative egos, such as Lagerfeld, and its French owners,

the Wertheimer family, whose two brothers are deeply involved in the business. They shun any public exposure and closely guard Chanel's financials. Analysts peg revenues at just over $3 billion. . . .

Intense competition in the luxury business led the family to create a global leadership position. Larger established brands like Louis Vuitton and Gucci have deep-pocketed, publicly traded parents that own many hot, smaller brands like upstart Bottega Veneta. These giants have been more centrally controlled than Chanel, whose five regional heads have had a fair degree of autonomy, insiders say. That's given the big players an edge in running more consistent global brands. Now Chanel's presidents report directly to Chiquet. "It tightens the consistency and speed of decision making," says Arie L Kopelman, Chanel's vice chairman. "When you factor in a far more competitive world, this is the only way to go."

Chiquet seemed destined for the job. She was the oldest of three sisters, and her father, a corporate lawyer, had a passion for French culture and spoke French fluently. By high school, speaking French was a major part of Chiquet's identity. At 16 she went to live with a French family in the town of Calvisson, near Nîmes, for four weeks. "I didn't want to have an accent," Chiquet says. "I wanted someone not to know I was American."

Chiquet attended Yale University, where she concentrated in literature, film, and theater. . . .

After graduation, Chiquet got an entry-level job in Paris at French consumer product maker L'Oréal. It wasn't long before she became a brand manager and made presentations to the CEO. Chiquet says she secretly dated a French manager, Antoine Chiquet, in the marketing department. But when he was promoted to a new post in Asia she didn't want to follow. They decided to quit, get married, and move to San Francisco without jobs.

She landed as a trainee at Gap, and over the next 15 years rose to major merchandising positions at the company. At its Old Navy division, she was No. 2 under former head Jenny Ming. Besides being the best merchant Ming had ever seen in identifying styles shoppers would want, her ex-boss says, Chiquet knew every lever in expanding a business: "She could connect all the pieces." She became president of Gap's Banana Republic unit in 2002, and won the Chanel job in 2003.

To claim it, Chiquet beat out more than 10 executives from the consumer-product, retailing, and luxury-goods industries. Kopelman says she had the best mix of business analytics combined with an ability to think creatively, a must to articulate the vision of Chanel's creative leaders. Chiquet's father negotiated her employment contract. "He was the best lawyer I knew," she quips. . . .

By all accounts, Chiquet has hit it off with her French colleagues. She's been careful to listen and learn. During her Paris stint, she says, "I spent nine months with a piece of tape on my mouth." Lyle Saunders, vice-president of US creative, recalls meeting a few months ago in Paris with his French counterpart who was surprised to learn Chiquet was American. He knew she lived in the States, "but assumed she was French born and raised." Chiquet's father would be proud.[1]

FOR DISCUSSION

Why is Maureen Chiquet a good prototype for the modern "global" manager?

We hear a lot about the global economy these days. Signs and symptoms of economic globalization making headlines in recent years have been the controversial North American Free Trade Agreement, riots at World Trade Organization meetings, complaints about the offshoring of jobs, trade imbalances, foreign sweatshops, and intellectual property abuses.[2] Meanwhile, US imports rose from 12% of gross national product in 1995 to 17% in 2006 ($2.2 trillion).[3] No less than a global economic earthquake is underway:

> For more than half a century, Americans could take for granted that the world economy would orbit around them. No longer. . . .
>
> "The change is from globalization going one way to globalization going every way. It's as much about what developing countries are doing as developed countries," said Mark Foster, a London-based Accenture consultant.
>
> Assuming continued economic growth in the developing world, the ranks of the global middle class are expected to triple by 2030 to 1.2 billion, according to the World Bank.

Today, a bit more than half of that free-spending group resides in developing countries. By 2030, almost all of it, 92%, will call the developing world home.

For multinational corporations, that means paying ever more attention to what's happening outside the United States and especially in Asia, Latin America, parts of the Middle East and Africa.[4]

Global managers such as Chanel's Maureen Chiquet, who can move comfortably from one culture to another while conducting business, have an advantage in the new global economy.[5] Indeed, according to one study, US multinational companies headed by CEOs with international assignments on their résumés tended to outperform the competition.[6] Even managers and employees who stay in their native country will find it hard to escape today's global economy. Many will be thrust into international relationships by working for foreign-owned companies or by dealing with foreign suppliers, customers, and co-workers. *Management Review* offered this helpful perspective:

> It's easy to think that people who have lived abroad or who are multilingual have global brains, while those who still live in their hometowns are parochial. But both notions are fallacies. Managers who have never left their home states can have global brains if they are interested in the greater world around them, make an effort to learn about other people's perspectives, and integrate those perspectives into their own way of thinking.[7]

The global economy is a rich mix of cultures, and the time to prepare to work in it is now. Accordingly, the purpose of this chapter is to help you take a step in that direction by exploring the impacts of culture in today's increasingly internationalized organizations. This chapter draws upon the area of cultural anthropology. We begin with a model that shows how societal culture and organizational culture (covered in Chapter 3) combine to influence work behavior. Next, we examine key dimensions of societal culture with the goal of enhancing cross-cultural awareness. Practical lessons from cross-cultural management research are then reviewed. The chapter concludes by exploring the challenge of accepting a foreign assignment.

Courtesy of Vahan Shirvanian
www.cartoonstock.com

Culture and Organizational Behavior

How would you, as a manager, interpret the following situations?

> An Asian executive for a multinational company, transferred from Taiwan to the Midwest, appears aloof and autocratic to his peers.

> A West Coast bank embarks on a "friendly teller" campaign, but its Filipino female tellers won't cooperate.

> A white manager criticizes a black male employee's work. Instead of getting an explanation, the manager is met with silence and a firm stare.[8]

If you attribute the behavior in these situations to personalities, three descriptions come to mind: arrogant, unfriendly, and hostile. These are reasonable conclusions.

Unfortunately, they are probably wrong, being based more on prejudice and stereotypes than on actual fact. However, if you attribute the behavioral outcomes to *cultural* differences, you stand a better chance of making the following more valid interpretations: "As it turns out, Asian culture encourages a more distant managing style, Filipinos associate overly friendly behavior in women with prostitution, and blacks as a group act more deliberately, studying visual cues, than most white men."[9] One cannot afford to overlook relevant cultural contexts when trying to understand and manage organizational behavior.

Societal Culture Is Complex and Multilayered

Culture

Beliefs and values about how a community of people should and do act.

In Chapter 3, we discussed *organizationa*l culture. Here, the focus is more broadly on *societal* culture. "**Culture** is a set of beliefs and values about what is desirable and undesirable in a community of people, and a set of formal or informal practices to support the values."[10] So culture has both prescriptive (what people should do) and descriptive (what they actually do) elements. Culture is passed from one generation to the next by family, friends, teachers, and relevant others. Most cultural lessons are learned by observing and imitating role models as they go about their daily affairs or as observed in the media.[11]

Culture is difficult to grasp because it is multilayered. International management experts Fons Trompenaars (from the Netherlands) and Charles Hampden-Turner (from Britain) offered this instructive analogy in their landmark book, *Riding the Waves of Culture:*

> Culture comes in layers, like an onion. To understand it you have to unpeel it layer by layer.
>
> On the outer layer are the products of culture, like the soaring skyscrapers of Manhattan, pillars of private power, with congested public streets between them. These are expressions of deeper values and norms in a society that are not directly visible (values such as upward mobility, "the more-the-better," status, material success). The layers of values and norms are deeper within the "onion," and are more difficult to identify.[12]

Consequently, the September 11, 2001, destruction of the New York World Trade Center towers by terrorists was as much an attack on American culture as it was on lives and property. That deepened the hurt and made the anger more profound for Americans and their friends around the world. In both life and business, culture is a serious matter.

Culture Is a Subtle but Pervasive Force

Culture generally remains below the threshold of conscious awareness because it involves *taken-for-granted assumptions* about how one should perceive, think, act, and feel. Cultural anthropologist Edward T Hall put it this way:

> Since much of culture operates outside our awareness, frequently we don't even know what we know. We pick ... [expectations and assumptions] up in the cradle. We unconsciously learn what to notice and what not to notice, how to divide time and space, how to walk and talk and use our bodies, how to behave as men or women, how to relate to other people, how to handle responsibility, whether experience is seen as whole or fragmented. This applies to all people. The Chinese or the Japanese or the Arabs are as unaware of their assumptions as we are of our own. We each assume that they're part of human nature. What we think of as "mind" is really internalized culture.[13]

In sum, it has been said: "you are your culture, and your culture is you." As part of the growing sophistication of marketing practices in the global economy, companies are hiring anthropologists to decipher the cultural roots of customer needs and preferences.[14]

Culture Overrides National Boundaries

The term *societal* culture is used here instead of national culture because the boundaries of many nation-states were not drawn along cultural lines. Instead, they evolved through conquest, migration, treaties, and geopolitics. The former Soviet Union, for example, included 15 republics and more than 100 ethnic nationalities, many with their own distinct language.[15] Also, English-speaking Canadians in Vancouver are culturally closer to Americans in Seattle than to their French-speaking compatriots in Quebec.

Nancy McKinstry, the American CEO of Wolters Kluwer, a multinational Dutch publishing company with 20,000 employees, has noticed a blurring of national boundaries. In a recent interview, she made this observation about the United States and Europe:

> There's a new kind of multiregional culture which combines the best of both worlds.... There are actually more similarities between the US, Germany and Holland than there are between those countries and southern Europe. In southern Europe decision-making is more collaborative, and developing long-term business relationships is essential to success.[16]

If we could redraw the world map along cultural lines instead of along geographical and political lines, we would end up with something very strange and different.[17] The point is, when preparing to live and work in a different country, be sure to consider more than national boundaries—study the culture.[18]

A Model of Societal and Organizational Cultures

As illustrated in Figure 4–1, culture influences organizational behavior in two ways. Employees bring their societal culture to work with them in the form of customs and language. Organizational culture, a by-product of societal culture, in turn affects the individual's values/ethics, attitudes, assumptions, and expectations. Societal culture is shaped by the various environmental factors listed in the left-hand side of Figure 4–1.

Figure 4–1   *Cultural Influences on Organizational Behavior*

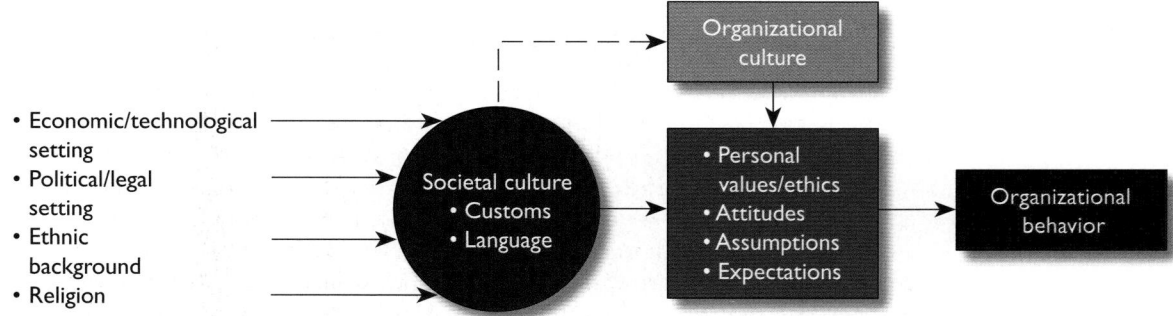

Once inside the organization's sphere of influence, the individual is further affected by the *organization's* culture. Mixing of societal and organizational cultures can produce interesting dynamics in multinational companies. For example, with French and American employees working side by side at General Electric's medical imaging production facility in Waukesha, Wisconsin, unit head Claude Benchimol has witnessed some culture shock:

> The French are surprised the American parking lots empty out as early as 5 PM; the Americans are surprised the French don't start work at 8 AM. Benchimol feels the French are more talkative and candid. Americans have more of a sense of hierarchy and are less likely to criticize. But they may be growing closer to the French. Says Benchimol: "It's taken a year to get across the idea that we are all entitled to say what we don't like to become more productive and work better."[19]

Same company, same company culture, yet GE's French and American co-workers have different attitudes about time, hierarchy, and communication. They are the products of different societal cultures.[20]

When managing people at work, the individual's societal culture, the organizational culture, and any interaction between the two need to be taken into consideration. For example, American workers' cultural orientation toward quality improvement differs significantly from the Japanese cultural pattern.

> Unlike Japanese workers, Americans aren't interested in making small step-by-step improvements to increase quality. They want to achieve the breakthrough, the impossible dream. The way to motivate them: Ask for the big leap, rather than for tiny steps.[21]

2 Ethnocentrism: A Cultural Roadblock in the Global Economy

Ethnocentrism

Belief that one's native country, culture, language, and behavior are superior.

Ethnocentrism, the belief that one's native country, culture, language, and modes of behavior are superior to all others, has its roots in the dawn of civilization. First identified as a behavioral science concept in 1906, involving the tendency of groups to reject outsiders,[22] the term *ethnocentrism* generally has a more encompassing (national or societal) meaning today. Worldwide evidence of ethnocentrism is plentiful. (See the Real World/Real People feature for a recent case in point.)[23] Militant ethnocentrism led to deadly "ethnic cleansing" in Bosnia and Kosovo and genocide in the African nations of Rwanda, Burundi, and Sudan.

Less dramatic, but still troublesome, is ethnocentrism within managerial and organizational contexts. Experts on the subject framed the problem this way:

> [Ethnocentric managers have] a preference for putting home-country people in key positions everywhere in the world and rewarding them more handsomely for work, along with a tendency to feel that this group is more intelligent, more capable, or more reliable. . . . Ethnocentrism is often not attributable to prejudice as much as to inexperience or lack of knowledge about foreign persons and situations. This is not too surprising, since most executives know far more about employees in their home environments. As one executive put it, "At least I understand why our own managers make mistakes. With our foreigners, I never know. The foreign managers may be better. But if I can't trust a person, should I hire him or her just to prove we're multinational?"[24]

Muslim-Americans Feel the Sting of Ethnocentrism

Background Information:

Muslims . . . around the country are the objects of suspicion and in some cases prejudice, especially since the attacks of September 11, 2001. But as a group, they offer a model of assimilation and material success. An astounding 59% of Muslim adults in the US have a college degree, compared with only 28% of all American adults. Surveys show that median family income among America's Muslims exceeds the national figure of $55,800. And four out of five eligible Muslims are registered to vote, slightly higher than the overall rate.

The duality of Muslim-American life often surfaces in the tension between allegiance to an adopted land and to causes back in the old country that most Americans view as dangerous.*

Ethnocentrism in Action:

Not so funny.

Keith Dennis came to that reckoning after a radio ad planned by his Ohio car dealership was criticized as anti-Muslim and refused by several radio stations.

The commercial called for "jihad on the automotive market." It said salespeople would be wearing burqas, a traditional garment in some Muslim nations, and kids would get rubber swords on "fatwa Friday."

"Our prices are lower than the evildoers' every day," the script said. "Just ask the pope!"

"Jihad," an Islamic term for an utmost struggle, is sometimes used to mean a religious war. A "fatwa," a legal pronouncement in Islam, can be a declaration of war. "This was simply an attempt at humor that fell flat," Dennis, owner of Dennis Mitsubishi in Columbus, said in a statement apologizing "to anyone who was offended."**

What are the ethical implications of any ethnocentric comments you have made and/or heard from others recently?

SOURCES: *P M Barrett, "They're Muslims, And Yankees, Too," *BusinessWeek*, January 15, 2007, p 51. **W Koch, "Ads Are Yanked as Offensive to Arabs, Muslims," *USA Today*, September 26, 2006, p 3A.

Research suggests ethnocentrism is bad for business. A survey of 918 companies with home offices in the United States (272 companies), Japan (309), and Europe (337) found ethnocentric staffing and human resource policies to be associated with increased personnel problems. Those problems included recruiting difficulties, high turnover rates, and lawsuits over personnel policies. Among the three regional samples, Japanese companies had the most ethnocentric human resource practices and the most international human resource problems.[25]

Current and future managers, and people in general, can effectively deal with ethnocentrism through education, greater cross-cultural awareness, international experience, and a conscious effort to value cultural diversity.

Toward Greater Cross-Cultural Awareness and Competence

This section explores basic ways of describing and comparing cultures. As a foundation, we discuss cultural stereotyping and paradoxes and the need for cultural intelligence. Next we contrast high-context and low-context cultures and introduce nine cultural dimensions identified in the GLOBE project. Then our attention turns to examining cross-cultural differences in terms of individualism, time, space, and religion.

Cultural Paradoxes Require Cultural Intelligence

An important qualification needs to be offered at this juncture. All of the cultural differences in this chapter and elsewhere need to be viewed as *tendencies* and *patterns* rather than as absolutes.[26] As soon as one falls into the trap of assuming all Italians are this, and *all* Koreans will do that, and so on, potentially instructive generalizations become mindless stereotypes. A pair of professors with extensive foreign work experience advises: "As teachers, researchers, and managers in cross-cultural contexts, we need to recognize that our original characterizations of other cultures are best guesses that we need to modify as we gain more experience."[27] Consequently, they contend, we will be better prepared to deal with inevitable *cultural paradoxes.* By paradox, they mean there are always exceptions to the rule; individuals who do not fit the expected cultural pattern. A good example is the head of Canon. "By Japanese CEO standards, Canon Inc.'s Fujio Mitarai is something of an anomaly. For starters, he's fast and decisive—a far cry from the consensus builders who typically run Japan Inc."[28] One also encounters lots of cultural paradoxes in large and culturally diverse nations such as the United States and Brazil. This is where the need for cultural intelligence arises.

Cultural intelligence

The ability to interpret ambiguous cross-cultural situations accurately.

Cultural intelligence, the ability to accurately interpret ambiguous cross-cultural situations, is an important skill in today's diverse workplaces. Two OB scholars explain:

> A person with high cultural intelligence can somehow tease out of a person's or group's behavior those features that would be true of all people and all groups, those peculiar to this person or this group, and those that are neither universal nor idiosyncratic. The vast realm that lies between those poles is culture.[29]

High-context cultures

Primary meaning derived from nonverbal situational cues.

Those interested in developing their cultural intelligence need to first develop their emotional intelligence, discussed in detail in Chapter 5, and then practice in ambiguous cross-cultural situations. Of course, as in all human interaction, there is no adequate substitute for really getting to know, listen to, and care about others.

The career paths for Brian McCann (left) and Jennifer Chang (right) at PricewaterhouseCoopers took a detour recently through this factory in the Central American country of Belize. The pair participated in the accounting and consulting firm's Ulysses Program, whereby up-and-coming leaders are sent to developing countries for eight weeks to do volunteer work on business development projects. For more on this win-win exercise in developing cultural intelligence, see the OB in Action Case Study at the end of this chapter.

High-Context and Low-Context Cultures

This is a broadly applicable and useful cultural distinction[30] (see Figure 4–2). People from **high-context cultures**—including China, Korea, Japan, Vietnam, Mexico, and Arab cultures—rely heavily on situational cues for meaning when perceiving and communicating with others. Nonverbal cues such as one's official position, status, or family connections convey messages more powerfully than do spoken words. In China, for example, one's actions—observed over extended periods of time—do indeed speak louder than words[31] (see the Real World/Real People feature on page 102).

Figure 4–2   *Contrasting High-Context and Low-Context Cultures*

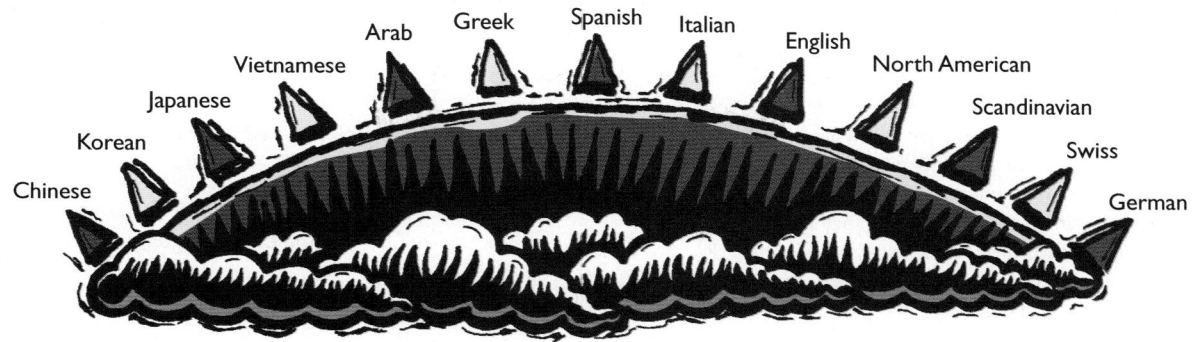

High-Context
- Establish social trust first
- Value personal relations and goodwill
- Agreement by general trust
- Negotiations slow and ritualistic

Low-Context
- Get down to business first
- Value expertise and performance
- Agreement by specific, legalistic contract
- Negotiations as efficient as possible

SOURCE: Reprinted from *Business Horizons*, vol. 36, No. 3, M Munter, "Cross-Cultural Communication for Managers," p 72, © 1993, with permission from Elsevier.

go to the Web for the Group Exercise: Looking into a Cultural Mirror

Reading the Fine Print in Low-Context Cultures
In low-context **cultures,** written and spoken words carry the burden of shared meanings. Low-context cultures include those found in Germany, Switzerland, Scandinavia, North America, and Great Britain. True to form, Germany has precise written rules for even the smallest details of daily life.[32] In *high*-context cultures, agreements tend to be made on the basis of someone's word or a handshake, after a rather prolonged get-acquainted and trust-building period. Low-context Americans and Canadians, at least those with cultural roots in Northern Europe, see the handshake as a signal to get a signature on a detailed, lawyer-approved, ironclad contract.

Low-context cultures

Primary meaning derived from written and spoken words.

Avoiding Cultural Collisions
Misunderstanding and miscommunication often are problems in international business dealings when the parties are from high- versus low-context cultures. A Mexican business professor made this instructive observation:

> Over the years, I have noticed that across cultures there are different opinions on what is expected from a business report. US managers, for instance, take a pragmatic, get-to-the-point approach, and expect reports to be concise and action-oriented. They don't have time to read long explanations: "Just the facts, ma'am."
>
> Latin American managers will usually provide long explanations that go beyond the simple facts. . . .
>
> I have a friend who is the Latin America representative for a United States firm and has been asked by his boss to provide regular reports on sales activities. His reports are long, including detailed explanations on the context in which the events he is

Relationships and *Guanxi* Matter When Doing Business in China

For the Chinese, the concept of *guanxi* plays a large role in successful relationships. While there is no precise English translation, *guanxi* involves personal connections based on mutually obligated dependency and lifelong commitment—a kind of mutual back scratching, which in the United States might be viewed as a form of nepotism or "a good old boys" network. . . .

As a consequence, you can't simply drop into China, give a series of banquets, and suddenly become a trusted colleague; you must demonstrate a sincere interest and commitment to an individual on an ongoing basis. A particularly important aspect of Chinese networking is that when out for a business meal, it is one person who pays; you don't split the check. The practice is reflective of a mind-set focused on the kind of mutual obligation in which costs will equal out across time.

How would the typical time-conscious American businessperson deal with this Chinese tradition of prolonged relationship building?

SOURCE: B Koenig, P Z Tith, and S Ludlum, "Engaging China," *Association Management*, December 2004, p 65.

reporting on occur and the possible interpretations that they might have. His boss regularly answers these reports with very brief messages, telling him to "cut the crap and get to the point!"[33]

Awkward situations such as this can be avoided when those on both sides of the context divide make good-faith attempts to understand and accommodate their counterparts. Here are some practical tips:

- People on both sides of the context barrier must be trained to make adjustments.
- A new employee should be greeted by a group consisting of his or her boss, several colleagues who have similar duties, and an individual located near the newcomer.
- Background information is essential when explaining anything. Include the history and personalities involved.
- Do not assume the newcomer is self-reliant. Give explicit instructions not only about objectives, but also about the process involved.
- High-context workers from abroad need to learn to ask questions outside their department and function.
- Foreign workers must make an effort to become more self-reliant.[34]

 3 Nine Cultural Dimensions from the GLOBE Project

Project GLOBE (Global Leadership and Organizational Behavior Effectiveness) is the brainchild of University of Pennsylvania professor Robert J House.[35] It is a massive and ongoing attempt to "develop an empirically based theory to describe, understand, and predict the impact of specific cultural variables on leadership and organizational processes and the effectiveness of these processes."[36] GLOBE has evolved into a network of more than 150 scholars from 62 societies since the project was launched in Calgary, Canada, in 1994. Most of the researchers are native to the particular cultures they study, thus greatly enhancing the credibility of the project. During the first two phases of the GLOBE project, a list of nine basic cultural dimensions was developed and statistically validated. Translated questionnaires based on the nine dimensions were administered to thousands of managers in the banking, food, and telecommunications industries around the world to build a database. Results are being published on a regular basis. Much work and many years are needed if the project's goal, as stated above, is to be achieved. In the meantime, we have been given a comprehensive, valid, and up-to-date tool for better understanding cross-cultural similarities and differences.

The nine cultural dimensions from the GLOBE project are

- *Power distance.* How much unequal distribution of power should there be in organizations and society?
- *Uncertainty avoidance.* How much should people rely on social norms and rules to avoid uncertainty and limit unpredictability?
- *Institutional collectivism.* How much should leaders encourage and reward loyalty to the social unit, as opposed to the pursuit of individual goals?
- *In-group collectivism.* How much pride and loyalty should individuals have for their family or organization?
- *Gender egalitarianism.* How much effort should be put into minimizing gender discrimination and role inequalities?
- *Assertiveness.* How confrontational and dominant should individuals be in social relationships?
- *Future orientation.* How much should people delay gratification by planning and saving for the future?
- *Performance orientation.* How much should individuals be rewarded for improvement and excellence?
- *Humane orientation.* How much should society encourage and reward people for being kind, fair, friendly, and generous?[37]

What about Your Culture? Take a short break from your reading and go to the web to complete the Self Exercise. It will help you better comprehend the nine GLOBE cultural dimensions. Can you trace your cultural profile to family history and country of origin of your ancestors? For example, one of your author's German roots are evident in his cultural profile. What are the personal implications of any cultural "gaps" that surfaced?

go to the Web for the Self-Exercise: What Is Your Cultural Profile?

Country Profiles and Practical Implications How do different countries score on the GLOBE cultural dimensions? Data from 18,000 managers yielded the profiles in Table 4–1. A quick overview shows a great deal of cultural diversity around the world. But thanks to the nine GLOBE dimensions, we have more precise understanding of *how* cultures vary. Closer study reveals telling cultural *patterns,* or cultural fingerprints for nations. The US managerial sample, for instance, scored high on assertiveness and performance orientation. Accordingly, Americans are widely perceived as pushy and hardworking. Switzerland's high scores on uncertainty avoidance and future orientation help explain its centuries

Table 4–1   *Countries Ranking Highest and Lowest on the GLOBE Cultural Dimensions*

DIMENSION	HIGHEST	LOWEST
Power distance	Morocco, Argentina, Thailand, Spain, Russia	Denmark, Netherlands, South Africa— black sample, Israel, Costa Rica
Uncertainty avoidance	Switzerland, Sweden, Germany— former West, Denmark, Austria	Russia, Hungary, Bolivia, Greece, Venezuela
Institutional collectivism	Sweden, South Korea, Japan, Singapore, Denmark	Greece, Hungary, Germany—former East, Argentina, Italy
In-group collectivism	Iran, India, Morocco, China, Egypt	Denmark, Sweden, New Zealand, Netherlands, Finland
Gender egalitarianism	Hungary, Poland, Slovenia, Denmark, Sweden	South Korea, Egypt, Morocco, India, China
Assertiveness	Germany—former East, Austria, Greece, US, Spain	Sweden, New Zealand, Switzerland, Japan, Kuwait
Future orientation	Singapore, Switzerland, Netherlands, Canada—English speaking, Denmark	Russia, Argentina, Poland, Italy, Kuwait
Performance orientation	Singapore, Hong Kong, New Zealand, Taiwan, US	Russia, Argentina, Greece, Venezuela, Italy
Humane orientation	Philippines, Ireland, Malaysia, Egypt, Indonesia	Germany—former West, Spain, France, Singapore, Brazil

SOURCE: Adapted from M Javidan and R J House, "Cultural Acumen for the Global Manager: Lessons from Project GLOBE," *Organizational Dynamics*, Spring 2001, pp 289–305.

of political neutrality and world-renowned banking industry. Singapore is known as a great place to do business because it is clean and safe and its people are well educated and hardworking. This is no surprise, considering Singapore's high scores on social collectivism, future orientation, and performance orientation. In contrast, Russia's low scores on future orientation and performance orientation could foreshadow a slower than hoped for transition from a centrally planned economy to free enterprise capitalism. These illustrations bring us to an important practical lesson: *Knowing the cultural tendencies of foreign business partners and competitors can give you a strategic competitive advantage.*

Individualism versus Collectivism

Have you ever been torn between what you personally wanted and what the group, organization, or society expected of you? If so, you have firsthand experience with a fundamental and important cultural distinction: individualism versus collectivism. This source of cultural variation—represented by two of the nine GLOBE dimensions—deserves a closer look. As might be expected with an extensively researched topic, individualism–collectivism has many interpretations.[38] Let us examine the basic concept for greater cultural awareness.

Individualistic cultures, characterized as "I" and "me" cultures, give priority to individual freedom and choice. Accordingly, they emphasize *personal* responsibility for one's affairs. This is no small matter in an aging society:

> A strong feeling of "social solidarity," as [Johns Hopkins University professor Gerald F] Anderson sees it, makes Europeans inclined to be generous to older people, more willing to support them. "Their attitude is, we're older and we'll need some help," he says. "The US attitude is, we're all rugged individualists and we're going to take care of ourselves, not others."[39]

This cultural distinction was borne out in a recent survey of the quality-of-life among senior citizens in 16 industrialized nations. The Netherlands was number one and the United States ranked number 13.[40]

Collectivist cultures, oppositely called "we" and "us" cultures, rank shared goals higher than individual desires and goals. People in collectivist cultures are expected to subordinate their own wishes and goals to those of the relevant social unit. A worldwide survey of 30,000 managers by Trompenaars and Hampden-Turner, who prefer the term communitarianism to collectivism, found the highest degree of individualism in Israel, Romania, Nigeria, Canada, and the United States. Countries ranking lowest in individualism—thus qualifying as collectivist cultures—were Egypt, Nepal, Mexico, India, and Japan. Brazil, China, and France also ended up toward the collectivist end of the scale.[41]

A Business Success Factor   Of course, one can expect to encounter both individualists and collectivists in culturally diverse countries such as the United States. For example, imagine the frustration of Dave Murphy, a Boston-based mutual fund salesperson, when he tried to get Navajo Indians in Arizona interested in saving money for their retirement. After several fruitless meetings with groups of Navajo employees, he was given this cultural insight by a local official: "If you come to this environment, you have to understand that money is different. It's there to be spent. If you have some, you help your family."[42] (This suggests Navajos would score high on in-group collectivism and low on future orientation on the GLOBE scale.) To traditional Navajos, enculturated as collectivists, saving money is an unworthy act of selfishness. Subsequently, the sales pitch was tailored to emphasize the *family* benefits of individual retirement savings plans.

Allegiance to Whom?   The Navajo example brings up an important point about collectivist cultures. Specifically, which unit of society predominates? For the Navajos, family is the key reference group. But, as Trompenaars and Hampden-Turner observe, important differences exist among collectivist (or communitarian) cultures:

> For each single society, it is necessary to determine the group with which individuals have the closest identification. They could be keen to identify with their trade union, their family, their corporation, their religion, their profession, their nation, or the state apparatus. The French tend to identify with *la France, la famille, le cadre;* the Japanese with the corporation; the former eastern bloc with the Communist Party; and Ireland with the Roman Catholic Church. Communitarian goals may be good or bad for industry depending on the community concerned, its attitude and relevance to business development.[43]

This observation validates GLOBE's distinction between institutional and in-group collectivism.

Individualistic culture
Primary emphasis on personal freedom and choice.

Collectivist culture
Personal goals less important than community goals and interests.

Cultural Perceptions of Time

In North American and Northern European cultures, time seems to be a simple matter. It is linear, relentlessly marching forward, never backward, in standardized chunks. To the American who received a watch for his or her third birthday, time is like money. It is spent, saved, or wasted.[44] A prime example is stockbroker Chris Gardner, whose rags-to-riches story was portrayed by actor Will Smith in the hit movie *The Pursuit of Happyness*. Gardner "wears two watches, one on each wrist, to make sure he's always on time."[45] Gardner's Hollywood opposite is actor Johnny Depp. According to a *Newsweek* reporter, "He seems like a man who has never rushed to, or from, anywhere in his life. He is chronically late for interviews—sometimes four or five hours, sometimes days—but this time around a gentlemanly 50 minutes."[46] Kentucky-born Depp certainly doesn't fit the stereotypical American who shows up 10 minutes early for appointments. When working across cultures, time becomes a very complex matter. Imagine a New Yorker's chagrin when left in a waiting room for 45 minutes, only to find a Latin American government official dealing with three other people at once. The North American resents the lack of prompt and undivided attention. The Latin American official resents the North American's impatience and apparent self-centeredness.[47] This vicious cycle of resentment can be explained by the distinction between **monochronic time** and **polychronic time:**

> The former is revealed in the ordered, precise, schedule-driven use of public time that typifies and even caricatures efficient Northern Europeans and North Americans. The latter is seen in the multiple and cyclical activities and concurrent involvement with different people in Mediterranean, Latin American, and especially Arab cultures.[48]

Monochronic time
Preference for doing one thing at a time because time is limited, precisely segmented, and schedule driven.

Polychronic time
Preference for doing more than one thing at a time because time is flexible and multidimensional.

A Matter of Degree Monochronic and polychronic are relative rather than absolute concepts. Generally, the more things a person tends to do at once, the more polychronic that person is.[49] Thanks to the Internet and advanced telecommunications systems, highly polychronic managers can engage in "multitasking."[50] For example, it is possible to talk on the telephone, read and respond to e-mail, print a report, check an instant message, *and* eat a stale sandwich all at the same time. Unfortunately, this extreme polychronic behavior too often is not as efficient as hoped and, as discussed in Chapter 18, can be very stressful. Monochronic people prefer to do one thing at a time. What is your attitude toward time?

Practical Implications Low-context cultures, such as that of the United States, tend to run on monochronic time, while high-context cultures, such as that of Mexico, tend to run on polychronic time. People in polychronic cultures view time as flexible, fluid, and multidimensional. The Germans and Swiss have made an exact science of monochronic time. In fact, a radio-controlled watch made by a German company, Junghans, is "guaranteed to lose no more than one second in 1 million years."[51] Many a visitor has been a minute late for a Swiss train, only to see its taillights leaving the station. Time is more elastic in polychronic cultures. During the Islamic holy month of Ramadan in Middle Eastern nations, for example, the faithful fast during daylight hours, and the general pace of things markedly slows. Managers need to reset their mental clocks when doing business across cultures.

Interpersonal Space

Anthropologist Edward T Hall noticed a connection between culture and preferred interpersonal distance. People from high-context cultures were observed standing

Figure 4–3 *Interpersonal Distance Zones for Business Conversations Vary from Culture to Culture*

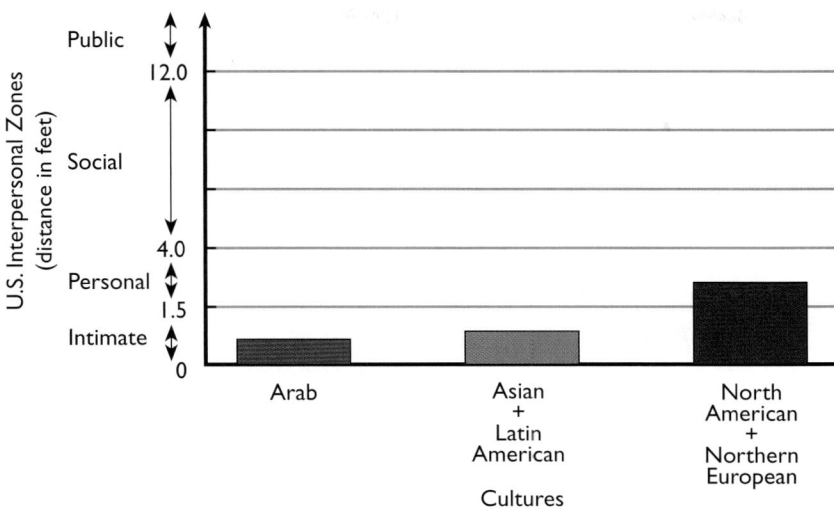

close when talking to someone. Low-context cultures appeared to dictate a greater amount of interpersonal space. Hall applied the term **proxemics** to the study of cultural expectations about interpersonal space.[52] He specified four interpersonal distance zones. Some call them space bubbles. They are *intimate* distance, *personal* distance, *social* distance, and *public* distance. Ranges for the four interpersonal distance zones are illustrated in Figure 4–3, along with selected cultural differences.

North American business conversations normally are conducted at about a three- to four-foot range, within the personal zone in Figure 4–3. A range of approximately one foot is common in Latin American and Asian cultures, uncomfortably close for Northern Europeans and North Americans. Some Arabs like to get even closer. Mismatches in culturally dictated interpersonal space zones can prove very distracting for the unprepared. Hall explains,

Proxemics

Hall's term for the study of cultural expectations about interpersonal space.

> Arabs tend to get very close and breathe on you. It's part of the high sensory involvement of a high-context culture....
>
> The American on the receiving end can't identify all the sources of his discomfort but feels that the Arab is pushy. The Arab comes close, the American backs up. The Arab follows, because he can only interact at certain distances. Once the American learns that Arabs handle space differently and that breathing on people is a form of communication, the situation can sometimes be redefined so the American relaxes.[53]

Asian and Middle-Eastern hosts grow weary of having to seemingly chase their low-context guests around at social gatherings to maintain what they feel is proper conversational range. Backing up all evening to keep conversational partners at a proper distance is an awkward experience as well. Awareness of cultural differences, along with skillful accommodation, are essential to productive intercultural business dealings.

Religion

Religious beliefs and practices can have a profound effect on cross-cultural relations. A comprehensive treatment of different religions is beyond the scope of our current discussion.[54] However, we can examine the relationship between religious affiliation and work-related values. A study of 484 international students at a midwestern US university uncovered wide variability. The following list gives the most important work-related value for each of five religious affiliations:

Catholic—Consideration ("Concern that employees be taken seriously, be kept informed, and that their judgments be used.")

Protestant—Employer effectiveness ("Desire to work for a company that is efficient, successful, and a technological leader.")

Buddhist—Social responsibility ("Concern that the employer be a responsible part of society.")

Muslim—Continuity ("Desire for stable environment, job longevity, reduction of uncertainty.")

No religious preference—Professional challenge ("Concern with having a job that provides learning opportunities and opportunities to use skills well.")[55]

Thus, there was virtually *no agreement* across religions about the primary work value. This led the researchers to conclude: "Employers might be wise to consider the impact that religious differences (and more broadly, cultural factors) appear to have on the values of employee groups."[56] Of course, in the United States and other selected countries, equal employment opportunity laws forbid managers from basing employment-related decisions on an applicant's religious preference.

Practical Insights from Cross-Cultural Management Research

Cross-cultural management

Understanding and teaching behavioral patterns in different cultures.

Nancy Adler, an international OB specialist at Canada's McGill University, has offered the following definition: "**Cross-cultural management** explains the behavior of people in organizations around the world and shows people how to work in organizations with employee and client populations from many different cultures."[57] Historically, cross-cultural management research has focused almost exclusively on cultural differences.[58] But GLOBE researchers Mansour Javidan and Robert J House recommend studying *similarities* as well. They believe tracking cultural similarities will help us judge how applicable specific management practices are in foreign cultures. "For example, leadership theories developed in the US are probably more easily generalizable to UK managers (another member of the Anglo cluster) than to managers in an Arab country."[59] In this section we will examine two different streams of cross-cultural management research. Both offer useful lessons for today's managers.

5 The Hofstede Study: How Well Do US Management Theories Apply in Other Countries?

The short answer to this important question: *not very well.* This answer derives from a landmark study conducted 30 years ago by Dutch researcher Geert Hofstede. His unique cross-cultural comparison of 116,000 IBM employees from 53 countries worldwide focused on four cultural dimensions:

- *Power distance.* How much inequality does someone expect in social situations?
- *Individualism–collectivism.* How loosely or closely is the person socially bonded?

- *Masculinity–femininity.* Does the person embrace stereotypically competitive, performance-oriented masculine traits or nurturing, relationship-oriented feminine traits?
- *Uncertainty avoidance.* How strongly does the person desire highly structured situations?

The US sample ranked relatively low on power distance, very high on individualism, moderately high on masculinity, and low on uncertainty avoidance.[60]

The high degree of variation among cultures led Hofstede to two major conclusions: (1) Management theories and practices need to be adapted to local cultures. This is particularly true for made-in-America management theories (e.g., Maslow's need hierarchy) and Japanese team management practices. *There is no one best way to manage across cultures.*[61] (2) Cultural arrogance is a luxury individuals, companies, and nations can no longer afford in a global economy.

Welcome to the Gateway Language Village, a total immersion English language school in Zhuhai, China. Students from China and elsewhere are forbidden to converse in anything but English when they set foot on campus. GLV was founded by Ping Hong who grew up in China and holds a master's degree from Purdue University in the US. He and his Colombian wife have a boy and a girl who speak Chinese, Spanish, and English. They will be well-equipped to succeed in the global economy.

6 Leadership Lessons from the GLOBE Project

In phase 2, the GLOBE researchers set out to discover which, if any, attributes of leadership were universally liked or disliked. They surveyed 17,000 middle managers working for 951 organizations across 62 countries. Their results, summarized in Table 4–2, have important implications for trainers and present and future global managers.[62] Visionary and inspirational *charismatic leaders* who are good team builders generally do the best. On the other hand, *self-centered leaders* seen as loners or face-savers generally receive a poor reception worldwide. (See Chapter 16 for a comprehensive treatment of leadership.) Local and foreign managers who heed these results are still advised to use a contingency approach to leadership after using their cultural intelligence to read the local people and culture. David Whitwam, the longtime CEO of appliance maker Whirlpool, recently framed the challenge this way:

> Leading a company today is different from the 1980s and '90s, especially in a global company. It requires a new set of competencies. Bureaucratic structures don't work anymore. You have to take the command-and-control types out of the system. You need to allow and encourage broad-based involvement in the company. Especially in consumer kinds of companies, we need a diverse workforce with diverse leadership. You need strong regional leadership that lives in the culture. We have a North American running the North American business, and a Latin American running the Latin American business.[63]

Table 4–2   *Leadership Attributes Universally Liked and Disliked across 62 Nations*

UNIVERSALLY POSITIVE LEADER ATTRIBUTES	UNIVERSALLY NEGATIVE LEADER ATTRIBUTES
Trustworthy	Loner
Just	Asocial
Honest	Noncooperative
Foresight	Irritable
Plans ahead	Nonexplicit
Encouraging	Egocentric
Positive	Ruthless
Dynamic	Dictatorial
Motive arouser	
Confidence builder	
Motivational	
Dependable	
Intelligent	
Decisive	
Effective bargainer	
Win–win problem solver	
Administrative skilled	
Communicative	
Informed	
Coordinator	
Team builder	
Excellence oriented	

SOURCE: Excerpted and adapted from P W Dorfman, P J Hanges, and F C Brodbeck, "Leadership and Cultural Variation: The Identification of Culturally Endorsed Leadership Profiles," in *Culture, Leadership, and Organizations: The GLOBE Study of 62 Societies,* eds R J House, P J Hanges, M Javidan, P W Dorfman, and V Gupta (Thousand Oaks, CA: Sage, 2004), Tables 21.2 and 21.3, pp 677–78.

go to the Web for the Self-Exercise: How Do Your Work Goals Compare Internationally?

Preparing Employees for Successful Foreign Assignments

As the reach of global companies continues to grow, many opportunities for living and working in foreign countries will arise. Imagine, for example, the opportunities for foreign duty and cross-cultural experiences at Siemens, the German electronics giant. "While Siemens' corporate headquarters is near Munich, nearly 80% of the firm's business is international. Worldwide the company has 470,000 employees, including 75,000 in the United States and 25,000 in China."[64] Siemens and other global players need a vibrant and growing cadre of employees who are willing and able to do business across cultures.[65] Thus, the purpose of this final section is to help you prepare yourself and others to work successfully in foreign countries, because a foreign assignment can be a real résumé builder these days. In fact, when *Fortune* magazine recently listed "Five Ways to Ignite Your Career," the number one suggestion was the following:

> Go global. International operations aren't a backwater—they're a way to prove you get it. "You don't have to go live in Bangalore [India] for three years," says Brian Sullivan of executive recruiters Christian & Timbers. But you "need more than just superficial knowledge. Get involved with customers, manufacturing technologies, and employees in different cultures."[66]

 ## 7 Why Do US Expatriates Fail on Foreign Assignments?

As we use the term here, **expatriate** refers to anyone living or working outside their home country. Hence, they are said to be *expatriated* when transferred to another country and *repatriated* when transferred back home. US expatriate managers, now at more than 300,000,[67] usually are characterized as culturally inept and prone to failure on international assignments. Research supports this view. A pair of international management experts offered this assessment:

> Over the past decade, we have studied the management of expatriates at about 750 US, European, and Japanese companies. We asked both the expatriates themselves and the executives who sent them abroad to evaluate their experiences. In addition, we looked at what happened after expatriates returned home. . . .
>
>   Overall, the results of our research were alarming. We found that between 10% and 20% of all US managers sent abroad returned early because of job dissatisfaction or difficulties in adjusting to a foreign country. Of those who stayed for the duration, nearly one-third did not perform up to the expectations of their superiors. And perhaps most problematic, one-fourth of those who completed an assignment left their company, often to join a competitor, within one year after repatriation. That's a turnover rate double that of managers who did not go abroad.[68]

A more recent study of why expatriate employees returned home early found the situation to be slowly improving. Still, *personal and family adjustment problems* (36.6%) and *homesickness* (31%) were found to be major stumbling blocks for American managers working in foreign countries.[69] A survey asking 72 human resource managers at multinational corporations to identify the most important success factor in a foreign assignment provided this insight: "Nearly 35% said cultural adaptability: patience, flexibility, and tolerance for others' beliefs."[70]

US multinational companies clearly need to do a better job of preparing employees and their families for foreign assignments, particularly in light of the high costs involved:

> The tab for sending an executive who earns $160,000 in the US, plus a spouse and two children, to India for two years is about $900,000, says Jacqui Hauser, vice president of consulting services for Cendant Mobility, a relocation-services firm in Danbury, Conn.

Expatriate

Anyone living or working in a foreign country.

This includes housing and cost-of-living allowances, foreign- and hardship-pay premiums, tax-assistance, education and car allowances and paid transportation home each year for the entire family.[71]

8 A Bright Spot: North American Women on Foreign Assignments

Historically, a woman from the United States or Canada on a foreign assignment was a rarity. Things are changing, albeit slowly. A review of research evidence and anecdotal accounts uncovered these insights:

- The proportion of corporate women from North America on foreign assignments grew from about 3% in the early 1980s to between 11% and 15% in the late 1990s.
- Self-disqualification and management's assumption that women would not be welcome in foreign cultures—not foreign prejudice, itself—are the primary barriers for potential female expatriates.
- Expatriate North American women are viewed first and foremost by their hosts as being foreigners, and only secondarily as being female.
- North American women have a very high success rate on foreign assignments.[72]

Considering the rapidly growing demand for global managers today,[73] self-disqualification by women and management's prejudicial policies are counterproductive. For their part, women and others who desire a foreign assignment need to take affirmative steps (see Table 4–3). The CEO of tobacco giant Reynolds American is a

Table 4–3   *Tips for Women (and Men) for Landing a Foreign Assignment*

- While still in school, pursue foreign study opportunities and become fluent in one or more foreign languages.
- Starting with the very first job interview, clearly state your desire for a foreign assignment.
- Become very knowledgeable about foreign countries where you would like to work (take vacations there).
- Network with expatriates (both men and women) in your company to uncover foreign assignment opportunities.
- Make sure your family fully supports a foreign assignment.
- Get your boss's support by building trust and a strong working relationship.
- Be visible: make sure upper management knows about your relevant accomplishments and unique strengths.
- Stay informed about your company's international strategies and programs.
- Polish your cross-cultural communication skills daily with foreign-born co-workers.

SOURCES: Based on discussions in A Varma, L K Stroh, and L B Schmitt, "Women and International Assignments: The Impact of Supervisor-Subordinate Relationships," *Journal of World Business,* Winter 2001, pp 380–88; T Wilen, "Women Working Overseas," *Training and Development,* May 2001, pp 120–22; and E Gundling, *Working GlobeSmart: 12 People Skills for Doing Business across Borders* (Palo Alto, CA.: Davies-Black Publishing, 2003).

Figure 4–4 *The Foreign Assignment Cycle (with OB Trouble Spots)*

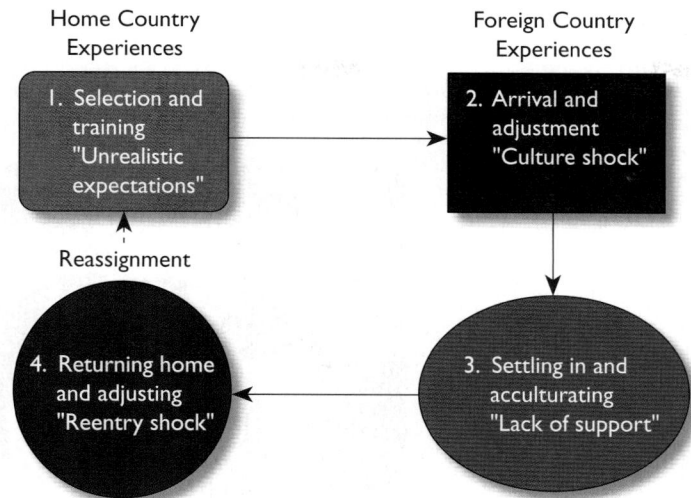

good case in point: "Susan Ivey says her big break came in 1990, when she was asked to take an overseas assignment and given 48 hours to decide. She went for it. The experience, Ivey says, was 'broadening in every way.'"[74]

 9 Avoiding OB Trouble Spots in Foreign Assignments

Finding the right person (often along with a supportive and adventurous family) for a foreign position is a complex, time-consuming, and costly process.[75] For our purposes, it is sufficient to narrow the focus to common OB trouble spots in the foreign assignment cycle. As illustrated in Figure 4–4, the first and last stages of the cycle occur at home. The middle two stages occur in the foreign or host country. Each stage hides an OB-related trouble spot that needs to be anticipated and neutralized. Otherwise, the bill for another failed foreign assignment will grow.

Avoiding Unrealistic Expectations with Cross-Cultural Training

Realistic job previews (RJPs) have proven effective at bringing people's unrealistic expectations about a pending job assignment down to earth by providing a realistic balance of good and bad news. People with realistic expectations tend to quit less often and be more satisfied than those with unrealistic expectations. RJPs are a must for future expatriates. In addition, cross-cultural training is required.

Cross-cultural training is any type of structured experience designed to help departing employees adjust to a foreign culture. The trend is toward more such training in the United States. But there is a great deal of room for improvement, as indicated by the results of a *Training* magazine survey. Only 12% rated cross-cultural/diversity training as "very important" for preparing employees for international assignments.[76] Experts believe that cross-cultural training, although costly, is less expensive than failed foreign assignments. Programs vary widely in type and also in rigor. Of course, the greater the difficulty, the greater the time and expense:

Cross-cultural training

Structured experiences to help people adjust to a new culture/country.

- *Easiest.* Predeparture training is limited to informational materials, including books, lectures, films, videos, and Internet searches.

A Taste of India in Silicon Valley

[In August 2004], Intel software manager Connie Martin arrived for work and received a new identity. She was handed some fake rupees and a nametag that read "Rekha Gupta," and was told that she now hailed from a northern Indian trading family. For the next eight hours, she hit the books, studying the subtle dietary differences between Jainism and Hinduism, Indian political history, and Bollywood movies. At the end of the day, she was given a test on it all, which she aced. . . .

A North Carolina native, Martin is a graduate of "Working with India," an optional training class that Intel began offering to employees in 2002. With an estimated 400,000 Indian nationals in Silicon Valley—and roughly a third of the 65,000 new H-1B visas issued by the United States in 2004 allocated for Indians—companies such as Adaptec, AMD, Intuit, and Rockwell Automation have also held similar sessions during the past year. "Indian cultural training is at the top of the radar screen right now," says [a cross-cultural trainer].

What are the pros and cons of this approach to developing cross-cultural competence?

SOURCE: R Rosmarin, "Mountain View Masala," *Business 2.0*, March 2005, p 54.

- *Moderately difficult.* Experiential training is conducted through case studies, role playing, simulations such as that in the Real World/Real People feature above, and introductory language instruction.
- *Most difficult.* Departing employees are given some combination of the preceding methods plus comprehensive language instruction and field experience in the target culture. As an example of the latter, PepsiCo Inc. transfers "about 25 young foreign managers a year to the US for one-year assignments in bottling plants."[77]

Which approach is the best? Research to date does not offer a final answer. One study involving US employees in South Korea led the researcher to recommend a *combination* of informational and experiential predeparture training.[78] As a general rule of thumb, the more rigorous the cross-cultural training, the better. Ideally, trainees should walk away with the nine cross-cultural competencies in Table 4–4.

Our personal experience with teaching OB to foreign students both in the United States and around the world reminds us there really is no substitute for an intimate knowledge of the local culture, language, customs, and etiquette.[79] Who will likely have the language advantage as the global economy evolves, given these recent figures? According to the US Department of Education, 24,000 American children are studying Chinese, while 200 million Chinese are studying English.[80] Meanwhile, nearly 81% of all Americans speak only English.[81]

Culture shock

Anxiety and doubt caused by an overload of new expectations and cues.

Avoiding Culture Shock Have you ever been in a totally unfamiliar situation and felt disoriented and perhaps a bit frightened? If so, you already know something about culture shock. According to anthropologists, **culture shock** involves anxiety

Table 4–4   *Key Cross-Cultural Competencies*

CROSS-CULTURAL COMPETENCY CLUSTER	KNOWLEDGE OR SKILL REQUIRED
Building relationships	Ability to gain access to and maintain relationships with members of host culture
Valuing people of different cultures	Empathy for difference; sensitivity to diversity
Listening and observation	Knows cultural history and reasons for certain cultural actions and customs
Coping with ambiguity	Recognizes and interprets implicit behavior, especially nonverbal cues
Translating complex information	Knowledge of local language, symbols or other forms of verbal language, and written language
Taking action and initiative	Understands intended and potentially unintended consequences of actions
Managing others	Ability to manage details of a job including maintaining cohesion in a group
Adaptability and flexibility	Views change from multiple perspectives
Managing stress	Understands own and other's mood, emotions, and personality

SOURCE: Excerpted from Y Yamazaki and D C Kayes, "An Experiential Approach to Cross-Cultural Learning: A Review and Integration of Competencies for Successful Expatriate Adaptation," *Academy of Management Learning and Education,* December 2004, Table 2, p 372.

and doubt caused by an overload of unfamiliar expectations and social cues.[82] College freshmen often experience a variation of culture shock. An expatriate manager, or family member, may be thrown off balance by an avalanche of strange sights, sounds, and behaviors. Among them may be unreadable road signs, strange-tasting food, inability to use your left hand for social activities (in Islamic countries, the left hand is the toilet hand), or failure to get a laugh with your surefire joke. For the expatriate manager trying to concentrate on the fine details of a business negotiation, culture shock is more than an embarrassing inconvenience. It is a disaster! Like the confused college freshman who quits and goes home, culture-shocked employees often panic and go home early.

The best defense against culture shock is comprehensive cross-cultural training, including intensive language study. Once again, the best way to pick up subtle—yet important—social cues is via the local language.

Support during the Foreign Assignment Especially during the first

six months, when everything is so new to the expatriate, a support system needs to be in place.[83] *Host-country sponsors,* assigned to individual managers or families, are recommended because they serve as "cultural seeing-eye dogs." In a foreign country, where even the smallest errand can turn into an utterly exhausting production, sponsors can get things done quickly because they know the cultural and geographical territory. Honda's Ohio employees, for example, enjoyed the help of family sponsors when training in Japan:

> Honda smoothed the way with Japanese wives who once lived in the US. They handled emergencies such as when Diana Jett's daughter Ashley needed stitches in her chin.

When task force senior manager Kim Smalley's daughter, desperate to fit in at elementary school, had to have a precisely shaped bag for her harmonica, a Japanese volunteer stayed up late to make it.[84]

Avoiding Reentry Shock

Strange as it may seem, many otherwise successful expatriate managers encounter their first major difficulty only after their foreign assignment is over. Why? Returning to one's native culture is taken for granted because it seems so routine and ordinary. But having adjusted to another country's way of doing things for an extended period of time can put one's own culture and surroundings in a strange new light. Three areas for potential reentry shock are work, social activities, and general environment (e.g., politics, climate, transportation, food). Ira Caplan's return to New York City exemplifies reentry shock:

> During the past 12 years, living mostly in Japan, he and his wife had spent their vacations cruising the Nile or trekking in Nepal. They hadn't seen much of the US. They are getting an eyeful now....
>
> Prices astonish him. The obsession with crime unnerves him. What unsettles Mr Caplan more, though, is how much of himself he has left behind.
>
> In a syndrome of return no less stressful than that of departure, he feels displaced, disregarded, and diminished....
>
> In an Italian restaurant, crowded at lunchtime, the waiter sets a bowl of linguine in front of him. Mr Caplan stares at it. "In Asia, we have smaller portions and smaller people," he says.
>
> Asia is on his mind. He has spent years cultivating an expertise in a region of huge importance. So what? This is New York.[85]

Work-related adjustments were found to be a major problem for samples of repatriated Finnish, Japanese, and American employees.[86] Upon being repatriated, a 12-year veteran of one US company said: "Our organizational culture was turned upside down. We now have a different strategic focus, different 'tools' to get the job done, and different buzzwords to make it happen. I had to learn a whole new corporate 'language.'"[87]Reentry shock can be reduced through employee career counseling and home-country sponsors. Simply being aware of the problem of reentry shock is a big step toward effectively dealing with it.[88]

Overall, the key to a successful foreign assignment is making it a well-integrated link in a career chain rather than treating it as an isolated adventure.

Summary of Key Concepts

1. *Define the term* culture, *and explain how societal culture and organizational culture combine to influence on-the-job behavior.* Culture is a set of beliefs and values about what is desirable and undesirable in a community of people, and a set of formal or informal practices to support the values. Culture has both prescriptive and descriptive elements and involves taken-for-granted assumptions about how to think, act, and feel. Culture overrides national boundaries. Key aspects of societal culture, such as customs and language, are brought to work by the

individual. Working together, societal and organizational culture influence the person's values, ethics, attitudes, and expectations.

2. *Define* ethnocentrism, *and distinguish between high-context and low-context cultures.* Ethnocentrism is the belief that one's native culture, language, and ways of doing things are superior to all others. People from low-context cultures infer relatively less from situational cues and extract more meaning from spoken and written words. In high-context cultures such as China and Japan, managers prefer slow negotiations and trust-building meetings, which tend to frustrate low-context Northern Europeans and North Americans who prefer to get right down to business.

3. *Identify and describe the nine cultural dimensions from Project GLOBE.* (1) Power distance—How equally should power be distributed? (2) Uncertainty avoidance—How much should social norms and rules reduce uncertainty and unpredictability? (3) Institutional collectivism—How much should loyalty to the social unit override individual interests? (4) In-group collectivism—How strong should one's loyalty be to family or organization? (5) Gender egalitarianism—How much should gender discrimination and role inequalities be minimized? (6) Assertiveness—How confrontational and dominant should one be in social relationships? (7) Future orientation—How much should one delay gratification by planning and saving for the future? (8) Performance orientation—How much should individuals be rewarded for improvement and excellence? (9) Humane orientation—How much should individuals be rewarded for being kind, fair, friendly, and generous?

4. *Distinguish between individualistic and collectivist cultures, and explain the difference between monochronic and polychronic cultures.* People in individualistic cultures think primarily in terms of "I" and "me" and place a high value on freedom and personal choice. Collectivist cultures teach people to be "we" and "us" oriented and to subordinate personal wishes and goals to the interests of the relevant social unit (such as family, group, organization, or society). People in monochronic cultures are schedule driven and prefer to do one thing at a time. To them, time is like money; it is spent wisely or wasted. In polychronic cultures, there is a tendency to do many things at once and to perceive time as flexible and multidimensional.

Polychronic people view monochronic people as being too preoccupied with time.

5. *Specify the practical lesson from the Hofstede cross-cultural study.* There is no one best way to manage across cultures. Management theories and practices need to be adapted to the local culture.

6. *Explain what Project GLOBE researchers discovered about leadership.* Across 62 cultures, they identified leader attributes that are universally liked and universally disliked. The universally liked leader attributes—including trustworthy, dynamic, motive arouser, decisive, and intelligent—are associated with the charismatic/transformational leadership style that is widely applicable. Universally disliked leader attributes—such as noncooperative, irritable, egocentric, and dictatorial—should be avoided in all cultures.

7. *Explain why US managers have a comparatively high failure rate on foreign assignments.* American expatriates are troubled by personal and family adjustment problems and homesickness. A great deal of money is wasted when expatriates come home early. More extensive cross-cultural training is needed.

8. *Summarize the research findings about North American women on foreign assignments, and tell how to land a foreign assignment.* The number of North American women on foreign assignments is still small, but growing. Self-disqualification and prejudicial home-country supervisors and staffing policies are largely to blame. Foreigners tend to view North American women primarily as foreigners and secondarily as women. North American women have a high success rate on foreign assignments. Foreign language skills, a strong and formally announced desire, foreign experience, networking, family and supervisory support, and visibility with upper management can increase the chances of getting a desired foreign assignment for both women and men.

9. *Identify four stages of the foreign assignment cycle and the OB trouble spot associated with each stage.* Stages of the foreign assignment cycle (with OB trouble spots) are (1) selection and training (unrealistic expectations); (2) arrival and adjustment (culture shock); (3) settling in and acculturating (lack of support); and (4) returning home and adjusting (reentry shock).

Key Terms

Culture 96
Ethnocentrism 98
Cultural intelligence 100
High-context cultures 100
Low-context cultures 101
Individualistic culture 105
Collectivist culture 105

Monochronic time 106
Polychronic time 106
Proxemics 107
Cross-cultural management 108
Expatriate 111
Cross-cultural training 113
Culture shock 114

It Takes a Village—and a Consultant[89]

BusinessWeek [In the summer of 2004], accounting-and-consulting giant PricewaterhouseCoopers tapped partner Tahir Ayub for a consulting gig unlike anything he had done before. His job: helping village leaders in the Namibian outback grapple with their community's growing AIDS crisis. Faced with language barriers, cultural differences, and scant access to electricity, Ayub, 39, and two colleagues had to scrap their PowerPoint presentations in favor of a more low-tech approach: face-to-face discussion. The village chiefs learned that they needed to garner community support for programs to combat the disease, and Ayub learned an important lesson as well: Technology isn't always the answer. "You better put your beliefs and biases to one side and figure out new ways to look at things," he said.

Ayub may never encounter as extreme a cultural disconnect at PwC as he did in Namibia. But for the next generation of partners, overcoming barriers and forging a connection with clients the world over will be a crucial part of their jobs. It's those skills that PwC hopes to foster in partners who take part in the Ulysses Program, which sends top mid-career talent to the developing world for eight-week service projects. For a fairly modest investment—$15,000 per person, plus salaries—Ulysses both tests the talent and expands the worldview of the accounting firm's future leaders. Since the company started the program four years ago, it has attracted the attention of Johnson & Johnson, Cisco Systems, and other big companies considering their own programs.

While results are hard to quantify, PwC is convinced that the program works. All two dozen graduates are still working at the company. Half of them have been promoted, and most have new responsibilities. Just as important, all 24 people say they have a stronger commitment to PwC—in part because of the commitment the firm made to them and in part because of their new vision of the firm's values. Says Global Managing Partner Willem Bröcker: "We get better partners from this exercise."

The Ulysses Program is PwC's answer to one of the biggest challenges confronting professional services companies: identifying and training up-and-coming leaders who can find unconventional answers to intractable problems. By tradition and necessity, new PwC leaders are nurtured from within. But with 8,000 partners, identifying those with the necessary business savvy and relationship-building skills isn't easy. Just as the program gives partners a new view of PwC, it also gives PwC a new view of them, particularly their ability to hold up under pressure.

For mid-career partners who were weaned on e-mail and the Blackberry, this was no walk in the park. They had become accustomed to a world of wireless phones, sleek offices, and Chinese take-out—so the rigors of the developing world came as quite a shock. Brian P McCann, 37, a mergers and acquisitions expert from PwC's Boston office, had never been to a Third World country before his stint in Belize, where he encountered dirt-floored houses, sick children, and grinding poverty.

Ayub, having been born in Africa, considered himself worldly. Even so, long days spent among Africa's exploding HIV-positive population took their psychological toll. With his work confined to daylight hours—there was often no electricity—Dinu Bumbacea, a 37-year-old partner in PwC's Romanian office who spent time in Zambia working with an agricultural center, had plenty of time to dwell on the misery all around him. "Africa is poor, and we all know that," says Bumbacea. "But until you go there, you don't understand how poor it is. We take so much for granted."

For more than 15 years, companies have used social-responsibility initiatives to develop leaders. But PwC takes the concept to a new level. Participants spend eight weeks in developing countries lending their business skills to local aid groups—from an ecotourism collective in Belize to small organic farmers in Zambia to AIDS groups in Namibia. Ulysses also presents participants with the challenge of collaborating across cultures with local clients as well as with PwC colleagues from other global regions. Ayub, for example, was paired with partners from Mexico and the Netherlands.

Beyond Accounting

PWC says the program, now in its third cycle, gives participants a broad, international perspective that's crucial for a company that does business around the world. Traditional executive education programs turn out men and women who have specific job skills but little familiarity with issues outside their narrow specialty, according to Douglas Ready, director of the International Consortium for Executive Development Research. PwC says Ulysses helps prepare participants for challenges that go beyond the strict confines of accounting or consulting and instills values such as community involvement that are fundamental to its corporate culture.

Ulysses is also a chance for partners to learn what they can accomplish without their usual resources to lean on. The program forces them to take on projects well outside their expertise. In the summer of 2003, for example, McCann developed a business plan for an ecotourism group in Belize. The experience was an eye-opener. McCann's most lasting memory is a dinner he shared in the home of a Mayan farmer after they spent a day discussing their plan. "He didn't even have electricity," McCann recalls, "but he made do."

PwC partners say they've already adapted their experiences to the task of managing people and clients. Malaysian partner Jennifer Chang says her team noticed a shift in her managerial style after the Belize trip. She listened more and became more flexible. "Once you see how slowly decisions are made in other places, you gain patience for the people you work with," she says. Ayub, who was promoted in June, now manages 20 partners. He says he favors face-to-face conversations over e-mail because the low-tech approach builds trust. "It made the difference in Namibia," he says.

If insights like those ripple out across the firm, Ulysses will be more than a voyage of personal discovery for a handful of partners. It could help build leaders capable of confronting the challenges of an increasingly global business. And that, says PwC, is the whole point.

Questions for Discussion

1. If you were the CEO of PricewaterhouseCoopers, how would you defend the Ulysses Program to shareholders concerned about spending?

2. What benefit would the Ulysses Program be to PwC employees who would not seek or take a foreign assignment?

3. How do the facts of this case confirm the GLOBE project's research findings about leadership? Explain.

4. Using Table 4–4 as a guide, what cross-cultural competencies were developed among the people featured in this case study? Explain.

5. Would you like to participate in this type of leadership development program? Why or why not?

Ethical Dilemma

3M Tries to Make a Difference in Russia[90]

Russian managers aren't inclined . . . to reward people for improved performance. They spurn making investments for the future in favor of realizing immediate gains. They avoid establishing consistent business practices that can reduce uncertainty. Add in the country's high political risk and level of corruption, and it's no wonder that many multinationals have all but given up on Russia. . . .

The Russian business environment can be corrupt and dangerous; bribes and protection money are facts of life. But unlike many international companies, which try to distance themselves from such practices by simply banning them, 3M Russia actively promotes not only ethical behavior but also the personal security of its employees. . . .

3M Russia also strives to differentiate itself from competitors by being an ethical leader. For example, it holds training courses in business ethics for its customers.

Should 3M export its American ethical standards to Russia?

1. If 3M doesn't like the way things are done in Russia, it shouldn't do business there. Explain your rationale.

2. 3M should do business in Russia but not meddle in Russian culture. "When in Russia, do things the Russian way." Explain your rationale.

3. 3M has a basic moral responsibility to improve the ethical climate in foreign countries where it does business. Explain your rationale.

4. 3M should find a practical middle ground between the American and Russian ways of doing business. How should that happen?

5. Invent other options. Discuss.

Web Resources

For study material and exercises that apply to this chapter, visit our Web site,

www.mhhe.com/kreitner

Part 2

Individual Behavior in Organizations

CHAPTER 5

Self-Concept, Personality, Abilities, and Emotions

LEARNING OBJECTIVES

When you finish studying the material in this chapter, you should be able to:

1   Define *self-esteem,* and explain how it can be improved with Branden's six pillars of self-esteem.

2   Define *self-efficacy,* and explain its sources.

3   Contrast high and low self-monitoring individuals, and discuss the ethical implications of organizational identification.

4   Identify and describe the Big Five personality dimensions, and specify which one is correlated most strongly with job performance.

5   Describe the proactive personality, and explain the need to balance an internal locus of control with humility.

6   Identify at least five of Gardner's eight multiple intelligences, and explain "practical intelligence."

7   Distinguish between positive and negative emotions, and explain how they can be judged.

8   Identify the four key components of emotional intelligence, and discuss the practical significance of emotional contagion and emotional labor.

Student Resources for Studying Chapter 5

The Web site for your text includes resources that will help you master the concepts in this chapter. As you read, you'll want to visit the site for these helpful tools:

- Your online Study Guide includes learning objectives, a chapter summary, a glossary of key terms, and discussion questions.
- Take a practice quiz and test your knowledge!
- Scroll through a PowerPoint presentation with key concepts for this chapter.

Your instructor might also direct you to the Web site for these exercises:

- Self-assessments that correspond with the chapter content and a Group Exercise.
- You'll also find Video Cases and Internet Exercises for this chapter online.

www.mhhe.com/kreitner

BusinessWeek Five months ago, Gretchen Tonnesen was carrying the ball, analyzing defenses, and leading her teammates as a flying halfback and captain on Princeton University's women's rugby team. And she was doing it all on a wobbly knee, following six months of rehabilitation after a painful injury. Today, her team is JPMorgan Chase & Company, where she's equally busy scrutinizing technology, media, and telecommunications companies for the investment bank.

Tonnesen, who majored in religion, was chosen not so much for her academic interests as for her proven passion for rugby. Recruiters are noticing that college athletes have a slew of qualities that not only lead to business success but are also often lacking in new recruits: leadership, competitiveness, and an almost obsessive focus on goals. Such employees can have the drive and stamina that make them near-perfect matches for the 80-hour high-pressure workweeks of many Wall Street jobs. "I love the work," says Tonnesen. "I love the fast-paced atmosphere."

Tonnesen is one of many young professionals who have come to Wall Street by way of the Alumni Athlete Network, founded by former Harvard University basketball captain Ronald P Mitchell. Each year the program whittles roughly 500 applications from college athletes down to 150 interview candidates, of which about 45 are placed in internships at banks such as Citigroup, Goldman Sachs, and Merrill Lynch, among others. The best part: A remarkable 87% of the interns, like Tonnesen, go on to land full-time jobs on the Street.

Scott Harrington, managing director at JPMorgan and sponsor for the Alumni Athlete Network, believes the program is a great opportunity for the firm to hire talent that is both driven and diverse. Title IX, the 1972 law that prohibits educational discrimination based on gender, may be responsible for some of that mix. In fact, few talent pools are as diverse as those of student athletes. Says Harrington of the former jocks: "We have more breadth in recruiting than we ever had before."

When Mitchell created the network, he knew that student athletes like himself would make good matches for the intense environment. Team responsibility, time management, and dedication all go a long way in the industry, and student athletes have these virtues in spades. "There is a winner and a loser every day on the trading floor," he says. And the dumb-jock stereotype? Forget it. Students in the program have an average GPA of 3.6 and an average SAT score of 1320—that's 300 points higher than the national average.[1]

FOR DISCUSSION

In terms of personality traits, abilities, and emotions, how can athletic experience pave the way to career success?

As the world's population continues to grow (more than 6.5 billion at the time of this writing),[2] many of us seek a unique identity that sets us apart from the crowd. This makes understanding and managing people and trying to please them increasingly difficult. For instance, consider Cold Stone Creamery's ice cream stores, where customer-selected mix-ins and toppings make more than 11.5 million variations possible![3] What's your favorite? Likewise, how do you express yourself in the workplace? Are you a go-getter, like the former college athletes featured in the opening vignette, or a slacker? Are you a loner or highly social? Do you see yourself as master of your own fate, or a victim of circumstances? Are you emotional or calm and cool? Is your job satisfaction through the roof or stuck in the basement? Thanks to a vast array of individual differences such as these, modern organizations have a rich and interesting human texture. On the other hand, individual differences make the manager's job endlessly challenging. In fact, according to research, "variability among workers is substantial at all levels but increases dramatically with job complexity. In life insurance sales, for example, variability in performance is around six times as great as in routine clerical jobs."[4]

Growing workforce diversity compels managers to view individual differences in a fresh new way. Rather than limiting diversity, as in the past, today's managers need to better understand and accommodate employee diversity and individual differences.[5]

Both this chapter and the next explore the key individual differences portrayed in Figure 5–1. The figure is intended to be an instructional road map showing the bridges between self-concept and self-expression. This chapter focuses on self-concept, personality, abilities, and emotions. Personal values, attitudes, and job satisfaction are covered in Chapter 6. Taken as an integrated whole, all these factors provide a foundation for better understanding each organizational contributor as a unique and special individual.

Self-Concept

When you look in the mirror, you recognize who it is. You see your*self*.[6] This is a remarkable talent in the animal kingdom, according to scientists. Only humans, apes, dolphins, and elephants can recognize themselves in a mirror.[7] But what exactly do you know about that person in the mirror? People ages 16 to 70 were asked what they would do differently if they could live life over again; 48% chose the response category "Get in touch with self."[8] Toward that end, this section helps you get in better touch with yourself on the way to better understanding and managing yourself and others in the workplace. Former General Electric CEO Jack Welch tells us: "You've got to be comfortable with yourself to make a good boss."[9]

Self-concept

Person's self-perception as a physical, social, spiritual being.

Sociologist Viktor Gecas defines **self-concept** as "the concept the individual has of himself as a physical, social, and spiritual or moral being."[10] In other words, because you have a self-concept, you recognize yourself as a distinct human being.

Figure 5–1   *An Instructional Road Map for the Study of Individual Differences in Chapters 5 and 6*

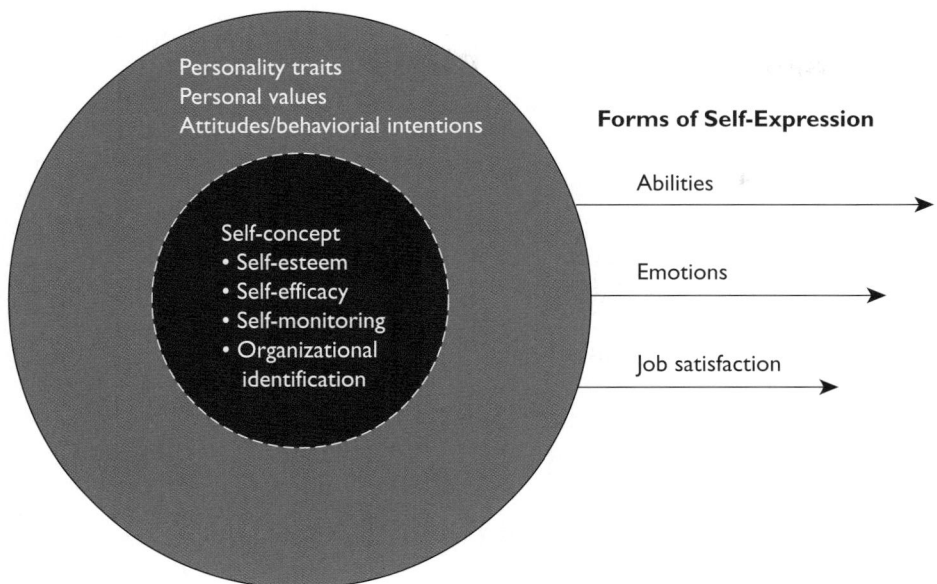

A self-concept would be impossible without the capacity to think. This brings us to the role of cognitions. **Cognitions** represent "any knowledge, opinion, or belief about the environment, about oneself, or about one's behavior."[11] Among many different types of cognitions, those involving anticipation, planning, goal setting, evaluating, and setting personal standards are particularly relevant to OB.

Our attention now turns to three topics invariably mentioned when behavioral scientists discuss self-concept. They are self-esteem, self-efficacy, and self-monitoring. We also consider the ethical implications of organizational identification, a social aspect of self. A social learning model of self-management can be found in Learning Module A (Learning Module A can be found on our Web site at www.mhhe.com/kreitner) to serve as a practical capstone for this section. Each of these areas deserves a closer look by those who want to better understand and effectively manage themselves and others.

Cognitions

A person's knowledge, opinions, or beliefs.

 Self-Esteem

Self-esteem is a belief about one's own self-worth based on an overall self-evaluation.[12] Self-esteem is measured by having survey respondents indicate their agreement or disagreement with both positive and negative statements. A positive statement on one general self-esteem survey is: "I feel I am a person of worth, the equal of other people."[13] Among the negative items is: "I feel I do not have much to be proud of."[14] Those who agree with the positive statements and disagree with the negative statements have high self-esteem. They see themselves as worthwhile, capable, and acceptable. People with low self-esteem view themselves in negative terms. They do not feel good about themselves and are hampered by self-doubts.[15]

Self-esteem

One's overall self-evaluation.

IT'S ALWAYS 'GOOD DOG'- NEVER 'GREAT DOG'.

www.cartoonbank.com

Employment and Self-Esteem

What researchers call *organization-based self-esteem* makes paid employment a prime determinant of overall self-esteem in modern life.[16] Consequently, unemployment can have a devastating impact on one's self-esteem. Consider these instructive remarks from Arthur J Fiacco, a 56-year-old executive who was laid off without any warning during the tech downturn in 2001:

> I had never felt so lonely and helpless. I had been working since I was 16 years old. . . .
> A job isn't just about working. A job helps define who we are. It is what we talk with our neighbors about. It is the place we go. It is how we are introduced. It is one of the first things people ask about when we meet them. And most important, we measure ourselves from our very first job onward. Without a job, I felt I had lost my identity.[17]

Fiacco eventually turned things around by building a successful consulting business. He says now, "I am making a contribution and feel good. . . . I have learned to listen to what others are trying to tell me."[18]

Self-Esteem across Cultures

What are the cross-cultural implications for self-esteem, a concept that has been called uniquely Western? In a survey of 13,118 students from 31 countries worldwide, a moderate positive correlation was found between self-esteem and life satisfaction. But the relationship was stronger in individualistic cultures (e.g., United States, Canada, New Zealand, Netherlands) than in collectivist cultures (e.g., Korea, Kenya, Japan). The researchers concluded that individualistic cultures socialize people to focus more on themselves, while people in collectivist cultures "are socialized to fit into the community and to do their duty. Thus, how a collectivist feels about him- or herself is less relevant to . . . life satisfaction."[19] Global managers need to remember to deemphasize self-esteem when doing business in collectivist ("we") cultures, as opposed to emphasizing it in individualistic ("me") cultures.

Can General Self-Esteem Be Improved?

The short answer is yes (see Table 5–1). More detailed answers come from research. In one study, youth-league baseball coaches who were trained in supportive teaching techniques had a positive effect on the self-esteem of young boys. A control group of untrained coaches had

Table 5–1   *Branden's Six Pillars of Self-Esteem*

What nurtures and sustains self-esteem in grown-ups is not how others deal with us but how we ourselves operate in the face of life's challenges—the choices we make and the actions we take.

    This leads us to the six pillars of self-esteem.

1. *Live consciously.* Be actively and fully engaged in what you do and with whom you interact.
2. *Be self-accepting.* Don't be overly judgmental or critical of your thoughts and actions.
3. *Take personal responsibility.* Take full responsibility for your decisions and actions in life's journey.
4. *Be self-assertive.* Be authentic and willing to defend your beliefs when interacting with others, rather than bending to their will to be accepted or liked.
5. *Live purposefully.* Have clear near-term and long-term goals and realistic plans for achieving them to create a sense of control over your life.
6. *Have personal integrity.* Be true to your word and your values.

    Between self-esteem and the practices that support it, there is reciprocal causation. This means that the behaviors that generate good self-esteem are also expressions of good self-esteem.

SOURCE: Excerpted and adapted from Nathaniel Branden, *Self-Esteem at Work: How Confident People Make Powerful Companies* (San Francisco: Jossey-Bass, 1998), pp 33–36. Reprinted with permission of John Wiley & Sons, Inc.

no such positive effect.[20] Meanwhile, middle-school teachers in the United States reportedly are correcting papers with purple ink rather than the traditional red in an effort to boost self-esteem. "We cannot keep purple pens in stock," says Robert Silberman, vice president of marketing for Pilot Pen in Connecticut. "It's a major move for teachers, moving away from red and going to a kinder, gentler color."[21] (Hmmm, will the next generation come to hate purple as much as their parents dislike red?) Another study led to this conclusion: "Low self-esteem can be raised more by having the person think of *desirable* characteristics *possessed* rather than of undesirable characteristics from which he or she is free."[22] This approach can help neutralize the self-defeating negative thoughts among those with low self-esteem.

2 Self-Efficacy

Self-confidence is important in today's demanding workplaces. In fact, when 2,500 managers and executives in the United States were recently polled by *BusinessWeek,* 72% of the women and 66% of the men said *self-confidence* was the most important quality for succeeding in business.[23] Self-confidence involves more than high self-esteem; it also requires self-efficacy.[24] **Self-efficacy** is a person's belief about his or her chances of successfully accomplishing a specific task. According to one OB writer, "Self-efficacy arises from the gradual acquisition of complex cognitive, social, linguistic, and/or physical skills through experience."[25] Heroic role models can inspire us to build self-efficacy (see the Real World/Real People feature on page 128).

Self-efficacy

Belief in one's ability to do a task.

The Cardiologist with a Big Heart

Stephen Oesterle, M.D., 55, senior vice president for medicine and technology, Medtronic:

It's rare that you find a way to combine your profession with your avocation. But Medtronic's mission and mine as a physician are the same: We strive to restore lives. I couldn't think of a better way to make that mission manifest than to invite people living with devices to come run the Twin Cities Marathon. It was one of the easiest things I ever sold at the company.

Thirteen chronically ill individuals came to this September's race from all over the globe—we called them Global Heroes. They came to us with a variety of problems, from heart disease to an overactive bladder, but they were all runners before they fell ill. We knew that they could endure the marathon—and send a message to people living with chronic disease.

Sure enough, one of my patients, Jason Burke, ran with an insulin pump for juvenile diabetes. I had been way ahead of him, but at the halfway point, he came burning by me, patted me on the back, and said, "How ya doing?" He took off, and I didn't see him again until after the race.

But at the end of the day, it's not really about running a marathon. It's about an exclamation of full life. We want people in Strasbourg, France, or Muncie, Indiana, to see pictures of our Global Heroes and say, "I can get up. I can do this. I can do anything."

Are you inspired by this unique expression of corporate social responsibility?

SOURCE: K Tuggle, "Fast Talk: Marathon Man," *Fast Company,* February 2007, pp 54–55.

The relationship between self-efficacy and performance is a cyclical one. Efficacy → performance cycles can spiral upward toward success or downward toward failure.[26] Researchers have documented strong linkages between high self-efficacy expectations and success in widely varied physical and mental tasks, anxiety reduction, addiction control, pain tolerance, illness recovery, avoidance of seasickness in naval cadets, physical exercise, and stress avoidance.[27] Oppositely, those with low self-efficacy expectations tend to have low success rates. Although self-efficacy sounds like some sort of mental magic, it operates in a very straightforward manner, as a model will show.

What Are the Mechanisms of Self-Efficacy? A basic model of self-efficacy is displayed in Figure 5–2. It draws upon the work of Stanford psychologist Albert Bandura. Let us explore this model with a simple illustrative task. Imagine you have been told to prepare and deliver a 10-minute talk to an OB class of 50 students on the workings of the self-efficacy model in Figure 5–2. Your self-efficacy calculation would involve cognitive appraisal of the interaction between your perceived capability and situational opportunities and obstacles.

As you begin to prepare for your presentation, the four sources of self-efficacy beliefs would come into play. Because prior experience is the most potent source, according to Bandura, it is listed first and connected to self-efficacy beliefs with a solid line.[28] Past success in public speaking would boost your self-efficacy. But bad experiences with delivering speeches would foster low self-efficacy. Regarding behavior models as a source of self-efficacy beliefs, you would be influenced by the success

Figure 5–2   *A Model of How Self-Efficacy Beliefs Can Pave the Way for Success or Failure*

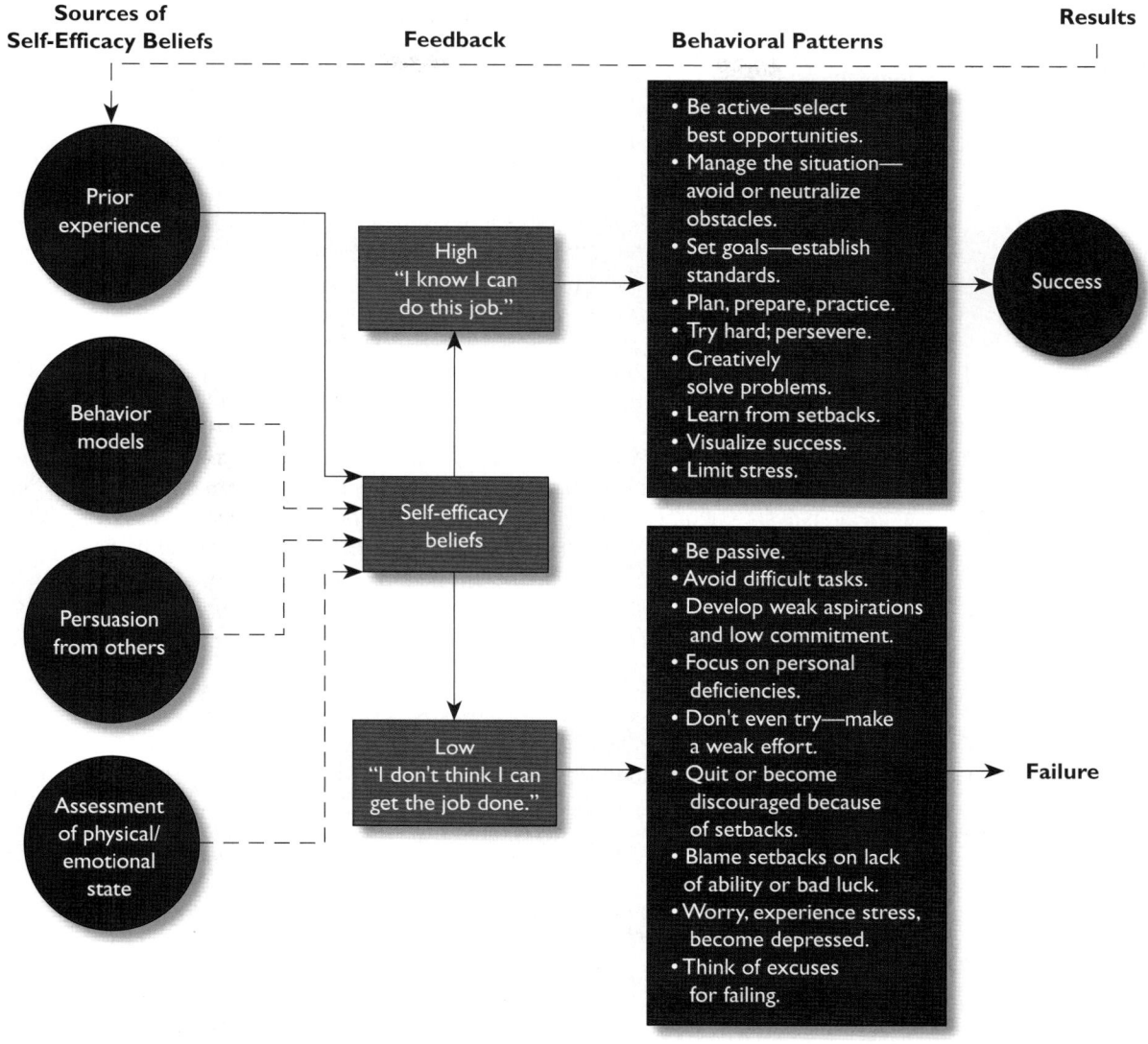

SOURCES: Adapted from discussion in A Bandura, "Regulation of Cognitive Processes through Perceived Self-Efficacy," *Developmental Psychology,* September 1989, pp 729–35; and R Wood and A Bandura, "Social Cognitive Theory of Organizational Management," *Academy of Management Review,* July 1989, pp 361–84.

or failure of your classmates in delivering similar talks. Their successes would tend to bolster you (or perhaps their failure would if you were very competitive and had high self-esteem). Likewise, any supportive persuasion from your classmates that you will do a good job would enhance your self-efficacy. Physical and emotional factors also might affect your self-confidence. A sudden case of laryngitis or a bout of stage fright could cause your self-efficacy expectations to plunge. Your cognitive evaluation of the situation then would yield a self-efficacy belief—ranging from high to low expectations for success. Importantly, self-efficacy beliefs are not merely boastful statements based on bravado; they are deep convictions supported by experience.

Moving to the *behavioral patterns* portion of Figure 5–2, we see how self-efficacy beliefs are acted out. In short, if you have high self-efficacy about giving your 10-minute speech you will work harder, more creatively, and longer when preparing for your talk than will your low-self-efficacy classmates. The results would then take shape accordingly. People program themselves for success or failure by enacting their self-efficacy expectations. Positive or negative results subsequently become feedback for one's base of personal experience. Bob Schmonsees, a software entrepreneur, is an inspiring example of the success pathway through Figure 5–2:

> A contender in mixed-doubles tennis and a former football star, Mr Schmonsees was standing near a ski lift when an out-of-control skier rammed him. His legs were paralyzed. He would spend the rest of his life in a wheelchair.
>
> Fortunately, he discovered a formula for his different world: Figure out the new rules for any activity, then take as many small steps as necessary to master those rules. After learning the physics of a tennis swing on wheels and the geometry of playing a second bounce (standard rules), he became the world's top wheelchair player over age 40.[29]

Self-Efficacy Implications for Managers

On-the-job research evidence encourages managers to nurture self-efficacy, both in themselves and in others. In fact, a meta-analysis encompassing 21,616 subjects found a significant positive correlation between self-efficacy and job performance.[30] Self-efficacy can be boosted in the workplace through careful hiring, challenging assignments, training and coaching, goal setting, supportive leadership and mentoring, and rewards for improvement. Boeing's CEO, James McNerney, recently offered this perspective:

> [S]uccess and achievement can feed on themselves. It feels good to keep succeeding. It feels great to see the people you work with grow and achieve. Maybe the ignition happens when you're younger, and then it feeds on itself. The next question is how you give it to people who weren't fortunate enough to have it given to them when they were young. It gets back to leadership attributes—expect a lot, inspire people, ask them to take the values that are important to them at home or at church and bring them to work.[31]

3 Self-Monitoring

Consider these contrasting scenarios:

1. You are rushing to an important meeting when a co-worker pulls you aside and starts to discuss a personal problem. You want to break off the conversation, so you glance at your watch. He keeps talking. You say, "I'm late for a big meeting." He continues. You turn and start to walk away. The person keeps talking as if they never received any of your verbal and nonverbal signals that the conversation was over.
2. Same situation. Only this time, when you glance at your watch, the person immediately says, "I know, you've got to go. Sorry. We'll talk later."

In the first all-too-familiar scenario, you are talking to a "low self-monitor." The second scenario involves a "high self-monitor." But more is involved here than an irritating situation. A significant and measurable individual difference in self-expression behavior, called self-monitoring, is highlighted. **Self-monitoring** is the extent to which a person observes their own self-expressive behavior and adapts it to the demands of the situation. Experts on the subject offer this explanation:

> Individuals high in self-monitoring are thought to regulate their expressive self-presentation for the sake of desired public appearances, and thus be highly responsive to social and interpersonal cues of situationally appropriate performances. Individuals

Self-monitoring

Observing one's own behavior and adapting it to the situation.

low in self-monitoring are thought to lack either the ability or the motivation to so regulate their expressive self-presentations. Their expressive behaviors, instead, are thought to functionally reflect their own enduring and momentary inner states, including their attitudes, traits, and feelings.[32]

In organizational life, both high and low monitors are subject to criticism. High self-monitors are sometimes called *chameleons,* who readily adapt their self-presentation to their surroundings. Low self-monitors, on the other hand, often are criticized for being on their own planet and insensitive to others. Former US housing secretary and 1996 vice presidential candidate Jack Kemp frustrated his political handlers with his low self-monitoring ways:

> Bush administration veterans recall windy lectures on US urban policy during cabinet meetings, and friends say Kemp will debate anything with anyone, any time. "We used to laugh at him for going to Iowa, where he'd wind up talking the gold standard with two farmers, three hogs, and two dogs," a former staffer says. "Everyone else had left."[33]

Importantly, within an OB context, self-monitoring is like any other individual difference—not a matter of right or wrong or good versus bad, but rather a source of diversity that needs to be adequately understood by present and future managers.

A Matter of Degree Self-monitoring is not an either-or proposition. It is a matter of degree; a matter of being relatively high or low in terms of related patterns of self-expression. What are your self-monitoring tendencies?

go to the Web for the Self-Exercise: What Are Your Self-Monitoring Tendencies?

Research Findings and Practical Recommendations A meta-analysis encompassing 23,191 subjects in 136 samples found self-monitoring to be relevant and useful when dealing with job performance and emerging leaders.[34] According to field research, there is a positive relationship between high self-monitoring and career success. Among 139 MBA graduates who were tracked for five years, high self-monitors enjoyed more internal and external promotions than did their low self-monitoring classmates.[35] Another study of 147 managers and professionals found that high self-monitors had a better record of acquiring a mentor (someone to act as a personal career coach and professional sponsor).[36] These results mesh well with an earlier study that found managerial success (in terms of speed of promotions) tied to political savvy (knowing how to socialize, network, and engage in organizational politics).[37]

The foregoing evidence and practical experience lead us to make these practical recommendations:

For high, moderate, and low self-monitors: Become more consciously aware of your self-image and how it affects others.

For high self-monitors: Don't overdo it by evolving from a successful chameleon into someone who is widely perceived as insincere, dishonest, phoney, and untrustworthy. You cannot be everything to everyone.

For low self-monitors: You can bend without breaking, so try to be a bit more accommodating while being true to your basic beliefs. Don't wear out your welcome when communicating. Practice reading and adjusting to nonverbal cues in various public situations. If your conversation partner is bored or distracted, stop—because he or she is not really listening.

Organizational Identification: A *Social* Aspect of Self-Concept with Ethical Implications

The dividing line between self and others is not a neat and precise one. A certain amount of blurring occurs, for example, when an employee comes to define him- or herself with a *specific* organization—a psychological process called *organizational identification.* According to an expert on this evolving OB topic, "**organizational identification** occurs when one comes to integrate beliefs about one's organization into one's identity."[38] Organizational identification goes to the heart of organizational culture and socialization (recall our discussion in Chapter 3).

Organizational identification

Organizational values or beliefs become part of one's self-identity.

Managers put a good deal of emphasis today on organizational mission, philosophy, and values with the express intent of integrating the company into each employee's self-identity. Hopefully, as the logic goes, employees who identify closely with the organization will be more loyal, more committed, and harder working.[39] For example, consider this recent business press clipping about American Express:

> Credit card behemoth breeds loyalty: Nearly a quarter of employees have been with the company more than 15 years. "It is my honor to serve my brand, my creed, my company," says one.[40]

Some companies, such as consultant McKinsey & Company, go so far as to cultivate organizational identification among *former* employees through corporate alumni networks. Former employees who still identify strongly with the company are potential customers, as well as informal marketers and goodwill ambassadors.[41] As an extreme case in point, organizational identification among employees at Harley-Davidson's motorcycle factories is so strong many have had the company logo tattooed on their bodies.[42] Working at Harley is not just a job, it is a lifestyle. (Somehow, your authors have a hard time imagining an employee with a General Motors or Burger King tattoo!)

A company tattoo may be a bit extreme, but the ethical implications of identifying too closely with one's employer are profound. Phyllis Anzalone, a former Enron employee, is a good case in point. She admitted that Enron *was* her self-identity and she ended up with emotional scars:

> What did working at Enron do for Anzalone? For one thing, it made her a lot of money, so much that the company's failure cost her about $1 million. More important, it made her. It took her from being a reasonably successful facilities management salesperson from rural Louisiana and propelled her into the ranks of sales superstars. It changed her view of herself; it confirmed what she thought she could achieve. "Enron had a profound effect on my life," she says. As devastating as it was, I'm glad I did it. It was like being on steroids every day."
>
> And what does Anzalone think of the executives who ran Enron—and then ran it into the ground? "They are scum," she says, "They are crooks, and they are traitors. They betrayed many people's trust, including mine."[43]

Anzalone distanced herself from Enron's most unsavory characters during her years with the company. But some of her colleagues, with equally strong organizational identification, evidently turned their backs on their personal ethical standards and values when working on clearly illegal deals. When employees suspend their critical thinking and lose their objectivity, unhealthy groupthink can occur and needed constructive conflict does *not* occur. (Groupthink is covered in Chapter 10 and functional conflict is discussed in Chapter 13.) Whistle-blowing, as defined in Chapter 1, is unlikely to occur when organizational identification is excessive. Company loyalty and dedication are one thing, blind obedience to unethical leaders is quite another.[44]

Personality: Concepts and Controversy

Individuals have their own way of thinking and acting, their own unique style or *personality.* **Personality** is defined as the combination of stable physical and mental characteristics that give the individual his or her identity.[45] These characteristics or traits—including how one looks, thinks, acts, and feels—are the product of interacting genetic and environmental influences.[46] In this section, we introduce the Big Five personality dimensions, explore the proactive personality, issue some cautions about workplace personality testing, and examine an important personality factor called locus of control.

Personality

Stable physical and mental characteristics responsible for a person's identity.

 ## 4 The Big Five Personality Dimensions

Decades of research produced cumbersome lists of personality traits. In fact, one recent study identified 1,710 English-language adjectives used to describe aspects of personality.[47] Fortunately, this confusing situation has been statistically distilled to the Big Five.[48] They are extraversion, agreeableness, conscientiousness, emotional stability, and openness to experience (see Table 5–2 for descriptions). Standardized personality tests determine how positively or negatively a person scores on each of the Big Five. For example, someone scoring negatively on extraversion would be an introverted person prone to shy and withdrawn behavior. Someone scoring negatively on emotional security would be nervous, tense, angry, and worried. Appropriately, the negative end of the emotional stability scale is labeled neuroticism.

A person's scores on the Big Five reveal a personality profile as unique as his or her fingerprints. One's personality profile is relatively durable, too. Extraversion and conscientiousness were found to be the most stable of the Big Five, according to data on 799 people covering the 40 years between their elementary-school days and midlife.[49] So don't be surprised when many of your high-school classmates seem pretty much the same at your 20th reunion, except for some extra pounds and thinning hair, of course.

But one important question lingers: Are personality models ethnocentric or unique to the culture in which they were developed? At least as far as the Big Five

Table 5–2   *The Big Five Personality Dimensions*

PERSONALITY DIMENSION	CHARACTERISTICS OF A PERSON SCORING POSITIVELY ON THE DIMENSION
1. Extraversion	Outgoing, talkative, sociable, assertive
2. Agreeableness	Trusting, good-natured, cooperative, softhearted
3. Conscientiousness	Dependable, responsible, achievement oriented, persistent
4. Emotional stability	Relaxed, secure, unworried
5. Openness to experience	Intellectual, imaginative, curious, broad-minded

SOURCE: Adapted from M R Barrick and M K Mount, "Autonomy as a Moderator of the Relationships between the Big Five Personality Dimensions and Job Performance," *Journal of Applied Psychology,* February 1993, pp 111–18.

Employers Like Conscientious Military Veterans

"When you look at our employee base and you see the guys who are very conscientious, who are always early for work, who are clean-cut, have a smile on their face, get the job done and just have a great attitude, many of those guys come from the military," says Jeff Owens, president of Advanced Technology Services in Peoria, Ill. . . .

Employers are impressed by the veterans' strong work ethic and training. Home Depot has found that veterans stay with the company longer than those without military experience, says Marion Sullivan, senior director of staffing.

Stacie Bearden, who served in the Marines for 22 years while on both active duty and in the reserves, has been with Home Depot since 1999. She says former military members make good employees because they have been tested in ways other people haven't.

SOURCE: Excerpted from B Hagenbaugh, "More Employers Recruit the Military Work Ethic," *USA Today*, February 16, 2007, pp 1B–2B.

What is the ethical argument for hiring military veterans?

---

model goes, cross-cultural research evidence points in the direction of no. Specifically, the Big Five personality structure held up very well in one study of women and men from Russia, Canada, Hong Kong, Poland, Germany, and Finland and a second study (85% male) of South Korean managers and stockbrokers.[50] A recent comprehensive analysis of Big Five studies led the researchers to this conclusion: "To date, there is no compelling evidence that culture affects personality structure."[51]

Those interested in OB want to know the connection between the Big Five and job performance. Ideally, Big Five personality dimensions that correlate positively and strongly with job performance would be helpful in the selection, training, and appraisal of employees. A meta-analysis of 117 studies involving 23,994 subjects from many professions offers guidance.[52] Among the Big Five, *conscientiousness* had the strongest positive correlation with job performance and training performance. According to the researchers, "those individuals who exhibit traits associated with a strong sense of purpose, obligation, and persistence generally perform better than those who do not."[53] (See the Real World/Real People feature above.) Not surprisingly, entrepreneurs score high on conscientiousness.[54] Another recent finding: Extraversion (an outgoing personality) correlated positively with promotions, salary level, and career satisfaction. And, as one might expect, neuroticism (low emotional stability) was associated with low career satisfaction.[55]

go to the Web for the Self-Exercise: How Do You Score on the Big Five Personality Factors?

5 The Proactive Personality

As suggested by the previous discussion, someone who scores high on the Big Five dimension of conscientiousness is probably a good worker. Thomas S Bateman and J Michael Crant took this important linkage an additional step by formulating the concept of the proactive personality. They define and characterize the **proactive personality** in these terms: "someone who is relatively unconstrained by situational forces and who effects environmental change. Proactive people identify opportunities and act on them, show initiative, take action, and persevere until meaningful change occurs."[56] In short, people with proactive personalities are "hardwired" to change the status quo. In a review of relevant studies, Crant recently found the proactive personality to be positively associated with individual, team, and organizational success.[57]

> **Proactive personality**
> Action-oriented person who shows initiative and perseveres to change things.

Successful entrepreneurs exemplify the proactive personality. An inspiring example is this 18-year-old who immigrated with his family to New York City from Bangladesh at age nine:

> Omar Faruk believes that social entrepreneurship can make the world a better place. He's CEO of BlueStream, a Web management company that specializes in helping nonprofits with limited resources. The business grossed $40,000 in 2006 and earned Faruk the Youth Entrepreneur of the Year award given out by Ernst & Young and the National Foundation for Teaching Entrepreneurship. "Make a difference first, make the money later," Faruk says.[58]

People with proactive personalities truly are valuable *human capital,* as defined in Chapter 1. Those wanting to get ahead would do well to cultivate the initiative, drive, courage, and perseverance of someone with a proactive personality—and managers would do well to hire them.[59]

Employees with a proactive personality typically exhibit **resiliency,** a desirable trait in today's fast-changing world. "Individuals with high-level resiliency skills hold up well under pressure, orient quickly to new demands, adapt to changing circumstances, and can work without an updated job description."[60] Resilient people bounce back or rebound quickly from mistakes, failures, and personal and career disasters.[61]

> **Resiliency**
> The ability to handle pressure and quickly bounce back from personal and career setbacks.

Issue: What about Personality Testing in the Workplace?

Personality testing as a tool for making decisions about hiring, training, and promotion is commonplace. "According to the Association of Test Publishers, overall employment testing, including personality tests, has been growing at a rate of 10% to 15% in each of the past three years."[62]

Unfortunately, there is the issue of *sloppy administration.* Annie Murphy Paul, author of the new book *The Cult of Personality,*[63] explains:

> You hear a lot from psychologists who are supportive of personality testing, and sometimes from testing companies, that there are ideal ways to use these tests. An example would be to bring in a psychologist to do a study of the job itself and design or tailor a test specifically for that position, and then have it administered by a psychologist, and have the results remain confidential. I think the way these tests are actually used is that they're usually bought off the shelf, they're given indiscriminately, often by people who aren't trained or qualified, and then the results aren't kept confidential or private at all. For all the talk about standards on how [these tests] should be used, the way they're used in the real world is more hit-or-miss.[64]

Table 5–3   *Advice and Words of Caution about Personality Testing in the Workplace*

Researchers, test developers, and organizations that administer personality assessments offer the following suggestions for getting started or for evaluating whether tests already in use are appropriate for forecasting job performance:

- Determine what you hope to accomplish. If you are looking to find the best fit of job and applicant, analyze the aspects of the position that are most critical for it.
- Look for outside help to determine if a test exists or can be developed to screen applicants for the traits that best fit the position. Industrial psychologists, professional organizations, and a number of Internet sites provide resources.
- Insist that any test recommended by a consultant or vendor be validated scientifically for the specific purpose that you have defined. Vendors should be able to cite some independent, credible research supporting a test's correlation with job performance.
- Ask the test provider to document the legal basis for any assessment: Is it fair? Is it job-related? Is it biased against any racial or ethnic group? Does it violate an applicant's right to privacy under state or federal laws? Vendors should provide a lawyer's statement that a test does not adversely affect any protected class, and employers may want to get their own lawyer's opinion, as well.
- Make sure that every staff member who will be administering tests or analyzing results is educated about how to do so properly and keeps results confidential. Use the scores on personality tests in tandem with other factors that you believe are essential to the job—such as skills and experience—to create a comprehensive evaluation of the merits of each candidate, and apply those criteria identically to each applicant.

SOURCE: S Bates, "Personality Counts," *HR Magazine*, February 2002, p 34. Reprinted with the permission of HR Magazine, published by the Society for Human Resource Management, Alexandria, VA.

The practical tips in Table 5–3 can help managers avoid abuses and costly discrimination lawsuits when using personality and psychological testing for employment-related decisions. Another alternative for employers is to eliminate personality testing altogether. At Microsoft, where 12,000 résumés stream in every month, recruits are screened with challenging interviews but no psychological tests. When *Fortune* magazine asked David Pritchard, Microsoft's director of recruiting, about the standard practice of screening recruits with psychological tests, Pritchard replied, "It doesn't really interest me much. In the end, you end up with a bunch of people who answer the questions correctly, and that's not always what you want. How can a multiple-choice test tell whether someone is creative or not?"[65] The growing use of job-related skills testing and behavioral interviewing is an alternative to personality testing.

Let us take a look at locus of control, another important job-related personality factor.

Locus of Control: Self or Environment?

Individuals vary in terms of how much personal responsibility they take for their behavior and its consequences. Julian Rotter, a personality researcher, identified a dimension of personality he labeled *locus of control* to explain these differences. He proposed that people tend to attribute the causes of their behavior primarily to either themselves or environmental factors.[66] This personality trait produces distinctly different behavior patterns.

People who believe they control the events and consequences that affect their lives are said to possess an **internal locus of control.** For example, such a person tends to attribute positive outcomes, such as getting a passing grade on an exam, to her or his own abilities. Similarly, an "internal" tends to blame negative events, such as failing an exam, on personal shortcomings—not studying hard enough, perhaps. Many entrepreneurs and corporate executives eventually succeed because their internal locus of control helps them overcome setbacks and disappointments. An internal locus of control fosters their resiliency. They see themselves as masters of their own fate and not simply lucky.[67] But, as *Fortune*'s Jaclyn Fierman humorously noted, luck is a matter of interpretation and not always a bad thing:

> For those of us who believe we are the masters of our fate, the captains of our soul, the notion that a career might hinge on random events is unthinkable. Self-made men and women are especially touchy on this subject. If they get all the breaks, it's because they're smarter and harder working than everyone else. If they know the right people, it's because they network the nights away. Luck? Many successful people think it diminishes them.
>
> Hard workers do get ahead, no doubt about it. . . . But then there are folks like Ringo Starr. One day he was an obscure drummer of limited talent from Liverpool; the next day he was a Beatle.
>
> Nobody demonstrates better than Ringo that true luck is accidental, not inevitable.[68]

On the other side of this personality dimension are those who believe their performance is the product of circumstances beyond their immediate control. These individuals are said to possess an **external locus of control** and tend to attribute outcomes to environmental causes, such as luck or fate. Unlike someone with an internal locus of control, an "external" would attribute a passing grade on an exam to something external (an easy test or a good day) and attribute a failing grade to an unfair test or problems at home. Later on, as people move up the career ladder, externals may be plagued by the **imposter syndrome.** This personality disorder involves chronic feelings of being a fake because all of one's accomplishments are attributed to external factors. Consider this case, for example:

> By most definitions, Bud Stockwell has hit the personal-fulfillment trifecta. At 53, he owns as profitable $2 million health food store called Cornucopia. His business is a beloved institution in Northampton, Massachusetts. . . .
>
> When a reporter called to interview the owner for an article about . . . [a prestigious award], Stockwell readily answered her questions. But then he told no one. Not his wife. Not his daughter. Not one of his 23 employees. "The magazine came out two months later and it was almost like I was embarrassed by it," says Stockwell. "I didn't feel like I deserved it. I think we have a great business, but how much of that was because of me and how much is because of our location or the staff?" . . .
>
> "Some people, the more successful they become, the more they feel like frauds," says Valerie Young, [a corporate trainer]. . . . "They feel as though they're fooling people. There's a dissonance between self-image and external reality."[69]

A career counselor or coach can help moderate the imposter syndrome by getting the individual to realistically balance internal and external success factors.

Internal locus of control
Attributing outcomes to one's own actions.

External locus of control
Attributing outcomes to circumstances beyond one's control.

Impostor syndrome
Failing to take any credit for one's success and feeling like a fake.

Research Findings on Locus of Control Researchers have found important behavioral differences between internals and externals:

- Internals display greater work motivation.
- Internals have stronger expectations that effort leads to performance.
- Internals exhibit higher performance on tasks involving learning or problem solving, when performance leads to valued rewards.
- There is a stronger relationship between job satisfaction and performance for internals than for externals.
- Internals obtain higher salaries and greater salary increases than externals.
- Externals tend to be more anxious than internals.[70]

Tempering an Internal Locus of Control with *Humility* Do you have an internal locus of control? Odds are high that you do, judging from the "typical" OB student we have worked with over the years. Good thing, because it should pay off in the workplace with opportunities, raises, and promotions. But before you declare yourself Grade A executive material, here is one more thing to toss into your tool kit: a touch of humility. **Humility** is "a realistic assessment of one's own contribution and the recognition of the contribution of others, along with luck and good fortune that made one's own success possible."[71] Humility has been called the silent virtue. How many truly humble people brag about being humble? Two OB experts recently offered this instructive perspective:

> Humble individuals have a down-to-earth perspective of themselves and of the events and relationships in their lives. Humility involves a capability to evaluate success, failure, work, and life without exaggeration. Furthermore, humility enables leaders to distinguish the delicate line between such characteristics as healthy self-confidence, self-esteem, and self-assessment, and those of over-confidence, narcissism, and stubbornness. Humility is the mid-point between the two negative extremes of arrogance and lack of self-esteem. This depiction allows one to see that a person can be humble and competitive or humble and ambitious at the same time, which contradicts common—but mistaken—views about humility.[72]

We now shift our focus to abilities and intelligence.

Humility
Considering the contributions of others and good fortune when gauging one's success.

---

go to the Web for the Self-Exercise: Where Is Your Locus of Control?

Abilities (Intelligence) and Performance

Individual differences in abilities and accompanying skills are a central concern for managers because nothing can be accomplished without appropriately skilled personnel. An **ability** represents a broad and stable characteristic responsible for a person's maximum—as opposed to typical—performance on mental and physical tasks. A **skill,** on the other hand, is the specific capacity to physically manipulate objects. Consider this difference as you imagine yourself being the only passenger on a small commuter airplane in which the pilot has just passed out. As the plane nose-dives, your effort and abilities will not be enough to save yourself and the pilot if you do not possess flying skills. As shown in Figure 5–3 successful performance (be it landing

Ability
Stable characteristic responsible for a person's maximum physical or mental performance.

Skill
Specific capacity to manipulate objects.

Figure 5–3   *Performance Depends on the Right Combination of Effort, Ability, and Skill*

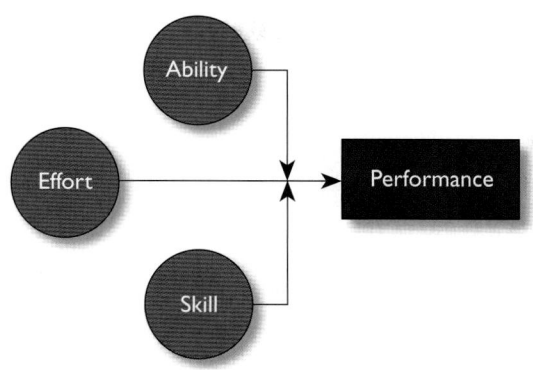

an airplane or performing any other job) depends on the right combination of effort, ability, and skill.

Abilities and skills are getting a good deal of attention in management circles these days. The more encompassing term *competencies* is typically used. According to the head of a New Jersey consulting firm,

> In the past decade, thousands of organizations throughout the world have joined the quest for competencies. Often, they spend a year or more conducting competency studies—identifying "clusters" of knowledge, attitudes, and skills needed to perform various jobs. The competencies turned up by these studies become the basis for decisions about hiring, training, promotions, and other human resource issues.[73]

Among the many desirable competencies are oral communication, initiative, decisiveness, tolerance, problem solving, adaptability, and resilience. Importantly, our cautions about on-the-job personality testing extend to ability, intelligence, and competency testing and certification.

Before moving on, we need to say something about a modern-day threat to abilities, skills, and general competence. That threat, according to public health officials, is *sleep deprivation*.[74]

Abilities and the Need for Sleep

In a recent survey of 1,506 adults in the United States, only 49% reported getting a "good night's sleep" every night or almost every night.[75] If you are routinely short-changing your basic sleep needs, you are likely to be less effective and more stressed (see Chapter 18) than you should be. Habitually sleep-deprived people need to be aware of this stunning fact: "Staying awake 24 hours impairs cognitive psychomotor performance to the same degree as having a 0.1 percent blood alcohol level. . . . That is above many states' legal driving limits."[76] Select employers are taking corrective action: "Today, Nike and Deloitte Consulting are among those that encourage employees to add a midday snooze to their to-do lists."[77] According to sleep researcher Sara Mednick:

> Without sleep you don't learn. My research shows that people deteriorate during the day. It's difficult to sustain productivity. Naps can add back to the sleep you're deprived of at night. And a nap enhances productivity even if you have enough nocturnal sleep. . . .

> A 20-minute nap in the afternoon, between 1 PM and 3 PM, right after lunch, would be ideal. You don't want to get into deep sleep, because you need to be alert. This nap will allow you to be as productive right after the nap as you were before. That's what a lot of businesspeople need for on-your-feet thinking.[78]

The balance of this section explores intelligence, specific cognitive abilities, and the controversial idea of multiple intelligences.

Intelligence and Cognitive Abilities

Intelligence

Capacity for constructive thinking, reasoning, problem solving.

Although experts do not agree on a specific definition, **intelligence** represents an individual's capacity for constructive thinking, reasoning, and problem solving.[79] Historically, intelligence was believed to be an innate capacity, passed genetically from one generation to the next. Research since has shown, however, that intelligence (like personality) also is a function of environmental influences.[80] Organic factors have more recently been added to the formula as a result of mounting evidence of the connection between alcohol and drug abuse by pregnant women and intellectual development problems in their children.[81]

Researchers have produced some interesting findings about abilities and intelligence in recent years. A unique five-year study documented the tendency of people to "gravitate into jobs commensurate with their abilities."[82] This prompts the vision of the labor market acting as a giant sorting or sifting machine, with employees tumbling into various ability bins. Meanwhile, a steady and significant rise in average intelligence among those in developed countries has been observed over the last 70 years. Why? Experts at an American Psychological Association conference concluded, "Some combination of better schooling, improved socioeconomic status, healthier nutrition, and a more technologically complex society might account for the gains in IQ scores."[83] So if you think you're smarter than your parents and your teachers, you're probably right!

Two Types of Abilities Human intelligence has been studied predominantly through the empirical approach. By examining the relationships between measures of mental abilities and behavior, researchers have statistically isolated major components of intelligence. Using this empirical procedure, pioneering psychologist Charles Spearman proposed in 1927 that all cognitive performance is determined by two types of abilities. The first can be characterized as a general mental ability needed for *all* cognitive tasks. The second is unique to the task at hand.[84] For example, an individual's ability to complete crossword puzzles is a function of his or her broad mental abilities as well as the specific ability to perceive patterns in partially completed words.

Seven Major Mental Abilities Through the years, much research has been devoted to developing and expanding Spearman's ideas on the relationship between cognitive abilities and intelligence. One research psychologist listed 120 distinct mental abilities. Table 5–4 contains definitions of the seven most frequently cited mental abilities. Of the seven abilities, personnel selection researchers have found verbal ability, numerical ability, spatial ability, and inductive reasoning to be valid predictors of job performance for both minority and majority applicants.[85]

6 Do We Have Multiple Intelligences?

Howard Gardner, a professor at Harvard's Graduate School of Education, offered a new paradigm for human intelligence in his 1983 book *Frames of Mind: The Theory of Multiple Intelligences*.[86] He has subsequently identified eight different intelligences

Table 5–4   *Mental Abilities Underlying Performance*

ABILITY	DESCRIPTION
1. Verbal comprehension	The ability to understand what words mean and to readily comprehend what is read.
2. Word fluency	The ability to produce isolated words that fulfill specific symbolic or structural requirements (such as all words that begin with the letter *b* and have two vowels).
3. Numerical	The ability to make quick and accurate arithmetic computations such as adding and subtracting.
4. Spatial	Being able to perceive spatial patterns and to visualize how geometric shapes would look if transformed in shape or position.
5. Memory	Having good rote memory for paired words, symbols, lists of numbers, or other associated items.
6. Perceptual speed	The ability to perceive figures, identify similarities and differences, and carry out tasks involving visual perception.
7. Inductive reasoning	The ability to reason from specifics to general conclusions.

SOURCE: Adapted from MD Dunnette, "Aptitudes, Abilities, and Skills," in *Handbook of Industrial and Organizational Psychology,* ed MD Dunnette (Skokie, IL: RandMcNally, 1976), pp 478–83. Copyright © 1976. Used with permission of the author.

that vastly broaden the long-standing concept of intelligence. Gardner's concept of multiple intelligences (MI) includes not only cognitive abilities but social and physical abilities and skills as well:

- *Linguistic intelligence:* potential to learn and use spoken and written languages.
- *Logical-mathematical intelligence:* potential for deductive reasoning, problem analysis, and mathematical calculation.
- *Musical intelligence:* potential to appreciate, compose, and perform music.
- *Bodily-kinesthetic intelligence:* potential to use mind and body to coordinate physical movement.
- *Spatial intelligence:* potential to recognize and use patterns.
- *Interpersonal intelligence:* potential to understand, connect with, and effectively work with others.
- *Intrapersonal intelligence:* potential to understand and regulate oneself.
- *Naturalist intelligence:* potential to live in harmony with one's environment.[87]

Many educators and parents have embraced MI because it helps explain how a child could score poorly on a standard IQ test yet be obviously gifted in one or more ways (e.g., music, sports, relationship building). Moreover, they believe the concept of MI underscores the need to help each child develop in his or her own unique way and at his or her own pace. They say standard IQ tests deal only with the first two intelligences on Gardner's list. Meanwhile, most academic psychologists and

"Enough with the Beethoven, Mom! How about some Jay-Z?" Some parents strive to develop their baby's multiple intelligences by exposing them to unconventional stimuli. Research tells us the vote is still out on whether or not they are wasting their time. Hmmm. Come to think of it, Tiger Woods' Dad had him playing golf at a very young age.

intelligence specialists continue to criticize Gardner's model as too subjective and poorly integrated. They prefer the traditional model of intelligence as a unified variable measured by a single test.

While the academic debate continues, we can draw some practical benefits from Gardner's notion of MI. Already, in Chapter 4, we discussed *cultural intelligence*. In the final section of this chapter, you will encounter the concept of *emotional intelligence*. Yale's Robert J Sternberg recently applied Gardner's "naturalist intelligence" to the domain of leadership under the heading *practical intelligence*. He explains,

Practical intelligence is the ability to solve everyday problems by utilizing knowledge gained from experience in order to purposefully adapt to, shape, and select environments. It thus involves changing oneself to suit the environment (adaptation), changing the environment to suit oneself (shaping), or finding a new environment within which to work (selection). One uses these skills to (*a*) manage oneself, (*b*) manage others, and (*c*) manage tasks.[88]

Others believe MI has important implications for employee selection and training.[89] One-size-fits-all training programs fall short when MI diversity is taken into consideration. We look forward to breakthroughs in this area as MI attracts OB researchers and practicing managers.

Emotions: An Emerging OB Topic

In the ideal world of management theory, employees pursue organizational goals in a logical and rational manner. Emotional behavior seldom is factored into the equation.[90] Yet day-to-day organizational life shows us how prevalent and powerful emotions can be. Anger and jealousy, both potent emotions, often push aside logic and rationality in the workplace. Managers use fear and other emotions to both motivate and intimidate. For example, consider Microsoft CEO Steve Ballmer's management style prior to his recent efforts to become a kinder, gentler leader: "Ballmer shouts when he gets excited or angry—his voice rising so suddenly that it's like an electric shock. . . . By the early 1990s, Ballmer had to have throat surgery to fix problems brought on by shouting."[91]

Less noisy, but still emotion laden, is John Chambers's tightrope act as CEO of Cisco Systems:

Any company that thinks it's utterly unbeatable is already beaten. So when I begin to think we're getting a little bit too confident, you'll see me emphasizing the paranoia side. And then when I feel that there's a little bit too much fear and apprehension, I'll just jump back to the other side. My job is to keep those scales perfectly balanced.[92]

These admired corporate leaders would not have achieved what they have without the ability to be logical and rational decision makers *and* be emotionally charged. Too much emotion, however, could have spelled career and organizational disaster for either of them.

In this final section, our examination of individual differences turns to defining emotions, reviewing a typology of 10 positive and negative emotions, exploring emotional intelligence and maturity, and focusing on the interesting topics of emotional contagion and emotional labor.

7 Positive and Negative Emotions

Richard S Lazarus, a leading authority on the subject, defines **emotions** as "complex, patterned, organismic reactions to how we think we are doing in our lifelong efforts to survive and flourish and to achieve what we wish for ourselves."[93] The word *organismic* is appropriate because emotions involve the *whole* person—biological, psychological, and social. Importantly, psychologists draw a distinction between *felt* and *displayed* emotions.[94] For example, a person might feel angry (felt emotion) at a rude co-worker but not make a nasty remark in return (displayed emotion). As discussed in Chapter 18, emotions play roles in both causing and adapting to stress and its associated biological and psychological problems. The destructive effect of emotional behavior on social relationships is all too obvious in daily life.

Lazarus's definition of emotions centers on a person's goals. Accordingly, his distinction between positive and negative emotions is goal oriented. Some emotions are triggered by frustration and failure when pursuing one's goals. Lazarus calls these *negative* emotions. They are said to be goal incongruent. For example, which of the six negative emotions in Figure 5–4 are you likely to experience if you fail the final exam in a required course? Failing the exam would be incongruent with your goal of graduating on time. On the other

Emotions

Complex human reactions to personal achievements and setbacks that may be felt and displayed.

Figure 5–4   *Positive and Negative Emotions*

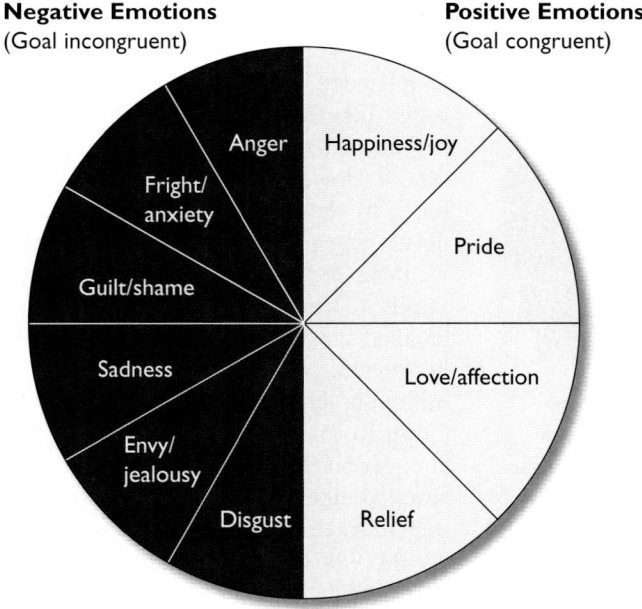

Negative Emotions
(Goal incongruent)

Positive Emotions
(Goal congruent)

Anger

Happiness/joy

Fright/anxiety

Pride

Guilt/shame

Sadness

Love/affection

Envy/jealousy

Disgust   Relief

SOURCE: Adapted from discussion in R S Lazarus, *Emotion and Adaptation* (New York: Oxford University Press, 1991), Chs. 6, 7.

hand, which of the four *positive* emotions in Figure 5–4 would you probably experience if you graduated on time and with honors? The emotions you would experience in this situation are positive because they are congruent (or consistent) with an important lifetime goal. The individual's goals, it is important to note, may or may not be socially acceptable. Thus, a positive emotion, such as love/affection, may be undesirable if associated with sexual harassment. Oppositely, slight pangs of guilt, anxiety, and envy can motivate extra effort.[95] On balance, the constructive or destructive nature of a particular emotion must be judged in terms of both its intensity and the person's relevant goal.

For a dramatic real-life example of the interplay between negative and positive emotions, consider the situation Kenneth I Chenault faced just 10 months after becoming CEO of American Express. The September 11, 2001, terrorist attacks claimed the lives of 11 employees, and the firm's headquarters building, across the street from ground zero in Lower Manhattan, had to be abandoned for what turned out to be eight months of repairs.

Chenault gathered 5,000 American Express employees at the Paramount Theater in New York on September 20 for a highly emotional "town hall meeting." During the session, Chenault demonstrated the poise, compassion, and decisiveness that vaulted him to the top. He told employees that he had been filled with such despair, sadness, and anger that he had seen a counselor. Twice, he rushed to spontaneously embrace grief-stricken employees. Chenault said he would donate $1 million of the company's profits to the families of the AmEx victims. "I represent the best company and the best people in the world," he concluded." In fact, you are my strength, and I love you."[96]

Thus, Chenault masterfully used positive emotions to cope with profound negative emotions.

8 Developing Emotional Intelligence

People cope with powerful emotions in lots of different ways. Take Taryn Rose, for example. She followed in her physician father's footsteps by attending medical school. However, near the end of her residency, she was bitten by the entrepreneurial bug and set her sights on developing and selling stylish shoes that would not ruin women's feet. But she did not want to disappoint her family. "I feared regret more than I feared failure,"[97] she recalled for *Fast Company* magazine, so she followed her dream. Now that she is the CEO of her own $20-million-a-year company, her family understands. For Taryn Rose, it took a good idea and determination to conquer her fears. Another way to deal effectively with fear and other emotions is to become more emotionally mature by developing emotional intelligence.

In 1995, Daniel Goleman, a psychologist turned journalist, created a stir in education and management circles with the publication of his book *Emotional Intelligence.* Hence, an obscure topic among psychologists became mainstream. Building upon Howard Gardner's concept

Talk about baptism by fire. Just 10 months after being named CEO of American Express, Kenneth I Chenault addressed 5,000 of his co-workers in an emotional meeting to begin the healing process following the September 11, 2001, terrorist attacks. The tragedy claimed the lives of 11 AmEx employees and closed the firm's New York headquarters for eight months of repairs. Chenault, seen here presiding over AmEx's May 13, 2002, headquarters homecoming celebration, reportedly handled the post-9/11 meeting with great skill and compassion.

of interpersonal intelligence, Goleman criticizes the traditional model of intelligence (IQ) for being too narrow, thus failing to consider interpersonal competence. Goleman's broader agenda includes "abilities such as being able to motivate oneself and persist in the face of frustrations; to control impulse and delay gratification; to regulate one's moods and keep distress from swamping the ability to think; to empathize and to hope."[98] Thus, **emotional intelligence** is the ability to manage oneself and one's relationships in mature and constructive ways. Referred to by some as EI and others as EQ, emotional intelligence is said to have four key components: self-awareness, self-management, social awareness, and relationship management. The first two constitute *personal competence;* the second two feed into *social competence* (see Table 5–5).

Emotional intelligence

Ability to manage oneself and interact with others in mature and constructive ways.

Table 5–5 *Developing Personal and Social Competence through Emotional Intelligence*

Personal Competence: These capabilities determine how we manage ourselves.

Self-Awareness

- *Emotional self-awareness:* Reading one's own emotions and recognizing their impact; using "gut sense" to guide decisions.
- *Accurate self-assessment:* Knowing one's strengths and limits.
- *Self-confidence:* A sound sense of one's self-worth and capabilities.

Self-Management

- *Emotional self-control:* Keeping disruptive emotions and impulses under control.
- *Transparency:* Displaying honesty and integrity; trustworthiness.
- *Adaptability:* Flexibility in adapting to changing situations or overcoming obstacles.
- *Achievement:* The drive to improve performance to meet inner standards of excellence.
- *Initiative:* Readiness to act and seize opportunities.
- *Optimism:* Seeing the upside in events.

Social Competence: These capabilities determine how we manage relationships.

Social Awareness

- *Empathy:* Sensing others' emotions, understanding their perspective, and taking active interest in their concerns.
- *Organizational awareness:* Reading the currents, decision networks, and politics at the organizational level.
- *Service:* Recognizing and meeting follower, client, or customer needs.

Relationship Management

- *Inspirational leadership:* Guiding and motivating with a compelling vision.
- *Influence:* Wielding a range of tactics for persuasion.
- *Developing others:* Bolstering others' abilities through feedback and guidance.
- *Change catalyst:* Initiating, managing, and leading in a new direction.
- *Conflict management:* Resolving disagreements.
- *Building bonds:* Cultivating and maintaining a web of relationships.
- *Teamwork and collaboration:* Cooperation and team building.

SOURCE: D Goleman, R Boyatzis, and A McKee, *Primal Leadership: Realizing the Power of Emotional Intelligence* (Boston: Harvard Business School Press, 2002), p 39. Copyright © 2002 by the Harvard Business School Publishing Corporation; All rights reserved.

Let Them See You Sweat

Pamela Thomas-Graham:

About two months into my tenure as CEO of CNBC, I asked Jack Welch for some feedback on how I was doing. He said I was doing great in terms of outlining a strategy for the network and how we would succeed in a tough economic climate. But he said I needed to let my team "see me sweat." Having been a consultant at McKinsey for 10 years, I was highly analytical, very calm and collected. I was used to having a poker face and never letting anyone see me get rattled, no matter how tough the challenge. Jack's advice was to do the opposite. His point was that, particularly in times of rapid change, people need to visibly see the urgency and passion of their leader if they're going to fully engage. Being analytical and strategic is great, but to get a team motivated during tough times, you also have to show your passion—you have to break a sweat so they understand at an emotional level what's really at stake. It was a vital leadership lesson as I made the transition from consultant to general manager, and I'm using that learning now in trying to turn around the Liz Claiborne apparel business

What does the term passionate leadership *mean to you and how useful is emotion in today's workplace?*

SOURCE: "Let Them See You Sweat," *Business 2.0,* December 2006, p 104.

go to the Web for the Group Exercise: Anger Control Role Play

As an integrated package, the proactive personality discussed earlier and the characteristics listed in Table 5–5 constitute a challenging self-development agenda for each of us. Indeed, Goleman and his followers believe greater emotional intelligence can boost individual, team, and organizational effectiveness[99] (see the Real World/Real People feature above).

Practical Research Insights about Emotional Contagion and Emotional Labor

Two streams of OB research on emotions are beginning to yield interesting and instructive insights:

- *Emotional contagion.* Have you ever had someone's bad mood sour your mood? That person could have been a parent, supervisor, co-worker, friend, or someone serving you in a store or restaurant. Appropriately, researchers call this *emotional contagion.* We, quite literally, can catch another person's bad mood or displayed negative emotions. This effect was documented in a recent study of 131 bank tellers (92% female) and 220 exit interviews with their customers. Tellers who expressed positive emotions tended to have more satisfied customers.[100] Two field studies with nurses and accountants as subjects found a strong linkage between the work group's collective mood and the individual's mood.[101] Both foul moods and good moods turned out to be contagious. Perhaps more managers should follow the lead of this German executive:

  After arriving at his Munich office in the morning, Ulrich Schumacher likes to pop a CD into a player on his desk and blast a track by singer James Brown. Nothing like the godfather of soul shouting "I feel good!" to get a manager psyched up for the day ahead, says Schumacher, 43, CEO of German semiconductor maker Infineon Technologies.[102]

- *Emotional labor.* Although they did not have the benefit of a catchy label or a body of sophisticated research, generations of managers have known about the power of emotional contagion in the marketplace. "Smile, look happy for the customers" employees are told over and over. But what if the employee is having a rotten day? What if they have to mask their true feelings and emotions? What if they have to fake it? Researchers have begun studying the dynamics of what they call *emotional labor.* A pair of authors, one from Australia the other from the United States, recently summarized the research lessons to date:

  > Emotional labor can be particularly detrimental to the employee performing the labor and can take its toll both psychologically and physically. Employees . . . may bottle up feelings of frustration, resentment, and anger, which are not appropriate to express. These feelings result, in part, from the constant requirement to monitor one's negative emotions and express positive ones. If not given a healthy expressive outlet, this emotional repression can lead to a syndrome of emotional exhaustion and burnout.[103]

Interestingly, a pair of laboratory studies with US college students as subjects found no gender difference in *felt* emotions. But the women were more emotionally *expressive* than the men.[104] This stream of research on emotional labor has major practical implications for productivity and job satisfaction, as well as for workplace anger, aggression, and violence.[105] Clearly, managers need to be attuned to (and responsive to) the emotional states and needs of their people. This requires emotional intelligence.

Summary of Key Concepts

1. *Define self-esteem, and explain how it can be improved with Branden's six pillars of self-esteem.* Self-esteem is how people perceive themselves as physical, social, and spiritual beings. Branden's six pillars of self-esteem are live consciously, be self-accepting, take personal responsibility, be self-assertive, live purposefully, and have personal integrity.

2. *Define self-efficacy, and explain its sources.* Self-efficacy involves one's belief about his or her ability to accomplish specific tasks. Those extremely low in self-efficacy suffer from learned helplessness. Four sources of self-efficacy beliefs are prior experience, behavior models, persuasion from others, and assessment of one's physical and emotional states. High self-efficacy beliefs foster constructive and goal-oriented action, whereas low self-efficacy fosters passive, failure-prone activities and emotions.

3. *Contrast high and low self-monitoring individuals, and discuss the ethical implications of organizational identification.* A high self-monitor strives to make a good public impression by closely monitoring his or her behavior and adapting it to the situation. Very high self-monitoring can create

   a "chameleon" who is seen as insincere and dishonest. Low self-monitors do the opposite by acting out their momentary feelings, regardless of their surroundings. Very low self-monitoring can lead to a one-way communicator who seems to ignore verbal and nonverbal cues from others. People who supplant their own identity with that of their organization run the risk of blind obedience and groupthink because of a failure to engage in critical thinking and not being objective about what they are asked to do.

4. *Identify and describe the Big Five personality dimensions, and specify which one is correlated most strongly with job performance.* The Big Five personality dimensions are extraversion (social and talkative), agreeableness (trusting and cooperative), conscientiousness (responsible and persistent), emotional stability (relaxed and unworried), and openness to experience (intellectual and curious). Conscientiousness is the best predictor of job performance.

5. *Describe the proactive personality, and explain the need to balance an internal locus of control with humility.* Someone

with a proactive personality shows initiative, takes action, and perseveres to bring about change. People with an internal locus of control, such as entrepreneurs, believe they are masters of their own fate. Humility helps "internals" factor the contributions of others and good fortune into their perceived success.

6. *Identify at least five of Gardner's eight multiple intelligences, and explain "practical intelligence."* Harvard's Howard Gardner broadens the traditional cognitive abilities model of intelligence to include social and physical abilities. His eight multiple intelligences include: linguistic, logical-mathematical, musical, bodily-kinesthetic, spatial, interpersonal, intrapersonal, and naturalist. Someone with practical intelligence, according to Sternberg, is good at solving everyday problems and learning from experience by adapting to the environment, reshaping their environment, and selecting new environments in which to work.

7. *Distinguish between positive and negative emotions, and explain how they can be judged.* Positive emotions—happiness/joy, pride, love/affection, and relief—are personal reactions to circumstances congruent with one's goals.

Negative emotions—anger, fright/anxiety, guilt/shame, sadness, envy/jealousy, and disgust—are personal reactions to circumstances incongruent with one's goals. Both types of emotions need to be judged in terms of intensity and the appropriateness of the person's relevant goal.

8. *Identify the four key components of emotional intelligence, and discuss the practical significance of emotional contagion and emotional labor.* Goleman's model says the four components are self-awareness, self-management, social awareness, and relationship management. People can, in fact, catch another person's good or bad moods and expressed emotions, much as they would catch a contagious disease. Managers and others in the workplace need to avoid spreading counterproductive emotions. People in service jobs who are asked to suppress their own negative emotions and display positive emotions, regardless of their true feelings at the time, pay a physical and mental price for their emotional labor. Managers who are not mindful of emotional labor may experience lower productivity, reduced job satisfaction, and possibly aggression and even violence.

Key Terms

Self-concept 124	Internal locus of control 137
Cognitions 125	External locus of control 137
Self-esteem 125	Impostor syndrome 137
Self-efficacy 127	Humility 138
Self-monitoring 130	Ability 138
Organizational identification 132	Skill 138
Personality 133	Intelligence 140
Proactive personality 135	Emotions 143
Resiliency 135	Emotional intelligence 145

OB in Action Case Study

Wendy Kopp: The Recruiter

BusinessWeek Sitting in a lunchroom at Columbia University with the school's star students—the senior class president, the student council VP, the premed triple major and 15 other superachievers—Wendy Kopp is begging them to shelve their career plans to teach in America's most troubled public schools. "This problem has to be this generation's issue," she tells the future grads. "We know we can solve it if we get enough true leaders."

Kopp is talking with prospective recruits for Teach for America, the Peace Corps-like program that she dreamed up 17 years ago when she was a senior at Princeton. As she speaks, she frequently covers her mouth with her right hand, a nervous gesture. But the students too are nervous about the job Kopp is asking them to do. Seniors who compete

to be Teach for America corps members must endure hours of interviews and tests designed to assess their organizational skills, perseverance and resiliency—critical traits since recruits receive only five weeks of teacher training (albeit grueling) before they get plopped into a classroom in the South Bronx or some other impoverished locale. As the students voice their qualms about TFA "What if I fail? Won't poor kids reject Ivy League teachers?" Kopp doesn't sugarcoat the obstacles: "It can be really overwhelming and depressing," she warns. "We all have bad days, and people who teach in Teach for America probably have more bad days than most."

Kopp's pitch is part challenge and part cautionary tale, yet the combination has been a winning one. . . . [In 2006],

19,000 college students—including 10% of the senior classes at Yale and Dartmouth, 9% at Columbia, and 8% at Duke and the University of Chicago—applied to Teach for America. (While local school districts cover the salaries of TFA teachers, TFA screens and trains them—and requires a two-year commitment.) "We recruit insanely aggressively," says Kopp, 39, who accepted 2,400 of those 19,000 applicants this year. That makes Kopp's nonprofit one of the largest hirers of college seniors, according to CollegeGrad.com—bigger than Microsoft, Procter & Gamble, Accenture, or General Electric.

Kopp, in fact, has built such a mighty recruiting machine that corporations are angling to work with TFA to buff their own images on campus. . . .

"One of the few jobs that people pass up Goldman Sachs offers for is Teach for America," says Edie Hunt, Goldman's co-COO [chief operating officer] of human-capital management. (First-year pay at Goldman averages $65,000, about twice what a TFA corps member makes.) . . .

Wendy Kopp never wanted to be a corporate role model. She just wanted to reform public education. Growing up in Dallas (where her parents owned a travel-guide business), she moved from parochial school to public school in sixth grade and went on to be valedictorian of her high school. Her interest in the failures of America's public schools began at Princeton, where she helped organize a conference on education reform during the fall of her senior year. Her senior thesis was entitled "A Plan and Argument for the Creation of a National Teacher Corps," and she wrote a letter to then-President George H W Bush, urging him to establish such a two-year service program. "I received a job-rejection letter in response," she recalls.

Rejection spurred her on. Failing to land a job after college (she was turned down by Morgan Stanley, Goldman, McKinsey, Bain, and P&G), she decided to launch the teaching corps herself. Though she describes herself as "very shy," Kopp drummed up the courage to cold-call scores of CEOs and foundation leaders. A Mobil executive named Rex Adams agreed to give her a seed grant of $26,000, and Dick Fisher, then-CEO of Morgan Stanley (and a Princeton alum), donated office space. A letter to the chairman of Hertz got her six cars for TFA's skeleton crew of recruiters (who included Richard Barth, now Kopp's husband). Other early believers—Merck, Union Carbide, Apple Computer, Young & Rubicam, and fellow Texan Ross Perot—chipped in, building her first-year budget to $2.5 million. That was enough to recruit, train, and place 500 teachers. . . .

Kopp wants to double TFA's corps to 8,000 by 2010. "We're trying to be the top employer of recent grads in the country," she says. "Size gives us leverage to have a tangible impact on school systems."[106]

Questions for Discussion

1. How would you describe Wendy Kopp's success, based on what you have learned in this chapter?

2. Relative to the concepts you have just read about, what traits and characteristics would describe the "ideal" TFA candidate? Explain your rationale for selecting each characteristic.

3. Ranked 1 = most important to 8 = least important, which of Gardner's eight multiple intelligences are most critical to a successful TFA assignment? Explain your ranking.

4. Using Table 5–5 as a guide, how important are the specific emotional intelligence competencies to the success of a TFA participant? Explain.

5. Do you have what it takes to be a successful TFA teacher? Explain in terms of the concepts in this chapter.

6. Will you apply for a TFA job? What are the ethical implications of your answer?

Ethical Dilemma

Can We Talk about Your Body Art?

As tattoos and piercings gain popularity with a younger generation of employees, interviewers and supervisors are developing new dress code criteria.

While there are industries and companies that are tolerant of body art, it is still more common for businesses to hold a hard line, especially in jobs that require frequent customer interaction.

For example, at the Fairmont Scottsdale Princess in Scottsdale [Arizona], recruitment specialist Melisa Leserance said the company has definitive guidelines about on-the-job appearances and applicants are told during the interview process what is acceptable. . . .

Leserance recalled one employee who had a tattoo across his wrist. "He wore a jacket, but you could still see it. And as long as he worked here, he wore a bandage over the tattoo."

"If the company has a written or stated dress code," . . . [says an employment attorney], then "the company gets to determine what constitutes a professional image or appearance."[107]

How should employers deal with self-expression through body art?

1. Many businesses have carefully cultivated images to protect, so they have a moral responsibility to their shareholders to monitor their employees' appearance. Explain.

2. Companies may have the legal right to force people to look a certain way, but they don't have the moral right to stifle self-expression in arbitrary ways. Explain.

3. The style of a new generation calls for new employment policies. Where should lines be drawn about employees' personal appearance?

4. The business case for diversity declares that an organization's employees should look like its customer base.

If a growing number of customers have body art, why can't employees? Should this vary by industry or type of business? Explain.

5. Today's discrimination against those with body art is equivalent to now-illegal racial and gender discrimination years ago. Do you agree or disagree? Explain.

6. Invent other options. Discuss.

Web Resources

For study material and exercises that apply to this chapter, visit our Web site,

www.mhhe.com/kreitner

CHAPTER 6

Values, Attitudes, and Job Satisfaction

Hard work and opportunities for growth are givens at New York-based accounting firm Pricewaterhouse-Cooper (PwC), but so is help maintaining balance. The company's learning team uses targeted programming to keep an eye on its driven workforce, coupling skill development with an emphasis on staying well rounded.

Workers, who more senior employees feel are at risk of losing that precarious work/life balance, are identified relatively early—just several years into their career at PwC. Through a program known as "Turning Point," these young staffers are given the opportunity to attend facilitator-led sessions to return their equilibrium.

"At that point in one's career you're faced with a lot of challenges," Chief Learning Officer Tom Evans says of the late 20s/early 30s age range most of the program's participants fall in. "A combination of forces have come into play—family, career, community." Instead of choosing one priority over another, the program teaches the importance of making time for all of it, and provides tips on balancing responsibilities. Launched about a year and a half ago, the program is open to any employee who's been with the company four to six years. "It's something we're very proud of because it's not linked to a specific role in the firm, or learning new technical information," says Evans. "It's a very unique, personal experience for the individual that says, 'This is about

leadership in life, where you have to deal with these converging forces.'"

About 100 workers at a time are identified for the program, which divides participants into "heavily coached" discussion groups of roughly five, Evans explains. Last year, approximately 800 employees participated in Turning Point. Success stories, Evans points out, include employees who say they lost weight, became more social, and re-engaged with peers following participation in the program. "It's not about economics, but the return to the firm has been enormous," he says. The coaches who facilitate the discussion sessions include both PwC executives as well as external

Employees at PricewaterhouseCooper are given the opportunity to participate in programs that encourage a healthy work/life balance.

experts, such as social psychologists. Participants, who are spurred by these coaches to reflect on and share their challenges, sometimes feel unburdened just knowing others at the company feel the same pressures, says Evans.[1]

FOR DISCUSSION

Why would PwC's program help reduce employee turnover?

The chapter-opening vignette highlights how PricewaterhouseCooper used its Turning Point program to enhance employee productivity and retention. This emphasis is one reason *Fortune* ranked PwC as the 58th best company to work for in 2007. Unfortunately, results from a nationwide survey of 8,044 people by Monster.com suggest that employee retention might become more of a problem in the future; 93% of the respondents indicated that they planned to job-hop next year even though they were not optimistic about the job market.[2] As discussed later in this chapter, employees quit their jobs for or a variety of reasons. That said, however, research indicates that employees are less likely to quit when their personal values are consistent with the organization's values, when they have positive attitudes about the work environment, and when they are satisfied with their jobs.[3] This is why progressive companies like Genentech, Container Store, Network Appliance, American Century Invest, and Microsoft are offering programs and benefits such as day care, flexible work schedules, paternal leaves, generous tuition reimbursement, wellness programs, telecommuting, concierge services, and mentoring to a wider segment of the workforce.[4]

The overall goal of this chapter is to continue our investigation of individual differences from Chapter 5 so that you can get a better idea of how managers and organizations can use knowledge of individual differences to attract, motivate, and retain quality employees. We explore and discuss the impact of personal values and attitudes on important outcomes such as job satisfaction, performance, and turnover.

Personal Values

Value system

The organization of one's beliefs about preferred ways of behaving and desired end-states.

When discussing organizational culture in Chapter 3, we defined *values* as desired ways of behaving or desired end-states. Accordingly, pioneering values researcher Milton Rokeach defined a person's **value system** as an "enduring organization of beliefs concerning preferable modes of conduct or end-states of existence along a continuum of relative importance."[5] Our focus in Chapter 3 was on collective or shared values; here the focus shifts to *personal* values.

Extensive research supports Rokeach's contention that differing value systems go a long way toward explaining individual differences in behavior. Value → behavior connections have been documented for a wide variety of behaviors, ranging from weight loss, shopping selections, and political party affiliation to religious involvement and choice of a college major.[6]

Let us learn more about personal values by distinguishing between instrumental and terminal values, discussing three types of value conflict, and examining the timely value-related topic of work versus family life conflicts.

Terminal values

Personally preferred end-states of existence.

Instrumental and Terminal Values

Rokeach proposed that personal values can be categorized along two dimensions: terminal and instrumental.[7] **Terminal values,** such as a sense of accomplishment, happiness, pleasure, salvation, and wisdom, are desired end-states or life goals. These values represent the things we want to achieve or accomplish during our lives. For example, if you value family more than career success, you are more likely to work fewer hours and to spend more time with your family than someone who values career success. These values can also change over time depending on what is happening in our lives. Brenda Barnes, for instance, resigned as CEO of Pepsi-Cola's $7.7 billion North America division in 1997 in order to spend more time raising her three children, who were 7, 8, and 10 at the time. She obviously felt that it was more important to be with her children at that time rather than leading a multibillion dollar business. Two years later, however, Brenda returned to an executive position with Starwood Hotels & Resorts, and today she is the chairman and CEO of Sara Lee.[8]

Instrumental values are alternative behaviors or means by which we achieve our terminal values or desired end-states. Sample instrumental values include ambition, honesty, independence, love, and obedience. The key thing to remember about instrumental values is that they direct us in determining how we should behave in the pursuit of our goals. For example, someone who values the instrumental value of honesty is less likely to lie and cheat in order to accomplish a terminal value associated with a sense of accomplishment than someone who does not value honesty.

> **Instrumental values**
>
> Personally preferred ways of behaving.

Value Conflicts

There are three types of value conflict that are related to an individual's attitudes, job satisfaction, turnover, and potentially performance. They are *intra*personal value conflict, *inter*personal value conflict, and individual–organization value conflict. These sources of conflict are, respectively, from inside the person, between people, and between the person and the organization.

Intrapersonal Value Conflict

Inner conflict and resultant stress typically are experienced when highly ranked instrumental and terminal values pull the individual in different directions. This is somewhat akin to role conflict, as discussed in Chapter 10. The main difference is locus of influence: Role conflict involves *outside* social expectations; intrapersonal value conflict involves *internal* priorities. For employees who want balance in their lives, a stressful conflict arises when one values, for example, "being ambitious" (instrumental value) and "ending up happy" (terminal value). Dan Rosensweig, chief operating officer at Yahoo!, is experiencing intrapersonal value conflict in his current job. He commented about this to a reporter from *Fast Company* by noting that his "biggest challenge is when you're given an opportunity like this, how do you give it everything you have because it deserves it, and also recognize and appreciate that the most important things in your life are your wife and daughters. I'm envious of people who have been able to find better balance."[9] In general, people are happier and less stressed when their personal values are aligned.

Interpersonal Value Conflict

This type of value conflict often is at the core of personality conflicts, and such conflicts can negatively affect one's career. Consider the case of Jeffrey Johnson. He was fired by the owner of the *Los Angeles Times*—the Tribune—when his values collided with those possessed by senior management. Senior management wanted Johnson to improve the paper's financial results by cutting costs. Johnson then was asked to eliminate employees from the payroll. The conflict for Mr. Johnson was that he did not believe that the newspaper's problems would be solved by employee layoffs. He wanted to improve the newspaper's financial status by exploring creative ways to generate revenue as opposed to cutting costs.[10]

Anne Mulcahy "Fits In" at Xerox

I'm what you call a "lifer" at Xerox; I've been with the company for 30 years. I joined the company because it offered me a chance to compete in a meritocracy as a salesperson where performance is fact-based—you're either selling or you're not. I stayed because I became enthralled by a culture that broadly defines "citizenship" to include how you treat your people, your customers, your suppliers, and the communities where we work and live. It wasn't talk, it was action, and still is. More than 40 years ago, our founder, Joe Wilson, spelled out a set of core values that cover how we engage with employees and customers, how we deliver value, and how we behave. Every decision I make is aligned with those values.

How would you describe Anne Mulcahy's terminal and instrumental values?

SOURCE: "Stay Tuned to Your Values," *Business 2.0*, December 2006, p 98.

This example highlights how important it is to carefully evaluate the pros and cons of handling interpersonal value conflicts with our superiors.

Individual–Organization Value Conflict As we saw in Chapter 3, companies actively seek to embed certain values into their corporate cultures. Conflict can occur when values espoused and enacted by the organization collide with employees' personal values. OB researchers refer to this type of conflict as value congruence or person–culture fit.[11] **Value congruence or person–culture fit** reflects the similarity between an individual's personal values and the cultural value system of an organization. This is an important type of conflict to consider when accepting future jobs because positive outcomes such as satisfaction, commitment, performance, career success, reduced stress, and lower turnover intentions are realized when an individual's personal values are similar or aligned with organizational values.[12] The Real World/Real People feature above illustrates high-value congruence for Anne Mulcahy, chairman and CEO of Xerox.

> **Value congruence or person–culture fit**
>
> The similarity between personal values and organizational values.

Handling Value Conflicts through Values Clarification For intrapersonal conflict, a Toronto management writer and consultant recommends getting out of what she calls "the busyness trap" by asking these questions:

- Is your work really meeting your most important needs?
- Are you defining yourself purely in terms of your accomplishments?
- Why are you working so hard? To what personal ends?
- Are you making significant sacrifices in favor of your work?
- Is your work schedule affecting other people who are important in your life?[13]

Another approach for dealing with all forms of value conflict is a career-counseling and team-building technique called *values clarification*. The goal of this technique is to reduce value conflict through discussion. Conflicting parties are encouraged to identify and talk about personal values to establish common ground as a basis for teamwork and conflict avoidance/resolution (as discussed in Chapters 11 and 13).

go to the Web for the Self-Exercise: Personal Values Clarification

2 Work versus Family Life Conflict

A complex web of demographic and economic factors makes the balancing act between job and life very challenging for most of us. Demographically, there are more women in the workforce, more dual-income families, more single working parents, more international travel, and an aging population that gives mid-career employees day care or elder care responsibilities, or both.[14] On the economic front, years of downsizing and corporate cost-cutting have given employees heavier workloads. Meanwhile, an important trend was recently documented in a unique 25-year study of values in the United States: "employees have become less convinced that work should be an important part of one's life or that working hard makes one a better person."[15] Something has to give in this collision of trends. Too often family life suffers. The experience of Michael Hickey and Karen Ambrose Hickey is a sign of the times.

> Michael Hickey knows better than to try to start a conversation with his wife when she gets home from work.
>
> After a hard day at the office, "I'm definitely too tired to talk at night," says Karen Ambrose Hickey of Palo Alto, Calif., a senior marketing director. "I put up a brick wall." Michael, an engineer, says he's resigned: Regardless of what's on his mind when Karen comes home, he says, "you just have to wait" until later. Finding time to talk is "an ongoing struggle."[16]

Experts estimate that almost 45% of high-income individuals experience conversational dead zones after a busy day at work.[17]

In this section, we seek to better understand work versus family life conflict by introducing a values-based model and discussing practical research insights. Importantly, our goal here is to get a firmer grasp on this difficult area, not offer quick-and-easy solutions with little chance of success.

A Values-Based Model of Work/Family Conflict Building upon the work of Rokeach, Pamela L Perrewé and Wayne A Hochwarter constructed the model in Figure 6–1. On the left, we see one's general life values feeding into one's family-related values and work-related values. Family values involve enduring beliefs about the importance of family and who should play key family roles (e.g., child rearing, housekeeping, and income earning). Work values center on the relative importance of work and career goals in one's life. *Value similarity* relates to the degree of consensus among family members about family values. When a housewife launches a business venture despite her husband's desire to be the sole breadwinner, lack of family value similarity causes work/family conflict. *Value congruence,* on the other hand, involves the amount of value agreement between employee and employer. If, for example, refusing to go on a business trip to stay home for a child's birthday is viewed as disloyalty to the company, lack of value congruence can trigger work/family conflict.

In turn, "work-family conflict can take two distinct forms: work interference with family and family interference with work."[18] For example, suppose two managers in the same department have daughters playing on the same soccer team. One manager

Figure 6-1   *A Values Model of Work/Family Conflict*

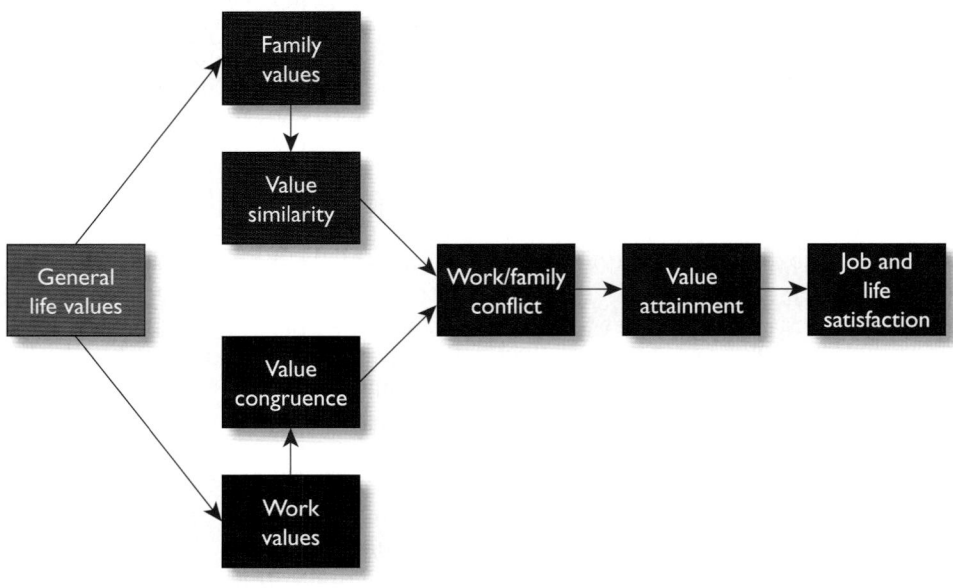

SOURCE: Pamela L Perrewé and Wayne A Hochwarter, "Can We Really Have It All? The Attainment of Work and Family Values," *Current Directions in Psychological Science*, February 2001, p 30. Published by Blackwell Publishers, Inc. © American Psychological Society.

misses the big soccer game to attend a last-minute department meeting; the other manager skips the meeting to attend the game. Both may experience work/family conflict, but for different reasons.

The last two boxes in the model—value attainment and job and life satisfaction—are a package deal. Satisfaction tends to be higher for those who live according to their values and lower for those who do not. Overall, this model reflects much common sense. How does *your* life track through the model? Sadly, it is a painful trip for many these days.

go to the Web for the Self-Exercise: Are Your Values and Commitments Aligned?

Practical Research Insights about Work/Family Conflict This is a new but very active area of OB research. Typically, the evidence comes from field surveys of real people in real jobs, rather than from contrived laboratory studies. Recent practical findings include

- *Work/family balance begins at home.* Historically, women shouldered the majority of the standard household chores and child-rearing responsibilities. Fortunately, there is some data suggesting that men are beginning to share more of the work associated with running a home. A national survey revealed that male Gen Xers, people born between 1965 and 1979, were equally involved with spouses in taking care of children. Males also were more focused on spending time with family.[19] This is a promising result in light of a recent study of 223 men and 113 women. Findings showed that people had greater life satisfaction when they were committed to their marriage and to their children.[20]

- *An employer's family-supportive philosophy is more important than specific programs.* Many employers offer family-friendly programs today, including child and elder day care assistance, parental leave, telecommuting, and flexible work schedules. However, if employees are afraid or reluctant to take advantage of those programs because the organization's culture values hard work and long hours above all else, families will inevitably suffer. To be truly family-friendly, the organization needs to provide programs and back them up with a family-supportive philosophy and culture.[21]

Great companies recognize that the ability to take care of family concerns is an important part of an employee's job satisfaction. How can a company's policies reflect a family-supportive philosophy?

- *Informal flexibility in work hours and in allowing people to work at home is essential to promoting work/family balance.* Quite simply, flexibility allows people to cope more effectively with competing demands across their personal and work lives. Dell Inc., for example, is allowing some work teams to eliminate "firm office hours and handing employees control over when and how they achieve goals." Bristol-Myers Squibb similarly tried to enhance worker flexibility by enabling people to choose one of six different work schedules.[22]

- *Mentors can help.* A field survey of 502 graduates of a US university (63% men), yielded this result: "The results indicate that having a mentor is significantly related to lower levels of work-family conflict. . . . Such findings suggest another potential benefit of mentoring: a source of social support to reduce employee stress caused by conflicts between the work and family domains."[23]

- *Take a proactive approach to managing work/family conflict.* Two recent meta-analyses of more than 60 different studies and 43,000 people demonstrated that an individual's personal life spills over to his or her work life and vice versa. This means that employees' job satisfaction, organizational commitment, and intentions to quit are significantly related to the amount of work/family conflict that exists in their lives.[24] We thus encourage you to identify and manage the sources of work/family conflict.

- *Being your own boss is no panacea.* Self-employment turns out to be a good news/bad news proposition, when compared to standard organizational employment. Among the benefits of being self-employed are a stronger sense of autonomy, a higher level of job involvement, and greater job satisfaction. But self-employed people report higher levels of work/family conflict and lower levels of family satisfaction.[25]

Organizational Response to Work/Family Issues
Organizations have implemented a variety of family-friendly programs and services aimed at helping employees to balance the interplay between their work and personal lives. Although these programs are positively received by employees, experts now believe that such efforts are partially misguided because they focus on balancing work/family issues rather than integrating them. Balance is needed for opposites, and work and family are not opposites. Rather, our work and personal lives should be a well-integrated whole. A team of researchers arrived at the following conclusion regarding the need to integrate versus balance work/life issues.

Gendered assumptions and stereotypes based in the separation of [occupational and family] spheres constrain the choices of both women and men. Our vision of gender equity is to relax these social norms about separation so that men and women are free to experience these two parts of their lives as integrated rather than as separate domains that need to be "balanced." Integration would make it possible for both women and men to perform up to their capabilities and find satisfaction in both work and personal life, no matter how they allocate their time commitment between the two. To convey this goal, we speak of integrating work and personal life rather than balancing. This terminology expresses our belief in the need to diminish the separation between these two spheres of life in ways that will *change both,* rather than merely reallocating—or "balancing"—time between them as they currently exist.[26]

go to the Web for the Self-Exercise: How Family-Supportive Is Your Employer?

3 Attitudes

Hardly a day goes by without the popular media reporting the results of another attitude survey. The idea is to take the pulse of public opinion. What do we think about candidate X, terrorism, the war on drugs, gun control, or abortion? In the workplace, meanwhile, managers conduct attitude surveys to monitor such things as job and pay satisfaction. All this attention to attitudes is based on the realization that our attitudes influence our behavior. For example, research demonstrated that seniors with a positive attitude about aging had better memory, better hearing, and lived longer than those with negative attitudes.[27] In a work setting, a recent meta-analysis involving more than 50,000 people revealed that overall job attitudes were positively related to performance and negatively associated with indicators of withdrawal—lateness, absenteeism, and turnover.[28] In this section, we discuss the components of attitudes and examine the connection between attitudes and behavior.

The Nature of Attitudes

Attitude

Learned predisposition toward a given object.

An **attitude** is defined as "a learned predisposition to respond in a consistently favorable or unfavorable manner with respect to a given object."[29] Consider your attitude toward chocolate ice cream. You are more likely to purchase a chocolate ice cream cone if you have a positive attitude toward chocolate ice cream. In contrast, you are more likely to purchase some other flavor, say vanilla caramel swirl, if you have a positive attitude toward vanilla and a neutral or negative attitude toward chocolate ice cream. Let us consider a work example. If you have a positive attitude about your job (i.e., you like what you are doing), you would be more willing to extend yourself at work by working longer and harder. These examples illustrate that attitudes propel us to act in a specific way in a specific context. That is, attitudes affect behavior at a different level than do values. While values represent global beliefs that influence behavior across *all* situations, attitudes relate only to behavior directed toward *specific* objects, persons, or situations. Values and attitudes generally, but not always, are in harmony. A manager who strongly values helpful behavior may have a negative attitude toward helping an unethical co-worker. The difference between attitudes and values is clarified by considering the three components of attitudes: affective, cognitive, and behavioral.[30] It is important to note that your overall attitude toward someone or something is a function of the combined influence of all three components.

Affective Component

The **affective component** of an attitude contains the feelings or emotions one has about a given object or situation. For example, how do you *feel* about people who talk on cell phones in restaurants? If you feel annoyed or angry with such people you are expressing negative affect or feelings toward people who talk on cell phones in restaurants. In contrast, the affective component of your attitude is neutral if you are indifferent about people talking on cell phones in restaurants.

Cognitive Component

What do you *think* about people who talk on cell phones in restaurants? Do you believe this behavior is inconsiderate, productive, completely acceptable, or rude? Your answer represents the cognitive component of your attitude toward people talking on cell phones in restaurants. The **cognitive component** of an attitude reflects the beliefs or ideas one has about an object or situation.

Behavioral Component

The **behavioral component** refers to how one intends or expects to act toward someone or something. For example, how would you intend to respond to someone talking on a cell phone during dinner at a restaurant if this individual were sitting in close proximity to you and your guest? Attitude theory suggests that your ultimate behavior in this situation is a function of all three attitudinal components. You are unlikely to say anything to someone using a cell phone in a restaurant if you are not irritated by this behavior (affective), if you believe cell phone use helps people to manage their lives (cognitive), and you have no intention of confronting this individual (behavioral).

Affective component

The feelings or emotions one has about an object or situation.

Cognitive component

The beliefs or ideas one has about an object or situation.

Behavioral component

How one intends to act or behave toward someone or something.

What Happens When Attitudes and Reality Collide?
Cognitive Dissonance

What happens when a strongly held attitude is contradicted by reality? Suppose you are extremely concerned about getting AIDS, which you believe is transferred from contact with body fluids, including blood. Then you find yourself in a life-threatening accident in a foreign country and need surgery and blood transfusions—including transfusions of blood (possibly AIDS-infected) from a blood bank with unknown quality control. Would you reject the blood to remain consistent with your beliefs about getting AIDS? According to social psychologist Leon Festinger, this situation would create cognitive dissonance.

Cognitive dissonance represents the psychological discomfort a person experiences when his or her attitudes or beliefs are incompatible with his or her behavior.[31] Festinger proposed that people are motivated to maintain consistency between their attitudes and beliefs and their behavior. He therefore theorized that people will seek to reduce the "dissonance" or psychological tension through one of three main methods.

Cognitive dissonance

Psychological discomfort experienced when attitudes and behavior are inconsistent.

1. *Change your attitude or behavior, or both.* This is the simplest solution when confronted with cognitive dissonance. Returning to our example about needing a blood transfusion, this would amount to either (1) telling yourself that you can't get AIDS through blood and take the transfusion or (2) simply refusing to take the transfusion.

2. *Belittle the importance of the inconsistent behavior.* This happens all the time. In our example, you could belittle the belief that you can get AIDS from the foreign blood bank. (The doctor said she regularly uses blood from that blood bank.)

3. *Find consonant elements that outweigh dissonant ones.* This approach entails rationalizing away the dissonance. You can tell yourself that you are taking the transfusion because you have no other options. After all, you could die if you don't get the required surgery.

How Stable Are Attitudes?

In one landmark study, researchers found the *job* attitudes of 5,000 middle-aged male employees to be very stable over a five-year period. Positive job attitudes remained positive; negative ones remained negative. Even those who changed jobs or occupations tended to maintain their prior job attitudes.[32] More recent research suggests the foregoing study may have overstated the stability of attitudes because it was restricted to a middle-aged sample. This time, researchers asked: What happens to attitudes over the entire span of adulthood? *General* attitudes were found to be more susceptible to change during early and late adulthood than during middle adulthood. Three factors accounted for middle-age attitude stability: (1) greater personal certainty, (2) perceived abundance of knowledge, and (3) a need for strong attitudes. Thus, the conventional notion that general attitudes become less likely to change as the person ages was rejected. Elderly people, along with young adults, can and do change their general attitudes because they are more open and less self-assured.[33]

Because our cultural backgrounds and experiences vary, our attitudes and behavior vary. Attitudes are translated into behavior via behavioral intentions. Let us examine an established model of this important process.

Attitudes Affect Behavior via Intentions

Building on Leon Festinger's work on cognitive dissonance, Icek Ajzen and Martin Fishbein further delved into understanding the reason for discrepancies between individuals' attitudes and behavior. Ajzen ultimately developed and refined a model focusing on intentions as the key link between attitudes and planned behavior. His theory of planned behavior in Figure 6–2 shows three separate but interacting determinants of one's intention (a person's readiness to perform a given behavior) to exhibit a specific behavior.

Importantly, this model only predicts behavior under an individual's control, not behavior due to circumstances beyond one's control. For example, this model can predict the likelihood of someone skipping work if the person says his intention is to stay in bed tomorrow morning. But it would be a poor model for predicting getting to work on time, because uncontrolled circumstances such as traffic delays or an accident could intervene.

Determinants of Intention Ajzen has explained the nature and roles of the three determinants of intention as follows:

> The first is the *attitude toward the behavior* and refers to the degree to which a person has a favorable or unfavorable evaluation or appraisal of the behavior in question. The second predictor is a social factor termed *subjective norm;* it refers to the perceived social pressure to perform or not to perform the behavior. The third antecedent of intention is the degree of *perceived behavior control,* which . . . refers to the perceived ease or difficulty of performing the behavior and it is assumed to reflect past experience as well as anticipated impediments and obstacles.[34]

To bring these three determinants of intention to life, let us return to our lazy soul who chose to stay in bed rather than go to work. He feels overworked and underpaid

Figure 6–2   *Ajzen's Theory of Planned Behavior*

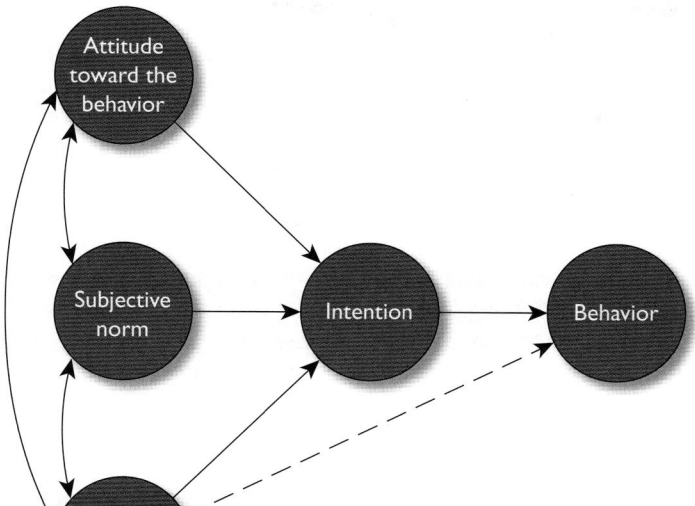

SOURCE: Reprinted from I Ajzen, "The Theory of Planned Behavior," *Organizational Behavior and Human Decision Processes*, Figure 1, p 182. Copyright 1991, with permission from Elsevier Science.

and thus has a favorable attitude about skipping work occasionally. His perceived subjective norm is favorable because he sees his co-workers skipping work with no ill effects (in fact, they collect sick pay). Regarding perceived behavior control, he is completely in charge of acting on his intention to skip work today. So he turns off the alarm clock and pulls the covers over his head. Sweet dreams!

Intentions and Behavior Research Lessons and Implications

According to the model of planned behavior, someone's intention to engage in a given behavior is a strong predictor of that behavior. For example, the quickest and possibly most accurate way of determining whether an individual will quit his or her job is to have an objective third party ask if he or she intends to quit. A meta-analysis of 34 studies of employee turnover involving more than 83,000 employees validated this direct approach. The researchers found stated behavioral intentions to be a better predictor of employee turnover than job satisfaction, satisfaction with the work itself, or organizational commitment.[35] A recent study took these findings one step further by considering whether or not job applicants' intention to quit a job before they were hired would predict voluntary turnover six months after being hired. Results demonstrated that intentions to quit significantly predicted turnover.[36]

Research has demonstrated that Ajzen's model accurately predicted intentions to buy consumer products, have children, and choose a career versus becoming a homemaker. Weight loss intentions and behavior, voting for political candidates, using Internet services to facilitate the shipping of products, nurses' willingness to work with older patients, attending on-the-job training sessions, condom use, and reenlisting in the National Guard also have been predicted successfully by the model.[37] The theory of planned behavior also was found to explain the behavior of people from Turkey and the Netherlands.[38]

From a practical standpoint, the theory of planned behavior has important managerial implications. Managers are encouraged to use prescriptions derived from the model to implement interventions aimed at changing employees' behavior. According to this model, changing behavior starts with the recognition that behavior is modified through intentions, which in turn are influenced by three different determinants (see Figure 6–2). Managers can thus influence behavioral change by doing or saying things that affect the three determinants of employees' intentions to exhibit a specific behavior: attitude toward the behavior, subjective norms, and perceived behavioral control.[39] This is accomplished by modifying the specific beliefs that foster each of these determinants. For example, behavioral beliefs, normative beliefs, and control beliefs directly affect attitude toward the behavior, subjective norms, and perceived behavioral control, respectively. As a case in point, a study showed that employees had lower perceptions of job security and more negative attitudes toward temporary workers when they had the behavioral belief that temporaries posed a threat to their jobs.[40] Ultimately, managers change both attitudes and behavior by changing employees' beliefs.

Employee beliefs can be influenced through the information management provides on a day-by-day basis, organizational cultural values, role models, and rewards that are targeted to reinforce certain beliefs. For instance, management can foster the belief that teamwork is valued by setting and rewarding team-based goals instead of individual goals. Beliefs can also be modified through education and training. Finally, the socialization tactics discussed in Chapter 3 (see Table 3–2) can be used to shape or change employees' beliefs.

Key Work Attitudes

Work attitudes such as organizational commitment, job involvement, and job satisfaction have a dual interest to managers. On the one hand, they represent important outcomes that managers may want to enhance. On the other, they are symptomatic of other potential problems. For example, low job satisfaction may be a symptom of an employee's intention to quit. It thus is important for managers to understand the causes and consequences of key work attitudes.

What is your attitude toward work? Is work something meaningful that defines and fulfills you, or is it just a way to pay the bills? Interestingly, attitudes toward work have changed significantly throughout recorded history (see Figure 6–3). Note the difference between the early Greeks' attitude toward work and the current perspective. Having fun at work clearly beats slavery! While everyone does not agree about having fun at work, organizations such as Southwest Airlines have turned it into a strategic competitive advantage. Key employee selection factors at Southwest Airlines are a keen sense of humor and a general positive attitude. Consider how CEO Bob Pike's positive attitude toward work would set the tone for his employees at Creative Training Techniques International, Inc.:

> It is not a choice between fun and work, it is a choice for fun and work. I find it depressing that so many people spend 8 hours a day at work and 16 hours trying to forget that they did! It's time for us to replace the common definition of work: if it is not dull and boring then it can't be work! Work should be about passion, it should have a sense of purpose, it should be about involvement and participation. High-performing teams who do challenging work also know how to have fun. They have an attitude that says they enjoy what they do and that they belong to a diverse group of committed individuals who know the mission, values, and vision of the team. And they look forward to making a contribution.

Figure 6-3 *Timeline of Work Values and Attitudes*

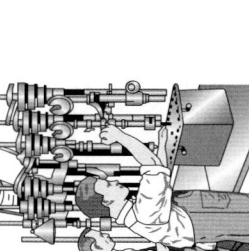
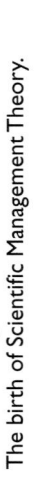

Early Greeks
Focus not on work but on personal development. The emergence of the concept of "liberal arts," and the pursuit of knowledge.

The trades
Working with your hands as a skilled artisan is highly prized. Payment provided for work. With the onset of the Renaissance, work and art are merged.

Calvin and Luther
Work as a commandment and moral obligation. The evolution of the Protestant Work Ethic.

Ben Franklin
Advocates work as a virtue; not a means to amass wealth but as a contribution of self. America is the land of opportunity. Work becomes the key to wealth.

Craftsmen vs Professionals
Separation between people who work with their hands and professionals who work with their heads. The bias is that working with your head is a more esteemed vocation.

Industrial Age
The birth of Scientific Management Theory.

Unions
Unions help workers defend their ability to earn a livelihood against managers and owners who see employees as objects.

1950s
The beginning of understanding of the culture of work in terms of Theory X and Theory Y. Loyalty to the organization becomes the expected norm.

1970s
Democracy comes to the workplace. Sexes and races begin to assume more equal roles in all aspects of work environments.

1980s
Gurus abound. How to make work meaningful. TQM becomes the newest program of the corporate culture.

1990s
Empowerment, Building the Team, and Reengineering begin the decade. Downsizing at the end of the decade completes the near total loss of loyalty as an organizational value.

2000s
Because we spend more time at work than at any other activity, we begin to question whether we live to work or work to live. The beginning of the Fun/Work Fusion.

SOURCE: Reprinted with permission of the publisher. From *Fun Works: Creating Places Where People Love to Work*, Copyright © 2001 by L Yerkes, Berrett-Koehler Publishers, Inc., San Francisco, CA. All rights reserved. www.bkconnection.com.

Chuck Carothers and Irene Tse Commit to Their Jobs, Careers, and the Thrill of Achievement

In the realm of extreme sports, Chuck Carothers is a champ. One of the world's leading motocross riders, he has broken 21 bones in his career. Yet he keeps competing, describing the rush he gets from sailing through the air on a motorbike as a "complete addiction." In a weird way, Irene Tse, the 34-year-old head of the government bond-trading desk at Goldman Sachs—Jon Corzine's old job—understands Carothers's passion. "I've done this for 10 years," she says. "And I can count on the fingers of one hand the number of days in my career when I didn't want to come to work. Every day I wake up and I can't wait to get here."

The bond market hasn't exactly been a lot of laughs during that decade. And overseeing a desk that trades billions of dollars daily, with profits and losses in the millions—Wall Street's equivalent of Carothers's famous flying barrel roll—can be hair-raising. "There

are days when you make a lot, and other days where you lose so much you're just stunned by what you've done," Tse admits. But the exhilaration of her work, and the challenge of figuring out what forces are likely to next roil the markets, has kept her motivated through a decade of 80-hour weeks.

Indeed, there's an addictive quality to her work that has rewired her body. There are no broken bones, but Tse says she hasn't slept through the night in years, typically getting up two or three times to check on global market activity. "Through time, your body clock just wakes up when London opens," she says.

What is driving Chuck and Irene's commitment?

SOURCE: Excerpted from L Tischler, "Extreme Jobs," *Fast Company*, April 2005, p 56. © 2005 Gruner & Jahr USA Publishing. First published in *Fast Company* Magazine. Reprinted with permission.

> Understand that there will always be both fun-loving and fun-killing people. Fun-killers don't actually object to the fun; they feel that the fun isn't relevant to the work and therefore not important.[41]

How would you like to work for Bob Pike?

People have a multitude of attitudes about things that happen to them at work, but OB researchers have focused on a limited number of them. This section specifically examines two work attitudes—organizational commitment and job involvement—that have important practical implications. Job satisfaction, the most frequently studied work attitude, is thoroughly discussed in the final section of this chapter.

5 Organizational Commitment

Before discussing a model of organizational commitment, it is important to consider the meaning of the term *commitment*. What does it mean to commit? Common sense suggests that commitment is an agreement to do something for yourself, another individual, group, or organization.[42] Formally, OB researchers define commitment as "a force that binds an individual to a course of action of relevance to one or more targets."[43] This definition highlights that commitment is associated with behavior and that commitment can be aimed at multiple targets or entities. For example, an individual can be committed to his or her job, family, girl- or boyfriend, faith, friends, career, organization, or a variety of professional associations. Chuck Carothers and Irene Tse are good examples of individuals who commit to multiple targets (see the Real World/Real People feature above). Let us now consider the application of commitment to a work organization.

Organizational commitment reflects the extent to which an individual identifies with an organization and is committed to its goals. It is an important work attitude because committed individuals are expected to display a willingness to work harder to achieve organizational goals and a greater desire to stay employed at an organization.

Organizational commitment

Extent to which an individual identifies with an organization and its goals.

Figure 6–4   *A Model of Organizational Commitment*

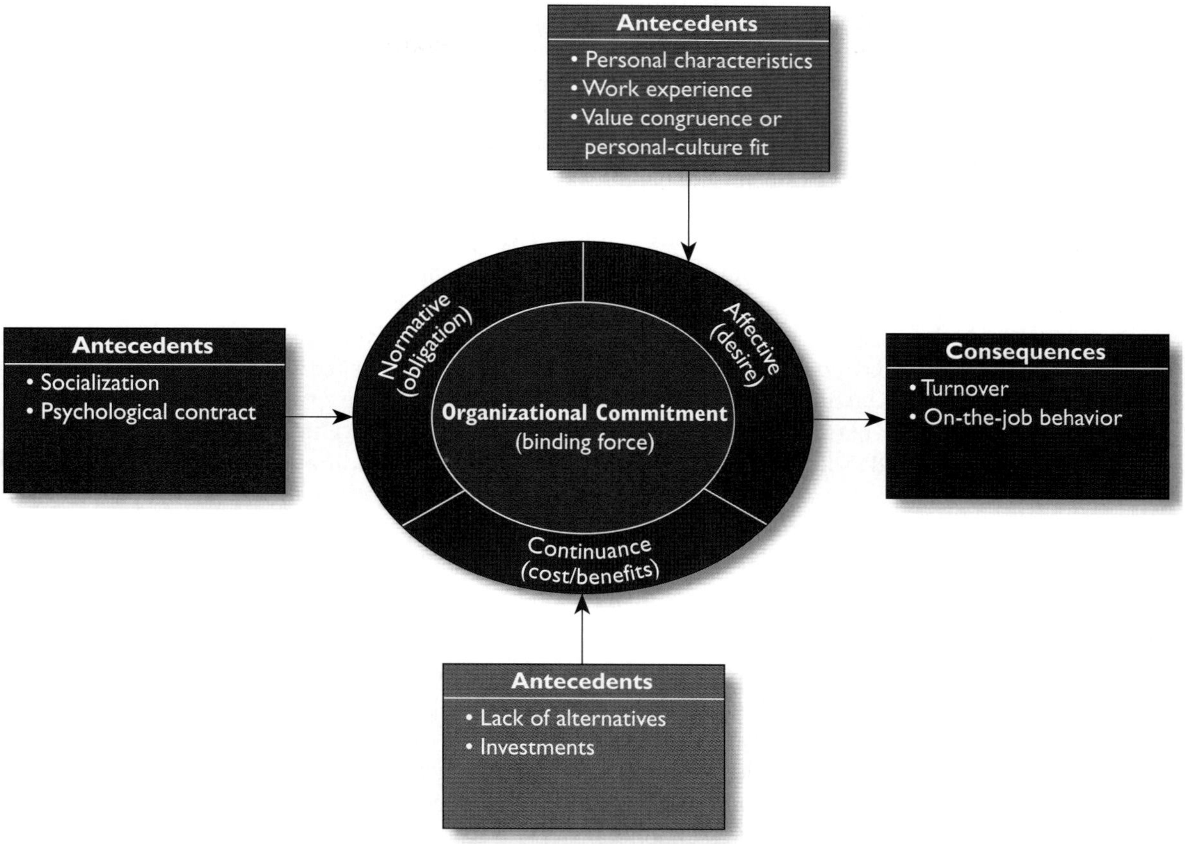

SOURCE: Adapted from J P Meyer and L Herscovitch, "Commitment in the Workplace: Toward a General Model," *Human Resource Management Review,* Autumn 2001, p 317.

Figure 6–4 presents a model of organizational commitment that identifies its causes and consequences.

A Model of Organizational Commitment   Figure 6–4 shows that organizational commitment is composed of three separate but related components: affective commitment, normative commitment, and continuance commitment. John Meyer and Natalie Allen, a pair of commitment experts, define these components as follows:

> *Affective commitment* refers to the employee's emotional attachment to, identification with, and involvement in the organization. Employees with a strong affective commitment continue employment with an organization because they *want* to do so. *Continuance commitment* refers to an awareness of the costs associated with leaving the organization. Employees whose primary link to the organization is based on continuance commitment remain because they *need* to do so. Finally, normative commitment reflects a feeling of obligation to continue employment. Employees with a high level of normative commitment feel that they *ought* to remain with the organization.[44]

Figure 6–4 also reveals that these three components combine to produce a binding force that influences the consequences of employee turnover and on-the-job behavior such as performance, absenteeism, and organizational citizenship, which is discussed later in this chapter.

Each component of commitment is influenced by a separate set of antecedents (see Figure 6–4). In the current context, an antecedent is something that causes the component of commitment to occur. For example, affective commitment is related to a variety of personal characteristics such as personality and locus of control (recall our discussion in Chapter 5), past work experience, and value congruence, which was discussed earlier in this chapter.[45] Because continuance commitment reflects a ratio of the costs and benefits associated with leaving an organization, antecedents are anything that affects the costs and benefits of leaving. Examples are a lack of job/career alternatives and the amount of real and psychological investments a person has in a particular organization or community. Continuance commitment would be high if an individual has no job alternatives, is actively involved in his or her church, has many friends in the community, and needs medical benefits for a family of five. Finally, normative commitment is influenced by the socialization process discussed in Chapter 3 and what is termed the psychological contract. **Psychological contracts** represent an individual's perception about the terms and conditions of a reciprocal exchange between him- or herself and another party.[46] In a work environment, the psychological contract represents an employee's beliefs about what he or she is entitled to receive in return for what he or she provides to the organization.

Psychological contract

An individual's perception about the terms and conditions of a reciprocal exchange with another party.

Research and Practical Applications
Organizational commitment matters. A meta-analysis of 183 studies and almost 26,000 individuals uncovered a significant and strong positive relationship between organizational commitment and job satisfaction.[47] This finding encourages managers to increase job satisfaction in order to elicit higher levels of commitment. In turn, another meta-analysis involving 26,344 individuals revealed organizational commitment was significantly correlated with job performance.[48] This is an important finding because it implies managers can increase productivity by enhancing employees' organizational commitment.

Finally, a third meta-analysis summarizing results across 67 studies and 27,500 people uncovered a significant, negative relationship between organizational commitment and turnover.[49] This finding underscores the importance of paying attention to employees' organizational commitment because high commitment helps reduce the costs of employee turnover. In summary, managers are encouraged to focus on improving employees' organizational commitment.

Interestingly, companies use a variety of methods to increase employees' organizational commitment. Consider the different approaches used by Genentech and the Container Store. Genentech provides employees with a six-week paid sabbatical for every six years of service, and the Container Store pays employees 50% to 100% higher than the industry average. The Container Store also relies on a flexible schedule that allows parents to drop off and pick up their children at day care or school.[50] All told, people are more likely to be committed to their organizations when they believe that the organization truly cares about their welfare and well-being.

Managers can also increase the components of employee commitment through the following activities:

- Affective commitment is enhanced by hiring people whose personal values are consistent with the organization's values. A positive, satisfying work environment should also increase employees' desire to stay. Harley-Davidson is following this advice. "Employee surveys show 90% strongly identify with the company's riding culture. Some employees get to work at biker rallies at Harley's expense."[51]

- Continuance commitment is enhanced by offering employees a variety of progressive benefits and human resource programs. For instance, Aflac will pay up to $20,000 per year in tuition reimbursement for an employee's college-age children or grandchildren who maintain a GPA of 2.5 or higher. QuikTrip also has a policy of promoting from within, and it provides part-time employees with tuition reimbursement and health coverage.[52]

- Normative commitment can be increased by making sure that management follows up on its commitments and by trying to enhance the level of trust throughout the organization. We provide specific recommendation for building and maintaining trust in Chapter 11.

go to the Web for the Group Exercise: The Paper Airplane Contest

6 Job Involvement

Job involvement is defined as "the degree to which one is cognitively preoccupied with, engaged in, and concerned with one's present job."[53] This work attitude manifests itself through the extent to which people are immersed in their job tasks. Take Vinton Studios' animator/directors Sean Burns and Doug Aberle for example. (Vinton Studios trademarked an animation process known as Claymation.® The process has been used in television commercials involving the California Raisins and M&Ms and the television series *The PJs.*) Sean says, "This is a great place to work. We work on truly interesting and cutting-edge stuff. Plus I get to work on things that interest me. Each project is a new situation every time. We suggest interesting twists, new ideas."[54] Doug is involved in his work. "At the end of the day, you've never been so tired—or had so much fun! There's a lot of variety in working on a TV show. There's something different every day."[55] This suggests it is important for managers to understand the causes and consequences of job involvement because of its association with motivation and satisfaction. Let us now consider results from a meta-analytic study involving thousands of people, to learn more about job involvement.[56]

Job involvement was positively associated with job satisfaction, organizational commitment, and intrinsic motivation, and negatively related to intentions to quit. There are three key managerial implications associated with these results. First, managerial attempts to improve either of the two work attitudes discussed in this section are likely to positively affect the other work attitude. Second, managers can increase employees' job involvement by providing work environments that fuel intrinsic

Job involvement

Extent to which an individual is immersed in his or her present job.

Although this little Claymation character seems a bit skeptical, the artists at Vinton Studios exhibit high job involvement. They love working on creative projects that hold their interest and turn hard work into fun. Task variety also is a big plus. An added bonus: their uncooperative subjects can be tossed back into the clay bucket.

motivation. Specific recommendations for doing this are discussed in the section on intrinsic motivation in Chapter 9. Third, improving job involvement can reduce employee turnover.

Past results pertaining to the relationship between job involvement and performance are controversial. While the earlier meta-analysis failed to uncover a significant relationship between job involvement and performance, poor measures of job involvement used in past studies may have biased the results. A more recent study corrected this problem and found a positive relationship between job involvement and performance.[57] Managers thus are encouraged to increase employees' job involvement as a viable strategy for improving job performance.

Results from three recent studies shed additional insight about the importance of job involvement. First, job involvement was found to remain relatively stable over five years. This suggests that managers may want to include an assessment of an individual's job involvement during the hiring process.[58] Second, job involvement was negatively associated with an individual's psychological detachment from his or her work.[59] Individuals thus are more likely to stay productive and focused at work when they possess high job involvement. Finally, job involvement was significantly associated with absenteeism when employees were dissatisfied with their jobs.[60] This finding underscores the importance of the interrelationship among key work attitudes. Managers are encouraged to consider the interplay among organizational commitment, job involvement, and job satisfaction when trying to motivate and retain employees. Let us now turn our attention to job satisfaction, the work attitude that is most frequently investigated by OB researchers.

Job Satisfaction

Job satisfaction

An affective or emotional response to one's job.

Job satisfaction essentially reflects the extent to which an individual likes his or her job. Formally defined, **job satisfaction** is an affective or emotional response toward various facets of one's job. This definition implies job satisfaction is not a unitary concept. Rather, a person can be relatively satisfied with one aspect of his or her job and dissatisfied with one or more other aspects. For example, researchers at Cornell University developed the Job Descriptive Index (JDI) to assess one's satisfaction with the following job dimensions: work, pay, promotions, co-workers, and supervision.[61] Researchers at the University of Minnesota concluded there are 20 different dimensions underlying job satisfaction. Although researchers do not have consensus about the exact number of dimensions that constitute job satisfaction, they do agree that it has five predominant causes. It is important to understand these various causes because each one offers a different solution toward stopping the decline in job satisfaction uncovered in recent employee surveys.[62] We believe that knowledge about the causes of job satisfaction can assist managers in using a multifaceted approach toward increasing this key work attitude. Let us now examine the causes of job satisfaction.

7 The Causes of Job Satisfaction

Five predominant models of job satisfaction focus on different causes. They are need fulfillment, discrepancy, value attainment, equity, and dispositional/genetic components. A brief review of these models provides insight into the variety of methods that can be used to increase employees' job satisfaction.[63]

Need Fulfillment These models propose that satisfaction is determined by the extent to which the characteristics of a job allow an individual to fulfill his or her needs.

Trane's Commercial Systems Distribution Unit Uses Surveys to Assess Employees' Job Satisfaction

John Conover, president of Trane's Commercial Systems Distribution unit says the survey process his company used yields information about managers that they may not enjoy hearing. . . .

And once you get the feedback, he says, you have to move on it. "If associates give you the input and see you doing something about it, reacting to it, that's powerful; it will have a strong impact."

Dan Tyler, HR leader for Trane's Latin American Territory, was surprised at the relative ease with which many of the managerial shortcomings revealed on the Human Capital Capability Scorecard (HCCS) could be addressed. "It was low-hanging fruit; there were things we could do easily that will improve the scores next time. For example, in Santiago, Chile, within the Leadership Practices index, we scored low on communications; employees said there was too much isolation. The solution was easy; we instituted a newsletter to keep people informed."

Do you think employees will honestly answer a job satisfaction survey? Explain.

SOURCE: Excerpted from R J Grossman, "Measuring the Value of HR," *HR Magazine*, December 2006, p 47.

For example, a survey of 30 Massachusetts law firms revealed that 35 to 50% of law-firm associates left their employers within three years of starting because the firms did not accommodate family needs. This example illustrates that unmet needs can affect both satisfaction and turnover.[64] Organizations are aware of the premise associated with this model of satisfaction and have responded by providing creative benefits to help satisfy employees' needs. A recent survey of 975 employers, for example, revealed the percentage of companies that provided the following services on the premises to make employees' lives easier: ATM (41%), banking services (24%), dry cleaning/laundry service (21%), credit union (19%), travel services (18%), company store (16%), entertainment discounts and ticket purchase (15%), and mail services (14%).[65] Although need fulfillment models generated a great degree of controversy, it is generally accepted that need fulfillment is correlated with job satisfaction.[66]

Discrepancies These models propose that satisfaction is a result of met expectations. **Met expectations** represent the difference between what an individual expects to receive from a job, such as good pay and promotional opportunities, and what he or she actually receives. When expectations are greater than what is received, a person will be dissatisfied. In contrast, this model predicts that an individual will be satisfied when he or she attains outcomes above and beyond expectations. A meta-analysis of 31 studies that included 17,241 people demonstrated that met expectations were significantly related to job satisfaction.[67] Many companies use employee attitude or opinion surveys to assess employees' expectations and concerns (see the Real World/Real People feature above).

Met expectations
The extent to which one receives what he or she expects from a job.

Value Attainment The idea underlying **value attainment** is that satisfaction results from the perception that a job allows for fulfillment of an individual's important work values.[68] For example, a survey by Salary.com showed that 53% of the respondents valued time off more than a raise of $5,000. These results suggest that organizations should stop measuring productivity in the number of hours people work and that they should encourage employees to take their vacations and turn off the technology while at home.[69] In general, research consistently supports the prediction that value fulfillment is positively related to job satisfaction. Managers can thus enhance

Value attainment
The extent to which a job allows fulfillment of one's work values.

employee satisfaction by structuring the work environment and its associated rewards and recognition to reinforce employees' values.

Equity In this model, satisfaction is a function of how "fairly" an individual is treated at work. Satisfaction results from one's perception that work outcomes, relative to inputs, compare favorably with a significant other's outcomes/inputs. A meta-analysis involving 190 studies and 64,757 people supported this model. Employees' perceptions of being treated fairly at work were highly related to overall job satisfaction.[70] Managers thus are encouraged to monitor employees' fairness perceptions and to interact with employees in such a way that they feel equitably treated. Chapter 8 explores this promising model in more detail.

Dispositional/Genetic Components
Have you ever noticed that some of your co-workers or friends appear to be satisfied across a variety of job circumstances, whereas others always seem dissatisfied? This model of satisfaction attempts to explain this pattern.[71] Specifically, the dispositional/genetic model is based on the belief that job satisfaction is partly a function of both personal traits and genetic factors. As such, this model implies that stable individual differences are just as important in explaining job satisfaction as are characteristics of the work environment. Although only a few studies have tested these propositions, results support a positive, significant relationship between personal traits and job satisfaction over time periods ranging from 2 to 50 years.[72] Genetic factors also were found to significantly predict life satisfaction, well-being, and general job satisfaction.[73] Overall, researchers estimate that 30% of an individual's job satisfaction is associated with dispositional and genetic components.[74] Pete and Laura Wakeman, founders of Great Harvest Bread Company, have used this model of job satisfaction while running their company for more than 25 years.

These employees appear to be enjoying their jobs. Research suggests that they are more likely to enjoy their job based on genetic factors and personal traits.

Our hiring ads say clearly that we need people with "strong personal loves as important as their work." This is not a little thing. You can't have a great life unless you have a buffer of like-minded people all around you. If you want to be nice, you can't surround yourself with crabby people and expect it to work. You might stay nice for a while, just because—but it isn't sustainable over years. If you want a happy company, you can do it only by hiring naturally happy people. You'll never build a happy company by "making people happy"—you can't really "make" people any way that they aren't already. Laura and I want to be in love with life, and our business has been a good thing for us in that journey.[75]

Although Pete and Laura's hiring approach is consistent with the dispositional and genetic model of job satisfaction, it is important to note that hiring "like-minded" people can potentially lead to discriminatory decisions. Managers are advised not to discriminate on the basis of race, gender, religion, color, national origin, and age.

go to the Web for the Self-Exercise: How Satisfied Are You with Your Present Job?

8 Major Correlates and Consequences of Job Satisfaction

This area has significant managerial implications because thousands of studies have examined the relationship between job satisfaction and other organizational variables. Because it is impossible to examine them all, we will consider a subset of the more important variables from the standpoint of managerial relevance.

Table 6–1 summarizes the pattern of results. The relationship between job satisfaction and these other variables is either positive or negative. The strength of the relationship ranges from weak (very little relationship) to strong. Strong relationships imply that managers can significantly influence the variable of interest by increasing job satisfaction. Let us now consider eight key correlates of job satisfaction.

Motivation A recent meta-analysis of nine studies and 1,739 workers revealed a significant positive relationship between motivation and job satisfaction. Because satisfaction with supervision also was significantly correlated with motivation managers are advised to consider how their behavior affects employee satisfaction.[76] Managers can potentially enhance employees' motivation through various attempts to increase job satisfaction.

Job Involvement Job involvement represents the extent to which an individual is personally involved with his or her work role. A meta-analysis involving 27,925 individuals from 87 different studies demonstrated that job involvement was moderately related with job satisfaction.[77] Managers are thus encouraged to foster satisfying work environments in order to fuel employees' job involvement.

Table 6–1   *Correlates of Job Satisfaction*

VARIABLES RELATED WITH SATISFACTION	DIRECTION OF RELATIONSHIP	STRENGTH OF RELATIONSHIP
Motivation	Positive	Moderate
Job involvement	Positive	Moderate
Organizational commitment	Positive	Moderate
Organizational citizenship behavior	Positive	Moderate
Absenteeism	Negative	Weak
Tardiness	Negative	Weak
Withdrawal cognitions	Negative	Strong
Turnover	Negative	Moderate
Heart disease	Negative	Moderate
Perceived stress	Negative	Strong
Pro-union voting	Negative	Moderate
Job performance	Positive	Moderate
Life satisfaction	Positive	Moderate
Mental health	Positive	Moderate

Organizational Citizenship Behavior Organizational citizenship behaviors (OCBs) consist of employee behaviors that are beyond the call of duty. Examples include "such gestures as constructive statements about the department, expression of personal interest in the work of others, suggestions for improvement, training new people, respect for the spirit as well as the letter of housekeeping rules, care for organizational property, and punctuality and attendance well beyond standard or enforceable levels."[78] Managers certainly would like employees to exhibit these behaviors. A meta-analysis covering 7,031 people and 21 separate studies revealed a significant and moderately positive correlation between organizational citizenship behaviors and job satisfaction.[79] Moreover, additional research demonstrated that employees' citizenship behaviors were determined more by leadership and characteristics of the work environment than by an employee's personality.[80] It thus appears that managerial behavior significantly influences an employee's willingness to exhibit citizenship behaviors. This relationship is important to recognize because employees' OCBs were positively correlated with their conscientiousness at work, organizational commitment, performance ratings and promotions.[81] Another recent study demonstrated a broader impact of OCBs on organizational effectiveness. Results revealed that the amount of OCBs exhibited by employees working in 28 regional restaurants was significantly associated with each restaurant's corporate profits one year later.[82] Because employees' perceptions of being treated fairly at work are related to their willingness to engage in OCBs, managers are encouraged to make and implement employee-related decisions in an equitable fashion. More is said about this in Chapter 8.

Absenteeism Absenteeism is not always what it appears to be, and it can be costly. For example, a survey of 700 managers indicated that 20% of them called in sick because they simply did not feel like going to work that day. The top three reasons given for the bogus excuse of being sick were doing personal errands, catching up on sleep, and relaxing.[83] While it is difficult to provide a precise estimate of the cost of absenteeism, one study projected it to be $789 per employee.[84] This would suggest that absenteeism costs $236,700 for a company with 300 employees. Imagine the costs for a company with 100,000 employees! Because of these costs, managers are constantly on the lookout for ways to reduce it: Read the Real World/Real People feature on page 176 for a description of what McDonald's is doing. One recommendation has been to increase job satisfaction. If this is a valid recommendation, there should be a strong negative relationship (or negative correlation) between satisfaction and absenteeism. In other words, as satisfaction increases, absenteeism should decrease. A researcher tracked this prediction by synthesizing three separate meta-analyses containing a total of 74 studies. Results revealed a weak negative relationship between satisfaction and absenteeism.[85] It is unlikely, therefore, that managers will realize any significant decrease in absenteeism by increasing job satisfaction.

Withdrawal Cognitions Although some people quit their jobs impulsively or in a fit of anger, most go through a process of thinking about whether or not they should quit.[86] **Withdrawal cognitions** encapsulate this thought process by representing an individual's overall thoughts and feelings about quitting. What causes an individual to think about quitting his or her job? Job satisfaction is believed to be one of the most significant contributors. For example, a study of managers, salespersons, and auto mechanics from a national automotive retail store chain demonstrated that job dissatisfaction caused employees to begin the process of thinking about quitting. In turn, withdrawal cognitions had a greater impact on employee turnover than job satisfaction in this sample.[87] Results from this study imply that managers can indirectly help to reduce employee turnover by enhancing employee job satisfaction.

Turnover Recent statistics show that turnover is on the rise for managers, salespeople, manufacturing workers, and chief financial officers.[88] This is a problem because turnover disrupts organizational continuity and is very costly. Costs of turnover fall into two categories: separation costs and replacement costs.

> Separation costs may include severance pay, costs associated with an exit interview, outplacement fees, and possible litigation costs, particularly for involuntary separation. Replacement costs are the well-known costs of a hire, including sourcing expenses, HR processing costs for screening and assessing candidates, the time spent by hiring managers interviewing candidates, travel and relocation expenses, signing bonuses, if applicable, and orientation and training costs.[89]

Experts estimate that the cost of turnover for an hourly employee is roughly 30% of annual salary, whereas the cost can range up to 150% of yearly salary for professional employees.[90]

Although there are various things a manager can do to reduce employee turnover, many of them revolve around attempts to improve employees' job satisfaction.[91] This trend is supported by results from a meta-analysis of 67 studies covering 24,556 people. Job satisfaction obtained a moderate negative relationship with employee turnover.[92] Given the strength of this relationship, managers are advised to try to reduce employee turnover by increasing employee job satisfaction.

Perceived Stress Stress can have very negative effects on organizational behavior and an individual's health. Stress is positively related to absenteeism, turnover, coronary heart disease, and viral infections. Based on a meta-analysis of 32 studies covering 11,063 individuals, Table 6–1 reveals that perceived stress has a strong, negative relationship with job satisfaction.[93] It is hoped that managers would attempt to reduce the negative effects of stress by improving job satisfaction.

Job Performance One of the biggest controversies within OB research centers on the relationship between job satisfaction and job performance. Although researchers have identified eight different ways in which these variables are related, the dominant beliefs are either that satisfaction causes performance or performance causes satisfaction.[94] A team of researchers recently attempted to resolve this controversy through a meta-analysis of data from 312 samples involving 54,417 individuals.[95] There were two key findings from this study. First, job satisfaction and performance are moderately related. This is an important finding because it supports the belief that employee job satisfaction is a key work attitude managers should consider when attempting to increase employees' job performance. Second, the relationship between job satisfaction and performance is much more complex than originally thought. It is not as simple as satisfaction causing performance or performance causing satisfaction. Rather, researchers now believe both variables indirectly influence each other through a host of individual differences and work-environment characteristics.[96] There is one additional consideration to keep in mind regarding the relationship between job satisfaction and job performance.

Researchers believe the relationship between satisfaction and performance is understated due to incomplete measures of individual-level performance. For example, if performance ratings used in past research did not reflect the actual interactions and interdependencies at work, inaccurate measures of performance served to lower the

McDonald's Creative Approach for Reducing Absenteeism

To help reduce absenteeism and turnover—chronic problems for fast-food managers—McDonald's is testing an unusual program at some of its 1,250 British restaurants. Employees from the same immediate family can fill in for one another without clearing it with the boss, a new twist on job-sharing, according to Mercer Human Resources Consulting.

The so-called Family Contract is a response to surveys in which workers described juggling work and other duties as stressful. It permits family members—including same-sex partners—to sign on in pairs and take each other's shifts.

Do you see any problems with the approach being used by McDonald's? Discuss.

SOURCE: Excerpted from M Arndt, "The Family that Flips Together ..." *Business Week*, April 17, 2006, p 14.

reported correlations between satisfaction and performance. Examining the relationship between *aggregate* measures of job satisfaction and organizational performance is one solution to correct this problem. In support of these ideas, a team of researchers conducted a recent meta-analysis of 7,939 business units in 36 companies. Results uncovered significant positive relationships between business-unit-level employee satisfaction and business-unit outcomes of customer satisfaction, productivity, profit, employee turnover, and accidents.[97] It thus appears managers can positively affect a variety of important organizational outcomes, including performance, by increasing employee job satisfaction.

Summary of Key Concepts

1. *Distinguish between terminal and instrumental values, and describe three types of value conflict.* A terminal value is an enduring belief about a desired end-state (e.g., happiness). An instrumental value is an enduring belief about how one should behave. Three types of value conflict are intrapersonal, interpersonal, and individual–organization.

2. *Describe the values model of work/family conflict, and specify at least three practical lessons from work/family conflict research.* General life values determine one's values about family and work. Work/family conflict can occur when there is a lack of value similarity with family members. Likewise, work/family conflict can occur when one's own work values are not congruent with the company's values. When someone does not attain his or her values because of work/family conflicts, job or life satisfaction, or both, can suffer. Six practical lessons from work/family conflict research are (1) work/family balance begins at home, (2) an employer's family-supportive philosophy is more important than specific programs, (3) informal flexibility in work hours and in allowing people to work at home is essential to promoting work/ family balance, (4) mentors can help, (5) take a proactive approach to managing work/family conflict, and (6) self-employment has its rewards, but it is associated with higher work/family conflict and lower family satisfaction.

3. *Identify the three components of attitudes and discuss cognitive dissonance.* The three components of attitudes are affective, cognitive, and behavioral. The affective component represents the feelings or emotions one has about a given object or situation. The cognitive component reflects the beliefs or ideas one has about an object or situation. The behavioral component refers to how one intends or expects to act toward someone or something. Cognitive dissonance represents the psychological discomfort an individual experiences when his or her attitudes or beliefs are incompatible with his or her behavior. There are three main methods for reducing cognitive dissonance: change an attitude or behavior, belittle the importance of the inconsistent behavior, and find consonant elements that outweigh dissonant ones.

4. *Explain how attitudes affect behavior in terms of Ajzen's theory of planned behavior.* Intentions are the key link

between attitudes and behavior in Ajzen's model. Three determinants of the strength of an intention are one's attitude toward the behavior, subjective norm (social expectations and role models), and the perceived degree of one's control over the behavior. Intentions, in turn, are powerful determinants of behavior.

5. *Describe the model of organizational commitment.* Organizational commitment reflects how strongly a person identifies with an organization and is committed to its goals. Organizational commitment is composed of three related components: affective commitment, continuance commitment, and normative commitment. In turn, each of these components is influenced by a separate set of antecedents: An antecedent is something that causes the component of commitment to occur.

6. *Define the work attitudes of job involvement and job satisfaction.* Job involvement is the extent to which a person is preoccupied with, immersed in, and concerned with their job. Job satisfaction reflects how much people like or dislike their jobs.

7. *Identify and briefly describe five alternative causes of job satisfaction.* They are need fulfillment (the degree to which one's own needs are met), discrepancies (satisfaction depends on the extent to which one's expectations are met), value attainment (satisfaction depends on the degree to which one's work values are fulfilled), equity (perceived fairness of input/outcomes determines one's level of satisfaction), and dispositional/genetic (job satisfaction is dictated by one's personal traits and genetic makeup).

8. *Identify eight important correlates/consequences of job satisfaction, and summarize how each one relates to job satisfaction.* Eight major correlates/consequences of job satisfaction are motivation (moderate positive relationship), job involvement (moderate positive), organizational citizenship behavior (moderate positive), absenteeism (weak negative), withdrawal cognitions (strong negative), turnover (moderate negative), perceived stress (strong negative), and job performance (moderate positive).

Key Terms

Value system 154
Terminal values 154
Instrumental values 155
Value congruence or person-culture fit 156
Attitude 160
Affective component 161
Cognitive component 161
Behavioral component 161
Cognitive dissonance 161

Organizational commitment 166
Psychological contract 168
Job involvement 169
Job satisfaction 170
Met expectations 171
Value attainment 171
Organizational citizenship behaviors (OCBs) 174
Withdrawal cognitions 174

OB in Action Case Study

Domino's Is Trying to Reduce Employee Turnover[98]

When Rob Cecere became regional manager for eight Domino's Pizza stores in New Jersey four years ago, his boss gave him a mission: slow down turnover.

Store managers in the region were leaving every three to six months. Without a steady boss, workers there who answered phones, made pizzas and delivered orders had a turnover rate as high as 300% a year.

Turnover is a chronic and costly headache for fast-food businesses, which rely on an army of low-paid workers. A harsh boss, a mean colleague, or a boring day can cause workers who earn around the minimum wage—which is $5.15 an hour nationally but slightly higher in some states—to quit for similar pay elsewhere. Average turnover for most large and midsize companies is about 10% to 15%. But at fast-food chains, rates as high as 200% a year for hourly workers aren't unusual.

Some companies are tackling the problem with a higher starting wage. Starbucks Corp. says it pays hourly store workers more than minimum wage, although the rate varies in different markets. The company says its turnover rate for such workers is 80% to 90%. Starbucks says it also focuses on friendly workplaces and good managers, but higher wages make a difference. "If we did all these other things, but we paid minimum wages, I bet our turnover would be higher," says Dave Pace, Starbucks executive vice president for partner resources.

Domino's has a different view. The company is willing to try all sorts of tactics to retain hourly employees—except paying them significantly more. "If we had increased every body's pay 20%, could we have moved the needle a little bit to buy a little loyalty? Maybe, but that's not a long-term solution," says Domino's chief executive officer David A Brandon.

He says that while pay is a factor, "you can't overcome a bad culture by paying people a few bucks more." He believes the way to attack turnover is by focusing on store managers—hiring more selectively, coaching them on how to create better workplaces, and motivating them with the promise of stock options and promotions.

High turnover hurts the bottom line. It costs money to recruit, hire and train people, and undercuts service when inexperienced employees don't work as efficiently. It costs Domino's about $2,500 each time an hourly store worker leaves and about $20,000 each time a store manager quits, the company estimates.

Domino's turnover crusade started in 1999 when Mr Brandon was named CEO. His first day at Domino's he asked about the company's turnover rate. He was told it was 158%. "Honest to God, I almost fainted," he says.

After doing some math, he realized Domino's was recruiting, hiring and training 180,000 people a year at the time, including those at franchise stores.

Mr Brandon vowed to change things. He renamed the human resources department "People First."

Mr Brandon commissioned research that showed the most important factor in a store's success wasn't neighborhood demographics, packaging or marketing, but the quality of its store manager. "When that position is turning over at a high rate, the ripple effect of that is enormous," he says.

His strategy seems to be working. By last year, the company's overall turnover had declined to 107%.

Domino's has about 15,000 employees; another 135,000 work at its franchisees. Many are part-timers—students or workers with other jobs who need extra income and a flexible schedule.

Store managers oversee people in three entry positions: assistant managers (who earn about $8 to $10 an hour); those who answer phones (and earn an average of $6.15 an hour); and drivers, most of whom make minimum wage. Drivers, who provide their own cars and gas, also get tips and an 82-cent reimbursement for each trip they make.

All the employees make the food, including managers and drivers. . . .

Hoping to pick better managers, Domino's implemented a new test. Those seeking promotion to that job have to take a 30-minute online evaluation of their financial skills and management style. Do they understand terms such as "break even" and "cash flow"? How would they manage a poorly performing employee? Candidates then receive training on their weak points.

To help managers keep track of their best and worst performers, Domino's rolled out a new in-store computer system. The screens, which everyone in the store can see, constantly update statistics such as the average order size for each employee and how long it's taking to get a pizza out the door.

Better financial incentives helped, too. Mr Brandon introduced a program that grants stock options to about 15% of store managers, based on criteria such as sales growth and customer service. This is in addition to profit-linked bonuses that Domino's already had, which traditionally average about 30% of managers' compensation. Today store managers' base salaries start at about $32,000. . . .

Domino's also stresses to store managers that most of its franchise owners came up through the ranks. The company has about 7,603 stores worldwide, with about 10% company-owned. Franchisees must train their workers to meet the same food-making standards and use the same training materials.

When Mr Cecere was promoted to regional manager for eight Domino's stores in New Jersey in 2001, he says his boss told him: "Once you get some stability in the management ranks here, these stores will do much better."

Pep Talk

Mr Cecere, a 14-year Domino's veteran who started as a driver after high school and continued working at the company through college, knew improvements were needed. His stores were averaging $8,500 each in sales a week, about $3,000 less than the chain's current average. He gathered his managers together and gave a pep talk. "How do we get to $15,000? How do we get to $20,000? Where do you start from?" he recalls saying. "It's got to start with people. We've got to hire people and keep people."

Questions for Discussion

1. What are your thoughts about the different approaches taken by Starbucks and Domino's to reduce turnover? Given these strategies, which company will be more effective in the long term? Explain your rationale.

2. Why do you think a store manager has greater impact on employee turnover than neighborhood demographics, packaging, or marketing?

3. How would you describe David Brandon's affective, cognitive, and behavioral components of his attitude toward turnover? Be specific.

4. Use Ajzen's theory of planned behavior (Figure 6–2) to analyze how managers can reduce voluntary turnover. Be sure to explain what managers can do to affect each aspect of the theory.

5. Based on what you learned in this chapter, what advice would you give Mr Cecere to increase employees' organizational commitment and job satisfaction? Be specific.

What Is the Impact of the Old College Grind on Personal Values?[99]

BusinessWeek Does an MBA change a person's values? According to a new study, the answer is yes—and perhaps not for the better. The nonprofit Aspen Institute found that students enter B-school with relatively idealistic ambitions, such as creating quality products. By the time they graduate, these goals have taken a backseat to such priorities as boosting share prices.

Sound a lot like MBAs Jeffrey Skilling (Harvard, 1979) and Andrew Fastow (Northwestern, 1987) at Enron? Indeed. The study included 1,978 MBAs who graduated in 2001 from 13 leading B-schools. It asked what a company's priorities should be: 75% said maximizing shareholder value; 71% chose satisfying customers; 33% said producing high-quality goods and services. Only 5% thought environmentalism should be a top goal; just 25% said creating value for their communities.

But two years earlier, when the students started B-school, 68% cited shareholder value; 75%, customer satisfaction; and 43%, quality goods and services.

MBAs also said they would leave companies whose values they can't stomach rather than stay and try to change them. "The Enron fiasco is showing that there are going to be serious cases where an organization's values are disputed, or disregarded," says Jennifer Welsh, Oxford University lecturer and manager of the research project. "We want them to stick up for their values and try to resolve the conflict."

One sure way to get MBAs keen on ethics: Put a number on how much good values add to earnings. Priscilla Wisner, a professor at Thunderbird who links corporate responsibility to profitability, says until that happens, B-schools are unlikely to go beyond the stray ethics course. That means the philosophy MBAs live by is less likely to be "Doing well by doing good" than "Show me the money."

Are your values for sale?

1. Yes, show me the money! What are the broader implications of this approach?
2. No, I have been true to my values through college and will continue to be. Explain.
3. No, I think it's possible to be true to your values and still make a good living. Explain.
4. Maybe, it depends on the situation. Explain.
5. I'm not sure, because I'm not as idealistic as I was when I started college. Explain.
6. Invent other options. Discuss.

Web Resources

For study material and exercises that apply to this chapter, visit our Web site,

www.mhhe.com/kreitner

CHAPTER 7

Social Perception and Attributions

LEARNING OBJECTIVES

When you finish studying the material in this chapter, you should be able to:

1. Describe perception in terms of the information-processing model.

2. Identify and briefly explain seven managerial implications of social perception.

3. Discuss stereotypes and the process of stereotype formation.

4. Summarize the managerial challenges and recommendations of sex-role, age, racial and ethnic, and disability stereotypes.

5. Describe and contrast the Pygmalion effect, the Galatea effect, and the Golem effect.

6. Discuss how the self-fulfilling prophecy is created and how it can be used to improve individual and group productivity.

7. Explain, according to Kelley's model, how external and internal causal attributions are formulated.

8. Contrast the fundamental attribution bias and the self-serving bias.

Why do China and America have such difficulty communicating?

Sure, the two nations are half a world apart, geographically, historically, and politically. But the cause of their at times cacophonous discourse could lie in something less obvious: the strikingly different academic training of their political leaders.

The majority of American senators and congressmen were schooled as lawyers. But each of China's senior leaders—all nine members of the Politburo's Standing Committee—was trained as an engineer: President Hu in hydropower, Premier Wen Jiabao in geological structure, for instance. Perhaps the difficulties between China and the US lie less with dissimilar languages, cultures, and histories, and more with the divergent ways of thinking between lawyers and engineers.

This is no small difference. Engineers strive for "better," while lawyers prepare for the worst. Failing to appreciate the implications of these different approaches (and the relating styles they engender) can lead to missed signals.

Such miscommunication occurred when a US plane accidentally bombed the Chinese embassy in Belgrade,

Yugoslavia, in 1999. When the Chinese government bused students from college campuses across Beijing to the US Embassy to protest, American politicians assumed that Chinese leaders orchestrated the demonstrations to whip up nationalistic fervor. (To lawyers, the evidence was prima facie.) In truth, the Chinese leaders—the engineers—worried that if protesting students were allowed to march through the city, their ranks would swell with workers and ordinary citizens, creating an even larger, less manageable problem. So busing them contained, rather than exacerbated, the volatile situation.

Another dichotomy: More than 90% of Chinese, including professionals often critical of their government, saw the bombing as deliberate. But most Americans believed the bombing had been, as US

China's president Hu Jintao on a recent history-making visit to the United States.

officials claimed, an accident due to the use of "old maps."

Why such disparity? The Chinese have an idealized picture of the U.S. as so technologically advanced that it would have been impossible for it to make such a stupid mistake. Americans, on the other hand, are quite used to their government's stupid mistakes.

More worrisome, most Americans perceive China as an economic predator concerned solely about its own welfare. Beijing does not deny its policies benefit its own people, as any legitimate government's would.

But it asserts that in a global economy, China's stability and development are essential for world peace and prosperity. Disturb the former, it warns, and you disrupt the latter. Given that consequence, it's time the lawyers and engineers began communicating better.[1]

FOR DISCUSSION

Why do people from China and the United States have different perceptions of the same events? Explain.

How important is the perception process? As highlighted in the chapter-opening vignette, perception can be the source of communication distortion and conflict between people from different cultures. Our perceptions and feelings are influenced by information we receive from newspapers, magazines, television, radio, family, and friends. You see we all use information stored in our memories to interpret the world around us, and our interpretations, in turn, influence how we respond and interact with others. As human beings, we constantly strive to make sense of our surroundings. The resulting knowledge influences our behavior and helps us navigate our way through life. Think of the perceptual process that occurs when meeting someone for the first time. Your attention is drawn to the individual's physical appearance, mannerisms, actions, and reactions to what you say and do. You ultimately arrive at conclusions based on your perceptions of this social interaction. The brown-haired, green-eyed individual turns out to be friendly and fond of outdoor activities. You further conclude that you like this person and then ask him or her to go to a concert, calling the person by the name you stored in memory.

The reciprocal process of perception, interpretation, and behavioral response also applies at work. Consider the experience of Lisa Bromiley Meier after losing her job at Enron. She told a reporter from *BusinessWeek* that "she endured six-months of potential employers asking her the same question: 'So, were you corrupt or were you stupid?'"[2] Interviewers apparently assumed or perceived that Lisa was either a crook or stupid because she worked for Enron. They could not have been more wrong. Today Lisa is the CFO of Flotek Industries, Inc., a maker of chemicals and drilling tools for the oil industry.

The perception process influences much more than the impressions people make about each other. For example, companies use knowledge about perceptions when designing and marketing their products, and political candidates use it to get elected.[3] The Transportation Security Administration also uses research about perception to design training programs aimed at helping airport security screeners to detect threatening objects more accurately.[4] An error in the perception process in this context can lead to catastrophic consequences!

Moreover, inaccurate perceptions and stereotypes can influence whether or not you get hired, promoted, or fired. Perceptions also impact the grade you receive when giving an oral presentation in class, and whether or not some person wants to date or marry you. Finally, the Real World/Real People feature on page 183 shows how some realtors are using the perception process to mislead home buyers. The point we are trying to make is that the perception process influences a host of managerial activities, organizational processes, and quality-of-life issues. We have written

Real Estate Agents Make Old Listings Appear New

Real estate agent Ross Simone wasn't attracting any potential buyers for a house in Mechanicsville, Md., that had sat on the market for months, so last November he took action. He pulled the house out of the regional database of active listings and then immediately reinserted it, changing the property ID number used to track properties over time. The result: The house appeared to be hitting the market for the first time, "It's in the best interests of my client [the seller]," Simone said in a November interview. "I started doing it consistently this year. I do it as much as I can." . . .

Fresh listings attract attention and can fetch higher prices because buyers are less likely to make lowball offers. Real estate is largely self-regulated. In most of the US, agents are responsible for entering information about the homes they're selling into a database that is maintained by the local Multiple Listing Service. Each of the 900-plus MLSs sets its own rules. The trick of making old listings appear new is against the rules of Simone's MLS, although he said later that he didn't know it at the time.

Should Ross Simone be fined or penalized for his behavior? Explain.

SOURCE: P Coy, "Real Estate: New Listing! (Sort Of)," *BusinessWeek*, January 22, 2007, p 44.

---

this chapter with this conclusion in mind. You will gain a thorough understanding of how perception works and how you can use it to enhance your future personal and professional success.

Let us now begin our exploration of the perceptual process and its associated outcomes. In this chapter we focus on (1) an information-processing model of perception, (2) stereotypes, (3) the self-fulfilling prophecy, and (4) how causal attributions are used to interpret behavior.

An Information-Processing Model of Perception

Perception is a cognitive process that enables us to interpret and understand our surroundings. Recognition of objects is one of this process's major functions. For example, both people and animals recognize familiar objects in their environments. You would recognize a picture of your best friend; dogs and cats can recognize their food dishes or a favorite toy. Reading involves recognition of visual patterns representing letters in the alphabet. People must recognize objects to meaningfully interact with their environment.[5] But since OB's principal focus is on people, the following discussion emphasizes *social* perception rather than object perception.

The study of how people perceive one another has been labeled *social cognition* and *social information processing*. In contrast to the perception of objects,

> Social cognition is the study of how people make sense of other people and themselves. It focuses on how ordinary people think about people and how they think they think about people. . . .
>
> Research on social cognition also goes beyond naive psychology. The study of social cognition entails a fine-grained analysis of how people think about themselves and others, and it leans heavily on the theory and methods of cognitive psychology.[6]

Let us now examine the fundamental processes underlying perception.

Perception
Process of interpreting one's environment.

Figure 7–1   *Perception: An Information-Processing Model*

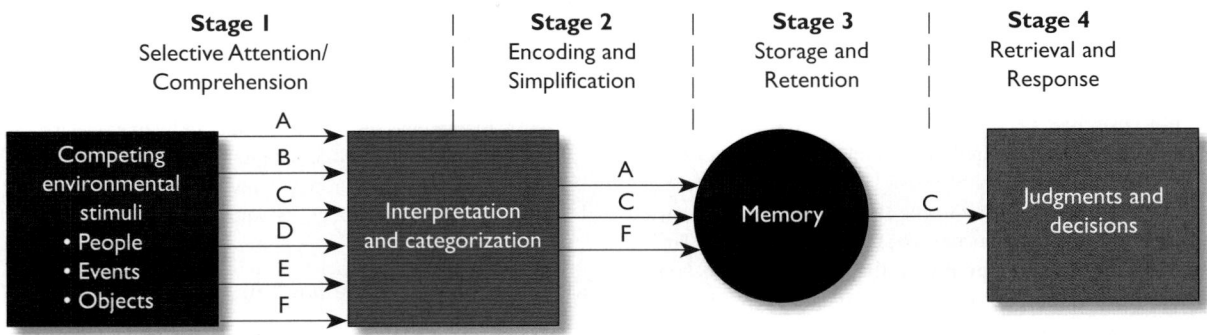

Four-Stage Sequence and a Working Example

Perception involves a four-stage information-processing sequence (hence, the label "information processing"). Figure 7–1 illustrates a basic information-processing model of perception. Three of the stages in this model—selective attention/comprehension, encoding and simplification, and storage and retention—describe how specific information and environmental stimuli are observed and stored in memory. The fourth and final stage, retrieval and response, involves turning mental representations into real-world judgments and decisions.

Keep the following everyday example in mind as we look at the four stages of perception. Suppose you were thinking of taking a course in, say, personal finance. Three professors teach the same course, using different types of instruction and testing procedures. Through personal experience, you have come to prefer good professors who rely on the case method of instruction and essay tests. According to the information-processing model of perception, you would likely arrive at a decision regarding which professor to take as follows:

Stage 1: Selective Attention/Comprehension

People are constantly bombarded by physical and social stimuli in the environment. Since they do not have the mental capacity to fully comprehend all this information, they selectively perceive subsets of environmental stimuli. This is where attention plays a role. **Attention** is the process of becoming consciously aware of something or someone. Attention can be focused on information either from the environment or from memory. Regarding the latter situation, if you sometimes find yourself thinking about totally unrelated events or people while reading a textbook, your memory is the focus of your attention. Research has shown that people tend to pay attention to salient stimuli.

Attention

Being consciously aware of something or someone.

Salient Stimuli Something is salient when it stands out from its context. For example, a 250-pound man would certainly be salient in a women's aerobics class but not at a meeting of the National Football League Players' Association. One's needs and goals often dictate which stimuli are salient. For a driver whose gas gauge is on empty, an Exxon or Mobil sign is more salient than a McDonald's or Burger King sign. The reverse would be true for a hungry driver with a full gas tank. Moreover, research shows that people have a tendency to pay more attention to negative than positive information. This leads to a negativity bias.[7] This bias helps explain the gawking factor that slows traffic to a crawl following a car accident.

Back to Our Example You begin your search for the "right" personal finance professor by asking friends who have taken classes from the three professors. You also may interview the various professors who teach the class to gather still more relevant information. Returning to Figure 7–1, all the information you obtain represents competing environmental stimuli labeled A through F. Because you are concerned about the method of instruction (e.g., line A in Figure 7–1), testing procedures (e.g., line C), and past grade distributions (e.g., line F), information in those areas is particularly salient to you. Figure 7–1 shows that these three salient pieces of information thus are perceived, and you then progress to the second stage of information processing. Meanwhile, competing stimuli represented by lines B, D, and E in Figure 7–1 fail to get your attention and are discarded from further consideration.

Stage 2: Encoding and Simplification

Observed information is not stored in memory in its original form. Encoding is required; raw information is interpreted or translated into mental representations. To accomplish this, perceivers assign pieces of information to **cognitive categories.** "By *category* we mean a number of objects that are considered equivalent. Categories are generally designated by names, e.g., *dog, animal*."[8] People, events, and objects are interpreted and evaluated by comparing their characteristics with information contained in schemata (or schema in singular form).

Cognitive categories
Mental depositories for storing information.

Schemata A **schema** represents a person's mental picture or summary of a particular event or type of stimulus. For example, what is your mental picture of the sequence of events that occur when you go out to dinner in a restaurant? Your memory probably is quite similar to the restaurant schema shown in Table 7–1.

Schema
Mental picture of an event or object.

Cognitive-category labels are needed to make schemata meaningful. For example, picture your image of a sports car. Does it contain a smaller vehicle with two doors? Is it red? If you answered yes, you would tend to classify all small, two-door, fire-engine-red vehicles as sports cars because this type of car possesses characteristics that are consistent with your "sports car schema."

Encoding Outcomes We use the encoding process to interpret and evaluate our environment. Interestingly, this process can result in differing interpretations and evaluations of the same person or event. Varying interpretations of what we observe occur due to four key reasons.

First, people possess different information in the schemata used for interpretation. For instance, a recent meta-analysis of 62 studies revealed women and men had different opinions about what type of behaviors constituted sexual harassment. Women defined a broader range of behaviors as harassing.[9] Second, our moods and emotions influence our focus of attention and evaluations of others.[10]

Is this consistent with your "sports car schema?" If it is, you'll likely classify all small, two-door, red vehicles as sports cars. Can you think of another example of a common schema in today's culture?

Table 7–1   *Restaurant Schema*

Schema: Restaurant.
Characters: Customers, hostess, waiter, chef, cashier.
Scene 1: Entering.
    Customer goes into restaurant.
    Customer finds a place to sit.
      He may find it himself.
      He may be seated by a hostess.
        He asks the hostess for a table.
        She gives him permission to go to the table.
Scene 2: Ordering.
    Customer receives a menu.
    Customer reads it.
    Customer decides what to order.
    Waiter takes the order.
      Waiter sees the customer.
      Waiter goes to the customer.
      Customer orders what he wants.
    Chef cooks the meal.
Scene 3: Eating.
    After some time the waiter brings the meal from the chef.
    Customer eats the meal.
Scene 4: Exiting.
    Customer asks the waiter for the check.
    Waiter gives the check to the customer.
    Customer leaves a tip.
      The size of the tip depends on the goodness of the service.
    Customer pays the cashier.
    Customer leaves the restaurant.

SOURCE: From D Rumelhart, *Introduction to Human Information Processing* (New York: John Wiley & Sons, Inc., 1977). Reprinted by permission of John Wiley & Sons, Inc.

Third, people tend to apply recently used cognitive categories during encoding. For example, you are more likely to interpret a neutral behavior exhibited by a professor as positive if you were recently thinking about positive categories and events.[11] Fourth, individual differences influence encoding. Pessimistic or depressed individuals, for instance, tend to interpret their surroundings more negatively than optimistic and happy people. The point is that we should not be surprised when people interpret and evaluate the same situation or event differently. Researchers are currently trying to identify the host of factors that influence the encoding process.

Back to Our Example Having collected relevant information about the three personal finance professors and their approaches, you compare this information with other details contained in schemata. This leads you to form an impression and evaluation of what it would be like to take a course from each professor. In turn, the relevant information contained on paths A, C, and F in Figure 7–1 are passed along to the third stage of information processing.

go to the Web for the Self-Exercise: Does a Schema Improve the Comprehension of Written Material?

Stage 3: Storage and Retention

This phase involves storage of information in long-term memory. Long-term memory is like an apartment complex consisting of separate units connected to one another. Although different people live in each apartment, they sometimes interact. In addition, large apartment complexes have different wings (such as A, B, and C). Long-term memory similarly consists of separate but related categories. Like the individual apartments inhabited by unique residents, the connected categories contain different types of information. Information also passes among these categories. Finally, long-term memory is made up of three compartments (or wings) containing categories of information about events, semantic materials, and people.[12]

Event Memory This compartment is composed of categories containing information about both specific and general events. These memories describe appropriate sequences of events in well-known situations, such as going to a restaurant (refer back to Table 7–1), going on a job interview, going to a food store, or going to a movie.

Semantic Memory Semantic memory refers to general knowledge about the world. In so doing, it functions as a mental dictionary of concepts. Each concept contains a definition (e.g., a good leader) and associated traits (outgoing), emotional states (happy), physical characteristics (tall), and behaviors (works hard). Just as there are schemata for general events, concepts in semantic memory are stored as schemata. Given our previous discussion of managing diversity in Chapter 2 and International OB in Chapter 4, it should come as no surprise that there are cultural differences in the type of information stored in semantic memory. This was illustrated in the chapter-opening vignette.

Person Memory Categories within this compartment contain information about a single individual (your supervisor) or groups of people (managers). The manner in which Yukihiro Yamazaki, chief Lexus GS technician for dynamic evaluation, does his job provides a good example of using all three compartments of long-term memory. Yamazaki's role is to evaluate the performance of a new car (see the Real World/Real People feature on page 188). His evaluation is based on comparing characteristics he observes about a new car against information stored in memory.

Back to Our Example As the time draws near for you to decide which personal finance professor to take, your schemata of them are stored in the three categories of long-term memory. These schemata are available for immediate comparison or retrieval.

Yukihiro Yamazaki Uses Information in Long-Term Memory to Evaluate a Vehicle's Performance

Yamazaki notes that he uses four senses to evaluate a car.

- **Sight:** I observe everything—the overall tone of the car, its shape and color, whether everything matches. I look for anything that may look unusual.
- **Sound:** I listen for any kind of out-of-place noise, such as a ticking, that might indicate the presence of a mechanical or assembly problem.

- **Smell:** I study the scent of the leather seats, air from the air conditioning, the exhaust gas—and try to detect any anomalies.
- **Touch:** I feel the interior and exterior of the car—the contour of the sheet metal, the action of the button and switches. When I'm driving, I use my entire body to feel the road and other vibrations.

SOURCE: Excerpted from A Taylor III, "Test Driver," *Fortune,* October 30, 2006, p 106.

Stage 4: Retrieval and Response

People retrieve information from memory when they make judgments and decisions. Our ultimate judgments and decisions are either based on the process of drawing on, interpreting, and integrating categorical information stored in long-term memory or on retrieving a summary judgment that was already made.

Concluding our example, it is registration day and you have to choose which professor to take for personal finance. After retrieving from memory your schemata-based impressions of the three professors, you select a good one who uses the case method and gives essay tests (line C in Figure 7–1). In contrast, you may choose your preferred professor by simply recalling the decision you made two weeks ago.

2 Managerial Implications

Social cognition is the window through which we all observe, interpret, and prepare our responses to people and events. A wide variety of managerial activities, organizational processes, and quality-of-life issues are thus affected by perception. Consider, for example, the following implications.

Hiring Interviewers make hiring decisions based on their impression of how an applicant fits the perceived requirements of a job. Unfortunately, many of these decisions are made on the basis of implicit cognition. **Implicit cognition** represents any thoughts or beliefs that are automatically activated from memory without our conscious awareness. The existence of implicit cognition leads people to make biased decisions without an understanding that it is occurring.[13] This tendency has been used as an explanation of alleged discriminatory behavior at Wal-Mart, FedEx, Johnson & Johnson, and Cargill. Experts recommend two solutions for reducing this problem.[14] First, managers can be trained to understand and reduce this type of hidden bias. For example, one study demonstrated that training improved interviewers' ability to obtain high-quality, job-related information and to stay focused on the interview task. Trained interviewers provide more balanced judgments about applicants than did nontrained

Implicit cognition
Any thought or belief that is automatically activated without conscious awareness.

interviewers.[15] Second, bias can be reduced by using structured as opposed to unstructured interviews, and by relying on evaluations from multiple interviewers rather than just one or two people.

Performance Appraisal Faulty schemata about what constitutes good versus poor performance can lead to inaccurate performance appraisals, which erode work motivation, commitment, and loyalty. For example, a study of 166 production employees indicated that they had greater trust in management when they perceived that the performance appraisal process provided accurate evaluations of their performance.[16] Therefore, it is important for managers to accurately identify the behavioral characteristics and results indicative of good performance at the beginning of a performance review cycle. These characteristics then can serve as the standards for evaluating employee performance. The importance of using objective rather than subjective measures of employee performance was highlighted in a meta-analysis involving 50 studies and 8,341 individuals. Results revealed that objective and subjective measures of employee performance were only moderately related. The researchers concluded that objective and subjective measures of performance are not interchangeable.[17] Managers are thus advised to use more objectively based measures of performance as much as possible because subjective indicators are prone to bias and inaccuracy. In those cases where the job does not possess objective measures of performance, however, managers should still use subjective evaluations. Furthermore, because memory for specific instances of employee performance deteriorates over time, managers need a mechanism for accurately recalling employee behavior.[18] Research reveals that individuals can be trained to be more accurate raters of performance.[19]

Leadership Research demonstrates that employees' evaluations of leader effectiveness are influenced strongly by their schemata of good and poor leaders. A leader will have a difficult time influencing employees when he or she exhibits behaviors contained in employees' schemata of poor leaders. A team of researchers investigated the behaviors contained in our schemata of good and poor leaders. Good leaders were perceived as exhibiting the following behaviors: (1) assigning specific tasks to group members, (2) telling others that they had done well, (3) setting specific goals for the group, (4) letting other group members make decisions, (5) trying to get the group to work as a team, and (6) maintaining definite standards of performance. In contrast, poor leaders were perceived to exhibit these behaviors: (1) telling others that they had performed poorly, (2) insisting on having their own way, (3) doing things without explaining themselves, (4) expressing worry over the group members' suggestions, (5) frequently changing plans, and (6) letting the details of the task become overwhelming.[20]

Communication Managers need to remember that social perception is a screening process that can distort communication, both coming and going. Messages are interpreted and categorized according to schemata developed through past experiences and influenced by one's age, gender, and ethnic, geographic, and cultural orientations. Consider how Wal-Mart's German employees perceived and responded to the company's newly translated code of ethics:

> To American eyes, a new ethics manual is standard stuff. But when Wal-Mart Stores, Inc., distributed its newly translated ethics code to German employees a few weeks ago, it created a furor. They read a caution against supervisor–employee romances as a puritanical ban on interoffice relationships, while a call to report improper behavior

was seen as an invitation to play the rat. "They have to communicate better," says Ul-rich Dalibor, an official at the ver.di service-workers union, which represents German employees of the Bentonville (Arkansas)-based retailer.[21]

Wal-Mart clearly underestimated the German employees' perceptions and response, which was based on local customs. Effective communicators try to tailor their messages to the receiver's perceptual schemata. This requires well-developed listening and observational skills in addition to cross-cultural sensitivity.

Workplace Aggression and Antisocial Behavior Research revealed that aggressive and antisocial behavior at work were based on employees' perceptions of the work environment. Employees behaved aggressively toward co-workers and displayed antisocial behaviors such as swearing, making fun of someone, and taking home organizational property without consent when they believed that they were treated unfairly.[22] It is very important for managers to treat employees fairly, remembering that perceptions of fairness are in the eye of the beholder. Chapter 8 discusses how this can be done in greater detail.

Physical and Psychological Well-Being The negativity bias can lead to both physical and psychological problems. Specifically, research shows that perceptions of fear, harm, and anxiety are associated with the onset of illnesses such as asthma and depression.[23] We should all attempt to avoid the tendency of giving negative thoughts too much attention. Try to let negative thoughts roll off yourself just like water off a duck.

Designing Web Pages Researchers have recently begun to explore what catches viewers' attention on Web pages by using sophisticated eye-tracking equipment. This research can help organizations to spend their money wisely when designing Web pages. Kara Pernice Coyne, director of a research project studying Web page design, praised the Web pages of JetBlue Airways and Sears while noting problems with the one used by Agree Systems.[24] One expert provided the following recommendations for designing an effective Web page.

- Individuals read Web pages in an F pattern. They're more inclined to read longer sentences at the top of a page and less as they scroll down. That makes the first two words of a sentence very important.

- Surfers connect well with images of people looking directly at them. It helps if the person in the photo is attractive, but not too good looking.

- Images in the middle of a page can present an obstacle course.

- People respond to pictures that provide useful information, not just decoration.[25]

# 3 Stereotypes: Perceptions about Groups of People

While it is often true that beauty is in the eye of the beholder, perception does result in some predictable outcomes. Managers aware of the perception process and its outcomes enjoy a competitive edge. The Walt Disney Company, for instance, takes full advantage of perceptual tendencies to influence customers' reactions to waiting in long lines at its theme parks:

In Orlando, at Disney-MGM Studios, visitors waiting to get into a Muppet attraction watch tapes of Kermit the Frog on TV monitors. At the Magic Kingdom, visitors to the Extra Terrestrial Alien Encounter attraction are entertained by a talking robot before the show. At some rides, the company uses simple toys, like blocks, to help parents keep small children busy and happy during the wait.[26]

This example illustrates how the focus of one's attention influences the perception of standing in long lines.

Likewise, managers can use knowledge of perceptual outcomes to help them interact more effectively with employees. For example, Table 7–2 describes five common perceptual errors. Since these perceptual errors often distort the evaluation of job applicants and of employee performance, managers need to guard against them. This section examines one of the most important and potentially harmful perceptual outcomes associated with person perception: stereotypes. After exploring the process of stereotype formation and maintenance, we discuss sex-role stereotypes, age stereotypes, race stereotypes, disability stereotypes, and the managerial challenge to avoid stereotypical biases.

Stereotype Formation and Maintenance

"A **stereotype** is an individual's set of beliefs about the characteristics or attributes of a group."[27] Stereotypes are not always negative. For example, the belief that engineers are good at math is certainly part of a stereotype. Stereotypes may or may not be accurate. Engineers may in fact be better at math than the general population. In general, stereotypic characteristics are used to differentiate a particular group of people from other groups.[28]

Stereotype
Beliefs about the characteristics of a group.

It is important to remember that stereotypes are a fundamental component of the perception process and we use them to help process the large amount of information that bombards us daily. As such, it is not immoral or bad to possess stereotypes. That said, however, inappropriate use of stereotypes can lead to poor decisions; can create barriers for women, older individuals, people of color, and people with disabilities; and can undermine loyalty and job satisfaction.

Stereotyping is a four-step process. It begins by categorizing people into groups according to various criteria, such as gender, age, race, and occupation. Next, we infer that all people within a particular category possess the same traits or characteristics (e.g., all women are nurturing, older people have more job-related accidents, all African-Americans are good athletes, all professors are absentminded). Then, we form expectations of others and interpret their behavior according to our stereotypes. Finally, stereotypes are maintained by (1) overestimating the frequency of stereotypic behaviors exhibited by others, (2) incorrectly explaining expected and unexpected behaviors, and (3) differentiating minority individuals from oneself.[29] It is hard to stop people from using stereotypes because these four steps are self-reinforcing. The good news, however, is that researchers have identified a few ways to break the chain of stereotyping.

Research shows that the use of stereotypes is influenced by the amount and type of information available to an individual and his or her motivation to accurately process information.[30] People are less apt to use stereotypes to judge others when they encounter salient information that is highly inconsistent with a stereotype. For instance, you are unlikely to assign stereotypic "professor" traits to a new professor you have this semester if he or she rides a Harley-Davidson, wears leather pants to class, and has a pierced nose. People also are less likely to rely on stereotypes when they are motivated

Table 7–2   *Commonly Found Perceptual Errors*

PERCEPTUAL ERROR	DESCRIPTION	EXAMPLE	RECOMMENDED SOLUTION
Halo	A rater forms an overall impression about an object and then uses that impression to bias ratings about the object.	Rating a professor high on the teaching dimensions of ability to motivate students, knowledge, and communication because we like him or her.	Remember that an employee's behavior tends to vary across different dimensions of performance. Keep a file or diary to record examples of positive and negative employee performance throughout the year.
Leniency	A personal characteristic that leads an individual to consistently evaluate other people or objects in an extremely positive fashion.	Rating a professor high on all dimensions of performance regardless of his or her actual performance. The rater that hates to say negative things about others.	It does not help employees when they are given positive feedback that is inaccurate. Try to be fair and realistic when evaluating others.
Central tendency	The tendency to avoid all extreme judgments and rate people and objects as average or neutral.	Rating a professor average on all dimensions of performance regardless of his or her actual performance.	It is normal to provide feedback that contains both positive and negative information. The use of a performance diary can help to remember examples of employee performance.
Recency effects	The tendency to remember recent information. If the recent information is negative, the person or object is evaluated negatively.	Although a professor has given good lectures for 12 to 15 weeks, he or she is evaluated negatively because lectures over the last 3 weeks were done poorly.	It is critical to accumulate examples of performance that span the entire rating period. Keep a file or diary to record examples of performance throughout the year.
Contrast effects	The tendency to evaluate people or objects by comparing them with characteristics of recently observed people or objects	Rating a good professor as average because you compared his or her performance with three of the best professors you have ever had in college. You are currently taking courses from the three excellent professors.	It is important to evaluate employees against a standard rather than your memory of the best or worst person in a particular job.

to avoid using them. That is, accurate information processing requires mental effort. Stereotyping is generally viewed as a less effortful strategy of information processing. Let us now take a look at different types of stereotypes and consider additional methods for reducing their biasing effects.

4 Sex-Role Stereotypes

A **sex-role stereotype** is the belief that differing traits and abilities make men and women particularly well suited to different roles. A recent survey of 61,647 people—50% female and 50% male—sheds light on the sex-role stereotypes held by adults within the United States. Results revealed that women were labeled as moody, gossipy, emotional, and catty. A similar set of negative stereotypes was not uncovered when it came to perceptions about men. When asked who would be more likely to lead effectively, males were preferred by a 2 to 1 margin by both men and women.[31] Researchers suggest that this pattern of results is related to gender-based expectations or stereotypes that people have about men and women.[32] The key question, however, is whether or not these stereotypes influence the hiring, evaluation, and promotion of people at work.

A meta-analysis of 19 studies comprising 1,842 individuals found no significant relationships between applicant gender and hiring recommendations.[33] A second meta-analysis of 24 experimental studies revealed that men and women received similar performance ratings for the same level of task performance. Stated differently, there was no pro-male bias. These experimental results were further supported in a field study of female and male professors.[34] Unfortunately, results pertaining to promotion decisions are not as promising. A field study of 682 employees in a multinational *Fortune* 500 company demonstrated that gender was significantly related to promotion potential ratings. Men received more favorable evaluations than women in spite of controlling for age, education, organizational tenure, salary grade, and type of job.[35] Another study of 448 upper-level managers showed that gender bias influenced the performance ratings and promotional opportunities for women, particularly when women worked in nontraditional jobs. The researchers conducting this study concluded that sex-role stereotypes partially explained these findings.[36]

Sex-role stereotype
Beliefs about appropriate roles for men and women.

Age Stereotypes

Age stereotypes reinforce age discrimination because of their negative orientation. For example, long-standing age stereotypes depict older workers as less satisfied, not as involved with their work, less motivated, not as committed, less productive than their younger co-workers, and more apt to be absent from work. Older employees are also perceived as being more accident prone. As with sex-role stereotypes, these age stereotypes are based more on fiction than fact.

OB researcher Susan Rhodes sought to determine whether age stereotypes were supported by data from 185 different studies. She discovered that as age increases so do employees' job satisfaction, job involvement, internal work motivation, and organizational commitment. Moreover, older workers were not more accident prone.[37] Results are not as clear-cut regarding job performance. A meta-analysis of 96 studies representing 38,983 people and a cross section of jobs revealed that age and job performance were unrelated.[38] Some OB researchers, however, believe that this finding does not reflect the true relationship between age and performance. They propose that the relationship between age and performance changes as people grow older.[39] This idea was tested on data obtained from 24,219 individuals. In support of this hypothesis, results revealed that age was positively related to performance for younger employees (25 to 30 years of age) and then plateaued: Older employees were not less productive. Age and experience also predicted performance better for more complex jobs than other jobs, and job experience had a stronger relationship with performance than age.[40] Another study examined memory, reasoning, spatial relations, and dual tasking for 1,000 doctors, ages 25 to 92, and 600 other adults. The researchers concluded "that a large proportion of older individuals scored as well or better on aptitude tests as those in the prime of life. We call these intellectually vigorous individuals 'optimal agers.' "[41]

Dr. Michael DeBakey, recognized as one of the greatest surgeons ever, disconfirms many age-related stereotypes. He is very satisfied, committed, and involved with his job despite being 96 years old. Given the choice, would you allow Dr. DeBakey to operate on you?

Dr Michael DeBakey is a good example. In 1939, he was one of the first physicians to find a relationship between smoking and cancer and is recognized as one of the greatest surgeons ever. He was interviewed by a reporter from *The Wall Street Journal* to determine his secrets of health: He was still working at the age of 96.

Entering the room, Dr DeBakey looked only slightly older than he did in photographs taken decades ago. . . . Whatever subject I broached, his response reflected a quality that aging experts say is common among the long lived: optimism. Avian flu doesn't worry him: "We're lucky now to pick up those threats early," he says. He sees democracy prevailing over terrorism. . . . But here is what Dr DeBakey sees as the real secret to his longevity: work. He rises at five each morning to write in his study for two hours before driving to the hospital at 7:30 AM, where he stays until 6 PM. He returns to his library after dinner for an additional two to three hours of reading or writing before going to bed after midnight. He sleeps only four to five hours a night, as he always has.[42]

What about turnover and absenteeism? A meta-analysis containing 45 samples and a total of 21,656 individuals revealed that age and turnover were negatively related.[43] That is, older employees quit less often than did younger employees. Similarly, another meta-analysis of 34 studies encompassing 7,772 workers indicated that age was inversely related to both voluntary (a day at the beach) and involuntary (sick day) absenteeism.[44] Contrary to stereotypes, older workers are ready and able to meet their job requirements. Moreover, results from the two meta-analyses suggest managers should focus more attention on the turnover and absenteeism among younger workers than among older workers.

Tiger Woods Experiences Racial Bias

"I became aware of my racial identity on my first day of school, on my first day of kindergarten. A group of sixth graders tied me to a tree, spray-painted the word 'nigger' on me, and threw rocks at me. That was my first day at school. And the teacher really didn't do much of anything. I used to live across the street from school and kind of down the way a little bit. The teacher said, 'Okay, just go home.' So I had to outrun all these kids going home, which I was able to do. It was certainly an eye-opening experience, you know, being five years old. We were the only minority family in all of Cypress, California.

"When my parents moved in, before I was born, they used to have these oranges come through the window all the time. And it could have not been racially initiated or it could have been. We don't know. But it was very interesting, though people don't necessarily know it, that I grew up in the 1980s and still had incidents. I had a racial incident even in the 1990s at my home course where I grew up, the Navy golf course. And right before the 1994 US Amateur, I was 18 years old, I was out practicing, just hitting pitch shots and some guy just yelled over the fence and used the N word numerous times at me. That's in 1994."

Despite his international acclaim and reputation, Tiger Woods has battled racial stereotypes into the mid-90s. What can be done to stop the spread of racism and racial stereotypes?

SOURCE: C Barkley, *Who's Afraid of a Large Black Man?* (New York: Penguin Press, 2005), p 7.

Racial and Ethnic Stereotypes

There are many different racial and ethnic stereotypes that exist. For instance, African-Americans have been viewed as athletic, aggressive, and angry; Asians as quiet, introverted, smarter, and more quantitatively oriented; Hispanics as family oriented and religious; and Arabs as angry.[45] Racial and ethnic stereotypes are particularly problematic because they are automatically triggered and lead to racial bias without our conscious awareness.[46] These stereotypes are often activated by looking at someone's facial features or skin color.[47]

Negative racial and ethnic stereotypes are still apparent in many aspects of life and in many organizations. Consider the experience of Eldrick (Tiger) Woods. Tiger was raised in two different cultures. His mother was from Thailand and his father was African-American. Since becoming a professional golfer in 1996, Tiger has won 76 tournaments and he has more career victories than any other active player on the PGA Tour. He also is the only golfer in history to hold the title for all four major tournaments at the same time.[48] Unfortunately, Tiger has experienced a host of racial stereotypes and biases (see the Real World/Real People feature above). Let us now consider the following evidence regarding racial and ethnic stereotypes in organizations.

A meta-analysis of interview decisions from 31 studies with total samples of 4,169 African-Americans and 6,307 whites revealed that whites received higher interviewer evaluations. Another study of 2,805 interviews uncovered a same-race bias for Hispanics and African-Americans but not for whites. That is, Hispanics and African-American interviewers evaluated applicants of their own race more favorably than applicants of other races. White interviewers did not exhibit any such bias.[49] Performance ratings were found to be unbiased in two studies that used large samples of 21,547 and 39,537 rater-ratee pairs of African-American and white employees, respectively, from throughout the United States. These findings revealed that African-American and white managers did not differentially evaluate their employees based on race.[50] Finally, a study of 153 police officers' promotion decisions by panel interviews indicated a same-race rating effect. That is, candidates received higher evaluations when they were racially similar to the interviewers.[51] Given the increasing number of people of color that will enter the workforce over the next 10 years (recall our discussion in Chapter 2), employers should focus on nurturing and developing women and people of color as well as increasing managers' sensitivities to invalid racial stereotypes.

Disability Stereotypes

People with disabilities not only face negative stereotypes that affect their employability, but they also can be stigmatized by the general population. These trends create a host of problems for people with disabilities. For example, people with disabilities are more likely to be unemployed—62% unemployed in 2006—and to make less money than those without disabilities. People with disabilities also were found to be two-and-a half times as likely to live in poverty as people without disabilities.[52] The problem is even more pronounced for people with serious mental illness. This group of people had a 90% unemployment rate in 2006.[53] The American with Disabilities Act (ADA) was created in 1990 in response to these statistics. As mentioned in Chapter 2, this act prohibits discrimination against qualified employees with physical or mental disabilities or chronic illness and requires "reasonable accommodation" of disabled employees.[54]

go to the Web for the Self-Exercise: How Do Diversity Assumptions Influence Team Member Interactions?

Managerial Challenges and Recommendations

The key managerial challenge is to reduce the extent to which stereotypes influence decision making and interpersonal processes throughout the organization. We recommend that an organization first needs to inform its workforce about the problem of stereotyping through employee education and training. Training also can be used to equip managers with the skills needed to handle situations associated with managing employees with disabilities. The next step entails engaging in a broad effort to reduce stereotypes throughout the organization. Social scientists believe that "quality" interpersonal contact among mixed groups is the best way to reduce stereotypes because it provides people with more accurate data about the characteristics of other groups of people. As such, organizations should create opportunities for diverse employees to meet and work together in cooperative groups of equal status.

Another recommendation is for managers to identify valid individual differences (discussed in Chapter 5) that differentiate between successful and unsuccessful performers. As previously discussed, for instance, research reveals experience is a better predictor of performance than age. Research also shows that managers can be trained to use these valid criteria when hiring applicants and evaluating employee performance.[55]

Removing promotional barriers for men and women, people of color, and persons with disabilities is another viable solution to alleviating the stereotyping problem. This can be accomplished by minimizing the differences in job experience across groups of people. Similar experience, coupled with the accurate evaluation of performance, helps managers to make decisions that are less influenced by stereotypes.

In conclusion, it is important to obtain top management's commitment and support to eliminate the organizational practices that support or reinforce stereotyping and discriminatory decisions. Research clearly demonstrates that top management support is essential to successful implementation of the types of organizational changes being recommended.

5 Self-Fulfilling Prophecy: The Pygmalion Effect

Historical roots of the self-fulfilling prophecy are found in Greek mythology. According to mythology, Pygmalion was a sculptor who hated women yet fell in love with an ivory statue he carved of a beautiful woman. He became so infatuated with the statue that he prayed to the goddess Aphrodite to bring her to life. The goddess heard his prayer, granted his wish, and Pygmalion's statue came to life. The essence of the **self-fulfilling prophecy,** or Pygmalion effect, is that someone's high expectations for another person result in high performance for that person. A related self-fulfilling prophecy effect is referred to as the Galatea effect. The **Galatea effect** occurs when an individual's high self-expectations for him- or herself lead to high performance. The key process underlying both the Pygmalion and Galatea effects is the idea that people's expectations or beliefs determine their behavior and performance, thus serving to make their expectations come true. In other words, we strive to validate our perceptions of reality, no matter how faulty they may be. Thus, the self-fulfilling prophecy is an important perceptual outcome we need to better understand.

Self-fulfilling prophecy
Someone's high expectations for another person result in high performance.

Galatea effect
An individual's high self-expectations lead to high performance.

THIS ISN'T ONE OF THOSE DUMPS I'VE HEARD ABOUT WHERE THE COOK SPITS ON THE FOOD OF OBNOXIOUS CUSTOMERS, IS IT?

BERT'S SELF-FULFILLING PROPHECY...

SOURCE: NON-SEQUITUR © Wiley Miller. Dist. by Universal Press Syndicate. Reprinted with permission. All rights reserved.

Research and an Explanatory Model

The self-fulfilling prophecy was first demonstrated in an academic environment. After giving a bogus test of academic potential to students from grades 1 to 6, researchers informed teachers that certain students had high potential for achievement. In reality, students were randomly assigned to the "high potential" and "control" (normal potential) groups. Results showed that children designated as having high potential obtained significantly greater increases in both IQ scores and reading ability than did the

Oprah Winfrey is a great example of the Galatea effect. Born in Kosciusko, Mississippi, where she lived on a farm and was raised by her grandmother, she has evolved into one of the 100 Most Influential People of the 20th Century by *Time* magazine.

control students.[56] The teachers of the supposedly high potential group got better results because their high expectations caused them to give harder assignments, more feedback, and more recognition of achievement. Students in the normal potential group did not excel because their teachers did not expect outstanding results.

Research similarly has shown that by raising instructors' and managers' expectations for individuals performing a wide variety of tasks, higher levels of achievement/productivity can be obtained. Results from a meta-analysis of 17 studies involving 2,874 people working in a variety of industries and occupations demonstrated the Pygmalion effect was quite strong.[57] This finding implies that higher levels of achievement and productivity can be obtained by raising managers' performance expectations of their employees. Further, the performance enhancing Pygmalion effect was stronger in the military, with men, and for people possessing low performance expectations. It is important to note, however, that no study has determined whether or not female leaders can produce the self-fulfilling prophecy among subordinate men. Given the number of women in managerial roles, future research is needed to determine if the Pygmalion effect works in this context.

Figure 7–2 presents a model that integrates the self-fulfilling prophecy, the Galatea effect, and self-efficacy, which was discussed in Chapter 5. The model shows that the self-fulfilling process begins with a manager's expectations for his or her direct reports. In turn, these expectations influence the type of leadership used by a leader (linkage 1). Positive expectations beget positive and supportive leadership, which subsequently leads employees to develop higher self-expectations (linkage 2). The positive Galatea effect created by these higher expectations then motivates employees to exert more effort (linkage 3), ultimately increasing performance (linkage 4) and supervisory expectations (linkage 5). Successful performance also improves an employee's self-efficacy, which then fuels additional self-expectations of success (linkage 6). Researchers coined the term *Golem effect* to represent the negative side of the performance enhancing process depicted in Figure 7–2. The **Golem effect** is a loss in performance resulting from low leader expectations.[58] Let us consider how it works.

Golem effect

Loss in performance due to low leader expectations.

Say that an employee makes a mistake such as losing notes during a meeting or exhibits poor performance on a task—turning in a report a day late. A manager then begins to wonder if this person has what it takes to be successful in the organization. This doubt leads the manager to watch this person more carefully. The employee of course notices this doubt and begins to sense a loss of trust. The suspect employee then responds in one of two ways. He or she may doubt his or her own judgment and competence. This in turn leads the individual to become more risk averse and to decrease the amount of ideas and suggestions for the manager's critical review. The manager notices this behavior and interprets it as an example of less initiative. Oppositely, the

Figure 7–2   *A Model of the Self-Fulfilling Prophecy*

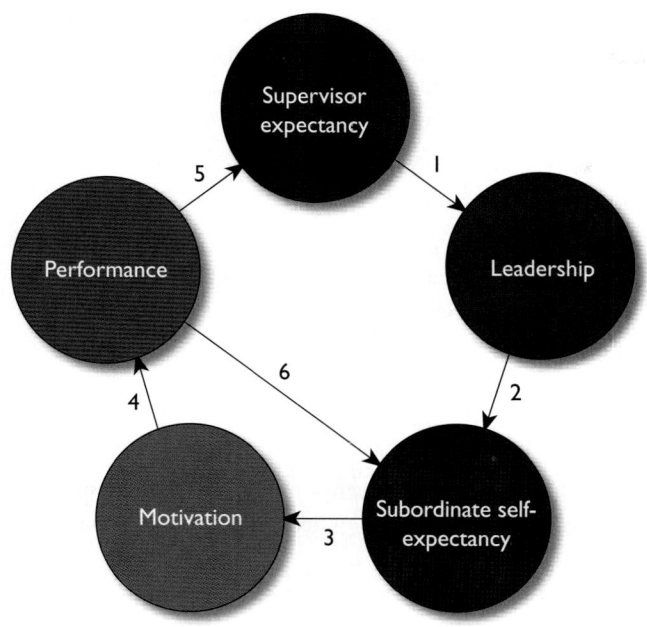

SOURCE: D Eden, "Self-Fulfilling Prophecy as a Management Tool: Harnessing Pygmalion," *Academy of Management Review,* January 1984, p 67. Reprinted by permission of The Academy of Management via The Copyright Clearance Center.

employee may take on more and more responsibility so that he or she can demonstrate his or her competence and worth. This is likely to cause the employee to screw up on something, which in turn reinforces the manager's suspicions. You can see that this process results in a destructive relationship that is fueled by negative expectations. The point to remember is that the self-fulfilling prophecy works in both directions. The next section discusses ideas for enhancing the Pygmalion effect and reducing the Golem effect.

Putting the Self-Fulfilling Prophecy to Work

Largely due to the Pygmalion effect, managerial expectations powerfully influence employee behavior and performance. Consequently, managers need to harness the Pygmalion effect by building a hierarchical framework that reinforces positive performance expectations throughout the organization.

Employees' self-expectations are the foundation of this framework.[59] In turn, positive self-expectations improve interpersonal expectations by encouraging people to work toward common goals. This cooperation enhances group-level productivity and promotes positive performance expectations within the work group. At Google, for example, employees routinely work long hours, especially when work groups are trying to meet deadlines for the launch of new products. Because Google is known for creating innovative products in a timely fashion, positive group-level expectations help create and reinforce an organizational culture of high expectancy for success.

This process then excites people about working for the organization, thereby reducing turnover.[60]

Because positive self-expectations are the foundation for creating an organization-wide Pygmalion effect, let us consider how managers can create positive performance expectations. This task may be accomplished by using various combinations of the following:

1. Recognize that everyone has the potential to increase his or her performance.
2. Instill confidence in your staff.
3. Set high performance goals.
4. Positively reinforce employees for a job well done.
5. Provide constructive feedback when necessary.
6. Communicate by using facial expressions, voice intonations, body language, and encouraging comments that reflect high expectations.
7. Provide employees with the input, information, and resources they need to achieve their goals.
8. Introduce new employees as if they have outstanding potential.
9. Become aware of your personal prejudices and nonverbal messages that may discourage others.
10. Encourage employees to visualize the successful execution of tasks.
11. Help employees master key skills and tasks.[61]

Causal Attributions

Causal attributions

Suspected or inferred causes of behavior.

Attribution theory is based on the premise that people attempt to infer causes for observed behavior. Rightly or wrongly, we constantly formulate cause-and-effect explanations for our own and others' behavior. Attributional statements such as the following are common: "Joe drinks too much because he has no willpower; but I need a couple of drinks after work because I'm under a lot of pressure." Formally defined, **causal attributions** are suspected or inferred causes of behavior. Even though our causal attributions tend to be self-serving and are often invalid, it is important to understand how people formulate attributions because they profoundly affect organizational behavior. For example, a supervisor who attributes an employee's poor performance to a lack of effort might reprimand that individual. However, training might be deemed necessary if the supervisor attributes the poor performance to a lack of ability.

Generally speaking, people formulate causal attributions by considering the events preceding an observed behavior. This section explores Harold Kelley's model of attribution, two important attributional tendencies, and related managerial implications.

Internal factors

Personal characteristics that cause behavior.

External factors

Environmental characteristics that cause behavior.

7 Kelley's Model of Attribution

Current models of attribution, such as Kelley's, are based on the pioneering work of the late Fritz Heider. Heider, the founder of attribution theory, proposed that behavior can be attributed either to **internal factors** within a person (such as ability and effort) or to **external factors** within the environment (such as task difficulty, help from others, and good/bad luck). This line of thought parallels the idea of an internal versus external locus of control, as discussed in Chapter 5. Building on Heider's work, Kelley attempted to pinpoint major antecedents of internal and external attributions. Kelley

Figure 7–3   *Performance Charts Showing Low and High Consensus, Distinctiveness, and Consistency Information*

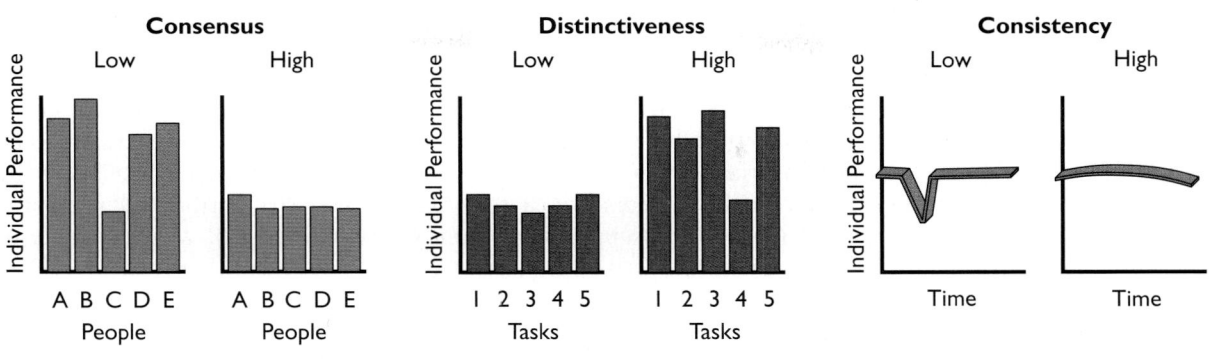

SOURCE: K A Brown, "Explaining Group Poor Performance: An Attributional Analysis," *Academy of Management Review*, January 1984, p 56. Reprinted by permission of The Academy of Management via The Copyright Clearance Center.

hypothesized that people make causal attributions after gathering information about three dimensions of behavior: consensus, distinctiveness, and consistency.[62] These dimensions vary independently, thus forming various combinations and leading to differing attributions.

Figure 7–3 presents performance charts showing low versus high consensus, distinctiveness, and consistency. These charts are now used to help develop a working knowledge of all three dimensions in Kelley's model.

- *Consensus* involves a comparison of an individual's behavior with that of his or her peers. There is high consensus when one acts like the rest of the group and low consensus when one acts differently. As shown in Figure 7–3, high consensus is indicated when persons A, B, C, D, and E obtain similar levels of individual performance. In contrast, person C's performance is low in consensus because it significantly varies from the performance of persons A, B, D, and E.

- *Distinctiveness* is determined by comparing a person's behavior on one task with his or her behavior on other tasks. High distinctiveness means the individual has performed the task in question in a significantly different manner than he or she has performed other tasks. Low distinctiveness means stable performance or quality from one task to another. Figure 7–3 reveals that the employee's performance on task 4 is highly distinctive because it significantly varies from his or her performance on tasks 1, 2, 3, and 5.

- *Consistency* is determined by judging if the individual's performance on a given task is consistent over time. High consistency implies that a person performs a certain task the same, time after time. Unstable performance of a given task over time would mean low consistency. The downward spike in performance depicted in the consistency graph of Figure 7–3 represents low consistency. In this case, the employee's performance on a given task varied over time.

It is important to remember that consensus relates to other *people,* distinctiveness relates to other *tasks,* and consistency relates to *time.* The question now is: How does information about these three dimensions of behavior lead to internal or external attributions?

Kelley hypothesized that people attribute behavior to *external* causes (environmental factors) when they perceive high consensus, high distinctiveness, and low consistency. *Internal* attributions (personal factors) tend to be made when observed behavior is characterized by low consensus, low distinctiveness, and high consistency. So, for example, when all employees are performing poorly (high consensus), when the poor performance occurs on only one of several tasks (high distinctiveness), and the poor performance occurs during only one time period (low consistency), a supervisor will probably attribute an employee's poor performance to an external source such as peer pressure or an overly difficult task. In contrast, performance will be attributed to an employee's personal characteristics (an internal attribution) when only the individual in question is performing poorly (low consensus), when the inferior performance is found across several tasks (low distinctiveness), and when the low performance has persisted over time (high consistency). Many studies have supported this predicted pattern of attributions in a work setting.[63] Most recently, the attribution process has been extended by marketing researchers to examine consumers' attributions about customer service, product characteristics, and advertising.[64]

go to the Web for the Group Exercise: Using Attribution Theory to Resolve Performance Problems

8 Attributional Tendencies

Fundamental attribution bias

Ignoring environmental factors that affect behavior.

Researchers have uncovered two attributional tendencies that distort one's interpretation of observed behavior—*fundamental attribution bias* and *self-serving bias.*

Fundamental Attribution Bias The **fundamental attribution bias** reflects one's tendency to attribute another person's behavior to his or her personal characteristics, as opposed to situational factors. This bias causes perceivers to ignore important environmental forces that often significantly affect behavior. For example, a study of 1,420 employees of a large utility company demonstrated that supervisors tended to make more internal attributions about worker accidents than did the workers. Interestingly, research also shows that people from Westernized cultures tend to exhibit the fundamental attribution bias more than individuals from East Asia.[65] A recent study of service encounters similarly showed that consumers attributed a poor service encounter to the service provider and not to situational factors.[66]

Kenneth Lay, the former CEO of Enron, entering the courthouse for his criminal fraud trial. He was ultimately found guilty and continually denied any involvement in a cover up of Enron's finances. Why do people exhibit the self-serving bias?

Self-Serving Bias The **self-serving bias** represents one's tendency to take more personal responsibility for success than for failure. The self-serving bias suggests employees will attribute their success to internal factors (high ability or hard work) and their failures to uncontrollable external factors (tough job, bad luck, unproductive co-workers, or an unsympathetic boss). Kenneth Lay, the former CEO of Enron, provides a good example of this bias based on his comments during his criminal fraud trial.

Self-serving bias

Taking more personal responsibility for success than failure.

> Lay told jurors there had been "a real conspiracy" against Enron. He asserted that one newspaper in particular, *The Wall Street Journal*, "was on a witch hunt" aimed at the company and its onetime chief financial officer, Andrew S Fastow. While also blaming Fastow, who has pled guilty to fraud and testified for the government, Lay zeroed in on articles the newspaper published in the fall of 2001 that he said "kicked off a run on the bank" that doomed the company. . . . He also lashed out at short sellers, investors who bet that the company's shares would fall.[67]

This example highlights how Lay blamed everyone beside himself for Enron's financial demise.

Much research has investigated the self-serving bias.[68] Two studies, for instance, examined whether or not senior executives fell prey to the self-serving bias when communicating with stockholders in their annual letter to shareholders. Results revealed executives in the United States and Singapore took credit for themselves when their companies did well and blamed negative outcomes on the environment.[69] Overall, however, research on the self-serving bias has produced inconsistent results. Two general patterns of attributions have been observed in past research. The first reveals that individuals make internal attributions for success as predicted by a self-serving bias. In contrast, people make both internal and external attributions for failure.[70] This means people do not automatically blame failure on external factors as originally expected from a self-serving bias. A team of researchers concluded, "When highly self-focused people feel that failure can be rapidly remedied, they will attribute failure to self; when the likelihood of improvement seems low, however, failure will be attributed externally."[71]

Managerial Application and Implications

Attribution models can be used to explain how managers handle poorly performing employees. One study revealed that managers gave employees more immediate, frequent, and negative feedback when they attributed their performance to low effort. This reaction was even more pronounced when the manager's success was dependent on an employee's performance. A second study indicated that managers tended to transfer employees whose poor performance was attributed to a lack of ability. These same managers also decided to take no immediate action when poor performance was attributed to external factors beyond an individual's control.[72]

The preceding discussion has several important implications for managers. First, men and women have different attributions regarding the causes of being promoted. Results from a recent survey of 140,000 people from 80 countries revealed that men and women had different attributions about what it takes to be promoted to a senior-level position. Men concluded that promotions were based on hard work whereas women reported that promotions were based more on luck and connections. These results, which were consistent across countries, suggest that women may not be as motivated to pursue senior-level positions as diligently as males because they view promotions as a chance event.[73] Managers can attack such beliefs by making sure to promote employees based on job-related criteria that are accurately measured.

Second, managers tend to disproportionately attribute behavior to *internal* causes.[74] This can result in inaccurate evaluations of performance, leading to reduced employee motivation. No one likes to be blamed because of factors they perceive to be beyond their control. Further, because managers' responses to employee performance vary according to their attributions, attributional biases may lead to inappropriate managerial actions, including promotions, transfers, layoffs, and so forth. This can dampen motivation and performance. Attributional training sessions for managers are in order. Basic attributional processes can be explained, and managers can be taught to detect and avoid attributional biases. Finally, an employee's attributions for his or her own performance have dramatic effects on subsequent motivation, performance, and personal attitudes such as self-esteem. For instance, people tend to give up, develop lower expectations for future success, and experience decreased self-esteem when they attribute failure to a lack of ability. Fortunately, attributional retraining can improve both motivation and performance. Research shows that employees can be taught to attribute their failures to a lack of effort rather than to a lack of ability.[75] This attributional realignment paves the way for improved motivation and performance. It also is important to remember the implications of the self-serving bias. If managers want employees to accept personal responsibility for failure and correspondingly modify their effort and behavior, it is essential for employees to believe that they can improve upon their performance in the future. Otherwise, employees are likely to attribute failure to external causes and they will not change their behavior.

Summary of Key Concepts

1. *Describe perception in terms of the information-processing model.* Perception is a mental and cognitive process that enables us to interpret and understand our surroundings. Social perception, also known as social cognition and social information processing, is a four-stage process. The four stages are selective attention/comprehension, encoding and simplification, storage and retention, and retrieval and response. During social cognition, salient stimuli are matched with schemata, assigned to cognitive categories, and stored in long-term memory for events, semantic materials, or people.

2. *Identify and briefly explain seven managerial implications of social perception.* Social perception affects hiring decisions, performance appraisals, leadership perceptions, communication processes, workplace aggression and antisocial behavior, physical and psychological well-being, and the design of Web pages. Inaccurate schemata or racist and sexist schemata may be used to evaluate job applicants. Similarly, faulty schemata about what constitutes good versus poor performance can lead to inaccurate performance appraisals. Invalid schemata need to be identified and replaced with appropriate schemata through coaching and training. Further, managers are advised to use objective rather than subjective measures of performance. With respect to leadership, a leader will have a difficult time influencing employees when he or she exhibits behaviors contained in employees' schemata of

poor leaders. Because people interpret oral and written communications by using schemata developed through past experiences, an individual's ability to influence others is affected by information contained in others' schemata regarding age, gender, ethnicity, appearance, speech, mannerisms, personality, and other personal characteristics. It is very important to treat employees fairly, as perceptions of unfairness are associated with aggressive and antisocial behavior. Try to let negative thoughts roll off yourself like water off a duck to avoid the physical and psychological effects of negative thoughts.

3. *Discuss stereotypes and the process of stereotype formation.* Stereotypes represent grossly oversimplified beliefs or expectations about groups of people. Stereotyping is a four-step process that begins by categorizing people into groups according to various criteria. Next, we infer that all people within a particular group possess the same traits or characteristics. Then, we form expectations of others and interpret their behavior according to our stereotypes. Finally, stereotypes are maintained by (a) overestimating the frequency of stereotypic behaviors exhibited by others, (b) incorrectly explaining expected and unexpected behaviors, and (c) differentiating minority individuals from oneself. The use of stereotypes is influenced by the amount and type of information available to an individual and his or her motivation to accurately process information.

4. *Summarize the managerial challenges and recommendations of sex-role, age, racial and ethnic, and disability stereotypes.* The key managerial challenge is to reduce the extent to which stereotypes influence decision making and interpersonal processes throughout the organization. Training can be used to educate employees about the problem of stereotyping and to equip managers with the skills needed to handle situations associated with managing employees with disabilities. Because mixed-group contact reduces stereotyping, organizations should create opportunities for diverse employees to meet and work together in cooperative groups of equal status. Hiring decisions should be based on valid individual differences, and managers can be trained to use valid criteria when evaluating employee performance. Minimizing differences in job opportunities and experiences across groups of people can help alleviate promotional barriers. It is critical to obtain top management's commitment and support to eliminate stereotyping and discriminatory decisions.

5. *Describe and contrast the Pygmalion effect, Galatea effect, and the Golem effect.* The Pygmalion effect, also known as the self-fulfilling prophecy, describes how someone's high expectations for another person result in high performance for that person. The Galatea effect occurs when an individual's high self-expectations lead to high self-

performance. The Golem effect is a loss of performance resulting from low leader expectations.

6. *Discuss how the self-fulfilling prophecy is created and how it can be used to improve individual and group productivity.* According to the self-fulfilling prophecy, high managerial expectations foster high employee self-expectations. These expectations in turn lead to greater effort and better performance and yet higher expectations.

7. *Explain, according to Kelley's model, how external and internal causal attributions are formulated.* Attribution theory attempts to describe how people infer causes for observed behavior. According to Kelley's model of causal attribution, external attributions tend to be made when consensus and distinctiveness are high and consistency is low. Internal (personal responsibility) attributions tend to be made when consensus and distinctiveness are low and consistency is high.

8. *Contrast the fundamental attribution bias and the self-serving bias.* Fundamental attribution bias involves emphasizing personal factors more than situational factors while formulating causal attributions for the behavior of others. Self-serving bias involves personalizing the causes of one's successes and externalizing the causes of one's failures.

Key Terms

OB in Action Case Study

Employees Use Cosmetic Surgery to Improve Their Image[76]

When the executive in the adjacent office returns from a two-week vacation minus any bags under his eyes or deep lines around his mouth, forget what he tells you about a certain Caribbean resort. Chances are, he has been under the knife.

Cosmetic surgery, botox and other de-aging skin treatments are becoming de rigueur for baby-boomer executives of both sexes who fear being judged as over the hill. For many, including some top CEOs who haven't yet gone public, plastic surgery is the next step in their rigorous fitness

and beauty regimens that include several hours a week at the gym, expensive personal trainers and diet consultants, and hair treatments. "I can't tell you the number of men I know who no longer are gray or who have covered bald spots with hair transplants," says Pat Cook, president of Cook & Co., a Bronxville, New York, executive-search firm.

In addition to vanity, these executives are driven by job insecurity. They believe that looking older in business now means looking vulnerable, not wise and experienced, as might have been the case in the past. So many 50-something managers have suffered layoffs and early retirement that survivors in this age bracket feel pressured to look and act as young as possible to hang onto their posts. And even 45-year-olds who are unemployed in today's tight market worry that wrinkles will cut them out of the running.

They ignore the financial expense (work on eyelids costs $3,000 to $6,000 and face-lifts, $15,000 to $25,000) and the medical risks (novelist Olivia Goldsmith died at the age of 54 during a chin-tuck operation).

A recent survey of senior executives by ExecuNet, a networking and job-search service, found that 82% consider age bias a "serious problem," up from 78% three years ago. And 94% of these respondents, who were mostly in their 40s and 50s, said they thought age had cost them a shot at a particular job.

"Ageism is unfortunate but it exists, and if you aren't looking good, you aren't a player, especially now when so many companies are run by younger executives," says Rick Miners, president of FlexCorp Systems, a New York business-process outsourcing company. "It isn't only women waiting for appointments with cosmetic surgeons, it's a lot of men, too, and not just senior executives but middle managers who want to stay competitive." . . .

It isn't something most executives want to discuss publicly, however. A 56-year-old public-relations manager at a New Jersey technology company, who had his lower eyelids done last April, says he was delighted when colleagues told him he looked more rested than they had ever seen him. But he didn't counter their belief that he had just returned from a cruise. "I didn't want to call attention to my age by saying I needed this to look younger," he says. But his new look has given him more confidence at work, prompting him to volunteer for new projects, he adds.

Even more executives are choosing less expensive and less invasive treatments, such as botox injections, which average several hundred dollars per session. Dr Diana Bihova, a New York dermatologist, *says 40% of her patients seeking botox and other cosmetic treatments, including chemical peels and collagen, are now men. . . .*

A major focus for both sexes is removing frown lines between the brows or on the forehead. One woman claimed that losing her worried look helped her land a new job.

Looking younger, however, isn't the most crucial way to counter ageism on the job. Managers who don't repeatedly rejuvenate their thinking—failing to stay informed about current events and popular culture—inevitably date themselves and limit their chances to advance.

Questions for Discussion

1. Would you go under the knife to enhance your career opportunities? Why or why not?

2. What negative stereotypes are fueling the use of cosmetic surgery to change one's appearance?

3. To what extent does the Pygmalion effect, Galatea effect, and Golem effect play a role in this case? Explain.

4. Based on this case and what you learned in this chapter, do the skills that come with age and experience count for less than appearance in today's organizations? Discuss your rationale.

Ethical Dilemma

Should Brain Scans Be Used to Craft Advertising?[77]

BusinessWeek IT MIGHT SOON BE time to redefine MRI machines as "market research imaging" devices. At Harvard's McLean Hospital not long ago, six male whiskey drinkers, ages 25 to 34, lined up to have their brains scanned for Arnold Worldwide. The Boston-based ad shop was using functional magnetic resonance imaging (fMRI) to gauge the emotional power of various images, including college kids drinking cocktails on spring break, twentysomethings with flasks around a campfire, and older guys at a swanky bar. The scans "help give us empirical evidence of the emotion of decision making," says Baysie Wightman, head of Arnold's new, science-focused Human Nature Dept. The results will help shape the 2007 ad campaign for client Brown-Forman, which owns Jack Daniels.

The idea of peeking into the brain for consumer insights isn't new. More than a dozen universities have been using fMRI to study how people respond to products (prompting Ralph Nader's Commercial Alert group to assert that "it's wrong to use a medical technology for marketing, not healing"). But now a few agencies like Arnold—whose clients also include McDonald's and Fidelity—and Digitas, another Boston-based shop, are offering fMRI research "Neuromarketing" consultants, like Los Angeles-based FKF Applied Research, are springing up, too, to link companies with hospitals seeking to lease time on their pricey MRI machines.

Should we allow companies to use brain scans to test advertising campaigns?

1. Absolutely not! Ralph Nader is right; it's wrong to use medical equipment for marketing.

2. Why not? People participate voluntarily in these studies and they get paid for the experience.

3. Ad campaigns are expensive, and it is good business sense to test their effectiveness with brain scans.

4. Using medical equipment in this way is a good way to share the costs of an expensive MRI. In the end, reducing the costs of medical equipment is good for society at large.

5. Invent other options.

Web Resources

For study material and exercises that apply to this chapter, visit our Web site, **www.mhhe.com/kreitner**

CHAPTER 8

Foundations of Motivation

When you finish studying the material in this chapter, you should be able to:

1   Contrast Maslow's, Alderfer's, and McClelland's need theories.

2   Explain the practical significance of Herzberg's distinction between motivators and hygiene factors.

3   Discuss the role of perceived inequity in employee motivation.

4   Explain the differences among distributive, procedural, and interactional justice.

5   Describe the practical lessons derived from equity theory.

6   Explain Vroom's expectancy theory, and review its practical implications.

7   Explain how goal setting motivates an individual, and review the four practical lessons from goal-setting research.

8   Review the mechanistic, motivational, biological, and perceptual-motor approaches to job design.

9   Specify issues that should be addressed before implementing a motivational program.

Student Resources for Studying Chapter 8

The Web site for your text includes resources that will help you master the concepts in this chapter. As you read, you'll want to visit the site for these helpful tools:

- Your online Study Guide includes learning objectives, a chapter summary, a glossary of key terms, and discussion questions.
- Take a practice quiz and test your knowledge!
- Scroll through a PowerPoint presentation with key concepts for this chapter.

Your instructor might also direct you to the Web site for these exercises:

- Self-assessments that correspond with the chapter content and a Group Exercise.
- You'll also find Video Cases and Internet Exercises for this chapter online.

www.mhhe.com/kreitner

A $2,600 bonus wasn't the only boost that Laurie Cunningham, a first-grade teacher, got from a new merit-pay plan at A.A. Nelson Elementary School in Lake Charles, La.

In addition to rewarding the 26-year-old teacher for improvements in student test scores, the school's compensation program also offered other important incentives: It matched Ms Cunningham with a more-experienced mentor and with a discussion group. As a result, she picked up classroom tips including a new word game, which she plays with students to help improve their vocabulary skills. "It gives you more specific information on what you should be doing," Ms Cunningham says of the program.

Teachers unions continue to oppose many merit-pay proposals, maintaining they expose members to arbitrary benchmarks set by school administrators. But many states and school districts are making headway in tying teacher pay to student achievement, ending the tradition of basing teachers' compensation almost entirely on seniority and academic degrees.

School districts in Florida and in Houston, Texas, have recently announced pay plans that closely link teacher pay and test scores. Denver, Colo., and districts in Minnesota have made test scores one of several criteria, along with performance assessments.

Merit-pay proponents have begun to defuse the opposition, by getting teachers involved in planning the systems and offering incentives and support that go beyond test scores. "I would say there is a lot of momentum," says Allan Odden, a professor of educational administration at the University of Wisconsin, Madison, and a supporter of merit pay. . . .

Yesterday, the Teaching Commission, a group that studies educator training and improvement, released a report saying governors in 20 states have proposed changes in how teachers are paid, including the use of

School systems are increasingly using merit-based pay systems to motivate teachers. Do you think this teacher would be more likely to improve her performance if her pay was tied to student achievement?

performance bonuses. The report says the increasing use of performance pay is a sign of progress. "We are seeing enough commitment to this idea that we have a chance to have it stick," says Louis Gerstner, the former International Business Machines Corp. chairman who formed the commission in 2003.

In Minnesota, school districts can become eligible for an extra $260-per-student in state aid if they sign up for the state's new "Q Comp" system, which requires districts to stop giving teachers automatic raises for seniority and instead base 60% of all pay increases on performance, as measured by test scores, classroom evaluations and other factors.

Districts hash out the details of their own pay plans, but they can't participate unless the teachers agree. So far, Minneapolis and eight other public school districts have signed up for the program, which was put in place last year; the state has received letters of intent from 134 others. Various plans offer bonuses ranging from as much as $600 per teacher for test-score gains to as much as

$3,000 a year for veteran teachers who agree to be mentors. . . .

Teacher-union opposition has doomed some performance pay measures. In 2002, Cincinnati teachers voted against accepting their district's merit-pay proposal amid concerns about the objectivity of the evaluation system driving it. In the late 1990s, similar concerns in the Colonial School District, outside Philadelphia, led some teachers to donate their $500 checks to charities rather than cash them. The district eventually dropped the program.

"Whether these plans work depends on whether the workforce buys into them," says Gayle Fallon, president of the Houston Federation of Teachers. "Nobody does passive-aggressive better than teachers."[1]

FOR DISCUSSION

What are the pros and cons of basing teachers' rewards on student achievement? Explain.

Effective employee motivation has long been one of management's most difficult and important duties. The opening vignette, for example, illustrates how challenging it is to apply motivational theories on teachers. Motivating teachers takes much more than simply linking pay to performance. As you will read in this chapter, an employee's motivation is a function of several components, including an individual's needs, the extent to which a work environment is positive and supportive, perceptions of being treated fairly, creating a strong relationship between performance and the receipt of valued rewards, the use of accurate measures of performance, and the setting of specific goals. As you study the various theories of motivation discussed in this chapter, keep in mind that each one offers different recommendations about how to motivate employees. We integrate these various recommendations in the final section of this chapter.

Motivation

Psychological processes that arouse and direct goal-directed behavior.

The term *motivation* derives from the Latin word *movere,* meaning "to move." In the present context, **motivation** represents "those psychological processes that cause the arousal, direction, and persistence of voluntary actions that are goal directed."[2] Researchers have proposed two general categories of motivation theories to explain the psychological processes underlying employee motivation: content theories and process theories. **Content theories of motivation** focus on identifying internal factors such as instincts, needs, satisfaction, and job characteristics that energize employee motivation. These theories do not explain how motivation is influenced by the dynamic interaction between an individual and the environment in which he or she works. This limitation led to the creation of process theories of motivation. **Process theories of motivation** focus on explaining the process by which internal factors and cognitions influence employee motivation.[3] Process theories are more dynamic than content theories.

Content theories of motivation

Identify internal factors influencing motivation.

Process theories of motivation

Identify the process by which internal factors and cognitions influence motivation.

The purpose of this chapter is to provide you with a foundation for understanding the complexities of employee motivation. After discussing the major content and process theories of motivation, this chapter provides an overview of job design methods used to motivate employees and concludes by focusing on practical recommendations for putting motivational theories to work.

Content Theories of Motivation

Most content theories of motivation revolve around the notion that an employee's needs influence motivation. **Needs** are physiological or psychological deficiencies that arouse behavior. They can be strong or weak and are influenced by environmental factors. Thus, human needs vary over time and place. The general idea behind need theories of motivation is that unmet needs motivate people to satisfy them. Conversely, people are not motivated to pursue a satisfied need. Let us now consider four popular content theories of motivation: Maslow's need hierarchy theory, Alderfer's ERG theory, McClelland's need theory, and Herzberg's motivator–hygiene model.

Needs

Physiological or psychological deficiencies that arouse behavior.

Maslow's Need Hierarchy Theory

In 1943, psychologist Abraham Maslow published his now-famous **need hierarchy theory** of motivation. Although the theory was based on his clinical observation of a few neurotic individuals, it has subsequently been used to explain the entire spectrum of human behavior. Maslow proposed that motivation is a function of five basic needs. These needs are

Need hierarchy theory

Five basic needs—physiological, safety, love, esteem, and self-actualization—influence behavior.

1. *Physiological.* Most basic need. Entails having enough food, air, and water to survive.
2. *Safety.* Consists of the need to be safe from physical and psychological harm.
3. *Love.* The desire to be loved and to love. Contains the needs for affection and belonging.
4. *Esteem.* Need for reputation, prestige, and recognition from others. Also contains need for self-confidence and strength.
5. *Self-actualization.* Desire for self-fulfillment—to become the best one is capable of becoming.

Maslow said these five needs are arranged in the prepotent hierarchy shown in Figure 8–1. In other words, he believed human needs generally emerge in a predictable stair-step fashion. Accordingly, when one's physiological needs are relatively satisfied, one's safety needs emerge, and so on up the need hierarchy, one step at a time. Once a need is satisfied it activates the next higher need in the hierarchy. This process continues until the need for self-actualization is activated.[4]

Figure 8–1   *Maslow's Need Hierarchy*

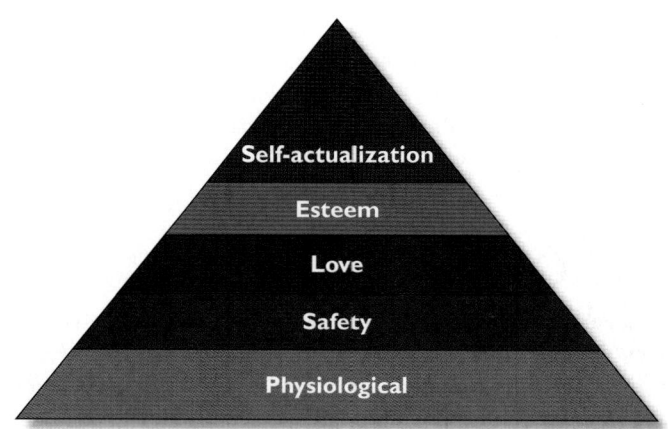

Table 8–1   *Employees' Needs and Desires Vary by Age*

	TOP FIVE NEEDS AND DESIRES
35 and younger	Compensation
	Other benefits
	Health care/medical benefits
	Job security
	Flexibility to balance work life issues
36 to 55	Compensation
	Health care/medical benefits
	Retirement benefits
	Other benefits
	Job security
56 and older	Feeling safe in the work environment
	Retirement benefits
	Other benefits
	Health care/medical benefits
	Meaningfulness of job

SOURCE: Data were reported in E Esen, *SHRM 2006 Job Satisfaction Survey Report* (Alexandria, VA: Society for Human Resource Management, 2006).

Although research does not clearly support this theory of motivation, two key managerial implications of Maslow's theory are worth noting. First, it is important for managers to focus on satisfying employee needs related to self concepts—self-esteem and self-actualization—because their satisfaction is significantly associated with a host of important outcomes such as academic achievement, physical illness, psychological well-being (e.g., anxiety disorders, depression), criminal convictions, drug abuse, marital satisfaction, money and work problems, and performance at work.[5]

Second, a satisfied need may lose its motivational potential. Therefore, managers are advised to motivate employees by devising programs or practices aimed at satisfying emerging or unmet needs. Many companies have responded to this recommendation by offering employees targeted benefits that meet their specific needs.[6] Results from a nationwide survey conducted by the Society for Human Resource Management can help in this pursuit. Findings revealed that employees' wants and desires varied by age. Table 8–1 summarizes the survey results by presenting the top five things employees are looking for from their jobs across three different age groups. Managers are encouraged to use customized surveys in order to assess the specific needs of their employees.[7]

Alderfer's ERG Theory

Clayton Alderfer developed an alternative theory of human needs in the late 1960s. Alderfer's theory differs from Maslow's in three major respects. First, a smaller set of core needs is used to explain behavior. From lowest to highest level they are *existence needs* (E)—the desire for physiological and materialistic well-being; *relatedness needs* (R)—the desire to have meaningful relationships with significant others; and growth needs (G)—the desire to grow as a human being and to use one's abilities to their fullest potential; hence, the label **ERG theory.** Second, ERG theory does not assume needs are related to each other in a stair-step hierarchy as does Maslow. Alderfer believes that more than one need may be activated at a time. Finally, ERG theory contains a frustration-regression component. That is, frustration of higher-order needs can influence the desire for lower-order needs.[8] For example, employees may demand higher pay or better benefits (existence needs) when they are frustrated or dissatisfied with the quality of their interpersonal relationships (relatedness needs) at work.

ERG theory
Three basic needs—existence, relatedness, and growth—influence behavior.

Research on ERG theory has provided mixed support for some of the theory's key propositions.[9] That said, however, there are two key managerial implications associated with ERG. The first revolves around the frustration-regression aspect of the theory. Managers should keep in mind that employees may be motivated to pursue lower-level needs because they are frustrated with a higher-order need. For instance, the solution for a stifling work environment may be a request for higher pay or better benefits. Second, ERG theory is consistent with the finding that individual and cultural differences influence our need states. People are motivated by different needs at different times in their lives. This implies that managers should customize their reward and recognition programs to meet employees' varying needs. Consider how Marc Albin, CEO of Albin Engineering Services, Inc., handles this recommendation.

> To identify which parts of individual employees' egos need scratching, Albin takes an unconventional approach. "My experience in managing people is, they're all different," says Albin. "Some people want to be recognized for their cheerful attitude and their ability to spread their cheerful attitude. Some want to be recognized for the quality of their work, some for the quantity of their work. Some like to be recognized individually; others want to be recognized in groups." Consequently, at the end of each employee-orientation session Albin e-mails his new hires and asks them how and in what form they prefer their strokes. "It helps me understand what they think of themselves and their abilities, and I make a mental note to pay special attention to them when they're working in that particular arena," he says. "No one has ever said, 'Just recognize me for anything I do well.'"[10]

McClelland's Need Theory

David McClelland, a well-known psychologist, has been studying the relationship between needs and behavior since the late 1940s. Although he is most recognized for his research on the need for achievement, he also investigated the needs for affiliation and power. Let us consider each of these needs.

The Need for Achievement
The **need for achievement** is defined by the following desires:

Need for achievement
Desire to accomplish something difficult.

> To accomplish something difficult. To master, manipulate, or organize physical objects, human beings, or ideas. To do this as rapidly and as independently as possible. To overcome obstacles and attain a high standard. To excel one's self. To rival and surpass others. To increase self-regard by the successful exercise of talent.[11]

Achievement-motivated people share three common characteristics: (1) a preference for working on tasks of moderate difficulty; (2) a preference for situations in which performance is due to their efforts rather than other factors, such as luck; and (3) they desire more feedback on their successes and failures than do low achievers.

Is the Need for Achievement Waning among Software Programming Students in the United States?

BEN MICKLE, MATT EDwards, and Kshipra Bhawalkar looked as though they had just emerged from a minor auto wreck. The members of Duke University's computer programming team had solved only one problem in the world finals of the ACM International Collegiate Programming Contest in San Antonio on Apr. 12. The winning team, from Saratov State University in Russia, solved six puzzles over the course of the grueling five-hour contest. Afterward, Duke coach Owen Astrachan tried to cheer up his team by pointing out that they were among "the best of the best" student programmers in the world. Edwards, 20, still distraught, couldn't resist a self-deprecating dig: "We're the worst of the best of the best."

Duke wasn't the only US school to be skunked at the prestigious computing contest. Of the home teams, only Massachusetts Institute of Technology ranked among the 12 highest finishers. Most top spots were seized by teams from Eastern Europe and Asia. Until the late 1990s, US teams dominated these contests. But the tide has turned. Last year not one was in the top dozen. . . .

It's not that foreign students are any smarter, say US university leaders. They just have relentless discipline. The team at Shanghai Jiao Tong University, which finished first last year and fifth this year, uses past participants to train each successive team. "We pile up experience year after year," says coach Yong Yu. The team practices year-round and puts in three hours a day during the months before the contest. US teams typically spend much less time preparing.

"Are We Hungry Enough?"

SOME TECH-INDUSTRY leaders are concerned that US students have become complacent. "There has to be a passion to be innovative," says Nicholas M Donofrio, executive vice-president for innovation and technology at IBM, which sponsors the ACM contest.

How would you increase the achievement motivation of programming students?

SOURCE: S Hamm, "A Red Flag in the Brain Game," *BusinessWeek*, May 1, 2006, pp 33–34.

Students competing in the ACM International Collegiate Programming Contest.

Interestingly, America's performance in an international contest of college-student programming suggests that US technical students' need for achievement may be waning (see the Real World/Real People feature above). Experts are concerned about this issue because programming and engineering are "the seed corn of the Information Economy."[12]

Need for affiliation

Desire to spend time in social relationships and activities.

Need for power

Desire to influence, coach, teach, or encourage others to achieve.

The Need for Affiliation People with a high **need for affiliation** prefer to spend more time maintaining social relationships, joining groups, and wanting to be loved. Individuals high in this need are not the most effective managers or leaders because they have a hard time making difficult decisions without worrying about being disliked.[13]

The Need for Power The **need for power** reflects an individual's desire to influence, coach, teach, or encourage others to achieve. People with a high need for power like to work and are concerned with discipline and self-respect. There is a positive and negative side to this need. The negative face of power is characterized by an "if I win, you lose" mentality. In contrast, people with a positive orientation to power focus on accomplishing group goals and helping employees obtain the feeling of competence. More is said about the two faces of power in Chapter 13. Because effective managers must positively influence others, McClelland proposes that top managers should have a high need for power coupled with a low need for affiliation. He also believes that individuals with high achievement motivation are *not* best suited for top management positions. Several studies support these propositions.[14]

Managerial Implications Given that adults can be trained to increase their achievement motivation,[15] organizations should consider the benefits of providing achievement training for employees. Moreover, achievement, affiliation, and power needs can be considered during the selection process, for better placement. For example, a study revealed that individuals' need for achievement affected their preference to work in different companies. People with a high need for achievement were more attracted to companies that had a pay-for-performance environment than were those with a low achievement motivation.[16] Finally, managers should create challenging task assignments or goals because the need for achievement is positively correlated with goal commitment and job involvement.[17] Moreover, challenging goals should be accompanied with a more autonomous work environment and employee empowerment to capitalize on the characteristics of high achievers.

 Herzberg's Motivator–Hygiene Theory

Frederick Herzberg's theory is based on a landmark study in which he interviewed 203 accountants and engineers.[18] These interviews sought to determine the factors responsible for job satisfaction and dissatisfaction. Herzberg found separate and distinct clusters of factors associated with job satisfaction and dissatisfaction. Job satisfaction

Motivators
Job characteristics associated with job satisfaction.

was more frequently associated with achievement, recognition, characteristics of the work, responsibility, and advancement. These factors were all related to outcomes associated with the *content* of the task being performed. Herzberg labeled these factors **motivators** because each was associated with strong effort and good performance. He hypothesized that motivators cause a person to move from a state of no satisfaction to satisfaction (see Figure 8–2). Therefore, Herzberg's theory predicts managers can motivate individuals by incorporating "motivators" into an individual's job.

Jesse Kiefer, a gumologist, is a good example of someone who is energized by the motivators contained in his job. Here is what he said to a reporter from *Fortune* about his job.

Jesse Kiefer (right) finds many rewards in his job as gumologist for Cadbury Schweppes, maker of Trident gum.

> Some days I don't blow any bubbles. Other days I have to blow a lot. It depends on what stage we are in the project. A piece of gum weighs just one to seven grams, but it's packed with a lot of different technology. It has to deliver a burst of flavor, a lot of sweetness, and a lot of tartness if it's a fruit gum. Our team figures out how to combine all those. For example, Trident Splash Strawberry

Figure 8–2   *Herzberg's Motivator–Hygiene Model*

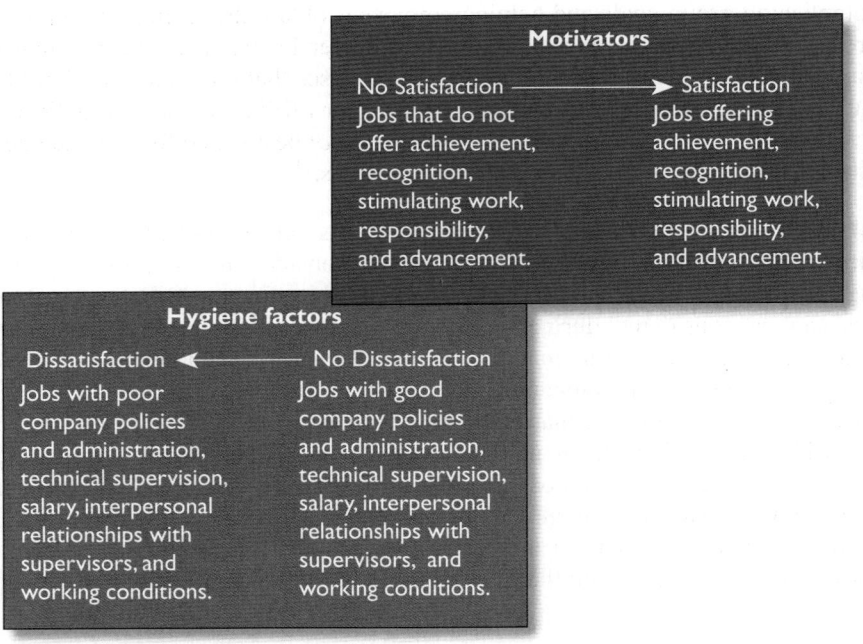

SOURCE: Adapted in part from D A Whitsett and E K Winslow, "An Analysis of Studies Critical of the Motivator–Hygiene Theory," *Personnel Psychology*, Winter 1967, pp 391–415.

with Lime—it's not easy to pick lime and strawberry flavors that complement each other. . . . When we work on the gum in its raw form, sometimes we use a hatchet to chop it up. I did my graduate work as a chemical engineer, and I started out working on detergent and soaps. But with gum there's just so many flavors! I find the job very stimulating.[19]

Herzberg found job *dissatisfaction* to be associated primarily with factors in the work *context* or environment. Specifically, company policy and administration, technical supervision, salary, interpersonal relations with one's supervisor, and working conditions were most frequently mentioned by employees expressing job dissatisfaction. Herzberg labeled this second cluster of factors **hygiene factors.** He further proposed that they were not motivational. At best, according to Herzberg's interpretation, an individual will experience no job dissatisfaction when he or she has no grievances about hygiene factors (refer to Figure 8–2). In contrast, employees like Katrina Gill are likely to quit when poor hygiene factors lead to job dissatisfaction.

Hygiene factors

Job characteristics associated with job dissatisfaction.

Katrina Gill, a 36-year-old certified nursing aide, worked in one of the premiere long-term care facilities near Portland, Oregon. From 10:30 PM to 7 AM, she was on duty alone, performing three rounds on the dementia ward, where she took care of up to 28 patients a night for $9.32 an hour. She monitored vitals, turned for bedsores, and changed adult diapers. There were the constant vigils over patients like the one who would sneak into other rooms, mistaking female patients for his deceased wife. Worse was the resident she called "the hitter" who once lunged at her, ripping a muscle in her back and laying her flat for four days. Last month, Gill quit and took another job for 68¢ an hour more, bringing her salary to $14,400 a year.[20]

The key to adequately understanding Herzberg's motivator–hygiene theory is recognizing that he believes that satisfaction is not the opposite of dissatisfaction. Herzberg concludes that "the opposite of job satisfaction is not job dissatisfaction, but rather no job satisfaction; and similarly, the opposite of job dissatisfaction is not job satisfaction, but no dissatisfaction."[21] Herzberg thus asserts that the dissatisfaction–satisfaction continuum contains a zero midpoint at which dissatisfaction and satisfaction are absent. Conceivably, an organization member who has good supervision, pay, and working conditions but a tedious and unchallenging task with little chance of advancement would be at the zero midpoint. That person would have no dissatisfaction (because of good hygiene factors) and no satisfaction (because of a lack of motivators).

Herzberg's theory has generated a great deal of research and controversy.[22] Research does not support the two-factor aspect of his theory nor the proposition that hygiene factors are unrelated to job satisfaction. On the positive side, however, Herzberg correctly concluded that people are motivated when their needs for achievement, recognition, stimulating work, and advancement are satisfied.[23] As you will learn in a later section of this chapter, Herzberg's theory has important implications for how managers can motivate employees through job design.

Process Theories of Motivation

Earlier in the chapter we discussed the difference between content theories of motivation, which focus on the impact of internal factors on motivation, and process theories. Process theories go one step further in explaining motivation by identifying the process by which various internal factors influence motivation. These models also are cognitive in nature. That is, they are based on the premise that motivation is a function of employees' perceptions, thoughts, and beliefs. We now explore the three most common process theories of motivation: equity theory, expectancy theory, and goal-setting theory.

Adams's Equity Theory of Motivation

Defined generally, **equity theory** is a model of motivation that explains how people strive for fairness and justice in social exchanges or give-and-take relationships. As a process theory of motivation, equity theory explains how an individual's motivation to behave in a certain way is fueled by feelings of inequity or a lack of justice. For example, Terry Garnett, currently chairman and CEO of Ingres Corporation, is powerfully motivated to seek revenge against Larry Ellison, CEO of Oracle, due to feelings of injustice (see the Real World/Real People feature on page 218). Psychologist J Stacy Adams pioneered application of the equity principle to the workplace. Central to understanding Adams's equity theory of motivation is an awareness of key components of the individual–organization exchange relationship. This relationship is pivotal in the formation of employees' perceptions of equity and inequity.

Equity theory
Holds that motivation is a function of fairness in social exchanges.

The Individual–Organization Exchange Relationship

Adams points out that two primary components are involved in the employee–employer exchange, *inputs* and *outcomes*. An employee's inputs, for which he or she expects a just return, include education/training, skills, creativity, seniority, age, personality traits, effort expended, and personal appearance. On the outcome side of

Terry Garnett Seeks Revenge against Larry Ellison

A former Oracle Corp. senior vice-president, Garnett spent the early 1990s traveling around the world with Ellison, Oracle's CEO. They hobnobbed with the likes of media moguls David Geffen and Barry Diller as the company tried to become a player in the interactive-TV business. Garnett and the software billionaire were so tight that Ellison even invited him and his wife to go along on a vacation to Kyoto in 1994. . . .

But what came next led to the bad blood that Garnett still tastes more than 12 years later. Within weeks of their return from Japan, Ellison summoned Garnett to this office. He scrapped the interactive-TV startup the two were planning and, Garnett claims, fired him without giving a clear reason. "It was pretty clinical," he recalls. "I tried to keep composed."

Feeling numb, Garnett returned to his office, not more than 30 feet away, and packed up. Afterward, he spent weeks trying to understand why he had been fired. Garnett later sued Ellison, accusing him of unfairly firing him, but then he dropped the claims. (Oracle officials declined to comment, but their reply to Garnett's suit cites his "declining productivity.") Brimming with anger, Garnett made a vow to himself: "There will be a day of reckoning."

What are your thoughts about Mr Garnett's feelings?

SOURCE: Excerpted from J McGregor, "Sweet Revenge," *BusinessWeek*, January 22, 2007, pp 65–66.

---

the exchange, the organization provides such things as pay/bonuses, fringe benefits, challenging assignments, job security, promotions, status symbols, and participation in important decisions.

Negative and Positive Inequity

On the job, feelings of inequity revolve around a person's evaluation of whether he or she receives adequate rewards to compensate for his or her contributive inputs. People perform these evaluations by comparing the perceived fairness of their employment exchange to that of relevant others. This comparative process, which is based on an equity norm, was found to generalize across countries.[24] People tend to compare themselves to other individuals with whom they have close interpersonal ties—such as friends—or to similar others—such as people performing the same job or individuals of the same gender or educational level—rather than dissimilar others. For example, do you consider the average CEO in the US a relevant comparison person to yourself? If not, then you should not feel inequity because the average CEO's pay rose 9% in 2006 whereas the average worker's pay decreased an estimated 0.3%. The average CEO earns about 300 times what the average worker is paid.[25]

Three different equity relationships are illustrated in Figure 8–3: equity, negative inequity, and positive inequity. Assume the two people in each of the equity relationships in Figure 8–3 have equivalent backgrounds (equal education, seniority, and so forth) and perform identical tasks. Only their hourly pay rates differ. Equity exists for an individual when his or her ratio of perceived outcomes to inputs is equal to the ratio of outcomes to inputs for a relevant co-worker (part A in Figure 8–3). Because equity is based on comparing *ratios* of outcomes to inputs, inequity will not necessarily be perceived just because someone else receives greater rewards. If the other person's additional outcomes are due to his or her greater inputs, a sense of equity may still exist. However, if the comparison person enjoys greater outcomes for similar inputs,

Figure 8–3   *Negative and Positive Inequity*

A. An Equitable Situation

B. Negative Inequity

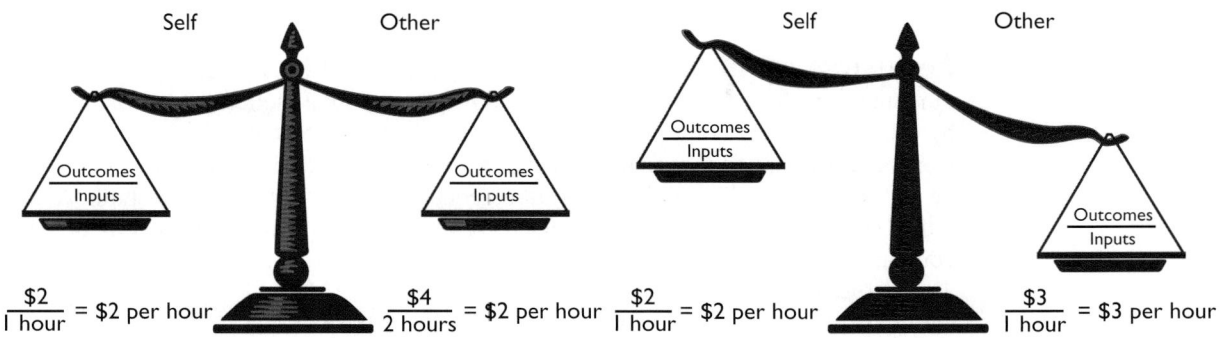

C. Positive Inequity

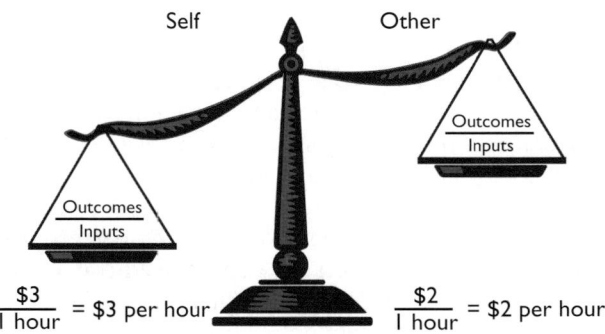

negative inequity will be perceived (part B in Figure 8–3). On the other hand, a person will experience **positive inequity** when his or her outcome to input ratio is greater than that of a relevant co-worker (part C in Figure 8–3).

Dynamics of Perceived Inequity

Managers can derive practical benefits from Adams's equity theory by recognizing that (1) people have varying sensitivities to perceived equity and inequity and (2) inequity can be reduced in a variety of ways.

Thresholds of Equity and Inequity

Have you ever noticed that some people become very upset over the slightest inequity whereas others are not bothered at all? Research has shown that people respond differently to the same level of inequity due to an individual difference called equity sensitivity. **Equity sensitivity** reflects an individual's "different preferences for, tolerances for, and reactions to the level of equity associated with any given situation."[26] Equity sensitivity spans a continuum ranging from benevolents to sensitives to entitled.

Benevolents are people who have a higher tolerance for negative inequity. They are altruistic in the sense that they prefer their outcome/input ratio to be lower than

Negative inequity

Comparison in which another person receives greater outcomes for similar inputs.

Positive inequity

Comparison in which another person receives lesser outcomes for similar inputs.

Equity sensitivity

An individual's tolerance for negative and positive equity.

ratios from comparison others. In contrast, equity *sensitives* are described as individuals who adhere to a strict norm of reciprocity and are quickly motivated to resolve both negative and positive inequity. Finally, *entitleds* have no tolerance for negative inequity. They actually expect to obtain greater output/input ratios than comparison others and become upset when this is not the case.[27]

Reducing Inequity Equity ratios can be changed by attempting to alter one's outcomes or adjusting one's inputs. For example, negative inequity might be resolved by asking for a raise or a promotion (i.e., raising outputs) or by reducing inputs (i.e., working fewer hours or exerting less effort). It also is important to note that equity can be restored by altering one's equity ratios behaviorally or cognitively, or both. A cognitive strategy entails psychologically distorting perceptions of one's own or one's comparison person's outcomes and inputs (e.g., conclude that comparison other has more experience or works harder).

 4 Expanding the Concept of Equity: Organizational Justice

Beginning in the late 1970s, researchers began to expand the role of equity theory in explaining employee attitudes and behavior. This led to a domain of research called *organizational justice.* Organizational justice reflects the extent to which people perceive that they are treated fairly at work. This, in turn, led to the identification of three different components of organizational justice: distributive, procedural, and interactional.[28] **Distributive justice** reflects the perceived fairness of how resources and rewards are distributed or allocated. **Procedural justice** is defined as the perceived fairness of the process and procedures used to make allocation decisions. Research shows that positive perceptions of distributive and procedural justice are enhanced by giving employees a "voice" in decisions that affect them. Voice represents the extent to which employees who are affected by a decision can present relevant information about the decision to others. Voice is analogous to asking employees for their input into the decision-making process.

The last justice component, **interactional justice**, relates to the "quality of the interpersonal treatment people receive when procedures are implemented."[29] This form of justice does not pertain to the outcomes or procedures associated with decision making, but rather it focuses on whether or not people feel they are treated fairly when decisions are implemented. Fair interpersonal treatment necessitates that managers communicate truthfully and treat people with courtesy and respect. Consider the role of interactional justice in how a manager of information-management systems responded to being laid off by a New Jersey chemical company. The man gained access to the company's computer systems from home by using another executive's password and deleted critical inventory and personnel files. The sabotage ultimately caused $20 million in damage and postponed a public stock offering that had been in the works. Why would a former employee do something like this?

> An anonymous note that he wrote to the company president sheds light on his motive. "I have been loyal to the company in good and bad times for over 30 years," he wrote. "I was expecting a member of top management to come down from his ivory tower to face us with the layoff announcement, rather than sending the kitchen supervisor with guards to escort us off the premises like criminals. You will pay for your senseless behavior."[30]

Distributive justice

The perceived fairness of how resources and rewards are distributed.

Procedural justice

The perceived fairness of the process and procedures used to make allocation decisions.

Interactional justice

Extent to which people feel fairly treated when procedures are implemented.

This employee's direct retaliation against the company was caused by the insensitive manner—interactional justice—in which employees were notified about the layoffs.

Many studies of organizational justice have been conducted over the last two decades. Fortunately, three meta-analyses of more than 200 studies help summarize what has been learned from this research.[31] The following trends were uncovered: (1) job performance was positively associated with both distributive and procedural justice, but procedural justice was the best predictor of this outcome, (2) all three forms of justice were positively correlated with job satisfaction, organizational commitment, organizational citizenship behaviors, and employees' trust, and negatively with employees' withdrawal cognitions and turnover, (3) distributive and procedural injustice were negatively related to negative emotions such as anger, and all three forms of justice were negatively associated with aggressive behavior at work.[32] These results suggest a host of practical lessons for managers.

5 Practical Lessons from Equity Theory

Equity theory has at least nine important practical implications. First, equity theory provides managers with yet another explanation of how beliefs and attitudes affect job performance. According to this line of thinking, the best way to manage job behavior is to adequately understand underlying cognitive processes. Indeed, we are motivated powerfully to correct the situation when our ideas of fairness and justice are offended.

Second, research on equity theory emphasizes the need for managers to pay attention to employees' perceptions of what is fair and equitable. No matter how fair management thinks the organization's policies, procedures, and reward system are, each employee's *perception* of the equity of those factors is what counts. For example, a recent nationwide study of 3,000 US workers revealed that 39% felt underpaid and only 37% reported feeling valued by their employer.[33] Managers thus are encouraged to make hiring decisions on merit-based, job-related information, and to make more attempts at providing positive recognition about employee behavior and performance. Moreover, because justice perceptions are influenced by the extent to which managers explain their decisions, managers are encouraged to explain the rationale behind their decisions.

Third, managers benefit by allowing employees to participate in making decisions about important work outcomes. In general, employees' perceptions of procedural justice are enhanced when they have a voice in the decision-making process.[34] For example, employees were more satisfied with their performance appraisals and resultant outcomes when they had a voice during the appraisal review.[35] Fourth, employees should be given the opportunity to appeal decisions that affect their welfare. Being able to appeal a decision fosters perceptions of distributive and procedural justice. In turn, perceptions of distributive and procedural justice promote job performance, job satisfaction, organizational commitment, and organizational citizenship behavior, and help reduce counterproductive work behavior, psychological distress, insomnia, absenteeism, and turnover.[36]

Fifth, employees are more likely to accept and support organizational change when they believe it is implemented fairly and when it produces equitable outcomes.

Sixth, managers can promote cooperation and teamwork among group members by treating them equitably. Research reveals that people are just as concerned with fairness in group settings as they are with their own personal interests.[37] Seventh, treating employees inequitably can lead to litigation and costly court settlements. Employees denied justice at work are more likely to turn to arbitration and the courts.

Whole Foods Market has over 190 stores in North America and the United Kingdom. The company's CEO, John Mackey (fourth from the left), has implemented a pay program that encourages equity among employees. What do you think about his decision to cut his pay?

Eighth, employees' perceptions of justice are strongly influenced by the leadership behavior exhibited by their managers (leadership is discussed in Chapter 16).[38] It thus is important for managers to consider the justice-related implications of their decisions, actions, and public communications. For example, John Mackey, CEO of Whole Foods Market, wrote a memo to all employees about the company's attempt to implement an equitable compensation system. He decided to create a salary cap that limits the pay of top executives at 19 times the average full-time employee salary and to grant 7% of all stock options to the top 16 executives. The other 93% are distributed to the remaining employees. He also reduced his salary to $1 and asked the board of directors to donate all of his future stock options to the company's charitable foundations.[39]

Finally, managers need to pay attention to the organization's climate for justice. For example, an organization's climate for justice was found to significantly influence employees' organizational commitment and job satisfaction.[40] Researchers also believe a climate of justice can significantly influence the type of customer service provided by employees. In turn, this level of service is likely to influence customers' perceptions of "fair service" and their subsequent loyalty and satisfaction.[41]

Managers can attempt to follow these practical implications by monitoring equity and justice perceptions through informal conversations, interviews, or attitude surveys. Researchers have developed and validated a host of surveys that can be used for this purpose.

go to the Web for the Self-Exercise: Measuring Perceived Fair Interpersonal Treatment

6 Vroom's Expectancy Theory

Expectancy theory

Holds that people are motivated to behaven in ways that produce valued outcomes.

Expectancy theory holds that people are motivated to behave in ways that produce desired combinations of expected outcomes. Generally, expectancy theory can be used to predict motivation and behavior in any situation in which a choice between two or more alternatives must be made. For instance, it can be used to predict whether to quit or stay at a job; whether to exert substantial or minimal effort at a task; and whether to major in management, finance, marketing, psychology, or communication.

Victor Vroom formulated a mathematical model of expectancy in his 1964 book *Work and Motivation*.[42] Vroom's theory has been summarized as follows:

The strength of a tendency to act in a certain way depends on the strength of an expectancy that the act will be followed by a given consequence (or outcome) and on the value or attractiveness of that consequence (or outcome) to the actor.[43]

Motivation, according to Vroom, boils down to the decision of how much effort to exert in a specific task situation. This choice is based on a two-stage sequence of expectations (effort→performance and performance→outcome). First, motivation is affected by an individual's expectation that a certain level of effort will produce the intended performance goal. For example, if you do not believe increasing the amount of time you spend studying will significantly raise your grade on an exam, you probably will not study any harder than usual. Motivation also is influenced by the employee's perceived chances of getting various outcomes as a result of accomplishing his or her performance goal. Finally, individuals are motivated to the extent that they value the outcomes received.

Vroom used a mathematical equation to integrate the above concepts into a predictive model of motivational force or strength. For our purposes however, it is sufficient to define and explain the three key concepts within Vroom's model—*expectancy, instrumentality*, and *valence.*

Expectancy

An **expectancy**, according to Vroom's terminology, represents an individual's belief that a particular degree of effort will be followed by a particular level of performance. In other words, it is an effort→performance expectation. Expectancies take the form of subjective probabilities. As you may recall from a course in statistics, probabilities range from 0 to 1. An expectancy of 0 indicates effort has no anticipated impact on performance.

Expectancy
Belief that effort leads to a specific level of performance.

For example, suppose you have not memorized the keys on a keyboard. No matter how much effort you exert, your perceived probability of typing 30 error-free words per minute likely would be 0. An expectancy of 1 suggests that performance is totally dependent on effort. If you decided to memorize the letters on a keyboard as well as practice a couple of hours a day for a few weeks (high effort), you should be able to type 30 words per minute without any errors. In contrast, if you do not memorize the letters on a keyboard and only practice an hour or two per week (low effort), there is a very low probability (say, a 20% chance) of being able to type 30 words per minute without any errors.

The following factors influence an employee's expectancy perceptions:

- Self-esteem.
- Self-efficacy (recall the discussion in Chapter 5).
- Previous success at the task.
- Help received from a supervisor and subordinates.
- Information necessary to complete the task.
- Good materials and equipment to work with.[44]

Instrumentality

An **instrumentality** is a performance→outcome perception. It represents a person's belief that a particular outcome is contingent on accomplishing a specific level of performance. Performance is instrumental when it leads to something else. For example, passing exams is instrumental to graduating from college.

Instrumentality
A performance→ outcome perception.

NCR Ties CEO William Nuti's Pay to Performance

Mr Nuti received a $1 million salary and $500,000 guaranteed bonus for 2005. But he loses 400,000 of his 650,000 options unless the Dayton, Ohio, maker of automated-teller machines and other products reaches an undisclosed level of cumulative net operating profit by Dec 31, 2008.

NCR directors embraced the idea of performance-linked options months before they recruited Mr Nuti because they felt a CEO only "should win when shareholders win," recalls Linda Fayne Levinson head of the board's compensation committee.

In another sign of the harder line some boards are taking toward CEO compensation, Mr Nuti's contract allows the board to fire him for cause if he and his family fail to relocate to Dayton by Aug 1 from their home on New York's Long Island. Until then, NCR is paying Mr Nuti to fly home weekly in the corporate jet.

What are the pros and cons of Mr. Nuti's pay plan?

SOURCE: Excerpted from J S Lublin, "Boards Tie CEO Pay More Tightly to Performance," *The Wall Street Journal,* February 21, 2006, p A14.

Instrumentalities range from −1.0 to 1.0. An instrumentality of 1.0 indicates attainment of a particular outcome is totally dependent on task performance. An instrumentality of 0 indicates there is no relationship between performance and outcome. For example, most companies link the number of vacation days to seniority, not job performance. Finally, an instrumentality of −1.0 reveals that high performance reduces the chance of obtaining an outcome while low performance increases the chance. For example, the more time you spend studying to get an A on an exam (high performance), the less time you will have for enjoying leisure activities. Similarly, as you lower the amount of time spent studying (low performance), you increase the amount of time that may be devoted to leisure activities.

The concept of instrumentality can be seen in practice by considering the national debate regarding CEO pay. Amid complaints that CEOs make too much money, more corporate boards are linking CEO pay to specific performance targets. For example, in 2005 "30 out of 100 major US corporations based a portion of the equity granted to their CEOs on performance targets, up from 23 in 2004 and 17 in 2003."[45] The Real World/Real People feature above illustrates how NCR Corporation has made pay based on performance for CEO William Nuti.

Farcus

by David Waisglass
Gordon Coulthart

CHICKEN OF THE MONTH

© 1994 Farcus Cartoons

WAISGLASS/COULTHART

"Frankly, I didn't think they'd go for this performance incentive stuff."

Valence

As Vroom used the term, **valence** refers to the positive or negative value people place on outcomes. Valence mirrors our personal preferences. For example, most employees have a positive valence for receiving additional money or recognition. In contrast, job stress and being laid off would likely result in negative valence for most individuals. In Vroom's expectancy model, *outcomes* refer to different consequences that are contingent on performance, such as pay, promotions, or recognition. An outcome's valence depends on an individual's needs and can be measured for research purposes with scales ranging from a negative value to a positive value. For example, an individual's valence toward more recognition can be assessed on a scale ranging from −2 (very undesirable) to 0 (neutral) to +2 (very desirable).

Valence
The value of a reward or outcome.

Vroom's Expectancy Theory in Action

Vroom's expectancy model of motivation can be used to analyze a real-life motivation program. Consider the following performance problem described by Frederick W Smith, founder and chief executive officer of Federal Express Corporation:

> [W]e were having a helluva problem keeping things running on time. The airplanes would come in and everything would get backed up. We tried every kind of control mechanism that you could think of, and none of them worked. Finally, it became obvious that the underlying problem was that it was in the interest of the employees at the cargo terminal—they were college kids, mostly—to run late, because it meant that they made more money. So what we did was give them all a minimum guarantee and say, "Look, if you get through before a certain time, just go home, and you will have beat the system." Well, it was unbelievable. I mean, in the space of about 45 days, the place was way ahead of schedule. And I don't even think it was a conscious thing on their part.[46]

How did Federal Express get its college-age cargo handlers to switch from low effort to high effort? According to Vroom's model, the student workers originally exerted low effort because they were paid on the basis of time, not output. It was in their best interest to work slowly and accumulate as many hours as possible. By offering to let the student workers *go home early if and when they completed their assigned duties,* Federal Express prompted high effort. This new arrangement created two positively valued outcomes: guaranteed pay plus the opportunity to leave early. The motivation to exert high effort became greater than the motivation to exert low effort.

Judging from the impressive results, the student workers had both high effort→ performance expectancies and positive performance→outcome instrumentalities. Moreover, the guaranteed pay and early departure opportunity evidently had strongly positive valences for the student workers.

Research on Expectancy Theory and Managerial Implications

Many researchers have tested expectancy theory. In support of the theory, a meta-analysis of 77 studies indicated that expectancy theory significantly predicted performance, effort, intentions, preferences, and choice.[47] Another summary of 16 studies revealed that expectancy theory correctly predicted occupational or organizational choice 63.4% of the time; this was significantly better than chance predictions.[48]

Table 8–2   *Managerial and Organizational Implications of Expectancy Theory*

IMPLICATIONS FOR MANAGERS	IMPLICATIONS FOR ORGANIZATIONS
Determine the outcomes employees value.	Reward people for desired performance; and do not keep pay decisions secret.
Identify good performance so appropriate behaviors can be rewarded.	Design challenging jobs.
Make sure employees can achieve targeted performance levels.	Tie some rewards to group accomplishments to build teamwork and encourage cooperation.
Link desired outcomes to targeted levels of performance.	Reward managers for creating, monitoring, and maintaining expectancies, instrumentalities, and outcomes that lead to high effort and goal attainment.
Make sure changes in outcomes are large enough to motivate high effort.	Monitor employee motivation through interviews or anonymous questionnaires.
Monitor the reward system for inequities.	Accommodate individual differences by building flexibility into the motivation program.

Nonetheless, expectancy theory has been criticized for a variety of reasons. For example, the theory is difficult to test, and the measures used to assess expectancy, instrumentality, and valence have questionable validity.[49] In the final analysis, however, expectancy theory has important practical implications for individual managers and organizations as a whole (see Table 8–2).

Managers are advised to enhance effort→performance expectancies by helping employees accomplish their performance goals. Managers can do this by providing support and coaching and by increasing employees' self-efficacy. It also is important for managers to influence employees' instrumentalities and to monitor valences for various rewards. This raises the issue of whether organizations should use monetary rewards as the primary method to reinforce performance. Although money is certainly a positively valent reward for most people, there are many issues to consider when deciding on the relative balance between monetary and nonmonetary rewards. For example, research shows that some workers value interesting work, recognition, and group welfare more than money.[50] These issues are discussed in Chapter 9.

In summary, there is no one best type of reward. Individual differences and need theories tell us that people are motivated by different rewards. Managers should therefore focus on linking employee performance to valued rewards regardless of the type of reward used to enhance motivation. Managers need to be careful or thoughtful, however, when implementing this suggestion. Consider the mistake made by a *Fortune* 500 insurance firm in California when it rewarded its top salespeople with tickets to a Christmas pageant at a local cathedral.

"The employees were upset and couldn't believe they would give them a gift like that," Davis says. [Helen Davis is president and CEO of Indaba Inc., a management consulting firm.] "What was supposed to be a reward became a disaster for the company." The workers ended up boycotting the firm for six months by bringing in only the minimum amount of sales on the insurance and investment products they sold. They wanted a formal apology from the CEO, but the executive was hoping the matter would just blow over. Although the CEO finally relented she says, it cost the firm nearly $750,000 in sales over that period and ultimately reached a loss of $1.5 million because many top producers left the firm as a result.[51]

Can you guess what caused the problem? A third of the firm's sales force was Jewish.

go to the Web for the Self-Exercise: What Outcomes Motivate Employees?

7 Motivation through Goal Setting

Regardless of the nature of their specific achievements, successful people tend to have one thing in common. Their lives are goal oriented. Consider Mike Proulx, for example. "When Mike Proulx was bagging groceries as a teenager in the 1960s, he decided he would become president of Bashas. [Bashas is a privately held grocery chain in Arizona with over 150 stores.] That's the job he has now held for three years . . . When I was 18 I made a series of goals that included by age such and such I would be a store manager, and by a certain age, I was going to be district manager and then vice president and then president."[52] As a process model of motivation, goal-setting theory explains how the simple behavior of setting goals activates a powerful motivational process that leads to sustained, high performance. This section explores the theory and research pertaining to goal setting, and Chapter 9 continues the discussion by focusing on the practical application of goal setting.

Goals: Definition and Background

Edwin Locke, a leading authority on goal setting, and his colleagues define a **goal** as "what an individual is trying to accomplish; it is the object or aim of an action."[53] The motivational effect of performance goals and goal-based reward plans has been recognized for a long time. At the turn of the century, Frederick Taylor attempted to scientifically establish how much work of a specified quality an individual should be assigned each day. He proposed that bonuses be based on accomplishing those output standards: Taylor's theory is discussed in the next section of this chapter. More recently, goal setting has been promoted through a widely used management technique called *management by objectives (MBO)*. The application of MBO is outlined in Chapter 9.

Goal
What an individual is trying to accomplish.

How Does Goal Setting Work?

Despite abundant goal-setting research and practice, goal-setting theories are surprisingly scarce. An instructive model was formulated by Locke and his associates. According to Locke's model, goal setting has four motivational mechanisms.

Goals Direct Attention Goals direct one's attention and effort toward goal-relevant activities and away from goal-irrelevant activities. If, for example, you have a term project due in a few days, your thoughts and actions tend to revolve around completing that project. For example, Robert Ruffolo, CEO of drugmaker Wyeth, used the power of goals to direct the attention of the company's research and development operation. The company now sets goals for how many drug compounds must be produced

Annika Sorenstam.

by each scientist. Prior to instituting this goal-setting program, Wyeth averaged the development of only four drug compounds per year. Since establishing the research and development goals, the company has averaged 12 per year with no increase in revenue. Ruffolo increased this goal to 15 in 2006.[54]

Goals Regulate Effort Not only do goals make us selectively perceptive, they also motivate us to act. The instructor's deadline for turning in your term project would prompt you to complete it, as opposed to going out with friends, watching television, or studying for another course. Generally, the level of effort expended is proportionate to the difficulty of the goal.

Goals Increase Persistence Within the context of goal setting, persistence represents the effort expended on a task over an extended period of time: It takes effort to run 100 meters; it takes persistence to run a 26-mile marathon. Persistent people tend to see obstacles as challenges to be overcome rather than as reasons to fail. A difficult goal that is important to an individual is a constant reminder to keep exerting effort in the appropriate direction. Annika Sorenstam is a great example of someone who persisted at her goal of being the best female golfer in the world. She has won 69 tournaments since starting the LPGA tour in 1994.

She already has qualified for the LPGA and World Golf Halls of Fame, has won a career Grand Slam, shot the only round of 59 in women's pro golf, and has won eight Player of the Year Titles.[55] Just like Tiger Woods, major titles and a single-season Grand Slam have become her focus. "Nobody else has done it, so I think that says it all," she said, "but I like to set high goals, I like to motivate myself. If you believe it in your mind, I think you can do it."[56]

Goals Foster the Development and Application of Task Strategies and Action Plans If you are here and your goal is out there somewhere, you face the problem of getting from here to there. For example, the person who has resolved to lose 20 pounds must develop a plan for getting from "here" (his or her present weight) to "there" (20 pounds lighter). Goals can help because they encourage people to develop strategies and action plans that enable them to achieve their goals. By virtue of setting a weight-reduction goal, the dieter may choose a strategy of exercising more, eating less, or some combination of the two.

Practical Lessons from Goal-Setting Research

Research consistently has supported goal setting as a motivational technique. Setting performance goals increases individual, group, and organizational performance. Further, the positive effects of goal setting were found in six other countries or regions: Australia, Canada, the Caribbean, England, West Germany, and Japan. Goal setting works in different cultures. Reviews of the many goal-setting studies conducted over the past few decades have given managers four practical insights:

1. *Specific high goals lead to greater performance.* **Goal specificity** pertains to the quantifiability of a goal. For example, a goal of selling nine cars a month is more specific than telling a salesperson to do his or her best. Results from more than 1,000 studies entailing over 88 different tasks and 40,000 people demonstrated that performance was greater when people had specific high goals.[57]

2. *Feedback enhances the effect of specific, difficult goals.* Feedback plays a key role in all of our lives. Feedback lets people know if they are headed toward their goals or if they are off course and need to redirect their efforts. Goals plus feedback is the recommended approach.[58] Goals inform people about performance standards and expectations so that they can channel their energies accordingly. In turn, feedback provides the information needed to adjust direction, effort, and strategies for goal accomplishment.

3. *Participative goals, assigned goals, and self-set goals are equally effective.* Both managers and researchers are interested in identifying the best way to set goals. Should goals be participatively set, assigned, or set by the employee him- or herself? A summary of goal-setting research indicated that no single approach was consistently more effective than others in increasing performance.[59] Managers are advised to use a contingency approach by picking a method that seems best suited for the individual and situation at hand.

4. *Goal commitment and monetary incentives affect goal-setting outcomes.* **Goal commitment** is the extent to which an individual is personally committed to achieving a goal. In general, an individual is expected to persist in attempts to accomplish a goal when he or she is committed to it. Researchers believe that goal commitment moderates the relationship between the difficulty of a goal and performance. That is, difficult goals lead to higher performance only when employees are committed to their goals. Conversely, difficult goals are hypothesized to lead to lower performance when people are not committed to their goals. A meta-analysis of 21 studies based on 2,360 people supported these predictions.[60] It also is important to note that people are more likely to commit to high goals when they have high self-efficacy about successfully accomplishing their goals.

Like goal setting, the use of monetary incentives to motivate employees is seldom questioned. Unfortunately, research uncovered some negative consequences when goal achievement is linked to individual incentives. Empirical studies demonstrated that goal-based bonus incentives produced higher commitment to easy goals and lower commitment to difficult goals. People were reluctant to commit to high goals that were tied to monetary incentives. People with high goal commitment also offered less help to their co-workers when they received goal-based bonus incentives to accomplish difficult individual goals. Individuals also neglected aspects of the job that were not covered in the performance goals.[61]

These findings underscore some of the dangers of using goal-based incentives, particularly for employees in complex, interdependent jobs requiring cooperation. Managers need to consider the advantages, disadvantages, and dilemmas of goal-based incentives prior to implementation.

8 Motivating Employees through Job Design

Job design is used when a manager suspects that the type of work an employee performs or characteristics of the work environment are causing motivational problems. **Job design,** also referred to as *job redesign,* "refers to any set of activities that involve the alteration of specific jobs or interdependent systems of jobs with

---

Goal specificity
Quantifiability of a goal.

Goal commitment
Amount of commitment to achieving a goal.

Job design
Changing the content or process of a specific job to increase job satisfaction and performance.

the intent of improving the quality of employee job experience and their on-the-job productivity."[62] A team of researchers examined the various methods for conducting job design and integrated them into an interdisciplinary framework that contains four major approaches: mechanistic, motivational, biological, and perceptual-motor.[63] As you will learn, each approach to job design emphasizes different outcomes. This section discusses these four approaches to job design and focuses most heavily on the motivational methods.

The Mechanistic Approach

The mechanistic approach draws from research in industrial engineering and scientific management and is most heavily influenced by the work of Frederick Taylor. Taylor, a mechanical engineer, developed the principles of scientific management while working at both Midvale Steel Works and Bethlehem Steel in Pennsylvania. He observed very little cooperation between management and workers and found that employees were underachieving by engaging in output restriction, which Taylor called "systematic soldiering." Taylor's interest in scientific management grew from his desire to improve upon this situation.

Scientific management

Using research and experimentation to find the most efficient way to perform a job.

Scientific management is "that kind of management which conducts a business or affairs by *standards* established by facts or truths gained through *systematic* observation, experiment, or reasoning."[64] Taylor's approach focused on using research and experimentation to determine the most efficient way to perform jobs. The application of scientific management involves the following five steps: (1) develop standard methods for performing jobs by using time and motion studies, (2) carefully select employees with the appropriate abilities, (3) train workers to use the standard methods and procedures, (4) support workers and reduce interruptions, and (5) provide incentives to reinforce performance.[65] Because jobs are highly specialized and standardized when they are designed according to the principles of scientific management, this approach to job design targets efficiency, flexibility, and employee productivity.

Designing jobs according to the principles of scientific management has both positive and negative consequences. Positively, employee efficiency and productivity are increased. On the other hand, research reveals that simplified, repetitive jobs also lead to job dissatisfaction, poor mental health, higher levels of stress, and low sense of accomplishment and personal growth.[66] These negative consequences paved the way for the motivational approach to job design.

Motivational Approaches

The motivational approaches to job design attempt to improve employees' affective and attitudinal reactions such as job satisfaction and intrinsic motivation as well as a host of behavioral outcomes such as absenteeism, turnover, and performance. We discuss four key motivational techniques: job enlargement, job enrichment, job rotation, and a contingency approach called the job characteristics model.

Job enlargement

Putting more variety into a job.

Job Enlargement This technique was first used in the late 1940s in response to complaints about tedious and overspecialized jobs. **Job enlargement** involves putting more variety into a worker's job by combining specialized tasks of comparable difficulty. Some call this *horizontally loading* the job. Researchers recommend using job enlargement as part of a broader approach that uses multiple motivational methods because it does not have a significant and lasting positive effect on job performance by itself.[67]

Job Rotation

As with job enlargement, job rotation's purpose is to give employees greater variety in their work. **Job rotation** calls for moving employees from one specialized job to another. Rather than performing only one job, workers are trained and given the opportunity to perform two or more separate jobs on a rotating basis. By rotating employees from job to job, managers believe they can stimulate interest and motivation while providing employees with a broader perspective of the organization. Other proposed advantages of job rotation include increased worker flexibility and easier scheduling because employees are cross trained to perform different jobs. Organizations also use job rotation as a vehicle to place new employees into jobs of their choice. The idea is that turnover is reduced and performance increases because people self-select their jobs. Ability Beyond Disability, an 800-person firm that provides health care for people with disabilities in more than 100 locations, is a good example.

> Within days after an interview, a successful applicant is on the payroll, undergoing extensive training and visiting the employer's group homes to see the real world of caring for people with disabilities. For about two months, sometimes three, the new hires—called intern floaters—are exposed to a wide variety of jobs in a variety of settings before they commit to a particular post.... New hires have choices and are urged to "try different areas" within the organization, to sample many types of direct care before taking a regular post.[68]

Managers at Ability Beyond Disability are happy with the results from the rotation program. Employee retention is up, turnover is down, and there is a reduction in staffing needs.

Despite positive experiences from companies like Ability Beyond Disability, it is not possible to draw firm conclusions about the value of job rotation programs because they have not been adequately researched.

Job rotation
Moving employees from one specialized job to another.

Job Enrichment

Job enrichment is the practical application of Frederick Herzberg's motivator–hygiene theory of job satisfaction that we discussed earlier in this chapter. Specifically, **job enrichment** entails modifying a job such that an employee has the opportunity to experience achievement, recognition, stimulating work, responsibility, and advancement. These characteristics are incorporated into a job through vertical loading. Rather than giving employees additional tasks of similar difficulty (horizontal loading), *vertical loading* consists of giving workers more responsibility. In other words, employees take on tasks normally performed by their supervisors.

Job enrichment
Building achievement, recognition, stimulating work, responsibility, and advancement into a job.

The Job Characteristics Model

Two OB researchers, J Richard Hackman and Greg Oldham, played a central role in developing the job characteristics approach. These researchers tried to determine how work can be structured so that employees are internally or intrinsically motivated. **Intrinsic motivation** occurs when an individual is "turned on to one's work because of the positive internal feelings that are generated by doing well, rather than being dependent on external factors (such as incentive pay or compliments from the boss) for the motivation to work effectively."[69] These positive feelings power a self-perpetuating cycle of motivation. As shown in Figure 8–4, internal work motivation is determined by three psychological states. In turn, these psychological states are fostered by the presence of five core job dimensions. The object of this approach is to promote high intrinsic motivation by designing jobs that possess the five core job characteristics shown in Figure 8–4. Let us examine the core job dimensions.

Intrinsic motivation
Motivation caused by positive internal feelings.

Figure 8–4   *The Job Characteristics Model*

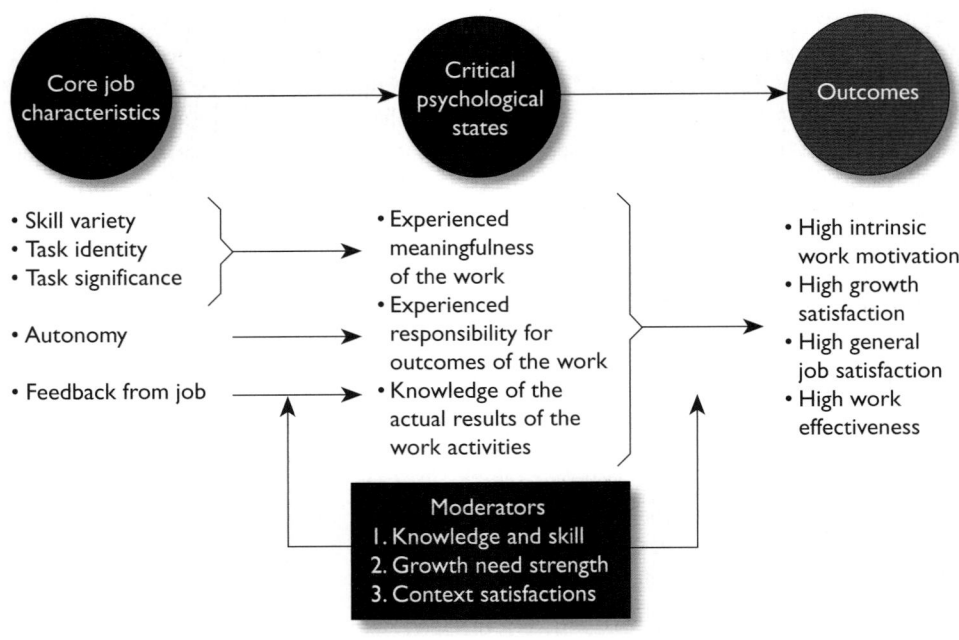

SOURCE: From J R Hackman and G R Oldham, *Work Redesign,* © 1980, p 90. Reprinted by permission of Pearson Education, Inc., Upper Saddle River, NJ.

Core job dimensions

Job characteristics found to various degrees in all jobs.

In general terms, **core job dimensions** are common characteristics found to a varying degree in all jobs. Three of the job characteristics shown in Figure 8–4 combine to determine experienced meaningfulness of work:

- *Skill variety.* The extent to which the job requires an individual to perform a variety of tasks that require him or her to use different skills and abilities.

- *Task identity.* The extent to which the job requires an individual to perform a whole or completely identifiable piece of work. In other words, task identity is high when a person works on a product or project from beginning to end and sees a tangible result.

- *Task significance.* The extent to which the job affects the lives of other people within or outside the organization.

Experienced responsibility is elicited by the job characteristic of autonomy, defined as follows:

- *Autonomy.* The extent to which the job enables an individual to experience freedom, independence, and discretion in both scheduling and determining the procedures used in completing the job.

Finally, knowledge of results is fostered by the job characteristic of feedback, defined as follows:

- *Feedback.* The extent to which an individual receives direct and clear information about how effectively he or she is performing the job.[70]

Hackman and Oldham recognized that everyone does not want a job containing high amounts of the five core job characteristics. They incorporated this conclusion

Table 8–3   *Steps for Applying the Job Characteristics Model*

1. Diagnose the work environment to determine if a performance problem is due to de-motivating job characteristics. Hackman and Oldham developed a self-report instrument for managers to use called the job diagnostic survey: It is shown and used in the Group Exercise, which can be found on the book's Web site. Diagnosis begins by determining whether the core job characteristics are low or high. If the job characteristics are lower than desired, a manager proceeds to step 2. If the performance problem is not due to low job characteristics, then a manager looks to apply another model of motivation or human behavior to solve the performance problem.

2. Determine whether job redesign is appropriate for a given group of employees. Job redesign is most likely to work in a participative environment in which employees have the necessary knowledge and skills to perform the enriched tasks and their job satisfaction is average to high.

3. Determine how to best redesign the job. The focus of this effort is to increase those core job characteristics that are low. Employee input is essential during this step to determine the details of a redesign initiative.

into their model by identifying three attributes that affect how individuals respond to job enrichment. These attributes are concerned with the individual's knowledge and skill, growth need strength (representing the desire to grow and develop as an individual), and context satisfactions (see the box labeled Moderators in Figure 8–4). Context satisfactions represent the extent to which employees are satisfied with various aspects of their job, such as satisfaction with pay, co-workers, and supervision.

There are several practical implications associated with using the job characteristics model to enhance intrinsic motivation: Steps for applying this model are shown in Table 8–3. Managers may want to use this model to increase employee job satisfaction. Research overwhelmingly demonstrates a moderately strong relationship between job characteristics and satisfaction.[71] Consistent with this finding, the Container Store in Coppell, Texas, and Principal Financial Group in Des Moines, Iowa, attempted to enhance employees' satisfaction by designing more autonomy into employees' jobs. Both organizations allow employees to select from a variety of work schedules that meets their needs. At Principal Financial Group, for example, 69% of the workers use flexible hours, 20% use compressed workweeks, and the remainder spends some portion of time working from home.[72] Research supports this investment, as autonomy has been found to be positively associated with job performance and proactive work behaviors.[73]

Moreover, research suggests that managers can enhance employees' intrinsic motivation, initiative, creativity, innovation, and commitment to their performance goals by increasing the core job characterstics.[74] Two separate meta-analyses also support the practice of using the job characteristics model to help managers reduce absenteeism and turnover.[75] On the negative side, however, job redesign appears to reduce the quantity of output just as often as it has a positive effect. Caution and situational appropriateness are advised. For example, one study demonstrated that job redesign works better in less complex organizations (small plants or companies).[76] Nonetheless, managers are likely to find noticeable increases in the quality of performance after a job redesign program. Results from 21 experimental studies revealed that job redesign resulted in a median increase of 28% in the quality of performance.[77]

go to the Web for the Group Exercise: Applying the Job Characteristics Model

Biological and Perceptual-Motor Approaches

The biological approach to job design is based on research from biomechanics, work physiology, and ergonomics and focuses on designing the work environment to reduce employees' physical strain, fatigue, and health complaints. For example, a host of companies, including Google, Bain & Company, and Sprint Nextel Corporation, are experimenting with the practice of allowing employees to sit on large rubber balls instead of traditional chairs. To date, researchers have identified both pros (e.g., improved posture and concentration) and cons (e.g., lower back strain, no arm support) for this technique.[78]

These Google employees seem to be enjoying their new work stations. Would you like to work with this type of office equipment?

The perceptual-motor approach is derived from research that examines human factors engineering, perceptual and cognitive skills, and information processing. This approach to job design emphasizes the reliability of work outcomes by examining error rates, accidents, and workers' feedback about facilities and equipment.[79] IBM and Steelcase are jointly developing a new interactive office system, labeled BlueSpace, that is based on this method of job design. Its features include

- *BlueScreen*. A touch screen that sits next to a user's computer monitor and puts users in control of their heat or cooling, ventilation, and light.

- *Everywhere Display*. A video projector that displays information on walls, floors, desktops, and other surfaces.

- *Monitor rail*. A moving rail that consists of a work surface that travels the length of a work space and a dual monitor arm that rotates to nearly a complete circle, letting users be positioned almost anywhere.

- *Threshold*. An L-shaped partial ceiling and wall on wheels that provides on-demand visual and territorial privacy to a user.[80]

The frequency of using both the biological and perceptual-motor approaches to job redesign is increasing in light of the number of workers who experience injuries related to overexertion or repetitive motion. **Repetitive motion disorders (RMDs)** are a family of muscular conditions that result from repeated motions performed in the course of normal work or daily activities. "RMDs include carpal tunnel syndrome, bursitis, tendonitis, epicondylitis, ganglion cyst, tenosynovitis, and trigger finger. RMDs are caused by too many uninterrupted repetitions of an activity or motion, unnatural or awkward motions such as twisting the arm or wrist, overexertion, incorrect posture,

Repetitive motion disorders (RMDs)

Muscular disorder caused by repeated motions.

or muscle fatigue."[81] Data from the US Department of Labor shows that RMDs result in the longest absences from work among the leading causes of absenteeism. The median time lost due to RMDs in 2005 was 23 days.[82] To combat this problem, the Occupational Safety and Health Administration (OSHA) implemented a new set of guidelines regarding ergonomic standards in the workplace due to this trend. The standards went into effect on October 14, 2001.

9 Putting Motivational Theories to Work

We started this chapter by noting that motivating employees is a key aspect of being an effective manager. That said, managers face two key challenges when trying to devise motivational programs. First, many managers are stretched in their job duties. They feel pulled in multiple dimensions and spend far too much time fighting fires instead of proactively focusing on employees' needs. This situation is frustrating and can lead to lower job satisfaction and motivation for managers. Although we feel sorry for people in this situation, it still is imperative for managers to find the time, and a positive attitude, to apply to the task of employee motivation. Second, managers may not know how to motivate people beyond the simple use of monetary rewards.[83] It is important for managers to use a broader or more integrated approach when trying to motivate employees. This approach should consider the various theories and models discussed in this chapter as well as concepts covered in previous chapters. Organizations can help managers by providing them with training and coaching that focuses on how they can improve their ability to "motivate others."[84]

With the aforementioned in mind, this section raises several issues to be considered when designing an integrated approach toward employee motivation. Our intent is not to discuss all relevant considerations but rather to highlight a few important ones.

Assuming a motivational program is being considered to improve productivity, quality, or customer satisfaction, the first issue revolves around the difference between motivation and performance. Motivation and performance are not one and the same. Motivation is only one of several factors that influence performance. For example, poor performance may be more a function of outdated or inefficient materials and machinery, not having goals to direct one's attention, a monotonous job, feelings of inequity, a negative work environment characterized by political behavior and conflict, poor supervisory support and coaching, or poor work flow. Motivation cannot make up for a deficient job context. Managers, therefore, need to carefully consider the causes of poor performance and employee misbehavior.

Individual differences represent one of the first causes of low motivation that should be considered. For example, low motivation may be due to issues associated with managing diversity (recall our discussion in Chapter 2). The individual differences discussed in Chapters 5 and 6 (self-esteem, self-efficacy, personality, locus of control, intelligence, mental abilities, emotions, values, and attitudes) also are important causes of employee motivation. Managers are advised to develop employees so they have the ability and job knowledge to perform their jobs effectively. In addition, attempts should be made to nurture positive employee characteristics such as self-esteem, self-efficacy, positive emotions, and the need for achievement.

Because motivation is goal directed, the process of developing and setting goals should be consistent with our previous discussion. Moreover, the method used to evaluate performance also needs to be considered. Without a valid performance appraisal system, it is difficult, if not impossible, to accurately distinguish good and poor performers.[85] Consider the approach that General Electric, rated as the most admired company to work for by *Fortune* in 2005, takes in terms of developing and evaluating its employees.

> The company takes a lot of heat for getting rid of the bottom 10% of its employees every year, but that's only the end point of a process of constant appraisal. The fired ones are not surprised when the ax comes down. . . . Dan Mudd is the president and CEO of Fannie Mae; as president and CEO of GE Capital Japan from 1999 to mid-2005, he saw this dynamic from the inside. "GE, like anywhere else, has a little bit of politics, a little bit of personal stuff and all that," he says, "but compared with all the other organizations I know, it's minimized. It's upfront. You know what you have to do to succeed." Most companies, frankly, don't have the stomach to give frequent, rigorous evaluations—and to fire those who need to be fired.[86]

Finally, it is important for organizations to train their managers to properly assess people. While GE clearly adheres to this suggestion, a recent survey of 96 human resource professionals suggests that many companies do not. Sixty-one percent of the respondents concluded that managers were not properly trained to conduct performance evaluations.[87]

Consistent with expectancy theory, managers should make extrinsic rewards contingent on performance. In doing so, however, it is important to consider two issues. First, managers need to ensure that performance goals are directed to achieve the "right" end-results. For example, too many organizations evaluate and reward employees for individual accomplishments or results when success is more a function of teamwork and collaboration.[88] Consider how Cisco Systems, the leading maker of computer networking equipment, focuses on the evaluation and reward of teamwork and collaboration.

> Cisco Systems . . . assesses the ability of employees and prospective hires to collaborate across departments and functions. "It is good for business," says Diane Adams, vice president, human resources, worldwide sales, "dramatically improving productivity and helping us to grow." Cisco, which has been cutting costs partly by streamlining and combining overlapping business groups, has made "teamwork and collaboration" a factor in its formula for computing management bonuses since 2003. Ms Adams says the assessment of managers' teamwork efforts "can impact their bonus by as much as 20% annually."[89]

Second, the promise of increased rewards will not prompt higher effort and good performance unless those rewards are clearly tied to performance and they are large enough to gain employees' interests or attention.

Moreover, equity theory tells us that motivation is influenced by employee perceptions about the fairness of reward allocations. Motivation is decreased when employees believe rewards are inequitably allocated. Rewards also need to be integrated appropriately into the appraisal system. If performance is measured at the individual level, individual achievements need to be rewarded. On the other hand, when performance is the result of group effort, rewards should be allocated to the group.

Feedback also should be linked with performance. Feedback provides the information and direction needed to keep employees focused on relevant tasks, activities, and goals. Managers should strive to provide specific, timely, and accurate feedback to employees.

Finally, we end this chapter by noting that an organization's culture (recall our discussion in Chapter 3) significantly influences employee motivation and behavior. A positive self-enhancing culture is more likely to engender higher motivation and commitment than a culture dominated by suspicion, faultfinding, and blame.

Summary of Key Concepts

1. **Contrast Maslow's, Alderfer's, and McClelland's need theories.** Maslow proposed that motivation is a function of five basic needs arranged in a prepotent hierarchy. The concept of a stair-step hierarchy has not stood up well under research. Alderfer concluded that three core needs explain behavior—existence, relatedness, and growth. He proposed that more than one need can be activated at a time and frustration of higher-order needs can influence the desire for lower-level needs. McClelland argued that motivation and performance vary according to the strength of an individual's need for achievement. High achievers prefer tasks of moderate difficulty, situations under their control, and a desire for more performance feedback than low achievers. Top managers should have a high need for power coupled with a low need for affiliation.

2. **Explain the practical significance of Herzberg's distinction between motivators and hygiene factors.** Herzberg believes job satisfaction motivates better job performance. His hygiene factors, such as policies, supervision, and salary, erase sources of dissatisfaction. On the other hand, his motivators, such as achievement, responsibility, and recognition, foster job satisfaction. Although Herzberg's motivator–hygiene theory of job satisfaction has been criticized on methodological grounds, it has practical significance for job enrichment.

3. **Discuss the role of perceived inequity in employee motivation.** Equity theory is a model of motivation that explains how people strive for fairness and justice in social exchanges. On the job, feelings of inequity revolve around a person's evaluation of whether he or she receives adequate rewards to compensate for his or her contributive inputs. People perform these evaluations by comparing the perceived fairness of their employment exchange with that of relevant others. Perceived inequity creates motivation to restore equity.

4. **Explain the differences among distributive, procedural, and interactional justice.** Distributive, procedural, and interactional justice are the three key components underlying organizational justice. Distributive justice reflects the perceived fairness of how resources and rewards are distributed. Procedural justice represents the perceived fairness of the process and procedures used to make allocation decisions. Interactional justice entails the perceived fairness of a decision maker's behavior in the process of decision making.

5. **Describe the practical lessons derived from equity theory.** Equity theory has at least nine practical implications. First, because people are motivated to resolve perceptions of inequity, managers should not discount employees' feelings and perceptions when trying to motivate workers. Second, managers should pay attention to employees' perceptions of what is fair and equitable. It is the employee's view of reality that counts when

trying to motivate someone, according to equity theory. Third, employees should be given a voice in decisions that affect them. Fourth, employees should be given the opportunity to appeal decisions that affect their welfare. Fifth, employees are more likely to accept and support organizational change when they believe it is implemented fairly and when it produces equitable outcomes. Sixth, managers can promote cooperation and teamwork among group members by treating them equitably. Seventh, treating employees inequitably can lead to litigation and costly court settlements. Eighth, perceptions of justice are influenced by the leadership behavior exhibited by managers. Finally, managers need to pay attention to the organization's climate for justice because it influences employee attitudes and behavior.

6. **Explain Vroom's expectancy theory, and review its practical implications.** Expectancy theory assumes motivation is determined by one's perceived chances of achieving valued outcomes. Vroom's expectancy model of motivation reveals how effort→performance expectancies and performance→outcome instrumentalities influence the degree of effort expended to achieve desired (positively valent) outcomes. Managers are advised to enhance effort→performance expectancies by helping employees accomplish their performance goals. With respect to instrumentalities and valences, managers should attempt to link employee performance and valued rewards.

7. **Explain how goal setting motivates an individual, and review the four practical lessons from goal-setting research.** Four motivational mechanisms of goal setting are as follows: (1) Goals direct one's attention, (2) goals regulate effort, (3) goals increase one's persistence, and (4) goals encourage development of goal-attainment strategies and action plans. Research identifies four practical lessons about goal setting. First, specific high goals lead to greater performance. Second, feedback enhances the effect of specific, difficult goals. Third, participative goals, assigned goals, and self-set goals are equally effective. Fourth, goal commitment and monetary incentives affect goal-setting outcomes.

8. **Review the mechanistic, motivational, biological, and perceptual-motor approaches to job design.** The mechanistic approach is based on industrial engineering and scientific management and focuses on increasing efficiency, flexibility, and employee productivity. Motivational approaches aim to improve employees' affective and attitudinal reactions and behavioral outcomes. Job enlargement, job enrichment, job-rotation, and a contingency approach called the job characteristics model are motivational approaches to job design. The biological approach focuses on designing the work environment to reduce employees' physical strain, fatigue, and health complaints. The perceptual-motor approach emphasizes the reliability of work outcomes.

9. *Specify issues that should be addressed before implementing a motivational program.* Managers need to consider the variety of causes of poor performance. Motivation is only one of several factors that influence performance. Managers should not ignore the many individual differences that affect motivation. The goal-setting process should be consistent with the four practical lessons derived from goal-setting research. The method used to evaluate performance as well as the link between performance and rewards must be examined. Performance must be accurately evaluated, and rewards should be equitably distributed. Rewards should also be directly tied to performance. Finally, managers should recognize that employee motivation and behavior are influenced by organizational culture.

Key Terms

OB in Action Case Study

Nucor Uses an Integrated Approach to Employee Motivation[90]

BusinessWeek It was about 2 P.M. on Mar. 9 when three Nucor Corp. electricians got the call from their colleagues at the Hickman (Ark.) plant. It was bad news: Hickman's electrical grid had failed. For a minimill steelmaker like Nucor, which melts scrap steel from autos, dishwashers, mobile homes, and the like in an electric arc furnace to make new steel, there's little that could be worse. The trio immediately dropped what they were doing and headed out to the plant. Malcolm McDonald, an electrician from the Decatur (Ala.) mill, was in Indiana visiting another facility. He drove down, arriving at 9 o'clock that night. Les Hart and Bryson Trumble, from Nucor's facility in Hertford County, N.C., boarded a plane that landed in Memphis at 11 P.M. Then they drove two hours to the troubled plant.

No supervisor had asked them to make the trip, and no one had to. They went on their own. Camping out in the electrical substation with the Hickman staff, the team worked 20-hour shifts to get the plant up and running again in three days instead of the anticipated full week. There wasn't any direct financial incentive for them to blow their weekends, no extra money in their next paycheck, but for the company their contribution was huge. Hickman went on to post a first-quarter record for tons of steel shipped. . . .

At Nucor, the art of motivation is about an unblinking focus on the people on the front line of the business. It's about talking to them, listening to them, taking a risk on their ideas, and accepting the occasional failure. It's a culture built in part with symbolic gestures. Every year, for example, every single employee's name goes on the cover of the annual report. And, like Iverson before him, DiMicco flies commercial, manages without an executive parking space, and really does make the coffee in the office when he takes the last cup. . . .

But Nucor's path is hard to follow. It requires managers to abandon the command-and-control model that has dominated American business for the better part of a century, trust their people, and do a much better job of sharing corporate wealth.

Money is where the rubber meets the road. Nucor's unusual pay system is the single most daring element of the company's model and the hardest for outsiders and acquired companies to embrace. An experienced steelworker at another company can easily earn $16 to $21 an hour. At Nucor the guarantee is closer to $10. A bonus tied to the production of defect-free steel by an employee's entire shift can triple the average steelworker's take-home pay.

With demand for steel scorching these days, payday has become a regular cause for celebration. Nucor gave out more than $220 million in profit sharing and bonuses to the rank and file in 2005. The average Nucor steelworker took home nearly $79,000 last year. Add to that a $2,000 one-time bonus to mark the company's record earnings and almost $18,000, on average, in profit sharing. Not only is good work rewarded, but bad work is penalized. Bonuses are calculated on every order and paid out every week. At the Berkeley mill in Huger, S.C., if workers make a bad batch of steel and catch it before it has moved on, they lose the bonus they otherwise would have made on that shipment. But if it gets to the customer, they lose three times that.

Managers don't just ask workers to put a big chunk of their pay at risk. Their own take-home depends heavily on results as well. Department managers typically get a base pay that's 75% to 90% of the market average. But in a great year that same manager might get a bonus of 75% or even 90%, based on the return on assets of the whole plant. "In average-to-bad years, we earn less than our peers in other companies. That's supposed to teach us that we don't want to be average or bad. We want to be good," says James M. Coblin, Nucor's vice-president for human resources.

Compared with other US companies, pay disparities are modest at Nucor. Today, the typical CEO makes more than 400 times what a factory worker takes home. Last year, Nucor's chief executive collected a salary and bonus precisely 23 times that of his average steelworker. [CEO Daniel] DiMicco did well by any reasonable standard, making some $2.3 million in salary and bonus (plus long-term pay equaling $4.9 million), but that's because Nucor is doing well. When things are bad, DiMicco suffers, too. In 2003, as the company was dealing with an industry downturn and barely squeaked out a profit, DiMicco made $1.4 million. . . .

Executive pay is geared toward team building. The bonus of a plant manager, a department manager's boss, depends on the entire corporation's return on equity. So there's no glory in winning at your own plant if the others are failing. . . .

This high-stakes teamwork can be the hardest thing for a newly acquired plant to get used to. David Hutchins, a frontline supervisor or "lead man" in the rolling mill at Nucor's first big acquisition, its Auburn (N.Y.) plant, describes the old way of thinking. The job of a rolling mill is to thin out the steel made in the hot mill furnace, preparing it to be cut into sheets. In the days before the Nucor acquisition, if the cutting backed up, Hutchins would just take a break. "We'd sit back, have a cup of coffee, and complain: 'Those guys stink,'" he says. "At Nucor, we're not 'you guys' and 'us guys.' It's all of us guys. Wherever the bottleneck is, we go there, and everyone works on it."

It took six months to convince Auburn workers that they would do better under Nucor's pay system. During that time the company paid people based on their old formula but posted what they would have received under Nucor's formula. Pretty soon the numbers became a powerful argument to switch. Hutchins saw his pay climb from $53,000 the year before the sale to $67,000 in 2001 and to $92,000 last year. "It's like I got a second job, and I'm doing the same one," he says. Today it has become standard procedure for a team of Nucor vets, including people who work on the plant floor, to visit with their counterparts in any acquisition. They explain the system eye to eye.

But to focus only on pay would be to miss something special about the culture Nucor has created. There's a healthy competition among facilities and even among shifts, balanced with a long history of cooperation and idea-sharing. Rick Ryan, the shipping department supervisor at the Auburn mill, has taken trips to study plants in Nebraska and South Carolina. Ryan had always used wood blocks as supports beneath the bundles of steel the plant produced. But after seeing other Nucor plants use steel blocks, he switched. Because they can be reused, Ryan figures the move saves $150,000 a year.

Since there's always room for improvement, plant managers regularly set up contests for shifts to try to outdo one another on a set goal, generally related to safety, efficiency, or output. Ryan says Nucor's Utah plant is the benchmark these days. It is the most profitable, with the lowest costs per ton. "They've got everything down to a science," says Ryan admiringly. "It gives you something to shoot for."

Questions for Discussion

1. How does Nucor's approach to motivation build on recommendations from Maslow's, Alderfer's, and McClelland's need theories? Explain.

2. To what extent are hygiene factors and motivators influencing employee behavior at Nucor?

3. What role does equity theory play in this case? Discuss.

4. To what extent is Nucor's approach to employee motivation consistent with expectancy theory? Explain.

5. What role does organizational culture play in this case?

6. Would it be easy for other companies to copy Nucor's approach to employee motivation? Why or why not?

Should Companies Donate Money to Charities to Help Land Business?[91]

In 2001, two J P Morgan Chase & Co investment bankers were looking for a way to get more work underwriting municipal bonds in Philadelphia. Then the bankers, Charles LeCroy and Anthony Snell, met one of the Philadelphia mayor's top fund-raisers, and their lives got complicated.

The fund-raiser was a folksy lawyer named Ronald A White. According to accounts later introduced in a trial in federal court in Philadelphia, Mr White suggested he could help the bank get bond work and also suggested various ways the bank could compensate him.

J P Morgan eventually gave $20,000 to fund a scholarship in Mr White's name. It also donated $70,000 to a charity of which he was co-chairman. And according to accounts later introduced in court, the bankers got J P Morgan to pay $50,000 to Mr White's tiny law firm for work that, it turned out, it never did.

Mr Snell, asked later about such events in a J P Morgan internal investigation, said that if Mr White "was going to use his contacts to help J P Morgan, he expected J P Morgan to help his friends." In big cities, Mr Snell added, according to J P Morgan lawyers' memo about the debriefing, "99.9% of the time there is a go-to guy" like Mr White.

What would you have done if you were Mr LeCroy or Mr Snell?

1. I would do what they did because Mr White was the go-to guy and this is the way to get the business.
2. I would donate to the scholarship and charity but not pay Mr White's law firm for services it did not provide.
3. I would tell Mr White that he is basically asking for a bribe and then would call the mayor directly.
4. I would sell the positive aspects of doing business with J P Morgan Chase and not donate any money.
5. Invent other options. Discuss.

Web Resources

For study material and exercises that apply to this chapter, visit our Web site,

www.mhhe.com/kreitner

CHAPTER 9

Improving Job Performance with Goals, Feedback, Rewards, and Positive Reinforcement

Student Resources for Studying Chapter 9

The Web site for your text includes resources that will help you master the concepts in this chapter. As you read, you'll want to visit the site for these helpful tools:

- Your online Study Guide includes learning objectives, a chapter summary, a glossary of key terms, and discussion questions.
- Take a practice quiz and test your knowledge!
- Scroll through a PowerPoint presentation with key concepts for this chapter.

Your instructor might also direct you to the Web site for these exercises:

- Self-assessments that correspond with the chapter content and a Group Exercise.
- You'll also find Video Cases and Internet Exercises for this chapter online.

www.mhhe.com/kreitner

Leigh Buchanan, Editor, *Inc.* Magazine:

The genius of Pat McGovern is the way he makes things all about you. That impressed me hugely, because when I first met Pat back in 1989 I wasn't the sort of person *anything* was all about. I was a new copy editor at *CIO* magazine; Pat was (still is) the founder and chairman of *CIO*'s parent, International Data Group, a then $400 million technology publishing and research empire. It hadn't occurred to me that the twain would meet, so I was startled (confused, marginally freaked) when a tall, ruddy man loomed in the entrance to my cubicle a few weeks before Christmas.

Pat thanked me for my contributions. He asked how things were going and looked vaguely disappointed when all I could muster was an unilluminating "Fine." Then he complimented me on a column I had ghostwritten for some technology honcho. The column was my most substantive accomplishment to date and the thing I was proudest of. But my name didn't appear on it anywhere, so how did he know? After three or four minutes, he handed me my bonus and proceeded to the next cubicle.

The formula for Pat's Christmas calls–expression of gratitude/request for feedback/congratulations on specific achievement/delivery of loot—never varied, even as IDG grew into the $2.4 billion global behemoth it is today. To personally thank most every person in every business unit in the US, more than 1,500 employees, takes almost four weeks, he told me years later: Managers provide him with a list of accomplishments for all their reports, and Pat memorizes them the night before his visits. He does this because he wants employees to know that he sees *them*—really sees them—as individuals, and that he considers what they do all day to be meaningful.

Not only does Pat care about his people; he also believes in them. His commitment to decentralization has created a constellation of motivated business units that make their own decisions about everything from how to reward staff to what new businesses to launch. He also treats his end customers—the readers of such publications as *Computerworld, PC World*, and *Macworld*—with consummate respect. At IDG the quality of content is

Pat McGovern is a master of "people" skills.

sacrosanct, a tough ideal to sustain when advertising pays so many of the bills.

Did I mention that he's giving $350 million to MIT to create an institute for brain research? Maybe I shouldn't: I don't want to lay it on too thick.

Another small-company tradition Pat has kept up over the years is taking each employee out for a meal at the Ritz on his or her 10th anniversary with IDG. I left *CIO* after only seven years (to work for *Inc.*, where I could write about people like Pat and not just work

for them), so I never got my anniversary dinner. Too bad—it would have been a class act. And I'm not talking about the restaurant.[1]

This final chapter of Part Two serves as a practical capstone for what we have learned so far in Parts One and Two. Our focus here is on improving individual job performance. We need to put to work what we have learned about cultural and individual differences, perception, and motivation. Some managers, such as Pat McGovern in the opening vignette, do a good job in this regard. His personal touch and supportive style triggered fond memories for a former employee. Unfortunately, research shows that most managers fall far short when it comes to carefully nurturing job performance. A consulting firm's ongoing study of more than 500 managers since 1993 led to this conclusion:

> Only one out of 100 managers provides every direct report with these five basics every day:
>
> - Performance requirements and standard operating procedures related to tasks and responsibilities.
> - Defined parameters, measurable goals and concrete deadlines for all work assignments for which the direct report will be held accountable.
> - Accurate monitoring, evaluation and documentation of work performance.
> - Specific feedback on work performance with guidance for improvement.
> - Fairly distributed rewards and detriments [penalties].[2]

Performance management

Continuous cycle of improving job performance with goal setting, feedback and coaching, and rewards and positive reinforcement.

The researchers call this situation "under-management." But the popular term these days for doing things the right way is performance management. **Performance management** is an organizationwide system whereby managers integrate the activities of goal setting, monitoring and evaluating, providing feedback and coaching, and rewarding employees on a continuous basis.[3] This contrasts with the haphazard tradition of annual performance appraisals,[4] a largely unsatisfying experience for everyone involved.[5] (See Learning Module B, on the book's Web site, for more on performance appraisal.) OB can shed valuable light on key aspects of performance management. Namely, goal setting, feedback and coaching, and rewards and positive reinforcement.

As indicated in Figure 9–1, job performance needs a life-support system. Like an astronaut drifting in space without the protection and support of a space suit, job performance will not thrive without a support system. First, people with the requisite abilities, skills, and job knowledge need to be hired. Joe Kraus, co-founder and CEO of Jotspot, a Web page hosting service, recently offered this blunt advice:

Never compromise on hiring. Every time I've compromised, I've come to regret it. You have to be tough, even if that means not hiring people who could turn out to be great, because of the damage one person who isn't great can do.

Nothing demotivates people like the equal treatment of unequals. When you hire a bozo and treat him the same as a rock star, it deflates the rock star.[6]

Figure 9–1   *Improving Individual Job Performance: A Continuous Process*

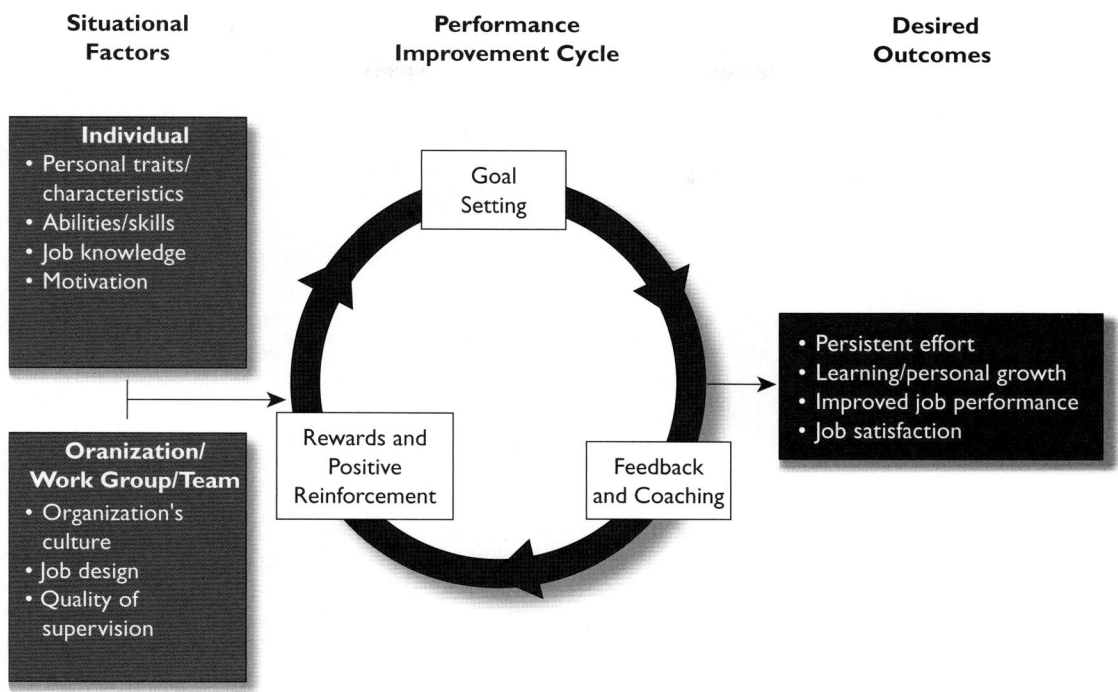

Next, training is required to correct any job knowledge shortfalls.[7] The organization's structure, culture, and job design and supervisory practices also can facilitate or hinder job performance. At the heart of the model in Figure 9–1 are the key aspects of the performance improvement cycle that we explore in depth in this chapter. Importantly, it is a dynamic and continuous cycle requiring management's day-to-day attention.

Goal Setting

Goal setting in the workplace could use an extreme makeover. According to a Franklin Covey survey of workers in the United States, 56% don't "clearly understand their organization's most important goals" and an astounding 81% "don't have clearly defined goals."[8] These figures could be cut in half and still represent a very unproductive situation. The missing element here is what goal-setting experts call line of sight. Employees with a clear **line of sight** understand the organization's strategic goals and know what actions they need to take, both individually and as team members.[9] Verizon Wireless, for example, achieves line of sight through its training programs:

> Trainers at the Basking Ridge, NJ-based communications company are expected to tie instruction directly to company objectives. This approach ensures executive buy-in, provides concrete benchmarks by which to measure success, and helps the company better serve its growing customer base, says Lou Tedrick, staff vice president, workforce development.
>
> "Training initiatives are not done unless there is a business reason to do it," she says.[10]

Line of sight

Employees know the organization's strategic goals and how they need to contribute.

This section gets things headed in that direction by distinguishing between two types of goals, discussing management by objectives, and explaining how to manage the goal-setting process.

Two Types of Goals

Performance outcome goal

Targets a specific end-result.

Learning goal

Encourages learning, creativity, and skill development.

Goal-setting researchers have drawn an instructive distinction between performance outcome goals and learning goals. A **performance outcome goal** targets a specific end-result. A **learning goal,** in contrast, strives to improve creativity and develop skills. Managers typically overemphasize the former and ignore the latter as they try to "motivate" greater effort and achieve final results. But for employees who lack the necessary skills, performance outcome goals are more frustrating than motivating. When skills are lacking, a developmental process is needed wherein learning goals precede performance outcome goals. Goal researchers Gerard Seijts and Gary Latham explain with a golfing analogy:

> A performance outcome goal often distracts attention from the discovery of task-relevant strategies. For example, focusing on a golf score of 95 by novices may prevent them from focusing on the mastery of the swing and weight transfer and using the proper clubs necessary for attaining that score. . . .
>
> In short, the novice golfer must learn how to play the game before becoming concerned with attaining a challenging performance outcome (e.g., score equals 95).[11]

Management by Objectives

Management by objectives

Management system incorporating participation in decision making, goal setting, and feedback.

The motivational impact of performance goals and goal-based reward plans has been recognized for a long time. More than a century ago, Frederick Taylor attempted to scientifically establish how much work of a specified quality an individual should be assigned each day. He proposed that bonuses be based on accomplishing those output standards. More recently, goal setting has been promoted through a widely used management technique called management by objectives (MBO). **Management by objectives** is a management system that incorporates participation in decision making, goal setting, and objective feedback.[12] A meta-analysis of MBO programs showed productivity gains in 68 of 70 different organizations. Specifically, results uncovered an average gain in productivity of 56% when top-management commitment was high. The average gain was only 6% when commitment was low. A second meta-analysis of 18 studies further demonstrated that employees' job satisfaction was significantly related to top management's commitment to an MBO implementation.[13] These impressive results are tempered by reports of ethical problems stemming from extreme pressure for results (see the Real World/Real People feature on page 247). Ethically sound MBO programs marry learning goals and performance outcome goals.

Managing the Goal-Setting Process

There are three general steps to follow when implementing a goal-setting program.[14] Serious deficiencies in one step cannot make up for strength in the other two. The three steps need to be implemented in a systematic fashion.

Step 1: Set Goals A number of sources can be used as input during this goal-setting stage. Time and motion studies are one source. Goals also may be based on the

Too Much Emphasis on Short-Term Financial Goals Causes Problems

Such an approach can easily backfire.

For one thing, employee loyalty and teamwork erode quickly, along with innovation and risk taking. So, in some cases, do business ethics. Managers and employees who fear they'll lose their jobs if they don't deliver their assigned numbers are more inclined to fudge results.

And companies that become fixated on hitting quarterly and even daily targets often don't produce sustainable profit growth. "It's hard to capture employees' hearts, and best efforts, with numbers alone," says [organizational psychologist Richard] Hagberg. In a recent study of 31 corporations, his staff found that the highest returns were achieved at companies whose CEOs set challenging financial goals but also articulated a purpose beyond profit making, such as creating a great product, and convinced employees their work mattered.

. . . [A] manager at a big global bank recently quit his job in Texas after observing how the pressure to hit targets under a new manager had backfired. "The pressure worked at first with increased sales, but now the territory, which used to be the top for our company, is one of the worst in the country," he wrote. "I left because it was tiresome seeing my co-workers getting beat on day in and day out about the number of checking accounts they had opened. When I left it wasn't because of poor performance—my numbers were in the top 1% of all reps in the country....I was on pace to make over $250,000." But, he added, "the environment they created made it a miserable place to work because teamwork had eroded along with morale."

What is your personal experience with the collision between pressure for results and ethics? At home? In school? On the job?

SOURCES: C Hymowitz, "When Meeting Targets Becomes the Strategy, CEO Is on Wrong Path," *The Wall Street Journal*, March 8, 2005, p B1; and C Hymowitz, "Readers Share Tales of Jobs Where Strategy Became Meeting Targets," *The Wall Street Journal*, March 22, 2005, p B1.

---

average past performance of job holders. Third, the employee and his or her manager may set the goal participatively, through give-and-take negotiation. Fourth, goals can be set by conducting external or internal benchmarking. Benchmarking is used when an organization wants to compare its performance or internal work processes to those of other organizations (external benchmarking) or to other internal units, branches, departments, or divisions within the organization (internal benchmarking). For example, a company might set a goal to surpass the customer service levels or profit of a benchmarked competitor. Finally, the overall strategy of a company (e.g., become the lowest-cost producer) may affect the goals set by employees at various levels in the organization.

In accordance with available research evidence, goals should be "SMART." SMART is an acronym that stands for specific, measurable, attainable, results oriented, and time bound. Table 9–1 contains a set of guidelines for writing SMART goals. There are two additional recommendations to consider when setting goals. First, for complex tasks, managers should train employees in problem-solving techniques and encourage them to develop a performance action plan. Action plans specify the strategies or tactics to be used in order to accomplish a goal.

Second, because of individual differences (recall our discussion in Chapter 5), it may be necessary to establish different goals for employees performing the same job. For example, a study of 103 undergraduate business students revealed that individuals high in conscientiousness had higher motivation, had greater goal commitment, and obtained higher grades than students low in conscientiousness.[15]

An individual's goal orientation is another important individual difference to consider when setting goals. Three types of goal orientations are a learning goal orientation, a performance-prove goal orientation, and a performance-avoid goal orientation.

Table 9–1   *Guidelines for Writing SMART Goals*

Specific	Goals should be stated in precise rather than vague terms. For example, a goal that provides for 20 hours of technical training for each employee is more specific than stating that a manager should send as many people as possible to training classes. Goals should be quantified when possible.
Measurable	A measurement device is needed to assess the extent to which a goal is accomplished. Goals thus need to be measurable. It also is critical to consider the quality aspect of the goal when establishing measurement criteria. For example, if the goal is to complete a managerial study of methods to increase productivity, one must consider how to measure the quality of this effort. Goals should not be set without considering the interplay between quantity and quality of output.
Attainable	Goals should be realistic, challenging, and attainable. Impossible goals reduce motivation because people do not like to fail. Remember, people have different levels of ability and skill.
Results oriented	Corporate goals should focus on desired end-results that support the organization's vision. In turn, an individual's goals should directly support the accomplishment of corporate goals. Activities support the achievement of goals and are outlined in action plans. To focus goals on desired end-results, goals should start with the word *to*, followed by verbs such as *complete, acquire, produce, increase,* and *decrease.* Verbs such as *develop, conduct, implement,* or *monitor* imply activities and should not be used in a goal statement.
Time bound	Goals specify target dates for completion.

SOURCE: A J Kinicki, *Performance Management Systems* (Superstition Mt., AZ: Kinicki and Associates Inc., 2005), pp 2–9. Reprinted with permission; all rights reserved.

A team of researchers described the differences and implications for goal setting in the following way:

> People with a high learning goal orientation view skills as malleable. They make efforts not only to achieve current tasks but also to develop the ability to accomplish future tasks. People with a high performance-prove goal orientation tend to focus on performance and try to demonstrate their ability by looking better than others. People with a high performance-avoid goal orientation also focus on performance, but this focus is grounded in trying to avoid negative outcomes.[16]

Although some studies showed that people set higher goals, exerted more effort, had higher self-efficacy, and achieved higher performance when they possessed a learning goal orientation as opposed to either a performance-prove or performance-avoid goal orientation, other research demonstrated a more complex series of relationships.[17]

The best we can conclude is that an individual's goal orientation influences the actions that he or she takes in the pursuit of accomplishing goals in specific situations. Thus, managers are encouraged to consider individual differences when setting goals.

Step 2: Promote Goal Commitment Obtaining goal commitment is important because employees are more motivated to pursue goals they view as reasonable, obtainable, and fair. Goal commitment may be increased by using one or more of the following techniques:

1. Provide an explanation for why the organization is implementing a goal-setting program.
2. Present the corporate goals, and explain how and why an individual's personal goals support them.
3. Have employees establish their own goals and action plans. Encourage them to set challenging, stretch goals. Goals should be difficult, but not impossible.[18]
4. Train managers in how to conduct participative goal-setting sessions, and train employees in how to develop effective action plans.
5. Be supportive, and do not use goals to threaten employees.
6. Set goals that are under the employees' control, and provide them with the necessary resources.
7. Provide monetary incentives or other rewards for accomplishing goals.[19]

Step 3: Provide Support and Feedback Step 3 calls for providing employees with the necessary support elements or resources to get the job done. This includes ensuring that each employee has the necessary abilities and information to reach his or her goals. As a pair of goal-setting experts succinctly stated, "Motivation without knowledge is useless."[20] Training often is required to help employees achieve difficult goals. Moreover, managers should pay attention to employees' perceptions of effort → performance expectancies, self-efficacy, and valence of rewards. Finally, as we discuss next, employees should be provided with timely, specific feedback (knowledge of results) on how they are doing.

Feedback

Numerous surveys tell us that employees' hearty appetite for feedback too often goes unfulfilled. For example, "43% of employees feel they don't get enough guidance to improve their performance, according to the *WorkUSA 2004* survey by Watson Wyatt Worldwide."[21] Achievement-oriented students also want feedback. Following a difficult exam, for instance, students want to know two things: how they did and how their peers did. By letting students know how their work measures up to grading and competitive standards, an instructor's feedback permits the students to adjust their study habits so they can reach their goals. Likewise, managers in well-run organizations follow up goal setting with a feedback program to provide a rational basis for adjustment and improvement. For example, consider the following remarks by Fred Smith, the founder and CEO of FedEx, the overnight delivery pioneer with over $29 billion in annual revenues and more than 215,000 employees.[22] Smith's experience as a US Marine company commander during the Vietnam War helped shape his leadership style.

My leadership philosophy is a synthesis of the principles taught by the marines and every organization for the past 200 years.

When people walk in the door, they want to know: What do you expect out of me? What's in this deal for me? What do I have to do to get ahead? Where do I go in this organization to get justice if I'm not treated appropriately? They want to know how they're doing. They want some feedback. And they want to know that what they are doing is important.

If you take the basic principles of leadership and answer those questions over and over again, you can be successful dealing with people.[23]

Feedback

Objective information about performance.

As the term is used here, **feedback** is objective information about individual or collective performance. Subjective assessments such as, "You're doing a poor job," "You're lazy," or "We really appreciate your hard work" do not qualify as objective feedback. But hard data such as units sold, days absent, dollars saved, projects completed, customers satisfied, and quality rejects are all candidates for objective feedback programs. Christopher D Lee, author of the new book *Performance Conversations: An Alternative to Appraisals,* clarifies the concept of feedback by contrasting it with performance appraisals:

> Feedback is the exchange of information about the status and quality of work products. It provides a road map to success. It is used to motivate, support, direct, correct and regulate work efforts and outcomes. Feedback ensures that the manager and employees are in sync and agree on the standards and expectations of the work to be performed.
>
> Traditional appraisals, on the other hand, discourage two-way communication and treat employee involvement as a bad thing. Employees are discouraged from participating in a performance review, and when they do, their responses are often considered "rebuttals."
>
> To reverse this, successful performance management must contain a healthy degree of feedback and employee involvement.[24]

 2 Two Functions of Feedback

Experts say feedback serves two functions for those who receive it, one is *instructional* and the other *motivational*. Feedback instructs when it clarifies roles or teaches new behavior. For example, an assistant accountant might be advised to handle a certain entry as a capital item rather than as an expense item. On the other hand, feedback motivates when it serves as a reward or promises a reward.[25] Having the boss tell you that a grueling project you worked on earlier has just been completed can be a rewarding piece of news. As documented by researchers, the motivational function of feedback can be significantly enhanced by pairing *specific,* challenging goals with *specific* feedback about results.[26] With these two functions of feedback in mind, we now explore the vital role of feedback recipients, some practical lessons from feedback research, 360-degree feedback, and how to give feedback for coaching purposes.

Are the Feedback Recipients Ready, Willing, and Able?

Conventional wisdom says the more feedback organizational members get, the better. An underlying assumption is that feedback works automatically. Managers simply need to be motivated to give it. According to a meta-analysis of 23,663 feedback incidents, however, feedback is far from automatically effective. While feedback did, in fact, have a generally positive impact on performance, performance actually *declined* in more than 38% of the feedback incidents.[27] Feedback also can be warped by nontask factors, such as race. A laboratory study at Stanford University focused on cross-race feedback on the content (subjective feedback) and writing mechanics (objective feedback) of written essays. White students gave African-American students *less* critical *subjective* feedback than they did to white students. This positive racial bias disappeared with objective feedback.[28] These results are a bright caution light for those interested in improving job performance with feedback. Subjective feedback is easily contaminated by situational factors. Moreover, if objective feedback is to work as intended, managers need to understand the interaction between feedback recipients and their environment.[29]

The Recipient's Characteristics

Personality characteristics such as self-esteem and self-efficacy can help or hinder one's readiness for feedback. Those having low self-esteem and low self-efficacy generally do not actively seek feedback that, unfortunately, would tend to confirm those problems. Needs and goals also influence one's openness to feedback. In a laboratory study, Japanese psychology students who scored high on need for achievement responded more favorably to feedback than did their classmates who had low need for achievement.[30] This particular relationship likely exists in Western cultures as well. For example, 331 employees in the marketing department of a large public utility in the United States were found to seek feedback on important issues or when faced with uncertain situations. Long-tenured employees from this sample also were less likely to seek feedback than employees with little time on the job.[31] High self-monitors, those chameleonlike people we discussed in Chapter 5, are also more open to feedback because it helps them adapt their behavior to the situation. Recall from Chapter 5 that high self-monitoring employees were found to be better at initiating relationships with mentors (who typically provide feedback).[32] Low self-monitoring people, in contrast, are tuned into their own internal feelings more than they are to external cues. For example, someone observed that talking to media kingpin Ted Turner, a very low self-monitor, was like having a conversation with a radio!

Researchers have started to focus more directly on the recipient's actual desire for feedback, as opposed to indirectly on personality characteristics, needs, and goals. Everyday experience tells us that not everyone really wants the performance feedback they supposedly seek. Restaurant servers who ask, "How was everything?" while presenting the bill, typically are not interested in a detailed reply.

The Recipient's Perception of Feedback

The *sign* of feedback, a term used in feedback research, refers to whether it is positive or negative. Generally, people tend to perceive and recall positive feedback more accurately than they do negative feedback.[33] But feedback with a negative sign (e.g., being told your performance is below average) can have a positive motivational impact. In fact, in one study, those who were told they were below average on a creativity test subsequently outperformed those who were led to believe their results were above average. The subjects apparently took the negative feedback as a challenge and set and pursued higher goals. Those receiving positive feedback apparently were less motivated to do better.[34] Nonetheless, feedback with a negative sign or threatening content needs to be administered carefully to avoid creating insecurity and defensiveness. Self-efficacy also can be damaged by negative feedback, as discovered in a pair of experiments with business students. The researchers concluded, "To facilitate the development of strong efficacy beliefs, managers should be careful about the provision of negative feedback. Destructive criticism by managers which attributes the cause of poor performance to internal factors reduces both the beliefs of self-efficacy and the self-set goals of recipients."[35]

The Recipient's Cognitive Evaluation of Feedback Upon receiving feedback, people cognitively evaluate factors such as its accuracy, the credibility of the source, the fairness of the system (e.g., performance appraisal system), their performance-reward expectancies, and the reasonableness of the standards. Any feedback that fails to clear one or more of these cognitive hurdles will be rejected or downplayed. Personal experience largely dictates how these factors are weighed. For instance, you would probably discount feedback from someone who exaggerates or from someone who performed poorly on the same task you have just successfully completed. In view of the "trust gap," discussed in Chapter 11, managerial credibility is an ethical matter of central importance today. According to the authors of the book *Credibility: How Leaders Gain and Lose It, Why People Demand It,* "without a solid foundation of personal credibility, leaders can have no hope of enlisting others in a common vision."[36] Managers who have proven untrustworthy and not credible have a hard time improving job performance through feedback.

Feedback from a source who apparently shows favoritism or relies on unreasonable behavior standards would be suspect.[37] Also, as predicted by expectancy motivation theory, feedback must foster high effort→performance expectancies and performance→reward instrumentalities if it is to motivate desired behavior.

go to the Web for the Self-Exercise: How Strong Is Your Desire for Performance Feedback?

Practical Lessons from Feedback Research

After reviewing dozens of laboratory and field studies of feedback, a trio of OB researchers cited the following practical implications for managers:

- The acceptance of feedback should not be treated as a given; it is often misperceived or rejected. This is especially true in intercultural situations.
- Managers can enhance their credibility as sources of feedback by developing their expertise and creating a climate of trust.
- Negative feedback is typically misperceived or rejected.
- Although very frequent feedback may erode one's sense of personal control and initiative, feedback is too *infrequent* in most work organizations.
- Feedback needs to be tailored to the recipient.
- While average and below-average performers need extrinsic rewards for performance, high performers respond to feedback that enhances their feelings of competence and personal control.[38]

More recent research insights about feedback include the following:

- Computer-based performance feedback leads to greater improvements in performance when it is received directly from the computer system rather than via an immediate supervisor.[39]
- Recipients of feedback perceive it to be more accurate when they actively participate in the feedback session versus passively receiving feedback.[40]
- Destructive criticism tends to cause conflict and reduce motivation.[41]
- "The higher one rises in an organization the less likely one is to receive quality feedback about job performance."[42]

Table 9–2   *Six Common Trouble Signs for Organizational Feedback Systems*

1. Feedback is used to punish, embarrass, or put down employees.
2. Those receiving the feedback see it as irrelevant to their work.
3. Feedback information is provided too late to do any good.
4. People receiving feedback believe it relates to matters beyond their control.
5. Employees complain about wasting too much time collecting and recording feedback data.
6. Feedback recipients complain about feedback being too complex or difficult to understand.

SOURCE: Adapted from C Bell and R Zemke, "On-Target Feedback," *Training*, June 1992, pp 36–44.

Managers who act on these research implications and the trouble signs in Table 9–2 can build credible and effective feedback systems.

Our discussion to this point has focused on traditional downward feedback. Let us explore a newer and interesting approach to feedback in the workplace.

 3 360-Degree Feedback

The concept of **360-degree feedback** involves letting individuals compare their own perceived performance with behaviorally specific (and usually anonymous) performance information from their manager, subordinates, and peers. Even outsiders may be involved in what is sometimes called full-circle feedback.[43]

A recent meta-analysis of twenty-four 360-degree feedback studies in which the recipients were rated two or more times prompted this helpful conclusion from the researchers:

> improvement is most likely to occur when feedback indicates that change is necessary, recipients have a positive feedback orientation, perceive a need to change their behavior, react positively to the feedback, believe change is feasible, set appropriate goals to regulate their behavior, and take actions that lead to skill and performance improvement.[44]

Top management support and an organizational climate of openness can help 360-degree feedback programs succeed. For example,

> Procter & Gamble CEO A G Lafley finds out what his employees really think about him when he receives the results of his 360-degree feedback evaluation.
>
> The human resources tool that assesses strengths and

360-degree feedback

Comparison of anonymous feedback from one's superior, subordinates, and peers with self-perceptions.

A G Lafley, CEO of Procter & Gamble, has the courage to handle 360-degree feedback and the common sense to make changes.

weaknesses can be brutally honest because it lets a circle of people from executives on down give him anonymous performance reviews. The results show that others at P&G think Lafley is impatient. Lafley must also test the patience of others, because he is excoriated for being chronically late to meetings.[45]

Research evidence and personal experience lead us to *favor* anonymity and *discourage* linking 360-degree feedback to pay and promotion decisions.

According to one expert, *trust* is the issue:

Trust is at the core of using 360-degree feedback to enhance productivity. Trust determines how much an individual is willing to contribute for an employer. Using 360 confidentially, for developmental purposes, builds trust; using it to trigger pay and personnel decisions puts trust at risk.[46]

Thus, 360-degree feedback definitely has a place in the development of managerial skills, especially in today's team-based organizations.

How to Give Feedback for Coaching Purposes and Organizational Effectiveness

Managers need to keep the following tips in mind when giving feedback as part of a comprehensive performance management program:

- Focus on *performance,* not personalities.
- Give *specific* feedback linked to learning goals and performance outcome goals.
- Channel feedback toward *key result areas* for the organization.
- Give feedback as *soon* as possible.
- Give feedback to coach *improvement,* not just for final results (see the Real World/Real People feature on page 255).
- Base feedback on *accurate* and *credible* information.
- Pair feedback with *clear expectations* for improvement.[47]

go to the Web for the Self-Exercise: What Kind of Feedback Are You Getting?

Organizational Reward Systems

Rewards are an ever-present and always controversial feature of organizational life. (Think of the ongoing debate over CEO compensation packages in the hundreds of millions of dollars.)[48] Some employees see their jobs as the source of a paycheck and little else. Others derive great pleasure from their jobs and association with co-workers. In fact, according to a Gallup survey, 55% of American workers said "they would continue to work even if they won a lottery jackpot to the tune of $10 million."[49] (How about you?) Even volunteers who donate their time to charitable organizations, such as the Red Cross, walk away with rewards in the form of social recognition and pride of having given unselfishly of their time. Hence, the subject of organizational rewards

Coaching for Employee Growth at PwC

Like any organization, joining New York-based accounting firm PricewaterhouseCoopers (PwC) comes with a lot of questions. To answer them, and make sure employees always have a more experienced peer to turn to, the company launched its Connectivity program four years ago.

When new hires arrive, they are immediately assigned a Connectivity partner who contacts them, arranging to meet for lunch, or in some other informal setting, to establish a relationship that will be ongoing as long as the new employee is with the company. Each PwC executive that has risen to the level of partner with the firm has about a dozen less-experienced workers he or she is advising as part of the program.

"We're very focused on our people, and their development, their unique needs, and milestones in their careers," says Chief Learning Officer Tom Evans, who, as a firm partner himself, has individuals assigned

to him through Connectivity. "At the entry-level, it's very important that we invest in them so they understand what our firm is about, the meaning of being associated with our brand, and the level of professionalism and responsibility that goes with that."

Connectivity partners pinpoint areas new hires need to develop, sometimes recommending them for specific corporate learning programs, supporting the new recruits throughout the programs. They also can act as career counselors. "If they [the new hire] want to change the focus of their career," says Evans, "a partner can become an advocate for that person to help them change."

From the perspective of a new college graduate, what are the pros and cons of this program?

SOURCE : M Weinstein, "Well-Connected," *Training*, March 2007, p 24.

includes, but goes far beyond, monetary compensation.[50] This section examines key components of organizational reward systems to provide a conceptual background for discussing the timely topic of pay for performance.

Despite the fact that reward systems vary widely, it is possible to identify and interrelate some common components. The model in Figure 9–2 focuses on three important components: (1) types of rewards, (2) distribution criteria, and (3) desired outcomes. Let us examine these components.

Figure 9–2   *A General Model of Organizational Reward Systems*

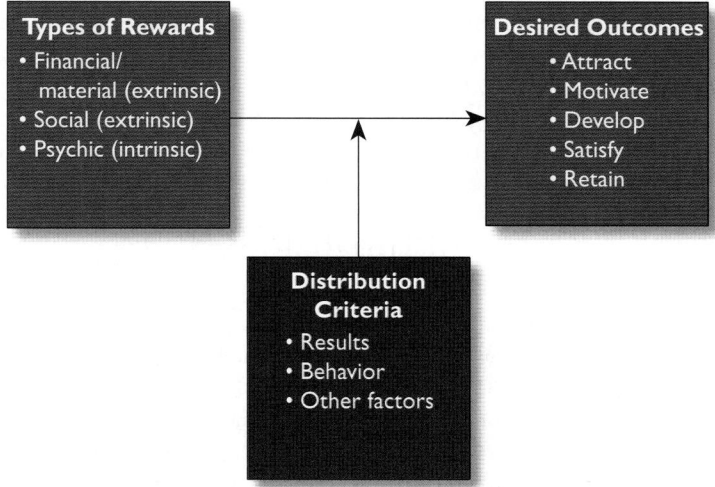

Types of Rewards

Financial, material, and social rewards qualify as **extrinsic rewards** because they come from the environment. Psychic rewards, however, are **intrinsic rewards** because they are self-granted. An employee who works to obtain extrinsic rewards, such as money or praise, is said to be extrinsically motivated. One who derives pleasure from the task itself or experiences a sense of competence or self-determination is said to be intrinsically motivated. The relative importance of extrinsic and intrinsic rewards is a matter of culture and personal tastes.[51]

Reward Distribution Criteria

According to one expert on organizational reward systems, three general criteria for the distribution of rewards are as follows:

- *Performance: results*. Tangible outcomes such as individual, group, or organization performance; quantity and quality of performance.

- *Performance: actions and behaviors*. Such as teamwork, cooperation, risk taking, creativity.

- *Nonperformance considerations*. Customary or contractual, where the type of job, nature of the work, equity, tenure, level in hierarchy, and so forth are rewarded.[52]

The trend today is toward performance criteria and away from nonperformance criteria such as seniority. For example, CEO Jeffrey Immelt is trying to bolster risk taking and innovation at General Electric by putting more emphasis on the second criterion listed above:

> To inspire the fresh thinking he's looking for, Immelt is wielding the one thing that speaks loud and clear: money. The GE chief is tying executives' compensation to their ability to come up with ideas, show improved customer service, generate cash growth, and boost sales instead of simply meeting bottom-line targets. As Immelt puts it, "you're not going to stick around this place and not take bets."[53]

Desired Outcomes of the Reward System

As listed in Figure 9–2, a good reward system should attract talented people and motivate and satisfy them once they have joined the organization. Further, a good reward system should foster personal growth and development and keep talented people from leaving. A prime example is Worthington Industries, the profitable steel processing firm in Columbus, Ohio, where the usual time clocks are not to be found. "Workers get profit-sharing payouts ranging from 40 to 70% of base pay, and the company pays 100% of health insurance premiums for employees and family members."[54] Worthington enjoys an industry-low turnover rate of 12% and a long line of job applicants.

The Building Blocks of Intrinsic Rewards and Motivation

As defined earlier, intrinsic rewards are self-granted. But this does not leave management out of the picture. Indeed, there is a great deal managers can do to create situations in which employees are more likely to experience intrinsic rewards and be intrinsically motivated.[55] Kenneth Thomas's model of intrinsic motivation provides helpful direction.[56] His model combines the job characteristics model of job design (discussed in Chapter 8), the concept of empowerment (discussed in Chapter 15), and

Figure 9–3   *Thomas's Building Blocks for Intrinsic Rewards and Motivation*

Choice	**Competence**
• Delegated authority • Trust in workers • Security (no punishment) for honest mistakes • A clear purpose • Information	• Knowledge • Positive feedback • Skill recognition • Challenge • High, noncomparative standards
Meaningfulness	**Progress**
• A non-cynical climate • Clearly identified passions • An exciting vision • Relevant task purposes • Whole tasks	• A collaborative climate • Milestones • Celebrations • Access to customers • Measurement of improvement

SOURCE: Reprinted with permission of the publisher. From K Thomas, *Intrinsic Motivation at Work: Building Energy and Commitment,* copyright © 2000 by K Thomas, Berrett-Koehler Publishers, Inc., San Francisco, CA. All rights reserved. www.bkconnection.com.

Edward Deci and Richard Ryan's cognitive evaluation theory. Deci and Ryan contend that people must satisfy their needs for autonomy and competence when completing a task for it to be intrinsically motivating.[57] Thomas uses the concept of *building blocks* to show managers how to construct the right conditions for four basic intrinsic rewards: meaningfulness, choice, competence, and progress (see Figure 9–3). Let us examine management's leadership challenges for each building block.

Leading for Meaningfulness Managers lead for meaningfulness by *inspiring* their employees and *modeling* desired behaviors. Figure 9–3 reveals managers can accomplish this by helping employees to identify their passions at work and creating an exciting organizational vision employees feel connected to. In support of this recommendation, results from Gallup poll surveys show that employees are more engaged and productive at work when they see the connection between their work and the organization's vision.[58] This connection creates a sense of purpose for employees. Imagine how intrinsically motivating it would be to work for Jay-Z, the rapper and president of Def Jam Records who finds great meaningfulness in his work:

With a roster that includes the likes of superstars Kanye West and Ludacris, and fresh

Rapper Jay-Z (right) can do it all: sing, get along with boss Russell Simmons (left), and *manage.*

acts such as Rihanna, Young Jeezy, and Rick Ross, the label has had plenty of hits. He says helping develop stars out of new artists is one of the rewards of the job.

"I love the process," he says. "Especially with a new artist, when somebody walks in and they don't understand what's going on and they are all wide-eyed. Then the next year, they are signing autographs and they're big, too."[59]

Leading for Choice

Managers lead for choice by *empowering* employees and *delegating* meaningful assignments and tasks. Consider how Gail Evans, an executive vice president at Atlanta-based CNN, and Judy Lewent, senior vice president and chief financial officer for pharmaceutical giant Merck & Co., feel about leading for choice.

> Gail Evans . . . says delegating is essential. If you refuse to let your staff handle their own projects, you're jeopardizing their advancement—because they aren't learning new skills and adding successes to their resume—and you're wasting your precious hours doing someone else's work. . . . For Lewent, delegating the responsibility of running staff meetings to one of her team members means she can sit back and observe her employees, an activity that helps her make decisions about their career development. It also lets her subordinates hone their leadership skills—a must as they move up the ladder. In fact, when asked for her single definition of a good boss, Lewent says, "someone who understands the true art of teamwork and delegation."[60]

Leading for Competence

Managers lead for competence by *supporting* and *coaching* their employees. Figure 9–3 provides examples of how this might be done. Managers first need to make sure employees have the knowledge needed to successfully perform their jobs. Deficiencies can be handled through training and mentoring. Providing positive feedback and sincere recognition can also be coupled with the assignment of a challenging task to fuel employees' intrinsic motivation.

Leading for Progress

Managers lead for progress by *monitoring* and *rewarding* others. Douglas R Conant, who in his six years as CEO of Campbell Soup Company has engineered a remarkable turnaround, is a good role model in this regard:

> The turnaround has been catalyzed by cost-cutting, smart innovations, and a concerted effort to reinvigorate the workforce. . . .
>
> Conant hasn't shaken up a complacent 137-year-old company by being in-your-face. He happily gives others credit and deflects praise. He's not brash. . . . In his time at Campbell, he has sent out more than 16,000 hand-written thank-you notes to staffers, from the chief investment officer to the receptionist at headquarters—notes often found hanging in people's offices or above their desks. "[In business] we're trained to find things that are wrong, but I try to celebrate what's right," says Conant.[61]

We now direct our attention to *extrinsic* rewards—money, opportunities, and recognition granted by others.

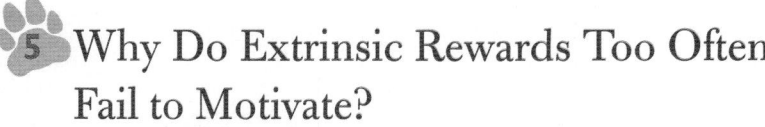

5 Why Do Extrinsic Rewards Too Often Fail to Motivate?

Despite huge investments of time and money for monetary and nonmonetary compensation, the desired motivational impact often is not achieved. A management consultant/writer offers these eight reasons:

1. Too much emphasis on monetary rewards.
2. Rewards lack an "appreciation effect."
3. Extensive benefits become entitlements.
4. Counterproductive behavior is rewarded. (For example, "a pizza delivery company focused its rewards on the on-time performance of its drivers, only to discover that it was inadvertently rewarding reckless driving."[62])
5. Too long a delay between performance and rewards.
6. Too many one-size-fits-all rewards.
7. Use of one-shot rewards with a short-lived motivational impact.
8. Continued use of demotivating practices such as layoffs, across-the-board raises and cuts, and excessive executive compensation.[63]

These stubborn problems have fostered a search for more effective extrinsic reward practices. While a thorough discussion of modern compensation practices[64] is way beyond our present scope, we can explore a general approach to boosting the motivational impact of monetary rewards—pay for performance.

Pay for Performance

Pay for performance is the popular term for monetary incentives linking at least some portion of the paycheck directly to results or accomplishments. Many refer to it simply as *incentive pay,* while others call it *variable pay.* "Broad-based variable pay programs are offered by 80% of US companies."[65] The general idea behind pay-for-performance schemes—including but not limited to merit pay, bonuses, and profit sharing—is to give employees an incentive for working harder or smarter. Pay

"HIGGINS, BOTH YOU AND FERGUSON WILL BE GOING AFTER THE SAME CARROT."

SOURCE: *Harvard Business Review,* September 2006, p 100.

Pay for performance
Monetary incentives tied to one's results or accomplishments.

for performance is something extra, compensation above and beyond basic wages and salaries. Proponents of incentive compensation say something extra is needed because hourly wages and fixed salaries do little more than motivate people to show up at work and put in the required hours.[66] The most basic form of pay for performance is the traditional piece-rate plan, whereby the employee is paid a specified amount of money for each unit of work. For example, 2,500 artisans at Longaberger's, in Frazeyburg, Ohio, are paid a fixed amount for each handcrafted wooden basket they weave. Together, they produce 40,000 of the prized maple baskets daily.[67] Sales commissions, whereby a salesperson receives a specified amount of money for each unit sold, is another long-standing example of pay for performance. Today's service economy is forcing management to creatively adapt and go beyond piece rate and sales commission plans to accommodate greater emphasis on product and service quality, interdependence, and teamwork.

Current Practices For an indication of current practices, see Table 9–3, which is based on a survey of 156 US executives. The lack of clear patterns in Table 9–3 is indicative of the still experimental nature of incentive compensation today. Much remains to be learned from research and practice.

These folks not only make really cool picnic baskets, they actually work *inside* one! Longaberger's headquarters building in Frazeyburg, Ohio, is a giant replica of the firm's famous maple wood baskets. Each day, 2,500 employees who are paid on a piece-rate basis weave 40,000 handcrafted baskets. This team of Longaberger employees recently won a prestigious quality award for cutting waste and improving productivity.

Research Insights According to available expert opinion and research results, pay for performance too often falls short of its goal of improved job performance. "Experts say that roughly half the incentive plans they see don't work, victims of poor design and administration."[68] In fact, one study documented how incentive pay had a *negative* effect on the performance of 150,000 managers from 500 financially distressed companies.[69] A meta-analysis of 39 studies found only a modest positive correlation between financial incentives and performance *quantity* and no impact on performance *quality*.[70] Other researchers have found only a weak statistical link between large executive bonuses paid out in good years and subsequent improvement in corporate profitability.[71] Also, in a survey of small business owners, more than half said their commission plans failed to motivate extra effort from their salespeople.[72] Linking teachers' merit pay to student performance, an exciting school reform idea, turned out to be a big disappointment: "The bottom line is that despite high hopes, none of the 13 districts studied was able to use teacher pay incentives to achieve significant, lasting gains in student performance."[73]

A recent study of variable pay plans by Hewitt Associates, a leading human resources consulting firm, uncovered this instructive pattern:

[M]ore than one-third (41%) of the companies with single-digit revenue growth said the cost outweighed the benefits for them. Not only have the plans failed to improve business results for a quarter of these organizations, they have actually led to adverse results for 26% of those surveyed.

The situation was reversed, however, for companies experiencing double-digit revenue growth. These companies reported that their programs achieved positive outcomes and contributed to business results. "We've found that companies achieving high-revenue growth have successful programs because they provide the appropriate amount of administrative, communication and monetary support," says Paul Shafer, a business leader for Hewitt. If not implemented well, he says, variable pay "will be seen as an entitlement by employees and a substantial loss to employers."[74]

Clearly, the pay-for-performance area is still very much up in the air.

6 Getting the Most out of Extrinsic Rewards and Pay for Performance

Based on what we have learned to date,[75] here is a workable plan for maximizing the motivational impact of extrinsic rewards:

- Tie praise, recognition, and noncash awards to *specific* results.
- Make pay for performance an integral part of the organization's basic strategy (e.g., pursuit of best-in-the-industry product or service quality).

Table 9–3   *The Use and Effectiveness of Modern Incentive Pay Plans*

PLAN TYPE	PRESENTLY HAVE	RATED HIGHLY EFFECTIVE
Annual bonus	74%	20%
Special one-time spot awards (after the fact)	42	38
Individual incentives	39	27
Long-term incentives (executive level)	32	44
Lump-sum merit pay	28	19
Competency-based pay	22	31
Profit-sharing (apart from retirement program)	22	43
Profit-sharing (as part of retirement program)	22	46
ESOP* stock plan	21	33
Suggestion/proposal programs	17	19
Team-based pay	15	29
Long-term incentives (below executive levels)	13	43
Skill-/knowledge-based pay	12	58
Group incentives (not team-based)	11	24
Pay for quality	9	29
Gainsharing	8	38
Special key-contributor programs (before the fact)	7	55

*Employee stock ownership plan.

SOURCE: Adapted from "Incentive Pay Plans: Which Ones Work . . . and Why?" From the April 2001 issue of IOMA's HR Focus newsletter. Used by permission.

- Base incentive determinations on objective performance data.
- Have all employees actively participate in the development, implementation, and revision of the performance-pay formulas.
- Encourage two-way communication so problems with the incentive plan will be detected early.
- Build pay-for-performance plans around participative structures such as suggestion systems or problem-solving teams.
- Reward teamwork and cooperation whenever possible.
- Actively sell the plan to supervisors and middle managers who may view employee participation as a threat to their traditional notion of authority.
- If annual cash bonuses are granted, pay them in a lump sum to maximize their motivational impact.
- Selectively use creative noncash rewards to create buzz and excitement (see the Real World/Real People feature on page 262).

go to the Web for the Group Exercise: Rewards, Rewards, Rewards

Good Job: Here Are the Keys to My BMW M3

What's the best way to keep a young company in the fast lane? Graham Weston, 42, co-founder and CEO of Rackspace Managed Hosting, based in San Antonio, hands top performers the keys to one of his cars, a BMW M3 convertible, for a week. Finding creative ways to recognize the stars on his 1,000-employee staff has helped Weston grow annual sales to $139 million at seven-year-old Rackspace, which hosts Web applications for other firms.

"I think it's one of the biggest bargains in business," Weston says. "If you gave somebody a $200 bonus, it wouldn't mean very much. When someone gets to drive my car for a week, they never forget it." For extra recognition, he offers workers the use of a guest house he owns on the Comal River in New Braunfels, Texas, where the water is 72 degrees year round.

Would these unique rewards motivate you to work harder and bolster your company loyalty?

SOURCE: Excerpted from E Pofeldt, "What Makes a Great Boss? Graham Weston, Rackspace," *Fortune*, October 16, 2006, pp 192[D]–192[F].

 ## 7 Positive Reinforcement

Feedback and extrinsic reward programs too often are ineffective because they are administered in haphazard ways.[76] For example, consider these scenarios:

- A young programmer stops e-mailing creative suggestions to his boss because she never responds.
- The office politician gets a great promotion while her more skilled co-workers scratch their heads and gossip about the injustice.

In the first instance, a productive behavior faded away for lack of encouragement. In the second situation, unproductive behavior was unwittingly rewarded. Feedback and rewards need to be handled more precisely. Fortunately, the field of behavioral psychology can help. Thanks to the pioneering work of Edward L Thorndike, B F Skinner, and many others, a behavior modification technique called *positive reinforcement* helps managers achieve needed discipline and desired effect when providing feedback and granting extrinsic rewards.

Thorndike's Law of Effect

Law of effect

Behavior with favorable consequences is repeated; behavior with unfavorable consequences disappears.

During the early 1900s, Edward L Thorndike observed in his psychology laboratory that a cat would behave randomly and wildly when placed in a small box with a secret trip lever that opened a door. However, once the cat accidentally tripped the lever and escaped, the animal would go straight to the lever when placed back in the box. Hence, Thorndike formulated his famous **law of effect,** which says *behavior with favorable consequences tends to be repeated, while behavior with unfavorable consequences tends to disappear.* [77] This was a dramatic departure from the prevailing notion a century ago that behavior was the product of inborn instincts.

Skinner's Operant Conditioning Model

Skinner refined Thorndike's conclusion that behavior is controlled by its consequences. Skinner's work became known as *behaviorism* because he dealt strictly with observable behavior.[78] As a behaviorist, Skinner believed it was pointless to explain behavior in terms of unobservable inner states such as needs, drives, attitudes, or thought processes.[79] He similarly put little stock in the idea of self-determination.

In his 1938 classic, *The Behavior of Organisms,* Skinner drew an important distinction between the two types of behavior: respondent and operant behavior.[80] He labeled unlearned reflexes, or stimulus–response (S–R) connections, **respondent behavior.** This category of behavior was said to describe a very small proportion of adult human behavior. Examples of respondent behavior would include shedding tears while peeling onions and reflexively withdrawing one's hand from a hot stove.[81] Skinner attached the label **operant behavior** to behavior that is learned when one "operates on" the environment to produce desired consequences. Some call this the response–stimulus (R–S) model. Years of controlled experiments with pigeons in "Skinner boxes" helped Skinner develop a sophisticated technology of behavior control, or operant conditioning. For example, he taught pigeons how to pace figure-eights and how to bowl by reinforcing the underweight (and thus hungry) birds with food whenever they more closely approximated target behaviors. Skinner's work spawned the field of behavior modification and has significant implications for OB because the vast majority of organizational behavior falls into the operant category.[82]

Renowned behavioral psychologist B F Skinner and your co-author Bob Kreitner met and posed for a snapshot at an Academy of Management meeting in Boston. As a behaviorist, Skinner preferred to deal with observable behavior and its antecedents and consequences in the environment rather than with inner states such as attitudes and cognitive processes. Professor Skinner was a fascinating man who left a permanent mark on modern psychology.

Contingent Consequences

Contingent consequences, according to Skinner's operant theory, control behavior in four ways: positive reinforcement, negative reinforcement, punishment, and extinction. The term contingent means there is a systematic if-then linkage between the target behavior and the consequence. Remember Mom (and Pink Floyd) saying something to this effect: "If you don't finish your dinner, you don't get dessert" (see Figure 9–4)? To avoid the all-too-common mislabeling of these consequences, let us review some formal definitions.

8 ⓿ Positive Reinforcement Strengthens Behavior Positive reinforcement is the process of strengthening a behavior by contingently presenting something pleasing. (Importantly, a behavior is strengthened when it increases in frequency and weakened when it decreases in frequency.) A design engineer who works overtime because of praise and recognition from the boss is responding to positive reinforcement.[83]

Similarly, people tend to return to businesses where they are positively reinforced with high-quality service. For example, Commerce Bank, based in Cherry Hill, New Jersey, owes part of its success and rapid growth to a culture based on positive reinforcement. Commerce tries hard to "wow" its customers with service innovations such as Sunday banking hours.

> Employees are praised for being "wowy." And every March, [CEO Vernon] Hill recognizes top performers at the companywide Wow Awards. " 'Wow' is more than a word

Respondent behavior

Skinner's term for unlearned stimulus–response reflexes.

Operant behavior

Skinner's term for learned, consequence-shaped behavior.

Positive reinforcement

Making behavior occur more often by contingently presenting something positive.

Figure 9–4 *Contingent Consequences in Operant Conditioning*

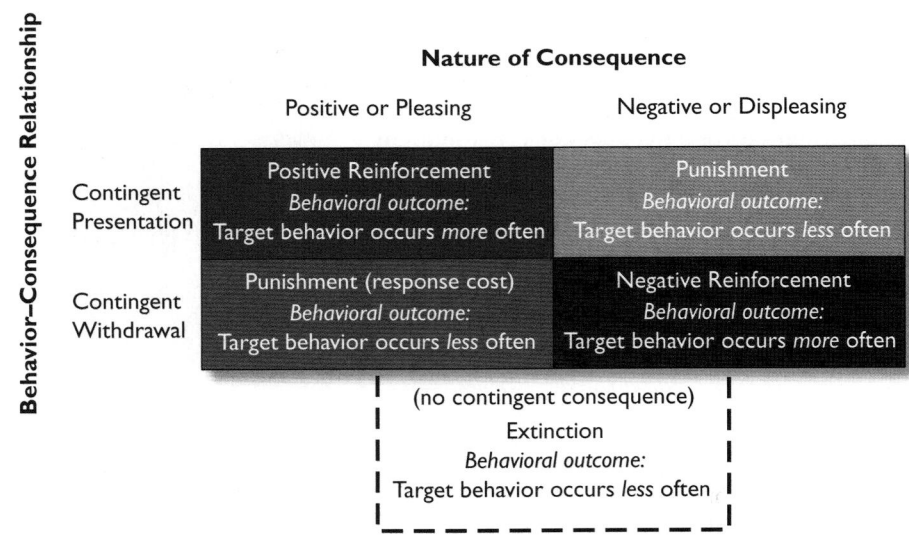

around here," says John Manning, vice president of—that's right—the Wow Department. "It's a feeling that you give and get."

That type of obsessive service culture starts with hiring the right people. "This is not the job for someone who's interested in being cool or indifferent," Manning says. And instead of the usual humdrum orientation class, every new employee attends a one-day course at Commerce University called Traditions. It's part game show, part training session, part common sense. Banks do all sorts of stupid things to customers, Manning tells new hires. That's why the company has a "Kill a Stupid Rule" program. "If you identify a rule that prevents you from wowing customers," Manning says, "we'll pay you 50 bucks."[84]

Negative reinforcement

Making behavior occur more often by contingently withdrawing something negative.

Negative Reinforcement Also Strengthens Behavior Negative reinforcement is the process of strengthening a behavior by contingently withdrawing something displeasing. For example, an army sergeant who stops yelling when a recruit jumps out of bed has negatively reinforced that particular behavior. Similarly, the behavior of clamping our hands over our ears when watching a jumbo jet take off is negatively reinforced by relief from the noise. Negative reinforcement is often confused with punishment. But the two strategies have opposite effects on behavior. Negative reinforcement, as the word *reinforcement* indicates, strengthens a behavior because it provides relief from an unpleasant situation.

Punishment

Making behavior occur less often by contingently presenting something negative or withdrawing something positive.

Punishment Weakens Behavior Punishment is the process of weakening behavior through either the contingent presentation of something displeasing or the contingent withdrawal of something positive. A manager assigning a tardy employee to a dirty job exemplifies the first type of punishment. Docking a tardy employee's pay is an example of the second type of punishment, called *response cost punishment*. Legal fines involve response cost punishment. Salespeople who must make up any

cash register shortages out of their own pockets are being managed through response cost punishment. Ethical questions can and should be raised about this type of on-the-job punishment.[85]

Extinction Also Weakens Behavior Extinction is the weakening of a behavior by ignoring it or making sure it is not reinforced. Getting rid of a former boyfriend or girlfriend by refusing to answer their phone calls is an extinction strategy. A good analogy for extinction is to imagine what would happen to your houseplants if you stopped watering them. Like a plant without water, a behavior without occasional reinforcement eventually dies. Although very different processes, both punishment and extinction have the same weakening effect on behavior.

Extinction

Making behavior occur less often by ignoring or not reinforcing it.

Schedules of Reinforcement

As just illustrated, contingent consequences are an important determinant of future behavior. The *timing* of behavioral consequences can be even more important. Based on years of tedious laboratory experiments with pigeons in highly controlled environments, Skinner and his colleagues discovered distinct patterns of responding for various schedules of reinforcement.[86]

Although some of their conclusions can be generalized to negative reinforcement, punishment, and extinction, it is best to think only of positive reinforcement when discussing schedules.

Continuous Reinforcement Every instance of a target behavior is reinforced when a **continuous reinforcement** (CRF) schedule is in effect. For instance, when your television set is operating properly, you are reinforced with a picture every time you turn it on (a CRF schedule). But, as with any CRF schedule of reinforcement, the behavior of turning on the television will undergo rapid extinction if the set breaks.

Continuous reinforcement

Reinforcing every instance of a behavior.

Intermittent reinforcement Unlike CRF schedules, **intermittent reinforcement** involves reinforcement of *some* but not all instances of a target behavior. Four subcategories of intermittent schedules are fixed and variable ratio schedules and fixed and variable interval schedules. Reinforcement in *ratio* schedules is contingent on the number of responses observed. *Interval* reinforcement is tied to the passage of time. Some common examples of the four types of intermittent reinforcement are as follows:

Intermittent Reinforcement

Reinforcing some but not all instances of behavior.

- *Fixed ratio*—piece-rate pay; bonuses tied to the sale of a fixed number of units.
- *Variable ratio*—slot machines that pay off after a variable number of lever pulls; lotteries that pay off after the purchase of a variable number of tickets.
- *Fixed interval*—hourly pay; annual salary paid on a regular basis.
- *Variable interval*—random supervisory praise and pats on the back for employees who have been doing a good job.

Scheduling Is Critical The schedule of reinforcement can more powerfully influence behavior than the magnitude of reinforcement. Although this proposition grew out of experiments with pigeons, subsequent on-the-job research confirmed it. Consider, for example, a field study of 12 unionized beaver trappers employed by a lumber company to keep the large rodents from eating newly planted tree seedlings.[87]

The beaver trappers were randomly divided into two groups that alternated weekly between two different bonus plans. Under the first schedule, each trapper earned his regular $7 per hour wage plus $1 for each beaver caught. Technically, this bonus was paid on a CRF schedule. The second bonus plan involved the regular $7 per hour wage plus a one-in-four chance (as determined by rolling the dice) of receiving $4 for each beaver trapped. This second bonus plan qualified as a variable ratio (VR-4) schedule. In the long run, both incentive schemes averaged out to a $1-per-beaver bonus. Surprisingly, however, when the trappers were under the VR-4 schedule, they were 58% more productive than under the CRF schedule, despite the fact that the net amount of pay averaged out the same for the two groups during the 12-week trapping season.

Work Organizations Typically Rely on the Weakest Schedule

Generally, variable ratio and variable interval schedules of reinforcement produce the strongest behavior that is most resistant to extinction. As gamblers will attest, variable schedules hold the promise of reinforcement after the next target response. For example, the following drama at a Laughlin, Nevada, gambling casino is one more illustration of the potency of variable ratio reinforcement:

> An elderly woman with a walker had lost her grip on the slot [machine] handle and had collapsed on the floor.
>
> "Help," she cried weakly.
>
> The woman at the machine next to her interrupted her play for a few seconds to try to help her to her feet, but all around her the army of slot players continued feeding coins to the machines.
>
> A security man arrived to soothe the woman and take her away.
>
> "Thank you," she told him appreciatively.
>
> "But don't forget my winnings."[88]

Organizations without at least some variable reinforcement are less likely to prompt this type of dedication to task. For example, consider this mix of fixed interval (going home early every Friday) and variable ratio (spot cash bonuses) at Kimley-Horn & Associates, a Cary, North Carolina, engineering firm: "[E]mployees typically work 7:30 to 5:30, Mondays through Thursdays, and leave at 11:30 AM on Fridays. And any employee can award a $50 on-the-spot bonus to a colleague."[89]

Despite the trend toward this sort of pay-for-performance, time-based pay schemes such as hourly wages and yearly salaries that rely on the weakest schedule of reinforcement (fixed interval) are still the rule in today's workplaces. (See the Ethical Dilemma at the end of this chapter for a controversial alternative.)

9 Behavior Shaping

Have you ever wondered how trainers at aquarium parks manage to get bottle-nosed dolphins to do flips, killer whales to carry people on their backs, and seals to juggle balls? The results are seemingly magical. Actually, a mundane learning process called shaping is responsible for the animals' antics.

Two-ton killer whales, for example, have a big appetite, and they find buckets of fish very reinforcing. So if the trainer wants to ride a killer whale, he or she reinforces very basic behaviors that will eventually lead to the whale being ridden. The killer whale is contingently reinforced with a few fish for coming near the trainer, then for being touched, then for putting its nose in a harness, then for being straddled, and eventually for swimming with the trainer on its back. In effect, the trainer systematically raises the behavioral requirement for reinforcement.[90] Thus, **shaping** is defined as the process of reinforcing closer and closer approximations to a target behavior.

Shaping works very well with people, too, especially in training and quality programs involving continuous improvement. Praise, recognition, and instructive and credible feedback cost managers little more than moments of their time. Yet, when used in conjunction with learning goals and a behavior-shaping program, these consequences can efficiently foster significant improvements in job performance.[91] The key to successful behavior shaping lies in reducing a complex target behavior to easily learned steps and then faithfully (and patiently) reinforcing any improvement. For example, Continental Airlines used a cash bonus program to improve its on-time arrival record from one of the worst in the industry to one of the best. Employees originally were promised a $65 bonus each month Continental earned a top-five ranking. Now it takes a second- or third-place ranking to earn the $65 bonus and a $100 bonus awaits employees when they achieve a number one ranking.[92] (Table 9–4 lists practical tips on shaping.)

Shaping
Reinforcing closer and closer approximations to a target behavior.

Table 9–4   *Ten Practical Tips for Shaping Job Behavior*

1. *Accommodate the process of behavioral change.* Behaviors change in gradual stages, not in broad, sweeping motions.
2. *Define new behavior patterns specifically.* State what you wish to accomplish in explicit terms and in small amounts that can be easily grasped.
3. *Give individuals feedback on their performance.* A once-a-year performance appraisal is not sufficient.
4. *Reinforce behavior as quickly as possible.*
5. *Use powerful reinforcement.* To be effective, rewards must be important to the employee—not to the manager.
6. *Use a continuous reinforcement schedule.* New behaviors should be reinforced every time they occur. This reinforcement should continue until these behaviors become habitual.
7. *Use a variable reinforcement schedule for maintenance.* Even after behavior has become habitual, it still needs to be rewarded, though not necessarily every time it occurs.
8. *Reward teamwork—not competition.* Group goals and group rewards are one way to encourage cooperation in situations in which jobs and performance are interdependent.
9. *Make all rewards contingent on performance.*
10. *Never take good performance for granted.* Even superior performance, if left unrewarded, will eventually deteriorate.

SOURCE: Adapted from A T Hollingsworth and D Tanquay Hoyer, "How Supervisors Can Shape Behavior," *Personnel Journal,* May 1985, pp 86, 88.

Summary of Key Concepts

1. *Define the term* performance management, *distinguish between learning goals and performance outcome goals, and explain the three-step goal-setting process.* Performance management is a continuous cycle of improving individual job performance with goal setting, feedback and coaching, and rewards and positive reinforcement. Learning goals encourage learning, creativity, and skill development. Performance outcome goals target specified end-results. The three-step goal-setting process includes (1) set goals that are SMART—specific, measurable, attainable, results oriented, and time bound; (2) promote goal commitment with clear explanations, participation, and supportiveness; (3) provide support and feedback by providing information, needed training, and knowledge of results.

2. *Identify the two basic functions of feedback, and specify at least three practical lessons from feedback research.* Feedback, in the form of objective information about performance, both instructs and motivates. Feedback is not automatically accepted as intended, especially negative feedback. Managerial credibility can be enhanced through expertise and a climate of trust. Feedback must not be too frequent or too scarce and must be tailored to the individual. Feedback directly from computers is effective. Active participation in the feedback session helps people perceive feedback as more accurate. The quality of feedback received decreases as one moves up the organizational hierarchy.

3. *Define 360-degree feedback, and summarize how to give good feedback in a performance management program.* A focal person receives anonymous 360-degree feedback from subordinates, the manager, peers, and selected others such as customers or suppliers. Good feedback is tied to performance goals and clear expectations, linked with specific behavior or results, reserved for key result areas, given as soon as possible, provided for improvement as well as for final results, focused on performance rather than on personalities, and based on accurate and credible information.

4. *Distinguish between extrinsic and intrinsic rewards, and explain the four building blocks of intrinsic rewards and motivation.* Extrinsic rewards—including pay, material goods, and social recognition—are granted by others. Intrinsic rewards are psychic rewards, such as a sense of competence or a feeling of accomplishment, that are self-granted and experienced internally. According to Thomas's model, the four basic intrinsic rewards are meaningfulness, choice, competence, and progress. Managers can boost intrinsic motivation by letting employees work on important whole tasks (meaningfulness), delegating and trusting (choice), providing challenge and feedback (competence), and collaboratively celebrating improvement (progress).

5. *Summarize the reasons why extrinsic rewards often fail to motivate employees.* Extrinsic reward systems can fail to motivate employees for these reasons: overemphasis on money, no appreciation effect, benefits become entitlements, wrong behavior is rewarded, rewards are delayed too long, use of one-size-fits-all rewards, one-shot rewards with temporary impact, and demotivating practices such as layoffs.

6. *Discuss how managers can generally improve extrinsic reward and pay-for-performance plans.* They need to be strategically anchored, based on quantified performance data, highly participative, actively sold to supervisors and middle managers, and teamwork oriented. Annual bonuses of significant size are helpful.

7. *State Thorndike's law of effect, and explain Skinner's distinction between respondent and operant behavior.* According to Edward L Thorndike's law of effect, behavior with favorable consequences tends to be repeated, while behavior with unfavorable consequences tends to disappear. B F Skinner called unlearned stimulus–response reflexes respondent behavior. He applied the term operant behavior to all behavior learned through experience with environmental consequences.

8. *Define* positive reinforcement, negative reinforcement, punishment, *and* extinction, *and distinguish between continuous and intermittent schedules of reinforcement.* Positive and negative reinforcement are consequence management strategies that strengthen behavior, whereas punishment and extinction weaken behavior. These strategies need to be defined objectively in terms of their actual impact on behavior frequency, not subjectively on the basis of intended impact.

    Every instance of a behavior is reinforced with a continuous reinforcement (CRF) schedule. Under intermittent reinforcement schedules—fixed and variable ratio or fixed and variable interval—some, rather than all, instances of a target behavior are reinforced. Variable schedules produce the most extinction-resistant behavior.

9. *Demonstrate your knowledge of behavior shaping.* Behavior shaping occurs when closer and closer approximations of a target behavior are reinforced. In effect, the standard for reinforcement is made more difficult as the individual learns. The process begins with continuous reinforcement, which gives way to intermittent reinforcement when the target behavior becomes strong and habitual.

OB in Action Case Study

A Real Stake in Your Customers[93]

BusinessWeek Nancy Kramer had a surprise up her sleeve. A few weeks before last January's annual meeting of Resource Interactive, the marketing agency she founded, Kramer sent an e-mail to her 140 employees. With mock seriousness, she said she needed some "VERRRRRRYYYYYY" important information before the meeting: their height in centimeters, favorite candy, shoe size, and favorite movie. Employees weren't thrown by the quirky message: Kramer, who co-produced the infamous Victoria's Secret online fashion show, once hired a pancake flipper to come to the office (employees caught their breakfast on a plate) and sometimes lies on the floor during meetings.

For the annual gathering, the only info she really needed was shoe size. Kramer and Kelly Mooney, with whom she runs the company, were about to introduce a new employee benefit called REEF, or Resource Employee Equity Fund, and were giving each staffer a pair of flip-flops by the surfwear brand REEF. The fund holds one share of stock per employee for each of Resource's publicly traded clients. Employees vest in the fund after a year.

Kramer's idea is an innovative approach to motivating employees and keeping them focused on their clients' businesses. "I wanted our employees to have the awareness of how clients are pressured," she says. "If [the stock price] does go down, what can we do to help?"

Ed Razek, Limited Brands' chief marketing officer, is impressed with Kramer's effort to turn her employees into shareholders. While other agencies might show their commitment by wearing clothes made by a client or driving its vehicles, he says, REEF is different. "It's ongoing, and it has value over time. Kelly and Nancy are telling their people very pointedly that what they do has to be measured."

Kramer's focus on results comes after 25 years of working with clients. She started out in media sales for an Ohio radio station, where she got to know a couple of manufacturers' sales reps. With them, Kramer launched Columbus-based Resource in 1981, at age 26. She eventually bought out her partners and built Resource into a full-service marketing firm with a growing Internet business.

Kramer got the idea for REEF in the late 1990s as she watched newly public bicoastal agencies toss stock options to their employees. But the boom went bust before Kramer could give REEF a try, and attracting talent was hardly her problem anymore. In early 2001, client bankruptcies erased half of her sales in 90 days.

But the idea stayed with her. As her company grew to $16 million in revenues and was ranked by *AdWeek* as one of the top 50 interactive agencies, Kramer decided to revisit it. She approached Merrill Lynch in 2004. "They said, 'It's too complicated,'" Mooney recalls. Merrill Lynch spokeswoman Jennifer Grigas says the adviser told Kramer the plan would be difficult to implement and described some of its financial implications. Kramer's tax advisers at PricewaterhouseCoopers also initially questioned the idea. After 18 months of planning, Kramer and Mooney laid out $1,337 per employee to buy one share of each of the firm's publicly traded clients (including Procter & Gamble and Hewlett-Packard). They also boosted associates' salaries the first year to offset any income tax hits.

Since its inception, the fund has done slightly better than the Standard & Poor's 500-stock index, which has returned just 0.3%. Still, there's more to the benefit than money, says John Kadlic, who joined Resource in May as executive director of business development. "Certainly, there was a financial interest," he says, noting that REEF, as well as Resource's reputation as a great place to work, was a factor in his decision to join. "But it was more about what it said to me about their values." There are few better ways to win a talent war than that.

Questions for Discussion

1. What role does the concept of "line of sight" play in this case? Is it a good motivational technique? Explain.

2. Is the REEF benefit an intrinsic or extrinsic reward? Explain.

3. In terms of Thomas's four building blocks in Figure 9–3, how would you rate Resource Interactive's potential for generating intrinsic motivation? Explain.

4. Is REEF an effective positive reinforcement program? Explain.

5. What is your personal view of REEF? Would it motivate you to be a harder working employee? Explain.

Ethical Dilemma

Care to Try Your Luck with This Incentive Program?

Most employee incentive programs are based on the presumed power of delayed gratification. Dangle a big prize or bonus in front of employees, the thinking goes, and they'll work hard for months to earn it.

A new kind of incentive program built around online gaming aims to change all that. Using Web-based software, the program allows employees to earn tokens for small accomplishments—coming back early from lunch, say, or shaving time off a sales call—and gamble for prizes, from iPods to prime parking spots. With its emphasis on immediate, rather than delayed, gratification, the system allows managers to skip the pep talks in favor of a kind of Pavlovian conditioning, says Brooks Mitchell, a management professor at the University of Wyoming and the founder of Snowfly, a software company in Laramie that designs such systems. "If you want your kid to get an A, don't give him 50 bucks at the end of the year," Mitchell says. "Instead, play soccer with him every day after he does his homework."

That argument makes sense to Fred Weiner, CEO of the Connection, a call-center operator based in Burnsville, Minnesota. For 25 years, Weiner has been searching for a way to motivate the customer service representatives at his five call centers, doling out incentive prizes such as cash and gift cards almost every month. But nothing seemed to work.

Last January, Weiner noticed a Snowfly brochure in an office trash can, fished it out, and gave Mitchell a call. Intrigued with what he heard, he decided to try the program. Now each time call center reps convert a sale, for example, they log on to their accounts, record their accomplishments, and receive a virtual token, which they can use as a wager in one of several games—such as a horse racing derby—that take seconds to complete. Employees can win up to 5,000 points at a time and redeem them for prizes, such as a 15-minute break (250 points) or a day off (7,600 points). And since they can't lose points, everyone's a winner.

Weiner has seen an improvement in measurable metrics, such as sales conversion, talk time, and attendance. "They are absolutely performing better," he says. The program has gotten a thumbs-up from staffers, as well. Mary Fournier, a supervisor in the Carlsbad, New Mexico, call center, works hard to earn tokens and plays games during downtime. She recently hoarded tokens for four months and used 11,000 points to buy a $100 Cuisinart, an item on the Connection's incentive list. "I enjoy the gambling aspect of it," she says. "It's a little bit of a rush."[94]

If your company was considering the Snowfly program, what would be your ethical evaluation?

1. No problem; it would introduce some harmless fun into the workplace. Explain your ethical reasoning.

2. This raises an ethical red flag because it encourages employees to gamble, including those who are against gambling for personal or religious reasons. Explain.

3. Ethics aside for the moment, this program is just another gimmick with poor prospects for long-term motivational effectiveness. Agree or disagree? Explain.

4. Invent other options. Explain and discuss.

Web Resources

For study material and exercises that apply to this chapter, visit our Web site, **www.mhhe.com/kreitner**

Part 3

Group and Social Processes

CHAPTER 10

Group Dynamics

LEARNING OBJECTIVES

When you finish studying the material in this chapter, you should be able to:

1   Identify the four sociological criteria of a group, and explain the role of equity in the Workplace Social Exchange Network (WSEN) model.

2   Describe the five stages in Tuckman's theory of group development, and discuss the threat of group decay.

3   Distinguish between role conflict and role ambiguity.

4   Contrast roles and norms, and specify four reasons norms are enforced in organizations.

5   Distinguish between task and maintenance roles in groups.

6   Summarize the practical contingency management implications for group size.

7   Discuss why managers need to carefully handle mixed-gender task groups.

8   Describe groupthink, and identify at least four of its symptoms.

9   Define social loafing, and explain how managers can prevent it.

Just when you think you've had a pretty good look at the office of Olson Sundberg Kundig Allen Architects, it shape-shifts. The pivoting walls in the conference room, you realize, are set at completely different angles than they were a few hours earlier. The huge white panel in the stairwell has suddenly been etched with a new abstraction of shadows. . . . And that skylight—that wasn't open before, was it? Even the staff itself scatters and shuffles. In fact, everything about this Seattle office is a work in progress, from the zealous use of raw materials to the firm's unique collaborative philosophy. It's never the same place twice. . . .

Like the cogs and wheels driving the skylight, the workings of the human machinery here are apparent as well. "This space shows our process of working rather than the finished product," [founder Jim] Olson says. "In our last space, we had all the interns in a back room, but now we've brought them out and put them right in the middle of everything. That's because this space itself is more like the back room."

The inside-out nature of the firm's culture is most evident during "the Crit," a Thursday afternoon tradition gathering the entire staff in one of the convertible cork-paneled conference rooms. The Crit allows staff members to explain their current projects, practice their presentation skills, or simply sort through a design problem using the studio's collective brain. The exploratory vibe helps the staff feel comfortable with their own less-than-perfect ideas. "There's nothing precious about this joint," says partner Rick Sundberg. "It's messy, it's dirty, it's funky. The process of creating is transparent, and it's right out there for everyone to see."[1]

FOR DISCUSSION

Why has it taken so long to fit workspaces to people, rather than vice versa?

The idea of marrying architecture and group dynamics, as illustrated in the opening vignette, promises to be fruitful in terms of more people-friendly workspaces and greater innovation. Organizations, by definition, are collections of people constantly interacting to achieve something greater than what can be achieved by individuals acting alone. Workspaces that encourage productive interaction leverage the social skills of organization members. Research consistently reveals the importance of social skills for both individual and organizational success.

For example, a recent study of 1,040 managers employed by 100 manufacturing and service organizations in the United States found 15 reasons why managers fail in the face of rapid change. The top two reasons were "ineffective communication skills/practices" and "poor work relationships/interpersonal skills."[2] Relationships *do* matter in the workplace, just as they do elsewhere.[3]

Table 10–1   *Key Social Skills Managers Need for Building Social Capital*

SOCIAL SKILL	DESCRIPTION	TOPICAL LINKAGES IN THIS TEXT
Social perception	Ability to perceive accurately the emotions, traits, motives, and intentions of others	• Individual differences, Chapters 5 and 6 • Emotional intelligence, Chapter 5 • Social perception, Chapter 7 • Employee motivation, Chapters 8 and 9
Impression management	Tactics designed to induce liking and a favorable first impression by others	• Impression management, Chapter 15
Persuasion and social influence	Ability to change others' attitudes or behavior in desired directions	• Influence tactics and social power, Chapter 15 • Leadership, Chapter 16
Social adaptability	Ability to adapt to, or feel comfortable in, a wide range of social situations	• Emotional intelligence, Chapter 5 • Managing change, Chapter 18

SOURCE: Columns 1 and 2 excerpted from R A Baron and G D Markman, "Beyond Social Capital: How Social Skills Can Enhance Entrepreneurs' Success," *Academy of Management Executive*, February 2000, table 1, p 110.

Management, as defined in Chapter 1, involves getting things done with and through others. Experts say managers need to build social capital with four key social skills: social perception, impression management, persuasion and social influence, and social adaptability (see Table 10–1).[4] How polished are your social skills? Where do you need improvement?

Let us begin by defining the term *group* as a prelude to examining types of groups, functions of group members, social exchanges in the workplace, and the group development process. Our attention then turns to group roles and norms, the basic building blocks of group dynamics. Effects of group structure and member characteristics on group outcomes are explored next. Finally, three serious threats to group effectiveness are discussed. (This chapter serves as a foundation for our discussion of teams and teamwork in the following chapter.)

Groups and Social Exchanges

Groups and teams are inescapable features of modern life.[5] College students are often teamed with their peers for class projects. Parents serve on community advisory boards at their local schools. Managers find themselves on product planning committees and productivity task forces. Productive organizations simply cannot function without gathering individuals into groups and teams. But as personal experience shows, group effort can bring out both the best and the worst in people. A marketing department meeting, where several people excitedly brainstorm and refine a creative new advertising campaign, can yield results beyond the capabilities of individual contributors. Conversely, committees have become the butt of jokes (e.g., a committee is a place where they take minutes and waste hours; a camel is a horse designed by a committee) because they all too often are plagued by lack of direction and by conflict. Modern managers need a solid understanding of groups and group processes so as to both avoid their pitfalls and tap

Figure 10–1   *Four Sociological Criteria of a Group*

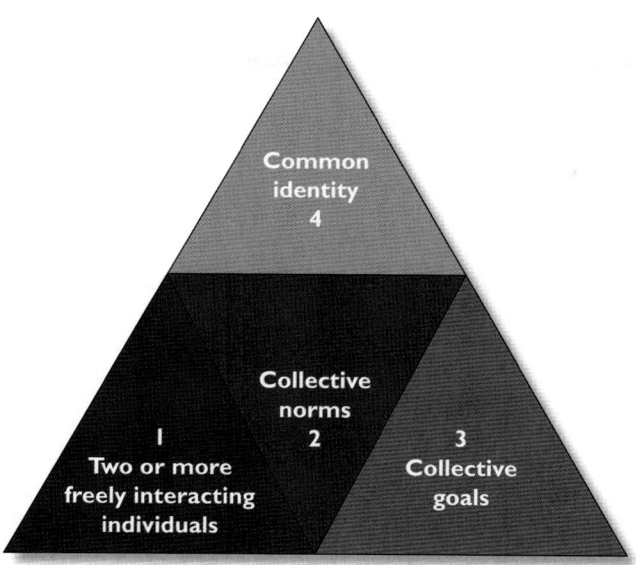

their vast potential. Moreover, the huge and growing presence of the Internet—with its own unique network of informal and formal social relationships—is a major challenge for profit-minded business managers.

Although other definitions of groups exist, we draw from the field of sociology and define a **group** as two or more freely interacting individuals who share collective norms and goals and have a common identity.[6] Figure 10–1 illustrates how the four criteria in this definition combine to form a conceptual whole. Organizational psychologist Edgar Schein shed additional light on this concept by drawing instructive distinctions between a group, a crowd, and an organization:

> The size of a group is thus limited by the possibilities of mutual interaction and mutual awareness. Mere aggregates of people do not fit this definition because they do not interact and do not perceive themselves to be a group even if they are aware of each other as, for instance, a crowd on a street corner watching some event. A total department, a union, or a whole organization would not be a group in spite of thinking of themselves as "we," because they generally do not all interact and are not all aware of each other. However, work teams, committees, subparts of departments, cliques, and various other informal associations among organizational members would fit this definition of a group.[7]

Take a moment now to think of various groups of which you are a member. Does each of your groups satisfy the four criteria in Figure 10–1?

Formal and Informal Groups

Individuals join groups, or are assigned to groups, to accomplish various purposes. If the group is formed by a manager to help the organization accomplish its goals, then it qualifies as a **formal group.** Formal groups typically wear such labels as work group, team, committee, corporate board, or task force. An **informal group** exists when the members' overriding purpose of getting together is friendship or common interests.[8]

Group

Two or more freely interacting people with shared norms and goals and a common identity.

Formal group

Formed by the organization.

Informal group

Formed by friends or those with common interests.

Although formal and informal groups often overlap, such as a team of corporate auditors heading for the tennis courts after work, some employees are not friends with their co-workers. The desirability of overlapping formal and informal groups is problematic. Some managers firmly believe personal friendship fosters productive teamwork on the job while others view workplace "bull sessions" as a serious threat to productivity. Both situations are common, and it is the manager's job to strike a workable balance, based on the maturity and goals of the people involved.[9]

Functions of Formal Groups

Researchers point out that formal groups fulfill two basic functions: *organizational* and *individual*. The various functions are listed in Table 10–2. Complex combinations of these functions can be found in formal groups at any given time.

For example, consider what Mazda's new American employees experienced when they spent a month working in Japan before the opening of the firm's Flat Rock, Michigan, plant:

> After a month of training in Mazda's factory methods, whipping their new Japanese buddies at softball and sampling local watering holes, the Americans were fired up. . . . [A maintenance manager] even faintly praised the Japanese practice of holding group calisthenics at the start of each working day: "I didn't think I'd like doing exercises every morning, but I kind of like it."[10]

While Mazda pursued the organizational functions it wanted—interdependent teamwork, creativity, coordination, problem solving, and training—the American workers benefited from the individual functions of formal groups. Among those benefits were affiliation with new friends, enhanced self-esteem, exposure to the Japanese social

Table 10–2 *Formal Groups Fulfill Organizational and Individual Functions*

ORGANIZATIONAL FUNCTIONS	INDIVIDUAL FUNCTIONS
1. Accomplish complex, interdependent tasks that are beyond the capabilities of individuals.	1. Satisfy the individual's need for affiliation.
2. Generate new or creative ideas and solutions.	2. Develop, enhance, and confirm the individual's self-esteem and sense of identity.
3. Coordinate interdepartmental efforts.	3. Give individuals an opportunity to test and share their perceptions of social reality.
4. Provide a problem-solving mechanism for complex problems requiring varied information and assessments.	4. Reduce the individual's anxieties and feelings of insecurity and powerlessness.
5. Implement complex decisions.	5. Provide a problem-solving mechanism for personal and interpersonal problems.
6. Socialize and train newcomers.	

SOURCE: Adapted from E H Schein, *Organizational Psychology*, 3rd ed (Englewood Cliffs, NJ: Prentice Hall, 1980), pp 149–51.

reality, and reduction of anxieties about working for a foreign-owned company. In short, Mazda created a workable blend of organizational and individual group functions by training its newly hired American employees in Japan.

Social Exchanges in the Workplace

Social relationships are complex, alive, and dynamic. Accordingly, we need dynamic models for realistic understanding. A team of researchers from Auburn University proposed the instructive model shown in Figure 10–2. They call it the Workplace Social Exchange Network (WSEN) because it captures multilevel social *exchanges* within organizations, along with the complex *network* of variables affecting those exchanges.[11]

The Exchange of Currencies The economic notion of exchange is at the heart of this model. In starkest economic terms, people exchange their time and labor

Figure 10–2   *The Workplace Social Exchange Network Model*

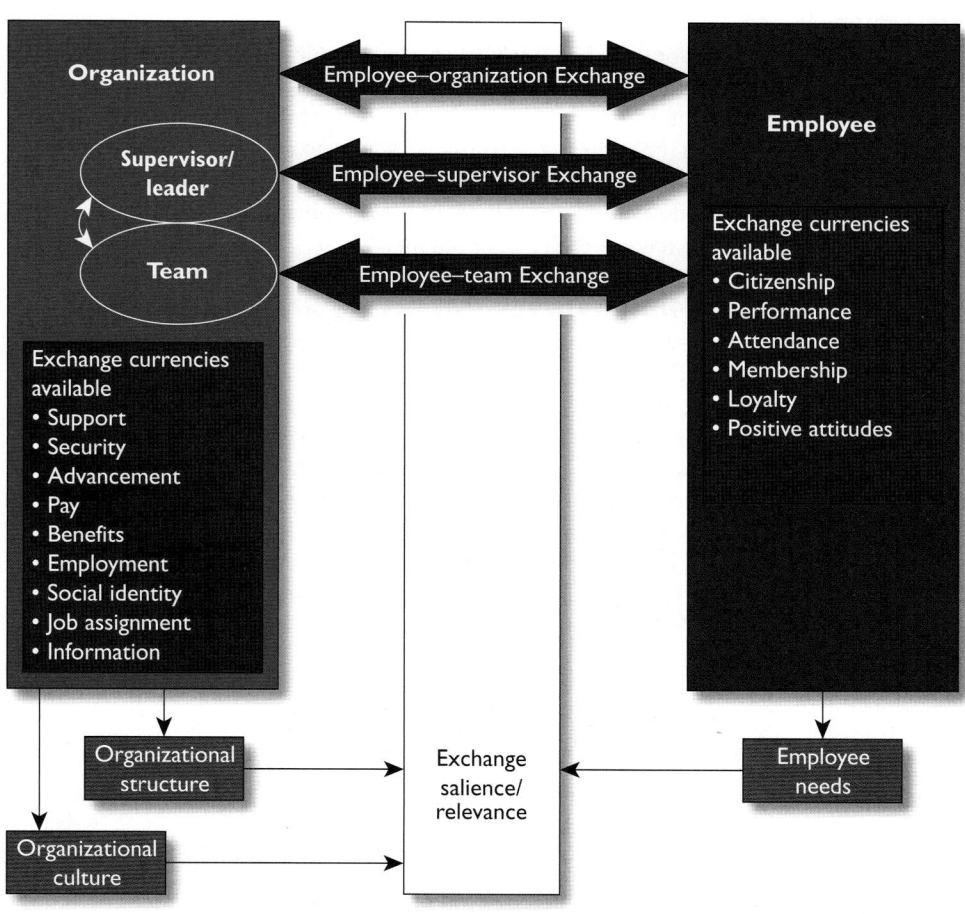

SOURCE: Adapted from M S Cole, W S Schaninger Jr, and S G Harris, "The Workplace Social Exchange Network: A Multilevel, Conceptual Examination," *Group & Organization Management,* March 2002, figure 1, p 148. Copyright © 2002 by Sage Publications. Reprinted by permission of Sage Publications.

for money when they take a job. But as this model realistically shows, there is much more at stake than just the exchange of time and labor for money. Individuals, organizations, and teams have many "currencies" they can grant or withhold.

Notably, the only social exchange currency that is not self-explanatory is "citizenship." As discussed in Chapter 6, *organizational citizenship* involves going above and beyond what is expected (e.g., voluntarily working late to finish an important project)—in short, being a good citizen.[12]

Three Types of Social Exchange According to the WSEN model, every employee has social exchanges on three levels: with the organization, with the boss, and with the work team as a whole. From the individual's perspective, exchanges at the various levels can be favorable or unfavorable. They can be motivating or de-motivating, depending on the perceived equity of the exchange. (Recall our discussion of equity motivation theory in Chapter 8.) For example, someone may have high-quality exchanges with his or her supervisor and work team, and thus want to be around them, be motivated to work hard for them, and be loyal to them. However, because the organization has a reputation for massive layoffs, the employee–organization exchange would be perceived unfavorably, thus fostering dissatisfaction and possibly poor performance and turnover.

Situational Factors The WSEN model includes three intervening factors: organizational structure, organizational culture, and employee needs. Structure—in the form of reporting relationships, policies, and work rules—shapes the individual's expectations about what is fair and what is unfair. So, too, cultural norms and traditions create a context for judging the fairness of social exchanges. The individual's need profile, as discussed in Chapter 8, will determine which of the organization's exchange currencies are motivating and which are not. People are motivated when they have a realistic chance of having their needs satisfied.

Is the Social Exchange Relevant? Finally, at the bottom center of the WSEN model is the individual's perceptual filter. Is the particular social exchange salient or relevant? Recall from the discussion of social perception in Chapter 7 that salient stimuli tend to capture and dominate one's attention. An exchange between the employee and his or her organization, leader, or team needs to be salient if it is to influence behavior. If, say, a marketing assistant is indifferent to her teammates on a special project, that particular exchange would not be salient or relevant for her.

Overall, the WSEN model does a good job of building a conceptual bridge between motivation theories and group dynamics. Also, it realistically indicates the multilevel nature of social relationships within organizations (see the Real World/Real People feature on page 279).

2 The Group Development Process

Groups and teams in the workplace go through a maturation process, such as one would find in any life-cycle situation (e.g., humans, organizations, products). While there is general agreement among theorists that the group development process occurs in identifiable stages, they disagree about the exact number, sequence, length, and nature of those stages.[13] One oft-cited model is the one proposed in 1965 by educational psychologist Bruce W Tuckman. His original model involved only four stages (forming, storming, norming, and performing). The five-stage model in Figure 10–3 (on page 280) evolved when Tuckman and a doctoral student added "adjourning"

How Can You Be Both a Manager and a Friend?

It's certainly nothing to be afraid of! Of course, you don't need to be friends with your subordinates, as long as you share the same values for the business. But if you are friends with them, lucky you. Working with people you really like for 8 or 10 hours a day adds fun to everything.

That said, remember that boss-subordinate friendships live or die because of one thing: complete, unrelenting candor. Candor is imperative in any working relationship, but it's especially necessary when there's a social aspect involved. You don't want your liking someone's personality to automatically communicate that you like his or her performance. You may, but performance evaluations have to come in a distinct and separate set of conversations at work—as often as four times a year—in which you sit down with your subordinate, put the shared laughs from last weekend's barbecue in the corner, and talk about what's expected and what has been delivered.

Do these candid conversations require a certain ability to compartmentalize? You bet they do. But when you recognize that fact and practice discipline, confident you're being fair to everyone, you should be able to enjoy one of work's best built-in perks: hanging out with friends.

Is it a good idea to be friends with your boss? Should managers be friends with those who report directly to them? Explain.

SOURCE: J Welch and S Welch, "From the Old, Something New," *BusinessWeek*, November 20, 2006, p 124.

in 1977.[14] A word of caution is in order. Somewhat akin to Maslow's need hierarchy theory, Tuckman's theory has been repeated and taught so often and for so long that many have come to view it as documented fact, not merely a theory. Even today, it is good to remember Tuckman's own caution that his group development model was derived more from group therapy sessions than from natural-life groups. Still, many in the OB field like Tuckman's five-stage model of group development because of its easy-to-remember labels and common-sense appeal.[15]

Five Stages

Let us briefly examine each of the five stages in Tuckman's model. Notice in Figure 10–3 how individuals give up a measure of their independence when they join and participate in a group. Also, the various stages are not necessarily of the same duration or intensity. For instance, the storming stage may be practically nonexistent or painfully long, depending on the goal clarity and the commitment and maturity of the members. You can make this process come to life by relating the various stages to your own experiences with work groups, committees, athletic teams, social or religious groups, or class project teams. Some group happenings that surprised you when they occurred may now make sense or strike you as inevitable when seen as part of a natural development process.

Stage 1: Forming During this ice-breaking stage, group members tend to be uncertain and anxious about such things as their roles, who is in charge, and the

Figure 10–3   *Tuckman's Five-Stage Theory of Group Development*

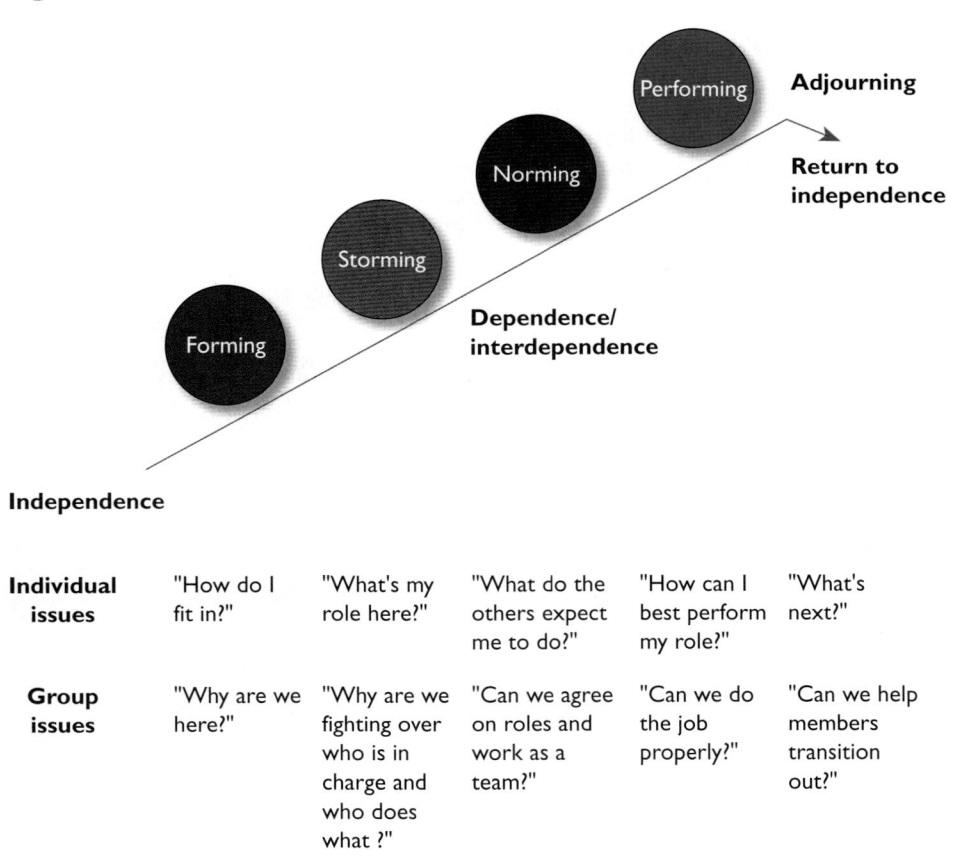

	Forming	Storming	Norming	Performing	Adjourning
Individual issues	"How do I fit in?"	"What's my role here?"	"What do the others expect me to do?"	"How can I best perform my role?"	"What's next?"
Group issues	"Why are we here?"	"Why are we fighting over who is in charge and who does what ?"	"Can we agree on roles and work as a team?"	"Can we do the job properly?"	"Can we help members transition out?"

group's goals. Mutual trust is low, and there is a good deal of holding back to see who takes charge and how. If the formal leader (e.g., a supervisor) does not assert his or her authority, an emergent leader will eventually step in to fulfill the group's need for leadership and direction. Leaders typically mistake this honeymoon period as a mandate for permanent control. But later problems may force a leadership change.[16]

Stage 2: Storming   This is a time of testing. Individuals test the leader's policies and assumptions as they try to determine how they fit into the power structure. Subgroups take shape, and subtle forms of rebellion, such as procrastination, occur. Many groups stall in stage 2 because power politics erupts into open rebellion.[17]

Stage 3: Norming   Groups that make it through stage 2 generally do so because a respected member, other than the leader, challenges the group to resolve its power struggles so something can be accomplished. Questions about authority and power are resolved through unemotional, matter-of-fact group discussion. A feeling of team spirit is experienced because members believe they have found their proper roles. **Group cohesiveness**, defined as the "we feeling" that binds members of a group together, is the principal by-product of stage 3.[18] (For a good laugh, see the golfing explanation below the photo).

Group cohesiveness

A "we feeling" binding group members together.

Stage 4: Performing Activity during this vital stage is focused on solving task problems. As members of a mature group, contributors get their work done without hampering others. There is a climate of open communication, strong cooperation, and lots of helping behavior. Conflicts and job boundary disputes are handled constructively and efficiently. Cohesiveness and personal commitment to group goals help the group achieve more than could any one individual acting alone. According to a pair of group development experts,

> the group structure can become flexible and adjust to fit the requirements of the situation without causing problems for the members. Influence can shift depending on who has the particular expertise or skills required for the group task or activity. Subgroups can work on special problems or subproblems without posing threats to the authority or cohesiveness of the rest of the group.[19]

Stage 5: Adjourning The work is done; it is time to move on to other things. Having worked so hard to get along and get something done, many members feel a compelling sense of loss. The return to independence can be eased by rituals celebrating "the end" and "new beginnings." Parties, award ceremonies, graduations, or mock funerals can provide the needed punctuation at the end of a significant group project. Leaders need to emphasize valuable lessons learned in group dynamics to prepare everyone for future group and team efforts.

Group Development: Research and Practical Implications

A growing body of group development research provides managers with some practical insights.

Extending the Tuckman Model: Group Decay
An interesting study of 10 software development teams, ranging in size from 5 to 16 members, enhanced the practical significance of Tuckman's model.[20] Unlike Tuckman's laboratory groups who worked together only briefly, the teams of software engineers worked on projects lasting *years*. Consequently, the researchers discovered more than

A *Fortune* article examined the question, Why do people love to mix golf and business? (Hint: It's all about group dynamics.):

> Ask people why they golf with business associates, and the answer is always the same: It's a great way to build relationships. They say this far more about golf than about going to dinner or attending a baseball game, and for good reason. Indeed, this may be the central fact about corporate golf, though it's rarely said: When people golf together, they see one another humiliated. At least 95% of all golfers are terrible, which means that in 18 holes everyone in the foursome will hit a tree, take three strokes in one bunker, or four-putt, with everyone else watching. Bonding is simply a matter of people jointly going through adversity, and a round of golf will furnish plenty of it. Of course it's only a game, but of course it isn't, so the bonds can be surprisingly strong. And what's that worth?

SOURCE: G Colvin, "Why Execs Love Golf," *Fortune*, April 30, 2001, p 46. Photo: (c) George Shelly/Corbis StockMarket

simply a five-stage group development process. Groups were observed actually shifting into reverse once Tuckman's "performing" stage was reached, in what the researchers called *group decay*. In keeping with Tuckman's terminology, the three observed stages of group decay were labeled "de-norming," "de-storming," and "de-forming." These additional stages take shape as follows:

- *De-norming*. As the project evolves, there is a natural erosion of standards of conduct. Group members drift in different directions as their interests and expectations change.

- *De-storming*. This stage of group decay is a mirror opposite of the storming stage. Whereas disagreements and conflicts arise rather suddenly during the storming stage, an undercurrent of discontent slowly comes to the surface during the de-storming stage. Individual resistance increases and cohesiveness declines.

- *De-forming*. The work group literally falls apart as subgroups battle for control. Those pieces of the project that are not claimed by individuals or subgroups are abandoned. "Group members begin isolating themselves from each other and from their leaders. Performance declines rapidly because the whole job is no longer being done and group members little care what happens beyond their self-imposed borders."[21]

The primary management lesson from this study is that group leaders should not become complacent upon reaching the performing stage. According to the researchers: "The performing stage is a knife edge or saddle point, not a point of static equilibrium."[22] Awareness is the first line of defense. Beyond that, constructive steps need to be taken to reinforce norms, bolster cohesiveness, and reaffirm the common goal—*even when work groups seem to be doing their best.*

Feedback Another fruitful study was carried out by a pair of Dutch social psychologists. They hypothesized that interpersonal feedback would vary systematically during the group development process. "The unit of feedback measured was a verbal message directed from one participant to another in which some aspect of behavior was addressed."[23] After collecting and categorizing 1,600 instances of feedback from four different eight-person groups, they concluded the following:

- Interpersonal feedback increases as the group develops through successive stages.

- As the group develops, positive feedback increases and negative feedback decreases.

- Interpersonal feedback becomes more specific as the group develops.

- The credibility of peer feedback increases as the group develops.[24]

These findings hold important lessons for managers. The content and delivery of interpersonal feedback among work group or committee members can be used as a gauge of whether the group is developing properly. For example, the onset of stage 2 (storming) will be signaled by a noticeable increase in *negative* feedback. Effort can then be directed at generating specific, positive feedback among the members so the group's development will not stall. Our discussion of feedback in Chapter 9 is helpful in this regard.

Deadlines Field and laboratory studies found uncertainty about deadlines to be a major disruptive force in both group development and intergroup relations. The practical implications of this finding were summed up by the researcher as follows:

Uncertain or shifting deadlines are a fact of life in many organizations. Interdependent organizational units and groups may keep each other waiting, may suddenly move deadlines forward or back, or may create deadlines that are known to be earlier than is necessary in efforts to control erratic workflows. The current research suggests that the consequences of such uncertainty may involve more than stress, wasted time, overtime work, and intergroup conflicts. Synchrony in group members' expectations about deadlines may be critical to groups' abilities to accomplish successful transitions in their work.[25]

Thus, effective group management involves clarifying not only tasks and goals, but schedules and deadlines as well. When group members accurately perceive important deadlines, the pacing of work and timing of interdependent tasks tend to be more efficient.

Leadership Styles Along a somewhat different line, experts in the area of leadership contend that different leadership styles are needed as work groups develop.

In general, it has been documented that leadership behavior that is active, aggressive, directive, structured, and task-oriented seems to have favorable results early in the group's history. However, when those behaviors are maintained throughout the life of the group, they seem to have a negative impact on cohesiveness and quality of work. Conversely, leadership behavior that is supportive, democratic, decentralized, and participative seems to be related to poorer functioning in the early group development stages. However, when these behaviors are maintained throughout the life of the group, more productivity, satisfaction, and creativity result.[26]

The practical punch line here is that managers are advised to shift from a directive and structured leadership style to a participative and supportive style as the group develops.[27]

go to the Web for the Self-Exercise: Is This a Mature Work Group or Team?

Roles and Norms: Social Building Blocks for Group and Organizational Behavior

Work groups transform individuals into functioning organizational members through subtle yet powerful social forces.[28] These social forces, in effect, turn "I" into "we" and "me" into "us." Group influence weaves individuals into the organization's social fabric by communicating and enforcing both role expectations and norms. We need to understand roles and norms if we are to effectively manage group and organizational behavior.

Roles

Four centuries have passed since William Shakespeare had his character Jaques speak the following memorable lines in Act II of *As You Like It:* "All the world's a stage, And all the men and women merely players; They have their exits and their entrances; And one man in his time plays many parts." This intriguing notion of all people as actors in a universal play was not lost on 20th-century sociologists who developed a

Figure 10–4   *A Role Episode*

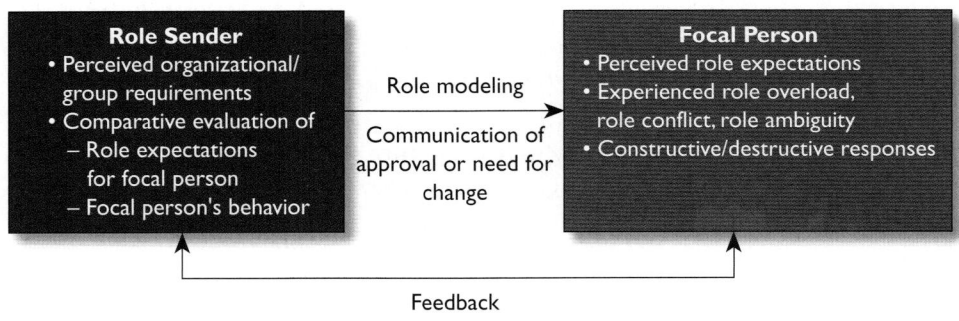

SOURCE: Adapted in part from R L Kohn, D M Wolfe, R P Quinn, and J D Snoek, *Organizational Stress: Studies in Role Conflict and Ambiguity*, 1981 ed. (Malabar, FL: Robert E Krieger Publishing, 1964), p 26.

Roles

Expected behaviors for a given position.

complex theory of human interaction based on roles. According to an OB scholar, "**roles** are sets of behaviors that persons expect of occupants of a position."[29] Role theory attempts to explain how these social expectations influence employee behavior. This section explores role theory by analyzing a role episode and defining the terms *role overload, role conflict,* and *role ambiguity.*

Role Episodes   A role episode, as illustrated in Figure 10–4, consists of a snapshot of the ongoing interaction between two people. In any given role episode, there is a role sender and a focal person who is expected to act out the role. Within a broader context, one may be simultaneously a role sender and a focal person. For the sake of social analysis, however, it is instructive to deal with separate role episodes.

Role episodes begin with the role sender's perception of the relevant organization's or group's behavioral requirements. Those requirements serve as a standard for formulating expectations for the focal person's behavior. The role sender then cognitively evaluates the focal person's actual behavior against those expectations. Appropriate verbal and behavioral messages are then sent to the focal person to pressure him or her into behaving as expected.[30] Consider how Westinghouse used a carrot-and-stick approach to communicate role expectations:

> The carrot is a plan, that … rewarded 134 managers with options to buy 764,000 shares of stock for boosting the company's financial performance.
>
> The stick is quarterly meetings that are used to rank managers by how much their operations contribute to earnings per share. The soft-spoken … [chairman of the board] doesn't scold. He just charts in green the results of the sectors that have met their goals and charts the laggards in red. Peer pressure does the rest. Shame "is a powerful tool," says one executive.[31]

On the receiving end of the role episode, the focal person accurately or inaccurately perceives the communicated role expectations and modeled behavior. Various combinations of role overload, role conflict, and role ambiguity are then experienced. (These three outcomes are defined and discussed in the following sections.) The focal person then responds constructively by engaging in problem solving, for example, or destructively because of undue tension, stress, and strain.[32]

Role overload

Others' expectations exceed one's ability.

Role Overload   According to organizational psychologist Edgar Schein, **role overload** occurs when "the sum total of what role senders expect of the focal person

AMD's CEO Prefers a Little Ambiguity

Hector Ruiz, CEO of the Sunnyvale, California, microprocessor maker:

We have gotten larger and more complex. By definition that means we're going to make some mistakes. I'm much more comfortable in an environment when I know that's going to happen. That means we're learning. An aura of confidence begins to develop around people who can make mistakes and learn and go forward. At employee meetings I say, "Please, go get speeding tickets. I don't want you to get parking tickets." . . .

Part of my job is to make people comfortable with change and ambiguity. That sounds counterintuitive. A lot of people think CEOs have to be absolutely crisp and perfect on what they want. Quite often my people push back. I don't like spelling out exactly what people need to do. I think that boxes them in.

What are the pros and cons of this management style?

SOURCE: Excerpted from D Kirkpatrick, "12 Peak Performers: Chief Executive," *Fortune*, October 30, 2006, p 118.

---

far exceeds what he or she is able to do."[33] Students who attempt to handle a full course load and maintain a decent social life while working 30 or more hours a week know full well the consequences of role overload. As the individual tries to do more and more in less and less time, stress mounts and personal effectiveness slips.

3 Role Conflict Have you ever felt like you were being torn apart by the conflicting demands of those around you? If so, you were a victim of role conflict. **Role conflict** is experienced when "different members of the role set expect different things of the focal person."[34] Managers often face conflicting demands between work and family, as discussed in Chapter 6. Although women tend to experience greater work-versus-family role conflict than men because they typically shoulder more of the household and child care duties, many men do not get a free pass.[35] Employees in single-person households have their own version of role conflict between work and outside interests.

Role conflict also may be experienced when internalized values, ethics, or personal standards collide with others' expectations. For instance, an otherwise ethical production supervisor may be told by a superior to "fudge a little" on the quality control reports so an important deadline will be met. The resulting role conflict forces the supervisor to choose between being loyal but unethical or ethical but disloyal. Tough ethical choices such as this mean personal turmoil, interpersonal conflict, and even resignation.[36] Consequently, experts say business schools should do a better job of weaving ethics education into their course requirements.

Role conflict
Others have conflicting or inconsistent expectations.

Role Ambiguity Those who experience role conflict may have trouble complying with role demands, but they at least know what is expected of them. Such is not the case with **role ambiguity,** which occurs when "members of the role set fail to communicate to the focal person expectations they have or information needed to perform the role, either because they do not have the information or because they deliberately withhold it."[37] In short, people experience role ambiguity when they do not know what is expected of them. Organizational newcomers often complain about unclear job descriptions and vague promotion criteria. According to role theory, prolonged role ambiguity can foster job dissatisfaction, erode self-confidence, and hamper job performance (see the Real World/Real People feature above).

Role ambiguity
Others' expectations are unknown.

As might be expected, role ambiguity varies across cultures. In a 21-nation study, people in individualistic cultures were found to have higher role ambiguity than people in collectivist cultures.[38] In other words, people in collectivist or "we" cultures had a clearer idea of others' expectations. Collectivist cultures make sure everyone knows their proper place in society. People in individualistic "me" cultures, such as the United States, may enjoy more individual discretion, but comparatively less input from others has its price—namely, greater role ambiguity.

As mentioned earlier, these role outcomes typically are experienced in some combination, usually to the detriment of the individual and the organization. In fact, a study in Israel documented lower job performance when employees experienced a combination of role conflict and role ambiguity.[39]

go to the Web for the Self-Exercise: Measuring Role Conflict and Role Ambiguity

🐾 4 Norms

Norm

Shared attitudes, opinions, feelings, or actions that guide social behavior.

Norms are more encompassing than roles. While roles involve behavioral expectations for specific positions, norms help organizational members determine right from wrong and good from bad. According to one respected team of management consultants: "A **norm** is an attitude, opinion, feeling, or action—shared by two or more people—that guides their behavior."[40] Although norms are typically unwritten and seldom discussed openly, they have a powerful influence on group and organizational behavior.[41] PepsiCo Inc., for instance, has evolved a norm that equates corporate competitiveness with physical fitness. According to observers,

> Leanness and nimbleness are qualities that pervade the company. When Pepsi's brash young managers take a few minutes away from the office, they often head straight for the company's physical fitness center or for a jog around the museum-quality sculptures outside of PepsiCo's Purchase, New York, headquarters.[42]

Ostracism

Rejection by other group members.

At PepsiCo and elsewhere, group members positively reinforce those who adhere to current norms with friendship and acceptance. On the other hand, nonconformists experience criticism and even **ostracism,** or rejection by group members. Anyone who has experienced the "silent treatment" from a group of friends knows what a potent social weapon ostracism can be.[43] Norms can be put into proper perspective by understanding how they develop and why they are enforced.

How Norms Are Developed Experts say norms evolve in an informal manner as the group or organization determines what it takes to be effective. Generally speaking, norms develop in various combinations of the following four ways:

1. *Explicit statements by supervisors or co-workers.* For instance, a group leader might explicitly set norms about not drinking (alcohol) at lunch.

2. *Critical events in the group's history.* At times there is a critical event in the group's history that establishes an important precedent. (For example, a key recruit may have decided to work elsewhere because a group member said too many negative things

about the organization. Hence, a norm against such "sour grapes" behavior might evolve.)

3. *Primacy.* The first behavior pattern that emerges in a group often sets group expectations. If the first group meeting is marked by very formal interaction between supervisors and employees, then the group often expects future meetings to be conducted in the same way.

4. *Carryover behaviors from past situations.* Such carryover of individual behaviors from past situations can increase the predictability of group members' behaviors in new settings and facilitate task accomplishment. For instance, students and professors carry fairly constant sets of expectations from class to class.[44]

We would like you to take a few moments and think about the norms that are currently in effect in your classroom. List the norms on a sheet of paper. Do these norms help or hinder your ability to learn? Norms can affect performance either positively or negatively.

Why Norms Are Enforced Norms tend to be enforced by group members when they

- Help the group or organization survive.
- Clarify or simplify behavioral expectations.
- Help individuals avoid embarrassing situations.
- Clarify the group's or organization's central values and/or unique identity.[45]

Working examples of each of these four situations are presented in Table 10–3.

Table 10–3   *Four Reasons Norms Are Enforced*

NORM	REASON FOR ENFORCEMENT	EXAMPLE
"Make our department look good in top management's eyes."	Group/organization survival	After vigorously defending the vital role played by the Human Resources Management Department at a divisional meeting, a staff specialist is complimented by her boss.
"Success comes to those who work hard and don't make waves."	Clarification of behavioral expectations	A senior manager takes a young associate aside and cautions him to be a bit more patient with co-workers who see things differently.
"Be a team player, not a star."	Avoidance of embarrassment	A project team member is ridiculed by her peers for dominating the discussion during a progress report to top management.
"Customer service is our top priority."	Clarification of central values/unique identity	Two sales representatives are given a surprise Friday afternoon party for having received prestigious best-in-the-industry customer service awards from an industry association.

Relevant Research Insights and Managerial Implications

Although instruments used to measure role conflict and role ambiguity have questionable validity,[46] two separate meta-analyses indicated that role conflict and role ambiguity negatively affected employees. Specifically, role conflict and role ambiguity were associated with job dissatisfaction, tension and anxiety, lack of organizational commitment, intentions to quit, and, to a lesser extent, poor job performance.[47]

The meta-analyses results hold few surprises for managers. Generally, because of the negative association reported, it makes sense for management to reduce both role conflict and role ambiguity. In this endeavor, managers can use feedback, formal rules and procedures, directive leadership, setting of specific (difficult) goals, and participation. Managers also can use the mentoring process discussed in Chapter 3 to reduce role conflict and ambiguity.

Regarding norms, a recent set of laboratory studies involving a total of 1,504 college students as subjects has important implications for workplace diversity programs. Subjects in groups where the norm was to express prejudices, condone discrimination, and laugh at hostile jokes tended to engage in these undesirable behaviors. Conversely, subjects tended to disapprove of prejudicial and discriminatory conduct when exposed to groups with more socially acceptable norms.[48] So, once again, Mom and our teachers were right when they warned us about the dangers of hanging out with "the wrong crowd." Managers who want to build strong diversity programs need to cultivate favorable role models and group norms.[49] Poor role models and antisocial norms need to be identified and weeded out.

Group Structure and Composition

Work groups of varying size are made up of individuals with varying ability and motivation.[50] Moreover, those individuals perform different roles, on either an assigned or voluntary basis. No wonder some work groups are more productive than others. No wonder some committees are tightly knit while others wallow in conflict. In this section, we examine three important dimensions of group structure and composition: (1) functional roles of group members, (2) group size, and (3) gender composition. Each of these dimensions alternatively can enhance or hinder group effectiveness, depending on how it is managed.

Functional Roles Performed by Group Members

As described in Table 10–4, both task and maintenance roles need to be performed if a work group is to accomplish anything.[51]

Task roles

Task-oriented group behavior.

Maintenance roles

Relationship-building group behavior.

5 **Task versus Maintenance Roles** Task roles enable the work group to define, clarify, and pursue a common purpose. Meanwhile, **maintenance roles** foster supportive and constructive interpersonal relationships. In short, task roles keep the group *on track* while maintenance roles keep the group *together*. A project team member is performing a task function when he or she stands at an update meeting and says, "What is the real issue here? We don't seem to be getting anywhere." Another individual who says, "Let's hear from those who oppose this plan," is performing a maintenance function. Importantly, each of the various task and maintenance roles

Table 10–4   *Functional Roles Performed by Group Members*

TASK ROLES	DESCRIPTION
Initiator	Suggests new goals or ideas.
Information seeker/giver	Clarifies key issues.
Opinion seeker/giver	Clarifies pertinent values.
Elaborator	Promotes greater understanding through examples or exploration of implications.
Coordinator	Pulls together ideas and suggestions.
Orienter	Keeps group headed toward its stated goal(s).
Evaluator	Tests group's accomplishments with various criteria such as logic and practicality.
Energizer	Prods group to move along or to accomplish more.
Procedural technician	Performs routine duties (e.g., handing out materials or rearranging seats).
Recorder	Performs a "group memory" function by documenting discussion and outcomes.

MAINTENANCE ROLES	DESCRIPTION
Encourager	Fosters group solidarity by accepting and praising various points of view.
Harmonizer	Mediates conflict through reconciliation or humor.
Compromiser	Helps resolve conflict by meeting others half way.
Gatekeeper	Encourages all group members to participate.
Standard setter	Evaluates the quality of group processes.
Commentator	Records and comments on group processes/dynamics.
Follower	Serves as a passive audience.

SOURCE: Adapted from discussion in K D Benne and P Sheats, "Functional Roles of Group Members," *Journal of Social Issues*, Spring 1948, pp 41–49.

may be played in varying combinations and sequences by either the group's leader or any of its members.

Checklist for Managers The task and maintenance roles listed in Table 10–4 can serve as a handy checklist for managers and group leaders who wish to ensure proper group development. Roles that are not always performed when needed, such as those of coordinator, evaluator, and gatekeeper, can be performed in a timely manner by the formal leader or assigned to other members. The task roles of initiator, orienter, and energizer are especially important because they are *goal-directed* roles. Research studies on group goal setting confirm the motivational power of challenging goals. As with individual goal setting (in Chapter 9), difficult but achievable goals are associated with better group results.[52] Also in line with individual goal-setting theory and research, group goals are more effective if group members clearly understand them and are both individually and collectively committed to achieving them. Initiators, orienters, and energizers can be very helpful in this regard.

International managers need to be sensitive to cultural differences regarding the relative importance of task and maintenance roles. In Japan, for example, cultural tradition calls for more emphasis on maintenance roles, especially the roles of harmonizer and compromiser:

> Courtesy requires that members not be conspicuous or disputatious in a meeting or classroom. If two or more members discover that their views differ—a fact that is tactfully taken to be unfortunate—they adjourn to find more information and to work toward a stance that all can accept. They do not press their personal opinions through strong arguments, neat logic, or rewards and threats. And they do not hesitate to shift their beliefs if doing so will preserve smooth interpersonal relations. (To lose is to win.)[53]

Group Size

How many group members is too many? The answer to this deceptively simple question has intrigued managers and academics for years. Folk wisdom says "two heads are better than one" but that "too many cooks spoil the broth." So where should a manager draw the line when staffing a committee? At 3? At 5 or 6? At 10 or more?[54] Researchers have taken two different approaches to pinpointing optimum group size: mathematical modeling and laboratory simulations. Let us briefly review research evidence from these two approaches.

The Mathematical Modeling Approach This approach involves building a mathematical model around certain desired outcomes of group action such as decision quality. Due to differing assumptions and statistical techniques, the results of this research are inconclusive. Statistical estimates of optimum group size have ranged from 3 to 13.[55]

The American Red Cross is a national society within the International Red Cross (shown here at an International Conference in Switzerland). The American Red Cross recently reduced its board membership from 50 to 28 people in response to criticism over handling of Katrina relief. How does the size of a group affect its ability to effectively work together?

The Laboratory Simulation Approach This stream of research is based on the assumption that group behavior needs to be observed firsthand in controlled laboratory settings. A laboratory study by respected Australian researcher Philip Yetton and his colleague, Preston Bottger, provides useful insights about group size and performance.[56]

A total of 555 subjects (330 managers and 225 graduate management students, of whom 20% were female) were assigned to task teams ranging in size from 2 to 6. The teams worked on the National Aeronautics and Space Administration moon survival exercise. (This exercise involves the rank ordering of 15 pieces of equipment that would enable a spaceship crew on the moon to survive a 200-mile trip between a crash-landing site and home base.)[57] After analyzing the relationships between group size and group performance, Yetton and Bottger concluded the following:

> It would be difficult, at least with respect to decision quality, to justify groups larger than five members. . . . Of course, to meet needs other than high decision quality, organizations may employ groups significantly larger than four or five.[58]

More recent laboratory studies exploring the brainstorming productivity of various size groups (2 to 12 people), in face-to-face versus computer-mediated situations, proved fruitful. In the usual face-to-face brainstorming sessions, productivity of ideas did not increase as the size of the group increased. But brainstorming productivity increased as the size of the group increased when ideas were typed into networked computers.[59] These results suggest that computer networks are helping to deliver on the promise of productivity improvement through modern information technology.

6 Managerial Implications Within a contingency management framework, there is no hard-and-fast rule about group size. It depends on the manager's objective for the group. If a high-quality decision is the main objective, then a three- to five-member group would be appropriate. However, if the objective is to generate creative ideas, encourage participation, socialize new members, engage in training, or communicate policies, then groups much larger than five could be justified. But even in this developmental domain, researchers have found upward limits on group size. According to a meta-analysis, the positive effects of team-building activities diminished as group size increased.[60] Managers also need to be aware of *qualitative* changes that occur when group size increases. A meta-analysis of eight studies found the following relationships: As group size increased, group leaders tended to become more directive, and group member satisfaction tended to decline slightly.[61]

Odd-numbered groups (e.g., three, five, seven members) are recommended if the issue is to be settled by a majority vote. Voting deadlocks (e.g., 2–2, 3–3) too often hamper effectiveness of even-numbered groups.[62]

7 Effects of Men and Women Working Together in Groups

As pointed out in Chapter 2, the female portion of the US labor force has grown significantly in recent decades. This demographic shift has impacted attitudes. For example, in a recent report about a longitudinal study of US executives, the researchers observed:

> Men and women are . . . responding similarly to the statement "I would feel comfortable working for a woman." Most female

One study suggests that females entering male-dominated fields, such as law enforcement, face greater challenges than do males entering female-dominated fields, such as nursing.

respondents continue to say they would, though there's been a slight drop since 1985. Of the men, 71% say they would. That figure is up significantly from 1965 (27%) and 1985 (47%).[63]

With more committees and teams requiring collaboration between women and men, some profound effects on group dynamics might be expected.[64] Let us see what researchers have found in the way of group gender composition effects and what managers can do about them.

Women Face an Uphill Battle in Mixed-Gender Task Groups

Laboratory and field studies paint a picture of inequality for women working in mixed-gender groups. Both women and men need to be aware of these often subtle but powerful group dynamics so corrective steps can be taken.

In a laboratory study of six-person task groups, a clear pattern of gender inequality was found in the way group members interrupted each other. Men interrupted women significantly more often than they did other men. Women, who tended to interrupt less frequently and less successfully than men, interrupted men and women equally.[65] A recent laboratory study involving Canadian college students found "both men and women exhibiting higher levels of interruption behavior in male-dominated groups."[66]

A field study of mixed-gender police and nursing teams in the Netherlands found another group dynamics disadvantage for women. These two particular professions— police work and nursing—were fruitful research areas because men dominate the former while women dominate the latter. As women move into male-dominated police forces and men gain employment opportunities in the female-dominated world of nursing, who faces the greatest resistance? The answer from this study was the women police officers. As the representation of the minority gender (either female police officers or male nurses) increased in the work groups, the following changes in attitude were observed:

> The attitude of the male majority changes from neutral to resistant, whereas the attitude of the female majority changes from favorable to neutral. In other words, men increasingly want to keep their domain for themselves, while women remain willing to share their domain with men.[67]

Again, managers are faced with the challenge of countering discriminatory tendencies in group dynamics.

The Issue of Sexual Harassment
According to an industry survey by a New York law firm specializing in workplace issues, the problem of sexual harassment refuses to go away:

> 63% of [234] respondents noted that they had handled a sexual harassment complaint at their company. That's up from 2003, when 57% said they had handled one. At least there was some good news here; that's way down from 1995, when 95% of respondents said that they'd handled one.[68]

Making matters worse, a recent field study of five organizations found sexual harassment compounded by ethnic discrimination. According to the researchers, "Women experienced more sexual harassment than men, minorities experienced more ethnic harassment than whites, and minority women experienced more harassment overall than majority men, minority men, and majority women."[69] Thus, it was double jeopardy for the minority women. On-the-job harassment is persistent because it is rooted in widespread abusive behavior among teenagers (both face-to-face and electronically).[70]

Table 10–5   *Behavioral Categories of Sexual Harassment*

CATEGORY	DESCRIPTION	BEHAVIORAL EXAMPLES
Derogatory attitudes— impersonal	Behaviors that reflect derogatory attitudes about men or women in general	Obscene gestures not directed at target Sex-stereotyped jokes
Derogatory attitudes— personal	Behaviors that are directed at the target that reflect derogatory attitudes about the target's gender	Obscene phone calls Belittling the target's competence
Unwanted dating pressure	Persistent requests for dates after the target has refused	Repeated requests to go out after work or school
Sexual propositions	Explicit requests for sexual encounters	Proposition for an affair
Physical sexual contact	Behaviors in which the harasser makes physical sexual contact with the target	Embracing the target Kissing the target
Physical nonsexual contact	Behaviors in which the harasser makes physical nonsexual contact with the target	Congratulatory hug
Sexual coercion	Requests for sexual encounters or forced encounters that are made a condition of employment or promotion	Threatening punishment unless sexual favors are given Sexual bribery

SOURCE: M Rotundo, D Nguyen, and P R Sackett, "A Meta-Analytic Review of Gender Differences in Perceptions of Sexual Harassment," *Journal of Applied Psychology*, October 2001, Article 914–922. Copyright © 2001 by the American Psychological Association. Reprinted with permission.

Another study of social-sexual behavior among 1,232 working men ($n = 405$) and women ($n = 827$) in the Los Angeles area found *nonharassing* sexual behavior to be very common, with 80% of the total sample reporting experience with such behavior. Indeed, according to the researchers, increased social contact between women and men in work groups and organizations has led to increased sexualization (e.g., flirting and romance) in the workplace.[71]

From an OB research standpoint, sexual harassment is a complex and multifaceted problem. For example, a meta-analysis of 62 studies found women perceiving a broader range of behaviors as sexual harassment (see Table 10–5), as opposed to what men perceived. Women and men tended to agree that sexual propositions and coercion qualified as sexual harassment, but there was less agreement about other aspects of a hostile work environment.[72]

Constructive Managerial Action Male and female employees can and often do work well together in groups. A survey of 387 male US government employees sought to determine how they were affected by the growing number of female co-workers. The researchers concluded, "Under many circumstances, including intergender interaction in work groups, frequent contact leads to cooperative and supportive social relations."[73] More recently, a field study of 1,158 US Air Force officers divided into mixed-gender teams for a five-week officer development program determined that "a higher female proportion within teams contributed to better team problem solving."[74] Still, managers need to take affirmative steps to ensure that the documented sexualization of work environments does not erode into sexual harassment. Whether perpetrated against women or men, sexual harassment is demeaning, unethical, and appropriately called "work environment pollution." Moreover, the US Equal Employment Opportunity Commission holds employers legally accountable for behavior it considers sexually harassing. An expert on the subject explains:

> What exactly is sexual harassment? The Equal Employment Opportunity Commission (EEOC) says that unwelcome sexual advances, requests for sexual favors, and other verbal or physical conduct of a sexual nature constitute sexual harassment when submission to such conduct is made a condition of employment; when submission to or rejection of sexual advances is used as a basis for employment decisions; or when such conduct creates an intimidating, hostile, or offensive work environment. These EEOC guidelines interpreting Title VII of the Civil Rights Act of 1964 further state that employers are responsible for the actions of their supervisors and agents and that employers are responsible for the actions of other employees if the employer knows or should have known about the sexual harassment.[75]

A *Training* magazine survey of 1,652 US companies with at least 100 employees found 91% conducting some sort of sexual harassment training and 68% doing so at least annually.[76] Given the disagreement between women and men about what constitutes sexual harassment, this type of education is very important.

Beyond avoiding lawsuits by establishing and enforcing antidiscrimination and sexual harassment policies, managers need to take additional steps. Workforce diversity training is a popular approach today. Gender-issue workshops are another option.

Threats to Group Effectiveness

Even when managers carefully staff and organize task groups, group dynamics can still go haywire. Forehand knowledge of three major threats to group effectiveness—the Asch effect, groupthink, and social loafing—can help managers take necessary preventive steps. Because the first two problems relate to blind conformity, some brief background work is in order.

Very little would be accomplished in task groups and organizations without conformity to norms, role expectations, policies, and rules and regulations. After all, deadlines, commitments, and product/service quality standards need to be established and adhered to if the organization is to survive. But conformity is a two-edged sword. Excessive or blind conformity can stifle critical thinking, the first line of defense against unethical conduct. Almost daily accounts in the popular media of executive misdeeds, insider trading scandals, price fixing, illegal dumping of hazardous wastes, and other unethical practices make it imperative that future managers understand the mechanics of blind conformity.

The Asch Effect

More than 50 years ago, social psychologist Solomon Asch conducted a series of laboratory experiments that revealed a negative side of group dynamics.[77] Under the guise of a "perception test," Asch had groups of seven to nine volunteer college students look at 12 pairs of cards such as the ones in Figure 10–5. The object was to identify the line that was the same length as the standard line. Each individual was told to announce his or her choice to the group. Since the differences among the comparison

Figure 10–5   *The Asch Experiment*

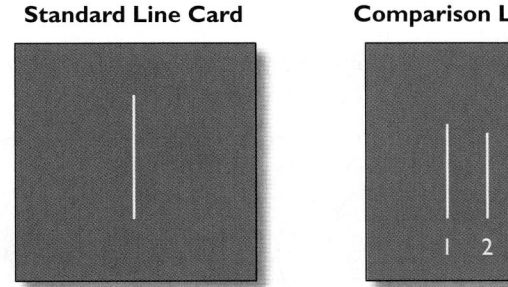

Standard Line Card   **Comparison Lines Card**

lines were obvious, there should have been unanimous agreement during each of the 12 rounds. But that was not the case.

A Minority of One All but one member of each group were Asch's confederates who agreed to systematically select the wrong line during seven of the rounds (the other five rounds were control rounds for comparison purposes). The remaining individual was the naive subject who was being tricked. Group pressure was created by having the naive subject in each group be among the last to announce his or her choice. Thirty-one subjects were tested. Asch's research question was: "How often would the naive subjects conform to a majority opinion that was obviously wrong?"

Only 20% of Asch's subjects remained entirely independent; 80% yielded to the pressures of group opinion at least once! And 58% knuckled under to the "immoral majority" at least twice. Hence, the **Asch effect,** the distortion of individual judgment by a unanimous but incorrect opposition, was documented. (See the Real World/Real People feature on page 296.)

Asch effect

Giving in to a unanimous but wrong opposition.

A Managerial Perspective Asch's experiment has been widely replicated with mixed results. Both high and low degrees of blind conformity have been observed with various situations and subjects. Replications in Japan and Kuwait have demonstrated that the Asch effect is not unique to the United States.[78] A 1996 meta-analysis of 133 Asch-line experiments from 17 countries found a *decline* in conformity among US subjects since the 1950s. Internationally, collectivist countries, where the group prevails over the individual, produced higher levels of conformity than individualistic countries.[79] The point is not precisely how great the Asch effect is in a given situation or culture, but rather, managers committed to ethical conduct need to be concerned that the Asch effect exists.

For Jeffrey Skilling, the now jailed former CEO of Enron, the Asch effect was something to cultivate and nurture. Consider this organizational climate for blind obedience:

> Skilling was filling headquarters with his own troops. He was not looking for "fuzzy skills," a former employee recalls. His recruits talked about a socialization process called "Enronizing." Family time? Quality of life? Forget it. Anybody who did not embrace the elbows-out culture "didn't get it." They were "damaged goods" and "shipwrecks," likely to be fired by their bosses at blistering annual job reviews known as rank-and-yank sessions. The culture turned paranoid: former CIA and FBI agents were hired to enforce security. Using "sniffer" programs, they would pounce on anyone e-mailing a potential competitor. The "spooks," as the former agents were called, were known to barge into offices and confiscate computers.[80]

An Asch Study Maverick Hits It Big as an Investor

What does it take to be an investing genius? For starters, you've got to have the guts to go against the herd. And that's a quality Ken Heebner of CGM Funds displayed as far back as college. As an undergrad at Amherst in the early 1960s, Heebner participated in a psychology-class experiment that was supposed to demonstrate how easily people can be swayed by the views of others. Heebner was asked for his impression of a painting and then ushered to another room where an "expert" offered an opposing viewpoint. Then Heebner was asked once again what he thought of the painting. Says Heebner: "They told me afterward that I was the only one who showed no evidence that other people's opinions had any effect whatsoever on what I thought."

That independent streak has helped make Heebner one of the most successful—and original—investors of his time.

How often do you turn your back on your better judgment just to be one of the crowd?

SOURCE: Excerpted from J Birger, "The Mad Genius of Mutual Funds," *Fortune*, June 26, 2006, pp 98–104.

Even isolated instances of blind, unthinking conformity seriously threaten the effectiveness and integrity of work groups and organizations. Functional conflict and assertiveness, discussed in Chapters 13 and 14, can help employees respond appropriately when they find themselves facing an immoral majority. Ethical codes mentioning specific practices also can provide support and guidance.

Groupthink

Janis's term for a cohesive in-group's unwillingness to realistically view alternatives.

8 Groupthink

Why did President Lyndon B Johnson and his group of intelligent White House advisers make some very *unintelligent* decisions that escalated the Vietnam War? Those fateful decisions were made despite obvious warning signals, including stronger than expected resistance from the North Vietnamese and withering support at home and abroad. Systematic analysis of the decision-making processes underlying the war in Vietnam and other US foreign policy fiascoes prompted Yale University's Irving Janis to coin the term *groupthink*.[81] Modern managers can all too easily become victims of groupthink, just like President Johnson's staff, if they passively ignore the danger.

Definition and Symptoms of Groupthink

Janis defines **groupthink** as "a mode of thinking that people engage in when they are deeply involved in a cohesive ingroup, when members' strivings for unanimity override their motivation to realistically appraise alternative courses of action."[82] He adds, "Groupthink refers to a deterioration of mental efficiency, reality testing, and moral judgment that results

"OUR LAST MEETING STARTED OUT WITH EVERYONE, EXCEPT MR. SIMMS, HEARTILY LAUGHING AT MR. BAINE'S JOKE..."

SOURCE: *Harvard Business Review*, September 2006, p 101.

Figure 10–6   *Symptoms of Groupthink Lead to Defective Decision Making*

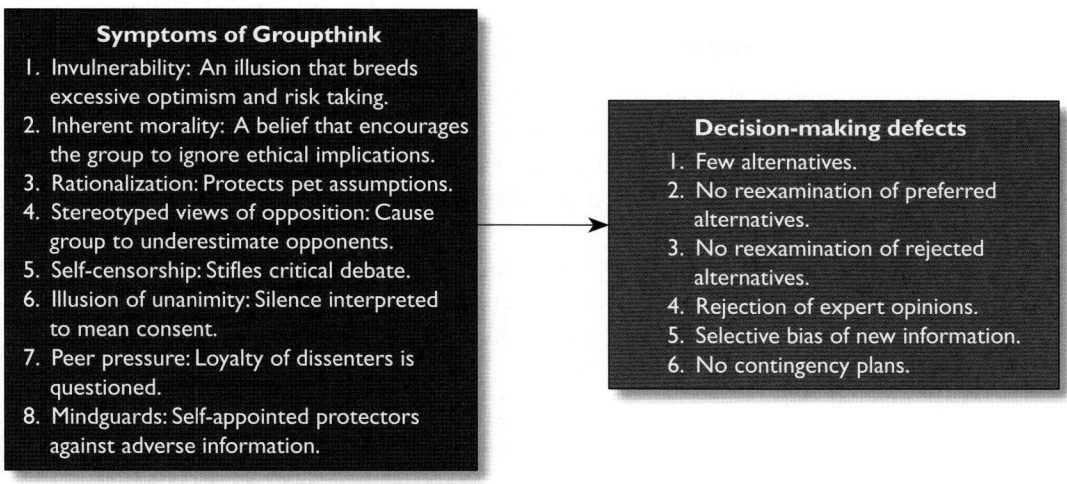

SOURCES: Symptoms adapted from I L Janis, *Groupthink: Psychological Studies of Policy, Decisions and Fiascoes* 2nd ed (Boston: Houghton Mifflin, 1982), pp 174–75. Copyright © 1982 by Houghton Mifflin Company. Used by permission. Defects excerpted from G Moorhead, "Groupthink: Hypothesis in Need of Testing," *Group & Organization Studies,* December 1982, p 434. Copyright © 1982 by Sage Publications. Reprinted by permission of Sage Publications.

from in-group pressures."[83] Unlike Asch's subjects, who were strangers to each other, members of groups victimized by groupthink are friendly, tightly knit, and cohesive.

The symptoms of groupthink listed in Figure 10–6 thrived in US corporate boardrooms of the past where cohesive directors too often caved in to strong-willed CEOs and signed off on bad decisions. But, as recently noted by *BusinessWeek*, circumstances have changed:

> A new era for directors dawned with the passage of the Sarbanes-Oxley Act of 2002. Then board members were hit with the frightening prospect of real financial liability in a smattering of lawsuits that followed the corporate crime wave. Now the heat on directors is growing more intense. Their reputations are increasingly at risk when the companies they watch over are tainted by scandal. Their judgment is being questioned by activist shareholders outraged by sky-high pay packages. And investors and regulators are subjecting their actions to higher scrutiny. Long gone are the days when a director could get away with a quick rubber-stamp of a CEO's plans. . . .
>
> The old rules of civility that discouraged directors from asking managers tough or embarrassing questions are eroding.[84]

Groupthink Research and Prevention Laboratory studies using college students as subjects validate portions of Janis's groupthink concept. Specifically, it has been found that

- Groups with a moderate amount of cohesiveness produce better decisions than low- or high-cohesive groups.
- Highly cohesive groups victimized by groupthink make the poorest decisions, despite high confidence in those decisions.[85]

Janis believes prevention is better than cure when dealing with groupthink. He recommends the following preventive measures:

1. Each member of the group should be assigned the role of critical evaluator. This role involves actively voicing objections and doubts.
2. Top-level executives should not use policy committees to rubber-stamp decisions that have already been made.
3. Different groups with different leaders should explore the same policy questions.
4. Subgroup debates and outside experts should be used to introduce fresh perspectives.
5. Someone should be given the role of devil's advocate when discussing major alternatives. This person tries to uncover every conceivable negative factor.
6. Once a consensus has been reached, everyone should be encouraged to rethink their position to check for flaws.[86]

These antigroupthink measures can help cohesive groups produce sound recommendations and decisions. A G Lafley, the widely respected CEO of Procter & Gamble, offers his own constructive twist:

> Some of the strongest, most courageous people are on the minority side of a decision. It doesn't mean they're wrong. It means they have the courage to speak. . . . I've been trying to change from an advocacy system to what I call an inquiry system. First, I make sure we have a clear definition of the problem. We hold off on the advocacy. We get all the possible solutions and sort through the options. Then, and only then, do we want people to advocate.[87]

Avoiding groupthink is a powerful argument in favor of *diversity;* not only racial and gender diversity, but diversity in age, background, religion, education, and world views as well.

 ## 9 Social Loafing

Is group performance less than, equal to, or greater than the sum of its parts? Can three people, for example, working together accomplish less than, the same as, or more than they would working separately? An interesting study conducted more than a half century ago by a French agricultural engineer named Ringelmann found the answer to be "less than."[88] In a rope-pulling exercise, Ringelmann reportedly found that three people pulling together could achieve only two and a half times the average individual rate. Eight pullers achieved less than four times the individual rate. This tendency for individual effort to decline as group size increases has come to be called **social loafing.**[89] Let us briefly analyze this threat to group effectiveness and synergy with an eye toward avoiding it.

Social loafing

Decrease in individual effort as group size increases.

Social Loafing Theory and Research

Among the theoretical explanations for the social loafing effect are (1) equity of effort ("Everyone else is goofing off, so why shouldn't I?"), (2) loss of personal accountability ("I'm lost in the crowd, so who cares?"), (3) motivational loss due to the sharing of rewards ("Why should I work harder than the others when everyone gets the same reward?"), and (4) coordination loss as more people perform the task ("We're getting in each other's way.").

Laboratory studies refined these theories by identifying situational factors that moderated the social loafing effect. Social loafing occurred when

- The task was perceived to be unimportant, simple, or not interesting.[90]
- Group members thought their individual output was not identifiable.[91]
- Group members expected their co-workers to loaf.[92]

But social loafing did *not* occur when group members in two laboratory studies expected to be evaluated.[93] Also, research suggests that self-reliant "individualists" are more prone to social loafing than are group-oriented "collectivists." But individualists can be made more cooperative by keeping the group small and holding each member personally accountable for results.[94]

Practical Implications These findings demonstrate that social loafing is not an inevitable part of group effort. Management can curb this threat to group effectiveness by making sure the task is challenging and perceived as important. Additionally, it is a good idea to hold group members personally accountable for identifiable portions of the group's task. One way to do this is with the *stepladder technique,* a group decision-making process proven effective by researchers (see Table 10–6). Compared with conventional groups, stepladder groups produced significantly better decisions in the same amount of time. "Furthermore, stepladder groups' decisions surpassed the quality of their best individual members' decisions 56% of the time. In contrast, conventional groups' decisions surpassed the quality of their best members' decisions only 13% of the time."[95] The stepladder technique could be a useful tool for organizations relying on any sort of teams, including self-managed and virtual teams (discussed in the next chapter).

Table 10–6   *How to Avoid Social Loafing in Groups and Teams: The Stepladder Technique*

The stepladder technique is intended to enhance group decision making by structuring the entry of group members into a core group. Increasing or decreasing the number of group members alters the number of steps. In a four-person group, the stepladder technique has three steps. Initially, two group members (the initial core group) work together on the problem at hand. Next, a third member joins the core group and presents his or her preliminary solutions for the same problem. The entering member's presentation is followed by a three-person discussion. Finally, the fourth group member joins the core group and presents his or her preliminary solutions. This is followed by a four-person discussion, which has as its goal the rendering of a final group decision.

The stepladder technique has four requirements. First, each group member must be given the group's task and sufficient time to think about the problem before entering the core group. Second, the entering member must present his or her preliminary solutions before hearing the core group's preliminary solutions. Third, with the entry of each additional member to the core group, sufficient time to discuss the problem is necessary. Fourth, a final decision must be purposely delayed until the group has been formed in its entirety.

SOURCE: Excerpted from S G Rogelberg, J L Barnes-Farrell, and C A Lowe, "The Stepladder Technique: An Alternative Group Structure Facilitating Effective Group Decision Making," *Journal of Applied Psychology* 77 (October 1992), p 731. Copyright © 1992 by the American Psychological Association. Reprinted with permission.

go to the Web for the Group Exercise: A Committee Decision

Summary of Key Concepts

1. *Identify the four sociological criteria of a group, and explain the role of equity in the Workplace Social Exchange Network (WSEN) model.* Sociologically, a *group* is defined as two or more freely interacting individuals who share collective norms and goals and have a common identity. The WSEN model identifies three levels of social exchange: employee–organization, employee–supervisor, and employee–team. Individuals judge each type of social exchange in terms of perceived equity or fairness. The greater the perceived fairness, the more loyal, motivated, and hard-working the individual will be. Lack of perceived fairness is demotivating.

2. *Describe the five stages in Tuckman's theory of group development, and discuss the threat of group decay.* The five stages in Tuckman's theory are forming (the group comes together), storming (members test the limits and each other), norming (questions about authority and power are resolved as the group becomes more cohesive), performing (effective communication and cooperation help the group get things done), and adjourning (group members go their own way). According to recent research, group decay occurs when a work group achieves the "performing" stage and then shifts into reverse. Group decay occurs through de-norming (erosion of standards), de-storming (growing discontent and loss of cohesiveness), and de-forming (fragmentation and breakup of the group).

3. *Distinguish between role conflict and role ambiguity.* Organizational roles are sets of behaviors persons expect of occupants of a position. One may experience role overload (too much to do in too little time), role conflict (conflicting role expectations), or role ambiguity (unclear role expectations).

4. *Contrast roles and norms, and specify four reasons norms are enforced in organizations.* While roles are specific to the person's position, norms are shared attitudes that differentiate appropriate from inappropriate behavior in a variety of situations. Norms evolve informally and are enforced because they help the group or organization survive, clarify behavioral expectations, help people avoid embarrassing situations, and clarify the group's or organization's central values.

5. *Distinguish between task and maintenance roles in groups.* Members of formal groups need to perform both task (goal-oriented) and maintenance (relationship-oriented) roles if anything is to be accomplished.

6. *Summarize the practical contingency management implications for group size.* Laboratory simulation studies suggest decision-making groups should be limited to five or fewer members. Larger groups are appropriate when creativity, participation, or socialization are the main objectives. If majority votes are to be taken, odd-numbered groups are recommended to avoid deadlocks.

7. *Discuss why managers need to carefully handle mixed-gender task groups.* Women face special group dynamics challenges in mixed-gender task groups. Steps need to be taken to make sure increased sexualization of work environments does not erode into illegal sexual harassment.

8. *Describe groupthink, and identify at least four of its symptoms.* Groupthink plagues cohesive in-groups that short-change moral judgment while putting too much emphasis on unanimity. Symptoms of groupthink include invulnerability, inherent morality, rationalization, stereotyped views of opposition, self-censorship, illusion of unanimity, peer pressure, and mindguards. Critical evaluators, outside expertise, and devil's advocates are among the preventive measures recommended by Irving Janis, who coined the term *groupthink*.

9. *Define social loafing, and explain how managers can prevent it.* Social loafing involves the tendency for individual effort to decrease as group size increases. This problem can be contained if the task is challenging and important, individuals are held accountable for results, and group members expect everyone to work hard. The stepladder technique, a structured approach to group decision making, can reduce social loafing by increasing personal effort and accountability.

Key Terms

Group 275
Formal group 275
Informal group 275
Group cohesiveness 280
Roles 284
Role overload 284
Role conflict 285
Role ambiguity 285

Norm 286
Ostracism 286
Task roles 288
Maintenance roles 288
Asch effect 295
Groupthink 296
Social loafing 298

Good Advice from GE's Retiring Human Resources Director

BusinessWeek General Electric Co.'s legendary reputation in talent management owes much to one man: William J. Conaty. In his 40 years at GE, including 13 as head of human resources, he helped to shape the modern face of HR. "The guy is spectacular," says former Chief Executive and *BusinessWeek* columnist Jack Welch. "He has enormous trust at every level. The union guys respect him as much as the senior managers."

Conaty took a department that's often treated as a support function and turned it into a high-level business partner, fostering a deep bench of talent and focusing attention on the need for continuous leadership development. Among other things, he helped manage the seamless transition from Welch to Jeffrey R. Immelt in 2001 and was critical in shaping a new vision of global leadership that emphasizes such traits as imagination and inclusiveness. At 61, Conaty is now easing into retirement, having passed the top job over to longtime HR colleague John Lynch earlier this year while agreeing to stay on to handle GE's labor union negotiations this summer. As he winds up affairs at GE, Conaty shared his advice for nurturing leaders.

Dare to Differentiate

Relentlessly assessing and grading employees build organizational vitality and foster a true meritocracy, in Conaty's view. Employees must be constantly judged, ranked, and rewarded or punished for their performance. Welch famously talked about cutting the bottom 10% of employees. Immelt doesn't like to fixate on hard targets. But Conaty insists that differentiation "is what still drives this company." There's nothing like a bit of anxiety and the knowledge that you're being measured against peers to boost performance. "We want to create angst in the system," he says. "We have evolved from being anal about what percent have to fall into each category. But you have to know who are the least effective people on your team—and then you have to do something about them."

Constantly Raise the Bar

Leaders continually seek to improve performance, both their own and their team members'. "The one reason executives fail at GE is they stop learning," says Conaty. "The job grows, the accountability grows, and the people don't grow with it." Continuous learning is so valued that GE training courses are considered high-profile rewards. Getting tapped to go to Crotonville, the 53-acre executive training center in New York's Hudson River Valley, is a signal that someone is poised to go to the next level. "Crotonville is one of the best tools we have in our arsenal," says Conaty. The company's extensive training programs are a powerful recruitment tool and help to stimulate midcareer employees. Moreover, GE uses Crotonville and other training centers worldwide as a way to recognize valued customers and business partners.

Don't Be Friends with the Boss

Too often, says Conaty, HR executives make the mistake of focusing on the priorities and needs of the CEO. That diminishes the powerful role of being an employee advocate. "If you just get closer to the CEO, you're dead," says Conaty. "The HR leader locks in with the CEO, and the rest of the organization thinks the HR leader isn't trustworthy and can't be a confidant."

Conaty tries to counteract that risk by distancing himself from Immelt in public settings. While few people spend more time with Immelt than Conaty, he deliberately socializes with other colleagues at functions. Moreover, Conaty says he is the one to "purposely throw the daggers at Jeff that the other guys don't dare do. He knows what I'm doing. I need to be independent. I need to be credible." He also makes a point of being candid with leaders in private. As Immelt recently remarked: "I call Bill the 'first friend' . . . the guy that could walk in my office and kick my butt when it needed to be." . . .

Become Easy to Replace

Great leaders develop great succession plans. Insecure leaders are intimidated by them. "I can go business by business and tell you where we're strongest and weakest on succession. It all comes down to having an executive who doesn't want to admit someone else could do their job," says Conaty. "If they kill two or three viable successors along the way, you have to start looking at the person who's doing the killing." At GE, leaders are judged on the strength of their team and are rewarded for mentoring people throughout the organization. Conaty, for one, takes pride in the fact that his own successor is someone that he helped develop within the HR function at GE. . . .

Keep It Simple

Most organizations require simple, focused, and disciplined communications. "You can't move 325,000 people with mixed messaging and thousands of initiatives," notes Conaty. Leaders succeed by being consistent and straightforward about a handful of core messages. And the best don't get derailed when times turn tough. "I'd say 70% of our leaders handle adversity well, and 30% let it overwhelm them," says Conaty. "If you can't take a punch and you don't have a sense of humor, you don't belong in this company. Everyone experiences failure now and then. It's how you handle it that matters."[96]

Questions for Discussion

1. What positive or negative impacts does GE's tough performance evaluation system potentially have on role conflict and role ambiguity? Explain.

2. Based on what you have just read, what particular norms are enforced at GE?

3. How did Conaty effectively prevent groupthink in his dealings with CEO Immelt?

4. Why is social loafing probably not a big problem at GE?

5. From a group dynamics standpoint, why is Conaty the right person to lead GE's negotiations with its unions?

Ethical Dilemma

Let's Have Our Business Meeting at a Strip Club

Nicolette Hart explains how she can make up to $2,500 a night with investment bankers and their clients in a Manhattan strip club's private rooms. . . .

Hart, who once worked for a venture-capital firm, always asks what brought the men together. They often say they're having a meeting.

"I say, 'You're having a *business meeting* in a *strip club*?'" Hart says in an interview in the dressing room at Rick's Cabaret here.

It's not just strippers who have questions. Some women on Wall Street want to know how it can be fair—or legal—for their managers and male colleagues to exclude them when they fraternize at strip clubs, often with the women's clients. Strip club clientele is hardly limited to Wall Street. Adult entertainment is enjoyed by men—and women—in most every industry in the USA, and it's a tax-deductible business expense allowed by the IRS.[97]

As a Top Executive, What Should Your Organization's Policy on this Practice Be?

1. Boys will be boys. Besides, there's nothing illegal about having business meetings in strip clubs. Take no action.

2. While the company doesn't officially support doing business in strip clubs, it can be an effective marketing tactic to loosen up clients, which the company should continue to ignore.

3. This is one good-old-boy tradition that should die because it demeans women in general and sends out the wrong signal for the company's fight against sexual harassment.

4. Having business meetings in strip clubs may be perfectly legal, but that doesn't make it right. The company should take an ethical stand by refusing to reimburse strip club business meeting expenses.

5. The company should be proactive by forbidding the practice and lobbying Congress to outlaw adult entertainment as a legitimate business expense.

6. Invent other interpretations or options. Discuss.

One study suggests that females entering male-dominated fields, such as law enforcement, face greater challenges than do males entering female-dominated fields, such as nursing.

Web Resources

For study material and exercises that apply to this chapter, visit our Web site,
www.mhhe.com/kreitner

CHAPTER 11

Teams and Teamwork

When you finish studying the material in this chapter, you should be able to:

1   Explain how a work group becomes a team.

2   Identify and describe four types of work teams.

3   Explain the model of effective work teams, and specify the two criteria of team effectiveness.

4   Identify five teamwork competencies team members need to possess.

5   Discuss why teams fail.

6   List at least four things managers can do to build trust.

7   Distinguish two types of group cohesiveness, and summarize cohesiveness research findings.

8   Define virtual teams and self-managed teams.

9   Describe high-performance teams.

BusinessWeek They share a title and a salary, a desk, a phone, and an e-mail account. Their résumés are nearly identical: For the past 15 years, Sharon Cercone, 48, and Linda Gladziszewski, 45, have been partners in seven human resources jobs at three different companies. They are now compensation consultants at PNC Financial Services Group in Pittsburgh, where one executive describes them in a way that might unnerve even the most collaborative among us: "I think of them as a single individual," says Valentine Przezdecki.

Successfully sharing a job is more demanding than pretty much any other flexible work arrangement. Partners have to trust each other with their careers. They receive the same recognition, and if one falters, both take the blame. They have to communicate the details of their days precisely and without fail. Theirs is an intricate ... [dance], requiring a certain familiarity and ease, and like most things in life, it can't be forced. "All of the stars have to be aligned. You have to be able to complete each other's sentences and have a manager who doesn't mind adding another level of complexity," says Kathleen C. D'Appolonia, a senior vice-president at PNC. "When it doesn't work, it is very disruptive, and it cannot work for all kinds of reasons. It's sort of like marriage." She says that nearly half of PNC's 25,000 employees have some kind of flexible arrangement; a total of 12 share jobs. . . .

After the birth of her first child, Sharon proposed sharing her job and was matched with another woman. When her partner left Mellon [Financial Corp.] to teach, Sharon asked Linda, who had just returned from maternity leave and wanted more time with her son, to apply for the job. In October 1991, they began to work together.

The practice of constant communication and intense organization that they developed then remains intact today, though made vastly easier by mobile phones and e-mail. Sharon works Mondays and Tuesdays, Linda Thursdays and Fridays; they alternate Wednesdays. They talk or exchange text messages several times a day, and more often on Wednesdays. They check in at night. They keep project notes and a phone log, and even describe the body language of those with whom they meet. "We overcompensate so people understand that we don't let anything fall through the cracks," says Sharon. "We make references to our notes when talking to others." The back-and-forth can add up to three hours to their workweeks, but, says Linda, "We know the arrangement could end at any time, so whatever we can do, we do." They even schedule face time; colleagues tease them about planning lunches weeks ahead. . . .

This spring, Sharon began working at home on her days off on an independent project for PNC. Her department is short-staffed, and she is ready to work more now that her kids are older. But she's uneasy about the new situation. "I'm not used to it, and I don't really like it," she says. "Linda and I are not as connected."[1]

FOR DISCUSSION

Why isn't job sharing more common?

The concept of *social capital,* covered in Chapter 1, really comes to life when our attention turns to teams and teamwork in today's organizations:

> It is the excitement of being part of something bigger than yourself and the thrill of building something—a product, a service, or a team. It is the fun of laughing, debating, sweating it out with fellow travelers—friends and allies in the never-ending competition for customers and profits. Say all you want about the joys of independence, but you can't claim that you and your BlackBerry on a plane can give you the same high as being in a room full of co-workers when word comes in that you've won a hard-fought contract. It just doesn't get any better.[2]

Cooperation, trust, and camaraderie, like that enjoyed by the job-sharing women in the opening vignette, energize organizations. Both women and younger employees, according to research, tend to thrive in team-oriented organizations.[3] Judging from a recent survey that asked corporate leaders to look ahead five years, we all need to polish our teamwork skills: "Teamwork/collaboration" (74%) was among the top three most important knowledge/skill areas, just behind "critical thinking/problem solving" (78%) and "information technology application" (77%).[4]

Emphasis in this chapter is on tapping the full and promising potential of work groups and teams. We will (1) identify different types of work teams, (2) look at what makes teams succeed or fail, (3) examine keys to effective teamwork, such as trust, (4) explore modern applications of the team concept, including virtual teams, and (5) discuss team building.

Work Teams: Types, Effectiveness, and Stumbling Blocks

Jon R Katzenbach and Douglas K Smith, management consultants at McKinsey & Company, say it is a mistake to use the terms *group* and *team* interchangeably. After studying many different kinds of teams—from athletic to corporate to military—they concluded that successful teams tend to take on a life of their own. Katzenbach and Smith define a **team** as "a small number of people with complementary skills who are committed to a common purpose, performance goals, and approach for which they hold themselves mutually accountable."[5] Relative to Tuckman's theory of group development in Chapter 10—forming, storming, norming, performing, and adjourning—teams are task groups that have matured to the *performing* stage (but not slipped into decay). Because of conflicts over power and authority and unstable interpersonal relations, many work groups never qualify as a real team.[6] Katzenbach and Smith clarified the distinction this way: "The essence of a team is common commitment. Without it, groups perform as individuals; with it, they become a powerful unit of collective performance."[7] (See Table 11–1.)

Team

Small group with complementary skills who hold themselves mutually accountable for common purpose, goals, and approach.

When Katzenbach and Smith refer to "a small number of people" in their definition, they mean between 2 and 25 team members. They found effective teams to typically have fewer than 10 members. This conclusion was echoed in a survey of 400 workplace team members in the United States and Canada: "The average North American team consists of 10 members. Eight is the most common size."[8]

2 A General Typology of Work Teams

Work teams are created for various purposes and thus face different challenges. Managers can deal more effectively with those challenges when they understand how teams differ. A helpful way of sorting things out is to consider a typology of work teams developed by Eric Sundstrom and his colleagues.[9] Four general types of work teams listed in Table 11–2

Table 11–1   *The Evolution of a Team*

A work group becomes a team when

1. Leadership becomes a shared activity.
2. Accountability shifts from strictly individual to both individual and collective.
3. The group develops its own purpose or mission.
4. Problem solving becomes a way of life, not a part-time activity.
5. Effectiveness is measured by the group's collective outcomes and products.

SOURCE: Condensed and adapted from J R Katzenbach and D K Smith, *The Wisdom of Teams: Creating the High-Performance Organization* (New York: HarperBusiness, 1999), p 214.

are (1) advice, (2) production, (3) project, and (4) action. Each of these labels identifies a basic *purpose.* For instance, advice teams generally make recommendations for managerial decisions. Less commonly do they actually make final decisions. In contrast, production and action teams carry out management's decisions.

Four key variables in Table 11–2 deal with technical specialization, coordination, work cycles, and outputs. Technical specialization is low when the team draws upon members' general experience and problem-solving ability. It is high when team members are required to apply technical skills acquired through higher education or extensive training. The degree of coordination with other work units is determined by the team's relative independence (low coordination) or interdependence (high coordination). Work cycles are the amount of time teams need to discharge their missions. The various outputs listed in Table 11–2 are intended to illustrate real-life impacts. A closer look at each type of work team is in order.[10]

Advice Teams   As their name implies, advice teams are created to broaden the information base for managerial decisions. Advice teams tend to have a low degree of technical specialization. Coordination also is low because advice teams work pretty much on their own. Ad hoc committees (e.g., the annual picnic committee) have shorter life cycles than standing committees (e.g., the grievance committee).

Production Teams   This second type of team is responsible for performing day-to-day operations. Minimal training for routine tasks accounts for the low degree of technical specialization. But coordination typically is high because work flows from one team to another. For example, railroad maintenance crews require fresh information about needed repairs from train crews, and the train crews, in turn, need to know exactly where maintenance crews are working.

Project Teams   Projects require creative problem solving, often involving the application of specialized knowledge. For example, this is how Motorola's popular RAZR cell phone came into being:

> [T]he RAZR—a play on a code name the geeks themselves dreamed up—was hatched in colorless cubicles in exurban Libertyville, an hour's drive north of Chicago. It was a skunkworks project whose tight-knit team repeatedly flouted Motorola's own rules for developing new products. They kept the project top-secret, even from their colleagues. They used materials and techniques Motorola had never tried before. After contentious internal battles, they threw out accepted models of what a mobile telephone should look and feel like. In short, the team that created the RAZR broke the mold, and in the process rejuvenated the company.[11]

Table 11–2   *Four General Types of Work Teams and Their Outputs*

TYPES AND EXAMPLES	DEGREE OF TECHNICAL SPECIALIZATION	DEGREE OF COORDINATION WITH OTHER WORK UNITS	WORK CYCLES	TYPICAL OUTPUTS
Advice Committees Review panels, boards Quality circles Employee involvement groups Advisory councils	Low	Low	Work cycles can be brief or long; one cycle can be team life span.	Decisions Selections Suggestions Proposals Recommendations
Production Assembly teams Manufacturing crews Mining teams Flight attendant crews Data processing groups Maintenance crews	Low	High	Work cycles typically repeated or continuous process; cycles often briefer than team life span.	Food, chemicals Components Assemblies Retail sales Customer service Equipment repairs
Project Research groups Planning teams Architect teams Engineering teams Development teams Task forces	High	Low (for traditional units) or High (for cross-functional units)	Work cycles typically differ for each new project; one cycle can be team life span.	Plans, designs Investigations Presentations Prototypes Reports, findings
Action Sports teams Entertainment groups Expeditions Negotiating teams Surgery teams Cockpit crews Military platoons and squads Police and fire teams	High	High	Brief performance events, often repeated under new conditions, requiring extended training or preparation.	Combat missions Expeditions Contracts, lawsuits Concerts Surgical operations Competitive events Disaster assistance

SOURCE: Excerpted and adapted from E Sundstrom, K P De Meuse, and D Futrell, "Work Teams," *American Psychologist,* February 1990, p 125. Copyright © 1990 by the American Psychological Association. Reprinted with permission.

This particular project had a low degree of coordination with other units, to escape interference. However, the trend in product development today is toward cross-functional teams that bring together specialists from production, marketing, and finance right from the start. Also, as illustrated in Real World/Real People, project teams can bring realism into academic settings.

Top-Ranked Global MBA Program Is Based on Project Teams

For this year's ranking of non-US MBA programs, *BusinessWeek* surveyed more than 2,000 students from 25 of the world's most competitive programs, as well as the recruiters who hire them, using the same methodology as the US ranking. For the first time since the launch of the international ranking in 2000, three Canadian schools top the list, led again by Queen's University in Kingston, Ont. In a year marked by a battle for differentiation among top international schools, Queen's took top honors with an unusual approach that treats students less like students and more like employees....

How does Queen's do it? For starters, it divides students into groups of five or six "participants," with each group consisting of several different personality types and nationalities so that conflict is almost guaranteed. Unlike most B-schools, where new teams form for each class, Queen's students belong to a single team for the whole program, much as they would on the job. Each team is assigned to a 15-by-20-foot "office" where each student has a cubicle and is expected to keep office-like hours. It's here that students spend a majority of their non-class time, discussing projects and working on assignments. And it's here where much of the magic happens. Students learn how to work as part of a team—resolving differences and solving problems—in a way that can't be taught in the classroom. "Students are treated like professionals, and they're expected to treat it like a job," says Alan Ridgeway, a 2006 Queen's grad.

What are the pros and cons of this team-based approach to education?

SOURCE: Excerpted from G Gloeckler, "The Best Global MBA Programs," *BusinessWeek*, October 23, 2006, pp 72–75.

Action Teams This last type of team is best exemplified by a baseball team. High specialization is combined with high coordination. Nine highly trained athletes play specialized defensive positions. But good defensive play is not enough because effective hitting is necessary. Moreover, coordination between the manager, base runners, base coaches, and the bull pen needs to be precise. So it is with airline cockpit crews, firefighters, hospital surgery teams, mountain-climbing expeditions, rock music groups, labor contract negotiating teams, and police SWAT teams, among others. A unique challenge for action teams is to exhibit peak performance on demand.[12]

This four-way typology of work teams is dynamic and changing, not static. Some teams evolve from one type to another. Other teams represent a combination of types. For example, consider the work of a team at General Foods: "The company launched a line of ready-to-eat desserts by setting up a team of nine people with the freedom to operate like entrepreneurs starting their own business. The team even had to oversee construction of a factory with the technology required to manufacture their product."[13] This particular team was a combination advice-project-action team. In short, the General Foods team did everything but manufacture the end product themselves (that was done by production teams).

3 Effective Work Teams

The effectiveness of athletic teams is a straightforward matter of wins and losses. Things become more complicated, however, when the focus shifts to work teams in today's organizations.[14] Figure 11–1 lists two effectiveness criteria for work teams: performance and viability. Conceptually, the first one is simple: Did the team get the job done? The second criterion is more subtle and easily ignored or overlooked, to the longer-term detriment of the organization. **Team viability** is defined as team members' satisfaction and continued willingness to contribute. Are the team members better or

Team viability

Team members satisfied and willing to contribute.

Figure 11–1   *Effective Work Teams*

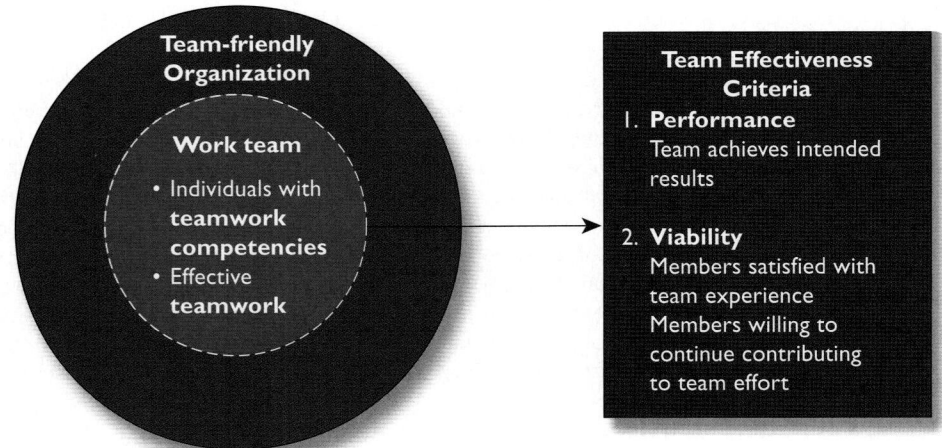

SOURCES: Adapted in part from E Sundstrom, K P DeMeuse, and D Futrell, "Work Teams," *American Psychologist,* February 1990, pp 120–33; and C A Beatty and B A Barker Scott, *Building Smart Teams: A Roadmap to High Performance* (Thousand Oaks, CA: Sage, 2004), pp 5–8.

worse off for having contributed to the team effort?[15] A work team is not truly effective if it gets the job done but self-destructs in the process and burns everyone out.

Also, as indicated in Figure 11–1, work teams require a team-friendly organization if they are to be effective. Work teams need a support system. They have a much greater chance of success if they are nurtured and facilitated by the organization. The team's purpose needs to be in concert with the organization's strategy. Similarly, team participation and autonomy require an organizational culture that values those processes. A good role model is Linda Hunt, president of St. Joseph's Hospital and Medical Center in Phoenix, Arizona. She recently noted,

> We live the model of collaboration. We promote it in our centers of excellence and in our teaching programs, and we incorporate teams into quality care wherever possible.[16]

Team members also need appropriate technological tools, *reasonable* schedules, and training. Teamwork needs to be rewarded by the organizational reward system.[17] Such is not the case when pay and bonuses are tied solely to individual output. For a positive example, consider what has taken place at Internet equipment maker Cisco Systems:

> [CEO John] Chambers took . . . steps to rein in Cisco's Wild West culture during 2002. Most pointedly, he made teamwork a critical part of top execs' bonus plans. He told them 30% of their bonuses for the 2003 fiscal year would depend on how well they collaborated with others. "It tends to formalize the discussion around how can I help you and how can you help me," says Sue Bostrom, head of Cisco's Internet consulting group.[18]

4 Contributors Need Teamwork Competencies Forming workplace teams and urging employees to be good team players are good starting points on the road to effective teams.[19] But much more is needed today. Jeff Zucker, president of NBC Universal Television Group, recently framed the issue this way:

My biggest challenge is getting the new team to maximize our potential and combine together into one culture. We have a bunch of people with strong personalities who are extremely good at what they do. I want them to feel they are the best, and yet have us work together as a team.[20]

In short, Zucker has a leadership group that has not yet melded into a true team, as defined earlier. He would do well to make sure his people possess the teamwork competencies in Table 11–3. Teamwork skills and competencies need to be role modeled and taught. For example, Jim Vesterman, an MBA student at the University of Pennsylvania's Wharton School, learned lifelong teamwork lessons as a combat US Marine serving in Iraq:

> We were one team. Our platoon commander would often quote Kipling to describe Marines: "The strength of the pack is the wolf, and the strength of the wolf is the pack." The Marine Corps recruits wolves. But its strength comes from training them to fight as a pack . . .
>
> When I'm working with a group now, I can honestly say that I think about the team first. The "I first" approach has been drilled out of me.[21]

Notice in Table 11–3 the importance of group problem solving, mentoring, and conflict management skills.

What Does Effective Teamwork Involve? Unfortunately, the terms *team* and *teamwork* are tossed around rather casually today. Many work groups are called teams when they are far from it. Real teamwork requires a concerted collective effort (see Table 11–4). It requires lots of tolerance, practice, and trial-and-error learning.[22] Using Table 11–4 as a guide, have you ever personally experienced real teamwork?

 # 5 Why Do Work Teams Fail?

Advocates of the team approach to management paint a very optimistic and bright picture. Yet there is a dark side to teams.[23] While exact statistics are not available, they can and often do fail. Anyone contemplating the use of team structures in the workplace needs a balanced perspective of advantages and limitations.

Common Management Mistakes with Teams The main threats to team effectiveness, according to the center of Figure 11–2 (on page 314), are *unrealistic expectations* leading to *frustration*. Frustration, in turn, encourages people to abandon teams. Both managers and team members can be victimized by unrealistic expectations.

On the left side of Figure 11–2 is a list of common management mistakes. These mistakes generally involve doing a poor job of creating a supportive environment for teams and teamwork.

Table 11–3   *How Strong Are Your Teamwork Competencies?*

Orients Team to Problem-Solving Situation

Assists the team in arriving at a common understanding of the situation or problem. Determines the important elements of a problem situation. Seeks out relevant data related to the situation or problem.

Organizes and Manages Team Performance

Helps team establish specific, challenging, and accepted team goals. Monitors, evaluates, and provides feedback on team performance. Identifies alternative strategies or reallocates resources to address feedback on team performance.

Promotes a Positive Team Environment

Assists in creating and reinforcing norms of tolerance, respect, and excellence. Recognizes and praises other team members' efforts. Helps and supports other team members. Models desirable team member behavior.

Facilitates and Manages Task Conflict

Encourages desirable and discourages undesirable team conflict. Recognizes the type and source of conflict confronting the team and implements an appropriate resolution strategy. Employs "win–win" negotiation strategies to resolve team conflicts.

Appropriately Promotes Perspective

Defends stated preferences, argues for a particular point of view, and withstands pressure to change position for another that is not supported by logical or knowledge-based arguments. Changes or modifies position if a defensible argument is made by another team member. Projects courtesy and friendliness to others while arguing position.

SOURCE: G Chen, L M Donahue, and R I Klimoski, "Training Undergraduates to Work in Organizational Teams," *Academy of Management Learning and Education,* March 2004, App. A, p 40. Copyright © 2004 by The Academy of Management. Reproduced by permission of The Academy of Management via The Copyright Clearance Center.

Problems for Team Members The lower-right portion of Figure 11–2 lists common problems for team members. Contrary to critics' Theory X contention about employees lacking the motivation and creativity for real teamwork, it is common for teams to take on too much too quickly and to drive themselves too hard for fast results. Important group dynamics and team skills get lost in the rush for results. Consequently, team members' expectations need to be given a reality check by management and team members themselves. Also, teams need to be counseled against quitting when they run into an unanticipated obstacle. Failure is part of the learning process with teams, as it is elsewhere in life. Comprehensive training in interpersonal skills can prevent many common teamwork problems.

Effective Teamwork through Cooperation, Trust, and Cohesiveness

As competitive pressures intensify, experts say organizational success increasingly will depend on teamwork rather than individual stars. No where is this more true than in hospitals. Imagine yourself or a loved one being in this terrible situation:

Table 11–4   *Characteristics of Effective Teamwork*

1. Clear purpose	The vision, mission, goal, or task of the team has been defined and is now accepted by everyone. There is an action plan.
2. Informality	The climate tends to be informal, comfortable, and relaxed. There are no obvious tensions or signs of boredom.
3. Participation	There is much discussion, and everyone is encouraged to participate.
4. Listening	The members use effective listening techniques such as questioning, paraphrasing, and summarizing to get out ideas.
5. Civilized disagreement	There is disagreement, but the team is comfortable with this and shows no signs of avoiding, smoothing over, or suppressing conflict.
6. Consensus decisions	For important decisions, the goal is substantial but not necessarily unanimous agreement through open discussion of everyone's ideas, avoidance of formal voting, or easy compromises.
7. Open communication	Team members feel free to express their feelings on the tasks as well as on the group's operation. There are few hidden agendas. Communication takes place outside of meetings.
8. Clear roles and work assignments	There are clear expectations about the roles played by each team member. When action is taken, clear assignments are made, accepted, and carried out. Work is fairly distributed among team members.
9. Shared leadership	While the team has a formal leader, leadership functions shift from time to time depending on the circumstances, the needs of the group, and the skills of the members. The formal leader models the appropriate behavior and helps establish positive norms.
10. External relations	The team spends time developing key outside relationships, mobilizing resources, and building credibility with important players in other parts of the organization.
11. Style diversity	The team has a broad spectrum of team-player types including members who emphasize attention to task, goal setting, focus on process, and questions about how the team is functioning.
12. Self-assessment	Periodically, the team stops to examine how well it is functioning and what may be interfering with its effectiveness.

SOURCE: G M Parker, *Team Players and Teamwork: The New Competitive Business Strategy* (San Francisco: Jossey-Bass, 1990), table 2, p 33. Copyright © 1990 Jossey-Bass Inc. Reprinted with permission of John Wiley & Sons, Inc.

A 67-year-old woman was admitted to the hospital for treatment of cerebral aneurysms—weakened blood vessels in the brain. Doctors examined her and sent her to her room.

   The next day, she was wheeled into cardiology, of all places, where a doctor had threaded a catheter into her heart before someone noticed he had the wrong patient. The procedure was stopped; the patient recovered.[24]

Analysis of this case by researchers revealed the need for better communication and teamwork.

   Whether in hospitals or the world of business, three components of teamwork receiving the greatest attention are cooperation, trust, and cohesiveness. Let us explore the contributions each can make to effective teamwork.

Figure 11–2   *Why Work Teams Fail*

Mistakes typically made by management

- Teams cannot overcome weak strategies and poor business practices.
- Hostile environment for teams (command-and-control culture; competitive/individual reward plans; management resistance).
- Teams adopted as a fad, a quick-fix; no long-term commitment.
- Lessons from one team not transferred to others (limited experimentation with teams).
- Vague or conflicting team assignments.
- Inadequate team skills training.
- Poor staffing of teams.
- Lack of trust.

Unrealistic expectations resulting in frustration

Problems typically experienced by team members

- Team tries to do too much too soon.
- Conflict over differences in personal work styles (and/or personality conflicts).
- Too much emphasis on results, not enough on team processes and group dynamics.
- Unanticipated obstacle causes team to give up.
- Resistance to doing things differently.
- Poor interpersonal skills (aggressive rather than assertive communication, destructive conflict, win-lose negotiation).
- Poor interpersonal chemistry (loners, dominators, self-appointed experts do not fit in).
- Lack of trust.

SOURCES: Adapted from discussion in S R Rayner, "Team Traps: What They Are, How to Avoid Them," *National Productivity Review,* Summer 1996, pp 101–15; L Holpp and R Phillips, "When Is a Team Its Own Worst Enemy?" *Training,* September 1995, pp 71–82; B Richardson, "Why Work Teams Flop—and What Can Be Done about It," *National Productivity Review,* Winter 1994/95, pp 9–13; and C O Longenecker and M Neubert, "Barriers and Gateways to Management Cooperation and Teamwork," *Business Horizons,* September–October 2000, pp 37–44.

Cooperation

Individuals are said to be cooperating when their efforts are systematically *integrated* to achieve a collective objective.[25] The greater the integration, the greater the degree of cooperation. Ritz-Carlton, the luxury hotel chain, effectively integrates cooperation into its service quality improvement strategy:

> The whole approach . . . depends upon identifying and correcting things that go wrong. To ensure that errors are reported rather than covered up, Ritz-Carlton tries hard to de-stigmatize them, shifting the focus from blame to correction. Mistakes are referred to as "Mr. BIVs," after a cartoon character whose name stands for breakdowns, inefficiencies, and variations. The point is that "a Mr. BIV occurred, and we want to surface it and get rid of it forever," explains [training director Diana] Oreck.

At the start of every shift, every day, at every Ritz-Carlton property, a 15-minute staff meeting takes place. Part of it is devoted to refresher training on one of the 12 "Service Values" incorporated into the company's Gold Standards. . . . Another part alerts the staff to Mr. BIVs that have arisen and the guests affected.[26]

Cooperation versus Competition

A widely held assumption among American managers is that "competition brings out the best in people." From an economic standpoint, business survival depends on staying ahead of the competition. But from an interpersonal standpoint, critics contend competition has been overemphasized, primarily at the expense of cooperation.[27] According to Alfie Kohn, a strong advocate of greater emphasis on cooperation in our classrooms, offices, and factories,

> My review of the evidence has convinced me that there are two . . . important reasons for competition's failure. First, success often depends on sharing resources efficiently, and this is nearly impossible when people have to work against one another. Cooperation takes advantage of all the skills represented in a group as well as the mysterious process by which that group becomes more than the sum of its parts. By contrast, competition makes people suspicious and hostile toward one another and actively discourages this process. . . .
>
> Second, competition generally does not promote excellence because trying to do well and trying to beat others simply are two different things. Consider a child in class, waving his arm wildly to attract the teacher's attention, crying, "Oooh! Oooh! Pick me!" When he is finally recognized, he seems befuddled. "Um, what was the question again?" he finally asks. His mind is focused on beating his classmates, not on the subject matter.[28]

Research Support for Cooperation

After conducting a meta-analysis of 122 studies encompassing a wide variety of subjects and settings, one team of researchers concluded that

1. Cooperation is superior to competition in promoting achievement and productivity.
2. Cooperation is superior to individualistic efforts in promoting achievement and productivity.
3. Cooperation without intergroup competition promotes higher achievement and productivity than cooperation with intergroup competition.[29]

Given the size and diversity of the research base, these findings strongly endorse cooperation in modern organizations. Cooperation can be encouraged by reward systems that reinforce teamwork, along with individual achievement.

Interestingly, cooperation can be encouraged by quite literally tearing down walls, or not building them in the first place. A recent study of 229 managers and professionals employed by eight small businesses proved insightful:

> The researchers looked at the effects of private offices, shared private offices, cubicles, and

Farcus   by David Waisglass / Gordon Coulthart

© 1995 Farcus Cartoons   WAISGLASS/COULTHART   www.farcus.com

team-oriented open offices on productivity, and found to their initial surprise that the small team, open-office configuration (desks scattered about in a small area with no partitions) to be significantly correlated with superior performance. In addition, they found that the open-office configuration was particularly favored by the youngest employees, who believe open offices provide them greater access to colleagues and the opportunity to learn from their more seasoned senior compatriots.[30]

There is a movement among architects and urban planners to design and build structures that encourage spontaneous interaction, cooperation, and teamwork.[31] A good example is Google's Mountain View, California, state-of-the-art headquarters building. This is what the firm's architect, Clive Wilkinson, recently told *Canadian Business* magazine:

Flexible building design and workspaces facilitate teamwork at Google's headquarters. How well can you perform in this sort of free-form environment?

They decided their ideal work module was this three- to four-person workroom. It was interesting that they didn't want total seclusion. So, we created the workroom as a glassed space equipped with highly flexible furniture. . . .

One great discovery we made is of the leveraged learning that Google practices. Continuous seminars are being delivered almost all day—in public locations, next to café spots, which are completely open. You walk through these spaces and there are people discussing formulas with colleagues.[32]

A study involving 84 male US Air Force trainees uncovered an encouraging link between cooperation and favorable race relations. After observing the subjects interact in three-man teams during a management game, the researchers concluded: "[Helpful] teammates, both black and white, attract greater respect and liking than do teammates who have not helped. This is particularly true when the helping occurs voluntarily."[33] These findings suggest that managers can enhance equal employment opportunity and diversity programs by encouraging *voluntary* helping behavior in interracial work teams. Accordingly, it is reasonable to conclude that voluntary helping behavior could build cooperation in mixed-gender teams and groups as well (see Real World/Real People).

Another study involving 72 health care professionals in a US Veterans Affairs Medical Center found a negative correlation between cooperation and team size. In other words, cooperation diminished as the health care team became larger.[34] Managers thus need to restrict the size of work teams if they desire to facilitate cooperation.

 Trust

These have not been good times for trust in the corporate world. Years of mergers, downsizings, layoffs, bloated executive bonuses, corporate scandals, and broken

Teaming Up to Fight Cancer

Wendi Pedicone, who works in internal communications, was diagnosed with breast cancer about two years ago. The mother of four credits her employer with leading to the diagnosis: The cancer was detected after her company, AstraZeneca, reminded her to schedule an annual on-site mammography and exam.

"I attribute my being alive to AstraZeneca," she says. She had chemotherapy, radiation, and surgery.

Pedicone says she was able to transition in and out of work by communicating clearly with team members and clients, sending bi-weekly updates about treatments to co-workers, and leaning on colleagues for practical assistance such as meals for her family.

Co-workers pitched in, she says, by delivering meals to her home for months. They even created a sign reading "executive nap in progress" that Pedicone, who works in Wilmington, Del, could use when she needed a brief rest on days she wasn't feeling well.

What can managers do to create a supportive climate for this sort of helping behavior among employees?

SOURCE: S Armour, "Cancer Patients Keep on Working," *USA Today*, November 20, 2006, p 4B.

---

promises have left many people justly cynical about trusting what management says and does.[35] For example, what does this news item do to your sense of fair play and trust?

> J.C.Penney fired Chief Operating Officer Catherine West on Dec. 28 [2006] after just five months on the job. . . . As a consolation, she'll reap a severance package of nearly $10 million.[36]

So it is no surprise that an international survey found only 25% of Americans saying information from CEOs is credible. Figures for other regions and countries were Europe, 21%; Japan, 29%; China, 43%; and Brazil, 57%.[37] Those who might be tempted to say "So what?" to these findings need to consider the results of another recent survey: "In a study of 500 business professionals, conducted by MasterWorks, Annandale, Virginia, 95% said the main factor in deciding to stay or leave their job was whether they had a trusting relationship with their manager."[38] Clearly, remedial action is needed to close the huge trust gap.

In this section, we examine the concept of trust and introduce six practical guidelines for building trust.

go to the Web for the Self-Exercise: How Trusting Are You?

Reciprocal Faith and a Cognitive Leap Trust is defined as reciprocal faith in others' intentions and behavior.[39] Experts on the subject explain the reciprocal (give-and-take) aspect of trust as follows:

> When we see others acting in ways that imply that they trust us, we become more disposed to reciprocate by trusting in them more. Conversely, we come to distrust those whose actions appear to violate our trust or to distrust us.[40]

In short, we tend to give what we get: trust begets trust; distrust begets distrust.

Trust

Reciprocal faith in others' intentions and behavior.

Figure 11–3   *Interpersonal Trust Involves a Cognitive Leap*

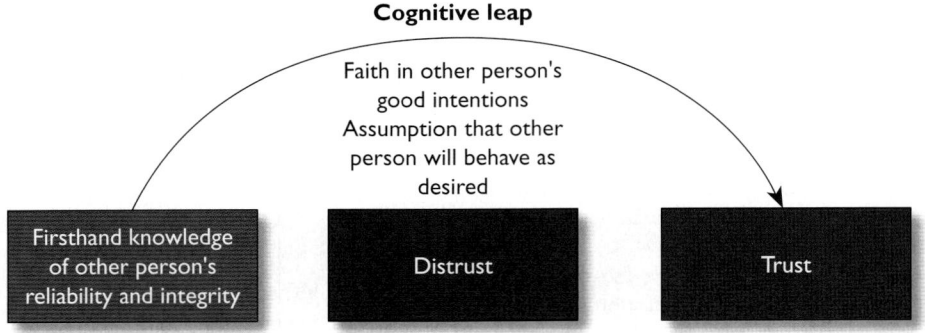

Propensity to trust

A personality trait involving one's general willingness to trust others.

A newer model of organizational trust includes a personality trait called **propensity to trust.** The developers of the model explain:

> Propensity might be thought of as the *general willingness to trust others.* Propensity will influence how much trust one has for a trustee prior to data on that particular party being available. People with different developmental experiences, personality types, and cultural backgrounds vary in their propensity to trust. . . . An example of an extreme case of this is what is commonly called blind trust. Some individuals can be observed to repeatedly trust in situations that most people would agree do not warrant trust. Conversely, others are unwilling to trust in most situations, regardless of circumstances that would support doing so.[41]

What is your propensity to trust? How did you develop that personality trait?

Trust involves "a cognitive 'leap' beyond the expectations that reason and experience alone would warrant"[42] (see Figure 11–3). For example, suppose a member of a newly formed class project team works hard, based on the assumption that her teammates also are working hard. That assumption, on which her trust is based, is a cognitive leap that goes beyond her actual experience with her teammates. When you trust someone, you have *faith* in their good intentions. The act of trusting someone, however, carries with it the inherent risk of betrayal.[43] Progressive managers believe that the benefits of interpersonal trust far outweigh any risks of betrayed trust. For example, Michael Powell, who founded the chain of bookstores bearing his name more than 25 years ago, built his business around the principles of open-book management, empowerment, and trust. Powell's propensity to trust was sorely tested when one of his employees stole more than $60,000 in a used-book purchasing scheme. After putting in some accounting safeguards, Powell's propensity to trust remains intact. He observed,

> The incident was a watershed for me and my staff, dispelling any naïveté we may have had about crime. We realized that not only *can* theft happen; it *will* happen. At the same time, dealing with the matter forced us to revisit our basic values and managerial philosophies. We believe that the modern demands of business call for an empowered and fully flexible staff, and we know that such a staff will often have to handle valuable commodities and money. We also believe that most people are not going to abuse our trust if they are put in a position with a reasonable amount of review and responsibility.[44]

How to Build Trust Management professor/consultant Fernando Bartolomé offers the following six guidelines for building and maintaining trust:

1. *Communication.* Keep team members and employees informed by explaining policies and decisions and providing accurate feedback. Be candid about one's own problems and limitations. Tell the truth.

2. *Support.* Be available and approachable. Provide help, advice, coaching, and support for team members' ideas.

3. *Respect.* Delegation, in the form of real decision-making authority, is the most important expression of managerial respect. Actively listening to the ideas of others is a close second. (Empowerment is not possible without trust.)[45]

4. *Fairness.* Be quick to give credit and recognition to those who deserve it. Make sure all performance appraisals and evaluations are objective and impartial.

5. *Predictability.* Be consistent and predictable in your daily affairs. Keep both expressed and implied promises.

6. *Competence.* Enhance your credibility by demonstrating good business sense, technical ability, and professionalism.[46]

Trust needs to be earned; it cannot be demanded.

 # Cohesiveness

Cohesiveness is a process whereby "a sense of 'we-ness' emerges to transcend individual differences and motives."[47] Members of a cohesive group stick together. They are reluctant to leave the group. Cohesive group members stick together for one or both of the following reasons: (1) because they enjoy each others' company or (2) because they need each other to accomplish a common goal. Accordingly, two types of group cohesiveness, identified by sociologists, are socio-emotional cohesiveness and instrumental cohesiveness.[48]

Cohesiveness
A sense of "we-ness" helps group stick together.

Socio-Emotional and Instrumental Cohesiveness

Socio-emotional cohesiveness is a sense of togetherness that develops when individuals derive emotional satisfaction from group participation. Most general discussions of group cohesiveness are limited to this type. However, from the standpoint of getting things accomplished in task groups and teams, we cannot afford to ignore instrumental cohesiveness. **Instrumental cohesiveness** is a sense of togetherness that develops when group members are mutually dependent on one another because they believe they could not achieve the group's goal by acting separately. A feeling of "we-ness" is *instrumental* in achieving the common goal. Team advocates generally assume both types of cohesiveness are essential to productive teamwork. But is this really true?

Socio-emotional cohesiveness
Sense of togetherness based on emotional satisfaction.

Instrumental cohesiveness
Sense of togetherness based on mutual dependency needed to get the job done.

Lessons from Group Cohesiveness Research

What is the connection between group cohesiveness and performance? A landmark meta-analysis of 49 studies involving 8,702 subjects provided these insights:

- There is a small but statistically significant cohesiveness → performance effect.

- The cohesiveness → performance effect was stronger for smaller and real groups (as opposed to contrived groups in laboratory studies).

- The cohesiveness → performance effect becomes stronger as one moves from nonmilitary real groups to military groups to sports teams.

Sergey Brin (left) and Larry Page have a lot to smile about these days. The Moscow and Michigan natives teamed up while pursuing graduate degrees at Stanford University and founded Google in 1998. Who says teamwork doesn't pay? Can you say "billionaire"?

- Commitment to the task at hand (meaning the individual sees the performance standards as legitimate) has the most powerful impact on the cohesiveness → performance linkage.

- The *performance → cohesiveness* linkage is stronger than the cohesiveness → performance linkage. Thus, success tends to bind group or team members together rather than closely knit groups being more successful.

- Contrary to the popular view, cohesiveness is not "a 'lubricant' that minimizes friction due to the human 'grit' in the system."[49]

- All this evidence led the researchers to this practical conclusion: "Efforts to enhance group performance by fostering interpersonal attraction or 'pumping up' group pride are not likely to be effective."[50]

A second meta-analysis found no significant relationship between cohesiveness and the quality of group decisions. However, support was found for Janis's contention that *groupthink* tends to afflict cohesive in-groups with strong leadership. Groups whose members liked each other a great deal tended to make poorer quality decisions.[51]

Getting Some Positive Impact from Group Cohesiveness Research tells us that group cohesiveness is no secret weapon in the quest for improved group or team performance. The trick is to keep task groups small, make sure performance standards and goals are clear and accepted, achieve some early successes, and follow the tips in Table 11–5. A good example is Westinghouse's highly automated military radar electronics plant in College Station, Texas. Compared with their counterparts at a traditional factory in Baltimore, each of the Texas plant's 500 employees produces eight times more, at half the per-unit cost:

> The key, says Westinghouse, is not the robots but the people. Employees work in teams of 8 to 12. Members devise their own solutions to problems. Teams measure daily how each person's performance compares with that of other members and how the team's performance compares with the plant's. Joseph L Johnson, 28, a robotics technician, says that is a big change from a previous hourly factory job where he cared only about "picking up my paycheck." Here, peer pressure "makes sure you get the job done."[52]

Self-selected work teams (in which people pick their own teammates) and off-the-job social events can stimulate socio-emotional cohesiveness.[53] The fostering of socio-emotional cohesiveness needs to be balanced with instrumental cohesiveness. The latter can be encouraged by making sure everyone in the group recognizes and appreciates each member's vital contribution to the group goal. While balancing the

Table 11–5   *Steps Managers Can Take to Enhance the Two Types of Group Cohesiveness*

Socio-Emotional Cohesiveness
Keep the group relatively small.
Strive for a favorable public image to increase the status and prestige of belonging.
Encourage interaction and cooperation.
Emphasize members' common characteristics and interests.
Point out environmental threats (e.g., competitors' achievements) to rally the group.

Instrumental Cohesiveness
Regularly update and clarify the group's goal(s).
Give every group member a vital "piece of the action."
Channel each group member's special talents toward the common goal(s).
Recognize and equitably reinforce every member's contributions.
Frequently remind group members they need each other to get the job done.

two types of cohesiveness, managers need to remember that groupthink theory and research cautions against too much cohesiveness.

8 Teams in Action: Virtual Teams and Self-Managed Teams

All sorts of interesting approaches to teams and teamwork can be found in the workplace today. A great deal of experimentation is taking place as organizations struggle to be more flexible and responsive. New information technologies also have spurred experimentation with team formats. This section profiles two different approaches to teams: virtual teams and self-managed teams. We have selected these particular types of teams for three reasons: (1) they have recognizable labels, (2) they have at least some research evidence, (3) they vary in degree of empowerment (refer to Figure 15–2 in Chapter 15).

As indicated in Table 11–6, the two types of teams are distinct but not totally unique. Overlaps exist. For instance, computer-networked virtual teams may or may

Table 11–6   *Basic Distinctions between Virtual Teams and Self-Managed Teams*

	VIRTUAL TEAMS	**SELF-MANAGED TEAMS**
Type of team (see Table 11–2)	Advice or project (usually project)	Production, project, or action
Type of empowerment (see Figure 15–2)	Consultation, participation, or delegation	Delegation
Members	Managers and technical specialists	Production/service, technical specialists
Basis of membership	Assigned (some voluntary)	Assigned
Relationship to organization structure	Parallel or integrated	Integrated
Amount of face-to-face communication	Periodic to none	Varies, depending on use of information technology

not have volunteer members and may or may not be self-managed. Another point of overlap involves the fifth variable in Table 11–6: relationship to organization structure. Teams are called *parallel* structures when they exist outside normal channels of authority and communication.[54] Self-managed teams, on the other hand, are *integrated* into the basic organizational structure. Virtual teams vary in this regard, although they tend to be parallel because they are made up of functional specialists (engineers, accountants, marketers, etc.) who team up on temporary projects. Keeping these basic distinctions in mind, let us explore virtual teams and self-managed teams.

This virtual team member has everything he needs at the local Starbucks: a table, cellphone, laptop computer, a broadband connection, project materials, and, oh yes, a hot coffee.

Virtual Teams

Virtual teams are a product of modern times. They take their name from *virtual reality* computer simulations, where "it's almost like the real thing." Thanks to evolving information technologies such as the Internet, e-mail, instant messaging, videoconferencing, groupware, and fax machines, you can be a member of a work team without really being there.[55] Traditional team meetings are location specific. Team members are either physically present or absent. Virtual teams, in contrast, convene electronically with members reporting in from different locations, different organizations, and even different time zones.

Virtual team

Information technology allows group members in different locations to conduct business.

Because virtual teams are relatively new, there is no consensual definition. Our working definition of a **virtual team** is a physically dispersed task group that conducts its business primarily through modern information technology.[56] Advocates say virtual teams are very flexible and efficient because they are driven by information and skills, not by time and location. People with needed information or skills can be team members, regardless of where or when they actually do their work. Virtual teams are second nature to many who grew up with the Internet. *USA Today* recently observed:

> Online communities have become so vital that close to half of those in the USA who participate—43%—say their online friends and associates are as important as groups they participate in face to face.[57]

On the negative side, lack of face-to-face interaction can weaken trust, communication, and accountability. Also, as covered in Chapter 1 under the discussion of e-leadership, leading and managing from a distance can be very challenging.[58]

Research Insights   As one might expect with a new and ill-defined area, research evidence to date is a bit spotty. Here is what we have learned so far from recent studies of computer-mediated groups:

- Virtual groups formed over the Internet follow a group development process similar to that for face-to-face groups.[59] (Recall our discussion of Tuckman's model in Chapter 10.)

How Many *Million* People Are on Your Personal Virtual Network?

Amid all the chatter about user-generated content and Web 2.0, another class of Web services has been quietly gaining momentum. Call it the "professional Web": online services designed explicitly to help you manage your career and do your job better. LinkedIn, for one, has been adding 120,000-plus members a week and now has almost 10 million total. Users of Jigsaw have compiled more than 5.3 million business contacts, adding 12,000 a day.

Right now, the most obvious value that these services provide is the opportunity to own (and control) your online identity. LinkedIn, as well as the services Ziggs and ZoomInfo, let you create a profile for free. (ZoomInfo also proactively aggregates Web info about professionals—34 million so far—and lets you verify your identity.) Search for a name and these profiles generally show up in a search engine's top 10. This is a low-stress way to control your image and, incidentally, make yourself a passive job seeker.

As an experiment, I imported 1,200 contacts into LinkedIn. Of those, about 350 were already members. I contacted all of them and asked them to connect. More than 230 have done so. But more interesting was the full gamut of responses to my request. It ranged from "Who are you, again?" to being thrilled to reconnect. Many people, justifiably, were protective of their contacts. "At some point, building a network just becomes an end in itself," was a recurring refrain, something I was clearly guilty of. Those folks understand LinkedIn's greatest value, and its greatest flaw: Let one pushy semioutsider into your network, and you've polluted it.

Is there a way to make this evolving professional Web work for you? LinkedIn is certainly useful for tracking your most trusted colleagues. But "use it for high-value items only," counsels Mikolaj Jan Piskorski, assistant professor at Harvard Business School, who has been studying social networks since 2003. That means: It ain't an everyday tool.

What useful lessons have you learned from social and professional networking on the Web?

SOURCE: D Lidsky, "It's Not Just Who You Know," *Fast Company*, May 2007, p 56.

- Internet chat rooms create more work and yield poorer decisions than face-to-face meetings and telephone conferences.[60]
- Successful use of groupware (software that facilitates interaction among virtual group members) requires training and hands-on experience.[61]
- Inspirational leadership has a positive impact on creativity in electronic brainstorming groups.[62]
- Conflict management is particularly difficult for *asynchronous* virtual teams (those not interacting in real time) that have no opportunity for face-to-face interaction.[63]

Practical Considerations Virtual teams may be in fashion, but they are not a cure-all. In fact, they may be a giant step backward for those not well versed in modern information technology. Managers who rely on virtual teams agree on one point: *Meaningful face-to-face contact, especially during early phases of the group development process, is absolutely essential.* Virtual group members need "faces" in their minds to go with names and electronic messages (see Real World/Real People). Periodic face-to-face interaction not only fosters social bonding among virtual team members, it also facilitates conflict resolution. Additionally, virtual teams cannot succeed without some old-fashioned factors such as top-management support, hands-on training, a clear mission and specific objectives, effective leadership, and schedules and deadlines.[64] (See the additional practical tips listed in Table 11–7.)

Self-Managed Teams

Have you ever thought you could do a better job than your boss? Well, if the trend toward self-managed work teams continues to grow as predicted, you just may get your

Table 11–7   *How to Manage Virtual Teams*

Establishing trust and commitment, encouraging communication, and assessing team members pose tremendous challenges for virtual team managers. Here are a few tips to make the process easier:

- Establish regular times for group interaction.
- Set up firm rules for communication.
- Use visual forms of communication where possible.
- Emulate the attributes of co-located teams. For example, allow time for informal chitchat and socializing, and celebrate achievements.
- Give and receive feedback and offer assistance on a regular basis. Be persistent with people who aren't communicating with you or each other.
- Agree on standard technology so all team members can work together easily.
- Consider using 360-degree feedback to better understand and evaluate team members.
- Provide a virtual meeting room via intranet, Web site or bulletin board.
- Note which employees effectively use e-mail to build team rapport.
- Smooth the way for an employee's next assignment if membership on the team, or the team itself, is not permanent.
- Be available to employees, but don't wait for them to seek you out.
- Encourage informal, off-line conversation between team members.

SOURCE: C Johnson, "Managing Virtual Teams," *HR Magazine*, June 2002, p 71. Reprinted with the permission of HR Magazine published by the Society for Human Resource Management, Alexandria, VA.

chance. Entrepreneurs and artisans often boast of not having a supervisor. The same generally cannot be said for employees working in offices and factories. But things are changing. In fact, an estimated half of the employees at *Fortune* 500 companies are working on teams.[65] A growing share of those teams are self-managing. For example, "At a General Mills cereal plant in Lodi, California, teams . . . schedule, operate, and maintain machinery so effectively that the factory runs with no managers present during the night shift."[66] More typically, managers are present to serve as trainers and facilitators. Self-managed teams come in every conceivable format today, some more autonomous than others.

Self-managed teams

Groups of employees granted administrative oversight for their work.

Self-managed teams are defined as groups of workers who are given administrative oversight for their task domains. Administrative oversight involves delegated activities such as planning, scheduling, monitoring, and staffing. These are chores normally performed by managers. In short, employees in these unique work groups act as their own supervisor. Accountability is maintained *indirectly* by outside managers and leaders. According to a study of a company with 300 self-managed teams, 66 "team advisers" relied on these four indirect influence tactics:

- *Relating.* Understanding the organization's power structure, building trust, showing concern for individual team members.
- *Scouting.* Seeking outside information, diagnosing teamwork problems, facilitating group problem solving.
- *Persuading.* Gathering outside support and resources, influencing team to be more effective and pursue organizational goals.
- *Empowering.* Delegating decision-making authority, facilitating team decision-making process, coaching.[67]

Self-managed teams are variously referred to as semiautonomous work groups, autonomous work groups, and superteams.

Managerial Resistance Something much more complex is involved than this apparently simple label suggests. The term *self-managed* does not mean simply turning workers loose to do their own thing. Indeed, an organization embracing self-managed teams should be prepared to undergo revolutionary changes in management philosophy, structure, staffing and training practices, and reward systems. Moreover, the traditional notions of managerial authority and control are turned on their heads. Not surprisingly, many managers strongly resist giving up the reins of power to people they view as subordinates. They see self-managed teams as a threat to their job security.

Cross-Functionalism A common feature of self-managed teams, particularly among those above the shop-floor or clerical level, is **cross-functionalism.**[68] In other words, specialists from different areas are put on the same team. For example, you can thank a cross-functional team for that little musical riff you hear every time you fire up Microsoft's Windows Vista operating system: "In the end, it took 18 months—and a team of 20 composers, sound designers, engineers, and developers."[69] Mark Stefik, a manager at the world-renowned Palo Alto Research Center in California, explains the wisdom of cross-functionalism:

Cross-functionalism
Team made up of technical specialists from different areas.

> Something magical happens when you bring together a group of people from different disciplines with a common purpose. It's a middle zone, the breakthrough zone. The idea is to start a team on a problem—a hard problem, to keep people motivated. When there's an obstacle, instead of dodging it, bring in another point of view: an electrical engineer, a user interface expert, a sociologist, whatever spin on the market is needed. Give people new eyeglasses to cross-pollinate ideas.[70]

As described in the Real World/Real People feature on page 309, cross-functionalism is seeping into university programs to help students see the big picture and polish their team skills.

Are Self-Managed Teams Effective? The Research Evidence

Among companies with self-managed teams, the most commonly delegated tasks are work scheduling and dealing directly with outside customers. The least common team chores are hiring and firing.[71] Most of today's self-managed teams remain bunched at the shop-floor level in factory settings. Experts predict growth of the practice in the managerial ranks and in service operations.[72]

Much of what we know about self-managed teams comes from testimonials and case studies. Fortunately, a body of higher quality field research is slowly developing. A review of three meta-analyses covering 70 individual studies concluded that self-managed teams had

- A positive effect on productivity.
- A positive effect on specific attitudes relating to self-management (e.g., responsibility and control).
- No significant effect on general attitudes (e.g., job satisfaction and organizational commitment).
- No significant effect on absenteeism or turnover.[73]

Although encouraging, these results do not qualify as a sweeping endorsement of self-managed teams. Nonetheless, experts say the trend toward self-managed work teams will continue upward in North America because of a strong cultural bias in favor of direct participation (see Table 11–8). Managers need to be prepared for the resulting shift in organizational administration.[74]

go to the Web for the Self-Exercise: Measuring Work Group Autonomy

Table 11–8   *There Are Many Ways to Empower Self-Managed Teams*

External Leader Behavior

1. Make team members responsible and accountable for the work they do.
2. Ask for and use team suggestions when making decisions.
3. Encourage team members to take control of their work.
4. Create an environment in which team members set their own team goals.
5. Stay out of the way when team members attempt to solve work-related problems.
6. Generate high team expectations.
7. Display trust and confidence in the team's abilities.

Production/Service Responsibilities

1. The team sets its own production/service goals and standards.
2. The team assigns jobs and tasks to its members.
3. Team members develop their own quality standards and measurement techniques.
4. Team members take on production/service learning and development opportunities.
5. Team members handle their own problems with internal and external customers.
6. The team works with a whole product or service, not just a part.

Human Resource Management System

1. The team gets paid, at least in part, as a team.
2. Team members are cross-trained on jobs within their team.
3. Team members are cross-trained on jobs in other teams.
4. Team members are responsible for hiring, training, punishment, and firing.
5. Team members use peer evaluations to formally evaluate each other.

Social Structure

1. The team gets support from other teams and departments when needed.
2. The team has access to and uses important and strategic information.
3. The team has access to and uses the resources of other teams.
4. The team has access to and uses resources inside and outside the organization.
5. The team frequently communicates with other teams.
6. The team makes its own rules and policies.

SOURCE: Reprinted from B L Kirkman and B Rosen, "Powering Up Teams," *Organizational Dynamics,* Winter 2000, ex 3, p 56, © 2000. Used by permission of Elsevier Science.

Team Building

Team building

Experiential learning aimed at better internal functioning of groups.

Team building is a catch-all term for a whole host of techniques aimed at improving the internal functioning of work groups. Whether conducted by company trainers or outside consultants, team-building workshops strive for greater cooperation, better communication, and less dysfunctional conflict. Rote memorization and lectures/

Do Team-Building Exercises Make the Grade?

Maury Dahn, who used to be a vice president for a contractor on an Apollo space project, was asked by HR to have his team participate in a role-playing game where the team had to return safely from the North Pole. They had managed helping astronauts return safely from space in real life, so the time and money spent on the exercise bugged him. "It just came across as a childish exercise," he says.

How's this for a corporate New Year's resolution: Lose the goofy team-building exercises. You can learn a lot from such company events, which take you out of the office and onto ropes courses, bowling alleys and white-water rafts. Research shows good team dynamics greatly improve performance, and these events can be meaningful metaphors for teamwork. But too often, the most memorable job metaphors include blindfolds, swamped boats and groin injuries. It's easy to do team-building poorly and easier to think it went really well.

After all, everyone in a "trust fall," falling backward blindfolded, lands safely in the arms of their colleagues. It proves only that colleagues prefer not to be sued.

Ron Roberts, an author and the president of Action Centered Training, offers a vast menu of team-building exercises, such as the "High Energy and Outdoor Challenges," which includes paintball (to teach teamwork and communication), white-water rescue of river guides (to help with management change). Nascar racing (for leadership and process improvement), a team-cuisine event in which people have to cook a seven-course meal without recipes (bonding) and Inflatable Olympics. That program includes bumper boats, obstacle courses, bungee cords and a full-body suit that allows you to hurl yourself against a Velcro wall and stick to it. The Velcro stick might do little for team building, but it's a good metaphor for the office.

Some participants find these outings amusing. "They make us feel good," says Margaret Neale, professor of organizational behavior at Stanford's Graduate School of Business. "What they don't do is improve team performance."

Team-building proponents counter that valuable principles operate in any number of games and can boost performance. Mr. Roberts says paintball may have little to do with an actual job, but it's powerful. Winning requires working as a team and communicating loudly. "If they don't work as a team, they get shot and experience pain. It's not for everybody," he adds. "But the principles of communication, teamwork, leadership and strategic planning are there."

If given the task by your manager, what specific team-building activity would you select and what would you do to make it an effective learning event?

SOURCE: J Sandberg, "Can Spending the Day Stuck to a Velcro Wall Help Build a Team?" *The Wall Street Journal*, December 26, 2006, p B1.

---

discussions are discouraged by team-building experts who prefer *active* versus passive learning. Greater emphasis is placed on *how* work groups get the job done than on the job itself. Experiential learning techniques such as interpersonal trust exercises, conflict-handling role-play sessions, and interactive games are common (see Real World/Real People).

Some prefer off-site gatherings to get participants away from their work and out of their comfort zones. An exotic (and expensive) case in point is Seagate Technology:

Plenty of companies try to motivate the troops, but few go as far as Seagate Technology. In February [2006] the $9.8 billion maker of computer storage hardware flew 200 staffers to New Zealand for

Seagate's CEO Bill Watkins "walks the talk" on off-site team building.

its sixth annual Eco Seagate—an intense week of team building topped off by an all-day race in which Seagaters had to kayak, hike, bike, swim, and rappel down a cliff. The tab? $9,000 per person. . . .

   This event, or social experiment, is [CEO Bill] Watkins' pet project. He dreamed up Eco Seagate as a way to break down barriers, boost confidence, and, yes, make staffers better team players. "Some of you will learn about teamwork because you have a great team," he . . . [said during his opening pep talk]. "Some of you will learn because your team is a disaster."[75]

Seagate's chief financial officer, Charles Pope, originally a nonparticipant who doubted the program's worth, has since joined in and now sees Eco Seagate as an investment, not a vacation.

The Bottom Line: Without clear goals, proper leadership, careful attention to details, and transfer of learning back to the job, both on-site and off-site team-building sessions can become an expensive disappointment.[76]

The University of Tennessee women's basketball team knows a lot about high-performance teamwork, thanks to 6'4" All-American Candace Parker and Coach Pat Summitt. Indeed, Tennessee's record seventh NCAA national championship in 2007 was made possible by individuals who stepped up to assume a leadership role at critical times. For example, an eight-point code of conduct introduced mid-season by junior center Nicky Anosike, and refined by her teammates, helped the Lady Vols solidify into a national championship team.

9 The Goal of Team Building: High-Performance Teams

Team building allows team members to wrestle with simulated or real-life problems. Outcomes are then analyzed by the group to determine what group processes need improvement. Learning stems from recognizing and addressing faulty group dynamics. Perhaps one subgroup withheld key information from another, thereby hampering group progress. With cross-cultural teams becoming commonplace in today's global economy, team building is more important than ever.[77]

A nationwide survey of team members from many organizations, by Wilson Learning Corporation, provides a useful model or benchmark of what we should expect of teams. The researchers' question was simply: "What is a high-performance team?"[78] The respondents were asked to describe their peak experiences in work teams. Analysis of the survey results yielded the following eight attributes of high-performance teams:

1. *Participative leadership.* Creating an interdependency by empowering, freeing up, and serving others.

2. *Shared responsibility.* Establishing an environment in which all team members feel as responsible as the manager for the performance of the work unit.

3. *Aligned on purpose.* Having a sense of common purpose about why the team exists and the function it serves.

4. *High communication.* Creating a climate of trust and open, honest communication.

5. *Future focused.* Seeing change as an opportunity for growth.
6. *Focused on task.* Keeping meetings focused on results.
7. *Creative talents.* Applying individual talents and creativity.
8. *Rapid response.* Identifying and acting on opportunities.[79]

These eight attributes effectively combine many of today's most progressive ideas on management, among them being participation, empowerment, service ethic, individual responsibility and development, self-management, trust, active listening, and envisioning. But patience and diligence are required. According to a manager familiar with work teams, "high-performance teams may take three to five years to build."[80] Let us keep this inspiring model of high-performance teams in mind as we conclude our discussion of team building.

go to the Web for the Group Exercise: Student Team Development Project

Developing Team Members' Self-Management Skills

A promising dimension of team building has emerged in recent years. It is an extension of the self-management approach discussed in Learning Module A (on the book's Web site). Proponents call it **self-management leadership,** defined as the process of leading others to lead themselves. An underlying assumption is that self-managed teams likely will fail if team members are not expressly taught to engage in self-management behaviors.[81] This makes sense because it is unreasonable to expect employees who are accustomed to being managed and led to suddenly manage and lead themselves. Transition training is required. A key transition to self-management involves *current managers* engaging in self-management leadership behaviors. This is team building in the fullest meaning of the term.

Six self-management leadership behaviors were isolated in a field study of a manufacturing company organized around self-managed teams. The observed behaviors were

Self-management leadership

Process of leading others to lead themselves.

1. *Encourages self-reinforcement* (e.g., getting team members to praise each other for good work and results).
2. *Encourages self-observation/evaluation* (e.g., teaching team members to judge how well they are doing).
3. *Encourages self-expectation* (e.g., encouraging team members to expect high performance from themselves and the team).
4. *Encourages self-goal-setting* (e.g., having the team set its own performance goals).
5. *Encourages rehearsal* (e.g., getting team members to think about and practice new tasks).
6. *Encourages self-criticism* (e.g., encouraging team members to be critical of their own poor performance).[82]

According to the researchers, Charles Manz and Henry Sims, this type of leadership is a dramatic departure from traditional practices such as giving orders or making sure everyone gets along. Empowerment, not domination, is the overriding goal.

Summary of Key Concepts

1. *Explain how a work group becomes a team.* A team is a mature group where leadership is shared, accountability is both individual and collective, the members have developed their own purpose, problem solving is a way of life, and effectiveness is measured by collective outcomes.

2. *Identify and describe four types of work teams.* Advice teams provide information for managerial decisions. Production teams perform an organization's day-to-day operations. Project teams apply specialized knowledge to solve problems needed to complete a specific project. Action teams are highly skilled and highly coordinated to provide peak performance on demand.

3. *Explain the model of effective work teams, and specify the two criteria of team effectiveness.* Work teams need three things: (*a*) a team-friendly organization to provide a support system; (*b*) individuals with teamwork competencies; and (*c*) effective teamwork. The two team effectiveness criteria are performance (getting the job done) and team viability (satisfied members who are willing to continue contributing to the team).

4. *Identify five teamwork competencies team members need to possess.* They are (*a*) orients team to problem-solving situation; (*b*) organizes and manages team performance; (*c*) promotes a positive team environment; (*d*) facilitates and manages task conflict; and (*e*) appropriately promotes perspective.

5. *Discuss why teams fail.* Teams fail because unrealistic expectations cause frustration and failure. Common management mistakes include weak strategies, creating a hostile environment for teams, faddish use of teams, not learning from team experience, vague team assignments, poor team staffing, inadequate training, and lack of trust.

Team members typically try too much too soon, experience conflict over differing work styles and personalities, ignore important group dynamics, resist change, exhibit poor interpersonal skills and chemistry, and display a lack of trust.

6. *List at least four things managers can do to build trust.* Six recommended ways to build trust are through communication, support, respect (especially delegation), fairness, predictability, and competence.

7. *Distinguish two types of group cohesiveness, and summarize cohesiveness research findings.* Cohesive groups have a shared sense of togetherness or a "we" feeling. Socio-emotional cohesiveness involves emotional satisfaction. Instrumental cohesiveness involves goal-directed togetherness. There is a small but significant relationship between cohesiveness and performance. The effect is stronger for smaller groups. Commitment to task among group members strengthens the cohesiveness-performance linkage. Success can build group cohesiveness. Cohesiveness is not a cure-all for group problems. Too much cohesiveness can lead to groupthink.

8. *Define virtual teams and self-managed teams.* Virtual teams are physically dispersed work groups that conduct their business via modern information technologies such as the Internet, e-mail, and videoconferences. Self-managed teams are work groups that perform their own administrative chores such as planning, scheduling, and staffing.

9. *Describe high-performance teams.* Eight attributes of high-performance teams are participative leadership, shared responsibility, aligned on purpose, high communication, future focused for growth, focused on task, creative talents applied, and rapid response.

Key Terms

OB in Action Case Study

In the Trenches at VF Boot Camp[83]

BusinessWeek **Nanette Byrnes,** *BusinessWeek* **reporter:** There were six of us, squinting down the length of a conference table at a single laptop. It was past 9 p.m., and what we could make out on the screen wasn't encouraging. We'd all met just 13 hours earlier—when I was thrown together with five fast-climbing executives at apparel maker VF Corp. for an exercise in management boot camp. Over the four days of the Leadership Institute, as VF calls it, we would face more important challenges, but what had us all flummoxed at the moment was a computer game at which we were failing spectacularly.

I'm a dyed-in-the-wool HR skeptic. So after a day of lectures on communication—and tossing around Nerf footballs to "loosen up"—I wasn't so sure why we were puzzling out "Launching a High-Risk Business," a simulation cooked up by two Harvard Business School academics. Another of our band, Rob Purvey, echoed my doubts. An executive at skateboard shoe brand Vans, Purvey had once been an entrepreneur himself and had raised $30 million of the real green stuff for one venture. We tried strategy after strategy. They all failed. But about a half-hour before our 10 p.m. deadline, something clicked. We partnered with the inventor, poured cash into marketing, and begged every virtual venture capitalist and bank for seed money. The offers started to trickle in, and soon our company was worth $5 million. We actually whooped with joy.

Score one for team bonding. Up to that point, sitting in that windowless, fluorescent-lit conference room, I'd wondered whether VF could possibly get enough from this program to justify taking 19 of its best people away from their day jobs for a week. As a reporter, I'm used to being an observer, operating solo. But when our fortunes turned that night, I was as elated as anyone else. That video game had broken down the normal reserve any group of distant colleagues would have, especially one with a journalist in its midst. . . .

The task of team-building has grown more complex lately for VF Chief Executive Mackey J. McDonald. The company, long known as the maker of traditional jeans brands Wrangler and Lee, has recently taken on a number of more fashion-forward brands, including Reef surfer wear, Vans, and The North Face outdoor gear. Hence the HR headache: getting the most out of a workforce of 52,500 employees spread over 40 different countries. But McDonald is doing something right: Good sales and profit growth at the $6.5 billion company have helped its stock return 47.6% over the past year. And the attrition rate for its top performers, both homegrown and acquired, is less than 5%.

Indeed, one of the goals of the Leadership Institutes, such as the one I attended in October, is to get top managers from all different parts of the company working together. Its "final exam" is a 45-minute, case-study presentation to McDonald, President Eric C. Wiseman, and other top brass. Four teams compete. A quarter of the graduates are promoted within 24 months. So it's no surprise that with so much ambition around, the atmosphere was at times intense and competitive. My team got an inkling of the challenge over beers after our late-breaking triumph at the computer game when we learned that the winning team had built a simulated company worth $100 million, twenty times the size of ours.

The next day, undaunted and even invigorated by our small victory, my teammates and I found ourselves on a luxury bus zipping off to an afternoon of research at a couple of local golf courses. In our laps was a case study, which would pose the session's capstone challenge: to kick-start the sportswear division of a company, beginning with the launch of a new golf apparel line.

We all had the same challenge, and the same research opportunities, but the four groups came up with completely different solutions. My team pitched a line of apparel for kids and parents to golf in together. The idea was to transform golf from something that split Dad from the family to one that brought them all together. Our field research on Wednesday was followed by a marathon Thursday working on our presentation. I was too busy to dwell on my growing hatred for our glum conference room, where we had all spent too much time over the boot camp's four days.

On the final morning, my team presented first. But not long into the third team's highly polished presentation, my heart began to sink. It seemed as if they had found another 24 hours to practice their parts. They had the most standard idea of all the teams, going after young men with a more fashionable look. The other two teams had zeroed in on women and environmentally-conscious urbanites. But the eventual victors had used the skills of each of their five presenters better than the rest of us. A marketing guy led the pitch, a dealmaker from the corporate M&A group presented the financial argument, and a jeanswear veteran pitched the product. "The combination of talent was really great," Doug Palladini, a member of the winning squad and Vans' vice-president for marketing, told me afterwards.

I knew the best team had won, but after the votes had been tallied, when McDonald asked me what I'd gotten out of the experience, I couldn't stop myself from shoehorning in a pitch for how good our idea was, even if our presentation wasn't tops. This was a competition after all, and I was surprisingly sad my team lost.

Questions for Discussion

1. Using Table 11–1 as a guide, did Nanette Byrnes's group deserve to be called a team after four days? Explain.

2. Should the participants in this program have been instructed ahead of time in the teamwork competencies listed in Table 11–3? Explain.

3. How important is trust in this sort of team building?

4. Which type of cohesiveness, socio-emotional or instrumental, is more important in this type of team building? Explain.

5. What role, if any, did cross-functionalism play in this case?

6. Is VF Corp.'s Leadership Institute an effective team building program? Is it money well spent? Explain.

Protects Like Armor, Fits Like Armani[84]

"Who here hasn't been shot?"

Miguel Caballero is walking around his company's showroom in Bogotá, Colombia, holding a .38-caliber revolver. "You!" he says, pointing to German Gonzalez, a 20-something salesman who's been on the job for just two weeks. "You're next."

Gonzalez wiggles nervously into an $850 brown suede winter jacket and zips it up to the collar. A foot or so away, the smiling Caballero lowers the weapon and takes aim.

"One!" Gonzalez takes a deep breath and stares up at the ceiling. "Two! . . ." A deafening blast sends Gonzalez lurching backward—and then screaming out in relief, clutching at the hole in the jacket where the bullet has come to a safe stop.

No, this isn't some cruel corporate hazing ritual. For Caballero, founder and CEO of the company that carries his name, this is just a showman's way of demonstrating his products. Caballero sells a line of armored clothing that fits like Armani but deflects point-blank gunfire like the Popemobile. Last year the 38-year-old entrepreneur sold an estimated $7 million worth of bulletproof trench coats, business suits, suede jackets, and denim casuals to executives, political leaders, undercover agents, and other VIPs—people who demand more than a bodyguard for protection and don't like the bulk or SWAT-team look of flak jackets and vests. "There are hundreds of companies that make bulletproof vests," Caballero says. "We make bulletproof fashion."

Situation: **The president of your company witnessed this demonstration on a recent visit to Colombia and now wants you, the marketing director, to develop a similar marketing campaign as a North American distributor. What is your response and its ethical implications?**

1. Talk about getting the customer's attention, this is great marketing! Let's go with live demonstrations. Who wants to take a bullet for the team?

2. A live demonstration is too dangerous and out of the question. Besides many cities have laws against firing guns within city limits. Let's go with a video demonstration. Who wants to take a bullet for the team?

3. What happens in Colombia should stay in Colombia. Have Miguel Caballero make a demonstration video, in Colombia, just like the one described above for use in foreign markets.

4. Live models in any sort of demonstration are out of the question. Too controversial. Let's create a promotional video in the safety of a shooting range with a mannequin wearing the bullet-proof jacket.

5. Invent other options. Discuss.

Web Resources

For study material and exercises that apply to this chapter, visit our Web site,

www.mhhe.com/kreitner

CHAPTER 12

Individual and Group Decision Making

When you finish studying the material in this chapter, you should be able to:

1   Compare and contrast the rational model of decision making, Simon's normative model, and the garbage can model.

2   Discuss eight decision-making biases.

3   Discuss knowledge management and techniques used by companies to increase knowledge sharing.

4   Explain the model of decision-making styles.

5   Explain the model of intuition and the ethical decision tree.

6   Summarize the pros and cons of involving groups in the decision-making process.

7   Contrast brainstorming, the nominal group technique, the Delphi technique, and computer-aided decision making.

8   Describe the stages of the creative process.

9   Explain the model of organizational creativity and innovation.

You would think the world's most successful Ford dealer might be in, say, Detroit or Los Angeles. Think again. Last year, New York Motors, on a commercial strip in southwest Moscow, sold more Fords than any other dealership in the world. All told, salesmen in the crowded showroom moved 10,060 vehicles, helping Ford race past rivals Hyundai, Toyota, and Chevrolet to become the top-selling auto nameplate in Russia. "This record has pleased and amazed everyone," says Andrey Pavlovich, general director of New York Motors. "Last year was a boom year."

The brand's success in Russia stands in striking contrast to Ford Motor Co.'s flagging fortunes elsewhere. The automaker clocked a global loss of $12.7 billion last year, but sales of Ford-branded vehicles in Russia soared 92%, to 115,985 cars and trucks, for some $2 billion in revenues. That's partly due to Russia's thriving economy, which has stoked strong demand for foreign models. Last year, foreign brands outsold domestic nameplates for the first time, topping 1 million—a 65% increase from 2005 and 20 times the level in 2000, according to the Association of European Businesses in Moscow.

Ford, though, has done more than simply ride the market wave. In 1999, Ford made a big bet on Russia, spending $150 million on a plant near St. Petersburg—the country's first foreign-owned auto factory. The facility opened in 2002, and last year production climbed to 62,400 Focus sedans, hatchbacks, and wagons. "When this decision was taken, in '99, it was of course very daring," says Henrik Nenzen, president of Ford Russia. "But Ford saw that this market would come. . . . And they knew that

they needed to enter [it]." Ford's growing network of dealerships is helping boost sales, too. The company now has 150 outlets, some as far away as Vladivostok on the Pacific coast and Murmansk in the far north.

Ford may face a bumpier ride from here on out. Competition is heating up as rivals copy Ford's strategy of local production. Volkswagen, Toyota, Nissan, GM, and Fiat have all announced plans to build plants in Russia. Worse, Ford workers in St. Petersburg, who earn about $650 per month, walked off the job for one day on Feb. 14 after rejecting an offer of a 14% to 20% pay raise, interest-free loans, and other benefits.[1]

FOR DISCUSSION

What role does risk taking play in Ford's decision to go after the Russian car market?

Ford's expansion into Russia has proved to be very profitable.

We all make decisions on a daily basis. From deciding what clothes to wear to whom we want to marry, our decisions impact our lives in many ways. Sometimes our choices are good and other times they are bad. At work, however, decision making is one of the primary responsibilities of being a manager, and the quality of one's decisions can have serious consequences. Consider Todd Thomson, for example. He was chief of Citigroup's wealth-management unit when he was forced out of his job by the company's CEO for lapses of judgment. These lapses ranged from the improper use of Citigroup's corporate jet to installing a wood-burning fireplace in his office.[2] In contrast, the chapter-opening vignette illustrates how decision making contributes to an organization's success. Although the decision to invest $150 million to open a plant in Russia while facing huge losses from domestic operations was risky, it certainly paid off for Ford.

The overall goal of this chapter is to provide you with a thorough understanding of decision making so that you can improve the quality of your personal and group-based decisions. To help in this pursuit, this chapter focuses on (1) models of decision making, (2) decision-making biases, (3) the dynamics of decision making, (4) group decision making, and (5) creativity.

 # Models of Decision Making

Decision making

Identifying and choosing solutions that lead to a desired end result.

Decision making entails identifying and choosing alternative solutions that lead to a desired state of affairs. For example, you may be reading this book as part of an online course that you decided to take because you are working full time. Alternatively, you may be a full-time student reading this book as part of a course being taken on campus. Identifying and sorting out alternatives like when and how to take a course is the process of decision making.

You can use two broad approaches to make decisions. You can follow a *rational model* or various *nonrational models*. Let us now consider how each of these approaches works. We begin by examining the rational model of decision making.

The Rational Model

Rational model

Logical four-step approach to decision making.

The **rational model** proposes that managers use a rational, four-step sequence when making decisions: (1) identifying the problem, (2) generating alternative solutions, (3) selecting a solution, and (4) implementing and evaluating the solution. According to this model, managers are completely objective and possess complete information to make a decision. Despite criticism for being unrealistic, the rational model is instructive because it analytically breaks down the decision-making process and serves as a conceptual anchor for newer models.[3] Let us now consider each of these four steps.

Problem

Gap between an actual and desired situation.

Identifying the Problem A **problem** exists when the actual situation and the desired situation differ. For example, a problem exists when you have to pay rent at the end of the month and don't have enough money. Your problem is not that you have to pay rent. Your problem is obtaining the needed funds. Consider the situation faced by Danny Burgin. (See the Real World/Real People feature on page 337.) He is one of four people working for American Airlines who has the responsibility for deciding whether or not to cancel flights. Danny's problem was determining which flights to cancel and which to reroute. The immediate cause of this problem was a snow storm that dropped 27 inches of snow along the East Coast.

Danny Burgin Has a Problem

It was 6 A.M., and already nearly 24,000 customers had seen their flights canceled. Facing Mr Burgin, 55, as he sat in front of a horseshoe-shaped command post, was a bank of computer screens full of blinking lights and data streams, feeding him constantly updating information. Tracking hundreds of flights across American's US and international maps, he had to decide which should be canceled or rerouted. . . .

Airline operations can be disrupted by anything from mechanical failures to political upheaval. But weather is the biggest cause of cancellations and delays. Compared with thunderstorms and other weather events, snowstorms can actually be simpler to handle; they're usually easier to predict and airline crews can work around them quickly with deicers and snowplows.

This weekend's blizzard, though, walloped the East Coast with an intensity no one had anticipated, shutting down airports earlier and for longer than expected, and affecting tens of thousands of travelers.

Why is decision making difficult for an air-traffic controller?

SOURCE: Excerpted from M Trottman, "Choices in Stormy Weather," *The Wall Street Journal,* February 15, 2006, p B1.

How do individuals such as Danny Burgin or companies as a whole know when a problem exists or is going to occur in the near future?

One expert proposed that managers use one of three methods to identify problems: historical cues, planning, and other people's perceptions:

1. Using historical cues to identify problems assumes that the recent past is the best estimate of the future. Thus, managers rely on past experience to identify discrepancies (problems) from expected trends. For example, a sales manager may conclude that a problem exists because the first-quarter sales are less than they were a year ago. This method is prone to error because it is highly subjective.

2. A planning approach is more systematic and can lead to more accurate results. This method consists of using projections or scenarios to estimate what is expected to occur in the future. A time period of one or more years is generally used. The **scenario technique** is a speculative, conjectural forecast tool used to identify future states, given a certain set of environmental conditions. Once different scenarios are developed, companies devise alternative strategies to survive in the various situations. This process helps to create contingency plans far into the future. For

"Our task, then, is to decide how to decide how to decide."

© 2002 Ted Goff. Used by permission.

Scenario technique

Speculative forecasting method.

337

example, the European Commission used the scenario technique to develop plans for how best to integrate European nations in the pursuit of economic adaptability in the future.[4] Companies like Royal Dutch/Shell, Fleet Financial Group, IBM, Pfizer, and Deutsche Bank are increasingly using the scenario technique as a planning tool.[5]

3. A final approach to identifying problems is to rely on the perceptions of others. A restaurant manager may realize that his or her restaurant provides poor service when a large number of customers complain about how long it takes to receive food after placing an order. In other words, customers' comments signal that a problem exists. Interestingly, companies frequently compound their problems by ignoring customer complaints or feedback.

Generating Solutions After identifying a problem, the next logical step is generating alternative solutions. For repetitive and routine decisions such as deciding when to send customers a bill, alternatives are readily available through decision rules. For example, a company might routinely bill customers three days after shipping a product. This is not the case for novel and unstructured decisions. Because there are no cut-and-dried procedures for dealing with novel problems, managers must creatively generate alternative solutions. Unfortunately, a recent study of 400 strategic decisions revealed that this recommendation is easier said than done. Results showed that managers fell prey to three decision-making blunders that restricted the number of solutions they considered when trying to solve a problem. These blunders were (1) rushing to judgment, (2) selecting readily available ideas or solutions, and (3) making poor allocation of resources to study alternative solutions. Decision makers thus are encouraged to slow down when making decisions, to evaluate a broader set of alternatives, and to invest in studying a greater number of potential solutions.[6]

Selecting a Solution Optimally, decision makers want to choose the alternative with the greatest value. Decision theorists refer to this as maximizing the expected utility of an outcome. This is no easy task. First, assigning values to alternatives is complicated and prone to error. Not only are values subjective, but they also vary according to the preferences of the decision maker. Research demonstrates that people vary in their preferences for safety or risk when making decisions. For example, a meta-analysis summarizing 150 studies revealed that males displayed more risk taking than females.[7] Evaluating alternatives assumes they can be judged according to some standards or criteria. This further assumes that (1) valid criteria exist, (2) each alternative can be compared against these criteria, and (3) the decision maker actually uses the criteria. As you know from making your own key life decisions, people frequently violate these assumptions. Finally, the ethics of the solution should be considered.

Implementing and Evaluating the Solution Once a solution is chosen, it needs to be implemented. After the solution is implemented, the evaluation phase assesses its effectiveness. If the solution is effective, it should reduce the difference between the actual and desired states that created the problem. If the gap is not closed, the implementation was not successful, and one of the following is true: Either the problem was incorrectly identified, or the solution was inappropriate. Assuming the implementation was unsuccessful, management can return to the first step, problem identification. If the problem was correctly identified, management should consider implementing one of the previously identified, but untried, solutions. This process can continue until all feasible solutions have been tried or the problem has changed.

Summarizing the Rational Model The rational model is prescriptive, outlining a logical process that managers should use when making decisions. As such, the rational model is based on the notion that managers optimize when making decisions. **Optimizing** involves solving problems by producing the best possible solution and is based on a set of highly desirable assumptions—having complete information, leaving emotions out of the decision-making process, honestly and accurately evaluating all alternatives, time and resources are abundant and accessible, and people are willing to implement and support decisions.[8] Practical experience, of course, tells us that these assumptions are unrealistic. As noted by Herbert Simon, a decision theorist who in 1978 earned the Nobel prize for his work on decision making, "The assumptions of perfect rationality are contrary to fact. It is not a question of approximation; they do not even remotely describe the processes that human beings use for making decisions in complex situations."[9]

Optimizing
Choosing the best possible solution.

That said, there are three benefits of trying to follow a rational process as much as realistically possible.

- The quality of decisions may be enhanced, in the sense that they follow more logically from all available knowledge and expertise.

- It makes the reasoning behind a decision transparent and available to scrutiny.

- If made public, it discourages the decider from acting on suspect considerations (such as personal advancement or avoiding bureaucratic embarrassment).[10]

Nonrational Models of Decision Making

In contrast to the rational model's focus on how decisions should be made, **nonrational models** attempt to explain how decisions actually are made. They are based on the assumption that decision making is uncertain, that decision makers do not possess complete information, and that it is difficult for managers to make optimal decisions. Two nonrational models are Herbert Simon's *normative* model and the *garbage can model*.

Nonrational models
Explain how decisions actually are made.

Simon's Normative Model Herbert Simon proposed this model to describe the process that managers actually use when making decisions. The process is guided by a decision maker's bounded rationality. **Bounded rationality** represents the notion that decision makers are "bounded" or restricted by a variety of constraints when making decisions. These constraints include any personal or environmental characteristics that reduce rational decision making. Examples are the limited capacity of the human mind, problem complexity and uncertainty, amount and timeliness of information at hand, criticality of the decision, and time demands.[11]

Bounded rationality
Constraints that restrict rational decision making.

Ultimately, these limitations result in the tendency to acquire manageable rather than optimal amounts of information. In turn, this practice makes it difficult for managers to identify all possible alternative solutions. In the long run, the constraints of bounded rationality cause decision makers to fail to evaluate all potential alternatives, thereby causing them to satisfice.

Satisficing consists of choosing a solution that meets some minimum qualifications, one that is "good enough." Satisficing resolves problems by producing solutions that are satisfactory, as opposed to optimal. Finding a radio station to listen to in your car is a good example of satisficing. You cannot optimize because it is impossible to listen to all stations at the same time. You thus stop searching for a station when you find one playing a song you like or do not mind hearing.

Satisficing
Choosing a solution that meets a minimum standard of acceptance.

A recent national survey by the Business Performance Management Forum underscores the existence of satisficing: only 26% of respondents indicated that their companies had formal, well-understood decision-making processes. Respondents noted that the most frequent causes of poor decision making included:

- Poorly defined processes and practices.
- Unclear company vision, mission, and goals.
- Unwillingness of leaders to take responsibility.
- A lack of reliable, timely information.[12]

The Garbage Can Model As is true of Simon's normative model, this approach grew from the rational model's inability to explain how decisions are actually made. It assumes that organizational decision making is a sloppy and haphazard process. This contrasts sharply with the rational model, which proposed that decision makers follow a sequential series of steps beginning with a problem and ending with a solution. According to the **garbage can model,** decisions result from a complex interaction between four independent streams of events: problems, solutions, participants, and choice opportunities.[13] The interaction of these events creates "a collection of choices looking for problems, issues and feelings looking for decision situations in which they might be aired, solutions looking for issues to which they might be the answer, and decision makers looking for work."[14] A similar type of process occurs in your kitchen garbage basket. We randomly discard our trash and it gets mashed together based on chance interactions. Consider, for instance, going to your kitchen trash container and noticing that the used coffee grounds are stuck to a banana peel. Can you explain how this might occur? The answer is simple: because they both got thrown in around the same time. Just like the process of mixing garbage in a trash container, the garbage can model of decision making assumes that decision making does not follow an orderly series of steps. Rather, attractive solutions can get matched up with whatever handy problems exist at a given point in time or people get assigned to projects because their work load is low at that moment. This model of decision making thus attempts to explain how problems, solutions, participants, and choice opportunities interact and lead to a decision.

The garbage can model has four practical implications.[15] First, many decisions are made by oversight or by the presence of a salient opportunity. For example, the Campbell Soup Company needed to find a way to motivate supermarkets to give them more space on the shelves. They thus decided to create a new shelving system that automatically slides soup cans to the front when a shopper picks up a can. The decision was a success. Customers bought more soup, increasing the revenue for both Campbell and the supermarkets, and the supermarkets reduced their restocking costs.[16]

Second, political motives frequently guide the process by which participants make decisions. It thus is important for you to consider the political ramifications of your decisions. Organizational politics are discussed in Chapter 15. Third, the decision-making process is sensitive to load. That is, as the number of problems increases, relative to the amount of time available to solve them, problems are less likely to be solved. Finally, important problems are more likely to be solved than unimportant ones because they are more salient to organizational participants.[17]

Garbage can model

Holds that decision making is sloppy and haphazard.

2 Decision-Making Biases

Judgmental heuristics

Rules of thumb or shortcuts that people use to reduce information-processing demands.

People make a variety of systematic mistakes when making decisions. These mistakes are generally associated with a host of biases that occur when we use judgmental heuristics. **Judgmental heuristics** represent rules of thumb or shortcuts that people use to reduce information-processing demands.[18] We automatically use them without conscious awareness. The use of heuristics helps decision makers to reduce the uncertainty inherent within the decision-making process. Because these shortcuts represent knowledge gained from past experience, they can help decision makers evaluate current problems. But they also can lead to systematic errors that erode the quality of decisions.

As you can see, there are both pros and cons to the use of heuristics. In this section we focus on discussing eight biases that affect decision making: (1) availability, (2) representativeness, (3) confirmation, (4) anchoring, (5) overconfidence, (6) hindsight, (7) framing, and (8) escalation of commitment. Knowledge about these biases can help you to avoid using them in the wrong situation.[19]

These stock traders make investment decisions in a pressure filled environment. What type of decision-making biases are likely to influence their decisions?

1. **Availability heuristic.** The availability heuristic represents a decision maker's tendency to base decisions on information that is readily available in memory. Information is more accessible in memory when it involves an event that recently occurred, when it is salient (e.g., a plane crash), and when it evokes strong emotions (e.g., a high-school student shooting other students). This heuristic is likely to cause people to overestimate the occurrence of unlikely events such as a plane crash or a high school shooting. This bias also is partially responsible for the recency effect discussed in Chapter 7. For example, a manager is more likely to give an employee a positive performance evaluation if the employee exhibited excellent performance over the last few months.

2. **Representativeness heuristic.** The representativeness heuristic is used when people estimate the probability of an event occurring. It reflects the tendency to assess the likelihood of an event occurring based on one's impressions about similar occurrences. A manager, for example, may hire a graduate from a particular university because the past three people hired from this university turned out to be good performers. In this case, the "school attended" criterion is used to facilitate complex information processing associated with employment interviews. Unfortunately, this shortcut can result in a biased decision. Similarly, an individual may believe that he or she can master a new software package in a short period of time because a different type of software was easy to learn. This estimate may or may not be accurate. For example, it may take the individual a much longer period of time to learn the new software because it involves learning a new programming language.

3. **Confirmation bias.** The confirmation bias has two components. The first is to subconsciously decide something before investigating why it is the right decision. This directly leads to the second component, which is to seek information that supports our point of view and to discount information that does not.

4. **Anchoring bias.** How would you answer the following two questions? Is the population of Iraq greater than 40 million? What's your best guess about the population of Iraq? Was your answer to the second question influenced by the number *40 million* suggested by the first question? If yes, you were affected by the anchoring bias. The anchoring bias occurs when decision makers are influenced by the first information received about a decision, even if it is irrelevant. This bias happens because initial information, impressions, data, feedback, or stereotypes anchor our subsequent judgments and decisions.

5. **Overconfidence bias.** The overconfidence bias relates to our tendency to be overconfident about estimates or forecasts. This bias is particularly strong when you are

asked moderate to extremely difficult questions rather than easy ones. Imagine the problem this bias might create for a sales manager estimating sales revenue for the next year. Research shows that overoptimism significantly influences entrepreneurs' decisions to start and sustain new ventures.[20]

6. **Hindsight bias.** Imagine yourself in the following scenario: You are taking an OB course that meets Tuesday and Thursday, and your professor gives unannounced quizzes each week. It's the Monday before a class, and you are deciding whether to study for a potential quiz or to watch Monday night football. Two of your classmates have decided to watch the game rather than study because they don't think there will be a quiz the next day. The next morning you walk into class and the professor says, "Take out a sheet of paper for the quiz." You turn to your friends and say, "I knew we were going to have a quiz; why did I listen to you?" The hindsight bias occurs when knowledge of an outcome influences our belief about the probability that we could have predicted the outcome earlier. We are affected by this bias when we look back on a decision and try to reconstruct why we decided to do something.

7. **Framing bias.** This bias relates to the manner in which a question is posed. Consider the following scenario: Imagine that the United States is preparing for the outbreak of an unusual Asian disease that is expected to kill 600 people. Two alternative programs to combat the disease have been proposed. Assume that the exact scientific estimates of the consequences of the programs are as follows:

   Program A: If Program A is adopted, 200 people will be saved.

   Program B: If Program B is adopted, there is a one-third probability that 600 people will be saved and a two-thirds probability that no people will be saved. Which of the two programs would you recommend?[21] Research shows that most people chose Program A even though the two programs produce the same results. This result is due to the framing bias. The framing bias is the tendency to consider risks about gains—saving lives–differently than risks pertaining to losses—losing lives. You are encouraged to frame decision questions in alternative ways in order to avoid this bias.

8. **Escalation of commitment bias.** The escalation of commitment bias refers to the tendency to stick to an ineffective course of action when it is unlikely that the bad situation can be reversed. Personal examples include investing more money into an old or broken car, waiting an extremely long time for a bus to take you somewhere when you could have walked just as easily, or trying to save a disruptive personal relationship that has already lasted 10 years. Case studies indicate that this bias is partially responsible for some of the worst financial losses experienced by organizations.[22] Researchers recommend the following actions to reduce the escalation of commitment:

   • Set minimum targets for performance, and have decision makers compare their performance against these targets.

   • Regularly rotate managers in key positions throughout a project.

   • Encourage decision makers to become less ego-involved with a project.

   • Make decision makers aware of the costs of persistence.[23]

Dynamics of Decision Making

Decision making is part science and part art. Accordingly, this section examines two dynamics of decision making—knowledge management and decision-making styles—that affect the "science" component. We also examine the "art" side of the equation by discussing the role of intuition in decision making and a decision tree for making ethical decisions. An understanding of these dynamics can help managers make better decisions.

3 Improving Decision Making through Effective Knowledge Management

Making good decisions is not easy in today's world. Managers are not only being asked to make faster decisions, but they also must process an overwhelming amount of information during the decision-making process.[24] Furthermore, the orientation toward collaborative decision making and flatter organizational structures necessitates that managers obtain timely information from others dispersed throughout the organization or the world.

Louise Anderson, owner of Anderson Performance Improvement Company, underscored this point by concluding that "knowledge sharing is key to APIC success. Basically that's how every job gets done. There is not one person in this company that delivers anything end-to-end to our customers. It is a team effort and that's how you improve and innovate."[25]

Have you ever had to make a decision with either too much or too little information? If you have, then you know the quality of a decision is only as good as the information used to make the decision. This realization has spawned a growing interest in the concept of knowledge management. **Knowledge management** (KM) is "the development of tools, processes, systems, structures, and cultures explicitly to improve the creation, sharing, and use of knowledge critical for decision making."[26] The effective use of KM helps organizations improve the quality of their decision making and correspondingly reduce costs and increase productivity.[27] In contrast, ineffective use of knowledge management can be very costly. For example, experts estimate that *Fortune* 500 companies lose at least $31.5 billion a year by failing to share knowledge.[28]

This section explores the fundamentals of KM so that you can use them to improve your decision making.

Knowledge Comes in Different Forms There are two types of knowledge that impact the quality of decisions: tacit knowledge and explicit knowledge. **Tacit knowledge** "entails information that is difficult to express, formalize, or share. It . . . is unconsciously acquired from the experiences one has while immersed in an environment."[29] Many skills, for example, such as swinging a golf club or writing a speech, are difficult to describe in words because they involve tacit knowledge. Tacit knowledge is intuitive and is acquired by having considerable experience and expertise at some task or job. We more thoroughly discuss the role of intuition in decision making later in this section. In contrast, **explicit knowledge** can easily be put into words and explained to others. This type of knowledge is shared verbally or in written documents or numerical reports. In summary, tacit knowledge represents private information that is difficult to share, whereas explicit knowledge is external or public and is more easily communicated. Although both types of knowledge affect decision making, experts suggest competitive advantages are created when tacit knowledge is shared among employees.[30] Let us now examine how companies foster this type of information sharing.

Knowledge Sharing Organizations increasingly rely on sophisticated KM software to share explicit knowledge. This software allows companies to amass large amounts of information that can be accessed quickly from around the world. In contrast, tacit

Knowledge management

Implementing systems and practices that increase the sharing of knowledge and information throughout an organization.

Tacit knowledge

Information gained through experience that is difficult to express and formalize.

Explicit knowledge

Information that can be easily put into words and shared with others.

Raving Brands Actively Pursues Knowledge Sharing

Chief Executive Martin Sprock talks a mile a minute and launches concepts nearly as fast. In the past five years, Sprock has unveiled six, including Fresh Mex, Asian fusion, and gourmet salads, and has another on the way. Raving Brands typically goes from finished concept to store opening in about a year. For some franchisers, it takes two years or more.

Raving Brands isn't so much a company as a SWAT team in chinos and polo shirts. Sprock meets with four or five senior partners every Monday to handle problems and talk over new ideas. They don't have a corporate office, so they gather at one of the restaurants. Sprock might come in with a new concept.

(The gourmet salad idea came after he saw fancy salads being custom-made for busy New York office workers.) They'll bat around ideas. Then they'll split up to handle their specialties—recipes, say, or real estate. If somebody needs a quick O.K., they get Sprock on his cell. "We take a lot of pride in moving quickly and not having a committee sitting around and planning things," he says.

How is Raving Brands fostering knowledge management?

SOURCE: Excerpted from S Hamm, "Speed Demons," *BusinessWeek,* March 27, 2006, pp 72–73.

---

knowledge is shared most directly by observing, participating, or working with experts or coaches. For example, organizations try to facilitate knowledge sharing at the highest levels by allowing retired CEOs to maintain offices in the corporate headquarters. This practice allowed Larry Kellner, CEO of Continental Airlines Inc., to consult regularly about the consolidation occurring in the airline industry with his predecessor, Gordon Bethune.[31] Mentoring, which was discussed in Chapter 3, is another method for spreading tacit knowledge. Finally, informal networking, periodic meetings, and the design of office space can be used to facilitate KM. Raving Brands, a restaurant franchiser in Atlanta, Georgia, uses a combination of these suggestions in order to fuel innovation and improve efficiency (see Real World/Real People feature above).

It is important to remember that the best-laid plans for increasing KM are unlikely to succeed without the proper organizational culture. Effective KM requires a knowledge-sharing culture that both encourages and reinforces the spread of tacit knowledge.[32]

4 General Decision-Making Styles

It should come as no surprise to learn that personal characteristics influence the manner in which we make decisions.[33] For example, a meta-analysis involving 14 studies and 3,338 individuals revealed that entrepreneurs had higher risk-taking propensities when making decisions than did managers.[34] This finding underscores the value of investigating the relationship between individual differences and decision making. This section therefore focuses on how an individual's decision-making style affects his or her approach to decision making. We believe this awareness can help you make better decisions.

A **decision-making style** reflects the combination of how an individual perceives and comprehends stimuli and the general manner in which he or she chooses to respond to such information.[35] A team of researchers developed a model of decision-making styles that is based on the idea that styles vary along two different dimensions: value orientation and tolerance for ambiguity.[36] *Value orientation* reflects

Decision-making style

A combination of how individuals perceive and respond to information.

Figure 12–1 *Decision-Making Styles*

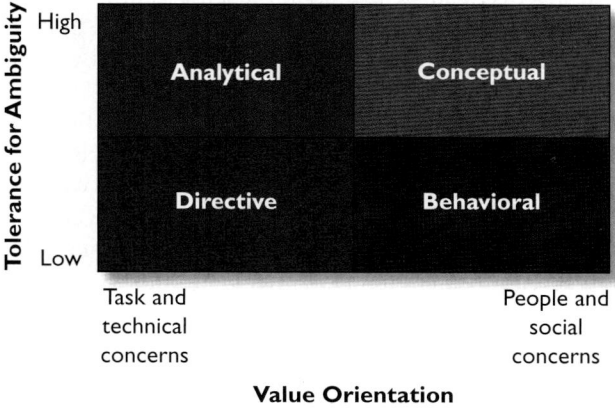

SOURCE: Based on discussion contained in A J Rowe and R O Mason, *Managing with Style: A Guide to Understanding, Assessing, and Improving Decision Making* (San Francisco: Jossey-Bass, 1987), pp 1–17.

the extent to which an individual focuses on either task and technical concerns or people and social concerns when making decisions. Some people, for instance, are very task focused at work and do not pay much attention to people issues, whereas others are just the opposite. The second dimension pertains to a person's *tolerance for ambiguity*. This individual difference indicates the extent to which a person has a high need for structure or control in his or her life. Some people desire a lot of structure in their lives (a low tolerance for ambiguity) and find ambiguous situations stressful and psychologically uncomfortable. In contrast, others do not have a high need for structure and can thrive in uncertain situations (a high tolerance for ambiguity). Ambiguous situations can energize people with a high tolerance for ambiguity. When the dimensions of value orientation and tolerance for ambiguity are combined, they form four styles of decision making (see Figure 12–1): directive, analytical, conceptual, and behavioral.

Directive People with a *directive* style have a low tolerance for ambiguity and are oriented toward task and technical concerns when making decisions. They are efficient, logical, practical, and systematic in their approach to solving problems. People with this style are action oriented and decisive and like to focus on facts. In their pursuit of speed and results, however, these individuals tend to be autocratic, exercise power and control, and focus on the short run.

Interestingly, a directive style seems well suited for an air-traffic controller. Here is what Paul Rinaldi had to say about his decision-making style to a reporter from *Fortune*.

> It's not so much analytical as it is making a decision quickly and sticking with it. You have to do that knowing that some of the decisions you're going to make are going to be wrong, but you're going to make that decision be right. You can't back out. You've constantly got to be taking into account the speed of the airplane, its characteristics, the climb rate, and how fast it's going to react to your instructions. You're taking all that in and processing it in a split second, hoping that it'll all work together. If it doesn't, then you go to plan B. ... The percentage of us that make it to retirement is not real high. It takes a toll on you. We can't make mistakes.[37]

Analytical This style has a much higher tolerance for ambiguity and is characterized by the tendency to overanalyze a situation. People with this style like to consider more information and alternatives than do directives. Analytic individuals are careful decision makers who take longer to make decisions but who also respond well to new or uncertain situations. They can often be autocratic.

Zhang Guangming is a good example of someone with an analytical style. "Zhang Guangming's car-buying synapses have been in overdrive for months. He has spent hours poring over Chinese car buff magazines, surfing Web sites to mine data on various models, and trekking out to a dozen dealerships across Beijing. Finally, Zhang settled on either a Volkswagen Bora or a Hyundai Sonata sedan. But with cutthroat competition forcing dealers to slash prices, he's not sure whether to buy now or wait."[38]

Conceptual People with a conceptual style have a high tolerance for ambiguity and tend to focus on the people or social aspects of a work situation. They take a broad perspective to problem solving and like to consider many options and future possibilities. Conceptual types adopt a long-term perspective and rely on intuition and discussions with others to acquire information. They also are willing to take risks and are good at finding creative solutions to problems. On the downside, however, a conceptual style can foster an idealistic and indecisive approach to decision making. Howard Stringer, Sony Corporation's first foreign-born CEO, possesses characteristics of a conceptual style.

> Mr Stringer's dilemma is that he is caught between different management styles and cultures. He says he recognizes the risk of falling behind amid breakneck changes in electronics. But he says there's an equal risk of moving too aggressively. "I don't want to change Sony's culture to the point where it's unrecognizable from the founder's vision," he says. . . . Mr Stringer, 65 years old, stuck with [an] executive team he inherited. He tried gently persuading managers to cooperate with one another and urged them to think about developing products in a new way.[39]

Behavioral This style is the most people oriented of the four styles. People with this style work well with others and enjoy social interactions in which opinions are openly exchanged. Behavioral types are supportive, receptive to suggestions, show warmth, and prefer verbal to written information. Although they like to hold meetings, people with this style have a tendency to avoid conflict and to be too concerned about others. This can lead behavioral types to adopt a wishy-washy approach to decision making and to have a hard time saying no to others and to have difficulty making difficult decisions.

Research and Practical Implications Research shows that very few people have only one dominant decision-making style. Rather, most managers have characteristics that fall into two or three styles. Studies also show that decision-making styles vary by age, occupations, job level, and countries.[40] You can use knowledge of decision-making styles in three ways. First, knowledge of styles helps you to understand yourself. Awareness of your style assists you in identifying your strengths and weaknesses as a decision maker and facilitates the potential for self-improvement. Second, you can increase your ability to influence others by being aware of styles. For example, if you are dealing with an analytical person, you should provide as much information as possible to support your ideas. This same approach is more likely to frustrate a directive type. Finally, knowledge of styles gives you an awareness of how people can take the same information and yet arrive at different decisions by using a variety of decision-making strategies. Different decision-making styles represent one likely source of interpersonal conflict at work (conflict is thoroughly discussed in Chapter 13). It is important to conclude with the caveat that there is not a best decision-making style that applies in all situations. We should all strive to achieve a "state of clarity" when making decisions. According to a decision-making expert, "The clarity state is characterized by a balance of physical, mental and emotional systems. . . . it is actually a measurable physical and emotional state of being relaxed, positive, and focused."[41]

go to the Web for the Self-Exercise: What Is Your Decision Making Style?

5 The Role of Intuition in Decision Making

Have you ever had a hunch or gut feeling about something? If yes, then you have experienced the effects of intuition. **Intuition** "is a capacity for attaining direct knowledge or understanding without the apparent intrusion of rational thought or logical inference."[42] As a process, intuition is automatic and involuntary. It is important to understand the sources of intuition and to develop your intuitive skills because intuition is as important as rational analysis in many decisions. Consider the following examples:

Intuition

Making a choice without the use of conscious thought or logical inference.

> Ignoring recommendations from advisers, Ray Kroc purchased the McDonald's brand from the McDonald brothers: "I'm not a gambler and I didn't have that kind of money, but my funny bone instinct kept urging me on." Ignoring numerous naysayers and a lack of supporting market research, Bob Lutz, former president of Chrysler, made the Dodge Viper a reality. "It was this subconscious, visceral feeling. And it just felt right." Ignoring the fact that 24 publishing houses had rejected the book and her own publishing house was opposed, Eleanor Friede gambled on a "little nothing book," called *Jonathan Livingston Seagull:* "I felt there were truths in this simple story that would make it an international classic."[43]

Unfortunately, the use of intuition does not always lead to blockbuster decisions such as those by Ray Kroc or Eleanor Friede. To enhance your understanding about the role of intuition in decision making, this section reviews a model of intuition and discusses the pros and cons of using intuition to make decisions.

A Model of Intuition Figure 12–2 presents a model of intuition. Starting at the far right of the model, you can see that there are two types of intuition: holistic hunches and automated experiences.[44] A *holistic hunch* represents a judgment that is based on a subconscious integration of information stored in memory. People using this form of intuition may not even be able explain or justify why they want to make a certain decision, but they conclude that the choice just "feels right." The previous examples of Ray Kroc and Bob Lutz represent this type of intuition. In contrast, *automated experiences* represent a choice that is based on a familiar situation and a partially subconscious application of previously learned information related to that situation. For example, in writing this book we have developed an intuitive sense for when an example is needed to clarify a concept, like the present situation. We intuitively know this based on our textbook-writing experiences. Driving a car and riding a bicycle are examples of the type of learning that underlies automated experiences.

Figure 12–2   *A Model of Intuition*

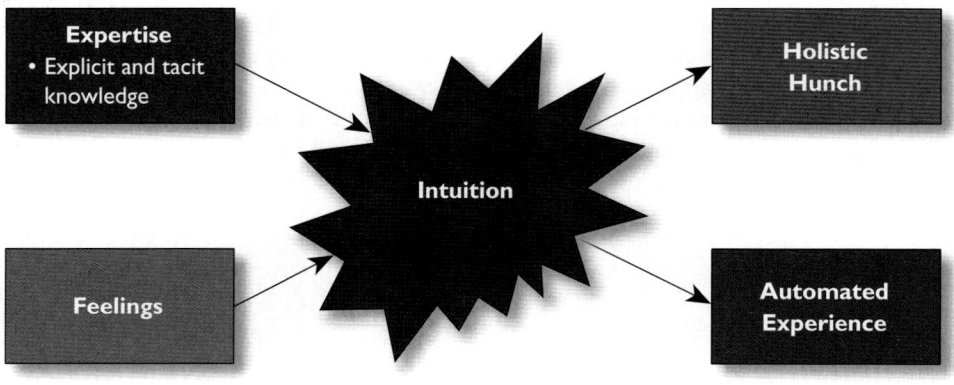

SOURCES: Based in part on E Sadler-Smith and E Shefy, "The Intuitive Executive: Understanding and Applying 'Gut Feel' in Decision-Making," *Academy of Management Executive,* November 2004, pp 76–91; and C C Miller and R D Ireland, "Intuition in Strategic Decision Making: Friend or Foe in the Fast-Paced 21st Century," *Academy of Management Executive,* February 2005, pp 19–30.

Returning to Figure 12–2, you can see that there are two sources of intuition: expertise and feelings. *Expertise* represents an individual's combined explicit and tacit knowledge regarding an object, person, situation, or decision opportunity. This source of intuition increases with age and experience. The *feelings* component of intuition simply reflects the automatic, underlying affect one experiences in response to an object, person, situation, or decision opportunity. Ultimately, an intuitive response is based on the interaction between one's expertise and feelings in a given situation. Consider the example of being cut off by another driver on the freeway. You may automatically get mad (intuitive feelings) but decide not to make any obscene hand gestures or tailgate because it may lead to road rage from the other individual (intuitive expertise).

Pros and Cons of Using Intuition When Making Decisions On the positive side, intuition can speed up the decision-making process.[45] Intuition thus can be valuable in the complex and ever-changing world we live in. Intuition also is a good approach to use when managers are faced with limited resources and tight deadlines. In contrast, intuition is subject to the same type of biases associated with rational decision making. For example, intuition is particularly susceptible to the availability and representativeness heuristics, which were previously discussed, as well as the overconfidence and the hindsight biases.[46] A final limitation involves the difficulty in convincing others that a hunch makes sense. In the end, a good intuitive idea may be ignored because people do not understand the idea's underlying logic.

Where does that leave us with respect to using intuition? We believe that intuition and rationality are complementary and that managers should attempt to use both when making decisions. For example, rational analysis can be used to verify or validate a hunch. We thus encourage managers to have the courage to use intuition when making decisions.[47] Chris De Buysscher, recognized as one of the best counterfeit goods inspectors in the world, follows this recommendation when doing his job at a port in Antwerp, Belgium (see the Real World/Real People feature on page 349). Thanks to

Chris De Buyssher Uses Intuition to Detect the Shipping of Counterfeit Goods

His skills are a low-tech blend of old-fashioned gumshoe detective work and intuition. On a recent trip to Algeria, Mr De Buysscher singled out a shipping container from China for checking at the port of Oran. It was supposed to contain shoes—and it did—fake Nikes. . . .

Part of his expertise comes from knowing brand-name goods. He visits outlet malls to study the products of Nike and Oscar de la Renta. He knows how things are packed in certain countries. . . . He's also up on fashion and can recognize 10 perfumes by nose alone, he says. "Chanel, Dior and Yves Saint Laurent smells are trademarked, just like the bottles they're in. . . .

The growth of the $500 billion counterfeit goods industry is one of the biggest economic challenges facing European and American companies as they relocate production to Asia.

Are there better ways to catch crooks than by using intuition?

SOURCE: J W Miller, "Gumshoe's Intuition: Spotting Counterfeits at Port of Antwerp," *The Wall Street Journal*, December 14, 2006, p A1.

Chris's outstanding work, Belgium has confiscated more counterfeit goods—about 40 million—than any country in the European Union.[48] Conversely, managers can use intuition to evaluate a rational choice by asking questions such as What does my experience suggest about this decision? You can develop your intuitive awareness by using the guidelines shown in Table 12–1.

Table 12–1 *Guidelines for Developing Intuitive Awareness*

RECOMMENDATION	DESCRIPTION
1. Open up the closet	To what extent do you experience intuition; trust your feelings; count on intuitive judgments; suppress hunches; covertly rely upon gut feel?
2. Don't mix up your I's	Instinct, insight, and intuition are not synonymous; practice distinguishing between your instincts, your insights, and your intuitions.
3. Elicit good feedback	Seek feedback on your intuitive judgments; build confidence in your gut feel; create a learning environment in which you can develop better intuitive awareness.
4. Get a feel for your batting average	Benchmark your intuitions; get a sense for how reliable your hunches are; ask yourself how your intuitive judgment might be improved.
5. Use imagery	Use imagery rather than words; literally visualize potential future scenarios that take your gut feelings into account.
6. Play devil's advocate	Test out intuitive judgments; raise objections to them; generate counter-arguments; probe how robust gut feel is when challenged.
7. Capture and validate your intuitions	Create the inner state to give your intuitive mind the freedom to roam; capture your creative intuitions; log them before they are censored by rational analysis.

SOURCE: E Sadler-Smith and E Shefy, "The Intuitive Executive: Understanding and Applying 'Gut Feel' in Decision-Making," *Academy of Management Executive*, November 2004, p 88. Reprinted with permission of The Academy of Management via The Copyright Clearance Center.

349

Road Map to Ethical Decision Making: A Decision Tree

In Chapter 1 we discussed the importance of ethics and the growing concern about the lack of ethical behavior among business leaders. For example, a US Roper poll revealed that 72% of respondents perceived that corporate wrongdoing was rampant, and only 2% believed that leaders of large organizations were trustworthy.[49] While this trend partially explains the passage of laws to regulate ethical behavior in corporate America, we believe that ethical acts ultimately involve individual or group decisions. It thus is important to consider the issue of ethical decision making. Harvard Business School professor Constance Bagley suggests that a decision tree can help managers to make more ethical decisions.[50] A **decision tree** is a graphical representation of the process underlying decisions and it shows the resulting consequences of making various choices. Decision trees are used as an aid in decision making.

Decision tree

Graphical representation of process underlying decision making.

Ethical decision making frequently involves trade-offs, and a decision tree helps managers to navigate through them. The decision tree shown in Figure 12–3 can be applied to any type of decision or action that an individual manager or corporation is contemplating. Looking at the tree, the first question to ask is whether or not the proposed action is legal. If the action is illegal, do not do it. If the action is legal, then consider the impact of the action on shareholder value. A decision maximizes shareholder value when it results in a more favorable financial position (e.g., increased profits) for an organization. Whether or not an action maximizes shareholder value, the decision tree shows that managers still need to consider the ethical implications of the decision or action. For example, if an action maximizes shareholder value, the next question to consider is whether or not the action is ethical. The answer to this question is based on considering the positive effect of the action on an organization's other key constituents (i.e., customers, employees, the community, the environment, and suppliers) against the benefit to the shareholders. According to the decision tree framework, managers should make the decision to engage in an action if the benefits to the shareholders exceed the benefits to the other key constituents. Managers should not engage in the action if the other key constituents would benefit more from the action than shareholders.

Figure 12–3 illustrates that managers use a slightly different perspective when their initial conclusion is that an action does not maximize shareholder value. In this case, the question becomes Would it be ethical not to take action? This question necessitates that a manager consider the *harm or cost* of an action to shareholders against the *costs or benefits* to other key constituents. If the costs to shareholders from a managerial decision exceed the costs or benefits to other constituents, the manager or company should not engage in the action. Conversely, the manager or company should take action when the perceived costs or benefits to the other constituents are greater than the costs to shareholders. Let us apply this decision tree to IBM's decision to raise the amount of money it required retirees to contribute to their health benefits.[51] The company made this decision in order to save money.

Is it legal for a company to decrease its contribution to retiree health care benefits while simultaneously raising retirees' contributions? The answer is yes. Does an organization maximize shareholder value by decreasing its retiree health care expenses? Again, the answer is yes. We now have to consider the overall benefits to shareholders against the overall benefits to other key constituents. The answer to this question is more complex than it appears and is contingent on an organization's corporate values.

Figure 12–3   *An Ethical Decision Tree*

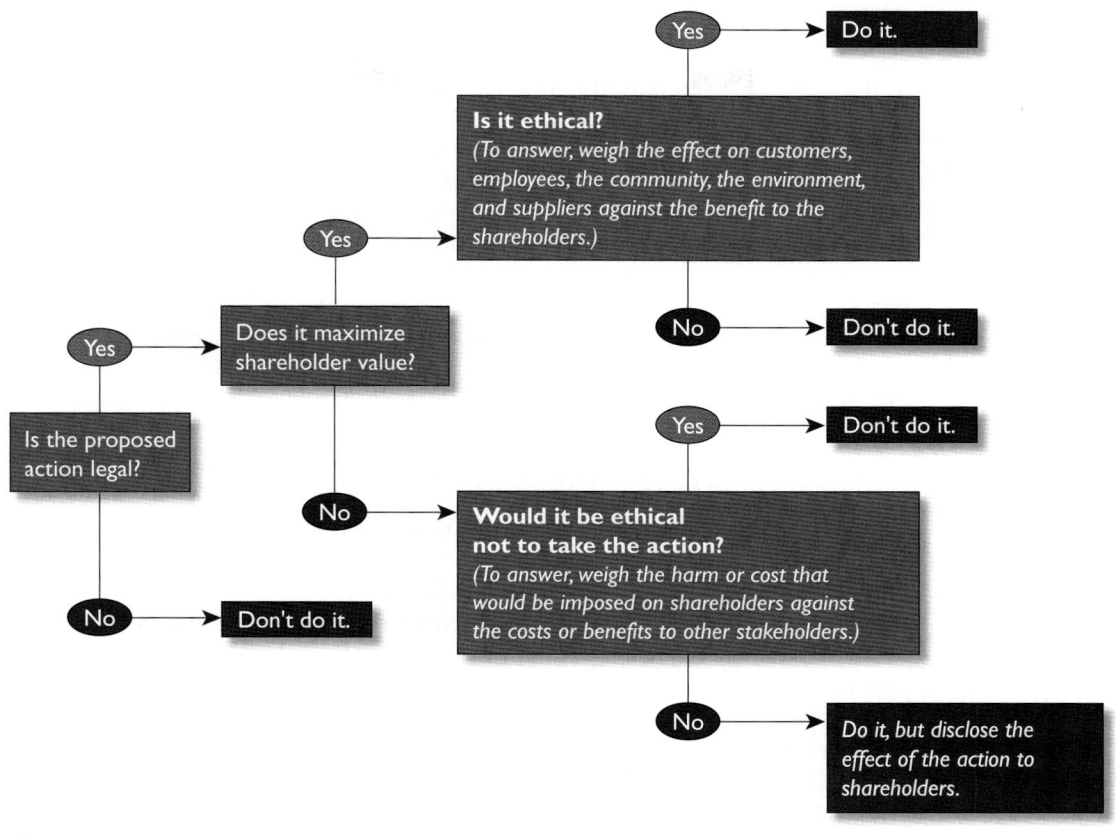

SOURCE: Reprinted by permission of *Harvard Business Review*. From Constance E Bagley, "The Ethical Leader's Decision Tree," *Harvard Business Review*. February 2003, p 19. Copyright © 2003 by the Harvard Business School Publishing Corporation; all rights reserved.

Consider the following two examples. In company one, the organization is losing money and it needs cash in order to invest in new product development. Management believes that new products will fuel the company's economic growth and ultimate survival. This company's statement of corporate values also reveals that the organization values profits and shareholder return more than employee loyalty. In this case, the company should make the decision to increase retirees' health care contributions. Company two, in contrast, is profitable and has been experiencing increased market share with its products. This company's statement of corporate values also indicates that employees are the most important constituent it has, even more than shareholders: Southwest Airlines is a good example of a company with these corporate values. In this case, the company should not make the decision to decrease its contribution to retirees' benefits.

It is important to keep in mind that the decision tree cannot provide a quick formula that managers and organizations can use to assess every ethical question. It does, however, provide a framework for considering the trade-offs between managerial and corporate actions and managerial and corporate ethics. Try using this decision tree the next time you are faced with a significant ethical question or problem.

go to the Web for the Group Exercise: Ethical Decision Making

Group Decision Making

Groups such as committees, task forces, project teams, or review panels often play a key role in the decision-making process. Are two or more heads always better than one? Do all employees desire to have a say in the decision-making process? To what extent are managers involving employees in the decision-making process? What techniques do groups use to improve their decision making? Are face-to-face meetings more effective than computer-aided decision making? This section provides the background for answering these questions. We discuss (1) group involvement in decision making, (2) advantages and disadvantages of group-aided decision making, and (3) group problem-solving techniques.

6 Group Involvement in Decision Making

Whether groups assemble in face-to-face meetings or rely on other technologically based methods to communicate, they can contribute to each stage of the decision-making process. In order to maximize the value of group-aided decision making, however, it is important to create an environment in which group members feel free to participate and express their opinions. Research sheds light on how managers can create such an environment.

A team of researchers conducted two studies to determine whether a group's innovativeness was related to *minority dissent,* defined as the extent to which group members feel comfortable disagreeing with other group members, and a group's level of participation in decision making. Results showed that the most innovative groups possessed high levels of both minority dissent and participation in decision making.[52] These findings encourage managers to seek divergent views from group members during decision making. They also support the practice of not seeking compliance from group members or punishing group members who disagree with majority opinion.

The aforementioned study reinforces the notion that the quality of group decision making varies across groups. This in turn raises the issue of how to best assess a group's decision-making effectiveness. Although experts do not agree on the one "best" criterion, there is agreement that groups need to work through various aspects of decision making in order to be effective. One expert proposed that decision-making effectiveness in a group is dependent on successfully accomplishing the following:[53]

1. Developing a clear understanding of the decision situation.
2. Developing a clear understanding of the requirements for an effective choice.
3. Thoroughly and accurately assessing the positive qualities of alternative solutions.
4. Thoroughly and accurately assessing the negative qualities of alternative solutions.

To increase the probability of groups making high-quality decisions, managers, team leaders, and individual group members are encouraged to focus on satisfying these four requirements.

go to the Web for the Self-Exercise: Assessing Participation in Group Decision Making

Advantages and Disadvantages of Group-Aided Decision Making

Including groups in the decision-making process has both pros and cons (see Table 12–2). On the positive side, groups contain a greater pool of knowledge, provide more varied perspectives, create more comprehension of decisions, increase decision acceptance, and create a training ground for inexperienced employees. These advantages must be balanced, however, with the disadvantages listed in Table 12–2. In doing so, managers need to determine the extent to which the advantages and disadvantages apply to the decision situation. The following three guidelines may then be applied to help decide whether groups should be included in the decision-making process.

1. If additional information would increase the quality of the decision, managers should involve those people who can provide the needed information.
2. If acceptance is important, managers need to involve those individuals whose acceptance and commitment are important.
3. If people can be developed through their participation, managers may want to involve those whose development is most important.[54]

Table 12–2   *Advantages and Disadvantages of Group-Aided Decision Making*

ADVANTAGES	DISADVANTAGES
1. **Greater pool of knowledge.** A group can bring much more information and experience to bear on a decision or problem than can an individual acting alone.	1. **Social pressure.** Unwillingness to "rock the boat" and pressure to conform may combine to stifle the creativity of individual contributors.
2. **Different perspectives.** Individuals with varied experience and interests help the group see decision situations and problems from different angles.	2. **Domination by a vocal few.** Sometimes the quality of group action is reduced when the group gives in to those who talk the loudest and longest.
3. **Greater comprehension.** Those who personally experience the give-and-take of group discussion about alternative courses of action tend to understand the rationale behind the final decision.	3. **Logrolling.** Political wheeling and dealing can displace sound thinking when an individual's pet project or vested interest is at stake.
4. **Increased acceptance.** Those who play an active role in group decision making and problem solving tend to view the outcome as "ours" rather than "theirs."	4. **Goal displacement.** Sometimes secondary considerations such as winning an argument, making a point, or getting back at a rival displace the primary task of making a sound decision or solving a problem.
5. **Training ground.** Less experienced participants in group action learn how to cope with group dynamics by actually being involved.	5. **Groupthink.** Sometimes cohesive in-groups let the desire for unanimity override sound judgment when generating and evaluating alternative courses of action. (Groupthink was discussed in Chapter 10.)

SOURCE: R Kreitner, *Management*, 8th ed (Boston: Houghton Mifflin, 2001), p 243. Copyright © 2001 by Houghton Mifflin Company. Used with permission.

These ad agency employees are conducting a brainstorming session. Brainstorming can be fun and is used to generate multiple ideas and solutions for solving problems.

Group versus Individual Performance Before recommending that managers involve groups in decision making, it is important to examine whether groups perform better or worse than individuals. After reviewing 61 years of relevant research, a decision-making expert concluded that "Group performance was generally qualitatively and quantitatively superior to the performance of the average individual."[55] Although subsequent research of small-group decision making generally supported this conclusion, there are five important issues to consider when using groups to make decisions:

1. Groups were less efficient than individuals. It thus is important to consider time constraints when determining whether to involve groups in decision making.

2. Groups were more confident about their judgments and choices than individuals. Because group confidence is not a surrogate for group decision quality, this overconfidence can fuel groupthink—groupthink was discussed in Chapter 10—and a resistance to consider alternative solutions proposed by individuals outside the group.

3. Group size affected decision outcomes. Decision quality was negatively related to group size.[56]

4. Decision-making accuracy was higher when (*a*) groups knew a great deal about the issues at hand and (*b*) group leaders possessed the ability to effectively evaluate the group members' opinions and judgments. Groups need to give more weight to relevant and accurate judgments while downplaying irrelevant or inaccurate judgments made by its members.[57]

5. The composition of a group affects its decision-making processes and ultimately performance. For example, groups of familiar people are more likely to make better decisions when members share a lot of unique information. In contrast, unacquainted group members should outperform groups of friends when most group members possess common knowledge.[58]

Additional research suggests that managers should use a contingency approach when determining whether to include others in the decision-making process. Let us now consider these contingency recommendations.

Practical Contingency Recommendations If the decision occurs frequently, such as deciding on promotions or who qualifies for a loan, use groups because they tend to produce more consistent decisions than do individuals. Given time constraints, let the most competent individual, rather than a group, make the decision. In the face of environmental threats such as time pressure and potential serious effects of a decision, groups use less information and fewer communication channels. This increases the probability of a bad decision. This conclusion underscores a general recommendation that managers should keep in mind: Because the quality of communication strongly affects a group's productivity, on complex tasks it is essential to devise mechanisms to enhance communication effectiveness.

Consensus
Presenting opinions and gaining agreement to support a decision.

🐾 7 Group Problem-Solving Techniques

Using groups to make decisions generally requires that they reach a consensus. According to a decision-making expert, a **consensus** "is reached when all members can say they either agree with the decision or have had their 'day in court' and were unable to convince the others of their viewpoint. In the final analysis, everyone agrees to support the outcome."[59] This definition indicates that consensus does not require unanimous agreement because group members may still disagree with the final decision but are willing to work toward its success.

Groups can experience roadblocks when trying to arrive at a consensus decision. For one, groups may not generate all relevant alternatives to a problem because an individual dominates or intimidates other group members. This can be overt or subtle. For instance, group members who possess power and authority, such as a CEO, can be intimidating, regardless of interpersonal style, simply by being present in the room. Moreover, shyness inhibits the generation of alternatives. Shy or socially anxious individuals may withhold their input for fear of embarrassment or lack of confidence. Satisficing is another hurdle to effective group decision making. As previously noted, groups satisfice due to limited time, information, or ability to handle large amounts of information. A management expert offered the following dos and don'ts for successfully achieving consensus: Groups should use active listening skills, involve as many members as possible, seek out the reasons behind arguments, and dig for the facts. At the same time, groups should not horse trade (I'll support you on this decision because you supported me on the last one), vote, or agree just to avoid "rocking the boat."[60] Voting is not encouraged because it can split the group into winners and losers.

Decision-making experts have developed three group problem-solving techniques—brainstorming, the nominal group technique, and the Delphi technique—to reduce the above roadblocks. Knowledge of these techniques can help current and future managers to more effectively use group-aided decision making. Further, the advent of computer-aided decision making enables managers to use these techniques to solve complex problems with large groups of people.

Brainstorming

Brainstorming Brainstorming was developed by A F Osborn, an advertising executive, to increase creativity.[61] **Brainstorming** is used to help groups generate multiple ideas and alternatives for solving problems. This technique is effective because it helps reduce interference caused by critical and judgmental reactions to one's ideas from other group members.

Brainstorming
Process to generate a quantity of ideas.

When brainstorming, a group is convened, and the problem at hand is reviewed. Individual members then are asked to silently generate ideas/alternatives for solving the problem. Silent idea generation is recommended over the practice of having group members randomly shout out their ideas because it leads to a greater number of unique ideas. Next, these ideas/alternatives are solicited and written on a board or flip chart. A recent study suggests that managers or team leaders may want to collect the brainstormed ideas anonymously. Results demonstrated that more controversial ideas and more nonredundant ideas were generated by anonymous than nonanonymous brainstorming groups.[62] Finally, a second session is used to critique and evaluate the alternatives. Managers are advised to follow the seven rules for brainstorming used by IDEO, a product design company[63]

1. *Defer judgment.* Don't criticize during the initial stage of idea generation. Phrases such as "we've never done it that way," "it won't work," "it's too expensive," and "our manager will never agree" should not be used.

2. *Build on the ideas of others.* Encourage participants to extend others' ideas by avoiding "buts" and using "ands."

3. *Encourage wild ideas.* Encourage out-of-the-box thinking. The wilder and more outrageous the ideas, the better.

4. *Go for quantity over quality.* Participants should try to generate and write down as many new ideas as possible. Focusing on quantity encourages people to think beyond their favorite ideas.

5. *Be visual.* Use different colored pens (e.g., red, purple, blue) to write on big sheets of flip chart paper, white boards, or poster board that are put on the wall.

6. *Stay focused on the topic.* A facilitator should be used for keeping the discussion on target.

7. *One conversation at a time.* The ground rules are that no one interrupts another person, no dismissing of someone's ideas, no disrespect, and no rudeness.

Brainstorming is an effective technique for generating new ideas/alternatives. It is not appropriate for evaluating alternatives or selecting solutions.

Nominal group technique

Process to generate ideas and evaluate solutions.

The Nominal Group Technique
The **nominal group technique** (NGT) helps groups generate ideas and evaluate and select solutions. NGT is a structured group meeting that follows this format:[64]

A group is convened to discuss a particular problem or issue. After the problem is understood, individuals silently generate ideas in writing. Each individual, in roundrobin fashion, then offers one idea from his or her list. Ideas are recorded on a blackboard or flip chart; they are not discussed at this stage of the process. Once all ideas are elicited, the group discusses them. Anyone may criticize or defend any item. During this step, clarification is provided as well as general agreement or disagreement with the idea. The "30-second soap box" technique, which entails giving each participant a maximum of 30 seconds to argue for or against any of the ideas under consideration, can be used to facilitate this discussion. Alternatively, groups can create an effort/benefit matrix to facilitate this discussion. This is done by identifying the amount of effort and the costs required to implement each idea and comparing these to the potential benefits associated with each idea.[65] Finally, group members anonymously vote for their top choices. The group leader then adds the votes to determine the group's choice. Prior to making a final decision, the group may decide to discuss the top ranked items and conduct a second round of voting.

The nominal group technique reduces the roadblocks to group decision making by (1) separating brainstorming from evaluation, (2) promoting balanced participation among group members, and (3) incorporating mathematical voting techniques in order to reach consensus. The NGT has been successfully used in many different decision-making situations and has been found to generate more ideas than a standard brainstorming session.[66]

Delphi technique

Process to generate ideas from physically dispersed experts.

The Delphi Technique
This problem-solving method was originally developed by the Rand Corporation for technological forecasting.[67] It now is used as a multipurpose planning tool. The **Delphi technique** is a group process that anonymously generates ideas or judgments from physically dispersed experts. Unlike the NGT, experts' ideas are obtained from questionnaires or via the Internet as opposed to face-to-face group discussions.

A manager begins the Delphi process by identifying the issue(s) he or she wants to investigate. For example, a manager might want to inquire about customer demand, customers' future preferences, or the effect of locating a plant in a certain region of the country. Next, participants are identified and a questionnaire is developed. The questionnaire is sent to participants and returned to the manager. In today's computer-networked environments, this often means that the questionnaires

Engineers at Starkey Laboratories Design Products with Information-Sharing Software

Starkey Laboratories Inc. is known for its high-end hearing aids, but until recently the process that engineers at the Eden Prairie (Minnesota) company used to design them was decidedly low-end. They would cook up a design concept and then e-mail it to colleagues so they could make changes. But because multiple copies of each design were circulating, there was a lot of confusion about which version was the most up-to-date.

Rather than wait for Starkey's tech department to deliver a solution, a group of frustrated engineers took matters into their own hands. They used Microsoft Corp. software to covertly set up an internal Web site for collaboration. They were able to go online to set common goals and deadlines, and to maintain one version of a design for their project that anyone could modify.

Are there any drawbacks to what the engineers did at Starkey?

SOURCE: Excerpted from J Greene, "Combat over Collaboration," *BusinessWeek,* April 18, 2005, p 64.

---

are e-mailed to participants. The manager then summarizes the responses and sends feedback to the participants. At this stage, participants are asked to (1) review the feedback, (2) prioritize the issues being considered, and (3) return the survey within a specified time period. This cycle repeats until the manager obtains the necessary information.

The Delphi technique is useful when face-to-face discussions are impractical, when disagreements and conflict are likely to impair communication, when certain individuals might severely dominate group discussion, and when groupthink is a probable outcome of the group process.[68]

Computer-Aided Decision Making The purpose of computer-aided decision making is to help managers make better decisions by reducing consensus roadblocks while collecting more information in a shorter period of time. Computerization is being used in two general ways. First, many organizations are using a variety of computer, software, and electronic devices to improve decision making. Hospitals and intensive care units are good examples. Computer-aided decision making has reduced the number of diagnostic errors and improved the delivery of patient care (see the Real World/Real People feature on page 358).[69] Wal-Mart also is well known for using computer-aided decision making to improve decision making. For example, Wal-Mart stores are using a new computerized system to schedule its 1.3 million workers. The system creates staffing levels for each store based on the number of customers in the store at any given point in time.[70]

The second general application of computer-aided decision making relates to the running of meetings. Two types of systems are used: chauffeur driven and group driven. Chauffeur-driven systems ask participants to answer predetermined questions on electronic keypads or dials. Live television audiences on shows such as *Who Wants to Be a Millionaire* are frequently polled with this system. The computer system tabulates participants' responses in a matter of seconds.

Group-driven electronic meetings are conducted in one of two major ways. First, managers can use e-mail systems, which are discussed in Chapter 14, or the Internet to collect information or brainstorm about a decision that must be made.

Sentara Healthcare Relies on Computer-Aided Decision Making

DAVID L. BERND HATES cold calls from salesmen, same as you do. But in 2000, the CEO of Sentara Healthcare felt he had to listen to a salesman who said he could use the Internet to transform intensive-care units at the nonprofit Norfolk (Va.) health system's seven hospitals. Those ICUs were costing the chain three times as much as its other units, and they were so short-staffed the hospitals routinely had to roust doctors out of bed to race in and handle late-night crises. Worst of all: At one Sentara ICU, 40% of patients, who stayed more than a week died. "Mortality is not a vague statistic. It's Do you save my life or not?" says Sentara Executive Vice-President Rodney F. Hochman.

That's how Sentara became the first client for the electronic ICU (eICU)—a technology that combines software, video feeds, and real-time patient information to let intensive-care specialists at Sentara Norfolk General Hospital cover 11 ICUs at six hospitals, spread 60 miles apart, around the clock. Today, the eICU is providing some of the most solid evidence that telemedicine, full of promise for years, is finally becoming real. . . .

The new face of telemedicine was on display one day in late May at Sentara Heart Hospital's eight-bed cardiac ICU in Norfolk. Charlotte Pipes, 56, was brought in after suffering a heart attack on May 21 at her home in Elizabeth City, N.C. Overseeing Pipes's care, from the eICU across the Norfolk General campus, was intensivist John T. Bowers III. Bowers works at a stand-up desk, where five screens gave him the basics about 69 patients in Sentara's wired ICUs that day. On one screen, their names appeared on a roster, color-coded by their condition. Newly admitted and gravely ill patients, including Pipes, had red lights next to their names. On other screens, Bowers toggled between video images of patients, test results, and treatment plans from patients' own doctors, and vital signs captured by monitors. He could also use the system's built-in reference database, which has the latest research on how to treat ICU complications.

What are the pros and cons of using computer-aided decision making in the context of health care?

SOURCE: Excerpted from T J Mullaney, "The Doctor Is (Plugged) In," *BusinessWeek*, June 26, 2006, pp 56, 58.

The second method of computer-aided, group-driven meetings is conducted in special facilities equipped with individual workstations that are networked to each other. Instead of talking, participants type their input, ideas, comments, reactions, or evaluations on their keyboards. The input simultaneously appears on a large projector screen at the front of the room, thereby enabling all participants to see all input. This computer-driven process reduces consensus roadblocks because input is anonymous, everyone gets a chance to contribute, and no one can dominate the process. Research demonstrated that computer-aided decision making produced greater quality and quantity of ideas than either traditional brainstorming or the nominal group technique for both small and large groups of people.[71]

Creativity

In light of today's need for fast-paced decisions, an organization's ability to stimulate the creativity and innovation of its employees is becoming increasingly important. Many organizations believe that creativity and innovation are the seeds of success.[72]

To gain further insight into managing the creative process, we begin by defining creativity and highlighting the stages underlying individual creativity. This section then presents a model of organizational creativity and innovation.

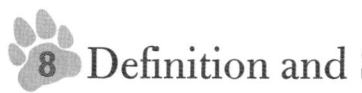 Definition and Stages

Although many definitions have been proposed, **creativity** is defined here as the process of using imagination and skill to develop a new or unique product, object, process, or thought.[73] It can be as simple as locating a new place to hang your car keys or as complex as developing a pocket-size microcomputer. This definition highlights three broad types of creativity. One can create something new (creation), one can combine or synthesize things (synthesis), or one can improve or change things (modification).

Researchers are not absolutely certain how creativity takes place. Nonetheless, we do know that creativity involves "making remote associations" between unconnected events, ideas, information stored in memory (recall our discussion in Chapter 7), or physical objects. At Nike, for example, engineers spent four weeks watching children play at school in order to generate ideas for designing new shoes.[74] Hasbro is trying to develop new games by allowing employees to play board games at work. "Some compete over Scrabble, Sorry, Clue, or more than a dozen other famous games invented decades ago and still manufactured at a factory here. Others play games sold by competitors, or enjoy their own childhood favorites no longer on store shelves."[75] Hasbro hopes that new ideas will spawn from playing old board games. Researchers, however, have identified five stages underlying the creative process: preparation, concentration, incubation, illumination, and verification. Let us consider these stages.

The *preparation* stage reflects the notion that creativity starts from a base of knowledge. Experts suggest that creativity involves a convergence between tacit or implied knowledge and explicit knowledge. During the *concentration* stage, an individual focuses on the problem at hand. Research shows that creative ideas at work are often triggered by work-related problems, incongruities, or failures.[76] This was precisely the case for aerospace engineer Walt Gillette when he was attempting to resolve aerodynamics problems for Boeing.

> Southwest Airlines Co. needed a small plane to break out of short hops and fly across the country. Gillette used an analytical method called computational fluid dynamics (CFD) to crack the toughest design problems, including figuring out how to sling powerful new engines on the wings of a small 737. "Every time we tried to put one of those big fat nacelles [engine enclosures] close to the wing, we got terrible aerodynamic interference between the nacelle and the wing," Gillette recalled. . . . Gillette and his team traveled the world, looked at every nacelle installation, studied them with CFD, and came up with a formula that changed aviation history. "We found five things, which remain trade secrets," he said in an interview, "five features that no one had used in such a combination. It let us shove a big nacelle really close to the wing."[77]

Interestingly, Japanese companies are noted for encouraging this stage as part of a quality improvement process more than American companies. For example, the average number of ideas per employee was 37.4 for Japanese workers versus .12 for US workers.[78]

Incubation is done unconsciously. During this stage, people engage in daily activities while their minds simultaneously mull over information and make remote associations. These associations ultimately are generated in the *illumination* stage. Finally, *verification* entails going through the entire process to verify, modify, or try out the new idea.

Let us examine the stages of creativity to determine why Japanese organizations propose and implement more ideas than do American companies. To address this issue, a creativity expert visited and extensively interviewed employees from five

Creativity

Process of developing something new or unique.

major Japanese companies. He observed that Japanese firms have created a management infrastructure that encourages and reinforces creativity. People were taught to identify problems (discontents) on their first day of employment. In turn, discontents were referred to as "golden eggs" to reinforce the notion that it is good to identify problems.

These organizations also promoted the stages of incubation, illumination, and verification through teamwork and incentives. For example, some companies posted the golden eggs on large wall posters in the work area; employees were then encouraged to interact with each other to execute the final three stages of the creative process. Employees eventually received monetary awards for any suggestions that passed all five phases of this process.[79] This research underscores the conclusion that creativity can be enhanced by effectively managing the creativity process and by fostering a positive and supportive work environment. Hewlett-Packard and Yahoo are well known for following this recommendation.[80]

9 A Model of Organizational Creativity and Innovation

Organizational creativity and innovation are relatively new topics within the field of OB despite their importance for organizational success. Rather than focus on group and organizational creativity, researchers historically examined the predictors of individual creativity. This final section examines a process model of organizational creativity. Knowledge of its linkages can help you to facilitate and contribute to organizational creativity.

Figure 12–4 illustrates the process underlying organizational creativity and innovation. It shows that organizational creativity is directly influenced by organizational characteristics and the amount of creative behavior that occurs within work groups. In turn, a group's creative behavior is influenced by group characteristics and the individual creative behavior/performance of its members. Individual creative behavior is directly affected by a variety of individual characteristics. The double-headed arrows between individual and group and between group and organizational characteristics indicate that the various characteristics all influence each other. Let us now consider the model's major components.

Individual Characteristics Creativity requires motivation. In other words, people make a decision whether or not they want to apply their knowledge and capabilities to create new ideas, things, or products. In addition to motivation, creative people typically march to the beat of a different drummer. They are highly motivated individuals who spend considerable time developing both tacit and explicit knowledge about their field of interest or occupation. But contrary to stereotypes, creative people are not necessarily geniuses or introverted nerds. In addition, they are not *adaptors*. "Adaptors are those who . . . prefer to resolve difficulties or make decisions in such a way as to have the least impact upon the assumptions, procedures, and values of the organization."[81] In contrast, creative individuals are dissatisfied with the status quo. They look for new and exciting solutions to problems. Because of this, creative organizational members can be perceived as disruptive and hard to get along with.[82] Further, research indicates that male and female managers do not differ in levels of creativity, and there are a host of personality characteristics that are associated with creativity.[83] These characteristics include, but are not limited to, those shown in Figure 12–4. This discussion comes to life by considering the following example.

Figure 12–4   *A Model of Organizational Creativity and Innovation*

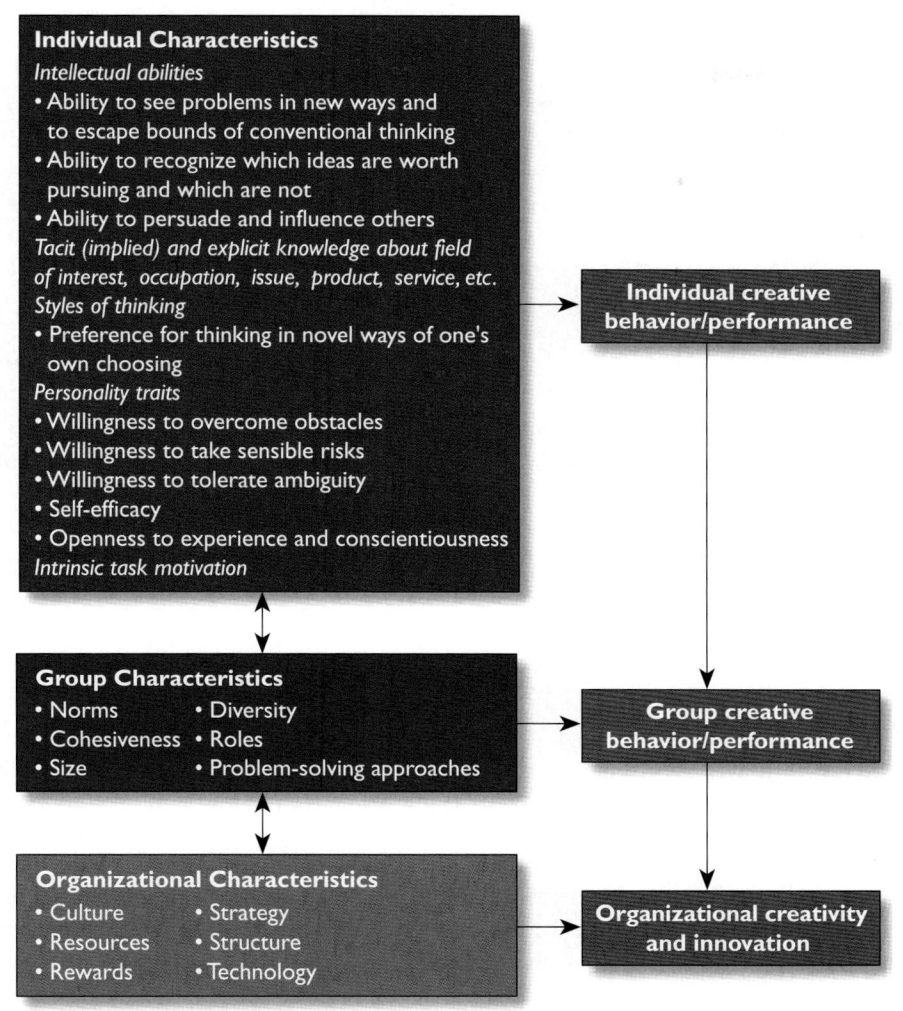

SOURCES: Based on discussion in R J Sternberg and R I Lubart, "Investing in Creativity," *American Psychologist*, July 1996, pp 677–88; and R W Woodman, J E Sawyer, and R W Griffin, "Toward a Theory of Organizational Creativity," *Academy of Management Review*, April 1993, pp 293–321.

The Post-it Notes story represents a good illustration of how the individual characteristics shown in Figure 12–4 promote creative behavior/performance. Post-it Notes are a $200 million-a-year product for 3M Corporation:

> The idea originated with Art Fry, a 3M employee who used bits of paper to mark hymns when he sat in his church choir. These markers kept falling out of the hymn books. He decided that he needed an adhesive-backed paper that would stick as long as necessary but could be removed easily. He soon found what he wanted in the 3M laboratory, and the Post-it Note was born.
>
> Fry saw the market potential of his invention, but others did not. Market-survey results were negative; major office-supply distributors were skeptical. So he began giving samples to 3M executives and their secretaries. Once they actually used the little pieces

Samsung Electronics Uses a Unique Process to Foster Innovation

LOCK 'EM UP	GUIDING HAND	MIX 'EM UP	SET A DATE	DO THE MATH
Daily routines can interrupt the flow of great ideas, so Samsung isolates its development teams in the VIP center— and requires all members to work there for weeks on end, until the project is completed.	Some 50 specialists work at the Center helping teams stay focused on the problems at hand, develop various alternative solutions, and reach a consensus when it's time to make a decision.	Brainstorming is most successful when a wide variety of viewpoints is represented. So Samsung gathers teams of engineers, designers and planners from across the company to develop new products.	Deadlines force teams to make tough choices and overcome disagreements that can slow down progress. Each team is given a timetable for progress and a fixed date for the project's completion.	Team members draw "values curves," graphs that rank attributes such as a product's sound or picture quality on a scale from 1 to 5. These help the team set priorities and differentiate Samsung's products from rivals.

What group problem-solving techniques are being used by Samsung?

SOURCE: Excerpted from M Ihlwan, "Camp Samsung," *BusinessWeek*, July 3, 2006, p 46.

of adhesive paper, they were hooked. Having sold 3M on the project, Fry used the same approach with other executives throughout the United States.[84]

Notice how Fry had to influence others to try out his idea. Figure 12–4 shows that creative people have the ability to persuade and influence others.

Group Characteristics Figure 12–4 also lists six characteristics that influence the level of creative behavior/performance exhibited by a work group. In general, group creativity is fueled by a cohesive environment that supports open interactions, diverse viewpoints, and playful surroundings.

Samsung Electronics represents a good example of how companies can use group characteristics to foster creativity. The company began this pursuit by creating the Value Innovation Program (VIP) center. "The facility is a sort of boiler room where people from across the company brainstorm day after day—and often through the night. Guided by one of 50 'value innovation specialists,' they study what rivals are offering, examine endless data on suppliers, components and costs, and argue over designs and technologies."[85] The Real World/Real People feature above reviews the five-step process that Samsung uses to develop products at the VIP center.

Organizational Characteristics Research and corporate examples clearly support the importance of organizational characteristics in generating organizational creativity.

Organizations such as Apple, Google, 3M, Toyota, Microsoft, General Electric, and IBM are all known as innovative companies that encourage creativity via the organizational characteristics shown in Figure 12–3.[86] It is particularly important for organizations to develop measures or metrics of innovation and to reward it accordingly. As discussed in Chapters 8 and 9, rewards for innovation must be large enough to motivate employee behavior.[87]

Summary of Key Concepts

1. *Compare and contrast the rational model of decision making, Simon's normative model, and the garbage can model.* The rational decision-making model consists of identifying the problem, generating alternative solutions, evaluating and selecting a solution, and implementing and evaluating the solution. Research indicates that decision makers do not follow the series of steps outlined in the rational model.

   Simon's normative model is guided by a decision maker's bounded rationality. Bounded rationality means that decision makers are bounded or restricted by a variety of constraints when making decisions. The normative model suggests that decision making is characterized by (*a*) limited information processing, (*b*) the use of judgmental heuristics, and (*c*) satisficing.

   The garbage can model is based on the assumption that decision making is sloppy and haphazard. Decisions result from an interaction between four independent streams of events: problems, solutions, participants, and choice opportunities.

2. *Discuss eight decision-making biases.* Decision-making bias occurs as the result of using judgmental heuristics. The eight biases that affect decision making include: (1) availability, (2) representativeness, (3) confirmation, (4) anchoring, (5) overconfidence, (6) hindsight, (7) framing, and (8) escalation of commitment.

3. *Discuss knowledge management and techniques used by companies to increase knowledge sharing.* Knowledge management involves the implementation of systems and practices that increase the sharing of knowledge and information throughout an organization. There are two types of knowledge that impact the quality of decisions: tacit knowledge and explicit knowledge. Organizations use computer systems to share explicit knowledge. Tacit knowledge is shared by observing, participating, or working with experts or coaches. Mentoring, informal networking, meetings, and design of office space also influence knowledge sharing.

4. *Explain the model of decision-making styles.* The model of decision-making styles is based on the idea that styles vary along two different dimensions: value orientation and tolerance for ambiguity. When these two dimensions are combined, they form four styles of decision making: directive, analytical, conceptual, and behavioral. People with a directive style have a low tolerance for ambiguity and are oriented toward task and technical concerns. Analytics have a higher tolerance for ambiguity and are characterized by a tendency to overanalyze a situation. People with a conceptual style have a high threshold for ambiguity and tend to focus on people or social aspects of a work situation. This behavioral style is the most people oriented of the four styles.

5. *Explain the model of intuition and the ethical decision tree.* Intuition consists of insight or knowledge that is obtained without the use of rational thought or logical inference. There are two types of intuition: holistic hunches and automated experiences. In turn, there are two sources of intuition: expertise, which consists of an individual's combined explicit and tacit knowledge regarding an object, person, situation, or decision opportunity; and feelings. Intuition is based on the interaction between one's expertise and feelings in a given situation.

   The ethical decision tree presents a structured approach for making ethical decisions. Managers work through the tree by answering a series of questions and the process leads to a recommended decision.

6. *Summarize the pros and cons of involving groups in the decision-making process.* There are both pros and cons to involving groups in the decision-making process. Although research shows that groups typically outperform the average individual, there are five important issues to consider when using groups to make decisions. (*a*) Groups are less efficient than individuals. (*b*) A group's overconfidence can fuel groupthink. (*c*) Decision quality is negatively related to group size. (*d*) Groups are more accurate when they know a great deal about the issues at hand and when the leader possesses the ability to effectively evaluate the group members' opinions and judgments. (*e*) The composition of a group affects its decision-making processes and performance. In the final analysis, managers are encouraged to use a contingency approach when determining whether to include others in the decision-making process.

7. *Contrast brainstorming, the nominal group technique, the Delphi technique, and computer-aided decision making.* Group problem-solving techniques facilitate better decision making within groups. Brainstorming is used to help groups generate multiple ideas and alternatives for solving problems. The nominal group technique assists groups both to generate ideas and to evaluate and select solutions. The Delphi technique is a group process that anonymously generates ideas or judgments from physically dispersed experts. The purpose of computer-aided decision making is to reduce consensus roadblocks while collecting more information in a shorter period of time.

8. *Describe the stages of the creative process.* Creativity is defined as the process of using imagination and skill to develop a new or unique product, object, process, or thought. There are five stages of the creative process: preparation, concentration, incubation, illumination, and verification.

9. *Explain the model of organizational creativity and innovation.* Organizational creativity is directly influenced by organizational characteristics and the creative behavior that occurs within work groups. In turn, a group's creative behavior is influenced by group characteristics and the individual creative behavior/performance of its members. Individual creative behavior is directly affected by a variety of individual characteristics. Finally, individual, group, and organizational characteristics all influence each other within this process.

Key Terms

OB in Action Case Study

IDEO Uses Its Creative Product Design Process to Help Companies Improve Their Products and Customer Service[88]

BusinessWeek From its inception, IDEO has been a force in the world of design. It has designed hundreds of products and won more design awards over the past decade than any other firm. . . . Now, IDEO is transferring its ability to create consumer products into designing consumer experiences in services, from shopping and banking to health care and wireless communication.

Yet by showing global corporations how to change their organizations to focus on the consumer, IDEO is becoming much more than a design company. Indeed, it is now a rival to the traditional purveyors of corporate advice: the management consulting companies such as McKinsey, Boston Consulting, and Bain. . . .

And IDEO works fast. That's because the company requires its clients to participate in virtually all the consumer research, analysis, and decisions that go into developing solutions. When the process is complete, there's no need for a buy-in: Clients already know what to do—and how to do it quickly. Unlike traditional consultants, IDEO shares its innovative process with its customers through projects, workshops, and IDEO U, its customized teaching program. In IDEO-speak, this is "open-source innovation." . . .

Corporate execs probably have the most fun simply participating in the IDEO Way, the design firm's disciplined yet wild-and-woolly five-step process that emphasizes empathy with the consumer, anything-is-possible brainstorming, visualizing solutions by creating actual prototypes, using technology to find creative solutions, and doing it all with incredible speed.

Here's how it works: A company goes to IDEO with a problem. It wants a better product, service, or space—no matter. IDEO puts together an eclectic team composed of members from the client company and its own experts who go out to observe and document the consumer experience. Often, IDEO will have top executives play the roles of their own customers. Execs from food and clothing companies shop for their own stuff in different retail stores and on the Web. Health care managers get care in different hospitals. Wireless providers use their own—and competing—services.

The next stage is brainstorming. IDEO mixes designers, engineers, and social scientists with its clients in a room where they intensely scrutinize a given problem and suggest possible solutions. It is managed chaos: a dozen or so very smart people examining data, throwing out ideas, writing potential solutions on big Post-its that are ripped off and attached to the wall.

IDEO designers then mock up working models of the best concepts that emerge. Rapid prototyping has always been a hallmark of the company. Seeing ideas in working, tangible form is a far more powerful mode of explanation than simply reading about them off a page. IDEO uses inexpensive prototyping tools—Apple-based iMovies to portray consumer experiences and cheap cardboard to mock up examination rooms or fitting rooms....

Like a law firm, IDEO specializes in different practices. The "TEX"—or technology-enabled experiences—aims to take new high-tech products that first appeal only to early adopters and remake them for a mass consumer audience. IDEO's success with the Palm V led AT&T Wireless to call for help on its mMode consumer wireless platform. The company launched mMode in 2002 to allow AT&T Wireless mobile-phone customers to access e-mail and instant messaging, play games, find local restaurants, and connect to sites for news, stocks, weather, and other information. Techies liked mMode, but average consumers were not signing up. "We asked [IDEO] to redesign the interface so someone like my mother who isn't Web savvy can use the phone to navigate how to get the weather or where to shop," says mMode's Hall.

IDEO's Game Plan

It immediately sent AT&T Wireless managers on an actual scavenger hunt in San Francisco to see the world from their customers' perspective. They were told to find a CD by a certain Latin singer that was available at only one small music store, find a Walgreen's that sold its own brand of ibuprofen, and get a Pottery Barn catalog. They discovered that it was simply too difficult to find these kinds of things with their mMode service and wound up using the newspaper or the phone directory instead. IDEO and AT&T Wireless teams also went to AT&T Wireless stores and videotaped people using mMode. They saw that consumers couldn't find the sites they wanted. It took too many steps and clicks. "Even teenagers didn't get it," says Duane Bray, leader of the TEX practice at IDEO.

After dozens of brainstorming sessions and many prototypes, IDEO and AT&T Wireless came up with a new mMode wireless service platform. The opening page starts with "My mMode," which is organized like a Web browser's favorites list and can be managed on a Web site. A consumer can make up an individualized selection of sites, such as ESPN or Sony Pictures Entertainment, and ring tones. Nothing is more than two clicks away.

An mMode Guide on the page allows people to list five places—a restaurant, coffee shop, bank, bar, and retail store—that GPS location finders can identify in various cities around the US. Another feature spotlights the five nearest movie theaters that still have seats available within the next hour. Yet another, My Locker, lets users store a large number of photos and ring tones with AT&T Wireless. The whole design process took only 17 weeks. "We are thrilled with the results," says Hall. "We talked to frog design, Razorfish, and other design firms, and they thought this was a Web project that needed flashy graphics. IDEO knew it was about making the cell phone experience better."

Questions for Discussion

1. Describe IDEO's creative design process.
2. Is IDEO's design process more characteristic of the rational normative or garbage can models of decision making? Discuss your rationale.
3. What type of decision-making styles are most and least consistent with IDEO's design process?
4. Is intuition more or less likely to be used during IDEO's design process? Explain.
5. To what extent does IDEO rely on the five stages of the creative process?

Ethical Dilemma

Should the Principal of Westwood High Allow an Exception to the Graduation Dress Code?[89]

This dilemma involves a situation faced by Helen Riddle, the principal of Mesa, Arizona's, Westwood High. "Westwood High has 225 Native American students, including 112 from the Salt River Pima-Maricopa Indian Community, most of which lies within the boundaries of the Mesa United School District." Districtwide, there are 452 Native American high school students, 149 of whom are from the Salt River Reservation. Here is the situation.

Native American students asked the principal for permission to wear eagle feathers during their graduation ceremony. While this may seem like a reasonable request given these students' customs and traditions, Westwood

High had a rule stating that "students were only allowed to wear a traditional cap and gown for graduation with no other adornments or clothing, including military uniforms. The rules were based on past practice and tradition at schools, not School Board policy."

Advocates for the Native American students argued that students should be allowed to wear the eagle feathers because they represent a significant achievement in the lives of those individuals. In contrast, one school board member opposed the exception to the rule because "it would open the door for other students wanting to display symbols of their own culture or background."

What Would You Do If You Were the Principal of Westwood High?

1. Allow the Native American students to wear the eagle feathers now and in the future. This shows an appreciation for diversity.

2. Not allow the Native American students to wear the eagle feathers because it violates an existing rule,

Allowing an exception opens the door for additional requests about changing the dress code. It would be difficult to defend one exception over another.

3. Allow the students to wear the eagle feathers only in this year's ceremony. Then form a committee to review the dress code requirements.

4. Invent other options. Discuss.

Web Resources

For study material and exercises that apply to this chapter, visit our Web site,
www.mhhe.com/kreitner

CHAPTER 13

Managing Conflict and Negotiation

Student Resources for Studying Chapter 13

The Web site for your text includes resources that will help you master the concepts in this chapter. As you read, you'll want to visit the site for these helpful tools:

- Your online Study Guide includes learning objectives, a chapter summary, a glossary of key terms, and discussion questions.
- Take a practice quiz and test your knowledge!
- Scroll through a PowerPoint presentation with key concepts for this chapter.

Your instructor might also direct you to the Web site for these exercises:

- Self-assessments that correspond with the chapter content and a Group Exercise.
- You'll also find Video Cases and Internet Exercises for this chapter online.

www.mhhe.com/kreitner

BusinessWeek When Robert Nardelli and James McNerney lost the horse race to succeed Jack Welch as head of General Electric, the two men had very different reactions. McNerney immediately swallowed his disappointment and told Welch that he had picked a great guy in Jeffrey Immelt. A devastated Nardelli pressed Welch to know why he didn't get the job. Didn't he have the best numbers? What did Immelt have on him? Why wasn't he the guy? The bitterness was palpable, say insiders.

Both moved on to lead underperforming companies. McNerney, 57, jumped to 3M and then Boeing. An angry Nardelli stormed into the top job at Home Depot. Both received big pay packages and delivered impressive numbers. But that's where the similarities end. While McNerney nurtured an environment of respect at his companies, Nardelli's tenure was marked by callousness and heavy-handedness. In the end, he couldn't even entertain a symbolic pay cut imposed by his board. [Nardelli resigned "by mutual agreement" from Home Depot in January 2007.] . . .

Consider how the former GE rivals approached their new jobs. Nardelli arrived at Home Depot full of bombast, standing up at one meeting to say "you guys don't know how to run a f——ing business," according to a former senior executive at Home Depot. In contrast, McNerney spent his first six months at Boeing talking to employees to better understand the businesses. He didn't yell or publicly humiliate anyone. And though the aerospace giant was reeling from a binge of corporate misconduct, McNerney didn't stuff the top ranks with his GE pals—as Nardelli did at Home Depot. McNerney called for teamwork and heaped credit on shunned CEO contender Alan Mulally. A modern-day Dale Carnegie, he even remembers low-level staffers' names. "Jim's problems have been as tough, or tougher, than the ones that Bob had to face," says a former GE peer. "But he has tried to solve them in a much more pleasant way. The guy is loved over there at Boeing—and that's got to make a difference."

With likability a buzzword among CEO headhunters, it can make all the difference. Nardelli clearly cared about Home Depot. When it came to measures like profitability, his push was paying off. What he neglected was the touchy-feely stuff: the enthusiasm of his people, a sense of humility before his board, the care and feeding of his shareholders. It all seems so soft and irrelevant, until the injured egos decide to fight back.[1]

FOR DISCUSSION

Why is this a classic case of "no surprise"?

How would you handle this situation?

Your name is Annie and you are a product development manager for Amazon.com. As you were eating lunch today in your cubicle, Laura, a software project manager with an office nearby, asked if she could talk to you for a few minutes. You barely know Laura and you have heard both good and bad things about her work habits. Although your mind was more on how to meet Friday's deadline than on lunch, you waved her in.

She proceeded to pour out her woes about how she is having an impossible time partnering with Hans on a new special project. He is regarded as a top-notch software project manager, but Laura has found him to be ill-tempered and uncooperative. Laura thought you and Hans were friends because she has seen the two of you talking in the cafeteria and parking lot. You told Laura you have a good working relationship with Hans, but he's not really a friend. Still, Laura pressed on. "Would you straighten Hans out for me?" she asked. "We've got to get moving on this special project."

"Why this?" "Why now?" "Why me?!!" you thought as your eyes left Laura and drifted back to your desk.

Write down some ideas about how to handle this all-too-common conflict situation. Set it aside. We'll revisit your recommendation later in the chapter. In the meantime, we need to explore the world of conflict because, as indicated in the opening vignette, the potential for conflict is an ever-present feature of modern life. After discussing a modern view of conflict and four major types of conflict, we learn how to manage conflict both as a participant and as a third party. The related topic of negotiation is examined next. We conclude with a contingency approach to conflict management and negotiation.

Conflict: A Modern Perspective

Make no mistake about it. Conflict is an unavoidable aspect of organizational life. These major trends conspire to make *organizational* conflict inevitable:

- Constant change.
- Greater employee diversity.
- More teams (virtual and self-managed).
- Less face-to-face communication (more electronic interaction).
- A global economy with increased cross-cultural dealings.

Dean Tjosvold, from Canada's Simon Fraser University, notes that "Change begets conflict, conflict begets change"[2] and challenges us to do better with this sobering global perspective:

> Learning to manage conflict is a critical investment in improving how we, our families, and our organizations adapt and take advantage of change. Managing conflicts well does not insulate us from change, nor does it mean that we will always come out on top or get all that we want. However, effective conflict management helps us keep in touch with new developments and create solutions appropriate for new threats and opportunities.
>
> Much evidence shows we have often failed to manage our conflicts and respond to change effectively. High divorce rates, disheartening examples of sexual and physical abuse of children, the expensive failures of international joint ventures, and bloody ethnic violence have convinced many people that we do not have the abilities to cope with our complex interpersonal, organizational, and global conflicts.[3]

But respond we must. As outlined in this chapter, tools and solutions are available, if only we develop the ability and will to use them persistently. The choice is ours: Be active managers of conflict, or be managed by conflict.

A comprehensive review of the conflict literature yielded this consensus definition: "**conflict** is a process in which one party perceives that its interests are being opposed or negatively affected by another party."[4] The word *perceives* reminds us that sources of conflict and issues can be real or imagined. The resulting conflict is the same. Conflict can escalate (strengthen) or deescalate (weaken) over time. "The conflict process unfolds

Conflict

One party perceives its interests are being opposed or set back by another party.

in a context, and whenever conflict, escalated or not, occurs the disputants or third parties can attempt to manage it in some manner."[5] Consequently, current and future managers need to understand the dynamics of conflict and know how to handle it effectively (both as disputants and as third parties). This call to action is bolstered by a recent survey asking employees what their manager's New Year's resolution should be. The number one response was "Deal with workplace conflicts faster."[6]

The Language of Conflict: Metaphors and Meaning

Conflict is a complex subject for several reasons. Primary among them is the reality that conflict often carries a lot of emotional luggage.[7] Fear of losing or fear of change quickly raises the emotional stakes in a conflict. Conflicts also vary widely in magnitude. Conflicts have both participants and observers. Some observers may be interested and active, others disinterested and passive. Consequently, the term *conflict* can take on vastly different meanings, depending on the circumstances and one's involvement. For example, consider these three metaphors and accompanying workplace expressions:

- *Conflict as war:* "We shot down that idea."
- *Conflict as opportunity:* "What are all the possibilities for solving this problem?"
- *Conflict as journey:* "Let's search for common ground."[8]

Anyone viewing a conflict as war will try to win at all costs and wipe out the enemy. For example, *BusinessWeek* recently quoted Donald Trump as saying, "In life, you have fighters and nonfighters. You have winners and losers. I am both a fighter and a winner."[9] Alternatively, those seeing a conflict as an opportunity and a journey will tend to be more positive, open-minded, and constructive. In a hostile world, combative and destructive warlike thinking often prevails. But typical daily workplace conflicts are *not* war. So when dealing with organizational conflicts, we are challenged to rely less on the metaphor and language of war and more on the metaphors and language of *opportunity* and *journey*. We need to monitor our choice of words in conflict situations carefully.[10]

While explaining the three metaphors, conflict experts Kenneth Cloke and Joan Goldsmith made this instructive observation that we want to keep in mind for the balance of this chapter:

> Conflict gives you an opportunity to deepen your capacity for empathy and intimacy with your opponent. Your anger transforms the "Other" into a stereotyped demon or villain. Similarly, defensiveness will prevent you from communicating openly with your opponents, or listening carefully to what they are saying. On the other hand, once you engage in dialogue with that person, you will resurrect the human side of their personality—and express your own as well.
>
> Moreover, when you process your conflicts with integrity, they lead to growth, increased awareness, and self-improvement. Uncontrolled anger, defensiveness, and shame defeat these possibilities. Everyone feels better when they overcome their problems and reach resolution, and worse when they succumb and fail to resolve them. It is a bitter truth that victories won in anger lead to long-term defeat. Those defeated turn away, feeling betrayed and lost, and carry this feeling with them into their next conflict.
>
> Conflict can be seen simply as a way of learning more about what is not working and discovering how to fix it. The usefulness of the solution depends on the depth of your understanding of the problem. This depends on your ability to listen to the issue as you would to a teacher, which depends on halting the cycle of escalation and searching for opportunities for improvement.[11]

In short, win–win beats win–lose in both conflict management and negotiation.

Figure 13–1   *The Relationship between Conflict Intensity and Outcomes*

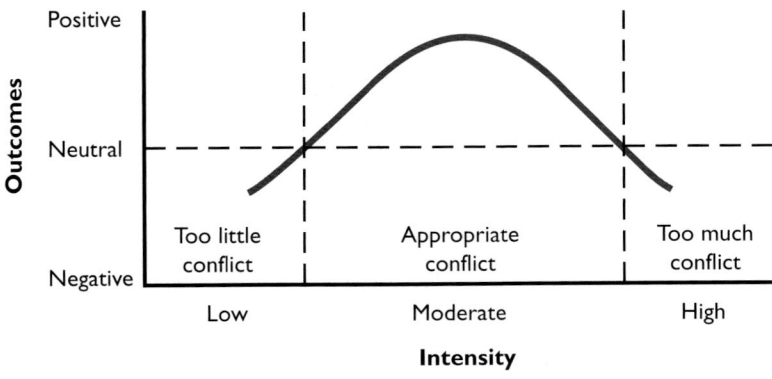

SOURCE: L D Brown, *Managing Conflict at Organizational Interfaces,* 1st edition, © 1983, p 8. Reprinted by permission of Pearson Education, Inc., Upper Saddle River, NJ.

A Conflict Continuum

Ideas about managing conflict underwent an interesting evolution during the 20th century. Initially, scientific management experts such as Frederick W Taylor believed all conflict ultimately threatened management's authority and thus had to be avoided or quickly resolved. Later, human relationists recognized the inevitability of conflict and advised managers to learn to live with it. Emphasis remained on resolving conflict whenever possible, however. Beginning in the 1970s, OB specialists realized conflict had both positive and negative outcomes, depending on its nature and intensity. This perspective introduced the revolutionary idea that organizations could suffer from *too little* conflict. Figure 13–1 illustrates the relationship between conflict intensity and outcomes.

Work groups, departments, or organizations experiencing too little conflict tend to be plagued by apathy, lack of creativity, indecision, and missed deadlines. Excessive conflict, on the other hand, can erode organizational performance because of political infighting, dissatisfaction, lack of teamwork, and turnover. Workplace aggression and violence can be manifestations of excessive conflict.[12] Appropriate types and levels of conflict energize people in constructive directions.[13]

 # 2 Functional versus Dysfunctional Conflict

Functional conflict
Serves organization's interests.

The distinction between **functional conflict** and **dysfunctional conflict** pivots on whether the organization's interests are served. According to one conflict expert,

> Some [types of conflict] support the goals of the organization and improve performance; these are functional, constructive forms of conflict. They benefit or support the main purposes of the organization. Additionally, there are those types of conflict that hinder organizational performance; these are dysfunctional or destructive forms. They are undesirable and the manager should seek their eradication.[14]

Dysfunctional conflict
Threatens organization's interests.

Functional conflict is commonly referred to in management circles as constructive or cooperative conflict.[15] In terms of what we just discussed about the language of conflict, those engaging in functional conflict apply a win–win attitude to solve problems and find common ground (see the Real World/Real People feature on the next page).

Functional Conflict Means "Courageous Communication" at Grand Circle Corporation

"We help change people's lives" proclaims a banner above the front desk in the offices of the Grand Circle Corp., an international travel company based in Boston. That's a pretty lofty goal, but it's one this company takes seriously. The lives that Grand Circle changes belong to both employees and customers. In addition to arranging "life-changing" trips to exotic locales for Americans age 50 and older, Grand Circle employees are expected to practice "open and courageous communication" in their dealings with each other and with management.

Grand Circle defines "open and courageous communication" as being willing to ask tough questions, give constructive feedback to others and accept such feedback without defensiveness. It's one of the values the company lives by. (Other core values include teamwork, risk taking, speed, quality and thriving in change.)

Marielle Arguello, a worldwide training manager at Grand Circle, admits the environment is not for everyone. "It's uncomfortable to be open and courageous," she says. In addition to giving and receiving feedback, "you can't just complain. You are expected to make recommendations for solutions" to the problems you identify.

Further, at monthly corporate meetings, Grand Circle employees are expected to bring up "non-discussables" (described by CEO Alan Lewis as "things you don't want to hear") and get answers to their questions from the executive team.

Nothing is off limits.

Why is "courageous communication" one of those easy-to-talk-about, but hard-to-do, organizational activities?

SOURCE: A Pomeroy, "Great Communicators, Great Communication," *HR Magazine*, July 2006, p 44.

Why People Avoid Conflict

Are you uncomfortable in conflict situations? Do you go out of your way to avoid conflict? If so, you're not alone. Many of us avoid conflict for a variety of both good and bad reasons. Tim Ursiny, in his entertaining and instructive book *The Coward's Guide to Conflict,* contends that we avoid conflict because we fear various combinations of the following things: "harm"; "rejection"; "loss of relationship"; "anger"; "being seen as selfish"; "saying the wrong thing"; "failing"; "hurting someone else"; "getting what you want"; and "intimacy."[16] This list is self-explanatory, except for the fear of "getting what you want." By this, Ursiny is referring to those who, for personal reasons, feel undeserving or fear the consequences of success, or both (so they tend to sabotage themselves).[17] For our present purposes, it is sufficient to become consciously aware of our fears and practice overcoming them. Reading, understanding, and acting upon the material in this chapter are steps in a positive direction.

3 Antecedents of Conflict

Certain situations produce more conflict than others. By knowing the antecedents of conflict, managers are better able to anticipate it and take steps to resolve it if it becomes dysfunctional. Among the situations tending to produce either functional or dysfunctional conflict are

- Incompatible personalities or value systems.
- Overlapping or unclear job boundaries.
- Competition for limited resources.
- Interdepartment/intergroup competition.
- Inadequate communication.

- Interdependent tasks (e.g., one person cannot complete his or her assignment until others have completed their work).
- Organizational complexity (conflict tends to increase as the number of hierarchical layers and specialized tasks increase).
- Unreasonable or unclear policies, standards, or rules.
- Unreasonable deadlines or extreme time pressure.
- Collective decision making (the greater the number of people participating in a decision, the greater the potential for conflict).
- Decision making by consensus.
- Unmet expectations (employees who have unrealistic expectations about job assignments, pay, or promotions are more prone to conflict).
- Unresolved or suppressed conflicts.[18]

Proactive managers carefully read these early warnings and take appropriate action.

Desired Conflict Outcomes

Within organizations, conflict management is more than simply a quest for agreement. If progress is to be made and dysfunctional conflict minimized, a broader agenda is in order. Tjosvold's cooperative conflict model calls for three desired outcomes:

1. *Agreement.* But at what cost? Equitable and fair agreements are best. An agreement that leaves one party feeling exploited or defeated will tend to breed resentment and subsequent conflict.
2. *Stronger relationships.* Good agreements enable conflicting parties to build bridges of goodwill and trust for future use. Moreover, conflicting parties who trust each other are more likely to keep their end of the bargain.
3. *Learning.* Functional conflict can promote greater self-awareness and creative problem solving. Like the practice of management itself, successful conflict handling is learned primarily by doing. Knowledge of the concepts and techniques in this chapter is a necessary first step, but there is no substitute for hands-on practice. In a contentious world, there are plenty of opportunities to practice conflict management.[19]

Types of Conflict

Certain antecedents of conflict, highlighted earlier, deserve a closer look. This section probes the nature and organizational implications of three basic types of conflict: personality conflict, intergroup conflict, and cross-cultural conflict. Our discussion of each type of conflict includes some practical tips and techniques.

Personality Conflict

We visited the topic of personalities in our Chapter 2 discussion of diversity. Also, recall the Big Five personality dimensions introduced in Chapter 5. Once again, your *personality* is the package of stable traits and characteristics creating your unique identity. According to experts on the subject:

Each of us has a unique way of interacting with others. Whether we are seen as charming, irritating, fascinating, nondescript, approachable, or intimidating depends in part on our personality, or what others might describe as our style.[20]

Given the many possible combinations of personality traits, it is clear why personality conflicts are inevitable. We define a **personality conflict** as interpersonal opposition based on personal dislike, disagreement, or different styles. For example, imagine the potential for a top-level personality conflict at EMC Corp., a leading maker of data storage equipment and services. Michael C Ruettgers, executive chairman of the Massachusetts-based firm, gave up his CEO position in January 2001 after running the company for nine years.

Personality conflict

Interpersonal opposition driven by personal dislike or disagreement.

> In a January [2002] interview, Ruettgers gave CEO Joseph M Tucci A's in innovation and strategic management, but F's in stock-price performance and financial management because the company lost $508 million in 2001. Ruettgers added that he was disappointed Tucci has attracted so little outside talent during his year at the helm. . . .
>
> At the same time, some former execs say, Tucci has wanted to move faster to cut costs, make acquisitions, and introduce new software but Ruettgers and EMC have slowed the pace of change. And Ruettgers, who had planned to be less active in daily affairs, has continued to attend weekly meetings to review operations. This has analysts and insiders speculating that Tucci could soon take the fall for EMC's poor performance. "In that culture, someone must fail," says a former EMC executive. "There will be a scapegoat." . . .
>
> The personal and management styles of Tucci, a salesman, and Ruettgers, who started at EMC as an operations expert, couldn't be more different. Tucci likes to build one-on-one relationships, while Ruettgers is more aloof. Tucci seems to be more willing than Ruettgers to make tough decisions quickly. Bill Scannell, EMC's senior vice president for global sales, says Tucci gives him an answer immediately when he asks for advice. Ruettgers tends to chew on things awhile. And Tucci praises and thanks his troops regularly, while Ruettgers once told a former executive that saying thank-you is a sign of weakness.[21]

A personality conflict with his former boss didn't keep EMC's CEO Joseph M Tucci from succeeding with a more people-friendly style of management.

Any way you look at it, Tucci was in a tough spot, and conflicting personalities only made it worse. How did things turn out? By 2006, Tucci's strategy and personal style were vindicated as EMC posted impressive results from hot new products.[22] Good guys don't always finish last!

Workplace Incivility: The Seeds of Personality Conflict Somewhat akin to physical pain, chronic personality conflicts often begin with seemingly insignificant irritations. A pair of OB researchers recently offered this cautionary overview of the problem and its consequences:

> Incivility, or employees' lack of regard for one another, is costly to organizations in subtle and pervasive ways. Although uncivil behaviors occur commonly, many organizations fail to recognize them, few understand their harmful effects, and most managers and executives are ill-equipped to deal with them. Over the past eight years, as we have learned about this phenomenon through interviews, focus groups, questionnaires, experiments, and executive forums with more than 2,400 people across the US and Canada, we have found that incivility causes its targets, witnesses, and additional stakeholders to act in ways that erode organizational values and deplete organizational resources. Because of their experiences of workplace incivility, employees decrease work effort, time on the job, productivity, and performance. Where incivility is not curtailed, job satisfaction and

It's Called "Cubicle Etiquette"

As office space gets tighter, the possibility of being annoyed by a co-worker increases dramatically. About 58% of offices throughout America now use an open layout or cubicles, and the lack of walls demands new etiquette for getting along with co-workers.

Noise is the biggest culprit, with cellphones, speakerphones, meetings in cubicles and eavesdropping irking the most workers. Thirty percent of workers say the annoying ringtones of others' cellphones are the most irritating part of the day, followed closely by loud talkers and improper use of speakerphones, according to a survey by Randstad USA, a staffing company.

Ellen A Kaye, leadership development expert and founder of Scottsdale-based Perfect Presentation, goes through the major rules. "No loud noises, no speakerphone, no radios, no meetings in cubicles, no hot food at your desk, no perfume," she said.

What are your pet peeves when it comes to incivility in public places such as offices, restaurants, public transportation, libraries, and classrooms?

SOURCE: E Ryan, "Courtesies Enhance Cubicle Life," *The Arizona Republic,* October 29, 2006, p D3.

---

organizational loyalty diminish as well. Some employees leave their jobs solely because of the impact of this subtle form of deviance.[23]

Vicious cycles of incivility need to be avoided, or broken early, with an organizational culture that places a high value on respect for co-workers (see the Real World/Real People feature above). This requires managers and leaders to act as caring and courteous role models. A positive spirit of cooperation, as opposed to one based on negativism and aggression, also helps. Proactive steps need to be taken because of these recent research insights:

- "Twenty-five percent to 30% of US employees are bullied and emotionally abused sometime during their work histories."[24]

- "The workplace is not a kinder or gentler place—at least when it comes to continued use of sexual, racial, ethnic, ageist and other slurs directed at co-workers."[25]

Day of contemplation

A one-time-only day off with pay to allow a problem employee to recommit to the organization's values and mission.

Some organizations have resorted to workplace etiquette training.[26] More specifically, constructive feedback or skillful behavior shaping can keep a single irritating behavior from precipitating a full-blown personality conflict (or worse). Another promising tool for nipping workplace incivility in the bud is a **day of contemplation,** defined as: "a *paid* day off where an employee showing lack of dedication to the job is granted the opportunity to rethink his commitment to working at your company."[27] This tactic, also called *decision-making leave,* is not part of the organization's formal disciplinary process, nor is it a traditional suspension without pay. A day of contemplation is a one-time-only-per-employee option.

Dealing with Personality Conflicts Personality conflicts are a potential minefield for managers. Let us frame the situation. Personality traits, by definition, are stable and resistant to change. Moreover, according to the American Psychiatric Association's *Diagnostic and Statistical Manual of Mental Disorders,* there are 410 psychological disorders that can and do show up in the workplace.[28] This brings up legal issues. Employees in the United States suffering from psychological disorders such as depression and mood-altering diseases such as alcoholism are protected from discrimination by the Americans with Disabilities Act.[29] (Other nations have similar laws.) Also, sexual harassment and other forms of discrimination can grow out of apparent personality conflicts. Finally, personality conflicts can spawn workplace aggression and violence.

Table 13–1   *How to Deal with Personality Conflicts*

TIPS FOR EMPLOYEES HAVING A PERSONALITY CONFLICT	TIPS FOR THIRD-PARTY OBSERVERS OF A PERSONALITY CONFLICT	TIPS FOR MANAGERS WHOSE EMPLOYEES ARE HAVING A PERSONALITY CONFLICT
• Communicate directly with the other person to resolve the perceived conflict (emphasize problem solving and common objectives, not personalities). • Avoid dragging co-workers into the conflict. • If dysfunctional conflict persists, seek help from direct supervisors or human resource specialists.	• Do not take sides in someone else's personality conflict. • Suggest the parties work things out themselves in a constructive and positive way. • If dysfunctional conflict persists, refer the problem to parties' direct supervisors.	• Investigate and document conflict. • If appropriate, take corrective action (e.g., feedback or behavior shaping). • If necessary, attempt informal dispute resolution. • Refer difficult conflicts to human resource specialists or hired counselors for formal resolution attempts and other interventions.

Note: All employees need to be familiar with and *follow* company policies for diversity, antidiscrimination, and sexual harassment.

Traditionally, managers dealt with personality conflicts by either ignoring them or transferring one party. In view of the legal implications, just discussed, both of these options may be open invitations to discrimination lawsuits. Table 13–1 presents practical tips for both nonmanagers and managers who are involved in or affected by personality conflicts. Our later discussions of handling dysfunctional conflict and alternative dispute resolution techniques also apply.

go to the Web for the Self-Exercise: What Is Your Primary Conflict-Handling Style?

5 Intergroup Conflict

Conflict among work groups, teams, and departments is a common threat to organizational competitiveness. For example, when Michael Volkema became CEO of Herman Miller in the mid-1990s, he found an inward-focused company with divisions fighting over budgets. He curbed intergroup conflict at the Michigan-based furniture maker by emphasizing collaboration and redirecting everyone's attention outward, to the customer.[30] Managers who understand the mechanics of intergroup conflict are better equipped to face this sort of challenge.

In-Group Thinking: The Seeds of Intergroup Conflict As we discussed in previous chapters, *cohesiveness*—a "we feeling" binding group members together—can be a good or bad thing. A certain amount of cohesiveness can turn a group of individuals into a smooth-running team. Too much cohesiveness, however, can breed groupthink because a desire to get along pushes aside critical thinking. The study of in-groups by small group researchers has revealed a whole package of

Talk about in-group thinking. Don't get between these rabid National Football League fans and their beloved Oakland Raiders.

changes associated with increased group cohesiveness. Specifically,

- Members of in-groups view themselves as a collection of unique individuals, while they stereotype members of other groups as being "all alike."
- In-group members see themselves positively and as morally correct, while they view members of other groups negatively and as immoral.
- In-groups view outsiders as a threat.
- In-group members exaggerate the differences between their group and other groups. This typically involves a distorted perception of reality.[31]

Avid sports fans who simply can't imagine how someone would support the opposing team exemplify one form of in-group thinking. Also, this pattern of behavior is a corm of ethnocentrism, discussed as a cross-cultural barrier in Chapter 4. Reflect for a moment on evidence of in-group behavior in your life. Does your circle of friends make fun of others because of their race, gender, nationality, religion, sexual preference, weight, or major in college?[32]

In-group thinking is one more fact of organizational life that virtually guarantees conflict. Managers cannot eliminate in-group thinking, but they certainly should not ignore it when handling intergroup conflicts.

Research Lessons for Handling Intergroup Conflict

Sociologists have long recommended the contact hypothesis for reducing intergroup conflict. According to the *contact hypothesis,* the more the members of different groups interact, the less intergroup conflict they will experience. Those interested in improving race, international, and union–management relations typically encourage cross-group interaction. The hope is that *any* type of interaction, short of actual conflict, will reduce stereotyping and combat in-group thinking. But research evidence has been mixed. A recent meta-analysis of 515 different studies did indeed support the contact hypothesis, with greater intergroup contact associated with less prejudice.[33] On the other hand, a field study of 83 health center employees (83% female) at a Midwest US university probed the specific nature of intergroup relations and concluded

> The number of *negative* relationships was significantly related to higher perceptions of intergroup conflict. Thus, it seems that negative relationships have a salience that overwhelms any possible positive effects from friendship links across groups.[34]

Intergroup contact and friendships are still desirable, as documented in many studies,[35] but they are readily overpowered by negative intergroup interactions. Thus, *priority number one for managers faced with intergroup conflict is to identify and root out specific negative linkages among groups.* A single personality conflict, for instance, may contaminate the entire intergroup experience. The same goes for an employee who voices negative opinions or spreads negative rumors about another group. Our updated contact model in Figure 13–2 is based on this and other research insights, such as the need to foster positive attitudes toward other groups. Also, notice how conflict within the group and negative gossip from third parties are threats that need to be neutralized if intergroup conflict is to be minimized.[36]

Figure 13–2   *An Updated Contact Model for Minimizing Intergroup Conflict*

Recommended actions:

Level of perceived intergroup conflict tends to increase when:

- Conflict within the group is high.
- There are negative interactions between groups (or between members of those groups).
- Influential third-party gossip about other group is negative.

- Work to eliminate *specific negative* interactions between groups (and members).
- Conduct team building to reduce *intra*group conflict and prepare employees for cross-functional teamwork.
- Encourage personal friendships and good working relationships across groups and departments.
- Foster positive attitudes toward members of other groups (empathy, compassion, sympathy).
- Avoid or neutralize negative gossip across groups or departments.

SOURCES: Based on research evidence in G Labianca, D J Brass, and B Gray, "Social Networks and Perceptions of Intergroup Conflict: The Role of Negative Relationships and Third Parties." *Academy of Management Journal,* February 1998, pp 55–67; C D Batson et al., "Empathy and Attitudes: Can Feeling for a Member of a Stigmatized Group Improve Feelings toward the Group?" *Journal of Personality and Social Psychology,* January 1997, pp 105–18; and S C Wright et al., "The Extended Contact Effect: Knowledge of Cross-Group Friendships and Prejudice," *Journal of Personality and Social Psychology,* July 1997, pp 73–90.

6 Cross-Cultural Conflict

Doing business with people from different cultures is commonplace in our global economy where cross-border mergers, joint ventures, and alliances are the order of the day.[37] Because of differing assumptions about how to think and act, the potential for cross-cultural conflict is both immediate and huge.[38] Success or failure, when conducting business across cultures, often hinges on avoiding and minimizing actual or perceived conflict. For example, consider this cultural mismatch:

> Mexicans place great importance on saving face, so they tend to expect any conflicts that occur during negotiations to be downplayed or kept private. The prevailing attitude in the [United States], however, is that conflict should be dealt with directly and publicly to prevent hard feelings from developing on a personal level.[39]

Nuclear disarmament talks with North Korea and other key players including China, Japan, and the US have been plagued by lots of cross-cultural conflict.

This is not a matter of who is right and who is wrong; rather it is a matter of accommodating cultural differences for a successful business transaction. Awareness of the GLOBE project's cross-cultural dimensions, discussed in Chapter 4, is an important first step. Stereotypes also need to be identified and neutralized. Beyond that, cross-cultural conflict can be moderated by using international consultants and building cross-cultural relationships.

International Consultants   In response to broad demand, there is a growing army of management consultants specializing in cross-cultural relations. Competency and fees vary widely, of course. But a carefully selected cross-cultural consultant can be helpful, as this illustration shows:

> [W]hen electronics-maker Canon planned to set up a subsidiary in Dubai through its Netherlands division, it asked consultant Sahid Mirza of Glocom, based in Dubai, to find out how the two cultures would work together.
>
> Mirza sent out the test questionnaires and got a sizeable response. "The findings were somewhat surprising," he recalls. "We found that, at the bedrock level, there were relatively few differences. Many of the Arab businessmen came from former British colonies and viewed business in much the same way as the Dutch."
>
> But at the level of behavior, there was a real conflict. "The Dutch are blunt and honest in expression, and such expression is very offensive to Arab sensibilities." … As a result of Mirza's research, Canon did start the subsidiary in Dubai, but it trained both the Dutch and the Arab executives first.[40]

Consultants also can help untangle possible personality and intergroup conflicts from conflicts rooted in differing national cultures. *Note:* Although we have discussed these three basic types of conflict separately, they typically are encountered in complex, messy bundles.

Building Cross-Cultural Relationships to Avoid Dysfunctional Conflict   Rosalie L Tung's study of 409 expatriates from US and Canadian multinational firms is very instructive.[41] Her survey sought to pinpoint success factors for the expatriates (14% female) who were working in 51 different countries worldwide. Nine specific ways to facilitate interaction with host-country nationals, as ranked from most useful to least useful by the respondents, are listed in Table 13–2. Good listening skills topped the list, followed by sensitivity to others and cooperativeness rather than competitiveness. Interestingly, US managers are culturally characterized as just the opposite: poor listeners, blunt to the point of insensitivity, and excessively competitive. Some managers need to add self-management to the list of ways to minimize cross-cultural conflict.

Managing Conflict

As we have seen, conflict has many faces and is a constant challenge for managers who are responsible for reaching organizational goals. Our attention now turns to the active management of both functional and dysfunctional conflict. We discuss how to stimulate functional conflict, how to handle dysfunctional conflict, and how third parties can deal effectively with conflict. Relevant research lessons also are examined.

Table 13–2   *Ways to Build Cross-Cultural Relationships*

BEHAVIOR	RANK
Be a good listener	1
Be sensitive to needs of others	2
Be cooperative, rather than overly competitive	2 > Tie
Advocate inclusive (participative) leadership	3
Compromise rather than dominate	4
Build rapport through conversations	5
Be compassionate and understanding	6
Avoid conflict by emphasizing harmony	7
Nurture others (develop and mentor)	8

SOURCE: Adapted from R L Tung, "American Expatriates Abroad: From Neophytes to Cosmopolitans," *Journal of World Business,* Summer 1998, table 6, p 136. © 1998, with permission from Elsevier.

Stimulating Functional Conflict

Sometimes committees and decision-making groups become so bogged down in details and procedures that nothing substantive is accomplished. Carefully monitored functional conflict can help get the creative juices flowing once again. Managers basically have two options. They can fan the fires of naturally occurring conflict—but this approach can be unreliable and slow. Alternatively, managers can resort to programmed conflict.[42] Experts in the field define **programmed conflict** as "conflict that raises different opinions *regardless of the personal feelings of the managers*."[43] The trick is to get contributors to either defend or criticize ideas based on relevant facts rather than on the basis of personal preference or political interests. This requires disciplined role playing. Two programmed conflict techniques with proven track records are devil's advocacy and the dialectic method. Let us explore these two ways of stimulating functional conflict.

Programmed conflict
Encourages different opinions without protecting management's personal feelings.

Devil's Advocacy   This technique gets its name from a traditional practice within the Roman Catholic Church. When someone's name came before the College of Cardinals for elevation to sainthood, it was absolutely essential to ensure that he or she had a spotless record. Consequently, one individual was assigned the role of *devil's advocate* to uncover and air all possible objections to the person's canonization. In accordance with this practice, **devil's advocacy** in today's organizations involves assigning someone the role of critic.[44] Recall from Chapter 10, Irving Janis recommended the devil's advocate role for preventing groupthink.

Devil's advocacy
Assigning someone the role of critic.

In the left half of Figure 13–3, note how devil's advocacy alters the usual decision-making process in steps 2 and 3. This approach to programmed conflict is intended to generate critical thinking and reality testing.[45] It is a good idea to rotate the job of devil's advocate so no one person or group develops a strictly negative reputation. Moreover, periodic devil's advocacy role-playing is good training for developing analytical and communication skills and emotional intelligence.

The Dialectic Method   Like devil's advocacy, the dialectic method is a time-honored practice. This particular approach to programmed conflict traces back to the

Figure 13–3 *Techniques for Stimulating Functional Conflict: Devil's Advocacy and the Dialectic Method*

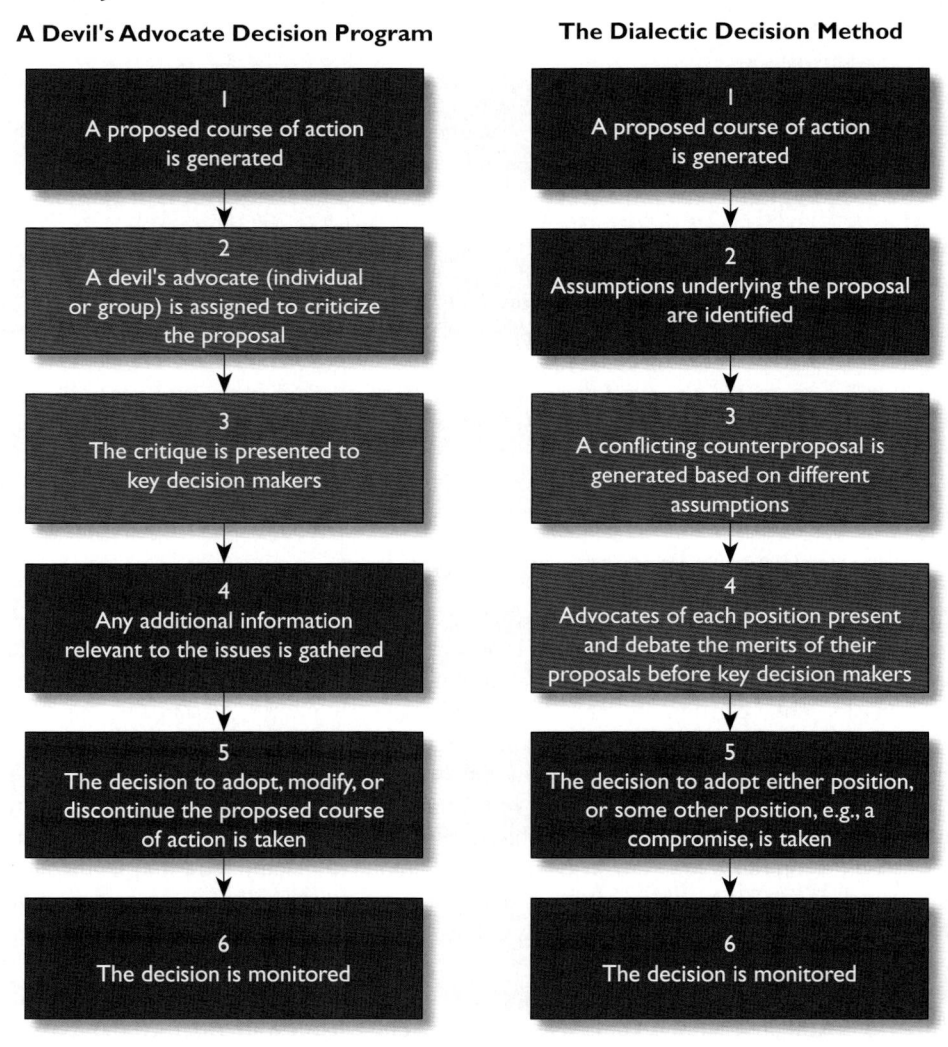

A Devil's Advocate Decision Program

1. A proposed course of action is generated
2. A devil's advocate (individual or group) is assigned to criticize the proposal
3. The critique is presented to key decision makers
4. Any additional information relevant to the issues is gathered
5. The decision to adopt, modify, or discontinue the proposed course of action is taken
6. The decision is monitored

The Dialectic Decision Method

1. A proposed course of action is generated
2. Assumptions underlying the proposal are identified
3. A conflicting counterproposal is generated based on different assumptions
4. Advocates of each position present and debate the merits of their proposals before key decision makers
5. The decision to adopt either position, or some other position, e.g., a compromise, is taken
6. The decision is monitored

SOURCE: R A Cosier and C R Schwenk, "Agreement and Thinking Alike: Ingredients for Poor Decisions," *Academy of Management Executive,* February 1990, pp 72–73. Reprinted with permission of The Academy of Management via The Copyright Clearance Center.

dialectic school of philosophy in ancient Greece. Plato and his followers attempted to synthesize truths by exploring opposite positions (called *thesis* and *antithesis*). Court systems in the United States and elsewhere rely on directly opposing points of view for determining guilt or innocence. Accordingly, today's **dialectic method** calls for managers to foster a structured debate of opposing viewpoints prior to making a decision.[46] Steps 3 and 4 in the right half of Figure 13–3 set the dialectic approach apart from the normal decision-making process. For an example of the dialectic method in action, see the Real World/Real People feature on the next page.

A major drawback of the dialectic method is that "winning the debate" may overshadow the issue at hand. Also, the dialectic method requires more skill training

Dialectic method

Fostering a debate of opposing viewpoints to better understand an issue.

How Toro Mows Down Bad Ideas

Toro, the $1.8 billion lawn-mower giant, knows how to curb the urge to merge. Anytime an M&A [merger and acquisition] pitch reaches the desk of CEO Mike Hoffman, he asks a due-diligence group to make the case to the company's board. But he also turns to the "contra team"—half a dozen vice presidents and directors—to deliver the voice of dissent. According to chairman Ken Melrose. . . . a few years ago the contras killed an eight-figure acquisition of a manufacturer that had pitched itself as a turnaround success. The contras' number crunching showed that its sector was facing a slump. The prospect's revenues have since tanked, while Toro has nearly doubled its sales. "Naysaying in corporate America isn't popular," Melrose says. "The contra team is a way to create negative views that are in the shareholders' best interest and the company's best interest."

What factors can limit the effectiveness of this technique?

SOURCE: Excerpted from P Kaihla, "Toro: The Contra Team," *Business 2.0,* April 2006, p 83.

---

than does devil's advocacy. Regarding the comparative effectiveness of these two approaches to stimulating functional conflict, however, a laboratory study ended in a tie. Compared with groups that strived to reach a consensus, decision-making groups using either devil's advocacy or the dialectic method yielded equally higher quality decisions.[47] But in a more recent laboratory study, groups using devil's advocacy produced more potential solutions and made better recommendations for a case problem than did groups using the dialectic method.[48]

In light of this mixed evidence, managers have some latitude in using either devil's advocacy or the dialectic method for pumping creative life back into stalled deliberations.[49] Personal preference and the role players' experience may well be the deciding factors in choosing one approach over the other. The important thing is to actively stimulate functional conflict when necessary, such as when the risk of blind conformity or groupthink is high. Joseph M Tucci, the CEO of EMC introduced previously, fosters functional conflict by creating a supportive climate for dissent:

> Good leaders always leave room for debate and different opinions. . . .
>
> The team has to be in harmony. But before you move out, there needs to be a debate. Leadership is not a right. You have to earn it.
>
> . . . . [E]very company needs a healthy paranoia. It's the CEO's job to keep it on the edge, to put tension in the system. You have to do the right thing for the right circumstances.[50]

This meshes well with the results of a pair of laboratory studies that found a positive relationship between the degree of minority dissent and team innovation, *but only when participative decision making was used.*[51]

Alternative Styles for Handling Dysfunctional Conflict

People tend to handle negative conflict in patterned ways referred to as *styles.* Several conflict styles have been categorized over the years. According to conflict specialist Afzalur Rahim's model, five different conflict-handling styles can be plotted on a 2 × 2 grid. High to low concern for *self* is found on the horizontal axis of the grid,

Figure 13–4   *Five Conflict-Handling Styles*

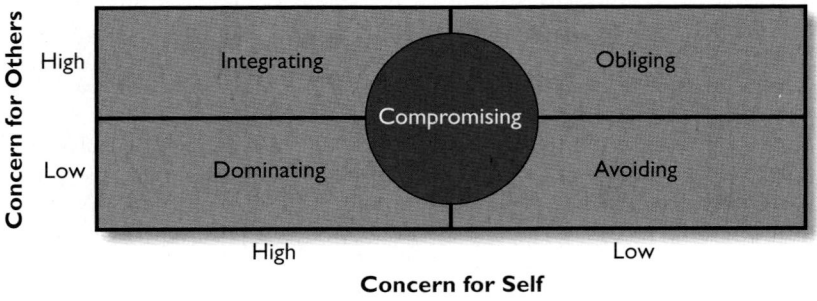

SOURCE: M A Rahim, "A Strategy for Managing Conflict in Complex Organizations," *Human Relations,* January 1985, p 84. Reprinted by permission of Sage Publications Ltd, Copyright (© The Tavistock Institute, 1985).

while low to high concern for *others* forms the vertical axis (see Figure 13–4). Various combinations of these variables produce the five different conflict-handling styles: integrating, obliging, dominating, avoiding, and compromising.[52] There is no single best style; each has strengths and limitations and is subject to situational constraints.

Integrating (Problem Solving) In this style, interested parties confront the issue and cooperatively identify the problem, generate and weigh alternative solutions, and select a solution. Integrating is appropriate for complex issues plagued by misunderstanding. However, it is inappropriate for resolving conflicts rooted in opposing value systems. Its primary strength is its longer lasting impact because it deals with the underlying problem rather than merely with symptoms. The primary weakness of this style is that it is very time consuming.

Obliging (Smoothing) "An obliging person neglects his or her own concern to satisfy the concern of the other party."[53] This style, often called *smoothing,* involves playing down differences while emphasizing commonalities. Obliging may be an appropriate conflict-handling strategy when it is possible to eventually get something in return. But it is inappropriate for complex or worsening problems. Its primary strength is that it encourages cooperation. Its main weakness is that it's a temporary fix that fails to confront the underlying problem.

Dominating (Forcing) High concern for self and low concern for others encourages "I win, you lose" tactics. The other party's needs are largely ignored. This style is often called *forcing* because it relies on formal authority to force compliance. Dominating is appropriate when an unpopular solution must be implemented, the issue is minor, a deadline is near, or a crisis looms. It can be awkward in an open and participative climate. Speed is its primary strength. The primary weakness of this domineering style is that it often breeds resentment. Interestingly, the National Center for Women and Policing cites this particular conflict-handling style as a reason for hiring more women.

> Women are 12.7% of the personnel in large police departments but account for 2% of excessive-force cases that are upheld. … the findings support their contention that women's negotiating and communication skills should prompt police departments to hire more women.[54]

Avoiding This tactic may involve either passive withdrawal from the problem or active suppression of the issue. Avoidance is appropriate for trivial issues or when the costs of confrontation outweigh the benefits of resolving the conflict. It is inappropriate for difficult and worsening problems. The main strength of this style is that it buys time in unfolding or ambiguous situations. The primary weakness is that the tactic provides a temporary fix that sidesteps the underlying problem.

Compromising This is a give-and-take approach involving moderate concern for both self and others. Compromise is appropriate when parties have opposite goals or possess equal power. But compromise is inappropriate when overuse would lead to inconclusive action (e.g., failure to meet important deadlines). The primary strength of this tactic is that it has no disgruntled losers, but it's a temporary fix that can stifle creative problem solving.[55]

go to the Web for the Group Exercise: Bangkok Blowup—A Role-Playing Exercise

 Third-Party Interventions

In a perfect world, people would creatively avoid conflict and handle actual conflicts directly and positively. Dream on! Organizational politics being what they are, we can find ourselves as unwilling (and often unready) third parties to someone else's conflict. Thus, a working knowledge of conflict triangles and alternative dispute resolution techniques, the focus of this section, is essential to effective management today.

Conflict Triangles Remember Annie, the Amazon.com manager at the start of this chapter? Her busy day was interrupted by her co-worker Laura's tale of a conflict situation. Laura was recruiting Annie to help settle the situation. This is a classic conflict triangle. A **conflict triangle** "occurs when two people are having a problem and, instead of addressing the problem directly with each other, one of them gets a third person involved."[56] As discussed under the heading of organizational politics, in Chapter 15, employees tend to form political *coalitions* because there is power in numbers. In Annie's case, Laura was engaged in a not-so-subtle attempt to gang up against her adversary, Hans. Moreover, Laura was using Annie to vent her pent-up frustrations. This is a common and often very disruptive situation in today's organizations. The question is, What to do?

> **Conflict triangle**
> Conflicting parties involve a third person rather than dealing directly with each other.

Those finding themselves in conflict triangles have a wide range of options, according to experts on the subject. Figure 13–5 shows how responses can promote either functional or dysfunctional conflict. Preferred options 1 and 2, called *detriangling,* involve the third party channeling the disputants' energy in a direct and positive manner, toward each other. Importantly, the third party avoids becoming part of a political coalition in options 1 and 2. Options 3 through 8 can be a slippery slope toward further counterproductive triangling. Also, political and ethical implications multiply as the third party progresses to option 3 and beyond.

Alternative Dispute Resolution (ADR) Disputes between employees, between employees and their employer, and between companies too often end up

Figure 13–5   *Third-Party Intervention Options for Handling Conflict Triangles*

Detriangling
(least political; low
risk of dysfunctional
conflict)

1. Reroute complaints by coaching the sender to find ways to constructively bring up the matter with the receiver. Do not carry messages for the sender.
2. Facilitate a meeting with the sender and receiver to coach them to speak directly and constructively with each other.
3. Transmit verbatim messages with the sender's name included and coach the receiver on constructive ways to discuss the message with the sender.
4. Carry the message verbatim but protect the sender's name.
5. Soften the message to protect the sender.

More triangling
(most political; high
risk of dysfunctional
conflict)

6. Add your spin to the message to protect the sender.
7. Do nothing. The participants will triangle in someone else.
8. Do nothing and spread the gossip. You will triangle in others.

SOURCE: List of options excerpted from P Ruzich, "Triangles: Tools for Untangling Interpersonal Messes," *HR Magazine,* July 1999, p 134.

in lengthy and costly court battles. For example, while discussing the steady rise in wrongful termination lawsuits, *BusinessWeek* recently cited these figures: "A company can easily spend $100,000 to get a meritless lawsuit tossed out before trial. And if a case goes to a jury, the fees skyrocket to $300,000, and often much higher."[57] A more constructive, less expensive approach called *alternative dispute resolution* has enjoyed enthusiastic growth in recent years.[58] In fact, the widely imitated People's Court–type television shows operating outside the formal judicial system are part of this trend toward what one writer calls "do-it-yourself justice."[59] **Alternative dispute resolution** (ADR), according to a pair of Canadian labor lawyers, "uses faster, more user-friendly methods of dispute resolution, instead of traditional, adversarial approaches (such as unilateral decision making or litigation)."[60] The following ADR techniques represent a progression of steps third parties can take to resolve organizational conflicts.[61] They are ranked from easiest and least expensive to most difficult and costly. A growing number of organizations have formal ADR policies involving an established sequence of various combinations of these techniques:

Alternative dispute resolution

Avoiding costly lawsuits by resolving conflicts informally or through mediation or arbitration.

- *Facilitation.* A third party, usually a manager, informally urges disputing parties to deal directly with each other in a positive and constructive manner. This can be a form of detriangling, as discussed earlier.

- *Conciliation.* A neutral third party informally acts as a communication conduit between disputing parties. This is appropriate when conflicting parties refuse to meet face to face. The immediate goal is to establish direct communication, with the broader aim of finding common ground and a constructive solution.

- *Peer review.* A panel of trustworthy co-workers, selected for their ability to remain objective, hears both sides of a dispute in an informal and confidential meeting. Any decision by the review panel may or may not be binding, depending on the company's ADR policy. Membership on the peer review panel often is rotated among employees.

- *Ombudsman.* Someone who works for the organization, and is widely respected and trusted by his or her co-workers, hears grievances on a confidential basis and attempts to arrange a solution. This approach, more common in Europe than North America, permits someone to get help from above without relying on the formal hierarchy chain.

- *Mediation.* "The mediator—a trained, third-party neutral—actively guides the disputing parties in exploring innovative solutions to the conflict. Although some companies have in-house mediators who have received ADR training, most also use external mediators who have no ties to the company."[62] Unlike an arbitrator, a mediator does *not* render a decision. It is up to the disputants to reach a mutually acceptable decision.

- *Arbitration.* Disputing parties agree ahead of time to accept the decision of a neutral arbitrator in a formal courtlike setting, often complete with evidence and witnesses. Participation in this form of ADR can be voluntary or mandatory, depending upon company policy or union contracts.[63] Statements are confidential. Decisions are based on legal merits. Trained arbitrators, typically from outside agencies such as the American Arbitration Association, are versed in relevant laws and case precedents.[64]

Practical Lessons from Conflict Research

Laboratory studies, relying on college students as subjects, uncovered the following insights about organizational conflict:

- People with a high need for affiliation tended to rely on a smoothing (obliging) style while avoiding a forcing (dominating) style.[65] Thus, personality traits affect how people handle conflict.

- Disagreement expressed in an arrogant and demeaning manner produced significantly more negative effects than the same sort of disagreement expressed in a reasonable manner.[66] In other words, *how* you disagree with someone is very important in conflict situations.

- Threats and punishment, by one party in a disagreement, tended to produce intensifying threats and punishment from the other party.[67] In short, aggression breeds aggression.

- As conflict increased, group satisfaction decreased. An integrative style of handling conflict led to higher group satisfaction than did an avoidance style.[68]

- Companies with mandatory or binding arbitration policies were viewed *less* favorably than companies without such policies.[69] Apparently, mandatory or binding arbitration policies are a turn-off for job applicants who dislike the idea of being forced to do something.

Field studies involving managers and real organizations have given us the following insights:

- Both intradepartmental and interdepartmental conflict decreased as goal difficulty and goal clarity increased. Thus, challenging and clear goals can defuse conflict.

- Higher levels of conflict tended to erode job satisfaction and internal work motivation.[70]

- Men and women at the same managerial level tended to handle conflict similarly. In short, there was no gender effect.[71]

- Conflict tended to move around the organization in a case study of a public school system.[72] Thus, managers need to be alerted to the fact that conflict often originates in one area or level and becomes evident somewhere else. Conflict needs to be traced back to its source if there is to be lasting improvement.

- Samples of Japanese, German, and American managers who were presented with the same conflict scenario preferred different resolution techniques. Japanese and German managers did not share the Americans' enthusiasm for integrating the interests of all parties. The Japanese tended to look upward to management for direction, whereas the Germans were more bound by rules and regulations. In cross-cultural conflict resolution, there is no one best approach. Culture-specific preferences need to be taken into consideration prior to beginning the conflict resolution process.[73]

As we transition from conflict to negotiation, take a short break from your reading and reflect on how you can better handle conflict in your daily life. Think win–win.

go to the Web for the Self-Exercise: The Conflict Iceberg

Negotiation

Negotiation
Give-and-take process between conflicting interdependent parties.

Formally defined, **negotiation** is a give-and-take decision-making process involving interdependent parties with different preferences.[74] Common examples include labor–management negotiations over wages, hours, and working conditions and negotiations between supply chain specialists and vendors involving price, delivery schedules, and credit terms. Self-managed work teams with overlapping task boundaries also need to rely on negotiated agreements. Negotiating skills are more important today than ever.[75] In fact, in a recent survey of 625 small business owners, 30% said they needed to develop their negotiation skills.[76]

"Never, EVER purr during the negotiating process, Derwood!"

Copyright Scott Arthur Masear. Reprinted with permission.

Two Basic Types of Negotiation

Negotiation experts distinguish between two types of negotiation—*distributive* and *integrative*. Understanding the difference requires a change in traditional fixed-pie thinking:

A *distributive* negotiation usually involves a single issue—a "fixed-pie"—in which one person gains at the expense of the other. For example, haggling over the price of a rug in a bazaar is a distributive negotiation. In most conflicts, however, more than one issue is at stake, and each party values the issues differently. The outcomes available are no longer a fixed-pie divided among all parties. An agreement can be found that is better for both parties than what they would have reached through distributive negotiation. This is an *integrative* negotiation.

Debra Lee, CEO of BET Networks, Doesn't Like to Burn Her Bridges

In my negotiations with business partners, I always maintain good relations whether the deal is successful or turns sour. You never know who you will be dealing with next or even who you may report to next. Philippe Dauman, who is now CEO of Viacom and to whom I report, once was a board member with me on a now defunct company. We had a terrific relationship, but who knew that several years later he would be my boss.

How often do you observe people doing just the opposite, and hurting themselves in the process?

SOURCE: Excerpted from C Hawn, S Hamner, and E Schonfeld, "How to Succeed in 2007," *Business 2.0*, December 2006, p 96.

However, parties in a negotiation often don't find these beneficial trade-offs because each *assumes* its interests *directly* conflict with those of the other party. "What is good for the other side must be bad for us" is a common and unfortunate perspective that most people have. This is the mind-set we call the *mythical* "fixed-pie."[77]

Distributive negotiation involves traditional win–lose thinking. Integrative negotiation calls for a progressive win–win strategy.[78] (see Real World/Real People). In a laboratory study of joint venture negotiations, teams trained in integrative tactics achieved better outcomes for *both* sides than did untrained teams.[79] North American negotiators generally are too short-term oriented and poor relationship builders when negotiating in Asia, Latin America, and the Middle East.[80] The added-value negotiation technique illustrated in Figure 13–6 is an integrative approach that can correct these shortcomings.

Ethical Pitfalls in Negotiation

The success of integrative negotiation, such as added-value negotiation, hinges to a large extent on the *quality* of information exchanged, as researchers have documented.[81] Telling lies, hiding key facts, and engaging in the other potentially unethical tactics listed in Table 13–3 erode trust and goodwill, both vital in win–win negotiations.[82] An awareness of these dirty tricks can keep good faith bargainers from being unfairly exploited.[83] Unethical negotiating tactics need to be factored into organizational codes of ethics.

Figure 13–6   *An Integrative Approach: Added-Value Negotiation*

Separately	Jointly
Step 1: Clarify interests	
• Identify tangible and intangible needs	• Discuss respective needs • Find *common ground* for negotiation
Step 2: Identify options	
• Identify *elements of value* (e.g., property, money, behavior, rights, risks)	• Create a *marketplace of value* by discussing respective elements of value
Step 3: Design alternative deal packages	
• Mix and match *elements of value* in various workable combinations • Think in terms of *multiple deals*	• Exchange *deal packages*
Step 4: Select a deal	
• Analyze deal packages proposed by other party	• Discuss and select from feasible deal packages • Think in terms of *creative agreement*
Step 5: Perfect the deal	
	• Discuss unresolved issues • Develop written agreement • *Build relationships* for future negotiations

SOURCE: Adapted from K Albrecht and S Albrecht, "Added Value Negotiating," *Training*, April 1993, pp 26–29. Used by permission of VNU Business Publications via The Copyright Clearance Center.

Practical Lessons from Negotiation Research

Laboratory and field studies have yielded these insights:

- Negotiators with fixed-pie expectations produced poor joint outcomes because they restricted and mismanaged information.[84]

- A meta-analysis of 62 studies found a *slight* tendency for women to negotiate more cooperatively than men. But when faced with a tit-for-tat bargaining strategy (equivalent countermoves), women were significantly more competitive than men.[85]

- Personality characteristics can affect negotiating success. Negotiators who scored high on the Big Five personality dimensions of extraversion and agreeableness (refer back to Table 5–2) tended to do poorly with distributive (fixed-pie; win–lose) negotiations.[86]

- Good and bad moods can have positive and negative effects, respectively, on negotiators' plans and outcomes.[87] So wait until both you and your boss are in a good mood before you ask for a raise.

Table 13–3   *Questionable/Unethical Tactics in Negotiation*

TACTIC	DESCRIPTION/CLARIFICATION/RANGE
Lies	Subject matter for lies can include limits, alternatives, the negotiator's intent, authority to bargain, other commitments, acceptability of the opponent's offers, time pressures, and available resources.
Puffery	Among the items that can be puffed up are the value of one's payoffs to the opponent, the negotiator's own alternatives, the costs of what one is giving up or is prepared to yield, importance of issues, and attributes of the products or services.
Deception	Acts and statements may include promises or threats, excessive initial demands, careless misstatements of facts, or asking for concessions not wanted.
Weakening the opponent	The negotiator here may cut off or eliminate some of the opponent's alternatives, blame the opponent for his own actions, use personally abrasive statements to or about the opponent, or undermine the opponent's alliances.
Strengthening one's own position	This tactic includes building one's own resources, including expertise, finances, and alliances. It also includes presentations of persuasive rationales to the opponent or third parties (e.g., the public, the media) or getting mandates for one's position.
Nondisclosure	Includes partial disclosure of facts, failure to disclose a hidden fact, failure to correct the opponents' misperceptions or ignorance, and concealment of the negotiator's own position or circumstances.
Information exploitation	Information provided by the opponent can be used to exploit his weaknesses, close off his alternatives, generate demands against him, or weaken his alliances.
Change of mind	Includes accepting offers one had claimed one would not accept, changing demands, withdrawing promised offers, and making threats one promised would not be made. Also includes the failure to behave as predicted.
Distraction	These acts or statements can be as simple as providing excessive information to the opponent, asking many questions, evading questions, or burying the issue. Or they can be more complex, such as feigning weakness in one area so that the opponent concentrates on it and ignores another.
Maximization	Includes demanding the opponent make concessions that result in the negotiator's gain and the opponent's equal or greater loss. Also entails converting a win–win situation into win–lose.

SOURCE: Reprinted from H J Reitz, J A Wall Jr, and M S Love, "Ethics in Negotiation: Oil and Water or Good Lubrication?" *Business Horizons*, May–June 1998, p 6. © 1998, with permission from Elsevier.

- Subjects in a recent study trained in goal setting and problem solving enjoyed more satisfying and optimistic dialogues on a controversial subject than did those with no particular strategy.[88] Practical implication: don't negotiate without being adequately prepared.
- Studies of negotiations between Japanese, between Americans, and between Japanese and Americans found less productive joint outcomes across cultures

than within cultures.[89] Less understanding of the other party makes cross-cultural negotiation more difficult than negotiations at home.

Conflict Management and Negotiation: A Contingency Approach

Three realities dictate how organizational conflict should be managed. First, various types of conflict are inevitable because they are triggered by a wide variety of antecedents. Second, too little conflict may be as counterproductive as too much. Third, there is no single best way of avoiding or resolving conflict. Consequently, conflict specialists recommend a contingency approach to managing conflict. Antecedents of conflict and actual conflict need to be monitored. If signs of too little conflict such as apathy or lack of creativity appear, then functional conflict needs to be stimulated. This can be done by nurturing appropriate antecedents of conflict or programming conflict with techniques such as devil's advocacy and the dialectic method. On the other hand, when conflict becomes dysfunctional, the appropriate conflict-handling style needs to be used. Realistic training involving role playing can prepare managers to try alternative conflict-handling styles.

Third-party interventions are necessary when conflicting parties are unwilling or unable to engage in conflict resolution or integrative negotiation. Integrative or added-value negotiation is most appropriate for intergroup and interorganizational conflict. The key is to get the conflicting parties to abandon traditional fixed-pie thinking and their win–lose expectations.

Managers can keep from getting too deeply embroiled in conflict by applying four lessons from recent research: (1) establish challenging and clear goals, (2) disagree in a constructive and reasonable manner, (3) do not get caught up in conflict triangles, and (4) refuse to get caught in the aggression-breeds-aggression spiral.

Summary of Key Concepts

1. *Define the term* conflict, *and put the three metaphors of conflict into proper perspective for the workplace.* Conflict is a process in which one party perceives that its interests are being opposed or negatively affected by another party. Conflict is inevitable but not necessarily destructive. Metaphorically, conflict can be viewed as war (win at all costs), an opportunity (be creative, grow, and improve), or a journey (a search for common ground and a better way). Within organizations, we are challenged to see conflicts as win–win opportunities and journeys rather than as win–lose wars.

2. *Distinguish between functional and dysfunctional conflict, and discuss why people avoid conflict.* Functional conflict enhances organizational interests while dysfunctional conflict is counterproductive. Three desired conflict outcomes are agreement, stronger relationships, and learning. People avoid conflict because of the following fears:

harm; rejection; loss of relationship; anger; being seen as selfish; saying the wrong thing; failing; hurting someone else; getting what we want; and intimacy.

3. *List six antecedents of conflict, and identify the desired outcomes of conflict.* Among the many antecedents of conflict are incompatible personalities or value systems; competition for limited resources; inadequate communication; unreasonable or unclear policies, standards, or rules; unreasonable deadlines or extreme time pressure; collective decision making; unmet expectations; and unresolved or suppressed conflicts. The three desired outcomes of conflict are agreement, stronger relationships, and learning.

4. *Define* personality conflicts, *and explain how managers should handle them.* Personality conflicts involve interpersonal opposition based on personal dislike or disagreement (or as an outgrowth of workplace incivility).

Care needs to be taken with personality conflicts in the workplace because of the legal implications of diversity, antidiscrimination, and sexual harassment. Managers should investigate and document personality conflict, take corrective actions such as feedback or behavior modification if appropriate, or attempt informal dispute resolution. Difficult or persistent personality conflicts need to be referred to human resource specialists or counselors.

5. *Discuss the role of in-group thinking in intergroup conflict, and explain what management can do about intergroup conflict.* Members of in-groups tend to see themselves as unique individuals who are more moral than outsiders, whom they view as a threat and stereotypically as all alike. In-group thinking is associated with ethnocentric behavior. According to the updated contact model, managers first must strive to eliminate negative relationships between conflicting groups. Beyond that, they need to provide team building, encourage personal friendships across groups, foster positive attitudes about other groups, and minimize negative gossip about groups.

6. *Discuss what can be done about cross-cultural conflict.* International consultants can prepare people from different cultures to work effectively together. Cross-cultural conflict can be minimized by having expatriates build strong cross-cultural relationships with their hosts (primarily by being good listeners, being sensitive to others, and being more cooperative than competitive).

7. *Explain how managers can stimulate functional conflict, and identify the five conflict-handling styles.* There are many antecedents of conflict—including incompatible person-

alities, competition for limited resources, and unrealized expectations—that need to be monitored. Functional conflict can be stimulated by permitting antecedents of conflict to persist or programming conflict during decision making with devil's advocates or the dialectic method. The five conflict-handling styles are integrating (problem solving), obliging (smoothing), dominating (forcing), avoiding, and compromising. There is no single best style.

8. *Explain the nature and practical significance of conflict triangles and alternative dispute resolution for third-party conflict intervention.* A conflict triangle occurs when one member of a conflict seeks the help of a third party rather than facing the opponent directly. Detriangling is advised, whereby the third-party redirects the disputants' energy toward each other in a positive and constructive manner. Alternative dispute resolution involves avoiding costly court battles with more informal and user-friendly techniques such as facilitation, conciliation, peer review, ombudsman, mediation, and arbitration.

9. *Explain the difference between distributive and integrative negotiation, and discuss the concept of added-value negotiation.* Distributive negotiation involves fixed-pie and win–lose thinking. Integrative negotiation is a win–win approach to better results for both parties. The five steps in added-value negotiation are as follows: step 1, clarify interests; step 2, identify options; step 3, design alternative deal packages; step 4, select a deal; and step 5, perfect the deal. Elements of value, multiple deal packages, and creative agreement are central to this approach.

Key Terms

OB in Action Case Study

Soaring Where Boeing Struggled[90]
(Who Says Union-Management Cooperation Can't Work?)

For union workers, a new corporate owner usually means one thing: mass layoffs. So it comes as quite a surprise that, after buying Boeing Co.'s Wichita aircraft plant, the Toronto private investment firm Onex Corp. kept on most of the 4,000 employees.

Of course, the Machinists union wasn't happy that more than 800 people lost their jobs. But the new owners helped ease the pain by giving the remaining workers $246 million in cash and stock options. The money was a reward for helping the company, now named Spirit AeroSystems, cut costs and pull off a successful initial public offering [by selling stock to the public]. "I can't tell you what a thrill it is to give our organized workforce nearly $250 million," says Seth M Mersky, an Onex managing director.

The comity between Spirit management and the International Association of Machinist & Aerospace Workers is partly a sign of the times. The commercial plane business is booming, which is why Spirit expects to post a 2007 profit of $260 million on projected revenues of $4.1 billion, up from about $3.2 billion in 2006. That won't last forever. But for now the unusual deal is being widely praised as a promising new labor model. No one is more bullish than the man who helped put it all together, former Democratic House Minority Leader Richard A Gephardt of Missouri. "It is what we are going to have to do in a lot of our industries to be globally competitive," says Gephardt, who is a consultant with Goldman, Sachs & Co. "It aligns [workers] with the company and gives them a fair reward for their contribution."

This improbable story began several years ago, when Boeing, in a bid to shed weak assets and outsource more of its manufacturing work, decided to sell its uncompetitive Wichita plant. Although it was Boeing's biggest internal supplier, cranking out fuselages and nose cones, it suffered from inflexible work rules, high wages, and testy labor relations.

Enter Mersky and fellow Onex Managing Director Nigel S Wright. Where Boeing executives saw lemons, the two turnaround specialists saw lemonade. They reasoned that if they could cut costs, make the plant more productive, and start working for Airbus, defense contractors, and regional jetmakers, the Wichita plant could become profitable.

But first Onex had to get costs under control. The firm saved $40 million annually by slashing corporate overhead costs inherited from Boeing. It negotiated price reductions from Spirit's suppliers and simplified the procurement process. It managed to reduce the complexity of work rules, reducing 160 job classifications to 13. Finally, it asked the unions for a 10% wage cut to better reflect the prevailing wages in the area and told them it would reduce the workforce by 15%. ...

Onex, which sought the union's support, lost the first vote with the Machinists. Many workers came from third- and fourth-generation Boeing families and wanted to stay with the giant. "It was tough on people," said Ron Eldridge, the Machinists' aerospace coordinator for Wichita. "It was like an ugly divorce." The managing directors approached R Thomas Buffenbarger, international president of the union. "They asked: 'What's it going to take?'" Buffenbarger recalls. "I said, 'If you want to share some of the pain, then give us a stake in the enterprise.' They warmed to it quickly."

A new deal was negotiated: For the wage and job cuts, Onex offered union members a 10% equity stake in an eventual IPO. The new owners sketched out a scenario where workers could earn some $30,000 in stock and cash over five years as long as the IPO was successful.

Now, 18 months later, the bargain has exceeded everyone's wildest dreams. An IPO on Nov. 21 raised $1.4 billion. Each Machinist is about to receive $61,440 in cash and stock. Given Boeing's backlog of orders, plus a surge of defense-related spending, analysts figure Spirit's stock will do well in the next few years. That should buy the company goodwill for when the industry hits the skids.

Questions for Discussion

1. Which conflict metaphor is evident in this case? Explain.
2. Which antecedents of conflict were problematic at the new Spirit AeroSystems? How were they handled?
3. Is the unusual degree of union-management cooperation in this case a result of good conflict management and negotiation, a healthy economy and good profits, or all of these factors working together? Explain.
4. What can both managers and union leaders in other industries learn about conflict management from this case? Explain.
5. In terms of the added-value negotiation model in Figure 13–6, what were the key "deal packages" in this case?

Break It Up!

At the company where I work—we make creative products for children—two of the top executives are at war with each other. They go off on rants, they use foul language, and from time to time they actually have shoving matches. Both of these men are top producers, I might add. What lies behind this behavior? And is there anything co-workers can do? We're appalled, but the boss won't step in.[91]

What Is the Right Thing to Do in This Situation? (What Are the Ethical Implications for Your Choice?)

1. These guys are simply high-spirited thoroughbreds who kick up some dust while helping us win the race. Just stay out of their way.

2. The good results these men get are more than offset by the negative impact their feud has on company productivity and morale. A coalition of employees needs to confront the boss with the facts and recommend corrective action.

3. In this obvious clash of personalities, one of these bullies must be fired. Or should the company fire both?

4. The boss is clueless, so someone needs to elevate the issue to the board of directors.

5. A brave co-worker who has the respect of these feuding men needs to take them aside for a little talk about workplace civility, to break the cycle of dysfunctional conflict. This would be a win–win option, where everyone could save face and upper management wouldn't be dragged into the fray.

6. Let's take sides in this feud and fight it out until there's a clear winner and loser.

7. Invent other options. Discuss.

Web Resources

For study material and exercises that apply to this chapter, visit our Web site, www.mhhe.com/kreitner

Part 4

Organizational Processes

CHAPTER | 4

Communication in the Internet Age

When you finish studying the material in this chapter, you should be able to:

1   Describe the perceptual process model of communication.

2   Describe the barriers to effective communication.

3   Contrast the communication styles of assertiveness, aggressiveness, and nonassertiveness.

4   Discuss the primary sources of nonverbal communication.

5   Review the five dominant listening styles and 10 keys to effective listening.

6   Describe the communication differences between men and women, and explain the source of these differences.

7   Discuss the formal and informal communication channels.

8   Explain the contingency approach to media selection.

9   Review the benefits and drawbacks of e-mail and summarize how e-mail can be more effectively managed.

10   Explain the information technology of Internet/intranet/extranet, handheld devices, blogs, videoconferencing, and group support systems, and explain the related use of teleworking.

Martin S Sorrell, CEO of advertising agency WPP Group, sues two blogging ex-colleagues for a Web hate campaign in which, he says, they smeared him and his former lover. *The Washington Post* grapples with a surge in online comments that read like the racist garbage on neo-Nazi Web sites. Home Depot's CEO goes into an emergency huddle with his crisis management team after 14,000 bilious customers storm an MSN comment room.

The venom of crowds isn't new. Ancient Rome was smothered in graffiti. But today the mad scrawls of everyday punters can coalesce into a sprawling, menacing mob, with its own international distribution system, zero barriers to entry, and the ability to ransack brands and reputations. No question, legitimate criticism about companies should get out. The wrinkle now is how often the threats, increasingly posted anonymously, turn savage. Even some A-list bloggers are wondering if the cranks are too often prevailing over cooler heads.

Most companies are wholly unprepared to deal with the new nastiness that's erupting online. That's worrisome as the Web moves closer to being the prime advertising medium—and reputational conduit—of our time. . . .

Trashing brands online can also be high theater. Rats cruising around a Greenwich Village KFC/Taco Bell on You Tube. MySpacers busting their employers' chops. Faux ads bashing the Chevy Tahoe as a gas-guzzling, global-warming monster. Millions of people watch this stuff—then join in and pile on. Is it any wonder companies lose control of the conversation?

When the Web turns against them, executives are faced with the problem of how to manage the blow-back. They have two choices: ignore the smaller furies and hope they won't metastasize, or respond outright to the attacks. It's rarely a good idea to lob bombs at the fire-starters. Preemption, engagement, and diplomacy are saner tools.

Companies such as Lenovo Group, Southwest Airlines, and Dell have specialists dedicated to engaging or co-opting their critics. Dell has made blogger outreach into such a discipline that the company's team, including refreshingly straight-talking blogger-in-chief Lionel Menchaca, recently sat down for drinks, nachos, and fried zucchini at an Austin (Tex.) pub with blogger Jeff Jarvis. He's the man who ignited the original Dell Hell customer-service crusade with his rants about the company. (Jarvis picked up his own tab.) "In a flash he transformed the borgish image of Dell for me," says Jarvis. That wasn't all. At Davos in January, Michael S Dell sought out Jarvis at a cocktail party and apologized to him. . . .

But what happens when the uproar grows so noisy that the mainstream media is bound to pick it up? That's exactly the position new Home Depot CEO Francis S Blake found himself in last month. MSN Money columnist Scott Burns accused Home Depot of being a "consistent abuser" of customers' time. Within hours, servers were caving under the weight of 10,000 angry e-mails and 4,000 posts, which took the company to task for pretty much everything. It was the biggest response in MSN Money's history. Blake's predecessor, Robert L Nardelli, the guy who famously didn't allow comments at the company's annual meeting, simply would have ignored the mob. But Blake knew the controversy could quickly mushroom.

Home Depot's reported poor service caused an avalache of Internet postings. CEO Francis Blake felt compelled to reply.

The only way over it, he decided, was through it. So Blake penned a heartfelt and repentant online letter to all Home Depot customers, essentially copping to the company's less-than-stellar service. He promised to increase staffing and begged for the chance to make good. He created a site to deal specifically with service. He thanked Scott Burns.

In crisis-management circles, the gamble was viewed as a win.[1]

FOR DISCUSSION

Are bloggers creating more harm than good for organizations?

In his best-selling book *The World Is Flat,* Thomas L Friedman concluded that information technology is transforming and connecting people's lives around the world. The chapter-opening vignette reinforces that claim. It shows how the Internet is being used to instantaneously communicate all types of information to anyone with access to a computer. Unfortunately, this information may be accurate or inaccurate. It thus is important for all of us to understand how information technology is affecting the way individuals communicate and how this technology influences organizational behavior as a whole. The final section of this chapter is devoted to examining these issues.

More broadly, the study of communication is important because every managerial function and activity involves some form of direct or indirect communication. Whether planning and organizing or directing and leading, managers find themselves communicating with and through others. This implies that everyone's communication skills affect both personal and organizational effectiveness.[2] For example, one study found that 70% of "preventable hospital mishaps" resulted from a lack of communication between employees, particularly during handoffs of patient care.[3] Another polling of 336 organizations revealed that 66% of the respondents did not know or understand their organization's mission and business strategy, which subsequently led them to feel disengaged at work. This apparent lack of communication is a problem because employee disengagement is associated with lower productivity and product quality, and higher labor costs and turnover.[4]

This chapter will help you to better understand how managers can both improve their communication skills and design more effective communication programs. We discuss (1) basic dimensions of the communication process, focusing on a perceptual process model and barriers to effective communication; (2) interpersonal communication; (3) organizational communication; and (4) communicating in the computerized information age.

Basic Dimensions of the Communication Process

Communication

Interpersonal exchange of information and understanding.

Communication is defined as "the exchange of information between a sender and a receiver, and the inference (perception) of meaning between the individuals involved."[5] Managers who understand this process can analyze their own communication patterns as well as design communication programs that fit organizational needs. This section reviews a perceptual process model of communication and discusses the barriers to effective communication.

 # Perceptual Process Model of Communication

Historically, the communication process was described in terms of a conduit model. This model depicts communication as a pipeline in which information and meaning are transferred from person to person. Today, communication experts have criticized the conduit model for being based on unrealistic assumptions. For example, the conduit model assumes communication transfers *intended meanings* from person to person. If this assumption was true, miscommunication would not exist and there would be no need to worry about being misunderstood. We could simply say or write what we want and assume the listener or reader accurately understands our intended meaning.

    As we all know, communicating is not that simple or clear-cut. Communication is fraught with miscommunication. In recognition of this, researchers have begun to examine communication as a form of social information processing (recall the discussion in Chapter 7) in which receivers interpret messages by cognitively processing information. This view led to development of a **perceptual model of communication** that depicts communication as a process in which receivers create meaning in their own minds. Let us consider the parts of this process and then integrate them with an example.

> **Perceptual model of communication**
> Process in which receivers create their own meaning.

Sender, Message, and Receiver
The sender is the person wanting to communicate information—the message—and the receiver is the person, group, or organization for whom the message is intended.

Encoding
Communication begins when a sender encodes an idea or thought. Encoding entails translating thoughts into a code or language that can be understood by others. This forms the foundation of the message. For example, if a professor wants to communicate to you about an assignment, he or she must first think about what information he or she wants to communicate. Once the professor resolves this issue in his or her mind (encoding), he or she can select a medium with which to communicate.

Selecting a Medium
Managers can communicate through a variety of media. Potential media include face-to-face conversations, telephone calls, electronic mail, voice mail, videoconferencing, written memos or letters, photographs or drawings, meetings, bulletin boards, computer output, and charts or graphs. Choosing the appropriate media depends on many factors, including the nature of the message, its intended purpose, the type of audience, proximity to the audience, time horizon for disseminating the message, and personal preferences.

    All media have advantages and disadvantages. Face-to-face conversations, for instance, are useful for communicating about sensitive or important issues and those requiring feedback and intensive interaction.[6] Telephones are convenient, fast, and private, but lack nonverbal information. Although writing memos or letters is time consuming, it is a good medium when it is difficult to meet with the other person, when formality and a written record are important, and when face-to-face interaction is not necessary to enhance understanding. More is said later in this chapter about choosing media.

Decoding and Creating Meaning Decoding occurs when receivers receive a message. It is the process of interpreting and making sense of a message. Returning to our example of a professor communicating about an assignment, decoding would occur among students when they receive the message from the professor.

In contrast to the conduit model's assumption that meaning is directly transferred from sender to receiver, the perceptual model is based on the belief that a receiver creates the meaning of a message in his or her mind. This means that the same message can be interpreted differently by different people. Consider the following example that occurred to a reporter from *The Wall Street Journal* when he was on assignment in China.

> I was riding the elevator a few weeks ago with a Chinese colleague here in the *Journal's* Asian headquarters. I smiled and said, "Hi." She responded, "You've gained weight." I might have been appalled, but at least three other Chinese co-workers also have told me I'm fat. I probably should cut back on the pork dumplings. In China, such an intimate observation from a colleague isn't necessarily an insult. It's probably just friendliness.[7]

This example highlights that decoding and creating the meaning of a message are influenced by cultural norms and values.

Noise

Interference with the transmission and understanding of a message.

Feedback Have you ever been on your cell phone and thought that you lost your connection with the person you were talking to? If yes, something like the following probably occurred. "Hello, Joyce are you there?" "Joyce, can you hear me?" The other person may say back, "Yes, I can hear you, but your voice is fading in and out." This is an example of feedback—the receiver expresses a reaction to the sender's message.

Trying to communicate via cell phone while sitting in an outside café is likely to be affected by noise. The person's cell phone conversation can also represent noise to someone trying to have a conversation at the next table.

Noise Noise represents anything that interferes with the transmission and understanding of a message. It affects all linkages of the communication process. Noise includes factors such as a speech impairment, poor telephone connections, illegible handwriting, inaccurate statistics in a memo or report, poor hearing and eyesight, and physical distance between sender and receiver.

For example, the Real World/Real People feature on page 403 illustrates how whistling can be a serious source of noise in an office environment. Nonverbal communication, which is discussed later in this chapter, also is a source of noise, as are cross-cultural differences between senders and receivers (recall our discussion in Chapter 4).

Figure 14-1 provides an example of the communication process. Notice the sequential nature of the communication process.

Barriers to Effective Communication

There are two key components of effective communication. First, senders need to accurately communicate their intended message. It is unlikely that a receiver will understand a message if this does not occur. Second, receivers need to correspondingly perceive and interpret the message accurately. Anything that gets in the way of the accurate transmission and reception of a message is a barrier to effective communication. It is important

Whistling Is a Serious Source of Noise in an Office Environment

There's no doubt Stewart Henderson is an accomplished whistler. Most of his colleagues in the office's open bullpen would just as soon never hear him whistle again. Part of the problem is that all manner of things seem to trigger his tunes, including conversations he's involved in, incidental snippets he overhears, and the sight of colleague Anne Baxter, who sits diagonally across from him and happens to be the daughter of a minister. When he sees her, he whistles Dusty Springfield's "Son of a Preacher Man."

"We love Stewart," Ms. Baxter says. "But if you're trying to concentrate and you're under the gun, [his whistling] penetrates in an inescapable way."

Other colleagues are less restrained. "It affects me so much that I threatened to rip his lips off one day," says Polly Sinesi, who says she has also thrown small office supplies at him.

How would you stop Stewart from whistling?

SOURCE: Excerpted from J Sandberg, "Office Minstrels Drive the Rest of Us Nuts But Are Hard to Silence," *The Wall Street Journal*, February 14, 2006, p B1.

---

for you to understand these barriers so that you can be aware of their existence and try to reduce their impact when you are communicating with others.

Some barriers are actually part of the communication process itself (see Table 14–1). The communication process will fail if any step in the communication process is blocked. From a practical point of view, however, there are three types of barriers that are likely to influence communication effectiveness: (1) personal barriers, (2) physical barriers, and (3) semantic barriers.

Personal Barriers Have you ever communicated with someone and felt totally confused? This may have led you to wonder: is it them or is it me? **Personal barriers** represent any individual attributes that hinder communication. Let's examine nine common personal barriers that foster miscommunication.

Personal barriers
Any individual attribute that hinders communication.

1. *Variable skills in communicating effectively.* Some people are simply better communicators than others. They have the speaking and listening skills, the ability to use

Figure 14–1 *Communication Process in Action*

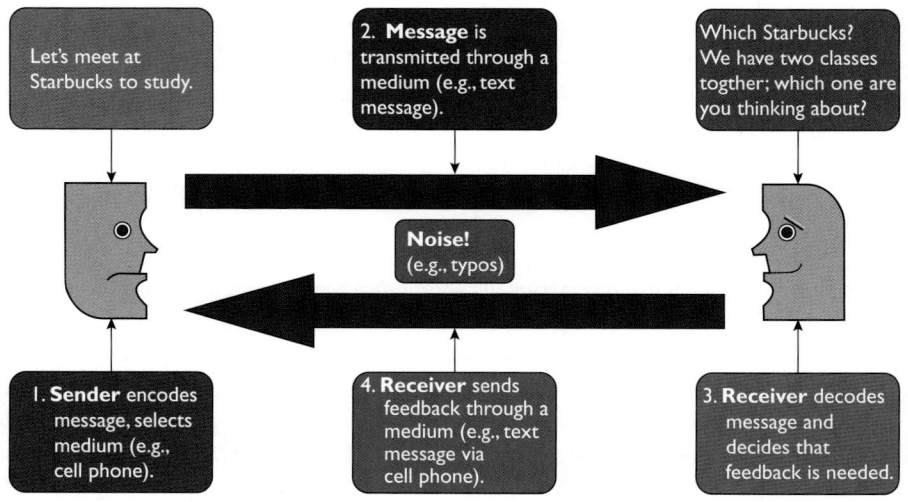

Let's meet at Starbucks to study.

2. **Message** is transmitted through a medium (e.g., text message).

Which Starbucks? We have two classes togther; which one are you thinking about?

Noise! (e.g., typos)

1. **Sender** encodes message, selects medium (e.g., cell phone).

4. **Receiver** sends feedback through a medium (e.g., text message via cell phone).

3. **Receiver** decodes message and decides that feedback is needed.

Table 14–1   *Barriers to Communication that Happen within the Communication Process*

- **Sender barrier—no message gets sent.** Have you ever had an idea but were afraid to voice it because (like Robert Suhoza) you feared criticism? Then obviously no message got sent.

  But the barrier need not be for psychological reasons. Suppose as a new manager you simply didn't realize (because you weren't told) that supervising your subordinates' expense accounts was part of your responsibility. In that case, it may be understandable why you never call them to task about fudging their expense reports—why, in other words, no message got sent.

- **Encoding barrier—the message is not expressed correctly.** No doubt you've sometimes had difficulty trying to think of the correct word to express how you feel about something. If English is not your first language, perhaps, then you may have difficulty expressing to a supervisor, co-worker, or subordinate what it is you mean to say.

- **Medium barrier—the communication channel is blocked.** You never get through to someone because his or her phone always has a busy signal. The computer network is down and the e-mail message you sent doesn't go through. These are instances of the communication medium being blocked.

- **Decoding barrier—the recipient doesn't understand the message.** Your boss tells you to "lighten up" or "buckle down," but because English is not your first language, you don't understand what the messages mean. Or perhaps you're afraid to show your ignorance when someone is throwing computer terms at you and says that your computer connection has "a bandwidth problem."

- **Receive barrier—no message gets received.** Because you were talking to a co-worker, you weren't listening when your supervisor announced today's work assignments, and so you have to ask him or her to repeat the announcement.

- **Feedback barrier—the recipient doesn't respond enough.** No doubt you've had the experience of giving someone street directions, but since they only nod their heads and don't repeat the directions back to you, you don't really know whether you were understood. The same thing can happen in many workplace circumstances.

SOURCE: A Kinicki and B Williams, *Management: A Practical Introduction*, 3rd ed. (Burr Ridge, IL: McGraw-Hill, 2008), p 493.

gestures for dramatic effect, the vocabulary to alter the message to fit the audience, the writing skills to convey concepts in simple and concise terms, and the social skills to make others feel comfortable.[8] In contrast, others lack these skills. Don't worry, communication skills can be enhanced with training.[9]

2. *Variations in how information is processed and interpreted.* Did you grow up in the country, in the suburbs, or in a city? Did you attend private or public school? What were your parents' attitudes about your doing chores and playing sports? Are you from a loving home or one marred with fighting, yelling, and lack of structure?

   Answers to these questions are relevant because they make up the different frames of references and experiences people use to interpret the world around them. As you may recall from Chapter 7, people selectively attend to various stimuli based on their unique frames of reference. This means that these differences affect our interpretations of what we see and hear.

3. *Variations in interpersonal trust.* Chapter 11 discussed the manner in which trust affects interpersonal relationships. Communication is more likely to be distorted when people do not trust each other. Rather than focusing on the message, a lack of

trust is likely to cause people to be defensive and question the accuracy of what is being communicated.

4. *Stereotypes and prejudices.* We noted in Chapter 7 that stereotypes are oversimplified beliefs about specific groups of people. They potentially distort communication because their use causes people to misperceive and recall information. It is important for all of us to be aware of our potential stereotypes and to recognize that they may subconsciously affect the interpretation of a message.

5. *Big egos.* Our egos, whether due to pride, self-esteem, superior ability, or arrogance, are a communication barrier. Egos can cause political battles, turf wars, and pursuit of power, credit, and resources. Egos influence how we treat others as well as our receptiveness to being influenced by others. Have you ever had someone put you down in public? Then you know how ego feelings can influence communication.

6. *Poor listening skills.* How many times have you been in class when one student asks the same question that was asked minutes earlier? How about going to a party and meeting someone who only talks about him or herself and never asks questions about you? This experience certainly doesn't make one feel important or memorable. It's hard to communicate effectively when one of the parties is not listening. We discuss listening skills in a later section of this chapter.

7. *Natural tendency to evaluate others' messages.* What do you say to someone after watching the latest movie in a theater? What did you think of the movie? He or she might say, "It was great, best movie I've seen all year." You then may say "I agree," or alternatively, "I disagree, that movie stunk." The point is that we all have a natural tendency, according to renowned psychologist Carl Rogers, to evaluate messages from our own point of view or frame of reference, particularly when we have strong feelings about the issue.[10]

8. *Inability to listen with understanding.* Listening with understanding occurs when a receiver can "see the expressed idea and attitude from the other person's point of view, to sense how it feels to him, to achieve his frame of reference in regard to the thing he is talking about."[11] Try to listen with understanding; it will make you less defensive and can improve your accuracy in perceiving messages.

9. *Nonverbal communication.* Communication accuracy is enhanced when one's facial expression and gestures are consistent with the intent of a message. Interestingly, people may not even be aware of this issue. More is said about this important aspect of communication later in this chapter.

Physical Barriers: Sound, Time, Space, and More
Have you ever been talking to someone on a cell phone while standing in a busy area with traffic noise and people talking next to you? You know what physical barriers are. Other such barriers include time-zone differences, telephone-line static, distance from others, and crashed computers. Office design is another physical barrier, which is why more organizations are hiring experts to design facilities that promote open interactions, yet provide space for private meetings.[12]

Semantic Barriers: When Words Matter
When your boss tells you, "We need to complete this project right away," what does it mean? Does "we" mean just you? You and your co-workers? Or you, your co-workers, and the boss? Does "right away" mean today, tomorrow, or next week? These are examples of semantic barriers. **Semantics** is the study of words.

Semantics

The study of words.

Wipro BPD Trains Employees to Reduce Semantic Barriers

In an American-culture training class at Wipro, students identify Indian stereotypes (superstitious, religious, and helpful) and American stereotypes (sports-loving, punctual, not as knowledgeable about computers as they think). The point is to identify shallow images as barriers to good communication so they can be overcome.

The class reviews cultural differences—big and small. As a "high-context" culture where what is communicated is more internalized (say, in a family), Indians can seem to be beating around the bush to Americans, who are part of a low-context culture in which communications need to be more explicit. "If you like to talk and you're dealing with a low-context person," explains the instructor, Roger George, "you might want to keep it simple and get to the point."

Will American-culture training improve customer service? Explain.

SOURCE: Excerpted from J Sandberg, "It Says Press Any Key. Where's the Any Key?" *The Wall Street Journal,* February 20, 2007, p B4.

Semantic barriers are more likely in today's multicultural workforce. Their frequency also is fueled by the growing trend to outsource customer service operations to foreign countries, particularly India. Unfortunately, some Americans are incensed over having to communicate with customer-service employees working in such call centers. Consider the message that Mitul Pandley, a specialist working in a call center located in India, received from a customer living in Mt. Pleasant, Pennsylvania. "I wish not to have anyone from India or any foreign country or anyone with an Indian accent or foreign accent continue handling my case."[13] Exchanges like this prompted Wipro BPO, Mitul's employer, to institute training programs aimed at reducing semantic barriers (see the Real World/Real People feature above).

Jargon

Language or terminology that is specific to a particular profession, group, or company.

Jargon is another key semantic barrier. **Jargon** represents language or terminology that is specific to a particular profession, group, or company. The use of jargon has been increasing as our society becomes more technologically oriented. (For example, "The CIO wants the RFP to go out ASAP" means "The Chief Information Officer wants the Request for Proposal to go out as soon as possible.") It is important to remember that words that are ordinary to you may be mysterious to outsiders. If we want to be understood more clearly, it is important to choose our language more carefully.[14]

go to the Web for the Self-Exercise: What Is Your Business Etiquette?

Interpersonal Communication

The quality of interpersonal communication within an organization is very important. People with good communication skills helped groups to make more innovative decisions and were promoted more frequently than individuals with less developed abilities.[15]

Communication competence

Ability to effectively use communication behaviors in a given context.

Although there is no universally accepted definition of **communication competence,** it is an individual's abilities to effectively use communication behaviors in a given context. Business etiquette, for example, is one component of communication competence.

While there are a host of communication abilities that influence communication competence, we focus on five that are under your control: assertiveness, aggressiveness, nonassertiveness, nonverbal communication, and active listening. We conclude this section by discussing gender differences in communication.

Table 14–2 *Communication Styles*

COMMUNICATION STYLE	DESCRIPTION	NONVERBAL BEHAVIOR PATTERN	VERBAL BEHAVIOR PATTERN
Assertive	Pushing hard without attacking; permits others to influence outcome; expressive and self-enhancing without intruding on others	Good eye contact Comfortable but firm posture Strong, steady, and audible voice Facial expressions matched to message Appropriately serious tone Selective interruptions to ensure understanding	Direct and unambiguous language No attributions or evaluations of other's behavior Use of "I" statements and cooperative "we" statements
Aggressive	Taking advantage of others; expressive and self-enhancing at other's expense	Glaring eye contact Moving or leaning too close Threatening gestures (pointed finger; clenched fist) Loud voice Frequent interruptions	Swear words and abusive language Attributions and evaluations of other's behavior Sexist or racist terms Explicit threats or put-downs
Nonassertive	Encouraging others to take advantage of us; inhibited; self-denying	Little eye contact Downward glances Slumped posture Constantly shifting weight Wringing hands Weak or whiny voice	Qualifiers ("maybe"; "kind of") Fillers ("uh," "you know," "well") Negaters ("It's not really that important"; "I'm not sure")

SOURCE: Adapted in part from J A Waters, "Managerial Assertiveness," *Business Horizons*, September–October 1982, pp 24–29.

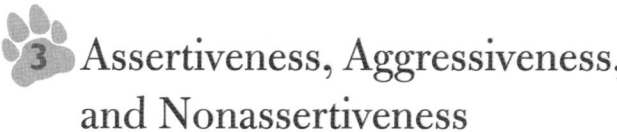 Assertiveness, Aggressiveness, and Nonassertiveness

Table 14–2 describes the styles of assertiveness, aggressiveness, and nonassertiveness and identifies the nonverbal and verbal behavior patterns associated with each one. In general, you can improve your communication competence by trying to be more assertive and less aggressive or nonassertive. Let's apply this recommendation in the context of saying no to someone.

We all get asked to do things that we really don't want to do. For example, you may have been asked by a friend to share a homework assignment so that your friend doesn't have to do the work or to purchase products you don't need. The communication goal in these cases is to say no in an assertive manner. Below are several tips for saying no.

- Don't feel like you have to provide a yes or no answer on the spot. You can ask for more time to think over the request.

- Be honest, and start your response with the word *no.* It's easier to be steadfast in your commitment to saying no if you start out by saying the word up front.

- Use nonverbal assertive behaviors to reinforce your words. For example, you can shake your head from side to side while saying no and you can look into the requester's eyes as you say no; don't glare.
- Use verbal assertive behaviors. Say no with a firm, direct tone. Use "I" statements when necessary. For example, "I feel it is unfair for me to give you my homework so that you can copy it."[16]

In closing, it is okay to say *no.* Remember, the more you say yes to others, the less time you have to yourself. Saying yes when you want to say no can lead to guilt, anger, resentment, and potentially failure.

go to the Web for the Group Exercise: Practicing Different Styles of Communication

4 Sources of Nonverbal Communication

Nonverbal communication

Messages sent outside of the written or spoken word.

Nonverbal communication is "Any message, sent or received independent of the written or spoken word . . . [It] includes such factors as use of time and space, distance between persons when conversing, use of color, dress, walking behavior, standing, positioning, seating arrangement, office locations and furnishing."[17]

Communication experts estimate that 65% of every conversation is partially interpreted through nonverbal communication.[18] It thus is important to ensure that your nonverbal signals are consistent with your intended verbal messages. Inconsistencies create noise and promote miscommunications.[19] Because of the prevalence of nonverbal communication and its significant impact on organizational behavior (including, but not limited to, perceptions of others, hiring decisions, work attitudes, and turnover), it is important that managers become consciously aware of the sources of nonverbal communication.

Body Movements and Gestures Body movements, such as leaning forward or backward, and gestures, such as pointing, provide additional nonverbal information that can either enhance or detract from the communication process. Open body positions such as leaning forward, communicate *immediacy,* a term used to represent openness, warmth, closeness, and availability for communication. *Defensiveness* is communicated by gestures such as folding arms, crossing hands, and crossing one's legs. Judith Hall, a communication researcher, conducted a meta-analysis of gender differences in body movements and gestures. Results revealed that women nodded their heads and moved their hands more than men. Leaning forward, large body shifts, and foot and leg movements were exhibited more frequently by men than women.[20] Although it is both easy and fun to interpret body movements and gestures, it is important to remember that body-language analysis is subjective, easily misinterpreted, and highly dependent on the context and cross-cultural differences. Thus, managers need to be careful when trying to interpret body movements. Inaccurate interpretations can create additional noise in the communication process.

Touch Touching is another powerful nonverbal cue. People tend to touch those they like. A meta-analysis of gender differences in touching indicated that women do more touching during conversations than men.[21] Of particular note, however, is the fact that

Advertisers Are Studying Facial Expressions

One frontier lies in tracking facial expressions without costly and cumbersome equipment. Advertisers, for example, would like to have the ability to read the changing expressions on their customers' faces as they browse Web sites—or shop at the corner store. In August 2006, Google Inc. acquired a small company called Neven Vision for an estimated $40 million. The startup has several patents on algorithms for tracking movements of key points on the face—the corner of the eye, the curves of the mouth—using a webcam, a mobile phone, or security cameras in bank machines and convenience stores. Google hasn't yet announced plans to create products based on these patents. But researchers at Stanford University have already come up with systems that can read such signs to tell whether a person is interested, happy, or annoyed.

Is the recording or our facial expressions for marketing purposes without our consent a violation of our privacy? Why or why not?

SOURCE: Excerpted from A McConnon, "The Mind-Bending New World of Work," *BusinessWeek,* April 2, 2007, p 52.

---

men and women interpret touching differently. Sexual harassment claims might be reduced by keeping this perceptual difference in mind.

Moreover, norms for touching vary significantly around the world. Consider the example of two males walking across campus holding hands. In the Middle East, this behavior would be quite normal for males who are friends or have great respect for each other. In contrast, this behavior is not commonplace in the United States.

Facial Expressions Facial expressions convey a wealth of information. Smiling, for instance, typically represents warmth, happiness, or friendship, whereas frowning conveys dissatisfaction or anger. Do you think these interpretations apply to different cross-cultural groups? If you said yes, it supports the view that there is a universal recognition of emotions from facial expressions. If you said no, this indicates you believe the relationship between facial expressions and emotions varies across cultures. A summary of relevant research revealed that the association between facial expressions and emotions varies across cultures.[22] A smile, for example, does not convey the same emotion in different countries. Therefore, managers need to be careful in interpreting facial expressions among diverse groups of employees.

Do you think advertisers can use information about facial expressions to help sell products? The answer is yes based on material presented in the Real World/Real People feature above.[23]

Eye Contact Eye contact is a strong nonverbal cue that serves four functions in communication. First, eye contact regulates the flow of communication by signaling the beginning and end of conversation. There is a tendency to look away from others when beginning to speak and to look at them when done. Second, gazing (as opposed to glaring) facilitates and monitors feedback because it reflects interest and attention. Third, eye contact conveys emotion. People tend to avoid eye contact when discussing bad news or providing negative feedback. Fourth, gazing relates to the type of relationship between communicators.

As is also true for body movements, gestures, and facial expressions, norms for eye contact vary across cultures. Westerners are taught at an early age to look at their parents when spoken to. In contrast, Asians are taught to avoid eye contact with a parent or superior in order to show obedience and subservience.[24] Once again, managers should be sensitive to different orientations toward maintaining eye contact with diverse employees.

Practical Tips It is important to have good nonverbal communication skills in light of the fact that they are related to the development of positive interpersonal relationships. Communication experts offer the following advice to improve nonverbal communication skills:[25]

Positive Nonverbal Actions That Help Communication

- Maintaining appropriate eye contact.
- Occasionally using affirmative nods to indicate agreement.
- Smiling and showing interest.
- Leaning slightly toward the speaker.
- Keeping your voice low and relaxed.
- Being aware of your facial expressions.

Actions to Avoid

- Licking your lips or playing with your hair or mustache.
- Turning away from the person you are communicating with.
- Closing your eyes and displaying uninterested facial expressions such as yawning.
- Excessively moving in your chair or tapping your feet.
- Using an unpleasant tone and speaking too quickly or too slowly.
- Biting your nails, picking your teeth, and constantly adjusting your glasses.

 **5** Active Listening

Some communication experts contend that listening is the keystone communication skill for employees involved in sales, customer service, or management. In support of this conclusion, listening effectiveness was positively associated with customer satisfaction and negatively associated with employee intentions to quit. Poor communication between employees and management also was cited as a primary cause of employee discontent and turnover.[26] Listening skills are particularly important for all of us because we spend a great deal of time listening to others.

Listening

Actively decoding and interpreting verbal messages.

Listening involves much more than hearing a message. Hearing is merely the physical component of listening. **Listening** is the process of *actively* decoding and interpreting verbal messages. Listening requires cognitive attention and information processing; hearing does not. With these distinctions in mind, we examine listening styles and offer some practical advice for becoming a more effective listener.

Listening Styles Communication experts believe that people listen with a preferred listening style. While people may lean toward one dominant listening style, we tend to use a combination of two or three. There are five dominant listening styles: appreciative, empathetic, comprehensive, discerning, and evaluative.[27] Let us consider each style.

An *appreciative* listener listens in a relaxed manner, preferring to listen for pleasure, entertainment, or inspiration. He or she tends to tune out speakers who provide no amusement or humor in their communications. *Empathetic* listeners interpret messages by focusing on the emotions and body language being displayed by the speaker as well as the presentation media. They also tend to listen without judging. A *comprehensive* listener makes sense of a message by first organizing specific thoughts and actions and then integrates this information by focusing on relationships among ideas. These listeners prefer logical presentations without interruptions. *Discerning* listeners attempt to understand the main message and determine important points. They like to take notes and prefer logical presentations. Finally, *evaluative* listeners listen analytically and continually formulate arguments and challenges to what is being said. They tend to accept or reject messages based on personal beliefs, ask a lot of questions, and can become interruptive.

You can improve your listening skills by first becoming aware of the effectiveness of the different listening styles you use in various situations. This awareness can then help you to modify your style to fit a specific situation. For example, if you are listening to a presidential debate, you may want to focus on using a comprehensive and discerning style. In contrast, an evaluative style may be more appropriate if you are listening to a sales presentation.

Becoming a More Effective Listener Effective listening is a learned skill that requires effort and motivation. That's right, it takes energy and desire to really listen to others. Unfortunately, it may seem like there are no rewards for listening, but there are negative consequences when we don't. Think of a time, for example, when someone did not pay attention to you by looking at his or her watch or doing some other activity such as typing on a keyboard. How did you feel? You may have felt put down, unimportant, or offended. In turn, such feelings can erode the quality of interpersonal relationships as well as fuel job dissatisfaction, lower productivity, and poor customer service. Listening is an important skill that can be improved by avoiding the 10 habits of bad listeners while cultivating the 10 good listening habits (see Table 14–3).

In addition, a communication expert suggests that we can all improve our listening skills by adhering to the following three fundamental recommendations:[28]

- Attending closely to what's being said, not to what you want to say next.
- Allowing others to finish speaking before taking our turn.
- Repeating back what you've heard to give the speaker the opportunity to clarify the message.

go to the Web for the Self-Exercise: Assessing Your Listening Skills

 # 6 Women and Men Communicate Differently

Women and men have communicated differently since the dawn of time. These differences can create communication problems that undermine productivity and interpersonal communication. Gender-based differences in communication are partly caused by linguistic styles commonly used by women and men. Deborah Tannen, a communication expert, defines **linguistic style** as follows:

> Linguistic style refers to a person's characteristic speaking pattern. It includes such features as directness or indirectness, pacing and pausing, word choice, and the use of such elements as jokes, figures of speech, stories, questions, and apologies. In other words, linguistic style is a set of culturally learned signals by which we not only communicate what we mean but also interpret others' meaning and evaluate one another as people.[29]

Linguistic style

A person's typical speaking pattern.

Table 14-3 *The Keys to Effective Listening*

KEYS TO EFFECTIVE LISTENING	THE BAD LISTENER	THE GOOD LISTENER
1. Capitalize on thought speed	Tends to daydream	Stays with the speaker, mentally summarizes the speaker, weighs evidence, and listens between the lines
2. Listen for ideas	Listens for facts	Listens for central or overall ideas
3. Find an area of interest	Tunes out dry speakers or subjects	Listens for any useful information
4. Judge content, not delivery	Tunes out dry or monotone speakers	Assesses content by listening to entire message before making judgments
5. Hold your fire	Gets too emotional or worked up by something said by the speaker and enters into an argument	Withholds judgment until comprehension is complete
6. Work at listening	Does not expend energy on listening	Gives the speaker full attention
7. Resist distractions	Is easily distracted	Fights distractions and concentrates on the speaker
8. Hear what is said	Shuts out or denies unfavorable information	Listens to both favorable and unfavorable information
9. Challenge yourself	Resists listening to presentations of difficult subject matter	Treats complex presentations as exercise for the mind
10. Use handouts, overheads, or other visual aids	Does not take notes or pay attention to visual aids	Takes notes as required and uses visual aids to enhance understanding of the presentation

SOURCES: Derived from N Skinner, "Communication Skills," *Selling Power*, July–August 1999, pp 32–34; and G Manning, K Curtis, and S McMillen, *Building the Human Side of Work Community* (Cincinnati: Thomson Executive Press, 1996), pp 127–54.

Linguistic style not only helps explain communication differences between women and men, but it also influences our perceptions of others' confidence, competence, and abilities. Increased awareness of linguistic styles can thus improve communication accuracy and your communication competence. This section strives to increase your understanding of interpersonal communication between women and men by discussing alternative explanations for differences in linguistic styles, various communication differences between women and men, and recommendations for improving communication between the sexes.

Why Do Linguistic Styles Vary between Women and Men?

Although researchers do not completely agree on the cause of communication differences between women and men, there are two competing explanations that involve the well-worn debate between *nature* and *nurture*. Some researchers believe that interpersonal differences between women and men are due to inherited biological differences between the sexes. More specifically, this perspective, which also is called the

Darwinian perspective or *evolutionary psychology,* attributes gender differences in communication to drives, needs, and conflicts associated with reproductive strategies used by women and men. For example, proponents would say that males communicate more aggressively, interrupt others more than women, and hide their emotions because they have an inherent desire to possess features attractive to females in order to compete with other males for purposes of mate selection. Although males may not be competing for mate selection during a business meeting, evolutionary psychologists propose that men cannot turn off their biologically based determinants of behavior.[30]

In contrast, social role theory is based on the idea that females and males learn ways of speaking as children growing up. Research shows that girls learn conversational skills and habits that focus on rapport and relationships, whereas boys learn skills and habits that focus on status and hierarchies. Accordingly, women come to view communication as a network of connections in which conversations are negotiations for closeness. This orientation leads women to seek and give confirmation and support more so than men. Men, on the other hand, see conversations as negotiations in which people try to achieve and maintain the upper hand. It thus is important for males to protect themselves from others' attempts to put them down or push them around. This perspective increases a male's need to maintain independence and avoid failure.[31]

Men and women possess different communication styles. Do you think that these differences can impede brainstorming sessions like the one shown here? If yes, what can be done to overcome this type of communication roadblock?

Gender Differences in Communication Research demonstrates that women and men communicate differently in a number of ways.[32] Table 14–4 illustrates 10 different communication patterns that vary between women and men. There are two important issues to keep in mind about the trends identified in Table 14–4. First, the trends identified in the table cannot be generalized to include all women and men. Some men are less likely to boast about their achievements, and some women are less likely to share the credit. The point is that there are always exceptions to the rule. Second, your linguistic style influences perceptions about your confidence, competence, and authority. These judgments may, in turn, affect your future job assignments and subsequent promotability. Consider, for instance, linguistic styles displayed by Greg and Mindy. Greg downplays any uncertainties he has about issues and asks very few questions. He does this even when he is unsure about an issue being discussed. In contrast, Mindy is more forthright at admitting when she does not understand something, and she tends to ask a lot of questions. Some people may perceive Greg as more competent than Mindy because he displays confidence and acts as if he understands the issues being discussed.

Improving Communication between the Sexes Author Judith Tingley suggests that women and men should learn to genderflex. **Genderflex** entails the temporary use of communication behaviors typical of the other gender in order to increase the potential for influence.[33]

Genderflex

Temporarily using communication behaviors typical of the other gender.

Table 14–4 *Communication Differences between Women and Men*

1. Men are less likely to ask for information or directions in a public situation that would reveal their lack of knowledge.
2. In decision making, women are more likely to downplay their certainty; men are more likely to downplay their doubts.
3. Women tend to apologize even when they have done nothing wrong. Men tend to avoid apologies as signs of weakness or concession.
4. Women tend to accept blame as a way of smoothing awkward situations. Men tend to ignore blame and place it elsewhere.
5. Women tend to temper criticism with positive buffers. Men tend to give criticism directly.
6. Women tend to insert unnecessary and unwarranted thank-you's in conversations. Men may avoid thanks altogether as a sign of weakness.
7. Women tend to ask "What do you think?" to build consensus. Men often perceive that question to be a sign of incompetence and lack of confidence.
8. Women tend to give directions in indirect ways, a technique that may be perceived as confusing, less confident, or manipulative by men.
9. Men tend to usurp [take] ideas stated by women and claim them as their own. Women tend to allow this process to take place without protest.
10. Women use softer voice volume to encourage persuasion and approval. Men use louder voice volume to attract attention and maintain control.

SOURCE: Excerpted from D M Smith, *Women at Work: Leadership for the Next Century* (Upper Saddle River, NJ: Prentice Hall, 2000), pp 26–32.

In contrast, Deborah Tannen recommends that everyone needs to become aware of how linguistic styles work and how they influence our perceptions and judgments. She believes that knowledge of linguistic styles helps to ensure that people with valuable insights or ideas get heard. Consider how gender-based linguistic differences affect who gets heard at a meeting:

> Those who are comfortable speaking up in groups, who need little or no silence before raising their hands, or who speak out easily without waiting to be recognized are far more likely to get heard at meetings. Those who refrain from talking until it's clear that the previous speaker is finished, who wait to be recognized, and who are inclined to link their comments to those of others will do fine at a meeting where everyone else is following the same rules but will have a hard time getting heard in a meeting with people whose styles are more like the first pattern. Given the socialization typical of boys and girls, men are more likely to have learned the first style and women the second, making meetings more congenial for men than for women.[34]

Knowledge of these linguistic differences can assist managers in devising methods to ensure that everyone's ideas are heard and given fair credit both in and out of meetings. Furthermore, it is useful to consider the organizational strengths and limitations of your linguistic style. You may want to consider modifying a linguistic characteristic that is a detriment to perceptions of your confidence, competence, and authority. In conclusion, communication between the sexes can be improved by remembering that women and men have different ways of saying the same thing.

Organizational Communication

Examining the broader issue of organizational communication is a good way to identify factors contributing to effective and ineffective management. We structure this discussion by focusing on the "who" and "how" of communication. For example, the first step in any type of communication is deciding who is going to be the recipient of the message. In work settings, you can communicate upward to your boss, downward to direct reports, horizontally with peers, and externally with customers and suppliers. We discuss the who of organizational communication by reviewing the various formal and informal channels used to communicate. We then delve into the how of communication by reviewing a contingency model for selecting medium. You will learn that communication effectiveness is determined by an appropriate match between the content of a message and the medium used to communicate—the how.

 7 Formal Communication Channels: Up, Down, Horizontal, and External

Formal communication channels follow the chain of command or organizational structure. Messages communicated on formal channels are viewed as official and are transmitted via one or more of three different routes: (1) vertical—either upward or downward, (2) horizontal, and (3) external.

Formal communication channels

Follow the chain of command or organizational structure.

Vertical Communication: Communicating Up and Down the Organization

Vertical communication involves the flow of information up and down the organization. As discussed later in this section, communication distortion is more likely to occur when a message passes through multiple levels of an organization.

- *Upward communication* involves sending a message to someone at a higher level in the organization. Employees commonly communicate information upward about themselves, co-workers and their problems, organizational practices and policies, and what needs to be done and how to do it. Organizations and managers are increasingly encouraging employees to communicate upward in the spirit of fostering organizational justice, intrinsic motivation, and empowerment. Upward communication also is a key component of organizational efforts to increase productivity and customer service because frontline employees generally know what it takes to get the job done. Managers encourage upward communication via employee attitude and opinion surveys, suggestion systems, formal grievance procedures, open-door communication policies, informal meetings, e-mail, and town hall meetings.[35]

- *Downward communication* occurs when someone at a higher level in the organization sends information or a message to someone at a lower level (or levels). Managers generally provide five types of information through downward communication: job instructions, job rationale, organizational procedures and practices, feedback about performance, and indoctrination of goals.

Because town hall meetings are increasingly used in organizations to facilitate vertical communication, tips for conducting them more effectively are offered below.

- The size of the meeting depends on the logistics of your workforce and the message being delivered. If you have good news to tell a number of employees, you can split them into more intimate groups if you like. But if the news is bad, it's better to have everyone hear it at the same time.

- Consider using speakers other than your senior executives.

- Broadcast town meetings so employees in other locations can participate. Taping allows absent employees to view the meeting later.

- When making a presentation, take the educational level of your audience into account.

- Don't make presentations too technical.

- Send invitations to all employees who are eligible to attend.

- Employees should be strongly encouraged to attend meetings, but attendance should not be mandatory. If your meeting is being held after business hours, consider paying employees for their time.[36]

Farcus

by David Waisglass
Gordon Coulthart

www.farcus.com

"... and just when I was about to give up on this company."

FARCUS® is reprinted with permission from LaughingStock Licensing Inc., Ottawa, Canada. All rights reserved.

Horizontal Communication: Communicating within and between Work Units

Horizontal communication flows within and between employees working in different work units, and its main purpose is coordination. During this sideways communication, employees share information and best practices, coordinate work activities and schedules, solve problems, offer advice and coaching, and resolve conflicts. Horizontal communication is facilitated by project teams, committees, team building (recall our discussion in Chapter 11), social gatherings, and matrix structures, which are discussed in Chapter 17.

Horizontal communication is impeded in three ways: (1) by specialization that causes people to work on their tasks and job alone; (2) by encouraging competition between people or work groups as it reduces the sharing of information; and (3) by an organizational culture that does not promote collaboration and cooperation.

External Communication: Communicating with Others outside the Organization

External communication flows between employees inside the organization and a variety of stakeholders outside the organization. External stakeholders include customers, suppliers, shareholder or owners, government officials, community residents, and so on. Many organizations create formal departments, such as public relations, to coordinate their external communications.

Informal communication channels

Do not follow the chain of command or organizational structure.

Grapevine

Unofficial communication system of the informal organization.

Informal Communication Channels

Informal communication channels do not follow the chain of command. They skip management levels and bypass lines of authority. Let us consider two commonly used informal channels: the grapevine and management by wandering around.

The Grapevine

The **grapevine** represents the unofficial communication system of the informal organization and encompasses all types of communication media.

For example, people can just as easily pass along information with e-mail, face-to-face conversations, or telephone calls. Although the grapevine can be a source of inaccurate rumors, it functions positively as an early warning signal for organizational changes, a medium for creating organizational changes, a medium for embedding organizational culture, a mechanism for fostering group cohesiveness, and a way of getting employee and customer feedback. For example, research shows that the grapevine is used by employees and consumers as a frequent source of information, and its use has increased with the advent of the Internet and instant messaging. Marketing experts refer to this as word-of-mouth advertising.[37]

People who consistently pass along grapevine information to others are called **liaison individuals** or gossips:

> About 10% of the employees on an average grapevine will be highly active participants. They serve as liaisons with the rest of the staff members who receive information but spread it to only a few other people. Usually these liaisons are friendly, outgoing people who are in positions that allow them to cross departmental lines. For example, secretaries tend to be liaisons because they can communicate with the top executive, the janitor, and everyone in between without raising eyebrows.[38]

Liaison individuals Those who consistently pass along grapevine information to others.

Effective managers monitor the pulse of work groups by regularly communicating with known liaisons.

In contrast to liaison individuals, **organizational moles** use the grapevine for a different purpose. They obtain information, often negative, in order to enhance their power and status. They do this by secretly reporting their perceptions and hearsay about the difficulties, conflicts, or failure of other employees to powerful members of management. This enables a mole to divert attention away from him- or herself and to position him- or herself as more competent than others. Management should attempt to create an open, trusting environment that discourages mole behavior because moles can destroy teamwork, create conflict, and impair productivity.

Organizational moles Those who use the grapevine to enhance their power and status.

Although research activity on this topic has slowed in recent years, past research about the grapevine provided the following insights: (1) it is faster than formal channels; (2) it is about 75% accurate; (3) people rely on it when they are insecure, threatened, or faced with organizational changes; and (4) employees use the grapevine to acquire the majority of their on-the-job information.[39]

The key managerial recommendation is to *monitor* and *influence* the grapevine rather than attempt to control it. Effective managers accomplish this by using a variety of media to communicate with employees on a regular basis. John Chambers, CEO of Cisco Systems, provides a good example of how this can be done (see the Real World/Real People feature on page 418).

Management by Walking Around (MBWA)

Management by walking around (MBWA) is the term used to describe a manager's literally walking around the organization and talking to people across all lines of authority.[40] It is an effective way to communicate because employees prefer to get information from their manager. Linda Dulye, a communications expert, concluded that employees "favor it more than e-mails, Web sites or intranet sites, or town hall meetings—even more than the grapevine. . . . The most effective channel for employees is the informal workplace 'walk-around'—having their manager come to their desk and sit an chat about work."[41] She offers the following tips for conducting MBWA:[42]

Management by walking around Managers literally walk around and talk to people across lines of authority.

1. Dedicate a certain amount of time each week for MBWA.
2. Don't take your cell phone. It is important to stay focused on the person/people you are talking with and to avoid distractions.

John Chambers Proactively Manages the Grapevine

I started off with classic communication methods when I got here 15 years ago. I'd walk around and talk to small groups and larger groups. I'd see who was here in the evening. To this day I can tell you whose car is out in the parking lot. Then e-mail became very effective because it gave me the ability to send a message to the whole group. But I'm a voice person, I communicate with emotion that way. I like to listen to emotion too. It's a lot easier to listen to a key customer if I hear how they're describing a problem to me. I'll leave 40 to 50 voicemails a day. I do them on the way to work and coming back from work. The newest thing for me is video on demand, which is my primary communication vehicle today. We have a small studio downstairs. We probably tape ten to 15 videos a quarter. That way employees and customers can watch them when they want.

As for how I hear from employees, I host a monthly birthday breakfast. Anybody who has a birthday in that month gets to come and quiz me for an hour and 15 minutes. No directors or VPs in the room. It's how I keep my finger on the pulse of what's working and what's not. It's brutal, but it's my most enjoyable session.

What is your reaction to Mr Chamber's approach to communication?

SOURCE: Excerpted from A Lashinsky, "Lights! Camera! Cue the CEO!" *Fortune,* August 2, 2006, p 27.

---

3. Use active listening and don't take the approach that business is the only available topic for discussion. Employees may enjoy some amount of casual conversation.
4. The experience should be a two-way conversation. Show interest in your employees' issues and concerns.
5. Don't hesitate to take a notepad and record things requiring follow-up. Don't bring formal charts and graphs; the goal is to maintain an informal conversation.
6. Thank the individual or group for their time and feedback.

8 Choosing Media: A Contingency Perspective

In this section we turn our attention to discussing the how of the communication process. Specifically, we examine how managers can determine the best method or medium to use when communicating across the various formal and informal channels of communication.

Managers can choose from many different types of communication media (telephone, e-mail, voicemail, cell phone, express mail, instant messaging, video, and so forth). Fortunately, research tells us that managers can help reduce information overload and improve communication effectiveness through their choice of communication media. If an inappropriate medium is used, managerial decisions may be based on inaccurate information, important messages may not reach the intended audience, and employees may become dissatisfied and unproductive. Consider Marnie Puritz Stone's reaction to the inappropriate use of e-mail.

"All communications regarding hiring and firings were sent via e-mail," Stone explains. Her managers may have felt they were being efficient, but she and her colleagues thought the managers were rude. "I think that callousness with which [some] e-mail delivers news—good or bad—is a poor way to show leadership," she says, "And it creates a lot of resentment."

Stone's manager created even more resentment when it came to providing feedback, which was done mostly through e-mail. "I was reprimanded via e-mail, which was really bad," she recalls, "Criticism via e-mail leaves you very belittled since you can't respond."[43]

This example illustrates that media selection is a key component of communication effectiveness. The following section explores a contingency model designed to help managers select communication media in a systematic and effective manner. Media selection in this model is based on the interaction between information richness and complexity of the problem/situation at hand.

Information Richness Respected organizational theorists Richard Daft and Robert Lengel define **information richness** in the following manner:

> Richness is defined as the potential information-carrying capacity of data. If the communication of an item of data, such as a wink, provides substantial new understanding, it would be considered rich. If the datum provides little understanding, it would be low in richness.[44]

Information richness
Information-carrying capacity of data.

As this definition implies, alternative media possess levels of information richness that vary from rich to lean.

Information richness is based on four factors: (1) feedback (ranging from fast to very slow), channel (ranging from the combined visual and audio characteristics of a video conference to the limited visual aspects of a computer report), (3) type of communication (ranging from personal to impersonal), and (4) language source (ranging from the natural body language and speech contained in a face-to-face conversation to the numbers contained in a financial statement).

Face-to-face is the richest form of communication. It provides immediate feedback and allows for the observation of multiple language cues such as body language and tone of voice. Although high in richness, the telephone and video conferencing are not as informative as the face-to-face medium. In contrast, newsletters, computer reports, and general e-mail are lean media because feedback is very slow, the channels involve only limited visual information, and the information provided is generic or impersonal.

Complexity of the Managerial Problem/Situation Managers face problems and situations that range from low to high in complexity. Low-complexity situations are routine, predictable, and managed by using objective or standard procedures. Calculating an employee's paycheck is an example of low complexity. Highly complex situations, like a corporate reorganization, are ambiguous, unpredictable, hard to analyze, and often emotionally laden. Managers spend considerably more time analyzing these situations because they rely on more sources of information during their deliberations. There are no set solutions to complex problems or situations.

Contingency Recommendations The contingency model for selecting media is graphically shown in Figure 14–2. As shown, there are three zones of communication effectiveness. Effective communication occurs when the richness of the

Figure 14–2 *A Contingency Model for Selecting Communication Media*

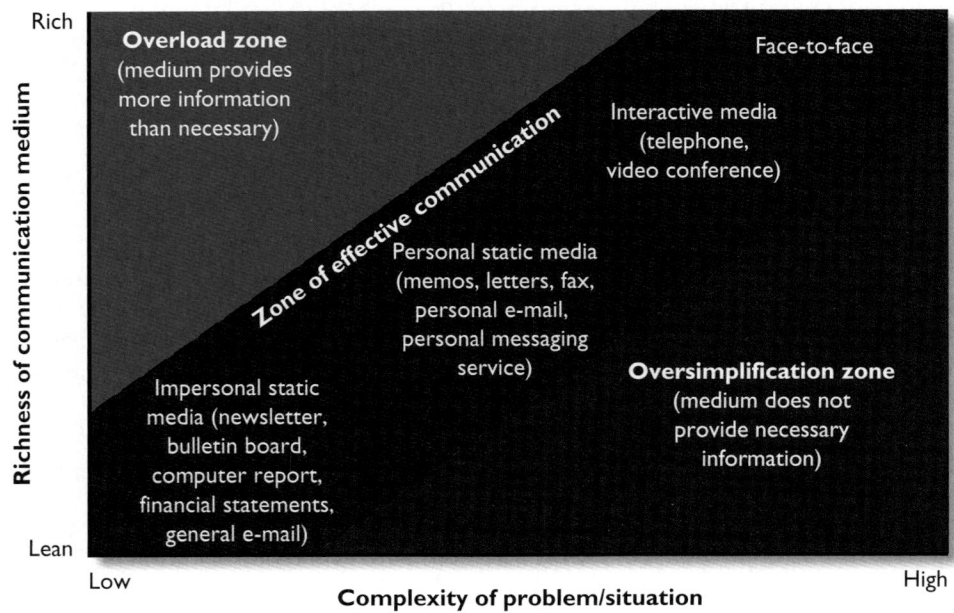

SOURCES: Adapted from R Lengel and R L Daft, "The Selection of Communication Media as an Executive Skill," *Academy of Management Executive,* August 1988, p 226, and R L Daft and R H Lengel, "Information Richness: A New Approach to Managerial Behavior and Organization Design," *Research in Organizational Behavior,* eds B M Staw and L L Cummings (Greenwich, CT: JAI Press, 1984), p 199.

medium is matched appropriately with the complexity of the problem or situation. Media low in richness—impersonal static and personal static—are better suited for simple problems; media high in richness—interactive media and face-to-face—are appropriate for complex problems or situations. Sun Microsystems, for example, followed this recommendation when communicating with employees about upcoming layoffs. The organization used a series of face-to-face sessions to deliver the bad news and provided managers with a set of slides and speaking points to help disseminate the necessary information.[45]

Conversely, ineffective communication occurs when the richness of the medium is either too high or too low for the complexity of the problem or situation. For example, a district sales manager would fall into the *overload zone* if he or she communicated monthly sales reports through richer media. Conducting face-to-face meetings or telephoning each salesperson would provide excessive information and take more time than necessary to communicate monthly sales data. The *oversimplification zone* represents another ineffective choice of communication medium. In this situation, media with inadequate richness are used to communicate about complicated or emotional issues. For example, Radio Shack Corporation used e-mail to notify 400 employees at its Texas headquarters that they were being let go. Worse yet, a London-based body-piercing and jewelry store used a text message to fire an employee. This choice of medium is ineffective in this context because it does not preserve privacy and it does not allow employees to ask questions. Further, dismissing employees in this manner can lower morale among remaining employees and damage a company's image.[46]

Research Evidence The relationship between media richness and problem/ situation complexity has not been researched extensively because the underlying theory is relatively new. Available evidence indicates that managers used richer sources when confronted with ambiguous and complicated events, and miscommunication was increased when rich media were used to transmit information that was traditionally communicated through lean media.[47] Moreover, a meta-analysis of more than 40 studies revealed that media usage was significantly different across organizational levels. Upper-level executives/managers spent more time in face-to-face meetings than did lower-level managers.[48] This finding is consistent with recommendations derived from the contingency model just discussed.

Communication in the Computerized Information Age

As discussed in Chapter 1, the use of computers and information technology is dramatically affecting many aspects of organizational behavior. Consider, for example, the process that employees use to clock in and out at Hilton Waterfront Beach Resort in Huntington Beach, California.

> Every morning when Romy Robb comes into work, she places her palm on a biometric hand reader that scans her hand, then she punches in a four-digit code and begins her job managing payroll for the other employees. . . . The reader take a 3-D reading of the size and shape of an employee's hand and verifies the user's identity in less than a second. Robb uses the system, which is manufactured by Ingersoll Rand, to clock herself in and out, and works with the system's software to calculate payroll for the hotel's 300 employees. She says she likes the system because it's easy to use, employees don't have a card to keep up with, and it eliminates the ability for one employee to clock another in and out.[49]

The use of biometrics is helping the hotel to cut its costs and to improve the accuracy of its payroll process. Biometrics tend to be used in health care, research labs, retail, and fast-food chains.

Companies are using information technology in a host of other ways. Companies such as Toyota, Quest Diagnostics, and SunTrust Bank conduct virtual job interviews and use online assessments and simulations during the hiring process. Both Quest Diagnostics and SunTrust Bank have reduced their recruitment costs and employee turnover as a result of using information technology during the selection process.[50] The Container Store and The Pennsylvania State University also have reduced their labor expenses by using an online system to enroll employees into their benefit programs.[51]

In this section we explore seven key components of information technology that influence organizational behavior: (1) the Internet along with intranets and extranets, (2) e-mail, (3) handheld device, (4) blogs, (5) videoconferencing, (6) group support systems, and (7) telecommuting.

Internet/Intranet/Extranet

The Internet, or more simply, the Net, is more than a computer network. It is a network of computer networks. The **Internet** is a global network of independently operating but interconnected computers. The Internet connects everything from supercomputers, to large mainframes contained in businesses, government, and universities, to the

Internet

A global network of computer networks.

Intranet

An organization's private Internet.

Extranet

Connects internal employees with selected customers, suppliers, and strategic partners.

personal computers in our homes and offices. Over 77% of American adults use the Internet on a regular basis and its use as a communication tool is growing around the world.[52] An **intranet** is nothing more than an organization's private Internet. Intranets also have *firewalls* that block outside Internet users from accessing internal information. This is done to protect the privacy and confidentiality of company documents. In contrast to the internal focus of an intranet, an **extranet** is an extended intranet in that it connects internal employees with selected customers, suppliers, and other strategic partners. Ford Motor Company, for instance, has an extranet that connects its dealers worldwide. Ford's extranet was set up to help support the sales and servicing of cars and to enhance customer satisfaction.

United Parcel Service estimated that productivity increased 35% after the implementation of high-speed wireless Internet access via Wi-Fi.[53] Employee training is another online application that has saved companies millions of dollars. For instance, Hewlett-Packard saved $50 million by using e-learning to help define the new corporate structure after the company merged with Compaq Computer Corp.[54]

In contrast to these positive case studies, a recent study by Harris Interactive revealed that 51% admitted using the Internet at work from one to five hours a week for personal matters. Another survey of 474 human resource professionals indicated that 43% found that employees were viewing pornography while at work.[55] All told, International Data Corp. estimated personal use of the Internet during work hours contributes to a 30 to 40% decrease in productivity.[56] Organizations are taking these statistics to heart and are attempting to root out cyberslackers by tracking employee behavior with electronic monitoring.

There is one last aspect of the Internet worth noting—cybercrime. It strikes individuals and organizations alike. For example, Figure 14–3 shows the amount of cybercrime committed for three categories of illegal behavior. All told, cyber-fraud cost businesses about $1.5 billion in 2005.[57] Interestingly, almost 50% of this criminal activity originates inside an organization. It may occur as the result of employee carelessness, for example, leaving a laptop unsecured or sending confidential, unencrypted information over the Internet. Alternatively, employees can steal trade secrets or sell customer information. Organizations can combat this problem by educating employees about security, classifying data as open or sensitive and confidential, using encryption for sensitive and confidential

Figure 14–3   *The Costs of Cybercrime*

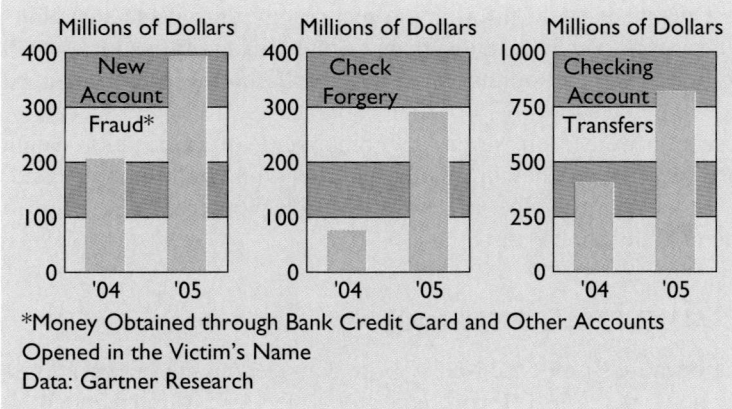

SOURCE: S E Ante and B Grow, "Meet the Hackers," *BusinessWeek,* May 29, 2006. p. 60.

information, monitoring employee activities, and holding employees accountable for failure to follow rules regarding information security.[58]

9 Electronic Mail

Electronic mail or e-mail uses the Internet/intranet to send computer-generated text and documents between people. The use of e-mail around the world has exploded due to four key benefits: (1) reduced costs of distributing information, (2) increased teamwork, (3) reduced paper costs, and (4) increased flexibility. On the other hand, there are four drawbacks: It can result in (1) wasted time and effort, as in dealing with spam and unsolicited junk mail; (2) information overload; (3) increased costs to organize, store, and monitor usage; and (4) neglect of other media (see Table 14–5).[59]

Electronic mail
Uses the Internet/ intranet to send computer-generated text and documents.

10 Handheld Devices

Handheld devices, which also are referred to as PDAs (personal digital assistants), offer users the portability to do work from any location. They are used by millions of people and were designed to allow users to multitask from any location. For example, PDAs can be used to make and track appointments, do word processing, crunch numbers on a spreadsheet, check out favorite tunes and video clips, receive and send e-mail, organize photos, play games, and complete a variety of other tasks.[60] The question from an OB perspective is whether or not these devices actually lead to higher productivity.

Although many people seem addicted to their handheld devices, some academics are skeptical about their real value. Consider the following comments made by several professors to a reporter from *BusinessWeek*.

> The idea that gadgets always make us more efficient, "is a scam, and illusion," says David Greenfield director of the Hartford-based Center for Internet Studies. That's because at their heart, gadgets enable multitasking. And a growing body of evidence suggests that multitasking can easily turn into multislacking. It also increases errors, short-circuits attention spans, induces air-traffic-controller-like stress, and elongates the time it takes to accomplish the most basic tasks by up to 50% or more, according to University of Michigan psychology professor David Meyer. . . .
>
> Gadgets also trigger cognitive overload, says Harvard Medical School psychiatry instructor Dr Edward M. Hallowell. . . . All that toggling back and forth "dilutes performance and increases irritability," says Hallowell, causing steady managers to become disorganized and underachievers.[61]

Given these considerations, we wonder why sales of handheld devices continue to explode. Dr Meyer offers one potential explanation. He notes that the use of PDAs activates our dopamine-reward system, which induces a pleasurable state for approximately 6% of the population. Dr Meyer says that this effect is clinically addictive.[62] Alternatively, people may view these devices as one way to cope with increasing pressures to accomplish more in the face of ever increasing informational demands.

Blogs

A **blog** is an online journal in which people write whatever they want about any topic. Blogging is one of the latest Internet trends. Experts estimate that there are

Blog
Online journal in which people comment on any topic.

Table 14–5   *E-Mail: Benefits, Drawbacks, and Suggestions for Managing It*

Benefits
- *Reduced costs of distributing information.* E-mail allows information to be sent electronically, thereby reducing the costs of sending information to employees and customers.
- *Increased teamwork.* Users can send messages to colleagues anywhere in the world and receive immediate feedback.
- *Reduced paper costs.* An expert estimates these savings at $9,000 per employee.
- *Increased flexibility.* Employees with laptops, cell phones, and handheld devices can access e-mail from anywhere.

Drawbacks
- *Wasted time and effort.* E-mail can distract people from completing their work responsibilities. People spend too much time searching.
- *Information overload.* The average corporate employee receives 171 messages a day, and 10 to 40% are unimportant.
- *Increased costs to organize, store, and monitor.* Systems are needed to protect privacy. The Federal Rules of Civil Procedures require organizations to keep tabs on e-mail and produce them in case of litigation.
- *Neglect of other media.* People unsuccessfully attempt to solve complex problems with e-mail. E-mail reduces the amount of face-to-face communication.

Managing E-Mail
- *Do not assume e-mail is confidential.* Employers are increasingly monitoring all e-mail. Assume your messages can be read by anyone.
- *Be professional and courteous.* Recommendations include: delete trailing messages, don't send chain letters and jokes, don't type in all caps—it's equivalent to shouting, don't respond immediately to a nasty e-mail, refrain from using colored text and background, don't expose your contact list to strangers, and be patient about receiving replies.
- *Avoid sloppiness.* Use a spell checker or reread the message before sending.
- *Don't use e-mail for volatile or complex issues.* Use a medium that is appropriate for the situation at hand.
- *Keep messages brief and clear.* Use accurate subject headings and let the reader know what you want right up front.
- *Save people time.* Type "no reply necessary" in the subject line or at the top of your message if appropriate.
- *Be careful with attachments.* Large attachments can crash someone's systems and use up valuable time downloading. Send only what is necessary, and get permission to send multiple attachments.

SOURCES: C Graham, "In-Box Overload," *The Arizona Republic,* March 16, 2007, p A14; M Totty, "Rethinking the Inbox," *The Wall Street Journal,* March 26, 2007, p R8; A Smith, "Federal Rules Define Duty to Preserve Work E-Mails," *HR Magazine,* January 2007, pp 27, 36; M Totty, "Letter of the Law," *The Wall Street Journal,* March 26, 2007, p R10; and "The Top 10 E-Mail Courtesy Suggestions," *Coachville Coach Training,* March 22, 2000, http://topten.org.content/tt.BN122.htm.

around 23.7 million blogs in existence, and 70,000 new ones pop up every day.[63] Current technology also allows people to blog on cell phones. The benefits of blogs include the opportunity for people to discuss issues in a casual format. These discussions serve much like a chat group and thus provide managers with insights from a wide segment of the employee and customer base as well as the general public.

The Blackstone Group Actively Uses Videoconferencing

A typical user is private equity star Blackstone Group. Several times a week, CEO Stephen A. Schwarzman gathers senior managing partners around a polished conference table in the firm's New York headquarters on Park Avenue for a five-way video call to talk about the sale of some real estate in the Northwest, say, or a bid for Tribune Co. On three wide, glistening, high-definition color screens appear executives from Blackstone's offices in such far-flung places as London, Hong Kong, Mumbai, or Paris. Blackstone has 40 video rooms stationed around the world. One executive is so enthralled with the system that he keeps the conference connection running in his office all day long. "We're big proponents of videoconferencing because of the way it enhances the quality of meetings," says Harry D Moseley, Blackstone's chief information officer.

Have you ever participated in a videoconference? What was your experience?

SOURCE: Excerpted from R O Crockett, "The 21st Century Meeting," *BusinessWeek*, February 26, 2007, p 76.

For example, Walt Disney, General Motors, McDonald's, Intel, Sun Microsystems, and Boeing are all using blogs for this purpose.[64] On a personal level, you can use blogs to help find a job and political candidates are using them to campaign. Watch for their use in the next election.[65]

Blogs also have pitfalls. One entails the lack of legal and organizational guidelines regarding what can be posted online. For example, flight attendant Ellen Simonetti and Google employee Mark Jen were both fired for information they included on their blogs. Simonetti posted suggestive pictures of herself in uniform, and Jen commented about his employer's finances.[66] Another involves the potential for employees to say unflattering things about their employer and to leak confidential information. Finally, one can waste a lot of time reading silly and unsubstantiated postings.

We cannot make any overall conclusion regarding blogs because there has not been any research into their effectiveness as a communication, marketing, or managerial tool.

Videoconferencing

Videoconferencing, also known as teleconferencing, uses video and audio links along with computers to enable people in different locations to see, hear, and talk with one another. This enables people from many locations to conduct a meeting without having to travel. (See the Real World/Real People feature above).

Videoconferencing can significantly reduce an organization's travel expenses. Many organizations set up special videoconferencing rooms or booths with specially equipped television cameras. More recent equipment enables people to attach small cameras and microphones to their desks or computer monitors. This enables employees to conduct long-distance meetings and training classes without leaving their office or cubicle.

Group Support Systems

Group support systems (GSSs) entail using state-of-the-art computer software and hardware to help people work better together. They enable people to share information without the constraints of time and space. This is accomplished by utilizing computer

Group support systems
Using computer software and hardware to help people work better together.

networks to link people across a room or across the globe. Collaborative applications include messaging and e-mail systems, calendar management, videoconferencing, computer teleconferencing, electronic whiteboards, and the type of computer-aided decision-making systems discussed in Chapter 12.

GSS applications have demonstrated increased productivity and cost savings. A recent meta-analysis of 48 experiments also revealed that groups using GSSs during brainstorming experienced greater participation and influence quality, a greater quantity of ideas generated, and less domination by individual members than did groups meeting face-to-face.[67]

Organizations that use full-fledged GSSs have the ability to create virtual teams (discussed in Chapter 11), who tend to use Internet/intranet systems, GSSs, and videoconferencing systems. These real-time systems enable people to communicate with anyone at anytime.

It is important to keep in mind that modern-day information technology only enables people to interact virtually; it doesn't guarantee effective communications. Interestingly, there are a whole host of unique communication problems associated with using the information technology needed to operate virtually.[68]

Teleworking

Teleworking

Doing work that is generally performed in the office away from the office using different information technologies.

Teleworking, also referred to as telecommuting, is a work practice in which an employee does part of his or her job in a remote location, typically at home, using a variety of information technologies. Teleworking involves receiving and sending work from a remote location via some form of information technology such as wireless devices, fax, or a home computer that is linked to an office computer. Teleworking is more common for jobs involving computer work, writing, and phone work that require concentration and limited interruptions. Experts estimate that 41 million people will telework from home at least one day a week by 2008.[69] Proposed benefits of teleworking include

1. *Reduction of capital costs.* IBM reported saving $100 million by letting 42% of its employees work from home.
2. *Increased flexibility and autonomy for workers.*
3. *Competitive edge in recruitment.* Arthur Andersen, Merrill Lynch, and Cisco used teleworking to increase their ability to keep and attract qualified personnel.
4. *Increased job satisfaction and lower turnover.* Employees like teleworking because it helps resolve work/family conflicts. AT&T's teleworkers had less absenteeism than traditional employees.
5. *Increased productivity.* Teleworking resulted in productivity increases of 25 and 35% for FourGen Software and Continental Traffic Services, respectively.
6. *Tapping nontraditional labor pools* (such as prison inmates and homebound disabled persons).[70]

There are two drawbacks to teleworking. First, it is not for everyone. Many people thoroughly enjoy the social camaraderie of an office setting. These individuals would not like to telecommute. Others lack the self-discipline needed to work at home. Second, teleworking can negatively affect your career. For example, a recent survey of 1,300 executives from 71 countries indicated that respondents believed that people who telework were less likely to get promoted.[71] Jack and Suzy Welch proposed that this drawback occurs because of a lack of "face time." They concluded that "what you can't do very well from home is lead. To lead, it's no good blowing into town for important meetings and showing up at retreats. You have to muddle in the muck in between. . . . Companies rarely promote people into leadership roles who haven't been consistently seen and measured."[72] We strongly encourage you to consider this drawback if and when you are debating whether or not to telework.

Summary of Key Concepts

1. *Describe the perceptual process model of communication.* Communication is a process of consecutively linked elements. Historically, this process was described in terms of a conduit model. Criticisms of this model led to development of a perceptual process model of communication that depicts receivers as information processors who create the meaning of messages in their own mind. Because receivers' interpretations of messages often differ from those intended by senders, miscommunication is a common occurrence.

2. *Describe the barriers to effective communication.* Every element of the perceptual model of communication is a potential process barrier. There are nine personal barriers that commonly influence communication: (1) variable skills in communicating effectively, (2) variations in how information is processed and interpreted, (3) variations in interpersonal trust, (4) stereotypes and prejudices, (5) big egos, (6) poor listening skills, (7) natural tendency to evaluate others' messages, (8) inability to listen with understanding, and (9) nonverbal communication. Physical barriers pertain to distance, physical objects, time, and work and office noise. Semantic barriers show up as encoding and decoding errors because these phases of communication involve transmitting and receiving words and symbols.

3. *Contrast the communication styles of assertiveness, aggressiveness, and nonassertiveness.* An assertive style is expressive and self-enhancing but does not violate others' basic human rights. In contrast, an aggressive style is expressive and self-enhancing but takes unfair advantage of others. A nonassertive style is characterized by timid and self-denying behavior. An assertive communication style is more effective than either an aggressive or nonassertive style.

4. *Discuss the primary sources of nonverbal communication.* There are several identifiable sources of nonverbal communication effectiveness. Body movements and gestures, touch, facial expressions, and eye contact are important nonverbal cues. The interpretation of these nonverbal cues significantly varies across cultures.

5. *Review the five dominant listening styles and 10 keys to effective listening.* The five dominant listening styles are appreciative, empathetic, comprehensive, discerning, and evaluative. Good listeners use the following 10 listening habits: (1) capitalize on thought speed by staying with the speaker and listening between the lines, (2) listen for ideas

rather than facts, (3) identify areas of interest between the speaker and listener, (4) judge content and not delivery, (5) do not judge until the speaker has completed his or her message, (6) put energy and effort into listening, (7) resist distractions, (8) listen to both favorable and unfavorable information, (9) read or listen to complex material to exercise the mind, and (10) take notes when necessary and use visual aids to enhance understanding.

6. *Describe the communication differences between men and women, and explain the source of these differences.* Men and women vary in terms of how they ask for information, express certainty, apologize, accept blame, give criticism and praise, say thank you, build consensus, give directions, claim ownership of ideas, and use tone of voice. There are two competing explanations for these differences. The biological perspective attributes gender differences in communication to inherited drives, needs, and conflicts associated with reproductive strategies used by women and men. The second explanation, which is based on social role theory, is based on the idea that females and males learn different ways of speaking as children growing up.

7. *Discuss the formal and informal communication channels.* Formal communication channels follow the chain of command and include vertical, horizontal, and external routes. Vertical communication involves the flow of information up and down the organization. Horizontal communication flows within and between employees working in different work units. External communication flows between employees inside the organization and a variety of stakeholders outside the organization. Informal communication channels do not follow the chain of command. The grapevine and management by walking around represent the two most commonly used informal channels.

8. *Explain the contingency approach to media selection.* Selecting media is a key component of communication effectiveness. Media selection is based on the interaction between the information richness of a medium and the complexity of the problem/situation at hand. Information richness ranges from low to high and is a function of four factors: speed of feedback, characteristics of the channel, type of communication, and language source. Problems/situations range from simple to complex. Effective communication occurs when the richness of the medium matches the complexity of the problem/situation. From a contingency

perspective, richer media need to be used as problems/situations become more complex.

9. *Review the benefits and drawbacks of e-mail and summarize how e-mail can be more effectively managed.* The benefits of e-mail include reduced costs of distributing information, increased teamwork, reduced paper costs, and increased flexibility. The drawbacks are wasted time and effort, information overload, increased costs to organize, store, and monitor, and neglect of other media. E-mail can be more effectively managed by doing the following: (1) do not assume e-mail is confidential, (2) be professional and courteous, (3) avoid sloppiness, (4) don't use e-mail for volatile or complex issues, (5) keep messages brief and clear, (6) save people time, and (7) be careful with attachments.

10. *Explain the information technology of Internet/intranet/extranet, handheld devices, blogs, videoconferencing, and group support systems, and explain the related use of teleworking.* The Internet is a global network of computer networks. An intranet is an organization's private Internet. It contains a firewall that blocks outside Internet users from accessing private internal information. An extranet connects an organization's internal employees with selected customers, suppliers, and strategic partners. The primary benefit of these "nets" is that they can enhance the ability of employees to find, create, manage, and distribute information. Handheld devices, also known as PDAs (personal digital assistants), offer users the portability to do work from any location. They serve as minicomputers and communication devices. A blog is an online journal in which people write whatever they want about any topic. Blogging is the latest Internet trend. Videoconferencing uses video and audio links along with computers to enable people located at different locations to see, hear, and talk with one another. GSSs use state-of-the-art computer software and hardware to help people work better together. Information is shared across time and space by linking people with computer networks. Teleworking involves doing work that is generally performed in the office away from the office using different information technologies.

Key Terms

Communication 400
Perceptual model of communication 401
Noise 402
Personal barriers 403
Semantics 405
Jargon 406
Communication competence 406
Nonverbal communication 408
Listening 410
Linguistic style 411
Genderflex 413
Formal communication channels 415
Informal communication channels 416

Grapevine 416
Liaison individuals 417
Organizational moles 417
Management by walking around 417
Information richness 419
Internet 421
Intranet 422
Extranet 422
Electronic mail 423
Blog 423
Group support systems 425
Teleworking 426

OB in Action Case Study

Companies in Korea and Japan Are Slow to Adopt Information Technology[73]

BusinessWeek MASANORI GOTO WAS in for a culture shock when he returned to Japan after a seven-year stint in New York. The 42-year-old public relations officer at cellular giant NTT DoCoMo logged many a late night at his Manhattan apartment, using his company laptop to communicate with colleagues 14 time zones away. Now back in Tokyo, Goto has a cell phone he can use to send quick e-mails after hours, but he must hole up at the office late into the night if he needs to do any serious work. The reason: His bosses haven't outfitted him with a portable computer. "I didn't realize that our people in Japan weren't using laptops," he says. "That was a surprise."

A few hundred miles to the west, in Seoul, Lee Seung-Hwa also knows what it's like to spend long hours chained to her desk. The 33-year-old recently quit her job as an executive assistant at a carmaker because, among other complaints, her company didn't let lower-level employees log on from outside the office. "I could have done all the work from home, but managers thought I was working hard only if I stayed late," says Lee. . . .

Why? Corporate culture in the Far East remains deeply conservative, and most businesses have been slow to mine the opportunities offered by newfangled communications technologies. One big reason is the premium placed on face time at the office. Junior employees are reluctant to leave work before the boss does for fear of looking like slackers. Also, Confucianism places greater stock on group effort and consensus-building than on individual initiative. So members of a team all feel they must stick around if there is a task to complete. "To reap full benefits from IT investment, companies must change the way they do business," says Lee Inn Chan, vice-president at SK Research Institute, a Seoul management think tank funded by cellular carrier SK Telecom. "What's most needed in Korea and Japan is an overhaul in business processes and practices."

Time, Not Task

In these countries, if you're not in the office, your boss simply assumes you're not working. It doesn't help that a lack of clear job definitions and performance metrics makes it difficult for managers to assess the productivity of employees working off site. "Performance reviews and judgments are still largely time-oriented here, rather than task-oriented as in the West," says Cho Burn Coo, a Seoul-based executive partner at business consulting firm Accenture Ltd.

Even tech companies in the region often refuse to untether workers from the office. Camera-maker Canon Inc. for instance, dispensed with flextime four years ago after employees said it interfered with communications, while Samsung stresses that person-to-person contact is far more effective than e-mail. In Japan, many companies say they are reluctant to send workers home with their laptops for fear that proprietary information might go astray. . . .

The result: Korean and Japanese white-collar workers clock long days at the office, often toiling till midnight and coming in on weekends. "In my dictionary there's no such thing as work life balance as far as

weekdays are concerned," says a Samsung Electronics senior manager who declined to be named. . . .

Still, a new generation of managers rising through the ranks may speed the transformation. These workers are tech-savvy and often more individualistic, having come from smaller families. Already, some companies are tinkering with changes to meet their needs. SK Telecom abolished titles for all midlevel managers in the hopes that this would spur workers to take greater initiative. Japan's NEC Corp. is experimenting with telecommuting for 2,000 of its 148,000 employees. And in Korea, CJ 39 Shopping, a cable-TV shopping channel, is letting 10% of its call-center employees work from home.

Foreign companies are doing their bit to shake things up. In Korea, IBM has outfitted all of its 2,600 employees with laptops and actively encourages them to work off site. The system, which was first introduced in 1995, has allowed the company to cut back on office space and reap savings of $2.3 million a year. One beneficiary is Kim Yoon Hee. The procurement specialist reports to the office only on Tuesdays and Thursdays. On other days, calls to her office phone are automatically routed to her laptop, so she can work from home. "It would have been difficult for me to remain employed had it not been for the telecommuting system," says Kim, 35, who quit a job at a big Korean company seven years ago because late nights at the office kept her away from her infant daughter. "This certainly makes me more loyal to my company."

Questions for Discussion

1. What is the core problem in this case? Provide rationale.
2. What are the root causes of the problem identified in question 1? Explain.
3. What role does organizational culture and national culture play in this case? Can anything be done about this?
4. What barriers to effective communication are apparent in this case?
5. Based on content you have learned in this course, what recommendations would you make to solve the core problem in this case? Explain your rationale.

Ethical Dilemma

Would You Stop Students from Making Malicious Classroom Videos?[74]

The videos started popping up last month on YouTube.

In one, secretly videotaped by a student, a teacher at Malibu High School in California loses control of class and raises his voice while students laugh at him. In another,

teenagers make fun of fellow students, who also appear to be unaware they're being taped. . . .

YouTube, Myspace, and other Web sites are sprinkled with videos taken in high-school classrooms around the

429

country—often, it appears, without permission of the subjects. One popular YouTube video called *The Angry Teacher* shows a male instructor increasingly losing his cool to a classroom of unruly students.

But policing these secret videos is proving a challenge for educators, who say they must balance protecting the rights of students to express themselves in this digital age while preventing them from holding classmates and teachers up to ridicule.

What Would You Do If You Were the Principal of a School in Which Students Were Found Making Malicious Videos?

1. This is a new issue. I would take time to study the issue and determine a response.
2. I would find out who made the videos and then punish them.
3. I would contact the students' parents and ask them to speak with their child.
4. I would create a policy that says students cannot use their phones in the classroom. I then would specify a consequence for anyone who breaks this rule.
5. I would invent other options.

Web Resources

For study material and exercises that apply to this chapter, visit our Web site,

www.mhhe.com/kreitner

CHAPTER 15

Influence, Empowerment, and Politics

When you finish studying the material in this chapter, you should be able to:

1   Explain the concept of mutuality of interest.

2   Name at least three "soft" and two "hard" influence tactics, and summarize the practical lessons from influence research.

3   Identify and briefly describe French and Raven's five bases of power, and discuss the responsible use of power.

4   Define the term *empowerment,* and explain why it is a matter of degree.

5   Explain why delegation is the highest form of empowerment, and discuss the connections among delegation, trust, and personal initiative.

6   Define *organizational politics,* and explain what triggers it.

7   Distinguish between favorable and unfavorable impression management tactics.

8   Explain how to manage organizational politics.

Julie Larson-Green had presented her work to Bill Gates earlier in her career, and like just about everyone in her shoes, had to manage some butterflies beforehand. But in January 2005, the stakes were higher. The 39-year-old program manager was out to persuade the company's chairman to radically overhaul one of the most profitable products in the history of mankind: Microsoft Office. The dropdown menus and toolbars that Gates had personally helped craft in the '80s had to go, she would tell him, to be replaced by an onscreen "ribbon" loaded with options that would dynamically change according to what you were poised to do next. Armed with results from extensive testing and already having convinced her intermediate bosses, she felt she had a strong case. But there was always the danger that Gates might think about the $11 billion that Office reaps annually and say that the change in this upgrade was too risky. Remember New Coke?

But at the end of the demo, Gates said the words Larson-Green had been waiting for: "I can't believe you convinced me to get rid of menus and toolbars."[1]

FOR DISCUSSION

What were the keys to this impressive case of persuasion?

At the very heart of interpersonal dealings in today's work organizations is a constant struggle between individual and collective interests. For example, Sid wants a raise, but his company doesn't make enough money to both grant raises and buy needed capital equipment. Preoccupation with self-interest is understandable. After all, each of us was born, not as a cooperating organization member, but as an individual with instincts for self-preservation. It took socialization in family, school, religious, sports, recreation, and employment settings to introduce us to the notion of mutuality of interest. Basically, **mutuality of interest** involves win–win situations in which one's self-interest is served by cooperating actively and creatively with potential adversaries. A pair of organization development consultants offered this managerial perspective of mutuality of interest:

> Nothing is more important than this sense of mutuality to the effectiveness and quality of an organization's products and services. Management must strive to stimulate a strong sense of shared ownership in every employee, because otherwise an organization cannot do its best in the long run. Employees who identify their own personal self-interest with the quality of their organization's output understand mutuality and strive to maintain it in their jobs and work relations.[2]

Mutuality of interest

Balancing individual and organizational interests through win–win cooperation.

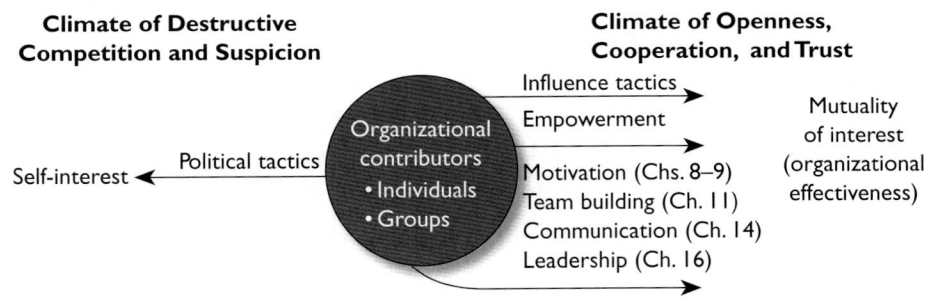

Figure 15–1 *The Constant Tug-of-War between Self-Interest and Mutuality of Interest Requires Managerial Action*

Figure 15–1 graphically portrays the constant tug-of-war between employees' self-interest and the organization's need for mutuality of interest. It also shows the linkage between this chapter—influence, empowerment, and politics—and other key topics in this book. Managers need a complete tool kit of techniques to guide diverse individuals, who are often powerfully motivated to put their own self-interests first, to pursue common objectives. At stake in this tug-of-war between individual and collective interests is no less than the ultimate survival of organizations such as Microsoft. (As for persuasive Julie Larson-Green, in our chapter-opening vignette, she received a big promotion: "she's in charge of interface for the next version of Windows, post-Vista.")[3]

Organizational Influence Tactics

How do you get others to carry out your wishes? Do you simply tell them what to do? Or do you prefer a less direct approach, such as promising to return the favor? Whatever approach you use, the crux of the issue is *social influence.* A large measure of interpersonal interaction involves attempts to influence others, including parents, bosses, co-workers, spouses, teachers, friends, and children. All of us need to sharpen our influence skills (see the inspiring story in the Real World/Real People feature on the next page). A good starting point is familiarity with the following research insights.

2 Nine Generic Influence Tactics

A particularly fruitful stream of research, initiated by David Kipnis and his colleagues in 1980, reveals how people influence each other in organizations. The Kipnis methodology involved asking employees how they managed to get either their bosses, co-workers, or subordinates to do what they wanted them to do.[4] Statistical refinements and replications by other researchers over a 13-year period eventually yielded nine influence tactics. The nine tactics, ranked in diminishing order of use in the workplace are as follows:

1. *Rational persuasion.* Trying to convince someone with reason, logic, or facts.
2. *Inspirational appeals.* Trying to build enthusiasm by appealing to others' emotions, ideals, or values.
3. *Consultation.* Getting others to participate in planning, making decisions, and changes.
4. *Ingratiation.* Getting someone in a good mood prior to making a request; being friendly, helpful, and using praise or flattery.

John Rice Has a Positive Influence on Minorities' Career Choices

There's a hole in higher education that you probably haven't heard about.

At American undergraduate schools, 23% of the students are black or Hispanic. At the top 20 colleges, they account for 14% of the student body. The top 20 law and medical schools? Fourteen to 15%....

But at the top 20 business schools, blacks and Hispanics represent just 7% of the student body. In the current second-year class, that's about 900 people.... So what's a diversity officer to do? You can't hire people who aren't there. So you have to find a way to get superstar minorities to go to the top MBA programs, where you can one day woo them. And there's only one program that does that....

Management Leadership for Tomorrow started out as an independent-study project at Harvard Business School. John Rice, a second-year student, wondered why there were so few nonwhite faces in the program. He found that many of the most talented minority graduates from elite colleges didn't even consider going to business school, mainly for cultural and sociological reasons. So he started a nonprofit organization to address those issues, introducing graduates to the business world through seminars, coaching, and test prep.

Today he has a monster hit on his hands. MLT is the No. 1 source of minorities for the top ten MBA programs.... "Talent is our most important asset," says Chuck Prince, CEO of longtime MLT partner Citigroup. "But unfortunately there's a very limited diversity pipeline in the US at the present time, so when someone comes up with a unique, innovative, and interesting new idea and brings the positive power that John does, it has the potential to have a dramatic impact in the next five, ten, 20 years."

Does this inspire you to enact one of your "big ideas" for making the world a better place?

SOURCE: Excerpted from N A Hira, "An Eye for Talent," *Fortune*, November 27, 2006, pp 200–208.

---

5. *Personal appeals.* Referring to friendship and loyalty when making a request.
6. *Exchange.* Making express or implied promises and trading favors.
7. *Coalition tactics.* Getting others to support your effort to persuade someone.
8. *Pressure.* Demanding compliance or using intimidation or threats.
9. *Legitimating tactics.* Basing a request on one's authority or right, organizational rules or policies, or express or implied support from superiors.[5]

These approaches can be considered *generic* influence tactics because they characterize social influence in all directions and in a wide variety of settings. Researchers have found this ranking to be fairly consistent regardless of whether the direction of influence is downward, upward, or lateral.[6]

Some call the first five influence tactics—rational persuasion, inspirational appeals, consultation, ingratiation, and personal appeals—*soft* tactics because they are friendlier and not as coercive as the last four tactics. Exchange, coalition, pressure, and legitimating tactics accordingly are called *hard* tactics because they involve more overt pressure. Margaret G McGlynn, president of Merck Vaccines, is a good role model for having made a career out of skillfully using rational persuasion:

An ability to argue her case in a "relentlessly logical and wonderfully intense way," as ex-boss David Anstice puts it, helped McGlynn rise rapidly....

McGlynn's powers of persuasion have also helped her achieve results on Capitol Hill. Last summer, after Merck won approval to market a vaccine for shingles—a painful disease that strikes the elderly—she started knocking on doors all over Capitol Hill. Turned out that the new Medicare Part D drug plan prevented doctors from getting fully paid to administer vaccines. "I explained to [policymakers] that shingles is a debilitating illness that causes a major impact on quality of life," she says. They seem to have listened: On Dec. 9, [2006], Congress passed a bill that fixes the Medicare payment shortfall, which the President signed.[7]

Three Possible Influence Outcomes

Put yourself in this familiar situation. It's Wednesday and a big project you've been working on for your project team is due Friday. You're behind on the preparation of your computer graphics for your final report and presentation. You catch a friend who is great at computer graphics as he heads out of the office at quitting time. You try this *exchange tactic* to get your friend to help you out: "I'm way behind. I need your help. If you could come back in for two to three hours tonight and help me with these graphics, I'll complete those spreadsheets you've been complaining about." According to researchers, your friend will engage in one of three possible influence outcomes:

1. *Commitment.* Your friend enthusiastically agrees and will demonstrate initiative and persistence while completing the assignment.
2. *Compliance.* Your friend grudgingly complies and will need prodding to satisfy minimum requirements.
3. *Resistance.* Your friend will say no, make excuses, stall, or put up an argument.[8]

The best outcome is commitment because the target person's intrinsic motivation will energize good performance. However, managers often have to settle for compliance in today's hectic workplace. Resistance means a failed influence attempt.

Practical Research Insights

Laboratory and field studies have taught us useful lessons about the relative effectiveness of influence tactics along with other instructive insights:

- Commitment is more likely when people rely on consultation, strong rational persuasion, and inspirational appeals and *do not* rely on pressure and coalition tactics.[9] Interestingly, in one study, managers were not very effective at *downward* influence. They relied most heavily on inspiration (an effective tactic), ingratiation (a moderately effective tactic), and pressure (an ineffective tactic).[10]

- A meta-analysis of 69 studies suggests ingratiation (making the boss feel good) can slightly improve your performance appraisal results and make your boss like you significantly more.[11]

- Commitment is more likely when the influence attempt involves something *important* and *enjoyable* and is based on a *friendly* relationship.[12]

- A recent field study of sales managers in the United States looked at how the quality of the working relationship between a manager and a team member affected willingness to help teammates. When the relationship was *not* good, inspirational appeals and exchange tactics actually *reduced* helping behavior, with lack of credibility being the likely culprit. On the other hand, exchange tactics increased helping behavior when the relationship was good. *Consultation* increased helping behavior, regardless of the quality of the relationship. This is a strong endorsement for participation, whereby managers and leaders solicit input from employees.[13]

- In a survey, 214 employed MBA students (55% female) tended to perceive their superiors' soft influence tactics as fair and hard influence tactics as unfair. *Unfair* influence tactics were associated with greater *resistance* among employees.[14]

- Another study probed male–female differences in influencing work group members. Many studies have found women to be perceived as less competent and less influential in work groups than men. The researchers had male and female work group leaders engage in either task behavior (demonstrating ability and task competence) or dominating behavior (relying on threats). For both women and men, task behavior was associated with perceived competence and effective influence. Dominating behavior was not effective. The following conclusion by the researchers has important practical implications for all current and future managers who desire to successfully influence others: "The display of task cues is an effective means to enhance one's status in groups and . . . the attempt to gain influence in task groups through dominance is an ineffective and poorly received strategy for both men and women."[15]

- Interpersonal influence is culture bound. The foregoing research evidence on influence tactics has a bias in favor of European–North Americans. Much remains to be learned about how to effectively influence others (without unintended insult) in today's diverse labor force and cross-cultural economy.[16]

Finally, Barbara Moses, consultant and author from Toronto, Canada, offers this advice on influencing your boss:

> If your boss doesn't understand the need for change, this might be partly your fault. You can't make change; you have to sell it. And the key to selling anything is to understand where the other person is coming from—rather than to assume that your boss is a complete jerk. But most of us communicate from an egocentric place. We construct an idea or a project mainly in terms of what makes sense to us. Instead, ask yourself: "What's most important to my boss?" "What are his greatest concerns?" Go forward only after you've answered these questions.[17]

Social Power

The term *power* evokes mixed and often passionate reactions. Citing recent instances of government corruption and corporate misconduct, many observers view power as a sinister force. To these skeptics, Lord Acton's time-honored statement that "power corrupts and absolute power corrupts absolutely" is as true as ever.[18] However, OB specialists remind us that, like it or not, power is a fact of life in modern organizations. According to one management writer,

> Power must be used because managers must influence those they depend on. Power also is crucial in the development of managers' self-confidence and willingness to support subordinates. From this perspective, power should be accepted as a natural part of any organization. Managers should recognize and develop their own power to coordinate and support the work of subordinates; it is powerlessness, not power, that undermines organizational effectiveness.[19]

Thus, power is a necessary and generally positive force in organizations. As the term is used here, **social power** is defined as "the ability to marshal the human, informational, and material resources to get something done."[20]

Importantly, the exercise of social power in organizations is not necessarily a downward proposition. Employees can and do exercise power upward and laterally. An example of an upward power play occurred at Alberto-Culver Company, the personal care products firm. Leonard Lavin, founder of the company, was under pressure to revitalize the firm because key employees were departing for more innovative competitors such as Procter & Gamble. Lavin's daughter Carol Bernick, and her husband Howard,

Social power

Ability to get things done with human, informational, and material resources.

both longtime employees, took things into their own hands:

> Even the Bernicks were thinking of jumping ship. Instead, in September 1994, they marched into Lavin's office and presented him with an ultimatum: Either hand over the reins as CEO or run the company without them. It was a huge blow for Lavin, forcing him to face selling his company to outsiders or ceding control to the younger generation. Unwilling to sell, he reluctantly stepped down, though he remains chairman.
>
> How does it feel to push aside your own father and wrest operating control of the company he created? "It isn't an easy thing to do with the founder of any company, whether he's your father or not," says Carol Bernick, 46, now vice chairman and president of Alberto-Culver North America.[21]

Howard Bernick became CEO, the firm's top-down management style was scrapped in favor of a more open culture, and Lavin reportedly is happy with how things have turned out.[22]

3 Dimensions of Power

While power may be an elusive concept to the casual observer, social scientists view power as having reasonably clear dimensions. Two dimensions of power that deserve our attention are (1) socialized versus personalized power and (2) the five bases of power.

Socialized power
Directed at helping others.

Personalized power
Directed at helping oneself.

Two Types of Power Behavioral scientists such as David McClelland contend that one of the basic human needs is the need for power (n Pwr), as discussed in Chapter 8. Because this need is learned and not innate, the need for power has been extensively studied. Historically, need for power was said to be high when subjects interpreted TAT pictures in terms of one person attempting to influence, convince, persuade, or control another. More recently, however, researchers have drawn a distinction between **socialized power** and **personalized power.**

> There are two subscales or "faces" in n Pwr. One face is termed "socialized" (s Pwr) and is scored in the Thematic Apperception Test (TAT) as "plans, self-doubts, mixed outcomes and concerns for others,…" while the second face is "personalized" power (p Pwr), in which expressions of power for the sake of personal aggrandizement become paramount.[23]

This distinction between socialized and personalized power helps explain why power has a negative connotation for many people.[24] Managers and others who pursue personalized power for their own selfish ends give power a bad name. For example, Nancy Traversy, cofounder and CEO of the successful children's book publisher Barefoot Books, recently related this story about how she came to be an entrepreneur:

> I was born in Canada to a family of artists. I studied business, which made me the black sheep. After college I worked for the banking division of Pricewaterhouse in London. One day I was wearing a suit. One of the partners said to me, "Women don't wear trousers" and sent me home to change. It was a formative experience.[25]

Abuse of power in the corporate world helped put Nancy Traversy on the road to entrepreneurial success.

A series of interviews with 25 American women elected to public office found a strong preference for socialized power. The following comments illustrate their desire to wield power effectively and ethically:

- "Power in itself means nothing. . . . I think power is the opportunity to really have an impact on your community."

- "My goal is to be a powerful advocate on the part of my constituents."[26]

Five Bases of Power
A popular classification scheme for social power traces back more than 45 years ago to the work of John French and Bertram Raven. They proposed that power arises from five different bases: reward power, coercive power, legitimate power, expert power, and referent power.[27] Each involves a different approach to influencing others:

- *Reward power.* A manager has **reward power** to the extent that he or she obtains compliance by promising or granting rewards. On-the-job behavior shaping, for example, relies heavily on reward power.

- *Coercive power.* Threats of punishment and actual punishment give an individual **coercive power.** For instance, consider this heavy-handed tactic by Wolfgang Bernhard, a Volkswagen executive: "A ruthless cost-cutter, Bernard, 46, has a favorite technique: He routinely locks staffers in meeting rooms, then refuses to open the doors until they've stripped $1,500 in costs from a future model."[28] Bathroom break, anyone?

- *Legitimate power.* This base of power is anchored to one's formal position or authority. Thus, individuals who obtain compliance primarily because of their formal authority to make decisions have **legitimate power.** Legitimate power may express itself in either a positive or negative manner in managing people. Positive legitimate power focuses constructively on job performance. Negative legitimate power tends to be threatening and demeaning to those being influenced. Its main purpose is to build the power holder's ego. Importantly, there is growing concern today about the limits of managers' legitimate power relative to privacy rights and off-the-job behavior.[29] (For example, see the Real World/Real People feature on page 440.)

- *Expert power.* Valued knowledge or information gives an individual **expert power** over those who need such knowledge or information. The power of supervisors is enhanced because they know about work schedules and assignments before their employees do. Skillful use of expert power played a key role in the effectiveness of team leaders in a study of three physician medical diagnosis teams.[30] Knowledge *is* power in today's high-tech workplaces.

- *Referent power.* Also called charisma, **referent power** comes into play when one's personality becomes the reason for compliance. Role models have referent power over those who identify closely with them.[31]

Regarding charisma, Jack and Suzy Welch recently offered this instructive perspective in their *BusinessWeek* column:

> [A]lmost everyone wonders at some point in his or her career how big a role charisma plays in success. So how big is it? In the short term, very. In the long term, very again—but not alone.
>
> Now, we're obviously not talking here about "bad" charisma, exuded without brains, vision, and character. That trait is useless, and even dangerous. In business, wow personalities with less-than-wow minds are called empty suits for good reason. Too many of these individuals manage to ho-ho-ho their way to the top, even to the CEO's office, but most self-destruct after looking great for a couple of years while achieving little. On a larger scale, darkly charismatic leaders have the power to wreck lives and nations. . . .

Reward power

Obtaining compliance with promised or actual rewards.

Coercive power

Obtaining compliance through threatened or actual punishment.

Legitimate power

Obtaining compliance through formal authority.

Expert power

Obtaining compliance through one's knowledge or information.

Referent power

Obtaining compliance through charisma or personal attraction.

Get Healthy. That's an Order!

Getting health insurance from your employer [in the United States] is sometimes seen as an entitlement, but the benefit owes its existence to a quirk of history. During World War II, employers desperate to attract workers began offering health insurance. Providing coverage has been an increasing burden for companies ever since. As a result, businesses have been forcing employees to shoulder more and more of the cost.

Some theorized that higher co-payments and pricier premiums would get people to take better care of themselves. It's not happening. "We have this notion that you can gorge on hot dogs, be in a pie-eating contest, and drink every day, and society will take care of you," says Harvard Business School Professor Michael E Porter, who coauthored *Redefining Health Care*. "We can't afford to let individuals drive up costs because they're not willing to address their health problems."

Hence the wellness fixation at companies as varied as IBM, Microsoft, Harrah's Entertainment, and Scotts. Employees who voluntarily sign up for such programs often receive discounts on health-care premiums, free weight-loss and smoking-cessation programs, gratis gym memberships, counseling for emotional problems, and prizes like vacations or points that can be redeemed for gift cards.

Companies save money. Employees get healthier. What's not to like? But the wellness craze raises important issues. One is that people could start blaming unhealthy colleagues for helping push up premiums. Then there are the privacy and discrimination issues: How far should managers intrude into employees' lives?

What is your position on this issue?

SOURCE: Excerpted from M Conlin, "Get Healthy—or Else," *BusinessWeek*, February 26, 2007, p 60.

But good charismatic leaders are everywhere, too, leading with magnetism plus integrity and intelligence. And for them, charisma just makes the job a whole lot easier. Why? Because leaders have always had to energize their people.[32]

go to the Web for the Self-Exercise: What Is Your Self-Perceived Power?

Where your name is on the building, you've got a lot of power. So it is with Bill Wrigley, Executive Chairman of Wm. Wrigley Jr. Co., the Chicago gum and candy giant. But contrary to skepticism about his wilingness to share power with Bill Perez (left), the firm's first outside CEO in 116 years, Bill Wrigley is proving to be a good team player.

Research Insights about Social Power

In one study, a sample of 94 male and 84 female non-managerial and professional employees in Denver, Colorado, completed TAT tests. The researchers found that the male and female employees had similar needs for power (n Pwr) and personalized power (p Pwr). But the women had a significantly higher need for socialized power (s Pwr) than did their male counterparts.[33] This bodes well for today's work organizations where women are playing an ever greater administrative role. Unfortunately, as women gain power in the workplace, greater tension between men and women has been observed. *Training* magazine offered this perspective:

[O]bservers view the tension between women and men in the workplace as a natural outcome of power inequities between the genders. Their argument is that men still have most of the power and are resisting any change as a way to protect their power base. [Consultant Susan L] Webb asserts that sexual harassment has far more to do with exercising power in an unhealthy way than with sexual attraction. Likewise, the glass ceiling, a metaphor for the barriers women face in climbing the corporate ladder to management and executive positions, is about power and access to power.[34]

Accordingly, "powerful women were described more positively by women than by men" in a study of 140 female and 125 male college students in Sydney, Australia.[35]

A reanalysis of 18 field studies that measured French and Raven's five bases of power uncovered "severe methodological shortcomings."[36] After correcting for these problems, the researchers identified the following relationships between power bases and work outcomes such as job performance, job satisfaction, and turnover:

- Expert and referent power had a generally positive impact.

- Reward and legitimate power had a slightly positive impact.

- Coercive power had a slightly negative impact.

The same researcher, in a follow-up study involving 251 employed business seniors, looked at the relationship between influence styles and bases of power. This was a bottom-up study. In other words, employee perceptions of managerial influence and power were examined. Rational persuasion was found to be a highly acceptable managerial influence tactic. Why? Because employees perceived it to be associated with the three bases of power they viewed positively: legitimate, expert, and referent.[37]

In summary, expert and referent power appear to get the best *combination* of results and favorable reactions from lower-level employees.[38]

Using Power Responsibly and Ethically

As democracy continues to spread around the world, one reality stands clear: Leaders who do not use their power responsibly risk losing it. This holds for corporations and nonprofit organizations as well as for government leaders and public figures. Case in point: On April 4, 2007, Radio Hall of Fame broadcaster Don Imus made a degrading comment about the Rutgers University women's basketball team. A ripple of public outcry about sexism and racism quickly turned into a tsunami of protest. Eight days later, with key sponsors defecting, CBS Radio fired Imus from his $10 million-a-year job.[39] A step in the right direction for managers who want to avoid such a turnaround and wield power responsibly is understanding the difference between commitment and mere compliance.

Responsible managers strive for socialized power while avoiding personalized power. In fact, in a survey, organizational commitment was higher among US federal government executives whose superiors exercised socialized power than among colleagues with "power-hungry" bosses. The researchers used the appropriate terms *uplifting power* versus *dominating power.*[40] How does this relate to the five bases of power? As with influence tactics, managerial power has three possible outcomes: commitment, compliance, or resistance. Reward, coercive, and negative legitimate power tend to produce *compliance* (and sometimes, resistance). On the other hand, positive legitimate power, expert power, and referent power tend to foster *commitment.* Once again, commitment is superior to compliance because it is driven by internal or intrinsic motivation.[41] Employees who merely comply require frequent "jolts" of power from the boss to keep them headed in a productive direction. Committed employees tend to be self-starters who do not require close supervision—a key success factor in today's flatter, team-oriented organizations.

4 Empowerment: From Power Sharing to Power Distribution

Empowerment

Sharing varying degrees of power with lower-level employees to tap their full potential.

An exciting trend in today's organizations centers on giving employees a greater say in the workplace. This trend wears various labels, including "high-involvement management," "participative management," and "open-book management." Regardless of the label one prefers, it is all about empowerment. Those who dismiss the employee empowerment trend as a passing fad need to see it as part of a much, much larger picture. Klaus Schwab, a respected Swiss businessman and philanthropist, recently offered this sweeping perspective:

Swiss power broker Klaus Schwab sees an erosion of traditional command-and-control structures in the Web 2.0 world.

[A] general issue will be the changing power equation, which means that everywhere in society and business, the power is moving from the center to the periphery. Vertical command-and-control structures are being eroded and replaced by communities and different platforms. We are moving into the Web 2.0 world, and this has tremendous implications on the national level and on business models.[42]

Management consultant and writer W Alan Randolph offers this definition: "**empowerment** is recognizing and releasing into the organization the power that people already have in their wealth of useful knowledge, experience, and internal motivation."[43] A core component of this process is pushing decision-making authority down to progressively lower levels. Steve Kerr, who has served as the "chief learning officer" at General Electric and now Goldman Sachs, adds this important qualification: "We say empowerment is moving decision making down to the lowest level *where a competent decision can be made*."[44] Of course, it is naive and counterproductive to hand power over to unwilling or unprepared employees.

A Matter of Degree

The concept of empowerment requires some adjustments in traditional thinking (see the Real Word/Real People feature on page 443). First, power is not a zero-sum situation where one person's gain is another's loss. Social power is unlimited. This requires win–win thinking. Frances Hesselbein, the woman credited with modernizing the Girl Scouts of the USA, put it this way: "The more power you give away, the more you have."[45] Authoritarian managers who view employee empowerment as a threat to their personal power are missing the point because of their win–lose thinking.

The second adjustment to traditional thinking involves seeing empowerment as *a matter of degree* not as an either–or proposition.[46] Figure 15–2 illustrates how power can be shifted to the hands of nonmanagers step by step. The overriding goal is to increase productivity and competitiveness in leaner organizations. Each step in this evolution increases the power of organizational contributors who traditionally were told what, when, and how to do things. A good role model for the spirit of empowerment is Motorola executive Greg Brown:

He boils his philosophy down to three words: listen, learn, lead. It means you need to understand your business down to the nuts and bolts, let your employees know you

Azim Premji, Head of India's Outsourcing Giant Wipro, Is Not "King"

One of Premji's most important accomplishments has been creating a sinewy management culture that thrives even under intense competitive pressure. He established two core principles that are instrumental in building the character of his leadership team. The first is rare among India's family-controlled companies: The chairman is not king. While Premji owns a controlling stake in Wipro, he shares authority and responsibility with his subordinates. The second key principle: Premji believes in a zero-politics culture. At Wipro, backstabbing, playing favorites, and kissing up to the boss—tactics that sap much of American executives' energy—simply don't work. Open and honest disagreements are not only tolerated, but also required—of everyone.

The chairman's style isn't just to encourage his lieutenants to debate one another: Premji insists that they debate him as well—or even take him to task for his decisions or actions. "The man takes frontal criticism, and it's celebrated. You can openly disagree with him," says [Subroto] Bagchi, the former Wipro executive who launched Wipro's U.S. business from his dining room table....

For Premji, openness is more than a personal style. It's a strategy. "I find that people excel when they're provided a fair, free, and apolitical environment," he says. "At Wipro we strive to provide an open culture that encourages diversity of opinions. An organizational ability to encourage and harness diversity of thought is a significant competitive advantage."

Playing the game of business according to Premji's rules has worked well for Wipro. It's expanding revenues consistently at some 30% annually, while the overall tech services industry is expanding at about 5% per year. Meanwhile, operating margins in its tech business top 20%—more than twice the level of large Western services outfits.

Think of Wipro's success as a wake-up call for Americans who are complacent about the future of their companies or their job security. With its work ethic and intense drive to win, Wipro is a reminder of the America of 100 years ago.

Would you thrive or struggle in this sort of organization?

SOURCE: Excerpted from S Hamm, "How This Tiger Got Its Roar," *BusinessWeek,* October 30, 2006, pp 92–100.

Figure 15–2   *The Evolution of Power: From Domination to Delegation*

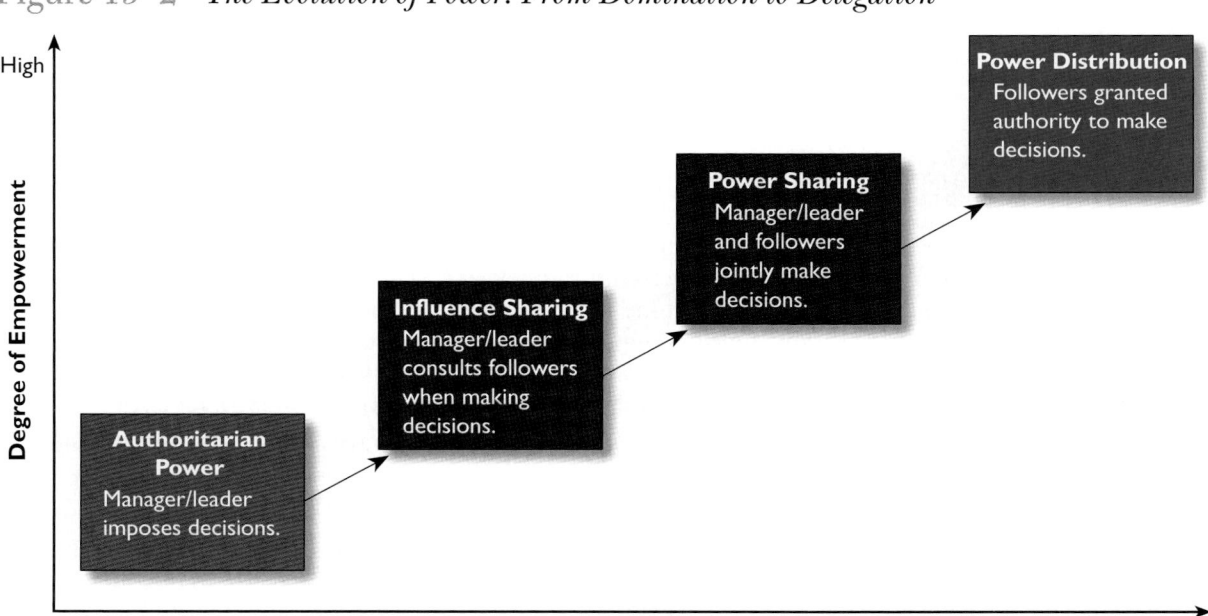

won't have all the answers, and focus on just a handful of truly crucial things, even though dozens seem as important.[47]

Participative Management

Confusion exists about the exact meaning of participative management (PM). Management experts have clarified this situation by defining **participative management** as the process whereby employees play a direct role in (1) setting goals, (2) making decisions, (3) solving problems, and (4) making changes in the organization. Participative management includes, but goes beyond, simply asking employees for their ideas or opinions.

Advocates of PM claim employee participation increases employee satisfaction, commitment, and performance. Consistent with both Maslow's need theory and the job characteristics model of job design (see Chapter 8), participative management is predicted to increase motivation because it helps employees fulfill three basic needs: (1) autonomy, (2) meaningfulness of work, and (3) interpersonal contact. Satisfaction of these needs enhances feelings of acceptance and commitment, security, challenge, and satisfaction. In turn, these positive feelings supposedly lead to increased innovation and performance.[48]

Participative management does not work in all situations. The design of work, the level of trust between management and employees, and the employees' competence and readiness to participate represent three factors that influence the effectiveness of PM. With respect to the design of work, individual participation is counterproductive when employees are highly interdependent on each other, as on an assembly line. The problem with individual participation in this case is that interdependent employees generally do not have a broad understanding of the entire production process. Participative management also is less likely to succeed when employees do not trust management. Finally, PM is more effective when employees are competent, prepared, and interested in participating. Northwest Airlines is a good case in point. Employees responded very positively to the company's new employee suggestion system because they were motivated to help the airline reduce operating costs in order to save jobs. The suggestion system resulted in $6 million in annual savings from workers' ideas.

> A flight attendant, for instance, noticed that too many coffeepots were being boarded on planes, so Northwest cut back and now saves $120,000 a year. A customer-service agent suggested that blanket folding and washing be done in-house, for savings of $205,000 annually. A manager in Minneapolis had an idea that resulted in an annual saving of $916,000 on maintenance on DC-10 thrust reversers.[49]

5 Delegation

The highest degree of empowerment is **delegation,** the process of granting decision-making authority to lower-level employees.[50] This amounts to *power distribution.* Delegation has long been the recommended way to lighten the busy manager's load while at the same time developing employees' abilities.[51] Importantly, delegation gives nonmanagerial employees more than simply a voice in decisions. It empowers them to make their own decisions. A prime example is the Ritz-Carlton Hotel chain:

> At Ritz-Carlton, every worker is authorized to spend up to $2,000 to fix any problem a guest encounters. Employees do not abuse the privilege. "When you treat people responsibly, they act responsibly," said Patrick Mene, the hotel chain's director of quality.[52]

Not surprising, then, that Ritz-Carlton has won national service quality awards.

Barriers to Delegation Delegation is easy to talk about, but many managers find it hard to actually do. A concerted effort to overcome the following common barriers to delegation needs to be made:

- Belief in the fallacy, "If you want it done right, do it yourself."
- Lack of confidence and trust in lower-level employees.
- Low self-confidence.
- Fear of being called lazy.
- Vague job definition.
- Fear of competition from those below.
- Reluctance to take the risks involved in depending on others.
- Lack of controls that provide early warning of problems with delegated duties.
- Poor example set by bosses who do not delegate.[53]

Delegation Research and Implications for Trust and Personal Initiative

Researchers at the State University of New York at Albany surveyed pairs of managers and employees and did follow-up interviews with the managers concerning their delegation habits. Their results confirmed some important common sense notions about delegation. Greater delegation was associated with the following factors:

1. Competent employee.
2. Employee shared manager's task objectives.
3. Manager had a long-standing and positive relationship with employee.
4. The lower-level person also was a supervisor.[54]

This delegation scenario boils down to one pivotal factor, *trust*.[55]

Managers prefer to delegate important tasks and decisions to the people they trust. As discussed in Chapter 11, it takes time and favorable experience to build trust. Of course, trust is fragile; it can be destroyed by a single remark, act, or omission. Ironically, managers cannot learn to trust someone without, initially at least, running the risk of betrayal. This is where the empowerment evolution in Figure 15–2 represents a three-step ladder to trust: consultation, participation, and delegation. In other words, managers need to start small and work up the empowerment ladder. They need to delegate small tasks and decisions and scale up as competence, confidence, and trust grow. Employees need to work on their side of the trust equation as well.[56] One of the best ways to earn a manager's trust is to show *initiative* (see Figure 15–3). Researchers in the area offer this instructive definition and characterization:

> **Personal initiative** is a behavior syndrome resulting in an individual's taking an active and self-starting approach to work and going beyond what is formally required in a given job. More specifically, personal initiative is characterized by the following aspects: it (1) is consistent with the organization's mission, (2) has a long-term focus, (3) is goal-directed and action-oriented, (4) is persistent in the face of barriers and setbacks, and (5) is self-starting and proactive.[57]

Personal initiative
Going beyond formal job requirements and being an active self-starter.

Recall our discussion of the *proactive personality* in Chapter 5.

Empowerment: The Research Record and Practical Advice

Like other widely heralded techniques—such as TQM, 360-degree reviews, teams, and learning organizations—empowerment has its fair share of critics and suffers from

Figure 15–3   *Personal Initiative: The Other Side of Delegation*

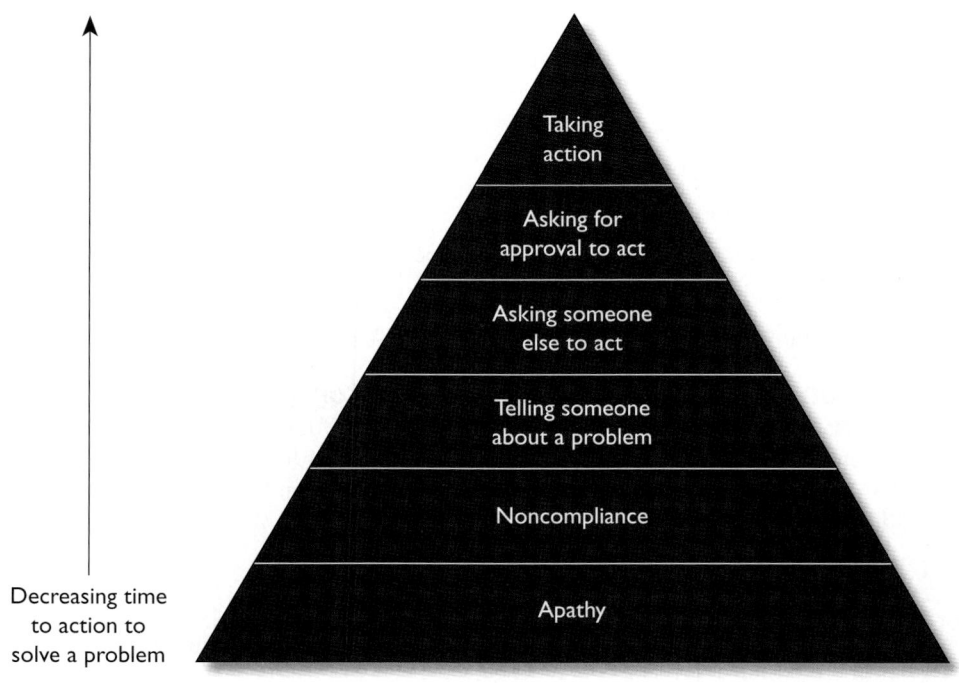

Decreasing time
to action to
solve a problem

Taking action

Asking for approval to act

Asking someone else to act

Telling someone about a problem

Noncompliance

Apathy

SOURCE: Figure from A L Frohman, "Igniting Organizational Change from Below: The Power of Personal Initiative," *Organizational Dynamics,* Winter 1997, p 46. © 1997, with permission from Elsevier.

unrealistic expectations.[58] Research results to date are mixed, with a recent positive uptrend:

- A meta-analysis encompassing 27 studies and 6,732 individuals revealed that employee participation in the performance appraisal process was positively related to an employee's satisfaction with his or her performance review, perceived value of the appraisal, motivation to improve performance after the review, and perceived fairness of the appraisal process.[59]

- Another meta-analysis of 86 studies involving 18,872 people demonstrated that participation had a small statistically significant positive impact on job performance but only a moderate positive effect on job satisfaction.[60]

- Relative to work teams, a recent field study of 102 hotels in the United States revealed that teams with empowering leadership tended to have more knowledge sharing, a greater sense of team efficacy, and better performance.[61]

- A study of 164 New Zealand companies employing at least 100 people found a positive correlation between high-involvement management practices and employee retention and company productivity.[62]

- A field study with 149 call center employees documented how "high-involvement work processes" more effectively boosted job performance (e.g., customer satisfaction), job satisfaction, and organizational commitment than did self-managed teams.[63]

- A recent study of 3,000 Canadian companies looked at the relationship between employee empowerment and layoffs. Productivity tended to drop after a layoff in high-involvement workplaces, *except* when the commitment to empowerment was continued during and after the layoff.[64]

We believe empowerment has good promise if managers go about it properly. Empowerment is a sweeping concept with many different definitions. Consequently, researchers use inconsistent measurements, and cause-effect relationships are fuzzy. Managers committed to the idea of employee empowerment need to follow the path of continuous improvement, learning from their successes and failures. Eight years of research with 10 "empowered" companies led Randolph to formulate the three-pronged empowerment plan in Figure 15–4. Notice how open-book management and active information sharing are needed to build the necessary foundation of trust. Beyond that, clear goals and lots of relevant training are needed. Noting that the empowerment process can take several years to unfold, Randolph offered this perspective:

> While the keys to empowerment may be easy to understand, they are hard to implement. It takes tremendous courage to start sharing sensitive information. It takes true strength to build more structure just at the point when people want more freedom of action. It takes real growth to allow teams to take over the management decision-making process. And above all, it takes perseverance to complete the empowerment process.[65]

Figure 15–4   *Randolph's Empowerment Model*

The Empowerment Plan

Share Information
- Share company performance information.
- Help people understand the business.
- Build trust through sharing sensitive information.
- Create self-monitoring possibilities.

Create Autonomy through Structure	**Let Teams Become the Hierarchy**
• Create a clear vision and clarify the little pictures.	• Provide direction and training for new skills.
• Create new decision-making rules that support empowerment.	• Provide encouragement and support for change.
• Clarify goals and roles collaboratively.	• Gradually have managers let go of control.
• Establish new empowering performance management processes.	• Work through the leadership vacuum stage.
• Use heavy doses of training.	• Acknowledge the fear factor.

**Remember: Empowerment is not magic;
it consists of a few simple steps and a lot of persistence.**

SOURCE: W A Randolph, "Navigating the Journey to Empowerment," *Organizational Dynamics,* Vol. 24, No. 3, p 46, © 1997, with permission from Elsevier.

6 Organizational Politics and Impression Management

Political wheeling and dealing occurs when contestants on *The Apprentice* strive to avoid being fired by Donald Trump. How would you handle yourself in such a stressful situation?

Most students of OB find the study of organizational politics intriguing. Perhaps this topic owes its appeal to the antics of Hollywood's corporate villains and contestants on *The Apprentice* stepping on each other to avoid Donald Trump's dreaded words, "you're fired!"[66] As we will see, however, organizational politics includes, but is certainly not limited to, dirty dealing. Organizational politics is an ever-present and sometimes annoying feature of modern work life. "Executives say that they spend 19% of their time dealing with political infighting with their staffs, according to a survey by OfficeTeam, a staffing services firm."[67] One expert recently observed, "Many 'new economy' companies use the acronym 'WOMBAT'—or waste of money, brains, and time—to describe office politics."[68] On the other hand, organizational politics can be a positive force in modern work organizations. Skillful and well-timed politics can help you get your point across, neutralize resistance to a key project, or get a choice job assignment.

Roberta Bhasin, a telephone company district manager, put organizational politics into perspective by observing the following:

> Most of us would like to believe that organizations are rationally structured, based on reasonable divisions of labor, a clear hierarchical communication flow, and well-defined lines of authority aimed at meeting universally understood goals and objectives.
>
> But organizations are made up of *people* with personal agendas designed to win power and influence. The agenda—the game—is called corporate politics. It is played by avoiding the rational structure, manipulating the communications hierarchy, and ignoring established lines of authority. The rules are never written down and seldom discussed.
>
> For some, corporate politics are second nature. They instinctively know the unspoken rules of the game. Others must learn. Managers who don't understand the politics of their organizations are at a disadvantage, not only in winning raises and promotions, but even in getting things *done*.[69]

To that end, 32% of 3,447 middle and senior managers responding to an Internet survey said they needed coaching in how to be more politically savvy at work.[70]

We explore this important and interesting area by (1) defining the term *organizational politics,* (2) identifying three levels of political action, (3) discussing eight specific political tactics, (4) considering a related area called *impression management,* and (5) examining relevant research and practical implications.

go to the Web for the Self-Exercise: How Political Are You?

Organizational politics

Intentional enhancement of self-interest.

Definition and Domain of Organizational Politics

"**Organizational politics** involves intentional acts of influence to enhance or protect the self-interest of individuals or groups."[71] An emphasis on *self-interest* distinguishes this form of social influence. Managers are constantly challenged to achieve a workable balance between employees' self-interests and organizational interests, as discussed at the beginning of this chapter. When a proper balance exists, the pursuit of self-interest may serve the organization's interests. Political behavior becomes a negative force when self-interests erode or defeat organizational interests. For example, researchers have documented the political tactic of filtering and distorting information flowing up to the boss. This self-serving practice put the reporting employees in the best possible light.[72]

Uncertainty Triggers Political Behavior

Political maneuvering is triggered primarily by *uncertainty*. Five common sources of uncertainty within organizations are

1. Unclear objectives.
2. Vague performance measures.
3. Ill-defined decision processes.
4. Strong individual or group competition.[73]
5. Any type of change.

Regarding this last source of uncertainty, organization development specialist Anthony Raia noted, "Whatever we attempt to change, the political subsystem becomes active. Vested interests are almost always at stake and the distribution of power is challenged."[74]

"STOP WHIMPERING AND SPIN THE WHEEL OF BLAME, LIPTON!"

SOURCE: *Harvard Business Review,* November 2003, p 86. © Scott A Masear. Reprinted by permission of the author.

Thus, we would expect a field sales representative, striving to achieve an assigned quota, to be less political than a management trainee working on a variety of projects. While some management trainees stake their career success on hard work, competence, and a bit of luck, many do not. These people attempt to gain a competitive edge through some combination of the political tactics discussed below. Meanwhile, the salesperson's performance is measured in actual sales, not in terms of being friends with the boss or taking credit for others' work. Thus, the management trainee would tend to be more political than the field salesperson because of greater uncertainty about management's expectations.

Because employees generally experience greater uncertainty during the earlier stages of their careers, are junior employees more political than more senior ones? The answer is yes, according to a survey of 243 employed adults in upstate New York. In fact, one senior employee nearing retirement told the researcher: "I used to play political games when I was younger. Now I just do my job."[75]

Three Levels of Political Action

Although much political maneuvering occurs at the individual level, it also can involve group or collective action. Figure 15–5 illustrates three different levels of political action: the individual level, the coalition level, and the network level.[76] Each level has its distinguishing characteristics. At the individual level, personal self-interests are pursued by the individual. The political aspects of coalitions and networks are not so obvious, however.

People with a common interest can become a political coalition by fitting the following definition. In an organizational context, a **coalition** is an informal group bound together by the *active* pursuit of a *single* issue. Coalitions may or may not coincide with formal group membership. When the target issue is resolved (a sexual-harassing supervisor is fired, for example), the coalition disbands. Experts note that political coalitions have "fuzzy boundaries," meaning they are fluid in membership, flexible in structure, and temporary in duration.[77]

Coalitions are a potent political force in organizations. Consider the situation Charles J Bradshaw faced in a finance committee meeting at Transworld Corporation. Bradshaw,

Coalition

Temporary groupings of people who actively pursue a single issue.

Figure 15–5   *Levels of Political Action in Organizations*

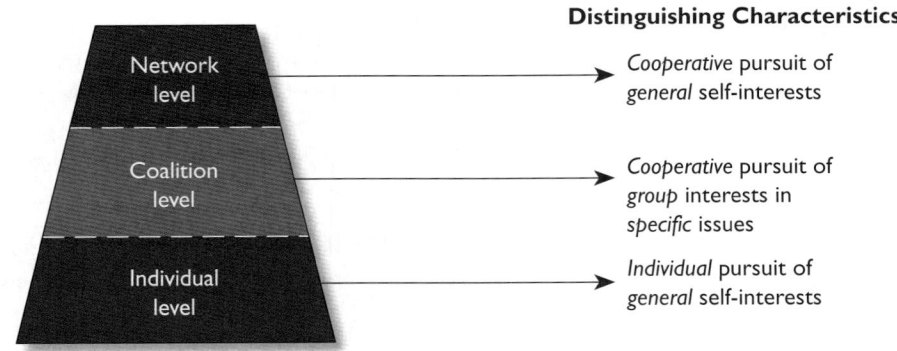

Distinguishing Characteristics

Network level → *Cooperative* pursuit of *general* self-interests

Coalition level → *Cooperative* pursuit of *group* interests in *specific* issues

Individual level → *Individual* pursuit of *general* self-interests

president of the company, opposed the chairman's plan to acquire a $93 million nursing home company:

> [The senior vice president for finance] kicked off the meeting with a battery of facts and figures in support of the deal. "Within two or three minutes, I knew I had lost," Bradshaw concedes. "No one was talking directly to me, but all statements addressed my opposition. I could tell there was a general agreement around the board table." . . .
> Then the vote was taken. Five hands went up. Only Bradshaw voted no.[78]

After the meeting, Bradshaw resigned his $530,000-a-year position, without as much as a handshake or good-bye from the chairman. In Bradshaw's case, the finance committee was a formal group that temporarily became a political coalition aimed at sealing his fate at Transworld. In recent years, coalitions on the corporate boards of Home Depot, Computer Associates, and Hewlett-Packard ousted the heads of those giant companies.

A third level of political action involves networks.[79] Unlike coalitions, which pivot on specific issues, networks are loose associations of individuals seeking social support for their general self-interests. Politically, networks are people oriented, while coalitions are issue oriented. Networks have broader and longer term agendas than do coalitions. For instance, Avon's Hispanic employees have built a network to enhance the members' career opportunities.[80]

Political Tactics

Anyone who has worked in an organization has firsthand knowledge of blatant politicking. Blaming someone else for your mistake is an obvious political ploy. But other political tactics are more subtle. Researchers have identified a range of political behavior.

One landmark study, involving in-depth interviews with 87 managers from 30 electronics companies in southern California, identified eight political tactics. Top-, middle-, and low-level managers were represented about equally in the sample. According to the researchers: "Respondents were asked to describe organizational political tactics and personal characteristics of effective political actors based upon their accumulated experience in *all* organizations in which they had worked."[81] Listed in descending order of occurrence, the eight political tactics that emerged were

1. Attacking or blaming others.
2. Using information as a political tool.

3. Creating a favorable image. (Also known as *impression management.*)

4. Developing a base of support.

5. Praising others (ingratiation).

6. Forming power coalitions with strong allies.

7. Associating with influential people.

8. Creating obligations (reciprocity).

Table 15–1 describes these political tactics and indicates how often each reportedly was used by the interviewed managers.

The researchers distinguished between reactive and proactive political tactics. Some of the tactics, such as scapegoating, were *reactive* because the intent was to *defend* one's self-interest. Other tactics, such as developing a base of support, were *proactive* because they sought to *promote* the individual's self-interest.

Table 15–1   *Eight Common Political Tactics in Organizations*

POLITICAL TACTIC	PERCENTAGE OF MANAGERS MENTIONING TACTIC	BRIEF DESCRIPTION OF TACTIC
1. Attacking or blaming others	54%	Used to avoid or minimize association with failure. Reactive when scapegoating is involved. Proactive when goal is to reduce competition for limited resources.
2. Using information as a political tool	54	Involves the purposeful withholding or distortion of information. Obscuring an unfavorable situation by overwhelming superiors with information.
3. Creating a favorable image (impression management)	53	Dressing/grooming for success. Adhering to organizational norms and drawing attention to one's successes and influence. Taking credit for others' accomplishments.
4. Developing a base of support	37	Getting prior support for a decision. Building others' commitment to a decision through participation.
5. Praising others (ingratiation)	25	Making influential people feel good ("apple polishing").
6. Forming power coalitions with strong allies	25	Teaming up with powerful people who can get results.
7. Associating with influential people	24	Building a support network both inside and outside the organization.
8. Creating obligations (reciprocity)	13	Creating social debts ("I did you a favor, so you owe me a favor").

SOURCE: Adapted from R W Allen, D L Madison, L W Porter, P A Renwick, and B T Mayes, "Organizational Politics: Tactics and Characteristics of Its Actors," *California Management Review*, Fall 1979, pp 77–83.

Table 15–2   *Are You Politically Naive, Politically Sensible, or a Political Shark?*

CHARACTERISTICS	NAIVE	SENSIBLE	SHARKS
Underlying attitude	Politics is unpleasant.	Politics is necessary.	Politics is an opportunity.
Intent	Avoid at all costs.	Further departmental goals.	Self-serving and predatory.
Techniques	Tell it like it is.	Network; expand connections; use system to give and receive favors.	Manipulate; use fraud and deceit when necessary.
Favorite tactics	None—the truth will win out.	Negotiate, bargain.	Bully; misuse information; cultivate and use "friends" and other contacts.

SOURCE: Reprinted from J K Pinto and O P Kharbanda, "Lessons for an Accidental Profession," *Business Horizons*, Vol. 38, No. 2, p 45, © 1995, with permission from Elsevier.

What is your attitude toward organizational politics? How often do you rely on the various tactics in Table 15–1? You can get a general indication of your political tendencies by comparing your behavior with the characteristics in Table 15–2. Would you characterize yourself as politically *naive,* politically *sensible,* or a political *shark?* How do you think others view your political actions? What are the career, friendship, and ethical implications of your political tendencies?[82]

 7 Impression Management

Impression management

Getting others to see us in a certain manner.

Impression management is defined as "the process by which people attempt to control or manipulate the reactions of others to images of themselves or their ideas."[83] This encompasses how one talks, behaves, and looks. Most impression management attempts are directed at making a *good* impression on relevant others. But, as we will see, some employees strive to make a *bad* impression. For purposes of conceptual clarity, we will focus on *upward* impression management (trying to impress one's immediate supervisor) because it is most relevant for managers. Still, it is good to remember that *anyone* can be the intended target of impression management. Parents, teachers, peers, voters, employees, and customers are all fair game when it comes to managing the impressions of others.

go to the Web for the Group Exercise: You Make Me Feel So Good!

A Conceptual Crossroads Impression management is an interesting conceptual crossroads involving self-monitoring, attribution theory, and organizational politics.[84] Perhaps this explains why impression management has gotten active research attention in recent years. High self-monitoring employees ("chameleons" who adjust to their surroundings) are likely to be more inclined to engage in impression management than would low self-monitors.[85] Impression management also involves the systematic manipulation of attributions. For example, a bank president will look good if the board of directors is encouraged to attribute organizational successes to her efforts and attribute problems and failures to factors beyond her control. Impression management definitely fits into the realm of organizational politics because of an overriding focus on furthering one's *self-interests*.

Making a Good Impression If you "dress for success," project an upbeat attitude at all times, and have polished a 15-second elevator speech for top executives, you are engaging in favorable impression management—particularly so if your motive is to improve your lot in life. Is it all worth the effort? In a recent survey of 2,198 employees, 56% said dressing for success paid off; 44% said no.[86] Too close to call. There are questionable ways to create a good impression, as well. For instance, Stewart Friedman, director of the University of Pennsylvania's Leadership Program, offered this gem:

> Last year, I was doing some work with a large bank. The people there told me a story that astounded me: After 7 PM, people would open the door to their office, drape a spare jacket on the back of their chair, lay a set of glasses down on some reading material on their desk—and then go home for the night. The point of this elaborate gesture was to create the illusion that they were just out grabbing dinner and would be returning to burn the midnight oil.[87]

Impression management can easily stray into unethical territory.

A statistical factor analysis of the influence attempts reported by a sample of 84 bank employees (including 74 women) identified three categories of favorable upward impression management tactics.[88] Favorable upward impression management tactics can be *job-focused* (manipulating information about one's job performance), *supervisor-focused* (praising and doing favors for one's supervisor), and *self-focused* (presenting oneself as a polite and nice person). A moderate amount of upward impression management is a necessity for the average employee today (see the Real World/Real People feature on page 454). Too little, and busy managers are liable to overlook some of your valuable contributions when they make job assignment, pay, and promotion decisions. Too much, and you run the risk of being branded a "schmoozer," a "phony," and other unflattering things by your co-workers. Excessive flattery and ingratiation can backfire by embarrassing the target person and damaging one's credibility. Also, the risk of unintended insult is very high when impression management tactics cross gender, racial, ethnic, and cultural lines. International management experts warn

> The impression management tactic is only as effective as its correlation to accepted norms about behavioral presentation. In other words, slapping a Japanese subordinate on the back with a rousing "Good work, Hiro!" will not create the desired impression in Hiro's mind that the expatriate intended. In fact, the behavior will likely create the opposite impression.[89]

Making a Poor Impression At first glance, the idea of consciously trying to make a bad impression in the workplace seems absurd. But an interesting new line of impression management research has uncovered both motives and tactics for making oneself look *bad*. In a survey of the work experiences of business students at a large northwestern US university, more than half "reported witnessing a case of someone intentionally looking bad at work."[90] Why? Four motives came out of the study:

> (1) *Avoidance:* Employee seeks to avoid additional work, stress, burnout, or an unwanted transfer or promotion. (2) *Obtain concrete rewards:* Employee seeks to obtain a pay raise or a desired transfer, promotion, or demotion. (3) *Exit:* Employee seeks to get laid off,

Advice for New College Graduates Who Want to Make a Good Impression on the Job

First of all, forget some of the most basic habits you learned in school. Once you are in the real world—and it doesn't make any difference if you are 22 or 62, starting your first job or your fifth—the way to look great and get ahead is to overdeliver. For years you've been taught the virtue of meeting specific expectations. And you've been trained to believe that an A-plus performance means fully answering every question the teacher asks. Those days are over.

To get an A-plus in business, you have to expand the organization's expectations of you and then exceed them, and you have to fully answer every question the "teachers" ask, plus a slew they didn't think of.

Your goal, in other words, should be to make your bosses smarter, your team more effective, and the whole company more competitive because of your energy, creativity, and insights. And you thought school was hard!

...give your boss shock and awe—something compelling that she can report to her bosses. In time, those kinds of ideas will move the company forward, and move you upward.

But be careful. People who strive to overdeliver can swiftly self-destruct if their exciting suggestions are seen by others as unfettered braggadocio, not-so-subtle ladder scaling, or both. That's right. Personal ambition can backfire.

Now, we're not saying curb your enthusiasm. But the minute you wear career lust on your sleeve, you run the risk of alienating people, in particular your peers. They will soon come to doubt the motives of your hard work. They will see any comments you make about, say, how the team could operate better, as political jockeying. And they will eventually peg you as an unrestrained striver, and, in the long run, that's a label that all the A-plus performing in the world can't overcome. So by all means, overdeliver—but keep your desire to distinguish yourself as a winner to yourself. You'll become one faster.

What do you do in the way of impression management in the workplace? And outside of work?

SOURCE: Excerpted from J Welch and S Welch, "Dear Graduate...," *BusinessWeek*, June 19, 2006, p 100.

---

fired, or suspended, and perhaps also to collect unemployment or workers' compensation. (4) *Power:* Employee seeks to control, manipulate, or intimidate others, get revenge, or make someone else look bad.[91]

Within the context of these motives, *unfavorable* upward impression management makes sense.

Five unfavorable upward impression management tactics identified by the researchers are as follows:

- *Decreasing performance*—restricting productivity, making more mistakes than usual, lowering quality, neglecting tasks.

- *Not working to potential*—pretending ignorance, having unused capabilities.

- *Withdrawing*—being tardy, taking excessive breaks, faking illness.

- *Displaying a bad attitude*—complaining, getting upset and angry, acting strangely, not getting along with co-workers.

- *Broadcasting limitations*—letting co-workers know about one's physical problems and mistakes, both verbally and nonverbally.[92]

Recommended ways to manage employees who try to make a bad impression can be found throughout this book. They include more challenging work, greater autonomy, better feedback, supportive leadership, clear and reasonable goals, and a less stressful work setting.

Research Evidence on Organizational Politics and Impression Management

Field research involving employees in real organizations rather than students in contrived laboratory settings has yielded these useful insights:

- In a study of 514 nonacademic university employees in the southwestern United States, white men had a greater understanding of organizational politics than did racial and ethnic minorities and white women. The researchers endorsed the practice of using mentors to help women and minorities develop their political skills.[93]

- Another study of 68 women and 84 men employed by five different service and industrial companies in the United States uncovered significant gender-based insights about organizational politics. In what might be termed the battle of the sexes,

   > it was found that political behavior was perceived more favorably when it was performed against a target of the opposite gender.... Thus subjects of both sexes tend to relate to gender as a meaningful affiliation group. This finding presents a different picture from the one suggesting that women tend to accept male superiority at work and generally agree with sex stereotypes which are commonly discriminatory in nature.[94]

- In a more recent survey of 172 team members in a large company's research and development unit, perceived higher levels of team politics were associated with lower organizational commitment, lower job satisfaction, poorer job performance, and lower unit effectiveness.[95]

The results of a cross-cultural laboratory study are noteworthy. A unique study of 38 Japanese Americans and 39 European Americans at the University of Utah showed how impression management can cause problems across cultures. Consistent with Japanese tradition, the Japanese Americans tended to publicly report their job performance in a self-effacing (or modest) way, *despite confiding in private that they had performed as well as the European Americans.* This Japanese cultural tendency toward understatement created a false impression for third-party European American evaluators (who were kept unaware of any cultural distinctions). According to the researchers, "Japanese American participants were seen as less competent and less likeable than their European American counterparts because of their tendency to downplay their performance."[96] The old American expression "It pays to toot your own horn" appears to be as true as ever. Too much tooting, however, can brand one as arrogant, self-centered, and overbearing. This sort of delicate cultural balancing act makes cross-cultural dealings very challenging.

go to the Web for the Self-Exercise: How Much Do You Rely on Upward Impression Management Tactics?

8 Managing Organizational Politics

Organizational politics cannot be eliminated. A manager would be naive to expect such an outcome. But political maneuvering can and should be managed to keep it constructive and within reasonable bounds. Harvard's Abraham Zaleznik put the issue

Table 15–3   *How to Keep Organizational Politics within Reasonable Bounds*

- Screen out overly political individuals at hiring time.
- Create an open-book management system.
- Make sure every employee knows how the business works and has a personal line of sight to key results with corresponding measurable objectives for individual accountability.
- Have nonfinancial people interpret periodic financial and accounting statements for all employees.
- Establish formal conflict resolution and grievance processes.
- As an ethics filter, do only what you would feel comfortable doing on national television.
- Publicly recognize and reward people who get real results without political games.

SOURCE: Adapted in part from discussion in L B MacGregor Server, "The End of Office Politics as Usual" (New York: American Management Association, 2002), pp 184–99.

this way: "People can focus their attention on only so many things. The more it lands on politics, the less energy—emotional and intellectual—is available to attend to the problems that fall under the heading of real work."[97]

An individual's degree of politicalness is a matter of personal values, ethics, and temperament. People who are either strictly nonpolitical or highly political generally pay a price for their behavior. The former may experience slow promotions and feel left out, while the latter may run the risk of being called self-serving and lose their credibility. People at both ends of the political spectrum may be considered poor team players. A moderate amount of prudent political behavior generally is considered a survival tool in complex organizations. Experts remind us that

> political behavior has earned a bad name only because of its association with politicians. On its own, the use of power and other resources to obtain your objectives is not inherently unethical. It all depends on what the preferred objectives are.[98]

With this perspective in mind, the practical steps in Table 15–3 are recommended. How many of the Enron- and WorldCom–type scandals could have been prevented with this approach? Remember: Measurable objectives are management's first line of defense against negative expressions of organizational politics.

Summary of Key Concepts

1. *Explain the concept of mutuality of interest.* Managers are constantly challenged to foster mutuality of interest (a win–win situation) between individual and organizational interests. Organization members need to actively cooperate with actual and potential adversaries for the common good.

2. *Name at least three "soft" and two "hard" influence tactics, and summarize the practical lessons from influence research.* Five soft influence tactics are rational persuasion, inspirational appeals, consultation, ingratiation, and personal appeals. They are more friendly and less coercive than the four hard influence tactics: exchange, coalition tactics, pressure, and legitimating tactics. According to research, soft tactics are better for generating commitment and are perceived as more fair than hard tactics. Ingratiation—making the boss feel good through compliments and being helpful—can slightly improve performance appraisal results and make the boss like you a lot more. Influence through domination is a poor strategy for both men and women. Influence is a complicated and situational process that needs to be undertaken with care, especially across cultures.

3. *Identify and briefly describe French and Raven's five bases of power, and discuss the responsible use of power.* French and

Raven's five bases of power are reward power (rewarding compliance), coercive power (punishing noncompliance), legitimate power (relying on formal authority), expert power (providing needed information), and referent power (relying on personal attraction). Responsible and ethical managers strive to use socialized power (primary concern is for others) rather than personalized power (primary concern for self). Research found higher organizational commitment among employees with bosses who used uplifting power than among those with power-hungry bosses who relied on dominating power.

4. **Define the term** empowerment, **and explain why it is a matter of degree.** Empowerment involves sharing varying degrees of power and decision-making authority with lower-level employees to tap their full potential. Empowerment is not an either-or, all-or-nothing proposition. It can range from merely consulting with employees, to having them actively participate in making decisions, to granting them decision-making authority through delegation

5. **Explain why delegation is the highest form of empowerment, and discuss the connections among delegation, trust, and personal initiative.** Delegation gives employees more than a participatory role in decision making. It allows them to make their own work-related decisions. Managers tend to delegate to employees they trust. Employees can get managers to trust them by demonstrating personal initiative (going beyond formal job requirements and being self-starters).

6. **Define organizational politics,** and explain what triggers it. Organizational politics is defined as intentional acts of influence to enhance or protect the self-interests of individuals or groups. Uncertainty triggers most politicking in organizations. Political action occurs at individual, coalition, and network levels. Coalitions are informal, temporary, and single-issue alliances.

7. **Distinguish between favorable and unfavorable impression management tactics.** Favorable upward impression management can be job-focused (manipulating information about one's job performance), supervisor-focused (praising or doing favors for the boss), or self-focused (being polite and nice). Unfavorable upward impression management tactics include decreasing performance, not working to potential, withdrawing, displaying a bad attitude, and broadcasting one's limitations.

8. **Explain how to manage organizational politics.** Since organizational politics cannot be eliminated, managers need to keep it within reasonable bounds. Measurable objectives for personal accountability are key. Participative management also helps, especially in the form of open-book management. Formal conflict resolution and grievance programs are helpful. Overly political people should not be hired, and employees who get results without playing political games should be publicly recognized and rewarded. The "how-would-it-look-on-TV" ethics test can limit political maneuvering.

Key Terms

OB in Action Case Study

How Bob Iger Unchained Disney[99]

BusinessWeek For the past year [2006–2007], the media-entertainment complex (aka Hollywood) has provided riveting theater. Summary firings at Viacom. A quixotic bid to break up Time Warner. News Corp.'s O J Simpson moment. But one entertainment colossus has been remarkably peaceful—so much so it's easy to forget that not long ago this place was a snake pit of warring egos, board intrigue, and assorted skullduggery.

That institution, of course, is Walt Disney Company. Not only has peace broken out since Robert A Iger settled into Michael D Eisner's throne at the pseudo-Tuscan

457

headquarters in Burbank, California, but the Mouse House also has been racking up enviable numbers. It's posting record earnings, and the stock price has been defying gravity like Disneyland's Big Thunder Mountain Railroad....

Behind the scenes he has upended Eisner's centrally planned company, hacking away at the bureaucracy and unshackling a group of veteran executives to plot their own courses. Putting Disney movies and ABC shows on the iPod is not just ground-breaking. It's a reflection of a faster-moving and more aggressive Disney....

Iger, who turn[ed] 56 on February 10, [2007] is a guy who says things like: "The story shouldn't be about me. It's about the team." Sounds like the false modesty of a media-trained CEO, no? But Iger really does prefer to hover in the background, letting the limelight stream over his lieutenants. He rules by consensus, not fiat. And rather than heaving Eisner's people overboard just because he could, Iger has kept the team largely intact....

And while Iger isn't without the vision thing, no one would call him a big strategic thinker. But by surrounding himself with smart people, including [Apple CEO Steve] Jobs and the Pixar crew, and letting them get on with it, Iger has recreated a can-do culture at Disney.

Iger, in short, is the Un-Eisner. He represents the new buttoned-down Hollywood—the anti-mogul in an industry where egos blot out the sunshine. "Bob lets [the person] who can handle the job get it done," says Jobs, who sits on the board and is Disney's single largest shareholder. "It's not [about grabbing] headlines. That's rare in that town."

Most Hollywood bigs either have mogul DNA (Rupert Murdoch) or lust for power and riches from Day One (Eisner). But Robert Iger wanted to be Walter Cronkite. Growing up on Long Island in Oceanside, N.Y., the son of a marketing executive father and librarian mother, Iger got the journalism bug early as sports editor of his high school newspaper. By 1972 a shaggy-haired Iger was hosting Ithaca College's ICB-TV show *Campus Probe,* tackling such breaking news as the school's new credit union. But the networks never came calling, and Iger accepted a job as a weatherman at a local TV station.

He might still be in Ithaca, N.Y., today had he not signed on as a schedule coordinator for ABC Sports in 1974. Soon after joining the network, Iger met the surrogate father who helped launch his career and instilled in him the management ethos he follows to this day. That man was Thomas S Murphy, founder of ABC's then-parent, CapCities. Murphy, now 80 and retired from the Disney board, was a legendary figure who gave young talent the freedom to experiment.

Iger calls it the Tom Murphy School of Management. "You put good people in jobs and give them room to run," he says. "You involve yourself in a responsible way, but not to the point where you are usurping their authority. I don't have the time or concentration—and you could argue maybe even the talent—to do that."

Disney acquired CapCities in 1996, and Iger, by then Murphy's heir apparent, found himself working for an entirely different species of boss. Eisner was everything Murphy wasn't: micromanaging, imperious, bullying....

To this day, Iger won't speak ill of Eisner. "I think fondly of Michael. I learned a lot from him," he says. "In a way, he founded the modern Walt Disney."

What Iger tactfully leaves unsaid is that during the final years of Eisner's otherwise brilliant two-decade run, Disney lost its animating spirit. To say the culture was poisonous doesn't begin to capture the company's dysfunction. Eisner left behind a place where division chiefs were afraid to make decisions—the last thing the company needed when such rivals as News Corp. and Viacom Inc. were boldly staking out territory on the Web.

Iger recognized that the problem wasn't the people running the show. It was the work environment—and he set about changing it. One of the first things Iger did was make the Monday morning meetings less autocratic. Where Eisner held court, Iger encourages a conversation. Even his office is more inviting. Out went the drabness of the Eisner years. In came airiness, family photos....

To encourage his executives to drop by, Iger also installed a door to a more heavily trafficked hallway. He moved studio chief Richard Cook up from the second floor to the sixth, where Iger has his office. And he made a point of visiting the troops—for example spending half a day at Buena Vista Games Inc. talking to game developers in town for a brainstorming session. "These are guys who'll go back to England or wherever with a sense that their ideas are getting heard," says game unit chief Graham Hopper. "That's tremendously empowering to a creative person." ...

Iger brings almost preternatural energy to the job. Every morning at 4:30 a personal trainer puts him through his paces at the Brentwood mansion (formerly owned by Michelle Pfeiffer and her TV writer husband, David E. Kelley) Iger shares with his wife, newscaster Willow Bay, and their two sons. By 6:45, Iger is at his desk, talking to New York.

It's what Iger doesn't do with his energy that is most telling. He doesn't dump on people's ideas. Eisner famously wrote: "Where's my wow?" on subordinates' proposals he didn't like. And where Eisner got involved in every aspect of the creative process, from the color of the carpets at the theme park hotels to Tuesday morning script sessions, Iger lets his people take the lead....

ABC chief [Anne] Sweeney recalls Iger dropping by her office not long after he took over to talk about the network's future. She suggested coming up with an ABC site where viewers could get TV shows whenever they want. "We had a really interesting discussion of how you'd construct your own [online] network," says Sweeney. "Bob's parting words were: "Go fast." A month later he announced the initiative at Disney's annual meeting.

Questions for Discussion

1. What are Eisner's and Iger's primary influence tactics in this case? Which man would do a better job of influencing and persuading you, if you worked for Disney?

2. Relative to running Disney, how does Iger's power base differ from Eisner's? What are the organizational implications of this difference?

3. What steps has Iger taken to create a culture of empowerment at Disney?

4. How do you score Iger on delegation? Explain.

5. Which management style, Eisner's or Iger's, would tend to prompt more political behavior at Disney? Explain.

Ethical Dilemma

You Say You Never Lie? That's a Lie!

It can be hard to get people to face the truth sometimes. Especially about lying.

You don't want your kids to eat too much, so you say all the cookies are gone.

You don't feel like going out, so you tell your date something important came up.

You're overloaded with errands, so you call in sick.

Lies, all of them, but we don't really like calling them that. In an Associated Press-Ipsos poll, more than half of respondents said lying was never justified. Yet in the same poll, up to two-thirds said it was OK to lie in certain situations, like protecting someone's feelings.

Apparently white lies are an acceptable, even necessary, part of many lives, even though we dislike the idea of lying. ...

Among the groups more likely to say lying was sometimes OK: people ages 18–29, college graduates and those with higher household incomes.[100]

When, If Ever, Is It Ethical for a Manager to Lie? Explain Your Moral Reasoning.

1. Never. A lie is a lie and it is immoral to deceive others, especially those for whom you are responsible.

2. Harmless "white lies" are okay when used to protect people's feelings. "Say, how do you like my new haircut?" "Do I look like I've gained some weight?"

3. True, it's wrong to lie. But life isn't perfect, so the truth needs to be bent a little bit sometimes. (When, and in what situations, exactly?)

4. Get real. Everyone lies one time or another. The trick is to do it skillfully and not overdo it.

5. A harmless white lie now and then is okay, but care needs to be taken because any sort of lying damages a manager's credibility.

6. Invent other options. Discuss.

Web Resources

For study material and exercises that apply to this chapter, visit our Web site, **www.mhhe.com/kreitner**

CHAPTER 16

Leadership

When you finish studying the material in this chapter, you should be able to:

1 Define the term *leadership*, and explain the difference between leading and managing.

2 Review trait theory research and the takeaways from this theoretical perspective.

3 Explain behavioral styles theory and its takeaways.

4 Explain, according to Fiedler's contingency model, how leadership style interacts with situational control, and discuss the takeaways from this model.

5 Discuss House's revised path–goal theory, and its practical takeaways.

6 Describe the difference between laissez-faire, transactional, and transformational leadership.

7 Discuss how transformational leadership transforms followers and work groups.

8 Explain the leader–member exchange model of leadership and the concept of shared leadership.

9 Review the Level 5 model of leadership and the principles of servant-leadership.

10 Describe the follower's role in the leadership process.

Student Resources for Studying Chapter 16

online **resources**

The Web site for your text includes resources that will help you master the concepts in this chapter. As you read, you'll want to visit the site for these helpful tools:

- Your online Study Guide includes learning objectives, a chapter summary, a glossary of key terms, and discussion questions.
- Take a practice quiz and test your knowledge!
- Scroll through a PowerPoint presentation with key concepts for this chapter.

Your instructor might also direct you to the Web site for these exercises:

- Self-assessments that correspond with the chapter content and a Group Exercise.
- You'll also find Video Cases and Internet Exercises for this chapter online.

www.mhhe.com/kreitner

Here is what Jack and Suzy Welch had to say about being successful in your first role as a leader.

> Being a leader means you will actually have to change how you act. Too often, people who are promoted to their first leadership position miss that point. And that failure probably trips up careers more than any other reason.
>
> Being a leader changes everything. Before you are a leader, success is all about you. It's about your performance. Your contributions. It's about raising your hand, getting called on, and delivering the right answer.
>
> When you become a leader, success is all about growing others. It's about making the people who work for you smarter, bigger, and bolder. Nothing you do anymore as an individual matters except how you nurture and support your team and help its members increase their self-confidence. Yes, you will get your share of attention from up above—but only inasmuch as your team wins. Put another way: Your success as a leader will come not from what you do but from the reflected glory of your team.
>
> Now, that's a big transition—and no question, it's hard. Being a leader basically requires a whole new mindset. You're no longer constantly thinking "How can I stand out?" but "How can I help my people do their jobs better?" Sometimes that requires undoing a couple of decades of momentum. After all, you probably spent your entire life, starting in grade school and continuing through your last job, as a contributor who excels at "raising your hand." But the good news is that you've been promoted because someone above you believes you have the stuff to make the leap from star player to successful coach.
>
> What does that leap actually involve? First and foremost, you need to actively mentor your people. Exude positive energy about life and the work that you are doing together, show optimism about the future, and care.

Jack and Suzy Welch.

Care passionately about each person's progress. Give your people feedback—not just at yearend and midyear performance reviews but after meetings, presentations, or visits to clients. Make every significant event a teaching moment. Discuss what you like about what they are doing and ways that they can improve. Your energy will energize those around you.

And there's no need for sugarcoating. Use total candor, which happens, incidentally, to be one of the defining characteristics of effective leaders.

Through it all, never forget—you're a leader now. It's not about you anymore. It's about them.[1]

FOR DISCUSSION

Why is it hard to go from being a high-performing individual to being a successful leader?

The chapter opening vignette highlights that effective leadership is all about focusing on others. This can be particularly difficult for overachievers. Overachieving leaders have been found to relentlessly push their direct reports, to the point of demanding and coercing, instead of coaching and empowering. This approach to leadership ultimately stifles employees.[2]

Someone once observed that a leader is a person who finds out which way the parade is going, jumps in front of it, and yells "Follow me!" The plain fact is that this approach to leadership has little chance of working in today's rapidly changing world. In short, successful leaders are those individuals who can step into a difficult situation and make a noticeable difference. But how much of a difference can leaders make in modern organizations?

OB researchers have discovered that leaders can make a difference. One study, for instance, revealed that leadership was positively associated with net profits from 167 companies over a time span of 20 years.[3] Research also showed that a coach's leadership skills affected the success of his or her team. Specifically, teams in both Major League Baseball and college basketball won more games when players perceived the coach to be an effective leader.[4] Rest assured, leadership makes a difference.

After formally defining the term *leadership,* this chapter focuses on the following areas: (1) trait and behavioral approaches to leadership, (2) alternative situational theories of leadership, (3) the full-range theory of leadership, and (4) additional perspectives on leadership. Because there are many different leadership theories within each of these areas, it is impossible to discuss them all. This chapter reviews those theories with the most research support.

What Does Leadership Involve?

Because the topic of leadership has fascinated people for centuries, definitions abound. This section presents a definition of leadership, reviews the different approaches or perspectives used to study leadership, and highlights the similarities and differences between leading and managing.

Leadership Defined

Disagreement about the definition of leadership stems from the fact that it involves a complex interaction among the leader, the followers, and the situation. For example, some researchers define leadership in terms of personality and physical traits, while others believe leadership is represented by a set of prescribed behaviors. In contrast, other researchers define leadership in terms of the power relationship between leaders and followers. According to this perspective, leaders use their power to influence followers' behavior. Leadership also can be seen as an instrument of goal achievement.

In other words, leaders are individuals who help others accomplish their goals. Still others view leadership from a skills perspective.

There are four commonalities among the many definitions of **leadership:** (1) leadership is a process between a leader and followers, (2) leadership involves social influence, (3) leadership occurs at multiple levels in an organization (at the individual level, for example, leadership involves mentoring, coaching, inspiring, and motivating; leaders also build teams, generate cohesion, and resolve conflicts at the group level; finally, leaders build culture and generate change at the organizational level),[5] and (4) leadership focuses on goal accomplishment.[6] Based on these commonalities, leadership is defined as "a process whereby an individual influences a group of individuals to achieve a common goal."[7]

Approaches to Leadership

Leadership is one of the most frequently investigated topics within the field of OB due to its importance to all organizations. As such, there are several different approaches or perspectives that have guided leadership research. While the popularity of these approaches has changed over time, knowledge of each one provides you with a better understanding of how the leadership process unfolds.

This chapter examines the different leadership approaches outlined in Table 16–1. OB researchers began their study of leadership in the early part of the 20th century by focusing on the traits associated with leadership effectiveness. This perspective was followed by attempts in the 1950s and 1960s to examine the behaviors or styles exhibited by effective leaders. This research led to the realization that there is not one best style of leadership, which in turn spawned various contingency approaches to leadership in the 1960s and 70s. Contingency approaches focused on identifying the types of leadership behaviors that are most effective in different settings. The transformational approach is the most popular perspective for studying leadership today. Research based on this approach began in the early 1980s and adheres to the idea that leaders transform employees to pursue organizational goals through a variety of leader behaviors. Finally, there are several emerging perspectives that examine leadership from new or novel points of view.

You would not believe how many different theories exist for each of these perspectives. There are literally a dozen or two. Moreover, the number of leadership theories exponentially increases if we count those proposed by managerial consultants. Rather than overwhelm you with all these theories of leadership, we focus on the historical ones that have received the most research support. We also discuss emerging perspectives that appear to have academic and practical application in the future. That said, we created a special learning module that contains descriptions of several leadership theories that are not covered in this chapter (see Learning Module C on the Web site for this book).

Leading versus Managing

It is important to appreciate the difference between leadership and management to fully understand what leadership is all about. Bernard Bass, a leadership expert, concluded that "leaders manage and managers lead, but the two activities are not synonymous."[8] Bass tells us that although leadership and management overlap, each entails a unique set of activities or functions. Broadly speaking, managers typically perform functions associated with planning, investigating, organizing, and control, and leaders deal with the interpersonal aspects of a manager's job. Leaders inspire others, provide emotional

Leadership

Process whereby an individual influences others to achieve a common goal.

Table 16–1   *Approaches to Studying Leadership*

1. Trait Approaches

- Stogdill and Mann's five traits—intelligence, dominance, self-confidence, level of energy, and task-relevant knowledge
- Leadership prototypes—intelligence, masculinity, and dominance
- Kouzes and Posner's four traits—honesty, forward-looking, inspiring, and competent
- Goleman—emotional intelligence
- Judge and colleagues—two meta-analyses: importance of extraversion, conscientiousness, and openness; importance of personality over intelligence
- Kellerman's bad traits—incompetent, rigid, intemperate, callous, corrupt, insular, and evil

2. Behavioral Approaches

- Ohio State studies—two dimensions: initiating structure behavior and consideration behavior
- University of Michigan studies—two leadership styles: job-centered and employee centered

3. Contingency Approaches

- Fiedler's contingency model—task-oriented style and relationship-oriented style; and three dimensions of situational control: leader–member relations, task structure, and position power
- House's path–goal revised theory—eight leadership behaviors clarify paths for followers' goals; and employee characteristics and environmental factors are contingency factors that influence the effectiveness of leadership behaviors

4. Transformational Approach

- Bass and Avolio's four transformational leadership behaviors—inspirational motivation, idealized influence, indivualized consideration, and intellectual stimulation
- Full-range theory of leadership—leadership varies along a continuum from laissez-faire leadership to transactional leadership to transformational leadership

5. Emerging Approaches

- Leader–member exchange (LMX) model—dyadic relationships between leaders and followers is critical
- Shared leadership—mutual influence process in which people share responsibility for leading
- Collins Level 5 leadership—leader has humility plus fearless will to succeed, plus four other capabilities
- Greenleaf's servant leadership—providing service to others not oneself
- Role of followers in leadership process—followers manage the leader–follower relationship

SOURCE: Adapted from A Kinicki and B Williams, *Management: A Practical Introduction,* 3rd ed (Burr Ridge, IL: McGraw-Hill/Irwin, 2008), p 453. Reprinted by permission of The McGraw-Hill Companies, Inc.

Table 16–2   *Characteristics of Being a Leader and a Manager*

BEING A LEADER MEANS	BEING A MANAGER MEANS
Motivating, influencing, and changing behavior	Practicing stewardship, directing and being held accountable for resources
Inspiring, setting the tone, and articulating a vision	Executing plans, implementing, and delivering the goods and services
Managing people	Managing resources
Being charismatic	Being conscientious
Being visionary	Planning, organizing, directing, and controlling
Understanding and using power and influence	Understanding and using authority and responsibility
Acting decisively	Acting responsibly
Putting people first; the leader knows, responds to, and acts for his or her followers	Putting customers first; the manager knows, responds to, and acts for his or her customers
Leaders can make mistakes when	Managers can make mistakes when
1. They choose the wrong goal, direction or inspiration, due to incompetence or bad intentions; or	1. They fail to grasp the importance of people as the key resource; or
2. They overlead; or	2. They underlead; they treat people like other resources, numbers; or
3. They are unable to deliver on, implement the vision due to incompetence or a lack of follow through commitment	3. They are eager to direct and to control but are unwilling to accept accountability

SOURCE: Reprinted from P Lorenzi, "Managing for the Common Good: Prosocial Leadership," *Organizational Dynamics*, vol. 33, no. 3, p 286, © 2004, with permission from Elsevier.

support, and try to get employees to rally around a common goal. Leaders also play a key role in creating a vision and strategic plan for an organization. Managers, in turn, are charged with implementing the vision and strategic plan. Table 16–2 summarizes the key characteristics associated with being a leader and a manager.[9]

There are several conclusions to be drawn from the information presented in Table 16–2. First, good leaders are not necessarily good managers, and good managers are not necessarily good leaders. Second, effective leadership requires effective managerial skills at some level. For example, good managerial skills turn a leader's vision into actionable items and successful implementation. Both Lou Gerstener, former CEO of IBM, and Larry Bossidy, former CEO of Allied Signal, endorsed this conclusion by noting that effective implementation is a key driver of organizational success.[10] Klaus Kleinfeld, former CEO of Siemens, is a good example. "He has pushed Siemens's 475,000 employees to make decisions faster and focus as much on customers as on technology. He spun off underperforming telecommunications-gear businesses and simplified the company's structure. And when one group of managers failed to deliver, he broke up an entire division.[11] All told then, organizational success requires a combination of effective leadership and management.

Ernst & Young and NextGen Use Multiple Programs to Develop Its Leaders

New York–based Ernst & Young's Transaction and Advisory practice addresses three critical business issues: succession planning, including building a pipeline of high-performing individuals to step into leadership roles and be better prepared to lead; increasing retention through stronger relationships with senior leaders; and increasing team-building opportunities for networking and collaboration across the firm. NextGen blends varied individual and team experiences, learning activities, case studies, and events to address five primary areas of leadership: personal, market, team, practice, and firm. The retention rate of NextGen participants was 13% higher, or 93% compared to the average of 80% overall, and 52% of the 77 participants were promoted to partner/principal.

Why would leadership training help reduce employee turnover?

SOURCE: Excerpted from "Best Practices and Outstanding Training Initiatives," *Training,* March 2007, p 85.

This in turn leads to the realization that today's leaders need to be effective at both leading and managing. While this may seem like a daunting task, the good news is that people can be taught to be more effective leaders and managers (see the Real World/Real People feature above).[12]

go to the Web for the Self-Exercise: How Ready Are You to Assume the Leadership Role?

 ## 2 Trait and Behavioral Theories of Leadership

This section examines the two earliest approaches used to explain leadership. Trait theories focused on identifying the personal traits that differentiated leaders from followers. Behavioral theorists examined leadership from a different perspective. They tried to uncover the different kinds of leader behaviors that resulted in higher work group performance. Both approaches to leadership can teach current and future managers valuable lessons about leading.

Trait Theory

Trait theory is the successor to what was called the "great man" theory of leadership. This approach was based on the assumption that leaders such as Abraham Lincoln, Martin Luther King, or Jack Welch were born with some inborn ability to lead. In contrast, trait theorists believed that leadership traits were not innate but could be developed through experience and learning. A **leader trait** is a physical or personality characteristic that can be used to differentiate leaders from followers.

Leader trait

Personal characteristics that differentiate leaders from followers.

Before World War II, hundreds of studies were conducted to pinpoint the traits of successful leaders. Dozens of leadership traits were identified. During the postwar period, however, enthusiasm was replaced by widespread criticism. This section reviews a series of studies that provide a foundation for understanding leadership traits. We conclude by integrating results across the various studies and summarizing the practical recommendations of trait theory.

Stogdill's and Mann's Findings

Ralph Stogdill in 1948 and Richard Mann in 1959 sought to summarize the impact of traits on leadership. Based on his review, Stogdill concluded that five traits tended to differentiate leaders from average followers: (1) intelligence, (2) dominance, (3) self-confidence, (4) level of energy and activity, and (5) task-relevant knowledge. Among the seven categories of personality traits examined by Mann, intelligence was the best predictor of leadership.[13] Unfortunately, the overall pattern of research findings revealed that both Stogdill's and Mann's key traits did not accurately predict which individuals became leaders in organizations. People with these traits often remained followers.

Leadership Prototypes: Do They Matter?

Yes! A **leadership prototype** is a mental representation of the traits and behaviors that people believe are possessed by leaders. It is important to understand the content of leadership prototypes because we tend to perceive that someone is a leader when he or she exhibits traits or behaviors that are consistent with our prototypes (recall our discussion of encoding and simplification in Chapter 7). Robert Lord and his colleagues attempted to identify employees' leadership prototypes by conducting a meta-analysis of past studies. Results demonstrated that people are perceived as leaders when they exhibit traits and behaviors associated with intelligence, masculinity, and dominance.[14] Another study of 6,052 middle-level managers from 22 European countries revealed that leadership prototypes are culturally based. In other words, leadership prototypes are influenced by national cultural values.[15] Researchers have not yet identified a set of global leadership prototypes.

Leadership prototype
Mental representation of the traits and behaviors possessed by leaders.

Kouzes and Posner's Research: Is Honesty the Most Critical Leadership Trait?

James Kouzes and Barry Posner attempted to identify key leadership traits by asking the following open-ended question to more than 20,000 people around the world: "What values (personal traits or characteristics) do you look for and admire in your superiors?" The top four traits included honesty, forward-looking, inspiring, and competent.[16] The researchers concluded that these four traits constitute a leader's credibility. This research suggests that people want their leaders to be credible and to have a sense of direction. That said, our discussion in Chapter 3 revealed that an organization's culture significantly influences the extent to which leaders encourage and reinforce integrity at work. This is one reason why credible leaders sometimes engage in questionable activities.[17] Anne Mulcahy, CEO of Xerox, is a good example of a leader who possesses credibility. She is known for being honest with employees and external constituents.[18]

Goleman's Research on Emotional Intelligence

We discussed Daniel Goleman's research on emotional intelligence in Chapter 5. Recall that *emotional intelligence* is the ability to manage oneself and one's relationships in mature and constructive ways: The six components of emotional intelligence are shown in Table 5–5. Given that leadership is an influence process between leaders and followers, it should come as no surprise that emotional intelligence is predicted to be associated with leadership effectiveness. While Goleman contends he has evidence to support this conclusion, he has not published it in any academic journals or professional magazine. We agree with others who contend that there presently is not enough research published in

OB journals to substantiate the conclusion that emotional intelligence is significantly associated with leadership effectiveness.[19]

Political intelligence is a recently proposed leadership trait and represents an offshoot of emotional intelligence. Politically intelligent leaders use power and intimidation to push followers in the pursuit of an inspiring vision and challenging goals. Although these leaders can be insensitive, hard to work with, and demanding, they tend to be effective when faced with stagnant and change-resistant situations.[20] Martha Stewart and Michael Eisner are two such examples. Consider how colleagues describe these leaders.

Martha Stewart's political intelligence has helped her amass $638 million in net worth and recognition as one of the most powerful women in business. She is an author, editor, homemaking guru, and former stockbroker.

She [Stewart] had the most amazing, well-organized and disciplined mind I've ever known. She grasped things instantly, and she had the ability to direct your attention to the single most important thing you should be thinking about or doing at that particular moment. She could be incredibly impatient and brusque if you were slow on the uptake—but if you could keep up with her, and perform to her standard, it was tremendously satisfying.

What is most lost in the stories about Mr. Eisner's arrogance, greed, and insensitivity is the more illuminating tale of how he transformed a faltering animation and amusement park company into one of the world's most successful entertainment companies. When he assumed command in 1984, Disney had a market value of $1.8 billion. Today its market value is $57.1 billion.[21]

Judge's Research: Is Personality More Important than Intelligence?

Tim Judge and his colleagues completed two meta-analyses that bear on the subject of traits and leadership. The first examined the relationship among the Big Five personality traits (see Table 5–2 for a review of these traits) and leadership emergence and effectiveness in 94 studies. Results revealed that extraversion was most consistently and positively related to both leadership emergence and effectiveness. Conscientiousness and openness to experience also were positively correlated with leadership effectiveness.[22] Judge's second meta-analysis involved 151 samples and demonstrated that intelligence was modestly related to leadership effectiveness. Judge concluded that personality is more important than intelligence when selecting leaders.[23]

Kellerman's Research: What Traits Are Possessed by Bad Leaders?

Thus far we have been discussing traits associated with "good leadership." Barbara Kellerman believes this approach is limiting because it fails to recognize that "bad leadership" is related to "good leadership." It also ignores the valuable insights that are gained by examining ineffective leaders. Kellerman thus set out to study hundreds of contemporary cases involving bad leadership and bad followers in search of the traits possessed by bad leaders. Her qualitative analysis uncovered seven key traits:[24]

- *Incompetent.* The leader and at least some followers lack the will or skill (or both) to sustain effective action. With regard to at least one important leadership challenge, they do not create positive change.

- *Rigid.* The leader and at least some followers are stiff and unyielding. Although they may be competent, they are unable or unwilling to adapt to new ideas, new information, or changing times.

Robert Nardelli Exhibits Characteristics of Bad Leaders While Jeff Immelt Displays Positive Traits

Mr Nardelli was old school. In an interview last fall, as his public-relations problems were compounding, he acknowledged he had gotten "too focused on the idea that you do your job, you take care of your numbers, and the rest will take care of itself." Some of Mr Nardelli's numbers were hard to argue with. In six years on the job, he doubled Home Depot's sales and more than doubled its earnings.

What Mr Nardelli missed, however, is that in the post-Enron world, CEOs have been forced to respond to a widening array of shareholder advocates, hedge funds, private-equity deal makers, legislators. . . . Today's CEO, in effect, has to play the role of politician, answering to varied constituents. And it's in that role that Mr Nardelli failed most spectacularly.

There were plenty of other reasons a board might want to dump him. He provided scant financial return to shareholders. He pursued a controversial strategy of expanding into the low-margin wholesale business. And he accepted an exorbitant pay package. . . .

Yet Mr Nardelli's extravagant pay became his biggest problem. It prompted an attack from shareholder advocates like Richard Ferlauto. . . . Mr Ferlauto helped organize protests at Home Depot's annual meeting last year, prompting Mr Nardelli to commit his gravest political error: Aware of the protests to come, he convinced other board members to stay away from the meeting, and restricted shareholders' questions to one minute. That sealed his public image as a callous and entrenched corporate leader. . . .

Mr Immelt has struggled with a languishing stock price. But in addition to generating good operating results, Mr Immelt has played the CEO's political role with great skill. He has tied his own pay closely to performance. He has eschewed the kind of employment contract that is now rewarding Mr Nardelli's failure. [Robert Nardelli walked away with $210 million.] He has reached out to a wide range of constituent groups. And he has adopted a number of popular initiatives, such as the "eco-imagination" program which, among other things, includes an effort to reduce GE's emissions of greenhouse gases.

Which of the seven key traits of bad leadership were exhibited by Robert Nardelli?

SOURCE: Excerpted from A Murray, "Executive's Fatal Flaw: Failing to Understand New Demands on CEOs," *The Wall Street Journal*, January 4, 2007, pp A1, A12.

- *Intemperate.* The leader lacks self-control and is aided and abetted by followers who are unwilling or unable effectively to intervene.
- *Callous.* The leader and at least some followers are uncaring and unkind. Ignored or discounted are the needs, wants, and desires of most members of the group or organization, especially subordinates.
- *Corrupt.* The leader and at least some followers lie, cheat, or steal. To a degree that exceeds the norm, they put self-interest ahead of the public interest.
- *Insular.* The leader and at least some followers minimize or disregard the health and welfare of "the other," that is, those outside the group or organization for which they are directly responsible.
- *Evil.* The leader and at least some followers commit atrocities. They use pain as an instrument of power. The harm done to men, women, and children is severe rather than slight. The harm can be physical, psychological, or both.[25]

Do you know leaders who possess any of these traits? Unfortunately, there are many examples. The Real World/Real People feature above illustrates how Robert Nardelli, former CEO of Home Depot, and Jeff Immelt, current CEO of GE, exhibited a host of leadership traits. While many people believe that both men are effective leaders, you will see that Nardelli exhibited several traits of bad leadership. This may be

Table 16–3 *Key Positive Leadership Traits*

POSITIVE TRAITS	
Intelligence	Sociability
Self-confidence	Problem-solving skills
Determination	Extraversion
Honesty/integrity	Conscientiousness

one reason why Home Depot's board of directors and Nardelli "mutually agreed" to his resignation in January 2007.[26]

Gender and Leadership The increase of women in the workforce has generated much interest in understanding the similarities and differences in female and male leaders. Three separate meta-analyses and a series of studies conducted by consultants across the country uncovered the following differences: (1) Men and women were seen as displaying more task and social leadership, respectively;[27] (2) women used a more democratic or participative style than men, and men used a more autocratic and directive style than women;[28] (3) men and women were equally assertive;[29] and (4) women executives, when rated by their peers, managers, and direct reports, scored higher than their male counterparts on a variety of effectiveness criteria.[30]

What Are the Takeaways from Trait Theory? We can no longer afford to ignore the implications of leadership traits. Traits play a central role in how we perceive leaders, and they ultimately impact leadership effectiveness. What can be learned from the previous research on traits? Integrating across past studies leads to the extended list of positive traits shown in Table 16–3.[31] This list, along with the negative traits identified by Kellerman, provides guidance regarding the leadership traits you should attempt to cultivate if you want to assume a leadership role. Personality tests, which were discussed in Chapter 5, and other trait assessments can be used to evaluate your strengths and weaknesses vis-à-vis these traits. Results can then be used to prepare a personal development plan. We encourage you to use an executive coach in this process.[32]

There are two organizational applications of trait theory. First, organizations may want to include personality and trait assessments into their selection and promotion processes. It is important to remember that this should only be done with valid measures of leadership traits. Second, management development programs can be used to enhance employees' leadership traits. For example, both small and large companies such as Schwan Food Corporation, PepsiCo, Inc., Bank of America, and Hasbro, Inc. send targeted groups of managers to developmental programs that include management classes, coaching sessions, trait assessments, and stretch assignments.[33] Many companies also are using information technology to offer developmental classes online.[34]

 3 Behavioral Styles Theory

This phase of leadership research began during World War II as part of an effort to develop better military leaders. It was an outgrowth of two events: the seeming inability of trait theory to explain leadership effectiveness and the human relations movement, an outgrowth of the Hawthorne Studies. The thrust of early behavioral leadership theory was to focus on leader behavior, instead of on personality traits. It was believed that leader behavior directly affected work group effectiveness. This led researchers to identify patterns of behavior (called *leadership styles*) that enabled leaders to effectively influence others.

The Ohio State Studies Researchers at Ohio State University began by generating a list of behaviors exhibited by leaders. At one point, the list contained 1,800 statements that described nine categories of leader behavior. Ultimately, the Ohio State researchers concluded there were only two independent dimensions of leader behavior: consideration and initiating structure. **Consideration** involves leader behavior associated with creating mutual respect or trust and focuses on a concern for group members' needs and desires. **Initiating structure** is leader behavior that organizes and defines what group members should be doing to maximize output. These two dimensions of leader behavior were oriented at right angles to yield four behavioral styles of leadership (see Figure 16–1).

It initially was hypothesized that a high-structure, high-consideration style would be the one best style of leadership. Through the years, the effectiveness of the high-high style has been tested many times.[35] Overall, results have been mixed and there has been very little research about these leader behaviors until just recently. Findings from a 2004 meta-analysis of 130 studies and more than 20,000 individuals demonstrated that consideration and initiating structure had a moderately strong, significant relationship with leadership outcomes. Results revealed that followers performed more effectively for structuring leaders even though they preferred considerate leaders.[36] All told, results do not support the idea that there is one best style of leadership, but they do confirm the importance of considerate and structuring leader behaviors. Follower satisfaction, motivation, and performance are significantly associated with these two leader behaviors. Future research is needed to incorporate them into more contemporary leadership theories.

Consideration
Creating mutual respect and trust with followers.

Initiating structure
Organizing and defining what group members should be doing.

Figure 16–1   *Four Leadership Styles Derived from the Ohio State Studies*

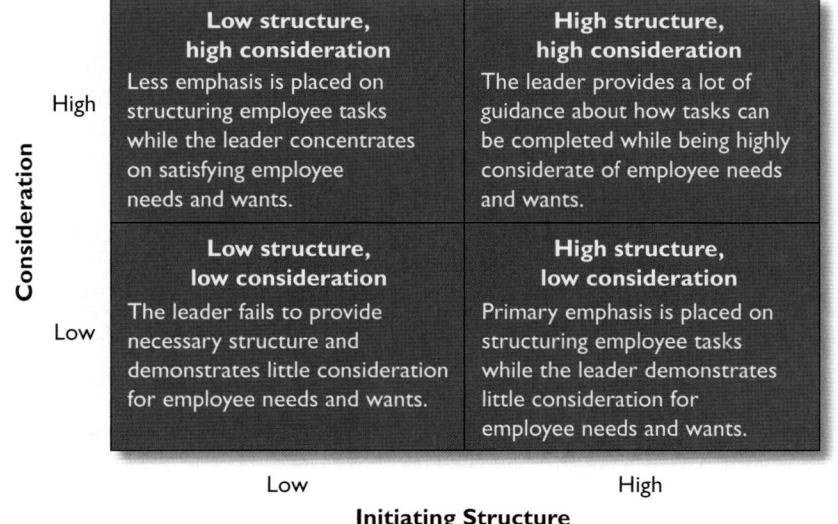

High (Consideration)	**Low structure, high consideration** Less emphasis is placed on structuring employee tasks while the leader concentrates on satisfying employee needs and wants.	**High structure, high consideration** The leader provides a lot of guidance about how tasks can be completed while being highly considerate of employee needs and wants.
Low (Consideration)	**Low structure, low consideration** The leader fails to provide necessary structure and demonstrates little consideration for employee needs and wants.	**High structure, low consideration** Primary emphasis is placed on structuring employee tasks while the leader demonstrates little consideration for employee needs and wants.
	Low	High

Initiating Structure

University of Michigan Studies As in the Ohio State studies, this research sought to identify behavioral differences between effective and ineffective leaders. Researchers identified two different styles of leadership: one was employee centered, the other was job centered. These behavioral styles parallel the consideration and initiating-structure styles identified by the Ohio State group. In summarizing the results from these studies, one management expert concluded that effective leaders (1) tend to have supportive or employee-centered relationships with employees, (2) use group rather than individual methods of supervision, and (3) set high performance goals.[37]

What Are the Takeaways from Behavioral Styles Theory? By emphasizing leader behavior, something that is learned, the behavioral style approach makes it clear that leaders are made, not born. This is the opposite of the trait theorists' traditional assumption. Given what we know about behavior shaping and model-based training, leader *behaviors* can be systematically improved and developed.[38]

Behavioral styles research also revealed that there is no one best style of leadership. The effectiveness of a particular leadership style depends on the situation at hand. For instance, employees prefer structure over consideration when faced with role ambiguity. Finally, research also reveals that it is important to consider the difference between how frequently and how effectively managers exhibit various leader behaviors. For example, a manager might ineffectively display a lot of considerate leader behaviors. Such a style is likely to frustrate employees and possibly result in lowered job satisfaction and performance. Because the frequency of exhibiting leadership behaviors is secondary in importance to effectiveness, managers are encouraged to concentrate on improving the effective execution of their leader behaviors.

Finally, Peter Drucker, an internationally renowned management expert and consultant, recommended a set of nine behaviors (see Table 16–4) managers can focus on

Table 16–4   *Peter Drucker's Tips for Improving Leadership Effectiveness*

1. Determine what needs to be done.
2. Determine the right thing to do for the welfare of the entire enterprise or organization.
3. Develop action plans that specify desired results, probable restraints, future revisions, check-in points, and implications for how one should spend his or her time.
4. Take responsibility for decisions.
5. Take responsibility for communicating action plans and give people the information they need to get the job done.
6. Focus on opportunities rather than problems. Do not sweep problems under the rug, and treat change as an opportunity rather than a threat.
7. Run productive meetings. Different types of meetings require different forms of preparation and different results. Prepare accordingly.
8. Think and say "we" rather than "I." Consider the needs and opportunities of the organization before thinking of your own opportunities and needs.
9. Listen first, speak last.

SOURCE: Reprinted by permission of *Harvard Business Review.* These recommendations were derived from P F Drucker, "What Makes an Effective Executive," *Harvard Business Review,* June 2004, pp 58–63. Copyright © 2004 by the Harvard Business School Publishing Corporation; all rights reserved.

to improve their leadership effectiveness. The first two practices provide the knowledge leaders need. The next four help leaders convert knowledge into effective action, and the last two ensure that the whole organization feels responsible and accountable. Drucker refers to the last recommendation as a managerial rule.

Situational Theories

Situational leadership theories grew out of an attempt to explain the inconsistent findings about traits and styles. **Situational theories** propose that the effectiveness of a particular style of leader behavior depends on the situation. As situations change, different styles become appropriate. This directly challenges the idea of one best style of leadership. Let us closely examine two alternative situational theories of leadership that reject the notion of one best leadership style.

Situational theories
Propose that leader styles should match the situation at hand.

 ## Fiedler's Contingency Model

Fred Fiedler, an OB scholar, developed a situational model of leadership. It is the oldest and one of the most widely known models of situational leadership. He labeled the model *contingency theory* because it is based on the premise that a leader's effectiveness is contingent on the extent to which a leader's style fits or matches characteristics of the situation at hand. To understand how this matching process works, we need to consider the key leadership styles identified by Fiedler and the situational variables that constitute what Fiedler labels *situational control*. We then review relevant research and managerial implications.[39]

Leadership Styles Fiedler believes that leaders have one dominant or natural leadership style that is resistant to change. A leader's style is described as either task-motivated or relationship-motivated. Task-motivated leaders focus on accomplishing goals, whereas relationship-motivated leaders are more interested in developing positive relationships with followers. These basic styles are similar to initiating structure/concern for production and consideration/concern for people that were previously discussed. To determine an individual's leadership style, Fiedler developed the least preferred co-worker (LPC) scale. High scores on the survey (high LPC) indicate that an individual is relationship-motivated, and low scores (low LPC) suggest a task-motivated style.

Situational Control Situational control refers to the amount of control and influence the leader has in her or his immediate work environment. Situational control ranges from high to low. High control implies that the leader's decisions will produce predictable results because the leader has the ability to influence work outcomes. Low control implies that the leader's decisions may not influence work outcomes because the leader has very little influence. There are three dimensions of situational control: leader–member relations, task structure, and position power. These dimensions vary independently, forming eight combinations of situational control (see Figure 16–2).

The three dimensions of situational control are defined as follows:

- **Leader–member relations** reflect the extent to which the leader has the support, loyalty, and trust of the work group. This dimension is the most important component of situational control. Good leader–member relations suggest that the leader can depend on the group, thus ensuring that the work group will try to meet the leader's goals and objectives.

Leader–member relations
Extent that leader has the support, loyalty, and trust of work group.

Figure 16–2   *Representation of Fiedler's Contingency Model*

Situational Control	High-Control Situations			Moderate-Control Situations				Low-Control Situations
Leader-member relations	Good	Good	Good	Good	Poor	Poor	Poor	Poor
Task structure	High	High	Low	Low	High	High	Low	Low
Position power	Strong	Weak	Strong	Weak	Strong	Weak	Strong	Weak
Situation	I	II	III	IV	V	VI	VII	VIII

Optimal Leadership Style	Task-Motivated Leadership	Relationship-Motivated Leadership	Task-Motivated Leadership

SOURCE: Adapted from F E Fiedler, "Situational Control and a Dynamic Theory of Leadership," in *Managerial Control and Organizational Democracy,* eds B King, S Streufert, and F E Fiedler (New York: John Wiley & Sons, 1978), p 114.

Task structure

Amount of structure contained within work tasks.

- **Task structure** is concerned with the amount of structure contained within tasks performed by the work group. For example, a managerial job contains less structure than that of a bank teller. Because structured tasks have guidelines for how the job should be completed, the leader has more control and influence over employees performing such tasks. This dimension is the second most important component of situational control.

Position power

Degree to which leader has formal power.

- **Position power** refers to the degree to which the leader has formal power to reward, punish, or otherwise obtain compliance from employees.

Linking Leadership Motivation and Situational Control

Fiedler suggests that leaders must learn to manipulate or influence the leadership situation in order to create a match between their leadership style and the amount of control within the situation at hand. These contingency relationships are depicted in Figure 16–2. The last row under the Situational Control column shows that there are eight different leadership situations. Each situation represents a unique combination of leader–member relations, task structure, and position power. Situations I, II, and III represent high-control situations. Figure 16–2 shows that task-motivated leaders are hypothesized to be most effective in situations of high control. Under conditions of moderate control (situations IV, V, VI, and VII), relationship-motivated leaders are expected to be more effective. Finally, the results orientation of task-motivated leaders is predicted to be more effective under the condition of very low control (situation VIII).

Research and Takeaways from Fiedler's Model On the positive side, two meta-analyses provided partial support for this model.[40] At the same time, this theory has generated much criticism and controversy. There are problems with the LPC scale and research does not clearly support all predictions derived from this model.[41] That said, there are three key takeaways from Fiedler's model.

First, this model emphasizes the point that leadership effectiveness goes beyond traits and behaviors. It is a function of the fit between a leader's style and the situational demands at hand. As a case in point, a team of researchers recently examined the effectiveness of 20 senior-level managers from GE who left the company for other positions. The researchers concluded that

> not all managers are equally suited to all business situations. The strategic skills required to control costs in the face of fierce competition are not the same as those required to improve the top line in a rapidly growing business or balance investment against cash flow to survive in a highly cyclical business.... We weren't surprised to find that relevant industry experience had a positive impact on performance in a new job, but that these skills didn't transfer to a new industry.[42]

This study leads to the conclusion that organizations should attempt to hire or promote people whose leadership styles *fit* or *match* situational demands.[43]

Second, this model explains why some people are successful in some situations and not in others. Leaders are unlikely to be successful in all situations (see the Real World/Real People feature on page 476). If a manager is failing in a certain context, management should consider moving the individual to another situation. Don't give up on a high-potential person simply because he or she was a poor leader in one context.

Third, leaders need to modify their style to fit a situation. Leadership styles are not universally effective. Martin Sullivan, CEO of American International Group, Inc., is a good example of someone who understands this conclusion. He told a reporter from *The Wall Street Journal*, "There's different ways of getting the best out of people. There are people you have to put your arm around and cajole to get better out of them. And there are others you seriously have to kick. I have an open style of management."[44] Mr Sullivan clearly changes his leadership style to fit the needs and values of the employee he is trying to motivate.

5 Path–Goal Theory

Path–goal theory was originally proposed by Robert House in the 1970s.[45] It was based on the expectancy theory of motivation discussed in Chapter 8. Recall that expectancy theory is based on the idea that motivation to exert effort increases as one's effort→performance→outcome expectations improve. Leader behaviors thus are expected to be acceptable when employees view them as a source of satisfaction or as paying the way to future satisfaction. In addition, leader behavior is predicted to be motivational to the extent it (1) reduces roadblocks that interfere with goal accomplishment, (2) provides the guidance and support needed by employees, and (3) ties meaningful rewards to goal accomplishment.

House proposed a model that describes how leadership effectiveness is influenced by the interaction between four leadership styles (directive, supportive, participative, and achievement-oriented) and a variety of contingency factors. **Contingency factors** are situational variables that cause one style of leadership to be more effective than another. Path–goal theory has two groups of contingency variables. They are employee

Contingency factors

Variables that influence the appropriateness of a leadership style.

Lack of Fit Affects Leadership Effectiveness for Successful Leaders

When Catherine West arrived at J.C. Penney Co.'s Plano (Tex.) offices in June as the new chief operating officer, she brought a gold-plated record. A veteran of credit-card giant Capital One Financial Corp., West had most recently run the company's $47 billion U.S. business. Penney CEO Myron E. Ullman called her a "world-class" executive. He was so confident she had what it would take to succeed that he gave her a contract guaranteeing a $10 million payment when she left the retailer, even in the remote event that she took off in less than a year.

That's just what happened. By Dec. 28, Ullman felt no holiday goodwill toward West. She was terminated "due to her failure to satisfy performance objectives," primarily "gaining an understanding of the company's operations," Penney reported to the Securities & Exchange Commission. In an e-mail message, West termed her months in Plano "an extraordinary developmental experience."

Perhaps, but her tenure was no success. Nor was it an isolated event. It caps off a steady march of other highfliers who have not lasted even a year. Some, like West, came from outside and fell short. Others have spent decades reaching for the gold ring, only to let go after it was in their grasp. At Wal-Mart Stores Inc., two marketing managers and the head of global procurement left, all in under 12 months. Home Depot Inc. lost its head of marketing and merchandising, Tom Taylor, in similarly short order. . . .

When a company ejects a high-profile hire in under a year, the problem is usually not one of ability but of style. The person clashes with the CEO, inspires resentment in co-workers, or pushes for too much change too quickly. Jeff Durocher, RHR's vice-president of market development, says his firm's research has found most fast failures come when managers haven't established a network of allies and confidants or adapted to the company's culture but instead see

Catherine West.

themselves as special and unique. "We call it tissue rejection," says Durocher. "They get no support from the people around them."

How can a company assess the fit between a leader's style and situational demands?

SOURCE: Excerpted from N Byrnes and D Kiley, "Hello, You Must Be Going," *BusinessWeek*, February 12, 2007, p 30.

characteristics and environmental factors. Five important employee characteristics are locus of control, task ability, need for achievement, experience, and need for clarity. Two relevant environmental factors are task structure (independent versus interdependent tasks) and work group dynamics. In order to gain a better understanding of how these contingency factors influence leadership effectiveness, we illustratively consider locus of control (see Chapter 5), task ability and experience, and task structure.

Employees with an internal locus control are more likely to prefer participative or achievement-oriented leadership because they believe they have control over the work environment. Such individuals are unlikely to be satisfied with directive leader behaviors that exert additional control over their activities. In contrast, employees with an external locus tend to view the environment as uncontrollable, thereby preferring the structure provided by supportive or directive leadership. An employee with high task ability and experience is less apt to need additional direction and thus would respond negatively to directive leadership. This person is more likely to be motivated and satisfied by participative and achievement-oriented leadership. Oppositely, an inexperienced employee would find achievement-oriented leadership overwhelming as he or she confronts challenges associated with learning a new job. Supportive and directive leadership would be helpful in this situation. Finally, directive and supportive leadership should help employees experiencing role ambiguity. However, directive leadership is likely to frustrate employees working on routine and simple tasks. Supportive leadership is most useful in this context.

There have been about 50 studies testing various predictions derived from House's original model. Results have been mixed, with some studies supporting the theory and others not.[46] House thus proposed a new version of path–goal theory in 1996 based on these results and the accumulation of new knowledge about OB.

A Reformulated Theory The revised theory is presented in Figure 16–3.[47] There are three key changes in the new theory. First, House now believes that leadership is more complex and involves a greater variety of leader behavior. He thus identified eight categories of leadership styles or behavior (see Table 16–5). The need for an expanded list of leader behaviors is supported by current research and descriptions of business leaders.

The second key change involves the role of intrinsic motivation (discussed in Chapter 9) and empowerment (discussed in Chapter 15) in influencing leadership effectiveness. House places much more emphasis on the need for leaders to foster intrinsic motivation through empowerment. Shared leadership represents the final change in the revised theory. That is, path–goal theory is based on the premise that an employee does not have to be a supervisor or manager to engage in leader behavior. Rather, House believes that leadership is shared among all employees within an organization. More is said about shared leadership in the final section of this chapter.

Figure 16–3   *A General Representation of House's Revised Path–Goal Theory*

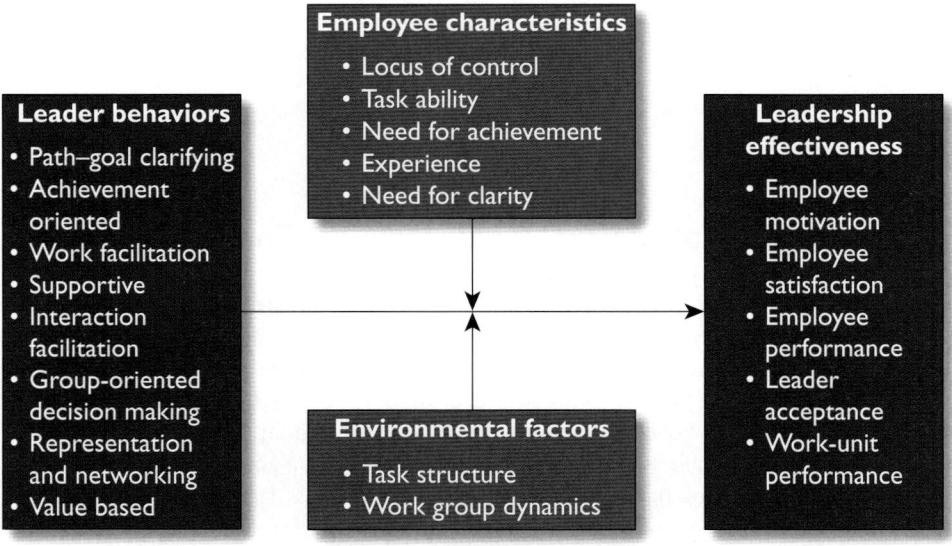

Table 16–5   *Categories of Leader Behavior within the Revised Path–Goal Theory*

CATEGORY OF LEADER BEHAVIOR	DESCRIPTION OF LEADER BEHAVIORS
Path–goal clarifying behaviors	Clarifying employees' performance goals; providing guidance on how employees can complete tasks; clarifying performance standards and expectations; use of positive and negative rewards contingent on performance
Achievement-oriented behaviors	Setting challenging goals; emphasizing excellence; demonstrating confidence in employees' abilities
Work-facilitation behaviors	Planning, scheduling, organizing, and coordinating work; providing mentoring, coaching, counseling, and feedback to assist employees in developing their skills; eliminating roadblocks; providing resources; empowering employees to take actions and make decisions
Supportive behaviors	Showing concern for the well-being and needs of employees; being friendly and approachable; treating employees as equals
Interaction-facilitation behaviors	Resolving disputes; facilitating communication; encouraging the sharing of minority opinions; emphasizing collaboration and teamwork; encouraging close relationships among employees
Group-oriented decision-making behaviors	Posing problems rather than solutions to the work group; encouraging group members to participate in decision making; providing necessary information to the group for analysis; involving knowledgeable employees in decision making
Representation and networking behaviors	Presenting the work group in a positive light to others; maintaining positive relationships with influential others; participating in organizationwide social functions and ceremonies; doing unconditional favors for others
Value-based behaviors	Establishing a vision, displaying passion for it, and supporting its accomplishment; demonstrating self-confidence; communicating high performance expectations and confidence in others' abilities to meet their goals; giving frequent positive feedback

SOURCE: Descriptions were adapted from R J House, "Path–Goal Theory of Leadership: Lessons, Legacy, and a Reformulated Theory," *Leadership Quarterly,* 1996, pp 323–52.

Research and Takeaways from House's Theory There are not enough direct tests of House's revised path–goal theory using appropriate research methods and statistical procedures to draw overall conclusions. Future research is clearly needed to assess the accuracy of this model. Nonetheless, there are three important takeaways from this theory. First, effective leaders possess and use more than one style of leadership. Managers are encouraged to familiarize themselves with the different categories of leader behavior outlined in path–goal theory and to try new behaviors when the situation calls for them. Second, the theory offers specific suggestions for how leaders can help employees. Leaders are encouraged to clarify the paths to goal accomplishment and to remove any obstacles that may impair an employee's ability to achieve his or her goals. In so doing, managers need to guide and coach employees during the pursuit of their goals. Third, a small set of employee characteristics (i.e., ability, experience, and need for independence) and environmental factors (task characteristics of autonomy, variety, and significance) are relevant contingency factors.[48] Managers are advised to modify their leadership style to fit these various employee and task characteristics.

6 The Full-Range Model of Leadership: From Laissez-Faire to Transformational Leadership

One of the most recent approaches to leadership is referred to as a *full-range model of leadership*.[49] The authors of this theory, Bernard Bass and Bruce Avolio, proposed that leadership behavior varied along a continuum from laissez-faire leadership (i.e., a general failure to take responsibility for leading) to transactional leadership to transformational leadership. Of course, laissez-faire leadership is a terrible way for any manager to behave and should be avoided. What gender do you think engages in more laissez-faire leadership? A meta-analysis revealed that men displayed more of this type of leadership than women.[50] It is important for organizations to identify managers who lead with this style and to train and develop them to use behaviors associated with transactional and transformational leadership. Both transactional and transformational are positively related to a variety of employee attitudes and behaviors and represent different aspects of being a good leader. Let us consider these two important dimensions of leadership.

Transactional leadership focuses on clarifying employees' role and task requirements and providing followers with positive and negative rewards contingent on performance. Further, transactional leadership encompasses the fundamental managerial activities of setting goals, monitoring progress toward goal achievement, and rewarding and punishing people for their level of goal accomplishment.[51] You can see from this description that transactional leadership is based on using extrinsic motivation (recall our discussion in Chapter 9) to increase employee productivity. Consider how Miller Brewing's CEO, Norman Adami, uses transactional leadership to improve organizational performance.

> Adami has made staff far more accountable with a performance system imported from SAB that rewards people for stepping up their game. (South African Breweries [SAB] is Miller's parent company.) The old system didn't challenge employees, says Adami, who once referred to the company as the "Socialist Republic of Miller." For example, in 2002, a year the business was in free-fall, 60% of managers got a four or five rating, the highest possible. Last year [2005] 50% of employees got three on a six-point scale, meaning they met their goals."[52]

In contrast, **transformational leaders** "engender trust, seek to develop leadership in others, exhibit self-sacrifice and serve as moral agents, focusing themselves and followers on objectives that transcend the more immediate needs of the work group."[53] Transformational leaders can produce significant organizational change and results because this form of leadership fosters higher levels of intrinsic motivation, trust, commitment, and loyalty from followers than does transactional leadership. That said, however, it is important to note that transactional leadership is an essential prerequisite to effective leadership and that the best leaders learn to display both transactional and

Transactional leadership

Focuses on clarifying employees' roles and providing rewards contingent on performance.

Transformational leadership

Transforms employees to pursue organizational goals over self-interests.

transformational leadership to various degrees. In support of this proposition, research reveals that transformational leadership leads to superior performance when it augments or adds to transactional leadership.[54] Let us return to the example of Norman Adami, CEO of Miller Brewing, to see how he augmented transactional leadership with transformational leadership shortly after taking over as CEO.

> Amid declining sales, management upheaval, and an uncertain outlook, Adami got plenty of criticism from staffers when he decided to turn some half-empty offices and storerooms into a bar for Miller's 900 headquarters employees in one of his first moves as CEO in 2003. But Adami considered opening Fred's Pub, named after company founder Frederick J Miller, an essential step in overhauling a moribund culture. He envisioned the pub as a place where the chief marketing officer could chat with an hourly worker in bottling, or a brand manager could have a casual team meeting.... His charm offensive, which includes touches like having flowers sent to his male executives' wives on birthdays, is paired with a demanding, no-BS management style.... Adami has instilled his sense of urgency into Miller. He'll often pick up the phone in a meeting to get the latest statistic. And after seeing an AB [Anheuser-Busch] commercial, he hustled to get a response ad launched within a week.[55]

We now turn our attention to examining the process by which transformational leadership influences followers.

7 How Does Transformational Leadership Transform Followers?

Mahatma Gandhi, India's "Father of the Nation," was a transformational leader. He helped fight poverty and tyranny through the use of non-violent civil disobedience.

Transformational leaders transform followers by creating changes in their goals, values, needs, beliefs, and aspirations. They accomplish this transformation by appealing to followers' self-concepts—namely their values and personal identity. Figure 16–4 presents a model of how leaders accomplish this transformation process.

Figure 16–4 shows that transformational leader behavior is first influenced by various individual and organizational characteristics. For example, research reveals that transformational leaders tend to have personalities that are more extraverted, agreeable, and proactive and less neurotic than nontransformational leaders.[56] Female leaders also were found to use transformational leadership more than male leaders.[57] It is important to note, however, that the relationship between personality traits and transformational leadership is relatively weak. This suggests that transformational leadership is less traitlike and more susceptible to managerial influence. This conclusion reinforces the notion that an individual's life experiences play a role in developing transformational leadership and that transformational leadership can be learned.[58] Finally, Figure 16–4 shows that organizational culture influences the extent to which leaders are transformational. Cultures that are adaptive and flexible rather than rigid and bureaucratic are more likely to create environments that foster the opportunity for transformational leadership to be exhibited.

Transformational leaders engage in four key sets of leader behavior (see Figure 16–4).[59] The first set, referred to as *inspirational motivation,* involves establishing an attractive vision of

Figure 16–4   *A Transformational Model of Leadership*

SOURCE: Based in part on D A Waldman and F J Yammarino, "CEO Charismatic Leadership: Levels-of-Management and Levels-of-Analysis Effects," *Academy of Management Review,* April 1999, pp 266–85; and B Shamir, R J House, and M B Arthur, "The Motivational Effects of Charismatic Leadership: A Self-Concept Based Theory," *Organization Science,* November 1993, pp 577–94.

the future, the use of emotional arguments, and exhibition of optimism and enthusiasm. A vision is "a realistic, credible, attractive future for your organization."[60] According to Burt Nanus, a leadership expert, the "right" vision unleashes human potential because it serves as a beacon of hope and common purpose. It does this by attracting commitment, energizing workers, creating meaning in employees' lives, establishing a standard of excellence, promoting high ideals, and bridging the gap between an organization's present problems and its future goals and aspirations.[61] Anne Mulcahy, Xerox's CEO, understands the importance of using a vision to energize the workforce. She used a vision, which was created by asking her top management team to write a story about how various constituents would describe the company in five years, to gain employees' commitment to needed and difficult organizational change. This process resulted in increased buy-in and support of a host of organizational changes that brought the company back from near bankruptcy.[62]

Idealized influence, the second set of leader behaviors, includes behaviors such as sacrificing for the good of the group, being a role model, and displaying high ethical standards. Through their actions, transformational leaders model the desired values, traits, beliefs, and behaviors needed to realize the vision. The Real World/Real People feature on page 482 provides an example of how Susan Lyne, CEO of Martha Stewart Living Omnimedia Inc., displayed idealized influence. Contrast her behavior with that of Frank Stronach, Magna International Inc.'s CEO. He earned an average of $34 million a year over the last five years, an amount that is several times what CEOs make from competing firms. He also supported cutting the shareholder dividend by 50%, and was behind Magna's purchase of two golf courses for $84 million from an entertainment company that Stronach also is running.[63] What behaviors and values is Stronach modeling?

Susan Lyne Is a Transformational Leader

Susan Lyne knows the power of a public statement. As chief executive of Martha Stewart Living Omnimedia Inc. since late 2004, she has run the company through Stewart's jail term and much publicized comeback. With ad pages in the flagship magazine up 44% last year and a flurry of new deals sparking optimism for the brand, Lyne got a cash bonus of $625,500 last year. Instead of pocketing it, though, she asked the board to give $200,000 to a bonus pool for employees and convert the rest into restricted shares that won't fully vest until 2009.

Lyne says she wanted to recognize the efforts of employees because her plan to boost the company's long-term health cut into annual bonuses. More important, she felt the gesture would be a potent symbol. "There was a period of time in the 1990s when the bigger your pay package, the more people respected you," says Lyne, who earned a $900,000 salary in 2005. "I think that has changed—dramatically. There's a very different sense of what makes a good leader of a public company."

At a time when most news on CEO pay spotlights wretched excess, Lyne's move is an example of something far rarer: executive sacrifice.

How would employees likely respond to Lyne's behavior?

SOURCE: Excerpted from D Brady, "No Hair Shirts, But Still ...," *BusinessWeek*, May 1, 2006, p 36.

The third set, *individualized consideration,* entails behaviors associated with providing support, encouragement, empowerment, and coaching to employees. *Intellectual stimulation,* the fourth set of leadership behaviors, involves behaviors that encourage employees to question the status quo and to seek innovative and creative solutions to organizational problems.

Research and Managerial Implications

Components of the transformational model of leadership have been the most widely researched leadership topic over the last decade. Overall, the relationships outlined in Figure 16–4 generally were supported by previous research. For example, transformational leader behaviors were positively associated with the extent to which employees identified with both their leaders and immediate work groups.[64] Followers of transformational leaders also were found to set goals that were consistent with those of the leader, to be more engaged in their work, to have higher levels of intrinsic motivation, and to have higher levels of group cohesion.[65] With respect to the direct relationship between transformational leadership and work outcomes, a meta-analysis of 49 studies indicated that transformational leadership was positively associated with measures of leadership effectiveness and employees' job satisfaction.[66] At the organizational level, a second meta-analysis demonstrated that transformational leadership was positively correlated with organizational measures of effectiveness.[67]

These results underscore four important managerial implications. First, the best leaders are not just transformational; they are both transactional and transformational, and they avoid a laissez-faire or "wait-and-see" style. This conclusion was reinforced by results from a recent meta-analysis. Findings demonstrated that transactional leadership was positively correlated with followers' job satisfaction, satisfaction with the leader, and motivation as well as group and organizational performance and measures of a leader's effectiveness. The opposite pattern was found for laissez-faire leadership.[68]

Second, transformational leadership not only affects individual-level outcomes like job satisfaction, organizational commitment, and performance, but it also influences group dynamics and group-level outcomes. Managers can thus use the four types of transformational leadership shown in Figure 16–4 as a vehicle to improve group dynamics and work-unit outcomes. This is important in today's organizations because most employees do not work in isolation. Rather, people tend to rely on the input and collaboration of others, and many organizations are structured around teams. The key point to remember is that transformational leadership transforms individuals as well as teams and work groups. We encourage you to use this to your advantage.

Third, employees at any level in an organization can be trained to be more transactional and transformational.[69] This reinforces the organizational value of developing and rolling out a combination of transactional and transformational leadership training for all employees. These programs, however, should be based on an overall corporate philosophy that constitutes the foundation of leadership development.

Fourth, transformational leaders can be ethical or unethical. Whereas ethical transformational leaders enable employees to enhance their self-concepts, unethical ones select or produce obedient, dependent, and compliant followers. Top management can create and maintain ethical transformational leadership by

1. Creating and enforcing a clearly stated code of ethics.
2. Recruiting, selecting, and promoting people who display ethical behavior.
3. Developing performance expectations around the treatment of employees—these expectations can then be assessed in the performance appraisal process.
4. Training employees to value diversity.
5. Identifying, rewarding, and publicly praising employees who exemplify high moral conduct.[70]

go to the Web for the Group Exercise: Exhibiting Leadership within the Context of Running a Meeting

Additional Perspectives on Leadership

This section examines five additional perspectives on leadership: leader–member exchange theory, shared leadership, Level 5 leadership, servant-leadership, and a follower perspective.

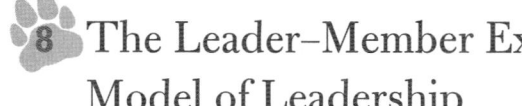

8 The Leader–Member Exchange (LMX) Model of Leadership

The leader–member exchange model of leadership revolves around the development of dyadic relationships between managers and their direct reports. This model is quite different from those previously discussed in that it focuses on the quality of relationships between managers and subordinates as opposed to the behaviors or traits of either leaders or followers. It also is different in that it does not assume that leader behavior is characterized by a stable or average leadership style as do the previously discussed models. In other words, most models of leadership assume a leader treats all employees in about the same way. In contrast, the LMX model is based on the assumption that leaders develop unique one-to-one relationships with each of the people reporting to them. Behavioral scientists call this sort of relationship a *vertical dyad.* The forming of vertical dyads is said to be a naturally occurring process, resulting from the leader's attempt to delegate and assign work roles. As a result of this process, two distinct types of leader–member exchange relationships are expected to evolve.[71]

In-group exchange

A partnership characterized by mutual trust, respect, and liking.

One type of leader–member exchange is called the **in-group exchange.** In this relationship, leaders and followers develop a partnership characterized by reciprocal influence, mutual trust, respect and liking, and a sense of common fates. In the second type of exchange, referred to as an **out-group exchange,** leaders are characterized as overseers who fail to create a sense of mutual trust, respect, or common fate.[72]

Out-group exchange

A partnership characterized by a lack of mutual trust, respect, and liking.

Research Findings If the leader–member exchange model is correct, there should be a significant relationship between the type of leader–member exchange and job-related outcomes. Research supports this prediction. For example, a positive leader–member exchange was positively associated with job satisfaction, job performance, goal commitment, trust between managers and employees, work climate, and satisfaction with leadership.[73] Results from a recent meta-analysis of 50 studies involving 9,324 people also revealed a moderately strong, positive relationship between LMX and organizational citizenship behaviors—recall our discussion in Chapter 6.[74] As you might imagine, positive LMXs were found to predict not only turnover but also career outcomes, such as promotability, salary level, and receipt of bonuses, over a seven-year period.[75] Finally, studies also have identified a variety of variables that influence the quality of an LMX. For example, LMX was related to personality similarity and demographic similarity.[76]

Managerial Implications There are three important implications associated with the LMX model of leadership. First, leaders are encouraged to establish high-performance expectations for all of their direct reports because setting high-performance standards fosters high-quality LMXs. Second, because personality and demographic similarity between leaders and followers is associated with higher LMXs, managers need to be careful that they don't create a homogeneous work environment in the spirit of having positive relationships with their direct reports. Our discussion of diversity in Chapter 2 clearly documented that there are many positive benefits of having a diverse workforce. The third implication pertains to those of us who find ourselves in a poor LMX. A management consultant offers the following tips for improving the quality of leader–member exchanges.[77]

1. Stay focused on your department's goals and remain positive about your ability to accomplish your goals. An unsupportive boss is just another obstacle to be overcome.
2. Do not fall prey to feeling powerless, and empower yourself to get things done.
3. Exercise the power you have by focusing on circumstances you can control and avoid dwelling on circumstances you cannot control.
4. Work on improving your relationship with your manager. Begin by examining the level of trust between the two of you and then try to improve it by frequently and effectively communicating. You can also increase trust by following through on your commitments and achieving your goals.

5. Use an authentic, respectful, and assertive approach to resolve differences with your manager. It also is useful to use a problem-solving approach when disagreements arise.

go to the Web for the Self-Exercise: Assessing Your Leader-Member Exchange

Shared Leadership

A pair of OB scholars noted that "there is some speculation, and some preliminary evidence, to suggest that concentration of leadership in a single chain of command may be less optimal than shared leadership responsibility among two or more individuals in certain task environments."[78] This perspective is quite different from the previous theories and models discussed in this chapter, which assume that leadership is a vertical, downward-flowing process. In contrast, the notion of shared leadership is based on the idea that people need to share information and collaborate to get things done at work. This in turn underscores the need for employees to adopt a horizontal process of influence or leadership. **Shared leadership** entails a simultaneous, ongoing, mutual influence process in which individuals share responsibility for leading regardless of formal roles and titles. The concept of shared leadership was first discussed in Chapter 11 when we reviewed the characteristics of high-performing teams. You may recall that *shared responsibility* is one of the eight attributes associated with high-performing teams.

> **Shared leadership**
> Simultaneous, ongoing, mutual influence process in which people share responsibility for leading.

Shared leadership is most likely to be needed when people work in teams, when people are involved in complex projects, and when people are doing knowledge work—work that requires voluntary contributions of intellectual capital by skilled professionals. Shared leadership also is beneficial when people are working on tasks or projects that require interdependence and creativity.[79] Despite these recommendations, it is important to remember that people vary in the preference for shared leadership. Some of these differences are culturally based (recall our discussion in Chapter 4). For example, we conducted a consulting project with a manufacturing company in Portugal and realized that many employees preferred a directive rather than collaborative approach toward decision making and leadership.

The concept of shared leadership is taking hold at the highest levels in organizations. We are seeing more and more cases in which a CEO and another executive, such as a chief operating officer or chief financial officer, share the overall responsibilities of running the business. A simple way to make this work is for one leader to focus on internal matters while the other is concerned with external issues. Organizations like Goldman Sachs (see the Real World/Real People feature on page 486), Adobe, PepsiCo, and others are using this form of leadership because they find that two people are more likely to possess the varied abilities that are needed to run an organization. The application of shared leadership in this manner also helps organizations build a leadership pipeline for executive-level positions.[80]

Researchers are just now beginning to explore the process of shared leadership, and results are promising. For example, shared leadership in teams was positively associated with group cohesion, group citizenship, and group effectiveness.[81] Table 16–6 contains a list of key questions and answers that managers should consider when determining how they can develop shared leadership.

Goldman Sachs Relies on Shared Leadership

The benefits and challenges of running an organization with leaders who play complementary roles can be seen at Goldman Sachs, where for decades many parts of the business—and sometimes the firm itself—have been headed by teams of two coleaders.

The practice emerged almost by chance. In 1976, when the senior managing director died, the firm decided to fill his position with two partners and members of the management committee, John Weinberg and John Whitehead, who had worked closely together for years. . . . Over time, the notion of coleadership became ingrained in the firm's culture. Although no formal policy mandates that certain businesses be run by more than one person, when a position opens, Cohen says [Jonathan Cohen is an advisory director], "you look over the best people for the job, and often there are two with complimentary strengths." . . . Perhaps the greatest benefit of coleadership is diversity of thought and talent.

What are the pros and cons of shared leadership?

SOURCE: Excerpted from S A Miles and M D Watkins, "The Leadership Team: Complementary Strengths or Conflicting Agendas?" *Harvard Business Review,* April 2007, p 93.

Level 5 Leadership

This model of leadership was not derived from any particular theory or model of leadership. Rather, it was developed from a longitudinal research study attempting to answer the following question: Can a good company become a great company and, if so, how? The study was conducted by a research team headed by Jim Collins, a former university professor who started his own research-based consulting company. He summarized his work in the best seller *Good to Great.*[82]

To answer the research question, Collins identified a set of companies that shifted from good performance to great performance. Great performance was defined as "cumulative stock returns at or below the general stock market for 15 years, punctuated by a transition point, then cumulative returns at least three times the market over the next 15 years."[83] Beginning with a sample of 1,435 companies on the *Fortune* 500 from 1965 to 1995, he identified 11 good-to-great companies: Abbot, Circuit City, Fannie Mae, Gillette, Kimberly-Clark, Kroger, Nucor, Philip Morris, Pitney Bowes, Walgreens, and Wells Fargo. His next step was to compare these 11 companies with a targeted set of direct-comparison companies. This comparison enabled him to uncover the drivers of good-to-great transformations. One of the key drivers was called Level 5 leadership (see Figure 16–5). In other words, every company that experienced good-to-great performance was led by an individual possessing the characteristics associated with Level 5 leadership. Let us consider this leadership hierarchy.

Figure 16–5 reveals that a Level 5 leader possesses the characteristics of humility and a fearless will to succeed. American president Abraham Lincoln is an example of such an individual. Although he was soft-spoken and shy, he possessed great will to accomplish his goal of uniting his country during the Civil War in the 1860s. This determination resulted in the loss of 250,000 Confederates, 360,000 Union soldiers, and ultimately to a united country. Being humble and determined, however, was not enough for Lincoln to succeed at his quest. Rather, a Level 5 leader must also possess the capabilities associated with the other levels in the hierarchy. Although an individual does not move up the hierarchy in a stair-step fashion, a Level 5 leader must possess the capabilities contained in Levels 1–4 before he or she can use the Level 5 characteristics to transform an organization.

It is important to note the overlap between the capabilities represented in this model and the previous leadership theories discussed in this chapter. For example,

Table 16–6   *Key Questions and Answers to Consider When Developing Shared Leadership*

KEY QUESTIONS	ANSWERS
What task characteristics call for shared leadership?	Tasks that are highly *interdependent*. Tasks that require a great deal of *creativity*. Tasks that are highly *complex*.
What is the role of the leader in developing shared leadership?	*Designing the team,* including clarifying purpose, securing resources, articulating vision, selecting members, and defining team processes. *Managing the boundaries* of the team.
How can organizational systems facilitate the development of shared leadership?	*Training and development systems* can be used to prepare both designated leaders and team members to engage in shared leadership. *Reward systems* can be used to promote and reward shared leadership. *Cultural systems* can be used to articulate and to demonstrate the value of shared leadership.
What vertical and shared leadership behaviors are important to team outcomes?	*Directive leadership* can provide task-focused directions. *Transactional leadership* can provide both personal and material rewards based on key performance metrics. *Transformational leadership* can stimulate commitment to a team vision, emotional engagement, and fulfillment of higher-order needs. *Empowering leadership* can reinforce the importance of self-motivation.
What are the ongoing responsibilities of the vertical leader?	The vertical leader needs to be able to step in and *fill voids* in the team. The vertical leader needs to continue to *emphasize the importance of the shared leadership approach,* given the task characteristics facing the team.

SOURCE: C L Pearce, "The Future of Leadership: Combining Vertical and Shared Leadership to Transform Knowledge Work," *Academy of Management Executive: The Thinking Manager's Source,* February 2004, p 48. Copyright 2004 by The Academy of Management. Reprinted by permission of The Academy of Management via The Copyright Clearance Center.

Levels 1 and 2 are consistent with research on trait theory. Trait research tells us that leaders are intelligent, self-confident, determined, honest, sociable, extroverted, and conscientious. Levels 3 and 4 also seem to contain behaviors associates with transactional and transformational leadership. Level 5 leadership thus appears to integrate components of trait theory and the full-range theory of leadership. The novel and unexpected component of this theory revolves around the conclusion that good-to-great leaders are not only transactional and transformational, but most important, they possess the traits of humility and determination. Robert Iger, CEO of Walt Disney Co., is a good example of someone who is driven and humble.

Iger . . . is a guy who says things like: "The story shouldn't be about me. It's about the team." Sounds like the false modesty of a media-trained CEO, no? But Iger really does prefer to hover in the background, letting the limelight stream over his lieutenants. He rules by consensus, not fiat. . . . Colleagues say they don't know much about Iger's

Figure 16–5   *The Level 5 Hierarchy*

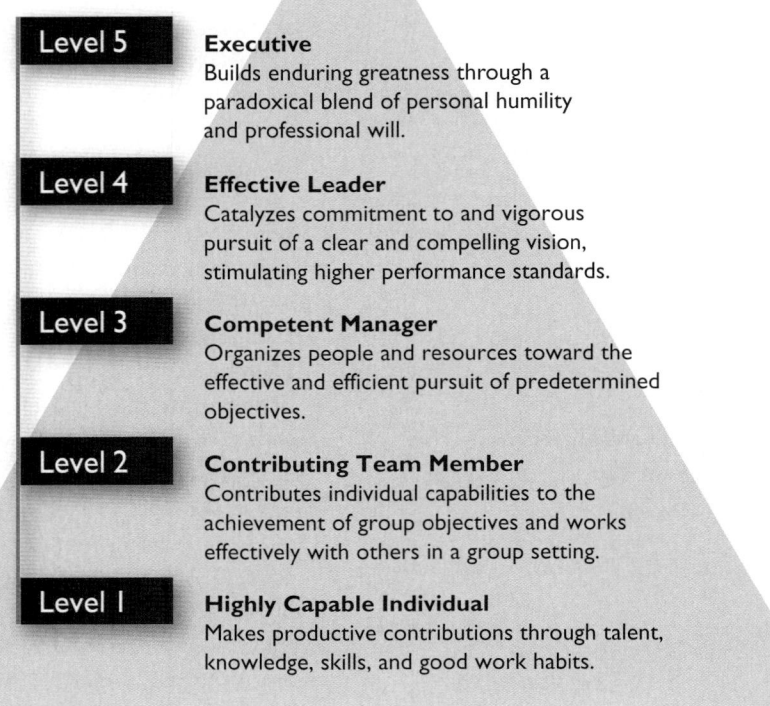

Level 5 **Executive**
Builds enduring greatness through a paradoxical blend of personal humility and professional will.

Level 4 **Effective Leader**
Catalyzes commitment to and vigorous pursuit of a clear and compelling vision, stimulating higher performance standards.

Level 3 **Competent Manager**
Organizes people and resources toward the effective and efficient pursuit of predetermined objectives.

Level 2 **Contributing Team Member**
Contributes individual capabilities to the achievement of group objectives and works effectively with others in a group setting.

Level I **Highly Capable Individual**
Makes productive contributions through talent, knowledge, skills, and good work habits.

SOURCE: Figure from J Collins, *Good to Great: Why Some Companies Make the Leap and Others Don't.* Copyright © 2001 by J Collins. Used by permission of the author.

personal life except that he's a basketball nut. And while Iger isn't without the vision thing, no one would call him a big strategic thinker. But by surrounding himself with smart people, including [Steve] Jobs and the Pixar crew, and letting them get on with it, Iger has recreated a can-do culture at Disney.[84]

There are three points to keep in mind about Level 5 leadership. First, Collins notes that there are additional drivers for taking a company from good to great other than being a Level 5 leader. Level 5 leadership enables the implementation of these additional drivers. Second, to date there has not been any additional research testing Collins's conclusions. Future research is clearly needed to confirm the Level 5 hierarchy. Finally, Collins believes that some people will never become Level 5 leaders because their narcissistic and boastful tendencies do not allow them to subdue their own ego and needs for the greater good of others.

Servant-Leadership

Servant-leadership

Focuses on increased service to others rather than to oneself.

Servant-leadership is more a philosophy of managing than a testable theory. The term *servant-leadership* was coined by Robert Greenleaf in 1970. Greenleaf believes that great leaders act as servants, putting the needs of others, including employees, customers, and community, as their first priority. **Servant-leadership** focuses on increased service to others rather than to oneself.[85] Because the focus of servant-leadership is serving others over self-interest, servant-leaders are less likely to engage in self-serving behaviors that hurt others (e.g., stockholders and employees).

More and more companies are trying to instill a philosophy of servant-leadership into their organizational cultures. Consider how Whole Foods Market CEO John Mackey is modeling servant-leadership. He e-mailed the following information to all employees in November 2006.

> The tremendous success of Whole Foods Market has provided me with far more money than I ever dreamed I'd have and far more than is necessary for either my financial security or personal happiness.... I am now 53 years old and have reached a place in my life where I no longer want to work for money, but simply for the job or the work itself and to better answer the call to service that I feel so clearly in my heart. Beginning on January 1, 2007, my salary will be reduced to $1, and I will no longer take any other cash compensation.... The intention of the board of directors is for Whole Foods Market to donate all of the future stock options I would be eligible to receive to our two company foundations.[86]

Whole Foods Market CEO John Mackey.

This example illustrates that it takes more than words to embed servant-leadership into an organization's culture. Servant-leadership must be reinforced through organizational structure, systems, and rewards for it to take hold. At the individual level, however, managers also need to commit to a set of behaviors underlying servant-leadership.

According to Jim Stuart, co-founder of the leadership circle in Tampa, Florida, "Leadership derives naturally from a commitment to service. You know that you're practicing servant-leadership if your followers become wiser, healthier, more autonomous—and more likely to become servant-leaders themselves."[87] Servant-leadership is not a quick-fix approach to leadership. Rather, it is a long-term, transformational approach to life and work. Table 16–7 presents 10 characteristics possessed by servant-leaders. One can hardly go wrong by trying to adopt these characteristics.

10 The Role of Followers in the Leadership Process

All of the previous theories discussed in this chapter have been leader-centric. That is, they focused on understanding leadership effectiveness from the leader's point of view. We conclude this chapter by discussing the role of followers in the leadership process. Although very little research has been devoted to this topic, it is an important issue to consider because the success of both leaders and followers is contingent on the dynamic relationship among the people involved.[88]

We begin our discussion by noting that both leaders and followers own the quality of their mutual relationship. If something is wrong with the relationship, one or the other needs to intervene. Poor relationships between leaders and followers are frequently caused by unmet expectations—recall our discussion of job satisfaction in Chapter 6. Let us thus consider the nature of leaders' and employees' expectations.

Table 16–7 *Characteristics of the Servant-Leader*

SERVANT-LEADERSHIP CHARACTERISTICS	DESCRIPTION
1. *Listening*	Servant-leaders focus on listening to identify and clarify the needs and desires of a group.
2. *Empathy*	Servant-leaders try to empathize with others' feelings and emotions. An individual's good intentions are assumed even when he or she performs poorly.
3. *Healing*	Servant-leaders strive to make themselves and others whole in the face of failure or suffering.
4. *Awareness*	Servant-leaders are very self-aware of their strengths and limitations.
5. *Persuasion*	Servant-leaders rely more on persuasion than positional authority when making decisions and trying to influence others.
6. *Conceptualization*	Servant leaders take the time and effort to develop broader based conceptual thinking. Servant-leaders seek an appropriate balance between a short-term, day-to-day focus and a long-term, conceptual orientation.
7. *Foresight*	Servant-leaders have the ability to foresee future outcomes associated with a current course of action or situation.
8. *Stewardship*	Servant-leaders assume that they are stewards of the people and resources they manage.
9. *Commitment to the growth of people*	Servant-leaders are committed to people beyond their immediate work role. They commit to fostering an environment that encourages personal, professional, and spiritual growth.
10. *Building community*	Servant-leaders strive to create a sense of community both within and outside the work organization.

SOURCE: These characteristics and descriptions were derived from L C Spears, "Introduction: Servant-Leadership and the Greenleaf Legacy," in *Reflections on Leadership: How Robert K Greenleaf's Theory of Servant-Leadership Influenced Today's Top Management Thinkers*, ed L C Spears (New York: John Wiley & Sons, 1995), pp 1–14.

Leaders want followers to be productive, reliable, honest, cooperative, proactive, and flexible.[89] Leaders do not benefit from followers who hide the truth, withhold information, fail to generate ideas, are unwilling to collaborate, provide inaccurate feedback, or are unwilling to take the lead on projects and initiatives.[90] In contrast, research shows that followers seek, admire, and respect leaders who foster three emotional responses in others: Followers want organizational leaders to create feelings of *significance* (what one does at work is important and meaningful), *community* (a sense of unity encourages people to treat others with respect and dignity and to work together in pursuit of organizational goals), and *excitement* (people are engaged and feel energy at work).[91] What then can followers do to enhance the achievement of these mutual expectations?

A pair of OB experts developed a four step process for followers to use in managing the leader–follower relationship.[92] First, it is critical for followers to understand their boss. Followers should attempt to gain an appreciation for their manager's leadership style, interpersonal style, goals, expectations, pressures, and strengths and weaknesses. Second, followers need to understand their own style, needs, goals, expectations, and strengths and weaknesses.[93] The next step entails conducting a gap analysis between the understanding a follower has about his or her boss and the understanding the follower has about him- or herself. With this information in mind, followers are ready to proceed to the final step of developing and maintaining a relationship that fits both parties' needs and styles.

This final step requires followers to build on mutual strengths and to adjust or accommodate the leader's divergent style, goals, expectations, and weaknesses.[94] For example, a follower might adjust his or her style of communication in response to the boss's preferred method for receiving information. Other adjustments might be made in terms of decision making. If the boss prefers a participative approach, then followers should attempt to involve their manager in all decisions regardless of the follower's decision-making style—recall our discussion of decision-making styles in Chapter 12. Good use of time and resources is another issue for followers to consider. Most managers are pushed for time, energy, and resources and are more likely to appreciate followers who save rather than cost them time and energy. Followers should not use up their manager's time discussing trivial matters.

There are two final issues to consider. First, a follower may not be able to accommodate a leader's style, expectations, or weaknesses and may have to seek a transfer or quit his or her job to reconcile the discrepancy. We recognize that there are personal and ethical trade-offs that one may not be willing to make when managing the leader–follower relationship. Second, we can all enhance our boss's leadership effectiveness and our employer's success by becoming better followers. Remember, it is in an individual's best interest to be a good follower because leaders need and want competent employees.

Summary of Key Concepts

1. *Define the term* leadership, *and explain the difference between leading and managing.* Leadership is defined as a process in which an individual influences a group of individuals to achieve a common goal. Although leadership and management overlap, each entails a unique set of activities or functions. Managers typically perform functions associated with planning, investigating, organizing, and control, and leaders deal with the interpersonal aspects of a manager's job. Table 16–2 summarizes the differences between leading and managing. All told, organizational success requires a combination of effective leadership and management.

2. *Review trait theory research and the takeaways from this theoretical perspective.* Historical leadership research did not support the notion that effective leaders possessed unique traits from followers. More recent research showed that effective leaders possessed the following traits: intelligence, self-confidence, determination, honesty/integrity, sociability, extraversion, conscientiousness and problem-solving skills. In contrast, bad leaders displayed the following characteristics: incompetence, rigid, intemperate, callous, corrupt, insular, and evil. Research

also demonstrated that men and women exhibited different styles of leadership. The takeaways from trait theory are that (a) we can no longer ignore the implications of leadership traits; traits influence leadership effectiveness; (b) organizations may want to include personality and trait assessments into their selection and promotion processes; and (c) management development programs can be used to enhance employees' leadership traits.

3. *Explain behavioral styles theory and its takeaways.* The thrust of behavioral styles theory is to identify the leader behaviors that directly affect work-group effectiveness. Researchers at Ohio State uncovered two key leadership behaviors: consideration and initiating structure. These behaviors are similar to the employee-centered and job-centered behaviors uncovered by researchers at the University of Michigan. The takeaways from this theoretical perspective are as follows: (a) leaders are made, not born; (b) there is no one best style of leadership; (c) the effectiveness of a particular style depends on the situation at hand; and (d) managers are encouraged to concentrate on improving the effective execution of their leader behaviors.

4. *Explain, according to Fiedler's contingency model, how leadership style interacts with situational control, and discuss the takeaways from this model.* Fiedler believes leader effectiveness depends on an appropriate match between leadership style and situational control. Leaders are either task motivated or relationship motivated. Situation control is composed of leader–member relations, task structure, and position power. Task-motivated leaders are effective under situations of both high and low control. Relationship-motivated leaders are more effective when they have moderate situational control. The three takeaways are: (a) leadership effectiveness goes beyond traits and behaviors, (b) leaders are unlikely to be successful in all situations, and (c) leaders need to modify their style to fit a situation.

5. *Discuss House's revised path–goal theory and its practical takeaways.* There are three key changes in the revised path–goal theory. Leaders now are viewed as exhibiting eight categories of leader behavior (see Table 16–5) instead of four. In turn, the effectiveness of these styles depends on various employee characteristics and environmental factors. Second, leaders are expected to spend more effort fostering intrinsic motivation through empowerment. Third, leadership is not limited to people in managerial roles. Rather, leadership is shared among all employees within an organization. There are three takeaways: (a) effective leaders possess and use more than one style of leadership, (b) the theory offers specific suggestions for how leaders can help employees, and (c) managers are advised to modify their leadership style to fit relevant contingency factors.

6. *Describe the difference between laissez-fair, transactional, and transformational leadership.* Laissez-faire leadership is the absence of leadership. It represents a general failure to take responsibility for leading. Transactional leadership focuses on clarifying employees' role and task requirements and providing followers with positive and negative rewards contingent on performance. Transformational leaders motivate employees to pursue organizational goals above their own self-interests. Transactional and transformational leadership are both important for organizational success.

7. *Discuss how transformational leadership transforms followers and work groups.* Individual characteristics and organizational culture are key precursors of transformational leadership, which is comprised of four sets of leader behavior. These leader behaviors in turn positively affect followers' and work-group goals, values, beliefs, aspirations, and motivation. These positive effects are then associated with a host of preferred outcomes.

8. *Explain the leader–member exchange model of leadership and the concept of shared leadership.* The LMX model revolves around the development of dyadic relationships between managers and their direct reports. These leader–member exchanges qualify as either in-group or out-group relationships. Research supports this model of leadership. Shared leadership involves a simultaneous, ongoing, mutual influence process in which individuals share responsibility for leading regardless of formal roles and titles. This type of leadership is most likely to be needed when people work in teams, when people are involved in complex projects, and when people are doing knowledge work. Shared leadership also is beneficial when people are working on tasks or projects that require interdependence and creativity.

9. *Review the Level 5 model of leadership and the principles of servant-leadership.* Level 5 leadership represents a hierarchy of leadership capabilities that are needed to lead companies in transforming from good to great. Servant-leadership is more a philosophy than a testable theory. It is based on the premise that great leaders act as servants, putting the needs of others, including employees, customers, and community, as their first priority.

10. *Describe the follower's role in the leadership process.* Followers can use a four-step process for managing the leader–follower relationship. Followers need to understand their boss and themselves. They then conduct a gap analysis between the understanding they have about their boss and themselves. The final step requires followers to build on mutual strengths and to adjust or accommodate the leader's divergent style, goals, expectations, and weaknesses.

Key Terms

Leadership 463
Leader trait 466
Leader prototype 467
Consideration 471
Initiating structure 471
Situational theories 473
Leader-member relations 473
Task structure 474

Position power 474
Contingency factors 475
Transactional leadership 479
Transformational leadership 479
In-group exchange 484
Out-group exchange 484
Shared leadership 485
Servant-leadership 488

A Crisis Causes Andrea Jung to Change Her Leadership Style[95]

In 2005, Avon Products Inc.'s success story turned ugly. After six straight years of 10%-plus growth and a tripling of earnings under CEO Andrea Jung, the company suddenly began losing sales across the globe. Developing markets such as Central Europe and Russia, the engine of Avon's amazing run, stumbled just as sales in the U.S. and Mexico stalled. The global diversity that had long propped up the company's performance suddenly began to weigh it down.

This dramatic turn of events hit investors by surprise. In May, Jung had predicted Avon would exceed Wall Street's already high expectations. By September, problems in China, Eastern Europe, and Russia were mounting, and Jung was backpedaling at full speed. Angry shareholders bailed out. The stock price, which had risen 181% during Jung's first 5½ years at the helm, plummeted 45% between April and October.

Over the past 18 months, Jung has tried to figure out what went wrong and how to fix it. While it's far too soon to celebrate at Avon, the company is emerging from Wall Street's doghouse....

An expert in building brands, Jung had no turnaround experience when she arrived in her job. At times she doubted that she could make the deep staff cuts needed to right the company. "I'd never done anything like that before," said the 48-year-old Jung on Feb. 15. "My first reaction was: 'I get it. I see the numbers, but I just don't know if I, or we, have the stomach for it.'"

One of Jung's most important moves has been forcing managers to make decisions based on fact rather than intuition. In the past year, she has reorganized Avon's management structure, taking away much of the autonomy from country managers, in favor of globalized manufacturing and marketing. Previously, Avon managers from Poland to Mexico ran their own plants, developed new products, and created their own ads, often relying as much on gut as numbers. In Jung's words they were "king or queen of every decision."

Now Jung has trimmed out seven layers of management, bringing the total from 15 down to 8, and finally launched the kind of numbers-heavy return-on-investment analysis that most large consumer products companies have been doing for decades. That analysis is directed from New York headquarters by an executive team stocked with more people from the outside. Recent recruits have come from larger, more analytical consumer-products companies such as Gillette, Procter & Gamble, PepsiCo, and Kraft. "When she speaks about what we have to do to achieve our goals, she is so much closer to the operations" now, says board member Paula Stern. "She has her hands directly on the levers that have to be moved."

At the height of Jung's problems, in December 2005, management guru Ram Charan gave her a piece of pivotal advice. He advised Jung to go home that Friday night and imagine she had been fired. Then, he said, return Monday morning with the mindset of someone brought in from the outside. "If you can be that objective and blend in your institutional knowledge and relationships, you're going to have an advantage," he told her. A month later Jung was flying around the globe on a CEO roadshow, addressing audiences of her top 1,000 global managers. Her message: By the end of this year, one-quarter of you will be gone. "I put a lot of people in those jobs," says Jung, "You can imagine it was the toughest time to walk the halls." ...

Avon's new data-centric approach isn't just about creating a good set of slides, however. It's also helping to change Avon's marketing and product development. Avon sells many thousands of products, and 1,000 of those have been introduced in the past 12 months. Savings from centralized manufacturing and other initiatives are being put into advertising and research and development, a strategy Jung hopes will get earnings climbing again.

Avon increased its ad budget from $136 million in 2005 to $249 million in 2006. This was a big factor in the company's 6% sales growth in 2006. Avon had planned to raise advertising to $200 million, but good returns on TV ads in Brazil, the US, and Russia, along with other marketing pushes, persuaded management to add a further $49 million, for a total increase of 83%. Avon is also doing more marketing to spark recruiting. Last year the company ran TV and newspaper ads supporting 1,400 recruiting events in China. In Russia the company sponsors a TV show featuring a character who sells Avon.

Jung's No. 1 role continues to be communicating the company's new strategy. In the weeks leading up to and just after the February analysts' gathering, Jung visited Bangkok, Hong Kong, London, São Paulo, Shanghai, and Warsaw. All that travel comes at a sacrifice. Jung has a daughter who will graduate from high school this spring and a son who is 9. She says she has completely prioritized her life in the past two years, skipping business dinners and formal evening affairs in order to be sure she sees them when she's in New York. But she also tells her children that she loves the company and the work, even if it has been grueling in recent months. "I think it's important they know that," she says. "Otherwise why would you do this?"

493

Questions for Discussion

1. Use Table 16–2 to evaluate the extent to which Andrea Jung displayed the characteristics associated with being a good leader and good manager.
2. Which different positive and negative leadership traits and styles were displayed by Jung. Cite examples.
3. What type of leadership did Jung rely upon to solve the financial problems facing Avon? Is this type of leadership consistent with prescriptions derived from both Fiedler's and House's models of leadership? Explain.
4. How could Jung have used more transformational leadership to help during the turnaround? Discuss.
5. What did you learn about leadership from this case?

Ethical Dilemma

Doug Durand's Staff Engages in Questionable Sales Activities[96]

In his 20 years as a pharmaceutical salesman, Douglas Durand thought he had seen it all. Then, in 1995, he signed on as vice president for sales at TAP Pharmaceutical Products Inc. in Lake Forest, Illinois. Several months later, in disbelief, he listened to a conference call among his sales staff: They were openly discussing how to bribe urologists. Worried about a competing drug coming to market, they wanted to give a 2% "administration fee" up front to any doctor who agreed to prescribe TAP's new prostate cancer drug, Lupron. When one of Durand's regional managers fretted about getting caught, another quipped: "How do you think Doug would look in stripes?" Durand didn't say a word. "That conversation scared the heck out of me," he recalls. "I felt very vulnerable." . . .

For years, TAP sales reps had encouraged doctors to charge government medical programs full price for Lupron they received at a discount or gratis. Doing so helped TAP establish Lupron as the prostrate treatment of choice, bringing in annual sales of $800 million, about a quarter of the company's revenues. . . .

Durand grew increasingly concerned. Colleagues told him he didn't understand TAP's culture. He was excluded from top marketing and sales meetings. Then came the crack about how he would look in stripes. Durand's stomach knotted in fear that he would become the company scapegoat. Yet he felt trapped: If he left within a year, he wouldn't be able to collect his bonus. He also doubted that anyone would hire him if he bolted so hastily.

What Would You Do If You Were Doug Durand?

1. It's a tough market, and giving kickbacks is nothing more than a form of building product loyalty. I wouldn't make a big issue about this practice.
2. I wouldn't do anything because I would not receive my bonus and it wouldn't look good on my résumé to leave the job within one year.
3. I would gather information about TAP and send it to a federal prosecutor. After all, TAP is giving kickbacks and it is encouraging doctors to charge full price for a drug they receive on a discount.
4. I would go to TAP's president and get his or her blessing for our sales activities.
5. Invent other options. Discuss.

Web Resources

For study material and exercises that apply to this chapter, visit our Web site,
www.mhhe.com/kreitner

CHAPTER 17

Creating Effective Organizations

LEARNING OBJECTIVES

When you finish studying the material in this chapter, you should be able to:

1   Describe the four characteristics common to all organizations, and explain the difference between closed and open systems.

2   Define the term *learning organization.*

3   Describe horizontal, hourglass, and virtual organizations.

4   Describe the four generic organizational effectiveness criteria, and discuss how managers can prevent organizational decline.

5   Explain what the contingency approach to organization design involves.

6   Describe the relationship between differentiation and integration in effective organizations.

7   Discuss Burns and Stalker's findings regarding mechanistic and organic organizations.

8   Define and briefly explain the practical significance of centralization and decentralization.

9   Discuss the effective management of organizational size.

Student Resources for Studying Chapter 17

The Web site for your text includes resources that will help you master the concepts in this chapter. As you read, you'll want to visit the site for these helpful tools:

- Your online Study Guide includes learning objectives, a chapter summary, a glossary of key terms, and discussion questions.
- Take a practice quiz and test your knowledge!
- Scroll through a PowerPoint presentation with key concepts for this chapter.

Your instructor might also direct you to the Web site for these exercises:

- Self-assessments that correspond with the chapter content and a Group Exercise.
- You'll also find Video Cases and Internet Exercises for this chapter online.

www.mhhe.com/kreitner

BusinessWeek For nearly five decades, Wal-Mart's signature "everyday low prices" and their enabler—low costs—defined not only its business model but also the distinctive personality of this proud, insular company that emerged from the Ozarks's backwoods to dominate retailing. Over the past year and a half, though, Wal-Mart's growth formula has stopped working. In 2006, its US division eked out a 1.9% gain in same-store sales—its worst performance ever—and this year [2007] has begun no better. By this key measure, such competitors as Target, Costco, Kroger, Safeway, Walgreen's, CVS, and Best Buy now are all growing two to five times faster than Wal-Mart.

Wal-Mart's botched entry into cheap-chic apparel is emblematic of the quandary it faces. Is its alarming loss of momentum the temporary result of disruptions caused by transitory errors ... and by overdue improvements such as the store remodeling program launched last year? Or is Wal-Mart doing lasting damage to its low-budget franchise by trying to compete with much hipper, nimbler rivals for the middle-income dollar? Should the retailer redouble its efforts to out-Target Target, or would it be better off going back to basics?

If Wal-Mart seems short of answers at the moment, it might well be because there aren't any good ones. Increasingly, it appears that America's largest corporation has steered itself into a slow-growth cul de sac from which there is no escape. "There are a lot of issues here, but what they add up to is the end of the age of Wal-Mart," contends Richard Hastings, a senior analyst for the retail rating agency Bernard Sands. "The glory days are over."

Simple mathematics suggests that a 45-year-old company in an industry growing no faster than the economy as a whole will struggle to sustain the speedy growth rates of its youth. In Wal-Mart's case, this difficulty is exacerbated by its great size and extreme dominance of large swaths of the US retail market. Wal-Mart already controls 20% of dry grocery, 29% of nonfood grocery, 30% of health and beauty aids, and 45% of general merchandise sales, according to ACNielsen.

However, the expansion impulse is as deeply embedded in Wal-Mart's DNA as its allegiance to cut-rate pricing. Wal-Mart was able to boost total US revenues by 7.2% last year by opening new stores at the prodigious rate of nearly one a day. According to Wal-Mart CEO H Lee Scott Jr, the company plans to sustain this pace for at least the next five years. In fact, he is on record saying that room remains in the US for Wal-Mart to add 4,000 Supercenters—the largest of its store formats by far—to the 2,000 it now operates.

Does Scott, 58, recognize any limits whatsoever to Wal-Mart's growth potential in the US, which accounted for 78% of its $345 billion in sales last year? "Actually, and I know it's going to sound naive to you, I don't," he replies. "The real issue is, are [we] going to be good enough to take advantage of the opportunities that exist?"[1]

FOR DISCUSSION

Can Wal-Mart grow its way to even greater success, or are its best days behind it?

Virtually every aspect of life is affected at least indirectly by some type of organization. We look to organizations to feed, clothe, house, educate, and employ us (in fact, Wal-Mart, with 1.9 million employees, is the largest employer in the United States).[2] Organizations attend to our needs for entertainment, police and fire protection, insurance, recreation, national security, transportation, news and information, legal assistance, and health care. Many of these organizations, such as Wal-Mart, seek a profit, others do not. Some are extremely large, others are tiny mom-and-pop operations. Despite this mind-boggling diversity, modern organizations have one basic thing in common. They are the primary context for organizational behavior. As mentioned in Chapter 1, organizations are the chessboard upon which the game of organizational behavior is played. Therefore, present and future organizational members need a working knowledge of modern organizations to improve their chances of making the right moves.

This chapter explores the changing shape, effectiveness, and design of today's organizations. Our overriding challenge is to build organizations capable of thriving in an environment characterized by rapid change and relentless global competition.

 # Organizations: Definition and Perspectives

As a necessary springboard for this chapter, we need to formally define the term *organization,* clarify the meaning of organization charts, and explore two open-system perspectives of organizations.

What Is an Organization?

Organization

System of consciously coordinated activities of two or more people.

According to Chester I Barnard's classic definition cited in Chapter 1, an **organization** is "a system of consciously coordinated activities or forces of two or more persons."[3] Embodied in the *conscious coordination* aspect of this definition are four common denominators of all organizations: coordination of effort, a common goal, division of labor, and a hierarchy of authority[4] (see Figure 17–1). Organization theorists refer to these factors as the organization's *structure.*

Coordination of effort is achieved through formulation and enforcement of policies, rules, and regulations. Division of labor occurs when the common goal is pursued by individuals performing separate but related tasks. The hierarchy of authority, also called the chain of command, is a control mechanism dedicated to making sure

Figure 17–1   *Four Characteristics Common to All Organizations*

the right people do the right things at the right time. Historically, managers have maintained the integrity of the hierarchy of authority by adhering to the unity of command principle. The **unity of command principle** specifies that each employee should report to only one manager. Otherwise, the argument goes, inefficiency would prevail because of conflicting orders and lack of personal accountability. (Indeed, these are problems in today's more fluid and flexible organizations based on innovations such as cross-functional, self-managed, and virtual teams.) Managers in the hierarchy of authority also administer rewards and punishments. When the four factors in Figure 17–1 operate in concert, the dynamic entity called an organization exists. At Starbucks, for example, where chairman Howard Schultz has declared an ambitious growth goal, just the right mix of factors in Figure 17–1 will be required for success:

Unity of command principle
Each employee should report to a single manager.

> By 2012, Schultz aims to nearly triple annual sales, to $23.3 billion. The company also plans to have 40,000 stores worldwide, up from 13,500 today, not long after that.[5]

Organization Charts

An **organization chart** is a graphic representation of formal authority and division of labor relationships. To the casual observer, the term *organization chart* means the family tree–like pattern of boxes and lines posted on workplace walls. Within each box one usually finds the names and titles of current position holders.[6] To organization theorists, however, organization charts reveal much more. The partial organization chart in Figure 17–2 reveals four basic dimensions of organizational structure: (1) hierarchy of authority (who reports to whom), (2) division of labor, (3) spans of control, and (4) line and staff positions.

Organization chart
Boxes-and-lines illustration showing chain of formal authority and division of labor.

Hierarchy of Authority As Figure 17–2 illustrates, there is an unmistakable hierarchy of authority.[7] Working from bottom to top, the 10 directors report to the two executive directors who report to the president who reports to the chief executive officer. Ultimately, the chief executive officer answers to the hospital's board of directors. The chart in Figure 17–2 shows strict unity of command up and down the line. A formal hierarchy of authority also delineates the official communication network.

Division of Labor In addition to showing the chain of command, the sample organization chart indicates extensive division of labor. Immediately below the hospital's president, one executive director is responsible for general administration while another is responsible for medical affairs. Each of these two specialities is further subdivided as indicated by the next layer of positions. At each successively lower level in the organization, jobs become more specialized.

Spans of Control The **span of control** refers to the number of people reporting directly to a given manager.[8] Spans of control can range from narrow to wide. For example, the president in Figure 17–2 has a narrow span of control of two. (Staff assistants usually are not included in a manager's span of control.) The executive administrative director in Figure 17–2 has a wider span of control of five. Spans of control exceeding 30 can be found in assembly-line operations where machine-paced and repetitive work substitutes for close supervision. Historically, spans of five to six were considered best. Despite years of debate, organization theorists have not arrived at a consensus regarding the ideal span of control.

Span of control
The number of people reporting directly to a given manager.

Generally, the narrower the span of control, the closer the supervision and the higher the administrative costs as a result of a higher manager-to-worker ratio. Recent emphasis

Figure 17–2   *Sample Organization Chart for a Hospital (executive and director levels only)*

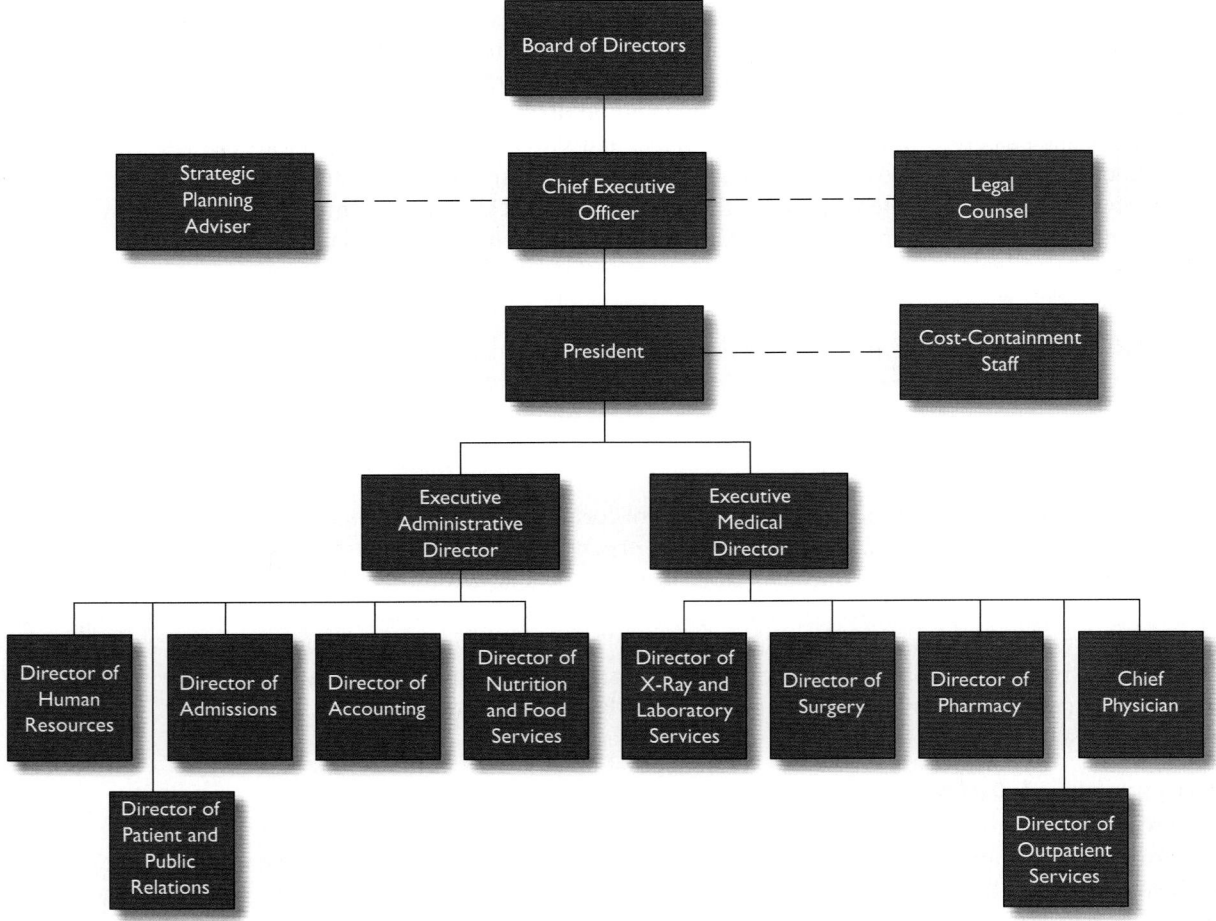

on leanness and administrative efficiency dictates spans of control as wide as possible but guarding against inadequate supervision and lack of coordination. Wider spans also complement the trend toward greater worker autonomy and empowerment.[9]

Line and Staff Positions   The organization chart in Figure 17–2 also distinguishes between line and staff positions. Line managers such as the president, the two executive directors, and the various directors occupy formal decision-making positions within the chain of command. Line positions generally are connected by solid lines on organization charts. Dotted lines indicate staff relationships. **Staff personnel** do background research and provide technical advice and recommendations to their **line managers,** who have the authority to make decisions. For example, the cost-containment specialists in the sample organization chart merely advise the president on relevant matters. Apart from supervising the work of their own staff assistants, they have no line authority over other organizational members. Modern trends such as cross-functional teams and reengineering are blurring the distinction between line and staff.

According to a study of 207 police officers in Israel, line personnel exhibited greater job commitment than did their staff counterparts.[10] This result was anticipated

Staff personnel
Provide research, advice, and recommendations to line managers.

Line managers
Have authority to make organizational decisions.

eBay Benefits from Open-System Thinking

In the olden days—before 2005—eBay was ambivalent about independent developers who ginned up applications to help buyers and sellers navigate its online auctions. In fact, it actually charged those developers fees, up to hundreds of thousands of dollars a year, based on the number of people who used the programs.

Which was, of course, crazy. Make auctions easier and more profitable for eBay's customers, and more people will bid, buy, and sell—meaning lots more revenue for eBay, which takes a cut from every auction.

Now "we want [the developers] to make money." Max Mancini says. "When they grow their business, they also grow ours." Mancini, 40, heads eBay's Disruptive Innovation team, formed last summer, he says, to identify "things that take the company forward the next 10, 20 years." He knows such brainstorms can come from outside as well as inside company walls—which is why he oversees the eBay Developers Program.

Where is the company's boundary in this case? Who is in charge?

SOURCE: C Salter, "Disruptors Welcome," *Fast Company*, May 2007, p 92.

---

because the line managers' decision-making authority empowered them and gave them comparatively more control over their work situations.

An Open-System Perspective of Organizations

To better understand how organizational models have evolved over the years, we need to know the difference between closed and open systems.[11] A **closed system** is said to be a self-sufficient entity. It is "closed" to the surrounding environment. In contrast, an **open system** depends on constant interaction with the environment for survival. The distinction between closed and open systems is a matter of degree.[12] Because every worldly system is partly closed and partly open, the key question is: How great a role does the environment play in the functioning of the system? For instance, a battery-powered clock is a relatively closed system. Once the battery is inserted, the clock performs its time-keeping function hour after hour until the battery goes dead. The human body, on the other hand, is a highly open system because it requires a constant supply of life-sustaining oxygen from the environment. Nutrients also are imported from the environment. Open systems are capable of self-correction, adaptation, and growth, thanks to characteristics such as homeostasis and feedback control.

Historically, management theorists downplayed the environment as they used closed-system thinking to characterize organizations as either well-oiled machines or highly disciplined military units. They believed rigorous planning and control would eliminate environmental uncertainty. But that proved unrealistic. Drawing upon the field of general systems theory that emerged during the 1950s, organization theorists suggested a more dynamic model for organizations.[13] The resulting open-system model likened organizations to the human body.[14] Accordingly, the model in Figure 17–3 reveals the organization to be a living organism that transforms inputs into various outputs. The outer boundary of the organization is permeable. People, information, capital, and goods and services move back and forth across this boundary. Moreover, each of the five organizational subsystems—goals and values, technical, psychosocial, structural, and managerial—is dependent on the others. Feedback about such things as sales and customer satisfaction or dissatisfaction enables the organization to self-adjust and survive despite uncertainty and change. In effect, the organization is alive (see the Real World/Real People feature above).

Closed system
A relatively self-sufficient entity.

Open system
Organism that must constantly interact with its environment to survive.

Figure 17–3   *The Organization as an Open System*

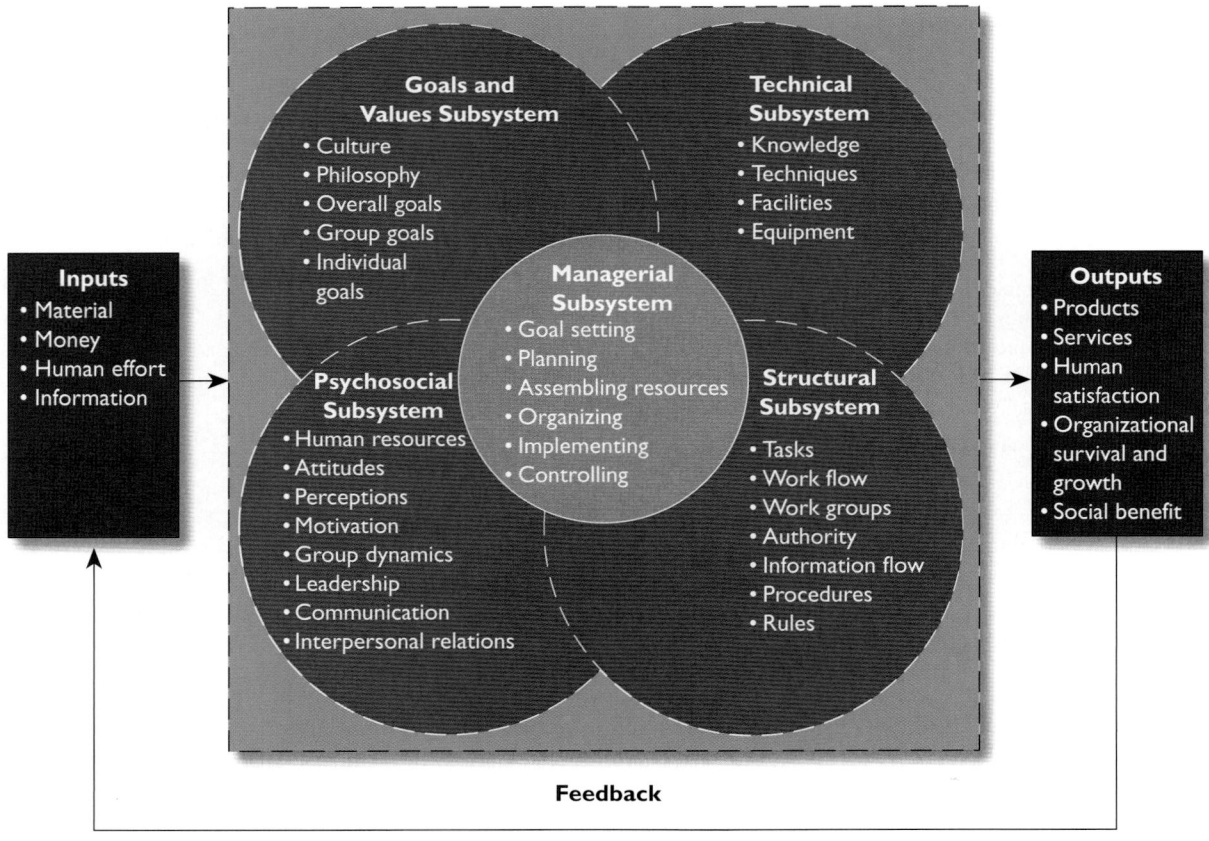

SOURCE: This model is a combination of Figures 5–2 and 5–3 in F E Kast and J E Rosenzweig, *Organization and Management: A Systems and Contingency Approach,* 4th ed (New York: McGraw-Hill, 1986), pp 112, 114. Copyright © 1986. Reprinted by permission of the McGraw-Hill Companies, Inc.

2 Learning Organizations

In recent years, organization theorists have extended the open-system model by adding a "brain" to the "living body." Organizations are said to have human-like cognitive functions, such as the abilities to perceive and interpret, solve problems, and learn from experience. Today, managers read and hear a good deal about learning organizations and knowledge management (as discussed in Chapter 12).[15] Peter Senge, a professor at the Massachusetts Institute of Technology, popularized the term *learning organization* in his best-selling book *The Fifth Discipline.* He described a learning organization as "a group of people working together to collectively enhance their capacities to create results that they truly care about."[16] A practical interpretation of these ideas results in the following definition. A **learning organization** is one that proactively creates, acquires, and transfers knowledge and that changes its behavior on the basis of new knowledge and insights.[17]

Learning organizations actively try to infuse their organizations with new ideas and information. They do this by constantly scanning their external environments, hiring new talent and expertise when needed, and by devoting significant resources to train

Learning organization

Proactively creates, acquires, and transfers knowledge throughout the organization.

and develop their employees. Next, new knowledge must be transferred throughout the organization. Learning organizations strive to reduce structural, process, and interpersonal barriers to the sharing of information, ideas, and knowledge among organizational members. Finally, behavior must change as a result of new knowledge. Learning organizations are results oriented. They foster an environment in which employees are encouraged to use new behaviors and operational processes to achieve corporate goals. A prime example of a learning organization is Cirque du Soleil. According to *BusinessWeek:*

> Niches are nice, but inventing a new market is a whole lot better. Former fire-eating street performer Guy Laliberté founded Canada's Cirque du Soleil 22 years ago on the notion of a unique combination of circus (but without the animals) and theater (but more acrobatic). Despite massive global expansion, with about $700 million in profitable annual sales, Cirque has no significant direct competitors.
>
> Cirque's [president Daniel] Lamarre attributes the company's edge to a stubborn resolve to "stay crazy" and keep "the suits" away from all creative decisions. To keep shows fresh and get a read on shifting public tastes, an in-house group called New Tendencies studies what's new in restaurants, car design, fashion, and other unrelated industries. One result: The group noticed the ascendance of Asian themes, so that flavor was injected into Cirque's hit [Las Vegas] MGM Grand show *Kà*.[18]

These *Cirque du Soleil* acrobats mirror the company's strategic adaptability and flexibility. But don't try this at home!

Now let us see how this evolution of ideas is reshaping organizations.

The Changing Shape of Organizations

Organizations are basically tools invented to get things done through collective action. As any carpenter or plumber knows, different jobs require different tools. So it is with organizations. When the situation changes significantly, according to contingency thinking, a different type of organization may be appropriate. The need for new organizations is greater than ever today because managers face revolutionary changes. *Fortune* magazine offered this perspective:

> We all sense that the changes surrounding us are not mere trends but the workings of large, unruly forces; the globalization of markets; the spread of information technology and computer networks; the dismantling of hierarchy, the structure that has essentially organized work since the mid-19th century. Growing up around these is a new, information-age economy, whose fundamental sources of wealth are knowledge and communication rather than natural resources and physical labor.[19]

What sorts of organizations will prosper in the age of the Internet and e-business? Will they be adaptations of the traditional pyramid-shaped organization? Or will they be radically different?[20] Let us put our imaginations to work by envisioning the shape of tomorrow's organizations, the rough outlines of which are visible today.

Table 17–1   *Profiles of the New-Style and Old-Style Organizations*

NEW	OLD
Dynamic, learning	Stable
Information rich	Information is scarce
Global	Local
Small and large	Large
Product/customer oriented	Functional
Skills oriented	Job oriented
Team oriented	Individual oriented
Involvement oriented	Command/control oriented
Lateral/networked	Hierarchical
Customer oriented	Job requirements oriented

SOURCE: J R Galbraith and E E Lawler III, "Effective Organizations: Using the New Logic of Organizing," in *Organizing for the Future: The New Logic for Managing Complex Organizations*, eds J R Galbraith, E E Lawler III, and Associates, p 298. Copyright 1993, John Wiley & Sons, Inc. Reprinted with permission of John Wiley & Sons, Inc.

New-Style versus Old-Style Organizations

Organization theorists Jay R Galbraith and Edward E Lawler III have called for a "new logic of organizing."[21] They recommend a whole new set of adjectives to describe organizations (see Table 17–1). Traditional pyramid-shaped organizations, conforming to the old-style pattern, tend to be too slow and inflexible today. Leaner, more flexible organizations are needed to accommodate today's strategic balancing act between cost, quality, and speed. These new-style organizations are customer focused, dedicated to continuous improvement and learning, and structured around teams. These qualities, along with computerized information technology, should enable big organizations to mimic the speed and flexibility of small organizations. Avon, for example, is making the tough transition from an old-style organization to a new-style organization. CEO Andrea Jung painted this strategic picture in a recent interview:

> We're in the middle of a turn-around. We've eliminated 10% of our workforce, cut almost 30% of our management, and reduced 15 layers to eight. This brings us closer to the market. It also helps us cut costs by almost $200 million annually....
>
> We're increasing ad spending more than 50% this year and will double it by 2008. Beyond that, we're investing in innovation: The game in beauty is

Andrea Jung, Avon's CEO, has streamlined her beauty products company to make it more adaptive to constant change.

Figure 17–4   *The Shape of Tomorrow's Organizations*

The Horizontal Organization

The Hourglass Organization   **The Virtual Organization**

   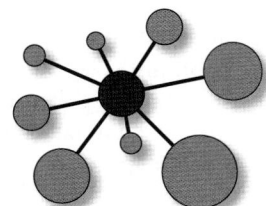

changing so much, if your product isn't high tech or can't make a unique performance claim—plump your lips, reduce your lines, look glossy, and stay on for 24 hours—you can't go to market today. I'm not just talking about a $20 lipstick, but a $5 lipstick! We've spent $100 million on a new R&D [research and development] center. . . .

Our IT [information technology] team has developed a global Internet platform, and I've put one of our top strategists full-time on the case.[22]

 # 3 Three New Organizational Patterns

Figure 17–4 illustrates three radical departures from the traditional pyramid-shaped organization. Each is the logical result of various trends that are evident today. In other words, we have exaggerated these new organizations for instructional purposes. You will likely encounter various combinations of these pure types in the years ahead. Let us imagine life in the organizations of tomorrow. (Importantly, these characterizations are not intended to be final answers. We simply seek to stimulate thoughtful discussion.)

Horizontal Organizations Despite the fact that *reengineering* became synonymous with huge layoffs and has been called a passing fad,[23] it will likely have a lasting effect on organization design. Namely, it helped refine the concept of a horizontally oriented organization. Unlike traditional vertically oriented organizations with functional units such as production, marketing, and finance, horizontal organizations are flat and built around core processes aimed at satisfying customers. *Fortune* magazine characterized horizontal organizations this way:

The horizontal corporation includes these potent elements: Teams will provide the foundation of organizational design. They will not be set up inside departments, like marketing, but around core processes, such as new-product development. Process owners, not department heads, will be the top managers, and they may sport wonderfully weird titles; GE Medical Systems has a "vice president of global sourcing and order to remittance."

Rather than focusing single-mindedly on financial objectives or functional goals, the horizontal organization emphasizes customer satisfaction. Work is simplified and hierarchy flattened by combining related tasks—for example, an account-management process that subsumes the sales, billing, and service functions—and eliminating work that does not add value. Information zips along an internal superhighway: The knowledge worker analyzes it, and technology moves it quickly across the corporation instead of up and down, speeding up and improving decision making.[24]

What will it be like to work in a horizontal organization?[25] It will be a lot more interesting than traditional bureaucracies with their functional ghettos. Most employees will be *close to the customer* (both internal and external)—asking questions, getting feedback, and jointly solving problems. Constant challenge also will come from being on cross-functional teams where co-workers with different technical specialties work side-by-side on projects. Sometimes people will find themselves dividing their time among several projects. Blurred and conflicting lines of authority will break the traditional unity-of-command principle. Project goals and deadlines will tend to replace the traditional supervisor role. Training in both technical and teamwork skills will be a top priority. Multiskilled employees at all levels will find themselves working on different teams and various projects during the year. Paradoxically, self-starters and team players will thrive. Because of the flatness of the organization, lateral transfers will be more common than traditional vertical promotions. This will be a source of discontent for many of those who want to move upward. Constant change will take its toll in terms of interpersonal conflict, personal stress, and burnout. Skill-based pay will supplement pay-for-performance.

Hourglass Organizations This pattern gets its name from the organization's pinched middle. Thanks to modern information technology, a relatively small executive group will be able to coordinate the efforts of numerous operating personnel who make goods or render services. Multiple and broad layers of middle managers who served as conduits for information in old-style organizations will be unnecessary in hourglass organizations. Competition for promotions among operating personnel will be intense because of the restricted hierarchy. Lateral transfers will be more common. Management will compensate for the lack of promotion opportunities with job rotation, skill training, and pay-for-performance. What few middle managers there are will be cross-functional problem solvers who also possess a number of technical skills. The potential for alienation between the executive elite and those at the base of the hourglass will be great, thus giving labor unions an excellent growth opportunity.

Virtual Organizations Like virtual teams, discussed in Chapter 11, modern information technology allows people in virtual organizations to get something accomplished despite being geographically dispersed.[26] Instead of relying heavily on face-to-face meetings, as before, members of virtual organizations send e-mail and voicemail messages, exchange project information over the Internet, and convene videoconferences among far-flung participants. In addition, cellular phones and the wireless broadband Internet have made the dream of doing business from the beach a reality! (See the Real World/Real People feature on page 507.) This disconnection between work and location is causing managers to question traditional assumptions

The Mighty Micro-Multinational

When working in the tropical sun becomes too much for Ivko Maksimovic, the lanky Serbian heads to one of the Dominican Republic's pristine white-sand beaches. He first gathers up a black hat, mosquito repellent, and a bottle of drinking water. Along with those essentials, he starts stuffing his black backpack with a tangle of computer cords, an extra laptop battery, a spare 160-gigabyte hard drive, and an EVDO card to connect to the Caribbean country's 3G broadband network. Finally, he adds a battered ThinkPad, a Skype-ready headset, and a cable lock to lash all the gear to a tree when he decides to take a swim. "It's very cool to think about important stuff while you fight the waves," Maksimovic says.

Maksimovic, 29, is the CTO [chief technology officer] of Vast.com, a startup search company based in San Francisco. He lives in the Dominican Republic because it's warm and far from Serbia's troubles. He works for Vast because his bosses think he's the best person for the job, and it doesn't matter much where he is physically as long as he has a broadband connection.

Between sessions in the surf pondering the arcana of coding on a May afternoon, Maksimovic chats with Vast's main development team in Belgrade by instant message and checks in with a colleague in Ireland through e-mail. The rest of the executive team dials in from San Francisco for a rare spoken conversation using a Skype-enabled speakerphone. . . .

Vast launched a year ago in its present form and now employs 25 people who work across five time zones, four nations, and two continents—all of which makes it a particularly striking example of a growing breed of startup that can best be described as a micro-multinational.

What does it take for someone to succeed in a virtual organization such as this?

SOURCE: Excerpted from M V Copeland, "The Mighty Micro-Multinational," *Business 2.0,* July 2006, pp 106–14.

about centralized offices and factories.[27] Why have offices for people who are never there because they are out finding and helping customers? Why have a factory when it is less expensive to contract out the work? Indeed, many so-called virtual organizations are really a *network* of several independent contractors or organizations hooked together contractually and electronically.

Here is how we envision life in the emerging virtual organizations and organizational networks. Things will be very interesting and profitable for the elite core of entrepreneurs and engineers who hit on the right business formula. Turnover among the financial and information have-nots—data entry, customer service, and production employees—will be high because of glaring inequities and limited opportunities for personal fulfillment and growth. Telecommuters who work from home will feel liberated and empowered (and sometimes lonely). Commitment, trust, and loyalty could erode badly if managers do not heed this caution by Charles Handy, a British management expert. According to Handy: "A shared commitment still requires personal contact to make the commitment feel real. *Paradoxically, the more virtual an organization becomes the more its people need to meet in person.*"[28] Independent contractors, both individuals and organizations, will participate in many different organizational networks and thus have diluted loyalty to any single one. Substandard

Starbucks' Founder and Chairman, Howard Schultz, Brewed Up a Grand Vision

I wanted to build a different kind of company—a company that had a conscience. So it wasn't only that I needed people with skills and discipline and business acumen that complemented my own qualities, but most important, I needed to attract and retain people with like-minded values. What tied us together was not our respective disciplines, and it was not chasing an exit strategy driven by money. What tied us together was the dream of building a company that would achieve the fragile balance of profitability, shareholder value, a sense of benevolence, and a social conscience.

SOURCE: As quoted in "The Best Advice I Ever Got," *Fortune*, March 21, 2005, p 98.

working conditions and low pay at some smaller contractors will make them little more than Internet-age sweatshops. Companies living from one contract to another will offer little in the way of job security and benefits. Opportunities to start new businesses will be numerous, but prolonged success could prove elusive at Internet speed.[29]

Be Prepared for Some Surprises The only certainty about tomorrow's organizations is they are not a cure-all and will produce their fair share of surprises. If you are a flexible and adaptable person who sees problems as opportunities, are a self-starter capable of teamwork, and are committed to life-long learning, don't worry. You will likely thrive in tomorrow's organizations.

4 Organizational Effectiveness (and the Threat of Decline)

How effective are you? If someone asked you this apparently simple question, you would likely ask for clarification before answering. For instance, you might want to know if they were referring to your grade point average, annual income, actual accomplishments, ability to get along with others, public service, or perhaps something else entirely. So it is with modern organizations. Effectiveness criteria abound. For example, see the Real World/Real People feature for Starbucks' unique vision of effectiveness.

Assessing organizational effectiveness is an important topic for an array of people, including managers, job hunters, stockholders, government agencies, and OB specialists. The purpose of this section is to introduce a widely applicable and useful model of organizational effectiveness; we will also deal with the related problem of organizational decline.

Generic Organizational-Effectiveness Criteria

A good way to better understand this complex subject is to consider four generic approaches to assessing an organization's effectiveness (see Figure 17–5). These effectiveness criteria apply equally well to large or small and profit or not-for-profit organizations. Moreover, as denoted by the overlapping circles in Figure 17–5, the four

Figure 17–5   *Four Ways to Assess Organizational Effectiveness*

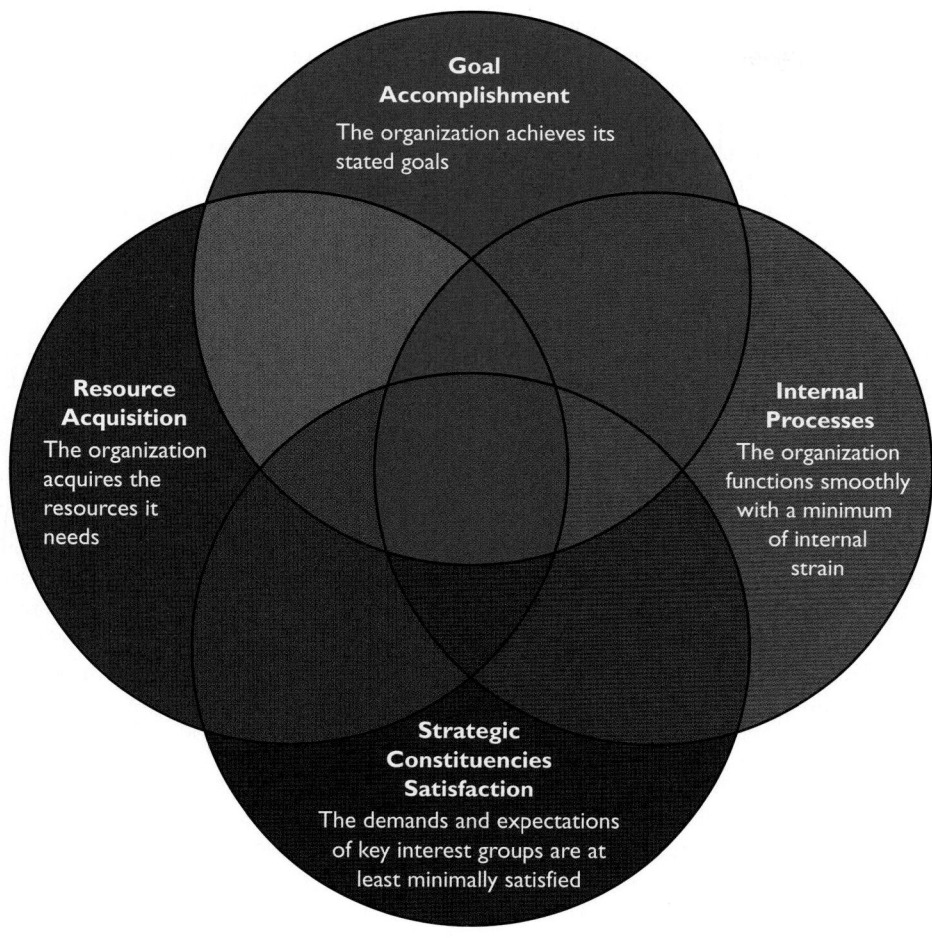

SOURCES: Adapted from discussion in K Cameron, "Critical Questions in Assessing Organizational Effectiveness," *Organizational Dynamics,* Autumn 1980, pp 66–80; and K S Cameron, "Effectiveness as Paradox: Consensus and Conflict in Conceptions of Organizational Effectiveness," *Management Science,* May 1986, pp 539–53.

effectiveness criteria can be used in various combinations. The key thing to remember is "no single approach to the evaluation of effectiveness is appropriate in all circumstances or for all organization types."[30] What do Coca-Cola and France Télécom, for example, have in common, other than being large profit-seeking corporations? Because a multidimensional approach is required, we need to look more closely at each of the four generic effectiveness criteria.

Goal Accomplishment   Goal accomplishment is the most widely used effectiveness criterion for organizations. Key organizational results or outputs are compared with previously stated goals or objectives. Deviations, either plus or minus, require corrective action. This is simply an organizational variation of the personal goal-setting process discussed in Chapter 9. Effectiveness, relative to the criterion of goal accomplishment, is gauged by how well the organization meets or exceeds its goals.

Productivity improvement, involving the relationship between inputs and outputs, is a common organization-level goal.[31] Goals also may be set for organizational efforts such as minority recruiting, pollution prevention, and quality improvement. Given today's competitive pressures and e-business revolution, *innovation* and *speed* are very important organizational goals worthy of measurement and monitoring.[32] A few years ago, Toyota gave us a powerful indicator of where things are going in this regard. The Japanese automaker announced it could custom-build a car in just five days! A customer's new Toyota would roll off the Ontario, Canada, assembly line just five days after the order was placed. A 30-day lag was the industry standard at the time.[33]

Resource Acquisition This second criterion relates to inputs rather than outputs. An organization is deemed effective in this regard if it acquires necessary factors of production such as raw materials, labor, capital, and managerial and technical expertise. Charitable organizations such as the Salvation Army judge their effectiveness in terms of how much money they raise from private and corporate donations.[34]

Internal Processes Some refer to this third effectiveness criterion as the "healthy systems" approach. An organization is said to be a healthy system if information flows smoothly and if employee loyalty, commitment, job satisfaction, and trust prevail.[35] Goals may be set for any of these internal processes. Healthy systems, from a behavioral standpoint, tend to have a minimum of dysfunctional conflict and destructive political maneuvering. M Scott Peck, the physician who wrote the highly regarded book *The Road Less Traveled,* characterizes healthy organizations in ethical terms:

> A healthy organization, Peck says, is one that has a genuine sense of community: It's a place where people are emotionally present with one another, and aren't afraid to talk about fears and disappointments—because that's what allows us to care for one another. It's a place where there is authentic communication, a willingness to be vulnerable, a commitment to speaking frankly and respectfully—and a commitment not to walk away when the going gets tough.[36]

Strategic Constituencies Satisfaction Organizations both depend on people and affect the lives of people. Consequently, many consider the satisfaction of key interested parties to be an important criterion of organizational effectiveness.

Strategic constituency

Any group of people with a stake in the organization's operation or success.

A **strategic constituency** is any group of individuals who have some stake in the organization—for example, resource providers, users of the organization's products or services, producers of the organization's output, groups whose cooperation is essential for the organization's survival, or those whose lives are significantly affected by the organization.[37]

Strategic constituencies (or *stakeholders*) generally have competing or conflicting interests.[38] For instance, when ExxonMobil's 2006 profits of $39.5 billion set a world record, customers at the gas pumps weren't cheering[39] (for more on this subject, see the OB in Action Case Study at the end of the chapter). Strategic constituents or stakeholders can be identified systematically through a stakeholder audit.[40] A **stakeholder audit** enables management to identify all parties significantly impacted by the organization's performance (see Figure 17–6). Conflicting interests and relative satisfaction among the listed stakeholders can then be dealt with.

Stakeholder audit

Systemic identification of all parties likely to be affected by the organization.

A never-ending challenge for management is to strike a workable balance among strategic constituencies so as to achieve at least minimal satisfaction on all fronts.

Figure 17–6   *A Sample Stakeholder Audit Identifying Strategic Constituencies*

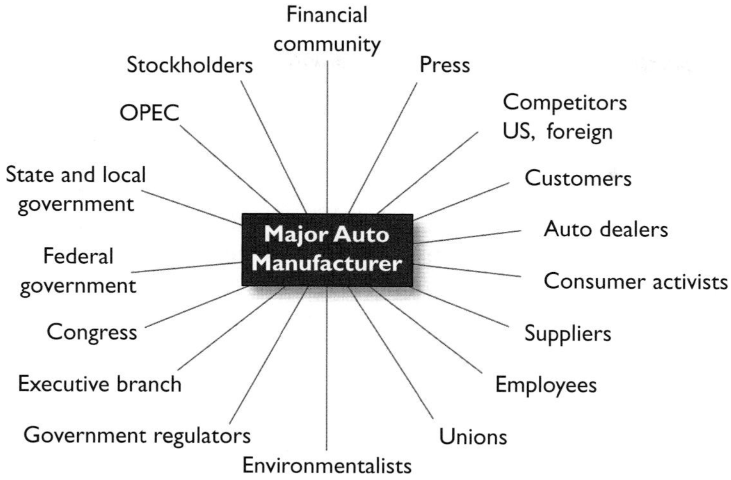

SOURCE: N C Roberts et al., "The Stakeholder Audit Goes Public," *Organizational Dynamics,* Winter 1989.
© 1989. Reprinted with permission from Elsevier Science.

Multiple Effectiveness Criteria:
Some Practical Guidelines

Experts on the subject recommend a multidimensional approach to assessing the effectiveness of modern organizations. This means no single criterion is appropriate for all stages of the organization's life cycle. Nor will a single criterion satisfy competing stakeholders. Well-managed organizations mix and match effectiveness criteria to fit the unique requirements of the situation.[41] For example, Jamie Dimon, CEO of J P Morgan Chase, is very goal oriented, an aggressive cost-cutter, and customer focused in his drive to grow the banking giant: "'What is growth?' says Dimon in his trademark staccato style. 'It's better service, better products, more hours. Growth to me is every budget review. It's 1,000 small steps.'"[42] Managers need to identify and seek input from strategic constituencies. This information, when merged with the organization's stated mission and philosophy, enables management to derive an appropriate *combination* of effectiveness criteria. The following guidelines are helpful in this regard:

- *The goal accomplishment approach* is appropriate when "goals are clear, consensual, time-bounded, measurable."[43]

- *The resource acquisition approach* is appropriate when inputs have a traceable effect on results or output. For example, the amount of money the World Wildlife Fund receives through donations dictates the level of services provided.

- *The internal processes approach* is appropriate when organizational performance is strongly influenced by specific processes (e.g., cross-functional teamwork).

- *The strategic constituencies approach* is appropriate when powerful stakeholders can significantly benefit or harm the organization.[44]

Keeping these basic concepts of organizational effectiveness in mind, we turn our attention to preventing organizational decline.

go to the Web for the Group Exercise: Stakeholder Audit Team

The Ever-Present Threat of Organizational Decline

Sadly, there are many examples of organizational decline and failure in the wake of the recent corporate scandals and the continuing pressure of globalization. (General Motors and Ford have been especially hard hit by the latter trend.)[45] Some failed because of illegal acts. Enron, for one, had the dubious honor of going from number seven on the 2001 *Fortune* 500 list to bankruptcy within a single year! During that time, Enron shareholders saw their shares plummet from $83 a share to 67 cents, when the stock was finally delisted. Thousands of Enron jobs evaporated and employee retirement plans and dreams were wiped out.[46] Other companies have tripped over strategic blunders and bad luck (see the Real World/Real People feature on page 513). Although the problems at these particular companies varied, both of them turned the corner from success to decline rather suddenly and dramatically.[47] Donald N Sull, a strategy professor at the London Business School, added this perspective:

> One of the most common business phenomena is also one of the most perplexing: when successful companies face big changes in their environment, they often fail to respond effectively. Unable to defend themselves against competitors armed with new products, technologies, or strategies, they watch their sales and profits erode, their best people leave, and their stock valuations tumble. Some ultimately manage to recover—usually after painful rounds of downsizing and restructuring—but many don't.[48]

Organizational decline

Decrease in organization's resource base (money, customers, talent, innovations).

Researchers call this downward spiral **organizational decline** and define it as "a decrease in an organization's resource base."[49] The term *resource* is used very broadly in this context, encompassing money, talent, customers, and innovative ideas and products. Managers seeking to maintain organizational effectiveness need to be alert to the problem because experts tell us "decline is almost unavoidable unless deliberate steps are taken to prevent it."[50] The first key step is to recognize the early warning signs of organizational decline.

Early Warning Signs of Decline

Short of illegal conduct, there are 14 early warning signs of organizational decline:

1. Excess personnel.
2. Tolerance of incompetence.
3. Cumbersome administrative procedures.
4. Disproportionate staff power (e.g., technical staff specialists politically overpower line managers, whom they view as unsophisticated and too conventional).
5. Replacement of substance with form (e.g., the planning process becomes more important than the results achieved).
6. Scarcity of clear goals and decision benchmarks.
7. Fear of embarrassment and conflict (e.g., formerly successful executives may resist new ideas for fear of revealing past mistakes).
8. Loss of effective communication.
9. Outdated organizational structure.[51]
10. Increased scapegoating by leaders.

Does Dell's Success Formula Need to Be Rebooted?

Dell's storied beginnings have given way to another classic business tale, one far less happy. Like many long-forgotten former champions, Dell succumbed to complacency in the belief that its business model would always keep it far ahead of the pack. While Dell broadened its product line, it never dealt with the vast improvement in the competition or used its lead in direct sales and the cash generated to invest in new business lines, talent, or innovation that could provide another competitive edge. "Dell is a textbook example of single-formula growth: 'We make PCs cheap. This is what we do, and we do it a lot,'" says Jim Mackey, managing director at the Billion Dollar Growth Network, a research consortium focused on large-company growth. "You can grow very fast when you're on a single formula, but when you get to a certain point, you don't have the ability to create new growth."

Long-term success demands constant reinvention. Research done by Mackey and others shows that most fast-growing companies hit a point somewhere over $50 billion in revenue at which they falter. By then, growing apace demands billions of new sales every year. Rarely is the original, unchanged business model up to the job. The only way around the challenge: Nurture the next growth platform long before it's needed. . . .

Michael Dell maintains that his company's business model is still its key advantage. Dell, he says, has acquired too much middle-aged fat and lost the intense focus and drive that made it an icon. In his internal e-mail explaining the recent departure of CEO Rollins, Dell's founder promised that the company will fix customer support problems, boost its services business, and focus more on small and midsize outfits in addition to the megacorporations that bring in the bulk of sales. While

he won't rule out big strategic shifts, such as a move into retail, Dell says: "I do think that Dell's core strengths historically will be its core strengths in the future."

How likely is a successful turnaround at Dell?

SOURCE: Excerpted from N Byrnes and P Burrows, "Where Dell Went Wrong," *Business Week*, February 19, 2007, pp 62–63.

Dell's Founder, Michael Dell, has returned to the CEO's role to get the firm back on track.

---

11. Resistance to change.
12. Low morale.
13. Special interest groups are more vocal.
14. Decreased innovation.[52]

Managers who monitor these early warning signs of organizational decline are better able to reorganize in a timely and effective manner.[53] However, research has uncovered a troublesome perception tendency among entrenched top management teams. In companies where there had been little if any turnover among top executives, there was a tendency to attribute organizational problems to *external* causes (e.g., competition, the government, technology shifts). Oppositely, *internal* attributions tended to be made by top management teams with *many* new members. Thus, proverbial "new blood" at the top appears to be a good insurance policy against misperceiving the early-warning signs of organizational decline.[54]

"Frankly, at this point in the flow chart, we don't know what happens to these people..."

SOURCE: Chris Wildt, *Harvard Business Review,* September 2004, p 86. © Chris Wildt. Used by permission.

Preventing Organizational Decline The time to start doing something about organizational decline is when everything is going *right.* For it is during periods of high success that the seeds of decline are sown.[55] *Complacency* is the number one threat because it breeds overconfidence and inattentiveness. As one management writer recently explained,

> In organizations, complacency is a side effect of success. Growth brings bloat, and bloat slows the organization's response to competitive threats. It is after sustained periods of success that organizations run the highest risk of getting hurt. At the moment of a company's greatest triumph, senior management's most important duty is to make sure that the butterflies are still fluttering in everybody's belly.[56]

Judging from what has been written about Enron, complacency also can breed arrogance and unethical or illegal conduct.[57]

Total quality management advocates remind us that *continuous improvement* is the first line of defense against organizational decline. Japan's Toyota is a world leader in this regard.

> Of all the slogans kicked around Toyota City, the key one is *kaizen,* which means "continuous improvement" in Japanese. While many other companies strive for dramatic breakthroughs, Toyota keeps doing lots of little things better and better. . . .
>
> One consultant calls Toyota's strategy "rapid inch-up": Take enough tiny steps and pretty soon you outdistance the competition. . . .
>
> In short, Toyota is the best carmaker in the world. And it keeps getting better. Says Iwao Isomura, chief of personnel: "Our current success is the best reason to change things." Extensive interviews with Toyota executives in the United States and Japan demonstrate the company's total dedication to continuous improvement. What is often mistaken for excessive modesty is, in fact, an expression of permanent dissatisfaction—even with exemplary performance.[58]

While General Motors and Ford shed 46,000 employees in 2006 alone, lost billions of dollars, and "announced the closing of 26 North American factories over the next five years," Toyota continued its steady march toward being the world's largest and most profitable automaker.[59] *Kaizen* works!

5 The Contingency Approach to Organization Design

Contingency approach to organization design

Creating an effective organization– environment fit.

According to the **contingency approach to organization design,** organizations tend to be more effective when they are structured to fit the demands of the situation.[60] A contingency approach can be put into practice by first assessing the degree of environmental uncertainty (see Figure 17–7).[61] Next, the contingency model calls for

Figure 17–7   *Assessing Environmental Uncertainty*

	Low	Moderate	High
1. How strong are social, political, and economic pressures on the organization?	Minimal	Moderate	Intense
2. How frequent are technological breakthroughs in the industry?	Infrequent	Occasional	Frequent
3. How reliable are resources and supplies?	Reliable	Occasional, predictable shortages	Unreliable
4. How stable is the demand for the organization's product or service?	Highly stable	Moderately stable	Unstable

SOURCE: R Kreitner, *Management,* 10th ed. Copyright © 2007 by Houghton Mifflin Company. Used with permission.

using various organization design configurations to achieve an effective organization–environment fit. Carol Bartz, the longtime CEO of Autodesk, captured the essence of the contingency approach with a sailboat metaphor. This is what she had to say in a *Fortune* magazine interview:

How do you explain your longevity as CEO?
I've turned this company around three times. It's like a sailboat. The weather changed, and I had to change. The economy changed, the technology changed, and luckily I had a patient board.

Autodesk started out making software for designers and architects. Where are your customers coming from these days?
About 35% of them are in manufacturing. . . . Another 30% is building and construction, 20% is infrastructure like roads and bridges, and 15% is media, like games and special effects. Our media division has software that layers the blood on Tom Cruise in *The Last Samurai.* Our customers have won the last nine Academy Awards for special effects—*Master and Commander, Titanic, Lord of the Rings*—you name it.[62]

Keeping this spirit of organizational flexibility and adaptability in mind,[63] let us review two classic contingency design studies.

6 Differentiation and Integration: The Lawrence and Lorsch Study

In their classic text *Organization and Environment,* Harvard researchers Paul Lawrence and Jay Lorsch explained how two structural forces simultaneously fragment the organization and bind it together. They cautioned that an imbalance between these two forces—labeled *differentiation* and *integration*—could hinder organizational effectiveness.

Figure 17–8   *Differentiation and Integration Are Opposing Structural Forces*

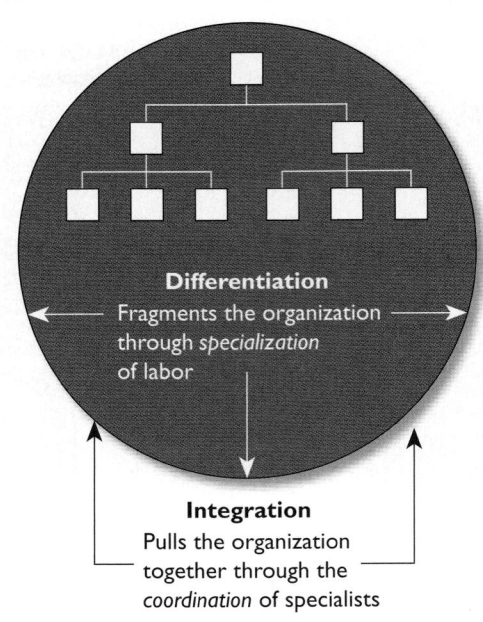

Differentiation Splits the Organization Apart Differentiation occurs through division of labor and technical specialization. A behavioral outcome of differentiation is that technical specialists such as computer programmers tend to think and act differently than specialists in, say, accounting or marketing. Excessive differentiation can cause the organization to bog down in inefficiency, miscommunication, conflict, and politics. Thus, differentiation needs to be offset by an opposing structural force to ensure needed *coordination*. This is where integration enters the picture (see Figure 17–8).

> **Differentiation**
> Division of labor and specialization that cause people to think and act differently.

Integration Binds the Organization Together Integration occurs when specialists cooperate to achieve a common goal. According to the Lawrence and Lorsch model, integration can be achieved through various combinations of the following six mechanisms: (1) a formal hierarchy; (2) standardized policies, rules, and procedures; (3) departmentalization; (4) committees and cross-functional teams; (5) human relations training; and (6) individuals and groups acting as liaisons between specialists.

> **Integration**
> Cooperation among specialists to achieve a common goal.

Achieving the Proper Balance When Lawrence and Lorsch studied successful and unsuccessful companies in three industries, they concluded the following: *As environmental complexity increased, successful organizations exhibited higher degrees of both differentiation and integration.* In other words, an effective balance was achieved. Unsuccessful organizations, in contrast, tended to suffer from an imbalance of too much differentiation and not enough offsetting integration. Managers need to fight this tendency if their growing and increasingly differentiated organizations are to be coordinated.

Lawrence and Lorsch also discovered that "the more differentiated an organization, the more difficult it is to achieve integration."[64] Managers of today's complex organizations need to strive constantly and creatively to achieve greater integration.[65] For example, how does 3M Company, with its dozens of autonomous divisions and more than 60,000 products, successfully maintain its competitive edge in technology? Among other things, 3M makes sure its technical specialists frequently interact with one another so cross-fertilization of ideas takes place. Art Fry, credited with inventing the now ubiquitous Post-it Notes, actually owes much of his success to colleague Spencer Silver, an engineer down the hall who created an apparently useless semi-adhesive. If Fry and Silver had worked in a company without a strong commitment to integration, we probably would not have Post-it Notes. 3M does not leave this sort of cross-fertilization of ideas to chance. It organizes for integration with such things as a Technology Council that regularly convenes researchers from various divisions and an annual science fair at which 3M scientists enthusiastically hawk their new ideas, not to customers, but to each other![66]

Mechanistic organizations
Rigid, command-and-control bureaucracies.

Organic organizations
Fluid and flexible networks of multitalented people.

7 Mechanistic versus Organic Organizations

A second landmark contingency design study was reported by a pair of British behavioral scientists, Tom Burns and G M Stalker. In the course of their research, they drew a very instructive distinction between what they called mechanistic and organic organizations. **Mechanistic organizations** are rigid bureaucracies with strict rules, narrowly defined tasks, and top-down communication. For example, when *BusinessWeek* correspondent Kathleen Deveny spent a day working in a McDonald's restaurant, she found a very mechanistic organization:

> Here every job is broken down into the smallest of steps, and the whole process is automated. . . .
>
> Anyone could do this, I think. But McDonald's restaurants operate like Swiss watches, and the minute I step behind the counter I am a loose part in the works. . . .
>
> I bag French fries for a few minutes, but I'm much too slow. Worse, I can't seem to keep my station clean enough. Failing at French fries is a fluke, I tell myself. . . .
>
> I try to move faster, but my co-workers are [leaving me behind].[67]

This sort of mechanistic structure is necessary at McDonald's because of the competitive need for uniform product quality, speedy service, and cleanliness. Oppositely, **organic organizations** are flexible networks of multitalented individuals who perform a variety of tasks.[68] W L Gore, maker of the popular Gore-Tex fabric found in outdoor gear, is the epitome of an organic organization. This is what Diane Davidson, a sales executive with 15 years of experience, encountered when she joined W L Gore:

> "I came from a very traditional male-dominated business—the men's shoe business," she recalls. "When I arrived at Gore, I didn't know who did what. I wondered how anything got done here. It was driving me crazy." Like all new hires, Davidson was given a "starting sponsor" at Gore—a mentor, not a boss. But she didn't know how to work without someone telling her what to do.

W L Gore, the maker of many products including the unique Gore-Tex fabric found in popular sportswear, is a very unique organization itself. Hierarchy, titles, and rank have been cast aside in favor of a highly organic and entrepreneurial culture in which teams, creativity, initiative, flexibility, open communication, and long-term thinking prevail. Under CEO Terri Kelly's (Pictured here) supportive guidance, Gore's employees even "celebrate" failures to encourage risk taking.

Table 17–2   *Characteristics of Mechanistic and Organic Organizations*

CHARACTERISTIC	MECHANISTIC ORGANIZATION		ORGANIC ORGANIZATION
1. Task definition and knowledge required	Narrow; technical	→	Broad; general
2. Linkage between individual's contribution and organization's purpose	Vague or indirect	→	Clear or direct
3. Task flexibility	Rigid; routine	→	Flexible; varied
4. Specification of techniques, obligations, and rights	Specific	→	General
5. Degree of hierarchical control	High	→	Low (self-control emphasized)
6. Primary communication pattern	Top-down	→	Lateral (between peers)
7. Primary decision-making style	Authoritarian	→	Democratic; participative
8. Emphasis on obedience and loyalty	High	→	Low

SOURCE: Adapted from discussion in T Burns and G M Stalker, *The Management of Innovation* (London: Tavistock, 1961), pp 119–25.

"Who's my boss?" she kept asking.

"Stop using the B-word," her sponsor replied....

"Secretly, there are bosses, right?" she asked.

There weren't. She eventually figured out that "your team is your boss, because you don't want to let them down. Everyone's your boss, and no one's your boss."

What's more, Davidson saw that people didn't fit into standard job descriptions. They had all made different sets of "commitments" to their team, often combining roles that remained segregated in different fiefdoms at conventional companies.[69]

A Matter of Degree   Importantly, as illustrated in Table 17–2, each of the mechanistic-organic characteristics is a matter of degree. Organizations tend to be *relatively* mechanistic or *relatively* organic. Pure types are rare because divisions, departments, or units in the same organization may be more or less mechanistic or organic. From an employee's standpoint, which organization structure would you prefer?

8 Different Approaches to Decision Making   Decision making tends to be centralized in mechanistic organizations and decentralized in organic organizations. **Centralized decision making** occurs when key decisions are made by top management. **Decentralized decision making** occurs when important decisions are made by middle- and lower-level managers. Generally, centralized organizations are more tightly controlled while decentralized organizations are more adaptive to changing situations.[70] Each has its appropriate use. For example, both Exxon and General Electric are very respected and successful companies, yet the former prefers centralization while the latter pushes decentralization.

Experts on the subject warn against extremes of centralization or decentralization. The challenge is to achieve a workable balance between the two extremes. A management consultant put it this way:

The modern organization in transition will recognize the pull of two polarities: a need for greater centralization to create low-cost shared resources; and, a need to improve

Centralized decision making

Top managers make all key decisions.

Decentralized decision making

Lower-level managers are empowered to make important decisions.

market responsiveness with greater decentralization. Today's winning organizations are the ones that can handle the paradox and tensions of both pulls. These are the firms that analyze the optimum organizational solution in each particular circumstance, without prejudice for one type of organization over another. The result is, almost invariably, a messy mixture of decentralized units sharing cost-effective centralized resources.[71]

Centralization and decentralization are not an either–or proposition; they are an *and–also* balancing act.

Relevant Research Findings
When they classified a sample of actual companies as either mechanistic or organic, Burns and Stalker discovered one type was not superior to the other. Each type had its appropriate place, depending on the environment. When the environment was relatively *stable and certain,* the successful organizations tended to be *mechanistic. Organic* organizations tended to be the successful ones when the environment was *unstable and uncertain.*[72]

In a study of 103 department managers from eight manufacturing firms and two aerospace organizations, managerial skill was found to have a greater impact on a global measure of department effectiveness in organic departments than in mechanistic departments. This led the researchers to recommend the following contingencies for management staffing and training:

> If we have two units, one organic and one mechanistic, and two potential applicants differing in overall managerial ability, we might want to assign the more competent to the organic unit since in that situation there are few structural aids available to the manager in performing required responsibilities. It is also possible that managerial training is especially needed by managers being groomed to take over units that are more organic in structure.[73]

Another interesting finding comes from a study of 42 voluntary church organizations. As the organizations became more mechanistic (more bureaucratic) the intrinsic motivation of their members decreased. Mechanistic organizations apparently undermined the volunteers' sense of freedom and self-determination. Additionally, the researchers believe their findings help explain why bureaucracy tends to feed on itself: "A mechanistic organizational structure may breed the need for a more extremely mechanistic system because of the reduction in intrinsically motivated behavior."[74] Thus, bureaucracy begets greater bureaucracy.

Field research in two factories, one mechanistic and the other organic, found expected communication patterns. Command-and-control (downward) communication characterized the mechanistic factory. Consultative or participative (two-way) communication prevailed in the organic factory.[75]

Most recently, a study of Internet service companies facing very turbulent circumstances during their first five years of existence led the researchers to this conclusion: "Whereas mature organizations with well-defined structure and embedded practices typically need to become more organic and flexible in order to adapt to dynamic environments, the opposite is true for new ventures."[76] This brings to mind a life-cycle concept of organizations where it is important to learn how to walk (via mechanistic characteristics) before attempting to run (trying to be more organic).

Both Mechanistic and Organic Structures Are Needed
Although achievement-oriented students of OB typically express a distaste for mechanistic organizations, not all organizations or subunits can or should be organic. For example, as mentioned earlier, McDonald's could not achieve its admired quality and service

standards without extremely mechanistic restaurant operations. Imagine the food and service you would get if McDonald's employees used their own favorite ways of doing things and worked at their own pace! On the other hand, mechanistic structure alienates some employees because it erodes their sense of self-control.

go to the Web for the Self-Exercise: Organization Design Field Study

9 Three Important Contingency Variables: Technology, Size, and Strategic Choice

Both contingency theories just discussed have one important thing in common. Each is based on an *environmental imperative,* meaning the environment is said to be the primary determinant of effective organizational structure. Other organization theorists disagree. They contend that factors such as the organization's core technology, size, and corporate strategy hold the key to organizational structure. This section examines the significance of these three additional contingency variables.

The Effect of Technology on Structure— Woodward and Beyond

Joan Woodward proposed a *technological imperative* in 1965 after studying 100 small manufacturing firms in southern England. She found distinctly different structural patterns for effective and ineffective companies based on technologies of low, medium, or high *complexity.* Effective organizations with either low- or high-complexity technology tended to have an organic structure. Effective organizations based on a technology of medium complexity tended to have a mechanistic structure. Woodward concluded that technology was the overriding determinant of organizational structure.[77]

Since Woodward's landmark work, many studies of the relationship between technology and structure have been conducted. Unfortunately, disagreement and confusion have prevailed. For example, a comprehensive review of 50 studies conducted between 1965 and 1980 found six technology concepts and 140 technology-structure relationships.[78] A statistical analysis of those studies prompted the following conclusions:

- The more the technology requires *interdependence* between individuals or groups, the greater the need for integration (coordination).
- "As technology moves from routine to nonroutine, subunits adopt less formalized and [less] centralized structures."[79]

Additional insights can be expected in this area as researchers coordinate their definitions of technology and refine their methodologies.[80]

Organizational Size and Performance

Size is an important structural variable subject to two schools of thought. According to the first school, economists have long extolled the virtues of economies of scale. This approach, often called the "bigger is better" model, assumes the per-unit cost of production decreases as the organization grows. In effect, bigger is said to be more efficient.[81] For example, on an annual basis, Honda supposedly can produce its 100,000th car less expensively than its 10th car.

The second school of thought pivots on the law of diminishing returns. Called the "small is beautiful" model,[82] this approach contends that oversized organizations and subunits tend to be plagued by costly behavioral problems. Large and impersonal organizations are said to breed apathy and alienation, with resulting problems such as turnover and absenteeism. Two strong advocates of this second approach are the authors of the book *In Search of Excellence:*

> In the excellent companies, small in *almost every case* is beautiful. The small facility turns out to be the most efficient; its turned-on, motivated, highly productive worker, in communication (and competition) with his peers, outproduces the worker in the big facilities time and again. It holds for plants, for project teams, for divisions—for the entire company.[83]

Is Complexity the Issue? (A Case against Mergers?)

Recent research suggests that when designing their organizations, managers should follow a middle ground between "bigger is better" and "small is beautiful" because both models have been oversold. Indeed, a newer perspective says *complexity,* not size, is the central issue.[84] British management teacher and writer Charles Handy, cited earlier, offered this instructive perspective:

> Growth does not have to mean more of the same. It can mean better rather than bigger. It can mean leaner or deeper, both of which might improve rather than expand the current position. Businesses can grow more profitable by becoming better, or leaner, or deeper, more concentrated, without growing bigger. Bigness, in both business and life, can lead to a lack of focus, too much complexity and, in the end, too wide a spread to control. We have to know when big is big enough.[85]

We do not have a definite answer to the question of how big is too big, but the excessive complexity argument is compelling. This argument may also help explain why many mergers have been disappointing in recent years. According to *Business Week,* the "historic surge of consolidations and combinations is occurring in the face of strong evidence that mergers and acquisitions, at least over the past 35 years or so, have hurt more than helped companies and shareholders."[86] A prime case in point is the Newell Rubbermaid merger. According to *Harvard Business Review,*

> When Newell's top managers approached their counterparts at Rubbermaid in 1999 about the possibility of a merger, it looked like a deal from heaven....
>
> Because Newell and Rubbermaid both sold household products through essentially the same sales channels, the cost synergies from the combination loomed large....
>
> Eager to seize the opportunity, Newell rushed to close the $5.8 billion megamerger—a deal ten times larger than any it had done before.
>
> But the deal from heaven turned out, to use *Business Week*'s phrase, to be the "merger from hell." Instead of lifting Newell to a new level of growth, the acquisition dragged the company down. In 2002, Newell wrote off $500 million in goodwill, leading its former CEO and chairman, Daniel Ferguson, to admit, "We paid too much." By that time, Newell shareholders had lost 50% of the value of their investment; Rubbermaid shareholders had lost 35%.[87]

A much better outcome resulted from the people-centered approach to a major bank merger[88] (see the Real World/Real People feature on page 522).

A Patient, People-Centered Approach Helps Norwest-Wells Fargo Merger Work

In most big bank mergers, the new CEO announces massive layoffs to achieve a large, one-time cost savings, then promises to produce 15% growth within a year or so.

In announcing the merger with Wells Fargo, [Norwest's CEO Richard] Kovacevich said layoffs would be kept to a minimum, and it would probably take as long as three years to return to Norwest's pre-merger growth rates.

"The investment community threw up when we announced that," he says with a laugh. Citibank had promised savings of 30% for its deal, and Bank of America predicted a hefty bonus from layoffs. There would be no such short-term gains at Wells Fargo.

But over time, the merger would prove to be more successful than the other deals struck in 1998.

Why is this approach the exception, rather than the rule, today?

SOURCE: G Farrell, "Banking on Success as a One-Stop Shop," *USA Today*, March 26, 2007, p 5B

Research Insights Researchers measure the size of organizations and organizational subunits in different ways. Some focus on financial indicators such as total sales or total asset value. Others look at the number of employees, transactions (such as the number of students in a school district), or capacity (such as the number of beds in a hospital). A meta-analysis[89] of 31 studies conducted between 1931 and 1985 that related organizational size to performance found

- Larger organizations (in terms of assets) tended to be more productive (in terms of sales and profits).
- There were "no positive relationships between organizational size and efficiency, suggesting the absence of net economy of scale effects."[90]
- There were zero to slightly negative relationships between *subunit* size and productivity and efficiency.

A more recent study examined the relationship between organizational size and employee turnover over a period of 65 months. Turnover was unrelated to organizational size.[91]

Striving for Small Units in Big Organizations In summary, bigger is not necessarily better and small is not necessarily beautiful. Hard-and-fast numbers regarding exactly how big is too big or how small is too small are difficult to come by. Management consultants offer some rough estimates (see Table 17–3). Until better evidence is available, the best that managers can do is monitor the productivity, quality, and efficiency of divisions, departments, and profit centers. Unwieldy and overly complex units need to be promptly broken into ones of more manageable size. The trick is to *create smallness within bigness.*[92]

Strategic Choice and Organizational Structure

In 1972, British sociologist John Child rejected the environmental imperative approach to organizational structure. He proposed a *strategic choice* model based on behavioral rather than rational economic principles.[93] Child believed structure resulted from a political process involving organizational power holders. According to the strategic choice model that has evolved from Child's work,[94] an organization's structure is determined largely by a dominant coalition of top-management strategists.[95]

Table 17–3   *Organizational Size: Management Consultants Address the Question of How Big Is Too Big?*

Peter F Drucker, well-known management consultant:

The real growth and innovation in this country has been in medium-size companies that employ between 200 and 4,000 workers. If you are in a small company, you are running all out. You have neither the time nor the energy to devote to anything but yesterday's crisis.

A medium-sized company has the resources to devote to new products and markets, and it's still small enough to be flexible and move fast. And these companies now have what they once lacked—they've learned how to manage.

Thomas J Peters and Robert H Waterman Jr, best-selling authors and management consultants:

A rule of thumb starts to emerge. We find that the lion's share of the top performers keep their division size between $50 and $100 million, with a maximum of 1,000 or so employees each. Moreover, they grant their divisions extraordinary independence—and give them the functions and resources to exploit.

SOURCES: Excerpted from J A Byrne, "Advice from the Dr Spock of Business," *BusinessWeek,* September 28, 1987, p 61; and T J Peters and R H Waterman Jr, *In Search of Excellence* (New York: Harper & Row, 1982), pp 272–73.

A Strategic Choice Model As Figure 17–9 illustrates, specific strategic choices or decisions reflect how the dominant coalition perceives environmental constraints and the organization's objectives. These strategic choices are tempered by the decision makers' personal beliefs, attitudes, values, and ethics. For example, put yourself in the shoes of Jeffrey Immelt, CEO of General Electric. Your company was number five on the 2007 *Fortune* 500 list, with $168 billion in revenues, and 319,000 employees.[96] How do you fuel innovation at this industrial giant, especially in the direction of your passion for products that are both environmentally friendly and profitable? In a recent interview with *Harvard Business Review,* Immelt explained his unique approach:

If you want to have growth, you've got to make sure that there are tough projects being done and you shine a light on them. We created imagination breakthroughs to pull some ideas out of the pile that we thought were really important and could possibly generate $100 million in new sales over a three-year horizon. Imagination breakthroughs are a protected class of ideas—safe from the budget slashers because I've blessed each one. . . .

An example of an imagination breakthrough project is the hybrid locomotive. It's got a program manager

CEO Jeff Immelt's personal values are clearly evident in the "greening" of General Electric.

Figure 17–9   *The Relationship between Strategic Choice and Organizational Structure*

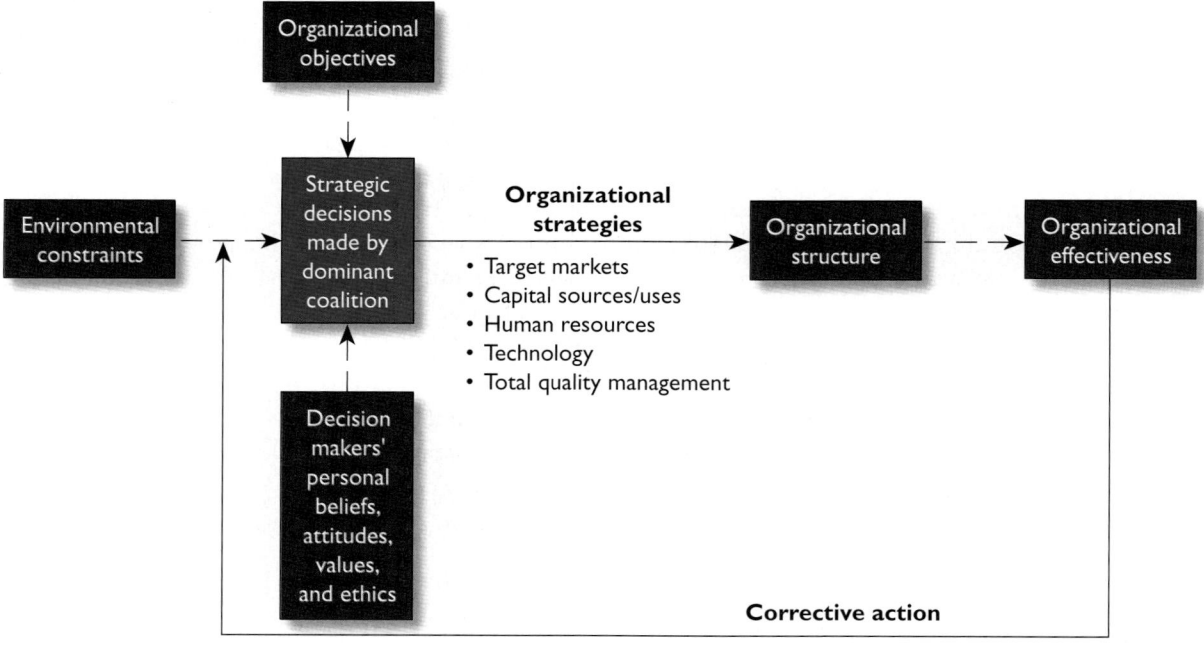

who's been selected by me, it's funded, and every best practice we know of in the company is going to be applied to it. I'm going to look at it once a month, in terms of status, and see to it that what is being learned in the project is disseminated. What we're trying to do with imagination breakthroughs is take risks, using my point of view.[97]

Thus, in line with the model in Figure 17–9, Immelt's dominant coalition is translating "green" values into an innovation strategy that requires a project-oriented structure. Corrective actions will be necessary as the imagination breakthrough projects evolve and obstacles are encountered.

Research and Practical Lessons In a study of 97 small and midsize companies in Quebec, Canada, strategy and organizational structure were found to be highly interdependent. Strategy influenced structure and structure influenced strategy. This was particularly true for larger, more innovative, and more successful firms.[98]

Strategic choice theory and research teaches managers at least two practical lessons. First, the environment is just one of many codeterminants of structure. Second, like any other administrative process, organization design is subject to the byplays of interpersonal power and politics.

Summary of Key Concepts

1. *Describe the four characteristics common to all organizations, and explain the difference between closed and open systems.* They are coordination of effort (achieved through policies and rules), a common goal (a collective purpose), division of labor (people performing separate but related tasks),

and a hierarchy of authority (the chain of command). Closed systems, such as a battery-powered clock, are relatively self-sufficient. Open systems, such as the human body, are highly dependent on the environment for survival. Organizations are said to be open systems.

2. *Define the term* learning organization. A learning organization is one that proactively creates, acquires, and transfers knowledge and changes its behavior on the basis of new knowledge and insights.

3. *Describe horizontal, hourglass, and virtual organizations.* Horizontal organizations are flat structures built around core processes aimed at identifying and satisfying customer needs. Cross-functional teams and empowerment are central to horizontal organizations. Hourglass organizations have a small executive level; a short and narrow middle-management level (because information technology links the top and bottom levels), and a broad base of operating personnel. Virtual organizations typically are families of interdependent companies. They are contractual and fluid in nature.

4. *Describe the four generic organizational effectiveness criteria, and discuss how managers can prevent organizational decline.* They are goal accomplishment (satisfying stated objectives), resource acquisition (gathering the necessary productive inputs), internal processes (building and maintaining healthy organizational systems), and strategic constituencies satisfaction (achieving at least minimal satisfaction for all key stakeholders). Because complacency is the leading cause of organizational decline, managers need to create a culture of continuous improvement. Decline automatically follows periods of great success if preventive steps are not taken to avoid the erosion of organizational resources (money, customers, talent, and innovative ideas).

5. *Explain what the contingency approach to organization design involves.* The contingency approach to organization design calls for fitting the organization to the demands of the situation. Environmental uncertainty can be assessed in terms of social, political, economic, technological, resource, and demand factors.

6. *Describe the relationship between differentiation and integration in effective organizations.* Harvard researchers Lawrence and Lorsch found that successful organizations achieved a proper balance between the two opposing structural forces of differentiation and integration. Differentiation forces the organization apart. Through a variety of mechanisms—including hierarchy, rules, teams, and liaisons—integration draws the organization together.

7. *Discuss Burns and Stalker's findings regarding mechanistic and organic organizations.* British researchers Burns and Stalker found that mechanistic (bureaucratic, centralized) organizations tended to be effective in stable situations. In unstable situations, organic (flexible, decentralized) organizations were more effective. These findings underscored the need for a contingency approach to organization design.

8. *Define and briefly explain the practical significance of centralization and decentralization.* Because key decisions are made at the top of centralized organizations, they tend to be tightly controlled. In decentralized organizations, employees at lower levels are empowered to make important decisions. Contingency design calls for a proper balance.

9. *Discuss the effective management of organizational size.* Regarding the optimum size for organizations, the challenge for today's managers is to achieve smallness within bigness by keeping subunits at a manageable size.

Key Terms

Organization 498
Unity of command principle 499
Organization chart 499
Span of control 499
Staff personnel 500
Line managers 500
Closed system 501
Open system 501
Learning organization 502
Strategic constituency 510

Stakeholder audit 510
Organizational decline 512
Contingency approach to organization design 514
Differentiation 516
Integration 516
Mechanistic organizations 517
Organic organizations 517
Centralized decision making 518
Decentralized decision making 518

OB in Action Case Study

Exxon: "The Defiant One"[99]

Rex Tillerson is way out of line, and he knows it. "They want us to join the parade," he says, referring to assorted environmentalists, scientists, politicians, investors, and others who've been lambasting him and the company he heads, ExxonMobil. He knows what they're saying about him, and he repeats it: "Get in line. You're outta

525

line right now—get in line." Why Tillerson refuses to run Exxon the way other CEOs are running other giant oil companies is for many people the most baffling and even infuriating question about the world's most profitable corporation.

The basic model for managing an oil company in this eco-conscious age became clear a few years ago when Britain's BP loudly declared itself to be "beyond petroleum." The other supermajors are all proclaiming their greenness and investing in biofuels, wind power, and solar power. Exxon isn't. It only recently acknowledged publicly that—brace yourself—the world is warming. Beyond petroleum? At Exxon it's all petroleum.

It does seem strange that such a high-profile corporation could be so egregiously not with the program. The pressure to conform arguably increases because Exxon is doing so well. In 2006 it earned higher profits than any company in history: $39.5 billion. That's more than the GDP of Yemen and Bahrain combined.

A year to remember in financial terms, but in other ways Exxon had to endure some truly miserable moments. Reports of former CEO Lee Raymond's exit package, worth some $400 million, stoked outrage across the political spectrum. Senators Jay Rockefeller (D-West Virginia) and Olympia Snowe (R-Maine) sent Tillerson a long letter berating the company for funding groups dubious of global warming. (The irony of a Rockefeller attacking Exxon ensured extra attention for the story: Exxon is a descendant of Standard Oil, source of the Rockefeller family fortune.) Legislators in Washington, D.C., and several states proposed windfall-profit taxes on oil companies; the notion stood little chance of becoming law but signaled powerful hostility. Through it all, Tillerson remained defiantly, even proudly, out of line.

And maybe he's not nuts.

His company is shaped above all by a rigorous analytical culture. "ExxonMobil is not a fun place to work," says Fadel Gheit, the Oppenheimer & Co. oil industry analyst widely considered Wall Street's best. "They're not in the fun business," he explains. "They're in the profit business."

Remember that. It means that Exxon understands the essence of capitalism: earning a return on capital that exceeds the cost of that capital. At this supremely important job, it is a world champion. All the major oil companies bear about the same capital cost, just over 6%. . . . Exxon earns a return that trounces its competitors.

The reasons are many. Partly it's the portfolio of locations—some acquired in the Middle East decades ago—at which Exxon can pump oil for less than $1 a barrel. Partly it's wise business bets on building refineries and petrochemical plants as vast single units that achieve tremendous efficiencies; most other big oil companies separate refineries from chemical plants. Partly it's that intensely focused corporate culture. Gheit, who worked for Mobil long before the companies merged, recalls being mystified by Exxon's X factor. "We [Mobil] could be pumping oil from the same platform, and they'd make more money on it than us," he says. "It was like taking the same train to work, but they got to the office first."

Exxon not only earns better returns on capital than its competitors, but also deploys more capital than any of them (although Royal Dutch Shell is close). That combination—higher returns on more capital—yields Exxon way more money than its competitors that it can use to invest in future projects or reward shareholders directly by paying dividends and buying back stock. And it is why Exxon has become the most valuable company on earth, with a current market cap of about $440 billion.

As a financial picture, it's a thing of beauty. Alas, it is one that needs constant attention: Investors expect Exxon to keep performing at that level. The price of any stock is based on an evaluation of the future. Exxon's high price (about $77, up almost 30% in the past year) means the market is counting on it to continue its run. If Exxon even hints that it might stumble, the stock could collapse. As Tillerson says during an interview in his Houston office, "We're only going to invest our shareholders' money where we think they can get the kind of returns they expected when they invested their money with ExxonMobil."

Which brings us to the biggest beef Exxon's critics have: Why isn't the company investing in less polluting energy sources like biofuels, wind, and solar? Remembering that Exxon is above all in the profit business, we know where to look for the answer. As a place to earn knockout returns on capital, alternative energy looks wobbly. For example, the darling of the moment, ethanol, is nowhere near economically competitive with gasoline (and may not be better environmentally, because it is fuel- and land-intensive to produce). Take out the 51-cents-a-gallon federal subsidy, and the true cost of U.S. produced ethanol is equivalent to paying $6 a gallon for the same energy as gasoline, calculates Michael B McElroy, Harvard professor of environmental studies. Even subsidies granted for national security reasons can come and go. To a disciplined investor, such a product is not especially attractive. "I don't have a lot of technology to add to moonshine," says Tillerson of ethanol.

It's a similar story for alternative fuels for power generation. Solar-generated electricity is still way costlier than juice from traditional coal- and gas-fueled plants. Wind power is narrowing the gap but is difficult to scale up. Hydro and biomass are clean and fully competitive on cost—but Exxon just doesn't know much about building dams or burning agricultural waste. Its expertise is in oil and gas, as exemplified by its world-class Upstream Research Center in Houston: the company is happy to leave the alternative stuff to others. "What are we going to bring to this area to create value for our shareholders that's differentiating?" asks Tillerson. "Because to just go in and invest like everybody else—well, why would a shareholder want to own ExxonMobil?"

At least one group of investors thinks Tillerson is missing the bigger picture. By not investing in new energy technologies, Exxon "lags far behind its competitors in developing a strategy to plan for and manage" the potential impact of climate change, argued a group of pension fund chiefs in a letter to the board. If governments around the world begin to bear down on Exxon's oil-based business—through heavier regulation or taxation—then the company's return-on-investment calculations get turned upside down. Its whole future would be in jeopardy.

That will not happen, says Exxon, because it cannot happen. Exxon is certain that oil, gas, and coal will remain the world's dominant energy sources for decades to come.

That belief drives the company's critics crazy. . . .

Maybe Tillerson will be proved wrong. Maybe wind or solar or "moonshine" will turn into huge businesses in which Exxon will lag far behind. Maybe retail customers will abandon its products out of irritation. But Tillerson is convinced that his judgments, which may seem out of line today, are not risky at all. And when you do the analysis from the perspective of a company in the profit business, it's hard to say he's wrong.

Questions for Discussion

1. How do the four generic organizational effectiveness criteria appear to rank at ExxonMobil? What are both the short-run and long-run (5 years plus) implications of the company's priorities?
2. Using Figure 17–6 as a guide, what would a stakeholder audit of ExxonMobil look like?
3. How would you rate the effectiveness of ExxonMobil? Explain.
4. How does the strategic choice model in Figure 17–9 help explain ExxonMobil's current strategic direction?
5. Relative to making progress in developing alternative energy sources, what could ExxonMobil learn from General Electric's Jeffrey Immelt, as detailed in our discussion of strategic choice?
6. Where would you place ExxonMobil on Carroll's global corporate social responsibility pyramid (Figure 1–3, back in Chapter 1 on page 21)? Explain your reasoning and implications.

Ethical Dilemma

Is Yahoo Helping to Suppress Political Dissent in China?

San Francisco, April 18 [2007]—A Chinese political prisoner and his wife sued Yahoo in federal court Wednesday, accusing the company of abetting the commission of torture by helping Chinese authorities identify political dissidents who were later beaten and imprisoned.

The suit, filed under the Alien Tort Claims Act and the Torture Victims Protection Act, is believed to be the first of its kind against an Internet company for its activities in China.

Wang Xiaoning, who according to the suit is serving a 10-year prison sentence in China; his wife, Yu Ling; and other unnamed defendants seek damages and an injunction barring Yahoo from identifying dissidents to Chinese authorities.

"I hope to be able to have Yahoo promise that in the future they will stop this kind of wrongdoing," said Ms. Yu, speaking through an interpreter in a telephone interview from San Francisco.

Yahoo said it had not yet seen the suit, filed in the Federal District Court for the Northern District of California, and could not comment on the allegations.

"Companies doing business in China are forced to comply with Chinese law," said Jim Cullinan, a Yahoo spokesman. When government officials present the company with a lawful request for information about a Yahoo user, he said, "Yahoo China will not know whether the demand for information is for a legitimate criminal investigation or is going to be used to prosecute political dissidents."

Several American Internet companies, including Cisco Systems, Google, and Microsoft, have come under fire, with some politicians and human rights groups accusing them of helping the government monitor and censor the Internet in China.

But Yahoo has come under particularly sharp criticism. Human rights groups say that Yahoo has helped identify at least four people, including the journalist Shi Tao in 2004, who have since been imprisoned for voicing dissent in cyberspace.

"Our concern is that Yahoo, as far as we know, is continuing this practice," said Morton Sklar, executive director of the World Organization for Human Rights USA and a lawyer for the plaintiffs.

According to the suit, Mr. Wang distributed online several journal articles calling for democratic reform and a multiparty system in China. He did so anonymously by posting the articles in a Yahoo Group in 2000 and 2001. The suit contends that Yahoo HK, a wholly owned Yahoo subsidiary based in Hong Kong, provided police with information linking Mr. Wang to the postings.

Mr. Cullinan of Yahoo disputed those claims. "Yahoo HK does not exchange info with Yahoo China or give information to mainland Chinese security forces," he said. Yahoo transferred its mainland China operations to Alibaba.com in 2005, and owns a minority stake in that company, which is based in China.[100]

To Be an Ethical Organization, What Should Yahoo Do?

1. Being sued is not the same as being guilty. Yahoo is simply following host country laws. Yahoo would be irresponsible to *not* do business in one of world's fastest-growing economies. Stay the course.

2. Because it has access to sensitive personal information, Yahoo should not do business in any country with a poor record on human rights. Explain your ethical reasoning.

3. Yahoo's credibility and ethical reputation are damaged when it hides behind Alibaba.com, a company it partially owns. It should review, clarify, and publish its information privacy policy for China to warn of the risk of disclosure.

4. For Yahoo, it's all about the huge potential payoff in China's burgeoning economy. Pursue business opportunities in China more aggressively.

5. If Yahoo violates individual privacy rights in China, can it be trusted to protect private information in other countries? Yahoo should cut its ties to China to salvage its credibility.

6. Invent other options. Discuss.

Web Resources

For study material and exercises that apply to this chapter, visit our Web site,
www.mhhe.com/kreitner

CHAPTER 18

Managing Change and Stress

LEARNING OBJECTIVES

When you finish studying the material in this chapter, you should be able to:

1 Discuss the external and internal forces that create the need for organizational change.

2 Describe Lewin's change model and the systems model of change.

3 Discuss Kotter's eight steps for leading organizational change.

4 Define *organization development* (OD), and demonstrate your familiarity with its four identifying characteristics.

5 Summarize the 11 reasons employees resist change.

6 Discuss the five personal characteristics related to resistance to change.

7 Identify alternative strategies for overcoming resistance to change.

8 Define the term *stress,* and describe the model of occupational stress.

9 Discuss the stress moderators of social support, hardiness, and Type A behavior.

10 Discuss employee assistance programs (EAPs) and a holistic approach toward stress reduction.

Student Resources for Studying Chapter 18

The Web site for your text includes resources that will help you master the concepts in this chapter. As you read, you'll want to visit the site for these helpful tools:

- Your online Study Guide includes learning objectives, a chapter summary, a glossary of key terms, and discussion questions.
- Take a practice quiz and test your knowledge!
- Scroll through a PowerPoint presentation with key concepts for this chapter.

Your instructor might also direct you to the Web site for these exercises:

- Self-assessments that correspond with the chapter content and a Group Exercise.
- You'll also find Video Cases and Internet Exercises for this chapter online.

www.mhhe.com/kreitner

BusinessWeek As China guns it from planned to market economy, the professional class is starting to display the same symptoms of modern angst that appear daily in the corridors of America's office towers. Burnout. Eating disorders. Depression. Substance abuse. "For China, it's as if the world has completely flipped on its axis," says Russ Hagen, CEO of employee assistance firm Chestnut Global Partners.

The radical structural changes in the Chinese economy have left many workers suspended between the old world and the new. The pressure to compete for one's precarious place at work is straining relations with colleagues. Performance reviews once based on effort are now about results. Family used to rule. Now making money does. "There's this sense of frenzy," says Richard Xu, who runs a human resources association in Beijing. "People don't want to stop, because they could lose out on an opportunity."

If this were North America or Europe, a visit to the family shrink or company counselor might be in order. But this is China, where psychological therapy has long been anathema. Admitting you need help is just not done in a face-saving culture. That may explain in part the newfound spirituality among professionals in a land that still officially frowns on religion. Buddhism in particular is experiencing a revival among stressed-out urbanites seeking respite from the pressures of the office. So far, Beijing tolerates the trend.

The distrust of all things psychological hasn't deterred Western firms from trying to convince Chinese that a little therapy can go a long way. For several years multinationals have offered counseling to their expatriate managers. Increasingly, they're extending such benefits to local hires. The services range from helping employees find child care to relationship counseling to dealing with credit-card debt.[1]

FOR DISCUSSION

Why are the Chinese resistant to seeking counseling when dealing with stress?

Increased global competition, startling breakthroughs in information technology, and calls for greater corporate ethics are forcing companies to change the way they do business. Employees want satisfactory work environments, customers are demanding greater value, and investors want more integrity in financial disclosures. The rate of organizational and societal change is clearly accelerating.

As exemplified in the chapter-opening vignette, organizations must change in order to satisfy customers and shareholders. That said, change is more likely to succeed when it is proactive rather than reactive. Peter Senge, a well-known expert on the topic of organizational change, made the following comment about organizational change during an interview with *Fast Company* magazine:

> When I look at efforts to create change in big companies over the past 10 years, I have to say that there's enough evidence of success to say that change is possible—and enough evidence of failure to say that it isn't likely.[2]

If Senge is correct, then it is all the more important for current and future managers to learn how they can successfully implement organizational change. This final chapter was written to help managers navigate the journey of change.

Specifically, we discuss the forces that create the need for organization change, models of planned change, resistance to change, and how managers can better manage the stress associated with organizational change.

 Forces of Change

How do organizations know when they should change? What cues should an organization look for? Although there are no clear-cut answers to these questions, cues signaling the need for change are found by monitoring the forces for change.

Organizations encounter many different forces for change. These forces come from external sources outside the organization and from internal sources. This section examines the forces that create the need for change. Awareness of these forces can help managers determine when they should consider implementing an organizational change. The external and internal forces for change are presented in Figure 18–1.[3]

External Forces

External forces for change

Originate outside the organization.

External forces for change originate outside the organization. Because these forces have global effects, they may cause an organization to question the essence of what business it is in and the process by which products and services are produced. Let us now consider the five key external forces for change: demographic characteristics, technological advancements, market changes, social and political pressures, and a crisis.

Demographic Characteristics Chapter 2 provided a detailed discussion of demographic changes occurring in the US workforce. We concluded that organizations need to effectively manage diversity if they are to receive maximum contribution and commitment from employees. Consider the implications associated with hiring the 80 million people dubbed the Net or Echo-Boom Generation—people born between 1977 and 1997.

> Employers will have to face the new realities of the Net Generation's culture and values, and what it wants from work if they expect to attract and retain those talents and align them with corporate goals.... The new wave of 80 million young people entering the workforce during the next 20 years are technologically equipped and, therefore, armed

Figure 18–1   *The External and Internal Forces for Change*

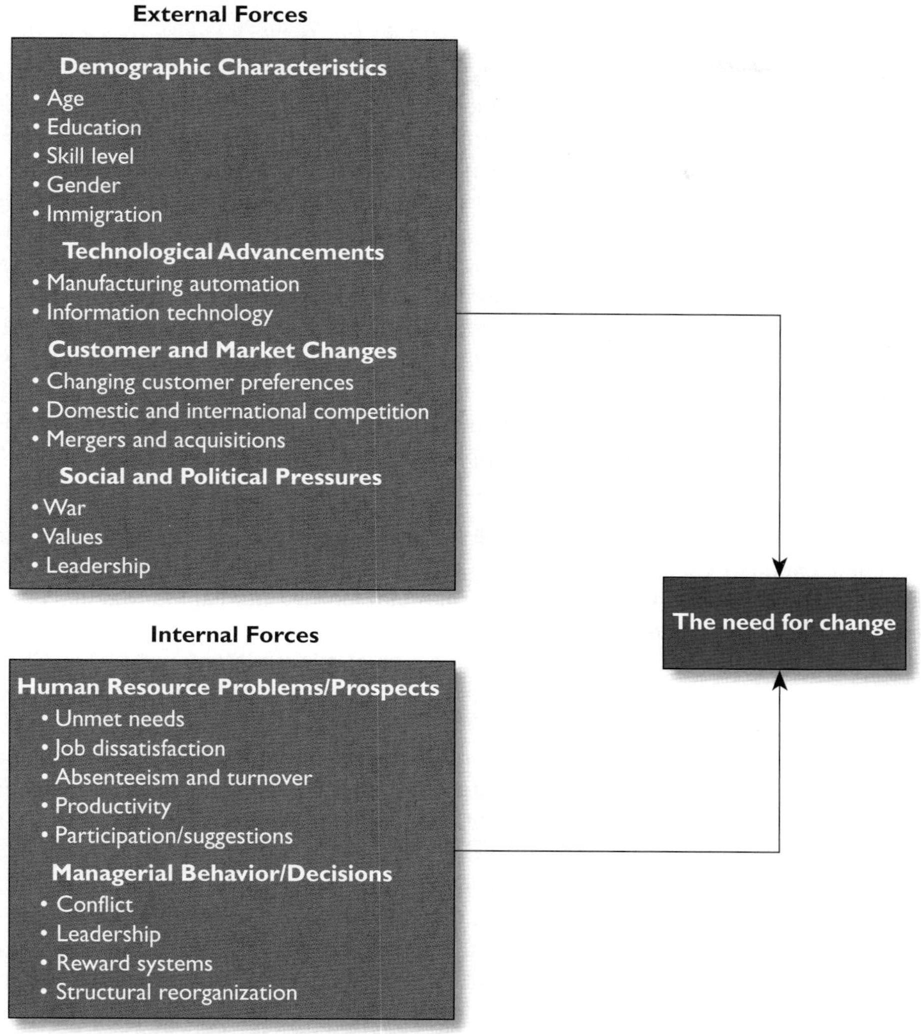

External Forces

Demographic Characteristics
- Age
- Education
- Skill level
- Gender
- Immigration

Technological Advancements
- Manufacturing automation
- Information technology

Customer and Market Changes
- Changing customer preferences
- Domestic and international competition
- Mergers and acquisitions

Social and Political Pressures
- War
- Values
- Leadership

Internal Forces

Human Resource Problems/Prospects
- Unmet needs
- Job dissatisfaction
- Absenteeism and turnover
- Productivity
- Participation/suggestions

Managerial Behavior/Decisions
- Conflict
- Leadership
- Reward systems
- Structural reorganization

The need for change

with the most powerful tools for business. That makes their place in history unique: No previous generation has grown up understanding, using, and expanding on such a pervasive instrument as the PC.[4]

Technological Advancements Both manufacturing and service organizations are increasingly using technology as a means to improve productivity, competitiveness, and customer service while also cutting costs. Microsoft and ExxonMobil are good examples. Microsoft hired Ray Ozzie, a renowned software expert who designed Lotus Notes, to "webify" all of Microsoft's products. To do this, "Microsoft must build a global network of server farms that will cost 'staggering' amounts of money, says Ozzie."[5] Microsoft is pursuing this change strategy in response to technological changes occurring within the global software industry. In contrast to Microsoft, ExxonMobil is already ahead of the game due to its application of technology. "Despite Big Oil's reputation as an old-economy industry, Exxon likes to think of itself as a technology company, pointing to systems like its brand-new Fast Drill Press that have allowed it to reduce the time it takes to drill wells by 35%, saving hundred of millions of dollars annually."[6] There is no question that the development and use of technological advancements is probably one of the biggest forces for change.[7]

Customer and Market Changes Increasing customer sophistication is requiring organizations to deliver higher value in their products and services. Customers are simply demanding more now than they did in the past. Moreover, customers are more likely to shop elsewhere if they do not get what they want because of lower customer switching costs. Michael Jackson, CEO of AutoNation Inc., the largest chain of auto dealers in the United States, is trying to combat this problem within the auto industry. He is putting pressure on US automakers to adopt a different approach for producing cars (see the Real World/Real People feature on page 535).[8]

With respect to market changes, service companies are experiencing increased pressure to obtain more productivity because competition is fierce and prices have remained relatively stable. Further, the emergence of a global economy is forcing companies to change the way they do business.[9] US companies have been forging new partnerships and alliances with their suppliers and potential competitors in order to gain advantages in the global marketplace.[10]

Social and Political Pressures These forces are created by social and political events. For example, the collapse of Enron and major accounting scandals at companies like WorldCom, American International Group, and Fannie Mae have created increased focus on the process by which organizations conduct financial reporting. This in turn has fueled boards of directors to pay more attention to what CEOs are doing and to exert more power and control into the manner in which organizations are being operated.

In general, social and political pressure is exerted through legislative bodies that represent the American populace.[11] Political events and legal decisions can create substantial change. For example, the Supreme Court made a decision in April 2007 that carbon dioxide is a "pollutant" under the Clean Air Act. This decision has implications for organizational responses to global warming. It may result in increased costs for automakers and utilities, for instance, as they attempt to lower their emissions.[12] Although it is difficult for organizations to predict changes in political forces, many organizations hire lobbyists and consultants to help them detect and respond to social and political changes.

Organizational Crises An organizational crisis may result from an accident, ignored problems that build over time, acts of nature, and criminal acts. Consider, for example, the operational meltdown that occurred at JetBlue Airways.

> David Neeleman, JetBlue's founder and chief executive, said a Valentine's Day storm exposed the airline's inability to manage in the face of bad weather, contributing to a thousand canceled flights and an overwhelmed reservations system that stranded thousands of travelers through the Presidents Day weekend. It suggested that the Forest Hills, N Y, airline may have expanded too fast. "We lost control," Mr. Neeleman said in an interview in which he vowed to make changes that would make JetBlue a better airline.[13]

Bad weather caused havoc for JetBlue's customers. Have you ever experienced a situation like this?

Auto Nation Puts Pressure on US Automakers to Change the Way It Produces Cars

One of the toughest problems facing the ailing US car industry stems from Detroit's century-old business model, which dates to Henry Ford's mass production of millions of largely identical Model T's. Rather than build cars to suit customer tastes, US automakers churn out what makes sense for their plants, and then use incentives and rebates to lure buyers. . . .

At the Detroit auto show last month, Mr Jackson had private meetings with the chiefs of General Motors Co., Ford Motor Co., and Chrysler . . . and offered to

help. Last year, AutoNation began sifting through its trove of data to identify the best-selling configurations of every vehicle on the market. He wants GM, Ford, and Chrysler to join the effort and use the information to produce vehicles customers actually want.

Why are US automakers resistant to change?

SOURCE: Excerpted from N E Boudette, "Big Dealer to Detroit: Fix How You Make Cars," *The Wall Street Journal*, February 9, 2007, pp A1, A8.

This crisis caused JetBlue to change some of its policies, to upgrade its communications system, to train more people in crew-handling procedures, and to implement a customer bill of rights. Only time and another storm will tell if these changes are effective.[14]

Internal Forces

Internal forces for change come from inside the organization. These forces may be subtle, such as low job satisfaction, or can manifest in outward signs, such as low productivity and conflict. Internal forces for change come from both human resource problems and managerial behavior/decisions.

Internal forces for change
Originate inside the organization.

Human Resource Problems/Prospects
These problems stem from employee perceptions about how they are treated at work and the match between individual and organization needs and desires. Chapter 6 highlighted the relationship between an employee's unmet needs and job dissatisfaction. Dissatisfaction is a symptom of an underlying employee problem that should be addressed. Dell, for example, instituted a process of semiannual employee surveys to determine employees' job satisfaction and to assess the quality of managers' leadership skills. A manager's effectiveness ratings are tied to compensation, promotions, and attendance at management training.[15] Unusual or high levels of absenteeism and turnover also represent forces for change. Organizations might respond to these problems by using the various approaches to job design discussed in Chapter 8, by reducing employees' role conflict, overload, and ambiguity (recall our discussion in Chapter 10), and by removing the different stressors discussed in the final section of this chapter. Prospects for positive change stem from employee participation and suggestions.

Managerial Behavior/Decisions
Excessive interpersonal conflict between managers and their subordinates is a sign that change is needed. Both the manager and the employee may need interpersonal skills training, or the two individuals may simply need to be separated. For example, one of the parties might be transferred to a new department. Inappropriate leader behaviors such as inadequate direction or support may result in human resource problems requiring change. As discussed in Chapter 16,

leadership training is one potential solution for this problem. Inequitable reward systems—recall our discussion in Chapters 8 and 9—and the type of structural reorganizations discussed in Chapter 17 are additional forces for change. Finally, managerial decisions are a powerful force for change. As discussed in detail in Chapter 8, the perceived organizational justice of management's decisions can do everything from fuel or crush employee motivation, satisfaction, and performance.

Models and Dynamics of Planned Change

American managers are criticized for emphasizing short-term, quick-fix solutions to organizational problems. When applied to organizational change, this approach is doomed from the start. Quick-fix solutions do not really solve underlying problems, and they have little staying power. Researchers and managers alike have thus tried to identify effective ways to manage the change process. This section sheds light on their insights. After discussing different types of organizational changes, we review Lewin's change model, a systems model of change, Kotter's eight steps for leading organizational change, and organizational development.

Types of Change

A useful three-way typology of change is displayed in Figure 18–2.[16] This typology is generic because it relates to all sorts of change, including both administrative and technological changes. Adaptive change is lowest in complexity, cost, and uncertainty. It involves reimplementation of a change in the same organizational unit at a later time or imitation of a similar change by a different unit. For example, an adaptive change for a department store would be to rely on 12-hour days during the annual inventory week. The store's accounting department could imitate the same change in work hours during tax preparation time. Adaptive changes are not particularly threatening to employees because they are familiar.

Innovative changes fall midway on the continuum of complexity, cost, and uncertainty. An experiment with flexible work schedules by a farm supply warehouse company qualifies as an innovative change if it entails modifying the way other firms in the industry already use it. Unfamiliarity, and hence greater uncertainty, make fear of change a problem with innovative changes.

Figure 18–2   *A Generic Typology of Organizational Change*

At the high end of the continuum of complexity, cost, and uncertainty are radically innovative changes. Changes of this sort are the most difficult to implement and tend to be the most threatening to managerial confidence and employee job security. At the same time, however, radically innovative changes potentially realize the greatest benefits. Sony's CEO, Sir Howard Stringer, is well aware of this trade-off. He is trying to right the "financial ship" at Sony by implementing deep cost cuts, selling assets, and changing the reward system from one that emphasized seniority to one that rewards performance.[17] Importantly, radical changes like this must be supported by an organization's culture. Organizational change is more likely to fail if it is inconsistent with any of the three levels of organizational culture: observable artifacts, espoused values, and basic assumptions (see the discussion in Chapter 3).

2 Lewin's Change Model

Most theories of organizational change originated from the landmark work of social psychologist Kurt Lewin. Lewin developed a three-stage model of planned change which explained how to initiate, manage, and stabilize the change process.[18] The three stages are unfreezing, changing, and refreezing. Before reviewing each stage, it is important to highlight the assumptions underlying this model:[19]

1. The change process involves learning something new, as well as discontinuing current attitudes, behaviors, or organizational practices.
2. Change will not occur unless there is motivation to change. This is often the most difficult part of the change process.
3. People are the hub of all organizational changes. Any change, whether in terms of structure, group process, reward systems, or job design, requires individuals to change.
4. Resistance to change is found even when the goals of change are highly desirable.
5. Effective change requires reinforcing new behaviors, attitudes, and organizational practices.

Let us now consider the three stages of change.

Unfreezing The focus of this stage is to create the motivation to change. In so doing, individuals are encouraged to replace old behaviors and attitudes with those desired by management. Managers can begin the unfreezing process by disconfirming the usefulness or appropriateness of employees' present behaviors or attitudes. In other words, employees need to become dissatisfied with the old way of doing things. Managers frequently create the motivation for change by presenting data regarding levels of effectiveness, efficiency, or customer satisfaction. For example, Mark Hurd, CEO of Hewlett-Packard (HP), unfroze the organization about the need to restructure by using information he obtained from corporate customers and HP employees. Customers told Hurd that HP's structure was so confusing that they did not know whom to call for help. HP salespeople complained that they spent only 33% of their time with customers because they were required to complete so much administrative paperwork.[20]

Benchmarking is a technique that can be used to help unfreeze an organization. **Benchmarking** "describes the overall process by which a company compares its performance with that of other companies, then learns how the strongest-performing companies achieve their results."[21] For example, one company for which we consulted discovered through benchmarking that their costs to develop software were twice as high as the best companies in the industry, and the time it took to get a new product

Benchmarking
Process by which a company compares its performance with that of high-performing organizations.

to market was four times longer than the benchmarked organizations. These data were ultimately used to unfreeze employees' attitudes and motivate people to change the organization's internal processes in order to remain competitive. Managers also need to devise ways to reduce the barriers to change during this stage.

Changing Organizational change, whether large or small, is undertaken to improve some process, procedure, product, service, or outcome of interest to management. Because change involves learning and doing things differently, this stage entails providing employees with new information, new behavioral models, new processes or procedures, new equipment, new technology, or new ways of getting the job done. How does management know what to change?

There is no simple answer to this question. Organizational change can be aimed at improvement or growth, or it can focus on solving a problem such as poor customer service or low productivity. Change also can be targeted at different levels in an organization. For example, sending managers to leadership training programs can be a solution to improving individuals' job satisfaction and productivity. In contrast, installing new information technology may be the change required to increase work group productivity and overall corporate profits. The point to keep in mind is that change should be targeted at some type of desired end-result. The systems model of change, which is the next model to be discussed, provides managers with a framework to diagnose the target of change.

Refreezing Change is stabilized during refreezing by helping employees integrate the changed behavior or attitude into their normal way of doing things. This is accomplished by first giving employees the chance to exhibit the new behaviors or attitudes. Once exhibited, positive reinforcement is used to reinforce the desired change. Additional coaching and modeling also are used at this point to reinforce the stability of the change. Extrinsic rewards, particularly monetary incentives (recall our discussion in Chapter 9), are frequently used to reinforce behavioral change.

A Systems Model of Change

A systems approach takes a "big picture" perspective of organizational change. It is based on the notion that any change, no matter how large or small, has a cascading effect throughout an organization.[22] For example, promoting an individual to a new work group affects the group dynamics in both the old and new groups. Similarly, creating project or work teams may necessitate the need to revamp compensation practices. These examples illustrate that change creates additional change. Today's solutions are tomorrow's problems.

A systems model of change offers managers a framework or model to use for diagnosing *what* to change and for determining *how* to evaluate the success of a change effort. To further your understanding about this model, we first describe its components and then discuss a brief application. The four main components of a systems model of change are inputs, strategic plans, target elements of change, and outputs (see Figure 18–3).

Mission statement

Summarizes "why" an organization exists.

Inputs All organizational changes should be consistent with an organization's mission, vision, and resulting strategic plan. A **mission statement** represents the "reason" an organization exists, and an organization's *vision* is a long-term goal that describes "what" an organization wants to become. Consider how the difference between mission and vision affects organizational change. Your university probably

Figure 18–3   *A Systems Model of Change*

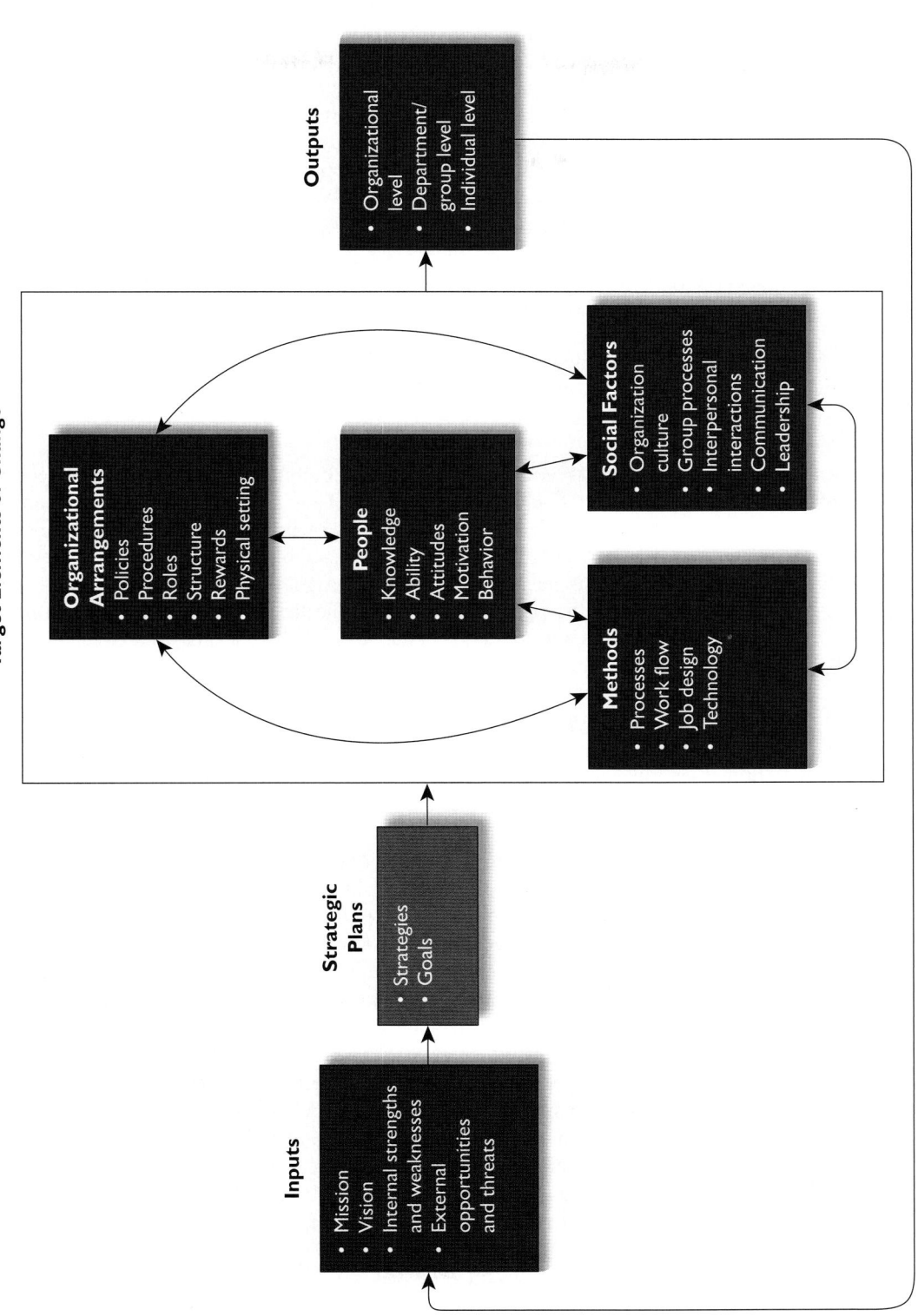

SOURCES: Adapted from D R Fuqua and D J Kurpius, "Conceptual Models in Organizational Consultation," *Journal of Counseling and Development*, July–August 1993. pp 602–18; and D A Nadler and M L Tushman, "Organizational Frame Bending: Principles for Managing Reorientation," *Academy of Management Executive*, August 1989, pp 194–203.

has a mission to educate people. This mission does not necessarily imply anything about change. It simply defines the university's overall purpose. In contrast, the university may have a vision to be recognized as the "best" university in the country. This vision requires the organization to benchmark itself against other world-class universities and to create plans for achieving the vision. For example, the vision of the W P Carey School of Business at Arizona State University is to be among the top 25 business schools in the world. An assessment of an organization's internal strengths and weaknesses against its environmental opportunities and threats (SWOT) is another key input within the systems model. This SWOT analysis is a key component of the strategic planning process.

Strategic Plans A strategic plan outlines an organization's long-term direction and the actions necessary to achieve planned results. Among other things, strategic plans are based on results from a SWOT analysis. This analysis aids in developing an organizational strategy to attain desired goals such as profits, customer satisfaction, quality, adequate return on investment, and acceptable levels of turnover and employee satisfaction and commitment.

Target elements of change

Components of an organization that may be changed.

Target Elements of Change Target elements of change are the components of an organization that may be changed. They essentially represent change levers that managers can push and pull to influence various aspects of an organization. The choice of which lever to pull, however, is based on a diagnosis of a problem, or problems, or the actions needed to accomplish a goal: A problem exists when managers are not obtaining the results they desire. The target elements of change are used to diagnose problems and to identify change-related solutions.

As shown in Figure 18–3, there are four targeted elements of change: organizational arrangements, social factors, methods, and people.[23] Each target element of change contains a subset of more detailed organizational features. For instance, the "social factors" component includes consideration of an organization's culture, group processes, interpersonal interactions, communication, and leadership. There are two final issues to keep in mind about the target elements of change shown in Figure 18–3. First, the double-headed arrows connecting each target element of change convey the message that change ripples across an organization. For example, changing a reward system to reinforce team rather than individual performance (an organizational arrangement) is likely to impact organizational culture (a social factor). Second, the "people" component is placed in the center of the target elements of change box because all organizational change ultimately impacts employees. Organizational change is more likely to succeed when managers proactively consider the impact of change on its employees.

Outputs Outputs represent the desired end-results of a change. Once again, these end-results should be consistent with an organization's strategic plan. Figure 18–3 indicates that change may be directed at the organizational level, department/group level, or individual level. Change efforts are more complicated and difficult to manage when they are targeted at the organizational level. This occurs because organizational-level changes are more likely to affect multiple target elements of change shown in the model.

Applying the Systems Model of Change There are two different ways to apply the systems model of change. The first is as an aid during the strategic planning process. Once a group of managers have determined their vision and strategic goals, the target elements of change can be considered when developing action plans to support the accomplishment of goals. For example, the management team at JP Morgan Chase & Co. established goals to increase revenue and decrease costs. They decided to cut 12,000 jobs (a people factor), decrease executive perks like country club memberships and first-class airfare (an organizational arrangements factor), and to invest heavily in information technology in order to redesign the work flow (a method factor).[24] The second application involves using the model as a diagnostic framework to determine the causes of an organizational problem and to propose solutions. We highlight this application by considering a consulting project in which we used the model.

We were contacted by the CEO of a software company and asked to figure out why the presidents of three divisions were not collaborating with each other—the problem. It turned out that two of the presidents submitted a proposal for the same $4 million project from a potential customer. Our client did not get the work because the customer was appalled at having received two proposals from the same company; hence the CEO's call to us. We decided to interview employees by using a structured set of questions that pertained to each of the target elements of change. For instance, we asked employees to comment on the extent to which the reward system, organizational culture, work flow, and physical setting contributed to collaboration across divisions. The interviews taught us that the lack of collaboration among the division presidents was due to the reward system (an organizational arrangement), a competitive culture and poor communications (social factors), and poor work flow (a methods factor). Our recommendation was to change the reward systems, restructure the organization, and redesign the work flow.

go to the Web for the Self-Exercise: Applying the Systems Model of Change

3 Kotter's Eight Steps for Leading Organizational Change

John Kotter, an expert in leadership and change management, believes that organizational change typically fails because senior management commits one or more of the following errors:[25]

1. Failure to establish a sense of urgency about the need for change.
2. Failure to create a powerful-enough guiding coalition that is responsible for leading and managing the change process.
3. Failure to establish a vision that guides the change process.
4. Failure to effectively communicate the new vision.
5. Failure to remove obstacles that impede the accomplishment of the new vision.
6. Failure to systematically plan for and create short-term wins. Short-term wins represent the achievement of important results or goals.
7. Declaration of victory too soon. This derails the long-term changes in infrastructure that are frequently needed to achieve a vision.
8. Failure to anchor the changes into the organization's culture. It takes years for long-term changes to be embedded within an organization's culture.

Table 18–1 *Steps to Leading Organizational Change*

STEP	DESCRIPTION
1. Establish a sense of urgency	Unfreeze the organization by creating a compelling reason for why change is needed.
2. Create the guiding coalition	Create a cross-functional, cross-level group of people with enough power to lead the change.
3. Develop a vision and strategy	Create a vision and strategic plan to guide the change process.
4. Communicate the change vision	Create and implement a communication strategy that consistently communicates the new vision and strategic plan.
5. Empower broad-based action	Eliminate barriers to change, and use target elements of change to transform the organization. Encourage risk taking and creative problem solving.
6. Generate short-term wins	Plan for and create short-term "wins" or improvements. Recognize and reward people who contribute to the wins.
7. Consolidate gains and produce more change	The guiding coalition uses credibility from short-term wins to create more change. Additional people are brought into the change process as change cascades throughout the organization. Attempts are made to reinvigorate the change process.
8. Anchor new approaches in the culture	Reinforce the changes by highlighting connections between new behaviors and processes and organizational success. Develop methods to ensure leadership development and succession.

SOURCE: The steps were developed by J P Kotter, *Leading Change* (Boston: Harvard Business School Press, 1996).

Based on these errors, Kotter proposed an eight-step process for leading change (see Table 18–1). Unlike the systems model of change, this model is not diagnostic in orientation. Its application will not help managers to diagnose *what* needs to be changed. Rather, this model is more like Lewin's model of change in that it prescribes *how* managers should sequence or lead the change process.

Each of Kotter's eight steps shown in Table 18–1 is associated with the eight fundamental errors just discussed. These steps also subsume Lewin's model of change. The first four steps represent Lewin's "unfreezing" stage. Steps 5, 6, and 7 represent "changing," and step 8 corresponds to "refreezing." The value of Kotter's steps is that it provides specific recommendations about behaviors that managers need to exhibit to successfully lead organizational change. It is important to remember that Kotter's research reveals that it is ineffective to skip steps and that successful organizational change is 70 to 90% leadership and only 10 to 30% management. Senior managers are thus advised to focus on leading rather than managing change.[26]

4 Creating Change through Organization Development

Organization development (OD) is different from the previously discussed models of change. OD does not entail a structured sequence as proposed by Lewin and Kotter, but it does possess the same diagnostic focus associated with the systems model of change. That said, OD is much broader in orientation than any of the previously discussed models. Specifically, a pair of experts in this field of study and practice defined **organization development** as follows:

> OD consists of planned efforts to help persons work and live together more effectively, over time, in their organizations. These goals are achieved by applying behavioral science principles, methods, and theories adapted from the fields of psychology, sociology, education, and management.[27]

Organization development
A set of techniques or tools used to implement planned organizational change.

As you can see from this definition, OD constitutes a set of techniques or interventions that are used to implement "planned" organizational change aimed at increasing "an organization's ability to improve itself as a humane and effective system." OD techniques or interventions apply to each of the change models discussed in this section. For example OD is used during Lewin's "changing" stage. It also is used to identify and implement targeted elements of change within the systems model of change. Finally, OD might be used during Kotter's steps 1, 3, 5, 6, and 7. In this section, we briefly review the four identifying characteristics of OD and its research and practical implications.[28]

OD Involves Profound Change Change agents using OD generally desire deep and long-lasting improvement. OD consultant Warner Burke, for example, who strives for fundamental *cultural* change, wrote: "By fundamental change, as opposed to fixing a problem or improving a procedure, I mean that some significant aspect of an organization's culture will never be the same."[29]

OD Is Value-Loaded Owing to the fact that OD is rooted partially in humanistic psychology, many OD consultants carry certain values or biases into the client organization. They prefer cooperation over conflict, self-control over institutional control, and democratic and participative management over autocratic management. In addition to OD being driven by a consultant's values, some OD practitioners now believe that there is a broader "value perspective" that should underlie any organizational change. Specifically, OD should always be customer focused. This approach implies that organizational interventions should be aimed at helping to satisfy customers' needs and thereby provide enhanced value of an organization's products and services[30].

OD Is a Diagnosis/Prescription Cycle OD theorists and practitioners have long adhered to a medical model of organization. Like medical doctors, internal and external OD consultants approach the "sick" organization, "diagnose" its ills, "prescribe" and implement an intervention, and "monitor" progress. Table 18–2 presents a list of several different OD interventions that can be used to change individual, group, or organizational behavior as a whole.

OD Is Process-Oriented Ideally, OD consultants focus on the form and not the content of behavioral and administrative dealings. For example, product design engineers and market researchers might be coached on how to communicate more

Table 18–2   *Some OD Interventions for Implementing Change*

- **Survey feedback:** A questionnaire is distributed to employees to ascertain their perceptions and attitudes. The results are then shared with them. The questionnaire may ask about such matters as group cohesion, job satisfaction, and managerial leadership. Once the survey is done, meaningful results can be communicated with employees so that they can then engage in problem solving and constructive changes.
- **Process consultation:** An OD consultant observes the communication process—interpersonal-relations, decision-making, and conflict-handling patterns—occurring in work groups and provides feedback to the members involved. In consulting with employees (particularly managers) about these processes, the change agent hopes to give them the skills to identify and improve group dynamics on their own.
- **Team building:** Work groups are made to become more effective by helping members learn to function as a team. For example, members of a group might be interviewed independently by the OD change agent to establish how they feel about the group, then a meeting may be held away from their usual workplace to discuss the issues. To enhance team cohesiveness, the OD consultant may have members work together on a project such as rock climbing, with the consultant helping with communication and conflict resolution. The objective is for members to see how they can individually contribute to the group's goals and efforts.
- **Intergroup development:** Intergroup development resembles team building in many of its efforts. However, intergroup development attempts to achieve better cohesiveness among several work groups, not just one. During the process, the change agent tries to elicit misperceptions and stereotypes that the groups have for each other so that they can be discussed, leading to better coordination among them.
- **Technostructural activities:** Technostructural activities are interventions concerned with improving the work technology or organizational design with people on the job. An intervention involving a work-technology change might be the introduction of e-mail to improve employee communication. An intervention involving an organizational-design change might be making a company less centralized in its decision making.

SOURCE: A Kinicki and B Williams, *Management: A Practical Introduction,* 3rd ed. (Burr Ridge: IL McGraw-Hill/Irwin, 2006), p 329.

effectively with one another without the consultant knowing the technical details of their conversations. In addition to communication, OD specialists focus on other processes, including problem solving, decision making, conflict handling, trust, power sharing, and career development.

OD Research and Practical Implications
Before discussing OD research, it is important to note that many of the topics contained in this book are used during OD interventions. For example, role analysis, which was discussed in Chapter 10, is used to enhance cooperation among work group members by getting them to discuss their mutual expectations. Team building also is commonly used as an OD technique. It is used to improve the functioning of work groups and was reviewed in Chapter 11. The point is that OD research has practical implications for a variety of OB applications previously discussed. OD-related interventions produced the following insights:

- A meta-analysis of 18 studies indicated that employee satisfaction with change was higher when top management was highly committed to the change effort.[31]

- A meta-analysis of 52 studies provided support for the systems model of organizational change. Specifically, varying one target element of change created changes in other target elements. Also, there was a positive relationship between individual behavior change and organizational-level change.[32]

- A meta-analysis of 126 studies demonstrated that multifaceted interventions using more than one OD technique were more effective in changing job attitudes and work attitudes than interventions that relied on only one human-process or technostructural approach.[33]

- A survey of 1,700 firms from China, Japan, the United States, and Europe revealed that (1) US and European firms used OD interventions more frequently than firms from China and Japan and (2) some OD interventions are culture free and some are not.[34]

There are four practical implications derived from this research. First, planned organizational change works. However, management and change agents are advised to rely on multifaceted interventions. As indicated elsewhere in this book, goal setting, feedback, recognition and rewards, training, participation, and challenging job design have good track records relative to improving performance and satisfaction. Second, change programs are more successful when they are geared toward meeting both short-term and long-term results. Managers should not engage in organizational change for the sake of change. Change efforts should produce positive results. Third, organizational change is more likely to succeed when top management is truly committed to the change process and the desired goals of the change program. This is particularly true when organizations pursue large-scale transformation. Finally, the effectiveness of OD interventions is affected by cross-cultural considerations. Managers and OD consultants should not blindly apply an OD intervention that worked in one country to a similar situation in another country.

Understanding and Managing Resistance to Change

Organizational change essentially represents a form of influence. That is, organizational change is management's attempt to get employees to behave, think, or perform differently. Viewing change from this perspective underscores what we discussed about influence techniques and outcomes in Chapter 15. You may recall that resistance is one of the three possible influence outcomes; the other two are commitment and compliance. Resistance to change thus represents a failed influence attempt. Let us consider one of the overriding causes of resistance to change.

We are all creatures of habit. It generally is difficult for people to try new ways of doing things. It is precisely because of this basic human characteristic that most employees do not have enthusiasm for change in the workplace. Rare is the manager who does not have several stories about carefully cultivated changes that died on the vine because of resistance to change. It is important for managers to learn to manage resistance because failed change efforts are costly. Costs include decreased employee loyalty, lowered probability of achieving corporate goals, a waste of money and resources, and difficulty in fixing the failed change effort. This section examines employee resistance to change, relevant research, and practical ways of dealing with the problem.

Ashok Kheny Encounters Extreme Resistance When Trying to Build a Highway in India

To understand why it's so hard to get things built in India, consider Ashok Kheny's quixotic quest. For 12 years he has sought to create a vision of modern India on the rolling, palm-dotted plains south of Bangalore. Along the way he has become entangled in India's unique blend of politics, bureaucracy, and corruption.

Kheny started off with high hopes. A native of Bangalore, he left home after college to get his master's degree in engineering at Worcester Polytechnic Institute in Massachusetts, then stayed on in America to work as a transportation contractor. In 1995 he returned to Bangalore with a bold proposal: to build a limited-access toll highway between Bangalore and neighboring Mysore, a ring road around half of Bangalore, and a handful of new townships nearby. The Karnataka state government approved the plan, so Kheny moved back—never suspecting that dynamiting the rocky terrain would turn out to be a snap compared with breaking through India's intransigent bureaucracy.

Officially, Kheny and his Nandi Infrastructure Corridor Enterprise Ltd. have been held up by land disputes and government reviews and approvals. But he claims the real problem is that he refuses to go along with the traditional way of getting things done in Karnataka. He won't pay bribes, and he won't buy off landowners or redraw his maps to accommodate them. Landowners and state agencies have filed more than 300 lawsuits against the project, and so far all have gone in Kheny's favor, including an appeal to the country's Supreme Court. But the battle isn't over. "I get letters and phone calls threatening to kill me and my family," he says—one reason his wife and children have remained behind in the U.S.

Will Ashok Kheny be able to accomplish his goals without doing business the traditional way? Explain.

SOURCE: Excerpted from S Hamm, "Change Agents: A Long and Winding Road," *BusinessWeek,* March 19, 2007, p 56.

go to the Web for the Self-Exercise: Does Your Commitment to a Change Initiative Predict Your Behavioral Support for the Change?

5 Why People Resist Change in the Workplace

No matter how technically or administratively perfect a proposed change may be, people make or break it (see the Real World/Real People feature above). Individual and group behavior following an organizational change can take many forms. The extremes range from acceptance to active resistance. **Resistance to change** is an emotional/behavioral response to real or imagined threats to an established work routine.

Resistance to change

Emotional/ behavioral response to real or imagined work changes.

Resistance can be as subtle as passive resignation and as overt as deliberate sabotage. Managers need to learn to recognize the manifestations of resistance both in themselves and in others if they want to be more effective in creating and supporting change. Let us now consider the reasons employees resist change in the first place. Eleven of the leading reasons are discussed below:[35]

I. *An individual's predisposition toward change.* This predisposition is highly personal and deeply ingrained. It is an outgrowth of how one learns to handle change and ambiguity as a child. Consider the hypothetical examples of Mary and Jim. Mary's parents were patient, flexible, and understanding. From the time Mary was weaned from a bottle, she was taught that there were positive compensations for the loss of immediate gratification. She learned that love and approval were associated with making changes. In contrast, Jim's parents were unreasonable, unyielding, and forced him to comply with their wishes. They forced him to take piano lessons even though he hated them. Changes were demands for compliance. This taught Jim to be distrustful and suspicious of change. These learned predispositions ultimately affect how Mary and Jim handle change as adults.

2. *Surprise and fear of the unknown.* When innovative or radically different changes are introduced without warning, affected employees become fearful of the implications. Grapevine rumors fill the void created by a lack of official announcements. Harvard's Rosabeth Moss Kanter recommends appointing a transition manager charged with keeping all relevant parties adequately informed.[36]

These striking employees are openly resisting change. Which of the 11 reasons why people resist change may be motivating these individuals?

3. *Climate of mistrust.* Trust, as discussed in Chapter 11, involves reciprocal faith in others' intentions and behavior. Mutual mistrust can doom to failure an otherwise well-conceived change. Mistrust encourages secrecy, which begets deeper mistrust. Managers who trust their employees make the change process an open, honest, and participative affair. Employees who, in turn, trust management are more willing to expend extra effort and take chances with something different.

4. *Fear of failure.* Intimidating changes on the job can cause employees to doubt their capabilities. Self-doubt erodes self-confidence and cripples personal growth and development. Recall our discussion about self-efficacy in Chapter 5.

5. *Loss of status or job security.* Administrative and technological changes that threaten to alter power bases or eliminate jobs generally trigger strong resistance. For example, most corporate restructuring involves the elimination of managerial jobs. One should not be surprised when middle managers resist restructuring and participative management programs that reduce their authority and status.

6. *Peer pressure.* Someone who is not directly affected by a change may actively resist it to protect the interests of his or her friends and co-workers.

7. *Disruption of cultural traditions or group relationships.* Whenever individuals are transferred, promoted, or reassigned, cultural and group dynamics are thrown into disequilibrium. For example, Nobuyuki Idei, former CEO of Sony Corp., was worried about employees' resistance to change when he named Sir Howard Stringer as the next chairman and CEO of Sony and asked six corporate officers to resign. Nobuyuki's concern, rightfully so, stemmed from the fact that Stringer's appointment is inconsistent with Sony's tradition of promoting an insider with technical background and resignations will create a majority board of foreigners.[37]

8. *Personality conflicts.* Just as a friend can get away with telling us something we would resent hearing from an adversary, the personalities of change agents can breed resistance.

9. *Lack of tact or poor timing.* Undue resistance can occur because changes are introduced in an insensitive manner or at an awkward time. Proposed organizational changes are more likely to be accepted by others when managers effectively explain or "sell" the value of their proposed changes. This can be done by explaining how a proposed change is strategically important to an organization's success.

10. *Nonreinforcing reward systems.* Individuals resist when they do not foresee positive rewards for changing. For example, an employee is unlikely to support a change effort that is perceived as requiring him or her to work longer with more pressure.

11. *Past success.* Success can breed complacency. It also can foster a stubbornness to change because people come to believe that what worked in the past will work in the future. Coca-Cola's strategic change initiatives were undermined by this form of resistance.

> For too long Coke has stayed stubbornly, defiantly rooted in its past, holding on to the belief that its business model was as good as gold: Make cola concentrate for pennies, then sell it for dollars through a global bottling system to a mass market that still pretty much drank what it saw on TV. When bottled water came along, one director called it a "low-margin road to nowhere." The company was late to the game in sports drinks, energy drinks, and coffee, regarding them as low volume distractions. . . . The irony, says analyst Matthew Reilly of Morningstar, is that until just recently, "Coke wasn't even a player in energy drinks—and it was the original energy drink."[38]

Research on Resistance to Change

The classic study of resistance to change was reported in 1948 by Lester Coch and John R P French. They observed the introduction of a new work procedure in a garment factory. The change was introduced in three different ways to separate groups of workers. In the "no participation" group, the garment makers were simply told about the new procedure. Members of a second group, called the "representative" group, were introduced to the change by a trained co-worker. Employees in the "total participation" group learned of the new work procedure through a graphic presentation of its cost-saving potential. Mixed results were recorded for the representative group. The no participation and total participation groups, meanwhile, went in opposite directions. Output dropped sharply for the no participation group, while grievances and turnover climbed. After a small dip in performance, the total participation group achieved record-high output levels while experiencing no turnover.[39] Since the Coch and French study, participation has been the recommended approach for overcoming resistance to change.

Empirical research uncovered five additional personal characteristics related to resistance to change. The first involves an employee's commitment to change. **Commitment to change** is defined as a mind-set "that binds an individual to a course of action deemed necessary for the successful implementation of a change initiative."[40] A series of studies showed that an employee's commitment to change was a significant and positive predictor of behavioral support for a change initiative.[41]

The second personal characteristic is resilience to change. **Resilience to change** is a composite characteristic reflecting high self-esteem, optimism, and an internal locus of control: Self-esteem and locus of control were discussed in Chapter 5. People with high resilience are expected to be more open and adaptable toward change.[42] In support of this prediction, a study of 130 individuals working in the areas of public housing and community development revealed that resilience to change was associated with respondents' willingness to accommodate or accept a specific organizational change. In turn, willingness to accept change was positively related to job satisfaction and negatively associated with work irritations and intentions to quit.[43]

The third and fourth characteristics were identified in a study of 514 employees from six organizations headquartered in four different continents (North America, Europe, Asia, and Australia). Results revealed that personal dispositions pertaining

Commitment to change

A mind-set of doing whatever it takes to effectively implement change.

Resilience to change

Composite personal characteristic reflecting high self-esteem, optimism, and an internal locus of control.

to having a "positive self-concept" and "tolerance for risk" were positively related to coping with change. That is, people with a positive self-concept and a tolerance for risk handled organizational change better than those without these dispositions.[44]

Finally, high levels of self-efficacy (recall our discussion in Chapter 5) were negatively associated with resistance to change.[45]

The preceding research is based on the assumption that individuals directly or consciously resist change. Some experts contend that this is not the case. Rather, there is a growing belief that resistance to change really represents employees' responses to obstacles in the organization that prevent them from changing.[46] For example, John Kotter, the researcher who developed the eight steps for leading organizational change that were discussed earlier in this chapter, studied more than 100 companies and concluded that employees generally wanted to change but were unable to do so because of obstacles that prevented execution. He noted that obstacles in the organization's structure or in a "performance appraisal system [that] makes people choose between the new vision and their own self-interests" impeded change more than an individual's direct resistance.[47] This new perspective implies that a systems model such as that shown in Figure 18–3 should be used to determine the causes of failed change. Such an approach would likely reveal that ineffective organizational change is due to faulty organizational processes and systems as opposed to employees' direct resistance. For example, employees frequently resist change because management has not effectively communicated the rationale to support the change.[48] In conclusion, a systems perspective suggests that people do not resist change, per se, but rather that individuals' anti-change attitudes and behaviors are caused by obstacles within the work environment.

go to the Web for the Self-Exercise: Assessing Your Organization's Readiness For Change

7 Alternative Strategies for Overcoming Resistance to Change

We previously noted that participation historically has been the recommended approach for overcoming resistance to change. More recently, however, organizational change experts criticized the tendency to treat participation as a cure-all for resistance to change. They prefer a contingency approach because resistance can take many forms and, furthermore, because situational factors vary (see Table 18–3). As shown in Table 18–3, participation + involvement does have its place, but it takes time that is not always available. Also as indicated in Table 18–3, each of the other five methods has its situational niche, advantages, and drawbacks. In short, there is no universal strategy for overcoming resistance to change. Managers need a complete repertoire of change strategies.

Moreover, there are four additional recommendations managers should consider when leading organizational change. First, an organization must be ready for change. Just as a table must be set before you can eat, so must an organization be ready for change before it can be effective.[49] Second, do not assume that people are consciously resisting change. Managers are encouraged to use a systems model of change to identify the obstacles that are affecting the implementation process. Third, radical innovative change is more likely to succeed when middle-level managers are highly involved in the change process.

Table 18–3   *Six Strategies for Overcoming Resistance to Change*

APPROACH	COMMONLY USED IN SITUATIONS	ADVANTAGES	DRAWBACKS
Education + communication	Where there is a lack of information or inaccurate information and analysis.	Once persuaded, people will often help with the implementation of the change.	Can be very time consuming if lots of people are involved.
Participation + involvement	Where the initiators do not have all the information they need to design the change and where others have considerable power to resist.	People who participate will be committed to implementing change, and any relevant information they have will be integrated into the change plan.	Can be very time consuming if participators design an inappropriate change.
Facilitation + support	Where people are resisting because of adjustment problems.	No other approach works as well with adjustment problems.	Can be time consuming, expensive, and still fail.
Negotiation + agreement	Where someone or some group will clearly lose out in a change and where that group has considerable power to resist.	Sometimes it is a relatively easy way to avoid major resistance.	Can be too expensive in many cases if it alerts others to negotiate for compliance.
Manipulation + co-optation	Where other tactics will not work or are too expensive.	It can be a relatively quick and inexpensive solution to resistance problems.	Can lead to future problems if people feel manipulated.
Explicit + implicit coercion	Where speed is essential and where the change initiators possess considerable power.	It is speedy and can overcome any kind of resistance.	Can be risky if it leaves people mad at the initiators.

Fourth, employees' perceptions or interpretations of a change significantly affect resistance. Employees are less likely to resist when they perceive that the benefits of a change overshadow the personal costs. At a minimum then, managers are advised to (1) provide as much information as possible to employees about the change, (2) inform employees about the reasons/rationale for the change, (3) conduct meetings to address employees' questions regarding the change, and (4) provide employees the opportunity to discuss how the proposed change might affect them.[50] These recommendations underscore the importance of communicating with employees throughout the process of change.

go to the Web for the Group Exercise: Creating Change at Best Buy

8 Dynamics of Stress

We all experience stress on a daily basis. Although stress is caused by many factors, researchers conclude that stress triggers one of two basic reactions: active fighting or passive flight (running away or acceptance), the so-called **fight-or-flight response.**[51] Physiologically, this stress response is a biochemical "passing gear" involving hormonal changes that mobilize the body for extraordinary demands. Imagine how our prehistoric ancestors responded to the stress associated with a charging saber-toothed tiger. To avoid being eaten, they could stand their ground and fight the beast or run away. In either case, their bodies would have been energized by an identical hormonal change, involving the release of adrenaline into the bloodstream.

Fight-or-flight response

To either confront stressors or try to avoid them.

In today's hectic urbanized and industrialized society, charging beasts have been replaced by problems such as deadlines, role conflict and ambiguity, financial responsibilities, information overload, technology, traffic congestion, noise and air pollution, family problems, and work overload. As with our ancestors, our response to stress may or may not trigger negative side effects, including headaches, ulcers, insomnia, heart attacks, high blood pressure, and strokes. The same stress response that helped our prehistoric ancestors survive has too often become a factor that seriously impairs our daily lives.

This lion has clearly created a flight response from its targeted prey. Have you ever run away from danger?

Because stress and its consequences are manageable, it is important for managers to learn as much as they can about occupational stress. After defining stress, this section provides an overview of the dynamics associated with stress by presenting a model of occupational stress, discussing moderators of occupational stress, and reviewing the effectiveness of several stress-reduction techniques.

Defining Stress

To an orchestra violinist, stress may stem from giving a solo performance before a big audience. While heat, smoke, and flames may represent stress to a firefighter, delivering a speech or presenting a lecture may be stressful for those who are shy. In short, stress means different things to different people. Managers need a working definition.

Formally defined, **stress** is "an adaptive response, mediated by individual characteristics and/or psychological processes, that is a consequence of any external action, situation, or event that places special physical and/or psychological demands

Stress

Behavioral, physical, or psychological response to stressors.

upon a person."[52] This definition is not as difficult as it seems when we reduce it to three inter-related dimensions of stress: (1) environmental demands, referred to as stressors, that produce (2) an adaptive response that is influenced by (3) individual differences.

Hans Selye, considered the father of the modern concept of stress, pioneered the distinction between stressors and the stress response. Moreover, Selye emphasized that both positive and negative events can trigger an identical stress response that can be beneficial or harmful. He referred to stress that is positive or produces a positive outcome as **eustress.** Receiving an award in front of a large crowd or successfully completing a difficult work assignment both are examples of stressors that produce eustress. He also noted that

- Stress is not merely nervous tension.
- Stress can have positive consequences.
- Stress is not something to be avoided.
- The complete absence of stress is death.[53]

These points make it clear that stress is inevitable. Efforts need to be directed at managing stress, not at somehow escaping it altogether.

A Model of Occupational Stress

Figure 18–4 presents an instructive model of occupational stress. The model shows that an individual initially appraises four types of stressors. This appraisal then motivates an individual to choose a coping strategy aimed at managing stressors, which, in turn, produces a variety of outcomes. The model also specifies several individual differences that moderate the stress process. A moderator is a variable that causes the relationship between two variables—such as stressors and cognitive appraisal—to be stronger for some people and weaker for others. Three key moderators are discussed in the next section. Let us now consider the remaining components of this model in detail.

Stressors Stressors are environmental factors that produce stress. Stated differently, stressors are a prerequisite to experiencing the stress response. Figure 18–4 shows the four major types of stressors: individual, group, organizational, and extra-organizational. Individual-level stressors are those directly associated with a person's job duties. The most common examples of individual stressors are job demands, work overload, role conflict, role ambiguity, everyday hassles, perceived control over events occurring in the work environment, job characteristics, and work/family conflict (recall our discussion in Chapter 6).[54] Losing one's job is another important individual-level stressor. Job loss is a very stressful event that is associated with decreased psychological and physical well-being.[55] Finally, sleep-related issues are important stressors. Research shows that most people need about seven hours of sleep per night and that alertness, energy, performance, creativity, and thinking are related to how much we sleep.[56] For example, a recent study revealed that employee fatigue costs US companies $136.4 billion annually in lost productivity.[57]

Group-level stressors are caused by group dynamics (recall our discussion in Chapter 10) and managerial behavior. Managers create stress for employees by (1) exhibiting inconsistent behaviors, (2) failing to provide support, (3) showing lack of concern, (4) providing inadequate direction, (5) creating a high-productivity environment, and (6) focusing on negatives while ignoring good performance. Sexual harassment experiences represent another group-level stressor. A recent meta-analysis

Eustress
Stress that is good or produces a positive outcome.

Stressors
Environmental factors that produce stress.

Figure 18–4   *A Model of Occupational Stress*

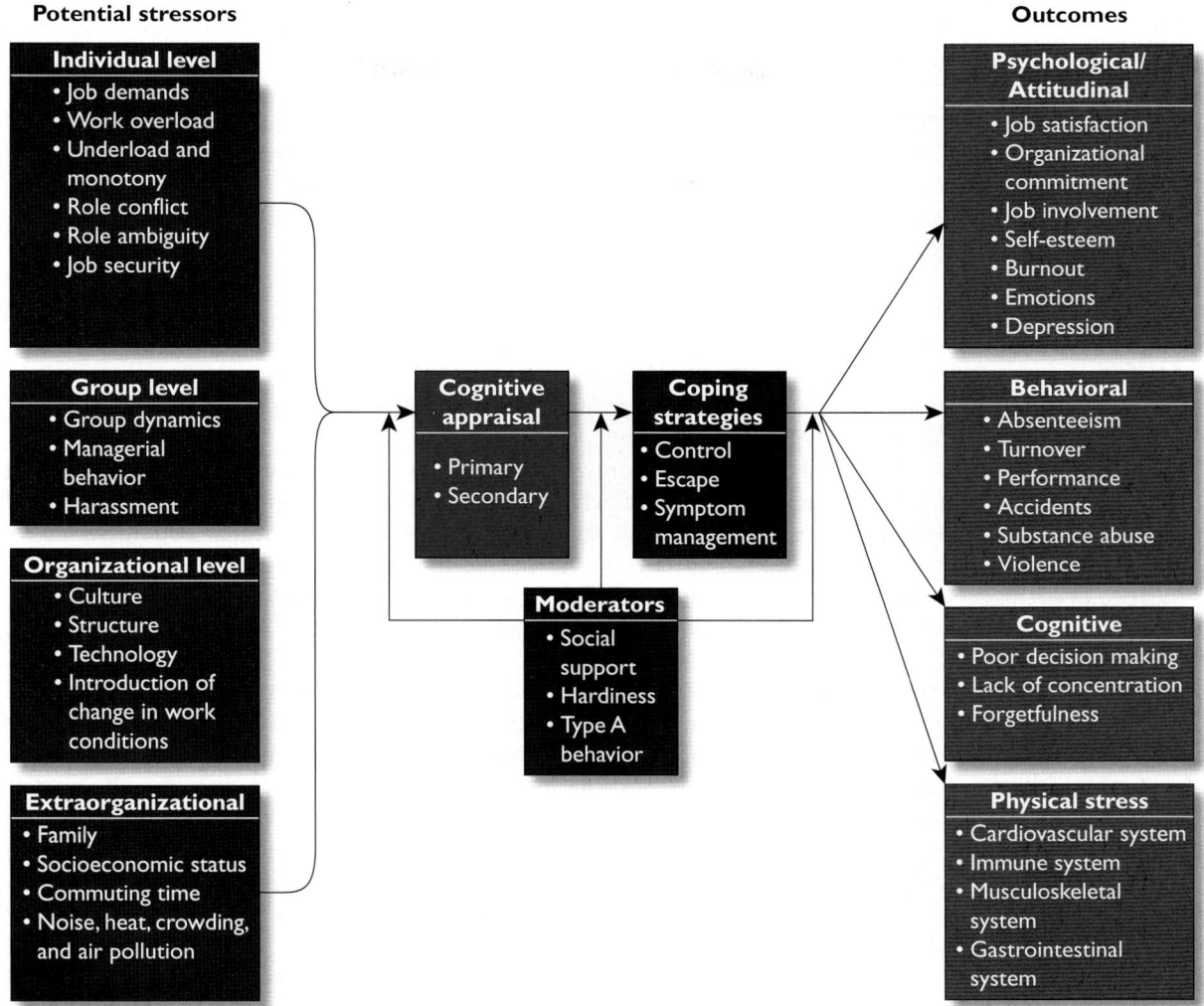

Potential stressors

Individual level
- Job demands
- Work overload
- Underload and monotony
- Role conflict
- Role ambiguity
- Job security

Group level
- Group dynamics
- Managerial behavior
- Harassment

Organizational level
- Culture
- Structure
- Technology
- Introduction of change in work conditions

Extraorganizational
- Family
- Socioeconomic status
- Commuting time
- Noise, heat, crowding, and air pollution

Cognitive appraisal
- Primary
- Secondary

Coping strategies
- Control
- Escape
- Symptom management

Moderators
- Social support
- Hardiness
- Type A behavior

Outcomes

Psychological/ Attitudinal
- Job satisfaction
- Organizational commitment
- Job involvement
- Self-esteem
- Burnout
- Emotions
- Depression

Behavioral
- Absenteeism
- Turnover
- Performance
- Accidents
- Substance abuse
- Violence

Cognitive
- Poor decision making
- Lack of concentration
- Forgetfulness

Physical stress
- Cardiovascular system
- Immune system
- Musculoskeletal system
- Gastrointestinal system

of 90 studies involving over 19,000 people demonstrated that harassing experiences were negatively associated with self-esteem, life and job satisfaction, organizational commitment, and positively with intentions to quit, absenteeism, anxiety, depression, and physical symptoms of stress.[58]

Organizational stressors affect large numbers of employees. Organizational culture, which was discussed in Chapter 3, is a prime example. For instance, a high-pressure environment that fuels employee fear about performing up to standard increases the stress response.[59] The increased use of information technology is another source of organizational stress, as is the air quality and ventilation found throughout the organization. The World Health Organization, for instance, reports that roughly 30% of all new and remodeled buildings have problems related to air quality, and air quality is associated with a variety of conditions such as headaches, dizziness, and the ability to concentrate.[60]

Extraorganizational stressors are those caused by factors outside the organization. For instance, in Chapter 6 we discussed how conflicts associated with balancing one's career and family life are stressful. Socioeconomic status is another extraorganizational stressor. Stress is higher for people with lower socioeconomic status, which represents a combination of (1) economic status, as measured by income, (2) social status, assessed by education level, and (3) work status, as indexed by occupation. These stressors are likely to become more important in the future.

Cognitive Appraisal of Stressors

Cognitive appraisal reflects an individual's overall perception or evaluation of a situation or stressor. It is an important component within the stress process because people interpret the same stressors differently. For example, some individuals perceive unemployment as a positive liberating experience, whereas others perceive it as a negative debilitating one.

Figure 18–4 shows that people make two types of appraisals when evaluating the potential impact of stressors on their lives: primary and secondary appraisals.[61] A **primary appraisal** results in categorizing a situation or stressor as irrelevant, positive, or stressful. Stress appraisals are obviously the most important in terms of our current discussion because they imply that a situation or stressor is perceived as harmful, threatening, or challenging.

A **secondary appraisal** only occurs in response to a stressful primary appraisal and entails an assessment of what might and can be done to reduce the level of perceived stress. During this evaluation a person considers which coping strategies are available and which ones are most likely to help resolve the situation at hand. Ultimately, the combination of an individual's primary and secondary appraisal influences the choice of coping strategies used to reduce stress.

Coping Strategies

Coping strategies are characterized by the specific behaviors and cognitions used to cope with a situation. People use a combination of three approaches to cope with stressors and stress (see Figure 18–4). The first, called a **control strategy,** consists of using behaviors and cognitions to directly anticipate or solve problems. A control strategy has a take-charge tone. Examples include talking to your boss about workload if you feel overwhelmed with your responsibilities, and confronting someone who is spreading negative rumors. Results from a meta-analysis of 34 studies and more than 4,000 people indicated that control coping was positively related to overall health outcomes.[62]

In contrast to tackling the problem head-on, an **escape strategy** amounts to avoiding the problem. Behaviors and cognitions are used to avoid or escape situations. Individuals use this strategy when they passively accept stressful situations or avoid them by failing to confront the cause of stress (an obnoxious co-worker, for instance). Finally, a **symptom management strategy** consists of using methods such as relaxation, meditation, medication, or exercise to manage the symptoms of occupational stress. A vacation, for example, can be a good way to reduce the symptoms of stress.[63]

Stress Outcomes

Theorists contend stress has psychological/attitudinal, behavioral, cognitive, and physical health consequences or outcomes. A large body of research supports the negative effects of perceived stress on many aspects of our lives. Workplace stress is negatively related to job satisfaction, organizational commitment, organizational citizenship behavior, positive emotions, performance, and turnover.[64] Research also shows that stress is associated with negative behaviors such as yelling and verbal abuse and violence toward others. These stress outcomes are very costly. The American Institute of Stress estimates that one million people miss work daily as a result of stress. All told, "the annual tab for all these lost hours due to absenteeism; reduced productivity; turnover; and medical, legal, and insurance costs comes to $300 billion or $7,500 per worker."[65] Finally, ample evidence supports the conclusion

Primary appraisal
Determining whether a stressor is irrelevant, positive, or stressful.

Secondary appraisal
Assessing what might and can be done to reduce stress.

Control strategy
Coping strategy that directly confronts or solves problems.

Escape strategy
Coping strategy that avoids or ignores stressors and problems.

Symptom management strategy
Coping strategy that focuses on reducing the symptoms of stress.

that stress negatively affects our physical health. Stress contributes to the following health problems: lessened ability to ward off illness and infection, high blood pressure, coronary artery disease, tension headaches, back pain, diarrhea, and constipation.[66] In fact, it's stressful to even think about all these problems!

9 Moderators of Occupational Stress

Moderators, once again, are variables that cause the relationships between stressors, perceived stress, and outcomes to be weaker for some people and stronger for others. Managers with a working knowledge of important stress moderators can confront employee stress in the following ways:

1. Awareness of moderators helps identify those most likely to experience stress and its negative outcomes. Stress-reduction programs then can be formulated for high-risk employees.

2. Moderators, in and of themselves, suggest possible solutions for reducing negative outcomes of occupational stress.

Keeping these objectives in mind, we will examine three important moderators: social support, hardiness, and Type A behavior.

Social Support Talking with a friend or taking part in a bull session can be comforting during times of fear, stress, or loneliness. For a variety of reasons, meaningful social relationships help people do a better job of handling stress. **Social support** is the amount of perceived helpfulness derived from social relationships. Importantly, social support is determined by both the quantity and quality of an individual's social relationships. We receive four types of social support from others:

Social support
Amount of helpfulness derived from social relationships.

- *Esteem support.* Providing information that a person is accepted and respected despite any problems or inadequacies.

- *Informational support.* Providing help in defining, understanding, and coping with problems.

- *Social companionship.* Spending time with others in leisure and recreational activities.

- *Instrumental support.* Providing financial aid, material resources, or needed services.[67]

Social support helps us deal with the ups and downs of life. A simple touch on the shoulder can be very comforting to someone in need.

Research shows that social support is negatively related to physiological processes and mortality. In other words, people with low social support tend to have poorer cardiovascular and immune system functioning and tend to die earlier than those with strong social support networks. Further, social support protects against the perception of stress, depression, psychological problems, pregnancy complications, anxiety, loneliness, high blood pressure, and a variety of other ailments. In contrast, negative social support, which amounts to someone undermining another person, negatively affects one's mental health.[68] We are well advised to avoid people who try to undermine us.

Social support research highlights two practical recommendations. First, managers are advised to keep employees informed about external and internal social support systems. Internally, managers can use all four forms of social support when employees experience a personal crisis. Coping with a divorce is a good example. Second, participative management programs and company-sponsored activities that make employees feel they are an important part of an extended family can be rich sources of social support. Employees need time and energy to adequately maintain their social relationships. If organizational demands are excessive, employees' social relationships and support networks will suffer, resulting in stress-related illness and decreased performance.[69]

Hardiness

Hardiness

Personality characteristic that neutralizes stress.

Suzanne Kobasa, a behavioral scientist, identified a collection of personality characteristics that neutralize occupational stress. This collection of characteristics, referred to as **hardiness,** involves the ability to perceptually or behaviorally transform negative stressors into positive challenges. Hardiness embraces the personality dimensions of commitment, locus of control, and challenge.[70]

Commitment reflects the extent to which an individual is involved in whatever he or she is doing. Committed people have a sense of purpose and do not give up under pressure because they tend to invest themselves in the situation. As discussed in Chapter 5, individuals with an *internal locus of control* believe they can influence the events that affect their lives. People possessing this trait are more likely to foresee stressful events, thereby reducing their exposure to anxiety-producing situations. Moreover, their perception of being in control leads "internals" to use proactive coping strategies. *Challenge* is represented by the belief that change is a normal part of life. Hence, change is seen as an opportunity for growth and development rather than a threat to security.

Research supports the moderating influence of hardiness on the stress process. For example, a five-year study of 259 managers from a public utility revealed that hardiness—commitment, locus of control, and challenge—reduced the probability of illness following exposure to stress.[71] The three components of hardiness also were found to directly influence how 276 members of the Israeli Defense Forces appraised stressors and ultimately coped with them. Hardy individuals interpreted stressors less negatively and were more likely to use control coping strategies than unhardy people.[72] Furthermore, additional research demonstrated that hardy individuals displayed lower stress, burnout, and psychological distress and higher job satisfaction than their less hardy counterparts.[73] Finally, a study of 73 pregnant women revealed that hardy women had fewer problems during labor and more positive perceptions about their infants than unhardy women.[74]

One practical offshoot of this research is organizational training and development programs that strengthen the characteristics of commitment, personal control, and challenge. For example, a team of researchers developed a hardiness training program based on this recommendation and tested it on a group of students and working adults. Results revealed that students' grade point average, retention, and health improved after the training. Training also resulted in increased performance, job satisfaction, and health for the working adults.[75] The hardiness concept also meshes nicely with job design. Enriched jobs are likely to fuel the hardiness components of commitment and challenge. A final application of the hardiness concept is as a diagnostic tool. Employees scoring low on hardiness would be good candidates for stress-reduction programs.

Type A Behavior Pattern

Type A behavior pattern

Aggressively involved in a chronic, determined struggle to accomplish more in less time.

According to Meyer Friedman and Ray Rosenman (the cardiologists who isolated the Type A syndrome in the 1950s):

Type A behavior pattern is an action-emotion complex that can be observed in any person who is aggressively involved in a chronic, incessant struggle to achieve more and more in less and less time, and if required to do so, against the opposing efforts of other things or persons. It is not psychosis or a complex of worries or fears or phobias or obsessions, but a socially acceptable—indeed often praised—form of conflict. Persons possessing this pattern also are quite prone to exhibit a free-floating but, extraordinarily well-rationalized hostility. As might be expected, there are degrees in the intensity of this behavior pattern.[76]

Table 18–4   *Type A Characteristics*

1. Hurried speech; explosive accentuation of key words.
2. Tendency to walk, move, and eat rapidly.
3. Constant impatience with the rate at which most events take place (e.g., irritation with slow-moving traffic and slow-talking and slow-to-act people).
4. Strong preference for thinking of or doing two or more things at once (e.g., reading this text and doing something else at the same time).
5. Tendency to turn conversations around to personally meaningful subjects or themes.
6. Tendency to interrupt while others are speaking to make your point or to complete their train of thought in your own words.
7. Guilt feelings during periods of relaxation or leisure time.
8. Tendency to be oblivious to surroundings during daily activities.
9. Greater concern for things worth *having* than with things worth *being*.
10. Tendency to schedule more and more in less and less time; a chronic sense of time urgency.
11. Feelings of competition rather than compassion when faced with another Type A person.
12. Development of nervous tics or characteristic gestures.
13. A firm belief that success is due to the ability to get things done faster than the other guy.
14. A tendency to view and evaluate personal activities and the activities of other people in terms of "numbers" (e.g., number of meetings attended, telephone calls made, visitors received).

SOURCE: Adapted from M Friedman and R H Rosenman, *Type A Behavior and Your Heart* (Greenwich, CT: Fawcett Publications, 1974), pp 100–2.

While labeling Type A behavior as "hurry sickness," Friedman and Rosenman noted that Type A individuals frequently tend to exhibit most of the behaviors listed in Table 18–4.

Because Type A behavior is a matter of degree, it is measured on a continuum. This continuum has the hurried, competitive Type A behavior pattern at one end and the more relaxed Type B behavior pattern at the other. Let us now consider the pros and cons of being Type A. OB research has demonstrated that Type A employees tend to be more productive than their Type B co-workers. For instance, Type A behavior yielded a significant and positive correlation with 766 students' grade point averages, the quantity and quality of 278 university professors' performance, and sales performance of 222 life insurance brokers.[77] On the other hand, Type A behavior is associated with some negative consequences.

A meta-analysis of 99 studies revealed that Type A individuals had higher heart rates, diastolic blood pressure, and systolic blood pressure than Type B people. Type A people also showed greater cardiovascular activity when they encountered the following situations:

1. Receipt of positive or negative feedback.

2. Receipt of verbal harassment or criticism.

3. Tasks requiring mental as opposed to physical work.[78]

Unfortunately for Type A individuals, these situations are frequently experienced at work. A second meta-analysis of 83 studies further demonstrated that the hard-driving and competitive aspects of Type A are related to coronary heart disease, but the speed and impatience and job involvement aspects are not. This meta-analysis also showed that feelings of anger, hostility, and aggression were more strongly related to heart disease than was Type A behavior.[79]

Do these results signal the need for Type A individuals to quit working so hard? Not necessarily. First off, the research indicated that feelings of anger, hostility, and aggression were more detrimental to our health than being Type A. We should all attempt to reduce these negative emotions. Second, researchers have developed stress-reduction techniques to help Type A people pace themselves more realistically and achieve better balance in their lives; they are discussed in the next section. Management can help Type A people, however, by not overloading them with work despite their apparent eagerness to take an everincreasing workload. Managers need to actively help rather than unthinkingly exploit Type A individuals.

go to the Web for the Self-Exercise: Where Are You on the Type A-B Behavior Continuum?

10 Stress-Reduction Techniques

Stress is very costly to organizations. The American Institute of Stress estimates that work stress costs US industries about $300 billion a year. It thus is not surprising that organizations are increasingly implementing a variety of stress-reduction programs to help employees cope with modern-day stress.[80]

There are many different stress-reduction techniques available. The four most frequently used approaches are muscle relaxation, biofeedback, meditation, and cognitive restructuring. Each method involves somewhat different ways of coping with stress (see Table 18–5).

Two teams of OB researchers reviewed the research on stress management interventions. Although much of the published research is methodologically weak, results offer preliminary support for the conclusion that muscle relaxation, biofeedback, meditation, and cognitive restructuring all help employees cope with occupational stress.[81]

Some researchers advise organizations not to implement these stress-reduction programs despite their positive outcomes. They rationalize that these techniques relieve *symptoms* of stress rather than eliminate stressors themselves.[82] Thus, they conclude that organizations are using a Band-Aid approach to stress reduction. This has led to the creation of much broader approaches toward stress reduction. The recommendation is for organizations to use employee assistance programs and for individuals to use a holistic wellness approach. Let us now consider each of these approaches toward stress reduction.

Employee assistance programs

Help employees to resolve personal problems that affect their productivity.

Employee Assistance Programs (EAPs) Employee assistance programs

consist of a broad array of programs aimed at helping employees to deal with personal problems such as substance abuse, health-related problems, family and marital issues, and other problems that negatively affect their job performance. EAPs are typically provided by employers or in combination with unions. Alternatively, referral-only EAPs simply provide managers with telephone numbers that they can distribute to employees in need of help. Employees then pay for these services themselves.

Holistic wellness approach

Advocates personal responsibility for healthy living.

Holistic Wellness Approach A holistic wellness approach encompasses and

goes beyond stress reduction by advocating that individuals strive for "a harmonious and productive balance of physical, mental, and social well-being brought about by

Table 18–5   *Stress-Reduction Techniques*

TECHNIQUE	DESCRIPTION	ASSESSMENT
Muscle relaxation	Uses slow, deep breathing and systematic muscle tension reduction.	Inexpensive and easy to use; may require a trained professional to implement.
Biofeedback	A machine is used to train people to detect muscular tension; muscle relaxation is then used to alleviate this symptom of stress.	Expensive due to costs of equipment; however, equipment can be used to evaluate effectiveness of other stress-reduction programs.
Meditation	The relaxation response is activated by redirecting one's thoughts away from oneself; a four-step procedure is used to attain passive stress-free state of mind.	Least expensive, simple to implement, and can be practiced almost anywhere.
Cognitive restructuring	Irrational or maladaptive thoughts are identified and replaced with those that are rational or logical.	Expensive because it requires a trained psychologist or counselor.
Holistic wellness	A broad, interdisciplinary approach that goes beyond stress reduction by advocating that people strive for personal wellness in all aspects of their lives.	Involves inexpensive but often behaviorally difficult lifestyle changes.

the acceptance of one's personal responsibility for developing and adhering to a health promotion program."[83] Five dimensions of a holistic wellness approach are as follows:

1. *Self-responsibility.* Take personal responsibility for your wellness (e.g., quit smoking, moderate your intake of alcohol, wear your seat belt, and eat less food). As a case in point, experts estimate that 50 to 70% of all diseases are caused by lifestyle choices under our control.[84]

2. *Nutritional awareness.* Because we are what we eat, try to increase your consumption of foods high in fiber, vitamins, and nutrients— such as fresh fruits and vegetables, poultry, and fish—while decreasing those high in sugar and fat.

3. *Stress reduction and relaxation.* Use techniques to relax and reduce the symptoms of stress.

4. *Physical fitness.* Exercise regularly to maintain strength, flexibility, endurance, and a healthy body weight. A review of employee fitness programs indicated that they were a

by David Waisglass
Gordon Coulthart

Farcus

© 1991 Farcus Cartoons   WAISGLASS/COULTHART

www.farcus.com

When stress management works too well.

cost-effective way to reduce medical costs, absenteeism, turnover, and occupational injuries. Fitness programs also were positively linked with job performance and job satisfaction.[85]

5. *Environmental sensitivity.* Be aware of your environment and try to identify the stressors that are causing your stress. A control coping strategy might be useful to eliminate stressors.

Summary of Key Concepts

1. *Discuss the external and internal forces that create the need for organizational change.* Organizations encounter both external and internal forces for change. There are five key external forces for change: demographic characteristics, technological advancements, customer and market changes, social and political pressures, and organizational crises. Internal forces for change come from both human resource problems and managerial behavior/decisions.

2. *Describe Lewin's change model and the systems model of change.* Lewin developed a three-stage model of planned change that explained how to initiate, manage, and stabilize the change process. The three stages were unfreezing, which entails creating the motivation to change, changing, and stabilizing change through refreezing. A systems model of change takes a big picture perspective of change. It focuses on the interaction among the key components of change. The three main components of change are inputs, target elements of change, and outputs. The target elements of change represent the components of an organization that may be changed. They include organizational arrangements, social factors, methods, and people.

3. *Discuss Kotter's eight steps for leading organizational change.* John Kotter believes that organizational change fails for one or more of eight common errors. He proposed eight steps that organizations should follow to overcome these errors. The eight steps are (1) establish a sense of urgency, (2) create the guiding coalition, (3) develop a vision and strategy, (4) communicate the change vision, (5) empower broad-based action, (6) generate short-term wins, (7) consolidate gains and produce more change, and (8) anchor new approaches in the culture.

4. *Define organization development (OD), and demonstrate your familiarity with its four identifying characteristics.* Organization development is a set of tools or techniques that are used to implement planned organizational change. OD is broader in focus and has a diagnostic focus. The identifying characteristics of OD are that it involves profound change, is value loaded, is a diagnosis/ prescription cycle, and is process oriented.

5. *Summarize the 11 reasons employees resist change.* Resistance to change is an emotional/behavioral response to real or imagined threats to an established work routine. Eleven reasons employees resist change are (1) an individual's predisposition toward change, (2) surprise and fear of the unknown, (3) climate of mistrust, (4) fear of failure, (5) loss of status or job security, (6) peer pressure, (7) disruption of cultural traditions or group relationships, (8) personality conflicts, (9) lack of tact or poor timing, (10) nonreinforcing reward systems, and (11) past success.

6. *Discuss the five personal characteristics related to resistance to change.* The first entails an employee's commitment to change, which reflects a mind-set of doing whatever it takes to effectively implement change. Resilience to change, a composite characteristic reflecting high self-esteem, optimism, and an internal locus of control, is the second personal characteristic. People with a positive self-concept and a tolerance for risk also handle change better than those without these two dispositions. High levels of self-efficacy also are negatively associated with resistance to change.

7. *Identify alternative strategies for overcoming resistance to change.* Organizations must be ready for change. Assuming an organization is ready for change, the alternative strategies for overcoming resistance to change are education + communication, participation + involvement, facilitation + support, negotiation + agreement, manipulation + co-optation, and explicit + implicit coercion. Each has its situational appropriateness and advantages and drawbacks.

8. *Define the term* stress *and describe the model of occupational stress.* Stress is an adaptive reaction to environmental demands or stressors that triggers a fight-or-flight response. This response creates hormonal changes that mobilize the body for extraordinary demands. According to the occupational model of stress, the stress process begins when an individual cognitively appraises stressors. This appraisal then motivates an individual to choose a coping strategy aimed at reducing stressors, which, in turn, results in a variety of stress outcomes.

9. *Discuss the stress moderators of social support, hardiness, and Type A behavior.* People use each of these moderators to help reduce the impact of stressors that are appraised as harmful, threatening, or challenging. Social support represents the amount of perceived helpfulness derived from social relationships. People use four types of support (esteem, informational, social, and instrumental) to reduce the impact of stress. Hardiness is a collection of personality characteristics that neutralize stress. It includes the characteristics of commitment, locus of control, and challenge. The Type A behavior pattern is characterized by someone who is aggressively involved in a chronic, determined struggle to accomplish more and more in less and less time. Management can help Type A individuals by not overloading them with work despite their apparent eagerness to take on an ever-increasing workload.

10. *Discuss employee assistance programs (EAPs) and a holistic approach toward stress reduction.* Employee assistance programs help employees to resolve personal problems that affect their productivity. EAPs are typically funded by organizations or in combination with unions. A holistic approach toward wellness goes beyond stress-reduction techniques by advocating that people strive for a harmonious balance among physical, mental, and social well-being. This approach to stress management has five key components: self-responsibility, nutritional awareness, stress reduction and relaxation, physical fitness, and environmental sensitivity.

Key Terms

OB in Action Case Study

Managers at Best Buy Covertly Created Organizational Change[86]

BusinessWeek At most companies, going AWOL during daylight hours would be grounds for a pink slip. Not at Best Buy. The nation's leading electronics retailer has embarked on a radical—if risky—experiment to transform a culture once known for killer hours and herd-riding bosses. The endeavor, called ROWE, for "results-only work environment," seeks to demolish decades-old business dogma that equates physical presence with productivity. The goal at Best Buy is to judge performance on output instead of hours. . . .

The official policy for this post-face-time, location-agnostic way of working is that people are free to work wherever they want, whenever they want, as long as they get their work done. "This is like TiVo for your work," says the program's co-founder, Jody Thompson. By the end of 2007, all 4,000 staffers working at corporate will be on ROWE. Starting in February, the new work environment will become an official part of Best Buy's recruiting pitch as well as its orientation for new hires. And the company plans to take its clockless campaign to its stores—a high-stakes challenge that no company has tried before in a retail environment.

Another thing about this experiment: It wasn't imposed from the top down. It began as a covert guerrilla action that spread virally and eventually became a revolution. So secret was the operation that Chief Executive Brad Anderson only learned the details two years after it began transforming his company. Such bottom-up, stealth innovation is exactly the kind of thing Anderson encourages. The Best Buy chief aims to keep innovating even when something is ostensibly working. "ROWE was an idea born and nurtured by a handful of passionate employees," he says. "It wasn't created as the result of some edict." . . .

The CEO may have bought in, but there has been plenty of opposition inside the company. Many execs wondered if the program was simply flextime in a prettier bottle. Others felt that working off-site would lead to longer hours and destroy forever the demarcation between work and personal time. Cynics thought it was all a PR stunt dreamed up by Machiavellian operatives in human resources. And as ROWE infected one department after the other, its supporters ran into old-guard saboteurs, who continue to plot an overthrow and spread warnings of a coming paradise for slackers.

Then again, the new work structure's proponents say it's helping Best Buy overcome challenges. And thanks to early successes, some of the program's harshest critics have become true believers. With gross margins on electronics under pressure, and Wal-Mart Stores Inc. and Target Corp. shouldering into Best Buy territory, the company has been moving into services, including its Geek Squad and "customer centricity" program in which salespeople act as technology counselors. But Best Buy was afflicted by stress, burnout, and high turnover. The hope was that ROWE, by freeing employees to make their own work-life decisions, could boost morale and productivity and keep the service initiative on track. . . .

ROWE may also help the company pay for the customer centricity campaign. The endeavor is hugely expensive because it involves tailoring stores to local markets and training employees to turn customer feedback into new business ideas. By letting people work off-campus, Best Buy figures it can reduce the need for corporate office space, perhaps rent out the empty cubicles to other companies, and plow the millions of dollars in savings into its services initiative. . . .

Jody Thompson and Cali Ressler are two HR people you actually don't hate. They groan over cultish corporate slogans like "Build Superior Organizational Capability." They disdain Outlook junkies who double-book and showboating Power Pointers, But it's flextime, or Big Business' answer to overwork, long commutes, and lack of work-family balance, that elicits the harshest verdict. "A con game," says Thompson. "A total joke," adds Ressler.

Flexible work schedules, they say, heap needless bureaucracy on managers instead of addressing the real issue: how to work more efficiently in an era of transcontinental teams and multiple time zones. They add that flextime also stigmatizes those who use it (the reason so few do) and keeps companies acting like the military (fixated on schedules) when they should behave more like MySpace (social networks where real-time innovation can flourish). Besides, they say, if people can virtually carry their office around in their pockets or pocket books, why should it matter where and when they work if they are crushing their goals? . . .

Outside the office, Thompson and Ressler couldn't help noticing how wireless broadband was turning the world into one giant work kibbutz. They talked about how managers were mired in analog-age inertia, often judging performance on how much they saw you, vs. how much you did. Ressler and Thompson recognized the danger-

ous, life-wrecking cocktail in the making: The always-on worker now also had to be always in.

The culture, not exactly Minnesota-nice, was threatening Best Buy's massive expansion plans. But Ressler and Thompson knew their solution was too radical to simply trot up to CEO Anderson. Nor, in the beginning, did they feel they could lobby their executive supervisors for official approval. Besides, they knew the usual corporate route of imposing something from the top down would bomb. So they met in private, stealthily strategizing about how to protect ROWE and then dribble it out under the radar in tiny pilot trials. Ressler and Thompson waited patiently for the right opportunity.

It came in 2003. Two managers—one in the properties division, the other in communications—were desperate. Top performers were complaining of unsustainable levels of stress, threatening business continuity just when Best Buy was rolling out its customer centricity campaign in hundreds of stores. They also knew from employee engagement data that workers were suffering from the classic work-life hex: jobs with high demands (always-on, transcontinental availability) and low control (always on-site, no personal life).

Ressler and Thompson saw their opening in these two vanguard managers. Would they be willing to partake in a private management experiment? The two outlined their vision. They explained how in the world of ROWE, there would be no mandatory meetings. No times when you had to physically be at work. Performance would be based on output, not hours. Managers would base assessments on data and evidence, not feelings and anecdotes. The executives liked what they heard and agreed.

The experiment quickly gained social networking heat. Waiting in line at Best Buy's on-site Caribou Coffee, in e-mails, and during drive-by's at friends' desks, employees in other parts of the company started hearing about this seeming antidote to megahour agita. A curious culture of haves and have-nots emerged on the Best Buy campus, with those in ROWE sporting special stickers on their laptops as though they were part of some cabal. Hance, the hunter, started taking conference calls in tree stands and exchanging e-mails from his fishing boat. When Wells wasn't following around Dave Matthews, chances were he was biking around Minneapolis' network of urban lakes, and digging into work only after night had fallen. Hourly workers were still putting in a full 40, but began doing so wherever and whenever they wanted.

At first, participants were loath to share anything about ROWE with higher-ups for fear the perk would be taken away or reversed. But by 2004, loftier and loftier levels of management began hearing about the experiment at about the time opposition to it grew more intense. Critics feared executives would lose control and co-workers would forfeit the collaboration born of proximity. If you can work anywhere, they asked, won't you always be working? Won't overbearing bosses start calling you in the middle of the night? Won't coasters see

ROWE as a way to shirk work and force more dedicated colleagues to pick up the slack? And there were generational conflicts: Some boomers felt they'd been forced to choose between work and life during their careers. So everyone else should, too.

Shari Ballard, Best Buy's executive vice-president for human capital and leadership (an analog title if ever there was one), was originally skeptical, although she eventually bought in. At first she couldn't figure out why managers needed a new methodology to help solve the work-life conundrum. "It wasn't hugs and smiles," she says of Ressler's and Thompson's campaign. "Managers in the old mental model were totally irritated." In the e-learning division, many of Wells's older co-workers (read 40-year-olds; the average age at Best Buy is 36) expressed resentment over the change, insisting that work relationships are better face-to-face, not screen-to-screen. "We have people in our group who are like, 'I'm not going to do it,'" says Wells, who likes to sleep in and doesn't own an alarm clock. "I'm like, 'that's fine, but I'm outta here.'" In enemy circles, Ressler and Thompson are known to this day as "those two" and "the subversives."

Yet ROWE continues to spread through the company. If intrigued nonparticipants work for progressive superiors, they usually talk up the program and get their bosses to agree to trials. If they toil under clock-watchers, they form underground networks and quietly lobby for outside support until there is usually no choice but for their boss to switch. It was only this past summer that CEO Anderson got a full briefing, and total understanding, about what was happening. "We purposely waited until the tipping point before we took it to him," says Thompson. Until then he wasn't well-versed on the 13 ROWE commandments. No. 1: People at all levels stop doing any activity that is a waste of their time, the customer's time, or the company's money. No. 7: Nobody talks about how many hours they work. No. 9: It's O.K. to take a nap on a Tuesday afternoon, grocery shop on Wednesday morning, or catch a movie on Thursday afternoon. . . .

Ressler and Thompson had convinced [Chad] Achen that ROWE would work. Now Achen would have to convince the general manager of BestBuy.com, senior vice-president John. "J.T." Thompson. That wasn't going to be easy. Thompson, a former General Electric Co. guy, was as old school as they come with his starched shirt, booming voice, and ramrod-straight posture. He came of age believing there were three 8-hour days in every 24 hours. He loved working in his office on weekends. At first, he pushed back hard. "I was not supportive," says Thompson, who was privately terrified about the loss of control. "He didn't want anything to do with it," says Achen "He was all about measurement, and he kept asking me, 'How are you going to measure this so you know you're getting the same productivity out of people?'"

That's where Achen's performance metrics came in handy. He could measure how many orders per hour his team was processing no matter where they were. He told

Thompson he'd reel everyone back to campus the minute he noticed a dip. Within a month, Achen could see that not only was his team's productivity up, but engagement scores, or measuring job satisfaction and retention, were the highest in the dotcom division's history.

For years, engagement had been a sore spot for Thompson. "I showed J.T. these scores, and his eyes lit up," says Achen. Thompson rushed to roll out ROWE to his entire department. Voluntary turnover among men dropped from 16.11% to 0. "For years I had been focused on the wrong currency," says Thompson. "I was always looking to see if people were here. I should have been looking at what they were getting done."

Today, Achen's commuting employee usually comes in once a week. Nearly three-quarters of his staff spend most of their time out of the office. Doesn't he worry that he loses some of the interoffice magic when they don't gather together all day, every day? What about the value in riffing on one another's ideas? What about teamwork and camaraderie? "You absolutely lose some of that," he says. "But what we get back far outweighs anything we've lost."

Achen says he would never go back. Orders processed by people who are not working in the office are up 13% to 18% over those who are. ROWE'ers are posting higher metrics for quality, too. Achen says he believes that's due to the new office paradox: Given the constant distractions, it sometimes feels impossible to get any work done at work. . . .

Next year Ressler and Thompson plan to pilot their boldest move yet, testing ROWE in retail stores among both managers and workers. How exactly they will do this in an environment where salespeople presumably need to put in regular hours, they won't say. And they acknowledge it won't be easy. Still, they are eager to try just about anything to help the company slash its 65% turnover rates in stores, where disgruntlement is common and workers form groups on MySpace with names like "Best Buy Losers Club!"

Questions for Discussion

1. What were the external and internal forces for change at Best Buy?
2. How did Jody Thompson and Cali Ressler use the three components of Lew's model of change to create change? Explain.
3. ROWE changed many aspects of organizational behavior. Which of the target elements of change within the Systems Model of Change were affected by ROWE? Explain.
4. Which of the 11 causes of resistance to change were apparent in this case? Discuss your rationale.
5. What are the key obstacles to implementing ROWE in Best Buy's retail stores? How might they be overcome?

Ethical Dilemma

What Would You Do If Your Boss Had a Serious Mental Illness?[87]

Paul Gottlieb was a 40-something rising star in the publishing world, sought after for top positions at major book publishers in New York City. In meetings with authors, business associates, and employees, he was a take-charge executive. No one realized that sometimes at the end of the day, Mr Gottlieb would sit at his desk, exhausted, and think about jumping out the window. . . .

Coping with employee depression is increasingly on the minds of workplace managers. But what happens when the boss is the one with a mental illness? The repercussions on a business, its employees and stockholders can be enormous if the illness interferes with a leader's performance. . . .

Securities laws require public companies to disclose anything that materially affects the company, and that can theoretically include serious health problems of key executives.

Assume That Your Boss Suffers from a Serious Mental Condition and He or She Is Trying to Withhold This Information from Others? What Would You Do?

1. Nothing. The boss's mental condition is none of my business.
2. I would not say a word because I could be ignored or punished for saying anything. Identify the pros and cons of this option.
3. Discuss the issue only with my boss and encourage him or her to get help. Explain your rationale.
4. Discuss the issue with someone from the human resources department. Explain your rationale.
5. Invent other options. Discuss.

Web Resources

For study material and exercises that apply to this chapter, visit our Web site,
www.mhhe.com/kreitner

Photo Credits

Page 291 The McGraw-Hill Companies, Inc./
Lars A. Niki, photographer

Page 296 Ruby Arguilla-Tull/Bloomberg News/Landov

CHAPTER 11

Page 311 Lance Cpl. Jeremy T. Ross/United States Marine Corp

Page 316 © Denis/REA/Redux

Page 320 © AP/Wide World Photos

Page 322 © Andrew Lichtenstein/Getty Images

Page 327 Courtesy of Seagate

Page 328 © AP/Wide World Photos

CHAPTER 12

Page 335 © ITAR-TASS/Landov

Page 337 © Ethan Miller/Reuters

Page 341 © Ryan McVay/Getty Images

Page 354 © Mark Romanelli/Jupiter Images

CHAPTER 13

Page 375 © PRAKASH SINGH/AFP/Getty Images

Page 378 © AP/Wide World Photos

Page 379 © Greg Baker/Reuters

Page 389 © Chad Buchanan/Getty Images

CHAPTER 14

Page 400 © AP/Wide World Photos

Page 402 © Brand X Pictures/PunchStock

Page 413 © Jon Feingersh/Getty Images

Page 418 © Robyn Twomey/Corbis Outline

CHAPTER 15

Page 438 © Bob O'Connor Photography

Page 440 © AP/Wide World Photos

Page 442 © REUTERS/ARC-Dominic Favre

Page 448 © TRUMP PROD./MARK BURNETT PROD./
THE KOBAL COLLECTION

CHAPTER 16

Page 461 © AP/Wide World Photos

Page 468 © NBC/Photofest

Page 476 © Adam Auel

Page 480 © J. Gaiger/Topical Press Agency/Getty Images

Page 482 © AP/Wide World Photos

Page 489 Courtesy of Whole Foods Market

CHAPTER 17

Page 503 © Reuters/Corbis

Page 504 © Getty Images

Page 507 RF/Corbis

Page 513 Courtesy of Dell

Page 517 © Brian Park

Page 523 © AP/Wide World Photos

CHAPTER 18

Page 531 © ImagineChina

Page 534 © AP/Wide World Photos

Page 547 The McGraw-Hill Companies, Inc./
Andrew Resek, photographer

Page 551 Digital Vision/Getty Images

Page 555 © Digital Vision

Endnotes

CHAPTER I

[1] Excerpted from S Hamm, "A Passion for the Planet," *BusinessWeek,* August 21–28, 2006, pp 92–94.

[2] Based on Jeffrey Pfeffer, *The Human Equation: Building Profits by Putting People First* (Boston: Harvard Business School Press, 1998); and Jeffrey Pfeffer and John F. Veiga, "Putting People First for Organizational Success," *Academy of Management Executive,* May 1999, pp 37–48.

[3] Data from Pfeffer and Veiga, "Putting People First for Organizational Success," p 47. Also see C A O'Reilly and Pfeffer, *Hidden Value: How Great Companies Achieve Extraordinary Results with Ordinary People* (Boston: Harvard Business School Press, 2000); and J Combs, Y Liu, A Hall, and D Ketchen, "How Much Do High-Performance Work Practices Matter? A Meta-Analysis of Their Effects on Organizational Performance," *Personnel Psychology,* Autumn 2006, pp 501–528.

[4] As quoted in G Colvin, "How One CEO Learned to Fly," *Fortune,* October 30, 2006, p 98.

[5] Many inspiring examples of people-centered and ethical organizational practices can be found in "50 Best Small and Medium Places to Work," *HR Magazine,* July 2006, pp 42–61; and R Levering and M Moskowitz, "Fortune 100 Best Companies to Work For: 2007," *Fortune,* January 22, 2007, pp 94–116. Also see K Gurchiek, "Show Workers Their Value, Study Says," *HR Magazine,* October 2006, p 40; J Welch and S Welch, "Avoiding Strikes—and Unions," *BusinessWeek,* January 15, 2007, p 92; and P Sellers, "A Kinder, Gentler Lehman Brothers," *Fortune,* January 22, 2007, pp 36, 38.

[6] C I Barnard, *The Functions of the Executive* (Cambridge, MA: Harvard University Press, 1938), p 73.

[7] F Zakaria, "The Education of Paul Wolfowitz," *Newsweek,* March 28, 2005, p 37. Also see A S Wellner, "Gary Heavin Is on a Mission from God," *Inc.,* October 2006, pp 116–23.

[8] Data frod J B Miner, "The Rated Importance, Scientific Validity, and Practical Usefulness of Organizational Behavior Theories: A Quantitative Review," *Academy of Management Learning and Education,* September 2003, pp 250–68. Also see M R Blood, "Only *You* Can Create Actionable Knowledge," *Academy of Management Learning and Education,* June 2006, pp 209–12; and G Symon and C Cassell, "Neglected Perspectives in Work and Organizational Psychology," *Journal of Occupational and Organizational Psychology,* September 2006, pp 307–14.

[9] E E Lawler III, *Treat People Right! How Organizations and Individuals Can Propel Each Other into a Virtuous Spiral of Success* (San Francisco: Jossey-Bass, 2003), p 19.

[10] Excerpted from J Welch and S Welch, "Growing Up but Staying Young," *BusinessWeek,* December 11, 2006, p 112.

[11] B S Lawrence, "Historical Perspective: Using the Past to Study the Present," *Academy of Management Review,* April 1984, p 307.

[12] See L T Benjamin Jr., "Hugo Munsterberg's Attack on the Application of Scientific Psychology," *Journal of Applied Psychology,* March 2006, pp 414–25.

[13] Evidence indicating that the original conclusions of the famous Hawthorne studies were unjustified may be found in RG Greenwood, A A Bolton, and R A Greenwood, "Hawthorne a Half Century Later: Relay Assembly Participants Remember," *Journal of Management,* Fall–Winter 1983, pp 217–31; and R H Franke and J D Kaul, "The Hawthorne Experiments: First Statistical Interpretation," *American Sociological Review,* October 1978, pp 623–43. For a positive interpretation of the Hawthorne studies, see J A Sonnenfeld, "Shedding Light on the Hawthorne Studies," *Journal of Occupational Behaviour,* April 1985, pp 111–30.

[14] See M Parker Follett, *Freedom and Coordination* (London: Management Publications Trust, 1949).

[15] See D McGregor, *The Human Side of Enterprise* (New York: McGraw-Hill, 1960).

[16] A manager's Theory X and Y management challenges are illustrated in A Fisher, "Changing Course," *Fortune,* November 27, 2006, p 278.

[17] S Bates, "Getting Engaged," *HR Magazine,* February 2004, pp 44, 46.

[18] See D W Organ, "Elusive Phenomena," *Business Horizons,* March–April 2002, pp 1–2.

[19] See, for example, R Zemke, "TQM: Fatally Flawed or Simply Unfocused?" *Training,* October 1992, p 8.

[20] R O Crockett, "Six Sigma Pays Off at Motorola," *BusinessWeek,* December 4, 2006, p 50. Also see K Richardson, "The 'Six Sigma' Factor for Home Depot," *The Wall Street Journal,* January 4, 2007, p C3; and B Hindo, "Six Sigma: So Yesterday?" Innovation Inside, *BusinessWeek,* June 2007, p 11.

[21] J McGregor, "The Performance Paradox," *Fast Company,* April 2005, pp 29–30. Also see A Levin, "Fewer Crashes Caused by Pilots," *USA Today,* March 2, 2004, p 1A.

[22] For example, see C Kalb, "Fixing America's Hospitals," *Newsweek,* October 16, 2006, pp 44–68; D M Berwick and L L Leape, "Perfect Is Possible," *Newsweek,* October 16, 2006, pp 70–71; and I Rowley, "Even Toyota Isn't Perfect," *BusinessWeek,* January 22, 2007, p 54.

[23] M Sashkin and K J Kiser, *Putting Total Quality Management to Work* (San Francisco: Berrett-Koehler, 1993), p 39.

[24] R J Schonberger, "Total Quality Management Cuts a Broad Swath—Through Manufacturing and Beyond," *Organizational Dynamics,* Spring 1992, p 18. Also see R Gulati and J B Oldroyd, "The Quest for Customer Focus," *Harvard Business Review,* April 2005, pp 92–101; and A Tilin, "Vespa Goes Back to School," *Business 2.0,* April 2005, p 24.

[25] Based on C Hui, S S K Lam, and J Schaubroeck, "Can Good Citizens Lead the Way in Providing Quality Service? A Field Quasi Experiment," *Academy of Management Journal,* October 2001, pp 988–95. Also See J Pfeffer, "How Companies Get Smart," *Business 2.0,* January–February 2005, p 74.

[26] Deming's landmark work is W E Deming, *Out of the Crisis* (Cambridge, MA: MIT, 1986).

[27] See M Trumbull, "What Is Total Quality Management?" *The Christian Science Monitor,* May 3, 1993, p 12; J Hillkirk, "World-Famous Quality Expert Dead at 93," *USA Today,* December 21, 1993, pp 1B–2B; and O Port, "The Kings of Quality," *BusinessWeek,* August 30, 2004, p 20.

[28] Based on discussion in M Walton, *Deming Management at Work* (New York: Putnam/Perigee, 1990).

[29] Ibid., p 20.

[30] Adapted from D E Bowen and E E Lawler III, "Total Quality-Oriented Human Resources Management," *Organizational Dynamics,* Spring 1992, pp 29–41.

[31] For details, see T J Douglas and W Q Judge Jr, "Total Quality Management Implementation and Competitive Advantage: The Role of Structural Control and Exploration," *Academy of Management Journal,* February 2001, pp 158–69; and K B Hendricks and V R Singhal, "The Long-Run Stock Price Performance of Firms with Effective TQM Programs," *Management Science,* March 2001, pp 359–68.

[32] See, for example, C Fishman, "No Satisfaction," *Fast Company,* January 2007, pp 82–92; and B Hindo, "A Dynamo Called Danaher," *BusinessWeek,* February 19, 2007, pp 56–60.

[33] See S Baker, "Wiser About the Web," *BusinessWeek,* March 27, 2006, pp 54–58; S Levy and B Stone, "The New Wisdom of the Web," *Newsweek,* April 3, 2006, pp 46–53; B Einhorn, "China: Falling Hard for Web 2.0," *BusinessWeek,* January 15, 2007, pp 66–67; and D Kirkpatrick, "It's Not a Game. The 3-D Online Experience Second Life Is a Hit with Users. IBM's Sam Palmisano and Other Tech Leaders Think It Could Be a Gold Mine," *Fortune,* February 5, 2007, pp 56–62.

[34] M J Mandel and R D Hof, "Rethinking the Internet," *BusinessWeek,* March 26, 2001, p 118. Also see G T Lumpkin and G G Dess, "E-Business Strategies and Internet Business Models: How the Internet Adds Value," *Organizational Dynamics,* no. 2, 2004, pp 161–73.

[35] A Bernasek, "Buried in Tech," *Fortune,* April 16, 2001, p 52.

[36] R D Hof, "Web 2.0: The New Guy at Work," *BusinessWeek,* June 19, 2006, p 58.

[37] See D Hartley, "Wireless Wonders," *Training and Development,* March 2006, pp 23–25; M Weinstein, "The Do's and Don'ts of E-Learning—the Initial Security Story," *Training,* June 2006, p 10; and K Kleps, "Virtual Sales Training Scores a Hit," *Training and Development,* December 2006, pp 63–64.

[38] See R J Grossman, "Blind Investment," *HR Magazine,* January 2005, pp 40–47; and A Pomeroy, "People Are Our Greatest Asset," *HR Magazine,* April 2005, p 20.

[39] For details on these trends, see G Toppo, "One in 20 U.S. Adults Lack Basic English Skills," *USA Today,* December 16, 2005, p 1A; D Brady, "Take This Job and Customize It," *BusinessWeek,* April 24, 2006, p 108; H Dolezalek, "Outta Here: Are You Ready for the Baby Boomers to Retire? You Should Be. . .," *Training,* September 2006, pp 19–23; and "Florida Findings," *Training,* January–February 2007, p 8.

[40] B E Becker, M A Huselid, and D Ulrich, *The HR Scorecard: Linking People, Strategy, and Performance* (Boston: Harvard Business School Press, 2001), p 4.

[41] See R E Ployhart, J A Weekley, and K Baughman, "The Structure and Function of Human Capital Emergence: A Multilevel Examination of the Attraction-Selection-Attrition Model," *Academy of Management Journal,* August 2006, pp 661–77; D A Griffith, "Human Capital in the Supply Chain of Global Firms," *Organizational Dynamics,* no. 3, 2006, pp 251–263; M Laff, "Talent Management: From Hire to Retire," *Training and Development,* November 2006, pp 42–48; S S R Datta, "Measuring Minds at Work," *Business 2.0,* November 2006, p 36; and H Dolezalek, "Got High Potential?" *Training,* January–February 2007, pp 18–22.

[42] See O Port, "Meet the Best and Brightest," *BusinessWeek,* March 28, 2005, pp 88–91. B Einhorn, "In China's Net Cafes, Intel Pours It On," *BusinessWeek,* November 6, 2006, p 52; and "Teen Scientists Awarded Siemens Prizes," *USA Today,* December 5, 2006, p 9D.

[43] Data from "The 100 Best Companies to Work For," *Fortune,* February 4, 2002, p 84.

[44] Inspired by P S Adler and S Kwon, "Social Capital: Prospects for a New Concept," *Academy of Management Review,* January 2002, pp 17–40. Also see H Oh, G Labianca, and M Chung, "A Multilevel Model of Group Social Capital," *Academy of Management Review,* July 2006, pp 569–82; N T Nguyen, C L Allen, and R L Godkin, "Recruiters' Assessment and Use of Social Capital in Resume Screening," *Journal of Applied Social Psychology,* August 2006, pp 1813–832; and M V Copeland, "The Missing Link," *Business 2.0,* December 2006, pp 118–24.

[45] L Prusak and D Cohen, "How to Invest in Social Capital," *Harvard Business Review,* June 2001, p 93.

[46] Data from "What Makes a Job OK," *USA Today,* May 15, 2000, p 1B.

[47] See B C Holtom, T R Mitchell, and T W Lee, "Increasing Human and Social Capital by Applying Job Embeddedness Theory," *Organizational Dynamics,* no. 4, 2006, pp 316–31.

[48] See W B Werther, "From Manager to Executive," *Organizational Dynamics,* no. 35, 2006, pp 196–204; M Fitzgerald, "Can You Ace This Test? A New Exam Forces Managers to Prove Their Mettle," *Fast Company,* February 2007, p 27; and J Welch and S Welch, "That's Management!" *BusinessWeek,* February 19, 2007, p 94.

[49] H Mintzberg, "The Manager's Job: Folklore and Fact," *Harvard Business Review,* July–August 1975, p 61. Also see J Gosling and H Mintzberg, "The Five Minds of

a Manager," *Harvard Business Review,* November 2003, pp 54–63; and H Mintzberg, "Third-Generation Management Development, *Training and Development,* March 2004, pp 28–38.

[50] M Adams, "Boeing Bounces Back Against Odds," *USA Today,* January 11, 2007, p 2b.

[51] See, for example, H Mintzberg, "Managerial Work: Analysis from Observation," *Management Science,* October 1971, pp B97–B110; and F Luthans, "Successful vs. Effective Real Managers," *Academy of Management Executive,* May 1988, pp 127–32. For an instructive critique of the structured observation method, see M J Martinko and W L Gardner, "Beyond Structured Observation: Methodological Issues and New Directions," *Academy of Management Review,* October 1985, pp 676–95. Also see N Fondas, "A Behavioral Job Description for Managers," *Organizational Dynamics,* Summer 1992, pp 47–58.

[52] See L B Kurke and H E Aldrich, "Mintzberg Was Right!: A Replication and Extension of *The Nature of Managerial Work,*" *Management Science,* August 1983, pp 975–84.

[53] For example, see L A Hill, "Becoming the Boss," *Harvard Business Review,* Special Issue: The Tests of a Leader, January 2007, pp 48–56.

[54] Validation studies can be found in E Van Velsor and J B Leslie, *Feedback to Managers, Volume II: A Review and Comparison of Sixteen Multi-Rater Feedback Instruments* (Greensboro, NC: Center for Creative Leadership, 1991); F Shipper, "A Study of the Psychometric Properties of the Managerial Skill Scales of the Survey of Management Practices," *Educational and Psychological Measurement,* June 1995, pp 468–79; and C L Wilson, *How and Why Effective Managers Balance Their Skills: Technical, Teambuilding, Drive* (Columbia, MD: Rockatech Multimedia Publishing, 2003).

[55] For example, see S D Bartram, "The Great Eight Competencies: A Criterion-Centric Approach to Validation," *Journal of Applied Psychology,* November 2005, pp 1185–203; and M Morrison, "The Very Model of a Modern Senior Manager," *Harvard Business Review,* Special Issue: The Tests of a Leader, January 2007, pp. 27–39.

[56] See F Shipper, "Mastery and Frequency of Managerial Behaviors Relative to Sub-Unit Effectiveness," *Human Relations,* April 1991, pp 371–88.

[57] Ibid.

[58] Data from F Shipper, "A Study of Managerial Skills of Women and Men and Their Impact on Employees' Attitudes and Career Success in a Nontraditional Organization," paper presented at the Academy of Management Meeting, August 1994, Dallas, Texas. The same outcome for on-the-job studies is reported in A H Eagly and B T Johnson, "Gender and Leadership Style: A Meta-Analysis," *Psychological Bulletin,* September 1990, pp 233–56.

[59] For instance, see J B Rosener, "Ways Women Lead," *Harvard Business Review,* November–December 1990, pp 119–25; and C Lee, "The Feminization of Management," *Training,* November 1994, pp 25–31.

[60] A similar finding is reported in J Kornik, "Bosses Say They're Great: Employees not So Sure," *Training,* October 2006, p 20.

[61] Based on F Shipper and J E Dillard Jr, "A Study of Impending Derailment and Recovery of Middle Managers across Career Stages," *Human Resource Management,* Winter 2000, pp 331–45. Also see K Sulkowicz, "When You're the Abusive Boss's Pet," *BusinessWeek,* January 15, 2007, p 14; B Grow, "Out at Home Depot," *BusinessWeek,* January 15, 2007, pp 56–62; and L Buchanan, "The Bully Rulebook: How to Deal with Jerks," *Inc.,* February 2007, pp 43–44.

[62] See B Morris, "The New Rules," *Fortune,* July 24, 2006, pp 70–87.

[63] Essential sources on reengineering are M Hammer and J Champy, *Reengineering the Corporation: A Manifesto for Business Revolution* (New York: HarperCollins, 1993); and J Champy, *Reengineering Management: The Mandate for New Leadership* (New York: HarperCollins, 1995). Also see "Anything Worth Doing Is Worth Doing from Scratch," *Inc.,* May 18, 1999 (20th Anniversary Issue), pp 51–52.

[64] See C A Beatty and B A Barker Scott, *Building Smart Teams: A Roadmap to High Performance* (Thousand Oaks, CA: Sage, 2004); G Colvin, "Why Dream Teams Fail," *Fortune,* June 12, 2006, pp 87–92; S Covey, "The Keys to Success," *Training,* September 2006, p 48; J Brett, K Behfar, M C Kern, "Managing Multicultural Teams," *Harvard Business Review,* November 2006, pp 83–91; and B Groysberg and R Abrahams, "Lift Outs: How to Acquire a High-Functioning Team," *Harvard Business Review,* December 2006, pp 133–40.

[65] See J E Mathieu, L L Gilson, and T M Ruddy, "Empowerment and Team Effectiveness: An Empirical Test of an Integrated Model," *Journal of Applied Psychology,* January 2006, pp 97–108; A Srivastava, K M Bartol, and E A Locke, "Empowering Leadership in Management Teams: Effects on Knowledge Sharing, Efficacy, and Performance," *Academy of Management Journal,* December 2006, pp 1239–251; and R Grover, "How Bob Iger Unchained Disney," *BusinessWeek,* February 5, 2007, pp 74–79.

[66] M Buckingham, "What Great Managers Do," *Harvard Business Review,* March 2005, pp 70–79. Also see M Buckingham, *One Thing You Need to Know: . . . About Great Managing, Great Leading, and Sustained Individual Success* (New York: Free Press, 2005); J J Salopek, "Leadership For a New Age," *Training and Development,* June 2006, pp 22–23; J Useem, "Five Levels of Excellence," *Fortune,* October 30, 2006, pp 176–77; and R S Kaplan, "What to Ask the Person in the Mirror," *Harvard Business Review,* Special Issue: The Tests of a Leader, January 2007, pp 86–95.

[67] As quoted in P LaBarre, "The Industrial Revolution," *Fast Company,* November 2003, pp 116, 118. The contingency approach was used in G E R Tummers, G G van Merode, and J A Landeweerd, "Organizational Characteristics as Predictors of Nurses' Psychological Work Reactions," *Organization Studies,* April 2006, pp 559–84.

[68] See G Johns, "The Essential Impact of Context on Organizational Behavior," *Academy of Management Review,* April 2006, pp 386–408.

[69] Data from N Varchaver, "Long Island Confidential," *Fortune,* November 27, 2006, pp 172–186. Also see M Orey, "Enron's Last Mystery," *BusinessWeek,* June 12, 2006, pp 28, 30; R W Clement, "Just How Unethical Is American Business?" *Business Horizons,* July-August 2006, pp 313–27; and H Maurer, "Hyundai's Black Eye," *BusinessWeek,* February 19, 2007, pp 30–31.

[70] See P Falcone, "Reporting for SOX Duty," *HR Magazine,* June 2006, pp 161–68; A Serwer, "Stop Whining About SarbOx!" *Fortune,* August 7, 2006, p 39; A L Nazareth, "Keeping SarbOx is Crucial," *BusinessWeek,* November 13, 2006, p 134; A Pomeroy, "Slashing SOX Costs Faster," *HR Magazine,* January 2007, pp 14, 16; and D Henry, "Not Everyone Hates SarbOx," *BusinessWeek,* January 29, 2007, p 37.

[71] Results can be found in "HR Poll Results," http://hr2.blr.com/index.cfm/Nav/11.0.0.0/Action/Poll_Question /qid/170, accessed April 8, 2005.

[72] Results can be found in Matthew Boyle, "By the Numbers: Liarliar!" *Fortune,* May 26, 2003, p 44.

[73] P Babcock, "Spotting Lies," *HR Magazine,* October 2003, p 47. Also see J Gill, "Smart Questions for Your Hiring Manager," *Inc.,* February 2007, p 47.

[74] See www.josephsoninstitute.org/pdf/workplace-flier_0604.pdf, accessed April 8, 2005.

[75] A discussion of ethics and financial performance is provided by R M Fulmer, "The Challenge of Ethical Leadership," *Organizational Dynamics,* August 2004, pp 307–17. Also see R Alsop, "How Boss's Deeds Buff a Firm's Reputation," *The Wall Street Journal,* January 31, 2007, pp B1–B2.

[76] Results can be found in "Tarnished Employment Brands Affect Recruiting," *HR Magazine,* November 2004, pp 16, 20.

[77] T M Jones, "Corporate Social Responsibility Revisited, Redefined," *California Management Review,* Spring 1980, pp 59–60. Also see P Engardio, "Beyond the Green Corporation," *BusinessWeek,* January 29, 2007, pp 50–64.

[78] See C M Sasse and R T Trahan, "Rethinking the New Corporate Philanthropy," *Business Horizons,* January–February 2007, pp 29–38.

[79] See, for example, E Iwata, "Businesses Grow More Socially Conscious," *USA Today,* February 14, 2007, p 3B.

[80] A B Carroll, "Managing Ethically with Global Stakeholders: A Present and Future Challenge," *Academy of Management Executive,* May 2004, p 118. Also see B W Husted and D B Allen, "Corporate Social Responsibility in the Multinational Enterprise: Strategic and Institutional Approaches," *Journal of International Business Studies,* November 2006, pp 838–49.

[81] Ibid., pp 117–18.

[82] T Kiuchi, "Fast Talk," *Fast Company,* January 2004, p 64.

[83] See C Gilligan, "In a Different Voice: Women's Conceptions of Self and Morality," *Harvard Educational Review,* November 1977, pp 481–517.

[84] Results can be found in S Jaffee and J Hyde, "Gender Differences in Moral Orientation: A Meta-Analysis," *Psychological Bulletin,* September 2000, pp 703–26.

[85] The following discussion is based on A J Daboub, A M A Rasheed, R L Priem, and D A Gray, "Top Management Team Characteristics and Corporate Illegal Activity," *Academy of Management Review,* January 1995, pp 138–70. Also see D A Waldman, M Sully de Luque, N Washburn, and R J House, "Cultural and Leadership Predictors of Corporate Social Responsibility Values of Top Management: a GLOBE Study of 15 Countries," *Journal of International Business Studies,* November 2006, pp 823–37.

[86] L Simpson, "Taking the High Road," *Training,* January 2002, p 38.

[87] Supporting results can be found in M E Schweitzer, L Ordóñez, and B Douma, "Goal Setting as a Motivator of Unethical Behavior," *Academy of Management Journal,* June 2004, pp 422–32.

[88] S Jayson, "Teens Face Up to Ethics Choices—If You Can Believe Them," *USA Today,* December 6, 2006, p 6D.

[89] Ibid.

[90] Supporting research can be found in J B Cullen, K P Parboteeah, and M Hoegl, "Cross-National Differences in Managers' Willingness to Justify Ethically Suspect Behaviors: A Test of Institutional Anomie Theory," *Academy of Management Journal,* June 2004, pp 411–21.

[91] Results can be found in T Jackson, "Cultural Values and Management Ethics: A 10-Nation Study," *Human Relations,* October 2001, pp 1267–302.

[92] The following discussion is based on Daboub et al., "Top Management Team Characteristics and Corporate Illegal Activity." Also see E White and T Herrick, "Ethical Breaches Pose Dilemma for Boards: When to Fire a CEO?" *The Wall Street Journal,* February 16, 2006, pp B1, B5.

[93] See Ch 6 in K Hodgson, *A Rock and a Hard Place: How to Make Ethical Business Decisions When the Choices Are Tough* (New York: AMACOM, 1992), pp 66–77.

[94] Adapted in part from W E Stead, D L Worrell, and J Garner Stead, "An Integrative Model for Understanding and Managing Ethical Behavior in Business Organizations," *Journal of Business Ethics,* March 1990, pp 233–42. Also see L Paine, R Deshpande, J D Margolis, and K E Bettcher, "Up to Code: Does Your Company's Conduct Meet World-Class Standards?" *Harvard Business Review,* December 2005, pp 122–33; E A Locke, "Business Ethics: A Way Out of the Morass," *Academy of Management Learning and Education,* September 2006, pp 324–32; and D C Kayes, D Stirling, and T M Nielsen, "Building Organizational Integrity," *Business Horizons,* January–February 2007, pp 61–70.

[95] For an excellent review of integrity testing, see D S Ones and C Viswesvaran, "Integrity Testing in Organizations," in *Dysfunctional Behavior in Organizations: Violent and Deviant Behavior,* eds R W Griffin et al. (Stamford, CT: JAI Press, 1998), pp 243–76. Also see J McGregor, "Background Checks That Never End," *BusinessWeek,* March 20, 2006, p 40.

[96] Guidelines for conducting ethics training are discussed by K Tyler, "Do the Right Thing," *HR Magazine,* February 2005, pp 99–101.

[97] See M Bartiromo, "The Ones Who Got Away," *BusinessWeek,* June 12, 2006, p 98; and C Rampell, "Whistle-Blowers Tell Cost of Conscience," *USA Today,* November 24, 2006, p 13A.

[98] As quoted in D Jones, "Military a Model for Execs," *USA Today,* June 9, 2004, p 4B.

[99] For a good discussion of values, see S D Steiner and M A Watson, "The Service Learning Component in Business Education: The Values Linkage Void," *Academy of Management Learning and Education,* December 2006, pp 422–34. For more on courage, see J McCain, "In Search of Courage," *Fast Company,* September 2004, pp 53–56; D Lidsky, "How Do You Rate? Take the Courage Quiz," *Fast Company,* September 2004, pp 107–09; and K K Reardon, "Courage," *Harvard Business Review,* Special Issue: The Tests of a Leader, January 2007, pp 58–64.

[100] Complete discussion of this technique can be found in J E Hunter, F L Schmidt, and G B Jackson, *Meta-Analysis: Cumulating Research Findings across Studies* (Beverly Hills, CA: Sage Publications, 1982); and J E Hunter and F L Schmidt, *Methods of Meta-Analysis: Correcting Error and Bias in Research Findings* (Newbury Park, CA: Sage Publications, 1990). Also see J Merrit and L Lavelle, "A Different Kind of Governance Guru," *BusinessWeek,* August 9, 2004, pp 46–47.

[101] Limitations of meta-analysis technique are discussed in P Bobko and E F Stone-Romero, "Meta-Analysis May Be Another Useful Tool, but It Is Not a Panacea, in *Research in Personnel and Human Resources Management,* vol. 16, ed G R Ferris (Stamford, CT: JAI Press, 1998), pp 359–97. Also see R A Peterson and S P Brown, "On the Use of Beta Coefficients in Meta-Analysis," *Journal of Applied Psychology.* January 2005, pp 175–81.

[102] L Tischler, "IBM's Management Makeover," *Fast Company,* November 2004, pp 112–13. For more on IBM, see S hamm, "Beyond Blue," *BusinessWeek,* April 18, 2005, pp 68–76. By Linda Tischler, © 2005 Gruner & Jahr USA Publishing. First published in *Fast Company* Magazine. Reprinted with permission.

[103] J Merritt, "You Mean Cheating Is Wrong?" *BusinessWeek,* December 9, 2002, p 8. Also see D L McCabe, K D Butterfield, and L K Treviño, "Academic Dishonesty in Graduate Business Programs: Prevalence, Causes, and Proposed Action," *Academy of Management Learning and Education,* September 2006, pp 294–305.

CHAPTER 2

[1] Excerpted from A Pomeroy, "She's Still Lovin' It," *HR Magazine,* December 2006, pp 59–60.

[2] L Wasmer Andrews, "Hard-Core Offenders," *HR Magazine,* December 2004, p 44.

[3] Excerpted from "Jury Awards $1.7M to Woman Spanked on Job," *USA Today,* May 16, 2006, http://www.usatoday.com/news/nation/2006-04-28-spanking-trial_x.htm.

[4] Taken from "Our Diversity Statement," February 21, 2007, http://sites.target.com/site/en/corporate/page.jsp?contentID=PRD03-002097.

[5] H Collingwood, "Who Handles a Diverse Work Force Best?" *Working Women,* February 1996, p 25.

[6] A description of Ford's program can be found in E Garsten, "Ford Muslim Workers Organize 'Islam,'" *Arizona Republic,* December 13, 2001, p D2.

[7] Excerpted from "Workforce Optimas Awards 2003," *Workforce,* March 2003, p 47.

[8] Information on equal employment opportunity legislation can be found in J R Mook, "Accommodation Paradigm Shifts," *HR Magazine,* January 2007, pp 115–20; A K Troutman, "Deja Review," *HR Magazine,* February 2007, pp 58–62; S Lau, V Neal, and L Albright, "Benefits Plan Eligibility, H-1B Visas, Job Offers," *HR Magazine,* February 2007, p 41; and J Deschenaux, "Insurers Required to Help Workers Quit Smoking," *HR Magazine,* February 2007, pp 25, 30.

[9] Results can be found in D A Harrison, D A Kravitz, D M Mayer, L M Leslie, and D Lev-Arey, "Understanding Attitudes Toward Affirmative Action Programs in Employment: Summary and Meta-Analysis of 35 Years of Research," *Journal of Applied Psychology,* September 2006, pp 1013–36.

[10] For a thorough review of relevant research, see M E Heilman, "Affirmative Action: Some Unintended Consequences for Working Women," in *Research in Organizational Behavior,* vol. 16, eds B M Staw and L L Cummings (Greenwich, CT: JAI Press, 1994), pp 125–69.

[11] Results from this study can be found in M E Heilman, W S Battle, C E Keller, and R A Lee, "Type of Affirmative Action Policy: A Determinant of Reactions to Sex-Based Preferential Selection?" *Journal of Applied Psychology,* April 1998, pp 190–205.

[12] A complete description of Wegmans' progressive managerial practices can be found in M Boyle, "The Wegmans Way," Fortune, January 24, 2005, pp 62–71. Also see R Levering and M Moskowitz, "100 Best Companies to Work for 2007: In Good Company," *Fortune,* January 22, 2007, p 94.

[13] A M Morrison, *The New Leaders: Guidelines on Leadership Diversity in America* (San Francisco: Jossey-Bass, 1992), p 78.

[14] Results can be found in N London-Vargas, *Faces of Diversity* (New York: Vantage Press, 1999).

[15] See S Capparell, "How Pepsi Opened Door to Diversity," *The Wall Street Journal,* January 9, 2007, pp B1–B2; and R Levering and M Moskowitz, "100 Best Companies to Work for 2007: In Good Company," *Fortune,* January 22, 2007, p 96.

[16] See R W Thompson, "Diversity among Managers Translates into Profitability," *HR Magazine,* April 1999, p 10; and M Jarman, "Glass Ceiling Hangs Low in Corporate Arizona," *The Arizona Republic,* March 4, 2007, pp A1, A21.

[17] See E Schine, "It's Fiesta Time at Goldman," *BusinessWeek,* February 5, 2007, p 9.

[18] These trends are discussed in "The New Commission on the Skills of the American Workforce," *Tough Choices or Tough Times* (San Francisco: Jossey-Bass, 2007); and "Immigration to the United States," *Wikipedia,* http://en.wikipedia.org/wiki/Immigration_to_the_United_States, last modified February 28, 2007.

[19] See "Florida Findings," *Training,* January/February 2007, p 8; "Comp and Hiring Landscape: Still Rocky in 2007, *HR Magazine,* February 2007, p 14; and S J Blakesley, "Hire Right the First Time," *Training,* November 2006, p 7.

[20] These statistics can be found in H Clark, "Are Women Happy Under the Glass Ceiling?" *Forbes,* March 8, 2006, http://www.forbes.com/ceonet/2006/03/07/glass-ceiling-opportunties–cx_hc_0308glass.html; and D Treftz, "Women Post Job Gains, Data Show," *The Wall Street Journal,* February 20, 2007, p A8.

[21] Results can be found in K S Lyness and D E Thompson, "Above the Glass Ceiling: A Comparison of Matched Samples of Female and Male Executives," *Journal of Applied Psychology,* June 1997, pp 359–75.

[22] This study was conducted by K S Lyness and M K Judiesch, "Are Women More Likely to Be Hired or Promoted into Management Positions?" *Journal of Vocational Behavior,* February 1999, pp 158–73.

[23] These statistics were obtained from B Fitzgerald, "Ms.-Fortune 500: Less Women Are Corporate Officers," *The Star Ledger,* February 22, 2007, http://www.nj.com/business/ledger/index.ssf?/base/business-5/1172123103202440.xml&c . . .; and "Women CEOs for Fortune 500 Companies," *CNNMoney.co,* http://money.cnn.com/magazines/fortune/fortune500/womenceos/, accessed February 28, 2007.

[24] Details of this study can be found in B R Ragins, B Townsend, and M Mattis, "Gender Gap in the Executive Suite: CEOs and Female Executives Report on Breaking the Glass Ceiling," *Academy of Management Review,* February 1998, pp 28–42.

[25] "Sara Lee Cleans Out Its Cupboards," *Fortune,* March 7, 2005, p 38.

[26] For details regarding these statistics, see G C Armas, "Almost Half of US Likely to be Minorities by 2050," *Arizona Republic,* March 18, 2004, p A5.

[27] Statistics are reported in "Job Type by Race in the U.S.," *MSN Encarta,* http://encarta.msn.com/media_461546975/Job_Type_by_Race_in_the_U_S.html, accessed March 1, 2007.

[28] These statistics were obtained from "Race-Based Charges FY 1997–2006," *The U.S. Equal Employment Opportunity Commission,* http://www.eeoc.gov/stats/race.html, last modified on January 31, 2007.

[29] See "Personal Income in the United States," *Wikipedia,* http://en.wikipedia.org/wiki/Personal_income_in_the_United_States, last modified February 20, 2007.

[30] Results were presented in S Jayson, "Young Blacks Feel the Sting," *USA Today,* February 1, 2007, p 6D. Also see "Accounting and Race: A Long Way to Go," *Training,* April 2006, p 15.

[31] Results can be found in E H James, "Race-Related Differences in Promotions and Support: Underlying Effects of Human and Social Capital," *Organization Science,* September–October 2000, pp 493–508.

[32] Representative studies were conducted by M S Bynum, E T Burton, and C Best, "Racism Experiences and Psychological Functioning in African American College Freshmen: Is Racial Socialization a Buffer?" *Cultural Diversity and Ethnic Minority Psychology,* January 2007, pp 64–71; A L Pieterse and R T Carter, "An Examination of the Relationship Between General Life Stress, Racism-Related Stress, and Psychological Health Among Black Men," *Journal of Counseling Psychology,* January 2007, pp 101–09; G M Walton and G L Cohen, "A Question of Belonging: Race, Social Fit, and Achievement," *Journal of Personality and Social Psychology,* January 2007, pp 82–96; and M G Constantine, "Racial Microaggressions Against African American Clients in Cross-Racial Counseling Relationships," *Journal of Counseling Psychology,* January 2007, pp 1–16.

[33] See E Vance, "College Graduates Lack Key Skills, Report Says," *The Chronicle of Higher Education,* February 2, 2007, p A30; T Minton-Eversole and K Gurchiek, "New Workers Not Ready for Prime Time," *HR Magazine,* December 2006, pp 28, 34.

[34] "Facts on Literacy," *National Literacy Facts,* August 27, 1998, www.svs.net/wpci/Litfacts.htm.

[35] Literacy statistics can be found in D Baynton, "America's $60 Billion Problem," *Training,* May 2001, pp 51–56.

[36] The New Commission on the Skills of the American Workforce, *Tough Choices or Tough Times* (San Francisco: Jossey-Bass, 2007), pp XVI, XVII.

[37] See the related discussion in Ibid; M Herbst, "Click for Foreign Labor," *BusinessWeek,* January 15, 2007, p 71; and J Hyatt, "Found in Translation: How to Make the Multicultural Work Force Work," *Inc. Magazine,* pp 40–42.

[38] See H London, "The Workforce, Education, and the Nation's Future," Summer 1998, www.hudson.org/american_outlook/articles_sm 98/london.htm.

[39] See P Engardio, C Matlack, G Edmondson, I Rowley, C Barraclough, and G Smith, "Now the Geezer Glut," *BusinessWeek,* January 31, 2005, pp 44–47; and D Roberts, "How Rising Wages Are Changing the Game in China," *BusinessWeek,* March 27, 2006, pp 32–36.

[40] Examples are provided by J Badal, "To Retain Valued Women Employees, Companies Pitch Flextime as Macho," *The Wall Street Journal,* December 11, 2006, pp B1–B3; and K Gurchiek, "Employers Urged to Make Workplace More 'Father Friendly'," *SHRM Home > HR News,* March 1, 2007, http://www.shrm.org/hrnews_published/articles/cms_020622.asp.

[41] See R Levering and M Moskowitz, "The 100 Best Companies to Work For," *Fortune,* January 24, 2005, p 76.

[42] See the discussion in C E Helfat, D Harris, and P J Wolfson, "The Pipeline to the Top: Women and Men in the Top Executive Ranks of U.S. Corporations," *Academy of Management*

Perspectives, November 2006, pp 42–64; and S E Needleman, "Path to the Top," *The Wall Street Journal,* October 9, 2006, p R7

[43] C Hymowitz, "Women Tell Women: Life in the Top Jobs Is Worth the Effort," *The Wall Street Journal,* November 20, 2006, p B1.

[44] See K Tyler, "Financial Fluencey," *HR Magazine,* July 2006, pp 76–81; and D R Avery, "Target Practice: An Organizational Impression Management Approach to Attracting Minority and Female Job Applicants," *Personnel Psychology,* pp 157–87.

[45] D A Thomas, "The Truth about Mentoring Minorities: Race Matters," Harvard *Business Review,* April 2001, p 107.

[46] See P Coy and J Ewing, "Where Are All The Workers?" *BusinessWeek,* April 9, 2007, p 28.

[47] See N Byrnes, "Get 'Em While They're Young," *Business-Week,* May 22, 2006, pp 86–87; and D S Onley, "Internship Program Dividends," *HR Magazine,* January 2006, pp 85–87.

[48] This statistic was presented in J Kornik, "A Numbers Game," *Training,* December 2006, p 4.

[49] This issue is discussed in the following articles: C Murray, "Intelligence in the Classroom," *The Wall Street Journal Online,* January 16, 2007, http://online.wsj.com/article_print/SB116892082599777371.html; C Murray, "What's Wrong with Vocational School?" *The Wall Street Journal Online,* January 17, 2007, http://online.wsj.com/article_print/SB116900815084478640.html; and C Murray, "On Education: Aztecs vs. Greeks," *The Wall Street Journal Online;* January 18, 2007, http://online.wsj.com/article_print/SB116909586869079981.html.

[50] These examples are discussed by J Barbian, "Get 'Em While They're Young," *Training,* January 2004, pp 44–46.

[51] PM Elsass and D A Ralston, "Individual Responses to the Stress of Career Plateauing," *Journal of Management,* Spring 1989, p 35.

[52] Supportive findings can be found in D R Ettington, "Successful Career Plateauing," *Journal of Vocational Behavior,* February 1998, pp 72–88. Also see J Wiltse, "You're Older? So Sell Your Wisdom," *BusinessWeek,* February 19, 2007, p 82.

[53] Approaches for handling elder care are discussed by T F Shea, "Help with Elder Care," *HR Magazine,* September 2003, pp 113–14, 116, 118.

[54] These recommendations were taken from G M McEvoy and M J Blahana, "Engagement or Disengagement? Older Workers and the Looming Labor Shortage," *Business Horizons,* September–October 2001, p 50.

[55] The cost of health care is reviewed by L A Weatherly, "The Rising Cost of Health Care: Strategic and Societal Considerations for Employees," 2004 *SHRM Research Quarterly,* 2004, pp 1–11.

[56] Additional examples are provided in M Conlin, "Get Healthy—or Else," *BusinessWeek,* February 26, 2007,

pp 58–69; and M Conlin, "More Micro, Less Soft," *BusinessWeek,* November 27, 2006, p 42.

[57] The cost of smoking and smoking cessation programs are discussed by K Gurchiek, "Study: Smoking Ban Improved Air," *HR Magazine,* January 2005, p 34.

[58] D van Knippenberg, C K W De Dreu, and A C Homan, "Work Group Diversity and Group Performance: An Integrative Model and Research Agenda," *Journal of Applied Psychology,* December 2004, p 1009.

[59] See ibid., pp 1008–22; and S E Jackson and A Joshi, "Diversity in Social Context: A Multi-Attribute, Multilevel Analysis of Team Diversity and Sales Performance," *Journal of Organizational Behavior,* September 2004, pp 675–702.

[60] See D Sandy and L Zhao, "The Effects of Cultural Diversity in Virtual Teams Versus Face-to-Face Teams," *Group Decision and Negotiation,* July 2006, p 389; and J L Berdahl and C Moore, "Workplace Harassment: Double Jeopardy for Minority Women," *Journal of Applied Psychology,* March 2006, pp 426–36.

[61] See Jackson and Joshi, "Diversity in Social Context."

[62] Results can be found in J M Sacco and N Schmitt, "A Dynamic Multilevel Model of Demographic Diversity and Misfit Effects," *Journal of Applied Psychology,* March 2005, pp 203–31; and H Liao, A Joshi, "Sticking Out Like a Sore Thumb: Employee Dissimilarity and Deviance at Work," *Personnel Psychology,* Winter 2004, pp 969–1000.

[63] van Knippenberg, De Dreu, and Homan, "Work Group Diversity and Group Performance," p 1009.

[64] These conclusions were derived from Jackson and Joshi, "Diversity in Social Context."

[65] Ibid.

[66] See S Schulz-Hardt, F C Brodbeck, A Mojzisch, R Kerschreiter, and D Frey, "Group Decision Making in Hidden Profile Situations: Dissent as a Facilitator for Decision Quality," *Journal of Personality and Social Psychology,* December 2006, pp 1080–93; and S R Sommers, "On Racial Diversity and Group Decision Making: Identifying Multiple Effects of Racial Composition on Jury Deliberations," *Journal of Personality and Social Psychology,* April 2006, pp 597–612.

[67] See R Moss-Kanter, *The Change Masters* (New York: Simon and Schuster, 1983); and L K Larkey, "Toward a Theory of Communicative Interactions in Culturally Diverse Workgroups," *Academy of Management Review,* April 1996, pp 463–91.

[68] See K Y Williams, "Demography and Diversity in Organizations: A Review of 100 Years of Research," in *Research in Organizational Behavior,* vol. 20, eds B M Staw and L L Cummings (Greenwich, CT: JAI Press, 1998), pp 77–140.

[69] This example was discussed by H Johnson, "Daring to Be Diverse," *Training,* March 2004, pp 34-35.

[70] Support groups are discussed by J T Arnold, "Employee Networks," *HR Magazine,* June 2006, pp 145–52; and C McGlothlen, "Inclusive, Exclusive or Outlawed?" *HR Magazine,* July 2006, pp 107–12.

[71] This recommendation was proposed by J A Chatman and CA O'Reilly, "Asymmetric Reactions to Work Group Sex and Diversity among Men and Women," *Academy of Management Journal,* April 2004, pp 193–208.

[72] These barriers were taken from discussions in M Loden, *Implementing Diversity* (Chicago: Irwin, 1996); E E Spragins, "Benchmark: The Diverse Work Force," *Inc.,* January 1993, p 33; and Morrison, *The New Leaders.*

[73] MG Danaher, "Prompt Response Avoids Liability for Hostile Work Environment," *HR Magazine,* June 2004, p 181.

[74] See the related results in L Torres and D Rollock, "Acculturation and Depression Among Hispanics: The Moderating Effect of Intercultural Competence," *Cultural Diversity and Ethnic Minority Psychology,* January 2007, pp 10–17.

[75] This example was taken from G Colvin, "Lafley and Immelt: In Search of Billions," *Fortune,* December 11, 2006, pp 70–72.

[76] This discussion is based on R R Thomas, Jr, *Redefining Diversity* (New York: AMACOM, 1996). Also see J Brett, K Behfar, and M C Kern, "Managing Multicultural Teams," *Harvard Business Review,* November 2006, pp 84–91.

[77] D J Gaiter, "Eating Crow: How Shoney's, Belted by a Lawsuit, Found the Path to Diversity," *The Wall Street Journal,* April 16, 1996, pp A, A11.

[78] P Dass and B Parker, "Strategies for Managing Human Resource Diversity: From Resistance to Learning," *Academy of Management Executive,* May 1999, p 69.

[79] Gaiter, "Eating Crow."

[80] E White, "Fostering Diversity to Aid Business," *The Wall Street Journal,* May 20, 2006, p B3.

[81] M Gunther, "Queer Inc.," *Fortune,* December 11, 2006, p 102.

[82] Gunter, "Queer Inc.," p 98.

[83] A good example is provided in D Brady, "The Holy Cross Fraternity," *BusinessWeek,* March 12, 2007, pp 70–76.

[84] Excerpted from A Pomeroy, "Cultivating Female Leaders," *HR Magazine,* February 2007, pp 46–48, 50.

[85] Excerpted from D Roberts and P Engardio, "Secrets, Lies, and Sweatshops," *BusiinessWeek,* November 27, 2006, pp 50, 52.

CHAPTER 3

[1] Excerpted from C Leung, "Culture Club," *Canadian Business,* October 9–22, 2006, pp 116–17.

[2] These companies are discussed in R Levering and M Moskowitz, "The 100 Best Companies to Work For," *Fortune,* January 22, 2007, p 94.

[3] See J Guinto, "Wheels Up," *Southwest Airlines Spirit,* June 2006, pp 109–17.

[4] See B Morris, "The Best Place toWork Now," *Fortune,* January 23, 2006, pp 79–86; and J Larson, "Maintaining Culture of Innovation," *The Arizona Republic,* April 13, 2006, pp D1, D3.

[5] E H Schein, "Culture: The Missing Concept in Organization Studies," *Administrative Science Quarterly,* June 1996, p 236.

[6] See the related discussion in L Buchanan, "The Office," *Inc. Magazine,* February 2007, p 120; and R Berner, "My Year at Wal-Mart," *BusinessWeek,* February 12, 2007, pp 70–74.

[7] E Byron, "Call Me Mike!" *The Wall Street Journal,* March 27, 2006, p B1.

[8] S H Schwartz, "Universals in the Content and Structure of Values: Theoretical Advances and Empirical Tests in 20 Countries," in *Advances in Experimental Social Psychology,* ed M P Zanna (New York: Academic Press, 1992), p 4.

[9] See P Engardio, "Beyond The Green Corporation," *BusinessWeek,* January 29, 2007, pp 50–64.

[10] Ibid, p 50–51.

[11] P Babcock, "Is Your Company Two-Faced?" *HR Magazine,* January 2004, p 43.

[12] Results are discussed in "Executing Ethics," *Training,* March 2007, p 8. Ethical cultures are also discussed by T M Jones, W Felps, and G A Bigley, "Ethical Theory and Stakeholder-Related Decisions: The Role of Stakeholder Culture," *Academy of Management Review,* January 2007, pp 137–55.

[13] Results can be found in S Clarke, "Perceptions of Organizational Safety: Implications for the Development of Safety Culture," *Journal of Organizational Behavior,* March 1999, pp 185–98.

[14] Statistics and data contained in the Southwest Airlines example can be found in the "Southwest Airlines Fact Sheet," updated February 20, 2007, www.southwest.com.

[15] K D Godsey, "Slow Climb to New Heights," *Success,* October 1996, p 21.

[16] Southwest's mission statement can be found in "The Mission of Southwest Airlines," March 2007, www.southwest.com.

[17] See C Ostroff, A Kinicki, and M Tamkins, "Organizational Culture and Climate," in *Handbook of Psychology,* vol. 12, eds W C Borman, D R Ilgen, and R J Klimoski (New York: Wiley and Sons, 2003), pp 565–93.

[18] See the related discussion in S Ten Have, W Ten Have, A F Stevens, M Vander Elst, and F Pol-Coyne, *Key Management Models: The Management Tools and Practices that will Improve Your Business* (San Francisco: Jossey-Bass, 2003); and P Kwan and A Walker, "Validating the Competing Values Model as a Representation of Organizational Culture Through Inter-Institutional Comparisons," *Organizational Analysis,* 2004, pp 21–37.

[19] A thorough description of the CVF is provided in K S Cameron, R E Quinn, J Degraff, and A V Thakor, *Creating Values Leadership* (Northampton, MA: Edward Elgar, 2006); and K S Cameron and R E Quinn, *Diagnosing and Changing Organizational Culture* (New York: Addison-Wesley, 1999).

[20] Excerpted from B Leonard, "Taking Care of Their Own," *HR Magazine,* June 2006, pp 113–14.

[21] Nucor's culture is discussed in N Byrnes, "The Art of Motivation," *BusinessWeek,* May 1, 2006, pp 57–62.

[22] Excerpted from J McGregor, "How Failure Breeds Success," *BusinessWeek,* July 10, 2006, pp 45–46. Also see N T Sheehan and G Vaidyanathan, "The Path to Growth," *The Wall Street Journal,* March 3–4, 2007, p R8.

[23] The Home Depot example was based on R Charan, "Home Depot's Blueprint for Culture Change," *Harvard Business Review,* April 2006, pp 61–71; B Grow, "Renovating Home Depot," *BusinessWeek,* March 6, 2006, pp 50–58; and "Nardelli Out at Home Depot," *BusinessWeek.com,* January 3, 2007; http:www.businessweek.com/bwdaily/dnflash/ccontent/jan2007/db20070103_534405.htm.

[24] See C Daniels, "Meet Mr. Nuke," *Fortune,* May 15, 2006, pp 140–46; and L Lee, "It's Dell vs. The Dell Way," *BusinessWeek,* March 6, 2006, pp 61–62.

[25] The Ritz Carlton's culture is discussed in J Gordon, "Redefining Elegance," *Training,* March 2007, pp 14–18.

[26] Results can be found in E A Goodman, R F Zammuto, and B D Gifford, "The Competing Values Framework: Understanding the Impact of Organizational Culture on the Quality of Work Life," *Organization Development Journal,* Fall 2001, 58–68; P A Balthazard, R A Cooke, and R E Potter, "Dysfunctional Culture, Dysfunctional Organization," *Journal of Managerial Psychology,* 2006, pp 709–32; and B Erdogan, R C Liden, and M L Kraimer, "Justice and Leader-Member Exchange: The Moderating Role of Organizational Culture," *Academy of Management Journal,* April 2006, pp 395–406.

[27] Supportive results can be found in C Ostroff, Y Shin, and A Kinicki, "Multiple Perspectives of Congruence: Relationships between Value Congruence and Employee Attitudes," *Journal of Organizational Behavior,* September 2005, pp 591–624; and W Arthur Jr., S T Bell, A J Villado, and D Doverspike, "The Use of Person-Organization Fit in Employment Decision Making: An Assessment of Its Criterion-Related Validity," *Journal of Applied Psychology,* July 2006, pp 786–801.

[28] Culture and performance was examined by M Škerlavaj, M I Štemberger, R Škrinjar, and V Dimovski, "Organizational Learning Culture—The Missing Link between Business Process Change and Organizational Learning," *International Journal of Production Economics,* April 2007, pp 346–67; A Xenikou and M Simosi, "Organizational Culture and Transformational Leadership as Predictors of Business Unit Performance," *Journal of Managerial Performance,* 2006, pp 566–79; T Igo and M Skitmore, "Diagnosing the Organizational Culture of an Australian Engineering Consultancy Using the Competing Values Framework," *Construction Innovation,* June 2006, pp 1221–139; and R Hauser and R Paul,

"IS Service Quality and Culture: An Empirical Investigation," *Journal of Computer Information Systems,* Fall 2006, pp 15–22.

[29] Results are reported in C W Hart, "Beating the Market with Customer Satisfaction," *Harvard Business Review,* March 2007, pp 30–31.

[30] Results can be found in J Combs, Y Liu, A Hall, and D Ketchen, "How Much Do High-Performance Work Practices Matter? A Meta-Analysis of Their Effects on Organizational Performance," *Personnel Psychology,* Autumn 2006, pp 501–28.

[31] Results can be found in J P Kotter and J L Heskett, *Corporate Culture and Performance* (New York: Free Press, 1992).

[32] The success rate of mergers is discussed in M J Epstein, "The Drivers of Success in Post-Merger Integration," *Organizational Dynamics,* May 2004, pp 174–89. Also see "Dealing with Cultural Misfits," *HR Magazine,* March 2007, pp 14, 16; and "Focus on the People During a Merger," *HR Magazine,* March 2007, p 16.

[33] See the related discussion in V Sathe and E J Davidson, "Toward a New Conceptualization of Culture Change," in *Handbook of Organizational Culture & Climate,* eds N M Ashkanasay, C P M Wilderom, and M F Peterson (Thousand Oaks, CA: Sage Publications, 2000), pp 279–96; and M Nunno, "The Effects of the ARC Organizational Intervention on Caseworker Turnover, Climate, and Culture in Children's Services Systems," *Child Abuse & Neglect,* August 2006, pp 849–54.

[34] W Disney, quoted in B Nanus, *Visionary Leadership: Creating a Compelling Sense of Direction for Your Organization* (San Francisco: Jossey-Bass, 1992), p 28; reprinted from B Thomas, *Walt Disney: An American Tradition* (New York: Simon & Schuster, 1976), p 247.

[35] D-A Durbin, "Ford Cuts Part of Culture Shift," *The Arizona Republic,* January 24, 2006, p D3.

[36] The mechanisms were based on material contained in E H Schein, "The Role of the Founder in Creating Organizational Culture," *Organizational Dynamics,* Summer 1983, pp 13–28.

[37] See N Byrnes, "The Art of Motivation," *BusinessWeek,* May 1, 2006, pp 57–62.

[38] Excerpted from D F Kuratko, R D Ireland, and J S Hornsby, "Improving Firm Performance through Entrepreneurial Actions: Acordia's Corporate Entrepreneurship Strategy," *Academy of Management Executive,* November 2001, p 67.

[39] S Holmes, "Cleaning Up Boeing," *BusinessWeek,* March 13, 2006, p 66.

[40] Ibid, p 68.

[41] T J Erickson and L Gratton, "What It Means to Work Here," *Harvard Business Review,* March 2007, p 111.

[42] S Tully, "Taking a Shot at the Title of World's Most Important Banker," *Fortune,* April 3, 2006, p 58.

[43] See "Calif. Charges Are Resolved in HP Spying Case," *The Arizona Republic,* March 15, 2007, p D1, D2; and P Burrows, "Controlling the Damage at HP," *BusinessWeek,* October 9, 2006, pp 36–44.

[44] "Training Rx'es," *Training,* July 2006, p 22.

[45] L Grensing-Pophal, "Building Service with a Smile," *HR Magazine,* November 2006, p 87.

[46] J Van Maanen, "Breaking In: Socialization to Work," in *Handbook of Work, Organization, and Society,* ed R Dubin (Chicago: Rand-McNally, 1976), p 67.

[47] E White, "Hiring Becomes Family Affair," *The Wall Street Journal,* March 5, 2007, p B4.

[48] Supportive evidence is provided by R W Griffeth and P W Hom, *Retaining Valued Employees* (Thousand Oaks, CA: Sage Publications, 2001), pp 46–65.

[49] See J M Phillips, "Effects of Realistic Job Previews on Multiple Organizational Outcomes: A Meta-Analysis," *Academy of Management Journal,* December 1998, pp 673–90.

[50] Onboarding programs are discusesd by J McGregor, "How to Take the Reins at Top Speed," *BusinessWeek,* February 5, 2007, pp 55–56; and J M Brodie, "Getting Managers On Board," *HR Magazine,* November 2006, pp 105–108.

[51] S J Wells, "Diving In," *HR Magazine,* March 2005, p 56.

[52] Reprinted by permission of *Harvard Business Review.* Excerpt from N M Tichy, "No Ordinary Boot Camp," April 2001. Copyright © 2001 by the Harvard Business School Publishing Corporation; all rights reserved.

[53] These results are presented in "Outsider Longer," *Training,* March 2007, p 6.

[54] See J P Slattery, T T Selvarajan, and J E Anderson, "Influences of New Employee Development Practices on Temporary Employee Work-Related Attitudes," *Human Resource Development Quarterly,* 2006, pp 279–303.

[55] See E H Offstein and R L Dufresne, "Building Strong Ethics and Promoting Positve Character Development: The Influence of HRM at the United States Military Academy at West Point," *Human Resource Management,* Spring 2007, pp 95–114.

[56] See D Cable and C Parsons, "Socialization Tactics and Person-Organization Fit," *Personnel Psychology,* Spring 2001, pp 1–23.

[57] R Levering and M Moskowitz, "The 100 Best Companies to Work For: And the Winners Are . . . " *Fortune,* January 23, 2006, p 94.

[58] A review of stage model research can be found in B E Ashforth, *Role Transitions in Organizational Life: An Identity-Based Perspective* (Mahwah, NJ: Lawrence Erlbaum Associates, 2001).

[59] See J A Gruman, A M Saks, and D I Zweig, "Organizational Socialization Tactics and Newcomer Proactive Behaviors: An Integrative Study," *Journal of Vocational Behavior,* August 2006, pp 90–104; and H D Cooper-Thomas and N Anderson, "Organizational Socialization," *Journal of Managerial Psychology,* 2006, pp 492–516.

[60] For a thorough review of research on the socialization of diverse employees with disabilities, see A Colella, "Organizational Socialization of Newcomers with Disabilities: A Framework for Future Research," in *Research in Personnel and Human Resources Management,* ed G R Ferris (Greenwich, CT: JAI Press, 1996), pp 351–417.

[61] This definition is based on the network perspective of mentoring proposed by M Higgins and K Kram, "Reconceptualizing Mentoring at Work: A Developmental Network Perspective," *Academy of Management Review,* April 2001, pp 264–88.

[62] Results can be found in T D Allen, L T Eby, M L Poteet, and E Lentz, "Career Benefits Associated with Mentoring for Protégés: A Meta-Analysis," *Journal of Applied Psychology,* February 2004, pp 127–36; and T D Allen, L T Eby, and E Lentz, "Mentorship Behaviors and Mentorship Quality Associated with Formal Mentoring Programs: Closing the Gap Between Research and Practice," *Journal of Applied Psychology,* May 2006, pp 567–78.

[63] Career functions are discussed in detail in K Kram, *Mentoring of Work: Developmental Relationships in Organizational Life* (Glenview, IL: Scott, Foresman, 1985).

[64] Excerpted from K Maher, "The Jungle: Focus on Retirement, Pay and Getting Ahead," *The Wall Street Journal,* February 24, 2004, p B8.

[65] This discussion is based on Higgins and Kram, "Reconceptualizing Mentoring at Work."

[66] Ibid.

[67] Supportive results can be found in T Allen, M Poteet, and J Russell, "Protégé Selection by Mentors: What Makes the Difference?" *Journal of Organizational Behavior,* May 2000, pp 271–82.

[68] Recommendations for improving your networking skills can be found in S Berfield, "Mentoring Can Be Messy," *BusinessWeek,* January 29, 2007, pp 80–81.

[69] Results can be found in "Leadership Needs Development," *Training,* February 2006, p 7.

[70] See S Tonidandel, D R Avery, and M G Phillips, "Maximizing Returns on Mentoring: Factors Affecting Subsequent Protégé Performance," *Journal of Organizational Behavior,* January 2007, pp 89–110.

[71] This recommendation was derived from J Welch and S Welch, "Ideas the WelchWay: Avoding Strikes—and Unions," *BusinessWeek,* January 15, 2007, p 92.

[72] Excerpted from A Lashinsky, "Search and Enjoy," *Fortune,* January 22, 2007, pp 70–82.

[73] Excerpted from S Reed, "BP Feels the Heat," *BusinessWeek,* January 22, 2007, pp 52–53.

CHAPTER 4

[1] Excerpted from R Berner, "Chanel's American in Paris," *BusinessWeek,* January 29, 2007, pp 70–71.

[2] See A Soota and M Courtney, "Open Debate: Offshoring Is Good for America," *Fast Company,* January–February 2006, p 108; D Roberts and P Engardio, "Secrets, Lies, and

Sweatshops," *BusinessWeek,* November 27, 2006, pp 50–58; P E Chaudhry, "Changing Levels of Intellectual Property Rights Protection for Global Firms: A Synopsis of Recent US and EU Trade Enforcement Strategies," *Business Horizons,* November–December 2006, pp 463–72; D J Lynch, "Enthusiasm for Globalization Ebbs," *USA Today,* January 15, 2007, pp 1B–2B; and D J Lynch, "U.S. Trade Deficit Hits New High for Fifth Year in a Row," *USA Today,* February 14, 2007, p 2B.

3 Data from M Mandel, "Can Anyone Steer This Economy?" *BusinessWeek,* November 20, 2006, pp 56–62.

4 D J Lynch, "Developing Nations Poised to Challenge USA as King of the Hill," *USA Today,* February 8, 2007, p 2B. Also see P Engardio, "Emerging Giants," *BusinessWeek,* July 31, 2006, pp 40–49; T Khanna and K G Palepu, "Emerging Giants: Building World-Class Companies in Developing Countries," *Harvard Business Review,* October 2006, pp 60–69; B Bremner, "The Dragon's Way or the Tiger's?" *BusinessWeek,* November 20, 2006, p 55; and C Chandler, "Vietnam Vrooooom. . . ," *Fortune,* December 11, 2006, pp 147–59.

5 Global executives are profiled in Z Olijnyk, "Global Leaders: Peter Beresford," *Canadian Business,* November 20–December 3, 2006, pp 44, 46; S Hamm and D Roberts, "China's First Global Capitalist," *BusinessWeek,* December 11, 2006, pp 52–58; and A Taylor III, "The World According to Ghosn," *Fortune,* December 11, 2006, pp 114–21.

6 Data from M A Carpenter, W G Sanders, and H B Gregersen, "Bundling Human Capital with Organizational Context: The Impact of International Assignment Experience on Multinational Firm Performance and CEO Pay," *Academy of Management Journal,* June 2001, pp 493–511. Also see H Maurer, "Kent Is It," *BusinessWeek,* January 1, 2007, p 32.

7 G Dutton, "Building a Global Brain," *Management Review,* May 1999, p 35.

8 M Mabry, "Pin a Label on a Manager—and Watch What Happens," *Newsweek,* May 14, 1990, p 43.

9 Ibid. Also see H S Kim and D K Sherman, "'Express Yourself:' Culture and the Effect of Self-Expression on Choice," *Journal of Personality and Social Psychology,* January 2007, pp 1–11.

10 M Javidan and R J House, "Cultural Acumen for the Global Manager: Lessons from Project GLOBE," *Organizational Dynamics,* Spring 2001, p 292. (Emphasis added.)

11 For instructive discussion, see J S Black, H B Gregersen, and M E Mendenhall, *Global Assignments: Successfully Expatriating and Repatriating International Managers* (San Francisco: Jossey-Bass, 1992), Ch 2. Also see A Mesoudi, A Whiten, and R Dunbar, "A Bias for Social Information in Human Cultural Transmission," *British Journal of Psychology,* August 2006, pp 405–23.

12 F Trompenaars and C Hampden-Turner, *Riding the Waves of Culture: Understanding Cultural Diversity in Global Business,* 2nd ed (New York: McGraw-Hill, 1998), pp 6–7. The concept of "cultural mosaic" is discussed in G T Chao and H Moon, "The Cultural Mosaic: A Metatheory for Understanding the

Complexity of Culture," *Journal of Applied Psychology,* November 2005, pp 1128–140. Also see C Wan, C Chiu, S Peng, and K Tam, "Measuring Cultures through Intersubjective Cultural Norms," *Journal of Cross-Cultural Psychology,* March 2007, pp 213–26.

13 "How Cultures Collide," *Psychology Today,* July 1976, p 69.

14 For example, see S Hamm, "Tech's Future," *BusinessWeek,* September 27, 2004, pp 82–89.

15 See C L Sharma, "Ethnicity, National Integration, and Education in the Union of Soviet Socialist Republics," *Journal of East and West Studies,* October 1989, pp 75–93; and R Brady and P Galuszka, "Shattered Dreams," *BusinessWeek,* February 11, 1991, pp 38–42.

16 As quoted in D Jones, "American CEO in Europe Blends Leadership Styles," *USA Today,* June 21, 2004, 4B.

17 See R Inglehart and W E Baker, "Modernization's Challenge to Traditional Values: Who's Afraid of Ronald McDonald?" *The Futurist,* March–April 2001, pp 16–21.

18 See S Kirchhoff, "Different Cultures Value Different Features," *USA Today,* August 5, 2004, p 2B; and W Gong, Z G Li, T Li, "Marketing to China's Youth: A Cultural Transformation Perspective," *Business Horizons,* November–December 2004, pp 41–50.

19 J Main, "How to Go Global—and Why," *Fortune,* August 28, 1989, p. 73.

20 For another cross-cultural GE example, see D Brady and K Capell, "GE Breaks the Mold to Spur Innovation," *BusinessWeek,* April 26, 2004, pp 88–89.

21 W D Marbach, "Quality: What Motivates American Workers?" *BusinessWeek,* April 12, 1993, p 93. Also see Y Kageyama, "Toyota Spreads Quality Globally," *The Arizona Republic,* April 16, 2006, p D5; C Fishman, "No Satisfaction," *Fast Company,* January 2007, pp 82–92; and I Rowley, "Even Toyota Isn't Perfect," *BusinessWeek,* January 22, 2007, p 54.

22 See G A Sumner, *Folkways* (New York: Ginn, 1906). Also see J G Weber, "The Nature of Ethnocentric Attribution Bias: Ingroup Protection or Enhancement?" *Journal of Experimental Social Psychology,* September 1994, pp 482–504.

23 See P Prengaman, "Niche Market for Swimsuits Lets Muslim Women Hit the Waves," *USA Today,* February 19, 2007, p 2B.

24 D A Heenan and H V Perlmutter, *Multinational Organization Development* (Reading, MA: Addison-Wesley, 1979), p 17. German ethnocentrism is discussed in J Ewing, "Siemen's Culture Clash," *BusinessWeek,* January 29, 2007, pp 42–46.

25 Data from R Kopp, "International Human Resource Policies and Practices in Japanese, European, and United States Multinationals," *Human Resource Management,* Winter 1994, pp 581–99. Also see G Balabanis, A Diamantopoulos, R D Mueller, and T C Melewar, "The Impact of Nationalism, Patriotism and Internationalism on Consumer Ethnocentric

Tendencies," *Journal of International Business Studies,* First Quarter 2001, pp 157–75.

²⁶ See The Global Deception Research Team, "A World of Lies," *Journal of Cross-Cultural Psychology,* January 2006, pp 60–74.

²⁷ J S Osland and A Bird, "Beyond Sophisticated Stereotyping: Cultural Sensemaking in Context," *Academy of Management Executive,* February 2000, p 67.

²⁸ "Fujio Mitarai: Canon," *BusinessWeek,* January 14, 2002. p 55.

²⁹ P C Earley and E Mosakowski, "Cultural Intelligence," *Harvard Business Review,* October 2004, p 140. Also see P C Earley and E Mosakowski, "Toward Culture Intelligence: Turning Cultural Differences into a Workplace Advantage," *Academy of Management Executive,* August 2004, pp 151–57; K Ng and P C Earley, "Culture + Intelligence: Old Constructs, New Frontiers," *Group and Organization Management,* February 2006, pp 4–19; H C Triandis, "Cultural Intelligence in Organizations," *Group and Organization Management,* February 2006, pp 20–26; and B J Fowers and B J Davidov, "The Virtue of Multiculturalism: Personal Transformation, Character, and Openness to the Other," *American Psychologist,* September 2006, pp 581–94.

³⁰ See "How Cultures Collide," pp 66–74, 97; and M Munter, "Cross-Cultural Communication for Managers," *Business Horizons,* May–June 1993, pp 69–78.

³¹ See N Lynton and K Hogh Thogersen, "How China Transforms an Executive's Mind," *Organizational Dynamics,* no. 2, 2006, pp 170–81; W McEwen, X Fang, C Zhang, and R Burkholder, "Inside the Mind of the Chinese Consumer," *Harvard Business Review,* March 2006, pp 68–76; P J Buckley, J Clegg, and H Tan, "Cultural Awareness in Knowledge Transfer to China—The Role of *Guanxi* and *Mianzi,*" *Journal of World Business,* September 2006, pp 275–88; and K Naughton, "The Great Wal-Mart of China," *Newsweek,* October 30, 2006, pp 50–52.

³² The German management style is discussed in R Stewart, "German Management: A Challenge to Anglo-American Managerial Assumptions," *Business Horizons,* May–June 1996, pp 52–54.

³³ I Adler, "Between the Lines," *Business Mexico,* October 2000, p 24.

³⁴ The tips were excerpted from R Drew, "Working with Foreigners," *Management Review,* September 1999, p 6.

³⁵ For background, see Javidan and House, "Cultural Acumen for the Global Manager," pp 289–305; the entire Spring 2002 issue of *Journal of World Business;* and R J House, P J Hanges, M Javidan, P W Dorfman, and V Gupta, eds *Culture, Leadership, and Organizations: The GLOBE Study of 62 Societies* (Thousand Oaks, CA: Sage, 2004).

³⁶ R House, M Javidan, P Hanges, and P Dorfman, "Understanding Cultures and Implicit Leadership Theories across the Globe: An Introduction to Project GLOBE," *Journal of World Business,* Spring 2002, p 4.

³⁷ Adapted from the list in ibid., pp 5–6. Also see M Javidan, G K Stahl, F Brodbeck, and C P M Wilderom, "Cross-Border Transfer of Knowledge: Cultural Lessons from Project GLOBE," *Academy of Management Executive,* May 2005, pp 59–76; and D A Waldman, M Sully de Luque, N Washburn, R J House, et al., "Cultural and Leadership Predictors of Corporate Social Responsibility Values of Top Management: a GLOBE Study of 15 Countries," *Journal of International Business Studies,* November 2006, pp 823–37.

³⁸ See D Oyserman, H M Coon, and M Kemmelmeier, "Rethinking Individualism and Collectivism: Evaluation of Theoretical Assumptions and Meta-Analyses," *Psychological Bulletin,* January 2002, pp 3–72; B Erdogan and R C Liden, "Collectivism as a Moderator of Responses to Organizational Justice: Implications for Leader-Member Exchange and Ingratiation," *Journal of Organizational Behavior,* February 2006, pp 1–17; and M Kemmelmeier, E E Jambor, and J Letner, "Individualism and Good Works: Cultural Variation in Giving and Volunteering Across the United States," *Journal of Cross-Cultural Psychology,* May 2006, pp 327–44.

³⁹ M Edwards, "As Good as It Gets," *AARP: The Magazine,* November–December 2004, p 48.

⁴⁰ See table in ibid., p 49.

⁴¹ Data from Trompenaars and Hampden-Turner, *Riding the Waves of Culture,* Ch 5. For recent research, see E G T Green and J Deschamps, "Variation of Individualism and Collectivism within and between 20 Countries," *Journal of Cross-Cultural Psychology,* May 2005, pp 321–39; J L Xie, J Roy, and Z Chen, "Cultural and Individual Differences in Self-Rating Behavior: An Extension and Refinement of the Cultural Relativity Hypothesis," *Journal of Organizational Behavior,* May 2006, pp 341–64; and H Z Li, Z Zhang, G Bhatt, and Y Yum, "Rethinking Culture and Self-Construal: China as a Middle Land," *The Journal of Social Psychology,* October 2006, pp 591–610.

⁴² As quoted in E E Schultz, "Scudder Brings Lessons to Navajo, Gets Some of Its Own," *The Wall Street Journal,* April 29, 1999, p C12.

⁴³ Trompenaars and Hampden-Turner, *Riding the Waves of Culture,* p 56.

⁴⁴ For related readings, see M Crossan, M P E Cunha, D Vera, and J Cunha, "Time and Organizational Improvisation," *Academy of Management Review,* January 2005, pp 129–45; and A C Bluedorn and R L Standifer, "Time and the Temporal Imagination," *Academy of Management Learning and Education,* June 2006, pp 196–206.

⁴⁵ J L Yang, " 'Happiness' for Sale," *Fortune,* September 18, 2006, p 56.

⁴⁶ S Smith, "A Pirate's Life," *Newsweek,* June 26, 2006, p 45.

⁴⁷ A good discussion of doing business in Mexico is G K Stephens and C R Greer, "Doing Business in Mexico: Understanding Cultural Differences," *Organizational Dynamics,* Summer 1995, pp 39–55. Also see P Seldon, *The Business Traveler's World Guide* (New York: McGraw-Hill, 1998), pp 311–17.

48 R W Moore, "Time, Culture, and Comparative Management: A Review and Future Direction," in *Advances in International Comparative Management,* vol. 5, ed S B Prasad (Greenwich, CT: JAI Press, 1990), pp 7–8.

49 See A C Bluedorn, C F Kaufman, and P M Lane, "How Many Things Do You Like to Do at Once? An Introduction to Monochronic and Polychronic Time," *Academy of Management Executive,* November 1992, pp 17–26.

50 See N Hellmich, "Most People Multitask, So Most People Don't Sit Down to Eat," *USA Today,* September 30, 2004, p 8D; S Jayson, "Sociability: It's All in Your Mind," *USA Today,* September 25, 2006, p 5D; and D H Freedman, "Why Interruption, Distraction, and Multitasking Are Not Such Awful Things After All," *Inc.,* February 2007, pp 67–68.

51 O Port, "You May Have to Reset This Watch—in a Million Years," *BusinessWeek,* August 30, 1993, p 65. Also see R F Howe, "Built for Speed," *Business 2.0,* June 2006, pp 104–10; L Petrecca, "Stores, Banks Go Speedy to Win Harried Customers," *USA Today,* December 1, 2006, p 1B; and C Palmeri, "Pass Go. Collect $200. Hurry," *BusinessWeek,* February 19, 2007, p 14.

52 See E T Hall, *The Hidden Dimension* (Garden City, NY: Doubleday, 1966).

53 "How Cultures Collide," p 72.

54 See A B Cohen and A Rankin, "Religion and the Morality of Positive Mentality," *Basic and Applied Social Psychology,* March 2004, pp 45–57; J Ginsburg, "Koran-Friendly Lenders," *BusinessWeek,* February 14, 2005, p 12; D Henry, "Returns Muslims Can Live With," *BusinessWeek,* July 17, 2006, p 9; A Smith, "Religious Beliefs Clash with Job Duties," *HR Magazine,* December 2006, pp 34, 36; and S Childress, "Ingrid Mattson," *Newsweek,* January 1, 2007, p 71.

55 Results adapted from and value definitions quoted from S R Safranski and I-W Kwon, "Religious Groups and Management Value Systems," in *Advances in International Comparative Management,* vol. 3, eds R N Farner and E G McGoun (Greenwich, CT: JAI Press, 1988), pp 171–83.

56 Ibid., p 180.

57 N J Adler, *International Dimensions of Organizational Behavior,* 4th ed (Cincinnati: South-Western, 2002), p 11. (Emphasis added.) Also see G Jones and T Khanna, "Bringing History (Back) into International Business," *Journal of International Business Studies,* July 2006, pp 453–68.

58 See D Matsumoto, R J Grissom, and D L Dinnel, "Do Between-Culture Differences Really Mean That People Are Different? A Look at Some Measures of Cultural Effect Size," *Journal of Cross-Cultural Psychology,* July 2001, pp 478–90.

59 M Javidan and R J House, "Leadership and Cultures around the World: Findings from GLOBE—An Introduction to the Special Issue," *Journal of World Business,* Spring 2002, p 1.

60 For complete details, see G Hofstede, *Culture's Consequences: International Differences in Work-Related Values,* abridged ed (Newbury Park, CA: Sage, 1984); G Hofstede, "The Interaction between National and Organizational Value Systems," *Journal of Management Studies,* July 1985, pp 347–57; and G Hofstede, "Management Scientists Are Human," *Management Science,* January 1994, pp 4–13. Also see M H Hoppe, "Introduction: Geert Hofstede's *Culture's Consequences: International Differences in Work-Related Values,*" *Academy of Management Executive,* February 2004, pp 73–74; M H Hoppe, "An Interview with Geert Hofstede," *Academy of Management Executive,* February 2004, pp 75–79; J W Bing, "Hofstede's Consequences: The Impact of His Work on Consulting and Business Practices," *Academy of Management Executive,* February 2004, pp 80–87; and B L Kirkman, K B Lowe, and C B Gibson, "A Quarter Century of *Culture's Consequences:* A Review of Empirical Research Incorporating Hofstede's Cultural Values Framework," *Journal of International Business Studies,* May 2006, pp 285–320.

61 A similar conclusion is presented in the following replication of Hofstede's work: A Merritt, "Culture in the Cockpit: Do Hofstede's Dimensions Replicate?" *Journal of Cross-Cultural Psychology,* May 2000, pp 283–301. Another extension of Hofstede's work can be found in S M Lee and S J Peterson, "Culture, Entrepreneurial Orientation, and Global Competitiveness," *Journal of World Business,* Winter 2000, pp 401–16.

62 For related reading, see E Van de Vliert, " Autocratic Leadership Around the World," *Journal of Cross-Cultural Psychology,* January 2006, pp 42–59; M Javidan, P W Dorfman, M Sully de Luque, and R J House, "In the Eye of the Beholder: Cross Cultural Lessons in Leadership from Project GLOBE," *Academy of Management Perspectives,* February 2006, pp 67–90; G B Graen, "In the Eye of the Beholder: Cross-Cultural Lesson in Leadership from Project GLOBE: A Response Viewed from the Third Culture Bonding (TCB) Model of Cross-Cultural Leadership," *Academy of Management Perspectives,* November 2006, pp 95–101; R J House, M Javidan, P W Dorfman, and M Sully de Luque, "A Failure of Scholarship: Response to George Graen's Critique of GLOBE," *Academy of Management Perspectives,* November 2006, pp 102–14; and E Cohen, "Developing Global Leaders the Satyam Way," *Training and Development,* January 2007, pp 39–41.

63 J Guyon, "David Whitwam," *Fortune,* July 26, 2004, p 174.

64 M Vande Berg, "Siemens: Betting That Big Is Once again Beautiful," *Milken Institute Review,* Second Quarter 2002, p 47.

65 See D Brady and D Roberts, "Management Grab," *BusinessWeek,* August 21–28, 2006, pp 88, 90; and G Gloeckler, "The Best Global MBA Programs," *BusinessWeek,* October 23, 2006, pp 72–75.

66 A Fisher, "Five Ways to Ignite Your Career," *Fortune,* February 6, 2006, p 50.

[67] Data from D Beck, "What Negotiating Tactics Reveal about Executives," February 11–17, 2002, www.careerjournal.com.

[68] J S Black and H B Gregersen, "The Right Way to Manage Expats," *Harvard Business Review,* March–April 1999, p 53. A more optimistic picture is presented in R L Tung, "American Expatriates Abroad: From Neophytes to Cosmopolitans," *Journal of World Business,* Summer 1998, pp 125–44. For interesting expatriate metaphors, see A Harzing, "Of Bears, Bumble-Bees, and Spiders: The Role of Expatriates in Controlling Foreign Subsidiaries," *Journal of World Business,* Winter 2001, pp 366–79.

[69] Data from G S Insch and J D Daniels, "Causes and Consequences of Declining Early Departures from Foreign Assignments," *Business Horizons,* November–December 2002, pp 39–48. Also see J P Shay and S A Baack, "Expatriate Assignment, Adjustment and Effectiveness: An Empirical Examination of the Big Picture," *Journal of International Business Studies,* May 2004, pp 216–32; and A E M Van Vianen, I E De Pater, A L Kristof-Brown, and E C Johnson, "Fitting In: Surface- and Deep-Level Cultural Differences and Expatriates' Adjustment," *Academy of Management Journal,* October 2004, pp 697–709.

[70] S Dallas, "Rule No. 1: Don't Diss the Locals," *BusinessWeek,* May 15, 1995, p 8. Also see S M Toh and A S DeNisi, "A Local Perspective to Expatriate Success," *Academy of Management Executive,* February 2005, pp 132–46. Also see M A Shaffer, D A Harrison, H Gregersen, J S Black, and L A Ferzandi, "You Can Take It with You: Individual Differences and Expatriate Effectiveness," *Journal of Applied Psychology,* January 2006, pp 109–25.

[71] P Capell, "Employers Seek to Trim Pay for US Expatriates," April 16, 2005, www.careerjournal.com. Also see E Krell, "Evaluating Returns on Expatriates," *HR Magazine,* March 2005, pp 60–65; and S P Nurney, "The Long and Short of It," *HR Magazine,* March 2005, pp 91–94.

[72] These insights come from Tung, "American Expatriates Abroad"; R L Tung, "Female Expatriates: The Model Global Manager?" *Organizational Dynamics,* no. 3, 2004, pp 243–53; A Varma, S M Toh, and P Budhwar, "A New Perspective on the Female Expatriate Experience: The Role of Host Country National Categorization," *Journal of World Business,* June 2006, pp 112–20; M Janssens, T Cappellen, and P Zanoni, "Successful Female Expatriates as Agents: Positioning Oneself through Gender, Hierarchy, and Culture," *Journal of World Business,* June 2006, pp 133–48; and A Pomeroy, "Outdated Policies Hinder Female Expats," *HR Magazine,* December 2006, p 16.

[73] A good resource book is M W McCall Jr and G P Hollenbeck, *Developing Global Executives: The Lessons of International Experience* (Boston: Harvard Business School Press, 2002).

[74] E Levenson, "Leaders of the Pack," *Fortune,* October 16, 2006, p 189. Also see D Foust, "Queen of Pop," *BusinessWeek,* August 7, 2006, pp 44–51.

[75] See S Jun and J W Gentry, "An Exploratory Investigation of the Relative Importance of Cultural Similarity and Personal Fit in the Selection and Performance of Expatriates," *Journal of World Business,* February 2005, pp 1–8.

[76] Data from "E-Pulse," *Training,* January 2002, p 60. Also see P Lehman, "The Evolution of a Diplomat," *BusinessWeek,* September 18, 2006, p 74.

[77] J S Lublin, "Younger Managers Learn Global Skills," *The Wall Street Journal,* March 31, 1992, p B1. For more on cross-cultural competence, see J P Johnson, T Lenartowicz, and S Apud, "Cross-Cultural Competence in International Business: Toward a Definition and a Model," *Journal of International Business Studies,* July 2006, pp 525–43; and J Ho-Ying Fu, "Spontaneous Inferences from Cultural Cues: Varying Responses of Cultural Insiders and Outsiders," *Journal of Cross-Cultural Psychology,* January 2007, pp 58–75.

[78] See P C Earley, "Intercultural Training for Managers: A Comparison of Documentary and Interpersonal Methods," *Academy of Management Journal,* December 1987, pp 685–98; J S Black and M Mendenhall, "Cross-Cultural Training Effectiveness: A Review and a Theoretical Framework for Future Research," *Academy of Management Review,* January 1990, pp 113–36; D Landis, J M Bennett, and M J Bennett, eds *Handbook of Intercultural Training,* 3rd ed (Thousand Oaks, CA: Sage, 2004); and M M L Wong, "Organizational Learning via Expatriate Managers: Collective Myopia as Blocking Mechanism," *Organization Studies,* 2005, pp 325–50.

[79] See Y Luo and O Shenkar, "The Multinational Corporation as a Multilingual Community: Language and Organization in a Global Context," *Journal of International Business Studies,* May 2006, pp 321–39; P Eyring, "Broadening Global Awareness," *Training and Development,* July 2006, pp 69–71; S Kang, "Measurement of Acculturation, Scale Formats, and Language Competence: Their Implications for Adjustment," *Journal of Cross-Cultural Psychology,* November 2006, pp 669–93; and R Willing, "U.S. Turns to Tech for Translators," *USA Today,* December 20, 2006, p 1A.

[80] Data from "USA Today Snapshots: Learning the Lingo," *USA Today,* January 26, 2006, p 1A. Also see B Kantrowitz and P Wingert, "English Spoken Here," *Newsweek,* July 24, 2006, p 41; B Walton, "Speak the Language of Youth," *USA Today,* January 10, 2007, p 8D; and A O'Connell, "Novartis's Great Leap of Trust," *Harvard Business Review,* March 2007, p 26.

[81] Data from "Diverse Landscape of Newest Americans," *USA Today,* December 4, 2006, p 8A.

[82] See E Marx, *Breaking through Culture Shock: What You Need to Succeed in International Business* (London: Nicholas Brealey Publishing, 2001). For more on cross-cultural adjustment, see Y Gong and J Fan, "Longitudinal Examination of the Role of Goal Orientation in Cross-Cultural Adjustment," *Journal of Applied Psychology,* January 2006, pp 176–84; and Y Gong and S Chang, "The Relationship of Cross-Cultural Adjustment with Dispositional Learning Orientation and Goal Setting: A Longitudinal Analysis," *Journal of Cross-Cultural Psychology,* January 2007, pp 19–25.

[83] See H H Nguyen, L A Messe, and G E Stollak, "Toward a More Complex Understanding of Acculturation and Adjustment," *Journal of Cross-Cultural Psychology,* January 1999, pp 5–31; S Jun, J W Gentry, and Y J Hyun, "Cultural Adaptation of Business Expatriates in the Host Marketplace," *Journal of International Business Studies,* Second Quarter 2001, pp 369–77; M Lazarova and P Caligiuri, "Retaining Repatriates: The Role of Organizational Support Practices," *Journal of World Business,* Winter 2001, pp 389–401; and S Overman, "Mentors without Borders," *HR Magazine,* March 2004, pp 83–85.

[84] K L Miller, "How a Team of Buckeyes Helped Honda Save a Bundle," *BusinessWeek,* September 13, 1993, p 68.

[85] B Newman, "For Ira Caplan, Re-Entry Has Been Strange," *The Wall Street Journal,* December 12, 1995, p A12.

[86] See Black, Gregersen, and Mendenhall, *Global Assignments,* p 227.

[87] Ibid., pp 226–27.

[88] See A B Bossard and R B Peterson, "The Repatriate Experience as Seen by American Expatriates," *Journal of World Business,* February 2005, pp 9–28; and K Tyler, "Retaining Repatriates," *HR Magazine,* March 2006, pp 97–102.

[89] J Hempel, "It Takes a Village—and a Consultant," *BusinessWeek,* September 6, 2004, pp 76–77.

[90] Excerpted from M V Gratchev, "Making the Most of Cultural Differences," *Harvard Business Review,* October 2001, pp 28, 30. For relevant background information, see C J Robertson, K M Gilley, and M D Street, "The Relationship between Ethics and Firm Practices in Russia and the United States," *Journal of World Business,* November 2003, pp 375–84; "Outrage of the Week," *BusinessWeek,* October 2, 2006, p 27; J Bush, "Russia: How Long Can the Fun Last?" *BusinessWeek,* December 18, 2006, pp 50–51; and M Bartiromo, "A Death in London," *BusinessWeek,* December 18, 2006, p 158.

CHAPTER 5

[1] J DeBruicker, "If You're a Jock, You Rock," *BusinessWeek,* September 18, 2006, p 67. Also see A S Wellner, "Eye on the Prize: Secrets of Entrepreneur Athletes," *Inc.,* January 2007, pp 40–41.

[2] Data from www.census.gov/main/www/popclock.html.

[3] Data from B Horovitz, "Ice Cream Shops Thaw Sales with Scoops of Fun," *USA Today,* June 9, 2006, pp 1B–2B.

[4] D Seligman, "The Trouble with Buyouts," *Fortune,* November 30, 1992, p 125.

[5] See A Joshi, H Liao, and S E Jackson, "Cross-Level Effects of Workplace Diversity on Sales Performance and Pay," *Academy of Management Journal,* June 2006, pp 459–61; J A Segal, "'Good Fit' Isn't Always Legit," *HR Magazine,* November 2006, pp 121–26; E H James and L P Wooten, "Diversity Crises: How Firms Manage Discrimination Lawsuits," *Academy of Management Journal,* December 2006, pp 1103–118; and

A Pomeroy, "Cultivating Female Leaders," *HR Magazine,* February 2007, pp 44–50.

[6] See R S Kaplan, "What to Ask the Person in the Mirror," *Harvard Business Review,* January 2007, pp 86–95; and "Young Adults Show More Self-Centeredness," *USA Today,* February 27, 2007, p 9D.

[7] Drawn from E Porter, "Mirror, Mirror on the Wall," *Best Friends Magazine,* January–February 2007, pp 8–9.

[8] Data from "If We Could Do It Over Again," *USA Today,* February 19, 2001, p 4D.

[9] As quoted in G Colvin, "Star Power," *Fortune,* February 6, 2006, p 56.

[10] V Gecas, "The Self-Concept," in *Annual Review of Sociology,* eds R H Turner and J F Short Jr (Palo Alto, CA: Annual Reviews Inc., 1982), vol. 8, p 3. Also see A E Kelly and R R Rodriguez, "Publicly Committing Oneself to an Identity," *Basic and Applied Social Psychology,* June 2006, pp 185–91; R E Boyatzis and K Akrivou, "The Ideal Self as the Driver of Intentional Change," *Journal of Management Development,* no. 7, 2006, pp 624–42; and S N Taylor, "Why the Real Self Is Fundamental to Intentional Change," *Journal of Management Development,* no. 7, 2006, pp 643–56.

[11] L Festinger, *A Theory of Cognitive Dissonance* (Stanford, CA: Stanford University Press, 1957), p 3. Also see G D Bromgard, D Trafimow, and I K Bromgard, "Valence of Self-Cognitions: The Positivity of Individual Self-Statements," *The Journal of Social Psychology,* February 2006, pp 85–94.

[12] Based in part on a definition found in Gecas, "The Self-Concept." Also see N Branden, *Self-Esteem at Work: How Confident People Make Powerful Companies* (San Francisco: Jossey-Bass, 1998). Two types of self-esteem—explicit and implicit—are discussed in A Dijksterhuis, "I Like Myself but I Don't Know Why: Enhancing Implicit Self-Esteem by Subliminal Evaluative Conditioning," *Journal of Personality and Social Psychology,* February 2004, pp 345–55.

[13] H W Marsh, "Positive and Negative Global Self-Esteem: A Substantively Meaningful Distinction or Artifacts?" *Journal of Personality and Social Psychology,* April 1996, p 819.

[14] Ibid.

[15] For more on self-esteem, see S Valentine, "Hispanics' Self-Esteem, Acculturation, and Skepticism of Women's Work," *Journal of Applied Social Psychology,* January 2006, pp 206–21; V L Vignoles, C Regalia, C Manzi, J Golledge, and E Scabini, "Beyond Self-Esteem: Influence of Multiple Motives on Identity Construction," *Journal of Personality and Social Psychology,* February 2006, pp 308–33; U Trautwein, O Ludtke, O Koller, and J Baumert, "Self-Esteem, Academic Self-Concept, and Achievement: How the Learning Environment Moderates the Dynamics of Self-Concept," *Journal of Personality and Social Psychology,* February 2006, pp 334–49; and W B Swann Jr., C Chang-Schneider, and K L. McClarty, "Do People's Self-Views Matter? Self-Concept and Self-Esteem in Everyday Life," *American Psychologist,* February–March 2007, pp 84–94.

[16] See D G Gardner, L Van Dyne, and J L Pierce, "The Effects of Pay Level on Organization-Based Self-Esteem and Performance: A Field Study," *Journal of Occupational and Organizational Psychology,* September 2004, pp 307–22.

[17] A J Fiacco, "Over 50? Keep Foot in Door," *Arizona Republic,* June 20, 2004, p D4.

[18] Ibid.

[19] E Diener and M Diener, "Cross-Cultural Correlates of Life Satisfaction and Self-Esteem," *Journal of Personality and Social Psychology,* April 1995, p 662. Also see D H Silvera and CR Seger, "Feeling Good about Ourselves," *Journal of Cross-Cultural Psychology,* September 2004, pp 571–85.

[20] Based on data in F L Smoll, R E Smith, N P Barnett, and JJ Everett, "Enhancement of Children's Self-Esteem through Social Support Training for Youth Sports Coaches," *Journal of Applied Psychology,* August 1993, pp 602–10.

[21] K Bland, "Purple Reigns: Teachers Spare Feelings by Rejecting Red Ink," *Arizona Republic,* February 19, 2005, p A19. Also see S Hofius, "A Spiritually Inclined Student Is a Happier Student," *USA Today,* October 27, 2004, p 7D.

[22] W J McGuire and C V McGuire, "Enhancing Self-Esteem by Directed-Thinking Tasks: Cognitive and Affective Positivity Asymmetries," *Journal of Personality and Social Psychology,* June 1996, p 1124.

[23] Data from P Coy, "The Competition Issue: The Poll," *BusinessWeek,* August 21–28, 2006, p 46.

[24] See G Chen, S M Gully, and D Eden, "General Self-Efficacy and Self-Esteem: Toward Theoretical and Empirical Distinction between Correlated Self-Evaluations," *Journal of Organizational Behavior,* May 2004, pp 375–95.

[25] M E Gist, "Self-Efficacy: Implications for Organizational Behavior and Human Resource Management," *Academy of Management Review,* July 1987, p 472. Also see A Bandura, "Self-Efficacy: Toward a Unifying Theory of Behavioral Change," *Psychological Review,* March 1977, pp 191–215; TJ Maurer and K D Andrews, "Traditional, Likert, and Simplified Measures of Self-Efficacy," *Educational and Psychological Measurement,* December 2000, pp 965–73; and S L Anderson and N E Betz, "Sources of Social Self-Efficacy Expectations: Their Measurement and Relation to Career Development," *Journal of Vocational Behavior,* February 2001, pp 98–117.

[26] Based on D H Lindsley, D A Brass, and J B Thomas, "Efficacy-Performance Spirals: A Multilevel Perspective," *Academy of Management Review,* July 1995, pp 645–78. Also see H Zhao, S E Seibert, and G E Hills, "The Mediating Role of Self-Efficacy in the Development of Entrepreneurial Intentions," *Journal of Applied Psychology,* November 2005, pp 1265–272; F Luthans, W Zhu, and B J Avolio, "The Impact of Efficacy on Work Attitudes Across Cultures," *Journal of World Business,* June 2006, pp 121–32; G B Yeo and A Neal, "An Examination of the Dynamic Relationship Between Self-Efficacy and Performance Across Levels of Analysis and Levels of Specificity," *Journal of Applied Psychology,* September 2006, pp 1088–101; and J B Vancouver and L N Kendall, "When Self-Efficacy Negatively Relates to Motivation and Performance in a Learning Context," *Journal of Applied Psychology,* September 2006, pp 1146–153.

[27] See, for example, V Gecas, "The Social Psychology of Self-Efficacy," in *Annual Review of Sociology,* eds W R Scott and J Blake (Palo Alto, CA: Annual Reviews, Inc., 1989), vol. 15, pp 291–316; C K Stevens, A G Bavetta, and M E Gist, "Gender Differences in the Acquisition of Salary Negotiation Skills: The Role of Goals, Self-Efficacy, and Perceived Control," *Journal of Applied Psychology,* October 1993, pp 723–35; D Eden and Y Zuk, "Seasickness as a Self-Fulfilling Prophecy: Raising Self-Efficacy to Boost Performance at Sea," *Journal of Applied Psychology,* October 1995, pp 628–35; S M Jex, P D Bliese, S Buzzell, and J Primeau, "The Impact of Self-Efficacy on Stressor-Strain Relations: Coping Style as an Explanatory Mechanism," *Journal of Applied Psychology,* June 2001, pp 401–9; and C A Shields, L B Brawley, and T I Lindover, "Self-Efficacy as a Mediator of the Relationship Between Causal Attributions and Exercise Behavior," *Journal of Applied Social Psychology,* November 2006, pp 2785–802.

[28] Research on this connection is reported in R B Rubin, M M Martin, S S Bruning, and D E Powers, "Test of a Self-Efficacy Model of Interpersonal Communication Competence," *Communication Quarterly,* Spring 1993, pp 210–20.

[29] T Petzinger Jr, "Bob Schmonsees Has a Tool for Better Sales, and It Ignores Excuses," *The Wall Street Journal,* March 26, 1999, p B1.

[30] Data from A D Stajkovic and F Luthans, "Self-Efficacy and Work-Related Performance: A Meta-Analysis," *Psychological Bulletin,* September 1998, pp 240–61.

[31] As quoted in G Colvin, "How One CEO Learned to Fly," *Fortune,* October 30, 2006, p 100.

[32] M Snyder and S Gangestad, "On the Nature of Self-Monitoring: Matters of Assessment, Matters of Validity," *Journal of Personality and Social Psychology,* July 1986, p 125.

[33] T Morganthau, "Throwing Long," *Newsweek,* August 19, 1996, p 29.

[34] Data from D V Day, D J Schleicher, A L Unckless, and N J Hiller, "Self-Monitoring Personality at Work: A Meta-Analytic Investigation of Construct Validity," *Journal of Applied Psychology,* April 2002, pp 390–401. Also see S W Gangestad and M Snyder, "Self-Monitoring: Appraisal and Reappraisal," *Psychological Bulletin,* July 2000, pp 530–55; and I M Jawahar, "Attitudes, Self-Monitoring, and Appraisal Behaviors," *Journal of Applied Psychology,* October 2001, pp 875–83.

[35] Data from M Kilduff and D V Day, "Do Chameleons Get Ahead? The Effects of Self-Monitoring on Managerial Careers," *Academy of Management Journal,* August 1994, pp 1047–60.

[36] Data from D B Turban and T W Dougherty, "Role of Protege Personality in Receipt of Mentoring and Career Success," *Academy of Management Journal,* June 1994, pp 688–702.

[37] See F Luthans, "Successful vs. Effective Managers," *Academy of Management Executive,* May 1988, pp 127–32. Also see F J Flynn and D R Ames, "What's Good for the Goose May Not Be as Good for the Gander: The Benefits of Self-Monitoring for Men and Women in Task Groups and Dyadic Conflicts," *Journal of Applied Psychology,* March 2006, pp 272–81; and F J Flynn, R E Reagans, E T Amanatullah, and D R Ames, "Helping One's Way to the Top: Self-Monitors Achieve Status by Helping Others and Knowing Who Helps Whom," *Journal of Personality and Social Psychology,* December 2006, pp 1123–137.

[38] M G Pratt, "To Be or Not to Be? Central Questions in Organizational Identification," in *Identity in Organizations,* eds D A Whetten and P C Godfrey (Thousand Oaks, CA: Sage Publications, 1998), p 172. Also see S H Chan, "Organizational Identification and Commitment of Members of a Human Development Organization," *Journal of Management Development,* no. 3, 2006, pp 249–68; D van Knippenberg and E Sleebos, "Organizational Identification Versus Organizational Commitment: Self-Definition, Social Exchange, and Job Attitudes," *Journal of Organizational Behavior,* August 2006, pp 571–84; M S Cole and H Bruch, "Organizational Identity Strength, Identification, and Commitment and Their Relationships to Turnover Intention: Does Organizational Hierarchy Matter?" *Journal of Organizational Behavior,* August 2006, pp 585–605; and S M B Thatcher and X Zhu, "Changing Identities in a Changing Workplace: Identification, Identity Enactment, Self-Verification, and Telecommuting," *Academy of Management Review,* October 2006, pp 1076–088.

[39] See T J Erickson and L Gratton, "What It Means to Work Here," *Harvard Business Review,* March 2007, pp 104–12.

[40] R Levering and M Moskowitz, "Fortune 100 Best Companies to Work For," *Fortune,* January 22, 2007, p 108.

[41] Based on C Sertoglu and A Berkowitch, "Cultivating Ex-Employees," *Harvard Business Review,* June 2002, pp 20–21.

[42] For more, see B Filipezak, "The Soul of the Hog," *Training,* February 1996, pp 38–42.

[43] C Fishman, "What if You'd Worked at Enron?" *Fast Company,* May 2002, pp 104, 106.

[44] For related discussion, see G E Kreiner, E C Hollensbe, and M L Sheep, "Where Is the 'Me' Among the 'We'? Identity Work and the Search for Optimal Balance," *Academy of Management Journal,* October 2006, pp 1031–057.

[45] For a good overview, see L R James and M D Mazerolle, *Personality in Work Organizations* (Thousand Oaks, CA: Sage Publications, 2002). Also see J D Mayer, "A Tale of Two Visions: Can a New View of Personality Help Integrate Psychology?" *American Psychologist,* May–June 2005, pp 294–307; and D P McAdams and J L Pals, "A New Big Five: Fundamental Principles for an Integrative Science

of Personality," *American Psychologist,* April 2006, pp 204–17.

[46] See S Yamagata, et al., "Is the Genetic Structure of Human Personality Universal? A Cross-Cultural Twin Study from North America, Europe, and Asia," *Journal of Personality and Social Psychology,* June 2006, pp 987–98.

[47] Data from M C Ashton, K Lee, and L R Goldberg, "A Historical Analysis of 1,710 English Personality-Descriptive Adjectives," *Journal of Personality and Social Psychology,* November 2004, pp 707–21.

[48] The landmark report is J M Digman, "Personality Structure: Emergence of the Five-Factor Model," *Annual Review of Psychology,* vol. 41, 1990, pp 417–40. Also see M R Barrick and M K Mount, "Autonomy as a Moderator of the Relationships between the Big Five Personality Dimensions and Job Performance," *Journal of Applied Psychology,* February 1993, pp 111–18; M R Mehl, S D Gosling, and J W Pennebaker, "Personality in Its Natural Habitat: Manifestations and Implicit Folk Theories of Personality in Daily Life," *Journal of Personality and Social Psychology,* May 2006, pp 862–77; D Nettle, "The Evolution of Personality Variation in Humans and Other Animals," *American Psychologist,* September 2006, pp 622–31; and C G DeYoung, "Higher-Order Factors of the Big Five in a Multi-Informant Sample," *Journal of Personality and Social Psychology,* December 2006, pp 1138–151.

[49] Based on S E Hampson and L R Goldberg, "A First Large Cohort Study of Personality Trait Stability Over the 40 Years Between Elementary School and Midlife," *Journal of Personality and Social Psychology,* October 2006, pp 763–79. Also see B W Roberts, K E Walton, and W Viechtbauer, "Patterns of Mean-Level Change in Personality Traits Across the Life Course: A Meta-Analysis of Longitudinal Studies," *Psychological Bulletin,* January 2006, pp 1–25; and D Watson and J Humrichouse, "Personality Development in Emerging Adulthood: Integrating Evidence from Self-Ratings and Spouse Ratings," *Journal of Personality and Social Psychology,* November 2006, pp 959–74.

[50] Data from S V Paunonen et al., "The Structure of Personality in Six Cultures," *Journal of Cross-Cultural Psychology,* May 1996, pp 339–53; and K Yoon, F Schmidt, and R Ilies, "Cross-Cultural Construct Validity of the Five-Factor Model of Personality among Korean Employees," *Journal of Cross-Cultural Psychology,* May 2002, pp 217–35.

[51] J Allik and R R McCrae, "Escapable Conclusions: Toomela (2003) and the Universality of Trait Structure," *Journal of Personality and Social Psychology,* August 2004, p 261. For more supporting evidence, see D P Schmitt, J Allik, R R McCrae, and V Benet-Martinez, "The Geographic Distribution of Big Five Personality Traits," *Journal of Cross-Cultural Psychology,* March 2007, pp 173–212.

[52] See M R Barrick and M K Mount, "The Big Five Personality Dimensions and Job Performance: A Meta-Analysis," *Personnel Psychology,* Spring 1991, pp 1–26. Also see R P Tett, D N Jackson, and M Rothstein, "Personality Measures as Predictors of Job Performance:

A Meta-Analytic Review," *Personnel Psychology,* Winter 1991, pp 703–42.

53 Barrick and Mount, "The Big Five Personality Dimensions and Job Performance," p 18. Also see N M Dudley, K A Orvis, J E Lebiecki, and J M Cortina, "A Meta-Analytic Investigation of Conscientiousness in the Prediction of Job Performance: Examining the Intercorrelations and the Incremental Validity of Narrow Traits," *Journal of Applied Psychology,* January 2006, pp 40–57; K Gurchiek, "U.S. Workers Continue to Leave Vacation Unused," *HR Magazine,* August 2006, p 35; C Peterson and N Park, "Character Strengths in Organizations," *Journal of Organizational Behavior,* December 2006, pp 1149–154; and T W H Ng, K L Sorensen, and D C Feldman, "Dimensions, Antecedents, and Consequences of Workaholism: A Conceptual Integration and Extension," *Journal of Organizational Behavior,* January 2007, pp 111–36.

54 See H Zhao and S E Seibert, "The Big Five Personality Dimensions and Entrepreneurial Status: A Meta-Analytical Review," *Journal of Applied Psychology,* March 2006, pp. 259–71.

55 Based on S E Seibert and M L Kraimer, "The Five-Factor Model of Personality and Career Success," *Journal of Vocational Behavior,* February 2001, pp 1–21.

56 J M Crant, "Proactive Behavior in Organizations," *Journal of Management,* 2000, p 439. Also see S K Parker, H M Williams, and N Turner, "Modeling the Antecedents of Proactive Behavior at Work," *Journal of Applied Psychology,* May 2006, pp 636–52; and D A Major, J E Turner, and T D Fletcher, "Linking Proactive Personality and the Big Five to Motivation to Learn and Development Activity," *Journal of Applied Psychology,* July 2006, pp 927–35.

57 Ibid., pp 439–41. Also see D Chan, "Interactive Effects of Situational Judgment Effectiveness and Proactive Personality on Work Perceptions and Work Outcomes," *Journal of Applied Psychology,* March 2006, pp 475–81; D J Brown, R T Cober, K Kane, P E Levy, and J Shalhoop, "Proactive Personality and the Successful Job Search: A Field Investigation with College Graduates," *Journal of Applied Psychology,* May 2006, pp 717–26; S W Spreier, M H Fontaine, and R L Malloy, "Leadership Run Amok: The Destructive Potential of Overachievers," *Harvard Business Review,* June 2006, pp 72–84; and J B Fuller, L E Marler, and K Hester, "Promoting Felt Responsibility for Constructive Change and Proactive Behavior: Exploring Aspects of an Elaborated Model of Work Design," *Journal of Organizational Behavior,* December 2006, pp 1089–120.

58 P J Sauer, "A Portfolio of Young Business Owners," *Inc.,* February 2007, p 24. Also see D Johnson, J B L Craig, and R Hildebrand, "Entrepreneurship Education: Towards a Discipline-Based Framework," *Journal of Management Development,* no. 1, 2006, pp 40–54; S Perman, "Where the Rubber Is the Roadside," *BusinessWeek,* December 11, 2006, p 76; L Tischler, "Fast Talk: Karen Walker," *Fast Company,* January 2007, pp 38–39.

59 See H Johnson, "Strength of Heart," *Training,* July 2004, p 16; D Lidsky, "Test Your Courage: How Do You Rate?" *Fast Company,* September 2004, pp 107–9; G P Hollenbeck and D T Hall, "Self-Confidence and Leader Performance," *Organizational Dynamics,* 2004, pp 254–69; and "Measuring Character," *Training,* October 2004, p 16.

60 A Siebert, "Develop Resiliency Skills," *Training and Development,* September 2006, pp 88–89.

61 See J A Sonnenfeld and A J Ward, "Firing Back: How Great Leaders Rebound After Career Disasters," *Harvard Business Review,* Special Issue: The Tests of a Leader, January 2007, pp 76–84; and G E Mangurian, "Realizing What You're Made Of," *Harvard Business Review,* March 2007, pp 125–30.

62 R Kurtz, "Testing, Testing," *Inc.,* June 2004, p 36. Also see A Overholt, "Personality Tests: Back with a Vengeance," *Fast Company,* November 2004, pp 115–17.

63 See A Murphy Paul, *The Cult of Personality: How Personality Tests Are Leading Us to Miseducate Our Children, Mismanage Our Companies, and Misunderstand Ourselves* (New York: Free Press, 2004).

64 H Dolezalek, "Tests on Trial," *Training,* April 2005, p 34. Also see R A Clay, "Assessing Assessment," *Monitor on Psychology,* January 2006, pp 44–46; S Clifford, "The New Science of Hiring," *Inc.,* August 2006, pp 90–98; S Birkman Fink, "10 Reasons to Test Personality Before Hiring," *Training,* November 2006, p 16; and C Palmeri, "Putting Managers To the Test," *BusinessWeek,* November 20, 2006, p 82.

65 R Lieber, "Wired for Hiring: Microsoft's Slick Recruiting Machine," *Fortune,* February 5, 1996, p 124.

66 For an instructive update, see J B Rotter, "Internal versus External Control of Reinforcement: A Case History of a Variable," *American Psychologist,* April 1990, pp 489–93. For relevant research updates, see W Johnson and R F Krueger, "Higher Perceived Life Control Decreases Genetic Variance in Physical Health: Evidence from a National Twin Study," *Journal of Personality and Social Psychology,* January 2005, pp 165–73; and C Tay, S Ang, and L Van Dyne, "Personality, Biographical Characteristics, and Job Interview Success: A Longitudinal Study of the Mediating Effects of Interviewing Self-Efficacy and the Moderating Effects of Internal Locus of Causality," *Journal of Applied Psychology,* March 2006, pp 446–54.

67 See D Freydkin, "For the Fresh Prince, Films Are Family Business," *USA Today,* December 6, 2006, pp 1A–2A; and "Moments of Truth: Global Executives Talk About the Challenges That Shaped Them as Leaders," *Harvard Business Review,* Special Issue: The Tests of a Leader, January 2007, pp 15–25.

68 J Fierman, "What's Luck Got to Do with It?" *Fortune,* October 16, 1995, p 149.

69 L Buchanan, "The Impostor Syndrome: Why Do So Many Successful Entrepreneurs Feel Like Fakes?" *Inc.,* September 2006, pp 37–38.

70 For an overall review of research on locus of control, see P E Spector, "Behavior in Organizations as a Function of Employee's Locus of Control," *Psychological Bulletin,*

May 1982, pp 482–97; for the linkage to motivation, see
T W H Ng, K L Sorensen, and L T Eby, "Locus of Control at
Work: A Meta-Analysis," *Journal of Organizational Behavior,*
December 2006, pp 1057–087; the relationship between locus
of control and performance and satisfaction is examined
in D R Norris and R E Niebuhr, "Attributional Influences on the
Job Performance–Job Satisfaction Relationship,"
Academy of Management Journal, June 1984, pp 424–31;
salary differences between internals and externals were
examined by P C Nystrom, "Managers' Salaries and Their
Beliefs about Reinforcement Control," *Journal of Social
Psychology,* August 1983, pp 291–92.

[71] Robert Solomon, as quoted in D Vera and A Rodriguez-
Lopez, "Strategic Virtues: Humility as a Source of
Competitive Advantage," *Organizational Dynamics,* no. 4,
2004, pp 394–95.

[72] Ibid., p 395. Also see A Stein Wellner, "Making Amends,"
Inc., June 2006, pp 41–42; and D Kirkpatrick, "Use Humility
as a Weapon: Hector Ruiz, CEO, AMD," *Fortune,* October 30,
2006, p 118.

[73] S B Parry, "The Quest for Competencies," *Training,*
July 1996, p 48. Also see S Meisinger, "Shortage of Skilled
Workers Threatens Economy," *HR Magazine,* November 2004,
p 12; and S Holt, "More Job Simulations," *Arizona Republic,*
February 26, 2005, p D3.

[74] See D Lidsky, "A Hard Day's Night," *Fast Company,*
September 2006, p 100; B Fryer, "Sleep Deficit: The
Performance Killer," *Harvard Business Review,* October
2006, pp 53–59; M Myser, "$20 Billion for a Good Night's
Rest," *Business 2.0,* October 2006, pp 57–59; and D Futrelle,
"Sleep Your Way to Success," *Money,* November 2006,
pp 136–39.

[75] Data from "People Rate How They Sleep," *USA Today,*
April 12, 2005, p 1A. Also see "Sleep Disorders Cost the USA
Billions," *USA Today,* April 5, 2006, p 6D.

[76] A Pomeroy, "Sleep Deprivation and Medical Errors,"
HR Magazine, February 2002, p 42.

[77] A Weintraub, "Napping Your Way to the Top," *BusinessWeek,*
November 27, 2006, p 98–99.

[78] As quoted in Ibid. Also see S Armour, "Companies Try
to Help Workers Sleep More," *USA Today,* August 22, 2006,
p 3B.

[79] For interesting reading on intelligence, see M Elias, "Mom's
IQ, Not Family Size, Key to Kids' Smarts," *USA Today,*
June 12, 2000, p ID; R Sapolsky, "Score One for Nature—or
Is It Nurture?" *USA Today,* June 21, 2000, p 17A; D Lubinski,
R M Webb, M J Morelock, and C P Benbow, "Top 1 in 10,000:
A 10-Year Follow-Up of the Profoundly Gifted," *Journal
of Applied Psychology,* Augus t 2001, pp 718–29; and
T A Judge, A E Colbert, and R Ilies, "Intelligence and
Leadership: A Quantitative Review and Test of Theoretical
Propositions," *Journal of Applied Psychology,* June 2004,
pp 542–52.

[80] For an excellent update on intelligence, including definitional
distinctions and a historical perspective of the IQ controversy, see
R A Weinberg, "Intelligence and IQ," *American Psychologist,*

February 1989, pp 98–104. Also see R Plomin and F M Spinath,
"Intelligence: Genetics, Genes, and Genomics," *Journal of
Personality and Social Psychology,* January 2004, pp 112–29;
C Arnst, "Getting Girls to the Lab Bench," *BusinessWeek,*
February 7, 2005, p 42; J J Salopek, "Nature and Nurture,"
Training and Development, April 2006, pp 26–27; M Elias, "After
60, the Crabbiest People Are the Smartest, Study Suggests," *USA
Today,* August 17, 2006, p 7D; and M Kripalani, "An Awakening
in Bihar," *BusinessWeek,* August 21–28, 2006, p 74.

[81] Weinberg, "Intelligence and IQ."

[82] S L Wilk, L Burris Desmarais, and P R Sackett,
"Gravitation to Jobs Commensurate with Ability: Longitudinal
and Cross-Sectional Tests," *Journal of Applied Psychology,*
February 1995, p 79.

[83] B Azar, "People Are Becoming Smarter—Why?" *APA Monitor,*
June 1996, p 20. Also see " 'Average' Intelligence Higher than It
Used to Be," *USA Today,* February 18, 1997, p 6D.

[84] See D Lubinski, "Introduction to the Special Section
on Cognitive Abilities: 100 Years after Spearman's (1904)
'General Intelligence, Objectively Determined and Measured,' "
Journal of Personality and Social Psychology, January 2004,
pp 96–111; and N L Vasilopoulos, J M Cucina, and
J M McElreath, "Do Warnings of Response Verification
Moderate the Relationship between Personality and Cognitive
Ability?" *Journal of Applied Psychology,* March 2005,
pp 306–22. Also see T Gallén, "Managers and Strategic
Decisions: Does the Cognitive Style Matter?" *Journal
of Management Development,* no. 2, 2006, pp 118–33;
J W Janove, "Turning Right in a Left-Brained World," *HR
Magazine,* August 2006, pp 111–14; and R L Jolles, "Think
Fast!" *Training and Development,* October 2006, pp 89–90.

[85] See F L Schmidt and J E Hunter, "Employment Testing: Old
Theories and New Research Findings," *American Psychologist,*
October 1981, p 1128. Also see Y Ganzach, "Intelligence
and Job Satisfaction," *Academy of Management Journal,*
October 1998, pp 526–39.

[86] See H Gardner, *Frames of Mind: The Theory of Multiple
Intelligences,* 10th anniversary ed (New York: Basic Books, 1993);
and H Gardner, *Intelligence Reframed: Multiple Intelligences for
the 21st Century* (New York: Basic Books, 2000).

[87] For a good overview of Gardner's life and work, see
M K Smith, "Howard Gardner and Multiple Intelligences,"
Encyclopedia of Informal Education, 2002, www.infed.org/
thinkers/gardner.htm. Also see B Fryer, "The Ethical Mind:
A Conversation with Psychologist Howard Gardner," *Harvard
Business Review,* March 2007, pp 51–56.

[88] R J Sternberg, "WICS: A Model of Leadership in
Organizations," *Academy of Management Learning and
Education,* December 2003, p 388. "Executive intelligence"
is discussed in J Menkes, "Hiring for Smarts," *Harvard Business
Review,* November 2005, pp 100–09 and "political intelligence"
is discussed in R M Kramer, "The Great Intimidators," *Harvard
Business Review,* February 2006, pp 88–96.

[89] See K Albrecht, "Social Intelligence: Beyond IQ," *Training,*
December 2004, pp 26–31; and AA Loort, "Multiple
Intelligences: A Comparative Study Between the Preferences

of Males and Females," *Social Behavior and Personality,* no.1, 2005, pp 77–88.

[90] See C D Fisher and N M Ashkanasy, "The Emerging Role of Emotions in Work Life: an Introduction," *Journal of Organizational Behavior,* March 2000, pp 123–29; P M Muchinsky, "Emotions in the Workplace: The Neglect of Organizational Behavior," *Journal of Organizational Behavior,* November 2000, pp 801–5; N M Ashkanasy and C S Daus, "Emotion in the Workplace: The New Challenge for Managers," *Academy of Management Executive,* February 2002, pp 76–86; A Molinsky and J Margolis, "The Emotional Tightrope of Downsizing: Hidden Challenges for Leaders and Their Organizations," *Organizational Dynamics,* no. 2, 2006, pp 145–59; P Tyre and J Scelfo, "Why Girls Will Be Girls," *Newsweek,* July 31, 2006, pp 46–47; and C T Fong, "The Effects of Emotional Ambivalence on Creativity," *Academy of Management Journal,* October 2006, pp 1016–030.

[91] S Hamm, "Bill's Co-Pilot," *BusinessWeek,* September 14, 1998, pp 85, 87.

[92] G Anders, "John Chambers after the Deluge," *Fast Company,* July 2001, p 108.

[93] R S Lazarus, *Emotion and Adaptation* (New York: Oxford University Press, 1991), p 6. Also see C Scott and K Myers, "The Socialization of Emotion: Learning Emotion Management at the Fire Station," *Journal of Applied Communication Research,* February 2005, pp 67–92.

[94] Based on discussion in R D Arvey, G L Renz, and T W Watson, "Emotionality and Job Performance: Implications for Personnel Selection," in *Research in Personnel and Human Resources Management,* vol. 16, ed G R Ferris (Stamford, CT: JAI Press, 1998), pp 103–47. Also see J M Diefendorff, E M Richard, and M H Croyle, "Are Emotional Display Rules Formal Job Requirements? Examinations of Employee and Supervisor Perceptions," *Journal of Occupational and Organizational Psychology,* June 2006, pp 273–98; and R Reisenzein, S Bordgen, T Holtbernd, and D Matz, "Evidence for Strong Dissociation Between Emotion and Facial Displays: The Case of Surprise," *Journal of Personality and Social Psychology,* August 2006, pp 295–315.

[95] See M Conlin, "Held Hostage By Health Care," *BusinessWeek,* January 29, 2007, p 82; and D Jones, "Could Insecurity Be the Secret to CEOs' Success?" *USA Today,* February 1, 2007, pp 1B–2B.

[96] J A Byrne and H Timmons, "Tough Times," *BusinessWeek,* October 29, 2001, p 66. Also see J E Dutton, P J Frost, MC Worline, J M Lilius, and J M Kanov, "Leading in Times of Trauma," *Harvard Business Review,* January 2002, pp 54–61; and J Creswell, "Ken Chenault Reshuffles His Cards," *Fortune,* April 18, 2005, pp 180–86.

[97] J McGregor, "#1 Taryn Rose," *Fast Company,* May 2005, p 69.

[98] D Goleman, *Emotional Intelligence* (New York: Bantam Books, 1995), p 34. For more, see S Cote and C T H Miners, "Emotional Intelligence, Cognitive Intelligence, and Job Performance," *Administrative Science Quarterly,* March 2006,

pp 1–28; S Jayson, "Sociability: It's All in Your Mind," *USA Today,* September 25, 2006, p 5D; M A Brackett, S E Rivers, S Shiffman, N Lerner, and P Salovey, "Relating Emotional Abilities to Social Functioning: A Comparison of Self-Report and Performance Measures of Emotional Intelligence," *Journal of Personality and Social Psychology,* October 2006, pp 780–95; and B Wall, "Being Smart Only Takes You So Far," *Training and Development,* January 2007, pp 64–68.

[99] See "What's Your EQ at Work," *Fortune,* October 26, 1998, p 298 and B Wall, *Coaching for Emotional Intelligence* (NY: AMACOM, 2006). For recent research, see K V Petrides and A Furnham, "The Role of Trait Emotional Intelligence in a Gender-Specific Model of Organizational Variables," *Journal of Applied Social Psychology,* February 2006, pp 552–69; J E Barbuto Jr. and M E Burbach, "The Emotional Intelligence of Transformational Leaders: A Field Study of Elected Officials," *The Journal of Social Psychology,* February 2006, pp 51–64; and E Engelberg and L Sjoberg, "Money Attitudes and Emotional Intelligence," *Journal of Applied Social Psychology,* August 2006, pp 2027–047.

[100] Data from S D Pugh, "Service with a Smile: Emotional Contagion in the Service Encounter," *Academy of Management Journal,* October 2001, pp 1018–27. Also see P B Barger and A A Grandey, "Service With a Smile and Encounter Satisfaction: Emotional Contagion and Appraisal Mechanisms," *Academy of Management Journal,* December 2006, pp 1229–238.

[101] Drawn from P Totterdell, S Kellett, K Teuchmann, and RB Briner, "Evidence of Mood Linkage in Work Groups," *Journal of Personality and Social Psychology,* June 1998, pp 1504–15. Also see A Singh-Manoux and C Finkenauer, "Cultural Variations in Social Sharing of Emotions: An Intercultural Perspective," *Journal of Cross-Cultural Psychology,* November 2001, pp 647–61; H H Tan, M D Foo, and M H Kwek, "The Effects of Customer Personality Traits on the Display of Positive Emotions," *Academy of Management Journal,* April 2004, pp 287–96; and T Sy, S Cote, and R Saavedra, "The Contagious Leader: Impact of the Leader's Mood on the Mood of Group Members, Group Affective Tone, and Group Processes," *Journal of Applied Psychology,* March 2005, pp 295–305.

[102] "Ulrich Schumacher," *BusinessWeek,* June 11, 2001, p 82.

[103] N M Ashkanasy and C S Daus, "Emotion in the Workplace: The New Challenge for Managers," *Academy of Management Executive,* February 2002, p 79. Also see J M Diefendorff, M H Croyle, and R H Gosserand, "The Dimensionality and Antecedents of Emotional Labor Strategies," *Journal of Vocational Behavior,* April 2005, pp 339–57; R H Gosserand and J M Diefendorff, "Emotional Display Rules and Emotional Labor: The Moderating Role of Commitment," *Journal of Applied Psychology*, November 2005, pp 1256–264; D E Rupp and S Spencer, "When Customers Lash Out: The Effects of Customer Interactional Injustice on Emotional Labor and the Mediating Role of Discrete Emotions," *Journal of Applied Psychology,* July 2006, pp 971–78; and D J Beal, J P Trougakos, H M Weiss, and S G Green, "Episodic Processes in Emotional Labor: Perceptions of Affective Delivery and Regulation

Strategies," *Journal of Applied Psychology,* September 2006, pp 1053–065.

[104] Data from A M Kring and A H Gordon, "Sex Differences in Emotions: Expressions, Experience, and Physiology," *Journal of Personality and Social Psychology,* March 1998, pp 686–703.

[105] See P J Frost, "Handling Toxic Emotions: New Challenges for Leaders and Their Organizations," *Organizational Dynamics,* no. 2, 2004, pp 111–27; T A Judge, B A Scott, and R Ilies, "Hostility, Job Attitudes, and Workplace Deviance: Test of a Multilevel Model," *Journal of Applied Psychology,* January 2006, pp 126–38; and S Sternberg, "Study: Angry People More Likely To Be Severely Hurt," *USA Today,* February 6, 2006, p 4D.

[106] Excerpted from P Sellers, "The Recruiter," *Fortune,* November 27, 2006, pp 87–88, 90.

[107] Excerpted from P Bathurst, "Workplace Policies on Body Art Differ," *The Arizona Republic,* October 22, 2006, p EC1.

CHAPTER 6

[1] Excerpted from M Weinstein, "Balancing Act," *Training,* March 2007, pp 22, 24.

[2] These results are presented in D E Lewis, "US Workers Making Plans to Job-Hop This Year," *Arizona Republic,* January 2, 2005, p D1. Turnover statistics are also presented in "Turnover Intel," *Training,* January/ February 2007, p 9.

[3] Research on turnover is summarized by P W Hom and R W Griffeth, *Employee Turnover* (Cincinnati, OH: Southwestern, 1995).

[4] Examples are provided in R Levering and M Moskowitz, "The 100 Best Companies to Work For," *Fortune,* January 22, 2007, pp 94–114.

[5] M Rokeach, *The Nature of Values* (New York: Free Press, 1973), p 5.

[6] See S H Schwartz and T Rubel, "Sex Differences in Value Priorities: Cross-Cultural and Multimethod Studies," *Journal of Personality and Social Psychology,* December 2005, pp 1010–28.

[7] See M Rokeach, *Beliefs, Attitudes, and Values* (San Francisco: Jossey-Bass, 1968).

[8] This example was taken from D Jones, "Sara Lee Biggest Company (for Now) with Female CEO," *USA Today,* February 11, 2005, p 43; and "Brenda C. Barnes Biography," www.saralee.com/home.aspx, accessed March 27, 2007.

[9] P B Brown, "What I Know Now," *Fast Company,* February 2005, p 96.

[10] This example was derived from D Lieberman, "L.A. Times' Publisher Forced Out Over Refusal to Cut Staff," *USA Today,* October 6, 2006, p 1B.

[11] For a thorough discussion of person-culture fit, see A L Kristof-Brown, R D Zimmerman, and E C Johnson,

"Consequences of Individuals' Fit at Work: A Meta-Analysis of Person-Job, Person-Organization, Person-Group, and Person-Supervisor Fit," *Personnel Psychology,* Summer 2005, pp 281–342.

[12] Supportive results can be found in H A Elfenbein and C A O'Reilly III, "Fitting In: The Effects of Relational Demography and Person-Culture Fit on Group Process and Performance," *Group & Organization Management,* February 2007, pp 109–42; and C Ostroff, Y Shin, and A Kinicki, "Multiple Perspectives of Congruence: Relationships between Value Congruence and Employee Attitudes," *Journal of Organizational Behavior,* September 2005, pp 591–624.

[13] B Moses, "The Busyness Trap," *Training,* November 1998.

[14] See P Sellers, "A Kinder, Gentler Lehman Brothers," *Fortune,* January 22, 2007, pp 36–38; K Gurchiek, "Give Us Your Sick," *HR Magazine,* January 2007, pp 91–93; and M J Frase, "International Commuters," *HR Magazine,* March 2007, pp 91–95.

[15] K W Smola and C D Sutton, "Generational Differences: Revisiting Generational Work Values for the New Millennium," *Journal of Organizational Behavior,* June 2002, p 379. (See P Engardio, C Matlack, G Edmondson, I Rowley, C Barraclough, and G Smith, "Now the Geezer Glut," *BusinessWeek,* January 31, 2005, pp 44–47; and A Park, "Between a Rocker and a High Chair," *BusinessWeek,* February 21, 2005, pp 86–88.)

[16] Excerpted from S Shellenbarger, "Dealing with the Dead Zone: Spouses Too Tired to Talk," *The Wall Street Journal,* February 22, 2007, p D1.

[17] See ibid.

[18] P L Perrewé and W A Hochwarter, "Can We Really Have It All? The Attainment of Work and Family Values," *Current Directions in Psychological Science,* February 2001, p 31.

[19] Results can be found in D Brady, "Hopping Aboard the Daddy Track," *BusinessWeek,* November 8, 2004, p 101.

[20] See L M Graves, P J Ohlott, and M N Ruderman, "Commitment to Family Roles: Effects on Managers' Attitudes and Performance," *Journal of Applied Psychology,* January 2007, pp 44–56.

[21] Examples can be found in S Shellenbarger, "Employers Step Up Efforts to Lure Stay-at-Home Mothers Back to Work," *The Wall Street Journal,* February 9, 2006, p D1.

[22] The need for flexibility is discussed by S Shellenbarger, "Reasons to Hold Out Hope for Balancing Work and Home," *The Wall Street Journal,* January 11, 2007, p D1; and S Shellenbarger, "Time on Your Side: Rating Your Boss's Flexible Scheduling," *The Wall Street Journal,* January 25, 2007, p D1.

[23] T R Nielson, D S Carlson, and M J Lankau, "The Supportive Mentor as a Means of Reducing Work-Family Conflict," *Journal of Vocational Behavior,* December 2001, pp 374–75.

[24] Results can be found in M T Ford, B A Heinen, and K L Langkamer, "Work and Family Satisfaction and

Conflict: A Meta-Analysis of Cross-Domain Relations," *Journal of Applied Psychology,* January 2007, pp 57–80; and W J Casper, L T Eby, C Cordeaux, A Lockwood, and D Lambert, "A Review of Research Methods in IO/OB Work-Family Research," *Journal of Applied Psychology,* January 2007, pp 28–43.

[25] Based on S Parasuraman and C A Simmers, "Type of Employment, Work-Family Conflict and Well-Being: A Comparative Study," *Journal of Organizational Behavior,* August 2001, pp 551–68.

[26] R Rapoport, L Bailyn, J K Fletcher, and B H Pruitt, *Beyond Work-Family Balance: Advancing Gender Equity and Workplace Performance* (San Francisco: Jossey-Bass, 2002), p 36.

[27] These results are discussed in L Winerman, "A Healthy Mind, a Longer Life," *Monitor on Psychology,* November 2006, pp 42–44.

[28] See D A Harrison, D A Newman, and P L Roth, "How Important Are Job Attitudes? Meta-Analytic Comparisons of Integrative Behavioral Outcomes and Time Sequences," *Academy of Management Journal,* April 2006, pp 305–25.

[29] M Fishbein and I Ajzen, *Belief, Attitude, Intention and Behavior: An Introduction to Theory and Research* (Reading, MA: Addison-Wesley Publishing, 1975), p 6.

[30] The components or structure of attitudes is thoroughly discussed by A P Brief, *Attitudes in and around Organizations* (Thousand Oaks, CA: Sage, 1998), pp 49–84.

[31] For details about this theory, see L Festinger, *A Theory of Cognitive Dissonance* (Stanford, CA: Stanford University Press, 1957). Also see J V Petrocelli, Z L Tormala, and D D Rucker, "Unpacking Attitude Certainty: Attitude Clarity and Attitude Correctness," *Journal of Personality and Social Psychology,* January 2007, pp 30–41; and S C Wheeler, P Briñol and A D Hermann, "Resistance to Persuasion As Self-Regulation: Ego-depletion and Its Effects on Attitude Change Processes," *Journal of Experimental Social Psychology,* January 2007, pp 150–56.

[32] See B M Staw and J Ross, "Stability in the Midst of Change: A Dispositional Approach to Job Attitudes," *Journal of Applied Psychology,* August 1985, pp 469–80. Also see J Schaubroeck, D C Ganster, and B Kemmerer, "Does Trait Affect Promote Job Attitude Stability?" *Journal of Organizational Behavior,* March 1996, pp 191–96.

[33] Data from P S Visser and J A Krosnick, "Development of Attitude Strength over the Life Cycle: Surge and Decline," *Journal of Personality and Social Psychology,* December 1998, pp 389–410.

[34] I Ajzen, "The Theory of Planned Behavior," *Organizational Behavior and Human Decision Processes,* vol. 50 (1991), p 188.

[35] See R P Steel and N K Ovalle II, "A Review and Meta-Analysis of Research on the Relationship between Behavioral Intentions and Employee Turnover," *Journal of Applied Psychology,* November 1984, pp 673–86.

[36] Results can be found in M R Barrick and R D Zimmerman, "Reducing Voluntary Turnover through Selection," *Journal of Applied Psychology,* January 2005, pp 159–66.

[37] Drawn from I Ajzen and M Fishbein, *Understanding Attitudes and Predicting Social Behavior* (Englewood Cliffs, NJ: Prentice Hall, 1980); and C-S Lu, K-H Lai, and T C E Cheng, "Application of Structural Equation Modeling to Evaluate the Intention of Shippers to Use Internet Services in Liner Shipping," *European Journal of Operational Research,* July 2007, pp 845–67; A McKinlay and S Cowan, " 'If You're Frail You've Had It': A Theory of Planned Behavior Study of Nurses' Attitudes Towards Working with Older Patients," *Journal of Applied Social Psychology,* April 2006, pp 900–17; J G Pesek, R D Raehsler, and R S Balough, "Future Professionals and Managers: Their Attitudes Toward Unions, Organizational Beliefs, and Work Ethic," *Journal of Applied Social Psychology,* June 2006, pp 1569–94; D Albarracín, B T Johnson, M Fishbein, and P A Muellerleile, "Theories of Reasoned Action and Planned Behavior as Models of Condom Use: A Meta Analysis," *Psychological Bulletin,* January 2001, pp 142–61; and P W Hom and C L Hulin, "A Competitive Test of the Prediction of Reenlistment by Several Models," *Journal of Applied Psychology,* February 1981, pp 23–39.

[38] Results can be found in E A J Hooft, M P Born, T W Taris, and H V D Flier, "The Cross-Cultural Generalizability of the Theory of Planned Behavior," *Journal of Cross-Cultural Psychology,* March 2006, pp 127–35.

[39] Supportive research is presented in T L Webb and P Sheeran, "Does Changing Behavioral Intentions Engender Behavior Change: A Meta-Analysis of the Experimental Evidence," *Psychological Bulletin,* March 2006, pp 249–68.

[40] Results can be found in M L Kraimer, S J Wayne, R C Liden, and R T Sparrowe, "The Role of Job Security in Understanding the Relationship between Employees' Perceptions of Temporary Workers and Employees' Performance," *Journal of Applied Psychology,* March 2005, pp 389–98.

[41] L Yerkes, *Fun Works: Creating Places Where People Love to Work* (San Francisco: Berrett-Koehler, 2001), p 73.

[42] The concept of commitment and its relationship to motivated behavior is thoroughly discussed by J P Meyer, T E Becker, and C Vandenberghe, "Employee Commitment and Motivation: A Conceptual Analysis and Integrative Model," *Journal of Applied Psychology,* December 2004, pp 991–1007.

[43] J P Meyer and L Herscovitch, "Commitment in the Workplace: Toward a General Model," *Human Resource Management Review,* Autumn 2001, p 301.

[44] J P Meyer and N J Allen, "A Three-Component Conceptualization of Organizational Commitment," *Human Resource Management Review,* Spring 1991, p 67.

[45] See R E Johnson and C-H Chang, "'I' Is to Continuance as 'We' Is to Affective: The Relevance of the Self-Concept For Organizational Commitment," *Journal of Organizational Behavior,* August 2006, pp 549–70; and J P Meyer, T E Becker, and R Van Dick, "Social Identities and Commitments at Work: Toward an Integrative Model," *Journal of Organizational Behavior,* August 2006, pp 665–83.

46 This definition was provided by D M Rousseau, "Psychological and Implied Contracts in Organizations," *Employee Responsibilities and Rights Journal,* June 1989, 121–39.

47 Results can be found in N P Podsakoff, J A LePine, M A LePine, "Differential Challenge Stressor-Hindrance Stressor Relationships with Job Attitudes, Turnover Intentions, Turnover, and Withdrawal Behavior: A Meta-Analysis," *Journal of Applied Psychology,* March 2007, pp 438–54.

48 Results can be found in M Riketta, "Attitudinal Organizational Commitment and Job Performance: A Meta-Analysis," *Journal of Organizational Behavior,* March 2002, pp 257–66.

49 Results can be found in R W Griffeth, P W Hom, and S Gaertner, "A Meta-Analysis of Antecedents and Correlates of Employee Turnover: Update, Moderator Tests, and Research Implications for the Next Millennium," *Journal of Management,* 2000, pp 463–88. Also see P F McKay, D R Avery, S Tonidandel, M A Morris, M Hernandez, and M R Hebl, "Racial Differences in Employee Retention: Are Diversity Climate Perceptions the Key?" *Personnel Psychology,* Spring 2007, pp 35–62.

50 These examples were discussed in R Levering and M Moskowitz, "The 100 Best Companies to Work For," *Fortune,* January 22, 2007, p 94.

51 R Levering and M Moskowitz, "The 100 Best Companies to Work For," *Fortune,* January 24, 2005, p 84.

52 Ibid, pp 80, 82. Also see M A S Al-Emadi and M J Marquardt, "Relationship between Employees' Beliefs Regarding Training Benefits and Employees' Organizational Commitment in a Petroleum Company in the State of Qatar," *International Journal of Training and Development,* March 2007, pp 49–70.

53 I M Paullay, G M Alliger, and E F Stone-Romero, "Construct Validation of Two Instruments Designed to Measure Job Involvement and Work Centrality," *Journal of Applied Psychology,* April 1994, p 224.

54 Yerkes, *Fun Works,* p 126.

55 Ibid.

56 Results can be found in S P Brown, "A Meta-Analysis and Review of Organizational Research on Job Involvement," *Psychological Bulletin,* September 1996, pp 235–55.

57 Results can be found in J M Diefendorff, D J Brown, A M Kamin, and R G Lord, "Examining the Roles of Job Involvement and Work Centrality in Predicting Organizational Citizenship Behaviors and Job Performance," *Journal of Organizational Behavior,* February 2002, pp 93–108.

58 Results can be found in N A Bowling, T A Beehr, and L R Lepisto, "Beyond Job Satisfaction: A Five-Year Prospective Analysis of the Dispositional Approach to Work Attitudes," *Journal of Vocational Behavior,* October 2006, pp 315–30.

59 See S Sonnentag and U Kruel, "Psychological Detachment from Work During Off-Job Time: The Role of Job Stressor, Job Involvement, and Recovery-Related Self-Efficacy," *European Journal of Work and Organizational Pscyhology,* June 2006, pp 197–17.

60 See J Wegge, K-H Schmidt, C Parkes, and R van Dick, "Taking a Sickie: Job Satisfaction and Job Involvement as Interactive Predictors of Absenteeism in a Public Organization," *Journal of Occupational and Organizational Psychology,* March 2007, pp 77–90.

61 For a review of the development of the JDI, see P C Smith, L M Kendall, and C L Hulin, *The Measurement of Satisfaction in Work and Retirement* (Skokie, IL: Rand McNally, 1969).

62 Supportive results can be found in "Job Satisfaction Palls Quickly for Most Workers," *HR Magazine,* March 2007, p 16; S Miller, "Satisfaction with Pay, Benefits Falling," *HR Magazine,* January 2007, pp 38–39; and "Middle Managers Unhappy," *HR Magazine,* July 2006, p 16.

63 For a review of these models, see Brief, *Attitudes in and around Organizations.*

64 See A R Karr, "Work Week: A Special News Report about Life on the Job—and Trends Taking Shape There," *The Wall Street Journal,* June 29, 1999, p A1.

65 The survey was conducted by Hewitt and Associates, and results were presented in J Saranow, "Anybody Want to Take a Nap?" *The Wall Street Journal,* January 24, 2005, p R5.

66 For a review of need satisfaction models, see E F Stone, "A Critical Analysis of Social Information Processing Models of Job Perceptions and Job Attitudes," *Job Satisfaction: How People Feel about Their Jobs and How It Affects Their Performance,* eds C J Cranny, P Cain Smith, and E F Stone (New York: Lexington Books, 1992), pp 21–52.

67 See J P Wanous, T D Poland, S L Premack, and K S Davis, "The Effects of Met Expectations on Newcomer Attitudes and Behaviors: A Review and Meta-Analysis," *Journal of Applied Psychology,* June 1992, pp 288–97.

68 A complete description of this model is provided by E A Locke, "Job Satisfaction," in *Social Psychology and Organizational Behavior,* eds M Gruneberg and T Wall (New York: John Wiley & Sons, 1984).

69 The results and recommendations can be found in J Chatzky, "Making Time for Time Off," *Money,* April 2005, pp 48, 50.

70 Results can be found in J Cohen-Charash and P E Spector, "The Role of Justice in Organizations: A Meta-Analysis," *Organizational Behavior and Human Decision Processes,* November 2001, pp 278–321.

71 A thorough discussion of this model is provided by C L Hulin, and T A Judge, "Job Attitudes," in *Handbook of Psychology,* vol. 12, eds W C Borman, D R Ilgen, and R J Klimoski (Hoboken, NJ: John Wiley & Sons, Inc., 2003), pp 255–76.

72 A summary and interpretation of this research is provided by B M Staw and Y Choen-Charash, "The Dispositional Approach

to Job Satisfaction: More than a Mirage, but Not Yet an Oasis," *Journal of Organizational Behavior,* February 2005, pp 59–78.

[73] See R D Arvey, T J Bouchard Jr, N L Segal, and L M Abraham, "Job Satisfaction: Environmental and Genetic Components," *Journal of Applied Psychology,* April 1989, pp 187–92. Also see S E Hammpson, L R Goldberg, T M Vogt, and J P Dubanoski, "Mechanisms by Which Childhood Personality Traits Influence Adult Health Status: Educational Attainment and Healthy Behaviors," *Health Psychology,* January 2007, pp 121–25.

[74] See C Dormann and D Zapf, "Job Satisfaction: A Meta-Analysis of Stabilities," *Journal of Organizational Behavior,* August 2001, pp 483–504.

[75] P Wakeman, "The Good Life and How to Get It," *Inc.,* February 2001, p 50.

[76] See A J Kinicki, F M McKee-Ryan, C A Schriesheim, and K P Carson, "Assessing the Construct Validity of the Job Descriptive Index: A Review and Meta-Analysis," *Journal of Applied Psychology,* February 2002, pp 14–32.

[77] See Brown, "A Meta-Analysis and Review of Organizational Research on Job Involvement."

[78] D W Organ, "The Motivational Basis of Organizational Citizenship Behavior," in *Research in Organizational Behavior,* eds B M Staw and L L Cummings (Greenwich, CT: JAI Press, 1990), p 46.

[79] Results can be found in B J Hoffman, C A Blair, J P Meriac, and D J Woehr, "Expanding the Criterion Domain? A Quantitative Review of the OCB Literature," *Journal of Applied Psychology,* March 2007, pp 555–66.

[80] Supportive results can be found in D Kamdar, D J McAllister, and D B Turban, " 'All in a Day's Work': How Follower Individual Differences and Justice Perceptions Predict OCB Role Definitions and Behavior," *Journal of Applied Psychology,* July 2006, pp 841–55; and B J Tepper, M K Duffy, J Hoobler, and M D Ensley, "Moderators of the Relationship between Coworkers' Organizational Citizenship Behavior and Fellow Employees' Attitudes," *Journal of Applied Psychology,* June 2004, pp 455–65.

[81] Supportive findings are presented in T D Allen, "Rewarding Good Citizens: The Relationship Between Citizenship Behavior, Gender, and Organizational Rewards," *Journal of Applied Social Psychology,* January 2006, pp 120–43; and T W Lee, T R Mitchell, C J Sablynski, J P Burton, and B C Holtom, "The Effects of Job Embeddedness on Organizational Citizenship, Job Performance, Volitional Absences, and Voluntary Turnover," *Academy of Management Journal,* October 2004, pp 711–22.

[82] Results can be found in D J Koys, "The Effects of Employee Satisfaction, Organizational Citizenship Behavior, and Turnover on Organizational Effectiveness: A Unit-Level, Longitudinal Study," *Personnel Psychology,* Spring 2001, pp 101–14.

[83] These results can be found in K Gurchiek, " 'I Can't Make It to Work Today, Boss . . . Gotta Round Up My Ostriches,'" *HR Magazine,* March 2005, p 30.

[84] These cost estimates are provided in E Robertson Demby, "Do Your Family-Friendly Programs Make Cents?" *HR Magazine,* January 2004, pp 74–78.

[85] See R D Hackett, "Work Attitudes and Employee Absenteeism: A Synthesis of the Literature," *Journal of Occupational Psychology,* 1989, pp 235–48.

[86] A thorough review of the cognitive process associated with quitting is provided in C P Maertz Jr and M A Campion, "Profiles in Quitting: Integrating Process and Content Turnover Theory," *Academy of Management Journal,* August 2004, pp 566–82.

[87] Results can be found in P W Hom and A J Kinicki, "Toward a Greater Understanding of How Dissatisfaction Drives Employee Turnover," *Academy of Management Journal,* October 2001, pp 975–87.

[88] Statistics are presented in A Fisher, "Playing For Keeps," *Fortune,* January 22, 2007, p 85; and "CFO: All Pain, No Gain," *Fortune,* February 5, 2007, pp 18.

[89] Y Lermusiaux, "Calculating the High Cost of Employee Turnover," www.ilogos.com/en/expertviews/articles/strategic/ 200331007_YL.html, accessed April 15, 2005, p 1. The various costs of employee turnover are also discussed by W G Bliss, "Cost of Employee Turnover," www.isquare.com/turnover.cfm, accessed April 15, 2005.

[90] See Lermusiaux, "Calculating the High Cost of Employee Turnover." An automated program for calculating the cost of turnover can be found at "Calculate Your Turnover Costs," www.keepemployees.com/turnovercalc.htm, accessed April 15, 2005.

[91] Techniques for reducing employee turnover are discussed by K Gurchiek, "Execs Take Exit Interview Seriously," *HR Magazine,* January 2007, p 34; and J Brandon, "Rethinking the Time Clock," *Business 2.0,* March 2007, p 24.

[92] Results can be found in Griffeth, Hom, and Gaertner, "A Meta-Analysis of Antecedents and Correlates of Employee Turnover."

[93] Results can be found in Podsakoff, LePine, and LePine, "Differential Challenge Stressor-Hindrance Stressor Relationships with Job Attitudes, Turnover Intentions, Turnover, and Withdrawal Behavior: A Meta-Analysis."

[94] The various models are discussed in T A Judge, C J Thoresen, J E Bono, and G K Patton, "The Job Satisfaction–Job Performance Relationship: A Qualitative and Quantitative Review," *Psychological Bulletin,* May 2001, pp 376–407.

[95] Results can be found in ibid.

[96] One example is provided by D J Schleicher, J D Watt, and G J Greguras, "Reexamining the Job Satisfaction–Performance Relationship: The Complexity of Attitudes," *Journal of Applied Psychology,* February 2004, pp 165–77.

[97] Results can be found in J K Harter, F L Schmidt, and T L Hayes, "Business-Unit-Level Relationship between Employee Satisfaction, Employee Engagement, and Business Outcomes: A Meta-Analysis," *Journal of Applied Psychology,* April 2002, pp 268–79.

[98] Excerpted from E White, "New Recipe: To Keep Employees, Domino's Decides It's Not All about Pay," *The Wall Street Journal,* February 17, 2005. Reprinted by permission of Dow Jones & Co Inc. via The Copyright Clearance Center.

[99] Excerpted from M Schneider, "How an MBA Can Bend Your Mind," *BusinessWeek,* April 1, 2002, p 12.

CHAPTER 7

[1] Excerpted from R L Kuhn, "A Problem of Perception," *BusinessWeek,* April 24, 2006, p 33.

[2] C Palmeri, *BusinessWeek,* February 6, 2006, p 53.

[3] Examples can be found in T Lowry, "'A McKinsey of Pop Culture'?" *BusinessWeek,* March 26, 2007, pp 104–08; and "Virtual Marketing Makes a False Impression," *BizEd,* March/April 2007, pp 54, 56.

[4] See L Winerman, "Screening Surveyed," *Monitor on Psychology,* January 2006, pp 28–29.

[5] Object perception is discussed by L J Rips, S Blok, and G Newman, "Tracing the Identity of Objects," *Psychological Bulletin,* January 2006, pp 1–30.

[6] ST Fiske and S E Taylor, *Social Cognition,* 2nd ed (Reading, MA: Addison-Wesley Publishing, 1991), pp 1–2.

[7] The negative bias was examined by N Kyle Smith, J T Larsen, T L Chartrand, J T Cacioppo, H A Katafiasz, and K E Moran, "Being Bad Isn't Always Good: Affective Context Moderates the Attention Bias Toward Negative Information," *Journal of Personality and Social Psychology,* February 2006, pp 210–220.

[8] E Rosch, C B Mervis, W D Gray, D M Johnson, and P BoyesBraem, "Basic Objects in Natural Categories," *Cognitive Psychology,* July 1976, p 383.

[9] Results can be found in M Rotundo, D-H Nguyen, and P R Sackett, "A Meta-Analytic Review of Gender Differences in Perceptions of Sexual Harassment," *Journal of Applied Psychology,* October 2001, pp 914–22. Also see J L Berdahl, "The Sexual Harassment of Uppity Women," *Journal of Applied Psychology,* March 2007, pp 425–37.

[10] See J Halberstadt, "Featural Shift in Explanation-Biased Memory for Emotional Faces," *Journal of Personality and Social Psychology,* January 2005, pp 38–49.

[11] See A J Kinicki, P W Hom, M R Trost, and K J Wade, "Effects of Category Prototypes on Performance-Rating Accuracy," *Journal of Applied Psychology,* June 1995, pp 354–70.

[12] For a thorough discussion about the structure and organization of memory, see L R Squire, B Knowlton, and G Musen, "The Structure and Organization of Memory," in *Annual Review of Psychology,* eds L W Porter and M R Rosenzweig (Palo Alto, CA: Annual Reviews Inc., 1993), vol. 44, pp 453–95.

[13] Implicit cognition is discussed by Y Dunham, A S Baron, and M R Banaji, "From American City to Japanese Village: A Cross-Cultural Investigation of Implicit Race Attitudes," *Child Development,* September 2006, pp 1268–81; and A G Greenwald and M R Banaji, "Implicit Social Cognition: Attitudes, Self-Esteem, and Stereotypes," *Psychological Review,* January 1995, pp 4–27.

[14] See M Orey, "White Men Can't Help It," *BusinessWeek,* May 15, 2006, pp 54, 57; and P Babcock, "Detecting Hidden Bias," *HR Magazine,* February 2006, pp 51–55.

[15] Details of this study can be found in C K Stevens, "Antecedents of Interview Interactions, Interviewers' Ratings, and Applicants' Reactions," *Personnel Psychology,* Spring 1998, pp 55–85.

[16] See R C Mayer and J H Davis, "The Effect of the Performance Appraisal System on Trust for Management: A Field Quasi-Experiment," *Journal of Applied Psychology,* February 1999, pp 123–36. Also see R P Wright, "Mapping Cognitions to Better Understand Attitudinal and Behavioral Responses in Appraisal Research," *Journal of Organizational Behavior,* May 2004, pp 339–74.

[17] Results can be found in W H Bommer, J L Johnson, G A Rich, P M Podsakoff, and S B Mackenzie, "On the Interchangeability of Objective and Subjective Measures of Employee Performance: A Meta-Analysis," *Personnel Psychology,* Autumn 1995, pp 587–605.

[18] See J I Sanchez and P D L Torre, "A Second Look at the Relationship between Rating and Behavioral Accuracy in Performance Appraisal," *Journal of Applied Psychology,* February 1996, pp 3–10.

[19] The effectiveness of rater training was supported by D V Day and L M Sulsky, "Effects of Frame-of-Reference Training and Information Configuration on Memory Organization and Rating Accuracy," *Journal of Applied Psychology,* February 1995, pp 158–67.

[20] Results can be found in J S Phillips and R G Lord, "Schematic Information Processing and Perceptions of Leadership in Problem-Solving Groups," *Journal of Applied Psychology,* August 1982, pp 486–92.

[21] J Ewing, "Wal-Mart: Local Pipsqueak," *BusinessWeek,* April 11, 2005, p 54.

[22] Results can be found in M Sandy Hershcovis, N Turner, J Barling, K A Arnold, K e Dupré, M Inness, M M Le Blanc, and N Sivanathan, "Predicting Workplace Aggression: A Meta-Analysis," *Journal of Applied Psychology,* January 2007, pp 228–38; and S Thau, K Aquino, and R Wittek, "An Extension of Uncertainty Management Theory to the Self: The Relationship between Justice, Social Comparison Orientation, and Antisocial Work Behaviors," *Journal of Applied Psychology,* January 2007, pp 250–58.

[23] See S Begley, "All In Your Head? Yes, and Scientists Are Figuring Out Why," *The Wall Street Journal,* March 17, 2006, p B1.

[24] See E C Baig, "Survey Offers a 'Sneak Peek' Into Net Surfers' Brains," *USA Today,* March 27, 2006, p 4B; and L Winerman, "Screening Surveyed," *Monitor on Psychology,* January 2006, pp 28–29.

[25] These recommendations were excerpted from Baig, "Survey Offers a 'Sneak Peek' Into Net Surfers' Brains," *USA Today,* March 27, 2006, p 4B.

[26] S Power, "Mickey Mouse, Nike Give Advice on Air Security," *The Wall Street Journal,* January 24, 2002, p B4.

[27] C M Judd and B Park, "Definition and Assessment of Accuracy in Social Stereotypes," *Psychological Review,* January 1993, p 110.

[28] For a thorough discussion of stereotype accuracy, see M C Ashton and V M Esses, "Stereotype Accuracy: Estimating the Academic Performance of Ethnic Groups," *Personality and Social Psychology Bulletin,* February 1999, pp 225–36.

[29] Stereotype formation and maintenance is discussed by J V Petrocelli, Z L Tormala, and D D Rucker, "Unpacking Attitude Certainty: Attitude Clarity and Attitude Correctness," *Journal of Personality and Social Psychology,* January 2006, pp 30–41.

[30] See S Madon, M Guyll, S J Hilbert, E Kyriakatos, and D L Vogel, "Stereotyping the Stereotypic: When Individuals Match Social Stereotypes," *Journal of Applied Social Psychology,* January 2006, pp 178–205.

[31] Results are presented in E Tahmincioglu, "Men Rule–At Least in Workplace Attitudes," *MSNBC,* http://www.msnbc.msn.com/id/17345308/, accessed March 6, 2007.

[32] See M E Heilman and T G Okimoto, "Why Are Women Penalized for Success at Male Tasks?: The Implied Communality Deficit," *Journal of Applied Psychology,* January 2007, pp 81–92.

[33] See J D Olian, D P Schwab, and Y Haberfeld, "The Impact of Applicant Gender Compared to Qualifications on Hiring Recommendations: A Meta-Analysis of Experimental Studies," *Organizational Behavior and Human Decision Processes,* April 1988, pp 180–95.

[34] Results from the meta-analyses are discussed in K P Carson, C L Sutton, and P D Corner, "Gender Bias in Performance Appraisals: A Meta-Analysis," paper presented at the 49th Annual Academy of Management Meeting, Washington, DC: 1989. Results from the field study can be found in T J Maurer and M A Taylor, "Is Sex by Itself Enough? An Exploration of Gender Bias Issues in Performance Appraisal," *Organizational Behavior and Human Decision Processes,* November 1994, pp 231–51.

[35] See J Landau, "The Relationship of Race and Gender to Managers' Ratings of Promotion Potential," *Journal of Organizational Behavior,* July 1995, pp 391–400.

[36] Results can be found in K S Lyness and M E Heilman, "When Fit Is Fundamental: Performance Evaluations and Promotions of Upper-Level Female and Male Managers," *Journal of Applied Psychology,* July 2006, pp 777–85.

[37] For a complete review, see S R Rhodes, "Age-Related Differences in Work Attitudes and Behavior: A Review and Conceptual Analysis," *Psychological Bulletin,* March 1983, pp 328–67. Also see S DeArmond, M Tye, P Y Chen, A Krauss, D A Rogers, and E Sintek, "Age and Gender Stereotypes:

New Challenges in a Changing Workplace and Workforce," *Journal of Applied Social Psychology,* September 2006, pp 2184–214.

[38] See G M McEvoy, "Cumulative Evidence of the Relationship between Employee Age and Job Performance," *Journal of Applied Psychology,* February 1989, pp 11–17.

[39] A thorough discussion of the relationship between age and performance is contained in D A Waldman and B J Avolio, "Aging and Work Performance in Perspective: Contextual and Developmental Considerations," in *Research in Personnel and Human Resources Management,* ed G R Ferris (Greenwich, CT: JAI Press, 1993), vol. 11, pp 133–62.

[40] For details, see B J Avolio, D A Waldman, and M A McDaniel, "Age and Work Performance in Nonmanagerial Jobs: The Effects of Experience and Occupational Type," *Academy of Management Journal,* June 1990, pp 407–22.

[41] D H Powell, "Aging Baby Boomers: Stretching Your Workforce Options," *HR Magazine,* July 1998, p 83.

[42] K Helliker, "The Doctor Is Still in: Secrets of Health from a Famed 96-Year-Old Physician," *The Wall Street Journal,* March 8, 2005, p D1.

[43] Results can be found in R W Griffeth, P W Hom, and S Gaertner, "A Meta-Analysis of Antecedents and Correlates of Employee Turnover: Update, Moderator Tests, and Research Implications for the Next Millennium," *Journal of Management,* 2000, pp 463–88.

[44] See J J Martocchio, "Age-Related Differences in Employee Absenteeism: A Meta-Analysis," *Psychology and Aging,* December 1989, pp 409–14.

[45] Racial stereotypes are studied and discussed by J K Maner, D T Kenrick, V D Becker, T E Robertson, B Hofer, and S Neuberg, "Functional Projection: How Fundamental Social Motives Can Bias Interpersonal Perception," *Journal of Personality and Social Psychology,* January 2005, pp 63–78; and N London-Vargas, *Faces of Diversity* (New York: Vantage Press, 1999).

[46] See J L Eberhardt, "Imaging Race," *American Psychologist,* February 2005, pp 181–90.

[47] Summaries of this research can be found in M Greer, "Automatic Racial Stereotyping Appears Based on Facial Features in Addition to Race," *Monitor on Psychology,* January 2005, p 14; and L Winerman, "Racial Stereotypes Can Speed Visual Processing," *Monitor on Psychology,* January 2005, p 15.

[48] This information was obtained from the official Web site of Tiger Woods, www.tigerwoods.com/defaultflash.spc, accessed April 1, 2007.

[49] Results from these studies can be found in A I Huffcutt and P L Roth, "Racial Group Differences in Employment Interview Evaluations," *Journal of Applied Psychology,* April 1998, pp 179–89; and T-R Lin, G H Dobbins, and J-L Farh, "A Field Study of Race and Age Similarity Effects on Interview Ratings in Conventional and Situational Interviews," *Journal of Applied Psychology,* June 1992, pp 363–71.

50 See D A Waldman and B J Avolio, "Race Effects in Performance Evaluations: Controlling for Ability, Education, and Experience," *Journal of Applied Psychology,* December 1991, pp 897–901; and E D Pulakos, L A White, S H Oppler, and W C Borman, "Examination of Race and Sex Effects on Performance Ratings," *Journal of Applied Psychology,* October 1989, pp 770–80.

51 Results can be found in Landau, "The Relationship of Race and Gender to Managers' Ratings of Promotion Potential."

52 These statistics were reported in C Komp, "Unemployment, Poverty Higher for People with Disabilities," *The New Standard,* October 4, 2006, http://newstandardnews.net/content/index. cfm/items/3727.

53 See "High Unemployment and Disability for People with Serious Mental Illness," *SAMHSA'S National Mental Health Information Center,* http://mentalhealth.samhsa. gov/publications/allpubs/NMH02-0144/unemployment.asp, accessed April 1, 2007; and R R Hastings, "Focus on Behavior, Not Psychiatric Condition," *HR Magazine,* November 2006, pp 26, 32.

54 The ADA and its associated accommodation requirements are discussed by D Cadrain, "Advocates for the Disabled Seek Overhaul of ADA," *HR Magazine,* February 2005, pp 27–31.

55 See Day and Sulsky, "Effects of Frame-of-Reference Training and Information Configuration on Memory Organization and Rating Accuracy"; and B B Baltes, C B Bauer, and P A Frensch, "Does a Structured Free Recall Intervention Reduce the Effect of Stereotypes on Performance Ratings and by What Cognitive Mechanism?" *Journal of Applied Psychology,* January 2007, pp 151–64.

56 The background and results for this study are presented in R Rosenthal and L Jacobson, *Pygmalion in the Classroom: Teacher Expectation and Pupils' Intellectual Development* (New York: Holt, Rinchart & Winston, 1968).

57 D B McNatt, "Ancient Pygmalion Joins Contemporary Management: A Meta-Analysis of the Result," *Journal of Applied Psychology,* April 2000, pp 314–22. Also see J R Shapiro, E B King, and M A Quiñones, "Expectations of Obese Trainees: How Stigmatized Trainee Characteristics Influence Training Effectiveness," *Journal of Applied Psychology,* January 2007, pp 239–49; and J Georgesen and M J Harris, "Holding Onto Power: Effects of Powerholders' Positional Instability and Expectancies on Interactions with Subordinates," *European Journal of Social Psychology,* July-August 2006, pp 451–68.

58 The Golem effect is defined and investigated by O B Davidson and D Eden, "Remedial Self-Fulfilling Prophecy: Two Field Experiments to Prevent Golem Effects among Disadvantaged Women," *Journal of Applied Psychology,* June 2000, pp 386–98.

59 The role of self-expectations in this process are discussed and tested by D B McNatt and T A Judge, "Boundary Conditions of the Galatea Effect: A Field Experiment and Constructive Replication," *Academy of Management Journal,* August 2004, pp 550–65.

60 The role of positive expectations at Google is discussed by A Lashinsky, "Search and Joy," *Fortune,* January 22, 2007, pp 70–82.

61 Pygmalion leadership training is discussed by D Eden, D Geller, A Gewirtz, R Gordon-Terner, I Inbar, M Liberman, Y Pass, I Salomon-Segev, and M Shalit, "Implanting Pygmalion Leadership Style through Workshop Training: Seven Field Experiments," *Leadership Quarterly,* Summer 2000, pp 171–210. Also see B Martinuzzi, "We Are What We Think We Are," *Canadian HR Reporter,* February 26, 2007, p 27;' and J Welch and S Welch, "The Welch Way," *BusinessWeek,* April 2, 2007, p 92.

62 Kelley's model is discussed in detail in H H Kelley, "The Processes of Causal Attribution," *American Psychologist,* February 1973, pp 107–28.

63 See K White, D R Lehman, K J Hemphill, D R Mandel, and A M Lehman, "Causal Attributions, Perceived Control, and Psychological Adjustment: A Study of Chronic Fatigue Syndrome," *Journal of Applied Social Psychology,* January 2006, pp 75–99; and S Taggar and M Neubert, "The Impact of Poor Performers on Team Outcomes: An Empirical Examination of Attribution Theory," *Personnel Psychology,* Winter 2004, pp 935–68.

64 Examples can be found in C Meyer and A Schwager, "Understanding Customer Experience," *Harvard Business Review,* February 2007, pp 117–26; and B Helm, "A Slick Pitch For 'Negative Calories,'" *BusinessWeek,* January 15, 2007, p 40.

65 Results from these studies can be found in D A Hofmann and A Stetzer, "The Role of Safety Climate and Communication in Accident Interpretation: Implications for Learning from Negative Events," *Academy of Management Journal,* December 1998, pp 644–57; and I Choi, R E Nisbett, and A Norenzayan, "Causal Attribution across Cultures: Variation and Universality," *Psychological Bulletin,* January 1999, pp 47–63.

66 Results can be found in E Cowley, "Views from Consumers Next in Line: The Fundamental Attribution Error in a Service Setting," *Academy of Marketing Science Journal,* Spring 2005, pp 139–52.

67 L Woellert, "The-Reporter-Did-It Defense," *BusinessWeek,* May 8, 2006, p 34.

68 See "To See Ourselves," *HR Magazine,* November 2006, p 16; and D R Collins and A A Stukas, "The Effects of Feedback Self-Consistency, Therapist Status, and Attitude Toward Therapy on Reaction To Personality Feedback," *Journal of Social Psychology,* August 2006, pp 463–83.

69 Results can be found in E W K Tsang, "Self-Serving Attributions in Corporate Annual Reports: A Replicated Study," *Journal of Management Studies,* January 2002, pp 51–65.

70 This research is summarized by T S Duval and P J Silvia, "Self-Awareness, Probability of Improvement, and the Self-Serving Bias," *Journal of Personality and Social Psychology,* January 2002, pp 49–61.

[71] Ibid., p 58.

[72] Details may be found in S E Moss and M J Martinko, "The Effects of Performance Attributions and Outcome Dependence on Leader Feedback Behavior following Poor Subordinate Performance," *Journal of Organizational Behavior,* May 1998, pp 259–74; and E C Pence, W C Pendelton, G H Dobbins, and J A Sgro, "Effects of Causal Explanations and Sex Variables on Recommendations for Corrective Actions Following Employee Failure," *Organizational Behavior and Human Performance,* April 1982, pp 227–40.

[73] Results are reported in M O'Neill, "Luck or Hard Work?" *Forbes,* February 26, 2007, p 38.

[74] See D Konst, R Vonk, and R V D Vlist, "Inferences about Causes and Consequences of Behavior of Leaders and Subordinates," *Journal of Organizational Behavior,* March 1999, pp 261–71.

[75] See M Miserandino, "Attributional Retraining as a Method of Improving Athletic Performance," *Journal of Sport Behavior,* August 1998, pp 286–97.

[76] Excerpted from C Hymowitz, "Top Executives Chase Youthful Appearance, but Miss Real Issue," *The Wall Street Journal,* February 17, 2004, p B1. Reprinted by permission of Dow Jones & Co. Inc. via The Copyright Clearance Center.

[77] Excerpted from A McConnon, "Mad Ave: If I Only Had a Brain Scan," *BusinessWeek,* January 22, 2007, p 19.

CHAPTER 8

[1] Exerpted from R Tomsho, "More Districts Pay Teachers For Performance," *The Wall Street Journal,* March 23, 2006, pp B1, B5.

[2] T R Mitchell, "Motivation: New Direction for Theory, Research, and Practice," *Academy of Management Review,* January 1982, p 81.

[3] A review of content and process theories of motivation is provided by R M Steers, R T Mowday, and D L Shapiro, "The Future of Work Motivation Theory," *Academy of Management Review,* July 2004, pp 379–87.

[4] For a complete description of Maslow's theory, see A H Maslow, "A Theory of Human Motivation," *Psychological Review,* July 1943, pp 370–96.

[5] See W B Swann Jr., C Chang-Schneider, and K L McClarty, "Do People's Self-Views Matter?" *American Pscyhologist,* February–March 2007, pp 84–94.

[6] See "Comp and Hiring Landscape: Still Rocky in 2007," *HR Magazine,* February 2007, p 14; R Wiles, "Tips Aimed to Help Debt-Ridden Workers, Boost Productivity," *The Arizona Republic,* March 3, 2007, p D1; and A Johnson, "4 Generations Can Challenge Management," *The Arizona Republic,* September 21, 2006, pp D1, D5.

[7] An example is provided by L Bassi and D McMurrer, "Maximizing Your Return on People," *Harvard Business Review,* March 2007, pp 115–24.

[8] For a complete review of ERG theory, see C P Alderfer, *Existence, Relatedness, and Growth: Human Needs in Organizational Settings* (New York: Free Press, 1972).

[9] See ibid., and J P Wanous and A Zwany, "A Cross-Sectional Test of Need Hierarchy Theory," *Organizational Behavior and Human Performance,* February 1977, pp 78–97.

[10] L Buchanan, "Managing One-to-One," *Inc.,* October 2001, p 87.

[11] H A Murray, *Explorations in Personality* (New York: John Wiley & Sons, 1938), p 164.

[12] See S Hamm, "A Red Flag in the Brain Game," *BusinessWeek,* May 1, 2006, pp 32–35.

[13] See the discussion in "Can't We All Just Get Along?" *HR Magazine,* April 2005, p 16.

[14] See G D Parsons and R T Pascale, "Crisis at the Summit," *Harvard Business Review,* March 2007, pp 80–89; and D K McNeese-Smith, "The Relationship between Managerial Motivation, Leadership, Nurse Outcomes and Patient Satisfaction," *Journal of Organizational Behavior,* March 1999, pp 243–59; A M Harrell and M J Stahl, "A Behavioral Decision Theory Approach for Measuring McClelland's Trichotomy of Needs," *Journal of Applied Psychology,* April 1981, pp 242–47.

[15] Evidence for the validity of motivation training can be found in H Heckhausen and S Krug, "Motive Modification," in *Motivation and Society,* ed A J Stewart (San Francisco: Jossey-Bass, 1982).

[16] Results can be found in D B Turban and T L Keon, "Organizational Attractiveness: An Interactionist Perspective," *Journal of Applied Psychology,* April 1993, pp 184–93.

[17] See T W H Ng, K L Sorensen, and D C Feldman, "Dimensions, Antecedents, and Consequences of Workaholism: A Conceptual Integration and Extension," *Journal of Organizational Behavior,* January 2007, pp 111–36.

[18] See F Herzberg, B Mausner, and B B Snyderman, *The Motivation to Work* (New York: John Wiley & Sons, 1959).

[19] Excerpted from J Mero, "Gumologist," *Fortune,* April 3, 2006, p 33.

[20] Excerpted from M Conlin and A Bernstein, "Working . . . and Poor," *BusinessWeek,* May 31, 2004, p 60.

[21] F Herzberg, "One More Time: How Do You Motivate Employees?" *Harvard Business Review,* January–February 1968, p 56.

[22] For a thorough review of research on Herzberg's theory, see C C Pinder, *Work Motivation: Theory, Issues, and Applications* (Glenview, IL: Scott, Foresman, 1984).

[23] Supportive results can be found in N R Lockwood, "Leveraging Employee Engagement for Competitive Advantage," *2007 SHRM Quarterly,* 2007, pp 1–11; and "Respect: Find Out What It Means to Employees," *Training,* June 2006, p 12.

[24] The generalizability of the equity norm was investigated by T M Begley, C Lee, and C Hui, "Organizational Level as a Moderator of the Relationship between Justice Perceptions and Work-Related Reactions," *Journal of Organizational Behavior,* September 2006, pp 705–21; and R Loi, N Hang-Yue, and S Foley, "Linking Employees' Justice Perceptions to Organizational Commitment and Intention to Leave: The Mediating Role of Perceived Organizational Support," *Journal of Occupational and Organizational Psychology,* March 2006, pp 101–20.

[25] These statistics were obtained from "Growth Rate of CEO Pay Continues to Slow, Rising 9.3% in 2006," CNBC. com, March 3, 2007, http://www.cnbc.com/id/17928232; and J Sahadi, "CEO Paychecks: $42,000 a day," CCCMoney. com, June 21, 2006, http://money.cnn.com/2006/06/21/news/companies/ceo_pay_epi/index.htm.

[26] M N Bing and S M Burroughs, "The Predictive and Interactive Effects of Equity Sensitivity in Teamwork-Oriented Organizations," *Journal of Organizational Behavior,* May 2001, p 271.

[27] Types of equity sensitivity are discussed by ibid., pp 271–90.

[28] For a thorough review of organizational justice theory and research, see R Cropanzano, D E Rupp, C J Mohler, and M Schminke, "Three Roads to Organizational Justice," in *Research in Personnel and Human Resources Management,* vol. 20, eds G R Ferris (New York: JAI Press, 2001), pp 269–329.

[29] J A Colquitt, D E Conlon, M J Wesson, C O L H Porter, and K Y Ng, "Justice at the Millennium: A Meta-Analytic Review of 25 Years of Organizational Justice Research," *Journal of Applied Psychology,* June 2001, p 426.

[30] E Tahmincioglu, "Electronic Workplace Vulnerable to Revenge," *Arizona Republic,* August 6, 2001, p D1.

[31] Results from these studies can be found in Y Cohen-Charash and P E Spector, "The Role of Justice in Organizations: A Meta-Analysis," *Organizational Behavior and Human Decision Processes,* November 2001, pp 278–321; Colquitt, Conlon, Wesson, Porter, and Ng, "Justice at the Millennium;" and M S Hershcovis, N Turner, J Barling, K A Arnold, K E Dupré, M Inness, M M LeBlanc, and N Sivanathan, "Predicting Workplace Aggression: A Meta-Analysis," *Journal of Applied Psychology,* January 2007, pp 228–38.

[32] For recent studies that support the impact of justice on a variety of individual and organizational outcomes see S Thau, K Aquino, and R Wittek, "An Extension of Uncertainty Management Theory to the Self: The Relationship between Justice, Social Comparison Orientation, and Antisocial Work Behaviors," *Journal of Applied Psychology,* January 2007, pp 250–58; A Barsky and S A Kaplan, "If You Feel Bad, It's Unfair: A Quantitative Synthesis of Affect and Organizational Justice Perceptions," *Journal of Applied Psychology*, January 2007, pp 286–95; and K Aquino, T M Tripp, and R J Bies, "Getting Even or Moving On? Power, Procedural Justice, and Types of Offense as Predictors

of Revenge, Forgiveness, Reconciliation, and Avoidance in Organizations," *Journal of Applied Psychology,* May 2006, pp 653–68.

[33] Results from this study were reported in K Gurchiek, "Show Workers Their Value, Study Says," *HR Magazine,* October 2006, p 40.

[34] See B W Heineman, Jr., "Avoiding Integrity Land Mines," *Harvard Business Review,* April 2007, pp 100–8.

[35] Supporting studies were conducted by D P Skarlicki, R Folger, and P Tesluk, "Personality as a Moderator in the Relationship between Fairness and Retaliation," *Academy of Management Journal,* February 1999, pp 100–8.

[36] Supportive results can be found in J Greenberg, "Losing Sleep Over Organizational Injustice: Attenuating Insomniac Reactions to Underpayment Inequity with Supervisory Training in Interactional Justice," *Journal of Applied Psychology,* June 2006, pp 58–69; D Kamdar, D J McAllister, and D B Turban, "'All in a Day's Work': How Follower Individual Differences and Justice Perceptions Predict OCB Role Definitions and Behavior," *Journal of Applied Psychology,* July 2006, pp 841–55; and C Spitzmüller D M Glenn, C D Barr, S G Rogelberg, and P Daniel, "'If You Treat Me Right, I Reciprocate': Examining the Role of Exchange in Organizational Survey Responses," *Journal of Organizational Behavior,* February 2006, pp 19–35.

[37] The impact of groups on justice perceptions was investigated by D A Jones and D P Skarlicki, "The Effects of Overhearing Peers to Discuss an Authority's Fairness Reputation on Reactions to Subsequent Treatment," *Journal of Applied Psychology,* March 2005, pp 363–72; and J A Colquitt, "Does the Justice of the One Interact with the Justice of the Many? Reactions to Procedural Justice in Teams," *Journal of Applied Psychology,* August 2004, pp 633–46.

[38] See B J Tepper, M K Duffy, C A Henle, and L S Lambert, "Procedural Injustice, Victim Precipitation, and Abusive Supervision," *Personnel Psychology,* Spring 2006, pp 101–23; and B Erdogan and R C Liden, "Collectivism As a Moderator of Responses to Organizational Justice: Implications for Leader-Member Exchange and Ingratiation," *Journal of Organizational Behavior,* February 2006, pp 1–17.

[39] See J Mackey, "'I No Longer Want to Work for Money,'" *Fast Company,* February 2007, p 112.

[40] Climate for justice was studied by H Liao and D E Rupp, "The Impact of Justice Climate and Justice Orientation on Work Outcomes: A Cross-Level Multifoci Framework," *Journal of Applied Psychology,* March 2005, pp 242–56.

[41] The relationship between organizational justice and customer service is discussed by D E Bowen, S W Gilliland, and R Folger, "HRM Service Fairness: How Being Fair with Employees Spills over to Customers," *Organizational Dynamics,* Winter 1999, pp 7–23.

[42] For a complete discussion of Vroom's theory, see V H Vroom, *Work and Motivation* (New York: John Wiley & Sons, 1964).

[43] E E Lawler III, *Motivation in Work Organizations* (Belmont, CA: Wadsworth, 1973), p 45.

[44] See C C Pinder, *Work Motivation* (Glenview, IL: Scott, Foresman, 1984), Ch 7.

[45] J S Lublin, "Boards Tie CEO Pay More Tightly to Performance," *The Wall Street Journal,* February 21, 2006, p A1.

[46] "Federal Express's Fred Smith," *Inc.,* October 1986, p 38.

[47] Results can be found in W van Eerde and H Thierry, "Vroom's Expectancy Models and Work-Related Criteria: A Meta-Analysis," *Journal of Applied Psychology,* October 1996, pp 575–86.

[48] See J P Wanous, T L Keon, and J C Latack, "Expectancy Theory and Occupational/Organizational Choices: A Review and Test," *Organizational Behavior and Human Performance,* August 1983, pp 66–86.

[49] See the discussion in T R Mitchell and D Daniels, "Motivation," in *Handbook of Psychology,* vol. 12, eds W C Borman, D R Ilgen, and R J Klimoski (Hoboken, NJ: John Wiley & Sons, Inc., 2003), pp 225–54.

[50] See "Insights on Maximizing the Value of Employee Awards," *The Power of Incentives,* 2006, pp 103–10; J Useem, "What's That Spell? Teamwork," *Fortune,* June 12, 2006, pp 65–66; and S J Dubner, "The Freaky Side of Business," *Training,* February 2006, pp 8–10.

[51] Excerpted from E Tahmincioglu, "Gifts That Gall," *Workforce Management,* April 2004, p 44.

[52] L Scott, "Grocery Bagger Set Course to Be President of Bashas," *The Arizona Republic,* February 11, 2007, p D2.

[53] E A Locke, K N Shaw, L M Saari, and G P Latham, "Goal Setting and Task Performance: 1969–1980," *Psychological Bulletin,* July 1981, p 126.

[54] This example is discussed in A Barrett, "Cracking the Whip at Wyeth," *BusinessWeek,* February 6, 2006, pp 70–71.

[55] Annika Sorenstam's biography can be found at www.lpga.com/player-career.aspx?id=29, accessed April 5, 2007.

[56] J Davis, "For Now, Sorenstam Feels She Still Has Peaks to Scale," *Arizona Republic,* March 18, 2004, p C14.

[57] See G P Latham and E A Locke, "Enhancing the Benefits and Overcoming the Pitfalls of Goal Setting," *Organizational Dynamics,* November 2006, pp 332–40.

[58] Supportive results can be found in K L Langeland, C M Johnson, and T C Mawhinney, "Improving Staff Performance in a Community Mental Health Setting: Job Analysis, Training, Goal Setting, Feedback, and Years of Data," *Journal of Organizational Behavior Management,* 1998, pp 21–43.

[59] See E A Locke and G P Latham, *A Theory of Goal Setting and Task Performance* (Englewood Cliffs, NJ: Prentice Hall, 1990).

[60] See J J Donovan and D J Radosevich, "The Moderating Role of Goal Commitment on the Goal Difficulty-Performance Relationship: A Meta-Analytic Review and Critical Reanalysis," *Journal of Applied Psychology,* April 1998, pp 308–15.

[61] See Latham and Locke, "Enhancing the Benefits and Overcoming the Pitfalls of Goal Setting."

[62] J L Bowditch and A F Buono, *A Primer on Organizational Behavior* (New York: John Wiley & Sons, 1985), p 210.

[63] This framework was proposed by M A Campion and P W Thayer, "Development and Field Evaluation of an Interdisciplinary Measure of Job Design," *Journal of Applied Psychology,* February 1985, pp 29–43.

[64] G D Babcock, *The Taylor System in Franklin Management,* 2nd ed (New York: Engineering Magazine Company, 1917), p 31.

[65] For a thorough discussion, see F B Copley, *Frederick W Taylor: The Principles of Scientific Management* (New York: Harper & Brothers, 1911).

[66] See the related discussion in S Wagner-Tsukamoto, "An Institutional Economic Reconstruction of Scientific Management: On the Lost Theoretical Logic of Taylorism," *Academy of Management Review,* January 2007, pp 105–17.

[67] This type of program was developed and tested by M A Campion and C L McClelland, "Follow-Up and Extension of the Interdisciplinary Costs and Benefits of Enlarged Jobs," *Journal of Applied Psychology,* June 1993, pp 339–51.

[68] T R Shea, "Quick-Decision Hiring," *HR Magazine,* September 2006, pp 123–24.

[69] J R Hackman, G R Oldham, R Janson, and K Purdy, "A New Strategy for Job Enrichment," *California Management Review,* Summer 1975, p 58.

[70] Definitions of the job characteristics were adapted from J R Hackman and G R Oldham, "Motivation through the Design of Work: Test of a Theory," *Organizational Behavior and Human Performance,* August 1976, pp 250–79.

[71] See F P Morgeson and S E Humphrey, "The Work Design Questionnaire (WDQ): Developing and Validating a Comprehensive Measure for Assessing Job Design and the Nature of Work," *Journal of Applied Psychology,* November 2006, pp 1321–339.

[72] These examples were taken from R Levering and M Moskowitz, "The 100 Best Companies to Work for 2007," *Fortune,* January 22, 2007, p 94; and R Levering and M Moskowitz, "The 100 Best Companies to Work For," *Fortune,* January 24, 2005, p 76.

[73] Supportive results were found by S K Parker, H M Williams, and N Turner, "Modeling the Antecedents of Proactive Behavior at Work," *Journal of Applied Psychology,* May 2006, pp 636–52; and J B Fuller, L E Marler, and K Hester, "Promoting Felt Responsibility for Constructive Change and Proactive Behavior: Exploring Aspects of an

Elaborated Model of Work Design," *Journal of Organizational Behavior,* December 2006, pp 1089–120.

74 See R F Piccolo and J A Colquitt, "Transformational Leadership and Job Behaviors: The Mediating Role of Core Job Characteristics," *Academy of Management Journal,* April 2006, pp 327–40; and S Ohly, S Sonnentag, and F Pluntke, "Routinization, Work Characteristics and Their Relationship with Creative and Proactive Behaviors," *Journal of Organizational Behavior,* May 2006, pp 257–79.

75 The turnover meta-analysis was conducted by R W Griffeth, P W Hom, and S Gaertner, "A Meta-Analysis of Antecedents and Correlates of Employee Turnover: Update, Moderator Tests, and Research Implications for the Next Millennium," *Journal of Management,* 2000, pp 463–88. Absenteeism results are discussed in Y Fried and G R Ferris, "The Validity of the Job Characteristics Model: A Review and Meta-Analysis," *Personnel Psychology,* Summer 1987, pp 287–322.

76 Results can be found in M R Kelley, "New Process Technology, Job Design, and Work Organization: A Contingency Model," *American Sociological Review,* April 1990, pp 191–208.

77 Productivity studies are reviewed in R E Kopelman, *Managing Productivity in Organizations* (New York: McGraw-Hill, 1986).

78 See A Athavaley, "The Ball's in Your Cubicle," *The Wall Street Journal,* February 27, 2007, pp D1, D3.

79 See R Malkin, S D Hudock, C Hayden, T J Lentz, J Topmiller, and R W Niemeier, "An Assessment of Occupational Safety and Health Hazards in Selected Small Business Manufacturing Wood Pallets—Part 1. Noise and Physical Hazards," *Journal of Occupational and Environmental Hygiene,* April 2005, pp D18–D21.

80 These descriptions were excerpted from J Prichard, "Reinventing the Office," *Arizona Republic,* January 16, 2002, p D1.

81 "NINDS Repetitive Motor Disorders Information Page," http://www.ninds.nih.gov/disorders/repetitive_motion/repetitive_motion.htm, last updated February 7, 2006.

82 See "Repetitive Motion Results in Longest Work Absences," *Bureau of Labor Statistics,* http://www.bls.gov/opub/ted/2004/mar/wk5/art02.htm, last updated March 30, 2005.

83 These suggestions were proposed by "Consultancy VP Offers Motivation Inspiration," *Training,* December 2006, p 12.

84 See L Grensing-Pophal, "Coaching HR," *HR Magazine,* February 2007, pp 95–99; and S Miller, "Kimberly-Clark Corp." *HR Magazine,* November 2006, pp 65–68.

85 Performance appraisal systems are discussed by C Winkler, "Peak Performance," *HR Magazine,* January 2007, pp 103–5.

86 G Colvin, "What Makes GE Great?" *Fortune,* March 6, 2006, p 96.

87 Results are reported in "Study: HR Execs Don't Trust Employee Evaluations," *Training,* April 2006, p 11.

88 See M Bolch, "Rewarding the Team," *HR Magazine,* February 2007, pp 91–93.

89 C Hymowitz, "Rewarding Competitors Over Collaborators No Longer Makes Sense," *The Wall Street Journal,* February 13, 2006, p B1.

90 N Byrnes, "The Art of Motivation," *BusinessWeek,* May 1, 2006, pp 57, 58, 60, 62.

91 Excerpted from M Whitehouse, "Closing the Deal: As Banks Bid for City Bond Work, 'Pay to Play' Tradition Endures," *The Wall Street Journal,* March 25, 2005, p A1. Reprinted by permission of Dow Jones & Co. Inc. via The Copyright Clearance Center.

CHAPTER 9

1 L Buchanan, "For Knowing the Power of Respect," *Inc.,* April 2004, p 143. By Leigh Buchanan, © 2005 Gruner & Jahr USA Publishing. First published in *Inc.* Magazine. Reprinted with permission.

2 B Tulgan, "The Under-Management Epidemic," *HR Magazine,* October 2004, p 119. For constructive ideas, see D Zielinski, "Best and Brightest," *Training,* January 2006, pp 11–16; S Berglas, "How to Keep A Players Productive," *Harvard Business Review,* September 2006, pp 104–12; D Ledingham, M Kovac, and H L Simon, "The New Science of Sales Force Productivity," *Harvard Business Review,* September 2006, pp 124–33; and M Weinstein, "Promoting Productivity," *Training,* March 2007, p 9.

3 See E E Lawler III, *Treat People Right! How Organizations and Individuals Can Propel Each Other into a Virtuous Spiral of Success* (San Francisco: Jossey-Bass, 2003); J A Algera, "Participation in the Design of Performance Management Systems: A Quasi-Experimental Field Study," *Journal of Organizational Behavior,* November 2004, pp 831–51; T Chastain, "Linking Performance Systems to Learning Systems," *Training and Development,* February 2006, pp 40–45; J Bersin, "Performance Management," *Training,* June 2006, p 7; and A Pomeroy, "Best Practices for Performance Management," *HR Magazine,* October 2006, p 16.

4 This distinction is drawn from G P Latham, J Almost, S Mann, and C Moore, "New Developments in Performance Management," *Organizational Dynamics,* no. 1, 2005, pp 77–87.

5 See K Tyler, "Performance Art," *HR Magazine,* August 2005, pp 57–63; J Welch and S Welch, "The Case for 20-70-10," *BusinessWeek,* October 2, 2006, p 108; and the second Q&A in J Welch and S Welch, "The Global Warming Wager," *BusinessWeek,* February 26, 2007, p 130.

6 As quoted in P B Brown, "What I Know Now," *Fast Company,* April 2005, p 104. Also see C Winkler, "Job Tryouts Go Virtual," *HR Magazine,* September 2006, pp 131–34; and J Gill, "Smart Questions for Your Hiring Manager," *Inc.,* February 2007, p 47.

[7] See B Cooper, "Training as an Operational Necessity," *Training,* April 2005, p 42; K Tyler, "Training Revs Up," *HR Magazine,* April 2005, pp 58–63; and "Best Practices and Outstanding Training Initiatives," *Training,* March 2007, pp 84–86.

[8] Adapted and quoted from "ThermoSTAT," *Training,* July–August 2003, p 16.

[9] Based on W R Boswell, J B Bingham, and A J S Colvin, "Aligning Employees Through 'Line of Sight,'" *Business Horizons,* November–December 2006, pp 499–509.

[10] M Weinstein, "Business Driven," *Training,* March 2007, pp 40, 42. Also see H Dolezalek, "Serving It Up: From Strategy to Execution, General Mills Aims for Real Customer Impact," *Training,* March 2007, pp 48–54.

[11] G H Seijts and G P Latham, "Learning versus Performance Goals: When Should Each Be Used?" *Academy of Management Executive,* February 2005, pp 126–27.

[12] A thorough discussion of MBO is provided by P F Drucker, *The Practice of Management* (New York: Harper, 1954); and PF Drucker, "What Results Should You Expect? A User's Guide to MBO," *Public Administration Review,* January–February 1976, pp 12–19.

[13] Results from both studies can be found in R Rodgers and J E Hunter, "Impact of Management by Objectives on Organizational Productivity," *Journal of Applied Psychology,* April 1991, pp 322–36; and R Rodgers, J E Hunter, and DL Rogers, "Influence of Top Management Commitment on Management Program Success," *Journal of Applied Psychology,* February 1993, pp 151–55.

[14] For a good update, see G P Latham and E A Locke, "Enhancing the Benefits and Overcoming the Pitfalls of Goal Setting," *Organizational Dynamics,* no. 4, 2006, pp 332–40.

[15] See J A Colquitt and M J Simmering, "Conscientiousness, Goal Orientation, and Motivation to Learn During the Learning Process: A Longitudinal Study," *Journal of Applied Psychology,* August 1998, pp 654–65.

[16] D VandeWalle, S P Brown, W L Cron, and J W Slocum Jr, "The Influence of Goal Orientation and Self-Regulated Tactics on Sales Performance: A Longitudinal Field Test," *Journal of Applied Psychology,* April 1999, p 250. Also see G H Seijts, G P Latham, K Tasa, and B W Latham, "Goal Setting and Goal Orientation: An Integration of Two Different yet Related Literatures," *Academy of Management Journal,* April 2004, pp 227–39; C L Porath and T S Bateman, "Self-Regulation: From Goal Orientation to Job Performance," *Journal of Applied Psychology,* January 2006, pp 185–86;

[17] For more, see Y Gong and J Fan, "Longitudinal Examination of the Role of Goal Orientation in Cross-Cultural Adjustment," *Journal of Applied Psychology,* January 2006, pp 176–84; J J Donovan and L G Hafsteinsson, "The Impact of Goal-Performance Discrepancies, Self-Efficacy, and Goal Orientation on Upward Goal Revision," *Journal of Applied Social Psychology,* April 2006, pp 1046–1069; S W J Kozlowski and B S Ball, "Disentangling Achievement Orientation and Goal Setting: Effects on Self-Regulatory Processes," *Journal*

of Applied Psychology, July 2006, pp 900–916; H J Klein, R A Noe, V J Fortunato and A M Goldblatt, "An Examination of Goal Orientation Profiles Using Cluster Analysis and Their Relationships With Dispositional Characteristics and Motivational Response Patterns," *Journal of Applied Social Psychology,* September 2006, pp 2150–2183; C Wang, "Motivation to Learn and Course Outcomes: The Impact of Delivery Mode, Learning Goal Orientation, and Perceived Barriers and Enablers," *Personnel Psychology,* Autumn 2006, pp 665–702 and S C Payne, S S Youngcourt, and J M Beaubien,"A Meta-Analytic Examination of the Goal Orientation Nomological Net," *Journal of Applied Psychology,* January 2007, pp 128–150.

[18] See S Kerr and S Landauer, "Using Stretch Goals to Promote Organizational Effectiveness and Personal Growth: General Electric and Goldman Sachs," *Academy of Management Executive,* November 2004, pp 134–38; and D A Nadler, "The CEO's 2nd Act," *Harvard Business Review,* Special Issue: The Tests of a Leader, January 2007, pp 66–72.

[19] See E A Locke, "Linking Goals to Monetary Incentives," *Academy of Management Executive,* November 2004, pp 130–33.

[20] E A Locke and G P Latham, *Goal Setting: A Motivational Technique That Works!* (Englewood Cliffs, NJ: Prentice Hall, 1984), p 79. Also see D C Kayes, "The Destructive Pursuit of Idealized Goals," *Organizational Dynamics,* no. 4, 2005, pp 391–401.

[21] K Tyler, "One Bad Apple," *HR Magazine,* December 2004, p 85. Also see M Weinstein, "Boss, Not Friend," *Training,* March 2007, p 10.

[22] Data from "2006 *Fortune* Global 500: World's Largest Corporations," *Fortune,* July 24, 2006, pp 114, 122.

[23] As quoted in C Fishman, "Fred Smith," *Fast Company,* June 2001, p 66.

[24] C D Lee, "Feedback, Not Appraisal," *HR Magazine,* November 2006, p 111. Also see J Gill, "How to Help an Underachiever," *Inc.,* March 2007, p 44.

[25] Both the definition of feedback and the functions of feedback are based on discussion in D R Ilgen, C D Fisher, and M S Taylor, "Consequences of Individual Feedback on Behavior in Organizations," *Journal of Applied Psychology,* August 1979, pp 349–71; and R E Kopelman, *Managing Productivity in Organizations: A Practical People-Oriented Perspective* (New York: McGraw-Hill, 1986), p 175. Also see Q M Roberson and M M Stewart, "Understanding the Motivational Effects of Procedural and Informational Justice in Feedback Processes," *British Journal of Psychology,* August 2006, pp 281–98.

[26] See P C Earley, G B Northcraft, C Lee, and T R Lituchy, "Impact of Process and Outcome Feedback on the Relation of Goal Setting to Task Performance," *Academy of Management Journal,* March 1990, pp 87–105. Also see D VandeWalle, W L Cron, and J W Slocum Jr, "The Role of Goal Orientation following Performance Feedback," *Journal of Applied Psychology,* August 2001, pp 629–40; J S Goodman, R E Wood, and M Hendrickx, "Feedback

Specificity, Exploration, and Learning," *Journal of Applied Psychology,* April 2004, pp 248–62; and J S Goodman and R E Wood, "Feedback Specificity, Learning Opportunities, and Learning," *Journal of Applied Psychology,* October 2004, pp 809–21.

27 Data from A N Kluger and A DeNisi, "The Effects of Feedback Interventions on Performance: A Historical Review, a Meta-Analysis, and a Preliminary Feedback Intervention Theory," *Psychological Bulletin,* March 1996, pp 254–84. Also see G Morse, "Feedback Backlash," *Harvard Business Review,* October 2004, p 28.

28 Data from K D Harber, "Feedback to Minorities: Evidence of a Positive Bias," *Journal of Personality and Social Psychology,* March 1998, pp 622–28.

29 See D M Herold and D B Fedor. "Individuals' Interaction with Their Feedback Environment: The Role of Domain-Specific Individual Differences," in *Research in Personnel and Human Resources Management,* vol. 16, ed G R Ferris (Stamford, CT: JAI Press, 1998), pp 215–54.

30 See T Matsui, A Okkada, and T Kakuyama, "Influence of Achievement Need on Goal Setting, Performance, and Feedback Effectiveness," *Journal of Applied Psychology,* October 1982, pp 645–48.

31 S J Ashford, "Feedback-Seeking in Individual Adaptation: A Resource Perspective," *Academy of Management Journal,* September 1986, pp 465–87. Also see D B Fedor, R B Rensvold, and S M Adams, "An Investigation of Factors Expected to Affect Feedback Seeking: A Longitudinal Field Study," *Personnel Psychology,* Winter 1992, pp 779–805; and M F Sully De Luque and S M Sommer, "The Impact of Culture on Feedback-Seeking Behavior: An Integrated Model and Propositions," *Academy of Management Review,* October 2000, pp 829–49.

32 See D B Turban and T W Dougherty, "Role of Protege Personality in Receipt of Mentoring and Career Success," *Academy of Management Journal,* June 1994, pp 688–702.

33 See B D Bannister, "Performance Outcome Feedback and Attributional Feedback: Interactive Effects on Recipient Responses," *Journal of Applied Psychology,* May 1986, pp 203–10; and JB Vancouver and E C Tischner, "The Effect of Feedback Sign on Task Performance Depends on Self-Concept Discrepancies," *Journal of Applied Psychology,* December 2004, pp 1092–98.

34 For complete details, see P M Podsakoff and J-L Farh, "Effects of Feedback Sign and Credibility on Goal Setting and Task Performance," *Organizational Behavior and Human Decision Processes,* August 1989, pp 45–67. Also see S J Ashford and AS Tsui, "Self-Regulation for Managerial Effectiveness: The Role of Active Feedback Seeking," *Academy of Management Journal,* June 1991, pp 251–80.

35 W S Silver, T R Mitchell, and M E Gist, "Responses to Successful and Unsuccessful Performance: The Moderating Effect of Self-Efficacy on the Relationship between Performance and Attributions," *Organizational Behavior and Human Decision Processes,* June 1995, p 297. Also see T A Louie, "Decision Makers' Hindsight Bias after Receiving Favorable and Unfavorable Feedback," *Journal of Applied Psychology,* February 1999, pp 29–41.

36 J M Kouzes and B Z Posner, *Credibility: How Leaders Gain and Lose It, Why People Demand It* (San Francisco: Jossey-Bass, 1993), p 25. For research support, see A J Kinicki, GE Prussia, B Wu, and F M McKee-Ryan, "A Covariance Structure Analysis of Employees' Response to Performance Feedback," *Journal of Applied Psychology,* December 2004, pp 1057–69.

37 See S E Moss and M J Martinko, "The Effects of Performance Attributions and Outcome Dependence on Leader Feedback Behavior Following Poor Subordinate Performance," *Journal of Organizational Behavior,* May 1998, pp 259–74; and K Leung, S Su, and M W Morris, "When Is Criticism *Not* Constructive? The Roles of Fairness Perceptions and Dispositional Attributions in Employee Acceptance of Critical Supervisory Feedback," *Human Relations,* September 2001, pp 1123–54.

38 Based on discussion in Ilgen, Fisher, and Taylor, "Consequences of Individual Feedback on Behavior in Organizations," pp 367–68. Also see A M O'Leary-Kelly, "The Influence of Group Feedback on Individual Group Member Response," in *Research in Personnel and Human Resources Management,* vol. 16, ed G R Ferris (Stamford, CT: JAI Press, 1998), pp 255–94.

39 See P C Earley, "Computer-Generated Performance Feedback in the Magazine-Subscription Industry," *Organizational Behavior and Human Decision Processes,* February 1988, pp 50–64.

40 See M De Gregorio and C D Fisher, "Providing Performance Feedback: Reactions to Alternate Methods," *Journal of Management,* December 1988, pp 605–16.

41 For details, see R A Baron, "Countering the Effects of Destructive Criticism: The Relative Efficacy of Four Interventions," *Journal of Applied Psychology,* June 1990, pp 235–45. Also see M L Smith, "Give Feedback, Not Criticism." *Supervisory Management,* February 1993, p 4.

42 C O Longenecker and D A Gioia, "The Executive Appraisal Paradox," *Academy of Management Executive,* May 1992, p 18. Also see M D Cannon and R Witherspoon, "Actionable Feedback: Unlocking the Power of Learning and Performance Improvement," *Academy of Management Executive,* May 2005, pp 120–134; and S B Silverman, C E Pogson, and A B Cober, "When Employees at Work Don't Get It: A Model for Enhancing Individual Employee Change in Response to Performance Feedback," *Academy of Management Executive,* May 2005, pp 135–47.

43 See J J Salopek, "Rethinking Likert," *Training & Development,* September 2004, pp 26–29; M Weinstein, "Study: HR Execs Don't Trust Employee Evaluations," *Training,* April 2006, p 11; M Carson, "Saying It Like It Isn't: The Pros and Cons of 360-Degree Feedback," *Business Horizons,* September–October 2006, pp 395–402; and T van Rensburg and G Prideaux, "Turning Professionals into Managers Using

Multisource Feedback," *Journal of Management Development,* no. 6, 2006, pp 561–71.

44 J W Smither, M London, and R R Reilly, "Does Performance Improve following Multisource Feedback? A Theoretical Model, Meta-Analysis, and Review of Empirical Findings," *Personnel Psychology,* Spring 2005, p 33. Also see Bono and A E Colbert, "Understanding Responses to Multi-Source Feedback: The Role of Core Self-Evaluations," *Personnel Psychology,* Spring 2005, pp 171–203.

45 D Jones, "It's Lonely—and Thin-Skinned—at the Top," *USA Today,* January 16, 2007, p 1B.

46 D E Coates, "Don't Tie 360 Feedback to Pay," *Training,* September 1998, pp 68–78. Also see A S Wellner, "Everyone's a Critic," *Inc.,* July 2004, pp 38, 41; and W C Byham, "Fixing the Instrument," *Training,* July 2004, p 50.

47 For more on coaching, see A Stein Wellner, "Do You Need a Coach?" *Inc.,* April 2006, pp 86–92; K Gurchiek, "Minority Employees Skipped for Coaching," *HR Magazine,* July 2006, pp 28, 36; and J Gordon, "The Coach Approach: Career Counseling Is on the Money at Deloitte," *Training,* October 2006, pp 26–30.

48 See M J Conyon, "Executive Compensation and Incentives," *Academy of Management Perspectives,* February 2006, pp 25–44; A Tergesen, "How Much Are Execs Really Paid?" *BusinessWeek,* March 20, 2006, pp 96–98; M Boyle, "They Didn't Earn It—They Should Return It," *Fortune,* May 15, 2006, p 35; "Scandal of the Week," *BusinessWeek,* June 5, 2006, p 25; and G Farrell, "President's Speech Shows CEO Pay Has Hit the Big Time," *USA Today,* February 5, 2007, p 1B.

49 "The Stat," *BusinessWeek,* October 4, 2004, p 16.

50 See, for example, D Jensen, T McMullen, and M Stark, *The Manager's Guide to Rewards* (New York; AMACOM, 2006).

51 See P Babcock, "Find What Workers Want," *HR Magazine,* April 2005, pp 50–56; and "So, What Do Employees *Really* Want?" *Training,* October 2006, p 17.

52 List adapted from J L Pearce and R H Peters, "A Contradictory Norms View of Employer–Employee Exchange," *Journal of Management,* Spring 1985, pp 19–30. Also see C Garvey, "Philosophizing Compensation," *HR Magazine,* January 2005, pp 73–76.

53 D Brady, "The Immelt Revolution," *BusinessWeek,* March 28, 2005, p 66.

54 "The 100 Best Companies to Work For," *Fortune,* February 4, 2002, p 90.

55 See E L Deci, R Koestner, and R M Ryan, "A Meta-Analytic Review of Experiments Examining the Effects of Extrinsic Rewards on Intrinsic Motivation," *Psychological Bulletin,* November 1999, pp 627–68; and R Eisenberger, W D Pierce, and J Cameron, "Effects of Reward on Intrinsic Motivation— Negative, Neutral, and Positive: Comment on Deci, Koestner, and Ryan (1999)," *Psychological Bulletin,* November 1999, pp 677–91.

56 See K W Thomas, *Intrinsic Motivation at Work: Building Energy and Commitment* (San Francisco: Berrett-Koehler Publishers, 2000).

57 See E L Deci and R M Ryan, "The 'What' and 'Why' of Goal Pursuits: Human Needs and Self-Determination of Behavior," *Psychological Inquiry,* December 2000, pp 227–68.

58 This study is summarized by S Ellingwood, "On a Mission," *Gallup Management Journal,* Winter 2001, pp 6–7.

59 S Jones, "Jay-Z Is a Very Busy Man," *USA Today,* November 21, 2006, p 5D. Also see J Durett, "Like Where You Work?" *Training,* August 2006, p 10.

60 M Littman, "Best Bosses Tell All," *Working Woman,* October 2000, p 55.

61 A Carter, "Lighting a Fire Under Campbell," *BusinessWeek,* December 4, 2006, p 96.

62 D R Spitzer, "Power Rewards: Rewards That Really Motivate," *Management Review,* May 1996, p 47. Also see S Kerr, "An Academy Classic: On the Folly of Rewarding A, while Hoping for B," *Academy of Management Executive,* February 1995, pp 7–14.

63 List adapted from discussion in Spitzer, "Power Rewards," pp 45–50. Also see W F Cascio, "The High Cost of Low Wages," *Harvard Business Review,* December 2006, p 23; and S Miller, "Satisfaction with Pay, Benefits Falling," *HR Magazine,* January 2007, pp 38–39.

64 See T B Wilson, *Innovative Reward Systems for the Changing Workplace,* 2nd ed. (New York: McGraw-Hill, 2002); and "Acculturate, Educate, and Motivate," *Training,* December 2004, pp 10–11.

65 "Performance-Based Pay Plans," *HR Magazine,* June 2004, p 22. Also see S J Wells, "No Results, No Raise," *HR Magazine,* May 2005, pp 76–80; J Sammer, "Figuring Incentive Plans' ROI," *HR Magazine,* July 2006, pp 83–86; S Ladika, "Rewarding Exempt Employees," *HR Magazine,* September 2006, pp 117–21; "The Power of Incentives," *HR Magazine,* Special Advertising Section, September 2006, pp 85–100.

66 For both sides of the "Does money motivate?" debate, see N Gupta and J D Shaw, "Let the Evidence Speak: Financial Incentives *Are* Effective!!" *Compensation & Benefits Review,* March–April 1998, pp 26, 28–32; A Kohn, "Challenging Behaviorist Dogma: Myths about Money and Motivation," *Compensation & Benefits Review,* March–April 1998, pp 27, 33–37; and B Ettorre, "Is Salary a Motivator?" *Management Review,* January 1999, p 8. Also see J Pfeffer, "Stopping the Talent Drain," *Business 2.0,* July 2006, p 80; M Weinstein, "A Win-Win in the Workplace: What Employees Really Care About," *Training,* August 2006, p 8; H Dolezalek, "You Get What You Pay For," *Training,* November 2006, pp 34–35.

67 Data from D Kiley, "Crafty Basket Makers Cut Downtime, Waste," *USA Today,* May 10, 2001, p 3B.

68 Data from N J Perry, "Here Come Richer, Riskier Pay Plans," *Fortune,* December 19, 1988, p 51. Also see W Zellner,

"Trickle-Down Is Trickling Down at Work," *BusinessWeek,* March 18, 1996, p 34.

[69] Data from M Bloom and G T Milkovich, "Relationships among Risk, Incentive Pay, and Organizational Performance," *Academy of Management Journal,* June 1998, pp 283–97.

[70] For details, see G D Jenkins Jr, N Gupta, A Mitra, and J D Shaw, "Are Financial Incentives Related to Performance? A Meta-Analytic Review of Empirical Research," *Journal of Applied Psychology,* October 1998, pp 777–87. Also see S J Peterson and F Luthans, "The Impact of Financial and Nonfinancial Incentives on Business-Unit Outcomes Over Time," *Journal of Applied Psychology,* January 2006, pp 156–165.

[71] See M J Mandel, "Those Fat Bonuses Don't Seem to Boost Performance," *BusinessWeek,* January 8, 1990, p 26; S F O'Byrne and S D Young, "Why Executive Pay Is Failing," *Harvard Business Review,* June 2006, p 28; and A Pomeroy, "Pay for Performance Is Working, Says a New Study," *HR Magazine,* January 2007, pp 14, 16.

[72] Based on discussion in R Ricklefs, "Whither the Payoff on Sales Commissions?" *The Wall Street Journal,* June 6, 1990, p B1.

[73] G Koretz, "Bad Marks for Pay-by-Results," *BusinessWeek,* September 4, 1995, p 28. Also see S Bates, "Now, the Downside of Pay for Performance," *HR Magazine,* March 2002, p 10; and R Grover and A Bernstein, "Arnold Gets Strict with the Teachers," *BusinessWeek,* May 2, 2005, pp 84–85.

[74] Performance-Based Pay Plans," p 22.

[75] See C Ginther, "Incentive Programs That Really Work," *HR Magazine,* August 2000, pp 117–20; and E A Locke, "Linking Goals to Monetary Incentives," *Academy of Management Executive,* November 2004, pp 130–33.

[76] See B E Litzky, K A Eddleston, and D L Kidder, "The Good, the Bad, and the Misguided: How Managers Inadvertently Encourage Deviant Behaviors," *Academy of Management Perspectives,* February 2006, pp 91–103.

[77] See E L Thorndike, *Educational Psychology: The Psychology of Learning, Vol. II* (New York: Columbia University Teachers College, 1913).

[78] Discussion of an early behaviorist who influenced Skinner's work can be found in P J Kreshel, "John B Watson at J Walter Thompson: The Legitimation of 'Science' in Advertising," *Journal of Advertising,* no. 2, 1990, pp 49–59. Recent discussions involving behaviorism include M R Ruiz, "B F Skinner's Radical Behaviorism: Historical Misconstructions and Grounds for Feminist Reconstructions," *Psychology of Women Quarterly,* June 1995, pp 161–79; J A Nevin, "Behavioral Economics and Behavioral Momentum," *Journal of the Experimental Analysis of Behavior,* November 1995, pp 385–95; and H Rachlin, "Can We Leave Cognition to Cognitive Psychologists? Comments on an Article by George Loewenstein," *Organizational Behavior and Human Decision Processes,* March 1996, pp 296–99.

[79] For recent discussion, see J W Donahoe, "The Unconventional Wisdom of B F Skinner: The Analysis-Interpretation Distinction," *Journal of the Experimental Analysis of Behavior,* September 1993, pp 453–56.

[80] See B F Skinner, *The Behavior of Organisms* (New York: Appleton-Century-Crofts, 1938).

[81] For modern approaches to respondent behavior, see B Azar, "Classical Conditioning Could Link Disorders and Brain Dysfunction, Researchers Suggest," *APA Monitor,* March 1999, p 17.

[82] For interesting discussions of Skinner and one of his students, see M B Gilbert and T F Gilbert. "What Skinner Gave Us," *Training,* September 1991, pp 42–48; and "HRD Pioneer Gilbert Leaves a Pervasive Legacy," *Training,* January 1996, p 14. Also see F Luthans and R Kreitner, *Organizational Behavior Modification and Beyond: An Operant and Social Learning Approach* (Glenview, IL: Scott, Foresman, 1985).

[83] The effect of praise is explored in C M Mueller and C S Dweck, "Praise for Intelligence Can Undermine Children's Motivation and Performance," *Journal of Personality and Social Psychology,* July 1998, pp 33–52. Also see C Garvey, "Meaningful Tokens of Appreciation," *HR Magazine,* August 2004, pp 101–6; K Hannon, "Praise Cranks Up Productivity," *USA Today,* August 30, 2004, p 6B; B Hindo, "Drive Green and Get Some Green," *BusinessWeek,* December 13, 2004, p 14; and D Jones, "Coach Says Honey Gets Better Results than Vinegar," *USA Today,* February 21, 2005, p 4B.

[84] C Salter, "Customer Service," *Fast Company,* May 2002, p 86. Also see R Kegan and L L Lahey, "More Powerful Communication: From the Language of Prizes and Praising to the Language of Ongoing Regard," *Journal of Organizational Excellence,* Summer 2001, pp 11–17.

[85] Research on punishment is reported in B P Niehoff, R J Paul, and J F S Bunch, "The Social Effects of Punishment Events: The Influence of Violator Past Performance Record and Severity of the Punishment on Observers' Justice Perceptions and Attitudes," *Journal of Organizational Behavior,* November 1998, pp 589–602; and L E Atwater, D A Waldman, J A Carey, and P Cartier, "Recipient and Observer Reactions to Discipline: Are Managers Experiencing Wishful Thinking?" *Journal of Organizational Behavior,* May 2001, pp 249–70.

[86] See C B Ferster and B F Skinner, *Schedules of Reinforcement* (New York: Appleton-Century-Crofts, 1957).

[87] See L M Saari and G P Latham, "Employee Reactions to Continuous and Variable Ratio Reinforcement Schedules Involving a Monetary Incentive," *Journal of Applied Psychology,* August 1982, pp 506–8.

[88] P Brinkley-Rogers and R Collier, "Along the Colorado, the Money's Flowing," *Arizona Republic,* March 4, 1990, p A12.

[89] R Levering and M Moskowitz, "*Fortune* 100 Best Companies to Work For: 2007," *Fortune,* January 22, 2007, p 96.

[90] See D Jones, "Training Workers the SeaWorld Way," *USA Today,* August 21, 2006, p 3B.

[91] See R F Gerson and R Gerson, "Effort Management: Why Reinforcing Results May Not Be Enough," *Training and Development,* June 2006, pp 26–27.

[92] Data from K L Alexander, "Continental Airlines Soars to New Heights," *USA Today,* January 23, 1996, p 4B; and M Knez and D Simester, "Making Across-the-Board Incentives Work," *Harvard Business Review,* February 2002, pp 16–17.

[93] J McGregor, "A Real Stake In Your Customers," *BusinessWeek,* June 19, 2006, p 70. For more, see J Fried, "Skin in the Game," *Inc.,* July 2006, pp 33–36.

[94] Excerpted from R McCarthy, "A New Kind of Perk: Online Gambling," *Inc.,* December 2006, p 38.

CHAPTER 10

[1] Excerpted from A Walker, "Space Shot: You Wish You Worked Here," *Fast Company*, April 2007, pp 102–07. Also see J Schlosser, "Another Space Race," *Fortune,* June 12, 2006, p 120.

[2] Drawn from C O Longenecker, M J Neubert, and L S Fink, "Causes and Consequences of Managerial Failure in Rapidly Changing Organizations," *Business Horizons*, March–April 2007, pp 145–55. Also see D Ancona, T W Malone, W J Orlikowski, and P M Senge, "In Praise of the Incomplete Leader," *Harvard Business Review*, February 2007, pp 92–100.

[3] See E de Nijs, "GRACE at Work," *Training and Development*, March 2006, pp 47–49; and D Goleman, *Social Intelligence: The New Science of Relationships* (New York: Bantam, 2006).

[4] See P S Adler and S Kwon, "Social Capital: Prospects for a New Concept," *Academy of Management Review,* January 2002, pp 17–40; and J Savage and S Kanazawa, "Social Capital and the Human Psyche: Why Is Social Life 'Capital'?" *Sociological Theory,* September 2004, pp 504–24.

[5] See G Lindemann, "The Analysis of the Borders of the Social World: A Challenge for Sociological Theory," *Journal for the Theory of Social Behaviour,* March 2005, pp 69–98.

[6] This definition is based in part on one found in D Horton Smith, "A Parsimonious Definition of 'Group': Toward Conceptual Clarity and Scientific Utility," *Sociological Inquiry,* Spring 1967, pp 141–67. Also see M S Poole, A B Hollingshead, J E McGrath, R L Moreland, and J Rohrbaugh, "Interdisciplinary Perspectives on Small Groups," *Small Group Research,* February 2004, pp 3–16; G M Wittenbaum, A B Hollingshead, P B Paulus, R Y Hirokawa, D G Ancona, R S Peterson, K A Jehn, and K Yoon, "The Functional Perspective as a Lens for Understanding Groups," *Small Group Research,* February 2004, pp 17–43; and G A Fine and B Harrington, "Tiny Publics: Small Groups and Civil Society," *Sociological Theory,* September 2004, pp 341–46.

[7] E H Schein, *Organizational Psychology,* 3rd ed (Englewood Cliffs, NJ: Prentice Hall, 1980), p 145. For more, see L R Weingart, "How Did They Do That? The Ways and Means of Studying Group Process," in *Research in Organizational Behavior,* vol. 19, eds L L Cummings and B M Staw (Greenwich, CT: JAI Press, 1997), pp 189–239.

[8] See J Labianca, "The Ties That Blind," *Harvard Business Review,* October 2004, p 19; J J Anove, "FOB: Friend of Boss," *HR Magazine,* June 2005, pp 153–56; E Levenson, "How the Office Really Works," *Fortune,* June 12, 2006, p 118; and D Jones, "March Madness Is Here, So Go Ahead and Goof Off?" *USA Today*, March 16, 2007, p 1B.

[9] See L Buchanan, "The Office: I Know Where You Live," *Inc.*, July 2006, p 124; C Wilbert, "You Schmooze, You Win," *Fast Company*, July–August 2006, p 109; and K Sulkowicz, "In Cupid's Cubicle," *BusinessWeek*, February 26, 2007, p 18.

[10] J Castro, "Mazda U.," *Time,* October 20, 1986, p 65.

[11] For more, see M S Cole, W S Schaninger Jr, and S G Harris, "The Workplace Social Exchange Network: A Multilevel, Conceptual Examination," *Group & Organization Management,* March 2002, pp 142–67. Also see J McGregor, "Game Plan: First Find the Leaders," *BusinessWeek*, August 21, 2006, pp 102–03; M Kilduff, W Tsai, and R Hanke, "A Paradigm Too Far? A Dynamic Stability Reconsideration of the Social Network Research Program," *Academy of Management Review*, October 2006, pp 1031–48; N Anand and J A Conger, "Capabilities of the Consummate Networker," *Organizational Dynamics,* no. 1, 2007, pp 13–27; C Meyer, "Breakthrough Ideas for 2007: The Best Networks Are Really Worknets," *Harvard Business Review*, February 2007, pp 47–48, 50; and L Young and P Lehman, "It's Not What You Know," *BusinessWeek*, February 26, 2007, p 14.

[12] See P Cardona, B S Lawrence, and P M Bentler, "The Influence of Social and Work Exchange Relationships on Organizational Citizenship Behavior," *Group & Organization Management,* April 2004, pp 219–47.

[13] For an instructive overview of five different theories of group development, see J P Wanous, A E Reichers, and S D Malik, "Organizational Socialization and Group Development: Toward an Integrative Perspective," *Academy of Management Review,* October 1984, pp 670–83.

[14] See B W Tuckman, "Developmental Sequence in Small Groups," *Psychological Bulletin,* June 1965, pp 384–99; and B W Tuckman and M A C Jensen, "Stages of Small-Group Development Revisited," *Group & Organization Studies,* December 1977, pp 419–27. An instructive adaptation of the Tuckman model can be found in L Holpp, "If Empowerment Is So Good, Why Does It Hurt?" *Training,* March 1995, p 56. Also see S A Furst, M Reeves, B Rosen, and R S Blackburn, "Managing the Life Cycle of Virtual Teams," *Academy of Management Executive,* May 2004, pp 6–20.

[15] Alternative group development models are discussed in L N Jewell and H J Reitz, *Group Effectiveness in Organizations* (Glenview, IL: Scott, Foresman, 1981), pp 15–20; and R S Wellins, W C Byham, and J M Wilson, *Empowered Teams: Creating Self-Directed Work Groups That Improve Quality,*

Productivity and Participation (San Francisco: Jossey-Bass, 1991). Also see H Arrow, M S Poole, K B Henry, S Wheelan, and R Moreland, "Time, Change, and Development," *Small Group Research,* February 2004, pp 73–105; K J Klein, B Lim, J L Saltz, and D M Mayer, "How Do They Get There? An Examination of the Antecedents of Centrality in Team Networks," *Academy of Management Journal,* December 2004, pp 952–63; and L A Erbert, G M Mearns, and S Dena, "Perceptions of Turning Points and Dialectical Interpretations in Organizational Team Development," *Small Group Research,* February 2005, pp 21–58.

[16] See E Gash, "More Training Than Camp," *Training,* December 2006, p 7; and G A Ballinger and F D Schoorman, "Individual Reactions to Leadership Succession in Workgroups," *Academy of Management Review,* January 2007, pp 118–136.

[17] For related research, see W Felps, T R Mitchell, and E Byington, "How, When, and Why Bad Apples Spoil the Barrel: Negative Group Members and Dysfunctional Groups," in *Research in Organizational Behavior: An Annual of Analytical Essays and Critical Reviews Research in Organizational Behavior*, vol. 27, ed B Staw (Amsterdam, Netherlands: Elsevier, 2006), pp 175–222; and J C Biesanz, S G West, and A Millevoi, "What Do You Learn About Someone Over Time? The Relationship Between Length of Acquaintance and Consensus and Self-Other Agreement in Judgments of Personality," *Journal of Personality and Social Psychology*, January 2007, pp 119–35.

[18] B L Riddle, C M Anderson, and M M Martin, "Small Group Socialization Scale: Development and Validity," *Small Group Research,* October 2000, pp 554–72; and M Van Vugt and C M Hart, "Social Identity as Social Glue: The Origins of Group Loyalty," *Journal of Personality and Social Psychology,* April 2004, pp 585–98.

[19] Jewell and Reitz, *Group Effectiveness in Organizations,* p 19. Also see C M Mason and M A Griffin, "Group Task Satisfaction: The Group's Shared Attitude to Its Task and Work Environments," *Group and Organization Management,* December 2005, pp 625–52.

[20] Based on J F McGrew, J G Bilotta, and J M Deeney, "Software Team Formation and Decay: Extending the Standard Model for Small Groups," *Small Group Research,* April 1999, pp 209–34.

[21] Ibid., p 232.

[22] Ibid., p 231.

[23] D Davies and B C Kuypers, "Group Development and Interpersonal Feedback," *Group & Organizational Studies,* June 1985, p 194.

[24] Ibid., pp 184–208.

[25] C J G Gersick, "Marking Time: Predictable Transitions in Task Groups," *Academy of Management Journal,* June 1989, pp 274–309.

[26] D K Carew, E Parisi-Carew, and K H Blanchard, "Group Development and Situational Leadership: A Model for Managing Groups," *Training and Development Journal,* June 1986, pp 48–49. For evidence linking leadership and group

effectiveness, see G R Bushe and A L Johnson, "Contextual and Internal Variables Affecting Task Group Outcomes in Organizations," *Group & Organization Studies,* December 1989, pp 462–82.

[27] See B George, P Sims, A N McLean, and D Mayer, "Discovering Your Authentic Leadership," *Harvard Business Review*, February 2007, pp 129–38; R Kark and D Van Dijk, "Motivation to Lead, Motivation to Follow: The Role of the Self-Regulatory Focus in Leadership Processes," *Academy of Management Review*, April 2007, pp 500–28; L Bossidy, "What Your Leader Expects of You: And What You Should Expect in Return," *Harvard Business Review*, April 2007, pp 58–65; and B George and W Kopp, "Resolved: The Hardest Person You Will Ever Have to Lead Is Yourself," *Fast Company*, April 2007, p 112.

[28] See C Anderson, S Srivastava, J S Beer, S E Spataro, and J A Chatman, "Knowing Your Place: Self-Perceptions of Status in Face-to-Face Groups," *Journal of Personality and Social Psychology*, December 2006, pp 1094–110; and D M Sluss and B E Ashforth, "Relational Identity and Identification Defining Ourselves Through Work Relationships," *Academy of Management Review*, January 2007, pp 9–32.

[29] G Graen, "Role-Making Processes within Complex Organizations," in *Handbook of Industrial and Organizational Psychology,* ed M D Dunnette (Chicago: Rand McNally, 1976), p 1201. Also see C G Soriano, "'Bored' By Her Kids, She's Getting It Full-Bore," *USA Today*, July 31, 2006, p 7D; and T Reay, K Golden-Biddle, and K Germann, "Legitimizing a New Role: Small Wins and Microprocesses of Change," *Academy of Management Journal*, October 2006, pp 977–98.

[30] Role modeling applications are covered in J Barbian, "A Little Help from Your Friends," *Training,* March 2002, pp 38–41. Also see A D Cast, "Role-Taking and Interaction," *Social Psychology Quarterly,* September 2004, pp 296–309.

[31] G L Miles, "Doug Danforth's Plan to Put Westinghouse in the 'Winner's Circle,'" *BusinessWeek,* July 28, 1986, p 75.

[32] For a review of research on the role episode model, see L A King and D W King, "Role Conflict and Role Ambiguity: A Critical Assessment of Construct Validity," *Psychological Bulletin,* January 1990, pp 48–64. Consequences of role perceptions are discussed in R C Netemeyer, S Burton, and M W Johnston, "A Nested Comparison of Four Models of the Consequences of Role Perception Variables," *Organizational Behavior and Human Decision Processes,* January 1995, pp 77–93.

[33] Schein, *Organizational Psychology,* p 198.

[34] Ibid. The relationship between interrole conflict and turnover is explored in P W Hom and A J Kinicki, "Toward a Greater Understanding of How Dissatisfaction Drives Employee Turnover," *Academy of Management Journal,* October 2001, pp 975–87.

[35] See A Park, "Between a Rocker and a High Chair," *BusinessWeek,* February 21, 2005, pp 86, 88; J Merritt, "MBA Family Values," *BusinessWeek,* March 14, 2005, pp 104–6; H T J Bainbridge, C Cregan, and C T Kulik, "The Effect of

Multiple Roles on Caregiver Stress Outcomes," *Journal of Applied Psychology*, March 2006, pp 490–97.

[36] See D C Kayes, D Stirling, and T M Nielsen, "Building Organizational Integrity," *Business Horizons*, January–February 2007, pp 61–70; M Weinstein, "Executing Ethics," *Training*, March 2007, p. 8; and B Leonard, "Blowing Whistle on Navy Recruitment Proves Costly," *HR Magazine*, March 2007, pp 25, 28.

[37] Schein, *Organizational Psychology*, p 198. Four types of role ambiguity are discussed in M A Eys and A V Carron, "Role Ambiguity, Task Cohesion, and Task Self-Efficacy," *Small Group Research*, June 2001, pp 356–73.

[38] Drawn from M Peterson et al., "Role Conflict, Ambiguity, and Overload: A 21-Nation Study," *Academy of Management Journal*, April 1995, pp 429–52.

[39] Based on Y Fried, H A Ben-David, R B Tiegs, N Avital, and U Yeverechyahu, "The Interactive Effect of Role Conflict and Role Ambiguity on Job Performance," *Journal of Occupational and Organizational Psychology*, March 1998, pp 19–27. Also see J Levin, "'This Topic Annoys Me,'" *Newsweek*, September 25, 2006, p 72; and B E Ashforth, G E Kreiner, M A Clark, and M Fugate, "Normalizing Dirty Work: Managerial Tactics for Countering Occupational Taint," *Academy of Management Journal*, February 2007, pp 149–74.

[40] R R Blake and J Srygley Mouton, "Don't Let Group Norms Stifle Creativity," *Personnel*, August 1985, p 28.

[41] See K Montgomery, K Kane, and C M Vance, "Accounting for Differences in Norms of Respect: A Study of Assessments of Incivility through the Lenses of Race and Gender," *Group & Organization Management*, April 2004, pp 248–68; A Spicer, T W Dunfee, and W J Bailey, "Does National Context Matter in Ethical Decision Making? An Empirical Test of Integrative Social Contracts Theory," *Academy of Management Journal*, August 2004, pp 610–20; and K S Cook, "Networks, Norms, and Trust: The Social Psychology of Social Capital," *Social Psychology Quarterly*, March 2005, pp 4–14.

[42] A Dunkin, "Pepsi's Marketing Magic: Why Nobody Does It Better," *BusinessWeek*, February 10, 1986, p 52.

[43] For related reading, see A J Towler and D J Schneider, "Distinctions among Stigmatized Groups," *Journal of Applied Social Psychology*, January 2005, pp 1–14; J K Maner, N DeWall, M Schaller, and R F Baumeister, "Does Social Exclusion Motivate Interpersonal Reconnection? Resolving the 'Porcupine Problem,'" *Journal of Personality and Social Psychology*, January 2007, pp 42–55; and J M Twenge, R F Baumeister, C N DeWall, N J Ciarocco, and J M Bartels, "Social Exclusion Decreases Prosocial Behavior," *Journal of Personality and Social Psychology*, January 2007, pp 56–66.

[44] D C Feldman, "The Development and Enforcement of Group Norms," *Academy of Management Review*, January 1984, pp 50–52. Also see S Maitlis and T B Lawrence, "Triggers and Enablers of Sensegiving in Organizations," *Academy of Management Journal*, February 2007, pp 57–84.

[45] Feldman, "The Development and Enforcement of Group Norms."

[46] See R G Netemeyer, M W Johnston, and S Burton, "Analysis of Role Conflict and Role Ambiguity in a Structural Equations Framework," *Journal of Applied Psychology*, April 1990, pp 148–57; and G W McGee, C E Ferguson Jr, and A Seers, "Role Conflict and Role Ambiguity: Do the Scales Measure These Two Constructs?" *Journal of Applied Psychology*, October 1989, pp 815–18.

[47] See S E Jackson and R S Schuler, "A Meta-Analysis and Conceptual Critique of Research on Role Ambiguity and Role Conflict in Work Settings," *Organizational Behavior and Human Decision Processes*, August 1985, pp 16–78.

[48] Based on C S Crandall, A Eshleman, and L O'Brien, "Social Norms and the Expression and Suppression of Prejudice: The Struggle for Internalization," *Journal of Personality and Social Psychology*, March 2002, pp 359–78. Also see B Leonard, "Gallup: Workplace Bias Still Prevalent," *HR Magazine*, February 2006, p 34; P Babcock, "Detecting Hidden Bias," *HR Magazine*, February 2006, pp 50–55; and M Orey, "White Men Can't Help It," *BusinessWeek*, May 15, 2006, pp 54, 57.

[49] See J A Segal, "'Good Fit' Isn't Always Legit," *HR Magazine*, November 2006, pp 121–26; and A Pomeroy, "Cultivating Female Leaders," *HR Magazine*, February 2007, pp. 44–50.

[50] See T Halfhill, E Sundstrom, J Lahner, W Calderone, and T M Nielsen, "Group Personality Composition and Group Effectiveness: An Integrative Review of Empirical Research," *Small Group Research*, February 2005, pp 83–105.

[51] See K D Benne and P Sheats, "Functional Roles of Group Members," *Journal of Social Issues*, Spring 1948, pp 41–49. Also see J Strijbos, R L Martens, W M G Jochems, and N J Broers, "The Effect of Functional Roles on Group Efficiency," *Small Group Research*, April 2004, pp 195–229.

[52] See G P Latham and E A Locke, "Enhancing the Benefits and Overcoming the Pitfalls of Goal Setting," *Organizational Dynamics*, no. 4, 2006, pp 332–40.

[53] A Zander, "The Value of Belonging to a Group in Japan," *Small Group Behavior*, February 1983, pp 7–8. Also see P R Harris and R T Moran, *Managing Cultural Differences*, 4th ed (Houston: Gulf Publishing, 1996), pp 267–76.

[54] See P R Laughlin, E C Hatch, J S Silver, and L Boh, "Groups Perform Better Than the Best Individuals on Letters-to-Numbers Problems: Effects of Group Size," *Journal of Personality and Social Psychology*, April 2006, pp 644–51; and J L Yang, "The Power of Number 4.6," *Fortune*, June 12, 2006, p 122.

[55] For example, see B Grofman, S L Feld, and G Owen, "Group Size and the Performance of a Composite Group Majority: Statistical Truths and Empirical Results," *Organizational Behavior and Human Performance*, June 1984, pp 350–59.

[56] See P Yetton and P Bottger, "The Relationships among Group Size, Member Ability, Social Decision Schemes, and Performance," *Organizational Behavior and Human Performance*, October 1983, pp 145–59.

[57] This copyrighted exercise may be found in J Hall, "Decisions, Decisions, Decisions," *Psychology Today,* November 1971, pp 51–54, 86, 88.

[58] Yetton and Bottger, "The Relationships among Group Size, Member Ability, Social Decision Schemes, and Performance," p 158.

[59] Based on R B Gallupe, A R Dennis, W H Cooper, J S Valacich, L M Bastianutti, and J F Nunamaker Jr, "Electronic Brainstorming and Group Size," *Academy of Management Journal,* June 1992, pp 350–69. Also see H Barki and A Pinsonneault, "Small Group Brainstorming and Idea Quality: Is Electronic Brainstorming the Most Effective Approach?" *Small Group Research,* April 2001, pp 158–205; and T J Kramer, G P Fleming, and S M Mannis, "Improving Face-to-Face Brainstorming through Modeling and Facilitation." *Small Group Research,* October 2001, pp 533–57.

[60] Data from E Salas, D Rozell, B Mullen, and J E Driskell, "The Effect of Team Building on Performance: An Integration," *Small Group Research,* June 1999, pp 309–29.

[61] Drawn from B Mullen, C Symons, L-T Hu, and E Salas, "Group Size, Leadership Behavior, and Subordinate Satisfaction," *Journal of General Psychology,* April 1989, pp 155–69. Also see P Oliver and G Marwell, "The Paradox of Group Size in Collective Action: A Theory of the Critical Mass, II.," *American Sociological Review,* February 1988, pp 1–8.

[62] For Example, see T Howard, "FTC Impasse Allows Pepsi, Quaker Deal," *USA Today,* August 2, 2001, p 1B.

[63] D S Carlson, K M Kacmar, and D Whitten, "What Men Think They Know About Executive Women," *Harvard Business Review,* September 2006, p 28.

[64] See E E Duehr and J E Bono, "Men, Women, and Managers: Are Stereotypes Finally Changing?" *Personnel Psychology,* Winter 2006, pp 815–46; S M Colarelli, J L Spranger, and M R Hechanova, "Women, Power, and Sex Composition in Small Groups: An Evolutionary Perspective," *Journal of Organizational Behavior,* March 2006, pp 163–84; and M Weinstein, "The Differences Between Boys and Girls . . . at the Office," *Training,* November 2006, p 8.

[65] See L Smith-Lovin and C Brody, "Interruptions in Group Discussions: The Effects of Gender and Group Composition," *American Sociological Review,* June 1989, pp 424–35.

[66] L Karakowsky, K McBey, and D L Miller, "Gender, Perceived Competence, and Power Displays: Examining Verbal Interruptions in a Group Context," *Small Group Research,* August 2004, p 407.

[67] E M Ott, "Effects of the Male-Female Ratio at Work," *Psychology of Women Quarterly,* March 1989, p 53.

[68] "Daily Downer," *Training,* April 2005, p 12. Also see S Armour, "More Men Say They Are Sexually Harassed at Work," *USA Today,* September 17, 2004, p 1B; M Conlin, "Harassers in High Places," *BusinessWeek,* November 13, 2006, p 44; E Hayes James and L Perry Wooten, "Diversity Crises: How Firms Manage Discrimination Lawsuits," *Academy of Management Journal,* December 2006, pp 1103–18; and J L Berdahl, "Harassment Based on Sex: Protecting Social Status in the Context of Gender Hierarchy," *Academy of Management Review,* April 2007, pp 641–58.

[69] J L Berdahl and C Moore, "Workplace Harassment: Double Jeopardy for Minority Women," *Journal of Applied Psychology,* March 2006, p 426. Also see M Orey, "Trouble at Toyota," *BusinessWeek,* May 22, 2006, pp 46–48.

[70] See S Jayson, "Abusive Teen Dating Behavior Goes High-Tech," *USA Today,* February 8, 2007, p 1D; and S Armour, "Companies Try to Educate Teen Workers about Harassment," *USA Today,* October 19, 2006, p 3B.

[71] Data from B A Gutek, A Groff Cohen, and A M Konrad, "Predicting Social-Sexual Behavior at Work: A Contact Hypothesis," *Academy of Management Journal,* September 1990, pp 560–77. Also see K Gurchiek, "Be Ready for Slings, Arrows of Cupid in the Cubicles," *HR Magazine,* March 2005, pp 27, 36–37; S Shellenbarger, "Employers Often Ignore Office Affairs, Leaving Co-Workers in Difficult Spot," *The Wall Street Journal,* March 10, 2005, p D1; and L Buchanan, "Isn't It Romantic," *Inc.,* August 2006, p 132.

[72] Data from M Rotundo, D Nguyen, and P R Sackett, "A Meta-Analytic Review of Gender Differences in Perceptions of Sexual Harassment," *Journal of Applied Psychology,* October 2001, pp 914–22. Also see M Barreto and N Ellemers, "The Perils of Political Correctness: Men's and Women's Responses to Old-Fashioned and Modern Sexist Views," *Social Psychology Quarterly,* March 2005, pp 75–88; L Bowes-Sperry and A M O'Leary-Kelly, "To Act or Not to Act: The Dilemma Faced by Sexual Harassment Observers," *Academy of Management Review,* April 2005, pp 288–306; and N A Bowling and T A Beehr, "Workplace Harassment from the Victim's Perspective: A Theoretical Model and Meta-Analysis," *Journal of Applied Psychology,* September 2006, pp 998–1012.

[73] S J South, C M Bonjean, W T Markham, and J Corder, "Female Labor Force Participation and the Organizational Experiences of Male Workers," *Sociological Quarterly,* Summer 1983, p 378.

[74] R R Hirschfeld, M H Jordan, H S Field, W F Giles, and A A Armenakis, "Teams' Female Representation and Perceived Potency as Inputs to Team Outcomes in a Predominantly Male Field Setting," *Personnel Psychology,* Winter 2005, p 893. Also see A M Konrad and V W Kramer, "How Many Women Do Boards Need?" *Harvard Business Review,* December 2006, p 22.

[75] B T Thornton, "Sexual Harassment, 1: Discouraging It in the Work Place," *Personnel,* April 1986, p 18. Also see R K Robinson, G M Franklin, and W J Davis, "Sexual Harassment Redux," *Business Horizons,* July–August 2004, pp 3–5; J W Janove, "Conclude and Communicate," *HR Magazine,* August 2004, pp 131–34; T O McCarthy, "Sexual Conduct: Equal Abuse Unequal Harm," *HR Magazine,* January 2005, pp 93–94; and J A Segal, "Deconstructing Documentation," *HR Magazine,* June 2006, pp 175–186.

[76] Data from T Galvin, "2001 Industry Report," *Training,* October 2001, pp 41, 54.

[77] For additional information, see S E Asch, *Social Psychology* (Englewood Cliffs, NJ: Prentice Hall, 1952), Ch. 16.

[78] See T P Williams and S Sogon, "Group Composition and Conforming Behavior in Japanese Students," *Japanese Psychological Research*, no. 4, 1984, pp 231–34; and T Amir, "The Asch Conformity Effect: A Study in Kuwait," *Social Behavior and Personality*, no. 2, 1984, pp 187–90.

[79] Data from R Bond and P B Smith, "Culture and Conformity: A Meta-Analysis of Studies Using Asch's (1952b, 1956) Line Judgment Task," *Psychological Bulletin*, January 1996, pp 111–37. Also see H Liao, A Joshi, and A Chuang, "Sticking Out Like a Sore Thumb: Employee Dissimilarity and Deviance at Work," *Personnel Psychology*, Winter 2004, pp 969–1000.

[80] J L Roberts and E Thomas, "Enron's Dirty Laundry," *Newsweek*, March 11, 2002, p 26. Also see G Farrell, "Pride at Root of Skilling's Downfall," *USA Today*, October 24, 2006, p 3B.

[81] For a comprehensive update on groupthink, see the entire February–March 1998 issue of *Organizational Behavior and Human Decision Processes* (12 articles). Also see W Schiano and J W Weiss, "Y2K All Over Again: How Groupthink Permeates IS and Compromises Security," *Business Horizons*, March-April 2006, pp 115–25.

[82] I L Janis, *Groupthink*, 2nd ed (Boston: Houghton Mifflin, 1982), p 9. Alternative models are discussed in K Granstrom and D Stiwne, "A Bipolar Model of Groupthink: An Expansion of Janis's Concept," *Small Group Research*, February 1998, pp 32–56; and A R Flippen, "Understanding Groupthink From a Self-Regulatory Perspective," *Small Group Research*, April 1999, pp 139–65.

[83] Ibid. For an alternative model, see R J Aldag and S Riggs Fuller, "Beyond Fiasco: A Reappraisal of the Groupthink Phenomenon and a New Model of Group Decision Processes," *Psychological Bulletin*, May 1993, pp 533–52. Also see A A Mohamed and F A Wiebe, "Toward a Process Theory of Groupthink," *Small Group Research*, August 1996, pp 416–30.

[84] N Byrnes and J Sasseen, "Board of Hard Knocks," *BusinessWeek*, January 22, 2007, pp 37–38. Also see J S Lublin and E White, "Drama in the Boardroom," *The Wall Street Journal*, October 2, 2006, pp B1, B3; and M Lubatkin, "One More Time: What Is a Realistic Theory of Corporate Governance?" *Journal of Organizational Behavior*, January 2007, pp 59–67.

[85] Details of this study may be found in M R Callaway and J K Esser, "Groupthink: Effects of Cohesiveness and Problem-Solving Procedures on Group Decision Making," *Social Behavior and Personality*, no. 2, 1984, pp 157–64. Also see C R Leana, "A Partial Test of Janis's Groupthink Model: Effects of Group Cohesiveness and Leader-Behavior on Defective Decision Making," *Journal of Management*, Spring 1985, pp 5–17; and G Moorhead and J R Montanari, "An Empirical Investigation of the Groupthink Phenomenon," *Human Relations*, May 1986, pp 399–410. A more modest indirect effect is reported in J N Choi and M U Kim, "The Organizational Application of Groupthink and Its Limitations in Organizations," *Journal of Applied Psychology*, April 1999, pp 297–306.

[86] Adapted from discussion in Janis, *Groupthink*, Ch. 11.

[87] D Jones, "P&G CEO Wields High Expectations But No Whip," *USA Today*, February 19, 2007, p 3B. Also see B Zhao and F Olivera, "Error Reporting in Organizations," *Academy of Management Review*, October 2006, pp 1012–30; and D Jones, "It's Lonely—and Thin-Skinned—at the Top," *USA Today*, January 16, 2007, pp 1B-2B.

[88] Based on discussion in B Latane, K Williams, and S Harkins, "Many Hands Make Light the Work: The Causes and Consequences of Social Loafing," *Journal of Personality and Social Psychology*, June 1979, pp 822–32; and D A Kravitz and B Martin, "Ringelmann Rediscovered: The Original Article," *Journal of Personality and Social Psychology*, May 1986, pp 936–41. Also see D Moyer, "First among Equals," *Harvard Business Review*, December 2004, p 152.

[89] See J A Shepperd, "Productivity Loss in Performance Groups: A Motivation Analysis," *Psychological Bulletin*, no. 1, 1993, pp 67–81; R E Kidwell Jr, and N Bennett, "Employee Propensity to Withhold Effort: A Conceptual Model to Intersect Three Avenues of Research," *Academy of Management Review*, July 1993, pp 429–56; S J Karau and K D Williams, "Social Loafing: Meta-Analytic Review and Theoretical Integration," *Journal of Personality and Social Psychology*, October 1993, pp 681–706; and S G Scott and W O Einstein, "Strategic Performance Appraisal in Team-Based Organizations: One Size Does Not Fit All," *Academy of Management Executive*, May 2001, pp 107–16.

[90] See S J Zaccaro, "Social Loafing: The Role of Task Attractiveness," *Personality and Social Psychology Bulletin*, March 1984, pp 99–106; J M Jackson and K D Williams, "Social Loafing on Difficult Tasks: Working Collectively Can Improve Performance," *Journal of Personality and Social Psychology*, October 1985, pp 937–42; and J M George, "Extrinsic and Intrinsic Origins of Perceived Social Loafing in Organizations," *Academy of Management Journal*, March 1992, pp 191–202.

[91] For complete details, see K Williams, S Harkins, and B Latane, "Identifiability as a Deterrent to Social Loafing: Two Cheering Experiments," *Journal of Personality and Social Psychology*, February 1981, pp 303–11.

[92] See J M Jackson and S G Harkins, "Equity in Effort: an Explanation of the Social Loafing Effect," *Journal of Personality and Social Psychology*, November 1985, pp 1199–206.

[93] Both studies are reported in S G Harkins and K Szymanski, "Social Loafing and Group Evaluation," *Journal of Personality and Social Psychology*, June 1989, pp 934–41. Also see R Hoigaard, R Safvenbom, and F E Tonnessen, "The Relationship Between Group Cohesion, Group Norms, and Perceived Social Loafing in Soccer Teams," *Small Group Research*, June 2006, pp 217–32.

[94] Data from J A Wagner III, "Studies of Individualism-Collectivism: Effects on Cooperation in Groups," *Academy of Management Journal*, February 1995, pp 152–72. Also see P W Mulvey and H J Klein, "The Impact of Perceived Loafing and Collective Efficacy on Group Goal Processes and Group Performance," *Organizational Behavior and Human*

Decision Processes, April 1998, pp 62–87; P W Mulvey, L Bowes-Sperry, and H J Klein, "The Effects of Perceived Loafing and Defensive Impression Management on Group Effectiveness," *Small Group Research,* June 1998, pp 394–415; L Karakowsky and K McBey, "Do My Contributions Matter? The Influence of Imputed Expertise on Member Involvement and Self-Evaluations in the Work Group," *Group & Organization Management,* March 2001, pp 70–92; and R C Liden, S J Wayne, R A Jaworski, and N Bennett, "Social Loafing: A Field Investigation," *Journal of Management,* no. 2, 2004, pp 285–304.

⁹⁵ S G Rogelberg, J L Barnes-Farrell, and C A Lowe, "The Stepladder Technique: An Alternative Group Structure Facilitating Effective Group Decision Making," *Journal of Applied Psychology,* October 1992, p 730.

⁹⁶ Excerpted from D Brady, "Secrets of An HR Superstar," *BusinessWeek*, April 9, 2007, pp 66–67.

⁹⁷ Excerpted from J O'Donnell, "Should Business Execs Meet at Strip Clubs?" *USA Today*, March 23, 2006, pp 1A–2A.

CHAPTER 11

¹ Excerpted from S Berfield, "Two for the Cubicle," *BusinessWeek,* July 24, 2006, pp 88–91.

² Jack Welch and Suzy Welch, "Company Man or Free Agent," *BusinessWeek,* February 12, 2007, p 106. Also see J Useem, "What's That Spell? Teamwork," *Fortune,* June 12, 2006, pp 65–66; R Davenport, "The Words of Legendary Coach John Wooden," *Training and Development,* August 2006, p 43; and S R Covey, "The Keys to Success," *Training,* September 2006, p 48.

³ See N Enbar, "What Do Women Want? Ask 'Em," *BusinessWeek,* March 29, 1999, p 8; and M Hickins. "Duh! Gen Xers Are Cool with Teamwork," *Management Review,* March 1999, p 7.

⁴ Data from "Creativity and Innovation," *Workplace Visions,* no. 1, 2007, Table 2, p 4. Also see C Palmeri, "Putting Managers To the Test," *BusinessWeek,* November 20, 2006, p 82; M B Marklein, "Panel Urges Collegians to Focus on Liberal Arts," *USA Today,* January 11, 2007, p 9D; and A Pomeroy, "Want to Disconnect? Build Your Team!" *HR Magazine,* February 2007, p 14.

⁵ J R Katzenbach, and D K Smith, *The Wisdom of Teams: Creating the High-Performance Organization* (New York: HarperBusiness, 1999), p 45. Also see "Company Is a Team, Not a Family," *HR Magazine,* April 2007, p 18; and S A Miles and M D Watkins, "The Leadership Team: Complementary Strengths or Conflicting Agendas?" *Harvard Business Review,* April 2007, pp 90–98.

⁶ For an interesting case study, see P F Levy. "The Nut Island Effect: When Good Teams Go Wrong," *Harvard Business Review,* March 2001, pp 51–59.

⁷ J R Katzenbach and D K Smith, "The Discipline of Teams," *Harvard Business Review,* March–April 1993, p 112.

⁸ "A Team's-Eye View of Teams." *Training,* November 1995, p 16.

⁹ See E Sundstrom, K P DeMeuse, and D Futrell, "Work Teams," *American Psychologist,* February 1990, pp 120–33.

¹⁰ For an alternative typology of teams, see S G Scott and Walter O Einstien, "Strategic Performance Appraisal in Team-Based Organizations: One Size Does Not Fit All," *Academy of Management Executive,* May 2001, pp 107–16. Also see H Minssen, "Challenges of Teamwork in Production: Demands of Communication," *Organization Studies,* January 2006, pp 103–24; T S Kiessling, L D Marino, and R G Richey, "Global Marketing Teams: A Strategic Option for Multinationals," *Organizational Dynamics,* no. 3, 2006, pp 237–50; J B Abbott, N G Boyd, and G Miles, "Does Type of Team Matter? An Investigation of the Relationships Between Job Characteristics and Outcomes Within a Team-Based Environment," *The Journal of Social Psychology,* August 2006, pp 485–507; and G B Graen C Hui, and E A Taylor, "Experienced-Based Learning About LMX Leadership and Fairness in Project Teams: A Dyadic Directional Approach," *Academy of Management Learning and Education,* December 2006, pp 448–60.

¹¹ A Lashinsky, "RAZR's Edge," *Fortune,* June 12, 2006, p 126.

¹² For a description of medical teams in action, see J Appleby and R Davis, "Teamwork Used to Be a Money Saver: Now It's a Lifesaver," *USA Today,* March 1, 2001, pp 1B–2B. Also see M A Prospero, "In Indy's Pits, It's More than Speed," *Fast Company,* August 2004, p 26.

¹³ P King, "What Makes Teamwork Work?" *Psychology Today,* December 1989, p 16.

¹⁴ See C A Beatty and Brenda A Barker Scott, *Building Smart Teams: A Roadmap to High Performance* (Thousand Oaks, CA: Sage, 2004); T A Timmerman, "Missing Persons in the Study of Groups," *Journal of Organizational Behavior,* February 2005, pp 21–36; J Vilaga, "The Teamster," *Fast Company,* April 2005, p 94; and M Cardinal and T O'Leary, "For Rewriting the Rules for Husband-and-Wife Teams," *Inc.,* April 2005, p 83.

¹⁵ For more on team-member satisfaction, see M A Griffin, M G Patterson, and M A West, "Job Satisfaction and Teamwork: The Role of Supervisor Support," *Journal of Organizational Behavior,* August 2001, pp 537–50; and C M Mason and M A Griffin, "Group Task Satisfaction: Applying the Construct of Job Satisfaction to Groups," *Small Group Research,* June 2002, pp 271–312.

¹⁶ "Collaboration Provides Edge," *Arizona Republic,* April 10, 2005, p 2. Also see L L Berry, "The Collaborative Organization: Leadership Lessons from Mayo Clinic," *Organizational Dynamics,* no. 3, 2004, pp 228–42.

¹⁷ See M Bolch, "Rewarding the Team," *HR Magazine,* February 2007, pp 91–93.

¹⁸ P Burrows, "Cisco's Comeback," *BusinessWeek,* November 24, 2003, p 124.

¹⁹ For more on the intersection between individuals and teams, see D K Sherman and H S Kim, "Is There an 'I' in 'Team'? The Role of the Self in Group-Serving Judgments," *Journal of Personality and Social Psychology,* January 2005, pp 108–20; T Halfhill, E Sundstrom, J Lahner, W Calderone,

and T M Nielsen, "Group Personality Composition and Group Effectiveness," *Small Group Research,* February 2005, pp 83–105; R R Hirschfeld, M H Jordan, H S Field, W F Giles, and A A Armenakis, "Becoming Team Players: Team Members' Mastery of Teamwork Knowledge as a Predictor of Team Task Proficiency and Observed Teamwork Effectiveness," *Journal of Applied Psychology,* March 2006, pp 467–74; and B D Edwards, E A Day, W Arthur Jr., and S T Bell, "Relationships Among Team Ability Composition, Team Mental Models, and Team Performance," *Journal of Applied Psychology,* May 2006, pp 727–36.

20 As quoted in P B Brown, "What I Know Now," *Fast Company,* January 2005, p 96.

21 J Vesterman, "From Wharton to War," *Fortune,* June 12, 2006, p 108.

22 For more on team effectiveness, see J E Mathieu, L L Gilson, and T M Ruddy, "Empowerment and Team Effectiveness: An Empirical Test of an Integrated Model," *Journal of Applied Psychology,* January 2006, pp 97–108; A Taylor and H R Greve, "Superman or the Fantastic Four? Knowledge Combination and Experience in Innovative Teams," *Academy of Management Journal,* August 2006, pp 723–40; and C B Gibson and P C Earley, "Collective Cognition in Action: Accumulation, Interaction, Examination, and Accommodation in the development and Operation of Group Efficacy Beliefs in the Workplace," *Academy of Management Review,* April 2007, pp 438–58.

23 For example, see G Colvin, "Why Dream Teams Fail," *Fortune,* June 12, 2006, pp 87–92; D H Freedman, "The Idiocy of Crowds: Collaboration Is the Hottest Buzzword in Business Today. Too Bad It Doesn't Work," *Inc.,* September 2006, pp 61–62; and J Durett, "There's No 'I' in Team, But Maybe There Should Be," *Training,* September 2006, p 12.

24 P Raeburn, "Whoops! Wrong Patient," *BusinessWeek,* June 17, 2002, p 85.

25 See M Weinstein, "The Good Part About It Being a Jungle Out There!" *Training,* September 2006, p 15; and C M Christensen, M Marx, and H H Stevenson, "The Tools of Cooperation and Change," *Harvard Business Review,* October 2006, pp 73–80.

26 J Gordon, "Redefining Elegance," *Training,* March 2007, p 20.

27 See M E Haskins, J Liedtka, and J Rosenblum, "Beyond Teams: Toward an Ethic of Collaboration," *Organizational Dynamics,* Spring 1998, pp 34–50; C C Chen, X P Chen, and J R Meindl, "How Can Cooperation Be Fostered? The Cultural Effects of Individualism-Collectivism," *Academy of Management Review,* April 1998, pp 285–304; and A Pomeroy, "Can't We All Just Get Along?" *HR Magazine,* April 2005, p 16.

28 A Kohn, "How to Succeed without Even Vying," *Psychology Today,* September 1986, pp 27–28. Sports psychologists discuss "cooperative competition" in S Sleek, "Competition: Who's the Real Opponent?" *APA Monitor,* July 1996, p 8.

29 D W Johnson, G Maruyama, R Johnson, D Nelson, and L Skon, "Effects of Cooperative, Competitive, and Individualistic Goal Structures on Achievement: A Meta-Analysis," *Psychological Bulletin,* January 1981, pp 56–57. An alternative interpretation of the foregoing study that emphasizes the influence of situational factors can be found in J L Cotton and M S Cook, "Meta-Analysis and the Effects of Various Reward Systems: Some Different Conclusions from Johnson et al.," *Psychological Bulletin,* July 1982, pp 176–83. Also see A E Ortiz, D W Johnson, and R T Johnson, "The Effect of Positive Goal and Resource Interdependence on Individual Performance," *Journal of Social Psychology,* April 1996, pp 243–49; and S L Gaertner, J F Dovidio, M C Rust, J A Nier, B S Banker, C M Ward, G R Mottola, and M Houlette, "Reducing Intergroup Bias: Elements of Intergroup Cooperation," *Journal of Personality and Social Psychology,* March 1999, pp 388–402.

30 R Zemke, "Office Spaces," *Training,* May 2002, p 24.

31 See M Lev-Ram, "How to Make Your Workspace Work Better," *Business 2.0,* November 2006, pp 58–60.

32 As quoted in C Campbell, "Inside the Googleplex," *Canadian Business,* November 6–19, 2006, pp 59–60.

33 S W Cook and M Pelfrey, "Reactions to Being Helped in Cooperating Interracial Groups: A Context Effect," *Journal of Personality and Social Psychology,* November 1985, p 1243. Also see G S Van Der Vegt, J S Bunderson, and A Oosterhof, "Expertness Diversity and Interpersonal Helping in Teams: Why Those Who Need the Most Help End Up Getting the Least," *Academy of Management Journal,* October 2006, pp 877–93.

34 See A J Stahelski and R A Tsukuda, "Predictors of Cooperation in Health Care Teams," *Small Group Research,* May 1990, pp 220–33. Also see K Aquino and A Reed II, "A Social Dilemma Perspective on Cooperative Behavior in Organizations," *Group & Organization Management,* December 1998, pp 390–413.

35 For example, see E Krell, "Do They Trust You?" *HR Magazine,* June 2006, pp 58–65; N Varchaver, "Long Island Confidential," *Fortune,* November 27, 2006, pp 172–186; and M Kessler, "Tech Companies Caught in Web of Ethics Issues," *USA Today,* April 11, 2007, p 8B.

36 M Arndt, "Sudden Exit at Penney," *BusinessWeek,* January 15, 2007, p 27.

37 Data from "US CEOs Rank Low in Trust," *USA Today,* March 22, 2005, p 1B. Also see D Z Levin, E M Whitener, and R Cross, "Perceived Trustworthiness of Knowledge Sources: The Moderating Impact of Relationship Length," *Journal of Applied Psychology,* September 2006, pp 1163–171; M Weinstein, "Trust Us—Really," *Training,* November 2006, p 14; and B W Heineman, Jr., "Avoiding Integrity Land Mines," *Harvard Business Review,* April 2007, pp 100–8.

38 J Barbian, "Short Shelf Life," *Training,* June 2002, p 52. See the second Q&A in Jack Welch and Suzy Welch, "The Blame Game—Forget It," *BusinessWeek,* March 5, 2007, p 92.

39 See K S Cook, "Networks, Norms, and Trust: The Social Psychology of Social Capital," *Social Psychology Quarterly,*

March 2005, pp 4–14; T C Earle and M Siegrist, "Morality Information, Performance Information, and the Distinction Between Trust and Confidence," *Journal of Applied Social Psychology,* February 2006, pp 383–416; D L Ferrin, K T Dirks, and P P Shah, "Direct and Indirect Effects of Third-Party Relationships on Interpersonal Trust," *Journal of Applied Psychology,* July 2006, pp 870–83; G A Ballinger and F D Schoorman, "Individual Reactions to Leadership Succession in Workgroups," *Academy of Management Review,* January 2007, pp 118–36; and F D Schoorman, R C Mayer, and J H Davis, "An Integrative Model of Organizational Trust: Past, Present, and Future," *Academy of Management Review,* April 2007, pp 344–54.

40 J D Lewis and A Weigert, "Trust as a Social Reality," *Social Forces,* June 1985, p 971. Trust is examined as an *indirect* factor in K T Dirks, "The Effects of Interpersonal Trust on Work Group Performance," *Journal of Applied Psychology,* June 1999, pp 445–55.

41 R C Mayer, J H Davis, and F D Schoorman, "An Integrative Model of Organizational Trust," *Academy of Management Review,* July 1995, p 715.

42 Lewis and Weigert, "Trust as a Social Reality," p 970. Also see R F Hurley, "The Decision to Trust," *Harvard Business Review,* September 2006, pp 55–62.

43 For an interesting trust exercise, see G Thompson and P F Pearce. "The Team-Trust Game," *Training & Development Journal,* May 1992, pp 42–43. Also see E C Tomlinson, B R Dineen, and R J Lewicki, "The Road to Reconciliation: Antecedents of Victim Willingness to Reconcile following a Broken Promise," *Journal of Management,* no. 2, 2004, pp 165–87; T Simons and R S Peterson, "When to Let Them Duke It Out," *Harvard Business Review,* June 2006, pp 23–24; and M Weinstein, "Office Trust Busters," *Training,* July 2006, pp 10–11.

44 M Powell, "Betrayal," *Inc.,* April 1996, p 24.

45 See M J Moye and A B Henkin, "Exploring Associations Between Employee Empowerment and Interpersonal Trust in Managers," *Journal of Management Development,* no. 2, 2006, pp 101–17; and E Kahane, "Trust and Powerful Learning," *Training and Development,* July 2006, pp 51–54.

46 Adapted from F Bartolomé, "Nobody Trusts the Boss Completely—Now What?" *Harvard Business Review,* March–April 1989, pp 135–42. Also see S M R Covey, *The Speed of Trust: The One Thing That Changes Everything* (New York: Free Press, 2006); "Dare to Be a Social Entrepreneur: Howard Schultz, Chairman, Starbucks," *Business 2.0,* December 2006, p 87; and M Williams, "Building Genuine Trust Through Interpersonal Emotion Management: A Threat Regulation Model of Trust and Collaboration Across Boundaries," *Academy of Management Review,* April 2007, pp 595–621.

47 W Foster Owen, "Metaphor Analysis of Cohesiveness in Small Discussion Groups," *Small Group Behavior,* August 1985, p 416. Also see M D Michalisin, S J Karau, and C Tangpong, "Top Management Team Cohesion and Superior Industry Returns: An Empirical Study of the Resource-Based View," *Group & Organization Management,* February 2004, pp 125–40; J Hardy, M A Eys, and A V Carron, "Exploring

the Potential Disadvantages of High Cohesion in Sports Teams," *Small Group Research,* April 2005, pp 166–87; and S M Burke et al., "Cohesion as Shared Beliefs in Exercise Classes," *Small Group Research,* June 2005, pp 267–88.

48 This distinction is based on discussion in A Tziner, "Differential Effects of Group Cohesiveness Types: A Clarifying Overview," *Social Behavior and Personality,* no. 2, 1982, pp 227–39.

49 B Mullen and C Copper, "The Relation between Group Cohesiveness and Performance: An Integration," *Psychological Bulletin,* March 1994, p 224.

50 Ibid. Additional research evidence is reported in P J Sullivan and D L Feltz, "The Relationship between Intrateam Conflict and Cohesion within Hockey Teams," *Small Group Research,* June 2001, pp 342–55; A Chang and P Bordia, "A Multidimensional Approach to the Group Cohesion–Group Performance Relationship," *Small Group Research,* August 2001, pp 379–405; and M I Norton, J H Frost, and D Ariely, "Less Is More: The Lure of Ambiguity, or Why Familiarity Breeds Contempt," *Journal of Personality and Social Psychology,* January 2007, pp 97–105.

51 Based on B Mullen, T Anthony, E Salas, and J E Driskell, "Group Cohesiveness and Quality of Decision Making: An Integration of Tests of the Groupthink Hypothesis," *Small Group Research,* May 1994, pp 189–204. Also see A V Carron et al., "Using Consensus as a Criterion for Groupness: Implications for the Cohesion–Group Success Relationship," *Small Group Research,* August 2004, pp 466–91; and P P Shah, K T Dirks, and N Chervany, "The Multiple Pathways of High Performing Groups: The Interaction of Social Networks and Group Processes," *Journal of Organizational Behavior,* May 2006, pp 299–317.

52 G L Miles, "The Plant of Tomorrow Is in Texas Today," *BusinessWeek,* July 28, 1986, p 76.

53 See, for example, P Jin, "Work Motivation and Productivity in Voluntarily Formed Work Teams: A Field Study in China," *Organizational Behavior and Human Decision Processes,* 1993, pp 133–55. Also see S Reysen, "Construction of a New Scale: The Reysen Likability Scale," *Social Behavior and Personality,* no. 2, 2005, pp 201–8.

54 Based on discussion in E E Lawler III and S A Mohrman, "Quality Circles: After the Honeymoon," *Organizational Dynamics,* Spring 1987, pp 42–54.

55 See D L Duarte and N Tennant Snyder, *Mastering Virtual Teams: Strategies, Tools, and Techniques,* 3rd ed (San Francisco, Calif.: Jossey-Bass, 2006).

56 For example, see M Conlin, "Square Feet. Oh, How Square!" *BusinessWeek,* July 3, 2006, pp 100–1; "Working from Home?" *Training,* January–February 2007, p 10; and A Danigelis, "Job Morph: Herding Cats," *Fast Company,* March 2007, p 32.

57 "Internet Use Grows in Importance, Time," *USA Today,* November 29, 2006, p 6D. Also see L Proserpio and D A Gioia, "Teaching the Virtual Generation," *Academy of Management Learning and Education,* March 2007, pp 69–80.

[58] See A Malhotra , A Majchrzak, and B Rosen, "Leading Virtual Teams," *Academy of Management Perspectives,* February 2007, pp 60–70; and M Derven, "The Remote Connection," *HR Magazine,* March 2007, pp 111–5.

[59] Based on P Bordia, N DiFonzo, and A Chang, "Rumor as Group Problem Solving: Development Patterns in Informal Computer-Mediated Groups," *Small Group Research,* February 1999, pp 8–28. Also see M L Baba, J Gluesing, H Ratner, and K H Wagner, "The Contexts of Knowing: Natural History of a Globally Distributed Team," *Journal of Organizational Behavior,* August 2004, pp 547–87.

[60] See K A Graetz, E S Boyle, C E Kimble, P Thompson, and J L Garloch, "Information Sharing in Face-to-Face, Teleconferencing, and Electronic Chat Groups," *Small Group Research,* December 1998, pp 714–43.

[61] Based on F Niederman and R J Volkema, "The Effects of Facilitator Characteristics on Meeting Preparation, Set Up, and Implementation," *Small Group Research,* June 1999, pp 330–60; and B Whitworth, B Gallupe, and R McQueen, "Generating Agreement in Computer-Mediated Groups," *Small Group Research,* October 2001, pp 625–65.

[62] Based on J J Sosik, B J Avolio, and S S Kahai, "Inspiring Group Creativity: Comparing Anonymous and Identified Electronic Brainstorming," *Small Group Research,* February 1998, pp 3–31. For practical advice on brainstorming, see C Caggiano, "The Right Way to Brainstorm," *Inc.,* July 1999, p 94. Also see S S Kahai, J J Sosik, and B J Avolio, "Effects of Participative and Directive Leadership in Electronic Groups," *Group and Organization Management,* February 2004, pp 67–105.

[63] Based on M M Montoya-Weiss, A P Massey, and M Song, "Getting It Together: Temporal Coordination and Conflict Management in Global Virtual Teams," *Academy of Management Journal,* December 2001, pp 1251–62. Also see B L Kirkman, B Rosen, P E Tesluk, and C B Gibson, "Enhancing the Transfer of Computer-Assisted Training Proficiency in Geographically Distributed Teams," *Journal of Applied Psychology,* May 2006, pp 706–16; J T Polzer, C B Crisp, S L Jarvenpaa, and J W Kim, "Extending the Faultline Model to Geographically Dispersed Teams: How Colocated Subgroups Can Impair Group Functioning," *Academy of Management Journal,* August 2006, pp 679–92; and S M B Thatcher and X Zhu, "Changing Identities in a Changing Workplace: Identification, Identity Enactment, Self-Verification, and Telecommuting," *Academy of Management Review,* October 2006, pp 1076–88.

[64] See "Setting Up a Training House," *Training,* October 2006, pp 14–15.

[65] Data from C Johnson, "Teams at Work," *HR Magazine,* May 1999, pp 30–36.

[66] B Dumaine, "Who Needs a Boss?" *Fortune,* May 7, 1990, p 52. Also see D Vredenburgh and I Y He, "Leadership Lessons from a Conductorless Orchestra," *Business Horizons,* September–October 2003. pp 19–24; and C A O'Reilly III and M L Tushman, "The Ambidextrous Organization," *Harvard Business Review,* April 2004, pp 74–81.

[67] Adapted from Table 1 in V U Druskat and J V Wheeler, "Managing from the Boundary: The Effective Leadership of Self-Managing Work Teams," *Academy of Management Journal,* August 2003, pp 435–57.

[68] See A E Randal and K S Jaussi, "Functional Background Identity, Diversity, and Individual Performance in Cross-Functional Teams," *Academy of Management Journal,* December 2003, pp 763–74; and L Fleming, "Perfecting Cross-Pollination," *Harvard Business Review,* September 2004, pp 22–24.

[69] L Tischler, "Twenty People, Four Notes: How Microsoft Created the Sound of Vista," *Fast Company,* February 2007, p 24.

[70] Excerpted from "Fast Talk," *Fast Company,* February 2004, p 50.

[71] See "1996 Industry Report: What Self-Managing Teams Manage," *Training,* October 1996, p 69.

[72] See L L Thompson, *Making the Team: A Guide for Managers* (Upper Saddle River, NJ: Prentice Hall, 2000).

[73] See P S Goodman, R Devadas, and T L Griffith Hughson, "Groups and Productivity: Analyzing the Effectiveness of Self-Managing Teams," in *Productivity in Organizations,* eds J P Campbell, R J Campbell, and Associates (San Francisco: Jossey-Bass, 1998), pp 295–327. Also see R C Liden, S J Wayne, and M L Kraimer, "Managing Individual Performance in Work Groups," *Human Resource Management,* Spring 2001, pp 63–72; R Batt, "Who Benefits from Teams? Comparing Workers, Supervisors, and Managers," *Industrial Relations,* January 2004, pp 183–209; H van Mierlo, C G Rutte, M A J Kompier, and H A C M Doorewaard, "Self-Managing Teamwork and Psychological Well-Being: Review of a Multilevel Research Domain," *Group & Organization Management,* April 2005, pp 211–35; and S Kauffeld, "Self-Directed Work Groups and Team Competence," *Journal of Occupational and Organizational Psychology,* March 2006, pp 1–21.

[74] See C Douglas and W L Gardner, "Transition to Self-Directed Work Teams: Implications of Transition Time and Self-Monitoring for Managers' Use of Influence Tactics," *Journal of Organizational Behavior,* February 2004, pp 47–65; and R G Perry and A Zender, "Let's Get Together," *Association Management,* July 2004, pp 28–33, 84.

[75] Excerpted from S Max, "Seagate's Morale-athon," *BusinessWeek,* April 3, 2006, pp 110–112.

[76] See B Frisch and L Chandler, "Off-Sites That Work," *Harvard Business Review,* June 2006, pp 117–126; M Laff, "Effective Team Building: More than Just Fun at Work," *Training and Development,* August 2006, pp 24–25; J Durett, "Make Music, Build Teams," *Training,* September 2006, pp 42–43; N H Woodward, "Make the Most of Team Building," *Training,* September 2006, pp 72–76; L Dressler, "Retreats That Make a Difference," *Training and Development,* December 2006, pp 27–28; and J Thilmany, "Acting Out," *HR Magazine,* January 2007, pp 95–100.

[77] See M Zellmer-Bruhn and C Gibson, "Multinational Organization Context: Implications for Team Learning and Performance," *Academy of Management Journal,* June 2006,

pp 501–18; and J Brett, K Behfar, and M C Kern, "Managing Multicultural Teams," *Harvard Business Review,* November 2006, pp 83–91.

[78] S Bucholz and T Roth, *Creating the High-Performance Team* (New York: John Wiley & Sons, 1987), p xi. Also see M F R Kets de Vries, "Leadership Group Coaching in Action: The Zen of Creating High-Performance Teams," *Academy of Management Executive,* February 2005, pp 61–76; B Groysberg and R Abrahams, "Lift Outs: How to Acquire a High-Functioning Team," *Harvard Business Review,* December 2006, pp 133–40; and M F R Kets de Vries, "Decoding the Team Conundrum: The Eight Roles Executives Play," *Organizational Dynamics,* no. 1, 2007, pp 28–44.

[79] Bucholz and Roth, *Creating the High-Performance Team,* p 14. Also see V U Druskat and S B Wolff, "Building the Emotional Intelligence of Groups," *Harvard Business Review,* March 2001, pp 80–90; and A Edmondson, R Bohmer, and G Pisano, "Speeding Up Team Learning," *Harvard Business Review,* October 2001, pp 125–32.

[80] P King, "What Makes Teamwork Work?" *Psychology Today,* December 1989, p 17.

[81] J Raelin, "Preparing for Leaderful Practice," *Training & Development,* March 2004, pp 65–70.

[82] Adapted from C C Manz and H P Sims Jr, "Leading Workers to Lead Themselves: The External Leadership of Self-Managing Work Teams," *Administrative Science Quarterly,* March 1987, pp 106–29. Also see C C Manz, *Mastering Self-Leadership: Empowering Yourself for Personal Excellence* (Englewood Cliffs, NJ: Prentice Hall, 1992); F Luthans, J B Avey, B J Avolio, S M Norman, and G M Combs, "Psychological Capital Development: Toward a Micro-Intervention," *Journal of Organizational Behavior,* May 2006, pp 387–93; J Useem, "Five Levels of Excellence," *Fortune,* October 30, 2006, pp 176–77; R S Kaplan, "What to Ask the Person in the Mirror," *Harvard Business Review,* January 2007, pp 86–95; and B George and W Kopp, "Resolved: The Hardest Person You Will Ever Have to Lead Is Yourself," *Fast Company,* April 2007, p 112.

[83] N Byrnes, "In the Trenches at VF Boot Camp," *BusinessWeek,* November 20, 2006, pp 93–94.

[84] Excerpted from S Brodzinsky, "Protects Like Armor, Fits Like Armani," *Business 2.0,* August 2006, p 60.

CHAPTER 12

[1] Excerpted from J Bush, "They've Driven a Ford Lately," *BusinessWeek,* February 26, 2007, p 52.

[2] M Langley, C Riley, and R Sidel, "In Citigroup Ouster, A Battle Over Expenses," *The Wall Street Journal,* January 24, 2007, p A1.

[3] Strengths and weaknesses of the rational model are discussed by M H Bazerman, *Judgment in Managerial Decision Making* (Hoboken, NJ: John Wiley & Sons, Inc., 2006).

[4] See K Gruber, "Scenario Technique: Scenarios Europe 2010," www.dbresearch.com/servlet/reweb2.ReWEB?rwkey=u436490, accessed March 28, 2005.

[5] The steps for conducting scenario planning are outlined by "Scenario Technique: Addressing Key Drivers in the Future," http://innovation.im-boot.org/modules.php?name=Content&pa=showpage&pid=153, accessed March 28, 2005.

[6] This study was conducted by P C Nutt, "Expanding the Search for Alternatives during Strategic Decision-Making," *Academy of Management Executive,* November 2004, pp 13–28.

[7] Results can be found in J P Bymes, D C Miller, and W D Schafer, "Gender Differences in Risk Taking: A Meta-Analysis," *Psychological Bulletin,* May 1999, pp 367–83.

[8] See S W Williams, *Making Better Business Decisions* (Thousand Oaks, CA: Sage Publications, 2002).

[9] H A Simon, "Rational Decision Making in Business Organizations," *American Economic Review,* September 1979, p 510.

[10] These conclusions were proposed by R Brown, *Rational Choice and Judgment* (Hoboken, NJ: John Wiley & Sons, Inc., 2005), p 9.

[11] Bounded rationality is discussed by M Bazerman and D Chugh, "Decisions Without Blinders," *Harvard Business Review,* January 2006, pp 88–97; and H A Simon, *Administrative Behavior,* 2nd ed (New York: Free Press, 1957).

[12] These conclusions were excerpted from "Poor Decisions Hurt Company Performance," *HR Magazine,* February 2007, p 16.

[13] The model is discussed in detail in M D Cohen, J G March, and J P Olsen, "A Garbage Can Model of Organizational Choice," *Administrative Science Quarterly,* March 1981; pp 1–25.

[14] Ibid., p 2.

[15] This discussion is based on material presented in J G March and R Weissinger-Baylon, *Ambiguity and Command* (Marshfield, MA: Pitman Publishing, 1986), pp 11–35.

[16] See A Carter, "Lighting a Fire Under Campbell," *BusinessWeek,* December 4, 2006, pp 96, 99.

[17] Garbage can processes are also discussed by J L Bower and C G Gilbert, "How Managers' Everyday Decisions Create or Destroy Your Company's Strategy," *Harvard Business Review,* February 2007, pp 72–79; and L G Shattuck and N L Miller, "Extending Naturalistic Decision Making to Complex Organizations: A Dynamic Model of Situated Cognition," *Organization Studies,* July 2006, pp 989–1009.

[18] Biases associated with using shortcuts in decision making are discussed by A Tversky and D Kahneman, "Judgment under Uncertainty: Heuristics and Biases," *Science,* September 1974, pp 1124–31.

[19] These biases are discussed by J S Hammond, R L Keeney, and H Raiffa, "The Hidden Traps in Decision Making," *Harvard Business Review,* January 2006, pp 118–26; S F Dingfelder, "Taking Stock of Your Stock," *Monitor on Psychology,* January 2007, pp 18–19; and Bazerman, *Judgment in Managerial Decision Making.*

[20] Results can be found in R A Lowe and A A Ziedonis, "Overoptimism and the Performance of Entrepreneurial Firms," *Management Science,* February 2006, pp 173–86.

[21] This scenario was taken from Bazerman, *Judgment in Managerial Decision Making,* p 41.

[22] See J Ross and B M Staw, "Organizational Escalation and Exit: Lessons from the Shoreham Nuclear Power Plant," *Academy of Management Journal,* August 1993, pp 701–32.

[23] Ibid. Also see J W Mullins, "Good Money After Bad?" *Harvard Business Review,* March 2007, pp 37–48.

[24] See the related discussion in S Hamm, "Speed Demons," *BusinessWeek,* March 27, 2006, pp 68–76.

[25] J V Rensselar, "Walking the Talk," *The Power of Incentives,* 2006, p 92.

[26] D W De Long and P Seemann, "Confronting Conceptual Confusion and Conflict in Knowledge Management," *Organizational Dynamics,* Summer 2000, p 33.

[27] Supportive research is reviewed by A C Inkpen and E W K Tsang, "Social Capital, Networks, and Knowledge Transfer," *Academy of Management Review,* January 2005, pp 146–65.

[28] These statistics can be found in P Babcock, "Shedding Light on Knowledge Management," *HR Magazine,* May 2004, pp 47–50.

[29] R Lubit, "Tacit Knowledge and Knowledge Management: The Keys to Sustainable Competitive Advantage," *Organizational Dynamics,* 2001, p 166.

[30] See M A McFadyen and A A Cannella Jr, "Social Capital and Knowledge Creation: Diminishing Returns of the Number and Strength of Exchange Relationships," *Academy of Management Journal,* October 2004, pp 735–46. Also see M A D'Eredita and C Barreto, "How Does Tacit Knowledge Proliferate? An Episode-Based Perspective," *Organization Studies,* December 2006, pp 1821–41.

[31] See J S Lublin, "Here Today, Here Tomorrow," *The Wall Street Journal,* January 22, 2007, pp B1, B3.

[32] See L Baird and D Griffin, "Adaptability and Responsiveness: The Case for Dynamic Learning," *Organizational Dynamics,* November 2006, pp 372–83.

[33] Individual differences and decision making are discussed by G Morse, "Decisions and Desire," *Harvard Business Review,* January 2006, pp 42–51; and S W Gangestad, C E Garver-Apgar, J A Simpson, and A J Cousins, "Changes in Women's Mate Preferences Across the Ovulatory Cycle," *Journal of Personality and Social Psychology,* January 2006, pp 151–63.

[34] Results can be found in W H Stewart Jr and P L Roth, "Risk Propensity Differences between Entrepreneurs and Managers: A Meta-Analytic Review," *Journal of Applied Psychology,* February 2001, pp 145–53.

[35] This definition was derived from A J Rowe and R O Mason, *Managing with Style: A Guide to Understanding, Assessing and Improving Decision Making* (San Francisco: Jossey-Bass, 1987).

[36] The discussion of styles was based on material contained in ibid.

[37] Excerpted from B Gimbel, "Keeping Planes Apart," *Fortune,* June 27, 2005, p 112.

[38] B Bremner and D Roberts, "A Billion Tough Sells," *BusinessWeek,* March 20, 2006, p 44.

[39] Y I Kane and P Dvorak, "Howard Stringer, Japanese CEO," *The Wall Street Journal,* March 3–4, 2007, p A1, A6.

[40] See Z Stambor, "Older Consumers Factor More Positives, Specifics into Product Choices," *Monitor on Psychology,* April 2005, p 10; and Rowe and Mason, *Managing with Style.*

[41] L Kopeikina, "The Elements of a Clear Decision," *MIT Sloan Management Review,* Winter 2006, p 19; and S G Barsade and D E Gibson, "Why Does Affect Matter in Organizations?" *Academy of Management Perspectives,* February 2007, pp 36–59.

[42] E Sadler-Smith and E Shefy, "The Intuitive Executive: Understanding and Applying 'Gut Feel' in Decision-Making," *Academy of Management Executive,* November 2004, p 77.

[43] Excerpted from C C Miller and R D Ireland, "Intuition in Strategic Decision Making: Friend or Foe in the Fast-Paced 21st Century," *Academy of Management Executive,* February 2005, p 20.

[44] Ibid., pp 19–30.

[45] See E Dane and M G Pratt, "Exploring Intuition and Its Role in Managerial Decision Making," *Academy of Management Review,* January 2007, pp 33–54.

[46] See D Begley, "You Might Help a Teen Avoid Dumb Behavior By Nurturing Intuition," *The Wall Street Journal,* November 3, 2006, p B1.

[47] Courage and intuition is discussed by K K Reardon, "Courage As a Skill," *Harvard Business Review,* January 2007, pp 58–64.

[48] Details on this example can be found at J W Miller, "Gumshoe's Intuition: Spotting Counterfeits At Port of Antwerp," *The Wall Street Journal,* December 14, 2006, pp A1, A18.

[49] Results were reported in "The Ethical Mind," *Harvard Business Review,* March 2007, pp 51–56.

[50] The decision tree and resulting discussion is based on C E Bagley, "The Ethical Leader's Decision Tree," *Harvard Business Review,* February 2003, pp 18–19.

[51] Details of this example can be found in E E Schultz and T Francis, "Financial Surgery: How Cuts in Retiree Benefits Fatten Companies' Bottom Lines," *The Wall Street Journal,* March 1, 2004, p A1.

[52] Results can be found in C K W De Dreu and M A West, "Minority Dissent and Team Innovation: The Importance of Participation in Decision Making," *Journal of Applied Psychology,* December 2001, pp 1191–201. Also see F S T Velden, B Beersma, and C K W De Dreu, "Majority and

Minority Influence in Group Negotiation: The Moderating Effects of Social Motivation and Decision Rules," *Journal of Applied Psychology,* January 2007, pp 259–68.

[53] These recommendations were derived from R Y Hirokawa, "Group Communication and Decision-Making Performance: A Continued Test of the Functional Perspective," *Human Communication Research,* October 1988, pp 487–515.

[54] These guidelines were derived from G P Huber, *Managerial Decision Making* (Glenview, IL: Scott, Foresman, 1980), p 149.

[55] G W Hill, "Group versus Individual Performance: Are N +1 Heads Better than One?" *Psychological Bulletin,* May 1982, p 535. Also see K Leung, K-K Tong, and E A Lind, "Realpolitik Versus Fair Process: Moderating Effects of Group Identification on Acceptance of Political Decisions," *Journal of Personality and Social Psychology,* March 2007, pp 476–89.

[56] J H Davis, "Some Compelling Intuitions about Group Consensus Decisions, Theoretical and Empirical Research, and Interpersonal Aggregation Phenomena: Selected Examples, 1950–1990," *Organizational Behavior and Human Decision Processes,* June 1992, pp 3–38.

[57] Supporting results can be found in J Hedlund, D R Ilgen, and J R Hollenbeck, "Decision Accuracy in Computer-Mediated versus Face-to-Face Decision-Making Teams," *Organizational Behavior and Human Decision Processes,* October 1998, pp 30–47.

[58] See J R Winquist and J R Larson Jr, "Information Pooling: When It Impacts Group Decision Making," *Journal of Personality and Social Psychology,* February 1998, pp 371–77.

[59] G M Parker, *Team Players and Teamwork: The New Competitive Business Strategy* (San Francisco, CA: Jossey-Bass, 1990).

[60] These recommendations were obtained from ibid.

[61] See A F Osborn, *Applied Imagination: Principles and Procedures of Creative Thinking,* 3rd ed (New York: Scribners, 1979).

[62] See W H Cooper, R Brent Gallupe, S Pollard, and J Cadsby, "Some Liberating Effects of Anonymous Electronic Brainstorming," *Small Group Research,* April 1998, pp 147–78;

[63] These recommendations and descriptions were derived from B Nussbaum, "The Power of Design," *BusinessWeek,* May 17, 2004, pp 86–94.

[64] An applications of the NGT can be found in M Utley, S Gallivan, M Mills, and M Mason, "A Consensus Process for Identifying a Prioritised List of Study Questions," *Health Care Management,* February 2007, pp 105–10.

[65] See M Redmond, "60 Minutes to a Solution," *Quality Progress,* February 2007, p 80.

[66] See L Thompson, "Improving the Creativity of Organizational Work Groups," *Academy of Management Executive,* February 2003, pp 96–109.

[67] See N C Dalkey, D L Rourke, R Lewis, and D Snyder, *Studies in the Quality of Life: Delphi and Decision Making* (Lexington, MA: Lexington Books: D C Heath and Co., 1972).

[68] An application of the Delphi technique can be found in H Eskandari, S Sala-Diakanda, S Furterer, and L Rabelo, "Enhancing the Undergraduate Industrial Engineering Curriculum; Defining Desired Characteristics and Emerging Topics," *Training,* 2007, pp 45–55.

[69] Examples are provided in L Landro, "Preventing the Tragedy of Misdiagnosis," *The Wall Street Journal,* November 29, 2006, pp D1, D5; and T J Mullaney, "The Doctor Is (Plugged) In," *BusinessWeek,* June 26, 2006, pp 56, 58.

[70] See K Maher, "Wal-Mart Seeks New Flexibility In Worker Shifts," *The Wall Street Journal,* January 3, 2007, pp A1, A11.

[71] Supportive results can be found in S S Lam and J Schaubroeck, "Improving Group Decisions by Better Polling Information: A Comparative Advantage of Group Decision Support Systems," *Journal of Applied Psychology,* August 2000, pp 565–73.

[72] See the related discussion in S Meisinger, "Education Gap Threatens U.S. Competitiveness," *HR Magazine,* March 2007, p 10; R Jana, "A Chorus of Voices Is Calling For An End to the Hype—and a Focus on What Really Drives Profitable Innovation," *IN,* March 2007, p 28.

[73] This definition was adapted from one provided by R K Scott, "Creative Employees: A Challenge to Managers," *Journal of Creative Behavior,* First Quarter, 1995, pp 64–71.

[74] See J Thilmany, "Acting Out," *HR Magazine,* January 2007, pp 95–100.

[75] C Hymowitz, "All Companies Need Innovation; Hasbro Finds a New Magic," *The Wall Street Journal,* February 26, 2007, p B1.

[76] See the discussion in O Janssen, E V De Vliert, and M West, "The Bright and Dark Sides of Individual and Group Innovation: A Special Issue Introduction," *Journal of Organizational Behavior,* March 2004, pp 129–45.

[77] S Holmes, "Just Plain Genius," *BusinessWeek,* April 17, 2006, p 20.

[78] Results can be found in E Tahmincioglu, "Gifts that Gall," *Workforce Management,* April 2004, p 45.

[79] Details of this study can be found in M Basadur, "Managing Creativity: A Japanese Model," *Academy of Management Executive,* May 1992, pp 29–42.

[80] See D M Zell, A M Glassman, and S A Duron, "The Short and Glorious History of Accelerated Decision Making at Hewlett-Packard," *Organizational Dynamics,* 2007, pp 93–104; and C Holahan, "Yahoo's Bid to Think Small," *BusinessWeek,* February 26, 2007, p 94.

[81] T A Matherly and R E Goldsmith, "The Two Faces of Creativity," *Business Horizons,* September–October 1985, p 9.

[82] This discussion is based on research reviewed in M A Collins and T M Amabile, "Motivation and Creativity," in *Handbook*

of Creativity, eds R J Sternberg (Cambridge, UK: Cambridge University Press, 1999), pp 297–311.

[83] Personality and creativity were investigated by M Baer and G R Oldham, "The Curvilinear Relations Between Experienced Creative Time Pressure and Creativity: Moderating Effects of Openness to Experience and Support for Creativity," *Journal of Applied Psychology,* July 2006, pp 963–70.

[84] J M Higgins, "Innovate or Evaporate: Seven Secrets of Innovative Corporations," *The Futurist,* September–October 1995, p 46.

[85] M Ihlwan, "Camp Samsung," *BusinessWeek,* July 3, 2006, p 46.

[86] Examples are provided in J McGregor, "The World's Most Innovative Companies," *BusinessWeek,* April 24, 2006, pp 63–74.

[87] The importance of rewards is discussed by G Carini and B Townsend, "$152,000 for Your Thoughts," *Harvard Business Review,* April 2007, p 23.

[88] Excerpted from B Nussbaum, "The Power of Design," *BusinessWeek,* May 17, 2004, pp 88, 90–92, 94. Reprinted by permission of The McGraw-Hill Companies, Inc.

[89] Excerpted from J Kelley, "Westwood Students Get OK for Eagle Feathers," *The Mesa Republic,* May 25, 2006, p 15.

CHAPTER 13

[1] D Brady, "'Being Mean Is So Last Millennium,'" *BusinessWeek,* January 15, 2007, p 61.

[2] D Tjosvold, *Learning to Manage Conflict: Getting People to Work Together Productively* (New York: Lexington Books, 1993), p xi.

[3] Ibid., pp xi–xii. Also see "'Peaceful' Ancient Humans Had a Dark Side," *USA Today,* August 9, 2004, p 6D.

[4] J A Wall Jr and R Robert Callister, "Conflict and Its Management," *Journal of Management,* no. 3 (1995), p 517.

[5] Ibid., p 544.

[6] D Stead, "The Big Picture," *BusinessWeek,* January 8, 2007, p 11.

[7] See M A von Glinow, D L Shapiro, and J M Brett, "Can We *Talk,* and Should We? Managing Emotional Conflict in Multicultural Teams," *Academy of Management Review,* October 2004, pp 578–92; C Palmeri, "Hair-Pulling in the Dollhouse," *BusinessWeek,* May 2, 2005, pp 76–77; and G Colvin, "CEO Knockdown," *Fortune,* April 4, 2005, pp 19–20.

[8] K Cloke and J Goldsmith, *Resolving Conflicts at Work: A Complete Guide for Everyone on the Job* (San Francisco: Jossey-Bass, 2000), pp 25, 27, 29.

[9] D Brady, "It's All Donald, All the Time," *BusinessWeek,* January 22, 2007, p 51.

[10] See P J Sauer, "Are You Ready for Some Football Clichés?" *Inc.,* October 2003, pp 97–100; and V P Rindova, M Becerra, and I Contardo, "Enacting Competitive Wars: Competitive Activity, Language Games, and Market Consequences," *Academy of Management Review,* October 2004, pp 670–86.

[11] Cloke and Goldsmith, *Resolving Conflicts at Work,* pp 31–32. Also see K Fackelmann, "Arguing Hurts the Heart in More Ways Than One," *USA Today,* March 6, 2006, p 10D; D Meyer, "The Saltshaker Theory," *Inc.,* October 2006, pp 69–70; J Welch and S Welch, "The Blame Game—Forget It," *BusinessWeek,* March 5, 2007, p 92; and J Welch and S Welch, "The Right Way to Say Goodbye," *BusinessWeek,* March 26, 2006, p 144.

[12] See M J Martinko, S C Douglas, and P Harvey, "Understanding and Managing Workplace Aggression," *Organizational Dynamics,* no. 2, 2006, pp 117–130; Z Stambor, "Bullying Stems From Fear, Apathy," *Monitor on Psychology,* July-August 2006, pp 72–78; T J Brown and K E Sumner, "Perceptions and Punishments of Workplace Aggression: The Role of Aggression Content, Context, and Perceiver Variables," *Journal of Applied Social Psychology,* October 2006, pp 2509–2531; and J Deschenaux, "Bills Prohibit Employer Bans on Firearms," *HR Magazine,* February 2007, pp 34, 39.

[13] See S Alper, D Tjosvold, and K S Law, "Interdependence and Controversy in Group Decision Making: Antecedents to Effective Self-Managing Teams," *Organizational Behavior and Human Decision Processes,* April 1998, pp 33–52; and T Simons and R S Peterson, "When to Let Them Duke It Out," *Harvard Business Review,* June 2006, pp 23–24.

[14] S P Robbins, "'Conflict Management' and 'Conflict Resolution' Are Not Synonymous Terms," *California Management Review,* Winter 1978, p 70. For examples of functional and dysfunctional conflict, see D Dahl, "Case Study: Michael Kalinsky Was Sick of Fighting with His Vice President, Who Was Also His Ex-Brother-in-Law. Was Firing Him Too Drastic?" *Inc.,* October 2006, pp 51–54; J S Lublin and E White, "Drama in the Boardroom," *The Wall Street Journal,* October 2, 2006, pp B1, B3; and S Clifford, "The Worst Case Scenario," *Inc.,* November 2006, p 111.

[15] Cooperative conflict is discussed in Tjosvold, *Learning to Manage Conflict: Getting People to Work Together Productively.* Also see A C Amason, "Distinguishing the Effects of Functional and Dysfunctional Conflict on Strategic Decision Making: Resolving a Paradox for Top Management Teams," *Academy of Management Journal,* February 1996, pp 123–48.

[16] Excerpted from T Ursiny, *The Coward's Guide to Conflict: Empowering Solutions for Those Who Would Rather Run than Fight* (Naperville, IL: Sourcebooks, 2003), p 27.

[17] See D Jones, "Could Insecurity Be the Secret to CEOs' Success?" *USA Today,* February 1, 2007, pp 1B–2B.

[18] Adapted in part from discussion in A C Filley, *Interpersonal Conflict Resolution* (Glenview, IL: Scott, Foresman, 1975), pp 9–12; and B Fortado, "The Accumulation of Grievance Conflict," *Journal of Management Inquiry,* December 1992, pp 288–303.

[19] Adapted from discussion in Tjosvold, *Learning to Manage Conflict,* pp 12–13.

[20] L Gardenswartz and A Rowe, *Diverse Teams at Work: Capitalizing on the Power of Diversity* (New York: McGraw-Hill, 1994), p 32.

[21] F Keenan, "EMC: Turmoil at the Top?" *BusinessWeek,* March 11, 2002, pp 58–60. Reprinted by permission of The McGraw-Hill Companies, Inc.

[22] For more, see S Hamm, "The Fine Art of Tech Mergers," *BusinessWeek*, July 10, 2006, pp 70, 72.

[23] C M Pearson and C L Porath, "On the Nature, Consequences and Remedies of Workplace Incivility: No Time for 'Nice'? Think Again," *Academy of Management Executive,* February 2005, p 7. Also see "When Bosses Attack," *Training,* May 2005, p 10; K Gurchiek, "Bullying: It's Not Just on The Playground," *HR Magazine,* June 2005, p 40; J Welch and S Welch, "Send the Jerks Packing," *BusinessWeek*, November 13, 2006, p 136; M Weinstein, "Are You Working for an 'Untouchable'?" *Training*, December 2006, p 13; and H Green, "How To Get Rid of the, Uh, Jerks," *BusinessWeek*, March 19, 2007, p 14.

[24] S Keeler, "Study Calls Out Workplace Bullies," *ASU Insight*, December 8, 2006, p U1. Also see J Rossi, "From the Bully Pulpit," *Training and Development*, April 2006, pp 12–13; L Meyers, "Still Wearing the 'Kick Me' Sign," *Monitor on Psychology*, July–August 2006, pp 68–70; L Buchanan, "The Bully Rulebook: How to Deal with Jerks," *Inc.*, February 2007, pp 43–44; and C M Dalton, "The Bully Down the Hall," *Business Horizons*, March-April 2007, pp 89–91.

[25] K Gurchiek, "Slurs at Work Are on the Rise, Survey Finds," *HR Magazine*, June 2006, pp 38, 42.

[26] See R Kurtz, "Is Etiquette a Core Value?" *Inc.,* May 2004, p 22; and D Weinstein, "Grace in Small Space: Cubicles Encourage New Era of Etiquette," *Arizona Republic,* March 12, 2005, p D3.

[27] P Falcone, "Days of Contemplation," *HR Magazine*, February 2007, p 107.

[28] Data from D Stamps, "Yes, Your Boss Is Crazy," *Training,* July 1998, pp 35–39. Also see J Keats, "Caution: Psychos at Work," *Business 2.0*, July 2006, p 32; S Armour, "Workplaces Quit Quietly Ignoring Mental Illness," *USA Today*, August 22, 2006, pp 1B–2B; R R Hastings, "Focus on Behavior, Not Psychiatric Condition," *HR Magazine*, November 2006, pp 26, 32; M Elias, "Conquering Depression Can Take Many Treatments," *USA Today*, November 1, 2006, p 9D; and J Scelfo, "Men and Depression: Facing Darkness," *Newsweek*, February 26, 2007, pp 42–49.

[29] See S Armour and D Jones, "Workers' Positive Drug Tests Decrease," *USA Today*, June 20, 2006, p 3B; and D M Owens, "EAPs for a Diverse World," *HR Magazine*, October 2006, pp 91–96.

[30] Drawn from J C McCune, "The Change Makers," *Management Review,* May 1999, pp 16–22.

[31] Based on discussion in G Labianca, D J Brass, and B Gray, "Social Networks and Perceptions of Intergroup Conflict: The Role of Negative Relationships and Third Parties," *Academy of Management Journal,* February 1998, pp 55–67. Also see

A Bizman and Y Yinon, "Intergroup Conflict Management Strategies as Related to Perceptions of Dual Identity and Separate Groups," *Journal of Social Psychology,* April 2004, pp 115–26; and R J Crisp and J K Nicel, "Disconfirming Intergroup Evaluations: Asymmetric Effects for In-Groups and Out-Groups," *Journal of Social Psychology,* June 2004, pp 247–71.

[32] See L A Rudman and S A Goodwin, "Gender Differences in Automatic In-Group Bias: Why Do Women Like Women More than Men Like Men?" *Journal of Personality and Social Psychology,* October 2004, pp 494–509; G Cowan, "Interracial Interactions at Racially Diverse University Campuses," *Journal of Social Psychology,* February 2005, pp 49–63; and G B Cunningham, "The Influence of Group Diversity on Intergroup Bias Following Recategorization," *The Journal of Social Psychology*, October 2006, pp 533–47.

[33] See T F Pettigrew and L R Tropp, "A Meta-Analytic Test of Intergroup Contact Theory," *Journal of Personality and Social Psychology*, May 2006, pp 751–83.

[34] Labianca, Brass, and Gray, "Social Networks and Perceptions of Intergroup Conflict," p 63 (emphasis added). Also see W Felps, T R Mitchell, and E Byington, "How, When, and Why Bad Apples Spoil the Barrel: Negative Group Members and Dysfunctional Groups," in *Research in Organizational Behavior: An Annual of Analytical Essays and Critical Reviews Research in Organizational Behavior*, vol. 27, ed B Staw (Amsterdam, Netherlands: Elsevier, 2006), pp 175–222.

[35] For example, see S C Wright, A Aron, T McLaughlin-Volpe, and S A Ropp, "The Extended Contact Effect: Knowledge of Cross-Group Friendships and Prejudice," *Journal of Personality and Social Psychology,* July 1997, pp 73–90.

[36] See C D Batson, M P Polycarpou, E Harmon-Jones, H J Imhoff, E C Mitchener, L L Bednar, T R Klein, and L Highberger, "Empathy and Attitudes: Can Feeling for a Member of a Stigmatized Group Improve Feelings toward the Group?" *Journal of Personality and Social Psychology,* January 1997, pp 105–18. Also see J N Shelton and J A Richeson, "Intergroup Contact and Pluralistic Ignorance," *Journal of Personality and Social Psychology,* January 2005, pp 91–107; B S Lowery, M M Unzueta, P A Goff, and E D Knowles, "Concern for the In-Group and Opposition to Affirmative Action," *Journal of Personality and Social Psychology*, June 2006, pp 961–74; A Karacanta and J Fitness, "Majority Support for Minority Out-Groups: The Roles of Compassion and Guilt," *Journal of Applied Social Psychology*, November 2006, pp 2730–49; and D A Butz and E A Plant, "Perceiving Outgroup Members as Unresponsive: Implications for Approach-Related Emotions, Intentions, and Behavior," *Journal of Personality and Social Psychology*, December 2006, pp 1066–79.

[37] For a good overview, see N J Adler and A Gundersen, *International Dimensions of Organizational Behavior*, 5th ed (Cincinnati: South-Western, 2007).

[38] See A L Molinsky, M A Krabbenhoft, N Ambady, and Y S Choi, "Cracking the Nonverbal Code: Intercultural Competence and Gesture Recognition across Cultures," *Journal of Cross-Cultural Psychology,* May 2005, pp 380–95; R Friedman, S Chi, and L A Liu, "An Expectancy Model

of Chinese-American Differences in Conflict-Avoiding," *Journal of International Business Studies*, January 2006, pp 76–91; and J Brett, K Behfar, and M C Kern, "Managing Multicultural Teams," *Harvard Business Review*, November 2006, pp 83–91.

[39] "Negotiating South of the Border," *Harvard Management Communication Letter*, August 1999, p 12.

[40] A Rosenbaum, "Testing Cultural Waters," *Management Review*, July–August 1999, p 43 © 1999 American Management Association International. Reprinted by permission of American Management Association International, New York, NY. All rights reserved. (www.amanet.org)

[41] See R L Tung, "American Expatriates Abroad: From Neophytes to Cosmopolitans," *Journal of World Business*, Summer 1998, pp 125–44.

[42] See J Weiss and J Hughes, "What Collaboration? Accept— and Actively Manage—Conflict," *Harvard Business Review*, March 2005, pp 92–101; G Colvin, "The Wisdom of Dumb Questions," *Fortune*, June 27, 2005, p 157; and M DuPraw, "Cut the Conflict with Consensus Building," *Training*, May 2006, p 8.

[43] R A Cosier and C R Schwenk, "Agreement and Thinking Alike: Ingredients for Poor Decisions," *Academy of Management Executive*, February 1990, p 71. Also see J P Kotter, "Kill Complacency," *Fortune*, August 5, 1996, pp 168–70; and S Caudron, "Keeping Team Conflict Alive," *Training & Development*, September 1998, pp 48–52.

[44] For example, see "Facilitators as Devil's Advocates," *Training*, September 1993, p 10. Also see K L Woodward, "Sainthood for a Pope?" *Newsweek*, June 21, 1999, p 65.

[45] Good background reading on devil's advocacy can be found in C R Schwenk, "Devil's Advocacy in Managerial Decision Making," *Journal of Management Studies*, April 1984, pp 153–68.

[46] See G Katzenstein, "The Debate on Structured Debate: Toward a Unified Theory," *Organizational Behavior and Human Decision Processes*, June 1996, pp 316–32.

[47] See D M Schweiger, W R Sandberg, and P L Rechner, "Experiential Effects of Dialectical Inquiry, Devil's Advocacy, and Consensus Approaches to Strategic Decision Making," *Academy of Management Journal*, December 1989, pp 745–72.

[48] See J S Valacich and C Schwenk, "Devil's Advocacy and Dialectical Inquiry Effects on Face-to-Face and Computer-Mediated Group Decision Making," *Organizational Behavior and Human Decision Processes*, August 1995, pp 158–73.

[49] Other techniques are presented in Cloke and Goldsmith, *Resolving Conflicts at Work*, pp 229–35.

[50] As quoted in D Jones, "CEOs Need X-Ray Vision in Transition," *USA Today*, April 23, 2001, p 4B. For an update, see K Maney, "EMC Chief Tucci Has Twice Led Turnarounds," *USA Today*, September 26, 2005, p 2B.

[51] Based on C K W De Dreu and M A West, "Minority Dissent and Team Innovation: The Importance of Participation in Decision Making," *Journal of Applied Psychology*, December 2001, pp 119–201.

[52] A statistical validation for this model can be found in M A Rahim and N R Magner, "Confirmatory Factor Analysis of the Styles of Handling Interpersonal Conflict: First-Order Factor Model and Its Invariance across Groups," *Journal of Applied Psychology*, February 1995, pp 122–32. Also see C K W De Dreu, A Evers, B Beersma, E S Kluwer, and A Nauta, "A Theory-Based Measure of Conflict Management Strategies in the Workplace," *Journal of Organizational Behavior*, September 2001, pp 645–68; and M A Rahim, *Managing Conflict in Organizations* (Westport, CT: Greenwood Publishing Group, 2001).

[53] M A Rahim, "A Strategy for Managing Conflict in Complex Organizations," *Human Relations*, January 1985, p 84.

[54] "Female Officers Draw Fewer Brutality Suits," *USA Today*, May 2, 2002, p 3A. Also see L W Andrews, "When It's Time for Anger Management," *HR Magazine*, June 2005, pp 131–36.

[55] For example, see M Arndt, "Back to Work at Goodyear," *Business Week*, January 15, 2007, p 26; and H Maurer, "Long and Winding Road of the Week," *BusinessWeek*, February 19, 2007, p 31.

[56] P Ruzich, "Triangles: Tools for Untangling Interpersonal Messes," *HR Magazine*, July 1999, p 129. Also see the first Q&A in Jack Welch and Suzy Welch, "Don't Play the Office Cop," *BusinessWeek*, December 4, 2006, p 144; and K Sulkowicz, "When You're the Abusive Boss's Pet," *BusinessWeek*, January 15, 2007, p 14.

[57] M Orey, "Fear of Firing," *Business Week*, April 23, 2007, p 54.

[58] For background, see D L Jacobs, "First, Fire All the Lawyers," *Inc.*, January 1999, pp 84–85; P S Nugent, "Managing Conflict: Third-Party Interventions for Managers," *Academy of Management Executive*, February 2002, pp 139–54; and F P Phillips, "Ten Ways to Sabotage Dispute Management," *HR Magazine*, September 2004, pp 163–68.

[59] See M Bordwin, "Do-It-Yourself Justice," *Management Review*, January 1999, pp 56–58.

[60] B Morrow and L M Bernardi. "Resolving Workplace Disputes," *Canadian Manager*, Spring 1999, p 17. For related research, see R Friedman, C Anderson, J Brett, M Olekalns, N Goates, and C C Lisco, "The Positive and Negative Effects of Anger on Dispute Resolution: Evidence from Electronically Mediated Disputes," *Journal of Applied Psychology*, April 2004, pp 369–76; C B Gibson and T Saxton, "Thinking Outside the Black Box: Outcomes of Team Decisions with Third-Party Intervention," *Small Group Research*, April 2005, pp 208–36; and J M Brett, M Olekalns, R Friedman, N Goates, C Anderson, and C Cherry Lisco, "Sticks and Stones: Language, Face, and Online Dispute Resolution," *Academy of Management Journal*, February 2007, pp 85–99.

[61] Adapted from discussion in K O Wilburn, "Employment Disputes: Solving Them Out of Court," *Management Review*, March 1998, pp 17–21; and Morrow and Bernardi, "Resolving Workplace Disputes," pp 17–19, 27. Also see W H Ross and D E Conlon, "Hybrid Forms of Third-Party Dispute Resolution:

Theoretical Implications of Combining Mediation and Arbitration," *Academy of Management Review,* April 2000, pp 416–27.

[62] Wilburn, "Employment Disputes," p 19. Also see B P Sunoo, "Hot Disputes Cool Down in Online Mediation," *Workforce,* January 2001, pp 48–52.

[63] For background on this contentious issue, see S Armour, "Arbitration's Rise Raises Fairness Issue," *USA Today,* June 12, 2001, pp 1B–2B; T J Heinsz, "The Revised Uniform Arbitration Act: An Overview," *Dispute Resolution Journal,* May–July 2001, pp 28–39; and J B Thelen, "Manager Who Refused to Sign Agreement Must Arbitrate," *HR Magazine*, January 2007, p 111.

[64] For example, see J B Thelen, "Agreements To Arbitrate USERRA Claims Approved," *HR Magazine*, August 2006, p 117; and M G Danaher, "Employee's Arbitration Victory Had Limits," *HR Magazine*, March 2007, p 116.

[65] See R E Jones and B H Melcher, "Personality and the Preference for Modes of Conflict Resolution," *Human Relations,* August 1982, pp 649–58.

[66] See R A Baron, "Reducing Organizational Conflict: An Incompatible Response Approach," *Journal of Applied Psychology,* May 1984, pp 272–79.

[67] See G A Youngs Jr, "Patterns of Threat and Punishment Reciprocity in a Conflict Setting," *Journal of Personality and Social Psychology,* September 1986, pp 541–46.

[68] For more details, see V D Wall Jr and L L Nolan, "Small Group Conflict: A Look at Equity, Satisfaction, and Styles of Conflict Management," *Small Group Behavior,* May 1987, pp 188–211. Also see S M Farmer and J Roth, "Conflict-Handling Behavior in Work Groups: Effects of Group Structure, Decision Processes, and Time," *Small Group Research,* December 1998, pp 669–713.

[69] Based on B Richey, H J Bernardin, C L Tyler, and N McKinney, "The Effects of Arbitration Program Characteristics on Applicants' Intentions toward Potential Employers," *Journal of Applied Psychology,* October 2001, pp 1006–13.

[70] See M E Schnake and D S Cochran, "Effect of Two Goal-Setting Dimensions on Perceived Intraorganizational Conflict," *Group & Organization Studies,* June 1985, pp 168–83. Also see O Janssen, E Van De Vliert, and C Veenstra, "How Task and Person Conflict Shape the Role of Positive Interdependence in Management Teams," *Journal of Management,* no. 2, 1999, pp 117–42.

[71] Drawn from L H Chusmir and J Mills, "Gender Differences in Conflict Resolution Styles of Managers: At Work and at Home," *Sex Roles,* February 1989, pp 149–63.

[72] See K K Smith, "The Movement of Conflict in Organizations: The Joint Dynamics of Splitting and Triangulation," *Administrative Science Quarterly,* March 1989, pp 1–20. Also see J B Olson-Buchanan, F Drasgow, P J Moberg, A D Mead, P A Keenan, and M A Donovan, "Interactive Video Assessment of Conflict Resolution Skills." *Personnel Psychology,* Spring 1998, pp 1–24; and D E Conlon and D P Sullivan, "Examining the Actions of Organizations in Conflict: Evidence from the Delaware Court of Chancery," *Academy of Management Journal,* June 1999, pp 319–29.

[73] Based on C Tinsley, "Models of Conflict Resolution in Japanese, German, and American Cultures," *Journal of Applied Psychology,* April 1998, pp 316–23; and S M Adams, "Settling Cross-Cultural Disagreements Begins with 'Where' Not 'How,'" *Academy of Management Executive,* February 1999, pp 109–10. Also see K Ohbuchi, O Fukushima, and J T Tedeschi, "Cultural Values in Conflict Management: Goal Orientation, Goal Attainment, and Tactical Decision," *Journal of Cross-Cultural Psychology,* January 1999, pp 51–71; and R Cropanzano, H Aguinis, M Schminke, and D L Denham, "Disputant Reactions to Managerial Conflict Resolution Tactics: A Comparison among Argentina, the Dominican Republic, Mexico, and the United States," *Group & Organization Management,* June 1999, pp 124–54.

[74] Based on a definition in M A Neale and M H Bazerman, "Negotiating Rationally: The Power and Impact of the Negotiator's Frame," *Academy of Management Executive,* August 1992, pp 42–51.

[75] See K Tyler, "Good-Faith Bargaining," *HR Magazine,* January 2005, pp 48–53; S Clifford, "Something for Nothing," *Inc.,* May 2005, pp 54, 56; L Stern, "Getting Your Slice," *Newsweek,* October 9, 2006, pp 66–67; P Bathurst, "Once Offered the Job, It Can Pay to Negotiate," *The Arizona Republic*, December 10, 2006, p EC 1; E Pooley, "Get a Killer Raise in 2007," Canadian Business, January 14, 2007, pp 61–62.

[76] Data from "Small-Business Owners Want Better Customer Service Skills," *USA Today*, January 16, 2007, p 1B.

[77] M H Bazerman and M A Neale, *Negotiating Rationally* (New York: Free Press, 1992), p 16. Also see G Cullinan, J Le Roux, and R Weddigen, "When to Walk Away from a Deal," *Harvard Business Review,* April 2004, pp 96–104; P B Stark and J Flaherty, "How to Negotiate," *Training & Development,* June 2004, pp 52–54; K Tyler, "The Art of Give-and-Take," *HR Magazine,* November 2004, pp 107–16; D Ertel, "Getting Past Yes: Negotiating as if Implementation Mattered," *Harvard Business Review,* November 2004, pp 60–68; and M Kaplan, "How to Negotiate Anything," *Money,* May 2005, pp 117–19.

[78] Good win–win negotiation strategies can be found in R R Reck and B G Long, *The Win–Win Negotiator: How to Negotiate Favorable Agreements That Last* (New York: Pocket Books, 1987); R Fisher and W Ury, *Getting to YES: Negotiating Agreement without Giving In* (Boston: Houghton Mifflin, 1981); and R Fisher and D Ertel, *Getting Ready to Negotiate: The Getting to YES Workbook* (New York: Penguin Books, 1995). Also see B Spector, "An Interview with Roger Fisher and William Ury," *Academy of Management Executive,* August 2004, pp 101–8; B Booth and M McCredie, "Taking Steps toward 'Getting to Yes' at Blue Cross and Blue Shield of Florida," *Academy of Management Executive,* August 2004, pp 109–12; C Woodyard, "Working Hand-in-Hand," *USA Today*, February 6, 2007, pp 1B–2B; E A Grant, "Playing Hard to Get," *Inc.*, March 2007, pp 104–9; and N Brodsky, "The Paranoia Moment. Are They Stalling? Is This Deal About to Fall Apart?" *Inc.*, April 2007, pp 67–68.

[79] See L R Weingart, E B Hyder, and M J Prietula, "Knowledge Matters: The Effect of Tactical Descriptions on Negotiation Behavior and Outcome." *Journal of Personality and Social Psychology,* June 1996, pp 1205–17.

[80] For more, see A Valenzuela, J Srivastava, and S Lee, "The Role of Cultural Orientation in Bargaining under Incomplete Information: Differences in Causal Attributions," *Organizational Behavior and Human Decision Processes,* January 2005, pp 72–88; K Lee, G Yang, and J L Graham, "Tension and Trust in International Business Negotiations: American Executives Negotiating with Chinese Executives," *Journal of International Business Studies,* September 2006, pp 623–41; and L E Metcalf, A Bird, M Shankarmahesh, Z Aycan, J Larimo, and D D Valdelamar, "Cultural Tendencies in Negotiation: A Comparison of Finland, India, Mexico, Turkey, and the United States," *Journal of World Business*, December 2006, pp 382–94.

[81] For supporting evidence, see J K Butler Jr, "Trust Expectations, Information Sharing, Climate of Trust, and Negotiation Effectiveness and Efficiency," *Group & Organization Management,* June 1999, pp 217–38.

[82] See H J Reitz, J A Wall Jr, and M S Love, "Ethics in Negotiation: Oil and Water or Good Lubrication?" *Business Horizons,* May–June 1998, pp 5–14; M E Schweitzer and Jeffrey L Kerr, "Bargaining under the Influence: The Role of Alcohol in Negotiations," *Academy of Management Executive,* May 2000, pp 47–57; and A M Burr, "Ethics in Negotiation: Does Getting to Yes Require Candor?" *Dispute Resolution Journal,* May–July 2001, pp 8–15.

[83] For related research, see A E Tenbrunsel, "Misrepresentation and Expectations of Misrepresentation in an Ethical Dilemma: The Role of Incentives and Temptation," *Academy of Management Journal,* June 1998, pp 330–39.

[84] Based on R L Pinkley, T L Griffith, and G B Northcraft, "'Fixed Pie' a la Mode: Information Availability, Information Processing, and the Negotiation of Suboptimal Agreements," *Organizational Behavior and Human Decision Processes,* April 1995, pp 101–12.

[85] Based on A E Walters, A F Stuhlmacher, and L L Meyer, "Gender and Negotiator Competitiveness: A Meta-Analysis," *Organizational Behavior and Human Decision Processes,* October 1998, pp 1–29.

[86] Based on B Barry and R A Friedman, "Bargainer Characteristics in Distributive and Integrative Negotiation," *Journal of Personality and Social Psychology,* February 1998, pp 345–59. Also see K J Sulkowicz, "The Psychology of the Deal," *BusinessWeek,* April 9, 2007, p 14.

[87] For more, see J P Forgas, "On Feeling Good and Getting Your Way: Mood Effects on Negotiator Cognition and Bargaining Strategies," *Journal of Personality and Social Psychology,* March 1998, pp 565–77. Also see G A van Kleef, C K W De Dreu, and A S R Manstead, "The Interpersonal Effects of Anger and Happiness in Negotiations," *Journal of Personality and Social Psychology,* January 2004, pp 57–76; and G A van Kleef, C K W De Dreu, and A S R Manstead, "The Interpersonal Effects of Emotions in Negotiations: A Motivated Information

Processing Approach," *Journal of Personality and Social Psychology,* October 2004, pp 510–28.

[88] Data from B Campbell and M M Marx, "Toward More Effective Stakeholder Dialogue: Applying Theories of Negotiation to Policy and Program Evaluation," *Journal of Applied Social Psychology*, December 2006, pp 2834–63.

[89] Drawn from J M Brett and T Okumura, "Inter- and Intracultural Negotiation: US and Japanese Negotiators," *Academy of Management Journal,* October 1998, pp 495–510. Also see W L Adair, T Okumura, and J M Brett, "Negotiation Behavior when Cultures Collide: The United States and Japan," *Journal of Applied Psychology,* June 2001, pp 37–85. More negotiation research is reported in K M O'Connor, J A Arnold, and E R Burris, "Negotiators' Bargaining Histories and Their Effects on Future Negotiation Performance," *Journal of Applied Psychology,* March 2005, pp 350–62; P H Kim and A R Fragale, "Choosing the Path to Bargaining Power: An Empirical Comparison of BATNAs and Contributions in Negotiation," *Journal of Applied Psychology,* March 2005, pp 373–81; J R Curhan, H A Elfenbein, and H Xu, "What Do People Value When They Negotiate? Mapping the Domain of Subjective Value in Negotiation," *Journal of Personality and Social Psychology*, September 2006, pp 493–512; and M D Henderson, Y Trope, and P J Carnevale, "Negotiation From a Near and Distant Time Perspective," *Journal of Personality and Social Psychology*, October 2006, pp 712–29.

[90] S Holmes, "Soaring Where Boeing Struggled," *BusinessWeek*, February 19, 2007, p 72.

[91] Excerpted from K Sulkowicz, "Sparring Execs Need a Time Out," *BusinessWeek*, December 18, 2006, p 18.

CHAPTER 14

[1] Excerpted from M Conlin, "Web Attack," *BusinessWeek,* April 16, 2007, pp 54, 56.

[2] See the related discussion in M Orey, "Fear of Firing," *BusinessWeek,* April 23, 2007, pp 52–62; and M D Hovanesian, "At CITI, More Heat on Chuck Prince," *BusinessWeek,* February 5, 2007, p 36.

[3] Results are reported in G Naik, "A Hospital Races to Learn Lessons of Ferrari Pit Stop," *The Wall Street Journal,* November 14, 2006, pp A1, A10.

[4] Results are summarized in "Why Am I Here," *Training,* April 2006, p 13. Also see J Robison, "An HCA Hospital's Miracle Workers," *Gallup Management Journal,* January 12, 2006, http:gmj.gallup.com/content/default.asp?ci=20707.

[5] J L Bowditch and A F Buono, *A Primer on Organizational Behavior,* 4th ed (New York: John Wiley & Sons, 1997), p 120.

[6] The appropriateness of using different media to terminate employees is discussed by J Welch and S Welch, "The Right Way to Say Goodbye," *BusinessWeek,* March 26, 2007, pp 144; and D Levine, A Maingault, and D Lacy, "Cobra, Evasive

Poor Performers, Illegal Workers," *HR Magazine,* March 2007, pp 41–42.

[7] G A Fowler, "In China's Offices, Foreign Colleagues Might Get an Earful," *The Wall Street Journal,* February 13, 2007, p B1.

[8] Ideas for improving personal communication skills are discussed by J S Lublin, "Improv Troupe Teaches Managers How to Give Better Presentations," *The Wall Street Journal,* February 6, 2007, p B1; and R Tucker, "Four Key Skills to Master Now," *Fortune,* October 30, 2006, p 123.

[9] See "Interpersonal Effectiveness Training: Beyond the Water Cooler," *Training,* April 2006, p 10.

[10] For a thorough discussion of these barriers, see C R Rogers and FJ Roethlisberger, "Barriers and Gateways to Communication," *Harvard Business Review,* July–August 1952, pp 46–52.

[11] Ibid., p 47.

[12] Physical barriers are discussed by S Shellenbarger, "Time-Zoned: Working Around the Round-the-Clock Workday," *The Wall Street Journal,* February 15, 2007, p D1; and E Woyke, "Wanted: A Clutter Cutter," *BusinessWeek,* April 9, 2007, p 12.

[13] J Sandberg, "'It Says Press Any Key. Where's the Any Key?'" *The Wall Street Journal,* February 20, 2007, p B1.

[14] The use of jargon is discussed by C Hymowitz, "Mind Your Language: To Do Business Today, Consider Delayering," *The Wall Street Journal,* March 27, 2006, p B1.

[15] Results can be found in J D Johnson, W A Donohue, C K Atkin, and S Johnson, "Communication, Involvement, and Perceived Innovativeness," *Group & Organization Management,* March 2001, pp 24–52; and B Davenport Sypher and T E Zorn Jr, "Communication-Related Abilities and Upward Mobility: A Longitudinal Investigation," *Human Communication Research,* Spring 1986, pp 420–31.

[16] These recommendations were adapted from J Yadegaran, "Just Say 'No,'" *The Arizona Republic,* September 14, 2006, p E3.

[17] This statistic was reported in R O Crockett, "The 21st Century Meeting," *Business Week,* February 26, 2007, pp 72–79.

[18] A study of decoding nonverbal cues was conducted by E L Cooley, "Attachment Style and Decoding of Nonverbal Cues," *North American Journal of Psychology,* 2005, pp 25–33.

[19] Related research is summarized by J A Hall, "Male and Female Nonverbal Behavior," in *Multichannel Integrations of Nonverbal Behavior,* eds A W Siegman and S Feldstein (Hillsdale, NJ: Lawrence Erlbaum, 1985), pp 195–226.

[20] Results can be found in ibid.

[21] See J A Russell, "Facial Expressions of Emotion: What Lies beyond Minimal Universality?" *Psychological Bulletin,* November 1995, pp 379–91; and Also see B Azar, "A Case for Angry Men and Happy Women," *Monitor on Psychology,* April 2007, pp 18–19.

[22] The use of nonverbal information in product development is discussed by A McConnon, "The Mind-Bending New World of Work," *BusinessWeek,* April 2, 2007, pp 46–54.

[23] Norms for cross-cultural eye contact are discussed by C Engholm, *When Business East Meets Business West: The Guide to Practice and Protocol in the Pacific Rim* (New York: John Wiley & Sons, 1991).

[24] These recommendations were adapted from those in P Preston, "Nonverbal Communication: Do You Really Say What You Mean?" *Journal of Healthcare Management,* March–April 2005, pp 83–86.

[25] See R D Ramsey, "Ten Things That Never Change for Supervisors," *SuperVision,* April 2007, pp 16–18; "CEOs Emphasize Listening to Employees," *HR Magazine,* January 2007, p 14; and M Marchetti, "Listen to Me!" *Sales and Marketing Management,* April 2007, p 12.

[26] The discussion of listening styles is based on "5 Listening Styles," www.crossroadsinstitute.org/listyle.html, accessed May 5, 2005; and J Condrill, "What Is Your Listening Style?" Authors Den.Com, July 7, 2005, http://www.authorsden.com/visit/viewarticle.asp?id=18707.

[27] These recommendations were excerpted from J Jay, "On Communicating Well," *HR Magazine,* January 2005, pp 87–88.

[28] D Tannen, "The Power of Talk: Who Gets Heard and Why," *Harvard Business Review,* September–October 1995, p 139.

[29] For a thorough review of the evolutionary explanation of sex differences in communication, see A H Eagly and W Wood, "The Origins of Sex Differences in Human Behavior," *American Psychologist,* June 1999, pp 408–23. A critique of evolutionary psychology was also provided by S Begley, "Evolutionary Psych May Not Help Explain Our Behavior after All," *The Wall Street Journal,* April 29, 2005, p B1.

[30] See Tannen, "The Power of Talk," pp 160–73; and D Tannen, *You Just Don't Understand: Women and Men in Conversation* (New York: Ballantine Books, 1990).

[31] See M Dainton and E D Zelley, *Applying Communication Theory for Professional Life: A Practical Introduction* (Thousand Oaks, CA: Sage, 2005); and "The Differences between Boys and Girls…At the Office," *Training,* November 2006, p 8.

[32] This definition was taken from J C Tingley, *Genderflex: Men and Women Speaking Each Other's Language at Work* (New York: American Management Association, 1994), p 16.

[33] A Stanton, "Mastering Communication: CEO Succeeds in Field of Mostly Men," *The Arizona Republic,* March 4, 2007, p D2.

[34] Tannen, "The Power of Talk," pp 147–48.

[35] The frequency of using upward communication techniques is discussed by A Pomeroy, "Great Communicators, Great Communication," *HR Magazine,* July 2006, pp 44–49.

[36] These recommendations were taken from N H Woodward, "Doing Town Hall Meetings Better," *HR Magazine,*

December 2006, p 70; also see S R Levine, "Make Meetings Less Dreaded," *HR Magazine,* January 2007, pp 107–9.

[37] See H Green, "Twitter: All Trivia, All the Time," *Business Week,* April 2, 2007, p 40; and "Word-of-Mouth: Heard It Through the Grapevine," *MarketingWeek,* September 28, 2006, p 42.

[38] H B Vickery III, "Tapping into the Employee Grapevine," *Association Management,* January 1984, pp 59–60.

[39] The most recent research is discussed by S M Crampton, J W Hodge, and J M Mishra, "The Informal Communication Network: Factors Influencing Grapevine Activity," *Public Personnel Management,* Winter 1998, pp 569–84, "Pruning the Company Grapevine," *Supervision,* September 1986, p 11; and R Half, "Managing Your Career: 'How Can I Stop the Gossip?'" *Management Accounting,* September 1987, p 27.

[40] Management by walking around is discussed by T Peters and N Austin, *A Passion for Excellence: The Leadership Difference* (New York: Random House, 1985).

[41] L Dulye, "Get Our of Your Office," *HR Magazine,* July 2006, p 99.

[42] These recommendations were adapted from ibid., pp 100–1.

[43] A C Poe, "Don't Touch That 'Send' Button!" *HR Magazine,* July 2001, pp 74–75.

[44] RL Daft and R H Lengel, "Information Richness: A New Approach to Managerial Behavior and Organizational Design," in *Research in Organizational Behavior,* eds B M Staw and L L Cummings (Greenwich, CT: JAI Press, 1984), p 196.

[45] Details of this example are provided in L Grensing-Pophal, "Spread the Word—Correctly," *HR Magazine,* March 2005, pp 83–88.

[46] See E Binney, "Is E-Mail the New Pink Slip?" *HR Magazine,* November 2006, pp 32, 38; and D M Cable and K Y T Yu, "Managing Job Seekers' Organizational Image Beliefs: The Role of Media Richness and Media Credibility," *Journal of Applied Psychology,* July 2006, pp 828–40.

[47] See B Barry and I S Fulmer, "The Medium and the Message: The Adaptive Use of Communication Media in Dyadic Influence," *Academy of Management Review,* April 2004, pp 272–92; and A F Simon, "Computer-Mediated Communication: Task Performance and Satisfaction," *The Journal of Social Psychology,* June 2006, pp 349–79.

[48] See R E Rice and D E Shook, "Relationships of Job Categories and Organizational Levels to Use of Communication Channels, Including Electronic Mail: A Meta-Analysis and Extension," *Journal of Management Studies,* March 1990, pp 195–229.

[49] E Agnvall, "Biometrics Clock In," *HR Magazine,* April 2007, p 103.

[50] These examples are discussed in C Winkler, "Job Tryouts Go Virtual," *HR Magazine,* September 2006, pp 131–34.

[51] See J T Arnold, "Enrolling Online," *HR Magazine,* December 2006, pp 89–92.

[52] See R D Hof, "Is Google Too Powerful," *Business Week,* April 9, 2007, pp 47–54; D Roberts, "China Mobile's Hot Signal," *BusinessWeek,* February 5, 2007, pp 42–44; and

D Kirkpatrick, "Life In a Connected World," *Fortune,* July 10, 2006, pp 98–100.

[53] This statistic was reported in H Green, S Rosenbush, R O Crockett, and S Holmes, "Wi-Fi Means Business," *BusinessWeek,* April 28, 2003, pp 86–92.

[54] Online training is discussed by S Overman, "Dow, Hewlett-Packard Put E-Learning to Work to Save Time and Money," *HR Magazine,* February 2004, pp 33.

[55] See M E Medland, "Time Squeeze," *HR Magazine,* November 2004, pp 66–70; and "X-Rated," *Training,* p 10.

[56] See D Buss, "Spies Like Us," *Training,* December 2001, pp 44–48.

[57] See B Grow, "The Mind Games Cybercrooks Play," *BusinessWeek,* April 17, 2006, pp 54, 58.

[58] Information security is discussed by A Blackman, "Foul Sents," *The Wall Street Journal,* March 26, 2007, p R8.

[59] Pros and cons of e-mail are discussed in C Graham, "In-Box Overload," *The Arizona Republic,* April 16, 2007, p A14; and J Saranow, "Deleting the Habit: How Email Junkies Do In Withdrawal," *The Wall Street Journal,* February 14, 2007, p A1, A18; and A Smith, "Federal Rules Define Duty to Preserve Work E-Mails," *HR Magazine,* January 2007, pp 27, 36.

[60] See descriptions in J E Vascellaro, "What's a Cellphone For?" *The Wall Street Journal,* March 26, 2007, p R5; J Schlosser, "Get Outta My Phone," *Fortune,* February 19, 2007, p 20.

[61] Excerpted from M Conlin, "Take a Vacation from Your BlackBerry," *BusinessWeek,* December 20, 2004, p 56.

[62] This issue is discussed by A Athavaley, "The New BlackBerry Addicts," *The Wall Street Journal,* January 23, 2007, pp D1, D2; and "Can't Disconnect? You Are Not Alone," *HR Magazine,* February 2007, p 14.

[63] These statistics were reported in J M Alterion, "IBM Taps into Blogosphere," *The Arizona Republic,* January 21, 2006, p D3.

[64] See S Holmes, "Into the Wild Blog Yonder," *BusinessWeek,* May 22, 2006, pp 84–86.

[65] These benefits are discussed by S E Needleman, "How Blogging Can Help You Get a New Job," *The Wall Street Journal,* April 10, 2007, p B7; and A Schatz, "Candidates Find a New Stump: the Blogosphere," *The Wall Street Journal,* February 14, 2007, pp B1, B2.

[66] A thorough discussion of video interviewing is provided by M Bolch, "Lights, Camera . . . Interview!" *HR Magazine,* March 2007, pp 99–102.

[67] Results can be found in S A Rains, "Leveling the Organizational Playing Field—Virtually: A Meta-Analysis of Experimental Research Assessing the Impact of Group Support System Use on Member Influence Behaviors," *Communication Research,* April 2005, pp 193–234.

[68] Challenges associated with virtual operations are discussed by S O'Mahony and S R Barley, "Do Digital Telecommunications Affect Work and Organization? The State of Our Knowledge," in *Research in Organizational*

Behavior, vol. 21, eds R I Sutton and B M Staw (Stamford, CT: JAI Press, 1999), pp 125–61.

[69] See A Donoghue, "2010: The Year of the Techie," ZDNet UK News, May 13, 2006, http://news.zdnet.co.uk/business/0,39020645,39269493,oo.htm. Also see S Meisinger, "Flexible Schedules Make Powerful 'Perks,'" *HR Magazine,* April 2007, p 12.

[70] See "the Virtual Workforce," *BusinessWeek,* March 5, 2007, p 6; and T D Golden, J F Veiga, and Z Simsek, "Telecommuting's Differential Impact on Work-Family Conflict: Is There No Place Like Home?" *Journal of Applied Psychology,* November 2006, pp 1240–350.

[71] Results are reported in K Gurchiek, "Telecommuting Could Hold Back Career," *HR Magazine,* March 2007, p 34.

[72] J Welch and S Welch, "The Importance of Being There," *BusinessWeek,* April 16, 2007, p 92.

[73] Excerpted from M Ihlwan and K Hall, "New Tech, Old Habits," *BusinessWeek,* March 26, 2007, pp 48–49.

[74] Excerpted from T Abdollah, "Malicious Classroom Videos Fuel Debate at High Schools," *The Arizona Republic,* February 11, 2007, p A10.

CHAPTER 15

[1] Excerpted from S Levy, "Moving Into a New Office," *Newsweek,* December 4, 2006, p 48. Also see J Greene, "The Soul of a New Microsoft," *BusinessWeek,* December 4, 2006, pp 56–66.

[2] H Malcolm and C Sokoloff, "Values, Human Relations, and Organization Development," in *The Emerging Practice of Organizational Development,* eds W Sikes, A Drexler, and J Gant (San Diego: University Associates, 1989), p 64.

[3] Levy, "Moving Into a New Office," p 48.

[4] See D Kipnis, S M Schmidt, and I Wilkinson, "Intraorganizational Influence Tactics: Explorations in Getting One's Way," *Journal of Applied Psychology,* August 1980, pp 440–52. Also see C A Schriesheim and T R Hinkin, "Influence Tactics Used by Subordinates: A Theoretical and Empirical Analysis and Refinement of the Kipnis, Schmidt, and Wilkinson Subscales," *Journal of Applied Psychology,* June 1990, pp 246–57; G Yukl and C M Falbe, "Influence Tactics and Objectives in Upward, Downward, and Lateral Influence Attempts," *Journal of Applied Psychology,* April 1990, pp 132–40; and G Yukl and B Tracey, "Consequences of Influence Tactics Used with Subordinates, Peers, and the Boss," in *Organizational Influence Processes,* eds L W Porter, H L Angle, and R W Allen (Armonk, NY: M E Sharpe, 2003), 2nd ed, pp 96–116.

[5] Based on Table 1 in G Yukl, C M Falbe, and J Y Youn, "Patterns of Influence Behavior for Managers," *Group & Organization Management,* March 1993, pp 5–28. An additional influence tactic is presented in B P Davis and E S Knowles, "A Disrupt-then-Reframe Technique of Social Influence," *Journal of Personality and Social Psychology,* February 1999, pp 192–99. For more on ingratiation, see D B Yoffie and M Kwak, "With Friends Like These: The Art of Managing Complementors," *Harvard Business Review,* September 2006, pp 88–98.

[6] For comprehensive coverage, see L W Porter, H L Angle, and R W Allen, eds *Organizational Influence Processes,* 2nd ed (Armonk, NY: M E Sharpe, 2003); and The Society for Human Resource Management and Harvard Business School Press, *The Essentials of Power, Influence, and Persuasion* (Boston: Harvard Business School Press, 2006).

[7] Excerpted from A Weintraub, "Making Her Mark at Merck," *BusinessWeek,* January 8, 2007, p 65.

[8] Based on discussion in G Yukl, H Kim, and C M Falbe, "Antecedents of Influence Outcomes," *Journal of Applied Psychology,* June 1996, pp 309–17.

[9] Data from ibid.

[10] Data from G Yukl and J B Tracey, "Consequences of Influence Tactics Used with Subordinates, Peers, and the Boss," *Journal of Applied Psychology,* August 1992, pp 525–35. Also see C M Falbe and G Yukl, "Consequences for Managers of Using Single Influence Tactics and Combinations of Tactics," *Academy of Management Journal,* August 1992, pp 638–52.

[11] Data from R A Gordon, "Impact of Ingratiation on Judgments and Evaluations: A Meta-Analytic Investigation," *Journal of Personality and Social Psychology,* July 1996, pp 54–70.

[12] Data from Yukl, Kim, and Falbe, "Antecedents of Influence Outcomes."

[13] Based on R T Sparrowe, B W Soetjipto, and M L Kraimer, "Do Leaders' Influence Tactics Relate to Members' Helping Behavior? It Depends on the Quality of the Relationship," *Academy of Management Journal,* December 2006, pp 1194–208. Also see S Sonenshein, "Crafting Social Issues at Work," *Academy of Management Journal,* December 2006, pp 1158–172.

[14] Data from B J Tepper, R J Eisenbach, S L Kirby, and P W Potter, "Test of a Justice-Based Model of Subordinates' Resistance to Downward Influence Attempts," *Group & Organization Management,* June 1998, pp 144–60. Also see M W Firmin, J M Helmick, B A Iezzi, and A Vaughn, "Say Please: The Effect of the Word 'Please' in Compliance-Seeking Requests," *Social Behavior and Personality,* no. 1, 2004, pp 67–72.

[15] J E Driskell, B Olmstead, and E Salas, "Task Cues, Dominance Cues, and Influence in Task Groups," *Journal of Applied Psychology,* February 1993, p 51. No gender bias was found in H Aguinis and S K R Adams, "Social-Role versus Structural Models of Gender and Influence Use in Organizations: A Strong Inference Approach," *Group & Organization Management,* December 1998, pp 414–46. Also see R J Green, J C Sandall, and C Phelps, "Effect of Experimenter Attire and Sex on Participant Productivity," *Social Behavior and Personality,* no. 2, 2005, pp 125–32.

[16] See P P Fu et al., "The Impact of Societal Cultural Values and Individual Social Beliefs on the Perceived Effectiveness of Managerial Influence Strategies: A Meso Approach," *Journal of International Business Studies,* July 2004, pp 284–305.

[17] B Moses, "You Can't Make Change; You Have to Sell It," *Fast Company,* April 1999, p 101. Also see J Kirby, "Just Trying to Help," *Harvard Business Review,* June 2006, pp 35–39; and J Welch and S Welch, "A Dangerous Division of Labor," *BusinessWeek,* November 6, 2006, p 122.

[18] For example, see K Gurchiek, "How To Defuse an Unreasonable Boss," *HR Magazine,* August 2006, pp 28, 30; S Berfield, "Don't Get Mad. Get Even," *BusinessWeek,* August 21–28, 2006, pp 64–65; and G Colvin, "Undercutting CEO Power," *Fortune,* March 5, 2007, p. 42.

[19] D Tjosvold, "The Dynamics of Positive Power," *Training and Development Journal,* June 1984, p 72. Also see "The Exercise of Power," *Harvard Business Review,* May 2002, p 136; G Colvin, "Power 25: The Most Powerful People in Business," *Fortune,* August 9, 2004, pp 90–106; and Ann Harrington and P Bartosiewicz, "50 Most Powerful Women: Who's Up? Who's Down?" *Fortune,* October 18, 2004, pp 181–98.

[20] M W McCall, Jr, *Power, Influence, and Authority: The Hazards of Carrying a Sword,* Technical Report No. 10 (Greensboro, NC: Center for Creative Leadership, 1978), p 5. For an excellent discussion, see J O Hagberg, *Real Power: Stages of Personal Power in Organizations,* 3rd ed (Salem, WI: Sheffield Publishing, 2003).

[21] D Weimer, "Daughter Knows Best," *BusinessWeek,* April 19, 1999, pp 132, 134. Also see "How to Stage a Coup," *Inc.,* March 2005, p 52.

[22] For an update, see C L Bernick, "When Your Culture Needs a Makeover," *Harvard Business Review,* June 2001, pp 53–61.

[23] L H Chusmir, "Personalized versus Socialized Power Needs among Working Women and Men," *Human Relations,* February 1986, p 149.

[24] See A Pomeroy, "Thanks, but No Thanks," *HR Magazine,* December 2004, p 18; and A Molinsky and J Margolis, "Necessary Evils and Interpersonal Sensitivity in Organizations," *Academy of Management Review,* April 2005, pp 245–68.

[25] As quoted in L Buchanan, "That's Quite a Story: How I Did It," *Inc.,* November 2006, p 113. Also see K Aquino, T M Tripp, and R J Bies, "Getting Even or Moving On? Power, Procedural Justice, and Types of Offense as Predictors of Revenge, Forgiveness, Reconciliation, and Avoidance in Organizations," *Journal of Applied Psychology,* May 2006, pp 653–68.

[26] D W Cantor and T Bernay, *Women in Power: The Secrets of Leadership* (Boston: Houghton Mifflin, 1992), p 40; and K Morris, "Trouble in Toyland," *BusinessWeek,* March 15, 1999, p 40.

[27] See J R P French and B Raven, "The Bases of Social Power," in *Studies in Social Power,* ed D Cartwright (Ann Arbor: University of Michigan Press, 1959), pp 150–67. Also see S M Farmer and H Aguinis, "Accounting for Subordinate Perceptions of Supervisor Power: An Identity-Dependence Model," *Journal of Applied Psychology,* November 2005, pp 1069–83.

[28] G Edmondson, "Power Play at VW," *BusinessWeek,* December 4, 2006, p 45. Also see M Weinstein, "Alpha Male on Your Hands: Here's How to Deal," *Training,* October 2006, p 16.

[29] See K Gurchiek, "Security Gets Under Employees' Skin," *HR Magazine,* April 2006, p 32; I Rowley, "Please Blow Gently Into the Phone," *BusinessWeek,* July 10, 2006, p 12; M Conlin, "More Micro, Less Soft," *BusinessWeek,* November 27, 2006, p 42; J B Thelen, "Smelling Smoke," *HR Magazine,* December 2006, pp 105–11; "Wellness—or Orwellness?" *BusinessWeek,* March 19, 2007, pp 82–83; and R Zeidner, "Using Chips to Track Workers Discouraged," *HR Magazine,* April 2007, p 34.

[30] Data from J R Larson Jr, C Christensen, A S Abbott, and T M Franz, "Diagnosing Groups: Charting the Flow of Information in Medical Decision-Making Teams," *Journal of Personality and Social Psychology,* August 1996, pp 315–30; Also see J Nebus, "Building Collegial Information Networks: A Theory of Advice Network Generation," *Academy of Management Review,* July 2006, pp 615–37.

[31] See M Maccoby, "Why People Follow the Leader: The Power of Transference," *Harvard Business Review,* September 2004, pp 76–85; and G R Weaver, L K Trevino, and B Agle, "'Somebody I Look Up To:' Ethical Role Models in Organizations," *Organizational Dynamics,* no. 4, 2005, pp 313–30.

[32] Excerpted from the first Q&A in J Welch and S Welch, "It's Not about Empty Suits," *BusinessWeek,* October 16, 2006, p 132. Also see the first Q&A in Jack Welch and Suzy Welch, "Turning Blasé Into Buy-In," *BusinessWeek,* April 9, 2007, p 106.

[33] Details may be found in Chusmir, "Personalized versus Socialized Power Needs among Working Women and Men," pp 149–59. For a review of research on individual differences in the need for power, see R J House, "Power and Personality in Complex Organizations," in *Research in Organizational Behavior,* ed B M Staw and L L Cummings (Greenwich, CT: JAI Press, 1988), pp 305–57.

[34] B Filipczak, "Is It Getting Chilly in Here?" *Training,* February 1994, p 27.

[35] Data from J Onyx, R Leonard, and K Vivekananda, "Social Perception of Power: A Gender Analysis," *Perceptual and Motor Skills,* February 1995, pp 291–96.

[36] P M Podsakoff and C A Schriesheim, "Field Studies of French and Raven's Bases of Power: Critique, Reanalysis, and Suggestions for Future Research," *Psychological Bulletin,* May 1985, p 388. Also see M A Rahim and G F Buntzman, "Supervisory Power Bases, Styles of Handling Conflict with Subordinates, and Subordinate Compliance and Satisfaction," *Journal of Psychology,* March 1989, pp 195–210; D Tjosvold, "Power and Social Context in Superior-Subordinate Interaction," *Organizational Behavior and Human Decision Processes,* June 1985, pp 281–93; and C A Schriesheim, T R Hinkin, and P M Podsakoff, "Can Ipsative and Single-Item Measures Produce Erroneous Results in Field Studies of French and Raven's (1950) Five Bases of Power? An Empirical Investigation," *Journal of Applied Psychology,* February 1991, pp 106–14.

[37] See T R Hinkin and C A Schriesheim, "Relationships between Subordinate Perceptions and Supervisor Influence Tactics and Attributed Bases of Supervisory Power," *Human*

Relations, March 1990, pp 221–37. Also see D J Brass and M E Burkhardt, "Potential Power and Power Use: An Investigation of Structure and Behavior," *Academy of Management Journal,* June 1993, pp 441–70; K W Mossholder, N Bennett, E R Kemery, and M A Wesolowski, "Relationships between Bases of Power and Work Reactions: The Mediational Role of Procedural Justice," *Journal of Management,* no. 4, 1998, pp 533–52; and J Sell, M J Lovaglia, E A Mannix, C D Samuelson, and R K Wilson, "Investigating Conflict, Power, and Status within and among Groups," *Small Group Research,* February 2004, pp 44–72.

[38] See J Scelfo, "10 Power Tips," *Newsweek,* September 25, 2006, p 78; and A Carter, "Curiously Strong Teamwork," *BusinessWeek,* February 26, 2007, pp 90, 92.

[39] See W Kosova, "The Power That Was," *Newsweek,* April 23, 2007, pp 24–31; and M Arndt and H Maurer, "Costly Comment of the Week," *BusinessWeek,* April 23, 2007, p 29.

[40] Based on P A Wilson, "The Effects of Politics and Power on the Organizational Commitment of Federal Executives," *Journal of Management,* Spring 1995, pp 101–18. For related research, see J B Arthur, "Effects of Human Resource Systems on Manufacturing Performance and Turnover," *Academy of Management Journal,* June 1994, pp 670–87.

[41] For related research, see L G Pelletier and R J Vallerand, "Supervisors' Beliefs and Subordinates' Intrinsic Motivation: A Behavioral Confirmation Analysis," *Journal of Personality and Social Psychology,* August 1996, pp 331–40.

[42] As quoted in M Bartiromo, "What to Expect at Davos," *BusinessWeek,* January 29, 2007, p 100. Also see G Mangurian, "Responsibility Junkie," *Harvard Business Review,* October 2006, p 30.

[43] As quoted in W A Randolph and M Sashkin, "Can Organizational Empowerment Work in Multinational Settings?" *Academy of Management Executive,* February 2002, p 104. (Emphasis added.) Also see J S Harrison and R E Freeman, "Special Topic: Democracy in and around Organizations: Is Organizational Democracy Worth the Effort?" *Academy of Management Executive,* August 2004, pp 49–53; J L Kerr, "The Limits of Organizational Democracy," *Academy of Management Executive,* August 2004, pp 81–97; and N R Lockwood, "Leveraging Employee Engagement for Competitive Advantage: HR's Strategic Role," 2007 SHRM Research Quarterly, *HR Magazine,* March 2007, pp 1–12.

[44] R M Hodgetts, "A Conversation with Steve Kerr," *Organizational Dynamics,* Spring 1996, p 71. For example, see B De Lollis, "Hotels Train Employees to Think Fast," *USAToday,* November 29, 2006, pp 1B–2B.

[45] L Shaper Walters, "A Leader Redefines Management," *Christian Science Monitor,* September 22, 1992, p 14. Also see B George, P Sims, A N McLean, and D Mayer, "Discovering Your Authentic Leadership," *Harvard Business Review,* February 2007, pp 129–38.

[46] For a 15-item empowerment scale, see Table 1 on p 103 of B P Niehoff, R H Moorman, G Blakely, and J Fuller, "The Influence of Empowerment and Job Enrichment on Employee Loyalty in a Downsizing Environment," *Group & Organization Management,* March 2001, pp 93–113.

[47] F Vogelstein, "Star Power: Greg Brown, Motorola," *Fortune,* February 6, 2006, p 57.

[48] For an extended discussion of this model, see M Sashkin, "Participative Management Is an Ethical Imperative," *Organizational Dynamics,* Spring 1984, pp 4–22.

[49] S Carey, "The Thrifty Get Thriftier," *The Wall Street Journal,* May 10, 2004, p R7.

[50] For more on delegation, see L Bossidy, "The Job No CEO Should Delegate," *Harvard Business Review,* March 2001, pp 46–49; F Dalton, "Delegation Pitfalls," *Association Management,* February 2005, pp 65–72; T Estep, "Devilish Delegation at the Department of Ominous Mechanical Mishaps," *Training & Development,* March 2005, pp 68–70; and J Janove, "A 3,500-Year-Old Lesson in Delegating," *HR Magazine,* March 2005, pp 109–12.

[51] See S Gazda, "The Art of Delegating," *HR Magazine,* January 2002, pp 75–78.

[52] M Memmott, "Managing Government Inc.," *USA Today,* June 28, 1993, p 2B. Also see R C Ford and C P Heaton, "Lessons from Hospitality That Can Serve Anyone," *Organizational Dynamics,* Summer 2001, pp 30–47.

[53] R Kreitner, *Management,* 10th ed (Boston: Houghton Mifflin, 2007), p 302. Also see C A Walker, "Saving Your Rookie Managers from Themselves," *Harvard Business Review,* April 2002, pp 97–102.

[54] Drawn from G Yukl and P P Fu, "Determinants of Delegation and Consultation by Managers," *Journal of Organizational Behavior,* March 1999, pp 219–32. Also see Z X Chen and S Aryee, "Delegation and Employee Work Outcomes: An Examination of the Cultural Context of Mediating Processes in China," *Academy of Management Journal,* February 2007, pp 226–38.

[55] See J Pfeffer, "It's Time to Start Trusting the Workforce," *Business 2.0,* December 2006, p 68; F D Schoorman, R C Mayer, and J H Davis, "An Integrative Model of Organizational Trust: Past, Present, and Future," *Academy of Management Review,* April 2007, pp 344–54; M Williams, "Building Genuine Trust Through Interpersonal Emotion Management: A Threat Regulation Model of Trust and Collaboration Across Boundaries," *Academy of Management Review,* April 2007, pp 595–621; and B W Heineman, Jr., "Avoiding Integrity Land Mines," *Harvard Business Review,* April 2007, pp 100–08.

[56] See the first Q&A in J Welch and S Welch, "Getting Back on the Radar," *BusinessWeek,* December 18, 2006, p 160.

[57] M Frese, W Kring, A Soose, and J Zempel, "Personal Initiative at Work: Differences between East and West Germany," *Academy of Management Journal,* February 1996, p 38. (Emphasis added.) For comprehensive updates, see D J Campbell, "The Proactive Employee: Managing Workplace Initiative," *Academy of Management Executive,* August 2000, pp 52–66; and M Frese and D Fay, "Personal Initiative: An Active Performance Concept for Work in the 21st Century," in *Research in Organizational Behavior,* vol. 23, eds B M Staw and R I Sutton (New York: JAI, 2001), pp 133–87.

58 See J A Belasco and R C Stayer, "Why Empowerment Doesn't Empower: The Bankruptcy of Current Paradigms," *Business Horizons,* March–April 1994, pp 29–41; and W A Randolph, "Re-thinking Empowerment: Why Is It So Hard to Achieve?" *Organizational Dynamics,* Fall 2000, pp 94–107.

59 Results can be found in B D Cawley, L M Keeping, and P E Levy, "Participation in the Performance Appraisal Process and Employee Reactions: A Meta-Analytic Review of Field Investigations," *Journal of Applied Psychology,* August 1998, pp 615–33.

60 Results are contained in J A Wagner III, C R Leana, E A Locke, and D M Schweiger, "Cognitive and Motivational Frameworks in US Research on Participation: A Meta-Analysis of Primary Effects," *Journal of Organizational Behavior,* 1997, pp 49–65.

61 Based on A Srivastava, K M Bartol, and E A Locke, "Empowering Leadership in Management Teams: Effects on Knowledge Sharing, Efficacy, and Performance," *Academy of Management Journal,* December 2006, pp 1239–251.

62 Based on J P Guthrie, "High-Involvement Work Practices, Turnover, and Productivity: Evidence from New Zealand," *Academy of Management Journal,* February 2001, pp 180–90.

63 Based on M Workman and W Bommer, "Redesigning Computer Call Center Work: A Longitudinal Field Experiment," *Journal of Organizational Behavior,* May 2004, pp 317–37.

64 Based on C D Zatzick and R D Iverson, "High-Involvement Management and Workforce Reduction: Competitive Advantage or Disadvantage?" *Academy of Management Journal,* October 2006, pp 999–1015.

65 W A Randolph, "Navigating the Journey to Empowerment," *Organizational Dynamics,* Spring 1995, p 31.

66 See D Jones, "America Loves to Hate Dastardly CEOs," *USA Today,* September 15, 2004, pp 1B–2B; D Jones and B Keveney, "10 Lessons of 'The Apprentice,'" *USA Today,* April 15, 2004, pp 1A, 5A; A Pomeroy, "Business Reality TV?" *HR Magazine,* January 2005, p 14; R Underwood, "Fast Talk: What I Learned on *The Apprentice,*" *Fast Company,* May 2005, pp 45–50; and M Orey, "Fear of Firing," *BusinessWeek,* April 23, 2007, pp 52–62.

67 D J Burrough, "Office Politics Mirror Popular TV Program," *Arizona Republic,* February 4, 2001, p EC1.

68 L B MacGregor Serven, *The End of Office Politics as Usual* (New York: American Management Association, 2002), p 5. Also see K J McGregor, "Sweet Revenge: The Power of Retribution, Spite, and Loathing in the World of Business," *BusinessWeek,* January 22, 2007, pp 64–70; D A Kaplan, "Suspicions and Spies in Silicon Valley," *Newsweek,* September 18, 2006, pp 40–47; J Fox, "Board Games," *Fortune,* October 2, 2006, pp 23–24, 26; G Anders and A Murray, "Behind H-P Chairman's Fall, Clash With a Powerful Director," *The Wall Street Journal,* October 9, 2006, pp A1, A14; and P Burrows, "Controlling the Damage at HP," *BusinessWeek,* October 9, 2006, pp 36–44.

69 R Bhasin, "On Playing Corporate Politics," *Pulp & Paper,* October 1985, p 175. Also see G R Ferris, P L Perrewé, W P Anthony, and D C Gilmore, "Political Skill at Work," *Organizational Dynamics,* Spring 2000, pp 25–37; R M Kramer, "When Paranoia Makes Sense," *Harvard Business Review,* July 2002, pp 62–69; J Barbian, "Office Politics: Swinging with the Sharks," *Training,* July 2002, p 16; L P Frankel, *Nice Girls Don't Get the Corner Office: Unconscious Mistakes Women Make That Sabotage Their Career* (New York: Warner, 2004); T Estep, "Winning the Rat Race," *Training & Development,* January 2005, pp 71–72; and S B Bacharach, "Politically *Proactive,*" *Fast Company,* May 2005, p 93; and R M Kramer, "The Great Intimidators," *Harvard Business Review,* February 2006, pp 88–96.

70 Data from M Weinstein, "Training Today: Q&A," *Training,* January–February 2007, p 7. Also see A Pomeroy, "Politics 101 for Women," *HR Magazine,* June 2006, pp 24, 26; and C Wilbert, "You Schmooze, You Win," *Fast Company,* July–August 2006, p 109.

71 R W Allen, D L Madison, L W Porter, P A Renwick, and B T Mayes, "Organizational Politics: Tactics and Characteristics of Its Actors," *California Management Review,* Fall 1979, p 77. A comprehensive update can be found in K M Kacmar and R A Baron, "Organizational Politics: The State of the Field, Links to Related Processes, and an Agenda for Future Research," in *Research in Personnel and Human Resources Management,* vol. 17, ed G R Ferris (Stamford, CT: JAI Press, 1999), pp 1–39. Also see K A Ahearn, G R Ferris, W A Hochwarter, C Douglas, and A P Ammeter, "Leader Political Skill and Team Performance," *Journal of Management,* no. 3, 2004, pp 309–27; P L Perrewé and D L Nelson, "Gender and Career Success: The Facilitative Role of Political Skill," *Organizational Dynamics,* no. 4, 2004, pp 366–78; G R Ferris, D C Treadway, R W Kolodinsky, W A Hochwarter, C J Kacmar, C Douglas, and D D Frink, "Development and Validation of the Political Skill Inventory," *Journal of Management,* no. 1, 2005, pp 126–52; and T B Lawrence, M K Mauws, B Dyck, and R F Kleysen, "The Politics of Organizational Learning: Integrating Power into the 4I Framework," *Academy of Management Review,* January 2005, pp 180–91.

72 See P M Fandt and G R Ferris, "The Management of Information and Impressions: When Employees Behave Opportunistically," *Organizational Behavior and Human Decision Processes,* February 1990, pp 140–58.

73 First four based on discussion in D R Beeman and T W Sharkey, "The Use and Abuse of Corporate Politics," *Business Horizons,* March–April 1987, pp 26–30. For supportive evidence, see C C Rosen, P E Levy, and R J Hall, "Placing Perceptions of Politics in the Context of the Feedback Environment, Employee Attitudes, and Job Performance," *Journal of Applied Psychology,* January 2006, pp 211–20.

74 A Raia, "Power, Politics, and the Human Resource Professional," *Human Resource Planning,* no. 4, 1985, p 203.

75 A J DuBrin, "Career Maturity, Organizational Rank, and Political Behavioral Tendencies: A Correlational Analysis of Organizational Politics and Career Experience," *Psychological Reports,* October 1988, p 535.

[76] This three-level distinction comes from A T Cobb, "Political Diagnosis: Applications in Organizational Development," *Academy of Management Review,* July 1986, pp 482–96.

[77] An excellent historical and theoretical perspective of coalitions can be found in W B Stevenson, J L Pearce, and L W Porter, "The Concept of 'Coalition' in Organization Theory and Research," *Academy of Management Review,* April 1985, pp 256–68.

[78] L Baum, "The Day Charlie Bradshaw Kissed off Transworld," *BusinessWeek,* September 29, 1986, p 68. Also see C J Loomis, "How the HP Board KO'd Carly," *Fortune,* March 7, 2005, pp 99–102.

[79] See H Ibarra and M Hunter, "How Leaders Create and Use Networks," *Harvard Business Review,* January 2007, pp 40–47; and N Anand and J A Conger, "Capabilities of the Consummate Networker," *Organizational Dynamics,* no. 1, 2007, pp 13–27.

[80] See J T Arnold, "Employee Networks," *HR Magazine,* June 2006, pp 145–52; and C McGlothlen, "Inclusive, Exclusive or Outlawed?" *HR Magazine,* July 2006, pp 107–12.

[81] Allen et al., "Organizational Politics," p 77. Also see D C Treadway, W A Hochwarter, C J Kacmar, and G R Ferris, "Political Will, Political Skill, and Political Behavior," *Journal of Organizational Behavior,* May 2005, pp 229–45.

[82] See the second Q&A in J Welch and S Welch, "Avoiding Strikes—and Unions," *BusinessWeek,* January 15, 2007, p 92; S Berfield, "Mentoring Can Be Messy," *BusinessWeek,* January 29, 2007, pp 80–81; and the second Q&A in J Welch and S Welch, "The Succession Opportunity," *BusinessWeek,* February 5, 2007, p 106.

[83] A Rao, S M Schmidt, and L H Murray, "Upward Impression Management: Goals, Influence Strategies, and Consequences," *Human Relations,* February 1995, p 147. Also see J A Clair, J E Beatty, and T L Maclean, "Out of Sight but Not out of Mind: Managing Invisible Social Identities in the Workplace," *Academy of Management Review,* January 2005, pp 78–95; S L Grover, "The Truth, the Whole Truth, and Nothing but the Truth: The Causes and Management of Workplace Lying," *Academy of Management Executive,* May 2005, pp 148–57; and A Semadar, G Robins, and G R Ferris, "Comparing the Validity of Multiple Social Effectiveness Constructs in the Prediction of Managerial Job Performance," *Journal of Organizational Behavior,* June 2006, pp 443–61.

[84] See W L Gardner and B J Avolio, "The Charismatic Relationship: A Dramaturgical Perspective," *Academy of Management Review,* January 1998, pp 32–58; L Wah, "Managing—Manipulating?—Your Reputation," *Management Review,* October 1998, pp 46–50; M C Bolino, "Citizenship and Impression Management: Good Soldiers or Good Actors?" *Academy of Management Review,* January 1999, pp 82–98; and W H Turnley and M C Bolino, "Achieving Desired Images while Avoiding Undesired Images: Exploring the Role of Self-Monitoring in Impression Management," *Journal of Applied Psychology,* April 2001, pp 351–60.

[85] See K Sulkowicz, "Me, Me, Me, Me, Me," *BusinessWeek,* April 23, 2007, p 14.

[86] Data from "Dressing for Success," *USA Today,* October 24, 2006, p 1B. Also see D Rosato, "The 'Oh, S#&%!' Moment," *Money,* February 2006, pp 126–30; S Westcott, "What's in a Job Title?" *Inc.,* July 2006, pp 31–33; J Lee-St. John, "It's a Brand-You World," *Time,* November 6, 2006, pp 60–61; M Weinstein, "Creative Titles… and Other Ways to Inflate Yourself," *Training,* December 2006, p 12; and S Grobart, "Allow Me to Introduce Myself (Properly)," *Money,* January 2007, pp 40–41.

[87] S Friedman, "What Do You Really Care About? What Are You Most Interested In?" *Fast Company,* March 1999, p 90. Also see E Woyke, "Another Busy Day at the Home Office," *BusinessWeek,* January 1, 2007, p 14.

[88] See S J Wayne and G R Ferris, "Influence Tactics, Affect, and Exchange Quality in Supervisor-Subordinate Interactions: A Laboratory Experiment and Field Study," *Journal of Applied Psychology,* October 1990, pp 487–99. For another version, see Table 1 (p 246) in S J Wayne and R C Liden, "Effects of Impression Management on Performance Ratings: A Longitudinal Study," *Academy of Management Journal,* February 1995, pp 232–60; Also see M C Bolino, J A Varela, B Bande, and W H Turnley, "The Impact of Impression-Management Tactics on Supervisor Ratings of Organizational Citizenship Behavior," *Journal of Organizational Behavior,* May 2006, pp 281–97.

[89] M E Mendenhall and C Wiley, "Strangers in a Strange Land: The Relationship between Expatriate Adjustment and Impression Management," *American Behavioral Scientist,* March 1994, pp 605–20.

[90] T E Becker and S L Martin, "Trying to Look Bad at Work: Methods and Motives for Managing Poor Impressions in Organizations," *Academy of Management Journal,* February 1995, p 191.

[91] Ibid., p 181. Also see M K Duffy, D C Ganster, and M Pagon, "Social Undermining in the Workplace," *Academy of Management Journal,* April 2002, pp 331–51; and M K Duffy, J D Shaw, B J Tepper, and K L Scott, "The Moderating Roles of Self-Esteem and Neuroticism in the Relationship Between Group and Individual Undermining Behavior," *Journal of Applied Psychology,* September 2006, pp 1066—77.

[92] Adapted from ibid., pp 180–81.

[93] Data from G R Ferris, D D Frink, D P S Bhawuk, J Zhou, and D C Gilmore, "Reactions of Diverse Groups to Politics in the Workplace," *Journal of Management,* no. 1, 1996, pp 23–44. For other findings from the same database, see G R Ferris, D D Frink, M C Galang, J Zhou, K M Kacmar, and J L Howard, "Perceptions of Organizational Politics: Prediction, Stress-Related Implications, and Outcomes," *Human Relations,* February 1996, pp 233–66.

[94] A Drory and D Beaty, "Gender Differences in the Perception of Organizational Influence Tactics," *Journal of Organizational Behavior,* May 1991, pp 256–57. Also see B A Pontari and B R Schlenker, "Helping Friends Manage Impressions: We Like Helpful Liars But Respect Nonhelpful Truth Tellers," *Basic and Applied Social Psychology,* June 2006, pp 177–83.

[95] Based on L A Witt, T F Hilton, and W A Hochwarter, "Addressing Politics in Matrix Teams," *Group & Organization*

Management, June 2001, pp 230–47. Also see D S Conner, "Human-Resource Professionals' Perceptions of Organizational Politics as a Function of Experience, Organizational Size, and Perceived Independence," *The Journal of Social Psychology,* December 2006, pp 717–32.

[96] S A Akimoto and D M Sanbonmatsu, "Differences in Self-Effacing Behavior between European and Japanese Americans," *Journal of Cross-Cultural Psychology,* March 1999, pp 172–73.

[97] A Zaleznik, "Real Work," *Harvard Business Review,* January–February 1989, p 60. Also see J Welch and S Welch, "Stop the B.S. Budgets," *BusinessWeek,* June 26, 2006, p 114; and S Sanghi, "How to Handle Boss Who Plays Politics," *The Arizona Republi*c, January 14, 2007, p D2.

[98] C M Koen, Jr, and S M Crow, "Human Relations and Political Skills," *HR Focus,* December 1995, p 11.

[99] Excerpted from R Grover, "How Bob Iger Unchained Disney," *BusinessWeek,* February 5, 2007, pp 74–79.

[100] Excerpted from J Noveck, "Poll: Lying Always Bad, But White Lies Are Frequent," *The Arizona Republic,* July 16, 2006, p A22.

CHAPTER 16

[1] Excerpted from J Welch and S Welch, "Ideas The Welch Way," *BusinessWeek,* January 30, 2006, p 120.

[2] This issue is discussed by S W Spreier, M H Fontaine, and R L Malloy, "Leadership Run Amok," *Harvard Business Review,* June 2006, pp 72–82.

[3] See S Lieberson and J F O'Connor, "Leadership and Organizational Performance: A Study of Large Corporations," *American Sociological Review,* April 1972, pp 117–30. The importance of leadership is also discussed by W Bennis, "The Challenges of Leadership in the Modern World," *American Psychologist,* January 2007, pp 2–5.

[4] Results can be found in K T Dirks, "Trust in Leadership and Team Performance: Evidence from NCAA Basketball," *Journal of Applied Psychology,* December 2000, pp 1004–12; and D Jacobs and L Singell, "Leadership and Organizational Performance: Isolating Links between Managers and Collective Success," *Social Science Research,* June 1993, pp 165–89.

[5] The multiple levels of leadership are discussed by F J Yammarino, F Dansereau, and C J Kennedy, "A Multiple-Level Multidimensional Approach to Leadership: Viewing Leadership through an Elephant's Eye," *Organizational Dynamics,* 2001, pp 149–63.

[6] The four commonalities were identified by P G Northouse, *Leadership: Theory and Practice,* 4th ed (Thousand Oaks, CA: Sage Publications, 2007), p 3.

[7] Ibid.

[8] B M Bass, *Bass & Stogdill's Handbook of Leadership: Theory, Research, and Managerial Applications,* 3rd ed. (New York: Free Press, 1990), p 383.

[9] For a discussion about the differences between leading and managing, see L A Hill, "Becoming the Boss," *Harvard Business Review,* January 2007, pp 49–56; and G Colvin, "Catch a Rising Star," *Fortune,* February 6, 2006, pp 46–50.

[10] See L V Gerstner Jr, *Who Says Elephants Can't Dance?* (New York: HarperBusiness, 2002); and L Bossidy and R Charan, *Execution: The Discipline of Getting Things Done* (New York: Crown Business, 2002).

[11] J Ewing, "Seimens' Culture Clash," *BusinessWeek,* January 29, 2007, p 42.

[12] Leadership development is discussed by H Dolezalek, "Got High Potentials?" *Training,* January–February 2007, pp 18–22; "Best Practices and Outstanding Training Initiatives," *Training,* March 2007, pp 84–86; and J Weber, "The Accidental CEO," *BusinessWeek,* April 23, 2007, pp 64–72.

[13] For complete details, see R M Stogdill, *Handbook of Leadership* (New York: Free Press, 1974); and R D Mann, "A Review of the Relationships between Personality and Performance in Small Groups," *Psychological Bulletin,* July 1959, pp 241–70.

[14] Results can be found in R G Lord, C L De Vader, and G M Alliger, "A Meta-Analysis of the Relation between Personality Traits and Leadership Perceptions: An Application of Validity Generalization Procedures," *Journal of Applied Psychology,* August 1986, pp 402–10. Leadership prototypes are also discussed by M K Ryan and S A Haslam, "The Glass Cliff: Exploring the Dynamics Surrounding the Appointment of Women to Precarious Leadership Positions," *Academy of Management Review,* April 2007, pp 549–72.

[15] Results from this study can be found in F C Brodbeck et al., "Cultural Variation of Leadership Prototypes across 22 European Countries," *Journal of Occupational and Organizational Psychology,* March 2000, pp 1–29.

[16] Results can be found in J M Kouzes and B Z Posner, *The Leadership Challenge* (San Francisco: Jossey-Bass, 1995).

[17] The relationship between culture and integrity is discussed by B W Heineman, Jr., "Avoiding Integrity Land Mines," *Harvard Business Review,* April 2007, pp 100–08.

[18] See W H Bulkeley, "The 50 Women to Watch: Anne Mulchay," *The Wall Street Journal,* November 20, 2006, p R4.

[19] See F J Landy, "Some Historical and Scientific Issues Related to Research on Emotional Intelligence," *Journal of Organizational Behavior,* June 2005, pp 411–24; and E A Locke, "Why Emotional Intelligence Is an Invalid Concept," *Journal of Organizational Behavior,* June 2005, pp 425–32.

[20] Political intelligence is discussed by R M Kramer, "The Great Intimidators," *Harvard Business Review,* February 2006, pp 88–96; An example can be found in C Hymowitz, "Two Football Coaches Have a Lot to Teach Screaming Managers," *The Wall Street Journal,* January 29, 2007, p B1. Supportive research is provided by A Semadar, G Robins, and G R Ferris, "Comparing the Validity of Multiple Social

Effectiveness Constructs in the Prediction of Managerial Job Performance," *Journal of Organizational Behavior,* June 2006, pp 443–61.

[21] Kramer, "The Great Intimidators," pp 95–96.

[22] Results can be found in T A Judge, J E Hono, R Ilies, and M W Gerhardt, "Personality and Leadership: A Qualitative and Quantitative Review," *Journal of Applied Psychology,* August 2002, pp 765–80.

[23] See T A Judge, A E Colbert, and R Ilies, "Intelligence and Leadership: A Quantitative Review and Test of Theoretical Propositions," *Journal of Applied Psychology,* June 2004, pp 542–52.

[24] Kellerman's research can be found in B Kellerman, *Bad Leadership* (Boston: Harvard Business School Press, 2004).

[25] The trait definitions were quoted from ibid. pp 40–46.

[26] The complete story is discussed in B Grow, "Out at Home Depot," *BusinessWeek,* January 15, 2007, pp 56–62; and J S Lublin, A Zimmerman, and C Terhune, "Behind Nardelli's Abrupt Exit," *The Wall Street Journal,* January 4, 2007, pp A1, A12.

[27] Gender and the emergence of leaders was examined by A H Eagly and S J Karau, "Gender and the Emergence of Leaders: A Meta-Analysis," *Journal of Personality and Social Psychology,* May 1991, pp 685–710; and R K Shelly and P T Munroe, "Do Women Engage in Less Task Behavior than Men?" *Sociological Perspectives,* Spring 1999, pp 49–67.

[28] See A H Eagly, S J Karau, and B T Johnson, "Gender and Leadership Style among School Principals: A Meta-Analysis," *Educational Administration Quarterly,* February 1992, pp 76–102.

[29] Supportive findings are contained in J M Twenge, "Changes in Women's Assertiveness in Response to Status and Roles: A Cross-Temporal Meta-Analysis, 1931–1993," *Journal of Personality and Social Psychology,* July 2001, pp 133–45.

[30] For a summary of this research, see R Sharpe, "As Leaders, Women Rule," *BusinessWeek,* November 20, 2000, pp 74–84. Also see "Avon, the Net, and Glass Ceilings," *BusinessWeek,* February 6, 2006, p 104.

[31] See S J Zaccaro, "Trait-Based Perspectives of Leadership," *American Psychologist,* January 2007, pp 6–16; and R Sternberg, "A Systems Model of Leadership," *American Psychologist,* January 2007, pp 34–42.

[32] Executive coaching is discussed by S Labadessa, "Now Go Out and Lead!" *BusinessWeek,* January 8, 2007, pp 72–73.

[33] Leadership development programs are discussed by E White, "Manager Shortage Spurs Small Firms to Grow Their Own," *The Wall Street Journal,* February 15, 2007, pp B1, B4; and G M Spreitzer, "Leading to Grow and Growing to Lead: Leadership Development Lessons from Positive Organizational Studies," *Organizational Dynamics,* November 2006, pp 305–15.

[34] See M Weinstein, "Virtually Integrated," *Training,* April 2007, pp 11–14.

[35] This research is summarized and critiqued by E A Fleishman, "Consideration and Structure: Another Look at Their Role in Leadership Research," in *Leadership: The Multiple-Level Approaches,* eds F Dansereau and F J Yammarino (Stamford, CT: JAI Press, 1998), pp 51–60.

[36] Results can be found in T A Judge, R F Piccolo, and R Ilies, "The Forgotten Ones? The Validity of Consideration and Initiating Structure in Leadership Research," *Journal of Applied Psychology,* February 2004, pp 36–51.

[37] See V H Vroom, "Leadership," in *Handbook of Industrial and Organizational Psychology,* ed M D Dunnette (Chicago: Rand McNally, 1976).

[38] Supportive results can be found in F Shipper, R C Hoffman, and D M Rotondo, "Does the 360 Feedback Process Create Actionable Knowledge Equally Across Cultures?" *Academy of Management Learning & Education,* March 2007, pp 33–50.

[39] For more on this theory, see F E Fiedler, "A Contingency Model of Leadership Effectiveness," in *Advances in Experimental Social Psychology,* vol. 1, ed L Berkowitz (New York: Academic Press, 1964); and F E Fiedler, *A Theory of Leadership Effectiveness* (New York: McGraw-Hill, 1967).

[40] See L H Peters, D D Hartke, and J T Pohlmann, "Fiedler's Contingency Theory of Leadership: An Application of the Meta-Analyses Procedures of Schmidt and Hunter," *Psychological Bulletin,* March 1985, pp 274–85. The meta-analysis was conducted by C A Schriesheim, B J Tepper, and L A Tetrault, "Least Preferred Co-Worker Score, Situational Control, and Leadership Effectiveness: A Meta-Analysis of Contingency Model Performance Predictions," *Journal of Applied Psychology,* August 1994, pp 561–73.

[41] See the related discussion in J R Hackman and R Wageman, "Asking the Right Questions about Leadership," *American Psychologist,* January 2007, pp 43–47; and V H Vroom and A G Jago, "The Role of the Situation in Leadership," *American Psychologist,* January 2007, pp 17–24.

[42] B Groysberg, A N McLean, and N Nohria, "Are Leaders Portable?" *Harvard Business Review,* May 2006, pp 95, 97.

[43] See B J Avolio, "Promoting More Integrative Strategies for Leadership Theory-Building," *American Psychologist,* January 2007, pp 25–33; and N Byrnes and D Kiley, "Hello, You Must Be Going," *BusinessWeek,* February 12, 2007, pp 30–32.

[44] L Pleven, "After the Storm at AIG," *The Wall Street Journal,* February 2, 2007, p B1.

[45] For more detail on this theory, see R J House, "A Path–Goal Theory of Leader Effectiveness," *Administrative Science Quarterly,* September 1971, pp 321–38.

[46] This research is summarized by R J House, "Path–Goal Theory of Leadership: Lessons, Legacy, and a Reformulated Theory," *Leadership Quarterly,* Autumn 1996, pp 323–52.

[47] See ibid.

[48] Results can be found in P M Podsakoff, S B MacKenzie, M Ahearne, and W H Bommer, "Searching for a Needle in a Haystack: Trying to Identify the Illusive Moderators of Leadership Behaviors," *Journal of Management,* 1995, pp 422–70.

[49] For a complete description of this theory, see B J Avolio and B M Bass, *A Manual for Full-Range Leadership Development* (Binghamton, NY: Center for Leadership Studies, 1991). The manual is now published by www.mindgarden.com.

[50] Results can be found in A H Eagly, M C Johannesen-Schmidt, and M L van Engen, "Transformational, Transactional, and Laissez-Faire Leadership Styles: A Meta-Analysis Comparing Women and Men," *Psychological Bulletin,* June 2003, pp 569–91.

[51] A definition and description of transactional leadership is provided by J Antonakis and R J House, "The Full-Range Leadership Theory: The Way Forward," in *Transformational and Charismatic Leadership: The Road Ahead,* eds B J Avolio and F J Yammarino (New York: JAI Press, 2002), pp 3–34.

[52] A Carter, "It's Norman Time," *BusinessWeek,* May 29, 2006, p 68.

[53] U R Dumdum, K B Lowe, and B J Avolio, "A Meta-Analysis of Transformational and Transactional Leadership Correlates of Effectiveness and Satisfaction: An Update and Extension," in *Transformational and Charismatic Leadership: The Road Ahead,* eds B J Avolio and F J Yammarino (New York: JAI Press, 2002), p 38.

[54] Supportive research is summarized by Antonakis and House, "The Full-Range Leadership Theory."

[55] Carter, "It's Norman Time," pp 65, 67.

[56] Supportive results can be found in T M Hautala, "The Relationship between Personality and Transformational Leadership," *Journal of Management Development,* 2006, pp 777–94; and J E Bono and T A Judge, "Personality and Transformational and Transactional Leadership: A Meta-Analysis," *Journal of Applied Psychology,* October 2004, pp 901–10.

[57] See Eagly, Johannesen-Schmidt, and van Engen, "Transformational, Transactional, and Laissez-Faire Leadership Style."

[58] See M Greer, "The Science of Savoir Faire," *Monitor on Psychology,* January 2005, pp 28–30; and T Divir, D Eden, B J Avolio, and B Shamir, "Impact of Transformational Leadership on Follower Development and Performance: A Field Experiment," *Academy of Management Journal,* August 2002, pp 735–44.

[59] These definitions are derived from R Kark, B Shamir, and C Chen, "The Two Faces of Transformational Leadership: Empowerment and Dependency," *Journal of Applied Psychology,* April 2003, pp 246–55.

[60] B Nanus, *Visionary Leadership* (San Francisco: Jossey-Bass, 1992), p 8.

[61] The visioning process is discussed by D Ancona, T W Malone, W J Orlikowski, and P M Senge, "In Praise of the Incomplete Leader," *Harvard Business Review,* February 2007, pp 92–100; and R S Kaplan, "What to Ask," *Harvard Business Review,* January 2007, pp 86–95.

[62] See W H Bulkeley, "Back from the Brink: Mulcahy Leads a Renaissance at Xerox by Emphasizing Color, Customers, and Costs," *The Wall Street Journal,* April 24, 2006, pp B1, B3.

[63] See D Welch, "How Sweet It Is at Magna," *BusinessWeek,* April 16, 2007, pp 36–37.

[64] Supportive research is summarized in R Kark and D V Dijk, "Motivation to Lead, Motivation to Follow: The Role of the Self-Regulatory Focus in Leadership Processes," *Academy of Management Review,* April 2007, pp 500–28.

[65] Supportive results can be found in B van Knippenberg and D Van Knippenberg, "Leader Self-Sacrifice and Leadership Effectiveness: The Moderating Role of Leader Prototypicality," *Journal of Applied Psychology,* January 2005, pp 25–37; Y Beson and B J Avolio, "Transformational Leadership and the Dissemination of Organizational Goals: A Case Study of a Telecommunication Firm," *Leadership Quarterly,* October 2004, pp 625–46.

[66] Results can be found in U R Dumdum, K B Lowe, and B J Avolio, "A Meta-Analysis of Transformational and Transactional Leadership Correlates of Effectiveness and Satisfaction: An Update and Extension," in *Transactional and Charismatic Leadership: The Road Ahead,* eds B J Avolio and F J Yammarino (New York: JAI, 2002), pp 35–66.

[67] See K B Lowe, K G Kroeck and N Sivasubramaniam, "Effectiveness Correlates of Transformational and Transactional Leadership: A Meta-Analytic Review of the MLQ Literature," *Leadership Quarterly,* 1996, pp 385–425.

[68] Results can be found in T A Judge and R F Piccolo, "Transformational and Transactional Leadership: A Meta-Analytic Test of Their Relative Validity," *Journal of Applied Psychology,* October 2004, pp 755–68.

[69] See A J Towler, "Effects of Charismatic Influence Training on Attitudes, Behavior, and Performance," *Personnel Psychology,* Summer 2003, pp 363–81; and M Frese and S Beimel, "Action Training for Charismatic Leadership: Two Evaluations of Studies of a Commercial Training Module on Inspirational Communication of a Vision," *Personnel Psychology,* Autumn 2003, pp 671–97.

[70] These recommendations were derived from J M Howell and B J Avolio, "The Ethics of Charismatic Leadership: Submission or Liberation?" *Academy of Management Executive,* May 1992, pp 43–54.

[71] See F Dansereau Jr, G Graen, and W Haga, "A Vertical Dyad Linkage Approach to Leadership within Formal Organizations," *Organizational Behavior and Human Performance,* February 1975, pp 46–78; and R M Dienesch and R C Liden, "Leader–Member Exchange Model of Leadership: A Critique and Further Development," *Academy of Management Review,* July 1986, pp 618–34.

[72] These descriptions were taken from D Duchon, S G Green, and T D Taber, "Vertical Dyad Linkage: A Longitudinal Assessment of Antecedents, Measures, and Consequences,"

Journal of Applied Psychology, February 1986, pp 56–60.

[73] Supportive results can be found in Z Chen, W Lam, and J A Zhong, "Leader-Member Exchange and Member Performance: A New Look at Individual-Level Negative Feedback-Seeking Behavior and Team-Level Empowerment Climate," *Journal of Applied Psychology,* January 2007, pp 202–12; R C Liden, B Erdogan, S J Wayne, and R T Sparrowe, "Leader-Member Exchange, Differentiation, and Task Interdependence: Implications for Individual and Group Performance," *Journal of Organizational Behavior,* September 2006, pp 723–46; and E K Pellegrini and T A Scandura, "Leader-Member Exchange (LMX), Paternalism, and Delegation in the Turkish Business Culture: An Empirical Investigation," *Journal of International Business Studies,* March 2006, pp 264–79.

[74] Results can be found in R Ilies, J D Nahrgang, and F P Morgeson, "Leader-Member Exchange and Citizenship Behaviors: A Meta-Analysis," *Journal of Applied Psychology,* January 2007, pp 269–77.

[75] A turnover study was conducted by G B Graen, R C Liden, and W Hoel, "Role of Leadership in the Employee Withdrawal Process," *Journal of Applied Psychology,* December 1982, pp 868–72. The career progress study was conducted by M Wakabayashi and G B Graen, "The Japanese Career Progress Study: A 7-Year Follow-Up," *Journal of Applied Psychology,* November 1984, pp 603–14.

[76] See D O Adebayo and I B Udegbe, "Gender in the Boss–Subordinate Relationship: A Nigerian Study," *Journal of Organizational Behavior,* June 2004, pp 515–25.

[77] These recommendations were derived from G C Mage, "Leading Despite Your Boss," *HR Magazine,* September 2003, pp 139–44.

[78] R J House and R N Aditya, "The Social Scientific Study of Leadership Quo Vadis?" *Journal of Management,* 1997, p 457.

[79] A thorough discussion of shared leadership is provided by C L Pearce "The Future of Leadership: Combining Vertical and Shared Leadership Transform Knowledge Work," *Academy of Management Executive,* February 2004, pp 47–59.

[80] Shared leadership is discussed by S A Miles and M D Watkins, "The Leadership Team: Complementary Strengths or Conflicting Agendas?" *Harvard Business Review,* April 2007, pp 90–98.

[81] This research is summarized in B J Avolio et al., "Leadership Models, Methods, and Application." Also see S J Zaccaro, A L Rittman, and M A Marks, "Team Leadership," *Leadership Quarterly,* 2001, pp 451–83.

[82] See J Collins, *Good to Great: Why Some Companies Make the Leap and Others Don't* (New York: Harper Business, 2001).

[83] J Collins, "Level 5 Leadership: The Triumph of Humility and Fierce Resolve," *Harvard Business Review,* January 2001, p 68.

[84] R Grover, "How Bob Iger Unchained Disney," *BusinessWeek,* February 5, 2007, p 75.

[85] An overall summary of servant-leadership is provided by L C Spears, *Reflections on Leadership: How Robert K Greenleaf's Theory of Servant-Leadership Influenced Today's Top Management Thinkers* (New York: John Wiley & Sons, 1995).

[86] J Mackey, "'I No Longer Want to Work for Money,'" *Fast Company,* February 2007, p 112.

[87] J Stuart, *Fast Company,* September 1999, p 114.

[88] The role of followers is discussed by J M Howell and B Shamir, "The Role of Followers in the Charismatic Leadership Process: Relationships and Their Consequences," *Academy of Management Review,* January 2005, pp 96–112.

[89] This point was made by J J Gabarro and J P Kotter, "Managing Your Boss," *Harvard Business Review,* January 2005, pp 92–99.

[90] See L Bossidy, "What Your Leader Expects of You and What You Should Expect in Return," *Harvard Business Review,* April 2007, pp 58–65.

[91] See R Goffee and G Jones, "Followership: It's Personal, Too," *Harvard Business Review,* December 2001, p 148.

[92] This checklist was proposed by Gabarro and Kotter, "Managing Your Boss."

[93] See the related discussion in B George, P Sims, A N McLean, and D Mayer, "Discovering Your Authentic Leadership," *Harvard Business Review,* February 2007, pp 129–38.

[94] The following suggestions were discussed by Gabarro and Kotter, "Managing Your Boss."

[95] Excerpted from N Byrnes, "Avon: More Than Cosmetic Changes," *BusinessWeek,* March 12, 2007, pp 62–63.

[96] Excerpted from C Haddad and A Barrett, "A Whistle-Blower Rocks an Industry," *BusinessWeek,* June 24, 2002, pp 126, 128.

CHAPTER 17

[1] Excerpted from A Bianco, "Wal-Mart's Midlife Crisis," *BusinessWeek,* April 30, 2007, pp 46–56. For more on Wal-Mart, see B Gimbel, "Attack of the Wal-Martyrs," *Fortune,* December 11, 2006, pp 125–30; J Birger, "The Unending Woes of Lee Scott," *Fortune,* January 22, 2007, pp 118–22; and D Leonard, "How Wal-Mart Got the Love E-mail," *Fortune,* April 30, 2007, p 52.

[2] Data from J Useem, "The Big . . . Get Bigger," *Fortune,* April 30, 2007, pp 81–84.

[3] C I Barnard, *The Functions of the Executive* (Cambridge, MA: Harvard University Press, 1938), p 73. Also see T Bakken and T Hernes, "Organizing IS Both a Verb and a Noun: Weick Meets Whitehead," *Organization Studies,* November 2006, pp 1599–616; and T R Schatzki, "On Organizations as They Happen," *Organization Studies,* December 2006, pp 1863–73.

[4] Drawn from E H Schein, *Organizational Psychology,* 3rd ed (Englewood Cliffs, NJ: Prentice Hall, 1980), pp 12–15.

5 B Helm, "Saving Starbucks' Soul," *BusinessWeek,* April 9, 2007, p 60. Also see A S Wellner, "Gary Heavin Is on a Mission from God," *Inc.,* October 2006, pp 116–123.

6 See M Cecere, "Drawing the Lines," *Harvard Business Review,* November 2001, p 24.

7 See H J Leavitt, "Why Hierarchies Thrive," *Harvard Business Review,* March 2003, pp 96–102; N Bennett and S A Miles, "Second in Command: The Misunderstood Role of the Chief Operating Officer," *Harvard Business Review,* May 2006, pp 71–78; see the first Q&A in J Welch and S Welch, "Are You a Boss-Hater?" *BusinessWeek,* July 3, 2006, p 136; and the first Q&A in J Welch and S Welch, "A Twisted Chain of Command," *BusinessWeek,* September 18, 2006, p 116.

8 For an excellent overview of the span of control concept, see D D Van Fleet and A G Bedeian, "A History of the Span of Management," *Academy of Management Review,* July 1977, pp 356–72. Also see E E Lawler III and J R Galbraith, "New Roles for the Staff: Strategic Support and Service," in *Organizing for the Future: The New Logic for Managing Complex Organizations,* eds J R Galbraith, E E Lawler III, and Associates (San Francisco: Jossey-Bass, 1993), pp 65–83.

9 A contrary example involving Southwest Airlines can be found in J Pfeffer, "How Companies Get Smart," *Business 2.0,* January–February 2005, p 74.

10 M Koslowsky, "Staff/Line Distinctions in Job and Organizational Commitment," *Journal of Occupational Psychology,* June 1990, pp 167–73.

11 For a discussion about organizational metaphors, see C Oswick and P Jones, "Beyond Correspondence? Metaphor in Organization Theory," *Academy of Management Review,* April 2006, pp 483–85; and J Cornelissen, "Metaphor in Organization Theory: Progress and the Past," *Academy of Management Review,* April 2006, pp 485–88.

12 For open-system perspectives, see G Sewell and J R Barker, "Coercion Versus Care: Using Irony to Make Sense of Organizational Surveillance," *Academy of Management Review,* October 2006, pp 934–61; A W Richter, M A West, R Van Dick, and J F Dawson, "Boundary Spanners' Identification, Intergroup Contact, and Effective Intergroup Relations," *Academy of Management Journal,* December 2006, pp 1252–69; and A Deutschman, "Open Wide: The Traditional Business Organization Meets Democracy," *Fast Company,* March 2007, pp 40–41.

13 A management-oriented discussion of general systems theory—an interdisciplinary attempt to integrate the various fragmented sciences—may be found in K E Boulding, "General Systems Theory—The Skeleton of Science," *Management Science,* April 1956, pp 197–208. For more recent systems-related ideas, see A M Webber, "How Business Is a Lot like Life," *Fast Company,* April 2001, pp 130–36; E Bonabeau and C Meyer, "Swarm Intelligence: A Whole New Way to Think about Business," *Harvard Business Review,* May 2001, pp 106–14; S Godin, "Survival Is Not Enough," *Fast Company,* January 2002, pp 90–94; E K Clemons and J A Santamaria, "Maneuver Warfare: Can Modern Military Strategy Lead You to Victory?" *Harvard Business Review,* April 2002, pp 56–65;

C Oswick, T Keenoy, and D Grant, "Metaphor and Analogical Reasoning in Organization Theory: Beyond Orthodoxy," *Academy of Management Review,* April 2002, pp 294–303; and D Ticoll, "Get Self-Organized," *Harvard Business Review,* September 2004, pp 18–19.

14 See L Buchanan, "No More Metaphors," *Harvard Business Review,* March 2005, p 19; and L Prusak, "The Madness of Individuals," *Harvard Business Review,* June 2005, p 22.

15 For updates, See A E Raz and J Fadlon, "Managerial Culture, Workplace Culture and Situated Curricula in Organizational Learning," *Organization Studies,* February 2006, pp 165–82; N Roome and F Wijen, "Stakeholder Power and Organizational Learning in Corporate Environmental Management," *Organization Studies,* February 2006, pp 235–63; N Ron, R Lipshitz, and M Popper, "How Organizations Learn: Post-Flight Reviews in an F-16 Fighter Squadron," *Organization Studies,* August 2006, pp 1069–89; J Frahm and K Brown, "Developing Communicative Competencies for a Learning Organization," *Journal of Management Development,* no. 3, 2006, pp 201–12; and L Baird and D Griffin, "Adaptability and Responsiveness: The Case for Dynamic Learning, *Organizational Dynamics,* no. 4, 2006, pp 372–83.

16 R M Fulmer and J B Keys, "A Conversation with Peter Senge: New Development in Organizational Learning," *Organizational Dynamics,* Autumn 1998, p 35.

17 This definition was based on D A Garvin, "Building a Learning Organization," *Harvard Business Review,* July–August 1993, pp 78–91.

18 R D Hof, "How to Hit a Moving Target," *BusinessWeek,* August 21–28, 2006, p 82. Also see P Galagan, "Old School Gets New Role," *Training and Development,* November 2006, pp 37–39.

19 T A Stewart, "Welcome to the Revolution," *Fortune,* December 13, 1993, p 66.

20 See B Morris, "The New Rules," *Fortune,* July 24, 2006, pp 70–87; B Demil and X Lecocq, "Neither Market nor Hierarchy nor Network: The Emergence of Bazaar Governance," *Organization Studies,* October 2006, pp 1447–66; K Gurchiek, "Robots Take on Roles in Public, Workforce," *HR Magazine,* February 2007, pp 26, 32; and R Kurzweil, "How to Predict the Future," *Inc.,* February 2007, pp 71–72.

21 See J R Galbraith and E E Lawler III, "Effective Organizations: Using the New Logic of Organizing," in *Organizing for the Future: The New Logic for Managing Complex Organizations,* eds J R Galbraith, E E Lawler III, and Associates (San Francisco: Jossey-Bass, 1993).

22 As quoted in P Sellers, "Now Is the Time to Invest," *Fortune,* October 16, 2006, p 142. For more on Avon's turnaround strategy, see N Byrnes, "Avon: More Than Cosmetic Changes," *BusinessWeek,* March 12, 2007, pp 62–63. Also see P Glader, "It's Not Easy Being Lean," *The Wall Street Journal,* June 19, 2006, pp B1, B3.

23 See D McGinn, "Re-engineering 2.0," *Newsweek,* November 22, 2004, p 59; and M Hammer, "The Process Audit," *Harvard Business Review,* April 2007, pp 111–23.

24 R Jacob, "The Struggle to Create an Organization for the 21st Century," *Fortune,* April 3, 1995, pp 91–92.

25 See S Sonnesyn Brooks, "Managing a Horizontal Revolution," *HR Magazine,* June 1995, pp 52–58; and M Hequet, "Flat and Happy," *Training,* April 1995, pp 29–34.

26 See J Hyatt, "The Soul of a New Team," *Fortune,* June 12, 2006, pp 134–41; T J Mullaney, "The Doctor Is (Plugged) In," *BusinessWeek,* June 26, 2006, pp 56, 58; M R della Cava, "Computers, Quiche, and Quiet," *USA Today,* October 5, 2006, pp 1D–2D; R Yu, "Work Away from Work Gets Easier with Technology," *USA Today,* November 28, 2006, p 8B; and K Maney, "Mass Collaboration Could Change Way Companies Operate," *USA Today,* December 27, 2006, p 4B.

27 For example, see A Fisher, "Playing for Keeps: Capital One (No. 84)," *Fortune,* January 22, 2007, p 87.

28 C Handy, *The Hungry Spirit* (New York: Broadway Books, 1998), p 186. (Emphasis added.)

29 See S Hamm, "Linux Inc.," *BusinessWeek,* January 31, 2005, pp 60–68; A R Winger, "Face-to-Face Communication: Is It Really Necessary in a Digitizing World?" *Business Horizons,* May–June 2005, pp 247–53; and D Ernst and J Bamford, "Your Alliances Are Too Stable," *Harvard Business Review,* June 2005, pp 133–41.

30 K Cameron, "Critical Questions in Assessing Organizational Effectiveness," *Organizational Dynamics,* Autumn 1980, p 70.

31 See, for example, R O Brinkerhoff and D E Dressler, *Productivity Measurement: A Guide for Managers and Evaluators* (Newbury Park, CA: Sage Publications, 1990); and J Bersin, "Organizational Effectiveness Is Within Your Reach," *Training,* August 2006, p 14.

32 See S Levy and B Stone, "The New Wisdom of the Web," *Newsweek,* April 3, 2006, pp 46–53; S D Anthony, M Eyring, and L Gibson, "Mapping Your Innovation Strategy," *Harvard Business Review,* May 2006, pp 104–113; D Kirkpatrick, "Life in a Connected World," *Fortune,* July 10, 2006, pp 98–100; and E Schonfeld, "Web 2.0 Around the World," *Business 2.0,* August 2006, pp 105–9.

33 Data from M Maynard, "Toyota Promises Custom Order in 5 Days," *USA Today,* August 6, 1999, p 1B.

34 See E Bazar, "Red Cross Announces Restructuring to Restore Image," *USA Today,* October 31, 2006, p 3A.

35 See M G Wilson, D M DeJoy, R J Vandenberg, H A Richardson, and A L McGrath, "Work Characteristics and Employee Health and Well-Being: Test of a Model of Healthy Work Organization," *Journal of Occupational and Organizational Psychology,* December 2004, pp 565–88; and the first Q&A in J Welch and S Welch, "How Healthy Is Your Company?" *BusinessWeek,* May 8, 2006, p 126.

36 "Interview: M Scott Peck," *Business Ethics,* March–April 1994, p 17. Also see B George, P Sims, A N McLean, and D Mayer, "Discovering Your Authentic Leadership," *Harvard Business Review,* February 2007, pp 129–38; and G E Mangurian, "Realizing What You're Made Of," *Harvard Business Review,* March 2007, pp 125–30.

37 Cameron, "Critical Questions in Assessing Organizational Effectiveness," p 67. Also see C Fishman, "The Wal-Mart You Don't Know," *Fast Company,* December 2003, pp 68–80; and A Reinhardt, "Will Rewiring Nokia Spark Growth?" *BusinessWeek,* February 14, 2005, pp 46–47.

38 See R J Martinez and P M Norman, "Whither Reputation? The Effects of Different Stakeholders," *Business Horizons,* September–October 2004, pp 25–32; T M Jones, W Felps, and G A Bigley, "Ethical Theory and Stakeholder-Related Decisions: The Role of Stakeholder Culture," *Academy of Management Review,* January 2007, pp 137–55; J Brugmann and C K Prahalad, "Cocreating Business's New Social Compact," *Harvard Business Review,* February 2007, pp 80–90; E Iwata, "Businesses Grow More Socially Conscious," *USA Today,* February 14, 2007, p 3B; and J Carey, "Hugging the Tree-Huggers," *BusinessWeek,* March 12, 2007, pp 66–68.

39 Data from M Krantz, "Exxon Posts World-Record Earnings," *USA Today,* February 2, 2007, p 3B.

40 See N C Roberts and P J King, "The Stakeholder Audit Goes Public," *Organizational Dynamics,* Winter 1989, pp 63–79; and I Henriques and P Sadorsky, "The Relationship between Environmental Commitment and Managerial Perceptions of Stakeholder Importance," *Academy of Management Journal,* February 1999, pp 87–99.

41 See C Ostroff and N Schmitt, "Configurations of Organizational Effectiveness and Efficiency," *Academy of Management Journal,* December 1993, pp 1345–61; and A Fisher, "America's Most Admired Companies," *Fortune,* March 6, 2006, pp 65–76.

42 M Der Hovanesian, "Dimon's Grand Design," *BusinessWeek,* March 28, 2005, p 98.

43 K S Cameron, "Effectiveness as Paradox: Consensus and Conflict in Conceptions of Organizational Effectiveness," *Management Science,* May 1986, p 542.

44 Alternative effectiveness criteria are discussed in ibid.; A G Bedeian, "Organization Theory: Current Controversies, Issues, and Directions," in *International Review of Industrial and Organizational Psychology,* eds C L Cooper and I T Robertson (New York: John Wiley & Sons, 1987), pp 1–33; and M Keeley, "Impartiality and Participant-Interest Theories of Organizational Effectiveness," *Administrative Science Quarterly,* March 1984, pp 1–25.

45 See S S Carty, "GM Offers Buyouts to 126,000," *USA Today,* March 23, 2006, p 1A; S S Carty, "Ford Cuts Output Way Back," *USA Today,* August 21, 2006, p 6B; and H Maurer, "*Et Tu,* Chrysler," *BusinessWeek,* February 26, 2007, p 36.

46 For an update, see S Armour, "Enron Woes Reverberate Through Lives," *USA Today,* January 26, 2006, pp 1B–2B.

47 For more on Dell's problems, see N Byrnes, P Burrows, and L Lee, "Dark Days at Dell," *BusinessWeek,* September 4, 2006, pp 26–29; L Lee and P Burrows, "Is Dell Too Big for Michael Dell?" *BusinessWeek,* February 12, 2007, p 33; M Bartiromo, "Will Dell Be a Comeback Kid?" *BusinessWeek,* February 26, 2007, p 128; and D Whitford, "Uh…Maybe I Should Drive," *Fortune,* April 30, 2007, pp 124–28.

48 D N Sull, "Why Good Companies Go Bad," *Harvard Business Review,* July–August 1999, pp 42–52. Also see H B Cohen, "The Performance Paradox," *Academy of Management Executive,* August 1998, pp 30–40.

49 M A Mone, W McKinley, and V L Barker III, "Organizational Decline and Innovation: A Contingency Framework," *Academy of Management Review,* January 1998, p 117.

50 P Lorange and R T Nelson, "How to Recognize—and Avoid—Organizational Decline," *Sloan Management Review,* Spring 1987, p 47. Also see M L Marks and K P De Meuse, "Resizing the Organization: Maximizing the Gain while Minimizing the Pain of Layoffs, Divestitures, and Closings," *Organizational Dynamics,* no. 1, 2005, pp 19–35.

51 Excerpted from ibid., pp 43–45. Also see E E Lawler III and J R Galbraith, "Avoiding the Corporate Dinosaur Syndrome," *Organizational Dynamics,* Autumn 1994, pp 5–17; and K Labich, "Why Companies Fail," *Fortune,* November 14, 1994, pp 52–68.

52 For details, see K S Cameron, M U Kim, and D A Whetten, "Organizational Effects of Decline and Turbulence," *Administrative Science Quarterly,* June 1987, pp 222–40. Also see, G Probst and S Raisch, "Organizational Crisis: The Logic of Failure," *Academy of Management Executive,* February 2005, pp 90–105.

53 For success stories, see B Stone, "Motorola's Good Call," *Newsweek,* March 14, 2005, pp 42–43; and Z Ruimin, "Raising Haier," *Harvard Business Review,* February 2007, pp 141–46.

54 Data from V L Barker III and P W Patterson Jr. "Top Management Team Tenure and Top Manager Causal Attributions at Declining Firms Attempting Turnarounds," *Group & Organization Management,* September 1996, pp 304–36. Also see J L Bower and C G Gilbert, "How Managers' Everyday Decisions Create or Destroy Your Company's Strategy," *Harvard Business Review,* February 2007, pp 72–79.

55 See H Ma and R Karri, "Leaders Beware: Some Sure Ways to Lose Your Competitive Advantage," *Organizational Dynamics,* no. 1, 2005, pp 63–76; and J Pfeffer, "The Agony of Victory," *Business 2.0,* January–February 2007, p 62.

56 B Treasurer, "How Risk-Taking Really Works," *Training,* January 2000, p 43.

57 See J L Roberts and E Thomas, "Enron's Dirty Laundry," *Newsweek,* March 11, 2002, pp 22–28; Also see N Varchaver, "Long Island Confidential," *Fortune,* November 27, 2006, pp 172–86.

58 A Taylor III, "Why Toyota Keeps Getting Better and Better and Better," *Fortune,* November 19, 1990, pp 66–67.

59 C Fishman, "No Satisfaction," *Fast Company,* January 2007, p 84. Also see H Maurer, "Detroit: Red Ink City," *BusinessWeek,* February 12, 2007, p 29; D Welch, "Why Toyota Is Afraid of Being Number One," *BusinessWeek,* March 5, 2007, pp 42–50; and I Rowley, "Fighting To Stay Humble," *BusinessWeek,* March 5, 2007, p 50.

60 For updates, see J M Pennings, "Structural Contingency Theory: A Reappraisal," *Research in Organizational Behavior* vol. 14 (Greenwich, CT: JAI Press, 1992), pp 267–309; M Goold and A Campbell, "Do You Have a Well-Designed Organization?" *Harvard Business Review,* March 2002, pp 117–24; and J A A Sillince, "A Contingency Theory of Rhetorical Congruence," *Academy of Management Review,* July 2005, pp 608–21.

61 See G J Lewis and B Harvey, "Perceived Environmental Uncertainty: The Extension of Miller's Scale to the Natural Environment," *Journal of Management Studies,* March 2001, pp 201–34.

62 D Kirkpatrick, "The Reigning Queen of Tech," *Fortune,* May 16, 2005, p 40.

63 See C B Gibson and J Birkinshaw, "The Antecedents, Consequences, and Mediating Role of Organizational Ambidexterity," *Academy of Management Journal,* April 2004, pp 209–26; C A O'Reilly III and M L Tushman, "The Ambidextrous Organization," *Harvard Business Review,* April 2004, pp 74–81; and E E Lawler III and C G Worley, *Built to Change: How to Achieve Sustained Organizational Effectiveness* (San Francisco: Jossey-Bass, 2006).

64 P R Lawrence and J W Lorsch, *Organization and Environment* (Homewood, IL: Richard D Irwin, 1967), p 157.

65 For example, see A Barrett, "J&J: Reinventing How It Invents," *BusinessWeek,* April 17, 2006, pp 60–61; and A Weintraub, "Under the Weather At J&J," *BusinessWeek,* April 23, 2007, pp 80, 82.

66 For more on 3M, see M Arndt, "3M's Rising Star," *BusinessWeek,* April 12, 2004, pp 62–74.

67 K Deveny, "Bag Those Fries, Squirt That Ketchup, Fry That Fish," *BusinessWeek,* October 13, 1986, p 86; Also see P Burrows, "Servers as High As an Elephant's Eye," *BusinessWeek,* June 12, 2006, pp 73–74.

68 See D A Morand, "The Role of Behavioral Formality and Informality in the Enactment of Bureaucratic versus Organic Organizations," *Academy of Management Review,* October 1995, pp 831–72; See the story on Google in A Lashinsky, "Chaos By Design," *Fortune,* October 2, 2006, pp 86–98.

69 A Deutschman, "The Fabric of Creativity," *Fast Company,* December 2004, p 59. Also see H Collingwood, "Peer-to-Peer Promotion," *Business 2.0,* April 2006, p 86.

70 See G P Huber, C C Miller, and W H Glick, "Developing More Encompassing Theories about Organizations: The Centralization-Effectiveness Relationship as an Example," *Organization Science,* no. 1, 1990, pp 11–40; and C Handy, "Balancing Corporate Power: A New Federalist Paper," *Harvard Business Review,* November–December 1992, pp 59–72. Examples of decentralization can be found in P Coy, "More Than One Way to Build a Home," *BusinessWeek,* April 3, 2006, p 74; D Brady, "The Reinvention of Martha Stewart," *BusinessWeek,* November 6, 2006, pp 76–80; and D Welch, "Looser Rules, Happier Clients," *BusinessWeek,* March 5, 2007, p 62.

71 P Kaestle, "A New Rationale for Organizational Structure," *Planning Review,* July–August 1990, p 22. Also see M E Raynor and J L Bower, "Lead from the Center: How to Manage Divisions Dynamically," *Harvard Business Review,* May 2001, pp 92–100; and R F Freeland, "When Organizational Messiness Works," *Harvard Business Review,* May 2002, pp 24–25.

[72] Details of this study can be found in T Burns and G M Stalker, *The Management of Innovation* (London: Tavistock, 1961); Also see N Nohria, "Survival of the Adaptive," *Harvard Business Review,* May 2006, p 23.

[73] D J Gillen and S J Carroll, "Relationship of Managerial Ability to Unit Effectiveness in More Organic versus More Mechanistic Departments," *Journal of Management Studies,* November 1985, pp 674–75.

[74] J D Sherman and H L Smith, "The Influence of Organizational Structure on Intrinsic versus Extrinsic Motivation," *Academy of Management Journal,* December 1984, p 883.

[75] See J A Courtright, G T Fairhurst, and L E Rogers, "Interaction Patterns in Organic and Mechanistic Systems," *Academy of Management Journal,* December 1989, pp 773–802.

[76] W D Sine, H Mitsuhashi, and D A Kirsch, "Revisiting Burns and Stalker: Formal Structure and New Venture Performance in Emerging Economic Sectors," *Academy of Management Journal,* February 2006, p 130.

[77] See J Woodward, *Industrial Organization: Theory and Practice* (London: Oxford University Press, 1965); and P D Collins and F Hull, "Technology and Span of Control: Woodward Revisited," *Journal of Management Studies,* March 1986, pp 143–64.

[78] See L W Fry, "Technology-Structure Research: Three Critical Issues," *Academy of Management Journal,* September 1982, pp 532–52.

[79] Ibid., p 548. Also see R Reese, "Redesigning for Dial Tone: A Socio-Technical Systems Case Study," *Organizational Dynamics,* Autumn 1995, pp 80–90.

[80] For example, see C C Miller, W H Glick, Y-D Wang, and G P Huber, "Understanding Technology-Structure Relationships: Theory Development and Meta-Analytic Theory Testing," *Academy of Management Journal,* June 1991, pp 370–99; and K H Roberts and M Grabowski, "Organizations, Technology and Structuring," in *Handbook of Organization Studies,* eds S R Clegg, C Hardy, and W R Nord (Thousand Oaks, CA: Sage Publications, 1996), pp 409–23.

[81] For interesting reading, see G B West, "Breakthrough Ideas for 2007: Innovation and Growth: Size Matters," *Harvard Business Review,* February 2007, pp 34–35. Also see C Edwards, "Intel Sharpens Its Offensive Game," *BusinessWeek,* July 31, 2007, p 60.

[82] The phrase "small is beautiful" was coined by the late British economist E F Schumacher. See E F Schumacher, *Small Is Beautiful: Economics as if People Mattered* (New York: Harper & Row, 1973).

[83] T J Peters and R H Waterman Jr, *In Search of Excellence* (New York: Harper & Row, 1982), p 321. Also see T Peters, "Rethinking Scale," *California Management Review,* Fall 1992, pp 7–29; P Ghemawat, "The Growth Boosters," *Harvard Business Review,* July–August 2004, pp 35–40; N J Mass, "The Relative Value of Growth," *Harvard Business Review,* April 2005, pp 102–12; and K Hannon, "Why Small Businesses Rock," *USA Today,* August 21, 2006, p 7B.

[84] See, for example, W McKinley, "Decreasing Organizational Size: To Untangle or Not to Untangle?" *Academy of Management Review,* January 1992, pp 112–23; W Zellner, "Go-Go Goliaths," *BusinessWeek,* February 13, 1995, pp 64–70; T Brown, "Manage 'BIG!'" *Management Review,* May 1996, pp 12–17; and E Shapiro, "Power, Not Size, Counts," *Management Review,* September 1996, p 61.

[85] Handy, *The Hungry Spirit,* pp 107–8. Also see C Handy, "The Doctrine of Enough," *Management Review,* June 1998, pp 52–54.

[86] P L Zweig, "The Case against Mergers," *BusinessWeek,* October 30, 1995, p 122. Also see B Hindo, "Tough Times for Leaders of the Pack," *BusinessWeek,* January 30, 2006, p 14; M L Marks, "Workplace Recovery After Mergers, Acquisitions, and Downsizings: Facilitating Individual Adaptation to Major Organizational Transitions," *Organizational Dynamics,* no. 4, 2006, pp 384–99; J M Shaver, "A Paradox of Synergy: Contagion Effects in Mergers and Acquisitions," *Academy of Management Review,* October 2006, pp 962–76; the first Q&A in J Welch and S Welch, "The Six Sins of M&A," *BusinessWeek,* October 23, 2006, p 148; A Pomeroy, "Focus on the People During a Merger," *HR Magazine,* March 2007, p 16; and D Harding and T Rouse, "Human Due Diligence," *Harvard Business Review,* April 2007, pp 124–31.

[87] D Harding and S Rovit, "Building Deals on Bedrock," *Harvard Business Review,* September 2004, pp 121–28.

[88] Another company's formula for successful mergers is discussed in B Hindo, "A Dynamo Called Danaher," *BusinessWeek,* February 19, 2007, pp 56–60.

[89] R Z Gooding and J A Wagner III, "A Meta-Analytic Review of the Relationship between Size and Performance: The Productivity and Efficiency of Organizations and Their Subunits," *Administrative Science Quarterly,* December 1985, pp 462–81.

[90] Ibid., p 477.

[91] Results are presented in P G Benson, T L Dickinson, and C O Neidt, "The Relationship between Organizational Size and Turnover: A Longitudinal Investigation," *Human Relations,* January 1987, pp 15–30. Also see M Yasai-Ardekani, "Effects of Environmental Scarcity and Munificence on the Relationship of Context to Organizational Structure," *Academy of Management Journal,* March 1989, pp 131–56.

[92] For research support, see P Puranam, H Singh, and M Zollo, "Organizing for Innovation: Managing the Coordination-Autonomy Dilemma in Technology Acquisitions," *Academy of Management Journal,* April 2006, pp 263–80.

[93] See J Child, "Organizational Structure, Environment and Performance: The Role of Strategic Choice," *Sociology,* January 1972, pp 1–22.

[94] See J Galbraith, *Organization Design* (Reading, MA: Addison-Wesley Publishing, 1977); J R Montanari, "Managerial Discretion: An Expanded Model of Organization Choice," *Academy of Management Review,* April 1978, pp 231–41; and H R Bobbitt, Jr, and J D Ford, "Decision-Maker Choice as a Determinant of Organizational Structure," *Academy of Management Review,* January 1980, pp 13–23.

[95] See D P Forbes, "Reconsidering the Strategic Implications of Decision Comprehensiveness," *Academy of Management Review,* April 2007, pp 361–76; and C Zook, "Finding Your Next Core Business," *Harvard Business Review,* April 2007, pp 66–75.

[96] Data from "Fortune 500 Largest U.S. Corporations," *Fortune,* April 30, 2007, pp F-1, F-37.

[97] As quoted in T A Stewart, "Growth as a Process," *Harvard Business Review,* June 2006, p 69. Also see S A Miles and M D Watkins, "The Leadership Team: Complementary Strengths or Conflicting Agendas?" *Harvard Business Review,* April 2007, pp 90–98.

[98] Details may be found in D Miller, "Strategy Making and Structure: Analysis and Implications for Performance," *Academy of Management Journal,* March 1987, pp 7–32. For more, see M W Peng and P S Heath, "The Growth of the Firm in Planned Economies in Transition: Institutions, Organizations, and Strategic Choice," *Academy of Management Review,* April 1996, pp 492–528; C M Beckman, "The Influence of Founding Team Company Affiliations on Firm Behavior," *Academy of Management Journal,* August 2006, pp 741–58; and P C Fiss and E J Zajac, "The Symbolic Management of Strategic Change: Sensegiving Via Framing and Decoupling," *Academy of Management Journal,* December 2006, pp 1173–93.

[99] Excerpted from G Colvin, "The Defiant One," *Fortune,* April 30, 2007, pp 86–92.

[100] Excerpted from M Helft, "Chinese Political Prisoner Sues in U.S. Court, Saying Yahoo Helped Identify Dissidents," *The New York Times,* April 19, 2007, http://www.nytimes.com/2007/04/19/technology/19yahoo.html?_r=1&adxnnl=1&oref=slogin&ref=technology&adxnnlx=1177614268-Q/jOPCdu/1EHi4nUIebeQw&pagewanted=print

CHAPTER 18

[1] Excerpted from M Conlin, "Go-Go Going To Pieces in China," *BusinessWeek,* April 23, 2007, p 88.

[2] A M Webber, "Learning for a Change," *Fast Company,* May 1999, p 180.

[3] Forces for change are thoroughly discussed by L R Beach, *Leadership and the Art of Change* (Thousand Oaks, CA: Sage, 2006).

[4] M L Alch, "Get Ready for the Net Generation," *Training & Development,* February 2000, pp 32, 34.

[5] D Kirkpatrick, "Microsoft's New Brain," *Fortune,* May 1, 2006, p 59.

[6] N D Schwartz, ". . . Is Also a Big Target," *Fortune,* April 17, 2006, p 87.

[7] An application within health care is provided by G Colvin, "Wiring the Medical World," *Fortune,* February 19, 2007, pp 90–94.

[8] See N E Boudette, "Big Dealer to Detroit: Fix How You Make Cars," *The Wall Street Journal,* February 9, 2007, pp A1, A8.

[9] Examples are provided by G Edmondson, "The Race to Build Really Cheap Cars," *BusinessWeek,* April 23, 2007, pp 44–48;

D Welch, "Why Toyota Is Afraid of Being Number One," *BusinessWeek,* March 5, 2007, pp 42–50.

[10] See the related discussion in J W Upson, D J Ketchen, Jr., and R D Ireland, "Managing Employee Stress: A Key to the Effectiveness of Strategic Supply Chain Management," *Organizational Dynamics,* 2007, pp 78–92.

[11] Examples are provided in J Lublin and P Dvorak, "How Five New Players Aid Movement to Limit CEO Pay," *The Wall Street Journal,* March 13, 2007, pp A1, A20; and A Tomisawa, "Matsushita Aims to Boost Quality, Guard Image with Suppliers Rules," *The Wall Street Journal,* March 30, 2007, p A12.

[12] This case is discussed in J Cary, "Lighting a Fire Under Global Warming," *BusinessWeek,* April 16, 2007, p 33.

[13] S Carey and D Aalund, "JetBlue Plans Overhaul As Snafus Irk Customers," *The Wall Street Journal,* February 20, 2007, p A11.

[14] See Ibid; and J A Clair and R L Dufresne, "How Companies Can Experience Positive Transformation from a Crisis," *Organizational Dynamics,* 2007, pp 63–77.

[15] This example was discussed in A Pomeroy, "Agent of Change," *HR Magazine,* May 2005, pp 52–56.

[16] This three-way typology of change was adapted from discussion in P C Nutt, "Tactics of Implementation," *Academy of Management Journal,* June 1986, pp 230–61.

[17] See M Gunther, "The Welshman, the Walkman, and the Salarymen," *Fortune,* June 12, 2006, pp 70-83.

[18] For a thorough discussion of the model, see K Lewin, *Field Theory in Social Science* (New York: Harper & Row, 1951).

[19] These assumptions are discussed in E H Schein, *Organizational Psychology,* 3rd ed (Englewood Cliffs, NJ: Prentice Hall, 1980).

[20] This example was derived from P-W Tam, "System Reboot: Hurd's Big Challenge at HP: Overhauling Corporate Sales," *The Wall Street Journal,* April 3, 2006, pp A1, A3; and A Lashinsky, "The Hurd Way," *Fortune,* April 17, 2006, pp 92–102.

[21] C Goldwasser, "Benchmarking: People Make the Process," *Management Review,* June 1995, p 40.

[22] See T A Stewart, "Architects of Change," *Harvard Business Review,* April 2006, p 10.

[23] A thorough discussion of the target elements of change can be found in M Beer and B Spector, "Organizational Diagnosis: Its Role in Organizational Learning," *Journal of Counseling and Development,* July–August 1993, pp 642–50; and M Hammer, "The Process Audit," *Harvard Business Review,* April 2007, pp 111–23.

[24] Details of this example can be found in M D Hovanesian, "Dimon's Grand Design," *BusinessWeek,* March 28, 2005, pp 96–99.

[25] These errors are discussed in J P Kotter, "Leading Change: When Transformation Efforts Fail," *Harvard Business Review,* January 2007, pp 96–103.

[26] See F Ostroff, "Change Management in Government," *Harvard Business Review,* May 2006, pp 141–47.

27 P G Hanson and B Lubin, "Answers to Questions Frequently Asked about Organization Development," in *The Emerging Practice of Organization Development,* ed W Sikes, A Drexler, and J Grant (Alexandria, VA: NTL Institute, 1989), p 16.

28 Over 60 different OD techniques are discussed by P Holman, T Devane, and S Cady, *The Change Handbook,* 2nd ed (San Francisco: Berrett-Kohler, 2007).

29 W W Burke, *Organization Development: A Normative View* (Reading, MA: Addison-Wesley Publishing, 1987), p 9.

30 See R Gulati, "Silo Busting: How to Execute on the Promise of Customer Focus," *Harvard Business Review,* May 2007, pp 98–108.

31 See R Rodgers, J E Hunter, and D L Rogers, "Influence of Top Management Commitment on Management Program Success," *Journal of Applied Psychology,* February 1993, pp 151–55.

32 Results can be found in P J Robertson, D R Roberts, and J I Porras, "Dynamics of Planned Organizational Change: Assessing Empirical Support for a Theoretical Model," *Academy of Management Journal,* June 1993, pp 619–34. Also see J M Hiatt, *ADKAR: A Model for Change in Business, Government and Our Community* (Loveland, CO: Prosci Learning Center Publications, 2006).

33 Results from the meta-analysis can be found in G A Neuman, J E Edwards, and N S Raju, "Organizational Development Interventions: A Meta-Analysis of Their Effects on Satisfaction and Other Attitudes," *Personnel Psychology,* Autumn 1989, pp 461–90.

34 Results can be found in C-M Lau and H-Y Ngo, "Organization Development and Firm Performance: A Comparison of Multinational and Local Firms," *Journal of International Business Studies,* First Quarter 2001, pp 95–114.

35 Adapted from R J Marshak, *Covert Processes at Work* (San Francisco: Berrett-Koehler Publishers, 2006); and A S Judson, *Changing Behavior in Organizations: Minimizing Resistance to Change* (Cambridge, MA: Blackwell, Inc., 1991).

36 See R Moss Kanter, "Managing Traumatic Change: Avoiding the 'Unlucky 13,'" *Management Review,* May 1987, pp 23–24.

37 Details of this example are provided by B Schlender, "Inside the Shakeup at Sony," *Fortune* April 4, 2005, pp 94–104.

38 B Morris, "Coke Gets a Jolt," *Fortune,* May 15, 2006, pp 77–78.

39 See L Coch and J R P French Jr, "Overcoming Resistance to Change," *Human Relations,* 1948, pp 512–32.

40 L Herscovitch and J P Meyer, "Commitment to Organizational Change: Extension of a Three-Component Model," *Journal of Applied Psychology,* June 2002, p 475.

41 Ibid., pp 474–87.

42 Research regarding resilience is discussed by K Kersting, "Resilience: The Mental Muscle Everyone Has," *Monitor on Psychology,* April 2005, pp 32–33; Also see G E Mangurian, "Realizing What You're Made Of," *Harvard Business Review,* March 2007, pp 125–130.

43 Results can be found in C R Wanberg and J T Banas, "Predictors and Outcomes of Openness to Changes in a Reorganizing Workplace," *Journal of Applied Psychology,* February 2000, pp 132–42.

44 Results from this study can be found in T A Judge, C J Thoresen, V Pucik, and T W Welbourne, "Managerial Coping with Organizational Change: A Dispositional Perspective," *Journal of Applied Psychology,* February 1999, pp 107–22.

45 See Wanberg and Banas, "Predictors and Outcomes of Openness to Changes in a Reorganizing Workplace," pp 132–42.

46 See the related discussion in E B Dent and S G Goldberg, "Challenging 'Resistance to Change,'" *Journal of Applied Behavioral Science,* March 1999, pp 25–41.

47 J P Kotter, "Leading Change: Why Transformation Efforts Fail," *Harvard Business Review,* 1995, p 64.

48 Communicating about organizational change is discussed in Z Ruimin, "Raising Haier," *Harvard Business Review,* February 2007, pp 141–46; and C M Christensen, M Marx, and H H Stevenson, "The Tools of Cooperation and Change," *Harvard Business Review,* October 2006, pp 73–81.

49 Readiness for change is examined by L T Eby, D M Adams, J E A Russell, and S H Gaby, "Perceptions of Organizational Readiness for Change: Factors Related to Employees' Reactions to the Implementation of Team-Based Selling," *Human Relations,* March 2000, pp 419–42.

50 See R Charan, "Home Depot's Blueprint for Culture Change," *Harvard Business Review,* April 2006, pp 61–70.

51 The stress response is thoroughly discussed by H Selye, *Stress without Distress* (New York: J B Lippincott, 1974).

52 J M Ivancevich and M T Matteson, *Stress and Work: A Managerial Perspective* (Glenview, IL: Scott, Foresman, 1980), pp 8–9.

53 See Selye, *Stress without Distress.*

54 See C Liu, P E Spector, and L Shi, "Cross-National Job Stress: A Quantitative and Qualitative Study," *Journal of Organizational Behavior,* January 2007, pp 209–239; T Deangelis, "American: A Toxic Lifestyle?" *Monitor on Psychology,* April 2007, pp 50–52; and C Hymowitz, "Executive Adopts Motto for Job Stress: Work Hard, Be Nice," *The Wall Street Journal,* April 16, 2007, p B1.

55 Supportive results can be found in F M McKee-Ryan, Z Song, C R Wanberg, and A J Kinicki, "Psychological and Physical Well-Being during Unemployment: A Meta-Analytic Study," *Journal of Applied Psychology,* January 2005, pp 53–76.

56 Sleep deprivation is discussed by C A Czeisler, "Sleep Deficit: The Performance Killer," *Harvard Business Review,* October 2006, pp 53–59.

57 This statistic was reported in "Study Finds Eye-Opening Cost Associated with Fatigued Workers," *HR Magazine,* March 2007, p 26.

58 Results are reported in N A Bowling and T A Beehr, "Workplace Harassment from the Victim's Perspective:

A Theoretical Model and Meta-Analysis," *Journal of Applied Psychology,* September 2006, pp 998–1012.

[59] See the related discussion in E M Hallowell, "Smart People Underperform," *Harvard Business Review,* January 2005, pp 55–62.

[60] The issue of environmental conditions is discussed by A Bruzzese, "Is Building Making You 'Sick' of Work?" *Arizona Republic,* January 29, 2005, p D3.

[61] The discussion of appraisal is based on R S Lazarus and S Folkman, *Stress, Appraisal, and Coping* (New York: Springer Publishing, 1984).

[62] Results are presented in J A Penley, J Tomaka, and J S Wiebe, "The Association of Coping to Physical and Psychological Health Outcomes: A Meta-Analytic Review," *Journal of Behavioral Medicine,* December 2002, pp 551–609; Also see M Fugate, A Kinicki, and G Prussia, "Employee Coping with Organizational Change: An Examination of Alternative Theoretical Perspectives and Models," 2007, manuscript under review.

[63] The impact of vacations are discussed by E White, "For Young Workers, Taking Time Off Can be Stressful," *The Wall Street Journal,* March 27, 2007, p B10; and C Fritz and S Sonnentag, "Recovery, Well-Being, and Performance-Related Outcomes: The Role of Workload and Vacation Experiences," *Journal of Applied Psychology,* July 2006, pp 936–45.

[64] Supportive results can be found in J R B Halbesleben and W M Bowler, "Emotional Exhaustion and Job Performance: The Mediating Role of Motivation," *Journal of Applied Psychology,* January 2007, pp 93–106; and J D Jonge and C Dormann, "Stressors, Resources, and Strain at Work: A Longitudinal Test of the Triple-Match Principle," *Journal of Applied Psychology,* November 2006, pp 1359–74.

[65] S Caminiti, "A New Health Care Prescription," *Fortune,* January 24, 2005, special advertising section, p S3.

[66] Supportive results can be found in G E Miller, E Chen, and E S Zhou, "If It Goes Up, Must It Come Down? Chronic Stress and the Hypothalamic-Pituitary-Adrenocortical Axis in Humans," *Psychological Bulletin,* January 2007, pp 25–45; and L Meyers, "Building a Stronger Heart," *Monitor on Psychology,* January 2007, pp 52–53.

[67] Types of support are discussed by S Cohen and T A Wills, "Stress, Social Support, and the Buffering Hypothesis," *Psychological Bulletin,* September 1985, pp 310–57.

[68] R A Clay, "One Heart-Many Threats," *Monitor on Psychology,* January 2007, pp 46–54; J-P Neveu, "Jailed Resources: Conservation of Resources Theory as Applied to Burnout Among Prison Guards," *Journal of Organizational Behavior,* January 2007, pp 21–42; and J R B Halbesleben, "Sources of Social Support and Burnout: A Meta-Analytic Test of the Conservation of Resources Model," *Journal of Applied Psychology,* September 2006, pp 1134–45.

[69] See P M L Blanc, J J Hox, T W Taris, and M C W Peeters, "Take Care! The Evaluation of a Team-Based Burnout Intervention Program for Oncology Care Providers," *Journal of Applied Psychology,* January 2007, pp 213–27.

[70] This pioneering research is presented in S C Kobasa, "Stressful Life Events, Personality, and Health: An Inquiry into Hardiness," *Journal of Personality and Social Psychology,* January 1979, pp 1–11.

[71] See S C Kobasa, S R Maddi, and S Kahn, "Hardiness and Health: A Prospective Study," *Journal of Personality and Social Psychology,* January 1982, pp 168–77.

[72] Results can be found in V Florian, M Mikulincer, and O Taubman, "Does Hardiness Contribute to Mental Health during a Stressful Real Life Situation? The Roles of Appraisal and Coping," *Journal of Personality and Social Psychology,* April 1995, pp 687–95.

[73] See C Robitschek and S Kashubeck, "A Structural Model of Parental Alcoholism, Family Functioning, and Psychological Health: The Mediating Effects of Hardiness and Personal Growth Orientation," *Journal of Counseling Psychology,* April 1999, pp 159–72.

[74] B Priel, N Gonik, and B Rabinowitz, "Appraisals of Childbirth Experience and Newborn Characteristics: The Role of Hardiness and Affect," *Journal of Personality,* September, 1993, pp 299–315.

[75] Results from this study are discussed in S R Maddi, "On Hardiness and Other Pathways to Resilience," *American Psychologist,* April 2005, pp 261–62.

[76] M Friedman and R H Rosenman, *Type A Behavior and Your Heart* (Greenwich, CT: Fawcett Publications, 1974), p 84. (Boldface added.)

[77] See C Lee, L F Jamieson, and P C Earley, "Beliefs and Fears and Type A Behavior: Implications for Academic Performance and Psychiatric Health Disorder Symptoms," *Journal of Organizational Behavior,* March 1996, pp 151–77; S D Bluen, J Barling, and W Burns, "Predicting Sales Performance, Job Satisfaction, and Depression by Using the Achievement Strivings and Impatience–Irritability Dimensions of Type A Behavior," *Journal of Applied Psychology,* April 1990, pp 212–16; and M S Taylor, E A Locke, C Lee and M E Gist, "Type A Behavior and Faculty Research Productivity: What Are the Mechanisms?" *Organizational Behavior and Human Performance,* December 1984, pp 402–18.

[78] Results from the meta-analysis are contained in S A Lyness, "Predictors of Differences between Type A and B Individuals in Heart Rate and Blood Pressure Reactivity," *Psychological Bulletin,* September 1993, pp 266–95.

[79] See T Q Miller, T W Smith, C W Turner, M L Guijarro, A J Hallet, "A Meta-Analytic Review of Research on Hostility and Physical Health," *Psychological Bulletin,* March 1996, pp 322–48; and N Geipert, "Don't Be Mad," *Monitor on Psychology,* January 2007, pp 50–51.

[80] See A Cynkar, "Whole Workplace Health," *Monitor on Psychology,* March 2007, pp 28–32; and S Miller, "CEOs Urged to Make Wellness A Strategy," *HR Magazine,* April 2007, pp 30, 36.

[81] See K Tyler, "Stress Management," *HR Magazine,* September 2006, pp 79–83; and J M Ivancevich, M T Matteson, S M Freedman, and J S Phillips, "Worksite Stress Management

Interventions," *American Psychologist,* February 1990, pp 252–61.

[82] An evaluation of stress-reduction programs is conducted by P A Landsbergis and E Vivona-Vaughan, "Evaluation of an Occupational Stress Intervention in a Public Agency," *Journal of Organizational Behavior,* January 1996, pp 29–48; and D C Ganster, B T Mayes, W E Sime, and G D Tharp, "Managing Organizational Stress: A Field Experiment," *Journal of Applied Psychology,* October 1982, pp 533–42.

[83] R Kreitner, "Personal Wellness: It's Just Good Business," *Business Horizons,* May–June 1982, p 28.

[84] This statistic was reported in "Meeting the Challenge of Motivating Employees to Embrace Wellness," *HR Magazine,*

May 2005, pp 15–17. Also see M Conlin, "Get Healthy—or Else," *BusinessWeek,* February 26, 2007, pp 58–69.

[85] See T Parker-Pope, "Doctor's Orders: Ways to Work Exercise Into a Busy Day," *The Wall Street Journal,* January 9, 2007, p D1; and M P McQueen, "Wellness Plans Reach Out to the Healthy," *The Wall Street Journal,* March 28, 2007, pp D1, D3.

[86] Excerpted from M Conlin, "Smashing the Clock," *BusinessWeek,* December 11, 2006, pp 60–68.

[87] Excerpted from E Tanouye, "What Happens When It's the Boss Who's Suffering?" *The Wall Street Journal,* June 13, 2001, pp B1, B6.

Glossary

ability   Stable characteristic responsible for a person's maximum physical or mental performance.

adhocracy culture   A culture that has an external focus and values flexibility.

affective component   The feelings or emotions one has about an object or situation.

affirmative action   Focuses on achieving equality of opportunity in an organization.

alternative dispute resolution   Avoiding costly lawsuits by resolving conflicts informally or through mediation or arbitration.

Americans with Disabilities Act   Prohibits discrimination against the disabled.

anticipatory socialization   Occurs before an individual joins an organization, and involves the information people learn about different careers, occupations, professions, and organizations.

Asch effect   Giving in to a unanimous but wrong opposition.

attention   Being consciously aware of something or someone.

attitude   Learned predisposition toward a given object.

benchmarking   Process by which a company compares its performance with that of high-performing organizations.

blog   Online journal in which people comment on any topic.

bounded rationality   Constraints that restrict rational decision making.

brainstorming   Process to generate a quantity of ideas.

care perspective   Involves compassion and an ideal of attention and response to need.

career plateauing   The end result when the probability of being promoted is very small.

case study   In-depth study of a single person, group, or organization.

causal attributions   Suspected or inferred causes of behavior.

centralized decision making   Top managers make all key decisions.

change and acquisition   Requires employees to master tasks and roles and to adjust to work group values and norms.

clan culture   A culture that has an internal focus and values flexibility rather than stability and control.

closed system   A relatively self-sufficient entity.

coalition   Temporary groupings of people who actively pursue a single issue.

coercive power   Obtaining compliance through threatened or actual punishment.

cognitions   A person's knowledge, opinions, or beliefs.

cognitive categories   Mental depositories for storing information.

cognitive dissonance   Psychological discomfort experienced when attitudes and behavior are inconsistent.

cohesiveness   A sense of "we-ness" helps group stick together.

collectivist culture   Personal goals less important than community goals and interests.

commitment to change   A mind-set of doing whatever it takes to effectively implement change.

communication   Interpersonal exchange of information and understanding.

communication competence   Ability to effectively use communication behaviors in a given context.

competing values framework   A framework for categorizing organizational culture.

conflict   One party perceives its interests are being opposed or set back by another party.

conflict triangle   Conflicting parties involve a third person rather than dealing directly with each other.

consensus   Presenting opinions and gaining agreement to support a decision.

consideration   Creating mutual respect and trust with followers.

content theories of motivation   Identify internal factors influencing motivation.

contingency approach   Using management tools and techniques in a situationally appropriate manner; avoiding the one-best-way mentality.

contingency approach to organization design   Creating an effective organization–environment fit.

contingency factors   Variables that influence the appropriateness of a leadership style.

continuous reinforcement   Reinforcing every instance of a behavior.

control strategy   Coping strategy that directly confronts or solves problems.

core job dimensions   Job characteristics found to various degrees in all jobs.

corporate social responsibility   The idea that corporations are expected to go above and beyond following the law and making a profit.

creativity   Process of developing something new or unique.

cross-cultural management   Understanding and teaching behavioral patterns in different cultures.

cross-cultural training   Structured experiences to help people adjust to a new culture/country.

cross-functionalism   Team made up of technical specialists from different areas.

cultural intelligence   The ability to interpret ambiguous cross-cultural situations accurately.

culture   Beliefs and values about how a community of people should and do act.

culture shock   Anxiety and doubt caused by an overload of new expectations and cues.

day of contemplation   A one-time-only day off with pay to allow a problem employee to recommit to the organization's values and mission.

decentralized decision making   Lower-level managers are empowered to make important decisions.

decision making   Identifying and choosing solutions that lead to a desired end result.

decision-making style   A combination of how individuals perceive and respond to information.

decision tree   Graphical representation of the process underlying decision making.

delegation   Granting decision-making authority to people at lower levels.

Delphi technique   Process to generate ideas from physically dispersed experts.

developmental relationship strength   The quality of relationships among people in a network.

devil's advocacy   Assigning someone the role of critic.

dialectic method   Fostering a debate of opposing viewpoints to better understand an issue.

differentiation   Division of labor and specialization that causes people to think and act differently.

discrimination   Occurs when employment decisions are based on factors that are not job related.

distributive justice   The perceived fairness of how resources and rewards are distributed.

diversity   The host of individual differences that make people different from and similar to each other.

diversity of developmental relationships   The variety of people in a network used for developmental assistance.

dysfunctional conflict   Threatens organization's interests.

e-business   Running the *entire* business via the Internet.

electronic mail   Uses the Internet/intranet to send computer-generated text and documents.

emotional intelligence   Ability to manage oneself and interact with others in mature and constructive ways.

emotions   Complex human reactions to personal achievements and setbacks that may be felt and displayed.

employee assistance programs   Help employees to resolve personal problems that affect their productivity.

empowerment   Sharing varying degrees of power with lower-level employees to tap their full potential.

enacted values   The values and norms that are exhibited by employees.

encounter phase   Employees learn what the organization is really like and reconcile unmet expectations.

equity sensitivity   An individual's tolerance for negative and positive equity.

equity theory   Holds that motivation is a function of fairness in social exchanges.

ERG theory   Three basic needs—existence, relatedness, and growth—influence behavior.

escape strategy   Coping strategy that avoids or ignores stressors and problems.

espoused values   The stated values and norms that are preferred by an organization.

ethics   Study of moral issues and choices.

ethnocentrism   Belief that one's native country, culture, language, and behavior are superior.

eustress   Stress that is good or produces a positive outcome.

expatriate   Anyone living or working in a foreign country.

expectancy   Belief that effort leads to a specific level of performance.

expectancy theory   Holds that people are motivated to behave in ways that produce valued outcomes.

expert power   Obtaining compliance through one's knowledge or information.

explicit knowledge   Information that can be easily put into words and shared with others.

external factors   Environmental characteristics that cause behavior.

external forces for change   Originate outside the organization.

external locus of control   Attributing outcomes to circumstances beyond one's control.

extinction   Making behavior occur less often by ignoring or not reinforcing it.

extranet   Connects internal employees with selected customers, suppliers, and strategic partners.

extrinsic motivation   Motivation caused by the desire to attain specific outcomes.

extrinsic rewards   Financial, material, or social rewards from the environment.

feedback   Objective information about performance.

field study   Examination of variables in real-life settings.

fight-or-flight response   To either confront stressors or try to avoid them.

formal communication channels   Follow the chain of command or organizational structure.

formal group   Formed by the organization.

functional conflict   Serves organization's interests.

fundamental attribution bias   Ignoring environmental factors that affect behavior.

Galatea effect   An individual's high self-expectations lead to high performance.

garbage can model   Holds that decision making is sloppy and haphazard.

genderflex   Temporarily using communication behaviors typical of the other gender.

glass ceiling   Invisible barrier blocking women and minorities from top management positions.

goal   What an individual is trying to accomplish.

goal commitment   Amount of commitment to achieving a goal.

goal specificity   Quantifiability of a goal.

Golem effect   Loss in performance due to low leader expectations.

grapevine   Unofficial communication system of the informal organization.

group   Two or more freely interacting people with shared norms and goals and a common identity.

group cohesiveness   A "we feeling" binding group members together.

group support systems   Using computer software and hardware to help people work better together.

groupthink   Janis's term for a cohesive in-group's unwillingness to realistically view alternatives.

hardiness   Personality characteristic that neutralizes stress.

hierarchy culture   A culture that has an internal focus and values stability and control over flexibility.

high-context cultures   Primary meaning derived from nonverbal situational cues.

holistic wellness approach Advocates personal responsibility for healthy living.

human capital   The productive potential of one's knowledge and actions.

humility   Considering the contributions of others and good fortune when gauging one's success.

hygiene factors   Job characteristics associated with job dissatisfaction.

implicit cognition   Represents any thoughts or beliefs that are automatically activated from memory without our conscious awareness.

impostor syndrome   Failing to take any credit for one's success and feeling like a fake.

impression management   Getting others to see us in a certain manner.

individualistic culture   Primary emphasis on personal freedom and choice.

informal communication channels Do not follow chain of command or organizational structure.

informal group   Formed by friends or those with common interests.

information/decision-making theory   Diversity leads to better task-relevant processes and decision making.

information richness   Information-carrying capacity of data.

in-group exchange   A partnership characterized by mutual trust, respect, and liking.

initiating structure   Organizing and defining what group members should be doing.

instrumental cohesiveness   Sense of togetherness based on mutual dependency needed to get the job done.

instrumental values   Personally preferred ways of behaving.

instrumentality   A performance → outcome perception.

integration   Cooperation among specialists to achieve a common goal.

intelligence   Capacity for constructive thinking, reasoning, problem solving.

interactional justice   Extent to which people feel fairly treated when procedures are implemented.

intermittent reinforcement Reinforcing some but not all instances of behavior.

internal factors   Personal characteristics that cause behavior.

internal forces for change Originate inside the organization.

internal locus of control   Attributing outcomes to one's own actions.

Internet   A global system of computer networks.

intranet   An organization's private Internet.

intrinsic motivation   Motivation caused by positive internal feelings.

intrinsic rewards   Self-granted, psychic rewards.

intuition   Making a choice without the use of conscious thought or logical inference.

jargon   Language or terminology that is specific to a particular profession, group, or company.

job design   Changing the content or process of a specific job to increase job satisfaction and performance.

job enlargement   Putting more variety into a job.

job enrichment   Building achievement, recognition, stimulating work, responsibility, and advancement into a job.

job involvement   Extent to which an individual is immersed in his or her present job.

job rotation   Moving employees from one specialized job to another.

job satisfaction   An affective or emotional response to one's job.

judgmental heuristics   Rules of thumb or shortcuts that people use to reduce information-processing demands.

justice perspective   Based on the ideal of reciprocal rights and driven by rules and regulations.

knowledge management Implementing systems and practices that increase the sharing of knowledge and information throughout an organization.

laboratory study   Manipulation and measurement of variables in contrived situations.

law of effect   Behavior with favorable consequences is repeated; behavior with unfavorable consequences disappears.

leader–member relations   Extent that leader has the support, loyalty, and trust of work group.

leader trait   Personal characteristics that differentiate leaders from followers.

leadership   Process whereby an individual influences others to achieve a common goal.

leadership prototype   Mental representation of the traits and behaviors possessed by leaders.

learning goal   Encourages learning, creativity, and skill development.

learning organization   Proactively creates, acquires, and transfers knowledge throughout the organization.

legitimate power   Obtaining compliance through formal authority.

liaison individuals   Those who consistently pass along grapevine information to others.

line managers   Have authority to make organizational decisions.

line of sight   employees know the company's strategic goals and how they need to contribute.

linguistic style   A person's typical speaking pattern.

listening   Actively decoding and interpreting verbal messages.

low-context cultures   Primary meaning derived from written and spoken words.

maintenance roles   Relationship-building group behavior.

management   Process of working with and through others to achieve organizational objectives efficiently and ethically.

management by objectives   Management system incorporating participation in decision making, goal setting, and feedback.

management by walking around   Managers actually walk around and talk to people across lines of authority.

managing diversity   Creating organizational changes that enable all people to perform up to their maximum potential.

market culture   A culture that has a strong external focus and values stability and control.

mechanistic organizations   Rigid, command-and-control bureaucracies.

mentoring   Process of forming and maintaining developmental relationships between a mentor and a junior person.

met expectations   The extent to which one receives what he or she expects from a job.

meta-analysis   Pools the results of many studies through statistical procedure.

mission statement   Summarizes "why" an organization exists.

monochronic time   Preference for doing one thing at a time because time is limited, precisely segmented, and schedule driven.

motivation   Psychological processes that arouse and direct goal-directed behavior.

motivators   Job characteristics associated with job satisfaction.

mutuality of interest   Balancing individual and organizational interests through win-win cooperation.

need for achievement   Desire to accomplish something difficult.

need for affiliation   Desire to spend time in social relationships and activities.

need for power   Desire to influence, coach, teach, or encourage others to achieve.

need hierarchy theory   Five basic needs—physiological, safety, love, esteem, and self-actualization—influence behavior.

needs   Physiological or psychological deficiencies that arouse behavior.

negative inequity   Comparison in which another person receives greater outcomes for similar inputs.

negative reinforcement   Making behavior occur more often by contingently withdrawing something negative.

negotiation   Give-and-take process between conflicting interdependent parties.

noise   Interference with the transmission and understanding of a message.

nominal group technique   Process to generate ideas and evaluate solutions.

nonrational model   Explains how decisions actually are made.

nonverbal communication   Messages sent outside of the written or spoken word.

norm   Shared attitudes, opinions, feelings, or actions that guide social behavior.

onboarding   Programs aimed at helping employees integrate, assimilate, and transition to new jobs.

open system   Organism that must constantly interact with its environment to survive.

operant behavior   Skinner's term for learned, consequence-shaped behavior.

optimizing   Choosing the best possible solution.

organic organizations   Fluid and flexible networks of multitalented people.

organization   System of consciously coordinated activities of two or more people.

organization chart   Boxes-and-lines illustration showing chain of formal authority and division of labor.

organization development   A set of techniques or tools used to implement organizational change.

organizational behavior   Interdisciplinary field dedicated to better understanding and managing people at work.

organizational citizenship behaviors (OCBs)   Employee behaviors that exceed work-role requirements.

organizational commitment   Extent to which an individual identifies with an organization and its goals.

organizational culture   Shared values and beliefs that underlie a company's identity.

organizational decline   Decrease in organization's resource base (money, customers, talent, innovations).

organizational identification   Organizational values or beliefs become part of one's self-identity.

organizational moles   Those who use the grapevine to enhance their power and status.

organizational politics Intentional enhancement of self-interest.

organizational socialization Process by which employees learn an organization's values, norms, and required behaviors.

ostracism Rejection by other group members.

out-group exchange A partnership characterized by a lack of mutual trust, respect, and liking.

participative management Involving employees in various aspects of decision making.

pay for performance Monetary incentives tied to one's results or accomplishments.

perception Process of interpreting one's environment.

perceptual model of communication Process in which receivers create their own meaning.

performance management Continuous cycle of improving job performance with goal setting, feedback and coaching, and rewards and positive reinforcement.

performance outcome goal Targets a specific end-result.

persistence Extent to which effort is expended on a task over time.

personal barriers Any individual attribute that hinders communication.

personal initiative Going beyond formal job requirements and being an active self-starter.

personality Stable physical and mental characteristics responsible for a person's identity.

personality conflict Interpersonal opposition driven by personal dislike or disagreement.

personalized power Directed at helping oneself.

polychronic time Preference for doing more than one thing at a time because time is flexible and multidimensional.

position power Degree to which leader has formal power.

positive inequity Comparison in which another person receives lesser outcomes for similar inputs.

positive reinforcement Making behavior occur more often by contingently presenting something positive.

primary appraisal Determining whether a stressor is irrelevant, positive, or stressful.

proactive personality Action-oriented person who shows initiative and perseveres to change things.

problem Gap between an actual and desired situation.

procedural justice The perceived fairness of the process and procedures used to make allocation decisions.

process theories of motivation Identify the process by which internal factors and cognitions influence motivation.

programmed conflict Encourages different opinions without protecting management's personal feelings.

propensity to trust A personality trait involving one's general willingness to trust others.

proxemics Hall's term for the study of cultural expectations about interpersonal space.

psychological contract An individual's perception about the terms and conditions of a reciprocal exchange with another party.

punishment Making behavior occur less often by contingently presenting something negative or withdrawing something positive.

rational model Logical four-step approach to decision making.

realistic job preview Presents both positive and negative aspects of a job.

referent power Obtaining compliance through charisma or personal attraction.

repetitive motion disorders (RMDs) Muscular disorder caused by repeating motions.

resiliency The ability to handle pressure and quickly bounce back from personal and career setbacks.

resilience to change Composite personal characteristic reflecting high self-esteem, optimism, and an internal locus of control.

resistance to change Emotional/ behavioral response to real or imagined work changes.

respondent behavior Skinner's term for unlearned stimulus–response reflexes.

reward power Obtaining compliance with promised or actual rewards.

role ambiguity Others' expectations are unknown.

role conflict Others have conflicting or inconsistent expectations.

role overload Others' expectations exceed one's ability.

roles Expected behaviors for a given position.

sample survey Questionnaire responses from a sample of people.

satisficing Choosing a solution that meets a minimum standard of acceptance.

scenario technique Speculative forecasting method.

schema Mental picture of an event or object.

scientific management Using research and experimentation to find the most efficient way to perform a job.

secondary appraisal Assessing what might and can be done to reduce stress.

self-concept Person's self-perception as a physical, social, spiritual being.

self-efficacy Belief in one's ability to do a task.

self-esteem One's overall self-evaluation.

self-fulfilling prophecy Someone's high expectations for another person result in high performance.

self-managed teams Groups of employees granted administrative oversight for their work.

self-management leadership Process of leading others to lead themselves.

self-monitoring Observing one's own behavior and adapting it to the situation.

self-serving bias Taking more personal responsibility for success than failure.

semantics The study of words.

servant-leadership Focuses on increased service to others rather than to oneself.

sex-role stereotype Beliefs about appropriate roles for men and women.   .

shaping Reinforcing closer and closer approximations to a target behavior.

shared leadership Simultaneous, ongoing, mutual influence process in which people share responsibility for leading.

situational theories Propose that leader styles should match the situation at hand.

skill Specific capacity to manipulate objects.

social capital The productive potential of strong, trusting, and cooperative relationships.

social categorization theory Similarity leads to liking and attraction.

social loafing Decrease in individual effort as group size increases.

social power Ability to get things done with human, informational, and material resources.

social support Amount of helpfulness derived from social relationships.

socialized power Directed at helping others.

socio-emotional cohesiveness Sense of togetherness based on emotional satisfaction.

span of control The number of people reporting directly to a given manager.

staff personnel Provide research, advice, and recommendations to line managers.

stakeholder audit Systematic identification of all parties likely to be affected by the organization.

stereotype Beliefs about the characteristics of a group.

strategic constituency Any group of people with a stake in the organization's operation or success.

stress Behavioral, physical, or psychological response to stressors.

stressors Environmental factors that produce stress.

sustainability Meeting humanity's needs without harming future generations.

symptom management strategy Coping strategy that focuses on reducing the symptoms of stress.

tacit knowledge Information gained through experience that is difficult to express and formalize.

target elements of change Components of an organization that may be changed.

task roles Task-oriented group behavior.

task structure Amount of structure contained within work tasks.

team Small group with complementary skills who hold themselves mutually accountable for common purpose, goals, and approach.

team building Experiential learning aimed at better internal functioning of groups.

team viability Team members satisfied and willing to contribute.

teleworking Doing work that is generally performed in the office away from the office using different information technologies.

terminal values Personally preferred end-states of existence.

theory A story defining key terms, providing a conceptual framework, and explaining why something occurs.

Theory Y McGregor's modern and positive assumptions about employees being responsible and creative.

360-degree feedback Comparison of anonymous feedback from one's superior, subordinates, and peers with self-perceptions.

total quality management An organizational culture dedicated to

training, continuous improvement, and customer satisfaction.

transactional leadership Focuses on interpersonal interactions between managers and employees.

transformational leadership Transforms employees to pursue organizational goals over self-interests.

trust Reciprocal faith in others' intentions and behavior.

Type A behavior pattern Aggressively involved in a chronic, determined struggle to accomplish more in less time.

unity of command principle Each employee should report to a single manager.

valence The value of a reward or outcome.

value attainment The extent to which a job allows fulfillment of one's work values.

value system The organization of one's beliefs about preferred ways of behaving and desired end-states.

value congruence or person–culture fit The similarity between personal values and organizational values.

values Enduring belief in a mode of conduct or end-state.

virtual team Information technology allows group members in different locations to conduct business.

vision Long-term goal describing "what" an organization wants to become.

whistle blowing Reporting unethical/illegal acts to outside third parties.

withdrawal cognitions Overall thoughts and feelings about quitting a job.

workforce demographics Statistical profiles of adult workers.

Name/Company Index

Subject Index

E

E-business, 12
E-commerce, 12
Economy, global, 94–95
Educational attainment, 47–52
Egos, as communication barrier, 405
85-15 rule (Deming), 10
E-leadership, 13
Electronic mail. *See* E-mail
E-mail, 423–424
Emotional contagion, 146
Emotional intelligence
    developing personal and social competence
        through, 145
    explanation of, 144–145
    function of, 146
    leadership and, 467–468
Emotional Intelligence (Goleman), 144
Emotional labor, 147
Emotions
    explanation of, 142–143
    positive and negative, 143–144
Employee assistance programs (EAPs), 558
Employees
    with disabilities, 196
    screening potential, 26
    turnover of, 175, 194
Employment. *See* Work
Empowerment. *See also* Power
    delegation and, 444–445
    explanation of, 442, 444
    participative management and, 444
    research on, 445–447
    of self-managed teams, 326
Empowerment Model (Randolph), 447
Enacted values, 68, 69
Encoding
    explanation of, 401
    outcomes of, 185–186
Encounter phase of socialization, 82
Encryption, 422–423
Environmental sensitivity, 560
Equal Employment Opportunity Commission
    (EEOC), 294
Equal employment opportunity (EEO)
    legislation, 39–41
Equity
    job satisfaction and, 172
    perception of, 221
    thresholds of, 219–220
Equity sensitivity, 219
Equity theory
    dynamics of perceived inequity and, 219–220
    explanation of, 217
    individual-organization exchange relationship
        and, 217–218
    negative and positive inequity
        and, 218–219
    organizational justice and, 220–221
    practical lessons from, 221–222

ERG theory, 212–213
Escalation of commitment bias, 342
Escape strategy, 554
Espoused values, 68, 69
Ethical behavior
    external organizational influences
        on, 22, 24
    general moral principles and, 24–27
    individual model of, 22–23
    internal organizational influences on, 22, 23
    methods to improve, 26
    neutralizing/enhancing factors related to, 24
    in organizations, 19–20
Ethical issues
    decision trees for, 350–351
    related to negotiation, 389
    related to power, 441
Ethics
    codes of, 23, 26
    in decision making, 350–351
    explanation of, 20
    global model of corporate social responsibility
        and, 21–22
Ethics training, 26
Ethnic stereotypes, 195–196
Ethnocentrism
    effects of, 55
    explanation of, 98–99
Eustress, 552
Event memory, 187
Exchange
    explanation of, 435
    social, 277–278
Expatriates, 111. *See also* Foreign assignments
Expectancy, 223
Expectancy theory
    application of, 225
    explanation of, 222–223
    instrumentality and, 223–224
    managerial implications for, 226–227
    research on, 225–226
    valence and, 225
Expert power, 439
Explicit knowledge, 343
External communication, 416
External factors of behavior, 200
External forces for change
    customer and market change as, 534
    demographic characteristics as, 532–533
    explanation of, 532
    organizational crises as, 534–535
    social and political pressures as, 534
    technological advances as, 533–534
External locus of control, 137
Extinction, 265
Extranet, 422
Extrinsic rewards. *See also* Rewards
    explanation of, 256
    failure of, 258–260, 262
    maximizing impact of, 260–261
Eye contact, 409